South Africa

written and researched by

Tony Pinchuck, Barbara McCrea,
Donald Reid and Greg Mthembu-Salter

with additional contributions by

Robert McCrea, Peta Lee and Bronwen Kaplan

**ROUGH
GUIDES**

D1167213

www.roughguides.com

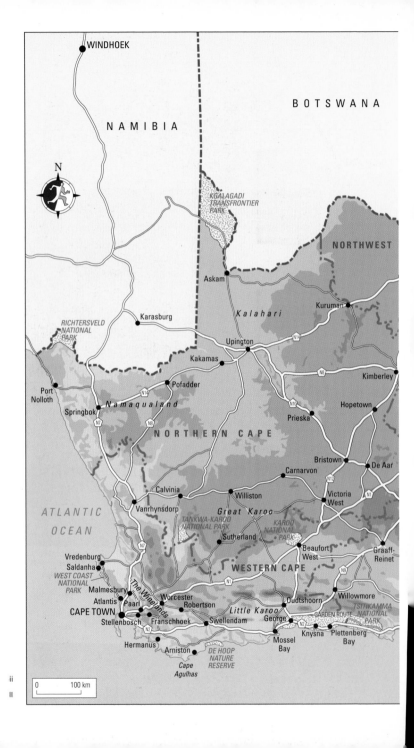

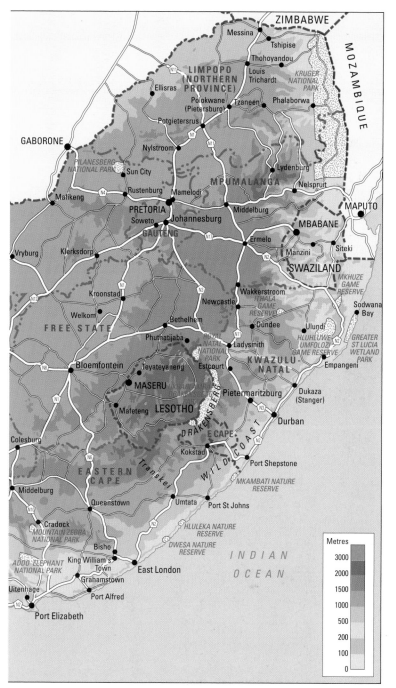

Introduction to
South Africa

South Africa is a large, diverse and incredibly beautiful country. The size of France and Spain combined, it varies from the picturesque Garden Route towns of the Western Cape to the raw stretch of subtropical coast in northern KwaZulu-Natal. It's also one of the great cultural meeting points of the African continent, a fact obscured by years of enforced racial segregation, but now manifest in the big cities. Yet South Africa is also something of an enigma; it has the best travel facilities on the African continent, but also the most difficult surface to scratch. After so long as an international pariah, the "rainbow nation" is still struggling to find its identity.

Many visitors are pleasantly surprised by South Africa's **excellent infrastructure**, which draws favourable comparison with countries such as Australia or the United States. Good air links and bus networks, excellent roads and a growing number of first-class B&Bs and guesthouses make South Africa a perfect touring country and – with the dramatic slide of the rand in 2001 – a cheap one too for visitors. For those on a budget, rapidly mushrooming **backpacker hostels** and backpacker buses provide an efficient means of exploring.

However, as a visitor, you'll have to make an effort to meet members of the country's African majority on equal terms. Apartheid may be dead, but its heritage continues to shape South Africa in a very physical way. The country was organized for the benefit of whites, so it's easy to get a very white-orientated experience of Africa. Nowhere is this more in evidence than in the layout of towns and cities, where African areas – often desperately poor – are usually tucked out of sight.

Fact file

- South Africa covers 1,219,090 square kilometres, with a **population** of 44 million. There are eleven official **languages**: Zulu, Xhosa, Afrikaans, Pedi, English, Ndebele, Sotho, Setswana, siSwati, Venda and Tsonga. The country's **religions** can be divided into Christianity (68 percent), Islam (2 percent), Hinduism (1.5 percent) and indigenous beliefs (28.5 percent).

- South Africa is a **multiparty democracy** within the Commonwealth. There are nine provinces, each with its own government; the head of state is President Thabo Mbeki. With the world's tenth-largest stock exchange and Africa's most advanced **economy**, South Africa is a middle-income country with a good infrastructure; it also has one of the greatest disparities of wealth in the world.

- **Lesotho** covers 30,355 square kilometres and has a population of 2 million. It is a parliamentary constitutional democracy within the Commonwealth, and the reigning monarch is King Letsie III. The official languages are Sesotho and English.

- The independent monarchy of **Swaziland** has an area of 17,363 square kilometres and a population of 1 million. The chief of state is King Mswati III, and the official languages are siSwati and English.

Some visitors are surprised to discover that South Africa's **population** doesn't reduce simply to black and white. The country's majority group are **Africans** (77 percent of the population); **whites** make up 11 percent, followed by **coloureds** (9 percent) – the descendants of white settlers, slaves and Africans, who speak English and Afrikaans and comprise the majority in the Western Cape. **Indians** (3 percent), most of whom live in KwaZulu-Natal, came to South Africa at the beginning of the twentieth century as indentured labourers.

Crime isn't the indiscriminate phenomenon that press reports suggest, but it is an issue. Really, it's a question of perspective – taking care but not becoming paranoid. Statistically, the odds of becoming a victim are highest in downtown Johannesburg, where violent crime is a daily reality. Other cities present a reduced risk – similar to, say, some parts of the United States; many country areas are safe by any standards.

Where to go

While you could circuit the whole of South Africa in a matter of weeks, a more satisfying approach is to focus your attention on one section of the country. Every one of the nine provinces (plus Lesotho and Swaziland) holds at least a couple of compelling reasons to visit, although, depending on the time of year and your interests, you'd be wise to concentrate on either the **west** or the **east**.

The **west**, best visited in the warmer months (Nov–April), has the outstanding attraction of **Cape Town**, worth experiencing for its matchless setting beneath Table Mountain, at the foot of the continent. Half a day's drive from here can take you to any other destination in the **Western Cape**, a province which owes its distinctive character to the fact that it has the longest-established colonial heritage in the country. You'll find gabled Cape Dutch architecture, historic towns and vineyard-covered mountains in the **Winelands**; forested coast along the **Garden Route**; and a dry interior punctuated by Afrikaner *dorps* in the **Little Karoo**.

If the west sounds a bit too pretty and you're after a more "African" experience, head for the **eastern** flank of the country, best visited in the cooler months (May–Oct). **Johannesburg** is likely to be your point of entry to this area: its frenetic street life, soaring office blocks and lively mix of people make it quite unlike anywhere else in the country. Half a day away by car lie the

Sun, sea and sweat

There are few countries in the world where the great outdoors is quite as great as in South Africa. You can, for example, catch the surf at Jeffrey's Bay or dive with white sharks, go scooting on a sailboard across Table Bay or kayaking up the Wild Coast. You can go rafting on the frothing Great Usutu River in Swaziland, or spend leisurely days drifting down the Orange. If you'd rather do something completely new, pick up a lilo and go kloofing in Suicide Gorge, or stick to basics and go walking (with or without rhinos). You can pony trek into Lesotho's Highlands, or mountain bike to Hell (Die Hel, to be precise). You can paraglide in the Northern Cape and balloon over baboons in Pilanesberg. If hair-raising descents are more your thing, you can abseil off Table Mountain, bungee at Bloukrans or even ski at Tiffendel – enough to leave you breathless.

Northern Province and Mpumalanga, which share the mighty **Kruger National Park**. Of South Africa's roughly two dozen major parks, the Kruger attracts the largest number of first-time visitors, and is unrivalled on the continent for its cross-section of mammal species.

A visit to Kruger combines perfectly with KwaZulu-Natal to the south, and an excellent short cut is to drive through tiny, landlocked **Swaziland**, which has attractions all of its own: a unique Swazi culture and a number of well-managed game parks. **KwaZulu-Natal** offers superb game and birdlife; **Hluhluwe-Umfolozi Park** is the best place in the world to see endangered rhinos and there are several other outstanding **small game reserves** nearby, such as Ithala, Mkhuze and Ndumo. For hiking and nature, nothing rivals the soaring **Drakensberg** range. After Cape Town, **Durban** remains the only city in South Africa worth visiting in its own right: a busy cultural melting pot with a bustling Indian district and lively beachfront. The long stretch of **beaches** north and south of Durban is the most developed in the country, but north towards the Mozambique border lies the wildest stretch of coast in South Africa.

Long sandy **beaches**, developed only in pockets, are characteristic of much of the 2500km of shoreline that curves from the cool Atlantic along

House of the spirits

For thousands of years, San Bushman shamans in South Africa decorated rockfaces with powerful religious images. These finely realized paintings include animals, people, and humans changing into animals, and are found in mountainous areas across South Africa. Archeologists now regard the images as metaphors for religious experiences, one of the most significant of which is the healing trance dance, still practised by the few surviving Bushman communities. Rockfaces can be seen as portals between the human and spiritual world: when we gaze at Bushman rock art, we are looking into the house of the spirits.

Long sandy beaches are characteristic of the 2500km of shoreline that curves from the cool Atlantic round to the subtropical Indian Ocean

the Northern Cape round to the subtropical Indian Ocean that foams onto KwaZulu-Natal's shores. **Jeffrey's Bay** on the Eastern Cape coast is reputed to be one of the world's top **surfing** spots. Much of the Eastern Cape coast is equally appealing, whether you just want to stroll, sunbathe or take in backdrops of mountains and hulking sand dunes. **Scubadiving**, especially in KwaZulu-Natal, opens up a world of coral reefs rich with colourful fish, and southeast of the Western Cape winelands, along the **Whale Coast**, is one of South Africa's unsung attractions – some of the best shore-based **whale-watching** in the world.

With time in hand, you might want to drive through the sparse but exhilarating **interior**, with its open horizons, switchback mountain passes, rocks, scrubby vegetation and isolated *dorps*. The **Northern Cape** and **Northwest Province** can reveal surprises. Visit the western section of the Northern Cape in August or September, and you'll be treated to a riot of colourful **wild flowers**. From the staunchly Afrikaner heartland of **Free State**, you're well poised to visit the undeveloped kingdom of **Lesotho**, set in the mountains between the Free State and KwaZulu-Natal. Lesotho has few vestiges of royalty left today, but it does offer plenty of spectacular highland scenery, best explored on a sturdy, sure-footed Lesotho pony.

When to go

South Africa is a predominantly sunny country, but when it does get cold you really feel it – indoor heating is limited, and everything is geared to fine weather. You'll need to pack with the weather in mind, especially in winter. Southern hemisphere seasons are the reverse of those in the north, with **midwinter** occurring in June and July and **midsummer** over December and January, when the country shuts down for its annual holiday.

South Africa has distinct climatic zones. **Cape Town** and the **Garden Route** coastal belt have a so-called Mediterranean climate, influenced by winds blowing in from the South Atlantic. Summers tend to be warm, mild and unpredictable; rain can fall at any time of the year and winter days can be cold and wet. Many Capetonians regard March to May as the perfect season, when the nagging winds drop, it's beautifully mild and the tourists have all gone home. Subtropical **KwaZulu-Natal** has warm, sunny winters, coral reefs and tepid seas; the province's Drakensberg range sees misty summer days and mountain snow in winter. **Johannesburg** and **Pretoria** lie on a plateau and have a near-perfect climate; summer days are hot, with none of the humidity of the KwaZulu-Natal coast, while the winters are dry with chilly nights. East of Johannesburg, the **Lowveld**, the low-lying wedge along the Mozambique border that includes the **Kruger National Park**, is subject to similar summer and winter rainfall patterns to the Highveld, but experiences far greater extremes of temperature because of its considerably lower altitude.

Average daily temperatures

	Jan	Feb	Mar	Apr	May	June	July	Aug	Sept	Oct	Nov	Dec
Cape Town												
Avg max °C	27	27	26	23	20	19	17	18	19	22	24	26
Durban												
Avg max °C	27	28	27	26	24	23	22	22	23	24	25	26
Johannesburg												
Avg max °C	26	26	24	22	19	16	16	20	23	25	25	26
Kimberley												
Avg max °C	33	31	28	25	21	19	19	22	25	28	30	32
Port Elizabeth												
Avg max °C	25	26	25	23	22	20	20	20	20	21	22	24
Skukuza (Kruger NP)												
Avg max °C	31	31	30	29	27	25	25	26	29	29	30	30
Maseru (Lesotho)												
Avg max °C	20	17	14	11	9	7	7	9	11	14	17	20
Mbabane (Swaziland)												
Avg max °C	25	25	24	23	21	19	19	21	23	24	24	25

24

things not to miss

It's not possible to see everything that South Africa has to offer in one trip – and we don't suggest you try. What follows is a selective and subjective taste of the country's highlights: outstanding national parks, spectacular wildlife, adventure sports, history and beautiful architecture. They're arranged in five colour-coded categories to help you find the very best things to see, do and experience. All entries have a page reference to take you straight into the guide, where you can find out more.

01 **Wild flowers** Page **332** • Following the winter rains, Namaqualand's normally bleak landscape explodes with colour in one of nature's most brilliant floral displays.

02 The Drakensberg Page **505** • Hike in the mysterious "dragon mountains", which border KwaZulu-Natal and Lesotho.

03 Robben Island
Page **122** • Visit the notorious off-shore jail where political prisoners, including Nelson Mandela, were incarcerated.

04 The Bo Kaap Page **116** • The streets of Cape Town's oldest residential area are filled with colourful Cape Dutch and Georgian architecture.

05 Traditional arts and crafts Page **742** • Highly skilled pottery and woodcarving remain an important part of life in the Northern Province's Venda region.

06 Rafting Page **817** • Swaziland's Great Usutu River offers some of the most exciting whitewater rafting in southern Africa.

07 Madikwe Game Reserve Page **655** • This massive game park sees remarkably few visitors, yet boasts excellent lodges and superb wildlife-spotting opportunities, from wild dogs to the Big Five.

08 Live music Page **613** • Johannesburg offers the best nightlife in South Africa, attracting top musical performers from around the country and abroad.

09 Cape Point Page **147** • The treacherous rocky promontory south of Cape Town, where many ships have come to grief since the fifteenth century.

10 Whales Page **142** • Regularly visiting the southern Cape Coast, whales often approach surprisingly close to the shore.

11 Table Mountain cableway Page **135** • The most spectacular way to ascend Cape Town's famous landmark is also the easiest – the revolving cable car.

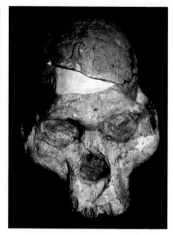

12 The Cradle of Humankind Page **621** • One of the world's major paleontological sites, the Sterkfontein Caves are home to "Mrs Ples", a female skull some 2.6 million years old.

13 Game lodges Page **700** • Indulge yourself at one of the Kruger National Park's luxurious and stylish lodges.

14 Wine routes Page **180** • The Western Cape's wine estates combine stunning scenery, Cape Dutch architecture and some fine and affordable vintages.

15 Pony trekking Page **755** • The perfect way to experience the ruggedly beautiful "mountain kingdom" of Lesotho.

16 **The Wild Coast** Page **417** • The Eastern Cape offers peace and seclusion along a remote and spectacular subtropical coastline.

17 **Soweto** Page **608** • Take a tour around the vast, sprawling township that became a world-famous symbol of resistance to apartheid.

18 **Vernacular architecture** Page **569** • Beautifully decorative Basotho huts are characteristic of the Eastern Free State's Highlands Route.

19 **Hluhluwe-Umfolozi Park** Page **516** • KwaZulu-Natal's finest game reserve offers an unsurpassed variety of wildlife-spotting activities, from night drives to self-guided walks and even donkey trails.

20 **Storms River Mouth** Page 277 • The Garden Route's most dramatic coastline, where the Storms River emerges from a gorge to meet the crashing surf.

21 **Swartberg Pass** Page 202 • The spectacular passes of the Little Karoo make for exciting drives and mountain biking.

22 **Indian culture** Page 463 • Durban's large Indian population has brought a rich cultural heritage to Africa's busiest port.

23 **Kgalagadi Transfrontier Park** Page 325 • View gemsbok and other desert dwellers amidst the harsh beauty of the Kalahari.

24 **Game trails** Page 703 • Combine adventure with wildlife-spotting on a guided hike in the mighty Kruger National Park, the most famous of South Africa's reserves.

The wildlife of East and Southern Africa

This field guide provides a quick reference to help you identify the larger mammals likely to be encountered in East and Southern Africa. It includes most species that are found throughout these regions, as well as a limited number whose range is more restricted. Straightforward photos show easily identified markings and features. The notes give you clear pointers about the kinds of habitat in which you are most likely to see each mammal; its daily rhythm (usually either nocturnal or diurnal); the kind of social groups it usually forms; and general tips about sighting it on safari, its rarity and its relations with humans. For further details and background, see p.667.

❀ HABITAT ◗ DAILY RHYTHM 🌿 SOCIAL LIFE ✓ SIGHTING TIPS

Baboon Papio cynocephalus

❀ open country with trees and cliffs; adaptable, but always near water

◐ diurnal

🌾 troops led by a dominant male

✓ common; several subspecies, including Yellow and Olive in East Africa and Chacma in Southern Africa; easily becomes used to humans, frequently a nuisance and occasionally dangerous

Eastern Black and White Colobus
Colobus guereza

❀ rainforest and well-watered savannah; almost entirely arboreal

◐ diurnal

🌾 small troops

✓ troops maintain a limited home territory, so easily located, but can be hard to see at a great height; not found in Southern Africa

Patas Monkey Erythrocebus patas

❀ savannah and forest margins; tolerates some aridity; terrestrial except for sleeping and lookouts

◐ diurnal

🌾 small troops

✓ widespread but infrequently seen; can run at high speed and stand on hind feet supported by tail; not found in Southern Africa

Vervet Monkey Cercopithecus aethiops

❀ most habitats except rainforest and arid lands; arboreal and terrestrial

◐ diurnal

🌾 troops

✓ widespread and common; occasionally a nuisance where used to humans

White-throated or Sykes' Monkey/Samango
Cercopithecus mitis/albogularis

 forests; arboreal and occasionally terrestrial

 diurnal

 families or small troops

✓ widespread; shyer and less easily habituated to humans than the Vervet

Aardvark Orycteropus afer

 open or wooded termite country; softer soil preferred

 nocturnal

 solitary

✓ rarely seen animal, the size of a small pig; old burrows are common and often used by warthogs

Spring Hare Pedetes capensis

 savannah; softer soil areas preferred

 nocturnal

🐾 burrows, usually with a pair and their young; often linked into a network, almost like a colony

✓ fairly widespread rabbit-sized rodent; impressive and unmistakable kangaroo-like leaper

Crested Porcupine
Hystrix africae-australis

🌸 adaptable to a wide range of habitats

🌙 nocturnal and sometimes active at dusk

🐾 family groups

✓ large rodent (up to 90cm in length), rarely seen, but common away from croplands, where it's hunted as a pest

🌸 HABITAT 🌙 DAILY RHYTHM 🐾 SOCIAL LIFE ✓ SIGHTING TIPS

Bat-eared Fox Otocyon megalotis

- 🌸 open country

- ◐ mainly nocturnal; diurnal activity increases in cooler months

- 🐾 monogamous pairs

- ✓ distribution coincides with termites, their favoured diet; they spend many hours foraging using sensitive hearing to pinpoint their underground prey

Blackbacked Jackal Canis mesomelas

- 🌸 broad range from moist mountain regions to desert, but drier areas preferred

- ◐ normally nocturnal, but diurnal in the safety of game reserves

- 🐾 mostly monogamous pairs; sometimes family groups

- ✓ common; a bold scavenger, the size of a small dog, that steals even from lions; black saddle distinguishes it from the shyer Side-striped Jackal

Hunting Dog or Wild Dog
Lycaon pictus

- 🌸 open savannah in the vicinity of grazing herds

- ◐ diurnal

- 🐾 nomadic packs

- ✓ extremely rare and rarely seen, but widely noted when in the area; the size of a large dog, with distinctively rounded ears

Honey Badger or Ratel
Mellivora capensis

- 🌸 very broad range of habitats

- ◐ mainly nocturnal

- 🐾 usually solitary, but also found in pairs

- ✓ widespread, omnivorous, badger-sized animal; nowhere common; extremely aggressive

---

🌸 HABITAT ◐ DAILY RHYTHM 🐾 SOCIAL LIFE ✓ SIGHTING TIPS

African Civet *Civettictis civetta*

 prefers woodland and dense vegetation

 mainly nocturnal

 solitary

✓ omnivorous, medium-dog-sized, short-legged prowler; not to be confused with the smaller genet

Common Genet *Genetta genetta*

 light bush country, even arid areas; partly arboreal

 nocturnal, but becomes active at dusk

 solitary

✓ quite common, slender, cat-sized omnivore, often seen at game lodges, where it easily becomes habituated to humans

Banded Mongoose *Mungos mungo*

 thick bush and dry forest

 diurnal

 lives in burrow colonies of up to thirty animals

✓ widespread and quite common, the size of a small cat; often seen in a group, hurriedly foraging through the undergrowth

Spotted Hyena *Crocuta crocuta*

tolerates a wide variety of habitat, with the exception of dense forest

nocturnal but also active at dusk; also diurnal in many parks

highly social, usually living in extended family groups

✓ the size of a large dog with a distinctive loping gait, quite common in parks; carnivorous scavenger and cooperative hunter; dangerous

Caracal Caracal caracal

🌸 open bush and plains; occasionally arboreal

🌓 mostly nocturnal

🦌 solitary

✓ lynx-like wild cat; rather uncommon and rarely seen

Cheetah Acionyx jubatus

🌸 savannah, in the vicinity of plains grazers

🌓 diurnal

🦌 solitary or temporary nuclear family groups

✓ widespread but low population; much slighter build than the leopard, and distinguished from it by a small head, square snout and dark "tear mark" running from eye to jowl

Leopard Panthera pardus

🌸 highly adaptable; frequently arboreal

🌓 nocturnal; also cooler daylight hours

🦌 solitary

✓ the size of a very large dog; not uncommon, but shy and infrequently seen; rests in thick undergrowth or up trees; very dangerous

Lion Panthera leo

🌸 all habitats except desert and thick forest

🌓 nocturnal and diurnal

🦌 prides of three to forty; more usually six to twelve

✓ commonly seen resting in shade; dangerous

🌸 HABITAT   🌓 DAILY RHYTHM   🦌 SOCIAL LIFE   ✓ SIGHTING TIPS

Serval *Felis serval*

 reed beds or tall grassland near water

 normally nocturnal but more diurnal than most cats

 usually solitary

✓ some resemblance to, but far smaller than, the cheetah; most likely to be seen on roadsides or water margins at dawn or dusk

Rock Hyrax or Dassie
Procavia capensis

 rocky areas, from mountains to isolated outcrops

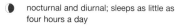 diurnal

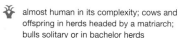 colonies consisting of a territorial male with as many as thirty related females

✓ rabbit-sized; very common; often seen sunning themselves in the early morning on rocks

African Elephant
Loxodonta africana

 wide range of habitats, wherever there are trees and water

 nocturnal and diurnal; sleeps as little as four hours a day

 almost human in its complexity; cows and offspring in herds headed by a matriarch; bulls solitary or in bachelor herds

✓ look out for fresh dung (football-sized) and recently damaged trees; frequently seen at water holes from late afternoon

Black Rhinoceros
Diceros bicornis

⚘ usually thick bush, altitudes up to 3500m

◐ active day and night, resting between periods of activity

⚘ solitary

✓ extremely rare and in critical danger of extinction; largely confined to parks where most individuals are known to rangers; distinctive hooked lip for browsing; small head usually held high; bad eyesight; very dangerous

White Rhinoceros Ceratotherium simum

⚘ savannah

◐ active day and night, resting between periods of activity

⚘ mother/s and calves, or small, same-sex herds of immature animals; old males solitary

✓ rare, restricted to parks; distinctive wide mouth (hence "white" from Afrikaans wijd) for grazing; large head usually lowered; docile

Burchell's Zebra Equus burchelli

⚘ savannah, with or without trees, up to 4500m

◐ active day and night, resting intermittently

⚘ harems of several mares and foals led by a dominant stallion are usually grouped together, in herds of up to several thousand

✓ widespread and common inside and out-side the parks; regional subspecies include granti (Grant's, East Africa) and chapmani (Chapman's, Southern Africa, left)

Grevy's Zebra Equus grevyi

⚘ arid regions

◐ largely diurnal

⚘ mares with foals and stallions generally keep to separate troops; stallions sometimes solitary and territorial

✓ easily distinguished from smaller Burchell's Zebra by narrow stripes and very large ears; rare and localized but easily seen; not found in Southern Africa

Warthog *Phacochoerus aethiopicus*

savannah, up to an altitude of over 2000m

diurnal

family groups, usually of a female and her litter

✓ common; boars are distinguishable from sows by their prominent face "warts"

Hippopotamus
Hippopotamus amphibius

slow-flowing rivers, dams and lakes

principally nocturnal, leaving the water to graze

bulls are solitary, but other animals live in family groups headed by a matriarch

✓ usually seen by day in water, with top of head and ears breaking the surface; frequently aggressive and very dangerous when threatened or when retreat to water is blocked

Giraffe *Giraffa camelopardalis*

wooded savannah and thorn country

diurnal

loose, non-territorial, leaderless herds

✓ common; many subspecies, of which Maasai (*G. c. tippelskirchi*, right), Reticulated (*G. c. reticulata*, bottom l.) and Rothschild's (*G. c. rothschildi*, bottom r.) are East African; markings of Southern African subspecies are intermediate between *tippelskirchi* and *rothschildi*

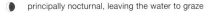
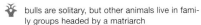

African or Cape Buffalo
Syncerus caffer

* wide range of habitats, always near water, up to altitudes of 4000m

* nocturnal and diurnal, but inactive during the heat of the day

* gregarious, with cows and calves in huge herds; young bulls often form small bachelor herds; old bulls are usually solitary

✓ very common; scent much more acute than other senses; very dangerous, old bulls especially so

Hartebeest Alcelaphus buselaphus

* wide range of grassy habitats

* diurnal

* females and calves in small, wandering herds; territorial males solitary

✓ hard to confuse with any other antelope except the topi/tsessebe; many varieties, distinguishable by horn shape, including Coke's, Lichtenstein's, Jackson's (left), and Red or Cape; common, but much displaced by cattle grazing

Blue or White-bearded Wildebeest Connochaetes taurinus

* grasslands

* diurnal, occasionally also nocturnal

* intensely gregarious; wide variety of associations within mega-herds which may number over 100,000 animals

✓ unmistakable, nomadic grazer; long tail, mane and beard

Topi or Tsessebe Damaliscus lunatus

* grasslands, showing a marked preference for moist savannah, near water

* diurnal

* females and young form herds with an old male

✓ widespread, very fast runners; male often stands sentry on an abandoned termite hill, actually marking the territory against rivals, rather than defending against predators

Gerenuk *Litocranius walleri*

 arid thorn country and semi-desert

 diurnal

 solitary or in small, territorial harems

✓ not uncommon; unmistakable giraffe-like neck; often browses standing upright on hind legs; the female is hornless; not found in Southern Africa

Grant's Gazelle *Gazella granti*

 wide grassy plains with good visibility, sometimes far from water

 diurnal

 small, territorial harems

✓ larger than the similar Thomson's Gazelle, distinguished from it by the white rump patch which extends onto the back; the female has smaller horns than the male; not found in Southern Africa

Springbok *Antidorcas marsupalis*

 arid plains

 seasonally variable, but usually cooler times of day

 highly gregarious, sometimes in thousands; various herding combinations of males, females and young

✓ medium-sized, delicately built gazelle; dark line through eye to mouth and lyre-shaped horns in both sexes; found only in Botswana, Namibia and South Africa

Thomson's Gazelle *Gazella thomsoni*

 flat, short-grass savannah, near water

 diurnal

 gregarious, in a wide variety of social structures, often massing in the hundreds with other grazing species

✓ smaller than the similar Grant's Gazelle, distinguished from it by the black band on flank; the female has tiny horns; not found in Southern Africa

 HABITAT   ● DAILY RHYTHM   SOCIAL LIFE   ✓ SIGHTING TIPS   xxvii

Impala *Aepyceros melampus*

 open savannah near light woodland cover

 diurnal

 large herds of females overlap with several male territories; males highly territorial during the rut when they separate out breeding harems of up to twenty females

✓ common, medium-sized, no close relatives; distinctive high leaps when fleeing; the only antelope with a black tuft above the hooves; males have long, lyre-shaped horns

Red Lechwe *Kobus leche*

 floodplains and areas close to swampland

 nocturnal and diurnal

 herds of up to thirty females move through temporary ram territories; occasionally thousand-strong gatherings

✓ semi-aquatic antelope with distinctive angular rump; rams have large forward-pointing horns; not found in East Africa

Common Reedbuck
Redunca arundinum

 reedbeds and tall grass near water

 nocturnal and diurnal

 monogamous pairs or family groups in territory defended by the male

✓ medium-sized antelope, with a plant diet unpalatable to other herbivores; only males have horns

Common or Defassa Waterbuck
Kobus ellipsiprymnus

 open woodland and savannah, near water

nocturnal and diurnal

territorial herds of females and young, led by dominant male, or territorial males visited by wandering female herds

✓ common, rather tame, large antelope; plant diet unpalatable to other herbivores; shaggy coat; only males have horns

Kirk's Dikdik  *Rhincotragus kirki*

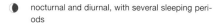 scrub and thornbush, often far from water

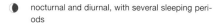 nocturnal and diurnal, with several sleeping periods

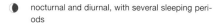 pairs for life, often accompanied by current and previous young

✓ tiny, hare-sized antelope, named after its alarm cry; only males have horns; not found in Southern Africa except Namibia

Common Duiker  *Sylvicapra grimmia*

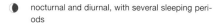 adaptable; prefers scrub and bush

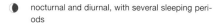 nocturnal and diurnal

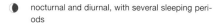 most commonly solitary; sometimes in pairs; occasionally monogamous

✓ widespread and common small antelope with a rounded back; seen close to cover; rams have short straight horns

Sitatunga 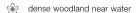 *Tragelaphus spekei*

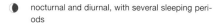 swamps

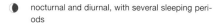 nocturnal and sometimes diurnal

 territorial and mostly solitary or in pairs

✓ very localized and not likely to be mistaken for anything else; usually seen half submerged; females have no horns

Nyala *Tragelaphus angasi*

 dense woodland near water

 primarily nocturnal with some diurnal activity

 flexible and non-territorial; the basic unit is a female and two offspring

✓ in size midway between the Lesser Kudu and Bushbuck, and easily mistaken for the latter; orange legs distinguish it; only males have horns; not found in East Africa

---

 HABITAT DAILY RHYTHM  SOCIAL LIFE ✓ SIGHTING TIPS

xxix

Bushbuck Tragelaphus scriptus

- 🌸 thick bush and woodland close to water
- ◐ principally nocturnal, but also active during the day when cool
- 🐾 solitary, but casually sociable; sometimes grazes in small groups
- ✓ medium-sized antelope with white stripes and spots; often seen in thickets, or heard crashing through them; not to be confused with the larger Nyala; the male has shortish straight horns

Eland Taurotragus oryx

- 🌸 highly adaptable; semi-desert to mountains, but prefers scrubby plains
- ◐ nocturnal and diurnal
- 🐾 non-territorial herds of up to sixty with temporary gatherings of as many as a thousand
- ✓ common but shy; the largest and most powerful African antelope; both sexes have straight horns with a slight spiral

Greater Kudu
Tragelaphus strepsiceros

- 🌸 semi-arid, hilly or undulating bush country; tolerant of drought
- ◐ diurnal when secure; otherwise nocturnal
- 🐾 territorial; males usually solitary; females in small troops with young
- ✓ impressively big antelope (up to 1.5m at shoulder) with very long, spiral horns in the male; very localized; shy of humans and not often seen

Lesser Kudu Tragelaphus imberbis

- 🌸 semi-arid, hilly or undulating bush country; tolerant of drought
- ◐ diurnal when secure; otherwise nocturnal
- 🐾 territorial; males usually solitary; females in small troops with young
- ✓ smaller than the Greater Kudu; only the male has horns; extremely shy and usually seen only as it disappears; not found in Southern Africa

🌸 HABITAT   ◐ DAILY RHYTHM   🐾 SOCIAL LIFE   ✓ SIGHTING TIPS

Gemsbok Oryx gazella gazella

🌸 open grasslands; also waterless wastelands; tolerant of prolonged drought

◐ nocturnal and diurnal

🐾 highly hierarchical mixed herds of up to fifteen, led by a dominant bull

✓ large antelope with unmistakable horns in both sexes; subspecies gazella is one of several similar forms, sometimes considered separate species; not found in East Africa

---

Fringe-eared Oryx
Oryx gazella callotis

🌸 open grasslands; also waterless wastelands; tolerant of prolonged drought

◐ nocturnal and diurnal

🐾 highly hierarchical mixed herds of up to fifteen, led by a dominant bull

✓ the callotis subspecies is one of two found in Kenya, the other, found in the northeast, being Oryx g. beisa (the Beisa Oryx); not found in Southern Africa

---

Roan Antelope Hippotragus equinus

🌸 tall grassland near water

◐ nocturnal and diurnal; peak afternoon feeding

🐾 small herds led by a dominant bull; herds of immature males; sometimes pairs in season

✓ large antelope, distinguished from the Sable by lighter, greyish colour, shorter horns (both sexes) and narrow, tufted ears

---

Sable Antelope Hippotragus niger

🌸 open woodland with medium to tall grassland near water

◐ nocturnal and diurnal

🐾 territorial; bulls divide into sub-territories, through which cows and young roam; herds of immature males; sometimes pairs in season

✓ large antelope; upper body dark brown to black; mask-like markings on the face; both sexes have huge curved horns

---

🌸 HABITAT　◐ DAILY RHYTHM　🐾 SOCIAL LIFE　✓ SIGHTING TIPS

Grysbok Raphicerus melanotis

🏵 thicket adjacent to open grassland

◐ nocturnal

🐾 rams territorial; loose pairings

✓ small, rarely seen antelope; two sub-species, Cape (*R. m. melanotis*, South Africa, left) and Sharpe's (*R. m. sharpei*, East Africa); distinguished from more slender Steenbok by light underparts; rams have short horns

Oribi Ourebia ourebi

🏵 open grassland

◐ diurnal

🐾 territorial harems consisting of male and one to four females

✓ localized small antelope, but not hard to see where common; only males have horns; the Oribi is distinguished from the smaller Grysbok and Steenbok by a black tail and dark skin patch below the eye

Steenbok Raphicerus campestris

🏵 dry savannah

◐ nocturnal and diurnal

🐾 solitary or (less often) in pairs

✓ widespread small antelope, particularly in Southern Africa, but shy; only males have horns

Klipspringer Oreotragus oreotragus

🏵 rocky country; cliffs and kopjes

◐ diurnal

🐾 territorial ram with mate or small family group; often restricted to small long-term territories

✓ small antelope; horns normally only on male; extremely agile on rocky terrain; unusually high hooves, giving the impression of walking on tiptoe

🏵 HABITAT   ◐ DAILY RHYTHM   🐾 SOCIAL LIFE   ✓ SIGHTING TIPS

contents

Using the Rough Guide

We've tried to make this Rough Guide a good read and easy to use. The book is divided into five main sections, and you should be able to find whatever you want in one of them.

colour section

The front colour section offers a quick tour of South Africa, Lesotho and Swaziland. The **introduction** aims to give you a feel for the place, with suggestions on where to go. We also tell you what the weather is like and include a basic country fact file. Next, our authors round up their favourite aspects of the region in the **things not to miss** section – whether it's great food, activities or amazing sights. Right after this comes a full **contents** list.

basics

The Basics section covers all the **pre-departure** nitty-gritty to help you plan your trip. This is where to find out which airlines fly to your destination, what paperwork you'll need, what to do about money and insurance, about internet access, food, security, public transport, car rental – in fact just about every piece of **general practical information** you might need.

guide

This is the heart of the Rough Guide, divided into user-friendly chapters, each of which covers a specific region. Every chapter starts with a list of **highlights** and an **introduction** that helps you to decide where to go, depending on your time and budget. Likewise, introductions to the various towns and smaller regions within each chapter should help you plan your itinerary. We start most town accounts with information on arrival and accommodation, followed by a tour of the sights, and finally reviews of places to eat and drink, and details of nightlife. Longer accounts also have a directory of practical listings. Each chapter concludes with **public transport** details for that region.

contexts

Read Contexts to get a deeper understanding of what makes South Africa tick. We include a brief history, sections on wildlife, literature, South African writers, books and music.

language

The **language** section gives useful guidance for getting by in South Africa and pulls together all the vocabulary you might need on your trip. Here you'll also find a glossary of words and terms peculiar to the country.

index + small print

Apart from a **full index**, which includes maps as well as places, this section covers publishing information, credits and acknowledgements, and also has our contact details in case you want to send in updates and corrections to the book – or suggestions as to how we might improve it.

Map and chapter list

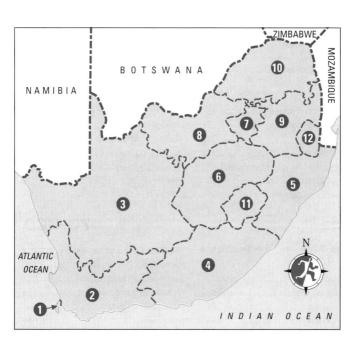

contents

contexts

821–908

language

909–916

index

917–931

map symbols

maps are listed in the full index using coloured text

Regional Maps

▪▫▪▫	International border	♛	Castle
▪▪▫▪▪	Province border	▣	Restaurant
▬ ▬ ▬	Chapter division boundary	◉	Accommodation
N1	National road	⚊	Campsite
R62	Regional road	⬠	Rest camp
M5	Metropolitan road	⊼	Picnic site
═══	Minor road	⚑	Museum
───	Untarred road	⚘	Public gardens
-----	Path		National park/nature reserve
▬▬▬	Railway		Beach
───	Waterway		
───	Wall		

Town Maps

♦	Border crossing post	▬▬▬	Pedestrianized roads
✈	Airport	⊞	Hospital
♦	Point of interest	⊛	Swimming pool
▲	Mountain peak	⚑	Golf course
⌃⌃	Mountain range	ⓘ	Information centre
⊻	Marshland	✉	Post office
⧈	Waterfall	★	Public transport stop
⚘	Viewpoint	✡	Synagogue
◗	Cave	☪	Mosque
✂	Battlefield	▬	Building
⚜	Vineyard	⊞	Church
▶	Hide	⬭	Stadium
∴	Ruins	⊞	Cemetery
⚲	Lighthouse		Park
▥	Monument		

basics

basics

Getting there

Most people travel to South Africa by air, and prices are kept competitive by the large number of scheduled flights aimed at both the holiday and business markets. A direct flight from the UK or North America makes the twelve-hour-plus journey a little more bearable, but there are cheaper flights via mainland Europe or Africa that involve a change of plane. Those not flying in normally arrive in South Africa at the end of an overland trip, often in a converted truck and often having started from East Africa.

Airfares depend on the **season**, with the highest prices and greatest demand occurring in the few weeks before Christmas. Prices remain high in the summer holiday season through January, February, and March; fares drop during the "shoulder" season from April to mid-July, but pick up again between late July and October, while you'll get the best prices during the low season in November and early December.

You can often cut costs by going through a **specialist flight agent** – either a consolidator, who buys up blocks of tickets from the airlines and sells them at a discount, or a **discount agent**, who in addition to dealing with discounted flights may also offer special student and youth fares and a range of other travel-related services such as travel insurance, rail passes, car rentals and tours. Some agents specialize in **charter flights**, which may be cheaper than scheduled flights, but departure dates are fixed and cancellation penalties are high.

A further possibility is to arrange a **courier flight**: in return for shepherding a parcel through customs, you get a heavily discounted ticket. However, you'll need a flexible schedule, and preferably be travelling alone with very little luggage, and there'll probably also be restrictions on the duration of your stay.

If South Africa is only one stop on a longer journey, it's worth considering a **round-the-world (RTW) ticket**. Some travel agents can sell you an "off-the-shelf" RTW ticket that will have you touching down in about half a dozen cities (Johannesburg is on many itineraries); others will have to assemble one for

you, which can be tailored to your needs but is likely to be more expensive. Expect to pay around $1800/£1200 for a RTW ticket including South Africa.

Booking online

Many airlines and discount travel websites offer you the opportunity to book your tickets online, cutting out the costs of agents and middlemen. Good deals can often be found through discount or auction sites, as well as through the airlines' own websites.

Online booking agents and general travel sites

ⓦ **www.cheapflights.com** Flight deals, travel agents, plus links to other travel sites.

ⓦ **www.cheaptickets.com** Discount flight specialists.

ⓦ **www.deckchair.com** Bob Geldof's online venture, drawing on a wide range of airlines.

ⓦ **www.etn.nl/discount.htm** A hub of consolidator and discount agent web links, maintained by the nonprofit European Travel Network.

ⓦ **www.expedia.com** Discount airfares, all-airline search engine and daily deals.

ⓦ **www.flyaow.com** Online air travel info and reservations site.

ⓦ **www.gaytravel.com** Gay online travel agent, concentrating mostly on accommodation.

ⓦ **www.hotwire.com** Bookings from the US only. Last-minute savings of up to forty percent on regular published fares. Travellers must be at least 18, and no refunds, transfers or changes are allowed. Log-in required.

ⓦ **www.innerafrica.co.za** InnerAfrica Holistic Holidays; specialist programmes run by Rough Guide author Barbara McCrea that include bodywork holidays in Cape Town and trips to the Cederberg mountains to learn about the ancient shamanic rock art of the Bushman. Also handpicked packages that include riding trails through Wild Coast villages and specialized safaris. From £685 for ten days excluding flights.

ⓦ **www.lastminute.com** Offers good last-minute holiday package and flight-only deals.

ⓦ **www.priceline.com** Bookings from the US only. A name-your-own-price website that has deals at around forty percent off standard fares. You cannot specify flight times (although you do specify dates) and the tickets are non-refundable, non-transferable and non-changeable.

ⓦ **www.princeton.edu/Main/air800.html** Has an extensive list of airline toll-free numbers and websites.

ⓦ **www.skyauction.com** Bookings from the US only. Auctions tickets and travel packages using a "second bid" scheme. The best strategy is to bid the maximum you're willing to pay, since if you win you'll pay just enough to beat the runner-up regardless of your maximum bid.

ⓦ **www.smilinjack.com/airlines.htm** An up-to-date compilation of airline website addresses.

ⓦ **http://travel.yahoo.com** Incorporates a lot of Rough Guide material in its coverage of destination countries and cities across the world, with information about places to eat and sleep etc.

ⓦ **www.travelocity.com** Destination guides, hot web fares and best deals for car rental, accommodation and lodging as well as fares. Provides access to the travel agent system SABRE, the most comprehensive central reservations system in the US.

ⓦ **www.travelshop.com.au** An Australian website offering discounted flights, packages, insurance, online bookings.

ⓦ **www.uniquetravel.com.au** Another Australian site with a good range of packages and good value flights.

Flights from the UK and Ireland

From London there are direct flights with British Airways and South African Airways (SAA) to Johannesburg, Cape Town and Durban, with prices starting around £650 for a return trip. Cheaper fares, rarely under £450 return, are available on charter flights and on European and African carriers, invariably involving changes of plane.

Airlines

Air France ☎0845/0845 111, in Republic of Ireland ☎01/605 0383, ⓦwww.airfrance.co.uk. Flights from or via Paris.

Air Namibia ☎020/8944 6181, ⓦwww.airnamibia .com. Often good-value flights to Windhoek, with connections from there to Cape Town and Johannesburg.

Britannia Airways ☎01582/424155, ⓦwww.britanniaairways.com. Charter flights to South Africa.

British Airways ☎0845/773 3377, in Republic of Ireland ☎0141/2222345, ⓦwww.britishairways .com. Direct overnight flights from London to Johannesburg and Cape Town.

Egyptair ☎020/7734 2395, ⓦwww.epyptair .com.eg.

Emirates Airlines ☎0870/243 2222, ⓦwww.emirates.com. Busy if indirect route from Europe via Dubai to Johannesburg.

Ethiopian Airlines ☎020/8987 7000, ⓦwww.flyethiopian.com.

Iberia Airlines ☎020/7830 0011, in Republic of Ireland ☎01/677 9846, ⓦwww.iberia.com.

Kenya Airways ☎01784/888222, ⓦwww.kenya-airways.com.

KLM ☎08705/074 074, in Northern Ireland ☎0990/074074, in Republic of Ireland ☎0345/445588, ⓦwww.klmuk.com. Direct flights from Amsterdam hub.

Lufthansa ☎0845/773 7747, in Republic of Ireland ☎01/844 5544, ⓦwww.lufthansa.com.

Olympic Airways ☎0870/606 0460, in Republic of Ireland ☎01/608 0090, ⓦwww.olympic -airways.co.uk.

South African Airways ☎020/7312 5000, ⓦwww.saa.co.za. Non-stop from Johannesburg and Cape Town to principal European airports.

Virgin Atlantic Airways ☎01293/747747, in Republic of Ireland ☎01/873 3388, ⓦwww.virgin-atlantic.com. London to Johannesburg and Cape Town non-stop.

Courier flights

Ben's Travel ☎020/7462 0022, ⓦwww.benstravel.co.uk.

International Association of Air Travel Couriers ☎0800/0746 481 or 01305/216 920, ⓦwww.aircourier.co.uk. Agent for many companies.

Flight and travel agents

Apex Travel Dublin ☎01/671 5933, ⓦwww.apextravel.ie.

Aran Travel International Galway ☎091/562595, ⓕ564581, ⓦwww.iol.ie/~aran/aranmain.htm.

Bridge the World ☎020/7911 0900, ⓦwww.bridgetheworld.com. Specializing in round-the-world tickets, with good deals aimed at the backpacker market.

CIE Tours International Dublin ☎ 01/703 1888, 🌐 www.cietours.ie.

Co-op Travel Care Belfast ☎ 028/9047 1717, ℻ 028/9047 1339.

Destination Group ☎ 020/7400 7000, 🌐 www.destination-group.com.

Flightbookers ☎ 020/7757 2444, 🌐 www.ebookers .com. Low fares on an extensive selection of scheduled flights.

Flynow ☎ 020/7835 2000, 🌐 www.flynow.com. Large range of discounted tickets; the official South African Airways agent.

Joe Walsh Tours Dublin ☎ 01/872 2555 or ☎ 01/676 3053, Cork ☎ 021/277959, 🌐 www .joewalshtours.ie. General budget fares agent.

Lee Travel Cork ☎ 021/277111, 🌐 www.leetravel.ie. Flights and holidays worldwide.

Liffey Travel Dublin ☎ 01/878 8322 or 878 8063. Package tour specialists.

The London Flight Centre ☎ 020/7244 6411, 🌐 www.topdecktravel.co.uk. A long-established agent dealing in discount flights.

McCarthy's Travel Cork ☎ 021/270127, 🌐 www.mccarthystravel.ie. A general flight agent.

North South Travel ☎ & ℻ 01245/608291, 🌐 www.northsouthtravel.co.uk. A friendly, competitive travel agency, offering discounted fares worldwide – the profits are used to support projects in the developing world, especially the promotion of sustainable tourism.

Premier Travel Derry ☎ 028/7126 3333, 🌐 www .premiertravel.uk.com. Discount flight specialists.

Quest Worldwide ☎ 020/8547 3322, 🌐 www .questtravel.com. Specialists in round-the-world and discount fares.

Rosetta Travel Belfast ☎ 028/9064 4996, 🌐 www .rosettatravel.com. Flight and holiday agent.

STA Travel ☎ 0870/160 6070, 🌐 www.statravel .co.uk. Worldwide specialists in low-cost flights and tours for students and under-26s, although other customers are welcome.

Trailfinders ☎ 020/7628 7628, in Republic of Ireland ☎ 01/677 7888, 🌐 www.trailfinders.com. One of the best-informed and most efficient agents for independent travellers, also producing a very useful quarterly magazine worth scrutinizing for round-the-world routes.

Travel Bag ☎ 0870/900 1350, 🌐 www.travelbag .co.uk. Discount flights worldwide.

Travel Cuts ☎ 020/7255 2082, 🌐 www.travelcuts .co.uk. A Canadian company specializing in budget, student and youth travel and round-the-world tickets.

Tour operators

Abercrombie and Kent ☎ 020/7730 9600, 🌐 www.abercrombiekent.com. Large upmarket

operator with comprehensive and professional programmes in southern Africa.

Africa Travel Centre ☎ 020/7387 1211, 🌐 www.africatravel.co.uk. Experienced and knowledgeable Africa specialists with a variety of tailor-made itineraries. Agents for many South Africa-based overland operators.

Bales Worldwide ☎ 0870/241 3208, tailor-mades ☎ 0870/241 3212, 🌐 www.balesworldwide .com. Family-owned company offering high-quality escorted tours to Africa, as well as tailor-made itineraries.

British Airways Holidays ☎ 0870/242 4245, 🌐 www.baholidays.co.uk. Offers an exhaustive range of package and tailor-made holidays, using British Airways and other quality international airlines.

Discover the World ☎ 01737/218800, 🌐 www.artic-discover.co.uk. A well-established wildlife holiday specialist, with groups led by naturalists. Fly-drives available.

Exodus ☎ 020/8675 5550, 🌐 www .thisamazingplanet.com. Adventure tour operators taking small groups for specialist programmes including walking, biking, overland, adventure and cultural trips.

Explore Worldwide ☎ 01252/760000, 🌐 www.explore.co.uk. Big range of small-group tours, treks, expeditions and safaris, staying mostly in small local hotels.

Hayes & Jarvis ☎ 0870/898 9890, 🌐 www.hayes-jarvis.com. Offers a wide variety of trips, including exotic weddings.

In the Saddle ☎ 01256/851665, 🌐 www.inthesaddle.com. Specializes in horse-riding safaris and expeditions across southern Africa.

Kuoni Travel ☎ 01306/742888, 🌐 www.kuoni.co.uk. Flexible package holidays including good family offers.

Nomad ☎ 01243/373929, 🌐 www .nomadafricantravel.co.uk. Guided tours in southern Africa for small groups as well as tailor-made tours, safaris and special interest holidays.

Okavango Tours and Safaris ☎ 020/8343 3283, 🌐 www.okavango.com. Old hands with on-the-ground knowledge of sub-Saharan Africa, offering fully flexible and individual tours across South Africa.

Rainbow Tours ☎ 020/7226 1004, 🌐 www .rainbowtours.co.uk. Very knowledgeable and sensitive South African specialists with trips emphasizing good-value guesthouses, game lodges and independent hotels, as well as eco-friendly and community-based tourism.

Safari Consultants ☎ 01787/228494, 🌐 www.safari-consultants.co.uk. Individually tailored and fairly upmarket holidays across southern Africa, with particular expertise in activity-based holidays, including walking safaris.

Sunvil Africa ☎020/8232 9777, ⦿www.sunvil
.co.uk. Specialists in good-quality
accommodation/flight deals.

Thomas Cook Holidays ☎01733/563200,
⦿www.thomascook.com. Range of flight and board
deals including fly-drive packages.

Tribes ☎01728/685971, ⦿www.tribes.co.uk.
Describing itself as "Fair Trade Travel", this company
offers unusual and off-the-beaten track safaris and
cultural tours in South Africa and Lesotho.

Twohigs Dublin ☎01/677 2666 or 01/670 9750,
⦿www.twohigs.ie. Ireland's largest long haul
specialist.

Wildlife Worldwide ☎020/8667 9158,
⦿www.wildlifeworldwide.com. Tailor-made trips for
wildlife and wilderness enthusiasts with a special
focus on Africa.

World Expeditions ☎020/8870 2600,
⦿www.worldexpeditions.co.uk. Australian-owned
adventure company. All expeditions are graded by
difficulty, from rugged adventure to itineraries tailored
to the over-50s; brochures available.

World Travel Centre Dublin ☎01/671 7155.
Centrally located travel agent specializing in long
haul flights and packages.

Worldwide Journeys and Expeditions
☎020/7386 4646. Imaginative and knowledgeable
tailor-made travel programmes by a company that
will steer you to the smaller, better-value options.

Flights from the USA and Canada

There are a handful of direct flights operated
by South African Airways (SAA) in partnership with American Airlines from New York
and Atlanta to South Africa, taking around
fifteen hours. Most other flights stop off in
Europe and involve a change of plane –
check the waiting time between connecting
flights to avoid a long layover. From Canada
you don't have much of a choice, with daily
services from Toronto or Vancouver to
Johannesburg operated by British Airways
via London, and KLM/Northwest via
Amsterdam.

Airlines

Air France ☎1-800/237-2747, in Canada ☎1-
800/667-2747, ⦿www.airfrance.com.

Air Zimbabwe ☎1-800/742-3006,
⦿www.airzimbabwe.com.

American Airlines ☎1-800/433-7300,
⦿www.aa.com.

British Airways ☎1-800/247-9297,
⦿www.british-airways.com.

Delta Air Lines domestic ☎1-800/221-1212,
international ☎1-800/241-4141, ⦿www.delta.com.

Emirates Air ☎1-800/777-3999, ⦿www.ekgroup
.com.

Iberia ☎1-800/772-4642, ⦿www.iberia.com.

KLM/Northwest US domestic ☎1-800/225-
2525, international ☎1-800/447-4747, in Canada
☎514/397-0775, ⦿www.klm.com.

Lufthansa ☎1-800/645-3880, in Canada ☎ 1-
800/563-5954, ⦿www.lufthansa-ca.com.

Northwest/KLM Airlines domestic ☎1-
800/225-2525, international ☎1-800/447-4747,
⦿www.nwa.com.

Olympic Airways ☎1-800/223-1226 or
212/735-0200, ⦿www.olympic-airways.gr.

South African Airways ☎1-800/722-9675,
⦿www.flysaa.com.

United Airlines domestic ☎1-800/241-6522,
international ☎1-800/538-2929, ⦿www.ual.com.

Virgin Atlantic Airways ☎1-800/862-8621,
⦿www.virgin-atlantic.com.

Courier flights

Air Courier Association ☎1-800/282-1202,
⦿www.aircourier.org. Courier flight broker.
Membership (1 year $49, 3 years $98) also entitles
you to twenty-percent discount on travel insurance
and name-your-own-price non-courier flights.

International Association of Air Travel
Couriers ☎561/582-8320, ⦿www.courier.org.
Courier flight broker with membership fee of $45 a
year.

Now Voyager ☎212/431-1616, ⦿www
.nowvoyagertravel.com. Courier flight broker and
consolidator.

Discount travel companies

Air Brokers International ☎1-800/883-3273 or
415/397-1383, ⦿www.airbrokers.com.
Consolidator and specialist in RTW and Circle Pacific
tickets.

Airtech ☎212/219-7000, ⦿www.airtech.com.
Standby seat broker, also dealing in consolidator
fares and courier flights.

Council Travel ☎1-800/226-8624 or ☎617/528-
2091, ⦿www.counciltravel.com. Nationwide
organization dealing largely – but not exclusively – in
student/budget travel.

Educational Travel Center ☎1-800/747-5551
or 608/256 5551, ⦿www.edtrav.com.
Student/youth discount agent.

High Adventure Travel ☎1-800/350-0612 or
415/912-5600, ⦿www.airtreks.com. The website
features an interactive database that lets you build
and price your own RTW itinerary.

Skylink US ☎1-800/AIR-ONLY or 212/573-8980, Canada ☎1-800/SKY-LINK. Consolidator.
STA Travel ☎1-800/777-0112 or 1-800/781-4040, ⊛www.sta-travel.com. Worldwide specialists in independent travel; also student IDs, travel insurance, car rental and rail passes.
TFI Tours International ☎1-800/745-8000 or 212/736-1140. Consolidator.
Travac ☎1-800/872-8800, ⊛www.thetravelsite.com. Consolidator and charter broker, with another office in Orlando.
Travel Avenue ☎1-800/333-3335, ⊛www.travelavenue.com. Full-service travel agent offering discounts in the form of rebates.
Travel Cuts in Canada ☎1-800/667-2887, in US ☎416/979-2406. Canadian student-travel organization.
Travelers Advantage Cendant Membership Services, Inc ☎1-877/259-2691, ⊛www.travelersadvantage.com. Discount travel club; annual membership fee required (currently $1 for three months' trial).
Worldtek Travel ☎1/800-243-1723, ⊛www.worldtek.com. Discount travel agency for worldwide travel.
Worldwide Discount Travel Club ☎305/534-2642. Discount travel club.

Tour operators

Abercrombie & Kent ☎1-800/323-7308 or 630/954-2944, ⊛www.abercrombiekent.com. Leading upscale operator with over thirty years of experience organizing African safaris.
Adventure Center ☎1-800/228-8747 or 510/654-1879, ⊛www.adventure-center.com. Wide variety of affordable South African packages including hiking and "soft adventure" options.
Adventures Abroad ☎1-800/665-3998 or 604/303-1099, ⊛www.adventures-abroad.com. Canada-based company offering small group and activity tours to South Africa and the neighbouring regions.
Backroads ☎1-800/462-2848 or 510/527-1555, ⊛www.backroads.com. Cycling, hiking and multi-sport tours.
Big Five Tours and Expeditions ☎1-888/244-3483, ⊛www.bigfive.com. Small group tours to wildlife destinations and other highlights.
Bushtracks ☎1-800/995-8689 or 650/326-8689, ⊛www.bushtracks.com. Upmarket, customized tours particularly good for travellers interested in wildlife photography.
Cox & Kings ☎1-800/999-1758, ⊛www.coxandkingsusa.com. Well-organized holidays including a Classic South Africa tour.

Global Exchange ☎1-800/497-1994, ⊛www.globalexchange.org. "Reality Tours", involving educational trips to non-touristy South Africa, Zimbabwe and elsewhere.
Himalayan Travel ☎1-800/225-2380 or ☎203/743-2349, ⊛www.himalayantravelinc.com. Adventure travel and small group tours.
International Gay & Lesbian Travel Association ☎1-800/448-8550, ⊛www.iglta.org.
Maupintour ☎1-800/255-4266 or ☎913/843-1211, ⊛www.maupintour.com. South African itineraries involving luxury train trips.
Nature Expeditions International ☎1-800/869-0639, ⊛www.naturexp.com. Compact, upmarket tours of South Africa and her neighbours.
Saga Holidays ☎1-877/265-6862, ⊛www.sagaholidays.com. Group and educational travel for senior citizens worldwide.
Vantage Travel ☎1-800/322-6677, ⊛www.vantagetravel.com. Specializes in group travel for senior citizens worldwide
Wilderness Travel ☎1-800/368-2794, ⊛www.wildernesstravel.com. Specialists in worldwide hiking, cultural and wildlife adventures.
Worldwide Adventures/Quest Nature Tours ☎1-800/387-1483, ⊛www.worldwidequest.com. Packages include a nineteen-day mixed-accommodation, hiking/game-viewing/cultural tour.

Flights from Australia and New Zealand

Southern Africa is an undeniably expensive destination for travellers from Australia and New Zealand. Fares are steep, and a ticket to Europe with a stopover in South Africa, or even a round-the-world (RTW) ticket, generally represents better value than a straightforward return. There are flights from the eastern states and Western Australia to Johannesburg and Cape Town, but New Zealanders fly via Sydney. South African Airways (SAA), Qantas, Air New Zealand and British Airways all fly to South Africa; some of the Asian and Middle Eastern airlines tend to be less expensive, but their routings often entail more stopovers.

Airlines

Air Botswana Australia ☎02/9956 6620.
Air Mauritius Australia ☎02/9267 7199, ⊛www.airmauritius.com.
Air Namibia Australia ☎02/9956 6620.
Air New Zealand Australia ☎13/24 76, New Zealand ☎0800/737 000 or 09/357 3000, ⊛www.airnz.com.

Air Zimbabwe Australia ☎02/9285 6822, New Zealand ☎09/309 8094, ⊛www.airzimbabwe.com.
British Airways Australia ☎02/8904 8800, New Zealand ☎09/356 8690, ⊛www.british-airways
.com.
Emirates Australia ☎02/9290 9700 or 1300/303 777, New Zealand ☎09/377 6004, ⊛www.emirates
.com.
Gulf Air Australia ☎02/9244 2199, New Zealand ☎09/308 3366, ⊛www.gulfairco.com.
Philippine Airlines Australia ☎02/9279 2020, ⊛www.philippineair.com.
Qantas Australia ☎13/13 13, New Zealand ☎09/357 8900 or 0800/808 767, ⊛www.qantas
.com.au.
Singapore Airlines Australia ☎13/10 11 or 02/9350 0262, New Zealand ☎09/303 2129 or 0800/808 909, ⊛www.singaporeair.com.
Sri Lanka Airlines Australia ☎02/9244 2234, New Zealand ☎09/308 3353, ⊛www.srilankan.com.
South African Airways Australia ☎02/9223 4402 or 1800/221 699, New Zealand ☎09/379 3708, ⊛www.saa-usa.com.

Travel agents

Anywhere Travel Australia ☎02/9663 0411 or 018/401 014, ℮eanywhere@ozemail.com.au.
Budget Travel New Zealand ☎09/366 0061 or 0800/808 040.
Destinations Unlimited New Zealand ☎09/373 4033.
Flight Centres Australia ☎02/9235 3522 or for nearest branch ☎13/16 00, New Zealand ☎09/358 4310, ⊛www.flightcentre.com.au.
Northern Gateway Australia ☎08/8941 1394, ℮oztravel@norgate.com.au.
STA Travel Australia ☎13/17 76 or 1300/360 960, New Zealand ☎09/309 0458 or 09/366 6673, ⊛www.statravel.com.au.
Student Uni Travel Australia ☎02/9232 8444, ℮Australia@backpackers.net.
Thomas Cook Australia ☎13/17 71 or 1800/801 002, New Zealand ☎09/379 3920, ⊛www.thomascook.com.au.
Trailfinders Australia ☎02/9247 7666.

Specialist agents

Adventure Specialists Australia ☎02/9261 2927. Overland and adventure tour agent.
Adventure World Australia ☎02/9956 7766 or 1300/363 055, New Zealand ☎09/524 5118, ⊛www.adventureworld.com.au. Agents for a vast array of international adventure travel companies that operate trips to every continent.

Africa Bound Holidays Australia ☎08/9361 2047, ℮africabound@citysearch.com.au. Travel consultant covering the whole of Africa.
Africa Travel Centre Australia ☎02/9249 5444 or 1800/000 447, New Zealand ☎09/520 2000, ⊛www.travel.com.au. Safaris, flights, transport and accommodation in Africa.
Birding Worldwide Australia ☎03/9899 9303, ⊛www.birdingworldwide.com.au. Organizes group trips around the globe for those wanting to glimpse typical, unique and rare species.
IT Adventures Australia ☎1800/804 277, ℮don@kumuku.co.uk. Agents for Kumuku, offering extended overland camping/hostelling expeditions worldwide, though specializing in South America.
Sydney International Travel Centre ☎02/9299 8000, ⊛www.sydneytravel.com.au. Flights, accommodation, city stays and car rental.

Tour operators

Abercrombie and Kent Australia ☎03/9699 9766 or 1800/331 429, New Zealand ☎09/579 3369, ⊛www.abercrombiekent.com. Upmarket tours of southern and eastern Africa.
The Adventure Travel Company New Zealand ☎09/379 9755, ℮advakl@hot.co.nz. NZ agent for Peregrine (see below).
African Wildlife Safaris Australia ☎03/9696 2899 or 1300/363 302, ℮office@africasafari.com
.au. Specialists in upmarket camping and lodge-based safaris to southern Africa.
Classic Safari Company Australia ☎1300/130 218, ⊛www.classicsafaricompany.com.au. Luxury, individually tailored safaris.
Peregrine Adventures Australia ☎03/9662 2700 or 1300/655 433, New Zealand see Adventure Travel Company, ⊛www.peregrine.net.au. Adventure tours.

Overland from neighbouring countries

Several overland operators run trans-Africa routes starting in Britain, Europe or Nairobi and working their way down to Cape Town. The most popular option is from Nairobi to Cape Town via Mount Kilimanjaro, Victoria Falls and Namibia – for an eight-week trip expect to pay around £1500, though shorter trips are available, some starting in Harare and taking in Zimbabwe, Botswana and Namibia before reaching South Africa.

Overland operators in the UK

Absolute Africa ☎020/8742 0226, ⊛www
.absoluteafrica.com. Adventure camping overland

trips including ten-week epics from Nairobi to Cape Town.

Acacia Expeditions ☎020/7706 4700, ⓦwww .acacia-africa.com. Camping-based trips along classic South African routes, with some trips including Swaziland, Mozambique and Namibia.

Dragoman ☎01728/861133, ⓦwww.dragoman .co.uk. Extended overland journeys in purpose-built expedition vehicles through Africa; also shorter camping and hotel-based safaris.

Drive Africa ☎020/8675 3974, ⓦwww.driveafrica .com. Guided and self-drive safaris in fully equipped 4WD vehicles.

Guerba Expeditions ☎01373/858956, ⓦwww.guerba.co.uk. Range of trans-African overland routes including a nineteen-day Discover South Africa package.

Kumuka Expeditions ☎020/7937 8855, ⓦwww .kumuka.co.uk. Seven-week journeys from Nairobi to Cape Town, and three-week trips from Victoria Falls to Cape Town, plus short tours around South Africa using local operators.

Oasis Overland ☎01258/471155, ⓦwww .oasisoverland.co.uk. One of the smaller overland companies, often running budget trips.

Phoenix Expeditions ☎01509/881818, ⓦwww .phoenixexpeditions.co.uk. Linking Africa to the Middle East, including a twenty-week Istanbul to Cape Town adventure.

Truck Africa ☎020/7731 6142, ⓦwww .truckafrica.com. Specialist in huge Pan-African overland expeditions, lasting as long as seven months.

Getting to South Africa by sea

It's possible to find a berth on cargo ships sailing between Europe or North America and South Africa, taking an average of one to three weeks, depending on itinerary. The unique Royal Mail Ship St Helena is half-cruise ship, half-container ship, and calls in at the remote mid-Atlantic island of St Helena, which has no airport.

The Cruise People ☎020/7723 2450, ⓦwww .cruisepeople.co.uk. Well informed about cruising berths available on freighters and banana boats, many of which stop in South Africa.

Maris Freighter Cruises Westport, CT, USA ☎1-203/222-1500 or 1-800/99-Maris, ⓦwww .freightercruises.com. An agent for worldwide trips aboard cargo ships.

Royal Mail Ship St Helena ☎01326/211466, ⓦwww.rms-st-helena.com. Comfortable cruises on the British Merchant Navy's last remaining Royal Mail ship, which plies a regular route between Britain, the Azores, St Helena and Cape Town. Yearly expedition to remote Tristan da Cunha.

Safmarine ☎023/8033 4415, ⓦwww.safmarine .co.uk. A busy South African freighter line well adapted to carrying passengers.

Visas and red tape

No visa is required by EU nationals, as well as those of the USA, Canada, Australia and New Zealand, to enter South Africa. As long as you carry a valid passport you will be granted a temporary visitors permit, which allows you to stay for up to three months in South Africa. All visitors should have a valid return ticket; without one, you may be required to deposit the equivalent of your fare home with customs (the money will be refunded to you after you have left the country). Visitors may also need to prove that they have sufficient funds to cover their stay.

Citizens of some African and former Eastern Bloc countries do require a visa to enter South Africa, and this must be purchased in advance, as visas are not issued on arrival. If you come under this category and plan on travelling to Lesotho and Swaziland during your trip, you'll need a multi-entry visa to get back into South Africa. If you don't have one, it will be issued free of charge on return, although this can be time-consuming. For longer stays in South Africa, applications for **extensions** to temporary residence permits must be made at one of the main offices of the Department of Home Affairs, where you will be quizzed about your intentions and your funds. In Cape Town, go to 56 Barrack St (℡021 462 4970); in Johannesburg, the office is at the corner of Plein and Harrison streets (℡011 836 3228); they also have offices in a number of towns – check in the telephone directory, and make sure that they are able to grant extensions.

Very few citizens need a **visa** to enter **Swaziland** – and those that do will be issued with one free of charge at the border. Visa requirements for **Lesotho** change from time to time, but the citizens of Commonwealth countries, most EU nations, the USA and Canada, are very unlikely to need a visa and should have no problem entering. For extended stays beyond the standard fourteen days granted at the border, contact the Department of Immigration and Passport Services, Kingsway, Maseru (℡31 7339) or the Lesotho High Commission in Pretoria (see p.637). Note that a brief visit to either Swaziland or Lesotho is not a reliable way of obtaining a new three-month temporary residence permit in South Africa – immigration officials will often only grant a limited stay on re-entry.

South African diplomatic missions abroad

Australia Rhodes Place, Yarralumla, Canberra, ACT 2600 ℡02/6273 2424, ✉www.rsa.emb.gov.au.
Botswana Plot 5131, Kopanyo House, Nelson Mandela Drive, Gaborone ℡304800.
Canada High Commission, 15 Sussex Drive, Ottawa, ON K1M 1M8 ℡613/744-0330, ✉www.docuweb.ca/SouthAfrica; Consulate General, Suite 2615, 1 Place Ville Marie, Montreal, Quebec H3B 4S3 ℡514/878-9217.
Ireland 2nd floor, Alexandra House, Earlssort Terrace, Dublin 2 ℡01/661 5553.

Malawi British High Commission Building, Convention Drive, Capital Hill, Lilongwe ℡783722.
Mozambique Avenue Eduardo Mondlane 41, Maputo ℡01/491614.
Namibia RSA House, corner of Jan Jonker and Nelson Mandela avenues, Windhoek ℡061/205 7111.
New Zealand No representative.
UK South Africa House, Trafalgar Square, London WC2N 5DP ℡020/7930 4488, ✉www.southafricahouse.com; Consular Section, 15 Whitehall ℡020/7925 8910.
USA Embassy, 3051 Massachusetts Ave NW, Washington, DC ℡202/232-4400, ✉usaembassy .southafrica.net; Consulates: 333 E38th St, 9th floor, New York, NY 10016 ℡212/213-5583, ✉www.southafrica-newyork.net; 200 South Michigan Ave, 6th floor, Chicago, IL 60604 ℡312/939-7929; 6300 Wilshire Boulevard, Los Angeles, CA 90048 ℡323/651-0902.
Zimbabwe 7 Elcombe St, Belgravia, Harare ℡04/753147.

Kingdom of Lesotho diplomatic missions abroad

South Africa 1 T. Edison St, Menlo Park, Pretoria ℡012 460 7648.
UK 7 Chesham Place, Belgravia, London SW1 8HN ℡020/7235 5686.
USA 2511 Massachusetts Ave NW, Washington DC 20008 ℡202/797-5533.

Kingdom of Swaziland diplomatic missions abroad

Canada 130 Albert St, Ottawa, Ontario ON K1P 5G4 ℡613 567-1480.
South Africa 715 Government Ave, Arcadia, Pretoria ℡012 344 1910.
UK 20 Buckingham Gate, London SW1E 6LB ℡020/7630 6611.
USA 3400 International Drive, Washington DC 20008 ℡202/362-6683.

Health

You can put aside most of the health fears that may be justified in some parts of Africa; run-down hospitals and bizarre tropical diseases aren't typical of South Africa. As in the rest of Africa, however, HIV is rampant, but there's little chance of catching it other than through intravenous drug taking or unprotected sex.

There are generally high standards of hygiene and safe **drinking water** in all tourist areas. The only hazard you're likely to encounter, and the one the majority of visitors are most blasé about, is the **sun**, which can cause short- and long-term illness. In some parts of the country there is a risk of **malaria**, and you will need to take precautions (see p.22).

Inoculations

Although no specific **inoculations** are compulsory if you arrive from the West, it's wise to ensure that your **polio** and **tetanus** vaccinations are up to date. A **yellow fever** vaccination certificate is necessary if you've come from a country where the disease is endemic, such as Kenya, Tanzania or tropical South America.

In addition to these, the Hospital for Tropical Diseases in London recommends a course of shots against **typhoid** and a Havrix injection against **hepatitis A**, which is caught from contaminated food or water. This is a worst-case scenario, as you probably won't be travelling in areas where these illnesses pose a serious threat. The cholera vaccination is unpleasant, pretty ineffective and not recommended unless you are going to be working for a period in very deprived areas. In any case, despite their terrible reputation, typhoid fever and cholera are both eminently curable and few, if any, visitors to South Africa ever catch them. Hepatitis B vaccine is essential only for people involved in health work. The disease is spread by the transfer of blood products, usually dirty needles, so most travellers need not worry about it.

If you decide to have an armful of jabs, start organizing them **six weeks** before departure. If you're going to another African country first and need the yellow fever jab, remember that a yellow fever certificate only becomes valid ten days after you've had the shot.

Medical resources for travellers

Websites

ⓦ **www.fitfortravel.scot.nhs.uk** UK NHS website carrying information about travel-related diseases and how to avoid them.

ⓦ **http://health.yahoo.com** Information on specific diseases and conditions, drugs and herbal remedies, as well as advice from health experts.

ⓦ **www.istm.org** The website of the International Society for Travel Medicine, with a full list of clinics specializing in international travel health.

ⓦ **www.travelclinic.co.za** Authoritative website of the SAA Netcare Travel Clinics, which provides health information for onward travel to other African countries, locations of travel clinics in SA, as well as excellent information on malaria in South Africa and the latest news on prophylaxis.

ⓦ **www.tripprep.com** Travel Health Online provides an online-only comprehensive database of necessary vaccinations for most countries, as well as destination and medical service provider information.

In the USA and Canada

Canadian Society for International Health 1 Nicholas St, Suite 1105, Ottawa, ON K1N 7B7 ☏613/241-5785, ⓦwww.csih.org. Distributes a free pamphlet, "Health Information for Canadian Travellers", which contains an extensive list of travel health centres in Canada.

Centers for Disease Control 1600 Clifton Rd NE, Atlanta, GA 30333 ☏1-800/311-3435 or 404/639-3534, ⓕ1-888/232-3299, ⓦwww.cdc.gov. Publishes outbreak warnings, suggested inoculations, precautions and other background information for travellers. Useful website plus International Travellers Hotline on ☏1-877/FYI-TRIP.

International Association for Medical Assistance to Travellers (IAMAT) 417 Center St, Lewiston, NY 14092 ☏716/754-4883, ⓦwww.sentex.net/~iamat and 40 Regal Rd, Guelph, ON N1K 1B5 ☏519/836-0102. A non-profit

19

∎

organization supported by donations, it can provide a list of English-speaking doctors in South Africa, climate charts and leaflets on diseases and inoculations.

International SOS Assistance Eight Neshaminy Interplex Suite 207, Trevose, USA 19053-6956 ☎1-800/523-8930, ⊛www.intsos.com. Members receive pre-trip medical referral info, as well as overseas emergency services designed to complement travel insurance coverage.

Travel Medicine ☎1-800/872-8633, ☏1-413/ 584-6656, ⊛www.travmed.com. Sells first-aid kits, mosquito netting, water filters, reference books and other health-related travel products.

Travellers Medical Center 31 Washington Square West, New York, NY 10011 ☎212/982-1600. Consultation service on immunizations and treatment of diseases for people travelling to developing countries.

In the UK and Ireland

British Airways Travel Clinics 28 regional clinics (call ☎01276/685040 for the nearest, or consult ⊛www.britishairways.com), with several in London (Mon–Fri 9.30am–5.15pm, Sat 10am–4pm), including 156 Regent St, London W1 (☎020/7439 9584, no appointment necessary). There are appointment-only branches at 101 Cheapside, London EC2 (☎020/7606 2977); and at the BA terminal in London's Victoria Station (☎020/7233 6661). All clinics offer vaccinations, tailored advice from an online database and a complete range of travel healthcare products.

Dun Laoghaire Medical Centre 5 Northumberland Ave, Dun Laoghaire, Co. Dublin ☎01/280 4996, ☏280 5603. Advice on medical matters abroad.

Hospital for Tropical Diseases Travel Clinic 2nd floor, Mortimer Market Centre, off Capper Street, London WC1E 6AU ☎020/7388 9600 (Mon–Fri 9am–5pm, by appointment only). A consultation costs £15 which is waived if you have your injections here. A recorded Health Line (☎09061/337 733; 50p per min) gives advice on hygiene and illness prevention as well as listing appropriate immunizations.

Malaria Helpline 24-hour recorded message (☎0891/600 350; 60p per minute).

MASTA (Medical Advisory Service for Travellers Abroad) London School of Hygiene and Tropical Medicine. Operates a pre-recorded 24-hour Travellers' Health Line (☎0906/822 4100, 60p per min; Republic of Ireland ☎01560/147000, 75p per minute), giving written information tailored to your journey by return of post.

Nomad Pharmacy Surgeries 40 Bernard St, London WC1; 3–4 Wellington Terrace, Turnpike Lane, London N8 (Mon–Fri 9.30am–6pm, 020/7833 4114 to book vaccination appointment). Free advice tailored to your travel needs if you go in person, or their telephone helpline is ☎09068/633 414 (60p per minute).

Trailfinders Immunization clinics (no appointments necessary) at 194 Kensington High St, London (Mon–Fri 9am–5pm except Thurs to 6pm, Sat 9.30am–4pm ☎020/7938 3999).

Travel Health Centre Dept of International Health and Tropical Medicine, Royal College of Surgeons in Ireland, Mercers Medical Centre, Stephen's Street Lower, Dublin ☎01/402 2337. Expert pre-trip advice and inoculations.

Travel Medicine Services PO Box 254, 16 College St, Belfast 1 ☎028/9031 5220. Offers medical advice before a trip and help afterwards in the event of a tropical disease.

Tropical Medical Bureau Grafton Buildings, 34 Grafton St, Dublin 2 ☎01/671 9200, ⊛www.iol.ie/-tmb.

In Australia and New Zealand

Travellers' Medical and Vaccination Centres:
27–29 Gilbert Place, Adelaide ☎08/8212 7522.
1/170 Queen St, Auckland ☎09/373 3531.
5/247 Adelaide St, Brisbane ☎07/3221 9066.
5/8–10 Hobart Place, Canberra ☎02/6257 7156.
147 Armagh St, Christchurch ☎03/379 4000.
5 Westralia St, Darwin ☎08/8981 2907.
270 Sandy Bay Rd, Sandy Bay, Hobart ☎03/6223 7577.
2/393 Little Bourke St, Melbourne ☎03/9602 5788.
5 Mill St, Perth ☎08/9321 1977, plus branch in Fremantle.
7/428 George St, Sydney ☎02/9221 7133, plus branches in Chatswood and Parramatta.
Shop 15, Grand Arcade, 14–16 Willis St, Wellington ☎04/473 0991.

Water – and stomach upsets

Stomach upsets from food are rare. Salad and ice – the danger items in many other Third World countries – are only found in hotels and restaurants, and both are perfectly safe. As anywhere, though, don't keep food for too long, be sure to wash fruit and vegetables as thoroughly as possible, and don't overindulge on fruit – no matter how tempting – when you first arrive.

If you do get a **stomach bug**, the best cure is lots of water and rest. Papayas, the flesh as well as the pips, are a good tonic to offset the

Medical kit

Most medicines and medical gear can be bought in pharmacies all over South Africa, so there's no need to lumber yourself with too heavy a **medical kit**. Only in deeply rural areas where few visitors ever go are you likely to be caught short. If you need specialized drugs bring your own supply, but any first-aid items can be easily replaced. A very **basic kit** should include:

❑ **Antibiotics** Potentially useful if you're heading off the beaten track; a broad-spectrum variety is best.

❑ **Antiseptic cream** Bacitracin is a reliable brand, while Nelson's natural calendula ointment is invaluable for stings, rashes, cuts, sores or cracked skin.

❑ **Bandages** One wide and one narrow.

❑ **Eyedrops** Wonderfully soothing if you're travelling on dusty roads.

❑ **Fine tweezers** Useful for removing thorns or glass.

❑ **Insect repellent** Essential in malarial areas (see p.22).

❑ **Paracetamol** For pain and fever relief.

❑ **Sticking plasters**

❑ **Lip salve/chapstick**

runs. Otherwise, most chemists should have name-brand anti-diarrhoea remedies. These – Lomotil, Codeine phosphate, etc. – shouldn't be overused.

Avoid jumping for **antibiotics** at the first sign of illness: keep them as a last resort – they don't work on viruses and annihilate your "gut flora" (most of which you want to keep), making you more susceptible next time round. Most upsets will resolve themselves by adopting a sensible fat-free diet for a couple of days, but if they do persist without improvement (or are accompanied by other unusual symptoms), then see a doctor as soon as possible.

The sun

The **sun** is likely to be the worst hazard you'll encounter in southern Africa, particularly if you're fair-skinned. The danger of overexposure to the sun is something white South Africans haven't yet caught onto, and locals still regard their tans as more important than their health.

The sun in the southern hemisphere is far more intense and transmits far more ultraviolet than it does in the north (even in the sunshine states of the USA). It's wise to limit your exposure to this major cause of **skin cancer**. If on returning home you notice any changes to any mole on your body you should see your doctor, as melanomas can be removed if caught early, but malignant melanomas can prove fatal if ignored.

Short-term effects of **overexposure** to the sun include burning, nausea and headaches. This usually comes from overeager tanning, which can leave you looking like a lobster. The fairer your skin, the slower you should take tanning. Start with short periods of exposure and **high protection suncreen** (at least SPF 15), gradually increasing your time in the sun and decreasing the factor of your screen. Many people with fair skins, especially those who freckle easily, should take extra care, starting with a very high factor screen (SPF 25–30) and continue using at least SPF 15 for the rest of their stay. There's no shame in smearing sensitive areas of your face with total block cream, which contains zinc and has been made fashionable by cricketers and skiers.

Overexposure to the sun can cause sunburn to the surface of the eye, inflammation of the cornea and can result in serious short- and long-term damage. Good **sunglasses** can reduce ultraviolet light exposure to the eye by fifty percent. Look for a pair that absorbs at least 95 percent of UVR (which is invisible to the human eye) as well as UVB. A **broad-brimmed hat** is also recommended.

These last measures are especially necessary for children, who should ideally be kept well covered at the seaside. Don't be lulled into complacency on cloudy days, as this is when UV levels can be especially high. UV-protective clothing is available locally, but it's best to buy before you arrive; some excellent ranges are made in Australia. If you don't come with this gear, make sure children wear T-shirts (preferably a close-weave fabric) at the beach, and use SPF 30 sun screen liberally and often.

AIDS and sexually transmitted diseases

Your biggest chance of catching **HIV** in South Africa is through unprotected sex. HIV/AIDS and other venereal diseases are widespread in southern Africa amongst both men and women, and the danger of catching the virus through sexual contact is very real. Follow the usual precautions regarding safer sex: abstain – or at the very least use a condom. There's no special risk from medical treatment in the country, but if you're travelling overland and you want to play it safe, take your own needle and transfusion kit.

Bilharzia

One ailment that you need to take seriously throughout sub-Saharan Africa is **bilharzia**, carried in most of South Africa's fresh waterways except in the mountains. Bilharzia (schistosomiasis) is spread by a tiny, waterborne parasite. These worm-like flukes leave their water-snail hosts and burrow into human skin to multiply in the bloodstream; they then work their way to the walls of the intestine or bladder, where they begin to lay eggs.

Avoid swimming in dams and rivers where possible. If you go canoeing or can't avoid the water, have a test when you return home. White water is no guarantee of safety; although the snails favour sheltered areas, the flukes can be swept downstream. The chances are you'll avoid bilharzia even if you swam in a suspect river, but it's best to be sure.

Symptoms may be no more than a feeling of lassitude and ill health. Once infection is established, abdominal pain and blood in the urine and stools are common. Fortunately, bilharzia is easily and effectively treated with praziquantel, although the drug can make you feel ill for a few days. No vaccine is available and none foreseen.

Malaria

Most of South Africa is free of **malaria**, a potentially lethal disease that is widespread in tropical and sub-tropical Africa, where it's a major killer. In South Africa there is a risk in **northern and northeastern Mpumalanga**, notably the **Kruger National Park**, as well as **northern KwaZulu-Natal**, in the border regions of **Northwest and Northern provinces**, and in low-lying areas of **Swaziland**. Protection against malaria is essential if you're planning on travelling to these areas.

The **highest risk** is during the hot, rainy months from **November to April**. The risk is reduced during the cooler, dry months from May to October, and some people decide not to take prophylaxis during this period.

Malaria is caused by a parasite carried in the saliva of the female anopheles mosquito. It has a variable incubation period of a few days to several weeks, so you can become ill long after being bitten. The first **symptoms** of malaria can be mistaken for flu, starting off relatively mildly with a variable combination that includes fever, aching limbs and shivering, which come in waves, usually beginning in the early evening. Deterioration can be rapid as the parasites in the bloodstream proliferate: get **medical help** without delay if you go down with flu-like symptoms within a week of entering or three months of leaving a malarial area. Malaria is not infectious, but it can be fatal if not treated quickly.

Prevention

No antimalarial drug is totally effective – your only sure-fire protection is to **avoid getting bitten**. Malaria-carrying mosquitoes are active between dusk and dawn, so try to avoid being out at this time, or at least cover yourself well.

Sleep under a **mosquito net** when possible, making sure to tuck it under the mattress, and burn **mosquito coils** (which you can buy everywhere) for a peaceful, if noxious, night. Whenever the mosquitoes are particularly bad – and that's not often – cover your exposed parts with **insect repellent**; those containing diethyltoluamide (deet) work well. Other locally produced repellents such as Peaceful Sleep are widely available.

Electric mosquito-destroyers which you fit with a pad every night are less pungent than mosquito coils, but require electricity. Mosquito "buzzers" are useless.

Doctors can advise on which kind of **anti-malarial tablets** to take. It's important to keep to the prescribed dose, which covers the period before and after your trip. The reliable SAA Netcare Travel Clinics (📍www.travelclinic.co.za), which constantly monitor malaria and its resistance to drugs in southern Africa, recommends mefloquine (marketed as Mefliam and Larium as well as under other trade names) or Doxycycline as providing the most effective protection against malaria. Mefloquine isn't recommended for anyone with a history of psychiatric problems or epilepsy; psychological effects such as paranoia and psychosis have been reported in some cases. Doxycycline should be avoided in pregnancy and by children. A combination of proguanil and chloriquine can also be taken, but it's more complicated and isn't believed to be as effective as the two drugs mentioned above.

Consult your doctor several weeks before you are due to leave for a malarial area, as you should start taking medication a week or two before entering the affected region. Whatever you decide to take be aware that none of these drugs offers a hundred percent protection and you should also adopt the other methods of protection described above.

Snakes, insects and other undesirables

Bites, stings and rashes in South Africa are comparatively rare. **Snakes** are present, but hardly ever seen as they move out of the way quickly. The sluggish puff and berg adders are the most dangerous, because they often lie in paths and don't move when humans approach – but they're seldom encountered by travellers. The best advice if you get bitten is to remember what the snake looked like and get yourself to a clinic or hospital. Most bites are not fatal and the worst thing is to panic: desperate measures with razor blades and tourniquets risk doing more harm than good.

Tick-bite fever is occasionally contracted from walking in the bush, particularly in long wet grass. The offending ticks can be minute and you may not spot them. Symptoms appear a week later – swollen glands and severe aching of the bones, backache and fever. Since it is a self-limiting disease, it will run its course in three or four days. Ticks you may find on yourself are not dangerous; just repulsive at first. Make sure you pull out the head as well as the body (it's not painful). A good way of removing small ones is to smear Vaseline or grease over them, making them release their hold.

Scorpions and spiders abound, but are hardly ever seen unless you turn over logs and stones. If you're collecting wood for a campfire, knock or shake it before picking it up. Contrary to popular myth, scorpion stings and spider bites are painful but almost never fatal. Most are harmless and should be left alone. A simple precaution when camping is to shake out your shoes and clothes in the morning before you get dressed.

Rabies is present throughout southern Africa. Be wary of strange animals and go immediately to a clinic if bitten. Rabies can be treated effectively with a course of injections.

Hospitals and doctors

Public **hospitals** in South Africa are fairly well equipped, but they are facing huge pressures under which their attempts to maintain standards are unfortunately buckling. Expect long waits and frequently indifferent treatment. Private hospitals or clinics, which are well up to British or North American standards, are usually a better option for travellers. You're likely to get more personal treatment and the costs are nowhere near as high as in the US; besides which, if you're adequately insured these shouldn't pose a problem. Private hospitals are given in the town and city listings throughout the Guide.

Teeth and eyes

Dental care in South Africa is well up to British and North American standards, and is generally no more expensive. You'll find **dentists** in all the cities and most smaller towns, listed after doctors at the beginning of each town in the telephone directory.

You can buy cleaning kit for most types of **contact lenses** in the larger centres.

Insurance

Before visiting South Africa, it's wise to take out an insurance policy to cover against theft, loss and illness or injury. Before paying for a new policy, however, it's worth checking whether you are already covered: some all-risks home insurance policies may cover your possessions when overseas, and many private medical schemes include cover when abroad. In Canada, provincial health plans usually provide partial cover for medical mishaps overseas, while holders of official student/teacher/youth cards in Canada and the US are entitled to meagre accident coverage and hospital in-patient benefits. Students will often find that their student health coverage extends during the vacations and for one term beyond the date of last enrolment.

After exhausting the possibilities above, you might want to contact a specialist travel insurance company, or consider the travel insurance deal offered by Rough Guides (see below). A typical travel insurance policy usually provides cover for the loss of baggage, tickets and – up to a certain limit – cash or cheques, as well as cancellation or curtailment of your journey. Most of them exclude so-called dangerous sports unless an extra premium is paid: in South Africa, this can mean scuba diving, whitewater rafting, windsurfing, horse-riding, bungee jumping and paragliding. In addition to these, it's well worth while checking to see if you are covered by your policy when you are hiking or trekking, kayaking, pony trekking or game viewing on safari, all activities people commonly take part in during a visit to South Africa. Many policies can be amended to exclude coverage you don't need – for example, sickness and accident benefits can often be excluded or included at will.

If you do take medical coverage, ascertain whether benefits will be paid as treatment proceeds or only after return home, and whether there is a 24-hour medical emergency number. When securing baggage cover, make sure that the per-article limit – typically under £500 – will cover your most valuable possession.

If you need to make a claim, you should

Rough Guide travel insurance

Rough Guides offers its own travel insurance, customized for our readers by a leading UK broker and backed by a Lloyds underwriter. It's available for anyone, of any nationality, travelling anywhere in the world.

There are two main Rough Guide insurance plans: **Essential**, for basic, no-frills cover; and **Premier** – with more generous and extensive benefits. Alternatively, you can take out **annual multi-trip insurance**, which covers you for any number of trips throughout the year (with a maximum of 60 days for any one trip). Unlike many policies, the Rough Guides schemes are calculated by the day, so if you're travelling for 27 days rather than a month, that's all you pay for. If you intend to be away for the whole year, the Adventurer policy will cover you for 365 days.

Each policy can be supplemented with a "Hazardous Activities Premium" if you plan to indulge in sports considered dangerous, such as skiing, scuba diving or trekking. Rough Guides also offers good deals for older travellers, and will insure you up to any age, at prices comparable to SAGA's.

For a policy quote, call the Rough Guide Insurance Line on UK freefone ☎0800/015 09 06; US toll free ☎1-866/220 5588, or, if you're calling from elsewhere ☎+44 1243/621 046. Alternatively, get an online quote or purchase a policy at ⊛www.roughguides.com/insurance.

keep receipts for medicines and medical treatment, and in the event you have anything stolen, you must obtain an official statement from the police.

Costs, money and banks

Visitors coming from Europe, North America or Australasia will find South Africa cheap by comparison. With the steady fifteen-percent average annual decline in the rand against sterling and the dollar – and an additional forty percent drop in the rand's value during 2001 – foreign visitors have found that their money goes a lot further here than at home. According to The Economist magazine's Big Mac index, at the end of 2001 one of the burgers cost US$2.89 in Britain, US$2.59 in America and US$0.82 in South Africa, making the rand the most undervalued currency in the world, which is good news for visitors.

What you spend obviously depends on the kind of trip you're planning. If you're prepared to stay in backpacker lodges, travel on public or backpacker transport and eat cheaply, you can get by on under **US$25/£16** a day – less if you're camping. If you stay in B&Bs and guesthouses, and eat out regularly, you should allow for anything between **US$25** and **US$50 (£16–35)** a day. In luxury hotels and game lodges, expect to pay upwards of **US$125/£85** per day. Extras such as car rental, scuba diving, horse-riding and safaris will add to these figures substantially.

You'll almost always find a very good **place to stay** for under US$20/£12 a night, especially if there are two of you. Backpacker lodges currently cost under US$4/£3 per person, and most B&Bs charge less than US$20/£12 per head for a couple. A hotel costing US$40/£25 or more per head should have something special to justify the price, although, in Cape Town particularly, this cannot be guaranteed. Prices tend to be highest over the Christmas and Easter holidays, especially at the coast.

Food and **drink** are both good value. Fresh fish and chips as well as fast food chicken and burgers need not set you back more than US$3/£2. Most **restaurants** cost in the region of US$7/£5 for a very good three-course meal. You'll eat well at the best gourmet restaurants for US$26/£12.

Despite the size of the country, **transport** is inexpensive, especially compared to Europe, Australia and the US. Even using luxury and tourist **bus** services won't set you back much, considering the distances that are usually involved. Expect to pay around US$125/£85 for a domestic **flight** between major centres provided you book two weeks in advance. **Driving** can be a relatively cheap way of getting around if there are two or more of you, and in many parts of the country it's the only realistic option. **Rental cars** usually cost US$25–40 (£15–25) a day. **Fuel**, though rising in price, is still relatively inexpensive at around US40¢/25p a litre.

What you'll pay **on safari** depends very much on whether you stay in government-run national parks, where accommodation in a rondavel can cost as little as US$12/£8 per night. If you prefer to be fully catered for on an upmarket private reserve, you'll find prices are around US$225/£150 a night.

While most **museums** and **art galleries** charge an entry fee, it's usually quite low: only the most sophisticated attractions charge more than US75¢/50p

Currency and exchange

South Africa's currency is the **rand** (R), often called the "buck". Notes come in R10, 20, 50, 100 and 200 denominations and there are coins of 1, 2, 5, 10, 20 and 50 cents, as well as R1, 2 and 5. At the time of writing, the **exchange rate** was hovering around

R17 to the pound sterling, R12 to the US dollar and R6 to the Australian dollar.

All but the tiniest settlement has a **bank** where you can **change money** swiftly and easily. **Banking hours** are Monday to Friday 9am to 3.30pm, and Saturday 9am to 11am; the banks in smaller towns usually close for lunch. In major cities, some banks operate bureaux de change that stay open until 7pm.

Outside banking hours, some hotels will change money, although you can expect to pay a fairly hefty commission. You can also change money at branches of American Express and Rennies Travel.

Traveller's cheques, cash and credit cards

Bank cards, useable at **automatic teller machines** (ATMs) throughout the country, are the most convenient way to carry your funds into South Africa. Visa, Mastercard and most international ATM cards (check with your bank before departing) can be used to withdraw money at ATMs, open 24 hours a day in the cities and elsewhere. Ask your bank which option you should choose for your card when the machine asks for the account type (cheque, savings, transmission or credit). Remember that all cash advances are treated as loans, with interest accruing daily from the date of withdrawal; there may be a transaction fee on top of this. Many debit cards can also be used to make withdrawals from ATMs in South Africa. These are not liable to interest payments, and the flat transaction fee is usually quite small – your bank will be able to advise on this. Make sure you have a personal identification number (PIN) that's designed to work overseas.

Traveller's cheques make a useful backup as they can be replaced if lost or stolen.

American Express, Visa and Thomas Cook are all widely recognized. However, they'll be useless if you're heading into remote areas, where you'll need to carry **cash**, preferably in a very safe place, such as a leather pouch under your waistband. The usual fee for traveller's cheque sales is one or two percent, though this fee may be waived if you buy the cheques through a bank where you have an account. It pays to get a selection of denominations. Make sure you keep the purchase agreement and a record of cheque serial numbers safe and separate from the cheques themselves. In the event that cheques are lost or stolen, the issuing company will expect you to report the loss forthwith to their office in South Africa; most companies claim to replace lost or stolen cheques within 24 hours. Both dollar and sterling cheques are accepted in South Africa.

Credit cards can come in very handy for hotel bookings and for paying for more mainstream and upmarket tourist facilities, and they are essential for car rental. Visa and Mastercard are the cards most widely accepted in major cities, while American Express is less widely accepted. Like traveller's cheques, credit cards won't be accepted in small *dorps* and rural areas such as the Wild Coast and Northern Cape, where you'll need cash for most transactions.

Wiring money

Getting money wired from home using one of the companies listed below is never convenient or cheap, and should be considered a last resort. It's also possible to have money wired directly from a bank in your home country to a bank in South Africa,

---

Visa Travel Money Ⓦwww.visa.com

This is a disposable debit card pre-paid with dedicated travel funds which you can access from over 457,000 Visa ATMs in 120 countries with a PIN that you select yourself. When your funds are depleted, you simply throw the card away. Since you can buy up to nine cards to access the same funds – useful for couples/families travelling together – it's recommended that you buy at least one extra as a back up in case your first is lost or stolen. There is a 24-hour Visa global customer assistance services centre which you can call from any of the 120 countries toll-free. From South Africa and its neighbours you should call Baltimore in the US collect on ☏410 581 9091. In the UK, many Thomas Cook outlets sell the card.

although this is somewhat less reliable because it involves two separate institutions. If you go this route, your home bank will need the address of the branch bank where you want to pick up the money and the address and telex number of the head office, which acts as the clearing house. Money wired this way normally takes two working days to arrive, and costs around £25/$40 per transaction.

Money-wiring companies

In the UK and Ireland

Moneygram ☎0800/018 0104, ⓦwww.moneygram.com.
Western Union Money Transfer ☎0800/833 833, ⓦwww.westernunion.com.
Thomas Cook ☎01733/318922, Belfast ☎028/9055 0030, Dublin ☎01/677 1721.

In North America

American Express Moneygram ☎1-800/926-9400, ⓦwww.moneygram.com.
Western Union ☎1-800/325-6000, ⓦwww.westernunion.com.
Thomas Cook US ☎1-800/287-7362, Canada ☎1-888 /8234-7328, ⓦwww.us.thomascook.com.

In Australia

American Express Moneygram ☎1800/230 100, ⓦwww.moneygram.com.
Western Union ☎1800/649 565, ⓦwww.westernunion.com.

In New Zealand

American Express Moneygram ☎09/379 8243 or 0800/262 263, ⓦwww.moneygram.com.
Western Union ☎09/270 0050, ⓦwww.westernunion.com.

Information, websites and maps

South Africa is experiencing a boom in tourism, and you should have no difficulty finding maps, books and brochures before you leave. South African Tourism (the official organization promoting the country) is reasonably efficient: if there's an office near you, it's worth visiting for their free map and information on hotels and organized tours. Alternatively, you can visit their website (http://southafrica.net) or check out South Africa's growing internet presence for up-to-date travel details, and maps you can print out.

Tourist information in South Africa

Nearly every town in South Africa, even down to the sleepiest *dorp*, has some sort of **tourist information office** – sometimes connected to the museum, municipal offices or library – where you can pick up local maps, lists of B&Bs and travel advice. In larger cities such as Cape Town and Durban, you'll find several branches offering everything from hotel bookings to organized safari trips.

We've given precise **opening hours** of tourist information offices in most cases; they generally adhere to a standard sched-

ule of 8.30am to 5pm, Monday to Friday, with many offices now also open on Saturdays and Sundays. In smaller towns, some close between 1pm and 2pm, while in the bigger centres some have extended hours.

In this fast-changing country, often the best way of finding out what's happening is by word of mouth, and for this **backpacker hostels** are invaluable. If you're planning on seeing South Africa on a budget, rest assured that the useful noticeboards, constant traveller traffic and largely helpful and friendly staff you'll encounter in the hostels will greatly smooth your travels.

South African Tourism offices

Head office Bojanala House, 12 Rivonia Rd, Illovo, Johannesburg ☏ 011 778 8000, @ www.southafricantourism.com.
Australia 6/285 Clarence St, Sydney, NSW 2000 ☏ 02/9261 3424, @ sydney@southafricantourism.com.
UK 5–6 Alt Grove, Wimbledon SW19 4DZ ☏ 020/8971 9350, @ uk.southafricantourism.com.
USA 500 Fifth Ave, Suite 2040, New York, NY 10110 ☏ 0212/730-2929, @ 764-1980, @ us.southafricantourism.com.

South Africa online

The tourism industry is one of the most vibrant adopters of online technology and its range is vast, from individuals posting their B&Bs to byzantine sites with vast numbers of links. Most of the sites listed here provide good information on practicalities and background, while others, such as the Ananzi and *Mail & Guardian* sites, are excellent lead-ins to other South African topics.

Only general websites are listed below. For online accommodation booking services see p.39; for websites for gay travellers see p.66; and you'll find websites relating to what's on and other information specific to a particular city or region listed in the relevant place in the Guide. For a comprehensive selection of the best on the web in Africa, weighted heavily in favour of South African coverage, see the *All-Africa Internet Guide* by Libby Young (M&G Books 2001).

Portals and search engines

Ananzi @ www.ananzi.co.za South Africa's premier search engine also has an easy-to-use directory organized by topic.
Mweb @ www.mweb.co.za The site of one of South Africa's biggest internet service providers offers news and information on a variety of topics including travel.
World Online @ www.worldonline.co.za Another of the large local ISPs is a slick affair, offering news and travel links.

News and current affairs

Daily Mail & Guardian @ www.mg.co.za The daily online presence of the intellectual heavyweight of South Africa's press, the *Mail and Guardian*, with extensive links from its JumpStart page to a vast variety of sites covering local issues.

IOL @ www.iol.co.za Probably the best web-based news service on the South African web is owned by Independent Newspapers, which operates in South Africa, Britain and Ireland.
Madiba's Legacy @ www.mg.co.za/mg /mandela A decent independent site on Mandela and his heritage, run by the *Mail and Guardian* with good links.
News 24 @ news24.co.za Another good source of local and international news.

Arts, culture and what's on

Artzone @ www.artzone.co.za South Africa's self-declared arts, culture and entertainment hub delivers with comprehensive coverage of what's happening in the arts, reviews and a searchable database of what's on.
Computicket @ ww.computicket.com Online booking site for cinema, live events, sport, festivals and bus tickets, with listings of what's on.
Museums online @ www.museums.org.za Hub for all South Africa's major museums provides links to their individual websites and lists institutions by alphabetical order or by region.
Rage @ www.rage.co.za An engine devoted to South African street culture with coverage of nightlife and *kwaito* and information about what's on in Cape Town, Durban and Gauteng.
Thunda @ ww.thunda.com Club culture site aimed at 18–24s, with coverage of Gauteng, Durban and Cape Town.
TicketWeb @ www.ticketweb.co.za The alternative to Computicket for online booking of events, shows and festivals (not bus tickets).
ZA@Play @ www.mg.co.za/mg/art/artmenu .htm Reviews and listings of what's on in Cape Town, Johannesburg, Durban and Pietermaritzburg.

General travel resources

Coast to Coast @ www.coastingafrica.com Website of *Coast to Coast*, the regularly updated backpackers' and budget travellers' guide to southern Africa.
Getaway @ www.getawaytoafrica.com Well-organized online presence of South Africa's biggest travel magazine with a searchable database of places and accommodation.
iAfrica @ www.iafrica.com One of the biggest South African portals has a comprehensive travel section with city and regional guides as well as specialist sections on topics such as surfing, safaris and budget travel.
Lonely Planet Thorn Tree @ thorntree .lonelyplanet.com Recommended and popular travellers' forums, divided into regions (eg Africa) and

topics (Traveling with Kids). A good place to look for travel companions, exchange information with other travellers or start a debate.

Rough Guides ⊛**www.roughguides.com** Interactive site for independent travellers with forums, bulletin boards, travel tips and features, plus online travel guides and special offers such as travel insurance.

South African Weather Bureau ⊛**www .weathersa.co.za** Temperatures and short- and long-term weather forecasts for the whole of South Africa.

Specialist travel topics

Prime Origins ⊛**www.primeorigins.co.za** An outstanding media and tourism initiative aimed at promoting South Africa's substantial prehistoric heritage. It provides excellent coverage of the origins of humanity in the subcontinent and information about the country's rock art sites and how to see them.

South African Astronomical Observatory ⊛**www.saao.ac.za** A good source of information about the southern sky, with a month-by-month guide and information about visiting South Africa's premier observatory at Sutherland in the Northern Cape Karoo.

Wildnet Africa ⊛**www.wildnetafrica.com** A commercial website devoted to coverage of wildlife and safaris in southern Africa, with the facility to find out more about specific destinations, accommodation and safari lodges.

SA regional tourism authorities

Eastern Cape ⊛www.ectourism.co.za.
Free State ⊛www.fstourism.co.za.
Gauteng ⊛www.gauteng.net.
KwaZulu-Natal ⊛www.tourism-kzn.org.
Mpumalanga ⊛www.mpumalanga.com.
North West ⊛www.tourismnorthwest.co.za.
Northern Cape ⊛www.northerncape.org.za.
Northern Province ⊛www.tourismboard.org.za.
Western Cape ⊛www.capetourism.org.

Lesotho and Swaziland tourism authorities

Swaziland ⊛www.mintour.gov.sz.
Lesotho ⊛www.ltb.org.ls.

Maps

Many place names in South Africa were changed after the 1994 elections – and changes are still being made – so if you buy a **map** before leaving home, make sure that it's up to date. Bartholomew produces an excellent map of **South Africa**, including

Lesotho and Swaziland (1:2,000,000), as part of their World Travel Map series. Also worth investing in are MapStudio's "Miniplan" maps of major cities such as Cape Town, Durban and Pretoria: these are a convenient size and have useful details, such as hotels, cinemas, post offices and hospitals. MapStudio also produces good regional maps, featuring scenic routes and street maps of major towns, and a fine Natal Drakensberg map which shows hiking trails, picnic spots, campsites and places of interest.

South Africa's motoring organization, the Automobile Association (AA) offers a wide selection of maps, free to members, which you can pick up from their offices.

Specialist book and map suppliers

USA and Canada

Adventurous Traveler Bookstore PO Box 64769, Burlington, VT 05406 ☎1-800/282-3963, ⊛www.AdventurousTraveler.com.
Book Passage 51 Tamal Vista Blvd, Corte Madera, CA 94925 ☎415/927-0960, ⊛www.bookpassage.com.
Elliot Bay Book Company 101 S Main St, Seattle, WA 98104 ☎206/624-6600 or 1-800/962-5311, ⊛www.elliotbaybook.com.
Forsyth Travel Library 226 Westchester Ave, White Plains, NY 10604 ☎1-800/367-7984, ⊛www.forsyth.com.
Globe Corner Bookstore 28 Church St, Cambridge, MA 02138 ☎1-800/358-6013, ⊛www.globecorner.com.
GORP Adventure Library Online only, ⊛www2.gorp.com.
Map Link Inc. 30 S La Patera Lane, Unit 5, Santa Barbara, CA 93117 ☎805/692-6777, ⊛www.maplink.com.
Phileas Fogg's Travel Center #87 Stanford Shopping Center, Palo Alto, CA 94304 ☎1-800/533-3644, ⊛www.foggs.com.
Rand McNally 444 N Michigan Ave, Chicago, IL 60611 ☎312/321-1751, 150 E 52nd St, New York, NY 10022 ☎212/758-7488; 595 Market St, San Francisco, CA 94105 ☎415/777-3131; around thirty stores across the US – call ☎1-800/333-0136 ext 2111 or check the website for the nearest store: ⊛www.randmcnally.com.
Travel Books & Language Center 4437 Wisconsin Ave, Washington, DC 20016 ☎1-800/220-2665, ⊛www.bookweb.org/bookstore /travellers.

The Travel Bug Bookstore 2667 West Broadway, Vancouver V6K 2G2 ☎604/737-1122, ⊛www.swifty.com/tbug.
World of Maps 118 Holland Ave, Ottawa, Ontario K1Y 0X6 ☎613/724-6776, ⊛www.itmb.com.
World Wide Books and Maps 1247 Granville St, Vancouver V6Z 1G3 ☎604/687-3320, ⊛www.worldofmaps.com.

In the UK and Ireland

Blackwell's Map and Travel Shop 53 Broad St, Oxford OX1 3BQ ☎01865/792792, ⊛www.bookshop.blackwell.co.uk.
Easons Bookshop 40 O'Connell St, Dublin 1 ☎01/873 3811, ⊛www.eason.ie.
Heffers Map and Travel 20 Trinity St, Cambridge CB2 1TJ ☎01223/568568, ⊛www.heffers.co.uk.
Hodges Figgis Bookshop 56–58 Dawson St, Dublin 2 ☎01/677 4754, ⊛www.hodgesfiggis.com.
James Thin Melven's Bookshop 29 Union St, Inverness IV1 1QA ☎01463/233500, ⊛www.jthin.co.uk.
John Smith and Sons (map department), Tiso Outdoor Experience, 50 Couper St, Glasgow G4 0DL ☎0141/552 4394, ⊛www.johnsmith.co.uk.
The Map Shop 30a Belvoir St, Leicester LE1 6QH ☎0116/247 1400.
National Map Centre 22–24 Caxton St, London SW1H 0QU ☎020/7222 2466, ⊛www.mapsnmc.co.uk.

Newcastle Map Centre 55 Grey St, Newcastle upon Tyne, NE1 6EF ☎0191/261 5622, ⊛www.traveller.ltd.uk.
Ordnance Survey of Northern Ireland Colby House, Stranmillis Ct, Belfast BT9 5BJ ☎028/9066 1244, ⊛www.osni.gov.uk.
Ordnance Survey Service Phoenix Park, Dublin 8 ☎01/820 6100, ⊛www.irlgov.ie/osi/.
Stanfords 12–14 Long Acre, London WC2E 9LP ☎020/7836 1321, ⊛www.stanfords.co.uk; maps by mail or phone order are available on this number and via ⓔsales@stanfords.co.uk. Other branches within British Airways offices at 156 Regent St, London W1R 5TA ☎020/7434 4744, and 29 Corn St, Bristol BS1 1HT ☎0117/929 9966.
The Travel Bookshop 13–15 Blenheim Crescent, London W11 2EE ☎020/7229 5260, ⊛www.thetravelbookshop.co.uk.

In Australia and New Zealand

The Map Shop 6 Peel St, Adelaide ☎08/8231 2033, ⊛www.mapshop.net.au.
Mapland 372 Little Bourke St, Melbourne ☎03/9670 4383, ⊛www.mapland.com.au.
Mapworld 173 Gloucester St, Christchurch ☎03/374 5399, ⓕ03/374 5633, ⊛www.mapworld.co.nz.
Perth Map Centre 1/884 Hay St, Perth ☎08/9322 5733, ⊛www.perthmap.com.au.
Speciality Maps 46 Albert St, Auckland ☎09/307 2217, ⊛www.ubd-online.co.nz/maps.

Getting around

Despite the large distances, travelling around most of South Africa is fairly straightforward, with a well-organized network of public transport, a good range of car rental companies, the best road system in Africa, and the continent's most comprehensive network of internal flights. The only weak point is public transport in urban areas, which is almost universally poor and often dangerous. Urban South Africans who can afford to do so tend to use private transport, and if you plan to spend much time in any one town you'd be well-advised to do the same. It's virtually impossible to get to the national parks and places off the beaten track by public transport; even if you do manage, you'll most likely need a car once you're there.

Buses

South Africa's three established **intercity bus companies** are Greyhound, Intercape and Translux; between them, they reach most towns in the country. Travel on these buses (commonly called coaches) is safe,

English/Afrikaans street names

Many towns have **bilingual street names** with English and Afrikaans alternatives sometimes appearing along the same road. This applies particularly in Afrikaans areas away from the large cities, where direct translations are sometimes used. Some common variations you may encounter are listed in "Language" (see p.912).

comfortable and good value. Fares vary according to distances covered. Generally, you can expect to pay a peak fare of roughly R375 (US$30/£22) from Johannesburg to Cape Town (1434km), and a similar amount from Cape Town to Durban (1639km). Peak fares correspond approximately to school holidays, and you can expect about thirty percent off at other times.

If you plan to make several long journeys, it's worth investing in a **pass**. By joining Greyhound's Travel Pass (fill in the form at one of their offices), each journey you make earns you points that can eventually buy you a free bus journey. Greyhound also offers a pass that gives seven days' unlimited travel over a thirty-day period for around R950 (US$80/£55); fifteen days over thirty days for

R1825 (US$150/£110); or thirty days over sixty days for R2890 (US$240/£170). At the time of writing Translux was planning a similar system of passes.

The **Baz Bus** operates an extremely useful hop-on/hop-off system aimed at backpackers and budget travellers. The Baz route runs up and down the coast in both directions between Cape Town and Durban. From Durban it goes to Johannesburg and Pretoria through Swaziland or via an alternative route that heads up along the Drakensberg. It picks up and drops off at backpacker accommodation, except in instances where the place is too remote – in which case the owner of the relevant backpackers' lodge generally comes to pick you up. The only drawback, apart from occa-

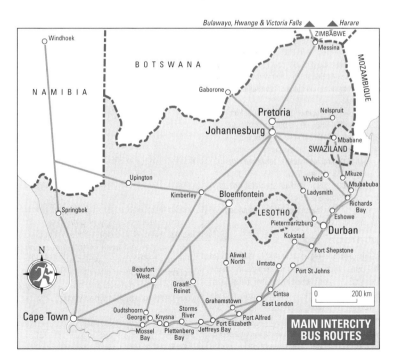

Bulawayo, Hwange & Victoria Falls ▲ ▲ Harare

MAIN INTERCITY BUS ROUTES

sionally erratic timing, is that the people you'll meet on them will almost exclusively be other backpackers, rather than locals.

As well as the major bus companies, there is a national network of **inexpensive buses**, some of which are operated by Translux's sister company Transcity (sometimes called Transtate), and others operated by a host of small private companies. It's difficult to get much information about them from travel agents and tourist information offices, though Translux offers some information about the Transcity service. To find out more – and to enquire about other private company services – enquire at the main bus station the day before you travel. Apart from saving money, travelling on these buses also enables you to meet black South African travellers, who are distinctly thin on the ground on the luxury coaches.

Intercity bus companies

Baz Bus National ☎021 439 2323, ☎021 439 2343. Bookings can also be made through hostels or the Baz offices at the central tourist information centres in Cape Town or Durban. Their website (☼www.bazbus.com) has route and pricing information.

Greyhound Cape Town ☎021 418 4310; Bloemfontein ☎051 430 2361; Durban ☎031 309 7830; Johannesburg ☎011 830 1301; Port Elizabeth ☎041 568 4879. Their website (☼www.greyhound.co.za) has contact information, routes and prices.

Intercape Cape Town ☎021 386 4400; Port Elizabeth ☎041/586 0055; Durban ☎031 307 2115; Pretoria ☎012 654 4114. Their website (☼www.intercape.co.za) has contact numbers.

Translux Central reservations Johannesburg ☎011 774 3333; Cape Town ☎021 449 3333; Durban ☎031 308 8111; East London ☎043 1700 1999; Port Elizabeth ☎041 507 1333. A useful website (☼www.translux.co.za) covers pricing, passes and routes.

Minibus taxis

Minibus taxis travel absolutely everywhere in South Africa, covering relatively short hops from town to town, commuter trips from township to town and back, and routes within larger towns and cities. However, the problems associated with them – unroadworthy vehicles, dangerous drivers and violent feuds between the different taxi associations competing for custom – mean that you should take local advice before using them. This is particularly true in cities, where minibus taxi ranks tend to be a magnet for petty criminals. The other problem with minibus taxis is that there is rarely much room to put luggage.

However, despite these drawbacks, don't rule out using this form of transport altogether. Without a car, minibus taxis will often be your only option for getting around in remote areas, where you're unlikely to encounter trouble. You should, however, be prepared for some long waits. **Fares** are very low. Try to have the exact change, and pass your fare to the row of passengers in front of you; eventually all the fares end up with the conductor, who dishes any change. There are no passes available for minibus taxis.

Trains

Travelling by **train** is just about the slowest way of getting around South Africa: the journey from Johannesburg to Cape Town, for example, takes 27 hours – compared to 19 hours by bus. Unless you've got a lot of time on your hands, you may be better off taking the bus, although rail travel does give you a free night's accommodation.

First- and second-class travel is in compartments equipped with washbasins and with seats that convert into bunks at night. The principal distinction between the two is that second-class cabins accommodate up to six people, while first-class takes a maximum of four, has a shower in each carriage and tends to be quieter. Coupés, which take two people in first or three people in second (although you pay for three if you want it to yourself), are ideal if you're travelling as a couple. Third-class travel isn't recommended. Seating in first and second classes is comfortable and so are the bunks, which offer the real possibility of getting a good night's sleep. If you don't have a sleeping bag, you can rent fresh cotton sheets and blankets for the night, which are brought around by a bedding attendant who'll make up your bed in the evening. It's best to buy your bedding voucher when you book your train ticket.

Spoornet (☼www.spoornet.co.za) runs most of the intercity rail services. **Ticket prices** for first-class seats are comparable to the cost of a bus journey over the same distance, with second-class compartments costing considerably less. Train tickets must be booked in advance at railway stations or at Spoornet offices in the large cities.

A word of warning about **security** on trains. Don't leave your valuables unattended in your compartment, unless you have some way of locking it, and make sure you close the window before you go, as thieves work the stations, especially around Gauteng. This may mean you won't want to eat in the dining car, so it's worth bringing your own food and drink, although someone usually comes round selling tea or coffee once or twice during the journey.

South Africa offers a handful of **luxury trains**; these are worth considering if you want to travel in plush surroundings, often through wonderful scenery, and don't mind paying through the nose for the privilege. The celebrated **Blue Train** runs from Pretoria to Cape Town, and from Pretoria to Victoria Falls. The full Pretoria–Cape Town fare is around R4500 for the 29-hour journey. Passengers must be dressed in "smart casual" clothes during the day, and have to change into formal wear for the evening meal. You can reserve a seat on this popular train by booking through Blue Train's central reservations in Pretoria (☎012 334 8459, ⓔbluetrain@transnet.co.za).

Another luxury rail option is offered by **Rovos Rail** (Pretoria ☎012 315 8242; Cape Town ☎021 421 4020; ⓦwww.rovos.co.za), which runs trips from Cape Town to: Pretoria for around R7500 (US$625/£440); George for R5000 (US$420/£295); or as far as Victoria Falls in Zimbabwe for R8000 (US$670/£470).

Internal flights

Flying between destinations in South Africa is an attractive option if time is short. While it's not particularly cheap, it compares favourably with the money you'll spend covering long distances in a rented car, stopping over at places en route. By far the biggest airline offering domestic flights is South African Airways (SAA) with its two associates SA Airlink and SA Express (reservations for the three go through SAA). There are a number of other smaller airlines of which the most significant are British Airways/Comair

and its budget internet-based subsidiary kulula.com.

Subject to availability, you can expect **discounts** of up to fifty percent for booking three weeks ahead. Booking through travel agents is the best idea, as they'll know of the cheapest available fares; there's little benefit shopping around different agents, as the only variation in price is going to be between airlines.

SAA and its associates have the most extensive flight network, serving the major hubs of Johannesburg, Cape Town and Durban, as well as Bloemfontein, East London, George, Kimberley, Margate, Mmabatho, Nelspruit, Phalaborwa, Pietermaritzburg, Pietersburg, Plettenberg Bay, Skukuza (Kruger National Park), Sun City, Ulundi, Umtata and Upington. As a rough guide, expect to pay just under R1500 (US$125/£90) for a one-way tourist-class fare from Johannesburg to Cape Town, or from Cape Town to Durban. The Johannesburg–Cape Town route has become particularly cheap since the arrival of kulula.com, which offers one-way fares as low as R500 (US$40/£30) and has forced SAA to offer some seats at similar prices. None of the airlines offers discounts for students or pensioners.

Travellers expecting to make more than four flights in and around South Africa will save considerably with the **African Explorer Pass**, available on SAA and SA Express internal and regional flights. To qualify for the pass, you need an international flight to South Africa on any airline, and must quote your ticket number to your travel agent or SAA. The pass, valid for 45 days from the date of issue, gives up to sixty percent savings when you book between four and eight flights, plus you save on VAT.

Airlines in South Africa

British Airways/Comair Offices are open daily 6am–9pm: Johannesburg (☎011 921 0222); Cape Town (☎021 936 9000); Durban (☎031 450 7000); Port Elizabeth (☎041 508 8000); ⓦwww.britishairways.com/regional/sa.
kulula.com ☎0861 585 852, ⓦwww.kulula.com.
South African Airways Central reservations is open daily 5am–11pm ☎0861 359 722, ⓦwww.flysaa.com.

Driving

South Africa is ideal for driving with a generally well-maintained network of highways and a high proportion of secondary and tertiary roads which are tarred and can be driven at speed. Some of the most interesting places off the beaten track are only accessible in your own vehicle, as buses tend to ply only the major routes. Short of joining a tour, the only way to get to national parks and remoter coastal areas is by car. The only real challenge you'll face on the roads is **other drivers**.

Renting a vehicle is not prohibitively expensive. In a small group, it can work out a cheap option, allowing you to explore areas in depth and at your own pace.

The usual **fuel** in coastal areas is **97** and **93 octane** on the highveld, with most filling stations also offering **unleaded**.

Filling stations are frequent on the major routes of the country, and usually open 24 hours a day, so it's hard to run out of fuel. Off the major routes, though, stations are less frequent, so do fill up regularly if you're on a long journey. Stations are rarely self-service; instead, poorly paid attendants fill up your car, check oil, water and tyre pressure if you ask them to, and often clean your windscreen even if you don't. A tip is always appreciated, though not obligatory.

Regulations and driving tips

Foreign **licences** are valid in South Africa for up to six months provided they are printed in English. If you don't have such a licence, you'll need to get an International Driving Permit before arriving in South Africa (available from national motoring organizations). When driving, make sure you have your driving licence and passport on you at all times.

You drive on the **left-hand side**; **speed limits** range from 60kph in built-up areas to 100kph on rural roads and 120kph on highways and major arteries. Note that traffic lights are called **robots** in South Africa.

In addition to roundabouts, which follow the British rule of giving way to the right, there are **four-way stops**, where the rule is that the person who got there first leaves first, and you are not expected to give way to the right.

South Africa has among the world's worst road accident statistics – the result of reck-

less driving, **drunken drivers** or defective, overloaded vehicles. Keep your distance from cars in front, as domino-style pile-ups are common. Watch out also for overtaking traffic coming towards you; overtakers often assume that you will head for the hard shoulder to avoid an accident – it is legal to drive on the hard shoulder, but it's also dangerous, so be careful. If you do pull into the hard shoulder to let a car overtake, the other driver will probably thank you by flashing the hazard lights. If oncoming cars flash their headlights at you, it probably means that there is a speed trap up ahead.

Other potential **hazards** include animals on the road in rural areas. This can be especially dangerous at night, so drive slowly at that time. Finally, the large **distances** between major towns means that falling asleep at the wheel, especially when travelling through long stretches of flat landscape in the Karoo or the Free State, is a real danger. Plan your car journeys carefully to include plenty of breaks and stopovers. Driving in Johannesburg, you risk the danger of being **car-jacked**; see p.62 for safety hints.

Motoring organizations

In South Africa

Automobile Association (AA) ☏ 0800 01 01 01, ⊛ www.aasa.co.za.

In North America

American Automobile Association (AAA) Each state has its own club – check the phone book for local address and phone number (or call ☏ 1-800/222-4357, ⊛ www.aaa.com).
Canadian Automobile Association (CAA) ☏ 613/247-0117, ⊛ www.caa.com. Each region has its own club – check the phone book for local address and phone number.

In the UK and Ireland

AA ☏ 0800/444500, ⊛ www.theaa.co.uk.
AA Travel Dublin ☏ 01/617 9988, ⊛ www.aaireland.ie.
RAC ☏ 0800/550055, ⊛ www.rac.co.uk.

In Australia and New Zealand

Australian Automobile Association ☏ 02/6247 7311.
New Zealand Automobile Association ☏ 09/377 4660.

Car rental

Renting a car is recommended if you want to travel widely without being governed by public transport timetables. Prebooking your car with a travel agent before flying out is the cheapest option, and will provide more favourable terms and conditions (such as unlimited mileage and lower insurance excesses). Don't rely on being able to just arrive at the airport and pick up a vehicle without pre-booking, as the rental firms do run out of cars, especially during the week.

The major car rental companies in South Africa are Avis (☎0861 02 1111, ⊛www.avis .co.za), Budget (☎0861 01 6622, ⊛www .budget.co.za), Europcar (☎0800 01 1344, ⊛www.europcar.co.za), Hertz (☎0861 60 0136, ⊛www.hertz.co.za), Imperial (☎0800 13 1000, ⊛www.imperial.ih.co.za) and Tempest (☎0800 03 1666, ⊛www.tempestcarhire .co.za) – see box on p.53 for international phone numbers. As a rough guideline, for a one-week rental you can expect to **pay** upwards of R1400 (US$120/£80) including ninety percent collision damage and theft waivers, as well as about 1400 free kilometres. Most companies stipulate that drivers must be a **minimum age** of 21.

The advantage of renting through major companies is that you don't have to return the car to where you hired it from, but can deposit it in some other major centre instead; though rental companies usually levy a charge for this. If you're planning on driving into **Lesotho** and **Swaziland**, check that the company allows it – some don't. Insurance often doesn't cover you if you drive off the tar, so check for this too. Local firms are almost always cheaper, but usually have restrictions on how far you can take the vehicle.

Camper vans can be a good idea for getting to remote places where accommodation is scarce. Expect to pay around R1000 (US$85/£60) per day for a vehicle that sleeps three. Some companies offer standby rates that knock fifteen to twenty percent off the price if you book at short notice (one week or less ahead). Vans come fully equipped with crockery, cutlery and linen and usually a toilet. The downside of camper vans is that they struggle up hills and guzzle a lot of fuel (15 litres per 100km in the smaller vans, and 20 litres per 100km in the larger ones), which could partly offset any savings on accommodation.

One of the biggest **camper-van rental companies** is Britz Africa whose head office is in Johannesburg (☎011 396 1860, ⊛www .britz.co.za), and which has branches in Cape Town (☎021 981 8947) and Durban (☎031 702 9326), and will pick you up from the airport and return you for about R100.

Rental agencies in North America

Auto Europe US ☎1-800/223-5555, Canada ☎1-888 /223-5555, ⊛www.autoeurope.com.
Avis US ☎1-800/331-1084, Canada ☎1-800/272-5871, ⊛www.avis.com.
Budget ☎1-800/527-0700, ⊛www.budgetrentacar.com.
Hertz US ☎1-800/654-3001, Canada ☎1-800/263 0600, ⊛www.hertz.com.
National ☎1-800/227-7368, ⊛www.nationalcar.com.

Rental agencies in Australia

Avis ☎13/6333, ⊛www.avis.com.
Budget ☎1300/362 848, ⊛www.budget.com.
Hertz ☎1800/550 067, ⊛www.hertz.com.
National ☎13/1908.

Rental agencies in New Zealand

Avis ☎09/526 5231 or 0800 655 111, ⊛www.avis.com.
Budget ☎0800/ 652 227 or 09/375 2270, ⊛www.budget.com.
Hertz ☎09/309 0989 or 0800 655 955, ⊛www.hertz.com.
National ☎09/537 2582.

Rental agencies in the UK

Autos Abroad ☎0870/066 7788, ⊛www.autosabroad.co.uk.
Avis ☎0870/606 0100, ⊛www.avisworld.com.
Budget ☎0800/181181, ⊛www.go-budget.co.uk.
Europcar ☎0845/722 2525, ⊛www.europcar.co.uk.
National ☎0870/536 5365, ⊛www.nationalcar.com.
Hertz ☎0870/844 8844, ⊛www.hertz.co.uk.
Holiday Autos ☎0870/400 0000, ⊛www.holidayautos.com.

Rental agencies in Ireland

Autos Abroad ☎0870/066 7788, ⊛www.autosabroad.com.
Avis Northern Ireland ☎028/9442 3333, Republic of Ireland ☎01/605 7555, ⊛www.avis.co.uk.

Budget Northern Ireland ☎028/9442, ✆www
.budget-ireland.co.uk. Republic of Ireland ☎01/
878 7814, ✆www.budgetcarrental.ie.
Cosmo Thrifty ☎028/9445 2565, ✆www.thrifty
.co.uk.
Europcar Northern Ireland ☎028/9442 3444,
Republic of Ireland ☎01/614 2800, ✆www
.europcar.ie.
Hertz Northern Ireland ☎028/9442 2533, Republic
of Ireland ☎0903/27711, ✆www.hertz.co.uk.
Holiday Autos ☎01/872 9366, ✆www
.holidayautos.ie.

Buying a car

Buying a used vehicle in South Africa is
more expensive than in most Western countries, and you will have to spend at least
R25,000 (US$2000/£1500) to be sure of
getting something reliable. However, you
should be able to get most of your money
back when you sell it, providing you haven't
paid over the odds for the vehicle in the first
place, although it can take a few weeks to
get the price you deserve.

Buying from a **dealer** will generally increase
the price by ten to twenty percent, but
should enable you to get a warranty for the
vehicle. Bear in mind that this is only worth
having if you are able to return the car to the
dealer who issued it, which is likely to be
tricky if you're travelling around the country.

Alternatively, you can buy a car through
the **small ads** in the newspapers or in the
growing number of free ads papers. If you
do this, it helps to know something about
the kind of vehicle you are buying, as no
guarantee will be offered for its roadworthi-
ness. If you don't trust your own mechanical
abilities, enlist the services of the AA, who
check out cars for about R400 (US$35/£25).
Go for a car that still has a few months of its
road tax left to save forking out for another
year's worth of tax when you register the car.

Beware of **rust**: cars from coastal regions,
particularly those from Cape Town, are most
likely to be on the rusty side.

When you buy, make sure you get the **registration document** from the previous
owner, as you'll need it when you come to
register the vehicle in your name. Make sure
you have a contact number for the previous
owner too, just in case the car turns out to
have been stolen. After buying the car, you

need to ensure that it's **roadworthy**. This
involves taking it to the nearest testing station and paying for it to be put through a
series of pretty basic tests. One possible
problem is that the engine serial numbers do
not all match up. If this happens, you'll have
to take the vehicle to a police testing station
where they run a series of computer checks
to see if the car has been stolen.

Once you've got the roadworthy certificate, head for the nearest vehicle registration centre with your certificate, registration
document, driving licence, passport and
about R120 (US$10/£7): this will procure
your own registration document for the vehicle.

Selling a vehicle is a lot more simple than
buying one. All you need is the registration
document to give to the new owner, a completed form for the transfer of ownership
(which you can pick up from any vehicle registration centre), and a photocopy of the new
owner's ID book or passport. Once you have
handed over the keys and the new owner
has driven away, you need to present the
completed form and photocopy to a vehicle
registration centre.

Most South Africans drive without any
form of **insurance**, but you would be foolish
to do the same. Aim to buy a third-party
insurance policy, preferably comprehensive,
as soon as you take charge of a new vehicle. **Joining the AA** is a good idea; a year's
membership costs about R350 (US$30/
£20), and their maps, travel advice and
emergency services can be invaluable.

Cycling

It's easy to see why **cycling** is popular in
South Africa: you can get to stunning destinations on good roads unclogged by traffic,
and many towns have decent cycle shops
for spares and equipment. You'll need to be
fit though, as South Africa is a hilly place,
and many roads have punishing gradients.
The weather can make life difficult too: if it
isn't raining, there is a good chance of it
being very hot, so carry plenty of liquids. An
increasing number of backpacker hostels
rent out mountain bikes for reasonable rates,
making it easy to do plenty of cycling without having to transport your bike into the
country. Cycling on the main roads is not
recommended.

Hitching

Generally speaking, **hitching** in most areas of South Africa is not a good idea, particularly in large towns and cities. Even in rural areas it's risky and, while you might encounter wonderful hospitality and interesting companions, it's advisable not to hitch at all.

If you must hitchhike, it's essential to take a number of precautions to maximize your safety. Avoid hitching alone, and being dropped off in isolated areas between *dorps*. Ask drivers where they are going before you say where you want to go, and keep your bags with you: having them locked in the boot makes a hasty escape more difficult. Check the notice boards in backpacker lodges for people offering or looking to share lifts – that way, you can meet the driver in advance.

Accommodation

Standards of accommodation in South Africa are generally very high and even the most modest backpacker lodge will provide a minimum of fresh sheets and clean rooms. Whatever your budget, you can pick up some real bargains. B&B prices are a lot cheaper than in Britain, particularly given the high standards you can expect. Apart from the very cheapest rooms, you'll almost always get a private bath or shower, and you'll often have the use of a garden or swimming pool. If you're looking for something special, South Africa has some outstanding boutique hotels, luxury guesthouses and country retreats – invariably in beautiful settings – at prices that would only get you a B&B room back home.

The continuing growth in **backpacker accommodation** means that you'll find a hostel in most areas, and many offer excellent facilities.

For **camping and self-catering**, you'll be spoilt for choice. This is the preferred form of holiday accommodation of South Africans themselves, and the country is well-supplied with caravan parks, camping resorts and self-catering apartments and cottages.

Advance booking is vital if you're planning on staying in a national park or in popular areas such as Cape Town or the Garden Route, or if you're travelling in the high season. South Africa's **peak season** is during the midsummer Christmas school holiday period (roughly Dec 4–Jan 21), which coincides with many foreign tourists piling in to catch their winter tan. The Easter school holiday (March 20–April 15) is a shorter and less intense period, when South African families migrate to the coast and inland resorts. At both Christmas and Easter, **prices** for budget and mid-priced accommodation (but not camping or backpacking) can double, and most places get booked up months ahead.

There's a lull in the midwinter **low season** (June–Aug), during which time you should have no problem finding plenty of good-value places to stay, often with hefty low-season discounts. This is the best time to go on safari in the Kruger National Park or KwaZulu-Natal when prices are at their lowest, malaria mosquitoes are dormant, temperatures are moderate and the game viewing is at its finest.

Hotels

Most of South Africa's cheaper **hotels** are throwbacks to the 1950s and 1960s and are being left behind by the growing profusion of guesthouses and B&Bs – many have degenerated into watering holes, earning most of their keep from their bar. Hotels are really only worth considering at the middle to the top end of the scale, and then only if you want plenty of facilities and luxurious accommodation. At some of the most expensive places you pay for the social cachet of the

Accommodation price codes

All the accommodation listed in the Guide has been categorized into one of nine price bands, as set out below. The rates quoted represent what you can expect to pay for much of the summer **per person**, and unless otherwise stated, are based on two sharing. Rooms are generally en suite. Expect prices in some areas to be significantly higher in peak season (Dec–Jan & Easter), and look out for discounts during the winter.

❶ **Up to R100** Dorms and doubles at backpackers' lodges, with shared washing and cooking facilities, basic B&Bs outside main centres and some self-catering accommodation.

❷ **R100–150** In this range you'll get decent budget hotels, very good self-catering accommodation on farms, at resorts and in towns, and pretty good en-suite B&Bs in less touristy areas. The most basic national parks accommodation in rondavels with shared washing and cooking facilities also fall into this range.

❸ **R150–200** Above-average B&Bs and guesthouses in popular areas, and exceptional places off the beaten track. This category also includes good mid-range hotels, and you can expect a garden and swimming pool. Most en-suite self-catering national parks chalets also fall within this range.

❹ **R200–300** You'll have no problem finding comfort and style in this range, whether in a guesthouse, hotel or country lodge. Expect spacious rooms, gardens with swimming pools, the occasional Jacuzzi, first-class service and above-average food.

❺ **R300–500** Luxurious country retreats in beautiful settings, exceptional guest-houses and some topnotch hotels, many of which can match those costing twice the price.

❻ **R500–750** Not much falls into this price range which includes the odd excellent hotel or guesthouse and some cheaper safari accommodation usually in less-sought-after private game areas.

❼ **R750–1000** Some exceptional boutique hotels fall into this range, as well as a few safari lodges in the private game reserves that are part of the Greater Kruger National Park.

❽ **R1000–2000** Standard rooms at South Africa's top hotels and mid-range (but still pretty luxurious) full-board accommodation, including game-viewing activities at safari lodges in the sought-after private game reserves integrated into the Greater Kruger National Park.

❾ **Over R2000** The sky's the limit here. Luxury suites at the top hotels and accommodation at the most expensive private game lodges in the Greater Kruger National Park fall into this category. We only recommend urban accommodation in this range if it's truly exceptional.

name, and may find the same facilities nearby far cheaper.

At the **bottom end** you can expect unremarkable en-suite rooms from around US$12/£8 per person. In smaller places off the tourist routes, you'll often have a choice of one or two hotels of this type, and these are rarely good value. There are exceptions of course: hotels with real charm in *dorps* where you'd least expect them, and we've included many of those in this guide.

Mid-range hotels usually charge US$20–35/£8–20, and you can expect decent – frequently excellent – standards, often in old and characterful refurbished buildings. Many hotels in this category are comparable to guesthouses for the same price, but they offer an acceptable alternative if you prefer hotel anonymity and facilities such as room service, private telephone and TV. Many mid-priced hotels – especially those on main routes in the interior – are fully booked during the week by travelling salesmen; but over the weekends, when they're often empty, you can usually negotiate reasonable discounts. Along the coastal holiday strips such as the Garden Route and southern KwaZulu-Natal and all the major seaside towns in between, medium-priced hotels are ubiquitous and frequently offer rooms right on the beachfront.

Prices at **upmarket** hotels start at a bargain U$40/£25 for real luxury, ranging up to US$125/£85 for places rated among the world's best. South Africa's main hotel chains include Holiday Inn, Protea, Southern Sun and Karos, all of which offer reliable but rather soulless upmarket accommodation. For the same money, you may be better off at one of the many pleasant country hotels with beautiful gardens tucked away in scenic parts of the country, such as the Garden Route and the KwaZulu-Natal Midlands. It's worth noting South Africa's idiosyncrasy over "smart casual" wear, which is demanded by many posher hotels after 6pm. The directive applies mainly to men, and in practice means you'll need a pair of slacks, a decent shirt with a collar and closed shoes.

Caravan parks, resorts and camping

Caravanning was once the favourite way of enjoying a cheap family holiday in South Africa, and this accounts for the very large number of caravan parks dotted across the length and breadth of the country. However,

their popularity has declined and with it the standard of many of the country's **municipal caravan parks and campsites**. Today, municipal campsites are generally pretty scruffy places, though you may find the odd pleasant one in rural areas, or near small *dorps*. Staying in a municipal campsite adjoining a city or large town is often more grief than it's worth; not only will facilities generally be run-down, but theft is a big risk. In most municipal sites you can expect to pay roughly US$5/£3 per tent.

All in all, you're best off heading for the better-organized **privately owned resorts**, where for roughly the same price you get greater comfort and far better facilities. Although private resorts sometimes give off a holiday-camp vibe, they usually provide good washing and cooking facilities, self-catering chalets, shops selling basic goods, braai stands and swimming pools.

Virtually all **national parks** in the country – and many provincial reserves – have campsites and in some of the really remote places, such as parts of KwaZulu-Natal, camping may be your only option. A site is unlikely to cost more than US$8/£5. At national parks you can expect well-maintained washing facilities and there are often communal kitchen areas or at the very least a braai stand and running water as well as decent communal shower, toilet and washing facilities (known locally as "ablutions").

Camping rough is not recommended anywhere in the country; with so many offi-

Booking accommodation online

Online accommodation booking in South Africa is still in its early stages and there's no single site that covers the whole market. The sites listed below cover distinct (and sometimes overlapping) niches. Many of the larger operators allow online booking through their individual sites which are listed in the Guide.

Book a Bed ⓦwww.bookabed.co.za. Self-catering and B&B.

Farm Stays ⓦwww.farmstay.co.za.

MT Beds ⓦwww.mtbeds.co.za. Standard rates and special offers for hotels and B&Bs.

Portfolio online ⓦwww.portfoliocollection.co.za. The industry leader in select accommodation directories with sections on B&Bs, country places and retreats.

South African Hotels ⓦwww.sahotels.com. Hotels, B&Bs and self-catering accommodation searchable by region or in alphabetical order.

Where to Stay ⓦwww.wheretostay.co.za. One of the most substantial directories of accommodation in all categories.

cial campsites, even in very remote areas, it's very unlikely you'll have to pitch a tent anywhere else.

Backpacker lodges and youth hostels

Backpacker lodges comprise the fastest-growing category of accommodation in South Africa, and their quality is improving all the time. Most offer basic hostel accommodation in a dormitory for under US$7/£4 per person, and many have some doubles, which cost a little more. They usually have communal kitchens, an on-site restaurant or café, TV, internet facilities and bike rental.

The lodges are invariably good meeting points, with large notice boards filled with advertisements for hostels and backpacker facilities, and a constant stream of travellers passing through. Many lodges operate reasonably priced excursions into the surrounding areas, and will pick you up from railway stations or bus stops (especially Baz Bus stops) if you phone in advance. The only drawback with staying in this kind of accommodation is that you tend to meet the same people over and over again as you travel around.

An **upmarket** variant on backpacker lodges is still something of a fledgling development, aimed at thirtysomethings who want reasonably priced, casual accommodation, but are looking for private rooms rather than dorms that are a little more stylish and sedate. At these places you'll get a very decent double for under US$10/£7, and can still expect congenial communal areas. They are still rare, so don't count on finding one in every town.

South Africa's **youth hostel** scene is on the small side, with around thirty backpackers' lodges affiliated to Hostelling International South Africa (HISA), part of the international Youth Hostel Association network. Located in all the major tourist centres, some of these can be prebooked and prepaid for through YHA offices in your country or on the internet. Apart from guaranteeing the standards of member hostels, which are vetted annually, membership of the YHA also provides ten percent discounts at member hostels as well as reductions on car rental, buses and a number of other facilities, which are detailed on their website (⊛www.hisa.org.za).

Youth hostel associations

South Africa

Hostelling International South Africa (HISA), 73 St George's Mall, Third floor, St George's House, Cape Town ☎021 424 2511, ⊛www.hisa.org.za. Annual membership R55 (no age limit) can be taken out through their head office, any member hostel or via their website and is valid throughout the world. Life membership, which is restricted to South Africans, costs R250.

England and Wales

Youth Hostel Association (YHA), Trevelyan House, 8 St Stephen's Hill, St Albans, Herts AL1 2DY ☎0870/870 8808, ⊛www.yha.org.uk and ⊛www.iyhf.org, ✉customerservices@yha.org.uk. Annual membership £12.50, for under-18s £6.25.

Scotland

Scottish Youth Hostel Association 7 Glebe Crescent, Stirling FK8 2JA ☎0870/1553 255, ⊛www.syha.org.uk. Annual membership £6, for under-18s £2.50.

Ireland

An Óige 61 Mountjoy St, Dublin 7 ☎01/8430 4555, ⊛www.irelandyha.org. Adult (and single parent) membership IR£10; family (2 parents and children under 16) IR£20; under-18s IR£4.
Hostelling International Northern Ireland 22–32 Donegall Rd, Belfast BT12 5JN ☎028/9032 4733, ⊛www.hini.org.uk. Adult membership £10; under-18s £6; family £20.

USA

Hostelling International-American Youth Hostels (HI-AYH), 733 15th St NW, Suite 840, PO Box 37613, Washington, DC 20005 ☎202/783-6161, ⊛www.hiayh.org. Annual membership for adults (18–55) is $25, for seniors (55 or over) is $15, and for under-18s is free. Lifetime membership costs $250.

Canada

Hostelling International/Canadian Hostelling Association Room 400, 205 Catherine St, Ottawa, ON K2P 1C3 ☎1-800/663-5777 or 613/237-7884, ⊛www.hostellingintl.ca. Rather than sell the traditional 1- or 2-year memberships, the association now sells one Individual Adult membership with a 28- to 16-month term. The length of the term depends on when the membership is sold, but a member can receive up to 28 months of membership for just $35. Membership is free for under-18s, and you can become a lifetime member for $175.

Australia

Australia Youth Hostels Association 422 Kent St, Sydney ☏ 02/9261 1111, ⊛ www.yha.com.au. Adult membership costs A$49 for the first twelve months and then A$32 each year after.

New Zealand

New Zealand Youth Hostels Association 173 Gloucester St, Christchurch ☏ 03/379 9970, ⊛ www.yha.co.nz. Adult membership costs NZ$40 for one year, NZ$60 for two and NZ$80 for three.

Self-catering

Away from the resorts, **self-catering accommodation** in cottages, apartments and small complexes provides the cheapest option outside of staying in a backpackers' lodge. A self-catering holiday seldom exceeds US$15/£10 per person per night for two people sharing. Apartments often sleep up to six, and because rates are mostly quoted for entire units, this can be very economical if you're travelling as a family or in a group. Even though you don't usually get breakfast (this is sometimes offered for a small extra charge), you can save a lot of money by cooking for yourself, and you'll get a sense of freedom and privacy missing from the nicest guesthouse or B&B.

Apart from chalets at the ropiest of municipal caravan parks, standards of self-catering accommodation are usually fairly high. Cottages or apartments generally come fully equipped with crockery and cutlery – and even microwaves and TVs in the more modern places. Linen and towels are often provided – but check before you book in.

One of the best things about self-catering is the wide choice of location. There are self-catering options on farms, near beaches, in forests and in wilderness areas, as well as in practically every town and city.

B&Bs, guesthouses and farmstays

More and more South Africans are opening their homes to visitors, and in some places you'll be spoilt for choice. The most basic **B&B** consists of just one or two rooms inside a house, where you share washing facilities with the owners and pay around about US$10/£7 per person. Far more common are the efficiently run B&Bs with en-

suite rooms, often in garden cottages or annexes to the main house, and frequently with tea-making facilities and the use of a garden; for these you can expect to pay around US$12–20/£8–12. It's worth asking to see your room first and get a feel for the place; South Africans are extremely hospitable, and at some B&Bs you run a real risk of being overwhelmed by attentive hosts and having little privacy.

For decades the homes of black South Africans were deliberately kept hidden from tourist trails, a situation that has changed dramatically with the proliferation of township tours. Since the late 1990s, township dwellers have begun offering accommodation, opening up new possibilities for experiencing South Africa. **Township B&Bs** are still few in number, but this is a sector that's growing, and we've tried to cover as many as possible that exist at the time of writing. Expect to pay US$10–12/£7–8 for this type of accommodation.

The defining line between a B&B and a **guesthouse** can seem a little hazy. According to the Tourism Grading Council of South Africa's definition a B&B is "usually provided in a family (private) home and the owner/manager lives in the house or on the property," whereas "a guesthouse is either a converted house, manor, etc adapted to accommodate overnight guests or it may be a purpose built facility". For practical purposes guesthouses fall somewhere between B&Bs and better hotels in facilities, atmosphere and cost. Prices start at around US$15/£10 per person and many offer half board.

Along many roads in the countryside you will see signs for "*Bed en Ontbyt*" (Afrikaans for "bed and breakfast") – this signals **farmstay** accommodation. As with urban B&Bs, you'll either be in rooms in the main homestead or in a cottage in its garden. On a farmstay, you can usually expect a hearty Afrikaner breakfast and prices a little below urban B&Bs. Some offer hiking, horse-riding, and other activities and excursions – there are some real gems dotted about, which we've listed in this guide. Tourist information bureaus will almost always have lists of farms in the area that rent out rooms or cottages.

National parks accommodation

Accommodation at national parks includes **campsites**, which cost about US$7/£4 per site; one-room **rondavels** with shared washing and cooking facilities for US$5–8/£3–5 per person; **safari tents** at some of the Kruger and some KwaZulu-Natal rest camps in the region of US$7/£4; and self-contained **chalets** with private bath or shower and cooking facilities, which cost around US$12–15/£8–10 per person. For groups of four there are self-contained **family cottages** with private bath and kitchen, where the price of the whole unit is around US$50/£35; and if there are five or six of you, you can aim for one of the **guest cottages** that go for US$50–75/£35–50 – this can work out fairly economical for a group.

In all national parks accommodation (apart from camping) you get bedding, towels, a fridge and basic cooking utensils. The ultimate wildlife accommodation is in the **private game reserves**, most of which are around the Kruger National Park. Here you pay big bucks, but get a far more intimate experience of the wild. Accommodation at this level is almost always luxurious and can be in large en-suite walk-in tents, small thatched rondavels, or plush rooms with air conditioning in the larger and most expensive lodges. Prices start with a handful of places charging US$60/£40 per person per night; but more commonly you can expect to pay upwards of US$125/£85, rising to several times that amount at the most fashionable spots. It's worth remembering that, high as these prices are, all your meals and game drives are included and you're essentially paying for an exclusive experience of the bush rather than for just a bed (see p.47 for more details).

Parks, reserves and wilderness areas

No other African country has as rich a variety of parks, reserves and wilderness areas as South Africa. Literally hundreds of game reserves and state forests pepper the terrain, creating a bewildering but enticing choice. While there are dozens of unsung treasures among these, the big destinations amount to some two dozen parks protecting the country's major game reserves and wilderness areas. With a few exceptions these fall under KwaZulu-Natal Wildlife, which controls most of the public reserves in KwaZulu-Natal, and the South African National Parks, which covers the rest of the country. When it comes to wildlife most people think about land mammals, but South Africa is also home to a number of marine mammals – and is one of the top destinations in the world for land-based whale watching.

It's important to realize that only some national parks are also game reserves; the chart on p.44–45 details what to expect from the major parks. While most people come for South Africa's superb **wildlife**, don't let the Big Five (buffalo, elephant, leopard, lion and rhino) blinker you into missing out on the marvellous **wilderness areas** that take in dramatic landscapes and less-publicized animal life. There are parks protecting marine and coastal areas, wetlands, endangered species, forests, deserts and mountains, usually with the added attraction of animals, birds, insects, reptiles or marine mammals.

If you had to choose just one of the country's top three parks, **Kruger**, stretching up the east flank of Mpumalanga and Northern Province, would lead the pack for its sheer size (it's larger than Wales), its range of

Park entry fees, reservations and enquiries

Entry fees into parks vary; some charge per vehicle, others per person. The most expensive place is the Kruger National Park, where you pay a one-off charge of R30 (US$3/£2) per vehicle plus R24 (US$2/£1.50) per person. Generally, you can expect to pay in the region of R20 (US$1.50/£1) per person. Most of South Africa's major national parks have accommodation that can be **booked** in advance (and in high season, this should be several months in advance) through South African National Parks, except for Pilanesberg, which should be booked through Pilanesberg National Park, and the KwaZulu-Natal reserves, which should be booked through the KwaZulu-Natal Conservation Services.

South African National Parks PO Box 787, Pretoria 0001; street address: 643 Leyds St, Muckleneuk, Pretoria ☏012 343 1991, ⊛www.parks-sa.co.za.

KwaZulu-Natal Wildlife Reservations, PO Box 13069, Cascades, Pietermaritzburg 3202 ☏033 845 1000, ⊛www.rhino.org.za.

animals, its varied lowveld habitats and unbeatable game-viewing opportunities. After Kruger, the **Tsitsikamma** in the Western Cape attracts large numbers of visitors for its ancient forests, cliff-faced oceans, the dramatic Storms River Mouth as well as its Otter Trail, South Africa's most popular **hike**. For epic mountain landscapes, nowhere in the country can touch the **Natal**

Drakensberg Park, which takes in a series of reserves on the KwaZulu-Natal border with Lesotho and offers gentle hikes along watercourses as well as ambitious mountaineering for serious climbers.

The unchallenged status of Kruger National Park as the place for packing in elephants, lions and casts of thousands of animals, tends to put the **KwaZulu-Natal parks** in

MAJOR PARKS AND WILDERNESS AREAS

Major parks and wildlife areas

KEY	PARK	PRINCIPAL FOCUS	DESCRIPTION & HIGHLIGHTS	DETAILS
WESTERN CAPE				
1	Agulhas NP	Marine and coastal	Rugged southernmost tip of Africa with rich plant biodiversity and significant archeological sites.	p.241
2	Bontebok NP	Endangered species	At the foot of rugged mountains provides refuge to bontebok and Cape mountain zebra.	P.229
3	Cape Peninsula NP	The natural areas of the peninsula	Extraordinarily rich and diverse flora and fauna that lives in the wild areas forming a large part of Cape Town, including Table Mountain and the Cape of Good Hope.	
4	Karoo NP	Desert reserve	Arid mountainous landscape with ancient fossils, herbivores and wild flowers in spring.	p.220
5	Knysna National Lake Area	Marine and coastal/ endangered species	Focused on the Knysna Lagoon and its dramatic Heads that open to the sea, the lake area protects the endangered Knysna seahorse.	p.257
6	Tsitsikamma NP	Marine and coastal	Cliff, tidal pools, deep gorges and evergreen forests. Snorkelling, scuba and forest trails.	p.275
7	West Coast NP	Marine and coastal	Wetland wilderness with birding and watersports.	p.284
8	Wilderness NP	Marine and coastal	Lakes, rivers, lagoons, forest, fynbos, beaches and the sea.	p.255
EASTERN CAPE				
9	Addo Elephant NP	Endangered species	Home to more than 200 elephants, Cape buffaloes and various antelopes.	p.360
10	Mountain Zebra NP	Endangered species	Dramatic hilly landscape in flat country with rare mountain zebras and other herbivores.	p.388
NORTHERN CAPE				
11	Augrabies Falls NP	Desert reserve	Orange River plummets down a deep ravine. Desert scenery, antelopes and prolific birdlife.	p.323
12	Kgalagadi Transfrontier Park NP	Desert/game reserve	Remote desert with rust-red dunes, desert lions, shy leopards and thousands of antelopes.	p.325
13	Namaqua NP	Marine and coastal/ wildflowers	Mountainous and coastal region renowned for its display of an estimated 3500 varieties of spring flowers.	p.335

BASICS | Parks, reserves and wilderness areas

KEY PARK	PRINCIPAL FOCUS	DESCRIPTION & HIGHLIGHTS	DETAILS
NORTHERN CAPE cont			
14 Richtersveld NP	Mountain and desert reserve	Craggy *kloofs*, high mountains and dramatic landscapes, sweeping inland from the Orange River, which sustain a remarkable range of reptiles, birds, mammals and plant life.	p.343
FREE STATE			
15 Golden Gate Highlands NP	Mountain enclave	Resort at the foot of rich sandstone formations in the heart of the Maluti Mountains. Trails.	p.571
NORTHWEST			
16 Pilanesberg GR	Game reserve	Mountain-encircled grassland trampled by the Big Five, accessible from Johannesburg.	p.651
NORTHERN PROVINCE/MPUMALANGA			
17 Kruger NP	Game reserve	The largest, best-stocked and most popular game reserve in the subcontinent.	p.693
18 Marakele NP	Game reserve	Striking landscape of peaks, plateaus and cliffs stocked with lions, elephants, rhinos and a variety of other mammals.	p.735
KWAZULU-NATAL			
19 Greater St Lucia	Coastal wetland	Vast patchwork of wetlands, wilderness, coast and game reserves.	p.520
20 Hluhluwe-Umfolozi GR	Game reserve	KwaZulu-Natal's hillier, smaller answer to Kruger is among the top African spots for rhinos.	p.516
21 Itala GR	Game reserve	Lesser-known small gem of a game reserve in mountainous country.	p.537
22 Mkuzi GR	Game/bird reserve	Top birding venue, excellent for rhinos and other herbivores. Walks in wild fig forest.	p.526
22 uKhMweni Valleyahlamba -Drajensberg Park	Mountain reserve	A series of parks covering the highest, most stirring and most dramatic peaks in SA.	p.499

45

the shade; quite undeservedly, as they have several points going for them. As well as offering the best places in the world for seeing **rhino**, these parks feel less developed than Kruger, often provide superior (but no more expensive) accommodation, and are just as accessible for self-driving. Both Kruger and KwaZulu-Natal parks offer guided **wildlife trails** and **night drives**, a popular way to catch sight of the elusive denizens that creep around after dark.

For accommodation in national parks, see p.42.

Safari

If it's **wildlife** you've come to see, you'll find South Africa hard to beat. The country has the best-managed **national parks** in Africa, with well-organized rest camps, developed over four decades to provide cheap holidays for white South African families, and offering reasonably priced accommodation, campsites and good self-catering facilities.

Game viewing isn't cheap, and mostly you get what you pay for. The **least expensive** way of experiencing a game park is by renting a car and **self-driving** around a national park, taking advantage of the self-catering and camping facilities. Nearby backpackers' lodges, and occasionally hotels and B&Bs, will often offer **safari excursions**. The disadvantages of these are that you miss out on the experience of waking up in the wild and you spend considerably more time on the road. But during South African school holidays, when Kruger, for example, is booked to capacity, you may have no other option. Another budget alternative for the Kruger, worth considering if you're alone and have no transport, is to stay outside the park and take game drives with a safari company into the park or a **budget tour** from Johannesburg or one of the gateway towns.

In addition to the state-run parks, there are expensive **private reserves**, frequently abutting onto them and sharing the same wildlife population. For your money you'll see the same animals, but under more exclusive conditions, staying at luxurious game lodges staffed by well-informed rangers who lead game-viewing outings in open-topped 4WDs. If you're new to the African bush and its wildlife, consider shelling out and spending at least two nights at one of the safari lodges on the private reserves abutting Kruger and then set out on your own. If money's no object, don't bother with self-driving at all.

A word of warning: be wary of any cheap deals on "safari farms" in the vicinity of Kruger. These are generally fine if you want to see animals in what are essentially huge zoos and make an acceptable overnight stop en route to Kruger, but are no substitute for a real wilderness experience – sooner or later you hit fences and gates on your game drive. Some of the better places in this category are given in the relevant chapters.

Spotting game takes skill and experience. It's easier than you'd think to mistake a rhino for a large boulder, or to miss the king of the beasts in the tall, lion-coloured grass – African game is after all designed with camouflage in mind. Don't expect the volume of animals you get in wildlife documentaries, which edit months of filming into half an hour: what you see is always a matter of luck, patience and skill. The section on Kruger National Park (see p.693) gives advice on how to go about spotting game and how to enjoy and understand what you do see – whether it's a brightly coloured lizard in a rest camp, head-butting giraffes at a waterhole or dust-kicking rhinos. For other **books** that can enhance your visit to a game reserve, see p.895.

Although the Kruger is the focus for most of South Africa's safari activity, particularly for venturing into the wilderness with skilled guides, the KwaZulu-Natal game reserves – foremost among them **Hluhluwe-Umfolozi**, **Mkuzi** and **Itala** – offer rewarding opportunities for self-drive touring. The same applies to the **Pilanesberg Game Reserve** in Northwest Province, while the remote **Kalahari-Gemsbok National Park** on the border of Botswana promises truly exciting wilderness driving. A number of extremely upmarket operations offer the whole game-lodge experience on private reserves, where your vehicle stays in the car park and you walk or are driven around by a guide. Among the most prestigious of these are **Phinda** in KwaZulu-Natal and **Tswalu** in the Northern Cape.

Self-drive safaris

Self-driving involves the thrill of spotting game yourself, rather than relying on a game ranger, and gives you the freedom to stick around for as long as you like. For people with **children** it's the principal way to get into a game reserve, as most of the upmarket lodges don't admit under-12s. You also have the advantage of going at your own pace, and may choose to cover a route that takes in both the Mpumalanga reserves and those in KwaZulu-Natal, just a few hours away – an appealing combination of one large and some more intimate reserves, which cover very different terrain.

As far as **accommodation** at the state reserves is concerned, you'll usually have a broad choice of camping; basic chalets with shared washing facilities; safari tents; or comfortable en-suite units (see p.42 for prices). En-suite accommodation is in serviced, thatched rondavels with linen provided. The cheaper units usually don't have their own kitchen, although everywhere you go will have a fridge, tea-making facilities and somewhere to braai. In several of the KwaZulu-Natal parks rest camps you aren't allowed to use the kitchen, but give your food to the camp chef and attendants who prepare your meal for you, serve you and wash up, at no extra cost. **Advance booking** is essential to secure a place to stay in a national park – this is especially true during holiday season.

Most game reserve rest camps have a **shop** selling supplies for picnics or braais, as well as a **restaurant**.

If you plan to self-drive, consider investing in good animal and bird field **guides**; once in the park, you'll find them indispensable for identification and learning about what you see. The same applies to a decent pair of **binoculars** – one pair per person is recommended if you want to keep your relationships on a friendly footing. Finally, whether you're cooking or not, it's worth taking a thermos for tea and a cool bag to keep water cold.

The one real disadvantage of self-driving is that you can end up jostling with other cars to get a view, especially when it comes to lion-watching. Also, you may not know what animal signs to look for; and unless you travel in a minibus or 4WD vehicle you're unlikely to be high enough off the ground to be able to see across the *veld*.

Private reserves and lodges

If you choose well, the ultimate South African game experience has to be in a **private reserve** or **lodge**. The advantage of private reserves is that you spend time in a small group and relax while your game-viewing activities are organized, and because you rarely see other visitors you get a stronger sense of the wild than you ever could at one of the big Kruger rest camps. Most of all, you get the benefit of knowledgeable rangers, who can explain the terrain and small-scale wildlife as they drive you around looking for game.

Nowhere are the private reserves more developed than along the west flank of the **Kruger**, where you'll find the top-dollar prestigious lodges as well as some places offering more bang for fewer bucks.

Smaller private reserves accommodate between ten and sixteen guests, which gives you very close contact with your hosts. Larger camps often cater to two or three times as many people, and resemble hotels in the bush, though you'll always have a game ranger and see the same quantity of game. Many safari lodges have their own waterholes, overlooked by the bar, from which you can watch animals drinking.

Accommodation is in luxurious safari tents with private bathrooms, or in a variety of chalets – some thatch and brick, some stylish luxury suites. A couple of places have "bush-showers" (a hoisted bucket of hot water with a shower nozzle attached) behind reed screens but open to the sky – one of the great treats of the bush is taking a shower under the southern sky. Some chalets or tents have gaslights or lanterns in the absence of electricity. **Food** is usually good and plentiful, and vegetarians can be catered for.

A **typical day** at a private camp or lodge starts at dawn for tea or coffee followed by guided game viewing on foot, or driving. After a mid-morning brunch/breakfast, there's the chance to spend time on a viewing platform or in a hide, quietly watching the passing scene. Late-afternoon game viewing is a repeat of early morning but culminates with sundowners as the light fades, and often turns into a night drive with spotlights out looking for nocturnal creatures.

Prices, which include accommodation,

meals and all game activities, vary widely. The ultra-expensive camps offer more luxury and social cachet, but not necessarily better game viewing. You might find the cheaper camps in the same areas more to your taste, their plainer and wilder atmosphere more in keeping with the bush.

Eating and drinking

South Africa doesn't really have a coherent indigenous cuisine, although attempts have been made to elevate Cape Cuisine to this status. The one element which seems to unite the country is a love of meat, and as a visitor you might struggle to keep in check the locals' assumption that meat and lots of it is the ideal choice for every meal. Having said that, South Africa is an ideal place to try out all kinds of interesting types of meat, from ostrich to giraffe, and good quality steaks are inexpensive and freely available. Alternatively, it's well worth paying attention to South Africa's vast array of seafood, which includes a wide variety of fish, lobster (crayfish), oysters and mussels. Locally grown fruit, vegetables and salads are generally of a high standard, and often available from markets and farm stalls in areas such as the Western Cape. Drinking is dominated by a handful of unmemorable lager beers and South Africa's often superb wines. In the cities, though less so beyond them, there are numerous excellent restaurants where you can taste a spectrum of international styles.

South African food

Although South Africa's indigenous offerings are few, you can still expect to eat well in this country. The variety of food available is huge, and context is always important – you may not want to eat *boerewors* at a restaurant; but at a braai under the stars, accompanied by a few beers, it's almost obligatory. Traditional African food tends to focus around stiff grain porridge called "pap" or "mielie pap" (similar to Italian polenta) accompanied by meat or vegetable-based sauces. Among white South Africans, Afrikaners have evolved a style of cooking known as *boerekos* ("farmer's food") that tends to be cholesterol-rich and can be heavy-going if you're not used to it (see box opposite). People of British extraction favour the traditional English style of meat and overcooked vegetables. As a snack, sun-dried meat called *biltong*, similar to beef jerky, is widely consumed.

Cape Cuisine

Styles of cooking brought by Asian slaves have evolved into **Cape Cuisine** (sometimes known as Cape Malay food – a misnomer given that few slaves came from Malaysia). Characterized by sweet aromatic curries, Cape Cuisine is worth sampling at least once, especially in Cape Town, where it developed and is associated with the Muslim community. Although it can be delicious, there isn't that much variety and few restaurants specialize in it. Despite this, most of the dishes considered as Cape Cuisine have actually crept into the South African diet, many becoming part of the Afrikaner culinary vocabulary.

Other ethnic and regional influences

Although South Africa doesn't really have distinct regional cuisines, you will find changes of emphasis and local specialities in different parts of the country. **KwaZulu-Natal**, for instance, particularly around Durban and Pietermaritzburg, is especially good for Indian food. The South African contribution to this great multifaceted tradition is the humble **bunny chow**, a cheap takeaway consisting of a hollowed out half-loaf of white bread originally filled with curried beans, but nowadays with anything from curried chicken to sardines.

Because of its proximity to Mozambique, **Portuguese food** made early inroads into South Africa, predominantly through the use of hot and spicy peri-peri seasoning, which goes extremely well with braais. The best-known example of this is delicious **peri-peri chicken**, which you will find all over. **Italian food** has also been around for a while, brought over with POWs from the North Africa campaign who were incarcerated here and stayed on after World War II. You'll find some excellent Italian restaurants in the cities, from small pizzerias to smarter restaurants going the whole hog. Eastern European **Jewish food** arrived with turn-of-the-century refugees and you'll find bagels, chopped liver and chopped herring at delis and some supermarkets.

Vegetarian food

While not quite a **vegetarian** paradise, South Africa is nevertheless vegetarian-savvy and you'll find at least one concession to meatless food on most menus. Even steakhouses will have something palatable on offer and generally offer the best salad bars around; especially at the Spur chain, where you can fill up on greens for not much more than US$2/£1.50. If you're self-catering in the larger cities, delicious dips and breads can be found at delis and Woolworths and Pick'n'Pay supermarkets. South Africa's wide choice of vegetables and fruit is mostly grown in the country and is inexpensive compared to Europe.

Eating out

Restaurants in South Africa offer outstanding value compared with Britain or North America. In every city you'll find places where you can eat a good main course for

The braai and boerekos

Braai (which rhymes with "dry") is an abbreviation of *braaivleis*, an Afrikaans word translated as "meat grill". More than simply the process of cooking over an outdoor fire, however, a braai is a cultural event arguably even more central to the South African identity than barbecues are to Australians. Despite its identification as part of quintessential white South Africa, braais are now popular across the races, and at any national park, nature reserve or resort you'll never be far from the distinctive odour of gently sizzling meat.

A braai is an intensely social event, usually amongst family and friends and accompanied by gallons of beer. It's also probably the only occasion you'll catch an unreconstructed white South African man cooking. You can braai anything, but a traditional barbecue meal consists of huge slabs of steak, lamb cutlets and **boerewors** ("farmer's sausage"), a deliciously spicy South African speciality. Potatoes and onions wrapped in aluminium foil and placed in the embers are a usual accompaniment. The real skill comes in knowing when the coals are hot enough to cook the meat and in concocting the marinades and sauces – in fact, discussion on the topic vies with rugby as the subject of the most intense conversation around a braai.

A variant on the braai is **potjiekos** – pronounced "poy-key-kos"– (pot food), in which the food is cooked, preferably outdoor over an open fire, in a three-legged cast-iron cauldron (the *potjie*). In a similar vein, but cooked indoors is **boerekos**, (literally "farmer's food"), a style of cooking enjoyed mainly by Afrikaners. Much of it is similar to English food, but taken to cholesterol-rich extremes, with even the vegetables prepared with sugar and butter. Should you spend the night on an Afrikaans farm, you could well find yourself waking up to a breakfast of several eggs, steak, piles of bacon and *boerewors*. *Boerekos* comes into its own in its variety of over-the-top desserts, including *koeksisters* (plaited doughnuts saturated with syrup) and *melktert* ("milk tart"), a solid rich custard in a flan case.

well under US$7/£4, and for US$15/£10 you can splurge on the best. Restaurants with imaginative menus are found in all the larger centres. **Franschhoek**, a small town in the Winelands, has established itself as a culinary centre for the country, where you'll find some fine eating places in extremely close proximity. As a rule, restaurants are licensed, but Muslim establishments serving Cape Cuisine don't allow alcohol at all.

An attractive phenomenon in the big cities, especially Cape Town, has been the rise of the continental-style **cafés** – easy-going, informal places where you can eat just as well as you would in a regular restaurant, but also drink coffee all night without feeling you're expected to order food. A reasonable meal in a café is unlikely to set you back more than US$5/£3. Café service tends to be slick and friendly, with long opening hours. Make sure you don't confuse this new type of café with the traditional South African café found in even the tiniest country town. The equivalent of a corner store elsewhere, they commonly sell a few magazines, soft drinks, sweets, crisps and an odd collection of tins and dry goods. Their only concession to ready-to-eat food is normally a meat pie heated in a microwave, or a leg of chicken that spent a little too long incubating in the warmer.

If popularity is the yardstick, then South Africa's real national cuisine is to be found in its **franchise restaurants**, which you'll find in every town of any size. The usual international names like KFC and Wimpy are omnipresent, but these are no match for South Africa's own home-grown American-style steakhouses, such as **Spurs**, **Steers** and **Saddles**, which project a wholesome Wild West image and remain popular with South African families. South Africa's great contribution to the world of fast food is the **Nando's Chickenland** chain, which grills excellent Portuguese-style chicken, served under a variety of spicy sauces. Expect to pay around US$3/£2 for a filling burger and chips or chicken meal at any of these places and around US$5/£3 for a good-sized steak.

Drinking

Although South Africa yearns to be a major wine-producing country, **beer** is indisputably the national drink. Beer is as much an emblem of South African manhood as the braai – and unlike the braai, it cuts through all race and class divisions. Pubs and bars are not the centres of social activity they are in the US or the UK, although in the African townships **shebeens** or informal bars do occupy this position; whites tend to do their drinking at home. In city centres, **bars** have traditionally been rough, men-only places, women being corralled into stiff lounges and ladies' bars attached to hotels. The **Irish/British-style pub** is beginning to make an appearance under the invasion of a series of franchised names, but has no deep roots in South African culture. Beer, wines and spirits can be bought at supermarkets and bottle stores (the equivalent of the British off-licence), which generally keep normal shopping hours, although some stay open until 6.30pm. Don't expect be able to buy liquor at night or on Sundays.

Beer

South Africans tend to be fiercely loyal to their brand of **beer**, though they all taste pretty much the same, given that virtually all beer in the country is produced by the huge South African Breweries monopoly. **Lager** is the predominant style, and to a British palate is likely to taste a bit thin and bland, though it can be wonderfully refreshing drunk ice-cold on a sweltering day. One or two micro-breweries have sprung up, best known of which is Mitchell's in Knysna, which produces some distinctive ales. These can be found at some bottle stores and bars between Cape Town and Port Elizabeth. **Imported beers** are starting to appear, but they're rather expensive compared to the local product.

Wine

South Africa's **wine industry** has emerged out of years in sanction-enforced doldrums, casting aside a 350-year-old tradition of trying to make French wine, and nailing its colours to the fresh, fruity style of New World wines. Production is rising all the time to meet the demands of the ever-growing export market, and a number of South African winemakers are achieving international recognition. While one or two labels produce some superb wines, in general, standards haven't reached those of Australian wine (yet). But make no mistake: this country produces some excellent wines at prices few visitors from overseas are likely to grumble about.

In general, South Africa's **white** wines such as Sauvingon Blanc and Reisling are a slightly better quality overall than its **red** wines, although among the reds you should look out for wines made from the **Pinotage** grape, a varietal unique to South Africa. **Port** is also made, though connoisseurs of the Portuguese equivalent will struggle to recognise the over-sweet, over-sticky South African style. On the other hand, a handful excellent **sparkling wines** are produced.

Prices for quaffable bottles start below US$4/£3 and the vast bulk of wines cost less than US$15/£10. For double this price you can expect the best, although anything over about US$8/£5 is considered outrageously expensive by locals. This means that anyone with an adventurous streak can indulge in a bacchanalia of sampling without breaking the bank. Wine is available throughout the country, although prices rise as you move out of the Western Cape.

The best way to sample wines is by visiting **wineries**, some of which charge a small tasting fee to discourage freeloading. The oldest and most rewarding wine-producing regions are the **Constantia estates** in Cape Town (see p.130) and the region known as the **Winelands** around the towns of Stellenbosch (see p.181), Paarl (see p.190) and Franschhoek (see p.197), which all have institutionalized wine routes. Other wine-producing areas include the Klein Karoo (see p.202), Robertson (see p.205), the Swartland (see p.282), the Orange River (see p.323) and Walker Bay (see p.236).

Soft drinks

There are no surprises when it comes to **soft drinks**, with all the usual names available. What does stand out is South African **fruit juice** the range is broad and includes what must be one of the most extensive selections of unsweetened juices in the world under the Liquifruit and Ceres labels.

Mail, telephones and internet access

Most towns of any size have a post office, generally open Monday to Friday 8.30am to 4.30pm and Saturday 8am to 11.30am (closing earlier in some places). The deceptively familiar feel of South African post offices can lull you into expecting an efficient British- or US-style service. In fact, post within the country is slow, erratic and unreliable, and money and valuables are frequently stolen en route. For important items, it makes sense to use one of the private courier services such as Federal Express, which are more expensive, but far more reliable.

Expect domestic delivery times from one city to another of about a week – longer if a rural town is involved at either end. **International airmail** deliveries are often quicker, especially if you're sending or receiving at Johannesburg, Cape Town or Durban – the cities with direct flights to London. By surface mail, you can expect your letter or package to take anything up to six weeks to get from South Africa to London. **Stamps** are available at post offices and newsagents, such as the CNA chain, and postage is relatively inexpensive compared to Britain or North America. You'll find **poste restante** facilities at the main post office in most larger centres, and in many backpackers' hostels.

Phones

South Africa's **telephone system**, operated by the state monopoly, Telkom, generally works well. Public phone booths are

Domestic phone numbers

Since 2001, all South African numbers have consisted of a ten-digit number that incorporates the area code. Wherever you are – whether inside or outside the area you are phoning – you must dial the entire number. For example, if you are in Cape Town and are phoning another number in the city you must include the 021 prefix.

found in every city and town, and many more are being installed in rural areas – a tangible result of the new government's policy of taking services to the people.

There are two types of Telkom phone: coin- or card-operated. While international calls can be made from virtually any phone, it helps to have a card, as you'll be lucky to stay on the line for more than a minute or two for R15. **Cards** are available at Telkom offices, post offices and newsagents, and come in R15, 20, 50, 100 and 200 denominations.

If you need to use the phone while staying at a **hotel**, be sure to ask what their rate is – the surcharge is often extortionate. In cities, you'll find **private phone bureaus**, where you can make your call on a normal phone and pay afterwards but, while it's more comfortable to sit down, these cost considerably more than a Telkom phone booth. Some of these bureaus will also send and receive **faxes** for you, which though expensive, may turn out cheaper than making a phone call. Many newsagents also offer fax services, advertised in their windows.

Mobile phones

Mobile phones (known locally as cellular or cell phones) operate on the GSM digital system. They're extremely well-established in South Africa, with more mobile than landline handsets now in use in the country. The two competing networks, Vodacom and MTN – with a third due to enter the market in 2002 – cover all the main areas and the national roads connecting them. If you want to use your GSM phone in South Africa you will need to arrange a **roaming agreement** with your provider at home – but be warned this

is likely to be expensive. If you don't need to be contacted on your normal number, a far cheaper alternative is to buy an inexpensive pay-as-you-go package which consists of a **local SIM card**, with which you replace your own one while you're in South Africa. The SIM card contains your new South African phone number, and you pay for airtime with **prepaid cards** that can be bought from the ubiquitous mobile phone shops and a number of other outlets including the CNA chain of newsagents and supermarkets. Before leaving home, check whether your phone has been network locked, in which case it will only work with your normal network. Keep your original SIM card safe, as you'll need to replace this when you return home.

Mobile phone **rental** can be arranged at the airports in the main cities as well as through other providers in town. US travellers will need a tri-band phone to use the South African network. For details of which mobiles will work outside the US, contact your mobile service provider. For further information about using your phone abroad, check out ⓦ www.telecomsadvice.org.uk /features/using_your_mobile_abroad.htm.

International calls

One of the most convenient ways of phoning home from abroad is via a **telephone charge card**. Using access codes for the particular country you are in and a PIN number, you can make calls from most hotel, public and private phones that will be charged to your own account. While rates are always cheaper from a residential phone at off-peak rates, that's normally not an option when you're travelling (if you do use a calling card in conjunction with a residential phone, when you're staying as a guest, for instance, you will be paying the calling card company's rates, which will usually be dearer than the local operator's). You may be able to use it to minimize hotel phone surcharges, but don't depend on it. However, the benefit of calling cards is mainly one of convenience, as rates aren't necessarily cheaper than calling from a public phone while abroad and can't compete with discounted off-peak times many local phone companies offer. But since most major charge cards are

Directory enquiries and international codes

Telkom operates an extremely useful **directory enquiry service** (☎1023). However, English is not the first language of many of the operators and, with standards of literacy quite a lot lower than in Europe or North America, be prepared to be patient and to help the operator with spelling. Also remember that the English accent people are accustomed to here may be very different to your own – so talk slowly and clearly.

International calls

To call southern Africa **from overseas**, dial the international access code (☎00 from the UK; ☎011 from the USA and Canada; ☎0011 from Australia; ☎00 from New Zealand) followed by the country code. Remember to leave out any zeros in front of domestic area codes. The international codes are:

South Africa ☎27   Lesotho ☎266   Swaziland ☎268

To dial **out of South Africa**, the international access code is ☎09. To dial **out of Lesotho and Swaziland**, the code is ☎00. Remember to omit any zeros in front of the city, town or area code of the place you're phoning. Outgoing international codes from South Africa include:

Australia ☎0961   Ireland 09353   New Zealand ☎0964

UK and Northern Ireland ☎0944   USA and Canada ☎091

free to obtain, it's certainly worth getting one at least for emergencies; enquire first though whether South Africa is covered.

In **the UK and Ireland**, British Telecom (☎0800/345144) will issue free to all BT customers the BT Charge Card, which can be used in South Africa; AT&T (Dial ☎0800/890 011, then ☎888 641 6123 when you hear the AT&T prompt to be transferred to the Florida Call Centre, free 24 hours) has the Global Calling Card; while Cable & Wireless (☎0500/100505) issues its own Global Calling Card, which can be used in more than sixty countries abroad, though the fees cannot be charged to a normal phone bill.

To call **Australia and New Zealand** from overseas, telephone charge cards such as Telstra Telecard or Optus Calling Card in Australia, and Telecom NZ's Calling Card can be used to make calls abroad, which are charged back to a domestic account or credit card. Apply to Telstra (☎1800/038 000), Optus (☎1300/300 937), or Telecom NZ (☎04/801 9000).

The cheapest time to make **international calls** is Monday to Friday 8pm to 8am and during the weekends. Collect or **reverse-charge calls** can be made from any phone through the International Operator Service (☎0900).

Internet access

One of the best ways to keep in touch while travelling is by email. Access in South Africa is widespread, with cybercafés found even in relatively small centres, and most **backpacker hostels** have internet and email facilities. The downside is that connecting with international sites can be slow, particularly in the afternoon when Americans come on line and gobble up bandwidth.

Before leaving home, you should check whether your existing **email account** offers a web-based service that enables you to pick up your email from any internet terminal in the world. This is becoming increasingly common and is very useful and straightforward, though it can sometimes be a bit slow. Failing this, you can set up a **free email address** that can be accessed from anywhere, for example YahooMail or Hotmail – accessible through ⓦwww.yahoo.com and ⓦwww.hotmail.com. Once you've set up an account, you can use these sites to pick up and send mail from any internet café, or hotel with internet access. ⓦwww.kropka .com is a useful website giving details of how to plug your laptop in when abroad, phone country codes around the world, and information about electrical systems in different countries.

The media

South Africa's press is rather parochial, with one or two notable exceptions. Unlike Britain, the country lacks a strong tradition of national papers and instead has many regional papers of varying quality. Television delivers a mix of imported programmes and home-grown soaps heavily modelled on US fare, as well as the odd home-grown reality TV show and one or two watchable documentary slots.

Radio is where South Africa is finding it easiest to meet the multicultural needs of a diverse and scattered audience. Deregulation of the airwaves has brought to life scores of new small stations.

Newspapers

Of the roughly twenty **newspapers**, most of which are published in English or Afrikaans, the only ones that qualify as nationals are the weeklies, the *Mail & Guardian*, the *Sunday Times* and the *Sunday Independent*. The *Mail & Guardian* is available throughout the country, and benefits enormously from its close association with the London *Guardian* (from which it draws most of its international coverage); it's unquestionably the country's intellectual heavyweight, although its dense reporting can be a bit stodgy.

The *Sunday Times* can attribute the fact that it has the biggest circulation in the country – roughly half a million copies – to its well-calculated mix of solid investigative reporting, gossip stories, material from the London Telegraph and tabloid sex.

The *Sunday Independent* is owned by Tony O' Reilly, whose press stable includes the London *Independent* and its Irish counterpart and projects a more thoughtful image than the *Sunday Times*, but is beginning to look a bit thin, with almost all its foreign news lifted from its sister papers.

The *Sowetan*, targeted at a mainly black Jo'burg audience, is also widely available across the country and provides a less exclusively white perspective on South African issues.

Of the English dailies, the *Star* in Johannesburg proves to offer less than one might hope for from the mouthpiece of the country's economic hub, while *Business Day*, with its solid coverage of local and international news as well as commerce, is South Africa's equivalent of the *Financial Times* or the *Wall Street Journal*.

Local papers are useful for listings; in Cape Town you'll find the *Cape Times*, and the *Cape Argus*, sister paper to the *Star*, which identifies itself with issues local to the mother city. Durban brings out the *Daily News* and the *Natal Mercury* in the morning and evening, while Port Elizabeth offers the *Eastern Province Herald* – a tacky broadsheet with the heart of a tabloid. Finally, East London has the *Daily Dispatch*, an Eastern Cape paper packed with local news, which earned some fame in the 1970s for its sympathetic coverage of black consciousness leader, Steve Biko.

The easiest places for **buying newspapers** are corner stores and newsagents, especially the CNA chain. These places also sell **international press**, such as *Time*, *Newsweek*, *The Economist* and the weekly editions of the London *Daily Mail*, the *Telegraph* and the *Express*.

Television

Every day twelve million South African adults tune into the SABC's three public **TV** channels, which churn out a mixed bag of domestic dramas, game shows, soaps and documentaries, filled out with lashings of familiar imports. **SABC 1**, **2** and **3** share the unenviable task of trying to deliver an integrated service, while having to split their time between the eleven official languages. This massive mission would tax the resources of even a rich, industrialized country, but for a Third World one like South Africa it's a crippling project. In practice, English turns out to be most widely used, with SABC 3 broad-

BBC World Service and VOA

The **BBC World Service** gives wider coverage than local South African stations, and broadcasts some excellent programmes in its **Africa Service**. Reception can vary considerably, so it's worth surfing the airwaves to find the sharpest frequency. As a rule of thumb, the short wave ones (below 7000kHz) tend to provide better reception from late afternoon and throughout the evening, while the higher ones are usually better during the early morning till about midday. **Frequencies** tend to change seasonally, so it's best to find out current wavelengths from the World Service's website (📶www.bbc.co.uk/worldservice/schedules/safrica.htm), or by simply experimenting.

The English-language service to Africa **Voice of America** broadcasts throughout the day on 909kHz (medium wave), as well as on a number of short-wave frequencies. A complete list of current schedules is available on their website (📶www.voa.gov /allsked.html).

casting almost exclusively in the language, while SABC 2 and SABC 1 spread themselves thinly across all the remaining ten languages with a fair amount of English creeping in even here.

A selection of sports, movies, news and specialist channels are available to subscribers to the **M-Net** satellite service, which you'll find piped into many hotels. South Africa's first and only free-to-air independent commercial channel **e.tv** won its franchise in 1998 on the promise of providing a showcase for local productions, a pledge it has signally failed to meet – its output has consisted substantially of uninspired and uninspiring imports.

Radio

Given South Africa's low literacy rate and widespread poverty, it's no surprise that **radio** is its most popular medium; receivers are cheap and broadcasts can penetrate into even the remotest rural area. The SABC operates a national radio station for each of the eleven official language groups. The

English-language service, **SAfm** is of a generally high standard; its best offerings are the highly polished evening and morning news programmes. SAfm's **Tim Modise Show** (Mon–Fri 8.30–10am), a current affairs phone-in and talkshow broadcast nationally, offers one of the best ways of plugging in to what ordinary South Africans are thinking. Modise has earned the respect of South Africans of all races for his gentle manner and his tolerance. His is one of the few programmes on the air where you'll hear the voices of members of all South Africa's ethnic groups engaging in dialogue or simply ranting and sounding off.

The SABC also runs **5FM Stereo**, a national pop station broadcasting Top 40 tracks, while their **Radio Metro** is targeted at black urban listeners. Apart from these, there are scores of regional, commercial and community stations, broadcasting a range of material, which makes surfing the airwaves an enjoyable experience, wherever you are in the country.

Opening hours and holidays

The working day starts and finishes early in South Africa: shops and businesses generally open on weekdays at 8.30am or 9am and close at 4.30pm or 5pm. In small towns, many places close for an hour over lunch. Many shops and businesses close around noon on Saturdays for the day, and most shops are closed on Sundays. However, in every neighbourhood, you'll find places – small shops and supermarkets – where you can buy groceries and essentials after hours.

Banking hours are generally Monday to Friday 8.30am to 3.30pm, Saturday 8am to 11am, but you'll find **bureaux de change** in the major cities open until at least 5pm (see "Listings" for each city for late openings) and open at the international airports to meet flights. Post offices are generally open 8.30am to 4.30pm on weekdays, and Saturdays 8am to 11.30am. Government departments are open 8am to 4pm weekdays.

Holidays

School holidays in South Africa can disrupt your plans, especially if you want to camp, or stay in the national parks and the cheaper end of accommodation (self-catering, cheaper B&Bs, etc), all of which are likely to be booked solid during that period. If you do travel to South Africa over the school holidays, book your accommodation well in advance, especially for the national parks.

The longest and busiest holiday period is **Christmas (summer)**, which for schools stretches from around December 4 to January 21. Flights and train berths can be hard to get from December 16 to January 2,

when many businesses and offices close for their annual break. You should book your flights – long-haul and domestic – as early as six months in advance for the Christmas period. The provinces stagger their school holidays, but as a general rule, the remaining school holidays cover the following periods: **Easter**, March 20–April 15; **winter**, June 20–July 21; and **spring**, Sept 19 –Oct 7.

South African public holidays

(For Lesotho and Swaziland public holidays, see p.754 & p.796).

January 1 New Year's Day
March 21 Human Rights Day
Good Friday
Easter Sunday
Easter Monday
April 27 Freedom Day
May 1 Workers' Day
June 16 Youth Day
August 9 National Women's Day
September 24 Heritage Day
December 16 Day of Reconciliation
Christmas Day
December 26 Day of Goodwill

Photography

South Africa is outstandingly photogenic; you don't need to be a professional to get striking photographs. What kind of camera you take depends on how much weight you're prepared to carry around, how much of a tourist you want to look, and whether or not you plan to photograph animals.

Small, compact cameras are handy for a quick shot, but they're hopeless for wildlife – a nearby lion will end up a furry speck in savannah. Compacts are also potentially dangerous – tales abound of tourists with little cameras sneaking up too close for comfort to big game and ending up hurt.

If you take your photography seriously, you'll probably want a single-lens reflex camera (SLR) and two or three lenses – a heavy and cumbersome option. For decent wildlife photography you definitely need a **telephoto lens**. A 300mm lens is a good all-rounder; any bigger and you'll need a tripod. The smallest you could get away with for animals is 200mm, while 400mm is the best for birds. All long lenses need fast film, or you'll find you're restricted to the largest apertures, and hence the narrowest depth of focus. If you simply want good snaps from your SLR, think about one well-chosen zoom lens.

Protecting your camera and film

The biggest problem can be **dust**, which tends to penetrate straight into a normal camera case or cloth bag. When travelling in dry, dusty regions, cameras need to be inside sealed plastic bags, or in some dust-proof container, and taken out only for the business of taking pictures. You'll need to carry a blower-brush to blow dust off lenses.

Another problem is South Africa's **heat**. Never leave your camera or films lying in the sun; the film in a camera left exposed on a car seat, for instance, will be completely ruined. Keep rolls of film cool in the middle of your clothes or sleeping bag.

Light reading

You really have to rely on a judicious combination of the camera's **light readings** and your own common sense. The contrast between light and shade can be huge, so expose for the subject and not the general scene. This can mean setting your camera to manual, approaching the subject to get a reading and then using that. With a zoom you can zoom in for a reading and then return. Some of the new multi-mode cameras will do much of this for you.

If you're photographing black people, especially in strong light, use more exposure than usual, otherwise they'll be underexposed; the light and your eyes (which are more sophisticated than any camera) can deceive you.

Early morning and late afternoon are the best times for photography. At midday, with the sun overhead, the light is flat and everything is lost in glare.

Film

Film is readily available in South Africa. Don't let anyone tell you it's unnecessary to have fast film because the sun is so bright in Africa. Even if you opt for a compact with a fast lens (ie one that's very light-sensitive) you'll need at least some 400 ASA film if you want to take pictures at dawn and dusk and in heavy cloud or forest. With long lenses on an SLR, fast film is essential.

Subjects and people

Photographing animals requires patience: avoid endless snaps of nothing happening. If you can't get close enough, don't waste your film. While taking photos, try keeping both eyes open and, in a vehicle, always turn off your engine.

You should always ask before taking photographs of **people** or, for example, of a dwelling decorated with colourful paintings. Some kind of interaction and exchange is customarily implied: people often ask for a copy of the photograph and you'll end up with several names and addresses and a list of promises.

Spectator sports

South Africa is a nation obsessed by sport, where heights of devotion are reached whenever local or international teams take to the field. Winning performances, controversial selections and scandals commonly dominate the front as well as the back pages of newspapers, and it can be hard to escape the domination of sport across radio, television and advertising media. The big spectator sports are soccer, rugby and cricket, and big matches involving the international team or big local clubs are well worth seeing live to experience the atmosphere and intensity of the crowd. Even on TV, however, the big games attract noisy gatherings in pubs and bars, adding to the excitement of watching them.

Soccer

Soccer is the country's most popular game, with a primarily black and coloured following, and it is only now starting to attract the kind of serious money that could one day see South Africa as one of the world's top soccer nations.

The professional season runs from August to May, with teams competing in the **Premier Soccer League** (PSL) and a couple of knock-out cup competitions. Unlike rugby teams, soccer teams do not own their own grounds and are forced to rent them for specific fixtures, which means that in Gauteng, the heartland of South African soccer, all the big clubs have to use the same grounds, which has prevented the development of the kind of terrace fan culture found elsewhere. Nonetheless, soccer crowds are generally witty and good-spirited, and while predominantly black, whites have no reason to feel uncomfortable going to a game.

The very big games, normally involving Johannesburg's big two teams, **Kaiser Chiefs** and **Orlando Pirates**, do simmer with underlying tension, though violence is rare. A tragic episode at a Chiefs–Pirates derby game at Ellis Park in Johannesburg in 2001, when a number of fans were trampled to death, was due to ticketing problems rather than fighting in the crowd. Although Chiefs and Pirates are both Sowetan clubs, they have a nationwide following, and their derbies are the highlight of the PSL's fixture list.

Games are played on weekday evenings (usually at 7.30pm or 8.30pm) and at 3pm on Saturdays, and cost about R25. The national squad, nicknamed **Bafana Bafana** (literally "boys boys" but connoting "our lads") are one of the stronger teams in Africa and have qualified for the World Cup finals in both 1998 and 2002. Bafana play typically South African soccer – imaginative and strong on spectacular athletic feats that have the crowd cheering, but less impressive when it comes to team work and resilience. Even games they should win have that element of unpredictability that makes for great spectator sport.

Rugby

Rugby is hugely popular with whites, especially Afrikaners, though attempts to broaden the game's appeal, particularly to a black audience, have struggled. The 1995 World Cup, hosted by South Africa, attracted fanatical attention nationwide, particularly when the national team, the Springboks, triumphed in the final and President Nelson Mandela donned a green Springbok jersey (long associated exclusively with whites) to present the cup to the winning side. Since then the goodwill has dissipated, to be replaced by an acrimonious struggle to transform the traditionally white sports (cricket and rugby) into something more representative of all race groups, particularly following the government's policy of enforcing racial quotas in national squads.

Despite this, the fact remains that South Africa is extraordinarily good at rugby, and you are likely to witness high-quality, if brutal play when you watch either inter-regional or international games. The main domestic competition has traditionally been the **Currie**

Cup, with games played on weekends from March to October. Admission is around R50. More recently this has been overshadowed by the **Super 12** competition, involving regional teams from South Africa, New Zealand and Australia. Matches are staged annually from late February to the end of May in all three countries, and in South Africa you'll catch a fair bit of action in the major centres of Johannesburg, Cape Town and Durban, though smaller places such as Port Elizabeth, East London, Bloemfontein and George sometimes get a look in. **International** fixtures involving the Springboks are dominated by visiting tours by northern hemisphere teams and the annual **Tri-Nations** competition, in which South Africa plays home and away fixtures against Australia and New Zealand. These are normally played from June to August, and are invariably popular, so you will need to get tickets well in advance.

Cricket

Cricket was for some years seen as the most progressive of the former white sports, with development programmes generating support and discovering talent among black and coloured communities. The sport was rocked to its foundations in 2000, however, when it was revealed that South African national captain Hansie Cronje had received money from betting syndicates hoping to influence the outcome of matches. Cronje was banned for life, but the credibility of the sport took a dive.

The domestic season of inter-provincial games runs from October to April, and the main one-day competition is the **Standard Bank Cup**. Games are played throughout the week, and admission is around R25 for standing and R35 for a seat. In the international standings, South Africa are one of the world's top teams, and you stand a good chance of being around for an international test or one-day series if you are in the country between November and March. South African cricket teams have historically been almost solidly white, but a few coloureds and Africans are now playing for their country.

Running

South Africa is very strong at **long distance running**, a tradition that reached its apotheosis at the 1996 Atlanta Olympics when Josiah Thugwane won the marathon, the first black South African ever to bag Olympic gold. The biggest single sports event in South Africa, the **Comrades Marathon**, attracts nearly 15,000 participants, among them some of the world's leading international ultra-marathon runners. The 90km course crosses the hilly country between Durban and Pietermaritzburg, with a drop of almost 800m between the town and the coast. Run annually on May 31, the race alternates direction each year and is notable for having been non-racial since 1975, although it took till 1989 for a South African, Samuel Tshabalala, to win it. Since then, black athletes have begun to dominate the front rankings.

Horse racing

You'll find huge interest among rich and poor South Africans in **horse racing**, with totes and tracks in all the main cities. Its popularity is partly due to the fact that for decades this was the only form of public gambling that South Africa's Afrikaner Calvinist rulers allowed – on the pretext that it involved skill not chance. The highlight of the racing calendar is the **Rothman's Durban July Handicap** held at Durban's Greyville racecourse. A flamboyant event, it attracts huge crowds, massive purses, socialites in outrageous headgear and vast amounts of media attention.

Activities and outdoor pursuits

South Africa's diverse landscape of mountains, forests, rugged coast and sandy beaches, as well as miles of veld and game-trampled national parks, make this supreme outdoor terrain. This fact hasn't been overlooked by South Africans themselves, who have been playing in the outdoors for decades. The result is a well-developed infrastructure for activities, an impressive national network of hiking trails and plenty of commercial operators selling adventure sports.

Hiking trails

Over the past twenty years, **hiking** has taken off in a big way in South Africa, which now has the most comprehensive system of footpaths in Africa (inspired by the US Appalachian Hiking Trail).

Wherever you are – even in the middle of Johannesburg – you won't be far from some sort of trail. The best ones are in wilderness areas, where you'll find waymarked paths that vary from half-hour strolls to major hiking expeditions of two to seven days that take you right into the heart of some of the most beautiful parts of the country.

Overnight hiking trails are normally well laid-out, with painted footprints or other markers to indicate the route and campsites or huts along the way (but you need to carry all your own equipment). Numbers are limited on most, and many trails are so popular that they become booked up many months in advance, so it's worth arranging these beforehand – although you can often find a place by just turning up and hoping for a cancellation.

If you want to do a fair amount of walking but don't want to launch out on a long expe-

dition, consider basing yourself in one of the wilderness areas such as the **Drakensberg**, where you can stay in chalets and set off on a series of day-walks, returning each night.

Unique to Africa are **guided wilderness trails**, where you walk in game country (such as the Kruger National Park), accompanied by an armed guide. These walks should be regarded as a way to get a feel for the wild rather than actually see any wildlife, as you'll encounter far fewer animals on foot than from a vehicle. Specialist trails include mountain biking, canoeing, horseback trails and camel trails. A handful of trails have also been set up specifically for **people with disabilities**, mostly for the visually impaired or people confined to wheelchairs.

Watersports

Don't expect balmy Mediterranean seas in South Africa: of its 2500km of coastline, only the stretch along the Indian Ocean seaboard of KwaZulu-Natal and the northern section of the Eastern Cape can be considered tropical, and along the entire coast an energetic surf pounds the shore. In **Cape Town**, sea bathing is only comfortable between November and March. Generally, the further

Trail books

Numerous books exist covering hikes in specific regions of South Africa, but these two general guides are extremely useful.

Jaynee Levy *The Complete Guide to Walks & Trails in Southern Africa* (Struik). Levy was important in helping establish the system of trails, and this is the most comprehensive guide to the region as a whole, with all the basic information and contact addresses you'll need to trail anywhere in the subcontinent.

Willie and Sandra Olivier *Hiking Trails of Southern Africa* (Southern). Covers less ground than Levy, dealing with only the 44 most important trails, but writes them up with greater depth and gives excellent natural history commentary on each trail.

east you go from here, the warmer the water becomes and the longer the bathing season. Sea temperatures that rarely drop below 18°C make the **KwaZulu-Natal** coast warm enough for a dip at any time of year. A word of warning: dangerous undertows and rip-tides are present along the coast and you should try to bathe where lifeguards are present. Failing that (and guards aren't that common away from main resorts out of season) you should follow local advice, never swim alone, and always treat the ocean with respect.

The pumping surf is of course precisely what makes South Africa among the world's finest spots for **surfing**. The country's perfect wave at **Jeffrey's Bay** was immortalized on celluloid in the Sixties cult movie *Endless Summer*, but any surfer will tell you that there are equal, if not better, breaks all the way along the coast from the Namibian to the Mozambique border. Surfers can be a cliquey bunch, but the South African community has a reputation for being among the friendliest in the world and, provided you pay your dues, you should find yourself easily accepted. Some of the world's top shapers work here, and you can pick up an excellent board at a fraction of European or US prices. If you can face the humiliation of being regarded by the pro-surfers as a "tea bag" or "doormat", boogie-boarding and body-surfing make easy alternatives to the real thing, require less skill or dedication and are great fun. **Windsurfing** (or sailboarding) is another popular sport you'll find at many resorts, where you can rent gear.

Scuba diving is a recreation that's growing in popularity, and South Africa is one of the cheapest places in the world to get an internationally recognized open-water certificate, with courses at all the coastal cities as well as a number of other resorts. The most rewarding diving is along the St Lucia Marine Reserve in northern KwaZulu-Natal coast, where 100,000 dives go under every year for its coral reefs and fluorescent fish. You won't find corals and bright colours along the Cape coast, but the huge number of sunken vessels makes wreck-diving popular and you can encounter the swaying rhythms of giant kelp forests.

KwaZulu-Natal is also good for

snorkelling and there are some underwater trails elsewhere in the country, most notable of which is in the Tsitsikamma National Park.

Fishing is another well-developed South African activity and the coasts yield 250 species caught through rock, bay or surf angling. The confluence of the warm Indian Ocean and cooler Atlantic east of the Cape Peninsula, brings one of the highest concentrations of game fish in the world, including longfin, tunny and marlin. Inland you'll find plenty of rivers and dams stocked with freshwater fish, while trout fishing is extremely well-established in Mpumalanga, the northern sections of the Eastern Cape and the KwaZulu-Natal Midlands.

If you want to find out how bait feels, there are a couple of places along the southern Cape and Garden Route where you can go on **shark-cage dives** and come face to face with deadly great whites.

On inland waterways, South African holiday-makers are keen **speedboaters**, an activity that goes hand in hand with **water-skiing**. **Kayaking** and **canoeing** are also very popular, and you can often rent craft at resorts or national parks that lie along rivers. For the more adventurous, there's **white-water rafting**, with some decent trips along the Tugela River in KwaZulu-Natal and on the Orange River.

Other activities

There are ample opportunities for aerial activities in South Africa. In the Winelands you can go **ballooning**, while **paragliding** offers a thrilling way to see Cape Town, by diving off Lion's Head and riding the thermals. More down-to-earth options include **mountaineering** and **rock climbing**, both of which have a huge following in South Africa. If you decide to go **skiing** at one or two resorts in the Eastern and Western Cape, you'll be able to go home with a quirky experience of Africa. And finally, if you can't choose between being airborne or earth-bound, you can always bounce between the two by **bungee jumping** off the Gouritz River Bridge near Mossel Bay – the world's highest commercial jump.

Horse-riding is a sport you'll find at virtually every resort, whether inland or along the coast, for two hours or two days. You can ride in the Drakensberg from the Natal parks, or go pony trekking for several days in Lesotho. Take your own hat, as not everyone provides them. **Bird-watching** is another activity you can do almost anywhere, either casually on your own, or as part of a guided trip with one of the several experts operating in South Africa. Among the very best bird-watching spots are Mkuzi and Ndumo game reserves in KwaZulu-Natal. **Golf** lovers will have a fabulous time in South Africa as courses are prolific and are frequently in stunningly beautiful locations.

Crime and the police

Despite horror stories of sky-high crime rates, most people visit South Africa without incident. This is not to minimize the problem – crime is probably the most serious problem facing the country. However, once you realize crime follows demographic patterns, the scale becomes less terrifying. The greatest proportion of violent crime takes place in the poorer areas – predominantly townships – and in Johannesburg, where the dangers are the worst in the country. Be careful, but don't be paranoid.

You'll notice that most middle-class homes subscribe to the services of armed, **private security firms** to protect their property. Protecting property and "security" are major national obsessions, and it's difficult to imagine what many South Africans would discuss at their dinner parties if the problem disappeared. The other obvious manifestation of this obsession is the huge number of alarms, bars, high walls and electronically controlled gates you'll find, not just in the suburbs, but even in less deprived areas of some townships.

Guns are openly carried by police – and often citizens. In many high streets you'll spot firearm shops rubbing shoulders with places selling clothes or books; and you'll come across notices asking you to deposit your weapon before entering the premises.

If you fall victim to a **mugging**, you should take very seriously the usual advice not to resist and do as you're told. The chances of this happening can be greatly minimized by using common sense and following a few simple rules. If you're staying in Johannesburg, it pays to be extra alert. For specific guidelines, see the box on p.63.

Police

For many black South Africans, the **South African National Police** (SANP) still carry strong associations of collaboration with apartheid and a lot of public relations work has yet to be done to turn the police into a genuine people's law enforcement agency. Poorly paid, shot at (and frequently hit), underfunded, badly equipped, barely respected and demoralized, the police keep a low profile. If you ever get stopped, at a roadblock for example (one of the likeliest encounters), always be courteous. And remember that under South African law if you're driving you are required to carry your **driver's licence** at all times. If you are robbed, don't expect too much crime-cracking enthusiasm (and don't expect to get your property back), but you will need to report the incident to the police, who should give you a case reference for insurance purposes.

Drugs, drinking and driving

Dagga (cannabis in dried leaf form) – pronounced like "dugger" with the "gg" pronounced gutterally as in the Scottish pronunciation of loch – is South Africa's most widely produced and widely used drug. The quality is generally good, but this doesn't alter the fact that it is illegal. Grown in hot regions like KwaZulu-Natal (the source of Durban Poison), Swaziland (Swazi Gold) and as a cash crop in parts of the former

Safety tips

In general
• Try not to look like a tourist.
• Dress down.
• Don't carry a camera or video openly visible in cities.
• Avoid wearing jewellery or expensive watches.
• Leave your expensive designer shades at home – they are sometimes pulled off people's faces.
• If you are robbed, remain calm and co-operative.

On foot
• Grasp bags firmly under your arm.
• Don't carry excessive sums of money on you (but have a small amount to satisfy a mugger).
• Don't put your wallet in your back trouser pocket.
• Always know where your valuables are.
• Don't leave valuables exposed (on a seat or the ground) while having a meal or drink.
• Develop an awareness of what people in the street around you are doing.
• Don't let anyone get too close to you – especially people in groups.
• In big cities, travel around in pairs or groups.

On the beach
• Take only the bare essentials to the beach.
• Don't leave valuables, especially cameras, unattended.
• Some people pin car keys to their swimming gear, or you can put them in a waterproof wallet or splash box and take them into the water with you.

On the road
• Lock all your car doors, especially in cities.
• Keep your rear windows sufficiently rolled up to keep out opportunistic hands.
• Never leave anything worth stealing in view when your car is unattended.

At cash machines
Automatic teller machines (ATMs) are favourite hunting grounds for sophisticated conmen who use cunning rather than force to steal money. Never underestimate their ability and don't get drawn into any interaction at an ATM, no matter how well spoken, friendly or distressed the other person appears. You can avoid trouble by following the pointers below.
• Never help anyone who claims to be having a problem with a cash machine – tell them to contact the bank.
• Never accept help from strangers if you have a problem at a cash machine.
• Don't allow people to crowd you while withdrawing money.
• If in doubt, go to another machine.
• Never allow anyone to see you punch in your personal identification number (PIN).
• If your card gets swallowed, report it without delay.

Transkei, it is fairly easily available. If you do decide to partake, you should take particular care when scoring, as visitors have run into trouble dealing with unfamilar local conditions.

Rave culture is big in South Africa, and together with **ecstasy** is principally a white, middle-class thing.

Strangely, for a country that sometimes seems to be on one massive binge, South Africa has laws that prohibit **drinking** in public – not that anyone pays any attention to them. The **drink-drive laws** are also routinely and brazenly flouted, making the country's roads the one real danger you should be concerned about. Levels of alcohol consumption go some way to explaining why during the Christmas holidays over a thousand people die in an annual orgy of carnage on the roads. People routinely stock up their cars with booze for long journeys and even at filling stations you'll find places selling liquor.

Women and sexual harassment

South Africa's extremely high incidence of **rape** doesn't as a rule affect tourists. In fact you're very unlikely to need to fend off the unwanted attentions of men. However, women should avoid travelling on their own, nor should they hitchhike or walk alone in deserted areas. This applies equally to cities,

the countryside or anywhere after dark. Minibus taxis should be ruled out as a means of transport after dark, especially if you're not exactly sure of local geography. **Sexual harassment** is rare, but you should nevertheless walk assertively in crowded areas such as minibus taxi termini in big cities. At heart the majority of the country's males, regardless of race, hold on to fairly sexist attitudes. Sometimes your eagerness to be friendly may be taken as a sexual overture – always be sensitive to potential crossed wires and unintended signals.

Travellers with disabilities

Facilities for disabled travellers in South Africa are not as sophisticated as those found in the First World, but overall they're sufficient to ensure you have a satisfactory visit.

By accident rather than design, you'll find pretty good accessibility to many buildings, as South Africans tend to build low (single-storey bungalows are the norm), with the result that you'll have to deal with fewer stairs than you may be accustomed to. Because the car is king, you'll frequently find that you can drive to, and park right outside, your destination.

A growing number of popular tourist attractions are being designed to facilitate **disabled access**. For example, the Kirstenbosch Botanical Gardens in Cape Town have Braille and wheelchair trails, while trails aimed specifically at disabled visitors are on offer at Kamberg Nature Reserve in the Drakensberg and in the Karoo National Park. The longest trail so far is a six-kilometre walk with a tapping rail and guide ropes in the Palmiet Nature Reserve in Durban. Cape Town's Waterfront, one of the top national attractions, has specially designed parking bays as well as ramps and broad walkways around the development itself. Sun City in Northwest Province, as well as a growing number of national parks, is also disability-friendly.

Planning a holiday

There are **organized tours** and holidays specifically for people with disabilities – the contacts on p.65 will be able to put you in touch with specialists for trips to South Africa. If you want to be more independent, it's important to know where you can expect help and where you must be self-reliant, especially regarding transport and accommodation. It's also vital to know your limitations, and to make sure others know them. If you do not use a wheelchair all the time but your walking capabilities are limited, remember that you are likely to need to cover greater distances while travelling (often over rougher terrain and in hotter temperatures) than you are used to. If you use a wheelchair, have it serviced before you go and take a repair kit with you.

Read your **travel insurance** small print carefully to make sure that people with a pre-existing medical condition are not excluded. Use your travel agent to make your journey as straightforward as possible; airline or bus companies can cope better if they are expecting you, with a wheelchair provided at airports and staff primed to help.

A **medical certificate** of your fitness to travel, provided by your doctor, is also extremely useful, and some airlines or insurance companies may insist on it. Make sure you have extra supplies of drugs – carried with you if you fly – and a prescription including the generic name in case of emergency. Carry spares of any clothing or equipment that might be hard to find; if there's an association representing people with your disability, contact them early in the planning process.

Contacts for travellers with disabilities

In South Africa

Eco-Access PO Box 1377, Roosevelt Park 2129 ☎011 477 3676, ⓦwww.eco-access.org. Non-profit agency working for improved facilities for disabled people to take part in eco-tourism in South Africa. Contact Rob and Julie Filmer.

Harvey World Travel Rondebosch Village PO Box 671, Rondebosch 7700, Cape Town ☎021 689 4151, ⓦwww.titchtours.co.za. Travel agent for physically disabled and visually impaired people.

Independent Living Centre PO Box 248, Auckland Park 2006, Johannesburg ☎011 482 5476, ⓔilcentre@icon.co.za. An organization that is compiling details of accessible holiday accommodation in South Africa, and can provide information on equipment, and also issue disabled parking permits for the Johannesburg area.

KwaZulu-Natal Conservation Services PO Box 13069, Cascades, Pietermaritzburg 3202 ☎033 845 1000, ⓦwww.rhino.org.za. Information about facilities in game reserves and parks in KwaZulu-Natal.

National Council for the Physically Disabled in South Africa PO Box 426, Melville 2109 ☎011 726 8040,ⓦwww.ncppdsa.co.za. Advice on where to rent wheelchairs and other equipment in the major cities.

South African National Parks PO Box 787, Pretoria 0001 ☎012 343 1991, ⓦwww.parks-sa .co.za. Up-to-date information about facilities at rest camps in the national parks.

In the UK and Ireland

Disability Action Group 2 Annadale Ave, Belfast BT7 3JH ☎028/9049 1011. Provides information about access for disabled travellers abroad.
ⓦ**www.everybody.co.uk** Provides a directory of airlines and details particular arrangements for disabled travellers.
Holiday Care 2nd floor, Imperial Building, Victoria Road, Horley, Surrey RH6 7PZ ☎01293/774535, Minicom ☎01293/776943, ⓦwww.holidaycare .org.uk. Provides a free information sheet on travel in South Africa with details of practical arrangements and accessible accommodation.
Irish Wheelchair Association Blackheath Drive, Clontarf, Dublin 3 ☎01/833 8241, ⓕ833 3873, ⓔiwa@iol.ie. Useful information provided about travelling abroad with a wheelchair.
RADAR (Royal Association for Disability and Rehabilitation) 12 City Forum, 250 City Rd, London EC1V 8AF ☎020/7250 3222, Minicom ☎020/7250 4119, ⓦwww.radar.org.uk. A general support organization with useful consultancy and information services, and a well-organized website.

In the USA and Canada

Access-Able ⓦwww.access-able.com. Online resource for travellers with disabilities.
Directions Unlimited 123 Green Lane, Bedford Hills, NY 10507 ☎1-800/533-5343 or 914/241-1700. A tour operator specializing in custom tours for people with disabilities.
Mobility International USA 451 Broadway, Eugene, OR 97401; voice and TDD ☎541/343-1284, ⓦwww.miusa.org. Provides information and referral services, access guides, tours and exchange programmes. Annual membership $35 (includes quarterly newsletter).
Society for the Advancement of Travellers with Handicaps (SATH) 347 5th Ave, New York, NY 10016 ☎212/447-7284, ⓦwww.sath.org. A non-profit educational organization that has actively represented travellers with disabilities since 1976.
Travel Information Service ☎215/456-9600. Telephone-only information and referral service.
Twin Peaks Press Box 129, Vancouver, WA 98661 ☎360/694-2462 or 1-800/637-2256, ⓦwww.twinpeak.virtualave.net. Publisher of the *Directory of Travel Agencies for the Disabled* ($19.95), listing more than 370 agencies worldwide; *Travel for the Disabled* ($19.95); the *Directory of Accessible Van Rentals* ($12.95) and *Wheelchair Vagabond* ($9.95), loaded with personal tips.
Wheels Up! ☎1-888/389-4335, ⓦwww.wheelsup.com. Provides discounted airfare, tour and cruise prices for disabled travellers, also publishes a free monthly newsletter and has a comprehensive website.

In Australia and New Zealand

ACROD (Australian Council for Rehabilitation of the Disabled) PO Box 60, Curtin ACT 2605 ☎02/ 6282 4333; 24 Cabarita Rd, Cabarita NSW 2137 ☎02/9743 2699. Provides lists of travel agencies and tour operators for people with disabilities.

Disabled Persons Assembly 4/173–175 Victoria St, Wellington, New Zealand ☎ 04/801 9100.
Resource centre with lists of travel agencies and tour operators for people with disabilities.

Transport

All the major **airlines** flying to South Africa can provide assistance for disabled passengers, but you should give them notice of your needs when booking. As far as domestic air travel is concerned, South African Airways provides passenger aid units at all principal airports.

Car rental of automatics with hand controls can be arranged for no extra charge through Avis or Budget (see p.35) at all the major centres, but a month's prior notice is recommended. Many garages along the main routes, especially along the N1 between Johannesburg and Cape Town, have wheelchair-accessible **toilets**. A Special Parking Disc, which allows **parking** concessions to people with severe mobility impairment, can be obtained for the Johannesburg area through the Independent Living Centre (see p.65) and for elsewhere in the country through the local traffic department. You

should bring any appropriate disc or badge from your home country, which can be used to get a temporary disc.

Accommodation

South Africa has a growing number of **hotels** with facilities for disabled people. South African Tourism publishes an accommodation guide, available from all their offices (see p.28), which includes up-to-date information about disability-friendly establishments. In the national parks, specially adapted huts are available in the Kruger and Karoo national parks. For further details of facilities in other parks, contact South African National and KwaZulu-Natal Nature Conservation (see p.43 for addresses).

Activities and tours

Activities and tours are opening up for disabled travellers to South Africa, ranging from the relatively sedate to the more energetic. Organized tours offer the possibility for wheelchair-bound visitors to take part in safaris, sport and a vast range of adventure activities, including whitewater rafting, horse-riding and parasailing. Tours can either be taken as self-drive trips or group packages.

Gay and lesbian travellers

South Africa has the world's first and only gay- and lesbian-friendly constitution, and Africa's most developed and diverse gay and lesbian scene. Not only is homosexuality legal between consenting adults of 18 or over, but the constitution outlaws any discrimination on the grounds of sexual orientation. This means that, for once, you have the law on your side.

Outside the big cities, however, South Africa is a pretty conservative place where open displays of public affection by gays and lesbians are unlikely to go down well; many whites will find it un-Christian, while blacks will think it un-African. South African Tourism (the official tourism organization), on the other hand, has recently woken up to the potential of pink spending power and is actively wooing gay travellers – an effort that is evidently paying off with the Spartacus gay

guide ranking Cape Town among the world's top five gay destinations. And although there are gay scenes in all the major cities, Cape Town is the one that is most developed.

There are a number of gay print **publications**, including *Exit* newspaper (www.exit .co.za) and *Rush* magazine (www.rush.co.za) both of which are available at newsagents in larger centres, and a substantial number of online publications (see resources listing on p.67). Cape Town and J'oburg have annual gay pride festivals (⊛www.sapride.org) and the Gay and Lesbian Film Festival (⊛www.oia.co.za) is screened in Cape Town, Johannesburg and Durban every year in February and March.

Contacts for gay and lesbian travellers

In South Africa

Gay and Lesbian Association of Cape Town Tourism ⊛www.galacttic.co.za. Gay listing of Cape Town businesses in the tourism industry; professionals, including dentists, doctors and lawyers; accommodation; clubs; restaurants; events and parties; and a gay chat room.

Gay, Lesbian and Bisexual Helpline ☏021 422 2500. Helpline of the Cape Town-based Triangle Project (see below). Phone their paging service and someone will call you back. Daily 1–9pm.

Gay Net ⊛www.gaynetsa.co.za. Gay directory that covers the country.

Gay South Africa ⊛www.gaysouthafrica.org.za. A slick and well-organized portal with links covering all topics of gay interest, with a dedicated section of erotica.

Lesbian and Gay Equality Project 36 Grafton Rd, Yeoville, Johannesburg ☏011 487 3811, ⊛www.equality.org.za. Johannesburg organization devoted mainly to lobbying and legal advice, but which can also provide basic information to gay visitors.

Q ⊛www.q.co.za. Excellent gay spin-off site of the *Daily Mail & Guardian*, with news and a variety of topics including a good travel section.

Triangle Project ☏021 448 3812, ⊛www.triangle.org.za. The Cape Town-based Triangle Project is the longest-established and most effective gay organization in South Africa and is a good first port of call for all types of help from information on gay clubs and bars to advice on where to go for medical testing and counselling. Office Mon–Fri 1–4.30pm.

In the UK

Also check out **adverts** in the weekly papers *Boyz* and *Pink Paper*, handed out free in gay venues.

Dream Waves Redcot High St, Child Okeford, Blandford, DT22 8ET ☏01258/861149, ⊜Dreamwaves@aol.com. Specializes in exclusively gay holidays, including skiing trips and summer sun packages.

⊛www.gaytravel.co.uk Online gay and lesbian travel agent, offering good deals on all types of holi-

day. Also lists gay- and lesbian-friendly hotels around the world.

Madison Travel 118 Western Rd, Hove, East Sussex NN3 1DB ☏01273/202532, ⊛www.madisontravel.co.uk. Established travel agent specializing in packages to gay- and lesbian-friendly mainstream destinations, and also to gay/lesbian destinations.

In the USA and Canada

Damron Company PO Box 422458, San Francisco CA 94142 ☏1-800/462-6654 or ☏415/255-0404, ⊛www.damron.com. Publisher of the *Men's Travel Guide*, a pocket-sized yearbook full of listings of hotels, bars, clubs and resources for gay men; the *Women's Traveler*, which provides similar listings for lesbians; the *Road Atlas*, which shows lodging and entertainment in major US cities; and *Damron Accommodations*, which provides detailed listings of over 1000 accommodations for gays and lesbians worldwide. All of these titles are offered at a discount on the website. There are no specific city guides – everything is incorporated in the yearbooks.

Ferrari Publications PO Box 37887, Phoenix, AZ 85069 ☏1-800/962-2912 or 602/863-2408, ⊛www.ferrariguides.com. Publishes *Ferrari Gay Travel A to Z*, a worldwide gay and lesbian guide; *Inn Places*, a worldwide accommodation guide; the guides *Men's Travel in Your Pocket* and *Women's Travel in Your Pocket*, and the quarterly *Ferrari Travel Report*.

International Gay/Lesbian Travel Association, 4331 N Federal Hwy, Suite 304, Ft Lauderdale, FL 33308 ☏1-800/448-8550, ⊛www.iglta.org. Trade group that can provide a list of gay- and lesbian-owned or friendly travel agents, accommodation and other travel businesses.

In Australia and New Zealand

Gay and Lesbian Travel ⊛www.galta.com.au. Directory and links for gay and lesbian travel in Australia and worldwide.

Gay Travel ⊛www.gaytravel.com. The site for trip planning, bookings, and general information about international travel.

Parkside Travel 70 Glen Osmond Rd, Parkside, SA 5063 ☏08/8274 1222 or 1800/888 501, ⊜hwtravel@senet.com.au. A gay travel agent associated with local branch of Hervey World Travel; all aspects of gay and lesbian travel worldwide.

Pinkstay ⊛www.pinkstay.com. Everything from visa information to finding accommodation and work around the world.

Silke's Travel 263 Oxford St, Darlinghurst, NSW 2010 ☏02/9380 6244 or ☏1800/807 860, ⊜silba @magna.com.au. Long-established gay and lesbian specialist, with the emphasis on women's travel. **Tearaway Travel** 52 Porter St, Prahan, VIC 3181 ☏03/9510 6344, ✉tearaway@bigpond.com. A gay-specific business dealing with international and domestic travel.

Cape Town

Cape Town is South Africa's – and indeed, the African continent's – gay capital. Cape Town Tourism's visitor centre in downtown Cape Town has good **information** on gay-friendly establishments in the city with a view to turning the mother city into an African Sydney. Their website (www.cape-town.org) has a substantial gay section. For information on **what's on** check out the gay section of the Western Cape listings magazine *Cape Review* or the gay supplement published on the last Thursday of the month in The *Cape Argus*, Cape Town's daily afternoon newspaper, both widely available at newsagents – or look at the websites listed under "Gay South Africa Online".

The city has a growing number of **gay-friendly businesses**: B&Bs, guesthouses, pubs, clubs, doctors, dentists and other professionals as well as cruise bars, video shows, restaurants with cabaret, strip shows and steam baths. Cape Town's **gay quarter** is concentrated along the entertainment strips of Somerset Road and Main Road in the adjoining inner-city suburbs of Green Point and Sea Point adjacent to the centre, where a number of establishments flaunt their pink credentials by flying a distinctive multi-coloured gay flag. *The Pink Map,* published by A&C Maps (☏021 685 4260, ⓦwww.capeinfo.com) lists gay-friendly and gay-owned places in Cape Town and is distributed at the visitor centre in town, the one in the Clock Tower at the V&A Waterfront, as well as the airport and hotels; they'll also send a copy free anywhere in the world on request.

Cape Town also hosts an annual **gay party**, organized by Mother City Queer Projects (ⓦwww.mcqp.co.za), a hugely popular event usually held in mid-December at the *River Club* (☏021 448 6117) in Observatory. People dress as outrageously as possible according to a theme (past ones have included "on safari", "underwater" and "farm fresh") and the event seeks to rival Sydney's Mardi Gras.

While in town, be sure to tune into Bush Radio's (89.5FM) gay programme, called **In the Pink**, every Thursday 8–10pm. Like many things in the city, Cape Town's gay scene is white-dominated, though there are a few gay-friendly clubs starting to emerge in the surrounding townships.

The rest of the country

The gay scene is a lot more multiracial in **Johannesburg**, especially in the clubs. If you're near Johannesburg in September, make sure you check out the **Pride Parade** through the streets of the city. The **Pretoria** gay and lesbian scene has grown enormously over the past few years and now outdoes Johannesburg. There are also gay scenes in **Port Elizabeth** and **Durban** and you'll find a growing number of gay-run or gay-friendly establishments in small towns all over the country.

Travelling with children

Holidaying with children is straightforward in South Africa, whether you want to explore a city, relax on the beach, or find peace in the mountains. You'll find people friendly, attentive and accepting of babies and young children. The following is aimed principally at families with under-5s.

Flying to South Africa with toddlers is the only considerable challenge, especially as the long-haul flight is bound to disrupt sleep-ing and eating routines. Although children up to 24 months only pay ten percent of the adult fare, the illusion that this is a bargain rapidly evaporates when you realize that they get no seat or baggage allowance. Given this, you'd be well advised to secure bulkhead seats and reserve a **basinet** or sky cot, which can be attached to the bulkhead. Basinets are usually allocated to babies under six months, though some airlines use weight (under 10kg) as the criterion. When you reconfirm your flights, check that your seat and basinet are still available. A child who has a seat will usually be charged fifty percent of the adult fare and is entitled to a full baggage allowance.

For getting to and from the aircraft, and for use during your stay, take a light-weight collapsible **buggy** – not counted as part of your luggage allowance. A child-carrier backpack is another useful accessory.

Given the size of the country, you're likely to be **driving** long distances, something you should think about carefully to avoid grizzly children. Aim to go slowly and plan a route that allows frequent stops – or perhaps take trains or flights between centres. The Garden Route, for example, is an ideal drive, with easy stops for picnics, particularly on the section between Mossel Bay and Storms River. The route between Johannesburg and Cape Town, conversely, is tedious.

Game viewing can also be boring for young children, since it too involves a lot of driving – and disappointment, should the promised beasts fail to put in an appearance. Plus, of course, toddlers won't particularly enjoy watching animals from afar and through a window. If they are old enough to enjoy the experience, make sure they have their own binoculars. To get in closer, some animal parks, such as Tshukudu near Kruger, have semi-tame animals, while snake and reptile parks are an old South African favourite.

Family accommodation is plentiful and hotels often have rooms with extra beds or interconnecting rooms. Kids usually stay for half price. Self-catering options are worth considering, as most such establishments have a good deal of space to play in, and there'll often be a pool. A number of resorts are specifically aimed at families with **older children**, with suitable activities offered. The pick of the bunch is the Aventura chain,

which has places in beautiful settings, including Keurboomstrand near Plettenberg Bay, and two close to the Blyde River Canyon in Mpumalanga. Another excellent option is full-board family hotels, of which there are a number along the Wild Coast (see p.417), where not only are there playgrounds to fool about on and canoes for paddling about lagoons, but most also provide nannies to look after the kids during meals or for the whole day if you want.

Note that many safari camps don't allow children under 12, so you'll have to self-cater or camp at the national parks and those in KwaZulu-Natal.

Eating out with a baby or toddler is easy, particularly if you go to an outdoor venue where they can get on unhindered with their exploration of the world. Some restaurants have highchairs and offer small portions. If in doubt, there's always the ubiquitous family-oriented chains such as Spur or Wimpy.

Breast feeding is practised by the majority of African mothers wherever they are, though you won't see many white women doing it in public. Be discreet, especially in more conservative white areas – which is most of the country outside middle-class Cape Town, Johannesburg or Durban. There are very few **baby rooms** in public places for changing or feeding.

You can buy disposable **nappies** wherever you go (imported brands are best), as well as wipes, bottles, formula and dummies. High-street chemists and the Clicks chain are the best places to buy baby goods. If you run out of **clothes**, Woolworths has good-quality stuff, but for trendy gear there are a number of creative children's clothes outlets, especially in Cape Town and Knysna.

Health and hygiene standards are high and there are plenty of good doctors and hospitals should you need them. **Malaria** affects only a small part of the country (see p.22), but think carefully about visiting such areas as the preventatives aren't recommended for under-2s. For toddlers, chloroquine is available as a syrup, while proguanil is only available in tablet form – not the easiest thing to get down little throats. Avoid most of the major game reserves, particularly the Kruger National Park and those in KwaZulu-Natal, Northwest and Northern provinces and Swaziland, and opt instead for malaria-free reserves in the Western and Eastern Cape, such as Addo Elephant National Park. Malarial zones carry a considerably reduced risk in winter, when it's unusual to find mosquitoes, so if you're set on going, this is the best time. Take mosquito nets, cover children from head to toe between dusk and dawn, and use a good repellent.

Tuberculosis (TB) is widespread in South Africa, mostly (but by no means exclusively) affecting the poor, so make sure your child has had a BCG jab.

For protection against **the sun**, see p.21.

Contacts for travellers with children

In the UK and Ireland

Club Med ☎0700/258 2633, ⓦwww.clubmed .com. Specializes in purpose-built holiday resorts, with kids' club, entertainment and sports facilities on site.
Mark Warner Holidays ☎020/7761 7000, ⓦwww.markwarner.co.uk. Holiday villages with children's entertainment and childcare laid on.

In the USA

Travel With Your Children 40 Fifth Ave, New York, NY 10011 ☎212/477 5524 or ☎1-888/822-4388. Publishes a regular newsletter, Family Travel Times (ⓦwww.familytraveltimes.com), as well as a series of books on travel with children including *Great Adventure Vacations With Your Kids.*

Directory

AIRPORT TAX An arrival tax is charged on all flights, but since it's already included in all air fares you will be unaware of it.

BARGAINING Haggling at markets and with street traders isn't a part of South African shopping culture. Most market traders are trying to earn an honest living and are generally not trying to rip you off, so bargaining just isn't expected.

BEGGING The coexistence of poverty and wealth in close proximity, and the absence of a social security safety net, make begging a widespread and inevitable phenomenon in South Africa. What you do when confronted by someone asking for money (or even food) is a sticky matter of conscience, but giving to every beggar you encounter is simply not a workable possibility. Your choices are to not give at all, to give selectively, or to make a donation to one of the recognized charities that is trying to alleviate the worst consequences of deprivation – the way many middle-class South Africans salve their consciences. An extension of begging is people offering services you may not have asked for. Common examples are self-appointed car

attendants who hang around parking places, direct you into your parking bay and offer to look after your vehicle while you're away – essentially an offer you can't refuse. Agree to pay when you return (around R3–5 should do the trick) provided they've done their job. Offers to clean your car are also very common (R10 is standard).

CONTRACEPTION Despite a serious HIV/AIDS problem, South Africa is remarkably coy about contraception and you shouldn't expect to find condoms anywhere other than in pharmacies. As far as the pill goes, this can also be bought through a pharmacy, but only with a doctor's prescription. The safest option is to bring your own supply.

ELECTRICITY Electricity runs on 220/230V, 50Hz AC and sockets take unique round-pinned plugs. Most hotel rooms have sockets that will take 110V electric razors, but for other appliances US visitors will need a transformer.

EMERGENCIES Police ☎10111, Ambulance ☎10177.

Metric conversion table

1 centimetre (cm) = 0.394in	1 hectare = 2.471 acres
1 inch (in) = 2.54cm	1 acre = 0.4 hectares
1 foot (ft) = 30.48cm	1 UK gallon (gal) = 4.55 litres
1 metre (m) = 100cm	1 litre = 0.26 US gal
1 metre = 39.37in	1 US gallon (gal) = 5.46 litres
1 yard (yd) = 0.91m	1 gramme (g) = 0.035oz
1 kilometre (km) = 1000m	1 ounce (oz) = 28.57 g
1 kilometre = 0.621 miles	1 kilogramme (kg) = 1000g
1 mile = 1610m	1 kilogramme = 2.2lb
1 hectare = 10,000 square metres	1 pound (lb) = 454g

LAUNDRIES Most towns have self-operated launderettes where for a reasonable sum you can also often have a serviced wash which can include ironing.

TAX Value-added tax (VAT) of fourteen percent is levied on most goods and services, though it's usually already included in any quoted price. Foreign visitors can claim back VAT on any goods over R250. To do this, you must present the tax invoice, a non-South African passport and the goods purchased at the airport just before you fly out. You need to complete a VAT refund control sheet (VAT 255) which is obtainable at international airports.

TIME There is only one time zone throughout the region, two hours ahead of GMT. If you're flying from anywhere in Europe, you shouldn't experience any jet lag, as you'll be travelling virtually due south, which won't affect your body clock.

TIPPING Ten to fifteen percent of the tab is the normal tip at restaurants and for taxis –

but don't feel obliged if the service has been shoddy. Keep in mind that many of the people who'll be serving you will be black South Africans, who rely on tips to supplement a meagre wage on which they support huge extended families. Porters at hotels normally get about R3 per bag. There are no self-service garages in South Africa; someone will always be on hand to fill your vehicle and clean your windscreen, for which you should tip around R3–5. It is also usual at hotels to leave some money for the person who services your room. Many establishments, especially private game lodges, take (voluntary) communal tips when you check out – by far the fairest system, which ensures that all the low-profile staff behind the scenes get their share.

WEIGHTS AND MEASURES South Africa is fully metricated, and kilometres, grammes, kilogrammes, litres and degrees Celsius are the norm. Shoe sizes follow the British system.

guide

guide

Cape Town
and the Peninsula

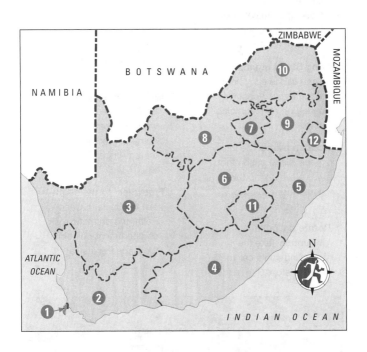

CHAPTER 1 # Highlights

✳ **Bo-Kaap** One of Cape Town's oldest residential areas, its streets characterized by colourful nineteenth-century Cape Dutch and Georgian terraces. See p.116

✳ **Golden Lion** Highlight of the Gold of Africa Museum, a major collection of historic African works of art. See p.117

✳ **Long Street nightlife** Party till the early hours along the city-centre's café, pub and nightclub strip. See p.119

✳ **Robben Island** The infamous island prison that was Nelson Mandela's home for nearly two decades. See p.122

✳ **Rotate up Table Mountain** Take the revolving cable car to the tabletop. See p.135

✳ **Sundowners on the Atlantic seaboard** Grab a bottle of Cape bubbly and make for Clifton, Camps Bay or Llandudno. See p.137

✳ **Train to Simon's Town** The Metrorail train from Muizenberg follows the False Bay coast, just metres from the crashing surf, with stunning mountain views across the water. See p.144

✳ **Swim with penguins** Boulders Beach offers wonderful bathing and is home to a colony of protected African penguins. See p.146

✳ **Freewheel to the southern tip** Cycle to Cape Point, the dramatic rocky southernmost point on the Cape Peninsula. See p.146

Cape Town and the Peninsula

CAPE TOWN is southern Africa's most beautiful, most romantic and most visited city. Indeed, few urban centres anywhere can match its setting along the mountainous **Cape Peninsula** spine, which slides into the Atlantic Ocean. By far the most striking – and famous – of its sights is **Table Mountain**, frequently shrouded by clouds, and rearing up from the middle of the city.

More than a scenic backdrop, Table Mountain is the solid core of Cape Town, dividing the city into distinct zones with public gardens, wilderness, forests, hiking routes, vineyards and desirable residential areas trailing down its lower slopes. Standing on the tabletop, you can look north for a giddy view of the **city centre**, its docks lined with matchbox ships. Looking west, beyond the mountainous Twelve Apostles, the drop is sheer and your eye will sweep across Africa's priciest real estate, clinging to the slopes along the chilly but spectacularly beautiful Atlantic seaboard. Turning south, the mountainsides are forested and several historic vineyards and the marvellous Botanical Gardens creep up the lower slopes. Beyond the oak-lined suburbs of Newlands and Constantia lies the warmer **False Bay seaboard**, which curves around towards **Cape Point**. Finally, relegated to the grim industrial east, are the coloured **townships** and black **ghettos**, spluttering in winter under the smoky pall of coal fires – your stark introduction to Cape Town when driving in.

To appreciate Cape Town you need to spend time **outdoors**, as Capetonians do, hiking, picnicking or sunbathing, or often choosing mountain bikes in preference to cars and turning **adventure activities** into an obsession. Sailboarders from around the world head for Table Bay for some of the world's best windsurfing, and the brave (or unhinged) jump off Lion's Head and paraglide down close to the Clifton beachfront. But the city offers sedate pleasures as well, along its hundreds of paths and 150km of beaches.

Cape Town's rich urban texture is immediately apparent in its diverse **architecture** (see p.130): an indigenous Cape Dutch style, rooted in the Netherlands, finds its apotheosis in the Constantia wine estates, which were themselves brought to new heights by French refugees in the seventeenth century; Muslim slaves, freed in the nineteenth century, added their minarets to the skyline; and the English, who invaded and freed these slaves, introduced Georgian and Victorian buildings. In the tightly packed terraces of twentieth-

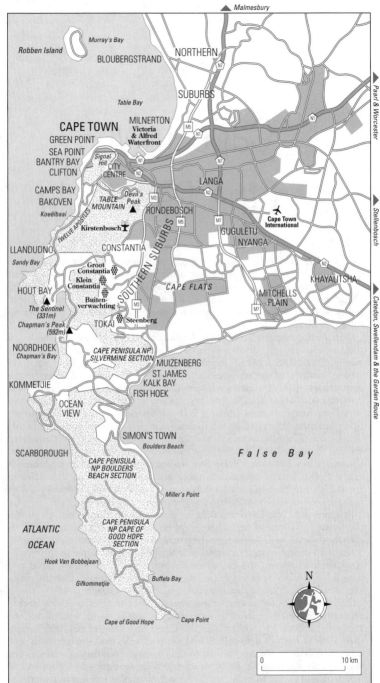

▲ Malmesbury

Robben Island

Murray's Bay

BLOUBERGSTRAND

NORTHERN

SUBURBS

Table Bay

MILNERTON

CAPE TOWN

Victoria
& Alfred
Waterfront

GREEN POINT

SEA POINT

BANTRY BAY

CLIFTON

Signal
Hill

CITY
CENTRE

CAMPS BAY

BAKOVEN

TABLE
MOUNTAIN

Devil's
Peak

Koeëlbaai

▲

TWELVE APOSTLES

Kirstenbosch ✝

RONDEBOSCH

LANGA

GUGULETU

NYANGA

Cape Town
International ✈

CONSTANTIA

LLANDUDNO

Sandy Bay

Groot
Constantia ❀

Klein
Constantia ❀

Buiten-
verwachting ❀

SOUTHERN SUBURBS

CAPE FLATS

KHAYALITSHA

HOUT BAY

The Sentinel
(331m)

Chapman's Peak
(592m) ▲

TOKAI

Steenberg ❀

MITCHELLS
PLAIN

NOORDHOEK

Chapman's Bay

KOMMETJIE

CAPE PENISULA NP
SILVERMINE SECTION

MUIZENBERG

ST JAMES

KALK BAY

FISH HOEK

OCEAN
VIEW

SIMON'S TOWN

Boulders Beach

F a l s e   B a y

SCARBOROUGH

CAPE PENISULA
NP BOULDERS
BEACH SECTION

Miller's Point

ATLANTIC

OCEAN

CAPE PENISULA
NP CAPE OF
GOOD HOPE
SECTION

Hoek Van Bobbejaan

Gifkommetjie

Buffels Bay

Cape of Good Hope

Cape Point

N

0   10 km

century Bo-Kaap and the tenements of District Six, coloured descendants of slaves evolved a unique brand of jazz, which is still played in the Cape Flats and some city-centre clubs.

Sadly, when most travellers expound the unarguable delights of the city, they are referring only to genteel Cape Town – the former whites-only areas. The harsh reality for most Capetonians is one of crowded **shantytowns**, sky-high murder rates, taxi wars, racketeering and gangland terror. In the late 1990s this violence has been characterized by a complex and bloody war between coloured gangs and Pagad (People Against Gangsterism and Drugs), a Cape Flats organization that started with the ostensible aim of stamping out crime. Fortunately, this conflict has remained largely restricted to the Cape Flats and isn't something tourists need be unduly concerned about. Having said that, petty crime is nonetheless a problem in central Cape Town, but it's a risk you can minimize by taking a few simple precautions.

Some history

San hunter-gatherers, South Africa's first human inhabitants, moved freely through the Cape Peninsula for tens of millennia before being edged into the interior some 2000 years ago by the arrival of sheep-herding **Khoikhoi** migrants from the north. Over the next 1600 years the Khoikhoi held sway over the Cape pastures. **Portuguese** mariners, in search of a stopoff point en route to East Africa and the East Indies, first rounded the Cape in the 1480s, and named it Cabo de Boa Esperanza (Cape of Good Hope), but their attempts at trading with the Khoikhoi were short-lived, and no Europeans seriously attempted to create a permanent stopping-off point until the **Dutch East India Company** (VOC) cruised into Table Bay in 1652 and set up shop.

The VOC, the world's largest corporation at the time, planned little more at the Cape than a halfway stop to provide fresh produce to their ships travelling between Europe and the East in search of spices, slaves and profit. Their small landing party, led by **Jan van Riebeeck**, built a mud fort where the Grand Parade now stands and established **vegetable gardens**, which they hoped to work with Khoikhoi labour.

The Khoikhoi were understandably reluctant to exchange their traditional lifestyle for the restrictions of formal employment, so van Riebeeck began to import **slaves** in 1658. The growth of the Dutch settlement alarmed the Khoikhoi, who declared war in 1659 in an attempt to drive the Europeans out; however, they were defeated and had to cede the Peninsula to the colonists.

During the early eighteenth century, Western Cape Khoikhoi society disintegrated, **German** and **French** religious refugees swelled the European population, and slavery became the economic backbone of the colony, which was now a minor colonial village of canals and low, whitewashed, flat-roofed houses. By 1750, Cape Town had become a town of over 1000 buildings, with 2500 inhabitants.

In 1795, **Britain**, deeply concerned by Napoleonic expansionism, grabbed Cape Town to secure the strategic sea route to the East. This move was not welcomed by the settlement's Calvinist Dutch burghers, but was better news for the substantially Muslim slave population, as Britain ordered the **abolition of slavery**. The British also allowed **freedom of religion**, and South Africa's first mosque was soon built by freed slaves, in Dorp Street in the Bo-Kaap.

By the turn of the nineteenth century, Cape Town had become one of the most cosmopolitan places anywhere and a sea port of major significance, growing under the influence of the British Empire. The Commercial Exchange was completed in 1819, followed by department stores, banks and insurance company buildings. In the 1860s the docks were begun, Victoria Road from the city to Sea Point was built, and the suburban railway line to Wynberg was laid. Since slavery had been abolished, Victorian Cape Town had to be built with **convict labour** and that of prisoners of war transported from the colonial frontier in Eastern Cape. Racial segregation wasn't far behind, and an outbreak of bubonic plague in 1901 gave the town council an excuse to establish **Ndabeni**, Cape Town's first black location, near Maitland.

In 1910, Cape Town was drawn into the political centre of the newly federated South Africa when it became the **legislative capital** of the Union. Africans and coloureds, excluded from the cosy deal between Boers and the British, had to find expression in the workplace. In 1919 they flexed their collective muscle on the docks, forming the mighty **Industrial and Commercial Union**, which boasted 200,000 members in its heyday.

Increasing industrialization brought an influx of black workers, who were housed in the locations of **Guguletu** and **Nyanga**, built in 1945. Three years later, the National Party came to power, promising a fearful white electorate that it would reverse the flow of Africans to the cities. In Cape Town it introduced a policy favouring coloureds for jobs, admitting only African men in employment, and forbidding the construction of family accommodation for Africans.

Langa township became a stronghold of the **Pan Africanist Congress** (PAC), which organized a peaceful anti-pass demonstration in Cape Town on April 8, 1960. Police fired on the crowd, killing three people and wounding many more. As a result, the government declared a state of emergency, and banned anti-apartheid opposition groups, including the PAC and ANC.

In 1966, the notorious **Group Areas Act** was used to uproot whole coloured communities from District Six and to move them to the desolate **Cape Flats**. Here, rampant gangsterism took vicious root and remains one of Cape Town's most pressing problems today. To compound the problem, the National Party stripped away coloured representation on the town council in 1972.

Eleven years later, at a huge meeting on the Cape Flats, the extra-parliamentary opposition defied government repression and re-formed as the **United Democratic Front**, heralding a period of intensified struggle to topple apartheid. In 1986, one of the major pillars crumbled when the government was forced to scrap influx control; blacks began pouring into Cape Town seeking work and erecting shantytowns, making Cape Town one of the fastest-growing cities in the world. On February 11, 1990, the city's history took a neat twist when, just hours after being released from prison, **Nelson Mandela** made his first public speech from the balcony of City Hall to a jubilant crowd spilling across the Grand Parade, the very site of the first Dutch fort. Four years later, he entered the formerly whites-only Parliament, 500m away, as South Africa's first democratically elected president.

Despite five years of non-racial democracy, on the eve of the 1999 elections, Cape Town remained a divided city. On the one hand, the whites still enjoyed a comfortable existence in the leafy suburbs along the two coasts and the slopes of Table Mountain, with the **V&A Waterfront** complex continuing to develop apace. On the desolate **Cape Flats**, however, some progress had been made in bringing electricity to the shantytowns, but the shacks were still there – and spreading. Despite white fears about crime, it was still blacks and coloureds who were overwhelmingly and disproportionately the victims of protracted violence, much of it gang-related.

Some attempts were made to foster cultural interaction and to forge a more integrated city. In 1999, the *Cape Times* launched a highly popular "One City, Many Cultures" campaign, featuring regular articles highlighting the rich

The language of colour

It's striking just how un-African Cape Town looks and sounds. The dominant language of the city is **Afrikaans** (a close relative of Dutch), the only "European" language to evolve outside Europe. Although English is universally spoken and understood, Afrikaans is the mother tongue of a large proportion of the city's **coloured** residents, as well as a good number of whites. The term "coloured" is fraught with confusion, but in South Africa doesn't have the same connotations as in Britain and the US; it refers to South Africans of mixed race, as opposed to indigenous Africans or whites of European ancestry. This comes as a surprise to most visitors, who assume that it's all black and white in South Africa, when in fact issues of ethnicity and language are extremely complex.

Most brown-skinned people in Cape Town (over fifty percent of the population), and many others throughout the country, are coloureds, with slave and Khoikhoi ancestry going back to the seventeenth to early nineteenth centuries. Lying halfway between East and West, Cape Town drew its population from Africa, Asia and Europe, and traces of all three continents are found in the genes, language, culture, religion and cuisine of South Africa's coloured population.

In the late nineteenth century, Afrikaans-speaking whites, fighting for an identity, sought to create a "racially pure" culture by driving a wedge between themselves and coloured Afrikaans-speakers. They reinvented Afrikaans as a "white man's language", eradicating the supposed stigma of its coloured ties by substituting Dutch words for those with Asian or African roots. In 1925, the white dialect of Afrikaans became an official language alongside English, and the dialects spoken by coloureds were treated as comical deviations from correct usage.

For Afrikaner nationalists this wasn't enough, and after the introduction of apartheid in 1948, they attempted to codify perceived racial differences. Under the **Population Registration Act**, all South Africans were classified as white, coloured or Bantu (the apartheid term for Africans). The underlying assumption was that these distinctions were based on objective criteria. For the apartheid authorities, it seemed fairly clear who was "Bantu" and who was white, but the coloureds posed particular problems. Firstly, they weren't homogenous so, to accommodate this, the **Coloured Proclamation Act** of 1959 defined eight categories of coloured: Cape Coloured; Malay (Muslim); Griqua; Chinese; Indian; Other Indian; Other Asiatic; and Other Coloured. For reasons of expediency related to trade, Japanese people were defined as "honorary white".

The second difficulty surrounding coloureds was the fact that their appearance spans the entire range, from those who are indistinguishable from whites to those who look like Africans. A number of coloureds managed successfully to reinvent themselves as whites, and apartheid legislation made provision for the racial reclassification of individuals. Between 1983 and 1990, nearly five thousand "Cape Coloureds" were reclassified as "white" and over two thousand Africans were reclassified as "Cape Coloured". Notorious tests were employed – one, for example, where a pencil would be placed in a person's hair and twirled; if the hair sprang back they would be regarded as coloured, but if it stayed twirled they were white.

Far more than mere semantics, these classifications became fundamental to what kind of life a person could expect. There are numerous cases of families in which one sibling was classified coloured, while another was termed white and then could live in comfortable white areas, enjoy good employment opportunities (many jobs were closed to coloureds), and have the right to send their children to better schools and universities. Many coloured professionals, on the other hand, were evicted from houses they owned in comfortable suburbs such as Claremont, which were overnight declared white.

With the demise of apartheid, residential boundaries are shifting – and so is the thinking on ethnic terminology. Some people now reject the term coloured because of its apartheid associations, and refuse any racial definitions; others, however, proudly embrace the term, as a means of acknowledging their distinct culture, with its slave and Khoikhoi roots.

diversity of Cape Town's ethnic and religious groups. To the same end, a restructuring of local government began. The city's 69 racially segregated bodies were rationalized into six councils that deliberately linked the wealthy and disadvantaged, and brought black, white and coloured areas under common administrations for the first time.

However, the **2000 local elections** proved just how divided a city Cape Town remains. The ANC had hoped its campaign for better services in poorer areas would capture the hearts and minds of the city's African and coloured township dwellers, and allow it to wrest control of the Western Cape and Cape Town city council from the National Party, which had now restyled itself as the **New National Party** (NNP), and was fronting itself with coloured candidates in an attempt to distance itself from its shabby apartheid past. But in the run-up to the election, the liberal Democratic Party, which for decades had been the only vociferous parliamentary opposition to the apartheid government, joined its NNP former-enemy to form the **Democratic Alliance** (DA), which won control of the city and the province. The NNP's Gerald Morkel and **Peter Marais** became the Western Cape provincial premier and Cape Town mayor respectively. Marais – described by the *Mail and Guardian* as "a buffoon of note" who "offers voters a curious mixture of American evangelism and H.F. Verwoerd" – proved to be a populist and erratic city leader, whose arbitrary behaviour, particularly over the street-renaming debacle (see box on p.107), led to his sacking in 2001 by the DA leader, Tony Leon. This in turn led to the swift collapse of the alliance, with Marais opting to stay with the NNP, while Morkel threw in his lot with the Democratic Party.

In a curious twist to the saga, the NNP then entered an alliance with the ANC. Formerly the bitterest of adversaries – the NNP's predecessors had, after all, incarcerated the ANC's leadership on Robben Island – they made unlikely bedfellows. In the farcical follow-up to the street renaming fiasco, the NNP in alliance with the ANC retained control of the province but the DA held on to Cape Town, with Morkel and Marais playing musical chairs. By the end of 2001, Marais had become the provincial premier and Morkel Cape Town mayor. This proved, if nothing else, how resourceful Western Cape politicians can be in preserving their jobs. What remains to be seen is whether they can apply those resources to running Cape Town.

Arrival and information

One of the world's great moments of **arrival** is cruising into Table Bay on a luxury liner. For most, however, the approach is much less picturesque – indeed, it can be something of a shock. Whether you come in by air or road, there's little chance of avoiding the grey, industrial sprawl and the miles of squatter camps lining the N2 into town.

The airport

Cape Town International Airport (flight information ☏021 934 0407) lies on the Cape Flats, 22km east of the city centre. Two **shuttle bus** companies, Legend Tours (☏021 936 2814) and Dumalisile (☏021 934 1660) have desks in the international arrivals hall outside the baggage reclaim area and run a door-to-door service throughout the Peninsula. Although they don't operate to a strict schedule (they try to take three or four passengers travelling on the same route), you shouldn't have to wait more than fifteen minutes for your minibus to leave. The fare from the airport into the city centre is R110 for the first person and R20 for each additional passenger; to Fish Hoek on the southern section of the Cape Peninsula it's R220 for the first person and R20 per each additional person. An alternative is the similarly priced Magic Bus (☎021 934 5455), which must be **prebooked** a day ahead; the bus will meet you at the airport and take you anywhere on the Peninsula.

Metered **taxis** operated by Touch Down Taxis, the company officially authorized by the airport, rank in reasonable numbers outside both terminals and charge about R150 per person for the trip into the city. Inside the international terminal, you'll find the **car rental** desks of the major car rental firms. Prebooking a vehicle is recommended, especially during the week when there is a big demand from domestic business travellers, and over the mid-December to mid-January and Easter peak seasons. There are no trains from the airport. A **bureau de change** is open to coincide with international arrivals.

Intercity buses and trains

Greyhound, Intercape and Translux **intercity buses**, and mainline **trains** from other provinces, all terminate in the centre of town around the interlinked central complex that includes the **train station** and **Golden Acre** shopping mall, at the junction of Strand and Adderley streets. Note that Intercape and Translux arrive on the northeast side of the station, off Adderley Street, while Greyhound arrives on the northwest side in Adderley itself. The Golden Acre shopping complex can be a confusing muddle, but this is where all rail and bus transport (both intercity and from elsewhere in the city) and most minibus taxis converge – if you use public transport at all, you're bound to find yourself here at some stage. Everything you need for your next move is within two or three blocks of here, including information. There's a **left-luggage** facility next to platform 24 at the train station (Mon–Fri 7am–4pm).

Information

The best source of information about the city is **Cape Town Tourism** (ⓦ www.cape-town.org), which has two excellent **information bureaux**: the city-centre visitor centre (March–Nov: Mon–Fri 8am–6pm, Sat 8.30am–1pm & Sun 9am–1pm; Dec–Feb: Mon–Fri 8am–7pm, Sat 8.30am–1pm & Sun 9am–1pm; ☎021 426 4260, ☎021 426 4266), at the corner of Burg and Castle streets, a five-minute walk two blocks northwest of the station; and the Clocktower Precinct visitor centre (daily 9am–9pm; ☎021 405 4500) in a fabulous office at the V&A Waterfront next to the Nelson Mandela Gateway to Robben Island overlooking the harbour. Both centres operate comprehensive accommodation and activity booking services, have a swanky coffee shop, a book shop and cybercafé as well as lots of brochures and very cheap city maps.

The best sources for weekly **events listings** are the *Top of the Times* supplement in Friday's *Cape Times*, and the *Good Weekend* pullout in the *Saturday Argus*, while the *Mail & Guardian* (Fridays) injects some attitude into its reviews and listings supplement. *Cape Review*, a monthly listings magazine with a passing resemblance to London's and New York's *Time Out*, gives a broad range of information on food, wine, gay venues, nightlife and sporting events.

If you're planning to explore beyond the confines of the city centre, you'll need to invest in a detailed **street atlas**, found at most bookshops, including the ubiquitous CNA chain. MapStudio's *A to Z Streetmap* is the cheapest; it's adequate for the centre and most of the suburbs, but doesn't cover Simon's Town. There are countless **guidebooks** on walks around Cape Town, hikes up Table Mountain, dive sites, fishing locations, surfing breaks and windsurfing spots. For the best-stocked shelves and nicest atmosphere, head for one of the Exclusive

Books stores, one in Claremont, one in Constantia and one at the Victoria Wharf at the V&A Waterfront; you'll also find some useful books on all aspects of South Africa at the second hand bookshops down Long Street (see p.169).

City transport

Although Cape Town's city centre is compact enough to get around on foot, many of the attractions are spread along the considerable length of the Peninsula. To make the most of your visit, you'll need to use **taxis**, **rent transport**, take a **tour**, or make do with the pretty skeletal public transport system. Inner-city areas west of the centre are better served by **buses** than other central suburbs, but transport north along the Atlantic coast is negligible. There is, however, a **train** service cutting through the southern suburbs and continuing all the way down to Simon's Town. It's fairly reliable and well-used, though the rolling stock is looking a little battered – vandals dismantle the train interiors to sell as scrap. A concerted programme is underway to upgrade and make the carriages vandal-proof.

Note that using public transport **after dark** is potentially risky. If in any doubt, make every effort to take metered taxis at night, and if you're forced to use public transport take sensible precautions, such as travelling in a group (especially women) and avoiding third-class carriages on trains.

Buses

The only frequent and reliable **bus** services are those from the centre to the Waterfront and Sea Point; infrequent buses also go down the Atlantic seaboard to Camps Bay and Hout Bay. Don't attempt to catch a bus to the southern sub-

---

City buses

There are two bus terminals in Cape Town: **Cape Town station**, Adderley Street: buses to Waterfront; and **Golden Acre Bus terminal**, off Strand Street, wedged between Golden Acre Shopping Centre, the station and the Grand Parade: buses to Green Point, Sea Point, Camps Bay and Hout Bay.

Note that the buses aren't numbered; you identify them from the destination on the front. All but the Waterfront buses are intended for use by workers, services beginning at 6.30am, and ending at 6.30pm. The Waterfront buses also start early, but continue until 10.30pm, and have the greatest frequency. State your destination to the driver, and pay when you get on.

City to:

Sea Point Golden Acre terminal– Mouille Point–Main Road Green Point–Main Road Sea Point. Mon–Sat at least 13 daily.

Waterfront Cape Town station–Riebeeck St–Buitengragt St–Waterfront. Mon–Fri every 10min, Sat & Sun every 15min.

Hout Bay Golden Acre terminal–Lower Plein St–Darling Rd–Adderley Mon–Sat 6 daily to Hout Bay, Sun 3 daily to Hout Bay. Services run via Green Point, Sea Point and Camps Bay and go to the beach and harbour, taking 60min from Golden Acre terminal.

V&A Waterfront to:

City V&A Waterfront–Cape Town station. Mon–Sat every 10min, Sun every 15min.

Sea Point V&A Waterfront–Mouille Point–Green Point–Three Anchor Bay– Beach Road Sea Point. Daily every 20min.

urbs: the train is much quicker and more efficient. All the principal terminals are around Adderley Street and Golden Acre (see box on p.84).

Tickets are sold on buses by the driver. A single ticket from the city to Sea Point costs around R3, and about R5 to Camps Bay. If you're planning on using buses frequently, consider buying a **Ten-Ride Clip Card**, which from the city costs R22 to Sea Point, and R35 to Camps Bay. Valid for fourteen days, the card saves you around 25 percent on the price of individual tickets. For **timetables**, enquire at the Golden Arrow **information booth** (toll-free ☎801 212 111, ⓦwww.gabs.co.za) at the Grand Parade central bus terminal. It's always advisable to check bus times and points of departure at the booth, as these can change without warning.

The official open-top bus tour of Cape Tourism, **the Cape Town Explorer**, is also an extremely useful, if slightly expensive (R60 per person per day), means of transport for negotiating the city-centre sights and the Atlantic seaboard beaches. There are two buses and you can hop on and off throughout the day wherever you please along the route (but you should tell the driver where you want to get on and off). **Departures** are hourly (Nov–Feb 9.40am–4.40pm, April–Sept 9.40am–1.40pm, Oct & March 9.40am–2.40pm) from behind the **V&A Waterfront** visitor centre in Dock Road. It arrives at the **Cape Town Tourism office** on the corner of Burg and Castle streets fifteen minutes' later; from here, it passes the **City Hall**, the **Castle of Good Hope**, **District Six**, **Parliament**, the **South African Museum**, the **Bo-Kaap**, **Kloofnek Road**, **Signal Hill**, **Sea Point** and the **Atlantic seaboard** beaches as far as Camps Bay.

Taxis, minibus taxis, shuttle buses and Rikki's

The term "**taxi**" is no less ambiguous in Cape Town than elsewhere in South Africa: it's used to refer to conventional metered cars, jam-packed minibuses and their more upmarket cousins, Rikki's.

Metered taxis

Metered taxis, regulated by the Cape Town Municipality, don't cruise up and down looking for fares; you'll need to go to the taxi ranks around town, including the Waterfront, the train station and Greenmarket Square. Alternatively, you can phone to be picked up (see p.173). Taxis must have the driver's name and identification clearly on display and the meter clearly visible. Fares work out at around R10 per kilometre, which although expensive compared with other forms of transport, is definitely worth it at night when metered taxis are the safest way of getting around.

Minibus taxis

Minibus taxis are cheap, frequent and bomb up and down the main routes at tearaway speeds. As well as the crazed driving, be prepared for pickpockets working the taxi ranks. Minibus taxis can be hailed from the street – you'll recognize them from the hooting, loud music and touting – or boarded at the central taxi rank, adjacent to the railway station. Once you've boarded, pay the *guardjie* (assistant), who sits near the driver, and tell him when you want to get off. Fares should be under R5 for most trips.

Shuttle buses

A growth area in Cape Town are **shuttle buses**, which are physically indistinguishable from minibus taxis, the difference being that they have to be booked, and they can pick you up from your accommodation. In some cases they run to a schedule, or can be chartered. They tend to be cheaper than metered taxis, but are more expensive than minibus taxis. One of the most useful services runs on demand in co-operation with Cape Town Tourism from their city centre and Waterfront visitor centres, during the bureaux opening hours, going from their office to Kirstenbosch National Botanical Gardens (R35 one way), and also to the lower cableway station and other points of interest.

Reliable operators you can charter include: Sun Tours & Shuttle (℡021 696 0596 or ℡083 270 5617, ℮suntours@iafrica.com), which offers a 24-hour service between any two points on the Peninsula, including the city to the airport (R140 for the first three passengers, then R30 per additional person); and the similarly priced Boogey Bus (℡082 495 5698), which specializes in taking passengers to clubs, including those on the Cape Flats.

Tours

Guided tours enable you to orientate yourself quickly and get to the highlights with a minimum of fuss. A growing number of smaller companies offer niche cultural tours; the most popular of these are **townships tours**, which can safely get you around the African and coloured areas that were created under apartheid. Apart from this, a number of other outfits, listed below, can help you scratch beneath Cape Town's surface.

City centre and Peninsula sights

Cape Town Explorer Cape Town Tourism ℡021 426 4260; Topless Tours ℡021 556 0700, ℗www.ticketweb.co.za. Cape Town Tourism's official bus tour is a two-hour circular ride in an open-top double-decker bus that follows a fixed route around the main central sights with a running commentary. It's also a useful, if expensive, form of transport for getting around the centre. See "Buses" on p.85 for times and route details; R60. They also run an all-day tour of the whole Peninsula as far as Cape Point, leaving Cape Tourism's city-centre office on the corner of Burg and Castle streets on Tues, Thurs & Sat at 9.30am and returning at about 6pm. Booking essential; R210.

City Walking Tour ℡021 426 4260. Operated by Cape Town Tourism (Mon–Fri 11am), this departs from their visitor centre, on the corner of Burg and Castle streets. The roughly two-

hour strolls don't go into any of the sites, but are good for orientation. R50.

Day Trippers ℡021 531 3274, ℗www.daytrippers.co.za. Cycling from Scarborough into the Cape of Good Hope Nature Reserve, with hikes down to Cape Point, as well as tours to the usual sights such as the Winelands. R265.

Hylton Ross Tours ℡021 511 1784, ℗www.hyltonross.co.za. Covers all the popular sights along the Cape Peninsula, and also scheduled guided day-tours to Hermanus (Wed & Sun), which cost R260.

Mother City Tours ℡021 448 3817, ℗021 448 3844. Half- and full-day tours of the city, Cape Point, Table Mountain and the Winelands. Half day from R245, full day R335. Also whale-watching trips in season, which is mainly from August to October (R350).

Cultural and township tours

AfriCultural Tours ℡021 423 3321. A comprehensive look at Cape Town's

"other side", not just the townships, but also a "Slave Route" tour, a visit to

Rikki's

Rikki's are more visitor-friendly versions of minibus taxis, carrying not more than eight passengers, and aimed principally at tourists. They are small open-backed vehicles, covered by a canopy but open at the rear; you need to book them by telephone. In Cape Town, Rikki's (7am–7pm; ☎021 423 4888) are restricted to the City Bowl, the Waterfront and the Atlantic seaboard as far as Camps Bay – they don't go into the suburbs. There is also a regular Rikki's service in Simon's Town, operating between the station and other points in the village on request. Fares are kept down by picking up and dropping off passengers along the way (R6–15). Rikki's also operate mini-tours to destinations including Cape Point and Stellenbosch, for which they charge about R85 an hour for the whole vehicle (maximum six people).

San rock art sites and visits to traditional music makers, dancers and artists. For a chance to experience the upbeat side of Cape Flats nightlife, join the "Vibey Jazz" tour. Half day R200, full day R280.

Grassroute Tours ☎021 706 1006, ⓦwww.grassroutetours.co.za. An alternative take on the traditional tour packages includes a visit to African and coloured townships. They also do walking tours of the Bo-Kaap, including the *kramats* (Muslim shrines). Half day R220, full day R380.

Kukummi Travel ☎083 267 7330, ⓦwww.kukummi.com. Day or overnight trips to rock art sites in the Western Cape, facilitated by archeology graduate and evironmental educator Catherine Price. Day-trips around R600 per person, including transport and meals; minimum two people.

Muse-Art Journeys ☎021 919 9168 or 082 921 1126, ⓔmuse-art@iafrica.com. Exciting cultural tours, including music outings (Wed & Fri eve; R350) that take in two or three nightclubs, and a craft route that visits township craftworkers; there are also special interest tours on request.

Our Pride ☎021 531 4291 or 082 446 7974, ⓔourpride@mweb.co.za. Highly recommended interactive tours, where you get to meet the people of the Bo-Kaap and District Six as well as the

African townships and squatter camps. They also do jazz outings in which you visit two clubs, and a "Township by Night" trip, which includes supper at a township restaurant and a visit to a *shebeen*. Half day R220.

Thuthuka Tours ☎021 439 2061 or 082 979 5831, ⓦwww.townshipcrawling .com. An outstanding range of scheduled township tours geared to individual interests, including Xhosa rituals, authentic consultations with a traditional healer and night-time music outings. Half-day trips Mon–Fri 9am–12.30pm & 1.30–4.30pm; R180. The full-day tour, which costs R360, runs Mon–Fri 1.30–10pm and incorporates some nightlife, such as a visit to a club or *shebeen*. On Saturday afternoons, half-day Xhosa Folklore tours allow you to witness traditional rituals still alive in the townships.

Western Cape Action Tours ☎021 461 1371, ⓦwww.dacpm.org. Led by former Umkhonto weSizwe (ANC armed wing) activists from Cape Town, these tours focus on the fight against apartheid and the post-apartheid scene. Visitors go to the townships, see sites of political resistance, as well as visiting a traditional healer, housing projects and township markets, where they are encouraged to make face-to-face contact with residents. Half day R200, full day R400.

Trains

Cape Town's **train** service (timetable information ☎0800 656 463), is a relatively reliable if slightly rundown urban line running from Cape Town station, through the southern suburbs and all the way down to Simon's Town. Highly recommended as an outing in its own right, and undoubtedly one of the great urban train journeys of the world, it reaches the False Bay coast at Muizenberg and continues south, sometimes so spectacularly close to the ocean that you can feel the spray and peer into rock pools. By far the nicest way to travel is in the **Biggsy's buffet car** (five times a day in each direction Mon–Fri, and four times Sat & Sun) which serves light snacks, beers and other refreshments.

Trains run overground, and there are no signposts to the stations on the streets, so if you're staying in the southern suburbs ask for directions at your accommodation; otherwise look at a map before you leave, or ask around. Tickets must be bought at the station before boarding. You're best off in the reasonably priced first-class carriages; curiously, there's no second class, and third class is not recommended.

A first-class single from Cape Town to Muizenberg is R10. Suburban trains tend to run pretty close to the **timetable**, with departures from the central station to the southern suburbs as far as Retreat leaving roughly every ten minutes at peak times (Mon–Fri 5.10–8.40am & 3.30–6pm). Services are slightly less frequent as far as Fish Hoek (about every 20 min Mon–Fri 5.10am–7.30pm & Sat 5.20am–6pm; every hour Sun 7.30am–6.30pm) and Simon's Town (about every 40 min Mon–Fri 5.10am–7.30pm & Sat 5.20am–6pm; every hour Sun 7.30am–6.30pm). From mid-December to the end of March there are additional Sunday trains.

Three other lines run east from Cape Town to **Strand** (through Bellville) and to the outlying towns of **Stellenbosch** and **Paarl**; however, the journeys aren't recommended, as they run through some less safe areas of the Flats.

Driving

Cape Town has good roads and several fast **freeways** that can whisk you across town in next to no time, except at peak hours (7–9am & 4–6.30pm). Take care approaching: the on-ramps frequently feed directly into the fast lane, and Capetonians have no compunction in exceeding the 100kph freeway and 120kph highway speed limits. There's often little warning of branches off to the suburbs, only the final destination of the freeway being given. Your best bet is to plan your journey, and make sure you know exactly where you're going. On the plus side, the obvious landmarks of Table Mountain and the two seaboards make orientation straightforward, particularly south of the centre, and there are some wonderful journeys, the most notable being the drives along the Atlantic seaboard to Hout Bay and Chapman's Peak Drive, a narrow winding cliff-edge route with the Atlantic breaking hundreds of metres below, and around the Cape Point Nature Reserve, returning from Cape Point along the False Bay seaboard. Note that Chapman's Peak is not expected to be open to motorized traffic till the middle of 2003, but you can get onto it on foot or by bike.

The usual precautions for defensive **driving** in South Africa are in order, especially since Cape Town has a few peculiarities all of its own. An unwritten rule of the road on the Peninsula is that **minibus taxis** have the right of way. Don't mess with them: their vehicles are bigger than yours, they may carry handguns and will routinely run through amber lights as they change to red – as will many Capetonians.

Car and motorbike rental

Given Cape Town's scant public transport, renting a vehicle is the only convenient way of exploring the Cape Peninsula. It needn't break the bank: there are dozens of competing **car rental** companies to choose from (see p.172). To find out who's currently operating and to get the best deal, either pick up one of the brochures at the Cape Town Tourism office (see p.83) or look in the Yellow Pages phone book. For one-way rental (to drive down the Garden Route and fly out of Port Elizabeth, for example), you'll have to rely on one of the bigger and pricier nationwide companies.

For **motorbike rental**, Le Cap Motorcycle Hire, 3 Carisbrook St (☎021 423 0823), provides all the necessary gear and rents out serious bikes (from R220 daily, plus 80c/km). African Buzz, (220 Long St in the city centre ☎021 423 0052) rents out 100cc **scooters** with all the gear you need for a fully inclusive R160 for 24 hours. They also provide a map of the Cape Peninsula, with suggested routes and points of interest.

One of the most popular – and hair-raising – road routes for cyclists is along the narrow hairpins of Chapman's Peak Drive (see p.141), which offer stupendous views of the Atlantic. There are also a number of dedicated mountain-biking routes in the Peninsula's nature reserves. For rental outlets, see p.87.

Accommodation

Cape Town has plenty of **accommodation** to suit all budgets, but to guarantee the kind of place you want, booking ahead is recommended, especially over the Christmas holidays (mid-December to mid-January). The greatest concentration of accommodation is in the areas that abut the city centre: the City Bowl and the Atlantic seaside strip as far as Sea Point. The City Bowl, spreading from the centre to the slopes of Table Mountain, comprises the city centre, Kloof Nek Road, the down-at-heel and lively suburb of Gardens, as well as the desirable inner-city suburbs of Tamboerskloof and Oranjezicht, which are close to the centre, sufficiently elevated to provide sea views and are only ten minutes' drive from the stunning Atlantic coast.

There are a few accommodation agencies that may be able to help if you're stuck. Cape Town Tourism (ⓦwww.cape-town.org) runs a Hotel and Accommodation Booking Desk (see p.83); Bed'n'Breakfast, PO Box 2739, Clareinch 7740, Claremont (☎021 683 3505, ⓔholtz@intekom.co.za) has places from R160–200 per person per night, while for self-catering accommodation during December and January, A–Z Holiday Accommodation, 15 Winton Crescent, Woodbridge Island 7441 (☎021 551 2785, ⓦwww.a-zholidayhomes.co.za) can provide accommodation, from a two-person apartment for R500 a day to a R8000 superluxury house. Roger and Kay's Travel Selection (☎021 715 7130, ⓦwww.travelselection.co.za) produces a South African accommodation guide, which lists a fair number of properties in Cape Town with rooms for R100 to 200 per person per night – choose your place and book directly with the host. The booklet is available free from South African Tourism offices worldwide, and can be posted (small charge for airmail, surface mail free), or check their website.

City centre

The city centre's accommodation is highly concentrated along **Long Street**, which is also the lively focus for restaurants, clubs and pubs. The heart of the

Robben Island ▲

CITY CENTRE AND SUBURBS

N

Table Bay

LIESBEEK PARKWAY

Rosebank
Mowbray
Observatory
MAIN RD
ROSEBANK
OBSERVATORY
SALT RIVER
Salt River
M5
PAARDEN EILAND
MARINE DRIVE
TABLE BAY BOULEVARD N1
WOODSTOCK
VICTORIA RD
EASTERN BOULEVARD N2
DE WAAL DRIVE M3
Rhodes
Memorial 🏛
Devil's Peak
(1000m)
M o u n t a i n

ZONNEBLOEM
(DISTRICT SIX)
THE FORESHORE
Duncan Dock
See Periphery & the Foreshore map
Victoria and Alfred Waterfront
See V&A Waterfront & De Waterkant map
Cape Town Central Station
Castle of Good Hope
CITY CENTRE
BO-KAAP
ADDERLEY ST
STRAND ST
LONG ST
BUITENGRACHT ST
BUITENKANT ST
TENNANT ST
SOMERSET RD
See Around Long St & the Company's Garden map
VREDEHOEK
ORANJEZICHT
GARDENS
Signal Hill
(350m)
TAMBOERSKLOOF
KLOOF NEK RD
KLOOF ST
Lion's Head
(669m)
MOUILLE POINT
BEACH RD
MAIN RD
HIGH LEVEL RD
KLOOF RD
THREE ANCHOR BAY
SEA POINT
BANTRY BAY
CLIFTON
VICTORIA RD
CAMPS BAY
See Mouille Point, Green Point, Sea Point & Clifton map
CAMPS BAY DRIVE
The Pipe Track hiking route
TAFELBERG RD
Kloof Nek Bus Terminus
See City Bowl Suburbs map
T a b l e
Cableway

0   1 km

city centre extends four blocks east to take in the **Company's Gardens**. Some accommodation and nightlife is also found in the far quieter city centre periphery, which extends for about five blocks east of Long Street and a similar distance west of the Company's Gardens to Zonnebloem (District Six). It also extends north away from Strand Street to take in the Foreshore. Most of these areas are a five-minute walk from Long Street and all the city-centre sites, and may be preferable to Long Street if you want to be central but don't plan to burn the midnight oil.

Around Long Street and the Company's Gardens

Accommodation here is marked on the map on p.92.

Cape Gardens Lodge Hotel 88 Queen Victoria St, Gardens ☎021 423 1260, ⓦwww .capegardenslodge.com. A smart multistorey hotel with 56 air-conditioned rooms with cable TV, baths and showers, bang in the centre, opposite the Gardens. Two minutes from the South African Museum and Art Gallery, and an easy and pleasant walk through the Company's Gardens to the city centre. ❹

Carnival Court Backpackers 255 Long St ☎021 423 9003, ⓔcarnivalcourt@freemail.absa .co.za. A clean, spacious and friendly establishment in an airy Victorian apartment building converted into a lodge. A buzzing bar makes this a good place for party animals. The rooms are clean but uninspiring, with twelve dorms, mostly sleeping four to six people, eight doubles and four singles. ❶

Cat & Moose 305 Long St ☎021 423 7638, ⓔcat&moose@hotmail.com. The most stylish of the Long Street lodges, housed in an eighteenth-century building a couple of doors from the steam baths at the south end of the city centre. Timber floors with Turkish-style rugs, exposed beams, earthy reds and ochres as well as some African masks imbue it with a warm ethnic feel. The six dorms, two triples and five double rooms are arranged around a small leafy courtyard, with a waterfall cascading into a plunge pool. ❶

Long Street Backpackers 209 Long St ☎021 423 0615, ⓔlongstbp@mweb.co.za. The oldest Long Street backpacker lodge, on the top two floors of an unexceptional three-storey former apartment block arranged around a courtyard with dorms, doubles and singles. Quieter than some of the other lodges in the vicinity, it's a well-organized, plain but clean place, with a laundry, internet facilities and a travel desk; there's also a lively bar and a kitchen. ❶

Overseas Visitors' Club Hostel 230 Upper Long St ☎021 424 6800, ⓦwww.ovc.co.za. A well-organized lodge above some shops, run more along the lines of a guesthouse than a hostel, it's small by Long Street standards, with three dorms (each sleeping six) with balconies. There are high ceilings and airy spaces, while the absence of a bar makes it more tranquil than most lodges in the vicinity. A TV lounge leads onto a wraparound balcony that offers views of the street. ❶

Simply the Best 187 Long St ☎021 424 8223, ⓦwww.backpackerslodge.co.za. A sizeable hostel with a party atmosphere, located on the top two floors of an undistinguished three-storey converted block of flats above a bar/bistro. Fully refurbished at the end of 2001, its great attraction is that the twelve dorms (sleeping a maximum of six) and five doubles are each self-contained, with their own kitchens and bathrooms. A good budget self-catering option in the city centre. ❶

Travellers' Inn 208 Long St ☎021 424 9272, ⓦwww.travellers-inn.co.za. Pleasant budget accommodation in a turn-of-the-century building above a cybercafé. With no bar and no backpacker scene, this could be a good bet for travellers wanting to avoid the hectic social atmosphere of the city-centre hostels. Apart from the light and spacious family rooms with twin beds and a double bunk, the rooms are small and sparely furnished, but clean and adequate, with shared bathroom facilities. Weekly and monthly discounts are available. ❶

Tudor Hotel 153 Longmarket St, Greenmarket Square ☎021 424 1335, ⓦwww.tudorhotel.co.za. Thirty en-suite B&B rooms in a very central and reasonably priced hotel overlooking cobbled Greenmarket Square, a five-minute walk from trendy Long Street. ❷

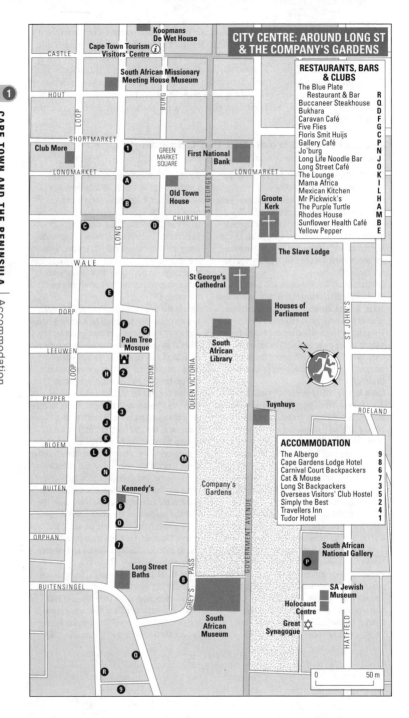

CAPE TOWN AND THE PENINSULA | Accommodation

Koopmans De Wet House

Cape Town Tourism Visitors' Centre (i)

CASTLE

HOUT

LOOP

BURG

South African Missionary Meeting House Museum

SHORTMARKET

Club More

❶

GREEN MARKET SQUARE

First National Bank

LONGMARKET

LONGMARKET

ST GEORGES

Ⓐ

Ⓑ

Old Town House

Groote Kerk

LONG

Ⓒ

Ⓓ

CHURCH

WALE

The Slave Lodge

St George's Cathedral

Ⓔ

DORP

Ⓕ Ⓖ

Palm Tree Mosque

LEEUWEN

LOOP

❷

Ⓗ

KEEROM

QUEEN VICTORIA

Houses of Parliament

South African Library

ST JOHN'S

N

PEPPER

Ⓘ ❸

Ⓙ

Ⓚ

BLOEM

Ⓛ ❹

Ⓜ

Ⓝ

Tuynhuys

ROELAND

BUITEN

Kennedy's

Ⓞ

Company's Gardens

GOVERNMENT AVENUE

ORPHAN

❺

❻

❼

South African National Gallery

BUITENSINGEL

Long Street Baths

GREY'S PASS

❽

Ⓟ

SA Jewish Museum

Holocaust Centre

Great Synagogue ✡

HATFIELD

South African Museum

Ⓠ

Ⓡ

❾

0   50 m

RESTAURANTS, BARS & CLUBS

The Blue Plate Restaurant & Bar	R
Buccaneer Steakhouse	Q
Bukhara	D
Caravan Café	F
Five Flies	G
Floris Smit Huijs	C
Gallery Café	P
Jo'burg	N
Long Life Noodle Bar	J
Long Street Café	O
The Lounge	K
Mama Africa	I
Mexican Kitchen	L
Mr Pickwick's	H
The Purple Turtle	A
Rhodes House	M
Sunflower Health Café	B
Yellow Pepper	E

ACCOMMODATION

The Albergo	9
Cape Gardens Lodge Hotel	8
Carnival Court Backpackers	6
Cat & Mouse	7
Long St Backpackers	3
Overseas Visitors' Club Hostel	5
Simply the Best	2
Travellers Inn	4
Tudor Hotel	1

City centre: periphery and the Foreshore

Accommodation here is marked on the map on p.94.

Cape Heritage Hotel 90 Bree St ℡ 021 424 4646, ⓦ www.capeheritage.co.za. An elegant and tastefully restored hotel located in a row of houses dating back to 1771, in Heritage Square, just below the Bo-Kaap. Fifteen spacious rooms are each furnished in a unique theme, among them African, Japanese and Dutch. Although there's no garden, there's a nice courtyard. ❻

City Slickers On the corner of 25 Rose and Hout streets ℡ 021 422 2357, ⓕ 021 422 2355. A lively lodge in the Bo-Kaap, five minutes from the city centre, whose roof garden has views to Table Mountain. The train-carriage style rooms have only one twin bunk, or a single or double bed in each. ❶

IKhaya Lodge Wandel Street, Dunkley Square ℡ 021 461 8880, ⓦ www.ikhayalodge.co.za. A guesthouse three short blocks away from the Company's Gardens and museums and walkable to all the city-centre sights. Its eleven standard rooms in the main guesthouse, five luxury loft suites and two self-catering apartments, done out in ethnically-inspired decor, have mountain or (cheaper) city views. The lodge's patio overlooks the outdoor eateries of trendy Dunkley Square. ❹–❺

St Paul's B&B Guest House 182 Bree St ℡ 021 423 4420 (7am–2pm), ⓕ 021 423 1580. A charming, well-managed and inexpensive guesthouse in a Georgian building (formerly a maternity hospital) in a calm street on the city-centre fringes, within easy striking distance of the sights. The rooms are large, comfortable and light with huge windows, with shared bathroom and kitchen facilities. ❷

V&A Waterfront and De Waterkant

In keeping with the gentrified ambience of the **Waterfront**, accommodation here tends to be upmarket; there are, however, a couple of reasonably priced places to stay, especially in the area just south of the V&A Waterfront and **De Waterkant**. Accommodation here is marked on the map on p.96.

Breakwater Lodge Portswood Road, Waterfront ℡ 021 406 1911 (ask for Lodge Reservations), ⓦ www.breakwaterlodge.co.za. The most affordable place to stay on the doorstep of the Waterfront, this is a sparkling white hotel linked to the Graduate School of Business, partially housed in a nineteenth-century prison building, a five-minute walk from the V&A Waterfront. Although it lacks personality, the lodge's 200 or so standard en-suite rooms are functional and come equipped with TVs and phones, while the 110 budget units share a bathroom with one other room. Rates exclude breakfast. ❸–❹

The Cape Grace West Quay, V&A Waterfront ℡ 021 410 7100, ⓦ www.capegrace.co.za. This is undoubtedly one of South Africa's most expensive and most exclusive hotels, and was Bill and Hillary Clinton's choice when they visited Cape Town in 1998. Spectacularly sited on a slender spit overlooking the V&A Waterfront's small vessel marina to one side and the Alfred Basin to the other, the hotel's 102 rooms have either harbour or Table Mountain views and are stylishly furnished in pared-back French period style. ❽

City Lodge On the corner of Alfred and Dock roads, Waterfront ℡ 021 419 9450, ⓦ www.citylodge.co.za. A rather austere but perfectly adequate hotel, part of a national chain, poised between the V&A Waterfront and the city centre, less than 1km from both. The rooms have TVs and there's a small swimming pool. While not as close to the V&A action as *Breakwater Lodge*, this is still one of the few reasonably priced places this close to the Waterfront. Friday–Sunday nights are cheaper, and you can pick up discounts of up to 75 percent on their auction site ⓦ www.bid2stay.co.za. ❹

St John's Waterfront Lodge 4–6 Braemar Rd, Green Point ℡ 021 439 1404, ⓦ www.stjohns.co.za. The closest hostel to the V&A Waterfront (a 15min walk away), well run by friendly and helpful staff. Accommodation is in four dorms sleeping eight to nine people, as well as some doubles, one of which is en suite. There are two swimming pools, a great garden and a bar, and the restaurant serves reasonably priced light meals till midnight. There's also internet access, a coin-operated washing machine and a travel centre. ❶

Victoria & Alfred Hotel Pierhead, Waterfront ℡ 021 419 6677, ⓦ www.vahotel.co.za. A four-star squeaky-clean hotel on North Quay, bang in the heart of the Waterfront, occupying a converted turn-of-the-century dock warehouse. It overlooks the Alfred Basin, within spitting distance of numerous bars and restaurants. Pricier rooms have stunning views of Table Mountain, while the decor is in the Cape Dutch Revival style. ❻–❼

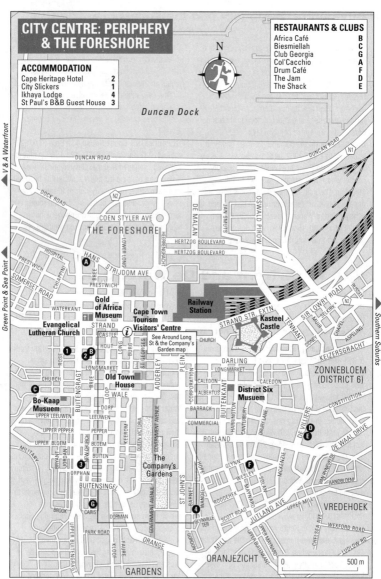

CITY CENTRE: PERIPHERY & THE FORESHORE

N

ACCOMMODATION

Cape Heritage Hotel	2
City Slickers	1
Ikhaya Lodge	4
St Paul's B&B Guest House	3

RESTAURANTS & CLUBS

Africa Café	B
Biesmiellah	C
Club Georgia	G
Col'Cacchio	A
Drum Café	F
The Jam	D
The Shack	E

Duncan Dock

DUNCAN ROAD
DUNCAN ROAD
N1

DOCK ROAD
N2

COEN STYLER AVE
THE FORESHORE

PRESTWICH
PRESTWICH
HANS STRIJDOM AVE
LOWER LONG
HERTZOG BOULEVARD
HERTZOG BOULEVARD
DE MALAN
JAN SMUTS
OSWALD PIROW
SIR LOWRY ROAD
N2

HOSPITAL
SOMERSET ROAD
CHIAPPINI
PRESTWICH
WATERKANT
BREE

Gold of Africa Museum
Cape Town Tourism Visitors' Centre
Railway Station
Kasteel Castle

Evangelical Lutheran Church
STRAND

See Around Long St & the Company's Garden map

CHURCH
STRAND STR. EXTN
TENNANT

ROSE
HOUT
CASTLE
BURG
ST GEORGES
ADDERLEY
PLEIN
DARLING
LONGMARKET
LONGMARKET
CALEDON
CALEDON

Old Town House

CHURCH
BREE
LOOP
CORPORATION
ALBERTUS

District Six Musuem

ZONNEBLOEM
(DISTRICT 6)
KEIZERSGRACHT
CONSTITUTION

Bo-Kaap Musuem
UPPER LEEUWEN
UPPER PEPPER
UPPER BLOEM
MILITARY
BRYANT
JORDAN
ORPHAN

BUITENGRAGT
WALE
DORP
LEEUWEN
PEPPER
KEEROM
BLOEM
BUITEN

BARRACK
COMMERCIAL
ROELAND

HARRINGTON
CANTERBURY
DRURY LANE
DE VILLIERS
DE WAAL DRIVE
D
E

QUEEN VICTORIA
GOVERNMENT AVENUE

The Company's Gardens

BUITENSINGEL
CARIS
DORMAN

BROOK
PARK ROAD
ORANGE
FAIRE
KLOOF

UPPER BUITENGRAGT

ST JOHN'S
BARNET
WANDEL
ROODEHEK

GLYNN
F
WESLEY
MYNHARDT

GLYNVILLE TER

GARDENS

ORANJEZICHT

SCOTT ROAD
MILL
JUTLAND AVE
UPPER MILL

MCKENZIE
VAN RYNEVELD
AANDBLOEM
VREDEHOEK
UPPER MYNHARDT
UPPER BUITENKANT
CHELSEA AVE
WEXFORD ROAD
LUDLOW RD.

0   500 m

▼ *Cable Station, Camps Bay & Atlantic Seaboard*

◄ *Green Point & Sea Point*
◄ *V & A Waterfront*
► *Southern Suburbs*

De Waterkant Village and De Waterkant House
1 Loader St, De Waterkant ☎021 422 2721,
Ⓦwww.dewaterkant.co.za. Sixty-five attractively
restored historic cottages in a villagey quarter of
the eighteenth-century Waterkant district of Green
Point, adjacent to the Bo-Kaap and less than 1km
from the V&A Waterfront and city centre. The luxury
cottages in Waterkant, Loader, Dixon and Napier
streets, have from one to three bedrooms; some
have garages, swimming pools and roof gardens
with harbour or mountain views. Also part of the
district is De Waterkant House, which has nine
rooms sharing a pool and terrace with views over
the V&A Waterfront. ❹

Mouille Point to Sea Point

Down the **Atlantic seaboard** lie the seaside suburbs of Mouille Point, Green Point, Three Anchor Bay and Sea Point. Historically Cape Town's hotel and high-rise land, this is now packed with accommodation from backpacker lodges to swish hotels, making it a good alternative to the City Bowl if you want to be close to the city centre. Accommodation here is marked on the map on p.98.

Inexpensive

Altona Lodge 19 Croxteth Rd, Green Point ☎021 434 2572, ⓦwww.altona.co.za. A quiet and friendly guesthouse with a homely atmpsphere in a Victorian house close to the city centre. Of the seventeen B&B rooms, five are en suite; the cheaper rooms share a bathroom, though each room has its own hand basin. The service is good, the rates very reasonable, and there's also a small garden. ❷

Carnaby the Backpacker 219 Main Rd, Three Anchor Bay ☎021 439 7410, ⓦwww.web.netactive .co.za/carnaby. An extraordinary and fun hostel, previously an old-fashioned three-star hotel, located about 100m from the sea (too rocky for swimming). The 1970s Spanish-style stucco decor has been retained for kitsch effect. A big attraction is that a number of its dorms (sleeping three to six) and double rooms are en suite and have phones which you can use to receive calls, but not make outgoing calls. There's even a honeymoon suite with its own TV, and a shady outdoor pool terrace, bar, pool table, pinball and travel centre. Dorms ❶, doubles ❷

Sunflower Stop 179 Main Rd, Green Point ☎021 434 6535, ⓦwww.sunflowerstop.co.za. A bright yellow backpacker lodge that claims to be the cleanest in Cape Town (it's serviced twice a day), in a two-storey 1940s house 1km from the Waterfront. Accommodation is in two dorms sleeping nine and twelve people, and fourteen doubles. This child-friendly lodge has a bar, pool room, swimming pool, a coin-operated washing machine, safe, travel centre and internet access. ❶

Waterfront Suites 153 Main Rd, Green Point ☎021 439 5020, ⓦwww.waterfront-suites.co.za. Small four-storey block quite close to the waterfront, with 26 modern, impersonal but extremely comfortable self-catering apartments offering brilliant value. The kitchens are well-equipped, rooms are serviced daily and you can have a continental breakfast in their cafeteria (not inclusive). ❷

Moderate

Brenda's Guest House 14 Pine Rd, Green Point ☎021 434 0902 or 083 627 5583, ⓦwww .brendas.co.za. Four rooms inside and another in the garden of a 1900s house, close to the

Waterfront. There's poolside seating on a bricked terrace, and rooms are brightly decorated with wicker furniture. ❹

Cape Town Ritz On the corner of Main and Camberwell roads, Three Anchor Bay ☎021 439 6010, ⓦwww.gk-hotels.co.za. An enormous 27-storey 1960s block, with 222 rooms and no balconies, best known for the revolving restaurant on the twenty-second floor. Less than 2km from the V&A Waterfront, it's in the heart of the Sea Point wining and dining district. Good value if you don't mind high-rise accommodation. ❹

Don Suite Hotel 249 Beach Rd, Sea Point ☎021 434 1083, ⓦwww.don.co.za. A five-storey block of 27 self-catering apartments across the road from the beachfront promenade, 300m from the lively Main Road restaurant strip and 4km from the V&A Waterfront. All the flats, studio and one- and two-bedroom units are modern and well-equipped; rates depend on whether or not you get a view. ❹

Dungarvin House 163 Main Rd, Green Point ☎021 434 0677, ⓦwww.kom.co.za. A grand Edwardian villa with moulded pediments on a busy road not far from the Sea Point restaurants, with gracious, well-appointed rooms. ❹

Jambo Guest House 1 Grove Rd, Green Point ☎021 439 4219, ⓦwww.jambo.co.za. Small atmospheric establishment with four double rooms in a quiet cul-de-sac off Main Road, just over 1km from the V&A Waterfront. Despite being in the inner-city suburbs, its lush leafy exterior and enclosed garden with pond are delightfully relaxing and the service is excellent. A luxury suite has a large sitting area, Jacuzzi and French doors opening onto the garden. ❹–❺

Lion's Head Lodge On the corner of Conifer and 319 Main Rd, Sea Point ☎021 434 4163, ⓦwww.lions-head-lodge.co.za. Plain but very comfortable en-suite hotel-style rooms that are clean and well maintained, despite the weather-worn exterior of the four-storey building. Some face the busy main road at the heart of Sea Point's restaurant strip, while quieter rooms overlook the courtyard. All have phones and TV, and the lodge also has a swimming pool, bar, beer terrace and an à la carte restaurant. Also offers fully equipped apartments that sleep two. ❸

◀ Mouille Point, Green Point & Sea Point

◀ Green Point & Sea Point

Mouille Point, Green Point & Sea Point ▶

▼ Bo Kaap

▼ City Centre

V&A WATERFRONT & DE WATERKANT

ACCOMMODATION

Breakwater Lodge	1
The Cape Grace	4
City Lodge	6
De Waterkant Village	5
St Johns Waterside Lodge	2
Victoria & Alfred Hotel	3

RESTAURANTS, BARS & CLUBS

Anatoli	L
Angels	M
Bar Code	S
Bayfront Blu	G
The Bronx	M
Café Manhattan	P
Caffé Balducci	D
Caffé San Marco	E
Chilli 'n' Lime	N
Club 55	K
Den Anker Restaurant	I
Emily's Bistro	J
The Green Dolphin	H
Mugg & Bean	B
On Broadway	O
Robert's Café & Cigar Bar	R
Rosie's	T
Sky	M
Tasca de Belém	F
Vasco Da Gama Tavern	Q
Willoughby & Co	C
Zerban's	A

Victoria Wharf B C

Victoria Wharf A

EAST PIER ROAD

JETTY WAY

BREAKWATER BOULEVARD

Victoria Basin

Agfa Amphitheatre

Telkom Exploratorium

Old Port Captain's Office

Swing Bridge

Nelson Mandela Gateway to Robben Island

Clock Tower Centre

Clock Tower & Waterfront Information Centre

Cape Town Tourism Visitors' Centre

Market Square

Waterfront Bus Stop

Alfred Mall

BMW Pavilion & IMAX Cinema

SA Maritime Museum

Two Oceans Aquarium

Waterfront Marina

PORTSWOOD ROAD

SOUTHARM ROAD

FISH QUAY ROAD

DOCK ROAD

PORT ROAD

EBENEZER ROAD

CARDIFF

BENNETT

BATTERY

HOSPITAL

PRESTWICH

ALFRED

CHIAPPINI

SOMERSET ROAD

NAPIER

DIXON

WATERKANT

LOADER

STRAND

VOS

HUDSON

COBERN

JARVIS

DE SMIDT

DE WATERKANT

GALLOWS HILL RD

HIGHFIELD ROAD

BEAUMONT

BOUNDARY ROAD

WESSELS ROAD

HILLSIDE TERRACE

UPPER PORTSWOOD ROAD

MAIN ROAD

VESPERDENE ROAD

BRAEMAR ROAD

0   100 m

Stonehurst Guest House 3 Frere Rd, Sea Point ☎021 434 9670, ✉stonehurstguesthouse@ absafreemail.co.za. An airy tin-roofed Victorian residence with original fittings, Cape furniture and a pleasant front garden. There's a kitchen and guest lounge. Some rooms have balconies, eleven are en suite and the remaining three cheaper ones share a bathroom. ❷–❸

Villa Rosa 277 High Level Rd, Sea Point ☎021 434 2768, ⊛www.villa-rosa.com. A friendly eight-room guesthouse in a salmon-pink two-storey Victorian house on the lower slopes of Signal Hill, two blocks from the beachfront promenade. Decorated with simplicity and style, all rooms have TVs, phones and safes, but only some on the upper floor have sea views. ❹

Expensive

Olaf's Guest House 24 Wisbeach Rd, Sea Point ☎021 439 8943, ⊛www.olafs.co.za. A clean, comfortable and pleasantly decorated Victorian bungalow with a friendly owner, 5min from the beachfront promenade and 3km from the city centre. Its eight en-suite rooms all have cable TV and telephones, and you can have breakfast on the patio beside the swimming pool. ❺

Winchester Mansions Hotel 221 Beach Rd, Sea Point ☎021 434 2351, ⊛www.winchester.co.za. A self-consciously colonial-style 1920s hotel, in a prime spot across the road from the seashore, with an atmosphere straight from the pages of Agatha Christie. Palm trees at the front of the three-storey Cape Dutch Revival building hint at the interior: rooms have ceiling fans, and a cool Italianate courtyard restaurant is overlooked by balconies draped in luxuriant creepers. ❺

City Bowl suburbs

The **City Bowl suburbs** are popular for accommodation, and the most southerly sections are just five to ten minutes' walk from the Gardens and museums. A few backpacker lodges can be found along Kloof Street, the continuation of trendy Long Street. The further up you go, the leafier the suburbs become, and you'll find the pricier and more comfortable B&Bs, guesthouses and hotels along the lower slopes of Table Mountain, overlooking the city centre and Duncan Dock. There's no public transport to the City Bowl Suburbs, but most accommodation listed is under 3km from Cape Town station. Accommodation here is marked on the map on p.100.

Inexpensive

African Sun 3 Florida Rd, Vredehoek ☎021 461 1601, ✉afpress@iafrica.com. A small, secluded, self-catering apartment, attached to a family house a little over 1km from the city centre. Furnished with pared-back ethnic decor, it's run by friendly, well-informed and interesting owners, one a novelist and children's author and the other a travel writer. A five-percent discount is offered if you produce this book. Great value. ❷

Ambleside Guesthouse 11 Forest Rd, Oranjezicht ☎021 465 2503, ☏021 465 3814. The guesthouse has been going for fifty years and comprises eight inexpensive, comfortable though slightly stuffy en-suite rooms, all with great views across the city to the harbour, and cable-car watching from the back patio. A hot breakfast is served in the rooms, and you can prepare your own meals in a communal kitchen. ❷

Ashanti Lodge and Guest House 11 Hof St, Gardens ☎021 423 8721, ⊛www.ashanti.com. King of the Cape Town lodges, this is a massive, superbly refurbished two-storey Victorian mansion a 5min walk from the Gardens. The details

that give it the edge are stripped timber, chic marbling and ethnic decor, soaring ceilings, a beautifully kept front garden, cosy TV lounge and a swimming pool with sun terrace. Twelve private rooms (twin or double beds) and ten dorms (sleeping six to eight) are furnished with custom-made wrought iron bunks and beds. They also have a quieter guesthouse around the corner in Union Street, with seven extremely well-priced en-suite double/twin rooms with TVs and a communal kitchen. ❶–❷

The Backpack 74 New Church St, Tamboerskloof ☎021 423 4530, ⊛www.backpackers.co.za. An excellent lodge in three interconnected houses, on the cusp of the City Bowl suburbs and the city centre, and easily walkable to both. Well-run and with excellent service, it's furnished with bold colours and ethnic fabrics, with plenty of outdoor space, including a pool terrace in its own private garden among banana trees. Accommodation is in four dorms (sleeping six to ten) and eleven private rooms (several of which are en suite); some rooms are suitable for families, although there's an unfenced pool. ❶–❷

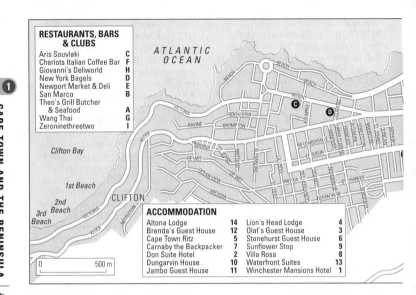

RESTAURANTS, BARS & CLUBS

Aris Souvlaki	C
Chariots Italian Coffee Bar	F
Giovanni's Deliworld	H
New York Bagels	D
Newport Market & Deli	E
San Marco	B
Theo's Grill Butcher & Seafood	
Wang Thai	A
Zeroninethreetwo	G I

ATLANTIC OCEAN

Clifton Bay

1st Beach

2nd Beach

3rd Beach

CLIFTON

ACCOMMODATION

Altona Lodge	14	Lion's Head Lodge	4
Brenda's Guest House	12	Olaf's Guest House	3
Cape Town Ritz	5	Stonehurst Guest House	6
Carnaby the Backpacker	7	Sunflower Stop	9
Don Suite Hotel	2	Villa Rosa	8
Dungarvin House	10	Waterfront Suites	13
Jambo Guest House	11	Winchester Mansions Hotel	1

0   500 m

Belmont House 10 Belmont Ave, Oranjezicht ☎021 461 5417, ⓦwww.capeguest.com. A tastefully restored 1920s house with seven fresh rooms, each with its own shower or bath. Either take the B&B option, or self-cater in their communal kitchen. A discount of five percent is offered if you produce this book. ❷–❸

Blencathra On the corner of De Hoop and Cambridge avenues, Tamboerskloof ☎021 424 9571, ⓦwww.geocities.com/blencathra_ct. Peaceful, spacious self-catering rooms, one of which is en suite, with stunning views in a large relaxed family house that attracts a young crowd who want to avoid the backpacker scene. On the slopes of Lion's Head, it's 2km from the city centre and 4km from the Atlantic seaboard beaches. There's a garden with outdoor seating and a swimming pool. ❶–❷

Cloudbreak Backpackers' Lodge 219 Upper Buitenkant St, Gardens ☎021 461 6892, ⓦwww.cloudbreakbackpackers.co.za. A friendly and fun place on a busy road, close to the large Gardens shopping centre. Eight doubles in a house with a garden, and three dorms sleeping six people in another house across the road. Surfing is a high priority, and daily trips are organized to good breaks and beaches. Free airport pick-up, and there's a travel and booking centre. ❶

Flower Street Villa Guest House 3 Flower St, Oranjezicht ☎ & ⓕ021 465 7517. Twenty spacious budget rooms in a former nursing home.

There's a small extra charge for breakfast, but guests have use of kitchen. Rooms sharing bathrooms ❶, en-suite rooms ❷

Oak Lodge 21 Breda St, Gardens ☎021 465 6182, ⓦwww.oaklodge.co.za. More an event than a lodge, this highly recommended hostel in an 1860s Victorian house has dramatic dungeons, dragon murals, and a lively atmosphere; it's also spacious, well-serviced and with an immaculate kitchen. There are four dorms and sixteen private rooms, one of which is en suite. ❶

Saasveld Lodge 73 Kloof St, Tamboerskloof ☎021 424 6169, ⓔsaasveld@icon.co.za. A clean but rather impersonal 1950s-style, four-storey guesthouse on a buzzing thoroughfare lined with good eating places, less than 1km from the centre. The rooms have TV and phone, and the rate excludes breakfast, offering reasonable value with no frills. ❷

Zebra Crossing 82 New Church St ☎021 422 1265, ⓔzebracross@intekom.co.za. Cape Town's only backpacker lodge that actually boasts about being quiet. On the northern edge of the City Bowl suburbs, it's an easy walk to the Kloof Street restaurants and pubs as well as those in the city centre. A café/bar serves full meals and decent coffee and there are two pleasant terraces under vines. Accommodation is in three spacious dorms (sleeping eight), eleven doubles and three singles; the best rooms are the three doubles in the annexe outside, with a balcony that has views of the mountain. Child-friendly. ❶

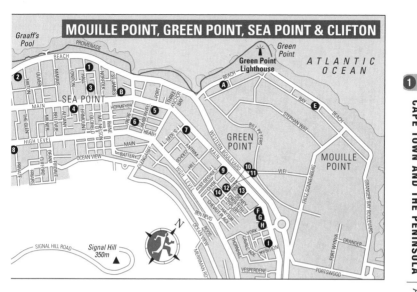

Graaff's Pool

PROMENADE

BEACH

Green Point

Green Point Lighthouse

ATLANTIC OCEAN

SEA POINT

MAIN

HIGH LEVEL

OCEAN VIEW

GREEN POINT

MOUILLE POINT

SIGNAL HILL ROAD

Signal Hill 350m

N

CAPE TOWN AND THE PENINSULA | Accommodation

Moderate to expensive

Cape Milner Hotel 2a Milner Rd, Tamboerskloof ☏021 426 1101, ⓦwwwcapemilner.co.za. A reasonably priced smart hotel, partly incorporating an early eighteenth-century building, at the foot of Signal Hill, about 1km from the centre. Totally refurbished in 2001 as a boutique hotel, it has 59 airy rooms, all with views of Table Mountain; the New York-style minimal decor gives rooms a light and pleasant atmosphere. There's also a swimming pool, restaurant and bar on the premises. ❺

Leeuwenvoet House 93 New Church St, Tamboerskloof ☏021 424 1133, ⓦwww .leeuwenvoet.co.za. A tranquil restored Victorian guesthouse, with eleven en-suite rooms kitted out with pine, wicker and all the hotel trimmings of TV, phone, fan and radio alarm. Situated on a major thoroughfare with secure parking, it's a fifteen-minute walk from the city centre, with airport transfers also available. ❹

Lezard Bleu 30 Upper Orange St, Oranjezicht ☏021 461 4601, ⓦwww.lezardbleu.co.za. Seven luxurious en-suite rooms, furnished with maple beds and cupboards in a spacious open-plan 1960s house. Sliding doors from each room open onto a garden. Located in a pleasant part of town, it's 1km from the centre and about half that distance to a nature reserve on the lower slopes of Table Mountain. A stand-alone timber cottage nestles among trees in the garden with views across the city; there's also a swimming pool and generous breakfasts. ❺

Mount Nelson Hotel 76 Orange St, Gardens ☏021 423 1000, ⓦwww.mountnelsonhotel.orient -express.com. Cape Town's grande dame: a fine and famous high-colonial Victorian hotel, built in 1899 (extended in the late-1990s in response to demand). Set in extensive established gardens, with arrival along a palm-lined colonnade, it takes itself terribly seriously and charges accordingly; the rate excludes breakfast. ❽

Underberg Guest House 6 Tamboerskloof Rd, Tamboerskloof ☏021 426 2262, ⓦwww.underbergguesthouse.co.za. Located on the doorstep of the city centre in the upmarket suburb of Tamboerskloof, this Victorian guesthouse offers excellent value. Its high ceilings and compact size (there are only eleven rooms) create an atmosphere that is both intimate and airy. ❹

Villa Belmonte Hotel 33 Belmont Ave, Oranjezicht ☏021 462 1576, ⓦwww.villabelmontehotel.co.za. The Western Cape's smallest five-star hotel, on the lower slopes of Table Mountain and 1km from the city centre, feels like an elegant Italian country villa. The fifteen rooms, some of which lead onto a lovely garden, are themed and prices vary according to size. Extremely good value, given the level of comfort and style. ❺–❻

Welgelegen Guest House 6 Stephen St, Gardens ☏021 426 2373, ⓦwww.welgelegen.co.za. Eight rooms in a Victorian guesthouse with mountain views furnished with considerable style – unsurprisingly, since the owner is an interior decorator. Despite being down a quiet cul de sac, it's just minutes from the Kloof Street restaurant and nightlife strip and an easy walk to the city-centre sights. ❺

99

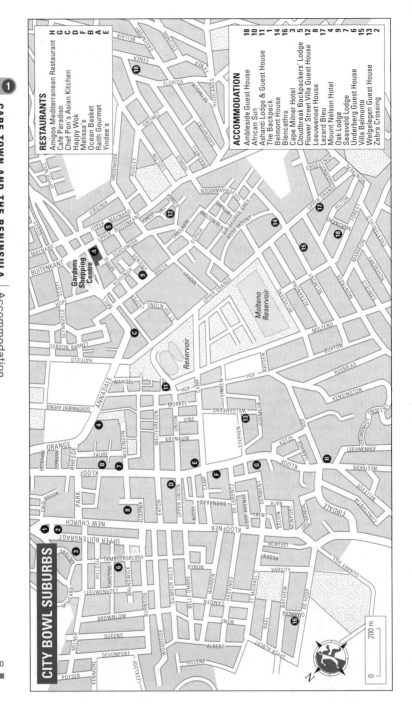

CITY BOWL SUBURBS

RESTAURANTS

Amigos Mediterranean Restaurant	H
Café Paradiso	G
Chef Pon's Asian Kitchen	C
Happy Wok	D
Melissa's	F
Ocean Basket	B
Raith Gourmet	A
Yindee's	E

ACCOMMODATION

Ambleside Guest House	18
African Sun	10
Ashanti Lodge & Guest House	11
The Backpack	1
Belmont House	14
Blencathra	16
Cape Milner Hotel	3
Cloudbreak Backpackers' Lodge	5
Flower Street Villa Guest House	12
Leeuwenoet House	8
Lezard Bleu	17
Mount Nelson Hotel	4
Oak Lodge	9
Saasveld Lodge	7
Underberg Guest House	6
Villa Belmonte	15
Welgelegen Guest House	13
Zebra Crossing	2

0   200 m

Southern suburbs

The **southern suburbs** – the formerly whites-only areas closest to the mountain – are convenient for the Simon's Town train line, providing easy access to both the city centre and the False Bay seaboard. Closest to town, Observatory (see p.125), with its streets of tightly packed Victorian cottages, large student population, congenial cafés and live music joints, can rival the city centre for eating places and nightlife. The more southerly suburbs of Rosebank, Claremont, Newlands and Rondebosch are leafier and quieter.

Carmichael House 11 Wolmunster Rd, Rosebank ☎021 689 8350, ⓦwww.carmichaelhouse.co.za. A turn-of-the-century two-storey guesthouse, with six big rooms equipped with phones, safes and hairdryers, with fax and email access. There's a peaceful garden, swimming pool and secure parking. It's a ten-minute walk to Rhodes Memorial and the Contour Path, while the Rondebosch shops are 1km away. ❹

The Courtyard Liesbeek Avenue, Mowbray ☎021 448 3929, ⓦwww.citylodge.co.za. Exceptional value, considering the high level of luxury. A beautiful early nineteenth-century Cape Dutch homestead under thatch, with terracotta floors, brass chandeliers and large lawns in a semi-rural setting. There's a hotel minibus (chargeable), and breakfast is extra. ❺

Gloucester House Bed & Breakfast 54 Weltevreden Ave, Rondebosch ☎ & ⓕ021 689 3894. A private house with two bedrooms, and a lounge/dining room for self-catering. Guests may use the large garden, swimming pool and barbecue area, and there's the plus of being close to Rondebosch station. The price excludes breakfast. ❹

The Green Elephant 57 Milton Rd, Observatory ☎021 448 6359, ⓦwww.hostels.co.za. Five basic dorms and six doubles in a large, vibey house just off Main Road, with a Jacuzzi, braai, solar-heated plunge pool and internet facilities. Camping is permitted in the garden, and the owner leads outdoor expeditions up Table Mountain and Lion's Head. ❶

Ivydene Off Glebe Road, Rondebosch ☎021 685 1747, ⓔivydene@mweb.co.za. Five flats in a delightful old Cape farmhouse near the universi-

ty, with a garden and swimming pool and an artistic and friendly atmosphere. There are discounts for stays over a week or more; if full, the helpful owner will recommend other places in the vicinity. ❹

Koornhoop Manor House Corner of Wrensch and Nuttal roads, Observatory ☎021 448 0595, ⓦwww.geocities.com/koornhoop. Pleasant rooms in a spacious Victorian house with a tranquil enclosed garden and small playground, close to the station, with secure parking and grounds. Besides B&B accommodation in seven double rooms, two of which are suitable for families, there's the option of a self-catering suite, which has three bedrooms and its own entrance. ❸

Riverview Lodge 5 Anson/Station roads, Observatory ☎021 447 9056, ⓔinfo@riverview.co.za. Huge professionally run lodge with 43 single, double and dorm rooms in a converted two-storey former apartment block, two minutes' walk from Observatory station. It tends to attract large groups, but has several small, comfortable lounges, outdoor spaces and quiet nooks if you need some solitude. A massive plus is the large breakfast included in the price. ❶

The Vineyard On the corner of Colinton and Protea roads, Newlands ☎021 683 3044, ⓦwww.vineyard.co.za. An excellent classy hotel that gives its snootier competitors a good run for their money at half the price. In a restored country villa built for Lady Anne Barnard in 1799, it's decorated in elegant Cape Dutch style, with an outstanding panorama of Table Mountain from the extensive garden. For the level of luxury, it offers outstanding value. ❻–❼

Constantia and Tokai

Lush **Constantia** is one of Cape Town's poshest suburbs, only twenty minutes' drive from either coast as well as the V&A Waterfront. Sharing the same valley is the adjoining suburb of **Tokai**, worth considering if you want to be well out of the centre; it's close to forest walks and ten minutes from the beach. Inexpensive accommodation is rare, but if money's no object and you're looking for somewhere exceptional and romantic, you might just find it here in a Cape Dutch manor house. A car is essential if you're staying in Constantia as there's no public transport; rental companies are listed on p.172.

Allandale Holiday Cottages 72 Zwaanswyk Rd, Tokai ☎ 021 715 3320, ⓦ www.allandale.co.za. Sixteen one-, two- and three-bedroom self-catering brick cottages on a smallholding adjoining Tokai Forest, on the slopes of Constantiaberg, two minutes from the motorway and twenty from Cape Town. Each cottage has a garden area with a braai and outdoor seating. Features a pool and tennis courts. ❹

Constantia Uitsig Country Hotel Spaanschemat River Road, Constantia ☎ 021 794 6500, ⓦ www.constantiauitsig.co.za. Sixteen custombuilt and luxurious Cape Dutch-style cottages, in a garden setting on Constantia Uitsig wine estate, next door to Steenberg. The hotel has two fabulous restaurants, *Constantia Uitsig* and *La Colombe* (see p.155). ❼

Elephant Eye Lodge 9 Sunwood Drive, Tokai ☎ 021 715 2432, ⓔ orsmond@iafrica.com. Six reasonably priced rooms at a friendly B&B family home in a converted Cape Dutch farmhouse, minutes' walk from Tokai Forest and with its own large grounds. Two rooms offer some basic selfcatering facilities, and you can get evening meals delivered. A baby's cot is also available and the swimming pool is safely fenced. ❸

Houtkapperspoort Hout Bay Road ☎ 021 794 5216, ⓦ www.houtkapperspoort.co.za. Twenty-four rustic one- and two-bedroom stone-and-brick selfcatering cottages set up against the Table Mountain Nature Reserve, close to Constantia Nek (around 5km from Hout Bay and 15km from the city centre). You can take paths straight from the estate up the mountain slopes, play tennis or take a dip in the solar-heated pool. Highly recommended. ❹

Little Ruo 11 Willow Rd, off Spaanschemat River Road, Constantia ☎ 021 794 2052, ⓦ www.littleruo .co.za. Two pretty B&B rooms at the home of friendly architect owners, plus three self-catering units set in a huge landscaped garden with willows, a stream and a saltwater pool. ❹

The Stables Chantercler Lane, Constantia ☎ & ⓕ 021 794 3653. Five en-suite doubles, each with their own entrance and patio, in converted stables. The six-course breakfasts are excellent, and you can relax around the pool in a large garden. ❹

Steenberg Corner Steenberg and Tokai roads ☎ 021 713 2222, ⓕ 021 713 2221, ⓦ www .steenberghotel.com. A luxurious place on South Africa's oldest wine estate at the foot of the Steenberg Mountain. Accommodation is in the original manor house and three other farm buildings (now national monuments), which are perfect examples of Cape Dutch architecture, dating back to 1682. Arranged around a large formal garden, the buildings have whitewashed walls, thatched roofs, ornate gables and are furnished with seventeenth- and eighteenth-century Cape antiques. ❼

Atlantic seaboard

Moving south from Sea Point along Victoria Drive, the luxury mountainside suburb of **Camps Bay** has soaring views over the Atlantic, with the advantage of being close to the city centre, and with its own restaurants and shops. Nearby **Llandudno** has similar vistas, no shops or restaurants, but a supremely beautiful beach with clusters of granite boulders at either end. **Hout Bay** is the main urban concentration along the lower half of the Peninsula, with a harbour, pleasant waterfront development and the only public transport beyond Camps Bay. South of Hout Bay is the semi-rural settlement of **Noordhoek**, close to the Cape of Good Hope Nature Reserve.

Bay Hotel Victoria Road ☎ 021 438 4444, ⓦ www.thebay.co.za. Luxurious, glitzy five-star hotel on the fashionable beachfront strip. Its late-1980s construction blends neo-Cape Dutch and Mediterranean styles and cane furniture, to conjure up a laidback colonial fantasy. Mountain-facing ❼, sea-facing and luxury suites ❽

Beach House Royal Avenue, Hout Bay ☎ 021 790 4228, ⓦ www.wk.co.za/beachhouse. A modern and friendly guesthouse with seven en-suite rooms, a five-minute walk from Mariner's Wharf and the beach. Features a patio with tables and chairs. ❹

Chapman's Peak Hotel Main Road, Hout Bay ☎ 021 790 1036, ⓕ 021 790 1089. The seaside setting overlooking Hout Bay Beach is impressive, though not all of the rather ordinary rooms are sea-facing. The pub-like restaurant does great calamari, though the other seafood is not particularly recommended. ❸

Leeukop 25 Sedgemoor Rd, Camps Bay ☎ 021 438 1361, ⓔ leeukopbb@hotmail.com. The most reasonably priced B&B accommodation in Camps Bay, near the beach and cafés, in two stylishly arty and comfortable apartments adjoining the cheerful proprietor's home. The flats, the bigger one being pricier, are fully equipped, and you can either self-cater or stay on a B&B basis. Studio apartment ④, larger apartment ⑤

Monkey Valley Resort Mountain Road, Noordhoek ☎ 021 789 1391, ⓦ www.monkeyvalleyresort.com. An attractive group of mainly wooden and thatched two-storey chalets spread over several acres of Chapman's Peak, overlooking the seven-kilometre Noordhoek Beach, 40km south of the city centre. Surrounded by indigenous vegetation and with no other houses in sight, there's an emphasis on natural products throughout. Either eat in the restaurant, self-cater or stay on a B&B basis. The cottages sleep six to eight people, and work out reasonably for a group. ⑤

False Bay seaboard

The Cape Town–Simon's Town Metrorail line runs through the southern suburbs to hit the coast at **Muizenberg**, the oldest of Cape Town's seaside suburbs. To its south are a series of settlements, including salubrious **St James**, **Kalk Bay** with its working harbour and great cafés, and **Fish Hoek**, which is known for the best swimming beach along the False Bay seaboard. At the end of the line is the handsome and historic village of Simon's Town (see p.144).

The Avenue Hotel 7 First Ave, Fish Hoek ☎ 021 782 6026, ⓦ www.inside.co.za. An unglamorous two-storey hotel within walking distance of the beach and shops, but with no sea view. Well-priced and perfectly adequate rooms make it popular with tour groups; there's a pool with loungers and umbrellas if it's too windy for the beach. ④

Chartfield Guest House On the corner of 30 Gatesville and Norman roads, Kalk Bay ☎ 021 788 3793, ⓦ www.chartfield.co.za. Unpretentious but newly refurbished accommodation, 100m from Kalk Bay station, in a well-kept rambling house halfway up the hill overlooking the harbour, with terrific panoramas of the Hottentots Holland Mountains across False Bay. The best rooms are the one in the loft with its own balcony and the two semicircular corner ones with 180 degree views. This good-value guesthouse has its own bistro and is three minutes' walk to the Kalk Bay restaurant strip. ②–③

Harbourside Backpackers 136 Main Rd, Kalk Bay ☎ 021 788 2943, ⓕ 021 788 6452. A popular hangout with a party atmosphere and views of the harbour. Two minutes' walk from the station, the hostel lies on the same road as several cafés and very browsable antique shops, and it's a ten-minute walk to the lovely Dalebrook tidal pool. ①

The Inn at Castle Hill 37 Gatesville Rd, Kalk Bay ☎ 021 788 2554, ⓦ www.castlehill.co.za. A stylishly restored two-storey Edwardian guesthouse up a hill with grand views of the sun rising across False Bay and whale watching in season. Five large bedrooms have high ceilings and timber floors. The best units are the Orca Whale and Humpback Whale rooms, which have French doors opening onto the upstairs verandah; avoid the small and viewless back room. ④–⑤

Nautilus Lodge 39 Simon's Town Rd, Fish Hoek ☎ 021 782 4168, ⓦ www.nautiluslodge.co.za. Three self-catering units next to Tudor House, on Jager's Walk leading to Fish Hoek Beach. Each unit has magnificent sea views and a patio with garden furniture. Two-bedroom unit R750, three-bedroom unit R850.

Sunny Cove Manor 72 Simon's Town Rd, Fish Hoek ☎ 021 782 2274, ⓔ sunnycovemanor @yahoo.com. This cheerful B&B, three minutes' walk to Sunny Cove station, offers outstanding sea views (except for the back room), with safe parking on the property. There are four suites, three of them with two bedrooms each, and if you cross the road and over the railway line, you're on Jager's walkway, which leads to Fish Hoek Beach. ④

Tudor House by the Sea 43 Simon's Town Rd, Fish Hoek ☎ 021 782 6238, ⓦ www.tudorhouse .co.za. Luxury self-catering apartments with slightly stuffy decor but excellent views of False Bay; each unit has its own balcony or garden. Sunny Cove station is two minutes away on foot, providing transport to both the city centre (35km) and Simon's Town (5km). It's a five-minute walk along a coastal path to the wide, safe and sandy Fish Hoek swimming beach. Book as far ahead as possible. ⑤

Simon's Town

Simon's Town (see p.144) is regarded by most Capetonians as a separate village, which it originally was, although it's now quite definitely part of the metropolis. During the day, all trains are met by Rikki's taxis, which will take you anywhere in the Simon's Town vicinity.

African township homestays

One of the best ways of getting a taste of the African townships is spending a night there. The number of township residents offering **B&B accommodation** in their homes is still small, but growing. You'll have a chance to experience the warmth of *ubuntu*, traditional African hospitality, by staying with a family with whom you'll generally eat breakfast and dinner; they can also usually take you around their area to *shebeens*, music venues or just to meet the neighbours.

To arrange **to get there**, you'll need to phone ahead. Many people are dropped off by tour operators, while a number of B&Bs will send someone to meet you at the airport; if you're self-driving, they'll give you detailed directions or arrange to meet you at a convenient landmark, such as a garage or police station. For information about other B&Bs in the townships, contact **Sivuyile Tourism Centre** in Guguletu (Mon–Fri 8am–5pm, Sat 8.30am–2pm, Sun 8.30am–1pm; ☎021 637 8449, ⓦwww.sivuyile.co.za) or Thuthuka Tours (☎021 439 2061 or 082 979 5831, ⓦwww.townshipcrawling.com), which, aside from running township tours, will also help with finding township accommodation.

Kopanong Khayelitsha ☎021 361 2084 or 082 476 1278. One of the most dynamic B&B operations in the township, run by the tireless Thope Lekau, who has a mission to replace gawping tourists in their buses with guests who engage with township life. Her house has three rooms and this former NGO worker will treat you to a history of the township, introduce you to local music and dish up a traditional family breakfast. A traditional dinner is available on request, as is a guided tour. B&B ❸

Majoro's Khayelitsha ☎021 361 3412 or 082 537 6882. Hosted by the charming Maria Maile in her family home, which has two rooms, which share a bath and toilet facilities. Dinner includes traditional food such as *mielie pap* (maize porridge), and you'll be treated to an English breakfast with a difference, which may include bacon and egg with fish cakes, sausage and homemade steamed bread. Half-board ❸

Malebo's Khayeletisha ☎021 361 2391. Three rooms sharing bath and toilet facilities in the welcoming home

of Lydea Masoleng and her husband. In the morning you'll be served a continental breakfast; dinners, which combine Western fare with traditional African food, are available on request. You're welcome to join your hosts on outings to a *shebeen* or to church on Sunday. B&B ❸

Maneo Langa ☎021 694 2504. B&B in Cape Town's oldest township, and the closest to the city centre, with two outside rooms and one inside the family house. The friendly hostess Thandi Peter will take guests to some of the township highlights, including a local *shebeen* where you may see singing and dancing, and you can go to *Eziko Catering,* a catering centre, for a bite. Since it's close to town, most visitors self-drive. B&B ❸

Vicky's Khayelitsha ☎021 387 7104 or 082 225 2986. Under the proprietorship of Vicky Ntozini, this three-room B&B was one of the first township homestays. Guests are offered a walking tour to meet local people. Half-board ❸

Ark Studio 4 Grant Ave, Boulders ☎021 786 2526 or 082 777 5562, ⓕ021 786 3512. Two luxurious and fully equipped self-catering units sleeping two to four people, with sweeping views across False Bay, a couple of minutes' walk from Boulders Beach. Guests have the use of the garden, a small heated plunge pool and off-street parking. Breakfast is available. ❹

Boulders Beach Guest House 4 Boulders Place,

Boulders Beach ☎021 786 1758, ⓕ021 786 1825, ⓔboulders@iafrica.com. Thirteen B&B rooms and two self-catering flats above the Boulders Beach car park, two minutes from Boulders Coastal Park and the African penguin colony. The self-catering units sleeping two to six people have patios for outdoor breakfasts, and braai facilities; meals are available at the adjacent restaurant (Mon–Sun 8am–9pm). ❹

British Hotel Apartments 90 St George's St ☎021 786 2214, ⓦwww.british-hotel.co.za. Three-bedroom self-catering apartments in a grand 1898 Victorian hotel, that once had Cecil Rhodes and the nineteenth-century explorer, Mary Kingsley, as guests. Part of a highly picturesque main street, this is an experience rather than just somewhere to stay, with Victorian colonial decor, high ceilings and huge balconies overlooking the street and the docks; there are also more modest doubles with baths. The *Victorian Rose* restaurant does breakfast and teas (9am–noon) in the courtyard. ❹

Kijabe Lodge 32 Disa Rd, Murdock Valley ☎ & ⓕ021 786 2433. Two en-suite bedrooms in the modern mountainside home of friendly Belgian owners, 5min by car from Simon's Town centre, and a ten-minute walk to Boulders Beach. The very reasonably priced rooms have good sea views, and there's a big pool with chairs and tables around it plus braai facilities. One of the rooms can accommodate parents and a child. ❷

Lord Nelson Inn 58 St George's St ☎021 786 1386, ⓦwww.simonstown/hotels/lordnelson. A comfortable and busy little inn, along the main road in the centre of town, whose name recalls the fact that Nelson once spent time convalescing in the harbour village. The best of the hotel's compact rooms, all furnished in country style with pine, have balconies and harbour views. Reasonable value. ❸

Oatlands Holiday Village Froggy Pond ☎021 786 1410, ⓦwww.caraville.co.za/oatlands.htm. A family resort across the road from the beach and near a golf course, 3km from Simon's Town and 1km from the Boulders Beach penguin colony. There are over twenty self-catering chalets of various sizes, sleeping two to six people. The cheapest of the lot are uncarpeted, without TV, and have bunks, while the best have all you need for a family holiday. The grounds are large, with a pool, playground and trampoline; there's also a pub and restaurant on the premises. ❸

Simon's Town Quayside Lodge St George's St, off Jubilee Square ☎021 786 3838, ⓦwww .quayside.co.za. A luxury hotel with 28 rooms, occupying a good part of the Simon's Town marina right in the centre of town, and with an annexe across the road above the post office. Views from the balconies of the sea-facing rooms take in the mountain-edged False Bay, the yacht basin and Naval dock yard; the hotel is awash with nautical artefacts. ❺

The City

Between two mountainous flanks, reaching away from the docks, through the intense city centre and up the mountain is the **City Bowl** (made up of the Upper and Lower city centres and the Waterfront), where lively areas, such as Long Street, the Bo-Kaap and Gardens rub shoulders with the serious new wealth of Tamboerskloof and Oranjezicht. Straggling south from the centre along the eastern slope of the mountain, the predominantly white **southern suburbs** become progressively more affluent as you move from arty Observatory through the comfortably middle-class districts of Rondebosch and Newlands, culminating with the Constantia wine estates. Along the coastal belt, the **Atlantic seaboard** is drier and sunnier, with the wealthiest areas like Clifton and Camps Bay clinging to the mountainside above the sea, white sands and rocky beaches. The **False Bay** coast is wetter and greener; the sea here is usually several degrees warmer than the western peninsula, making Muizenberg, Fish Hoek and Boulders Beach in Simon's Town the most popular bathing beaches in Cape Town. Curling northeast around Table Bay, the **northern suburbs**, taking in Parow, Milnerton and Bloubergstrand are exceptionally dull, with a traditional Afrikaans flavour. South of these, and extending seemingly endlessly along the N2 into the interior, the coloured **Cape Flats townships** jostle with the desolate, litter-strewn **African ghettos** of Nyanga, Langa and Guguletu, which relentlessly overflow into kilometre after kilometre of iron, wood and cardboard shantytowns.

The Upper City Centre

The **Upper City Centre**, the entire area from Strand Street to the southern foot of the mountain, is a collage of Georgian, Cape Dutch, Victorian and twentieth-century architecture (see p.130), as well as the place where Europe, Asia and Africa meet in markets, alleyways and mosques. Among the substantial drawcards here are **Parliament**, the **Botanical Gardens** and many of Cape Town's major **museums**.

Strand Street marks the edge of Cape Town's original beachfront (though you'd never guess it today), and all urban development to its north stands on reclaimed land. To its south, heading towards Table Mountain, are the remains of the city's 350-year-old historic core, which has survived the ravages of modernization and apartheid-inspired urban clearance to emerge with enough charm to make it South Africa's most pleasing city centre.

Adderley Street, slicing through the Upper City from the railway station in the north to the Gardens in the south, is the obvious orientation axis. To its east, and close to each other just off Strand Street, are the **Castle of Good Hope**, the site of **District Six**, the **Grand Parade** and the **City Hall**. The district to the west of Adderley Street is the closest South Africa gets to a European quarter – a tight network of streets with cafés, buskers, bookstores, street stalls and antique shops congregating around the pedestrianized **St George's Mall** and **Greenmarket Square**. The **Bo-Kaap**, or Muslim district, three blocks further west across Buitengragt (which means the Outer Canal, but is actually a street), exudes a piquant contrast to this, with its minarets, spice shops and cafés selling curried snacks.

South of Adderley Street, where it takes a sharp right into Wale Street, is the symbolic heart of Cape Town (and arguably South Africa), with **Parliament**, museums, archives and De Tuynhuys, the Western Cape office of the President, arranged around the **Botanical Gardens**.

Adderley Street

Once *the* place to shop in Cape Town, **Adderley Street**, lined with handsome buildings from several centuries, is still worth a stroll today, for what grand architecture remains. Its attractive streetscape has been wantonly blemished by a series of large 1960s shopping centres, but just minutes away from crowded malls, among the streets and alleys around Greenmarket Square, you can still find some human scale and historic texture.

Adderley Street was formerly the Heerengracht (Gentlemen's Canal) – a waterway that ran from the Botanical Gardens down to the sea. Low-walled channels, ditches, bridges and sluices ran through Cape Town and earned it the name Little Amsterdam. During the nineteenth century, the canals were buried underground, and in 1850 Heerengracht was renamed Adderley Street (see box on p.107). There's little evidence of the canals today, except in name – one section of the street is still called Heerengracht and a parallel street to its west is called Buitengragt (sometimes spelled Buitengracht, after the Dutch style).

The destruction of old Cape Town continued well into the twentieth century, with the razing of many of the older buildings. One of the ugliest newcomers is the **Golden Acre** shopping complex, built in the 1970s, and today Cape Town's unavoidable transport hub. Dominating the north (harbour) end of Adderley Street, Golden Acre employs an unfriendly network of subways and walkways to draw together all the major arrival points into town. The Metrorail urban transit and mainline stations, the central bus terminals, the taxi ranks and tiered parking garages all congregate around this huge and dark shopping mall.

The naming of Adderley Street

Although the Dutch used Robben Island (see p.122) as a political prison, the South African mainland only narrowly escaped becoming a second Australia, a **penal colony** where British felons and enemies of the state could be dumped. By the 1840s, "respectable Australians" were lobbying for a ban on the transportation of criminals to the Antipodes, and the British authorities responded by trying to divert convicts to the Cape.

In 1848, the British ship *Neptune* set sail from Bermuda for Cape Town with a cargo of 282 prisoners. When news of its departure reached Cape Town there was outrage. Five thousand citizens gathered on the Grand Parade the following year to hear prominent liberals denounce the British government, an event depicted in *The Great Meeting of the People at the Commercial Exchange* by Johan Marthinus Carstens Schonegevel, which hangs in the Rust-en-Vreugd Museum. When the ship docked in September 1849, governor Sir Harry Smith forbade any criminal from landing while, back in London, politician **Charles Adderley** successfully addressed the House of Commons in support of the Cape colonists. In February 1850, the *Neptune* set off for Tasmania, and grateful Capetonians renamed the city's main thoroughfare **Adderley Street**.

In 2001, there was a postscript to all this with yet another attempt to rename Adderley Street, this time by the populist National Party mayor **Peter Marais**. Marais announced that he wanted to alter its name to **Nelson Mandela Street** and the adjoining Wale Street, which runs through the Bo-Kaap, to **F.W. de Klerk Street** after South Africa's last National Party president. Most of the coloured residents of the Bo-Kaap were less than delighted about having their main street named after a former proponent of apartheid. Marais, himself a coloured, ran a purported "consultation exercise" which delivered a huge number of signatures in favour of the change. When later it turned out that many had been signed by the same hand, the renaming was shelved, Marais was sacked, and the Democratic-National Party coalition that ran Cape Town and the Western Cape collapsed. In the strangest twist in the tale, the National Party then formed a coalition with the ANC – once its bitterest enemy (see p.846) – and Marais became premier of the province, a position he still holds.

Inside sit the **Golden Acre Ruins**, the remains of southern Africa's oldest colonial structure – a reservoir built in 1663 by the Dutch. All that's left is a small bit of wall behind glass, and you might easily walk past and think that the builders who worked on the complex forgot to finish the plastering. Although the mall itself and its environs are anything but picturesque, you'll get an authentic taste of ordinary Capetonians doing their shopping, something you won't find at the sanitized Victoria and Alfred Waterfront. On Saturday mornings, if you exit through onto Adderley Street, you'll often encounter the spirited sounds of busking brass bands or choirs. Among the sidewalks and pedestrianized sections outside, which run down to the station, there's a closely packed **flea market** offering curios, crafts and electronic goods (but watch your wallet).

A little further south lies a **flower market**, run by members of the Bo-Kaap Muslim community. Two grandiose banks stand on opposite sides of Adderley Street; the fussier of the two is the **Standard Bank**, fronted by Corinthian columns and covered with a tall dome – a temple to the partnership of empire and finance. The **First National Bank**, completed in 1913, was the last South African building designed by Sir Herbert Baker (see box on p.602). Inside the banking hall, a solid timber circular writing desk, with the original inkwells still in place, resembles an altar.

At the top corner of Adderley Street, just as it veers sharply west into Wale Street, you'll find the **Slave Lodge** (Mon–Sat 9.30am–4.30pm; R7), previously known as the Cultural History Museum. The lodge houses an eclectic collection of antiquities and artefacts from around the world, as well as good displays on the Cape. The museum was renamed on Heritage Day, 1998, and is currently in the process of reinventing itself to portray South African social history, especially the bloodstained story of slavery.

For nearly two centuries – more than half its existence as an urban settlement – Cape Town's economic and social structures were founded on slavery (see box below), and the Slave Lodge was built in 1679 for the Dutch East India Company to house its human chattels. The Company was the largest single slaveowner at the Cape; by the 1770s, almost a thousand slaves were held at the lodge. Under Company administration, the lodge also became the Cape Colony's main brothel, its doors thrown open to all comers for an hour each night. Following the British takeover and the auctioning of the slaves, the lodge became the Supreme Court in 1810, and remained so until 1914. From 1914, the building was used as government offices, and in 1966 became a museum.

A couple of small but interesting displays can be found on the ground floor, to the left of the entrance hall. The first deals with **Khoisan hunter–gatherers**, the original inhabitants of the Cape (and South Africa), focusing on their knowledge of plants and herbs, many of which are still in use today. An adjacent room houses "**186 Years of Slavery**", centred around a model of the lodge as it was 300 years ago. A poignant memorial plaque on one wall lists, by first name only, the slaves who endured the appalling conditions of the fortress-like structure, and a map on another wall refers to sites in the city centre with slave connections: where they worked, worshipped, were sold, punished and executed.

Behind the Slave Lodge, on the traffic island in Spin Street, a simple and inconspicuous plinth marks the site of the **Old Slave Tree**, under which slaves were bought and sold.

Slavery at the Cape

Slavery was officially abolished at the Cape in 1838, but its legacy lives on in South Africa. The country's coloured inhabitants, who make up fifty percent of Cape Town's population, are largely descendants of slaves, and some historians argue that apartheid was a natural successor to slavery. Certainly, domestic service, still widespread throughout South Africa, and certain labour practices such as the "*dop* system" in which workers on some farms are partially paid in rations of cheap plonk, can be traced directly back to slavery.

By the end of the eighteenth century, the almost 26,000-strong slave population of the Cape exceeded that of the free burghers. Despite the profound impact this had on the development of social relations in South Africa, until the publication of a number of studies on slavery in the 1980s, it remained one of the most neglected topics of the country's history. There's still a reluctance on the part of most coloureds to acknowledge their slave origins.

Few if any slaves were captured at the Cape for export, making the colony unique in the African trade. Paradoxically, while people were being captured elsewhere on the continent for export to the Americas, the Cape administration, forbidden by the VOC from enslaving the local indigenous population, had to look further afield. Of the 63,000 slaves imported to the Cape before 1808, most came from East Africa, Madagascar, India and Indonesia, representing one of the broadest cultural mixes of any slave society. This diversity initially worked against the establishment of a unified group identity, but eventually a Creolized culture emerged which, among other things, played a major role in the development of the Afrikaans language.

Castle of Good Hope

From the outside, South Africa's oldest building looks somewhat miserable, and its position on Darling Street, behind the railway station and city bus terminal, does nothing to dispel this. Nevertheless the **Castle of Good Hope** (daily 9am–4pm; R15) is well worth the modest entrance fee; inside, a meticulous ten-year restoration has returned the decor to the British Regency style introduced in 1798.

The Castle, as it's commonly known, was built in accordance with seventeenth-century European principles of fortification, comprising strong bastions from which the outside walls could be protected by cross fire. Completed in 1679, it replaced van Riebeeck's earlier mud and timber fort, which stood on the site of the Grand Parade.

The construction of the Castle lasted over thirteen years, with work constantly coming to a standstill either because of labour shortages or insufficient materials. The original, seaward entrance had to be moved to its present position facing landward, because the spring tide sometimes came crashing in – a remarkable thought given how far aground it is now. This newer entrance is a fine example of seventeenth-century Dutch classicism, and the bell, cast in 1679 by Claude Fremy in Amsterdam, still hangs from its original wooden beams in the tower over the entrance.

For 150 years, the Castle remained the symbolic heart of the Cape administration, and the centre of social and economic life. In the late nineteenth century, when the colony had expanded far beyond its walls, there were at least three attempts by the authorities to demolish it, as it was regarded as a white elephant that was costly to maintain.

Inside the Castle are three interesting collections: the **Military Museum** has displays on the conflicts that dogged the early settlement; the **Secunde's House** has furnishings, paintings and *objets d'art* that filled the living space of the deputy governor; and the **William Fehr Collection**, one of the country's most important exhibits of decorative arts, includes paintings of the settlement, eighteenth- and nineteenth-century Dutch and Indonesian furniture, and seventeenth- and eighteenth-century Chinese and Japanese porcelain. **Free tours** (daily 11am, noon & 2pm) are useful for orientation and cover the main features, including the prison cells and dungeons, with their centuries-old graffiti painstakingly carved by prisoners. The Castle is also home to the Defence Force's Western Province Command; you may see armed soldiers marching through the elegant courtyard. There is also a very pleasant tea shop in the courtyard, with Table Mountain looming over the west wall.

The Grand Parade and the City Hall

The **Grand Parade**, to the west of the Castle, is where the residents of District Six used to come to trade. On Wednesdays and Saturdays it still transforms itself into a **market**, where you can buy a whole array of bargains ranging from used clothes to spicy food. The Grand Parade appeared on TV screens throughout the world on February 11, 1990, when 100,000 people gathered to hear **Nelson Mandela** make his first speech, from the balcony of City Hall, after being released from prison. The **City Hall** is a slightly fussy Edwardian building dressed in Bath stone which, despite its drab surroundings, looks impressive against Table Mountain.

District Six

South of the Castle, in the shadow of Devil's Peak, is a vacant lot shown on maps as the suburb of Zonnebloem. Before being demolished by the apartheid authorities two decades ago, it was an inner-city slum known as **District Six**, an impoverished but lively community of 55,000 predominantly coloured people. Once regarded as the soul of Cape Town, the district harboured a rich cultural life in its narrow alleys and crowded tenements. Along the cobbled streets, hawkers rubbed shoulders with prostitutes, gangsters, drunks and gamblers, while craftsmen plied their trade in small workshops. This was a rich place of the South African imagination, inspiring novels, poems, jazz and the blockbuster *District Six: The Musical*, by David Kramer, which in the late 1980s played to packed houses and spawned a series of hits.

In 1966, apartheid ideologues declared District Six a **White Group Area** and the bulldozers moved in, taking fifteen years to drive its presence from the skyline, leaving only the mosques and churches. But, in the wake of the demolition gangs, international and domestic outcry was so great that the area was never developed apart from a few luxury town houses on its fringes and the hefty Cape Technikon, a college that now occupies nearly a quarter of the former suburb. After years of negotiation, the original residents will be allowed to move back under a scheme to develop low-cost housing in the district.

The District Six Museum

On the northern boundary of District Six, on the corner of 25a Buitenkant and Albertus streets, is the compelling **District Six Museum** (Mon–Sat 10am–4.30pm; donation). The museum occupies the former **Central Methodist Mission Church**, which offered solidarity and ministry to the victims of forced removals right up to the 1980s, and became a venue for anti-apartheid gatherings. Today, it houses a series of fascinating displays that include everyday household items and tools of trades, such as hairdressing implements, as well as documentary photographs, which evoke the lives of the individuals who once lived here. Occupying most of the floor is a huge map of District Six as it was, annotated by former residents, who describe their memories, reflections and incidents associated with places and buildings that no longer exist. There's also an almost complete collection of original street signs, secretly retrieved at the time of demolition by the man entrusted with dumping them into Table Bay.

There are few places in Cape Town that speak more eloquently of the effect of apartheid on the day-to-day lives of ordinary people.

Long Street

Parallel to Adderley Street, **Long Street** aptly runs the full length of the city centre and continues as lively Kloof Street, which cuts through the City Bowl suburbs to Kloofnek, a junction that splays out to the lower cableway station, Sea Point, the Atlantic seaboard and Signal Hill. The buzzing artery itself is one of Cape Town's most diverse thoroughfares, a great place for leisurely exploration, with views of Table Mountain, Signal Hill and Lion's Head, as well as glimpses of the sea.

When it was first settled by Muslims some three hundred years ago, Long Street marked Cape Town's boundary; by the 1960s, it had become a sleazy alley of drinking holes and whorehouses. Miraculously, it's all still here, but with a whiff of gentrification. Mosques still coexist with bars, brothels above old-fashioned locksmiths, pawnbrokers alongside porn shops, while gun shops sit next to delicatessens, antique dealers, craft shops and cafés. There are also a number of excellent second hand and Africana bookshops, and more **backpacker lodges** per square metre than on any other street in Cape Town with, in their wake, a growing number of student travel agencies, cheap car-rental outfits and adventure-activity outlets.

The **Long Street Baths** (Mon–Fri 7am–8pm, Sat 7am–7pm, Sun 8am–6pm) occupy the top of the road, where it hits Buitensingel (Outer Crescent). A Cape Town institution, established in 1906, the steam rooms are great for relaxing on a winter's day and are open on separate days to women (Mon, Thurs & Sat) and men (Tues, Wed, Fri & Sun morning). A four-hour session (R55) gets you a private cubicle and towel, access to the dry or wet steam rooms, the plunge pool and a short massage. Swimming (R7) is communal.

Further north, an unmistakable landmark at no.185, the **Palm Tree Mosque** (not open to the public) is fronted by a lone palm tree, its fronds caressing the upper storey. Significant as the only surviving eighteenth-century house in the street, it was erected in 1780 by Carel Lodewijk Schot as a private dwelling. The house was bought in 1807 by Frans van Bengal, a member of the local Muslim community, and a freed slave, Jan van Boughies, who became its imam, turning the upper floor into a mosque and the lower into his living quarters.

Across Wale Street is one of Cape Town's most intriguing places for African crafts, and one of the easiest to miss. The inconspicuous frontage of the **Pan African Market** at no.76 belies the three-floor warren of passageways and rooms, which burst at the hinges with traders selling vast quantities of art and artefacts from all over the continent. Hidden amongst less inspiring offerings you'll find terrific masks from West Africa, brass leopards from Benin as well as textiles, contemporary South African art, CDs, musical instruments, leathersmiths, tailors, hair-braiders and a drum instructor.

Further towards the harbour end of Long Street at no.40, the **South African Missionary Meeting-House Museum** (Mon–Fri 9am–4pm; free) is an exceptional building with one of the most beautiful frontages in Cape Town. Broken into three bays by four slender Corinthian pilasters surmounted by a gabled pediment, its facade is dominated by its large windows. Inside, an impressive Neoclassical timber **pulpit** perches high above the congregation on a pair of columns, framing an inlaid image of an angel in flight. Completed in 1804 by the South African Missionary Society, it was the first missionary church in the country, where slaves were taught literacy and instructed in Christianity.

The society itself was founded in 1799 by Reverend Vos, who was alarmed that many slaveowners neglected the religious education of their property. Owners believed that, once baptized, their slaves' emancipation became obligatory – a misunderstanding of the law, which merely stated that Christian slaves couldn't be sold. Vos, himself a slaveowner, saw proselytization to those in bondage as a Christian duty, and even successfully campaigned to end the prohibition against selling Christian slaves, which he believed was "a great obstacle in this country to the progress of Christianity", because it encouraged owners to avoid baptizing their human chattels.

Greenmarket Square and around

Turning east from Long Street into Shortmarket Street, you'll skim the edge of **Greenmarket Square**, which is worth at least a little exploration to soak up the distinctly European atmosphere, with cobbled streets, coffee shops and grand buildings. As its name implies, the square started as a vegetable market, though it spent many ignominious years as a car park. Human life has returned, and it's now home to a flea market, selling crafts, jewellery and hippie clobber. This is also one of the few places in Cape Town to buy from Congolese traders, selling masks and malachite carvings. On the western side are the solid limewashed walls and small shuttered windows of the **Old Town House** (Feb–Dec daily 10am–5pm; free), entered from Longmarket Street. Built in the mid-1700s, this beautiful example of Cape Dutch architecture (see p.130), with its fine interior, has seen duty as a guard-house, a police station and Cape Town's city hall, and today houses the Michaelis collection of minor but interesting Dutch and Flemish landscape paintings. Small visiting exhibitions are also displayed, and good evening classical concerts are a regular event; pick up the town house's quarterly newsletter, which lists forthcoming events. Tickets are available at the door immediately prior to the shows.

Heading east of the square, you come to **St George's Mall**, a pedestrianized road that runs southwest from Thibault Square, near the train station, to Wale Street. Coffee shops, snack bars and lots of street traders and buskers make this a more pleasant route between the station and the Company's Gardens than parallel Adderley Street, while dancers, drummers, choirs and painters add a certain buzz to the place. **Church Street** (which crosses the mall towards its southern end) and its surrounding area abound with antique dealers, and on the pedestrianized section at its northeastern end you'll find an informal antique market. Prices are competitive and you may pick up unusual pieces of jewellery, bric-a-brac, Africana and even old sheet music. At the southern end of the mall, at Queen Victoria and Wale streets, **St George's Cathedral** is interesting more for its history than for its Herbert Baker Victorian Gothic design; on September 7, 1986, **Desmond Tutu** hammered on its doors symbolically demanding to be enthroned as South Africa's first black archbishop. Three years later, he heralded the last days of apartheid by leading 30,000 people from the Cathedral to the City Hall, where he coined his now famous slogan for the new order: "We are the rainbow people!" he told the crowd, "We are the new people of South Africa!"

Back in Greenmarket Square, if you head northeast down Shortmarket Street and cross Long Street, you'll come to **Cape Heritage Square**, three blocks up, the largest restoration project ever undertaken in Cape Town. Situated on the fringe of the Bo-Kaap, it's home to the *Cape Heritage Hotel* as well as a conglomeration of restaurants, wine merchants, art galleries, jewellers and fashion shops, many of which are housed in a complex dating back to 1771. Set around a courtyard, in which the oldest known (and still fruit-bearing) vine in South Africa continues to flourish, the square is worth visiting for a glimpse of the superb restoration work.

Government Avenue and the Company's Gardens

A stroll down **Government Avenue**, the southwest extension of Adderley Street, makes for one of the most serene walks in central Cape Town (all roads and paths in the Gardens are pedestrianized). This oak-lined boulevard runs past the rear of Parliament through the Gardens, and its benches are frequently occupied by snoring *bergies* (tramps).

Looming on your right as you enter the north end of the avenue, the **South African Library** (Mon–Fri 9am–6pm, Sat 9am–1pm; free) houses one of the country's best collections of antiquarian historical and natural history books, covering southern Africa. Built with the revenue from a tax on wine, it opened in 1822 as one of the first free libraries in the world.

Stretching from here to the South African Museum, the **Company's Gardens** were the initial *raison d'être* for the Dutch settlement at the Cape. Established in 1652 to supply fresh greens to Dutch East India Company ships travelling between the Netherlands and the East, the Gardens were initially worked by imported slave labour. This proved too expensive, as the slaves had to be shipped in, fed and housed, so the Company phased out its own farming and granted land to free burghers, from whom it bought fresh produce (see p.112). At the end of the seventeenth century, the gardens were turned over to botanical horticulture for Cape Town's growing colonial elite. Ponds, lawns, landscaping and a criss-cross web of oak-shaded walkways were introduced. Today, they are full of local plants, the result of long-standing European interest in Cape botany; experts have been sailing out since the seventeenth century to classify and name specimens.

The Gardens have an outdoor café, and remain a pleasant place to meander. You'll find a statue of Rhodes here; it was during a stroll in these gardens that Rhodes first plotted the invasion of Matabeleland and Mashonaland (both of which became Rhodesia and subsequently Zimbabwe). He also introduced an army of small, furry colonizers to the Gardens: the North American grey squirrels.

Continuing along Government Avenue from the South African Library, past the rear of Parliament, you can peer through an iron gate to see the grand buildings and tended flowerbeds of **De Tuynhuys**, the office (but not residence) of the president. During Mandela's presidency, one party of tourists stood amazed as the great man, who is renowned for his common touch, strolled across the lawns for a friendly chat.

A little further along, the tree-lined walkway opens out into a formal gravel area with ponds and statues, around which are sited the National Gallery, the Jewish Museum and the Great Synagogue to the east, and the South African Museum and Planetarium to the west.

The South African National Gallery

Not far from the southern end of Government Avenue, where it's joined by the tiny Gallery Lane, the **South African National Gallery** (Tues–Sun 10am–5pm; R5) is an essential port of call for anyone interested in the local art scene, and includes a small but excellent permanent collection of contemporary South African art. You'll also find a fine display of traditional works from the southeast of the continent, based around a small collection donated by the German government. The exhibits, which include beadwork, carvings and craft objects, were chosen for their aesthetic qualities and rarity, and represent the gallery's policy of focusing on neglected parts of South Africa's heritage. One room contains minor works by various British artists including Pre-Raphaelites, George Romney, Thomas Gainsborough and Joshua Reynolds. The gallery has a good café serving light lunches, snacks, coffees and cakes, as well as an excellent gallery shop.

The South African Jewish Museum

Next to the National Gallery but accessed from 84 Hatfield St, the **South African Jewish Museum** (Mon–Thurs & Sun 10am–5pm, Fri 10am–2pm; R20), is partially housed in South Africa's first synagogue, built in 1863. One of Cape Town's most ambitious permanent exhibitions, it tells the story of South African Jewry from its beginnings over 150 years ago to the present – a narrative which starts in the Old Synagogue from which visitors cross, via a gangplank, to the upper level of a new two-storey building, symbolically re-enacting the arrival by boat of the first Jewish immigrants at Table Bay harbour in the 1840s. Employing multimedia interactive displays, models and Judaica artefacts, the exhibition follows three threads: "**Memories**", looking at the roots and experiences of the immigrants; "**Reality**", covering their integration into South Africa; and "**Dreams**", examining a diversity of views about the role of Jews in South Africa, their relationship to Israel and their position in the world. Other displays examine anti-Semitism, apartheid and the Jews who opposed it, as well as Nelson Mandela's relationship with the Jewish community.

Jewish immigration to South Africa

Today there are around twenty thousand Jews in Cape Town, the majority descended from **Eastern European refugees** who fled discrimination and pogroms during the late nineteenth and early twentieth centuries.

Since 1795, when the occupying British introduced freedom of worship at the Cape, Jews in South Africa have faced few legal impediments. However, there were instances of semi-official anti-Semitism during the twentieth century, the most notable being the policy of the Nationalist Party while in opposition during the 1940s. Before World War II, elements in the party came under the influence of Nazi ideology, which was being poured into South Africa by the German foreign and propaganda offices, and began to attribute all the ills facing Afrikanerdom to a "British–Jewish capitalist" conspiracy. In 1941, the party adopted a policy of ending Jewish immigration and even repatriating "undesirable immigrants", as well as placing stronger controls over naturalization and the introduction of a "vocational permit" system to protect "the original white population against unfair competition".

Ironically, on the eve of taking power in 1947, the party of apartheid turned its back on anti-Semitism: one of its first acts after winning the 1948 election was to recognize the newly created state of Israel, with which it maintained links until it relinquished power in 1994.

Drawing parallels between Judaism and the ritual practices and beliefs of South Africa's other communities, the "**Culture among Cultures**" display covers topics such as birth, marriage, circumcision and death. The **basement level** houses a walk-through reconstruction of a Lithuanian *shtetl* or village (most South African Jews have their nineteenth-century roots in Lithuania), as well as the **Discovery Centre**, an interactive computer with a genealogy bank, a searchable database on Jewish life and culture and a "glimpse into Israel". A restaurant, shop and auditorium are also housed in the museum complex.

The Holocaust Exhibition and the Great Synagogue

Opened in 1999, the **Holocaust Exhibition** (Mon–Thurs & Sun 10am–5pm, Fri 10am–1pm; free), is one of the most moving and brilliantly executed museums in Cape Town. Housed upstairs in the Holocaust Centre (in the same complex as the Jewish Museum), it resonates sharply in a country that only recently emerged from an era of racial oppression – a connection that the exhibition makes explicitly. A densely layered narrative is related through text, photographs, artefacts (such as a concentration camp uniform), film clips, soundtracks, multimedia and interactive video, while the design uses modulated lighting, cobblestones reminiscent of the ghettos and pieces of barbed wire and railway track to evoke the death camps.

Exhibits trace the history of anti-Semitism in Europe, culminating with the Nazis' Final Solution; they also look at South Africa's Greyshirts, who were motivated by Nazi propaganda during the 1930s and were later absorbed into the National Party. There are accounts of heroism, often tragic, including acts of resistance by Jews, and a touch screen portrays many individuals in Europe who risked their lives to protect or rescue the victims of Nazism. To conclude, a twenty-minute video tells the story of survivors who eventually settled in Cape Town.

The **Great Synagogue** next door is one of Cape Town's outstanding religious buildings. Designed by the Scottish architects Parker & Forsyth and completed in 1905, it faces onto the Gardens. It features an impressive dome and two soaring towers after the style of central European Baroque churches. To see the arched interior and the alcove decorated with gilt mosaics, you need to ask at the Holocaust Centre, and may be asked to provide some form of identification.

The South African Museum and Planetarium

The nation's premier museum of natural history and human sciences, the **South African Museum and Planetarium** (daily 10am–5pm; museum R7, planetarium R10, combined R15) stands at 25 Queen Victoria St, west of Government Avenue and across the square from the National Gallery. The museum's **ethnographic galleries** contain some very good displays on the traditional arts and crafts of several African groups, some exceptional examples of rock art (entire chunks of caves sitting in the display cases), and casts of the stone birds found at Great Zimbabwe. Upstairs, the **natural history galleries** display mounted mammals, dioramas of prehistoric Karoo reptiles, and Table Mountain flora and fauna. The highlight is the four-storey "whale well", in which a collection of beautiful whale skeletons hang like massive mobiles, accompanied by the eerie strains of their song.

The attached **Planetarium** (shows Mon–Fri 1pm; Sat & Sun noon, 1pm & 2.30pm; Tues 8pm) is recommended if you want to see the constellations of the southern hemisphere accompanied by informed commentary. There's also a changing programme of shows covering topics such as San sky myths. Leaflets at the museum provide a list of forthcoming attractions, and you can buy a monthly chart of the current night sky – especially worthwhile if you're staying in an area without streetlights and can actually see the stars.

Bertram House

At the southernmost end of Government Avenue, you'll come upon **Bertram House** (Tues–Sat 9.30am–4.30pm; R5), whose beautiful two-storey brick facade looks out across a fragrant herb garden. Built in the 1840s, the museum is significant as the only surviving brick Georgian-style house in Cape Town, and displays typical furniture and objects of a well-to-do colonial British family in the first half of the nineteenth century.

The site was bought in 1839 by John Barker, a Yorkshire attorney who came to the Cape in 1823. He named the house after his wife, Ann Bertram Findlay, who died in 1838, and was responsible for building it. Declared a National Monument in 1962, Bertram House was extensively restored to its current state between 1983 and 1984. Imported face brick and Welsh slate were used to recreate the original facade, while the interior walls were redecorated in their earlier dark green and ochre, based on the evidence of paint scrapings. The reception rooms are decorated in the Regency style, while the porcelain is predominantly nineteenth-century English, although there are also some very fine Chinese pieces.

Houses of Parliament

South Africa's **Houses of Parliament**, east of Government Avenue, on Parliament Street, are a complex of interlinking buildings, with labyrinthine corridors connecting hundreds of offices, debating chambers and miscellaneous other rooms. Many of these are relics of the 1980s reformist phase of apartheid when, in the interests of racial segregation, there were three distinct legislative complexes sited here to cater to different "races".

The original wing, completed in 1885, is an imposing Victorian Neoclassical building which first served as the legislative assembly of the Cape Colony. After the Boer republics and British colonies amalgamated in 1910, it became the

Parliament of the Union of South Africa. This is the old Parliament, where over seven decades of repressive legislation, including apartheid laws, were passed. It's also where **Hendrik Verwoerd**, the arch-theorist of apartheid, met his bloody end, not at the hand of a political activist, but stabbed to death by Dimitri Tsafendas, a parliamentary messenger who inexplicably went off the rails, committing the act because, as he told police, "a tapeworm ordered me to do it." Due to his mental state, the assassin escaped the gallows to outlive apartheid – albeit in an institution. Verwoerd's portrait, depicting him as a man of vision and *gravitas*, used to hang over the main entrance to the dining room. In 1996 it was removed "for cleaning", along with paintings of generations of white parliamentarians.

The new chamber was built in 1983 as part of the **tricameral parliament**, P.W. Botha's attempt to avert majority rule by trying to co-opt Indians and coloureds – but in their own separate debating chambers. The "tricameral" chamber, where the three non-African "races" on occasions met together, is now the **National Assembly**, where you can watch sessions of Parliament. One-hour **tours** take in the old and new debating chambers, the library and museum, and should be booked in advance through the Tours Section (tours Mon–Fri 9am–1pm on the hour; free; booking essential ☏021 403 2201), which is also the place to contact for day tickets to watch the **debating sessions** – the most interesting of which is question time (Wed from 3pm), when you can hear ministers being quizzed by MPs if Parliament is sitting. To join a tour, go to the Plein Street entrance to Parliament, opposite the Receiver of Revenue (it's the more southerly of the two entrances in this street); go through a security check, where you should ask for directions to the Poorthuis entrance. From there you'll see arrows indicating the starting point for tours.

The ANC sits to the right of the speaker, so if you want to see them you should enter the gallery at the rear via the right entrance. The minority parties sit opposite. You're most unlikely to see the President, who is not a member of parliament and rarely attends sittings. When he does, for the opening of Parliament or for visits by foreign leaders, seats are invariably already snapped up.

The Bo-Kaap

Minutes from Parliament, on the slopes of Signal Hill, is the **Bo-Kaap**, one of Cape Town's oldest and most fascinating residential areas. Its streets are characterized by brightly coloured nineteenth-century Dutch and Georgian terraces, which conceal a network of alleyways that are the arteries of its **Muslim community**. The Bo-Kaap harbours its own strong identity, made all the more unique by the destruction of District Six, with which it had much in common. A particular dialect of Afrikaans is spoken here, although it is steadily being eroded by English, which has a higher social status and lacks the associations with apartheid.

Bo-Kaap residents are descended from dissidents and slaves imported by the Dutch in the sixteenth and seventeenth centuries. They became known collectively as "Cape Malays", a term you'll still hear, even though it's a complete misnomer: fewer than one percent of slaves actually came from Malaysia, and most originated from Africa, India, Madagascar and Sri Lanka.

The easiest way to get to the Bo-Kaap is by foot along Wale Street, which trails up from the south end of Adderley Street and across Buitengragt, to become the main drag of the Bo-Kaap. There's a deceptively quaint feel to the area; apart from Wale Street, this is not really a place to explore alone. A good place to head for is the **Bo-Kaap Museum**, 71 Wale St (Mon–Sat 9.30am–

4.30pm; R5), near the Buitengragt end. It consists mainly of the family house and possessions of Abu Bakr Effendi, a nineteenth-century religious leader brought out from Turkey by the British in 1862 as a mediator between feuding Muslim factions. He became an important member of the community, founded an Arabic school and wrote a book in the local vernacular – now regarded as possibly the first book to be published in what can be recognized as Afrikaans. The museum also has exhibits exploring the local brand of Islam, which has its own unique traditions and nearly two dozen *kramats* (shrines) dotted about the peninsula. One block south of the museum, at Dorp Street, is the **Auwal**, South Africa's first official mosque, founded in 1795 by Tuan Guru, a Muslim activist. Ten more mosques, whose minarets give spice to the quarter's skyline, now serve its 10,000 residents.

Modern, low-cost developments, looking down from the heights of Signal Hill onto the photogenic Bo-Kaap townscape, have helped alleviate the community's housing shortage, but have added nothing to the architectural charm of the protected historic core bounded by Dorp and Strand streets, and Buitengragt and Pentz streets. A small Muslim shantytown, tucked away next to the old quarry below the cemetery, brings the immediacy of South Africa's housing crisis right to the edge of the city centre.

The best way to explore the Bo-Kaap is on one of several **tours** that take in the museum and walk you around the district. The best (and cheapest) of these is the two-and-a-half hour walk, costing R55, run by Bo-Kaap Guided Tours (℡021 422 1554 or 082 423 6932) and operated by residents of the area, whose knowledge goes beyond the standard tour-guide script.

Strand Street

A major artery from the N2 freeway to the central business district, **Strand Street** neatly separates the Upper from the Lower city centre. Between the mid-eighteenth and mid-nineteenth centuries, Strand Street, because of its proximity to the shore, was one of the most fashionable streets in Cape Town, a fact that's now only discernible from the handful of quietly elegant National Monuments left standing amid the roar of traffic: Martin Melck House, which accommodates the **Gold of Africa Museum**, the **Evangelical Lutheran Church** and **Koopmans-De Wet House**.

Gold of Africa Museum

Since the discovery of gold near Johannesburg in the late nineteenth century, South Africa has been closely associated in the Western mind with the precious metal and the riches it represents. However, the outstanding **Gold of Africa Museum** (daily 10am–5pm; R20), 96 Strand St, just off Buitengragt, focuses on a completely different side to gold – the exquisite **artworks** crafted by nineteenth- and twentieth-century **African goldsmiths** from Mali, Senegal, Ghana and the Cote d'Ivoire. Arguably the most important such collection in the world, it was acquired in 2001 from the Barbier-Meuller Museum in Geneva. Now housed in the beautifully restored **Martin Melck House**, it traces Africa's ancient gold routes, and includes several hundred beautiful items – precious masks, crocodiles, birds, a gold crown and human figures; the highlight is the sculpted **Golden Lion** from Ghana that is the symbol of the museum. There's also a small auditorium with a continuous **film show**, a **wine cellar**, where you can have a snack, a coffee and quaff a glass of Cape wine in a beautiful courtyard garden, a **studio** where goldsmiths practise their art and a **shop** where you can buy postcards, gold leaf and beautiful little souvenirs.

Evangelical Lutheran Church

Next door to the Gold of Africa Museum, at the corner of Buitengragt, which marks the eastern boundary of the Bo-Kaap, and Strand Street, stands the **Evangelical Lutheran Church** (Mon, Wed & Fri 9am–noon; free). Converted by **Anton Anreith** (see box on p.130) in 1785 from a barn, its facade includes Classical details such as a broken pediment perforated by the clock tower, as well as Gothic features such as the arched windows. Inside, the magnificent **pulpit**, supported on two life-size Herculean figures, is one of Anreith's masterpieces; the white swan perched on the canopy is a symbol of Lutheranism.

The establishment of a Lutheran church in Cape Town struck a significant blow against the extreme **religious intolerance** that pervaded under VOC rule. Before 1771, when permission was granted to Lutherans to establish their own congregation, Protestantism was the only form of worship allowed and the Dutch Reformed Church held an absolute monopoly over saving people's souls. The Lutheran Church's congregation was dominated by Germans, who at the time constituted 28 percent of the colony's free burgher population.

Koopmans-De Wet House

Sandwiched between two office blocks, **Koopmans-De Wet House** (Tues–Sat 9.30am–4.30pm; R5), 35 Strand St, on the other side of the street to the Gold of Africa Museum and towards the station, is an outstanding eighteenth-century pedimented Neoclassical town house and museum, accommodating a very fine collection of antique furniture and rare porcelain. An inexpensive **guide** booklet gives interesting contextual background to the house and its history, while a separate brochure describes items in the collection: both are available at the entrance.

The earliest sections of the house were built in 1701 by **Reyner Smedinga**, a well-to-do goldsmith who imported the building materials from Holland. The house changed hands more than a dozen times over the following two centuries, with minor additions made in the 1760s and a second storey added between 1774 and 1790. In 1806, it came into the hands of the De Wet family, eventually becoming the home of **Marie Koopmans-De Wet** (1834–1906), a prominent figure on the Cape social and political circuit.

The building's **facade** has been attributed to Louis Thibault and Anton Anreith (see box on p.130), but there's no proof of this. Whoever was responsible, the house represents a fine synthesis of Dutch elements (sash windows and large entrance doors) with the demands of local conditions; the huge rooms, lofty ceilings and shuttered windows reflect the high summer temperatures, while the front *stoep* has plastered masonry seats at each end. The **lantern** in the fanlight of the entrance to the house was a feature of all Cape Town houses in the eighteenth and early nineteenth centuries, its purpose to shine light onto the street and thus hinder slaves from gathering at night to plot.

The Lower City Centre

The **Lower City Centre** has for centuries been a marginal area between Cape Town and the sea. The area stretches north of Strand Street to the shore, taking in the still-functional **Duncan Dock** and Cape Town's biggest shopping and entertainment complex at the **Victoria and Alfred Waterfront**. In the mid-nineteenth century, the city's middle classes viewed the quarter and its low-life activities with a mixture of alarm and excitement – a tension that remains today. **Lower Long Street** divides the area just inland from the docklands into two. To the east is The Foreshore, an ugly post-World War II wasteland of grey corporate architecture, among which is the **Artscape Centre**,

Cape Town's prestige arts complex. To the west, in sharp contrast, is **De Waterkant and Somerset Road**, the city's densely packed clubbing and pubbing area.

De Waterkant and Somerset Road

West of the Foreshore and rubbing up against the west side of the city centre and the V&A Waterfront to its north is Cape Town's thriving clubland, that incorporates **De Waterkant and Somerset Road**, the city's self-proclaimed "gay village". Frequented by sailors and dockers, Cape Town's former red-light district used to be a hard-drinking, drugged-up, apartheid-free zone where some of the city's best jazz was played and raids by the police were a regular part of the scene. These days, with its high density of **nightclubs** and **pubs**, the area around **Somerset Road**, which heads from the city centre into Green Point, has become the best place in Cape Town to club-crawl and one of the few places you're guaranteed action seven nights a week. Between **Somerset Road** and Signal Hill, parallel **Jarvis** and **Waterkant** streets are connected by the smaller **Hudson** and **Dixon** streets, which between them constitute the throbbing heart of Cape Town's clubland. For club details, see p.157.

The Foreshore

The Foreshore, an area of reclaimed land north of Strand Street, stretching to the docks, and east of Lower Long Street was developed in the late 1940s in a spirit of modernism – large highly planned urban spaces – that was sweeping the world. It was intended to turn Cape Town's harbour into a symbolic gateway to Africa; instead, it turned out as a series of large concrete boxes surrounded by acres of windswept tarmac parking lots.

Heerengracht, a truncated two-lane carriageway running from Adderley Street to the harbour, has massive roundabouts at each end solemnly guarded by statues of Jan van Riebeeck and Bartholomeu Dias. It was meant to be the ceremonial axis through this grand scheme, joining the city to the sea, but it never quite makes it to the water, coming to a disappointing standstill at the dock perimeter fence, before bearing east under the dismal shadow of the N1 and N2 flyovers.

The only building worth visiting here – when there's something on – is the **Artscape Complex** (previously known as the Nico Theatre Complex), Cape Town's major performance venue, in DF Malan Street just east of Heerengracht. Incorporating the large Main Theatre, it also houses the small Arena Theatre and an opera house. The complex is currently making attempts to throw off the burden of a long association with the apartheid establishment

The Foreshore redevelopment

The windswept Foreshore is at last being redeveloped with the construction of the **Cape Town International Convention Centre**, due for completion in the second half of 2003. A major conference facility – something Cape Town has notably lacked up to now – it will create a link between the city centre, the Duncan Dock and the V&A Waterfront. From the end of Heerengracht, the city's oldest throughfare, a **canal** planned for completion at the same time as the conference centre will be served by water-taxis and water-buses, modelled on those used in Amsterdam, and will link the Convention Centre with the V&A Waterfront. The developers say five key open spaces – the Grand Parade, Greenmarket Square, the area around the station, Artscape and the Convention Centre – will be linked to the proposed Harbour Square at the edge of the Duncan Dock, by a series of pedestrian walkways.

(its original name derived from Nico Malan, one-time Nationalist Party administrator). In 1999, to the dismay of traditional opera-, ballet- and theatre-goers, the complex shed its highbrow image and relaunched itself as a community arts centre.

Duncan Dock

North of the Foreshore, **Duncan Dock**, Cape Town's working harbour is a forbidding industrial landscape of large ships and towering cranes cut off from the city by an enormous perimeter fence. It's a fabulous place to photograph gigantic hulks against Table Mountain, and has an excellent Taiwanese restaurant, the *Jewel Tavern* (see p.153), but is not the kind of area you'd want to linger alone in.

Work started on the dock in 1938, swallowing the city beachfronts at Woodstock and Paarden Island to cater for the growing supertanker traffic that was outstripping the capacity of the Victoria and Alfred Docks.

The V&A Waterfront

The Victoria and Alfred Waterfront, usually known simply as the Waterfront, adjoins the west of Duncan Dock and is Cape Town's original Victorian harbour. After two decades of stagnation, it was redeveloped in the 1990s and is now the most popular attraction on the Peninsula, incorporating the city's central shopping area, its most fashionable eating and drinking venues, the site of an excellent aquarium and the Nelson Mandela Gateway – the embarkation point for trips to Robben Island. Authentic nineteenth-century buildings, imitation Victorian shopping malls, piers with waterside walkways and a functioning harbour complement the wide range of restaurants, outdoor cafés, pubs, clubs, cinemas, museums and outdoor entertainment, with magnificent Table Mountain rising beyond.

Arguments raged throughout the first half of the nineteenth century over the need for a proper dock. The Cape was often known as the **Cape of Storms** because of its vicious weather, which left Table Bay littered with wrecks. Many makeshift attempts were made, including the construction of a lighthouse in 1823, and work was begun on a jetty at the bottom of Bree Street in 1832. Clamour for a harbour grew in the 1850s, with the increase in sea traffic arriving at the Cape, reaching its peak in 1860, when the Lloyds insurance company refused the risk of covering ships dropping anchor in Table Bay.

The British colonial government dragged its heels due to the costs involved, but eventually conceded; on a suitably stormy September day in 1860, at a huge ceremony, the teenage Prince Alfred tipped the first batch of stones into Table Bay to begin the **Breakwater**, the westernmost arm of the harbour, which was subsequently completed with convict labour. In 1869, the dock – consisting of two main basins – was completed, and the sea was allowed to pour in.

Getting to and from the Waterfront

The Waterfront is one of the easiest points to reach in Cape Town by **public transport**. Waterfront shuttle buses leave from outside the train station in Adderley Street every ten minutes (daily 6.30am–10pm) and from Beach Road in Sea Point every twenty minutes (daily 6.30am–10pm), and terminate in Dock Road, at the back of the Waterfront Visitor Centre. Arriving by **car**, you'll find yourself well catered for, with several car parks and garages. If you want to leave by **taxi**, head for the taxi rank on Breakwater Boulevard. You can also catch shuttle buses from the V&A Waterfront branch of Cape Town Tourism's visitor centre at the Clock Tower Centre to major points of interest including the lower cableway station and Kirstenbosch.

The Marina and the Victoria and Alfred basins

Victoria Basin, the smaller **Alfred Basin** to its west, and the **Marina** beyond, create the northwestern half of the Waterfront's geography of piers and quays. The **Waterfront Visitor Centre**, set back from the Victoria Basin on Dock Road (daily 9am–9pm; ☎021 408 7600, ⓦwww.waterfront.co.za), provides maps and bookings for tours and taxis. They also have an office in the Clock Tower, adjacent to the Nelson Mandela Gateway, as does Cape Town Tourism.

North of the Visitor Centre, the outdoor action centres around **Market Square** and the **Agfa Amphitheatre**, where you can sometimes catch free rock, jazz or traditional African musical performances and occasionally hear the Cape Town Symphony Orchestra (details from the Visitor Centre). The shopping focus of the Waterfront is **Victoria Wharf**, an enormous flashy mall on two levels, extending along Quays Five and Six northeast of the amphitheatre. Inside the mall, you could be in any large city in the world, but the restaurants and cafés with outdoor seating on the mall's east side have fabulous views of Table Mountain across the busy harbour. On the west side of Victoria Wharf, the rather contrived **Red Shed Craft Workshop** (Mon–Sat 9am–9pm, Sun 10am–9pm) brings together craft workers such as glass-blowers, leatherworkers, township artists and jewellery-makers under one huge roof.

Head west from Market Square (away from the water) and you'll find yourself on Dock Road; 100m north along here is the **Imax Cinema** (information ☎021 419 7365, booking via Computicket ☎083 915 8000, ⓦwww .computicket.com; tickets at the door) at the BMW Pavilion on the corner of Portswood Road. It shows nature documentaries on topics such as African elephants, the Grand Canyon and the Amazon.

Adjacent to the Visitor Centre is one of Cape Town's best wine shops, Vaughan Johnson's. To the west, the **Telkom Exploratorium** in Union Castle Building is a small hands-on science museum, highly popular with kids. Southwest of the Alfred Basin's North Quay, **Alfred Mall Shopping Centre** is a complex of fifteen touristy curio shops, boutiques and restaurants. Further west lies the quite exceptional **Two Oceans Aquarium**.

East of the Alfred Shopping Mall, the Pierhead is dominated by the **Old Port Captain's Office**, a gabled Arts and Crafts building erected in 1904, with an imposing presence that reflected its status as the nerve centre of the harbour in the early twentieth century. It's now the headquarters of the Victoria and Alfred Waterfront Company.

Two Oceans Aquarium

One of Cape Town's highlights, the **Two Oceans Aquarium** (daily 9.30am–6pm; adults R45, children R20) on Dock Road at the Marina's North Wharf showcases the Cape's unique marine environment, where the warm Indian Ocean mingles with the cold Atlantic. Although you're not obliged to follow it, a designed route takes in the nine major galleries in sequence, starting on the **ground floor** with the **Indian Ocean**, where you'll see tank after tank of psychedelic fish. One of the most beautiful displays features scores of small gossamer-like jellyfish floating gently in their ultra-violet cylindrical tank like parachutists. To the rear of the ground floor, the **Diversity Hall**, as its name implies, contains an astonishing variety of strange marine creatures, including giant spider crabs, octopuses, sea horses and the deadly devil firefish, whose lacy beauty disguises lethal spines. Also on the ground floor, the **Agfa Auditorium** shows videos on South Africa's marine life and related topics (such as underwater photography).

The **basement** houses the **Alpha Activity Centre**, another good place to keep kids occupied, with free organized activities such as puppet shows and face painting, and computers which allow youngsters to explore marine ecology. The Centre is combined with the **Diving Animals** display, where you can watch a group of resident Cape fur seals frolicking underwater.

One of the aquarium highlights is the **shark feeding** every Sunday at 3.30pm, when you can watch *raggies* (ragged-tooth sharks) being hand-fed by divers. Smaller sharks, stingrays and turtles get their turn on Monday, Wednesday and Friday at 3.30pm.

The **top floor**, reached via a ramp, accommodates the **Story of Water**, which, in glorious reconstruction, traces the course of a river from its mouth to its source, via a salt marsh and lagoon. Not to everyone's taste, it features a small colony of African penguins (which you can see in their natural state at Boulders; see p.146), while captive sea birds fly about the rafters. In the **Kelp Forest** in an adjacent gallery, a dense jungle of giant seaweed sways hypnotically with the rhythmic surge of the water; you can sit in the small amphitheatre and gaze at beautiful shoals of silvery fish shimmering through sunlit sea. From here, a ramp takes you in a gentle downward spiral through the **Predators** exhibit, for many visitors the most compelling attraction of all. A massive tank, open to the ocean, houses some large resident ragged-toothed sharks, which glide past as you walk through a glass underwater tunnel; other species confined here include rays and giant turtles.

An **aquarium shop**, off the entrance foyer, with its plastic sharks, fluffy dolphins and souvenirs, may appear slightly banal, but stocks some interesting natural history books, CDs and videos.

The Clock Tower Precinct and Nelson Mandela Gateway to Robben Island

From the Pierhead you can use the **swing bridge** to cross to **Fish Quay**, the **Clock Tower Precinct** and the **Nelson Mandela Gateway** to Robben Island, a museum and the embarkation point for ferries to **Robben Island** (see below). As its name suggests, the swing bridge pivots to allow ships to pass through the narrow channel connecting the Victoria and Alfred basins. Rising up from Fish Quay, the **Clock Tower**, which houses a branch of the Waterfront Information Centre, is Cape Town's finest architectural folly. Built as the original Port Captain's office in 1882, this strange-looking octagonal structure with Gothic windows consists of three stacked rooms with a stairwell running through its core. The mirror room on the second floor enabled the Port Captain to survey all the activities of the harbour without leaving his office. Adjacent to the Clock Tower, the **Clock Tower Centre** is a compact two-storey shopping mall, with a substantial Cape Tourism visitor centre.

The Nelson Mandela Gateway to Robben Island

The **Nelson Mandela Gateway to Robben Island** (daily 7.30am–9pm; free), a two-storey building which looks out from its fabulous vantage point across the water to the island, incorporates a restaurant with a great view and a small museum with hi-tech interactive displays including a history of Robben Island, the voices of prisoners and resistance songs.

Robben Island

Lying only a few kilometres from the commerce of the Waterfront, flat and windswept **Robben Island** is suffused by a meditative, otherwordly silence. This key site of South Africa's liberation struggle was intended to silence

Tours to Robben Island

A number of vendors at the Waterfront sell tickets for cruises; while some of these may go close to the island, only the official ones sold at the **Nelson Mandela Gateway** will get you onto it. **Ferries** leave hourly (9am–3pm daily; ☎ 021 419 1300, ⓔ bookings@robben-island.org.za); the inclusive ferry fare, island entry fee and three-and-a-half hour tour costs R100.

The catamaran takes about half an hour to reach this potent symbol of apartheid, where ex-prisoners and ex-warders work as guides, sharing their experiences. The visit takes in Section B of the prison, which includes **Mandela's cell** as well as the horrifically crowded **dormitory cells**, which accommodated sixty to seventy prisoners in cramped and sometimes freezing conditions. A bus ride around the island takes in the **leper graveyard**, the **leper church** designed by Sir Herbert Baker, and the **lime quarry**, where Mandela and the other prisoners worked. Perhaps one of the saddest and most poignant sites is **Robert Sobukwe's house** (see p.124).

apartheid's domestic critics, but instead became an international focus for opposition to the regime. Measuring six square kilometres and sparsely vegetated by low scrub, this was Nelson Mandela's "home" for nearly two decades.

Some history

Nelson Mandela may have been the most famous Robben Island prisoner, but he certainly wasn't the first. In the seventeenth century the island became a place of banishment for those who offended the political order (initially the Dutch, later the British and the Afrikaner Nationalists). The island's first prisoner was the indigenous Khoikhoi leader **Autshumato**, who learnt English in the early seventeenth century and became an emissary of the British. After the Dutch settlement was established, he was jailed on the island in 1658 by Jan van Riebeeck. The rest of the seventeenth century saw a succession of East Indies political prisoners and Muslim holy men exiled here for opposing Dutch colonial rule.

During the nineteenth century, the **British** used Robben Island as a dumping ground for deserters, criminals and political prisoners, in much the same way as they used Australia. Captured **Xhosa leaders** who defied the Empire during the Frontier Wars of the early to mid-nineteenth century were transported by sea from the Eastern to the Western Cape to be imprisoned, and many ended up on Robben Island. In 1846, the island's brief was extended to include a whole range of the **socially marginalized**; criminals and political detainees were now joined by vagrants, prostitutes, lunatics and the chronically ill. All were victim to a regime of brutality and maltreatment, even in hospital. In the 1890s, a leper colony existed alongside the social outcasts. Lunatics were removed in 1921 and the lepers in 1930. During World War II, the **Defence Force** took over the island to set up defensive guns against a feared Axis invasion, which never came.

Robben Island's greatest era of notoriety began in 1961, when it was taken over by the **Prisons Department**. Prisoners arriving at the island prison were greeted by a slogan on the gate that read: "Welcome to Robben Island: We Serve with Pride." By 1963, when Nelson Mandela arrived, it had become a maximum security prison, and all the warders – and none of the prisoners – were white; prisoners were only allowed to send and receive one letter every six months; and common-law and political prisoners were housed together, until 1971 when they were separated in an attempt to further isolate the politicals. Harsh conditions, including routine beatings and forced hard labour, were exacerbated by geographical location; there's nothing but sea between the island and the South Pole, so icy winds routinely blow in from across the Atlantic – and inmates were made to wear shorts and flimsy jerseys. Like every other prisoner, Mandela slept on a thin mat on the floor (until 1973, when he was given a bed because he was ill) and was kept in a solitary confinement cell measuring two metres square for sixteen hours a day.

Amazingly, the prisoners found ways of **protesting**, through hunger strikes, publicizing conditions when possible (by visits from the International Committee of the Red Cross, for example) and, remarkably, by taking legal action against the prison authority to stop arbitrary punishments. They won improved conditions over the years, and the island also became a university behind bars, where people of different political views and generations met; it was not unknown for prisoners to give academic help to their warders. The last political prisoners were released from Robben Island in 1991 and the remaining common-law prisoners were transferred to the mainland in 1996. On January 1, 1997, control of Robben Island was transferred from the Department of Correctional Services to the Department of the Arts, Culture, Science and Technology, which has now established it as a museum. In December 1999 the entire island was declared a **UN World Heritage Site**.

The Island

Catamarans to the island take thirty minutes. After arrival at the tiny Murray's Bay harbour, you are taken on a **bus tour** around the island and a **tour of the prison**.

The bus tour stops off at several historical landmarks, the first of which is the **kramat**, a beautiful shrine built in memory of Tuan Guru, a Muslim cleric from present-day Indonesia who was imprisoned here by the Dutch in the eighteenth century. On his release, he helped to establish Islam among slaves in Cape Town, where it has flourished ever since. The tour also passes a **leper graveyard** and **church** designed by Sir Herbert Baker, both of which are quiet reminders that the island was a place of exile for leprosy sufferers in the early twentieth century.

Robert Sobukwe's house seems to echo with loneliness, and is perhaps the most affecting relic of incarceration on the island. It was here that Sobukwe, leader of the Pan Africanist Congress (a radical offshoot of the ANC was held in solitary confinement for nine years. He was initially sentenced to three years, but was regarded as so dangerous by the authorities that they passed a special law – the "Sobukwe Clause" – to keep him on Robben Island for a further six years. No other political prisoners were allowed to speak to him, but he would sometimes gesture his solidarity with other sons of the African soil by letting sand trickle through his fingers as they walked past. After his release in 1969, Sobukwe was restricted to Kimberley under house arrest, until his death from cancer in 1978.

Another stopoff is the **lime quarry** where Nelson Mandela and his fellow inmates spent countless hours of hard labour. The soft, pale stone is extremely bright under the summer sun, as a result of which Mandela and others have in later years suffered eye disorders. As the years passed, the lime quarry became a place of furtive study among the prisoners, with the help of sympathetic wardens.

The bus tour also takes in a stretch of coast dotted with shipwrecks and abundant seabirds, including the elegant **Egyptian sacred ibis**. You may also spot some of a recently expanded population of **antelope**: springbok, eland and bontebok.

The Maximum Security Prison

The **Maximum Security Prison**, a forbidding complex of unadorned H-blocks on the edge of the island, is introduced with the **Footsteps of Mandela** tour through the famous **B-Section**; you'll be guided by a former inmate, after which you're free to wander. B-Section is a small compound full of tiny rooms that has become legendary in South African history; initially a place of defeat for the resistance movement, it ironically came to incubate and concentrate the energies of liberation. **Mandela's cell** has been left exactly as it was, without embellishments or display, but the rest have been left locked and empty.

In the nearby **A-Section**, the "Cell Stories" exhibition skilfully suggests the sparseness of prison life; the tiny isolation cells contain personal artefacts loaned by former prisoners (including a functional saxophone made of found objects), plus quotations, recordings and photographs.

Towards the end of the 1980s, cameras were sneaked onto the island, and inmates took snapshots of each other, which have been enlarged to almost life size and mounted as the **Smuggled Camera Exhibition** in the D-Section communal cells. The jovial demeanour of the prisoners indicates their realization that the end was within sight; moreover, the warm camaraderie that evidently connects them suggests how people endured so many years of captivity. The **Living Legacy** tour in F-Section involves ex-political prisoner guides describing their lives here and answering your questions. **Overnight visits** are also planned.

The southern suburbs

Away from Table Mountain and the city centre, the bulk of Cape Town's residential sprawl extends east into South Africa's interior. It's here that the **southern suburbs**, the formerly whites-only residential areas, stretch out down the east side of Table Mountain, ending just before Muizenberg on the False Bay coast. All the main suburban attractions are concentrated in this area and, not surprisingly, the best shopping areas and cinemas.

From anywhere in the southern suburbs you can see Table Mountain rising above Cape Town. The area offers some quick escapes from the city heat into forests, gardens and vineyards, all hugging the eastern slopes of the mountain, and its extension, the Constantiaberg. The suburbs themselves are pleasant enough places to stay, eat and shop, but sights are thin on the ground.

Woodstock, Salt River and Observatory

First and oldest of the suburbs as you take an easterly exit from town is **Woodstock**, unleafy and windblown, but redeemed by some nice Victorian buildings, originally occupied by working-class coloureds, and now yuppifying.

To its east, **Salt River** is a harsh, industrial, mainly coloured area, built initially for workers and artisans, while **Observatory**, abutting its southern end, is generally regarded as Cape Town's bohemian hub, a reputation fuelled by its proximity to the University of Cape Town in Rondebosch and its large student population. Many of the houses here are student digs, but the narrow Victorian streets are also home to young professionals, hippies and arty types. The refreshingly unrestored peeling arcades on Observatory's Lower Main Road, and the streets off it, have some nice cafés and lively bars, as well as a wholefood shop, an African fabrics shop, and a couple of antiques emporiums. The huge Groote Schuur Hospital, which overlooks the freeway that sweeps through Observatory, was the site of the world's first heart transplant in 1967.

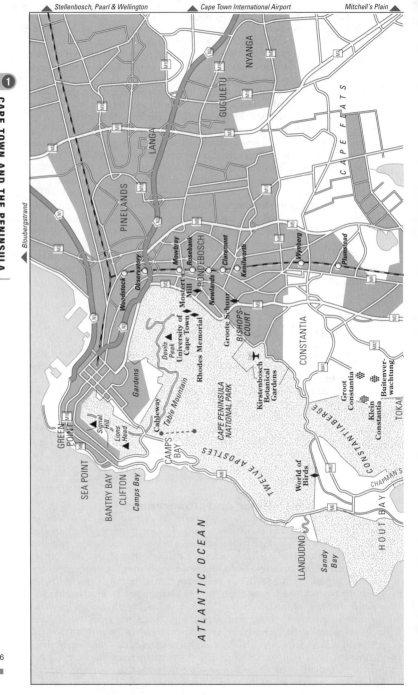

Blouubergstrand ▲

NYANGA

GUGULETU

LANGA

PINELANDS

CAPE FLATS

Woodstock

Observatory

Mowbray

Rosebank

RONDEBOSCH

Claremont

Wynberg

Plumstead

Mostert's Mill

Newlands

Kenilworth

Groote Schuur

BISHOPS-
COURT

Devil's Peak

University of
Cape Town

Rhodes Memorial

CONSTANTIA

Gardens

Table Mountain

Cableway

Signal
Hill

Lions
Head

CAPE PENINSULA
NATIONAL PARK

Kirstenbosch
Botanical
Gardens

CONSTANTIABERGE

Groot
Constantia

Klein
Constantia

Buitenver-
wachung

TOKAI

GREEN
POINT

SEA POINT

BANTRY BAY

CLIFTON

Camps Bay

CAMPS
BAY

TWELVE APOSTLES

World of
Birds

CHAPMAN'S

ATLANTIC OCEAN

LLANDUDNO

Sandy
Bay

HOUT BAY

SOUTHERN SUBURBS, FALSE BAY & ATLANTIC SEABOARD

CAPE TOWN AND THE PENINSULA

N

False Bay

Retreat

Muizenberg

St James

Kalk Bay

Clovelly

Fish Hoek

Glencairn

Simon's Bay

SIMON'S TOWN

Seaforth

The Boulders

CAPE PENINSULA NATIONAL PARK BOULDERS SECTION

CAPE PENINSULA NATIONAL PARK SILVERMINE SECTION

Steenberg

Tokai Forest

CAPE PENINSULA NATIONAL PARK

PEAK DRIVE

Chapman's Peak

NOORDHOEK

The Sentinel (331m)

Chapman's Bay

KOMMETJIE

OCEAN VIEW

CAPE PENINSULA NATIONAL PARK

SCARBOROUGH

Schuster's River Mouth

▶ Cape Point & Cape of Good Hope

M17

M5

M64

M6

M65

M64

M65

M6

M4

0   5 km

Mowbray and Rosebank

Heading along Station Road, away from the mountain and south of Observatory, is **Mowbray**, originally called Drie Koppen (Three Heads), after the heads of three slaves impaled there in 1724, but its name was sanitized in the 1840s. In the nineteenth century, this was the home of philologist Willem Bleek, who lived with a group of San convicts given up by the colonial authorities so that he could study their languages and attitudes. Bleek's pioneering work still forms the basis of much of what we know about traditional Khoisan life.

Rosebank, to Mowbray's south, has a substantial student community, some staying in the so-called Tampax Towers, the unmistakable circular residential blocks on Main Road. Just beyond them is the brown-bricked **Baxter Theatre**, one of Cape Town's premier arts complexes (see p.160).

Irma Stern Museum

Irma Stern is acknowledged as one of South Africa's pioneering artists of the twentieth century, more for the fact that she brought modern European ideas to the colonies than for any huge contribution she made to world art. The **UCT Irma Stern Museum**, Cecil Road, Rosebank (Tues–Sat 10am–5pm; R7), was the artist's home for 38 years until her death in 1966. The museum is definitely worth visiting to see Stern's collection of Iberian, African, Oriental and ancient artefacts. The whole house, in fact, reflects the artist's fascination with exoticism, starting with her own Gauguinesque paintings of "native types", the fantastic carved doors she brought back from Zanzibar, and the very untypical garden that brings a touch of the tropics to Cape Town with its exuberant bamboo thickets and palm trees.

Born in a backwater town in South Africa in 1894 to German Jewish parents, Stern studied at Germany's Weimar Academy. In reaction to the academy's conservatism, she adopted **expressionist distortion** in her paintings, some of which were included in the Neue Sezession Exhibition in Berlin in 1918. Although Stern's work was appreciated in Europe when she returned to South Africa after World War II, critics claimed that her style was simply a cover for technical incompetence. Stern went on several expeditions into Africa in the 1940s and 1950s, where she found the source for her intensely sensuous work that shocked contemporary South Africa, but has led historians to regard her as the towering figure of her generation.

Rondebosch and the Rhodes Memorial

South of Rosebank, neighbouring **Rondebosch** is home to the **University of Cape Town** (UCT), whose nineteenth-century buildings are handsomely festooned with creepers and sit grandly on the mountainside, overlooking Main Road and the M3 highway. Next to the campus north towards the city is the **Rhodes Memorial**, built to resemble a Greek temple, and grandiosely conspicuous against the slopes of Devil's Peak. The monument celebrates Cecil Rhodes' energy with a sculpture of a wildly rearing horse, and the empire-builder's bust is planted at the top of a towering set of stairs. His large estate, **Groote Schuur**, bordering on Main Road, became the official prime ministerial residence of the Cape, though Nelson Mandela preferred to stay at Genadendal, nearby (his private home is in Houghton, Johannesburg). Herds of wildebeest and zebra nonchalantly graze on the slopes around the Memorial, as cars fly past on the M3, and the **Tea Garden**, with terrific views of Cape Town. From here you can walk to the King's Blockhouse, formerly a signalling station to Muizenberg, and onto the Contour Path which follows the eastern side of the mountain, way above the southern suburbs to Constantia

Nek. Below the Memorial, alongside the M3, is the incongruous **Mostert's Mill**, built two centuries ago when there were wheat fields here instead of highways.

South of Rondebosch

Continuing **south from Rondebosch** along the Van der Stel Freeway or along the more congested Main Road, you pass some of Cape Town's most prestigious suburbs. **Newlands**, almost merging with Rondebosch, is home to the city's famous rugby and cricket stadiums, while the well-heeled suburb of **Claremont** to its south is becoming an alternative focus to the city centre for shopping and entertainment, with two cinema complexes and several malls. Alongside the high-quality shops, hawkers sell clothes, vegetables and herbs; closer to Claremont station, you can buy tasty *boerewors* rolls from women cooking them outdoors on *skottel braais* (braziers). A little further on, **Bishopscourt**, as its name suggests, is home to the Anglican bishop of Cape Town and it was in a mansion here that Archbishop Desmond Tutu lived even in the years when blacks weren't supposed to live in whites-only suburbs. Partly because of its prime siting – some plots have views of both Newlands Forest and the sea – this is one of the most prestigious areas in Cape Town; a number of consuls live here on huge properties behind the high walls that are about all you'll see passing the area. Further down the line, **Wynberg** is known for its Maynardville Shakespearean open-air theatre (see p.160) and quaint little row of shops and eating places.

Kirstenbosch National Botanical Gardens

Five kilometres south of Rondebosch, in Rhodes Avenue, are the **Kirstenbosch National Botanical Gardens** (daily: April–Aug 8am–6pm; Sept–March 8am–7pm; ☎021 762 1166; R15), the third most-popular tourist attraction in Cape Town (exceeded only by the Waterfront and the cable-car trip up Table Mountain). The gardens are magnificent, glorying in lush shrubs and exuberant blooms, which trail off into fynbos (see box on p.147), covering a huge expanse of the rugged eastern slopes and wooded ravines of Table Mountain. The setting is quite breathtaking – this is a great place to have tea and stroll around gazing up the mountain, or to wander onto the paths, which meander steeply to the top. If you're here in summer, one of the undoubted delights is to bring a picnic for a Sunday evening **open-air concert**, where you can lie back on the lawn, sip Cape wine and savour the mountain air and sunsets. There's a middling tea house here, open daily for breakfast, and lunch and teas, plus a restaurant and a coffee bar.

Kirstenbosch is the oldest and largest botanical garden in South Africa, created by Cecil Rhodes in 1895 (his camphor and fig trees are still here). Today, over 22,000 indigenous plants – and a research unit and library – attract researchers and botanists from all over the world. There's a nursery selling local plants, while characteristic Cape plants, found nowhere else in the world, are cultivated on the slopes. Little signboards and paved paths guide you through the highlights of the gardens, with trees and plants identified to enhance the rambling. The most interesting route is the one created for blind visitors, with labels in Braille and an abundance of aromatic and textured plants.

The cultivated gardens blend seamlessly into the mountainside, as there are no fences cutting off the way to the top of Table Mountain. From here, you can make your way up the mountain: two popular paths, starting from the Contour Path above Kirstenbosch, are Nursery Ravine and Skeleton Gorge (see p.137). Note that women should **not walk alone** in the isolated upper reaches of Kirstenbosch.

If you don't have a car and don't want to take an organized tour, the best way **to get to Kirstenbosch** is on one of the **buses** operated from Cape Town Tourism (☎021 426 4266; departures on demand during visitor centre opening hours; R35 one way). Alternatively, you'll have to rely on one of the local taxi services (see p.173). If you're driving, take the M5, and leave it at the signposted Rhodes Avenue turn-off. There is no train.

Constantia and its winelands

South of Kirstenbosch lie the elegant suburbs of **Constantia** and the Cape's oldest **winelands**. Luxuriating on the lower slopes of Table Mountain and the Constantiaberg, with tantalizing views of False Bay, the winelands are an easy drive from town, not more than ten minutes off the Van der Stel Freeway (the M3), which runs between the centre and Muizenberg.

Cape Dutch architecture

Cape Dutch style, which developed in the Western Cape countryside from the seventeenth to the early nineteenth century, is so distinctively rooted in the Winelands that it has become an integral element of the landscape. The dazzling limewashed walls look stunning in the midst of glowing green vineyards, while the thatched roofs and elaborate curvilinear gables seem to mirror the undulations of the surrounding mountains. The style was embraced in the twentieth century as part of white South African identity, and elements appear on the facades of many **suburban homes**.

The **Posthuys** (1673) in Main Road, Muizenberg, is thought to be the oldest colonial dwelling in South Africa. A rude thatch-roofed cottage consisting of a single rectangular space, its tiny windows served as a defence against feared attacks by the Khoikhoi, as well as protection from the fierce winds that lash the Peninsula. One of the few surviving examples of the so-called "**longhouse**", it represents the primitive language from which a rich vernacular **Cape Dutch** architecture evolved during the first two hundred years of colonial settlement.

Although there were important developments in the internal organization of Cape houses during this period, their most obvious element is the **gable**. End-gables were common in medieval northern European and particularly Dutch buildings, but central gables set into the long side of roofs were more unusual, and became the quintessential feature of the Cape Dutch style. Large numbers of buildings in central Cape Town had gables during the eighteenth century, but they had disappeared from the urban streetscape by the 1830s, to be replaced by buildings with flush facades and flat roofs.

Arson appears to be a major reason for these developments. There was a succession of town fires believed to have been started by slaves, including one that razed Stellenbosch in 1710 and Cape Town's **great fires** of 1736 and 1798; this led to a series of measures that shaped the layout of central Cape Town as well as the design of its houses. Flat roofs, clad in fireproof materials, became compulsory on all VOC buildings, as exemplified by the **Town House** (1755) off Greenmarket Square. After the 1798 conflagration, alarmed officials studied reports from London's Great Fire of 1666 and introduced legislation based on lessons learned from there. To retard the spread of flames, narrow alleys were provided between houses, there was a total ban on thatched roofs, and any protrusions on building exteriors – including shutters – were banned. This led to the flush facades and internal shutters that typify early nineteenth-century Cape town houses. With the disappearance of pitched roofs, the urban gable withered away, surviving symbolically in some instances as minimal roof decoration, one example being the **Bo-Kaap Museum** (1763–1768) in Wale Street, which sports a wavy parapet.

Rural homesteads developed from the plain longhouse to become increasingly elaborate over time. As landowners became more wealthy, the size of home-

The winelands started cultivated life in 1685 as the farm of **Simon van der Stel**, the governor charged with opening up the fledgling Dutch colony to the interior. Thrusting himself wholeheartedly into the task, he selected for his own use an enormous tract of the choicest land set against the Constantiaberg, the section of the Peninsula just south of Table Mountain. He named the estate after his daughter Constancia, and this is now (with a minor change of spelling) the name of Cape Town's oldest and most prestigious residential area. Exuding the easy ambience of landed wealth, Constantia is a green and pleasant place, shaded by oak forests and punctuated with farm stalls, riding schools, designer Cape Dutch-style shopping centres and, of course, the vineyards.

Constantia grapes have been making wine since van der Stel's first ouput in 1705. After his death in 1712, the estate was divided up and sold off as the modern **Groot Constantia**, **Klein Constantia** and **Buitenverwachting**. In

steads grew, and the house plan became more complex. The spread of fire from one building to another wasn't a major consideration in the countryside, where VOC building regulations carried little weight. Consequently, the pitched roof survived here. Gables, similarly, became the hallmark of country manors, being an important element of the facade, positioned above the front door to provide a window admitting light into the loft. Because they were just above the front door, they could also provide protection for the entrance against burning thatch. From these functional origins, gables evolved into important symbols of wealth, with landowners vying to erect the biggest, most elaborate and most fashionable examples.

Cape Dutch architects

Between 1750 and 1850 – the golden century of Cape architecture – three men were associated with some of the most highly regarded buildings in the colony. So elevated is their status that numerous apocryphal attributions exist, claiming their hand in various projects.

Anton Anreith (1754–1822) was born near Freiburg in Germany, where it is believed he was apprenticed to a Rococo master-sculptor. He joined the Dutch East India Company's army as a private in 1776, but quickly gained employment as a carpenter, later earning the commission to reconstruct the facade of the Lutheran Church in Strand Street. In 1786, he became the VOC's master-sculptor and was probably responsible for the Kat balcony at the castle.

Hermann Schutte (1761–1844), born in Bremen, was apprenticed to an architect in Germany for seven years. After joining the Dutch East India Company as a stonemason, he came to the Cape in 1790 and worked on the Robben Island quarries, where he lost an eye and a hand in a blasting accident. He was discharged from the VOC and became a private building contractor, benefiting from numerous commissions from the influential Louis Michel Thibault. Schutte designed the Groote Kerk in Adderley Street and is also believed to have been responsible for the Green Point Lighthouse, the first lighthouse erected along the South African coast.

Louis Michel Thibault (1750–1815), a highly trained architect, was born near Amiens in France. Having held the honour of premier student at l'Academie Royale d'Architecture in Paris, he joined the Dutch East India Company as Lieutenant of Engineers, effectively making him the colony's principle military engineer and government architect, in which capacity he designed most of the major public buildings in Cape Town. He designed the Good Hope Masonic Lodge, which served as the parliamentary debating chamber prior to 1884, the current facade of the Slave Lodge and the imposing gables at Groot Constantia.

1990, the nearby Steenberg Estate was bought up by a large Johannesburg mining conglomerate. All **four estates** are open to the public and offer tastings; they're definitely worth visiting if you aren't heading further afield to the Winelands proper.

There is no public **transport** to Constantia, but Groot Constantia features on most organized tours of Cape Town or the Peninsula. To get to the estates **by car**, take the signposted Groot Constantia exit from the M3 onto Ladies Mile Extension, and follow the signs to Groot Constantia. Buitenverwachting and Klein Constantia are on Klein Constantia Road, just off Ladies Mile Extension, and are clearly signposted.

Groot Constantia

The largest estate and the one most geared to tourists is **Groot Constantia**, Cape Town's fourth most-visited attraction. Its big pull is that it retains the rump of van der Stel's original estate, as well as the original buildings. Otherwise, there's a pretty average **museum** full of period furniture (museum daily 10am–5pm; R8), a gift shop, art gallery and two **restaurants**. **Cellar tours** start every hour on the hour (daily: April–Sept 11am & 3pm; Oct–March 10am–4pm; R20 booking essential ☎021 794 5128) and there's **wine tasting** (daily: May–Nov 10am–4.30pm; Dec–Apr 9am–6pm; R14).

Despite the commercialism, Groot Constantia is impressive, though its portrayal of life in a seventeenth-century colonial chateau makes scant reference to the slave labour that underpinned its operations. The **manor house**, a quintessential Cape Dutch building, was Van der Stel's original home, modified at the end of the eighteenth century by the French architect Thibault. Walking straight through it, down the ceremonial axis, you'll come to the cellar, fronted with a carved pediment, depicting a riotous bacchanalia, which represents fertility.

Klein Constantia and Buitenverwachting

Smaller in scale than Groot Constantia, Klein Constantia and Buitenverwachting both offer free wine tasting in less regimented conditions than at the bigger estate, and although the buildings are far humbler, the settings are equally beautiful. **Klein Constantia**, Klein Constantia Rd (free wine tasting & sales Mon–Fri 9am–5pm, Sat 9am–1pm; ☎021 794 5188) has a friendly atmosphere and produces some fine wines. Something of a curiosity is its **Vin de Constance**, the re-creation of an eighteenth-century Constantia wine that was a favourite of Napoleon, Frederick the Great and Bismarck. It's a delicious dessert wine, packaged in a replica of the original bottle, and makes an original souvenir. There's also wildlife here: look out for the guinea fowls that roam the estate munching on the beetles that attack young vine leaves; in summer, migrant steppe buzzards prey on unsuspecting starlings, which eat the grapes. **Buitenverwachting** (roughly pronounced: bay-tin-fur-vuch-ting, with the "ch" as in the Scottish rendition of loch), also on Klein Constantia Road (Mon–Fri 9am–5pm, Sat 9am–1pm; ☎021 794 5190; free) provides its workers with some of the best living conditions of any South African farm. Unusual labour practices include the provision of two social workers, weekly visits by a doctor to the farm clinic, and worker involvement in the selection of new staff. Buitenverwachting's expensive **restaurant** of the same name (Tues–Fri noon–3pm & Tues–Sat 7pm–midnight), is regularly voted one of South Africa's ten best. For a day out on the farm (they have cattle and horses, too), they also do luxury **picnic lunches** (Nov–Apr Mon–Sat 12.30–2.30pm; R65; booking essential – contact Sue ☎021 794 2122 or 082 973 8543), which you can enjoy under the oaks in their fabulous gardens.

Tokai

Effectively the southern extension of Constantia, forested **Tokai** is an excellent area for leafy recreation away from the centre, with some relaxed and child-friendly places for eating and drinking, and sheltered from the southeaster. You can also take in some wine tasting at the nearby **Steenberg Vineyards**, which incorporates a luxury golfing resort. Across the road is Pollsmoor Prison, where during the apartheid era numerous political prisoners, including Nelson Mandela towards the end of his period of incarceration, did time. To drive to Tokai from the centre of Cape Town, head south along the M3 and exit north onto Ladies Mile Road; continue for 100m before turning south into Spaanschemat River Road, which runs through the suburb. You can easily combine Tokai with a trip to the seaside, as the suburb is fifteen minutes' drive from the False Bay seaboard.

Tokai Forest

Most people come out to Tokai for the well-marked hiking paths and mountain-biking trails in the pine plantations of the **Tokai Forest**. You can get there along the M3 or Spaanschemat River Road (which becomes Orpen Road), turning west from either into Tokai Road, which leads straight to the forest. About 1.2km from the M3 or 500m from Spaanschemat River Road, the road first passes through a forested section, equipped with picnic tables, though this isn't the nicest part of the forest or the best place to picnic. Instead, keep on till you reach the Arboretum (see below).

A little further along the road from the picnic sites, you'll come to an opening in the forest occupied by **Tokai Manor House** (not open to the public). Designed by Louis Michel Thibault (see p.131) and built around 1795, this National Monument is an elegant gem of Cape Dutch architecture surrounded by trees, and combines the Cape Dutch style with the understated elegance of French Neoclassicism.

A hundred metres to its west lies the entrance to another National Monument, the historic tree plantation that constitutes the **Tokai Arboretum** (see p.164; daily dusk to dawn; R2 donation), which has a car park and is the best place to begin rambling or have tea and scones at the thatched **café** close to the entrance gate. The arboretum is the work of Joseph Storr Lister, who was a nineteenth-century Conservator of Forests for the Cape Colony. In 1885 he experimented with planting 150 species of trees from temperate countries, with oaks and eucalyptus featuring extensively as well as some beautiful California redwoods. Storr discovered that conifers were best suited to the Cape, which is why the plantation to the west of the arboretum, owned by the Safcol timber company, consists mainly of pines.

Several tracks and trails crisscross the arboretum and plantation providing easy walks and mountain-biking trails (bring your own bike). There are several longer hikes, including the walk from the entrance gate to **Elephant's Eye Cave** (6km). This can easily be completed in well under three hours, and passes through beautiful moist woodland, before opening into montane fynbos that covers the slopes of the Constantiaberg, eventually leading to the cave, which offers terrific panoramas. Ask for a map and directions at the entrance gate or, if this is unattended, at the adjacent café.

Steenberg Vineyards

In a fabulous location at the foot of Steenberg mountain, the **Steenberg Vineyards** (March–Aug Mon–Fri 8.30am–4.30pm; Sept–Feb Mon–Fri 8.30am–4.30pm, Sat 9am–1pm; free) comprise a fine Cape Dutch manor house and three other farm buildings, set around a large formal garden dating from 1695. This is South Africa's oldest wine estate: the lands were granted by Governor Simon van der Stel to the five-times widowed Catherina Michelse in 1682 and sold on in 1695 to Frederik Roussouw. That year, Roussouw erected the first buildings, and produced the first wine here. After his death, his widow Christina Diemer turned the estate into a highly profitable business, providing hospitality to travellers and provisions to the fleet (the VOC declared Simon's Town its winter port in 1741). Steenburg now boasts one of Cape Town's best country hotels, using the refurbished buildings that were declared a National Monument in 1996. Of their wines, the Merlot, Sauvignon Blanc and Semillon stand out.

Table Mountain

The icon that for hundreds of years and from hundreds of kilometres announced Cape Town to seafarers, **Table Mountain**, a 1087m flat-topped massif with dramatic cliffs and eroded gorges, dominates the northern end of the Peninsula. Its north face overlooks the city centre with the distinct formations of **Lion's Head** and **Signal Hill** to the west and **Devil's Peak** to the east. The west face is made up of a series of gabled formations known as the **Twelve Apostles**; the southwest towers over Hout Bay and the east over the southern suburbs.

Table Mountain safety

Make sure you:
- Don't climb alone.
- Inform someone you're going up the mountain.
- Tell them your route, when you're leaving and when you expect to be back.
- Leave early enough to give yourself time to complete your route during daylight.
- Don't try to descend via an unknown route. If you get lost in poor weather, seek shelter, keep warm and wait for help.
- Never leave even the tiniest scrap of litter on the mountain.
- Never make fires. No cooking is allowed, even on portable stoves.

Wear:
- Good footwear. Boots or running shoes are recommended.
- A broad-rimmed hat.

Take:
- A backpack.
- A water bottle. Allow two litres per person.
- Enough food: sandwiches, glucose sweets, nuts, raisins, juice.
- A warm jersey.
- A windbreaker.
- A raincoat.
- Sunglasses.
- High-factor sunscreen.
- Money for the cable car.
- Plasters for blisters.
- A map (available from Cape Union Mart at the Waterfront, or Cavendish Square Shopping Centre in Claremont).

The mountain is a compelling feature in the middle of the city, a wilderness where you'll find wildlife and a substantial 1400 species of **flora**. Indigenous mammals include baboons, dassies (see box on p.136) and porcupines, while the animals that resemble mountain goats are Himalayan tahrs, descended from specimens introduced by Cecil Rhodes onto his estate, and which escaped to flourish on the mountain.

Reckoned the most-climbed massif in the world, Table Mountain has suffered under the constant pounding of **hikers** and wanton vandalism – although the damage isn't always obvious, and certainly not from the dizzying vista at the top. Every year the mountain strikes back, taking its toll of lives. One of the commonest causes of difficulties is people losing the track (often due to sudden mist falling) and becoming trapped. If you plan on tackling one of the hundreds of walks and climbs on its slopes, go properly prepared (see box opposite); you might also like to take a guide (see "Participation sports" on p.166).

The cable car

The least challenging, but certainly not least interesting, way up the mountain, is via the highly popular **cable car**, which offers dizzying views across Table Bay and the Atlantic. To cope with half a million visitors jostling to ride the cable car to the top of the mountain (at the front of the western table), a state-of-the-art Swiss system was installed in 1997. The floor of the fishbowl-shaped car is designed to complete a 360-degree rotation on its way to the top, giving passengers a full panorama. Cars leave from the **lower cableway station** on Tafelberg Road (daily every 10–20 min: May–Oct 8.30am–6pm; Nov 7.30am–9pm; Dec–Jan 8am–10pm; Feb–Mar 8.30am–9pm; April 8.30am–7.30pm; ☎021 424 5148 or 021 424 8181; May–Oct R68 return; Nov–Apr R85 return).

To get there by public transport, take the shuttle bus that leaves from Cape Town Tourism's visitor centre, or take one of the minibus taxis that ply the route from Adderley Street to the lower cableway station (around R10 each way). If you're driving, you'll find parking along Tafelberg Road, the road that leads to the lower cableway station, but you may be in for a bit of a walk in peak season – the parking can stretch for several hundred metres in either direction.

Climbs and walks

Climbing the mountain will give you a greater sense of achievement than being ferried up by the cable car, but proceed with extreme caution: it may look sunny and clear when you leave, but conditions at the top could be very different. The weather is subject to rapid changes, both in general and in small localized areas. The main hazards are sun, mist and violent winds. Unless you're going with a knowledgeable guide, attempt only the simplest routes (the ones outlined here).

Signal Hill and Lion's Head

From the roundabout at the top of Kloofnek a road leads all the way along **Signal Hill** to a car park and lookout with good views over Table Bay, the docks and the city. A cannon was formerly used for sending signals to ships at anchor in the bay, and the Noon Gun, still fired from its slopes daily, sends a thunderous rumble through the Bo-Kaap below. Halfway along the road is a sacred Islamic *kramat* (shrine), one of several dotted around the Peninsula which "protect" the city. You can also walk up **Lion's Head**, an unstrenuous hike that seems to bring out half the population of Cape Town every full moon.

Dassies

The outsized fluffy guinea pigs you'll encounter at the top of Table Mountain are **dassies** or hyraxes (*Procavia capensis*) which, despite their appearance, aren't rodents at all, but the closest living relatives – some way back – of elephants. Their name (pronounced like "dusty" without the "t") is the Afrikaans version of *dasje*, meaning "little badger", given to them by the first Dutch settlers. Dassies are very widely distributed, having thrived in South Africa with the elimination of predators, and live in suitably rocky habitats all over the country.

Like reptiles, dassies have poor body control systems and rely on shelter against both hot sunlight and the cold. They wake up sluggish and first thing in the morning seek out rocks where they can catch the early morning sun – this is one of the best times to look out for them. One adult stands sentry against predators and issues a low-pitched warning cry in response to a threat. Dassies live in colonies of a dominant male and eight or more related females and their offspring.

Platteklip Gorge and Maclear's Beacon

The first recorded ascent to the summit of Table Mountain was by the Portuguese captain Antonio de Saldanha, in 1503. He wisely chose **Platteklip Gorge**, the gap visible from the front table (the north side) which, as it turned out, is the most accessible way up. A short and easy extension will get you to Maclear's Beacon which, at 1086m, is the highest point on the mountain. The Platteklip route has the added advantage of ending at the upper cableway station, so you can descend in a car.

The route starts out at the **lower cableway station**. From here, walk east along Tafelberg Road until you see a high embankment built from stone and maintained with wire netting. Just beyond and to the left of a small dam is a sign pointing to Platteklip Gorge. A steep fifteen-minute climb brings you onto the **Upper Contour Path**. About 25m east along this, take the path indicated by a sign reading "Contour Path/Platteklip Gorge". The path zigzags from here onwards and is very clear. The gorge is the biggest cleavage on the whole mountain, leading directly and safely to the top, but it's a very steep slog which will take **two to three hours** in total if you're reasonably fit. Once on top, turn right and ascend the last short section onto the **front table** for a breathtaking view of the city. A sign points the way to the **upper cableway station** – a fifteen-minute walk along a concrete path thronging with visitors.

Maclear's Beacon is about 35 minutes from the top of the Platteklip Gorge on a path leading eastward, with white squares on little yellow footsteps guiding you all the way. The path crosses the front table with Maclear's Beacon visible at all times. From the top you'll get views of False Bay and the Hottentots Holland Mountains to the east.

The Pipe Track

One of the most rewarding and easiest walks along the mountainside takes the **Pipe Track**, a service road which follows water pipes from the mountain reservoirs to Kloofnek. The track runs on the level for roughly 7km, on the west flank of Table Mountain, beneath the Twelve Apostles, following the mountain's contours and offering fantastic views of the Atlantic. The Pipe Track isn't a circular route, so you can turn back at any point. The whole walk can take up to three hours each way.

The route begins at some stone steps at Kloofnek opposite the bus terminus for the cable car, just to the west of the Tafelberg Road turn-off (if you're driving, park on Tafelberg Road). Steps lead up alongside forestry staff houses before the road levels off under some pines. The path intersects several climbs up the mountain, useful indicators as to how far you've come. The first, after about 45 minutes, is indicated by a sign to Blinkwater Ravine (closed to the public due to rockfalls). A further ten to fifteen minutes brings you to the Kasteelspoort ascent (signposted under gum trees) followed by Woody Ravine and the last, roughly 25 minutes after Kasteelspoort, at Slangolie Ravine, where the path ends. The rock bed on Slangolie is steep, unstable and to be avoided. Turn back when you see the first of the Woodhead Tunnel danger signs.

Skeleton Gorge and Nursery Ravine

You can combine a visit to the gardens at Kirstenbosch with an ascent up Table Mountain via one route and a descent down another, ending at the Kirstenbosch National Botanical Gardens' **restaurant** for tea. Starting at the restaurant, follow the **Skeleton Gorge** signs, which lead you onto the **Contour Path**. At the Contour Path, a plaque indicates that this is **Smuts' Track**, the route favoured by Jan Smuts, the Boer leader and South African prime minister (see p.283). The plaque marks the start of a broad-stepped climb up Skeleton Gorge, involving wooden steps, stone steps, wooden ladders and loose boulders. Be prepared for steep ravines and difficult rock climbs – and under no circumstances stray off the path. It requires reasonable fitness, but can take as little as an hour. Skeleton can be an unpleasant way down, especially in the wet season when it gets slippery.

Nursery Ravine is recommended for the descent. At the top of Skeleton Gorge, walk a few metres to your right to a sign indicating **Kasteelspoort**. It's just 35 minutes from the top of Skeleton along this path to the head of Nursery Ravine. The descent returns you to the 310-metre Contour Path, which leads back to Kirstenbosch. This entire walk lasts about five hours.

The Atlantic seaboard

Table Mountain's steep drop into the ocean along much of the western Peninsula forces the suburbs along the **Atlantic seaboard** into a ribbon of developments clinging dramatically to the slopes. The sea washing the west side of the Peninsula can be very chilly, far colder than on the False Bay seaboard. Although not ideal for bathing, the Atlantic offers mind-blowing views from some of the most incredible coastal roads in the world, particularly beyond **Sea Point**. The coast itself consists of a series of bays and white-sanded beaches edged with smoothly sculpted bleached rocks; inland, the Twelve Apostles, a series of rocky buttresses, gaze down onto the surf. The beaches are ideal for sunbathing, or sunset picnics – it's from this side of the Peninsula that you can watch the sun sink into the ocean, creating fiery reflections on the sea and mountains behind as it slips away.

Mouille Point and Green Point

Just to the west of the V&A Waterfront, Mouille Point and its close neighbour, Green Point, are among the suburbs closest to the city centre. **Mouille Point** is known principally for its squat rectangular Victorian lighthouse, commissioned in the 1820s, and painted like a children's picture-book lighthouse, with diagonal red and white stripes. The recent opening of entrances directly connecting Mouille Point with the Waterfront has helped regenerate the suburb and has integrated the Waterfront with its neighbouring suburbs with some seriously upmarket hotels along Granger Bay Street.

△ Fishermen and catch, Hout Bay

Mouille Point merges with the far larger suburb of **Green Point**, which continues both inland from it and west along the ragged Atlantic shore. Over the last couple of years Green Point's proximity to the Waterfront – an easy ten-or-so minutes' walk away – and its position along the coast has turned it from a sleazy district into a humming area of excellent accommodation, eating places and clubs.

Inland, at the foot of Signal Hill is **De Waterkant**, a quarter of terraced Cape cottages next to the Bo-Kaap, established in the 1700s to house artisans and freed slaves. About three blocks by three it has now turned into a trendy district of bright tourist accommodation, narrow streets and corner cafés. Defining its eastern edge, Somerset Road and its continuation, Main Road, in Green Point has become one of Cape Town's principal gay strips, where numerous establishments fly the multicoloured gay flag.

Sea Point and Bantry Bay

Continuing southwest along Main Road, Green Point merges with **Sea Point**, a long-established place for great restaurants. Middle-class couples, pram-pushing mothers, street kids, hookers and drunks create an uneasy blend of respectability and seediness that disappears as you move into Bantry Bay and the wealthier suburbs down the Atlantic seaboard.

The closest seaside to the city centre is a block down from Main Road, although it's too rocky for swimming. At the westernmost edge of Sea Point lies **Bantry Bay**, combining the density of Sea Point with the wealth of the Atlantic suburbs and consisting of large upmarket resort hotels and self-catering apartment blocks just far enough for comfort from the sleaze of Sea Point, but close enough should you want to walk to a restaurant. Halfway along the kilometre-long beach promenade, running alongside Beach Road, you'll catch views of **Graaff's Pool**, an institutionalized and exclusively male nudist spot, while at the westernmost end is the only place in the vicinity to swim, at the new Olympic-sized **saltwater pool**, alongside the crashing surf (see p.163).

Clifton to Sandy Bay

Suburbia proper begins south of Sea Point at Bantry Bay. Fashionable **Clifton**, on the next cove, is sheltered by Lion's Head. Sitting on the most expensive real estate in Africa, Clifton is studded with fabulous seaside apartments and four wonderful sandy **beaches**, reached via steep stairways. The sea here is good for surfing and safe for swimming, but bone-chillingly cold. First Beach (they're all numbered) is colonized by muscular ball-players, surfers and their female counterparts, so avoid it unless your tan is up to scratch. Second and Third beaches are split between the teenies and thirtysomethings, with beautiful men and some cruising on Third; if in doubt, head for Fourth, which has become the family beach because it has the fewest steps. Hout Bay **buses** go to Clifton from the city centre twelve times a day (a 30min journey).

A little to the south, **Camps Bay** suburb climbs the slopes of Table Mountain and is scooped into a small amphitheatre, bounded by the Lion's Head and the Twelve Apostles sections of the Table Mountain range. This, and the airborne views across the Atlantic, make Camps Bay one of the most desirable places to live in Cape Town. The main drag, Victoria Road, skirts the coast and is packed with trendy restaurants, while the wide sandy beach is accessible by bus and is consequently enjoyed by families of all shapes and colours. Lined by a row of palms and some grassy verges with welcome shade for picnics, Camps Bay beach is very busy around the Christmas and Easter breaks.

However, it's exposed to the southeaster, and there's the usual Atlantic chill and an occasional dangerous backwash.

There's little development between Camps Bay and the wonderful cove of **Llandudno**, 20km from Cape Town along Victoria Road (not served by public transport). A steep and narrow road winds down past smart homes to the shore, where the sandy beach is punctuated at either end by magnificent granite boulders and rock formations. This is a good sunbathing spot and a choice one for bring-your-own sundowners. The small car park frequently spills over into the suburban streets at peak periods.

Isolated **Sandy Bay**, Cape Town's main nudist beach, can only be reached via a twenty-minute walk from Llandudno. In the apartheid days, the South African police went to ingenious lengths to trap nudists, but nowadays the beach is relaxed, so feel free to come as undressed as feels comfortable. Among the dunes and fynbos (see box on p.147) there are no houses – in fact, no facilities whatsoever – so bring whatever supplies you may need. To get there, take the path from the south end of the Llandudno car park, through fynbos vegetation and across some rocks, to the beach. It's a fairly easy walk, but if you're barefoot watch out for broken glass.

Hout Bay

Although no longer the quaint fishing village it once was, **Hout Bay** still has a functioning fishing harbour and is the centre of the local crayfish industry. Leopards no longer stalk its *kranses* and *koppies*, but their former presence is recalled by a bronze statue looking down from Chapman's Peak Drive. Despite ugly modern development and a growing shantytown, the natural setting is quite awesome. Next to the harbour and car park, the little **Mariner's Wharf** waterfront development shelters the Seafood Emporium selling fresh fish and there's a decent restaurant upstairs. This is a good place to pick up fresh snoek, a Western Cape speciality, both at the restaurant and from the Emporium.

The sea off the long slender **beach** is no good for swimming; it's too cold, too close to the harbour and too prone to fish scales floating in its surf – but the beach is perfect for walking. Away from the harbour, the village is just managing to hang onto its historic ambience, with the **Hout Bay Museum**, 4 St Andrews Rd (Tues–Fri 8.30am–4.30pm; R5; ℡021 790 3270), offering good exhibits on Strandloper culture and the local fishing industry. Nearby **World of Birds**, Valley Rd (daily 9am–5pm; R30), requires at least two hours to see the more than 3000 birds and small animals housed in surprisingly pleasant and peaceful walk-through aviaries. You can watch penguins being fed at 11.30am and 3.30pm, pelicans at 12.30pm and birds of prey at 4.10pm daily except Mondays and Fridays. A large walk-in aviary open 11.30am–1pm & 2–3.30pm includes among its inhabitants cute squirrel monkeys; visitors can handle and play with them. There's a café and restaurant serving light lunches, or you can picnic at the Flamingo Terrace.

Hout Bay is at a convenient junction for the rest of the Peninsula and has the highest concentration of places to stay south of Sea Point, including the upmarket, country-style *Hout Bay Manor*. From Cape Town it's 20km along either the coast or inland via Constantia. At a push you can get there on public transport on one of the two **buses** (see p.84) leaving from Adderley Street every day along the latter route; you can also catch minibus taxis. Crossing the Peninsula spine from Simon's Town, it's 26km (on the Glencairn Expressway).

Chapman's Peak Drive to Scarborough

Continuing south along the coast, **Chapman's Peak Drive** is a thrilling journey along one of the most beautiful drives in the world. For 10km the road carves into the mountainside on the one side, dropping precipitously hundreds of metres to the ocean on the other. Unceasingly spectacular views take in the breadth of Hout Bay to the 331-metre-high sentinel on a curved outcrop. Viewpoints are provided along the route, but take care in high winds as it can be dangerous, with occasional rockfalls, although this doesn't seem to bother the scores of cyclists who sweat their way round, making considerate driving a necessity.

Noordhoek, a low-key settlement at the end of the descent from Chapman's Peak Drive, consists of smallholdings in a gentle valley with a long white untamed beach stretching 3km across Chapman's Bay to Kommetjie. The sands are fantastic for walking and horse-riding, but can resemble a sandblaster when the southeaster blows. Swimming is hazardous, though surfers relish the rough waters around the rocks to the north. For refreshment, the only place around here is the excellent *Red Herring* restaurant (see p.155) set back from the sea, about ten minutes on foot from the car park as you head away from the sea, with fine views from its outdoor deck.

Although only a few kilometres south of Noordhoek along the beach, getting to **Kommetjie** by road involves a fifteen-kilometre haul inland up the Peninsula spine south along Noordhoek Road, taking a west turn into Kommetjie Road, to descend again. The beach's small basin (*kommetjie*), which is always a few degrees above the surrounding sea temperature, is perfect for swimming. Just to its north, **Long Beach** is a favourite surfing spot, used by devotees even during the chilly winter months.

Almost 10km by road from Kommetjie, the developing village of **Scarborough** is the most far-flung suburb along the Peninsula. A long wide beach edges temptingly to its south just beyond Schusters River Lagoon – resist its potentially treacherous sea and stick to the lagoon.

The False Bay seaboard

In summer, the waters of **False Bay** are several degrees warmer than those on the Atlantic seaboard, which is why Cape Town's oldest and most popular seaside development is along this flank of the Peninsula. A series of village-like suburbs, backing onto the mountains, each served by a Metrorail Station, is dotted all the way south from **Muizenberg**, through **St James**, **Kalk Bay**, **Fish Hoek** and down to **Simon's Town**. Each has its own character with restaurants, shops and places to stay, while Simon's Town, one of South Africa's oldest settlements, is worth taking in as a day-trip and makes a useful base for visiting the **Cape of Good Hope Nature Reserve** and **Cape Point**.

Muizenberg

Once South Africa's most fashionable beachfront, today **Muizenberg**, (pronounced: mew-zin-burg) on the train line and one of the beaches closest to the populous Cape Flats, has become pretty rundown, although plans are in the pipeline to upgrade and restore it. Brightly coloured bathing boxes are reminders of a more elegant heyday, when it was visited by the likes of Agatha Christie, who enjoyed riding its waves while holidaying here in the 1920s: "Whenever we could steal time off," she wrote, "we got out our surf boards and went surfing."

Capetown's top whale spots

Cape Town's best **whale-watching spots** are on the warmer **False Bay** side of the Peninsula, from August to November, and you'll need binoculars. Along this side, look out for whale signboards, indicating good places for sightings. The commonest whales along this section of coast are southern rights, but it's worth noting that there are more spectacular spotting opportunities further east, especially around Hermanus (see p.231).

Boyes Drive, running along the mountainside behind Muizenberg and Kalk Bay, provides an outstanding vantage point. To get there **by car**, head out on the M3 from the city centre to Muizenberg, taking a sharp right into Boyes Drive, at Lakeside, from where the road begins to climb, descending finally to join Main Road between Kalk Bay and Fish Hoek. Alternatively, sticking close to the shore along Main Road, the stretch between **Fish Hoek** and **Simon's Town** is recommended, with a particularly nice spot above the rocks at the south end of Fish Hoek Beach, as you walk south towards Glencairn. **Boulders Beach** at the southern end of Simon's Town has a whale signboard, and smooth rocky outcrops above the sea to sit on and gaze out over the sea. Even better vantage points are further down the coast between Simon's Town and **Smitswinkel Bay**, where the road goes higher along the mountainside.

Without a car, it's easy enough to go **by train** to Fish Hoek or Simon's Town and whale-spot from the Jager's Walk beach path that runs along the coast from Fish Hoek to Sunny Cove, just below the railway line.

If you're on a **coach trip**, or **driving** around the Peninsula, you could also try your luck looking out to sea at **Chapman's Peak** towards Hout Bay, and between **Llandudno** and **Sea Point**, where the road curves along the ocean. Outside Cape Town, the best place of all is ninety minutes away, at **Hermanus** and the other towns dotted around Walker Bay.

Information on the exact location of whale sightings in the past 24 hours is available from the **Whale Watch Hotline** (toll-free ☏ 0800 22 8222).

Despite the slight air of tawdriness, Muizenberg's gently shelving, sandy **beach** is the most popular along the Peninsula for swimming; it's safe for bathing, the water tends to be flat and warm, and there's good surfing in its breakers. This is also the most developed of the Peninsula's beaches, with a pavilion complex around the car park featuring tea shops, a waterslide and minigolf. Along the beachfront and Main Road you'll also find downbeat shops, cafés and restaurants catering to the seaside trade.

Getting there is best done by train: from the centre it's a 45-minute journey – the train's first seaside stop as it trundles through the southern suburbs on its way to Simon's Town. By car, take the M3 through the posh suburbs, or the slightly quicker M5 via the less salubrious Cape Flats to Muizenberg. During peak season, finding a place to leave your vehicle can be near impossible.

The Historical Mile

South of Muizenberg, Main Road and the railway line hug the shore all the way to Simon's Town. A short stretch, starting at Muizenberg station, is known as the **Historical Mile**, dotted with a run of notable buildings and easily explored on foot. **Muizenberg station**, an Edwardian-style edifice completed in 1913, is now a National Monument, while further towards Simon's Town is the **Posthuys**, a rugged whitewashed and thatched building dating from 1673 and a fine example of the Cape vernacular style. **Rhodes' Cottage Museum** (Tues–Sun 10am–5pm; free; ☏ 021 788 1816), was bought in 1899 by the millionaire politician, who died here in 1902 before his grander dwelling next door (closed to the public) could be completed. Rhodes'

Cottage contains memorabilia painting a distinctly rosy portrait of the man, with photographs, a model of the Big Hole in Kimberley (where Rhodes made his fortune at the diamond diggings), and a curious diorama of World's View in Zimbabwe's Matopos Hills, where he lies buried.

Most idiosyncratic of the buildings along the Historical Mile, and closest to St James, is the **Natale Labia Museum** (Tues–Sun 10am–5pm; R5; ☎021 788 4106), completed in 1930 as the residence of the Italian Consul, now part of the National Gallery and housing a small collection of paintings, *objet's d'arts* and furniture. Built in eighteenth-century Venetian style, it sits incongruously amid the Main Road townscape. Inside, heavy lace obscures the magnificent view, but there's an excellent **restaurant**, which serves up breakfasts, light meals and teas in the ersatz-Baroque interior or outside on the Italianate patio.

St James

St James, 2km south of Muizenberg, and just one stop away by train, is more upmarket than its northern neighbour, and its pleasing, villagey feel makes it a nice place to hop off the train. The compact beach draws considerable character from its much-photographed Victorian-style bathing boxes, whose bright, primary colours catch your eye as you pass by road or rail. The rocky beaches here don't make for great sea swimming, although it's always sheltered from the wind and there's a fine **tidal pool** that is safe for toddlers and great for bathing at high tide, when enormous breakers crash over the sea wall. St James tends to be overcrowded at weekends and on school holidays, so is best avoided at these times. Instead, make for Danger Beach between St James and Kalk Bay. A paved one-kilometre **coastal path**, connected at intervals to the Historical Mile, runs along the ocean from Muizenberg to St James; as well as providing stupendous views across the bay, it leads conveniently to the Labia Museum (see above).

Kalk Bay

Moving south from Muizenberg, **Kalk Bay**, one of the most southerly and smallest of Cape Town's suburbs, is a lively **working harbour** with wooden fishing vessels, mountain views, and a shopping precinct packed with trendy coffee shops, antique dealers and curiosity shops.

Kalk Bay somehow managed to slip through the net of the Group Areas Act, making it one of the few places on the Peninsula with an intact coloured community. Apart from the larger Hout Bay, Kalk Bay is the only harbour settlement still worked by coloured fishermen. The settlement is arranged around the small docks, where you can watch the boats come in; you can also buy fresh fish, which are flung onto the quayside and sold in spirited and noisy auctions. The harbour is busiest on Saturdays and Sundays when Capetonians descend on the harbour to pick up something for a weekend braai or for lunch at *Kalky's*, an informal fish 'n' chips restaurant right in the lively working harbour. Perched on the harbour wall in the station building, pounded by waves, is the popular *Brass Bell* **restaurant**, one of Kalk Bay's biggest attractions and one of the few restaurants along the Peninsula where you can actually sit next to the sea (see p.156).

Rising up behind the Kalk Bay settlement is **Silvermine Nature Reserve**, which runs across the Peninsula's spine, almost stretching to the west side at Chapman's Peak. Part of the Table Mountain chain, it offers walks and drives with fabulous views of False Bay, the mountains, indigenous forest and montane fynbos (see box on p.147). It's most easily reached via the Ou Kaapseweg (Old Cape Road, the M64) through Tokai. Alongside Silvermine runs **Boyes Drive**, a high-level alternative to the main road between Fish Hoek and

Muizenberg offering spectacular views across False Bay to the Hottentots Holland Mountains on the east side of False Bay.

Fish Hoek

Fish Hoek, south of Kalk Bay, boasts one of the Peninsula's finest family **beaches** along the False Bay coast. The best and safest swimming is at its southern end, where the surf is moderately warm, tame and much enjoyed by boogie boarders. Facilities include changing rooms, toilets, fresh water, and a surprisingly good **restaurant** right on the beach, the *Fish Hoek Galley Seafood Restaurant*. Apart from this, it's one of the dreariest suburbs along the entire False Bay coast; an obscure by-law banning the sale of alcohol in supermarkets or bottle stores, boosts the town's image as the Mother Grundy capital of the Peninsula.

From behind the restaurant, a picturesque concrete pathway called **Jager's Walk** skirts the rocky shoreline above the sea for 1km to Sunny Cove; from there, it continues for 6km as an unpaved track to Simon's Town. The walkway provides a good vantage point for seeing whales.

The Cape Town to Simon's Town train stops at Fish Hoek station, just opposite the beach. If you're driving, Fish Hoek is well-placed for access to the Atlantic seaboard or for heading into the Constantia winelands. Just south of the suburb, you can strike west on the Glencairn Expressway (M6), or alternatively take the equally scenic Kommetjie Road (M65) about 4km further south (more convenient than the M6 if you're coming from Simon's Town). The two intersect halfway across the Peninsula at Sun Valley, where Kommetjie Road continues west, veering slightly south to the coastal suburban village of Noordhoek. At Sun Valley, the M6 strikes north and splits about a kilometre after the intersection. The northwesterly branch hits the coast at Chapman's Point, and continues along the precipitously beautiful Chapman's Peak Drive, which eventually reaches the City Bowl along the Atlantic shore. The northeasterly branch heads along the winding treelined Ou Kaapseweg (M64, becoming the M42), passing through the Silvermine Nature Reserve and the winelands.

Simon's Town

South Africa's principal naval base, **Simon's Town** isn't the hard-drinking, raucous place you might expect or hope for. Just 40km from Cape Town, the country's third-oldest European settlement is exceptionally pretty, with a near-perfectly preserved streetscape. It's slightly marred on the ocean side by the domineering **naval dockyard**, but this, and glimpses of naval squaddies square-bashing behind the high walls or strolling to the station in their crisp white uniforms, are what give the place its distinct character.

Roughly halfway down the coast to Cape Point, Simon's Town makes the perfect base for a mellow break along the Peninsula, offering easy day-trips by train to Cape Town. Just a few kilometres to the south is the rock-strewn **Boulders Beach**, with its colony of nonchalant African penguins – reason in themselves to venture here.

Founded in 1687 as the winter anchorage of the Dutch East India Company, Simon's Town was modestly named by **Governor Simon van der Stel** after himself. Its most celebrated visitor was Lord Nelson, who convalesced here as a midshipman while returning home from the East in 1776. Nineteen years later, the British sailed into Simon's Town and occupied it as a bridgehead for their first invasion and occupation of the Cape. After just seven years they left, only to return in 1806. Simon's Town remained a British base until 1957, when it was handed over to South Africa.

There are fleeting hints, such as the occasional mosque, that the town's exclusively white appearance isn't the whole story. In fact, the first **Muslims** arrived from the East Indies in the early eighteenth century, imported as slaves to build the Dutch naval base. After the British banning of the slave trade in 1807, ships were compelled to disgorge their human cargo at Simon's Town, where one district became known as Black Town. In 1967, when Simon's Town was declared a White Group Area, there were 1200 well-established coloured families descended from these slaves. By the early 1970s, the majority had been **forcibly removed** under the Group Areas Act (see p.834), to the desolate township of Ocean View (ironically, one of the few places along the Peninsula not to enjoy a sea vista). After their departure their dwellings were destroyed or allowed to rot, depriving the town of significant historic buildings. In 1973, town clerk Charles Chevalier complained that "the loss of the non-white population has had a depressing effect on the commercial life of the town".

Arrival and information

Trains run from Cape Town roughly every hour during the day. The trip takes an hour, the last twenty minutes from Muizenberg skirting the coast spectacularly close to the shoreline; it's worth going to Simon's Town just for the train ride. Trains are met at Simon's Town by Rikki's taxis (☎021 786 2136), which you can also book for excursions to Cape Point and Boulders. A great outing is to take one of the restaurant trains pulling *Biggsy's Restaurant Carriage & Wine Bar*, which serves lunches, salads and breakfasts. *Biggsy's* operates five return trips a day (Tues–Sat) from Platform 1 at Cape Town station, but space is limited so book ahead (☎021 449 3870). **By car**, the quickest way to get here from Cape Town is via the M3 or M5 freeways to Muizenberg, before following the coastal road to Simon's Town. There are no buses to Simon's Town.

The Town

A short way south of the station along King George's Street (the main drag through town), a signposted road to the left points to the museums. The **Simon's Town Museum**, Court Rd (Mon–Fri 9am–4pm, Sat 10am–4pm, Sun 11am–4pm; R5; ☎021 786 3046), is in the Old Residency built in 1772 for the Governor of the Dutch East India Company. It also served as the slave quarters (the dungeons are in the basement) and town brothel. The motley collection includes maritime material and an inordinate amount of information and exhibits on Able Seaman Just Nuisance, a much-celebrated seafaring Great Dane adopted as a mascot by the Royal Navy in World War II, and who enjoyed drinking beer with the sailors he accompanied into Cape Town. At the **South African Naval Museum** (daily 10am–4pm; free; ☎021 797 4653) next door, lively displays include the inside of a submarine, the bridge of a ship that simulates rocking, and a lot of official portraits of South African Naval commanders from 1922 to the present.

In the centre of Simon's Town, a little over a kilometre south of the station, lies **Jubilee Square**, a palm-shaded car park just off St George's Street, the main drag running through town. Flanked by some good cafés and shops, including a great fish and chips restaurant, its harbour-facing side has a broad walkway with a statue of the ubiquitous Able Seaman Just Nuisance. A couple of sets of stairs lead down to the **Marina**, a modest development of shops and a couple of good restaurants set right on the waterfront.

Long and Seaforth beaches

Nearest to the station, **Long Beach** offers no shade and is therefore little used. However, on windless days it can be pleasant for long walks, with views of the Hottentots Holland Mountains, and its tidal pool is safe for bathing. Access is by a number of gaps in a brick wall alongside the main road and about mid-way along the beach (opposite Hopkirk Way), by a flight of steps. There are changing rooms (free) and toilets nearby, and fresh water.

One of the best beaches for swimming is at **Seaforth**, where clear, deep waters lap around rocks. It's calm, protected and safe, but not pretty (bounded on one side by the looming grey mass of the naval base), but there's plenty of lawn shaded by palm trees.

Boulders

Two kilometres from the station towards Cape Point lies **Boulders**, the most popular local beach, which offers a number of places to stay. The area takes its name from the huge rounded rocks that create a cluster of little coves with sandy beaches and clear sea pools. However, the main reason people come to Boulders is for the **African penguins** (formerly known as jackass penguins), in the **Boulders section of the Cape Peninsula National Park** (open 24hr; R10 entry fee 8am–5pm), a fenced reserve on Boulders Beach. Passing sailors used to prey on the quirky birds and their eggs, and more recently they have fallen victim to vandals, and some locals who consider them pests; they're now protected by a guard. African penguins usually live on islands off the west side of the South African coast, the Boulders birds forming one of only two mainland colonies in the world. This is also the only place where the endangered species are actually increasing in numbers, and provides a rare opportunity to get a close look at them. To get there, take a Rikki's taxi from Simon's Town station.

Miller's Point and Smitswinkelbaai

Almost 5km to the south is the popular **Miller's Point** resort, which has a number of small sandy beaches and a tidal pool protected from the southeaster. A **campsite** at the caravan park offers great sea views. Along Main Road, the notable *Black Marlin* seafood **restaurant** attracts busloads of tourists, while the boulders around the point attract rock agama and black zonure lizards and dassies.

The last place before you get to the Cape of Good Hope Nature Reserve is **Smitswinkelbaai** (pronounced: smits-vin-cull-buy); this little cove has a small beach safe for swimming, but feels the full blast of the southeaster. It's not accessible by car, as local property-owners fiercely guard their privacy. To get there, you must park next to the road and walk down a seemingly endless succession of stairs.

Cape of Good Hope Nature Reserve

Most people come to **Cape of Good Hope Nature Reserve** (daily: April–Sept 7am–5pm; Oct–March 6am–6pm; R25; ☎021 780 9100) to see the southernmost tip of Africa and the place where the Indian and Atlantic oceans meet at **Cape Point**. In fact, it's the site of neither, but is nevertheless an awesomely dramatic spot, which should on no account be missed. The reserve sits atop massive sea cliffs with huge views, strong seas, and an even wilder wind,

Fynbos

Early Dutch settlers were alarmed by the lack of good timber on the Cape Peninsula's hillsides, which were covered by nondescript, scrubby bush they described as *fijn bosch* (literally "fine bush") and which is now known by its Afrikaans name **fynbos** (pronounced "fayn-bos"). The settlers planted exotics, like the oaks that now shade central Cape Town, and over the ensuing centuries their descendants established pine forests on the sides of Table Mountain in an effort to create a landscape that fulfilled their European idea of the picturesque. It's only relatively recently that Capetonians have come to proudly claim fynbos as part of the Peninsula's cultural heritage.

Fynbos is remarkable for its astonishing variety of plants, making up eighty percent of the vegetation of the **Cape Floral Kingdom**, the smallest and richest of the floral kingdoms; its 8500 species make it one of the world's biodiversity hot spots. Only the South American rainforests come anywhere near matching its concentration of diversity.

The Cape Peninsula alone, measuring less than 500 square kilometres, has 2256 plant species (nearly twice as many as Britain, which is 5000 times bigger). While the other five floral kingdoms cover vast areas such as Australia or the northern hemisphere, the entire Cape kingdom stretches across a relatively narrow coastal crescent from Niewoudville in the west, through Cape Town and across to Grahamstown in the east.

The four basic types of fynbos are: **proteas** (South Africa's national flower, sold in bouquets at the airport); **ericas**, amounting to 600 species of heather (against 26 in the rest of the world); **restios** or reeds; and **geophytes**, including ground orchids and the startling flaming red disas, which can be seen in flower on Table Mountain in late summer.

which whips off caps and sunglasses as visitors gaze southwards from the old lighthouse buttress. The continent's real tip is at **Cape Agulhas**, some 300km southeast of here, but Cape Point is a lot easier to get to than Agulhas and a lot more exciting.

There's no public transport to the reserve, although you can rent a Simon's Town **Rikki's** (℡021 786 2136) there and back. To get there **by car**, take the M3 to Muizenberg, continuing on the M4 via Simon's Town to the reserve gates, where you'll be given a good **map** that marks the main driving and walking routes, as well as the tidal pools and other facilities.

From the car park, the famous viewpoint is a short, steep walk, crawling with tourists, up to the original lighthouse. A **funicular** runs the less energetic to the top, where there's a curio shop. There's also a functional **restaurant** at the car park, which has outdoor seating (but it's usually too windy to be pleasant) and huge picture windows taking in the drop to the sea below. Most people come to the Point as part of a round-trip, returning via Kommetjie and the especially scenic Chapman's Peak Drive. Numerous **tours** spend a day stopping off at the Peninsula highlights; Day Trippers (℡021 531 3274) runs fun tours for R265 (including a picnic lunch), some of which give you the option of cycling part of the way. For general tours that take in the reserve see p.88.

Cape Point and around

Cape Point is the treacherous promontory of rocks, winds and swells braved by navigators since the Portuguese in the fifteenth century first "rounded the Cape." Plenty of wrecks lie submerged off its coast, and at **Olifantsbos** on the

Cape wildlife

Along with indigenous plants and flowers, you may well spot some of the **animals** living in the Cape of Good Hope Nature Reserve fynbos habitat. **Baboons** lope along the rocky shoreline and can be a menace; keep your car windows closed, it's not unknown for them to invade vehicles, and they're adept at slyly swiping picnics. There are also **bontebok**, **eland** and **red hartebeest**, as well as **Cape rhebok** and **grysbok** grazing on the heathery slopes. If you're very lucky, you may even see some of the extremely rare **Cape mountain zebras**.

Ostriches stride through the low fynbos, and occasionally **African penguins** come ashore. A distinctive bird on the rocky shores is the **black oystercatcher** with a bright red beak, jabbing limpets off the rocks. You'll also see **Cape cormorants** in large flocks on the beach or rocks, often drying their outstretched wings. Running up and down the water's edge are **white-fronted plovers** and **sanderlings**, probing for food left by the receding waves. Finally, as on any other beach walk in the Cape, you'll see piles of shiny brown **ecklonia kelp** on the beach or floating in dark beds in the wave-swells.

west side you can walk to two wrecks: one a US ship sunk in 1942, and the other a South African coaster which ran aground in 1965. The **Old Lighthouse**, built in 1860, was too often dangerously shrouded in cloud, and failed to keep ships off the rocks, so another was built lower down in 1914, not always successful in averting disasters, but still the most powerful light beaming onto the sea from South Africa.

From the Cape Point car park, the famous viewpoint is a steep walk, crawling with tourists, up to the old lighthouse. Alternatively, a **funicular** (R24 return) runs to the top, where there's a curio shop. The rather good *Two Oceans* restaurant at the car park has outdoor seating and huge picture windows taking in the drop to the sea below.

The sea and mountain scenery in the reserve are reason enough to travel the 66km from central Cape Town. Most visitors make a beeline for Cape Point, seeing the rest of the reserve through a vehicle window, but walking is the best way to appreciate indigenous **Cape flora**. At first glance the landscape appears rocky and bleak, with short, wind-cropped plants, but the vegetation is surprisingly rich – there are as many plant varieties in this small reserve as in the whole of Britain. Amazingly, many bright blooms in Britain and the US, such as geraniums, freesias, gladioli, daisies, lilies and irises, are hybrids grown from indigenous Cape plants.

Swimming and walking

There are several waymarked **walks** in the Cape of Good Hope Nature Reserve. If you're planning a big hike it's best to set out early, as shade is rare and the wind can be foul, especially during summer, often increasing in intensity as the day goes on. One of the most straightforward **hiking routes** is the signposted forty-minute trek from the car park at **Cape Point** to the more westerly **Cape of Good Hope**. For exploring the shoreline, a clear path runs down the Atlantic side from Hoek van Bobbejaan. A convenient place to join it is at **Gifkommetjie**, which is signposted off Cape Point Road. From the car park, several sandy tracks drop quite steeply down the slope across rocks, and through bushes and milkwood trees to the shore, along which you can walk in either direction. Alternatively, take a copy of the Government Printer's 1:50,000 map 3318 C.D. *Cape Town* for some more intrepid exploration. Take water on any walk in the reserve, as there are no reliable fresh sources.

You'll find the **beaches** along signposted sideroads branching out from Cape Point Road, the main route through the reserve, going from the entrance gate to the car park at Cape Point. The sea is too dangerous for swimming, but there are safe tidal pools at the adjacent **Buffels Bay** and **Bordjiesrif**, midway along the east shore. Both have braai stands, but more southerly Buffels Bay is the nicer, with big lawned areas and some sheltered spots to have a picnic.

Table Bay and the northern suburbs

The **northern suburbs**, middle-class and Afrikaner-dominated, curl around the edge of Table Bay, north from Duncan Dock, and east along the N2 freeway. Few tourists see more of this area than the strip along the coast from Milnerton to Blouberg, and with good reason: the main attraction here is the much-snapped view of Table Mountain across the bay, otherwise the northern suburbs are an unappetizing sprawl of starter homes and new developments (this is one of the few areas of Cape Town where there's room for expansion).

Nevertheless, the long sandy beaches are ideal for a sunset walk, when you can watch the glowing orb slip into the sea close to **Robben Island** (see p.122). The sea is cold, and often windy, but windsurfers and kite-fliers do well here. **Big Bay** (Grootbaai), close to the principal resort of **Bloubergstrand** (usually shortened to Blouberg and pronounced "blow-berg-strunt"), draws windsurfing enthusiasts from all over the world for annual competitions.

By car, take the N1 from the city centre and the Milnerton/Paarden Island exit to get onto Marina Drive which follows the coast to Milnerton, Tableview, Blouberg, Melkbosstrand, Koeberg nuclear power station and right on up the west coast to the Namibian border.

Milnerton to Melkbosstrand

The beachfront strip at **Milnerton**, closest to central Cape Town, is a banal, neon-lit fast-food haven, offering little reason to stop off, unless you're one of the surfing devotees who brave the water for the break off the lighthouse, undeterred by the debris floating across from the docks.

To the west is **Table View**, noted for its easy access to the beach, beachside parking and its classic view of Table Mountain. Nearby **Bloubergstrand**, 25km from the city, is the only place to draw you out to Table Bay. Once a fishing village, this is a good place to walk and take in the views, and you can sample one of Blouberg's outdoor restaurants for meals or tea.

By the time you get to **Melkbosstrand** and find yourself driving through dry, low scrub, you will feel well and truly out of Cape Town. Melkbos, 30km from Cape Town, has a caravan park and one or two places to stay, but few people choose to, perhaps because the settlement is so close to Koeberg, the country's only **nuclear power station**, which generates electricity for the Western Cape. It's said that the sea around Melkbos is a few degrees warmer than elsewhere around here, heated by the water used to cool the reactor. The radioactive waste itself is currently deposited 600km to the north at Vaalputs, but the national power company, Eskom, is negotiating to store spent fuel on site.

The Cape Flats and the African townships

East of the northern and southern suburbs, among the industrial smokestacks and the windswept Cape Flats, reaching well beyond the airport, is Cape Town's largest residential block, taking in the **coloured districts**, **African townships** and shantytown **squatter camps**, which are only visited on packaged township tours.

The **Cape Flats** are exactly that: flat, as well as being barren and windswept, stretching east from the former whites-only southern suburbs, with the M5 acting as a dividing line. Exclusively inhabited by Africans and coloureds in separate areas, the Flats can be both shocking and heartening, their abject poverty coexisting with a spirit of enterprise and stoicism.

The African townships were set up as dormitories to provide labour for white Cape Town, not as places to build a life, which is why they had no facilities and no real hub. The **men-only hostels**, another apartheid relic, are at the root of many of the area's social problems. During the 1950s, the government set out a blueprint to turn the tide of Africans flooding into Cape Town. No African was permitted to settle permanently in the Cape west of a line near the Fish River, the old frontier over 1000km from Cape Town; women were entirely banned from seeking work in Cape Town and men prohibited from bringing their wives to join them. By 1970 there were ten men for every woman in Langa.

In the end, apartheid failed to prevent the influx of work-seekers desperate to come to Cape Town. Where people couldn't find legal accommodation they set up the **squatter camps** of makeshift iron, cardboard and plastic sheeting. During the 1970s and 1980s, the government attempted to demolish these and destroy anything left inside – but no sooner had the police left than the camps reappeared, and they are now a permanent feature of the Cape Flats. One of the best known of all South Africa's squatter camps is **Crossroads**, whose inhabitants suffered campaigns of harassment that included killings by apartheid collaborators and police, and continuous attempts to bulldoze it out of existence. Through sheer determination and desperation its residents hung on, eventually winning the right to stay. Today, the government is making attempts to improve conditions in the shantytowns by introducing running water and sanitation; families and ad hoc traders are now moving in.

Tours and township stays

Several projects are underway to encourage tourists into the townships but, as a high proportion of Cape Town's nearly 2000 annual murders take place here, the recommended way to visit is on one of the **tours** listed on pp.88–89. All the tours recommended are operated by residents of the Cape Flats or in co-operation with local communities, and emphasize face-to-face encounters with ordinary people. They include visits to *shebeens*, nightclubs and a township restaurant, chats to residents of squatter camps and the Langa hostels, and meetings with traditional healers and music makers, township artists and craftworkers. Some tours also take in "sites of political struggle", where significant events in the fight against apartheid occurred. If you want to really get under the skin of the townships, there's no better way than staying with a family in one of the **township B&Bs** recommended on p.104.

Langa and Mitchell's Plain

Langa is the oldest and most central township, lying just east of the white suburb of Pinelands and north of the N2. In this relentlessly grey place, without the tiniest patch of green relief, you'll find women selling sheep and goats' heads, alongside state-of-the-art public phone bureaus run by enterprising township businessmen from inside recycled cargo containers. Nuclear families live in smart suburban houses while, not far away, there are former men-only hostels where as many as three families share one room.

South of the African ghettos is **Mitchell's Plain**, a coloured area stretching down to the False Bay coast, which you'll skirt if you take the M5 to Muizenberg. More salubrious than any of the African townships, Mitchell's Plain reflects how under apartheid lighter skins meant better conditions, even if you weren't quite white. But for coloureds the forced removals were no less tragic, many being summarily forced to vacate family homes because their suburb had been declared a White Group Area. Many families were relocated here when District Six was razed (see p.109), and their communities never fully recovered – one of the symptoms of dislocation are the violent gangs, which have become an everyday part of Mitchell's Plain youth culture.

Eating and drinking

Cape Town has fabulous food. There are a large number of relaxed and convivial restaurants, which generally serve imaginative and healthy food of a high standard. The range of styles is broad, with international cuisine readily available. The devalued South African rand means that many foreign visitors can eat in upmarket restaurants with outstanding chefs creating innovative food for the kind of money they'd spend on a pizza back home. This is the city to splash out on whatever takes your fancy, and you'll find the quality of meat and fish very high, with many vegetarian options.

While there is a local Cape cuisine, it's not the thing to concentrate on when you're choosing somewhere to eat. Some elements of Cape and African cuisine find their way onto fusion style menus at upmarket restaurants. If you are curious, there are a couple of restaurants dedicated to Cape cuisine, which is a spicy hybrid of the cooking styles brought to South Africa and adapted by slaves, principally from Asia and Madagascar. Mild and semi-sweet curries with a strong Indonesian influence predominate, and include: *bredie* (stew), of which *waterblommetjiebredie*, made using water hyacinths, is a speciality; *bobotie*, a spicy minced dish served under a savoury custard; and *sosaties*, a local version of kebab using mincemeat. For dessert, dates stuffed with almonds make a light and delicious end to a meal, while *malva* pudding is a rich combination of milk, sugar, cream and apricot jam.

As far as **seafood** goes, you can expect fresh fish at every good restaurant. Cape Town itself offers cold-water fish such as kingklip, hake and snoek. The cold waters up the West Coast yield quantities of crayfish and mussels, while fresh fish, oysters and prawns are flown in from warmer waters, including Mozambique. **Cape wines** are the obvious accompaniment to your meals, particularly when sampled under the gaze of Table Mountain.

As far as **prices** go, expect to pay under R40 for a main course at an inexpensive restaurant, up to R60 at a moderately priced one, and more than this at an expensive place.

City centre

Cape Town's city centre has recently enjoyed a renaissance, and its **restaurants** are being joined by plenty of continental-style **cafés**. Service tends to be efficient and friendly, and most cafés stay open till around 11pm.

Around Long Street and the Company's Gardens

The places listed below are shown on the map on p.92.

Africa Café 108 Shortmarket St, Heritage Square ☎021 422 0221. Probably the best restaurant in Cape Town for African cuisine, with a fantastic selection from around the continent. Given that you're served a communal feast of sixteen dishes and can have as many extra helpings as you like, its R105 per head price tag is pretty reasonable. Booking essential. Dinner Mon–Sat. Inexpensive–moderate.

Bukhara 33 Church St ☎021 424 0000. A popular upmarket North Indian restaurant, with green marble floors and a show kitchen where you can watch chefs at work. The food is superb, but not cheap. Booking is essential to get into one of the two sittings in the evening. Mon–Sat lunch and dinner, Sunday dinner. Moderate–expensive.

Caravan Café 167 Long St ☎021 426 4671. Small, inexpensive starters followed by huge dishes of cous cous and main courses such as fish in ginger and orange sauce and lamb tagine; there's also a hookah to smoke. Lunch and dinner Mon–Sat. Moderate.

Five Flies 14–16 Keerom St ☎021 424 4442. Wonderfully imaginative food, with a sophisticated blend of world cuisine which really works. The presentation delights, the ambience is elegant, but not formal. You won't find better in Cape Town. Mon–Fri lunch and dinner, Sat & Sun dinner. Moderate–expensive.

Floris Smit Huijs 55 Church St ☎021 423 3414. The beautiful decor in this eighteenth-century town house is as big an attraction as the eclectic international cuisine, which also features local specialities such as Malay chicken salad, and kudu venison served with a delicious apple sauce. Daily until 10.30pm, closed Sun all day, and Mon lunch. Moderate.

Gallery Café South African National Gallery, Government Avenue. Breakfast, lunch and tea with a small but good menu that includes pasta, salads and sandwiches in a pleasant space inside the gallery. Tues–Sun 10am–5pm. Inexpensive.

Long Life Noodle Bar 192 Long St ☎021 426 5805. A canteen-style eating place with long benches, offering a vast variety of tasty noodle dishes, from Thai-style broth to Japanese miso. Dinner Mon–Sat. Inexpensive to moderate.

Long Street Café 259 Long St. Cool bar/deli/restaurant in the city centre's most happening street, with tasteful open-plan decor and fresh continental-style food. Also good if you just want a drink. Mon–Sat 9.30am–midnight, Sun 6–11pm. Inexpensive.

Mama Africa 178 Long St ☎021 424 8634. Food from around the continent, including local Cape specialities and succulent Karoo lamb, served in a relaxed atmosphere. The highlight is a twelve-metre bar in the form of a sinuous green mamba. Dinner Mon–Sat. Moderate.

Mexican Kitchen Café 13 Bloem St ☎021 423 1541. An excellent casual restaurant serving good-value burritos, enchiladas, nachos and calamari fajitas, with some fine vegetarian options and deli-style takeaways. Daily until midnight. Inexpensive.

Mr Pickwick's 158 Long St. Hearty and cheap "tin-plate" meals, including a challenging range of hot and cold "foot-long" sandwiches. Mon & Tues 8am–2pm, Wed–Sat 8am–4pm. Inexpensive.

Sunflower Health Café 111 Long St. A vegetarian restaurant attached to a health food shop. The menu includes two hot meals each day, of the lentil bake or vegetable lasagne variety, as well as salads and tasty cold food. Mon–Fri 9.45am–5.30pm, Sat 9am–2pm. Inexpensive.

Yellow Pepper 138 Long St. A good lunch spot near town centre, featuring big plate-glass windows looking out at bustling Long Street, and decent pasta bakes. Mon–Sat 8.30am–5pm, plus dinner Fri & Sat. Inexpensive–moderate.

Periphery and the Foreshore

The places listed below are shown on the map on p.94.

Biesmiellah On the corner of Upper Wales and Pentz streets ☎021 423 0850. One of the oldest and best-known restaurants for traditional Cape cuisine; especially recommended are the spicy stews and wickedly rich *malva* pudding made with apricot jam and cream. No alcohol. Daily, except Sundays noon–3pm & 6–11pm. Moderate.

Col'Cacchio Seeff House, 42 Hans Strijdom Ave. An offbeat pizza restaurant, which also serves pasta, salads and often spills onto the pavement outside. Has over forty different and original pizza toppings, such as smoked salmon, sour cream and caviar, and bills itself as low fat and heart-friendly. No bookings. Lunch Mon–Fri, dinner daily. Inexpensive.

Jewel Tavern Off Vanguard Road, Duncan Docks ☎ 021 448 1977. An unpretentious Taiwanese sailors' eating house, now "discovered" by Cape Town's *bon viveurs*. Located in the middle of the docks, it serves superb food, including great hot and sour soup and spring rolls made while you watch. Daily mid-morning till 10pm. Moderate.

V&A Waterfront and De Waterkant

The **V&A Waterfront** offers a lot if you want to eat well and your budget is fairly generous, while **De Waterkant** offers some nice places in a gentrified historic quarter that has a more rooted urban character than the Waterfront. The places listed below are shown on the map on p.96.

V&A Waterfront

Bayfront Blu Two Oceans Aquarium ☎ 021 419 9068. All-day breakfasts and fine coffee in an unbeatable location attached to the aquarium, with seating on a quayside deck that gives views of boats cutting across the water and clouds drifting over Table Mountain. More substantial meals include traditional African food as well as Californian dishes, a good vegetarian selection and some exciting seafood options such as Swahili prawn curry. Daily 9am–11.30pm. Moderate–expensive.

Caffé Balducci Quay 6, V&A Waterfront ☎ 021 421 6002. An upmarket coffeeshop/restaurant with lovely views, offering interesting Californian/Italian food with South African overtones; the steak roll in peri-peri sauce is recommended. Daily 9am until midnight. Inexpensive.

Caffé San Marco Piazza level, Victoria Wharf, V&A Waterfront ☎ 021 418 5434. A coffee shop/bar with umbrellas on the piazza, serving an all-day breakfast menu, good sandwiches on Italian breads, grilled vegetable and fresh salads, hot food and delicious grilled calamari with garlic and chilli. They also offer 18 flavours of gelato and sorbet. Daily 9am–midnight. Inexpensive.

Emily's Bistro Shop 202, Clock Tower Centre, V&A Waterfront ☎ 021 421 1133. One of the Western Cape's finest restaurants (a cooking school is also based here), with flamboyant and chic South African creations and updated traditional Afrikaans dishes. Every table has a view of the water. Lunch daily. Mon–Sat dinner. Moderate–expensive.

Mugg & Bean Ground level, Victoria Wharf. A range of excellent coffees, and light meals including toasted sandwiches and salads; unfortunately, the location inside a shopping mall doesn't make the most of the Waterfront setting. Daily 9am–midnight. Inexpensive.

Tasca de Belem Shop 154, Piazza level, Victoria Wharf, Waterfront ☎ 021 419 3009. Portuguese specialities with funky outdoor seating in summer. The flame-grilled chicken is good, as are the peri-peri chicken livers. Daily 12.30–2.30pm & 6.30–10.30pm. Moderate.

Willoughby & Co Lower level, Victoria Wharf ☎ 021 418 6115. Excellent sushi created by master sushi makers. Buy fresh seafood in the deli section if you're cooking for yourself, or go for their Namibian oysters, crayfish or seafood platters. Daily lunch and dinner (sushi bar closed 3pm–6pm). Moderate.

Zerban's Victoria Wharf. The Waterfront incarnation of a Cape Town institution, previously known for its European-style cakes, bread and coffee, but now successfully branching out into breakfasts as well as brunch and lunch. Daily 8am–11pm. Inexpensive.

De Waterkant

Anatoli 24 Napier St ☎ 021 419 2501. A Turkish restaurant in a turn-of-the-century warehouse buzzing with atmosphere. Excellent *meze* include exceptionally delicious *dolmades*, and there are superb deserts such as pressed dates topped with cream. Tues–Sun until 11pm. Moderate.

Vasco da Gama Tavern 3 Alfred St ☎ 021 425 2157. Known locally as the "Portuguese embassy", this unpretentious restaurant with a blaring TV is a genuine working man's pub. Grilled tongue with bread, accompanied by wine mixed with Coke – a Portuguese "speciality" called *catemba* – are standard. It's also a great seafood restaurant at half the usual price, and better than many of the upmarket joints. Daily 10.45am–7.30pm. Inexpensive.

Mouille Point to Sea Point

The places listed below are shown on the map on p.98.

Mouille Point and Green Point

Chariots Italian Coffee Bar 107 Main Rd, Green Point. Stylish decor and great inexpensive food make this a fashionable haunt for Cape Town's yuppies; come for *foccaccia* and decent coffee. Mon–Sat until 11pm, Sun until 5pm. Inexpensive.

Giovanni's Deliworld 103 Main Rd, Green Point. With some indoor as well as pavement seating, this friendly Italian deli/coffee shop is handy for coffee, excellent made-to-order sandwiches, Italian food, take-out salads and dips, and pre-cooked hot meals. Daily 8am–9pm. Inexpensive–moderate.

Newport Market and Deli 47 Beach Rd, Mouille Point. A light, airy deli with views onto Table Bay, offering coffee, excellent sandwiches, salads and some hot dishes. Daily 7pm till late. Inexpensive.

Theo's Grill Butcher and Seafood Beach Road, Mouille Point. Upmarket, and right on the beachfront, *Theo's* offers superb Greek-style steaks and seafood. Lunch Mon–Fri, dinner Mon–Sat. Moderate.

Wang Thai 105 Main Rd, Green Point ☎ 021 439 6164. Cape Town's best Thai restaurant, serving hot and spicy prawn soup, Hanoi beef salad, steamed fish with lemon juice and chilli, or their special of thinly sliced, seared sirloin. Lunch daily except Sat. Dinner daily. Moderate.

Zeroninethreetwo 79 Main Rd, Exhibition Building, Green Point ☎ 021 439 6306. Belgian cuisine and beer, with mussels, excellent thin chips, prawns and salads in funky minimalist surroundings. Daily 11am till late. Moderate.

Sea Point

Aris Souvlaki 83a Regent Rd, Sea Point ☎ 021 439 6683. A reliable terrace restaurant for Greek *shwarma* and *souvlaki,* also takeaways. Daily until 11pm. Inexpensive.

New York Bagels 51 Regent Rd, Sea Point. A fantastic supermarket of a deli, with a sit-down section. Choose from a dizzying array of bagels and homemade fillings, from chopped liver to herring, plus stir-fry, pasta and pastries. Daily till late. Inexpensive.

Pizzeria Napoletana 178 Main Rd, Sea Point. A family business since 1956, this is the best pizza joint in Cape Town, and good value too. Try the veal parmigiano, or their crayfish. Closed Mon. Moderate.

San Marco 92 Main Rd, Sea Point ☎ 021 439 2758. Stunning Italian seafood as well as pasta; the grilled calamari tossed in chilli and garlic is wonderful, and their antipasto trolley is especially recommended for vegetarians. Lunch Sun, dinner daily except Tues. Moderate–expensive.

City Bowl suburbs

The places listed below are shown on the map on p.100.

Amigos Mediterranean Restaurant 158 Kloof St, Gardens ☎ 021 423 6805. A tasty mixture of Greek *meze* combined with Italian and Spanish food. This is a lively joint, with some tables outside and a loyal clientele. Lunch and dinner daily until midnight. Moderate.

The Blue Plate Restaurant and Bar 35 Kloof St, Gardens ☎ 021 424 1515. A spacious restaurant in an elegant Victorian home, with global cuisine, friendly and well-informed waiters and some outdoor seating along the sidewalk. Dinner daily till late, lunch Fri only. Moderate.

Buccaneer Steakhouse 64 Orange St, Gardens ☎ 021 424 4966. Swiss-owned eating place that does good steaks and great sauces. The atmosphere borders on dowdy, but it makes for a relaxed and low-cost evening. Dinner daily, lunch Mon–Fri. Inexpensive.

Café Paradiso 110 Kloof St, Gardens ☎ 021 423 8653. Good Greek and Mediterranean dishes, including a weigh-your-plate *meze* bar and outside

terrace with views up to the mountain and down over the city and docks. Daily lunch & dinner. Moderate.

Chef Pon's Asian Kitchen 12 Mill St, Gardens, next to the *Holiday Inn* ☎ 021 465 5846. A popular and noisy neighbourhood restaurant serving Thai, Vietnamese, Japanese and Chinese food. Lunch and dinner daily, except Sundays. Moderate.

Happy Wok 62a Kloof St, Gardens. An informal café-style eating place, serving a reliable range of dishes from China, Japan and Vietnam, plus self-service jasmine tea. Try their glass or Singapore noodles and peppered stir-fried beef. Daily 5.30pm–late, Mon–Fri noon–2.30pm. Inexpensive.

Melissa's 94 Kloof St, Gardens. In the food emporium you can buy freshly made Mediterranean fare, while the small café serves light meals and fine desserts. Weekdays 7.30am–9pm. Weekends 8am–9pm. Inexpensive.

Ocean Basket Southern Africa 75 Kloof St, Gardens ☎ 021 422 0322. Long queues and delicious aromas speak eloquently of the outstanding dishes – from fish'n'chips to prawns and calamari – at this slick quick-in, quick-out seafood chain. Lunch Mon–Sat & dinner every evening. Moderate.

Raith Gourmet Gardens Centre, Mill Street, Gardens. Meat-centred deli with an exceptional selection of foods; try one of their marvellous

sandwiches at the tables dotted between enticing comestibles. German specialities include sauerkraut fried with strips of bacon. Mon–Fri 8.30am until 6pm, Sat until 1pm. Moderate.

Yindees 22 Camp St, Tamboerskloof ☎021 422 1012. A popular Thai restaurant; try their brilliant spicy prawn soup served by dour waiters. Lunch and dinner Mon–Sat. Moderate.

Southern suburbs

Observatory, Wynberg and Newlands

Café Carte Blanche 42a Trill Rd, Observatory. A former curio shop decorated with Eastern artefacts, where you can sip wine under a hanging Persian carpet or quaff beer on a Mongolian bedspread. Small, unique and exotic. Inexpensive.

Enrica Rocca 19 Wolfe St, Wynberg ☎021 762 3855. An authentic Italian restaurant, with a vast antipasto spread followed by a limited range of interesting pasta dishes. The fixed-price set menu options are a good deal if you want the full works: antipasto, pasta, main dish and dessert. Mon–Sat lunch & dinner. Moderate–expensive.

Gardener's Cottage 31 Newlands Ave, Montebello Estate, Newlands. Set in a complex of old farm buildings under ancient pine trees, and serving hearty breakfasts and lunches as well as tea and coffee. Worthwhile if you want to browse through the neighbouring arts and crafts workshops. Tues–Fri 8am–4.30pm, Sat & Sun 8.30am–4.30pm. Inexpensive.

Obz Café 115 Lower Main Rd, Observatory. A trendy deli/café/bar, where you can get tasty deli meals, bacon-and-egg breakfasts and Danish pastries, or drink all evening. Daily all day till late. Inexpensive.

Pancho's Mexican Kitchen 127 Lower Main Rd, Observatory ☎021 447 4854. A highly popular

cantina-style restaurant serving Mexican dishes. Daily until late. Inexpensive.

Constantia

Buitenverwachting Buitenverwachting Estate, Klein Constantia Road ☎021 794 3522. One of South Africa's top restaurants, wonderfully located on the Buitenverwachting wine estate with views of the vineyards and mountains from the terrace. The food is imaginative, fusing international and Cape flavours, but can be uneven. Tues–Fri lunch & dinner, Sat lunch. Expensive.

Jonkershuis Groot Constantia Wine Estate, off Ladies Mile Extension, Constantia. A rustic informal place, where you can enjoy traditional Cape dishes or tea, surrounded by vineyards and mountains. A children's playground adjacent to outdoor seating makes this congenial and easygoing for a family outing. Breakfast, tea & lunch daily, dinner Tues–Sat. Inexpensive–moderate.

La Colombe Constantia Uitsig Wine Estate, Spaanschemat River Road, Constantia ☎021 794 2390. Airy restaurant, rated one of South Africa's best, overlooking a swimming pool and beautiful gardens. An imaginative Provençale menu dreamed up by the French chef varies from day to day, depending on what's in season. Book way in advance. Lunch & dinner; closed Sun dinner & all day Tues. Expensive.

Atlantic seaboard

Fish on the Rocks Beyond Mariner's Wharf, Hout Bay, drive through the dock and factory. Delicious fresh fish'n'chips, served under red umbrellas or eaten on the rocks overlooking the bay. In season it's also a fabulous place to watch whales. Daily 9am–7pm. Inexpensive.

La Cuccina Food Store Victoria Mall, Victoria Road, Hout Bay. Open for breakfast and lunch buffets with tea and cake in between. High-quality deli food in pleasant surrounds, though no views. Daily 8am–7pm. Inexpensive–moderate.

Mariners Wharf Bistro The Harbour, Hout Bay. A relaxed, well-run place with terrace seating overlooking the harbour. Good for seafood to eat in or

take away. Daily 10am–6pm. Inexpensive.

Primi Piatti 9 Victoria Rd, Camps Bay ☎021 438 3120. Pizza, pasta and salads in a noisy, busy restaurant on the bay. Daily lunch and dinner. Moderate.

Red Herring Beach Road/Pine Road, Noordhoek. Snacks and drinks on the upstairs deck, which offers marvellous sea and mountain views, attached to a country restaurant that does grilled meats that include springbok and kudu, plus a good choice of vegetarian options or fresh fish. Tues–Sun lunch & dinner. Moderate.

Theo's Grill Butcher and Seafood Promenade Building, Victoria Road, Camps Bay ☎021 438

3120. Brilliant steaks sold by weight, also seafood; the atmosphere is buzzy, and there's some outdoor seating. Daily lunch and dinner. Moderate.

Vilamoura 9 The Broadway, Victoria Road, Camps Bay ℡021 438 1850. Cape Town's best seafood restaurant doesn't come cheap, but makes a fine choice for a special occasion. Slick and modern, it has fantastic views, superb service and includes traditional Portuguese dishes like salt cod soup and Lourenço Marques chicken on the menu. Daily noon until after midnight. Expensive.

False Bay seaboard

Muizenberg and Kalk Bay

Artvark Gallery and Café Main Road, Kalk Bay. A relaxed café with sea views and upstairs seating, dominated by an old palm tree. Daily 9am–5pm. Inexpensive.

Brass Bell In Kalk Bay station building, Main Road, Kalk Bay. Primarily an unpretentious drinking spot, *Brass Bell* has arguably the best location on the Peninsula, with False Bay's waves breaking against the wall of its outdoor terrace. The views of both the Peninsula mountains and the Hottentots Holland peaks are unbeatable, but the seafood meals don't always match the magnificent setting. Daily until late. Moderate.

Gaylords Indian Cuisine 65 Main Rd, Muizenberg ℡021 788 5470. The tacky interior belies an imaginative menu, adapting great North Indian cooking and local ingredients to create something unique and reasonably priced; expect to wait for your food though. Dinner & lunch Wed–Sun, dinner only Mon. Inexpensive–moderate.

Harbour House Restaurant Kalk Bay Harbour ℡021 788 4133. Freshly caught seafood and Mediterranean fare, at a venue situated spectacularly on the breakwater of Kalk Bay Harbour; book a table with bay views. The winter specials are great value, and there's a fire inside. Lunch & dinner daily. Moderate–expensive.

Kalky's Kalk Bay Harbour. The best traditional fish and chips on the Peninsula, and also great-value seafood platters; fish is hauled off the boats and straight into the frying pan. This totally unpretentious harbourside eating place has been serving the fishing community for years; you sit at benches, or take away. Daily. Inexpensive.

The Olympia Café & Deli Main Road, Kalk Bay. One of the few places that draws parochial uptown Capetonians down the False Bay seaboard. Always buzzing, *Olympia* offers views of Kalk Bay harbour, and has become a regular village meeting spot for residents of Kalk Bay and St James. Great coffee or freshly squeezed orange juice can be accompanied by freshly baked Danish pastries, filled croissants or delicious homemade biscuits for breakfast, while imaginative gourmet lunch menus are chalked up on a board, with local fish always included. Tues–Sat 7am–7pm, Sun 7am–3pm. Inexpensive.

VegiTable 138 Main Rd, Kalk Bay. A spacious, friendly vegetarian café overlooking the harbour. There's also some groceries for sale, and live music some weekend evenings. Daily 8am–6pm. Thurs, Fri & Sat until 9pm. Inexpensive.

Simon's Town and around

Black Marlin Main Road, Miller's Point ℡021 786 1621. Recommeded for seafood, particularly the crayfish and fish kebabs. Lunch & dinner daily; closed Sun evening. Moderate.

The Meeting Place 98 St George's St, Simon's Town ℡021 786 1986. Chill out on the upstairs balcony on Simon's Town's main drag, and enjoy funky Mediterranean café food while viewing the harbour. Mon–Wed & Sun 9am–5pm, Thurs–Sat 9am–9pm. Inexpensive.

Nightlife and entertainment

Cape Town's **nightlife** has traditionally been a little sleepy compared with Johannesburg's, but this is changing. Things have become much more open and cosmopolitan in recent years, spiced up by thousands of African and European visitors and immigrants. A general loosening up of the city's staid personality has made Cape Town a diverse and exciting place to go out in.

Pubs and clubs

The city is passionate about music. Mainstream house is very popular, but there are also strong followings for drum'n'bass, trance, hip-hop, dub and Latin grooves, as well as **kwaito** (see p.897), the dance style of young black Jo'burg. Much more laid-back than European club sounds, *kwaito* can be described as slowed-down, bass-heavy house fused with township pop. Sexy and jubilant, it makes for a positive and uproarious party. Though *kwaito* is still predominately a black scene, coloured and white youth are gradually getting into it.

Many dance **clubs** have a short lifespan – and many of the best regular parties hop from venue to venue. Some of the more enduring clubs are listed below, but watch the press for up-to-the-minute information. The daily newspapers the *Cape Argus* and *Cape Times* run weekly club columns on Thursdays and Fridays respectively, and the monthly listings magazine *Cape Review* is also useful. Backpacker hostels are often the most up-to-date sources of party information – keep your ears open, as often the best parties get little promotion. Cover charges vary from R20 to over R100 for big events with international DJs. It's worth remembering that all drugs are illegal in South Africa, and aggressive police raids on clubs are by no means unknown.

Cape Town is well populated with **bars**, ranging from the hip to the eccentric to the seedy. Most liquor licences stipulate that the last round is served at 2am, but this is far from strictly followed. Expect a cover charge if live music is featured. Traditional pubs are not a big feature: where they do exist, they're generally either cod-Irish franchises or depressing empty dives.

Pop music and Cape Jazz

Cape Town's greatest musical treasure is **Cape Jazz**, a subgenre of South African township jazz. Its greatest exponent is the internationally acclaimed **Abdullah Ibrahim** (known as Dollar Brand before his conversion to Islam). Born and raised in District Six, Ibrahim is a supremely gifted pianist and composer, who for decades has produced a hypnotic fusion of African, American and Cape Muslim idioms. In his greatest recordings, *Mannenberg* and *African Marketplace*, the fluttering rhythms of *goema* – traditional Cape carnival music – are combined with the cascading call-and-answer structure of African gospel. This is emotional jazz, full of simple, euphoric melody and enchanting brass lines.

Other Cape Town jazz legends are the late Basil Coetzee, a phenomenal tenor saxophonist who played on *Mannenberg*; Robbie Jansen, another saxman with a raunchy, fiery style who worked with Afro-pop greats Juluka; and alto saxman Winston "Ngozi" Mankunku, an old-school hepcat whose gigs are an exercise in good vibes. Both Jansen and Mankunku can occasionally be heard live in the city – watch the press. Other veteran stars to look out for are guitarist Errol Dyers, pianist Hotep Galeta and bassist Spencer Mbadu.

Two young stars stand out as talented heirs to the Cape Jazz tradition: astronomically cool guitarist Jimmy Dludlu and subtle, mellow pianist Paul Hanmer; catch them live if you can. Also watch out for the powerful singer Judith Sephuma, and Jo'burg-based maestros Moses Molelekwa, McCoy Mrubata and Sipho Gumede. Check the press for upcoming performances and venues.

Cape Town is also well stocked with charismatic **rock**, **reggae** and **pop** bands. Notable exports include township bubblegum star Brenda Fassie, radical hip-hop crew Prophets Of Da City and R'n'B crooner Jonathan Butler. The best live acts are the Springbok Nude Girls, cheesy funk merchants The Honeymoon Suites, funk-reggae crew Firing Squad and the innovative live trance outfit Colorfields.

City centre and City Bowl suburbs

Club Georgia 30 Georgia St, off Buitensingel ☎021 422 0261. A lively over-25s club that celebrates music from across Africa, including *kwassa-kwassa, kwaito, ndombolo, rai, kizamba* and *makossa*. Tues–Sat 9.30pm–late.

Club More 74 Loop St ☎021 422 0544. Fresh and funky house music in a New York-style club. Wed, Fri & Sat 10pm till late. Entry R40.

Drum Café 32 Glynn St, Gardens ☎021 461 1305. Here you can hire a drum for a communal drumming session. Every Monday and Wednesday at 9pm there's a facilitated drum circle lead by a South African or West African drum teacher, suitable for all levels of experience; the smaller Monday groups are better if you're a complete novice, while the Saturday afternoon sessions at 3pm are for families. If you prefer to leave things to the professionals, there are often parties at the weekends; ring for the current schedule. Light meals available, and the café is fully licensed. Entrance R30, drums R20. Mon, Wed, Fri & Sat 8pm–late.

The Jam 43 De Villiers St, District Six ☎021 465 2106. Quality live music and underground hip-hop parties at a spacious minimalist venue. There's no rigid schedule, but there's an event on most nights – watch the press for details.

Jo'burg 218 Long St, City Centre ☎021 422 0142. Great decor, and a good place to schmooze to a funky soundtrack, in the company of a hip art-school and media crowd. Live music on Sunday nights. Daily 5pm–4am.

Kennedy's Restaurant and Cigar Lounge 251 Long St, City Centre ☎021 424 1212. A swanky cigar bar offering cigars from all over the world, with brilliant martinis and margueritas, good food, an older crowd, and live jazz every evening. Mon–Fri noon till late, Sat 7pm till late.

The Lounge 194 Long St, City Centre ☎021 424 7636. A trendy long-serving refuge for Cape Town's smart and glamorous. Upstairs, make for the superb balcony and grab a table overlooking vibrant Long Street. House and jungle dominate the turntables. Mon–Sat 8pm–2am.

Mama Africa 178 Long St, City Centre ☎021 424 8634. A relaxed and spacious restaurant-bar in the heart of Long Street clubland, *Mama Africa* boasts a twelve-metre bar in the form of a green mamba. Traditional percussion groups perform regularly, and it's popular with European and North American visitors. Mon–Sat 8.30pm–late.

The Purple Turtle On the corner of Shortmarket and Long streets, City Centre. A cavernous, vaguely seedy bar frequented by Goths, metalheads and other nocturnal creatures. Catch live music on Saturday nights, but don't expect easy listening. Daily 11am–late.

Rhodes House 60 Queen Victoria St ☎021 424 8844. A smart though relaxed and fashion-conscious place, with progressive, French and Deep House sounds and lounge suites. Themed parties with dress codes also happen – ring before turning up. Wed–Sat 10pm till late.

The Shack 45b De Villiers St, District Six ☎021 465 2106. A walk-through venue with a restaurant, bar and pool hall. The music here ranges from the 1960s to 1980s, while the adoining *Blue Lizard* plays acidy jazz house music and trip hop. Mon–Sat 1pm–early hours, Sun 6pm–early hours.

V&A Waterfront and De Waterkant

As well as its upmarket restaurants, the **V&A Waterfront** also offers reasonably good mainstream nightlife in safe surroundings: the area has an emphatically clean-cut atmosphere.

Chilli'n'Lime 23 Somerset Rd, De Waterkant ☎021 426 4469. Painfully stylish upmarket club with two dance floors and four bars, which hosts pulsing house and hip-hop parties. Frequented by a left-field student crowd, around the 20–28 age group. Tues–Sat 8am–4am.

Den Anker Restaurant and Bar Victoria and Alfred Pierhead. A smart busy pub and continental bistro-style restaurant, populated by tourists and well-heeled locals. Den Anker specializes in imported Belgian beers, both on tap and in a bottle. One of the livelier places to visit at the Waterfront. Daily 11am–midnight.

Green Dolphin Victoria and Alfred Pierhead ☎021 421 7471. A top-notch, though a tad chilly, jazz venue, serving excellent seafood and hosting quality jazz bands nightly at 8.15pm. Dinner is served from 6pm. R20 cover charge. Daily noon–midnight (music from 8.30pm).

On Broadway 21 Somerset Rd, De Waterkant ☎021 418 8338. Cabaret restaurant-bar, on the fringes of the city centre, with Mediterranean-style food and live performances for a mixed crowd every night. One of the few venues committed to the city's small cabaret scene. Drag shows on Sunday and Tuesday, feature shows Wednesday to Saturday, and satirist Pieter Dirk Uys performs on Monday evenings. Daily 7pm–late.

Southern suburbs

If you're on foot, **Observatory** is a good destination: in and around Lower Main Road is compact and safe. The buildings are old and characterful, the vibe is warm, mellow and multi-ethnic, and there's plenty of bohemian restaurants and bars. Of the neighbouring suburbs, **Woodstock** is similar, while upmarket **Newlands** and **Constantia** offer more sedate nightlife.

Bar 89 Woodstock 89 Roodebloem Rd, Woodstock. A friendly and intimate bar filled with elegant decor. Once an artisan's cottage, *89* offers a welcoming hearthfire in winter and – for the rest of the year – a great space to chill out in. Gay-friendly. Tues–Sun 6pm–2am.

Boer and Brit Pub *Alphen Hotel,* Alphen Drive, off the M41h Constantia. Tables and umbrellas under oaks at an historic Cape Dutch hotel, with bar meals and a fire indoors on cold nights in a cosy English-style pub. Gracious yet relaxed. Daily 10am–11pm.

Café Ganesh 66 Lower Main Rd/Trill Road, Observatory ☎021 448 3435. *Café Ganesh* is the cosmopolitan heart of Observatory, and *the* place to meet artists, writers, performers and students. Spontaneous *kwaito* parties sometimes break out. Tues–Sun 6pm–late; closed during July.

Don Pedros 113 Roodebloem Rd, Woodstock ☎021 447 4493. Since the 1980s, when it was a regular haunt for struggling activists, *Don Pedros* has been a place for good cheap food and scruffy Capetonian ambience – you can linger all evening

over a beer or coffee without feeling hassled. There are smoking and non-smoking rooms; it's also a gay-friendly place where people tend to hang out after shows. Daily 9am–late.

Foresters' Arms 52 Newlands Ave, Newlands. Preppie students and professionals gather to quaff draught beer at the very popular and busy "Forries", in the heart of leafy Newlands. A big wood-panelled pub in the Anglo-Celtic tradition, it boasts a beautiful hedged-in courtyard; grab a bench for a drowsy afternoon pint in the great out-doors. Mon–Sat 10am–11pm, Sun 9am–4pm.

Independent Armchair Theatre 135 Lower Main Rd, Observatory ☎021 447 1514. A spacious club with several lounge suites, the *Independent Armchair Theatre* is a stylish, innovative venue with a small art gallery attached. Cult and art-house films are screened on week nights, and a steady stream of notable bands plays here.

Pedlars on the Bend Spaanschemat River Road, Constantia. An upmarket bar at one of the posher restaurants in this ritzy suburb, with a delightful outdoor area shaded by oaks. Daily 11am–11pm.

Atlantic seaboard

Dizzy Jazz Café 41 Camps Bay Drive, Camps Bay ☎021 438 2686. A crowded and lively nightspot with a big verandah and sea views, serving draught beer and quality seafood, with various live music nightly. R20 cover charge. Daily noon–4am (music from 8.30pm).

La Med Bar and Restaurant Glen Country Club, Victoria Road, Clifton ☎021 438 5600. A great sundowner venue overlooking the rocks at Clifton Beach, this spot draws a sporty, mainstream

crowd; it's a favourite place for hang-gliders from Lion's Head to visit, after they've landed in the adjacent field. There's live music Wed, Fri and Sat. Daily noon till late

Red Herring On the corner of Pine and Beach roads, Noordhoek. A pub above a smart restaurant with an outdoor deck overlooking the panoramic Noordhoek valley. Busy on warm weekend after-noons, when a clean-cut 20-something crowd gathers. Tues–Sun 11am–midnight.

Cape Flats

Club Vibe Rigel Road/Castor Road, Lansdowne ☎021 762 8962. A vast nightclub catering mainly to a well-dressed coloured crowd. Features two dance floors (mainstream and uplifting house), a hundred television screens and a groundbreaking sound technology feature known as "The Earthquake". Security is strong, the door policy is smart–casual, and strictly no under-18s. Fri & Sat 9pm–late.

West End & Club Galaxy College Road, Rylands ☎021 637 9132. Definitely the most happening place on the Flats, with some good international

musicians appearing from time to time. There are two nightclubs in the one building; you can circu-late between them in the course of an evening. *West End* is a top jazz venue with a wine, dine and dance ambience. The last Sunday of every month sees several acts sharing the bill (call the club for details). Dress up, and book a good table if you want to be seated and see the stage. *Club Galaxy* is a straight-up dance club playing R'n'B and mainstream house to a young and smart crowd, with a party atmosphere for the 20-something crowd. Thurs, Fri & Sat 8pm–late.

Nightlife and entertainment

159

Theatre and live performance

Despite scarce resources (state funds have been redirected to more pressing areas), theatre and live performance in South Africa is making a valiant attempt to lift itself out of its post-democracy doldrums. Political protest theatre, a fertile genre in the oppressive 1970s and 1980s, is now obsolete and it's no longer seen as self-indulgent for plays to deal with personal rather than political issues. A steady trickle of new plays are being written and performed in Cape Town, some of them innovative and hard-hitting. As yet there is no real successor to the world-renowned playwright Athol Fugard, several of whose works were first staged here, but writers and directors to look out for include Brett Bailey, Marthinus Basson, Reza de Wet, Fiona Coyne, Roy Sargeant and the duo of Heinrich Rosehofer and Oscar Petersen.

On the **musical** front, David Kramer and Taliep Petersen have produced several hit shows celebrating the history and culture of Cape Town. Their latest, *Kat and the Kings*, took Broadway and London's West End by storm, bagging the 1999 Olivier Award for the best new musical. **Comedy**, too, is starting to shape up well with the annual Smirnoff International Comedy Festival, at the Baxter Theatre around October, showcasing global and local talent. Probably South Africa's best-known stage satirist is Pieter Dirk Uys, whose character Evita Bezuidenhout, South Africa's answer to Dame Edna Everidge, has relentlessly roasted South African society since apartheid days. New homegrown comedians to look out for include Marc Lottering, a coloured Capetonian, who derives his material from his own community, and David Kau, an African, who is as caustic about Jo'burg township dwellers as he is about white South Africans.

Artscape DF Malan Street ☎021 421 5470. Once the Camelot of state-funded white performing arts, Artscape has reinvented itself as a more popular, less elitist theatre. High-quality ballet and opera are still produced, while adventurous new dramas appear periodically. Don't be intimidated by the monumental 1970s architecture.

Baxter Theatre Centre Main Road, Rondebosch ☎021 685 7880. A mammoth brick theatre complex whose design was inspired by Soviet Moscow's central railway station. Mounts an eclectic programme of shows, ranging from innovative plays to comedy festivals, jazz concerts and kids' theatre.

Little Theatre University of Cape Town, Orange Street ☎021 480 7129. A showcase for innovative work from the University of Cape Town drama school; the productions range from self-indulgent to breathtaking. The drama school has a long tradition of producing fine actors, and counts Richard E. Grant among its graduates.

Maynardville Open Air Theatre On the corner of Church and Wolfe streets, Wynberg. Book through Artscape ☎021 421 5470. Every year in January and February, a Shakespeare comedy is staged under the summer stars in Maynardville Park. The setting is pure romance, and the plays are presented with great imagination by the cream of Cape Town's actors and designers.

Theatre On The Bay Link Street, Camps Bay ☎021 438 3300. An upmarket theatre catering to a mature establishment audience. The productions include contemporary mainstream plays, farces, musical tributes and revues – rather predictable fare, but generally good-quality performances.

The Warehouse 6 Dixon Rd, Green Point ☎021 421 0777. A 280-seat venue that provides a minimalist space for modern drama. One of the few genuinely adventurous, youth-oriented theatres in town.

Cinema

Despite the fact that Cape Town is booming as a film-production centre, local feature **films** are scarce. Mainstream Hollywood releases are shown at several commercial cinemas, all of which advertise daily in the *Cape Times* and *Cape Argus*, while a couple of independent cinemas include art-house films in their programmes. A handful of small film theatres posing as arthouse cinemas – the Ster-Kinekor Cinemas Nouveau and the Labia – show the odd subtitled movie and slightly less mainstream fare, but don't expect anything too exotic.

The **mainstream cinemas** most convenient for visitors are: the Nu-Metro (☎021 419 9700) and Ster-Kinekor Cinema Nouveau (☎021 425 8222) at the V&A Waterfront ; the Ster-Kinekor Cavendish Commercial (☎0860 300 222) at Cavendish Square Shopping Centre, Claremont; and, at the same shopping centre, the Ster-Kinekor Cinema Nouveau (☎021 683 4063). The Ster-Kinekor complex at the Blue Route Mall in Tokai (☎021 713 1280) is convenient if you're staying along the False Bay seaboard.

Independent cinemas are listed below. Tickets cost around R26, and many cinemas have discounted tickets one day a week, which you'll find advertised in the press.

Independent Armchair Theatre 135 Lower Main Rd, Observatory ☎021 447 1514. An adventurous club/cinema screening cult and art movies with a video projector – sprawl in one of the comfy couches with a drink whilst enjoying the show. Screenings are on Monday to Friday evenings; contact the venue for details.
The Labia 69 Orange St; and **Labia on Kloof**

Lifestyles on Kloof Centre, Kloof Street Gardens ☎021 424 5927. Formerly the flea-ridden temple of alternative cinema in Cape Town, the Labia has been spruced up in recent times and opened another cinema with two screens in 2002 just around the corner. It shows an intelligent mix of art films, cult classics and new releases on three screens, advertised in the daily papers.

Cape Town for kids

Cape Town is an excellent place to travel with children. The city enjoys fine weather, and activities in its many nature reserves, gardens and historic estates let under-10s work off some energy in a safe environment. Many activities for kids are either free or inexpensive, although renting a car is pretty well essential, given the poor public transport.

Where the prices in this section refer to children, they mean under-16s, unless specified.

Museums and sights

Cable Car Lower cableway station, Tafelberg Road ☻www. tablemountain.co.za. Shuttle bus from Cape Town Tourism. Cable car return fares: Nov to April R85, children R45; May to Oct R68, children R35, under-4s free. A ride in the cable car can't fail to thrill, and once on the tabletop there are views, pathways to explore, and outdoor and indoor refreshments, albeit expensive. The furry little dassies (see p.136) always provide some amusement, but they shouldn't be fed as they may bite.
Groot Constantia Groot Constantia Wine Estate, off Ladies Mile Extension, Constantia. ☎021 794 5128, ☻www.museums.org.za/grootcon. Museum daily 10am–5pm; R8. Cellar tours and wine tasting (booking essential ☎021 794 5128): April–Sept daily 11am & 3pm; Oct–March daily every hour 10am–4pm; R20. Wine tasting only: May–Nov daily 10am–4.30pm; Dec–April daily 9am–6pm; R14; grounds free. A beautiful seventeenth-century Cape Dutch manor house with large grounds ideal for a wander. The most child-friendly of the

Constantia wine estates, its congenial outdoor *Jonkershuis* restaurant has an adjoining playground.
SA Museum and Planetarium 25 Queen Victoria St ☎021 424 3330, ☻www.museums.org.za /sam. Cape Town central station. Daily 10am–5pm; adults: museum R8, planetarium R10, combined R15; kids: museum free, planetarium R5. Cape Town station. The museum is great for rainy days, especially for 5- to 12-year-olds, who'll enjoy the four-storey whale well and African animal dioramas, as well as the dinosaur displays. The museum's Discovery Room (Mon–Fri 10am–3pm, Sat & Sun 11am–4.30pm) features live ants, massive spiders, and a crocodile display. For cheap internet access (R8 for 30min), there are ten computers with natural-history websites bookmarked and interactive CD-ROMs. The Planetarium has special children's shows over weekends and in school holidays, while the adjoining Gardens are full of friendly squirrels.

Telkom Exploratorium Union Castle Building, V&A Waterfront ⓦ www.exploratorium.co.za. Waterfront buses. Daily 9am–9pm; R15, under-18s R9. An interactive science museum where kids over 4 are invited to let their itchy fingers loose on knobs, buttons and dials. Activities include stomach-turning rotation inside a gyroscope, simulated speeding at 315kph in a Ferrari, virtual-reality rides as well as fairground favourites such as distorting mirrors.

Two Oceans Aquarium V&A Waterfront ☎021 418 3823, ⓦ www.aquarium.co.za. Waterfront buses. Daily 9.30am–6pm; R45, kids R20. One of Cape Town's most rewarding museums (see p.121) has loads for kids to do, apart from the excitement of just looking at the weird and wonderful sea creatures. The touch pool provides the chance to handle a few species – sometimes this includes a small shark or sea urchins – while the Apha Activity Centre usually has puppet shows or face painting as well as computer terminals where older kids can learn about marine ecology.

Amusement and theme parks

Ratanga Junction N1 to Bellville, take exit 10 (Sable Street exit) ☎0861 200 300, ⓦ www.ratanga.co.za. Rides: Wed–Fri 10am–5pm, Sat 10am–6pm, Sun 10am–5pm; unlimited rides R75, unlimited rides for people under 1.3m R39; non-riders and under-2s free. A spectacular multi-million-rand theme park that recreates a mythological late nineteenth-century mining town, with loads of activities and places to eat. The real attractions are the 24 rides, which include family rides, thrill rides, steam trains and boats. The biggie is the Cobra, a towering spine-like rollercoaster which takes you 34m to the first drop, speeds you along at 100kph and delivers four-times gravity traction around the bends. A rider ticket entitles you to sample all the rides as many times as you wish; certain rides are restricted to people over 1.3m tall.

Scratch Patch and Mineral World Dido Valley Road, off Main Road, Simon's Town ☎021 786 2020; and V&A Waterfront ☎021 419 9429. Mon–Fri 9am–4.45pm, Sat & Sun 9am–5.15pm; R10–32, depending on size of container. Over-3s can fill a bag with the reject polished gemstones which literally cover the floor; you can then cross the catwalk to see one of the world's biggest gemstone tumbling plants in operation (Mon–Fri).

Spier 50km from Cape Town, along the R310 ☎021 809 1100, ⓦ www.spier.co.za. Daily 9am–5pm, free. A brilliant family outing that dovetails nicely with a tour of the Winelands, Spier is a historic manor house in vast grounds with a large lake. It's a good setting for picnics, with a kids' playground and space to run about, as well as guided pony rides (Sat & Sun 11am–4pm; R10 for ten minutes). Another highlight is the cheetah park, part of a breeding programme, where you can enter the enclosure to pet a purring big cat (viewing free; cheetah encounter R40, kids R20). You're not allowed to consume your own food on the estate, but their farmstall and coffee shop has a deli that bakes delicious fresh bread and pastries and sells cheeses, cold meats and dips, from which you can make your own picnic basket. There's also a choice of five places to eat: the *Jonkershuis Restaurant*, *Spier Café*, the *Taphuis Grill*, the *Riverside Pub* and *Figaro's* at the on-site hotel.

World of Birds Valley Road, Hout Bay ☎021 790 2730. Daily 9am–5pm, R30, kids R20, under-3s free. Over 3000 birds and small animals housed in peaceful walk-through aviaries (see p.140).

Beaches

Cape Town is literally surrounded by **beaches** – a classic and easy summer weekend family outing. This selection is particularly suitable for toddlers and smaller kids and generally also offers something for parents. Most beaches are pretty undeveloped, so it's best to take what you need in the way of food and drinks with you. Sea water and swimming pool temperatures are published each day in the weather section of the *Cape Times*. Get to the beach as early as possible so you can leave by 10–11am before the sun gets too strong, and to avoid the wind which often gusts up in the late morning.

False Bay seaboard

The warmer **False Bay seaboard** has the advantage of being accessible by Metrorail train from central Cape Town. By car, take the M3 in the direction of Muizenberg; it'll take about forty minutes from central Cape Town to Fish Hoek.

Boulders Beach 39km south of central Cape Town; entry R10, kids R5. One of the few beaches to visit when the southeaster is blowing, Boulders has safe, flat water, making it ideal for kids – and its resident penguin breeding colony. The granite boulders create a beautiful, protected setting, and there's some shade in the morning. It's an extremely popular beach, and fills up fast during the December school holidays, so go as early in the day as you can. There's a pleasant café with views across False Bay at the car park just outside the beach, but not at the beach itself.

Fish Hoek 30km south of central Cape Town. One of the best Peninsula beaches has gentle waves that are warm in summer, and a long stretch of sand. There's a playground, and a reasonable café on the beach, and with a pushchair you can stroll along Jager's Walk, a paved pathway along the rocky coast with beautiful views of the Hottentots Holland Mountains. When it's windy, the small grassy area next to the showers is the most protected area for sunbathing.

St James 38km south of central Cape Town. A safe tidal pool with a small sandy beach and photogenic bathing boxes. With a pushchair, you can walk to Muizenberg along a concrete coastal pathway, with views of the distant mountains across the water. St James can get overcrowded at weekends, and parking can be inadequate; it's always wise to be here as early as possible in the day. There are no tea shops on site, but you can get tea and scones at the Labia Museum on Main Road, between St James and Muizenberg, and there's an Italian restaurant across the road from St James station.

Atlantic seaboard

The **Atlantic seaboard** is too cold for serious swimming, but does have some lovely stretches of sand, boulders and rock pools – and astonishing scenery. Beaches are excellent for picnics, and on calm summer evenings idyllic for sundowners and sunsets. In the summer they're less windy than the False Bay beaches, but the afternoons are often baking hot. There's no public transport south of Hout Bay,.

Camps Bay 8km southwest of central Cape Town. A sandy beach with some grass and shady palm trees, lying below the impressive Twelve Apostles rampart. There's a tidal pool and small rock pools, and its easily reachable from the centre by car or bus. The road opposite the beach is lined with pavement cafés, restaurants and bars.

Noordhoek and Kommetjie 41km southwest of central Cape Town. The eight-kilometre stretch of white sand from Noordhoek to Kommetjie provides fine walking, kite-flying and horse-riding, with stupendous views of Chapman's Peak. Some good restaurants and farmstalls in the wooded Noordhoek area make for a pleasant outing, and if you're going to Kommetjie you can go camel-riding (see p.164). Kommetjie itself has some nice groves of milkwood trees, and rocks and pathways to explore. You'll need your own transport to get out here.

Sea Point Promenade 4km west of central Cape Town. Stretching 3km from the lighthouse in Mouille Point to Sea Point Pavilion, the paved promenade, bordered by lawns, hotels and apartment blocks hugs the rocky coastline. It's the closest stretch of coast to the centre, with several parking spots along the promenade, and it's ideal for pram pushing or roller-blading. There's also the draw of playgrounds and ice-cream sellers. While there are two little beaches strewn with slimy kelp, they're not safe for swimming, although you could take a bucket and spade to them. For swimming, head for the pool at the Sea Point Pavilion.

Swimming pools

Long Street Baths On the corner of Long Street and Buitensingel ☎021 400 3302. Mon–Fri 7am–8pm, Sat 7am–7pm, Sun 8am–6pm. R7, kids R4. Conveniently central, Cape Town's only heated indoor pool is recommended when the weather is poor.

Newlands Pool On the corner of Main Road and Sans Souci Road, Newlands ☎021 674 4197. Daily: April–Sept 9am–5pm; Oct–March 7am–6.30pm; R7, kids R4. An Olympic-sized unheated pool surrounded by lawns and mountain views. Its summer high temperature of 24ºC drops to an unappealing 15ºC in winter.

Sea Point Pool Sea Point Pavilion, Beach Road ☎021 434 3341. 5km west of central Cape Town. Daily: April–Sept 9am–5pm; Oct–March 7am–6.45pm; adults R7, kids R4. A marvellous Olympic-sized chlorinated seawater pool on the sea edge, with two paddling pools for children, and seagulls flapping about.

Outdoor and picnic spots

The Barnyard Farmstall Steenberg Road (M42), next to Steenberg Estate, between Tokai Road and the Ou Kaapse Weg. An excellent place for an outdoor snack or cup of coffee at a small farmyard, with ducks and chickens wandering around, and an unusually good kids' playground. The farmstall itself offers delectable breads, dips, baked goods and deli fare, and is a good stop if you're doing the Constantia winelands.

Imhoff Farm Kommetjie Road, opposite Ocean view turn-off ☏021 783 4545 or ☏083 735 5227. Camel rides are laid on daily between noon and 4pm at Imhoff Farm; R50 for thirty minutes. Walks lead into the surrounding trees and sandy areas, but not on the beach itself. Toddlers can ride with a parent in the same saddle, and 4-year-olds and upwards can do it alone.

Kirstenbosch National Botanical Gardens Rhodes Drive ☏021 799 8999. Daily April–Aug 8am–6pm, Sept–March 8am–7pm; R15, kids R5. Top of the list for a family outing, the extensive lawns here offer miles of space for running about, there are trees and rocks to climb and streams to paddle in. There's no litter, no dogs, it's extremely safe and you can push a pram all over the walkways; it's also great for picnics or to have tea outdoors at the café. For older kids there are short waymarked walks, the Stinkwood and Yellowwood trails (1.2km and 2.5km), or you can scale the mountain up Skeleton Gorge (see p.137). Their summer sunset concerts on Sundays are also recommended (see p.129).

Newlands Forest 9km south of the centre, off the M3 to Muizenberg. Dawn to dusk; free. Gentle walks in and around pine forests and streams on the wooded southern slopes of Table Mountain, with a flattish pathway suitable for pushchairs. It's good for picnics if you want to get out of the city and don't have time to go further afield. Safest at weekends and in the afternoons when the joggers and dog walkers are out. Use the access point off the M3 signposted "Forestry Office", where there's ample parking.

Noordhoek Farm Village Noordhoek Main Road, just before the road climbs up to Chapman's Peak ☏021 789 1317. Daily 8.30am–5.30pm. Very much geared to the tour buses en route to Cape Point via Chapman's Peak, but nevertheless a delightfully tranquil place under oak trees, where you can buy fresh produce, clothes, souvenirs and Zimbabwean sculpture. Best of all is the shady playground next to the café with outdoor seating, which can be a life-saver if you're doing Chapman's Peak with restless children in the car.

Silvermine Nature Reserve (see p.143) Ou Kaapse Weg (M64). Dawn to dusk; R10, kids R5. A beautiful nature reserve on the mountains above Muizenberg and Kalk Bay, about 25km from the centre, accessed from a signposted entry gate at the top of Ou Kaapseweg (M64). It's a good place to see fynbos vegetation at close quarters, stroll around the pine-fringed lake and picnic with small children; however, it is exposed, and not recommended in heavy winds or mist. With older children there are some mountain-top walks with relatively gentle gradients, which give spectacular views over both sides of the Peninsula. Friends of Silvermine (☏021 782 5079 or 021 785 1477) offers free walks with members at various times of the week.

Tokai Forest Arboretum Tokai Road; take the Tokai exit from the M3 towards Muizenberg, then head to the mountains at the end of Tokai Road, or access it from the signpost on the M42. Dawn to dusk; R2. A peaceful forest with trees from all over the world, established in 1885 on the slopes of Constantiaberg. A wonderful place to escape to when the southeast wind blows, it offers walks and mountain biking, as well as a thatched tea shop with outdoor seating. It's also a great place for young children to explore, with logs to jump off and a gentle walk to a stream.

Gay scene

Cape Town is South Africa's – and indeed, the African continent's – gay capital. The city has always had a strident and vibrant gay culture, and is on its way to becoming an African Sydney, attracting gay travellers from across the country and the globe. Cape Town's **gay quarter**, with B&Bs, guesthouses, pubs, clubs, cruise bars, video shows, restaurants with cabaret, strip shows and steam baths, is concentrated along the entertainment strips of Somerset Road and

Main Road in the interconnected inner-city suburbs of Green Point, Sea Point and De Waterkant, adjacent to the centre, where a number of establishments flaunt their pink credentials by flying a distinctive multicoloured gay flag.

Cape Town hosts an annual **gay party**, organized by Mother City Queer Projects (Ⓦ www.mcqp.co.za), a hugely popular event usually held in mid-December at the *River Club* (☎ 021 448 6117) in Observatory. People dress as outrageously as possible according to a theme (past ones have included "on safari", "underwater" and "farm fresh") and the event seeks to rival Sydney's Mardi Gras. There's also an annual **gay pride festival** (Ⓦ www.sapride.org) around the same time.

Clubs and pubs

Bar 89 Woodstock 89 Roodebloem Rd Woodstock ☎ 021 447 0982. An elegant, beautifully outfitted gay-friendly pub in a Victorian house. Nestled in increasingly trendy upper Woodstock, it strikes a refreshing chord, halfway between an intimate local and a sleekly cosmopolitan meeting-place. Tues–Sun 6pm–2am.

Bar Code 16 Hudson St, Green Point ☎ 021 421 5305. A leather uniform and jeans bar that attracts an older crowd, *Bar Code* has monthly underwear and fetish parties. The atmosphere is industrial hardcore with cruising areas, a darkroom, video, pool table and outdoor garden. Daily 9pm till late.

The Bronx, Angels and Sky 35 Somerset Rd, Green Point ☎ 021 419 9216. A complex of clubs that share a courtyard and a reputation as the heartbeat of Cape Town's gay nightlife. *Angels* and *Sky* are two cavernous dance venues, while *Bronx* is a hugely popular and energetic bar. The crowd here is mixed, unpretentious and committed to having a good time. Daily till late.

Café Manhattan 74 Waterkant St, Green Point ☎ 021 421 6666. A cultured, relaxed restaurant-bar which serves good affordable food (even Sunday roasts) and hosts live music every Thursday night (no cover charge). It also features an outside terrace beneath oak trees. Straight-friendly. Daily noon–late.

Club 55 22 Somerset Rd, Green Point ☎ 021 425 2739. A young and sassy theatre/club/bistro

attracting a cosmopolitan crowd. The decor can be described as "warehouse chic", and regular live entertainment includes drag shows (Wednesdays) and revues (Thursdays) – cover charge R35. It takes on its club persona on Fridays and Saturdays. Daily 10am till late.

On Broadway 21 Somerset Rd, Green Point ☎ 021 418 8338. A great cabaret restaurant-bar with Mediterranean-style food and live performances every night of the week. One of the few venues committed to the city's small but sassy cabaret scene. Top comic and satirist Pieter Dirk Uys performs every Monday night, there are feature shows Wednesdays to Sundays, and drag shows on Sundays and Tuesdays. All shows start at 9pm and cost R45. You can go earlier for dinner, but booking is essential. Mixed crowd, and definitely straight-friendly. Daily 7pm till late.

Robert's Café and Cigar Bar 74 Waterkant St, De Waterkant ☎ 021 425 2478. A relaxed and convivial place in De Waterkant gay village, where you can have good food and socialize at the bar; a nice place to eat out with a sexy, bluesey atmosphere. Daily noon–very late.

Rosie's 125a Waterkant St, De Waterkant, opposite *Manhattan* ☎ 021 250 7621. A small intimate pool bar attracting a bear crowd and leather boys, with a restaurant that's a popular after-work drinking spot with angels and demons. Tues–Fri 4pm–late, Sat & Sun 2pm–late

Steambaths

The Hothouse Steam and Leisure 18 Jarvis St, Green Point ☎ 021 418 3888, ℮ info@hothouse .co.za. A luxurious pleasure complex featuring Jacuzzis, sauna, a sundeck with a superb view, a full bar with a limited food menu, video room, fireplace and satellite TV. Luxury cabins R50. Entrance R35–50 depending on days and times. Mon–Fri noon–2am, Sat & Sun 24hr.

Steamers Corner Wembley and Solan roads, Gardens ☎ 021 461 6210, ℮ info@steamers.co .za. The ultimate cruise venue featuring a swimming pool, steam room, sauna, Jacuzzi, glory holes, leather room, cabins, voyeurs' room, sunbed and more. Feb–Nov daily noon–3am; Dec & Jan Mon–Fri noon–8am, Sat & Sun 24hr.

Outdoor activities

One of Cape Town's most remarkable features is the fact that it melds with the Cape Peninsula National Park, a patchwork of mountains, forests and coastline – all on the city's doorstep. There are few, if any, cities in the world where outdoor pursuits are so easily available and affordable. You can try activities such as sea kayaking, abseiling, rock climbing and scuba diving for little more than the price of a night out back home. Alternatively, just let everyone else get on with it while you sink a few beers and watch the cricket, rugby or soccer.

Spectator sports

Cricket This is keenly followed by a wide range of Capetonians. The city's cricketing heart is at Newlands Cricket Ground, 61 Campground Road, Newlands (☎021 674 4146, ⓦwww.cricket.org). One of the most beautiful grounds in the world, Newlands nestles beneath venerable oaks and the elegant profile of Devil's Peak. Provincial, test and one-day international matches are played here; **tickets** range from R25–45 for provincial matches to R60–175 for internationals.

Rugby The Western Cape is one of the world's rugby heartlands, and the game is followed religiously. Provincial, international and Super 12 contests are fought on the hallowed turf of Newlands Rugby Stadium, Boundary Road, Newlands (☎021 689 4921). The stadium becomes packed, and the atmosphere gets exhilarating; expect to pay R40–60 for stand **tickets** for lower profile events and up to R75 for crowd-pullers like the Super 12.

Soccer Though never as well attended as cricket or rugby, Cape Town **soccer** is burgeoning with talent. The dusty streets of the Cape Flats have produced superb young footballers such as Benni McCarthy (Ajax Amsterdam, Celta Vigo) and Quinton Fortune (Atletico Madrid, Manchester United). The most ambitious and professional club in the city is Ajax – pronounced "I-axe" – Cape Town (☎021 930 6001, ⓦwww.ajaxct.org), jointly owned by its Amsterdam namesake. The most exciting games to attend are those between a local outfit and either of the Soweto glamour teams, Orlando Pirates and Kaizer Chiefs: they draw a buzzing crowd wherever they play. Matches are at Green Point Stadium, off Beach Road; Athlone Stadium, off Klipfontein Road, Athlone; and Newlands Rugby Stadium (see above). Tickets for league matches are cheap at around R20.

Participation sports and activities

Abseiling and kloofing You can abseil off Table Mountain with Abseil Africa (☎021 424 1580) for around R200 for a half-day trip. They also do full-day trips twice a week to Kamikaze Canyon, that include kloofing, hiking and abseiling for R395.

Bird-watching The Peninsula's varied habitats attract nearly 400 different species of birds. Good places for bird-watching include Lion's Head, Kirstenbosch Gardens and the Cape of Good Hope Nature Reserve, as well as at Kommetjie and Hout Bay; you can find out about guided outings with knowledgeable guides through the Cape Bird Club (☎021 559 0726). For a more institutionalized experience, try the World of Birds (see p.140), Valley Road, Hout Bay (☎021 790 2730).

Golf The Milnerton golf course, Bridge Road, Milnerton (☎021 552 1047), is tucked in between a lagoon and Table Bay, and boasts classic views of Table Mountain. Other popular local courses are at Rondebosch Golf Club, Klipfontein Road, Rondebosch (☎021 689 4176), and Royal Cape Golf Club, 174 Ottery Rd, Wynberg (☎021 761 6551) Prices are around R160/R260 for 9/18 holes; clubs can be rented for R80; and caddy fees are R70. Booking is essential.

Gyms Virgin Active clubs are upmarket but well-appointed gyms dotted around the Peninsula. Contact their call centre (☎0860 200 911, ⓦwww.virginactive.co.za) to find out where the nearest one is to you and the cost of day rates.

Horse-riding Horse Trail Safaris, Indicator Lodge, Skaapskraal Road, Ottery (☎082 575 5669) offers riding through the dunes to Strandfontein and Muizenberg beaches; Sleepy Hollow Horse Riding, Sleepy Hollow Lane, Noordhoek (☎021 789 2341) covers the spectacular Noordhoek Beach. Both cost around R130 for 1hr 30min; two-hour sunset rides cost R160.

Inline skating (roller-blading) Especially popular along the long smooth promenade that runs from Mouille Point to Sea Point, inline skating is a growing activity. You can rent blades from Rent'n'Ride, 1 Park Rd, Mouille Point (☎021 434 1122; around R40 for 2hr).

Kite-flying The Kite Shop, Shop 110, Ground Floor, Main Shopping Complex, V&A Waterfront (☎021 421 6231), sells kites of all shapes, colours and sizes.

Mountain-biking Downhill Adventures, corner of Kloof and Orange streets in the city centre (☎082 459 2422), takes organized mountain-biking trips down Table Mountain, around Cape Point and through the Winelands (from R350 for a full day; R250 for a half day). Day Trippers (☎021 531 3274, ⓦwww.daytrippers.co.za) offers similar half-day trips, including one from Scarborough to Cape Point.

Paragliding Fun 2 Fly (☎021 557 9735) offers one-day, one-and-a-half day and full-licence paragliding courses, from R350 to R2500.

Road cycling Cycling (for rental outlets see p.172) is popular all over the Peninsula, and is a great way to take in the scenery. For information about the Cape Argus Pick'n'Pay Cycle Tour the largest individually timed bike race in the world, contact Pedal Power Associates (☎021 689 8420), which also organizes fun rides from September to May.

Rock climbing You can learn how to rock climb up Table Mountain's famous facade with the Cape Town School of Mountaineering (☎021 685 6972), which charges R600 for a two-day rock-climbing course, usually over weekends; they also guide experienced climbers. For other recommended climbing leaders.

Sea kayaking Real Cape Adventures (☎021 790 5611 or ☎082 556 2520, ⓦwww.seakayak.co.za) offers a range of half- or full-day packages that include trips around Cape Point, to the penguin colony at Boulders Beach and around Hout Bay. They also do trips of several days around the Peninsula, where you spend nights at guesthouses, and longer safaris all over South Africa and even further north. Half-days start at R180 per person.

Scuba diving While the Cape waters are cold, they're good for seeing wrecks, reefs and magnificent kelp forests. Because it's invariably warmer than the Atlantic seaboard, False Bay is preferred in winter. Dives cost from R180 for a short dive from the shore to around R220 from a boat; prices include dive gear. An internationally recognized PADI open-water diving qualification can be completed for around R1700. For information and arranging scuba-diving courses and equipment rental, contact: Ian's Scuba School, Master Mariners Sports Club, Stephan Way, Mouille Point (☎021 439 9322); Orca Industries, Herschel

Road/Bowwood Road, Claremont (☎021 671 9673); and Time Out Adventures, Avalon Building, 8 Mill St, Gardens (☎021 461 2709).

Surfing Top surfing spots include Big Bay at Bloubergstrand, where competitions are held every summer, Llandudno, Muizenberg, Kalk Bay and Long Beach at Kommetjie and Noordhoek. For further information, contact Surfing South Africa (☎021 674 2972); or surf the excellent ⓦwww.wavescape.co .za, the best place on the web for everything you want to know about surfing in SA.

Swimming There are surf lifesaver patrols on duty at Milnerton, Camps Bay, Llandudno, Muizenberg and Fish Hoek beaches. For pools, try Long Street Swimming Pool, Long Street (☎021 400 3302), Cape Town's only heated indoor pool; or Newlands Swimming Pool, corner of Main and San Souci roads, Newlands (☎021 467 4197), an Olympic-sized chlorinated pool. The excellent Sea Point Swimming Pool at Beach Road, Sea Point (☎021 434 3341) is an enormous sea-water pool.

Walking The best places for gentle strolls are Newlands Forest, up from Rhodes Memorial, and the beaches. For longer walks, head for anywhere on Table Mountain (see p.134), Tokai Forest, Silvermine Nature Reserve or Cape Point Nature Reserve.

Windsurfing and kitesurfing While most Capetonians moan about the howling southeaster in summer, it's handy if you're into windsurfing. Langebaan, 75 minutes' drive north of town, is one of the best spots; for further help, contact Cape Sport Centre, Langebaan (☎022 772 1114, ⓦwww.capesport.co.za), which also does kitesurfing. Prices for windsurfing start at $31 for two hours for rigs; windsurfing instruction for beginners starts at R195 and kitesurfing lessons at R220 inclusive of gear and teacher. Otherwise, the place to go in Cape Town is Bloubergstrand. The Blouberg Windsurf and Leisure (☎021 554 1663 or 082 420 2990, ⓔblouwind@mweb.co.za) rents equipment, cars with racks and has long-term accommodation at Bloubergstrand, as well as being able to offer general advice to its clients, such as information on which airlines offer free carriage of windsurfing equipment.

Shopping

The V&A Waterfront is the city's most popular shopping venue, with good reason: it has a vast range of shops, the setting on the harbour is lovely and there's a huge choice of places to eat and drink when you want to rest your feet – but expect to pay above the odds for everything. The city centre also offers variety and, for some people's taste, a grittier and more interesting venue for browsing, especially if you're looking for collectables, antiques and secondhand books. Cape Town's suburbanites tend to do their shopping closer to home at the upmarket Cavendish Square Mall in Claremont or one of the other shopping centres that include the monstrously outsized Tygerberg Mall and the pastiche-Venice Canal Walk in the northern suburbs. If you're staying in the inner-city suburbs of Green and Sea Point, adjacent to the V&A Waterfront, you'll find supermarkets and other functional shops along Main Road, and the City Bowl suburbs are served by the Gardens Shopping Centre. There are other smaller shopping areas dotted about the other suburbs.

Shopping hours have traditionally been Monday to Friday 8.30am–5pm, and Saturday till 1pm. But this has begun to change and lots of supermarkets, bookshops and other specialist outlets now open on Sundays and beyond 5pm.

Malls and shopping centres

South African shopping tends to follow an American rather than European model, with huge **malls** where you can browse in a bookshop as well as bank, buy clothes and groceries and go to the movies. They always have several coffee shops and restaurants.

Blue Route Mall Tokai Road, Tokai. A functional single-storey centre that's handy if you're staying in Constantia or along the False Bay, with branches of Pick'n'Pay and Woolworths. Mon–Fri 9am–5.30pm, Sat & Sun 9am–5pm.

Cavendish Square Vineyard Road, Claremont station, Claremont. An upmarket multistorey complex, the major shopping focus for the southern suburbs. Mon–Thurs 9am–6pm, Fri 9am–9pm, Sat 9am–6pm, Sun 10am–4pm.

Gardens Shopping Centre Mill Street, Gardens. Small shopping mall in the City Bowl, very close to the Company's Gardens and city centre, with a large supermarket, excellent deli and most of the

shops you'll need. Mon–Fri 9am–6pm, Sat 9am–3pm; selected shops Sun 10am–2pm.

Golden Acre Adderley Street, Cape Town station. A dark and not entirely pleasant complex linked by a walkway to the station. Handy if you're about to catch a train, but otherwise best avoided. Mall 6am–midnight; most shops 8.30am–5pm.

V&A Waterfront It would be possible to visit Cape Town and never leave the Waterfront complex, which has a vast range of upmarket shops packed into the Victoria Wharf Shopping Centre, including outlets of all the major South African chains, selling books, clothes, food and crafts. Mon–Sat 9am–9pm, Sun 10am–9pm.

Arts and crafts

Cape Town is not known for its indigenous **arts and crafts** in the way that Durban is, and many of the goods you'll buy here are from elsewhere in Africa, especially Zimbabwe and Zambia. There are several places in the city centre and the V&A Waterfront, but you'll often pick up the same arts and crafts for a lot less money at the sidewalk **markets** scattered around town. Don't expect exotic West African-style market places, however; Cape Town's venues are more like European or North American flea markets.

Shops

Africa Nova Main Road, Hout Bay ☏ 021 790 4454. A better than average selection of ethnic crafts and curios as well as contemporary African textiles and artwork, with an emphasis on the individual and handmade. Mon–Fri 9am–5pm, Sat & Sun 10am–2pm.

African Image Branches at the corner of Church and Burg streets ☏ 021 423 8385, Mon–Fri 9am–5pm, Sat 9am–1.30pm; and Shop 6228, Victoria Wharf, V&A Waterfront ☏ 021 419 0382, daily 9am–9pm. One of the best places for authen-

tic traditional and contemporary African arts and crafts, from fabrics and antique sculpture to beadwork, but goods are a little overpriced.

Ethno Bongo Mainstream Shopping Centre, Main Road, Hout Bay ☏ 021 790 0802. A charming shop in the main shopping centre in Hout Bay, selling wonderful and well-priced crafts, jewellery and accessories made from recycled metal and wood, and also quirky kaftans and ethnic clothing – highly recommended for unique gifts and souvenirs. Mon–Fri 9.30am–6pm, Sat 9.30am–4pm, Sun 10am–4pm.

Kalk Bay Gallery 62 Main Rd, Kalk Bay ☏ 021 788 1674. Graphics, engravings as well as African art and artefacts – good value, with the chance of picking up something very collectible. Mon–Fri 9am–5pm, Sat & Sun 9.30am–5pm.

Out of Africa Shop 125, Victoria Wharf, V&A Waterfront ☏ 021 418 5505. Expensive baskets, beads and African arts and antiques. Daily 9am–9pm.

Rose Korber Art Consultancy 48 Sedgemoor Rd, Camps Bay ☏ 021 438 9152. This should be the first stop for the serious collector, with an exceptional selection of contemporary art and craft, including ceramics and beadwork from around the continent. Mon–Fri 9am–5pm.

Yellow Door Upper floor, Gardens Centre, Gardens ☏ 021 465 4702. One of the largest and best selections of local crafts and design, including ceramics, fabrics, jewellery, basketry, metalwork and interior decor. Mon–Fri 9am–6pm, Sat 9am–4pm, Sun 10am–2pm.

Markets

Cape Town Station Forecourt, Adderley Street. Thronging ranks of market traders selling radios, leather goods and African crafts. Not principally aimed at tourists, so it's pretty authentic. Mon–Fri 8am–5pm, Sat 8am–2pm.

Constantia Craft Market Alphen Common, corner of Spaanschemat River and Ladies Mile roads, Constantia. Sizeable outdoor flea market where

you can pick up good local crafts and items from around the continent, ride a camel or a pony and have a cup of tea. First and last Sat and first Sun of the month.

Greenmarket Square Burg Street. An open-air market that's the best place in town for colourful handmade Cape Town beachwear, from T-shirts to shorts and sandals, as well as being a place to pick up knick-knacks. Mon–Fri 8am–5pm, Sat 8am–2pm.

The Pan African Market 76 Long St. A multicultural hothouse of township and contemporary art, artefacts, curios and crafts. There's music, a café specializing in African cuisine, a bookshop, a Cameroonian hairbraider and West African tailor. Mon–Fri 9am–5pm, Sat 9am–3pm.

The Red Shed Craft Workshop Victoria Wharf, V&A Waterfront. A market where some two dozen craftworkers make and sell ceramics, textiles, candles and jewellery, and you can see glass-blowers at work. Mon–Sat 9am–9pm, Sun 10am–9pm.

Sivuyile Craft Centre On the corner of NY1 and NY4, Guguletu, Cape Flats. A township market attached to an information centre close to the N2 freeway, where bead-workers, wire-workers and other artists make traditional and modern crafts. Mon–Fri 8am–5pm, Sat 8am–2pm, Sun 9am–1pm.

Victoria Road Market 1km south of Bakoven along the coast road. Carvings, beads, fabrics and baskets sold from a market spectacularly sited on a clifftop overlooking the Atlantic. Daily.

Books

South Africa produces a lot of **books** given the size of its reading population: you'll find scores of good locally produced novels and endless volumes on history, politics and natural history. For new books there are some pleasant places in the suburbs or at the Waterfront to browse for half an hour, while Upper Long Street has over half a dozen secondhand book and specialist comic shops in close proximity, interspersed with congenial cafés.

Clarke's Bookshop 211 Long St ☏ 021 423 5739. The best place in Cape Town for South African books, with a huge selection of locally published titles covering literature, history, politics, natural history and the arts, plus very well-informed staff. They also deal in collectors' editions of South African books. Mon–Fri 8.45am–5pm, Sat 9am–1pm.

Exclusive Books Branches at Victoria Wharf, V&A Waterfront ☏ 021 419 0905, Mon–Fri 9am–10.30pm, Sat 9am–11pm, Sun 10am–9pm; Lower Mall, Cavendish Square, Claremont ☏ 021 674 3030, Mon–Thurs 9am–9pm, Fri & Sat 9am–10.30pm, Sun 9.30am–9pm; Constantia Village Shopping Centre, Spaanschemat River Road, Constantia ☏ 021 794 7800, Mon–Sat 9am–8pm,

Sun 9am–5pm. A friendly bookshop, ideal for browsing; the well-stocked shelves include magazines and a wide choice of coffee-table books on Cape Town and South African topics.

Kirstenbosch Shop Kirstenbosch National Botanical Gardens ☏ 021 762 2510. An excellent selection of natural-history books, field guides and travel guides covering southern Africa, as well as a range of titles for kids. Daily 9am–7pm.

The Travellers Bookshop King's Warehouse, Victoria Wharf, V&A Waterfront ☏ 021 425 6880. Cape Town's only specialist travel bookshop stocks a good range of titles, mainly about South Africa and especially the Cape, covering history, politics, natural history and the arts as well as travel guides. Daily 9am–9pm.

Music

Most **music** is sold on CD, and the ubiquitous chains such as CNA and Musica tend to stock pretty unadventurous selections of mainly British and American sounds. For South African bands and music from the rest of the continent, the outlets listed below are by far the best.

African Music Store 90a Long St, City Centre ☎021 426 0867. A small very central shop specializing in African music. Mon–Fri 9am–5pm, Sat 9am–2pm.

Look & Listen Shop F14, Upper level, Cavendish Square, Claremont ☎021 683 1810. Africa's first music megastore, with late-night opening seven days a week and a vast selection of all kinds of music, including good local jazz and a respectable

selection from all over the African continent. Daily 9am–10.30pm.

Sessions Music Lower level, Victoria Wharf, V&A Waterfront ☎021 419 7892. One of the best places in Cape Town to buy music, with an extensive selection of South African and African sounds and helpful staff. Mon–Thurs & Sun 9am–9pm, Fri & Sat 9am–10pm.

Food and provisions

Self-catering is the cheapest way to eat in Cape Town, and it can also be good fun. Apart from **braais**, which happen anywhere with any excuse, there are countless places on beaches, in the forests or up Table Mountain where you can enjoy a terrific **picnic**, or you may just want to cook at your accommodation. Lots of delis can be found down Kloof Street and in Green Point and Sea Point. By far the most atmospheric places to buy seafood are the Hout Bay and Kalk Bay harbours (see p.140 & p.143 respectively).

Supermarkets

The easiest places to shop for food are at the big **supermarket** chains. The larger branches of the better supermarkets also have fishmonger counters where you can buy fresh fish.

Woolworths Branches at Adderley Street (Mon–Fri 8.30am–5.30pm, Sat 8am–2pm); V&A Waterfront (daily 9am–9pm); Cavendish Square Mall, Claremont, (Mon–Thurs 9am–6pm, Fri 8.30am–8pm, Sat 8am–6pm, Sun 9am–5pm); Blue Route Mall, Tokai (Mon–Thurs 9am–5.30pm, Fri 8.30am–7pm, Sat 8.30am–5pm, Sun 9am–2pm). The South African version of Britain's Marks & Spencer stores is excellent for quality fast-cook meals, fresh produce and cold foods, such as olives, houmus and various Mediterranean dips, but can be pricey.

Pick'n'Pay V&A Waterfront, daily 9am–8pm; Gardens Shopping Centre, Mill Street, Gardens (Mon–Thurs 8am–7pm, Fri 8am–9pm, Sat

8am–5pm, Sun 9am–2pm); Main Road, Camps Bay (daily 9am–7pm); Main Road, Observatory (Mon–Thurs 7am–8.30pm, Fri 7am–10pm, Sat 7am–10pm, Sun 8am–2pm); corner Main Road and Campground Road, Claremont (Mon–Thurs 8am–6pm, Fri 8am–7pm, Sat 8am–4pm, Sun 9am–2pm); Blue Route Mall, Tokai (Mon–Thurs 8.30am–6pm, Fri 8.30am–7pm, Sat 8am–2pm, Sun 9am–2pm). In a similar vein to Woolworths but considerably larger and cheaper, with a good deli counter and a choice of prepared meals, among which you'll find their excellent-value ready-grilled whole chickens. It's also one of the best places for all groceries.

Delis and farm stalls

Thanks to the city's cosmopolitan population, there are some excellent (if pricey) delicatessens, several of which are strung along Main Road, Green Point and Sea Point. You'll also find delicious food and some unusual fruit and vegetables at the more sophisticated farm stalls.

The Barnyard Farm Stall Steenberg Road, adjacent to the well-signposted Steenberg Wine Estate, Tokai. ☎021 712 6934. One of Cape Town's nicest farm stalls, with a selection of high-class cheeses, breads,

home-baked cakes, wines, patés, coffee beans and many other delights. There's also the major attraction of a very good outdoor café with a children's playground attached. Daily 8.30am–5.30pm.

Giovanni's 103 Main Rd, Green Point ⊕ 021 434 6893. Excellent breads and delicious Italian foods to take away and – if temptation overcomes you – there's always the option of sitting down for a coffee and a snack. Mon–Sun 8.30am–9pm.
Melissa's 94 Kloof St, Gardens ⊕ 021 424 5540. Expensive imported and local specialities, which you can either eat in or take away. Mon–Fri 7.30am–9pm, Sat & Sun 8am–9pm.
New York Bagel Deli 51 Regent Rd, Sea Point ⊕ 021 439 7523. The best bagels in town and a

great selection of Eastern European Jewish fillings – salt beef, gherkins, chopped liver and pickled herring – and an array of delicious pastries. Daily 7am–9pm.
Old Cape Farm Stall turn-off to Groot Constantia, on Constantia Nek Road ⊕ 021 794 7062. A good place to pick up a picnic, where you can choose from their delicious selection of dips and ready-made foods such as olive bread, couscous and other salads, as well as fresh fruit and vegetables. Daily 8.15am–6pm.

Fresh fish

Fish Market Mariner's Wharf, Hout Bay Harbour. Fresh seafood from South Africa's original waterfront emporium, but slicker and less atmospheric than Kalk Bay Harbour. Mon–Fri 9am–5.30pm, Sat & Sun 9am–6pm.

Kalk Bay Harbour Harbourside, Kalk Bay. Buy fresh fish directly from the fishermen and have it gutted and scaled on the spot. Availability is subject to weather.

Wine

Supermarkets tend to have decent **wine** at competitive prices, but for more interesting labels and well-informed staff, there are some first-rate specialist wine merchants in town.

Enoteca Branches on the corner of 125c Buitengragt and Bloem streets, Mon–Fri 9am–8pm, Sat 9am–6pm; and Castle Building, on the corner of Kildare Lane and Main Road, Newlands, Mon–Fri 10am–9pm, Sat 9am–7pm. An excellent selection of South African and foreign wines from a knowledgeable and helpful outfit.
Vaughan Johnson's Dock Road, V&A Waterfront

⊕ 021 419 2121. One of Cape Town's best-known wine shops, which has a huge range of labels from all over the country, but can be a bit pricey. Mon–Fri 9am–6pm, Sat 9am–5pm, Sun 10am–5pm.
Woolworths Branches at Adderley Street, Mon–Fri 8.30am–5.30pm, Sat 8am–2pm; V&A Waterfront, daily 9am–9pm; Cavendish Square Mall,

Holistic Cape Town

Cape Town is South Africa's alternative-culture and **holism** capital. To find out what's on, the best **publications** are *Link-Up*, a free listings magazine, and the glossier *Odyssey* (R15), which is also the place to track down sources of southern African crystals, gemstones and essential oils – disappointingly though, there are few oils from Cape plants except for geraniums. Both publications are available from health-food shops and alternative health venues.

Fields Health Store 84 Kloof St, Gardens ⊕ 021423 9587. Sells health and beauty products, with a juice bar serving a daily vegetarian lunch buffet and cakes. Upstairs you can get massage, shiatsu, acupuncture and the like, but appointments are essential. Mon–Fri 8am–7pm, Sat 8.30am–4pm.
Natural Remedies Pearce St, Claremont ⊕ 021 674 1692. The best place in the southern suburbs for homeopathic and herbal remedies, aromatherapy oils, beauty products and a range of health foods. Mon–Fri 9am–5.15pm, Sat 8.30am–1pm.

Sunflower Health Café 111 Long St, City Centre. Health food shop and vegetarian restaurant that sells a good selection of natural remedies, organic and whole foods. Mon–Fri 9.45am–5.30pm, Sat 9am–1pm.
White's Chemist 77 Plein Park, Plein St, City Centre ⊕ 021 465 3332. A long-established manufacturer and supplier of homeopathic remedies, powders, tinctures and books. They also sell homeopathic first-aid kits and herbal products. Mon–Fri 7.30am–5pm, Sat 8am–12.30pm.

Claremont, Mon–Thurs 9am–6pm, Fri 8.30am–8pm, Sat 8am–6pm, Sun 9am–5pm; Blue Route Mall, Tokai, Mon–Thurs 9am–5.30pm, Fri 8.30am–7pm, Sat 8.30am–5pm, Sun 9am–2pm. The own-label wines of South Africa's upmarket supermar-ket chain have come a long way since the days when you'd sneakily decant them so no one would know their source. Cognoscenti now happily flaunt these competitively priced good-quality wines.

Listings

Airlines British Airways ☎ 021 936 9000, ⊛ www.britishairways.com/regional/sa; KLM Royal Dutch Airlines ☎ 0860 247 747, ⊛ www.klm.com; Kulula.com ☎ 0861 585 852, ⊛ www.kulula.com; Lufthansa ☎ 021 934 8534, ⊛ www.lufthansa.com; Nationwide ☎ 021 936 2050, ⊛ www.nationwideair.co.za; Olympic Airways ☎ 021 423 0260, ⊛ www.olympic-air-ways.co.uk; Qantas ☎ 011 441 8550, ⊛ www.qantas.com.au; SA Airlink ☎ 021 936 1111, ⊛ www.saairlink.co.za; South African Airways ☎ 021 936 1111, ⊛ www.flysaa.com; Virgin Atlantic ☎ 011 340 3400, ⊛ www.virgin-atlantic.com.

American Express Thibault House, Thibault Square, City Centre ☎ 021 421 5586. Offers full Amex facilities, including help with lost cards.

Banks Main branches are easy to find in the shopping areas of the city centre, the middle-class suburbs and at the Waterfront (Mon–Fri 8.30am–3.30pm, Sat 8–11am). Wherever you find banks, you'll also find automatic teller machines (ATMs) that take cards on the Cirrus and Maestro networks.

Bike rental Mountain bikes are available from Rent'n'Ride, Park Road, Mouille Point (☎ 021 434 1122; R75 a day including helmet and lock; R1000 credit card deposit required). Downhill Adventures (☎ 021422 0388, ⊛ www.downhilladventures.co.za) offers similar rentals for R95 a day or R570 a week.

Bureaux de change For foreign-exchange trans-actions outside normal banking hours, try one of the following: American Express, Shop 11a, Alfred Mall, Waterfront (Mon–Fri 9am–7pm, Sat & Sun 9am–5pm; ☎ 021 419 3917); Rennies Foreign Exchange, Victoria Wharf, V&A Waterfront (Mon–Sat 9am–9pm, Sun 10am–9pm; ☎ 021 418 3744); Rennies Travel, Riebeeck Street, City Centre (Mon–Thurs 8.30am–5pm, Fri 9–11.30am, Sat 9am–noon; ☎ 021 425 2370); Absa Bank, Cape Town International Airport (Mon 7am–8pm, Tues 6am–8pm, Wed 7am–9pm, Thurs 7am–8m, Fri 7am–8pm, Sat 7am–8pm, Sun 6am–9pm; ☎ 021 934 0223).

Car parks These are dotted all over the place in this car-friendly city. There are pay-and-display car parks at street level all around the centre, where hustlers will offer to look after your car and clean it for a tip, especially on the Grand Parade and Loop and Church streets. If you want to park in peace, head for one of the multi-storey parking garages; there's one attached to the Golden Acre complex, and another at the north end of Lower Burg Street.

Car rental One of the cheapest is Discount Drive Car Hire (☎ 021 511 6802), which rents out vehi-cles for as little as R160 a day (including 200km a day free) on the basis of a one-week rental, while Berea Car and Bakkie Hire (☎ 021 386 4054) offers a rate of R260 a day for three to six days with 250km free a day. For one-way rental (to drive down the Garden Route and fly back from Port Elizabeth, for example), you'll have to rely on one of the bigger companies, such as Avis ☎ 0861 021 111, ⊛ www.avis.co.za; Budget ☎ 0861 016 622, ⊛ www.budget.co.za; Europcar ☎ 0800 011 344, ⊛ www.europcar.co.za; Hertz ☎ 0861 600 136, ⊛ www.hertz.co.za; Imperial ☎ 0800 131 000, ⊛ www.imperial.ih.co.za; Tempest ☎ 0800 031 666, ⊛ www.tempestcarhire.co.za. Although pricier, they have nationwide offices. You'll need a credit card to arrange car rental.

Dental care Dentists are listed in the Yellow Pages telephone directory and are well up to British and North American standards, and gener-ally no more expensive.

Educational tours For arranging specialist educa-tional exchanges, cultural visits or fact-finding missions, there are few better operators in Cape Town than Ida Cooper Associates (☎ 021 683 4648, ⓔ idaca@iafrica.com), who facilitate con-tacts with a wide range of South Africans, includ-ing leading academics, artists, writers and govern-ment ministers.

Embassies and consulates Canada, 60 St George's Mall ☎ 021 423 5240; UK, Southern Life Centre, 8 Riebeeck St ☎ 021 405 2400; USA, 4th floor, Broadway Centre, Heerengracht ☎ 021 421 4280. The main embassies for most countries are in Pretoria, South Africa's executive capital.

Emergencies Ambulance ⏲10177; Police (Flying Squad) ⏲10111; Rape Crisis ⏲021 447 9762.

Hospitals and doctors Doctors are listed in the telephone directory under "Medical" and hospitals under "Hospitals and Associated Institutions". The largest state hospital is Groote Schuur, Hospital Drive, Observatory (⏲021 404 9111), just off the M3. Somerset Hospital, Beach Road, Mouille Point (⏲021 402 6911), nearer the centre, has outpatient and emergency departments and is convenient for the City Bowl and Atlantic seaboard, although it's generally overcrowded, understaffed and seemingly under-equipped. If you have medical insurance you might prefer to be treated at one of the well-staffed and well-equipped private hospitals listed in the phone directory. The two largest hospital groups are the Netcare (emergency response ⏲082911) and Medi-clinic chains, with hospitals all over the Cape Peninsula. Most central is Netcare's Chris Barnard Memorial Hospital (formerly the City Park) on Loop Street (⏲021 480 6111).

Laundry Most backpacker hostels have coin-operated washing machines, while guesthouses, hotels and B&Bs will usually offer a laundry service for a charge. There are also laundries in the city centre and most suburban areas that will do a service wash for you.

Left luggage Virtually every backpacker hostel provides luggage storage facilities and most other accommodation will be happy to take care of your luggage for a day or two. The left-luggage facility next to platform 24 at the train station (Mon–Fri 7am–4pm) is inexpensive and convenient if you're arriving by intercity bus or train, or catching an airport shuttle into the city centre.

Mobile phone rental Available from Cellucity, Shop 6193, Victoria and Alfred Waterfront (⏲021 418 1306) for around R13 per day for the handset, with calls charged at a little under R2.50 per minute. For security reasons you'll need a credit card.

Pharmacies Chemists with extended opening hours include: Hypermed Pharmacy, corner York and Main roads, Green Point (Mon–Sat 8.30am–9pm, Sun 9am–9pm; ⏲021 434 1414); Sunset Pharmacy, Sea Point Medical Centre, Kloof Road, Sea Point (daily 8.30am–9pm; ⏲021 434 3333); Tamboerskloof Pharmacy, 16 Kloof Nek Road, Tamboerskloof (daily 9.30am–6pm; ⏲021 424 4450).

Police Head office: Caledon Square, Buitenkant Street ⏲021 467 8000.

Post office The main branch, on Parliament Street, City Centre (Mon–Tues & Thurs–Fri 8am–4.30pm, Wed 8.30am–4.30pm, Sat 8am–noon; ⏲021 464 1700), has a poste restante and enquiry desk.

Taxis There are a number of reliable companies, including Marine Taxi Hire (⏲021 434 0434), Sea Point Radio Taxis (⏲021 434 4444), Unicab (⏲021 448 1720) and Rikki's (⏲021 423 4892).

Ticket agencies Computicket (⏲021 915 8000, ⓦwww.computicket.com) and Ticketweb (ⓦwww.ticketweb.co.za) book most theatre, cinema and sporting events, as well as airline and bus tickets.

Travel agents The largest travel franchise in the country is Sure Travel, which has about two dozen centres across Cape Town; call ⏲0800 221 656 for the nearest office. Try also STA, 31 Riebeeck St ⏲021 418 6570.

Travel details

Cape Town's undisputed status as the tourism hub of South Africa has meant the development of an excellent network of connections to the rest of the country. **Flying** from Cape Town airport (flight information ⏲021 934 0407) is the quickest though most expensive way of getting around, and useful if you need to cover large distances. As far as overland travel goes, the **intercity express buses**, run by Greyhound (⏲021 418 4310), Intercape (⏲021 386 4400) and Translux (⏲021 449 3333), offer a frequent, comprehensive and inexpensive service connecting Cape Town to major centres in the coastal provinces of Northern, Western and Eastern Cape, and KwaZulu-Natal. All have good connections to Pretoria and Johannesburg, which are on the same route. Besides the intercity express buses detailed above, there are **Baz buses**, the cheapest way to get around; services run constantly to and fro from Cape Town. The Baz Bus (⏲021 439 2323) leaves Cape Town daily and runs along the coast as far as Port Elizabeth (a 14hr journey), with connections from there to Durban (also a 14hr journey) five times a week. The 24-hour journey from Cape Town to Johannesburg is worth considering, especially if you're a family, as children go free, and you get your own private compartment. Moreover, you can put a car on the train for R900 which saves the very long drive between the two centres (℡0860 008 888). However, you need to be a bit of a stalwart for the 36-hour journey between Cape Town and Durban.

Trains

Two useful **trains** are the Metrorail suburban services connecting Cape Town with Stellenbosch and Paarl (both 1hr). Outside peak morning and evening hours, trains are irregular but run at approximately two-hour intervals; check that they're running on time. Mainline trains are slow, but can provide a relaxing way of traversing long routes:

Cape Town to: Bloemfontein (every Mon; 23hr); Durban (every Mon; 36hr 25min); Johannesburg (1 daily; 24hr 55min); Kimberley (1 daily; 16hr 30min); Pietermaritzburg (every Mon; 34hr); Pretoria (1 daily; 26hr 20min).

Intercity buses

Cape Town to: Bloemfontein (5–6 daily; 13hr); Cradock (1 daily; 10hr); Durban (3 daily; 20hr); East London (3 daily; 15hr 40min); George (4 daily; 6hr); Graaff Reinet (1–2 daily; 9hr); Grahamstown (1 daily; 12hr 25min); Johannesburg (4 daily; 17hr); Kimberley (1 daily except Wed; 11hr 45min); Knysna (4 daily; 6hr 50min); Montagu (3 weekly; 4hr); Mossel Bay (4 daily; 5hr 15min); Oudtshoorn (3 weekly; 6hr 15min); Pietermaritzburg (2 daily; 18hr 40min); Plettenberg Bay (4 daily; 7hr 30min); Port Elizabeth (4 daily; 10hr); Pretoria (4 daily; 18hr); Sedgefield (4 weekly; 6hr 45min); Stellenbosch (1–2 daily; 1hr); Storms River (4 daily; 10hr 10min); Umtata (1 daily; 18hr); Upington (4 weekly; 10hr 30min); Wilderness (4 daily; 6hr 30min); Windhoek (4 weekly; 16hr 30min).

Flights

Cape Town to: Bloemfontein (2–3 daily; 2hr 20min); Durban (10 daily; 2hr); East London (4 daily; 2hr); George (3–4 daily; 1hr); Johannesburg (16 daily; 2hr); Kimberley (1 daily; 3hr); Port Elizabeth (4 daily; 1hr 30min); Upington (6 weekly; 1hr 45min); Walvis Bay (2 weekly; 2hr); Windhoek (5 weekly; 2hr).

The Western Cape

CHAPTER 2 # Highlights

✳ **The Winelands** Quaff fine vintages on some of South Africa's most beautiful wine estates. See p.180

✳ **Lamb burger** The lamb burgers are outstanding at *Le Quartier Français*, one of the best restaurants in Franschhoek, the culinary capital of the Western Cape. See p.201

✳ **Passes of the Little Karoo** Drive down one of the Cape's dozen or so spectacular mountain passes. See p.202

✳ **The Lodge** The Philippe Starck bathrooms are only one of the features making Plettenberg Bay's monument to minimalism the hippest small hotel in the country. See p.270

✳ **Ocean safaris** Learn about whales and dolphins around Plettenberg Bay on an ocean safari. See p.271

✳ **Storms River Mouth** One of the most dramatic sections of coast, where hillside forests drop away to rocky coastline and the Storms River surges out of a gorge into the thundering ocean. See p.277

✳ **Sevilla Trail** Hike along a series of nine rockfaces decorated with ancient Bushman rock paintings – part of a 6,000-year-old tradition predating the pyramids. See p.296

The Western Cape

The most mountainous and arguably the most beautiful of South Africa's provinces, the **Western Cape** is also the most popular area of the country for foreign tourists. Curiously, it's also the least African province. Visitors spend weeks here without exhausting its attractions, but frequently leave slightly disappointed, never having quite experienced an African beat. Of South Africa's nine provinces, only the Western Cape and the Northern Cape don't have an African majority; one person in five here is African, and the largest community, making up 55 percent of the population, are coloureds – people of mixed race descended from white settlers, indigenous Khoisan people and slaves from the East.

Although the Western Cape appears to conform more closely to the First World than any other part of the country, the impression is strictly superficial. Beneath the prosperous feel of the Winelands and the Garden Route lies a reality of Third World poverty in **squatter camps** on the outskirts of well-to-do towns and on some farms where nineteenth-century labour practices prevail, despite the end of apartheid.

Nevertheless, you can't fail to be moved by the sensuous physical beauty of the province's mountains, valleys and beaches. The **Winelands**, less than an hour from Cape Town, give full reign to the sybaritic pleasures of eating, drinking and visual feasting. Dutch colonial heritage reaches its peak in this region of gabled homesteads sitting among vineyards against a backdrop of slaty crags.

To the northeast lies the **Breede River Valley**, a region usually bypassed along the N1 en route to Johannesburg, but featuring among its faceless fruit-farming towns some hideaways, such as Greyton and McGregor, favoured by Capetonians as weekend retreats. Almost totally neglected by visitors in the past, some creative marketing has now literally put the region on the map as the **Route 62** – the intriguing R62 – a back road tracing its way through the interior linking **Little Karoo** towns between Cape Town and Port Elizabeth. The timeless landscapes of the Little Karoo, the curtain-raiser to the semi-desert covering one-third of South Africa's surface, is nowhere more rewarding nor more easily accessed than here. Less visited than it deserves, the Little Karoo is skirted by the N1 to its north and the N2 to its south, and offers a succession of dramatic – sometimes hair-raising – **passes** switch-backing across one mountain range after another.

Southeast of the Winelands, the **Overberg** – roughly the area between Arniston and Mossel Bay along the coast, and as far inland as Swellendam – is another region that remains hidden behind the mountains during a hasty journey east. The **Whale Coast**, an angry stretch of Indian Ocean to the south that has claimed hundreds of ships, is known for being the best area in the country

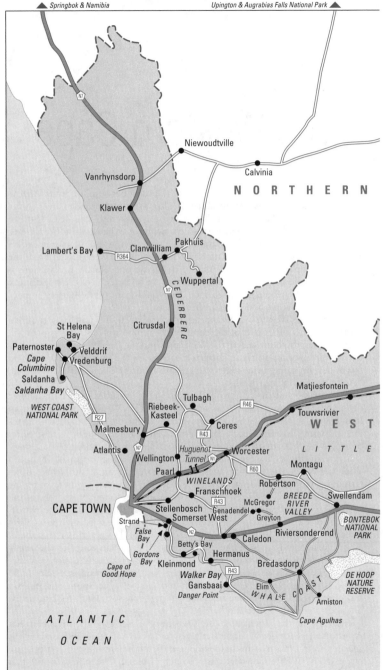

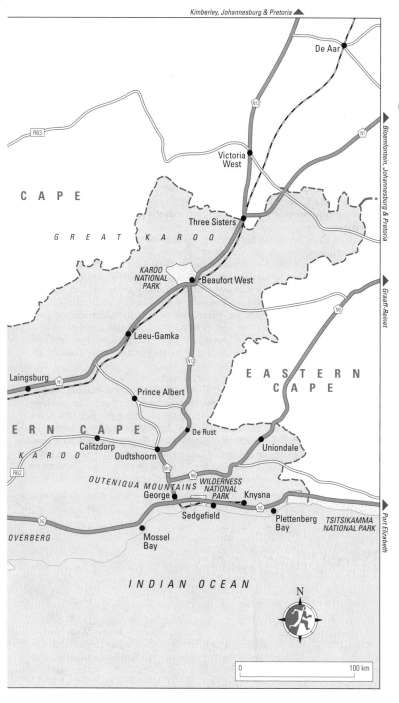

for shore-based **whale-watching**, and there are a couple of pleasant coastal towns off the main routes along here.

The best-known feature of the Western Cape is the **Garden Route**, a drive along the N2 that technically begins at **Mossel Bay**, where the freeway hits the coast, and continues east for 185km to **Storms River**. In reality it is taken as part of a journey between Cape Town and Port Elizabeth, simply because these are the easiest places to catch flights and to pick up and drop off rental cars. The Garden Route proper can be driven in half a day, but to cover it so quickly would mean missing its essence, which can be found off the road in its coastal towns, lagoons, mountains and ancient forests, the highlight being the **Tsitsikamma National Park**, where the dark Storms River opens spectacularly into the Indian Ocean. Partly because it lies along a single stretch of freeway, **public transport** along the Garden Route is better than anywhere in the country. Taking advantage of its accessibility and obvious natural charm, operators along the Garden Route have recently begun turning it into the country's most concentrated strip for packaged **adventure sports** and **outdoor activities**.

North of Cape Town, the less popular, remote and windswept **west coast** is usually explored during the wildflower months of August and September, when visitors converge on its centrepiece, the **West Coast National Park**. Its other major pull is the **Cederberg** mountain range, 200km north of Cape Town on the N7, a rocky wilderness with hikes and hidden rock-art sites.

Apart from the annual explosion of wild flowers in the north, the Western Cape, as South Africa's **fynbos province**, really scores on wilderness and flora. The plants you'll glimpse from afar all along the coast and up every mountainside look like a nondescript grey-green blur of vegetation, but on closer examination reveal a rich kingdom of delicate flowering species rivalling the Amazon rainforest for biodiversity.

Several national parks and nature reserves make excellent places to explore fynbos, as do all the hikes mentioned in this chapter, but you shouldn't expect to see much African wildlife here. Most reserves have a few zebra or antelope, but the big game disappeared many years ago – reflecting the fact that South Africa's longest-colonized province was also the first to taste the destructive power of firearms. By the same means, indigenous **Khoikhoi and San people** were virtually extinguished in the nineteenth century and **Africans** kept at a distance, some 1000km away on the "Eastern Frontier", which accounts for their relatively small numbers in the Western Cape.

The Winelands

South Africa has over a dozen recognized wine routes extending to the Karoo and way into the Northern Cape, but the area known as **the Winelands** is restricted to the oldest wineries outside the Peninsula, within a sixty-kilometre radius of Cape Town. The district contains the earliest European settlements at Stellenbosch, Paarl, Franschhoek and Somerset West, each with its own wine route. On the hillsides and in the valleys around these towns you'll find a flawless blending of traditional Cape Dutch **architecture** with the landscape.

The Winelands are best covered in your own car, as half the pleasure is the drive through the countryside. Without private transport, the best option is to head for **Stellenbosch**, which is served by regular trains from Cape Town. The most satisfying of the Wineland towns, Stellenbosch enjoys an easy elegance, beautiful streetscapes, a couple of decent museums and plenty of visitor facilities. If you're in a car, one of the region's scenic highlights is the drive along the R310 through the **Helshoogte Pass** between Stellenbosch and Paarl, which can also be reached on the Metrorail link from Cape Town. The workaday farming town of the region, Paarl is credited as the place where Afrikaans first sprang to recognition, and has an Afrikaans language monument and a museum to honour the fact. Smallest of the Wineland towns, **Franschhoek** has the most magnificent setting at the head of a narrow valley, and has established itself as the culinary capital of the Cape. By contrast, the sprawling town of **Somerset West** has only one drawcard, but it's an outstanding one – **Vergelegen**, by far the most stunning of all the Wineland estates, which can be tacked onto a tour of the Stellenbosch wine route.

Summer is the best time to visit, when days are longer, as are opening hours, the vines are in leaf and there's activity at the wineries. In winter the wine has been made, there are fewer cellar tours and there's not much going on. Several estates offer lunches, while some allow picnics in their grounds – a great idea if you're travelling with children or simply want to drink in the mountainous views in a bucolic haze.

Stellenbosch

Dappled avenues of three-century-old oaks are the defining feature of **STELLENBOSCH**, 46km east of Cape Town – a fact reflected in its Afrikaans nickname Die Eikestad (the oak city). Street frontages of the same vintage, sidewalk cafés, water furrows and a European town layout centred on the Braak, a large village green, add up to a well-rooted urban texture that invites casual exploration. The city is the undisputed heart of the Winelands, having more urban attractions than either Paarl or Franschhoek, while at the same time being at the hub of the largest and oldest of the Cape **wine routes**.

The city is also home to Stellenbosch University, Afrikanerdom's most prestigious educational institution, which does something to enliven the atmosphere. But even the heady promise of plentiful alcohol and thousands of students haven't changed the fact that at heart this is a conservative place, which was once the intellectual engine room of apartheid, and fostered the likes of Dr H.F. Verwoerd, the prime minister who dreamed up Grand Apartheid.

Some history

One of the first actions of **Simon van der Stel** after arriving at the Cape in November 1679 to take over as Dutch East India commander was to explore the area along the Eerste River (first river), where he came upon an enchanting little valley. Less than a month later it appeared on maps as Stellenbosch (Stel's bush), the first of several places dotted around the Cape, including Simonsberg overlooking the town, which the governor was to name after himself or members of his family.

Charged by the Dutch East India Company directors in the Netherlands with opening up the Cape interior, van der Stel soon settled the first **free**

Tackling the Winelands

With over one hundred estates in the **Winelands**, the big question is which ones to visit. Our selection covers wineries of general interest that feature beautiful architecture or scenery, or are entertaining in some way, not primarily because they produce the best wine (although some are in the first rank). When planning your trip, bear in mind that although all the wineries offer tastings, many offer a lot more, such as restaurants, picnics and horse-riding. Choose an area to explore and don't try to visit too many wineries in a day unless you want to return home in a dizzy haze. Remember that wine tasting and wine buying are supposed to be fun, so don't take it too seriously and don't take on too much. Even if you aren't a wine buff, you'll often find staff at tasting rooms are happy to talk you through a wine, which can be especially interesting once you begin to pick up the characteristics of different wines. Most estates will charge a fee of between R2 and R8 for a wine-tasting session. If you plan on anything more than the briefest of tours, think about buying the authoritative John Platter's *South African Wine Guide*, which provides up-to-date ratings of the produce of every winery in the country. *Wine* magazine, published every month and available from all newsagents, has useful features on wineries, places to eat, wine reviews, information on latest bottlings and a diary of events.

Rough Guide favourite estates

Boschendal Estate Franschhoek (see p.200). The best-organized estate aimed at tourists, offering conducted tours, beautiful buildings, shops and a choice of restaurants.

Cabrière Estate Franschhoek (see p.199). Here you can see the most eccentric uncorking using sabrage – slicing clean through the neck of a bubbly bottle with a sabre.

Delaire Stellenbosch (see p.189). Offering the best mountain view across the Helshoogte Pass.

Fairview Estate Paarl (see p.196). A great family venue with a famous goat

tower, peacocks, cheese and wine.

La Motte Estate Franschhoek (see p.199). The best tasting room, decorated with marble, glass and oak barrels.

Rhebokskloof Estate Paarl (see p.196). This estate offers the trendiest restaurant, overlooking a lake of swans.

Rustenberg Estate Stellenbosch (see p.188). The most bucolic setting, with a historic gabled milking shed.

Vergelegen Somerset West (see p.189). The estate that has it all: fabulous buildings, a small museum, beautiful gardens, good wines to taste and a choice of restaurants.

Rough Guide favourite labels

An A to Z of old favourites, rising stars and plain good value:

Old Favourites

Backsberg Paarl. Whites and reds.
Blaauwklippen Stellenbosch. Whites and reds.
Kanonkop Stellenbosch. Reds.
Lievland Stellenbosch. Reds.
Meerlust Stellenbosch. Whites and reds.
Overgaauw Paarl. Reds.
Rust en Vrede Stellenbosch. Reds.
Simonsig Stellenbosch. Whites and reds.
Villiera Paarl. Whites and reds.

Hot Tips

Brampton Rustenberg Estate, Stellenbosch. Whites and reds.
Fairview Paarl. Whites and reds.
Glen Carlou Paarl. Whites and reds.
Hartenberg Stellenbosch. Reds.
Klawervlei Stellenbosch. Reds.
Klein Constantia Constantia. Whites and reds.
Morgenhof Stellenbosch. Whites and reds.
Plaisir de Merle Simonsberg. Whites and reds.
Saxenburg Stellenbosch. Reds.
Veenwouden Paarl. Reds.

burghers in Stellenbosch. Within eight years, 60 freehold grants had been made; within the next two decades, Stellenbosch had established itself as a prosperous, semi-feudal society dominated by landowners, and in 1702 the Danish traveller, Abraham Bogaert, admired how it had "grown with fine dwellings, and how great a treasure of wine and grain is grown here". By the end of the century there were over 1000 houses and some substantial burgher estates in and around Stellenbosch, many of which still exist.

Arrival, information and getting around

Coming to Stellenbosch **by car** gives you the freedom to explore the surrounding wineries at your leisure. The drive from Cape Town takes under an hour along either the N1 or N2. Metrorail **trains** (℡021 449 2991) commute between Cape Town and Stellenbosch roughly every two hours during the day, and take about an hour. Infrequent (and expensive) intercity buses from Cape Town and Port Elizabeth pass through Stellenbosch, calling at the train station; again, it's around an hour's journey.

The busy **tourist information** bureau, about 1km from the station at 36 Market St (Mon–Fri 8am–6pm, Sat 9am–5pm, Sun 9.30am–4.30pm; ℡021 883 3584, Ⓦwww.istellenbosch.org.za), can provide basic information on local attractions, and can supply you with the *Discover Stellenbosch on Foot* leaflet, which describes a walking tour covering a daunting 62 sites.

The centre of Stellenbosch is small enough to explore on foot, but if you need to get further afield, contact Tazzis (℡072 210 7882), who provide transport in **tuk-tuks**. They also offer excursions to wineries for around R25 per person per farm.

For **Winelands tours**, Easy Rider Wine Tours, based at *Stumble Inn* backpacker lodge (see below) offers daytime packages (10.30am–5pm; R180) to five cellars; they also do reasonably priced pub crawls to five nightspots in town.

Accommodation

Stellenbosch has no shortage of **places to stay**, from backpacker lodges to total luxury. Apart from a handful of out-of-town farmstays and the luxurious *Lanzerac*, all the accommodation is within easy walking distance of the town centre.

Backpacker lodges

Backpackers Inn De Wet Centre, corner of Bird and Church streets ℡021 887 2020, Ⓔbacpac1@global.co.za. Stellenbosch's most central backpacker lodge has a squeaky-clean atmosphere, attracting travellers of all ages and making it highly suitable for families. Dorms and doubles ❶
Stumble Inn 12 Market St ℡ & Ⓕ021 887 4049, Ⓔstumble@iafrica.com). The town's best and oldest established hostel in two turn-of-the-century houses, with friendly, switched-on staff and a chilled atmosphere, just down the road from the tourist information bureau. The hostel offers doubles, dorms and camping, and is also noted for its good-value tours (see above). ❶

Guesthouses and hotels

Avenues Guest House 32 The Avenue ℡021 887 1843 or 082 390 6659, Ⓔtheavenues@mweb.co.za. A friendly B&B done out in airy yel-

lowwood and pine, with a twist of Laura Ashley. It's across the road from the Eerste River, an easy walk to the centre and university campus, where guests can use the swimming pool and three-storey gym. ❹
Blombosch Guest House 61 Plein St ℡021 883 3674, Ⓔernieb@netactive.co.za. A central guesthouse with eight budget B&B double rooms, some with balconies. ❶
Bonne Esperance 17 Van Riebeeck St ℡021 887 0225, Ⓦwww.bonneesperance.com. Colonial elegance in a terrific two-storey Victorian villa. Some larger rooms, good service, a verandah overlooking a lovely front garden, and a courtyard and swimming pool at the rear all help to justify the price. ❹
D'Ouwe Werf 30 Church St ℡021 887 1608, Ⓦwww.ouwewerf.com. Located in the middle of town, South Africa's oldest country inn dates back to the end of the nineteenth century. There are TVs

183 ▬

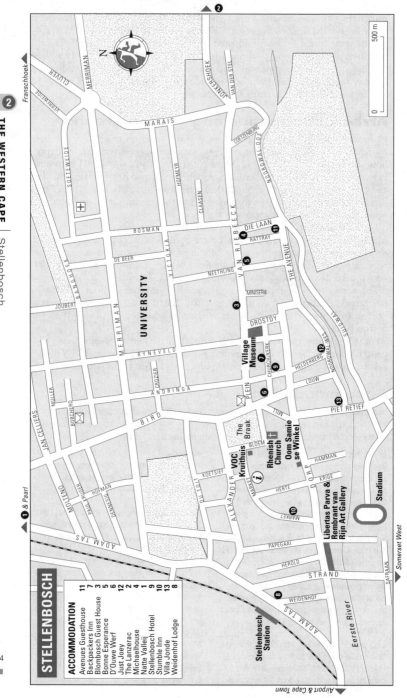

STELLENBOSCH

ACCOMMODATION

Avenues Guesthouse	11
Backpackers Inn	7
Blombosch Guest House	3
Bonne Esperance	5
D'Ouwe Werf	6
Just Joey	12
The Lanzerac	2
Michaelhouse	4
Natte Vallei	1
Stellenbosch Hotel	9
Stumble Inn	10
Villa Jonde	13
Weidenhof Lodge	8

and phones in every room, a swimming pool, and you can eat in their lovely courtyard (see p.186). **⑤**

Just Joey On the corner of 13 Noordwal-Wes and Helderberg streets ⓣ 021 887 1799, ⓔ justjoey@mweb.co.za. A peachy-pink guesthouse, with comfortable rooms glowing with rose-tinted frills and drapes. **❹**

The Lanzerac Jonkershoek Road, 1km east of town ⓣ 021 887 1132, ⓕ 021 887 2310, ⓦ www.lanzerac.co.za. The last word in Winelands luxury, this hotel wallows in a visual orgy of white-washed buildings surrounded by vineyards and mountains. **❽**

Michaelhouse 29 Van Riebeeck St ⓣ & ⓕ 021 886 6343. A guesthouse with modern cast-iron decor, with just a hint of the ethnic, offering a relief from the town's ubiquitous soft colours and floral prints. The rooms have showers or baths, while the garden terrace with trellised vines makes the perfect venue for a summery breakfast. **❸–❹**

Natte Valleij On the R44 Klapmuts Road, 12km north of town ⓣ 021 875 5171,

ⓔ milner@intekom.co.za. Guests have a choice of a large cottage sleeping six, or a smaller and less expensive family unit attached to an old white-washed homestead with a swimming pool and large gardens in the heart of the Winelands. Breakfast is served on the verandah. **❸**

Stellenbosch Hotel On the corner of Dorp and Andringa streets ⓣ 021 887 3644, ⓦ www.stellen-bosch.co.za/hotel. A smart town-centre hotel in a restored nineteenth-century house, now declared a National Monument, offering brass beds, capacious sofas, starched linen and atmosphere. Room only **⑤**

Villa Jonde 27 Noorwal-Wes ⓣ & ⓕ 021 883 3568. A rambling Edwardian house eccentrically furnished and generally unpretentious, surrounded by a huge jungle of a garden, and offering reasonable value. **❷**

Weidenhof Lodge 24 Weidenhof St ⓣ 021 886 4679, ⓕ 021 887 2397, ⓔ thys_haupt@hotmail.com. Good-value, compact self-catering apartments with showers, fully equipped kitchens, TVs and linen, accommodating two to four people. **❷**

The Town

Stellenbosch's attractions lie principally in its setting and streetscape; it's a lovely place to simply wander around. The tourist information bureau in the Rhenish Complex, Market Street, is a good place to start your explorations. Heading east up this road you'll soon reach a whitewashed block that was the **VOC Kruithuis** (Jan–May & Aug–Dec Mon–Fri 9.30am–1.30pm & 2–5pm) – the Dutch East India Company's powder magazine – which houses a small and unprepossessing collection of four British uniforms, assorted rifles, some intriguing, but unexplained, little laptop-sized cannons and some powder kegs. From here, a right turn south down the side of the **Braak**, the large green occupying the centre of town, will take you past the **Rhenish Church** in Bloem Street, built in 1823 as a school for slaves and coloured people.

The Village Museum

Head north up Ryneveld Street, and you'll encounter Stellenbosch's highlight, the extremely enjoyable **Village Museum**, 18 Ryneveld St (Mon–Sat 9am–4.45pm, Sun 2–4.45pm; R10; ⓣ 021 887 2902), which cuts a cross-section through the town's architectural and social heritage by means of a complex of four fortuitously adjacent historical dwellings from different periods. They're beautifully conserved and furnished in period style, and you'll meet the odd worker dressed in contemporary costume. Earliest of the houses is the homely **Shreuderhuis**, a vernacular cottage built in 1709, with a small courtyard garden filled with aromatic herbs, pomegranate bushes and vine-draped pergolas – bearing more resemblance to the early Cape settlement's European aesthetics than to modern South Africa. Across the garden, **Blettermanhuis**, built in 1789 for the last Dutch East India Company-appointed magistrate of Stellenbosch, is an archetypal eighteenth-century Cape Dutch house, built on an H-plan with six gables. **Grosvenor House**, opposite, was altered to its current form in 1803, reflecting the growing influence of English taste after the 1795 British occupation of the Cape. The Neoclassical facade, with fluted pilasters supporting a pedimented entrance, borrows from high fashion then current at the heart of the growing Empire. The more modest **O.M. Bergh House**, across the road, is a typical Victorian dwelling that was once similar to Blettermanhuis, but was "modernized" in the mid-nineteenth century on a rectangular plan with a simplified facade without gables.

Dorp Street and around

From the Village Museum, head back south into **Dorp Street**, Stellenbosch's best-preserved historic axis, well worth a slow stroll just to soak in the ambience of buildings, gables, oaks and roadside water furrows. Heading west along it, you'll spot the **Stellenbosch Wine Tasting Centre** on your left and next door the much-celebrated **Oom Samie se Winkel**, which amounts to little more than a jam-packed Victorian-style general dealer selling tourist knick-knacks, antiques, comestibles and wines, but is worth popping into if only to sample some fish biltong. On your right, look out for **Krige's Cottages**, an unusual terrace of historic town houses at nos. 37–51, between Aan-die-Wagen-Weg and Krige streets. The houses were built as Cape Dutch cottages in the first half of the nineteenth century, and later Victorian features were added, resulting in an interesting hybrid, with gables housing Victorian attic windows and decorative Victorian verandahs with filigree ironwork fronting the elegant simplicity of Cape Dutch facades.

A left turn into Strand Street brings you to **Libertas Parva**, a fine example of an H-plan Cape Dutch manor, and home to the **Rembrandt van Rijn Art Museum** (Mon–Fri 9am–12.45pm & 2–5pm, Sat 10am–1pm & 2–5pm; free). Don't let the name fool you into expecting Old Dutch Masters – the museum is funded by the Rembrandt tobacco multinational. The gallery has a small but stimulating collection of South African art, including a wonderful 360-degree panorama of Cape Town rendered in pen, ink and watercolour by Josephus Jones in 1808; *The Conservationists Ball*, an acerbic tryptich by William Kentridge, a leading light among the current generation of South African artists; and a number of Irma Stern paintings and drawings.

Eating and drinking

You'll be spoilt for choices of good places to eat in Stellenbosch, both in the centre and on some of the surrounding estates. Many places have outdoor seating, and in the evenings, the student presence ensures a relaxed and sometimes raucous drinking culture.

De Akker 90 Dorp St. Good spot for pub lunches and late nights (it hots up after 11pm, and the music is loud) in a buzzing joint enjoyed both by students and a not-so-young crowd.

Decameron 50 Plein St ☎021 883 3331. One of the best, though least exciting, restaurants in town, offering southern Italian food, including pasta, pizzas and gnocchi, as well as first-rate seafood. You can watch the street life from the glassed-in pavement tables. Daily 11am–11pm.

D'Ouwe Werf 30 Church St ☎021 887 1608. A restaurant in a beautiful courtyard with vines, offering traditional Cape Cuisine, including Karoo lamb, *bobotie* and oxtail stewed in red wine sauce. Outdoor lunches and teas are very appealing, as the ambience gets rather formal after dark.

The Fishmonger Sanlam Building, Ryneveld Street ☎021 887 7835. A superb seafood restaurant, centrally located, with outdoor seating. Open daily for lunch and dinner, it's not cheap, but reasonable value for what you get.

La Masseria Blaauwklippen Road off the R44 ☎021 880 0266. A converted winery that combines a deli and restaurant, offering good Italian food in an informal venue which is great for kids. If you get there for Sunday lunch or a dinner, you may find yourself listening to the patron's songs and joining in yourself. Lunch Tues–Sun 12.30–5pm; dinner (booking only) Fri and Sat.

Lanzerac Manor & Winery *Lanzerac Hotel*, Jonkershoek Road ☎021 887 1132. A formal restaurant in this grand historic homestead among the vineyards on the outskirts of town. Less intimidating are the light lunches on the terrace or in the pub. Winter lunches and cream teas are especially nice around a cosy fire.

Rustic Café 43a Bird St ☏021 883 3545. A cosy and popular evening place with bean bags, couches and music, offering cheap to moderately priced pizzas, nachos, and salads; open every evening.

Spice Café Church Street ☏021 883 8480. The *Spice Café* has friendly staff and a central location, with a relaxing garden setting and play area for kids. It's popular for weekend brunches, and also offers fresh cakes, sandwiches, salads and Mediterranean-based meals. Mon–Fri 9am–5pm, Sat 9am–2pm, Sun 10am–2pm.

The Terrace Shop 12, Drostdy Centre ☏021 887 1942. A central bar-cum-restaurant overlooking the Braak, where you can get pub lunches, burgers and light meals. Frequented by a young crowd, it's open from mid-morning to the early hours of the next day.

Volkskombuis & De Oewer Aan-de-Wagenweg, off Dorp Street ☏021 887 2121. A good place to sample Cape Cuisine, this venue with two separate menus, on the banks of the Eerste River, does Mediterranean fare at *De Oewer*, with a buffet in the garden and platters of reasonably priced Cape Cuisine specialities at *Volkskombuis*. Lunch daily, dinner Mon–Sat.

The Stellenbosch wine estates

Stellenbosch was the first locality in the country to wake up to the marketing potential of a **wine route** (where you travel from one estate to the next to taste the wines), which it launched in 1971. The tactic has been hugely successful and now draws tens of thousands of visitors from all over the world to the wineries, making this the most toured area in the Winelands. Although the region accounts for only fifteen percent of South Africa's land under vine, its wine route is the most extensive in the country and offers some of the Cape's best reds and overall the greatest diversity of wines. The wineries are all along a series of roads that radiate out from Stellenbosch; the selection below covers three of these roads, with the wineries arranged from Stellenbosch outwards, making each series easy to cover in a single journey. All the wineries have wine-route signposts along the main road.

Along the R44

North out of Stellenbosch towards the N1, Klapmuts Road (the **R44**) leads you after around 4km to **Morgenhof** (May–Oct Mon–Fri 9am–4.30pm, Sat 10am–3pm; Nov–Apr Mon–Thurs 9am–5.30pm, Fri 9am–5pm, Sat & Sun 10am–5pm; R10; ☏021 889 5510). A French-owned chateau-style complex overlooked by the vine-covered Simonsberg, Morgenhof has a light and airy tasting room with a bar. Delicious light lunches are served outside, topped off with ice cream on the lawns. Among the numerous top-ranking wines worth sampling are the Merlot, Cabernet Sauvignon, Pinotage, Sauvignon Blanc, Chardonnay and Chenin Blanc.

Drive north along the Klapmuts Road for about another 4km and you'll reach the left turn-off to **Simonsig**, located just over 2km down Kromme Rhee Road (Mon–Fri 8.30am–5pm, Sat 8.30am–4pm; cellar tours Mon–Fri 10am & 3pm, Sat 10am; R5; ☏021 888 4900). The winery has an outdoor tasting area under vine-covered pergolas, offering majestic views back to Stellenbosch of hazy stone-blue mountains and vineyards. Their first-class wines include a cutting-edge Pinotage Red Hill, a Kaapse Vonkel sparkling wine and an extremely good value Chardonnay.

Back on the main road, **Lievland** (Mon–Fri 9am–5pm, Sat 9am–1pm; ☏021 875 5226), 4.5km north of the Simonsig turn-off, is the last of the Stellenbosch wineries on this section of the R44 – after this they fall under Paarl (see p.190).

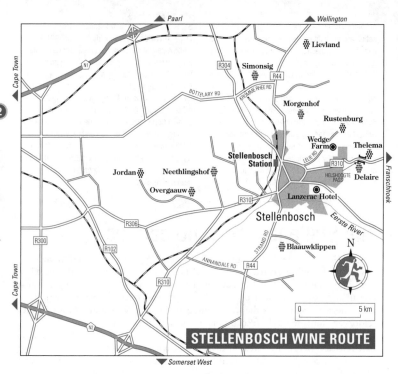

Paarl ▲   ▲ Wellington

Lievland

Cape Town ◀

N1

R304   Simonsig

R44

BOTTELARY RD   KROMME RHEE RD

Morgenhof

Rustenburg

Wedge Farm ●   Thelema

Stellenbosch Station

LELIE RD   R310

HELSHOOGTE PASS   Delaire

Jordan   Neethlingshof

Overgaauw

R310

Lanzerac Hotel

Stellenbosch

Eerste River

R306

R300

R102

Blaauwklippen   N

ANNANDALE RD   R44

STRAND RD

R310

Cape Town ◀

N2

0   5 km

STELLENBOSCH WINE ROUTE

Franschhoek ▶

Somerset West ▼

Lievland is an informal place, with a Cape Dutch tasting room which dates back to 1823. Its small variety of wines include an ace Shiraz and a DVB Bordeaux-style blend; for a good quaffer at a reasonable price, give their Lievlander red blend a shot.

Drive straight back through Stellenbosch, and 4km from town along the Strand Road (R44 south) you'll come to **Blaauwklippen** (Mon–Fri 9am–5pm, Sat 9am–1pm; R10; ☎021 880 0133), at the foot of the Stellenboschberg. Although big enough to take tour buses, Blaauwklippen isn't overly commercialized. Apart from the usual Cape Dutch buildings, there's a museum housing antique horse-drawn carriages; a little shop sells soft drinks and knick-knacks, and a coachman's lunch is served (Mon–Sat) on the verandah. Their wines are generally of middling quality, but include a celebrated Zinfandel, of which they are one of the few local producers.

If you continue south along the R44, you'll eventually reach Somerset West, centre of the Helderberg wine route, the highlight of which is **Vergelegen** (see p.189).

Along the R310

One of the closest wine estates to central Stellenbosch, **Rustenberg Wines** (Mon–Fri 9am–4.30pm, Sat 9am–12.30pm; ☎021 809 1200; free) is also one of the most alluring. To get there, join the R310 from the R44 to Paarl, just north of town. After just under 2km along the R310 to Franschhoek, turn into Ida's Valley along Lelie Road for a further 2km which, after a drive through orchards, sheep pastures and tree-lined avenues, brings you to the estate. An unassuming working farm, Rustenberg's romantic pastoral atmosphere stands in contrast to its high-tech tasting room. The first vines were planted here in 1692, but the viniculture looks to the future. Most of their wines under the Rustenberg label are worth tasting, but also look out for highly drinkable and less expensive reds and whites under the Brampton brand – their second label.

For the best views in the Winelands, head for **Delaire** (Mon–Sat 10am–5pm; R10; ☎021 885 1756), on the **Helshoogte Pass**, 6km east of Stellenbosch along the R310 to Franschhoek. The restaurant here has views through oaks across the Groot Drakenstein and Simonsig mountains and down into craggy valleys; in the tasting room, their flagship Merlot is particularly worth sampling.

Along the R306

Moddergat Road (the R310) heads southwest out of Stellenbosch beside the train tracks, branching off 5.5km later onto Polkadraai Road (the **R306**). Half a kilometre later you'll come to the driveway leading to **Neethlingshof** (Mon–Fri 9am–7pm, Sat & Sun 10am–6pm; tasting R20 including a glass you take away; ☎021 883 8988), which has a beautifully restored Cape Dutch manor dating back to 1814, and two good restaurants. The first vines were planted here in 1692 and Neethlingshof produces very good wines, consistently hitting the high notes with its stunning Noble Late Harvest sweet dessert wines. A further 500m along the R306 takes you to another turn-off to the north, along which after a short distance you'll reach **Overgaauw** (Mon–Fri 9am–12.30pm & 2–5pm, Sat 10am–12.30pm; ☎021 881 3815), notable for its elegant Victorian tasting room. A pioneering estate that produces reds and ports of excellent quality, Overgaauw was the first in the country to produce Merlots, and it's still the only one to make Sylvaner, a well-priced, easy-drinking dry white.

Further north along the same road, **Jordan Vineyards** (Mon–Fri 10am–4.30pm, Sat 9.30am–2.30pm; ☎021 881 3441; R7.50 refundable with purchases) is part of the new wave of Cape wineries, with a hi-tech cellar, modern tasting room and friendly service. The drive there is half the fun, taking you into a *kloof* bounded by vineyards that get a whiff of the seas from both False Bay and Table Bay, which has obviously done something for their outstanding Chardonnay and Blanc Fumé.

Somerset West and Vergelegen

The only compelling reason to trawl out to the unpromising town of **SOMERSET WEST**, 50km east of Cape Town along the N2, is for **Vergelegen** on Lourensford Road (daily 9.30am–4pm; entrance R10; tasting R5 for five wines; ☎021 847 1334), an absolute architectural treasure and an estate producing a stunning range of wines. Officially part of the Helderberg wine route, Vergelegen can easily be included as an extension to a visit to Stellenbosch, just 14km to the north.

Vergelegen represents a notorious episode of corruption and the arbitrary abuse of power at the Cape in the early years of Dutch East India Company rule. Built by Willem Adriaan van der Stel, who became governor in 1699 after the retirement of his father Simon, the estate formed a grand Renaissance complex in the middle of the wild backwater that was the Cape at the turn of the eighteenth century. Van der Stel acquired the land illegally and used Dutch East India Company slaves to build Vergelegen as well as Company resources to farm vast tracts of land in the surrounding areas. At the same time he abused his power as governor to corner most of the significant markets at the Cape.

When this was brought to the notice of the Dutch East India Company in the Netherlands, van der Stel was sacked and Vergelegen was ordered to be destroyed to discourage future miscreant governors. It's believed that the destruction was never fully carried out and the current building is thought to stand on the foundations of the original.

Vergelegen was the only wine estate visited by the British queen during her 1995 state visit to South Africa – a good choice, as there's enough here to occupy an easy couple of hours. The **interpretive centre**, just across the courtyard from the shop at the building entrance, provides a useful history and background to the estate. Next door, the **wine-tasting centre** (closed Sun in winter) offers a professionally run sampling with a brief talk through each label. The **homestead**, which was restored in 1917 to its current state by Lady Florence Phillips, wife of a Johannesburg mining magnate, can also be visited. Its pale facade with a classical triangular gable and pilaster-decorated doorways is reached along an axis through an octagonal garden that dances with butterflies in summer. Massive grounds planted with chestnuts and camphor trees and ponds around every corner make this one of the most serene places in the Cape.

Practicalities

Vergelegen is best reached **by car**. Although there are regular Metrorail trains between Cape Town and Somerset West, the estate is too far from town to make this a serious option, unless you're prepared to hitch. To reach Vergelegen from Cape Town, take the N2 east past the International Airport, and leave the freeway at exit 43, signposted to Somerset West. This brings you onto the R44, which you should follow into town. Once in Main Street, take the turn-off to Lourensford Road (if you hit the town centre you've missed the turn-off), and follow this for just over 3km to Vergelegen, on the right.

Given its proximity to far nicer Stellenbosch, there's no reason to stay overnight in Somerset West. For **eating and drinking**, Vergelegen offers two excellent choices: at the chintzy *Lady Phillips Tea Garden* (℡021 847 1346) you can take tea or eat country-cuisine lunches (booking essential) of pies, quiches and pastas with an international flavour, while the less formal *Rose Terrace* offers outdoor light lunches of sandwiches on home-baked bread, cheese platters and wine by the glass.

Paarl

Although **PAARL** is attractively ensconced in a fertile valley brimming with historical monuments, at heart it's a parochial *dorp*, lacking either the sophistication of Stellenbosch or the new-found trendiness of Franschhoek. It can claim some virtue, however, from being a prosperous farming centre that earns its keep from the agricultural light industries – grain silos, canneries and flour mills – on the north side of town, and the cornucopia of grapes, guavas, olives, oranges and maize grown on the surrounding farms. Despite its small-town feel, Paarl has the largest municipality in the Winelands, with its most exclusive areas on the vined slopes of **Paarl Mountain** overlooking the town. In stark contrast with the cliquey conservatism of the predominantly white centre, the coloured townships on its periphery bear racy American names such as Chicago and New Orleans.

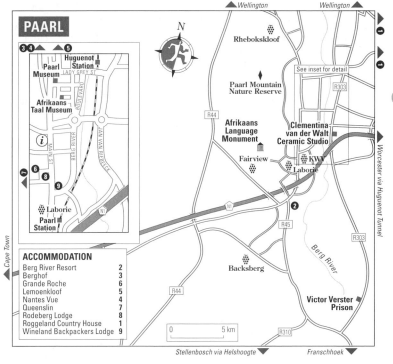

PAARL

Wellington — Wellington

Rheboksloof

Cape Town

See inset for detail

Paarl Mountain
Nature Reserve

R303

Afrikaans
Language
Monument

Clementina
van der Walt
Ceramic Studio

Fairview

KWV
Laborie

Worcester via Huguenot Tunnel

R44

R45

R303

Berg River

Huguenot
Station

Paarl
Museum

LADY GREY ST

Afrikaans
Taal Museum

BOULEVARD

MAIN ST

BERG RIVER

JAN VAN RIEBEECK

N1

Laborie
Paarl
Station

Backsberg

Victor Verster
Prison

ACCOMMODATION

Berg River Resort	2
Berghof	3
Grande Roche	6
Lemoenkloof	5
Nantes Vue	4
Queenslin	7
Rodeberg Lodge	8
Roggeland Country House	1
Wineland Backpackers Lodge	9

0   5 km

R44

R310

Stellenbosch via Helshoogte — *Franschhoek*

Some history

In 1657, just five years after the establishment of the Dutch East India Company refreshment station on the Cape Peninsula, a party under **Abraham Gabbema** arrived in the Berg River Valley to look for trading opportunities with the Khoikhoi, and search for the legendary gold of Monomotapa. They obviously had treasure on the brain, because on awaking after a rainy night to the sight of the silvery dome of granite dominating the valley, they dubbed it Peerlbergh (pearl mountain), which in its modified form, **Paarl**, became the name of the town.

Thirty years later, the commander of the Cape, Simon van der Stel, granted strips of the Khoikhoi lands on the slopes of Paarl Mountain to French Huguenot and Dutch settlers. By the time Paarl was officially granted town status in 1840, it was still an outpost at the edge of the Drakenstein Mountains, a flourishing wagon-making and last-stop provisioning centre. This status was enhanced when the first **train line** in the Cape connected it to the Peninsula in 1863. Following in the spirit of the first Dutch adventurers of 1657, thousands of treasure-seekers brought custom to Paarl as the gateway to the interior during the diamond rush of the 1870s and the gold fever of the 1880s.

The town holds deep historical significance for the two competing political forces that forged modern South Africa. **Afrikanerdom** regards Paarl as the hallowed ground on which their language movement was born in 1875 (see p.193), while for the **ANC** (and the international community), Paarl will be remembered as the place from which Nelson Mandela made the final steps of his long walk to freedom, when he walked out of **Victor Verster Prison** in 1990.

Arrival and information

Metrorail and Spoornet **trains** from Cape Town pull in at Huguenot Station in Lady Grey Street at the north end of town, near to the central shops. Greyhound and Intercape intercity **buses** stop at the Shell Garage, on the main road, at the south end of town, about 2km from the tourist information bureau.

Paarl's **tourist information** bureau, 216 Main St (Mon–Fri 9am–5pm, Sat 9am–1pm & Sun 10am–1pm; ℡021 872 3829, ℱ021 872 9376), has a selection of good **maps** and can help with finding accommodation.

Accommodation

Most places to stay in town are either along or just off Main Street, many in historic buildings, with camping and chalets just outside of town for the cheapest stay. At the other end of the scale, *Roggeland Country House*, which isn't far from central Paarl, is one of South Africa's most outstanding places to stay.

Berg River Resort 5km south of town on the R45 ℡021 863 1650, ℱ021 863 2583. A rambling, run-down family holiday resort on the banks of the Berg River, offering camping and chalets (bring your own towels). The resort has a swimming pool and restaurant, and also offers mini-golf and canoeing on the river. ❷

Berghof Monte Christo Avenue ℡021 871 1099, ✉afrikamail@aol.com. The 22 rooms in this large, modern guesthouse at the top of a hill, are done out in marble, glass and impersonal motel furniture, but the swimming pool commands one of the best sites in Paarl, with soaring views across town of the Drakenstein Mountains. ❸

De Waenhuis 8 Patriot St, on the corner of Second Street ℡021 872 6643, ℱ021 872 7921. A couple of blocks down from the tourist information bureau, and very central, this tiny but fully equipped self-catering cottage has TV, swimming pool and a private entrance. ❷

Grande Roche Plantasie Street ℡021 863 2727, ⓦwww.granderoche.com. A formal, seriously upmarket hotel in the centre of town, surrounded by vineyards up against Paarl Mountain, with service that is meticulous to a fault and a very good but expensive restaurant (see p.196). ❻

Lemoenkloof 396a Main St ℡021 872 3782, ✉lemkloof@adept.co.za. A comfortable and well-run guesthouse in a National Monument with 1820s' Cape Dutch and Victorian features, a TV and fridge in each room, and a swimming pool. ❹

Nantes Vue 56 Mill St ℡021 872 7311, ⓦwww.nantesvue.com. En-suite doubles decorated with artistic flair in a National Monument turned friendly Cape Dutch guesthouse where breakfast is served on the verandah overlooking a small garden. ❸

Queenslin 2 Queen St ℡ & ℱ021 863 1160 or ℡082 577 0635. Two en-suite rooms with their own entrances and garden spaces, in a split-level family home, and two free-standing garden rooms, set in a quiet part of town bounded on one side by vineyards and towered over by Paarl Rock. Limited self-catering is possible with a fridge, kettle, toaster, microwave and cutlery, but no cooker. Breakfast can be provided as an extra. Good value ❷

Rodeberg Lodge 74 Main St ℡021 863 3202, ⓦwww.rodeberglodge.co.za. Plain period furnishing gives this huge, centrally located Victorian town house a cool, spacious atmosphere. Ask for a room at the back if traffic noise bothers you. ❸

Roggeland Country House Roggeland Road, Dal Jospehat Valley (℡021 868 2501, ⓦwww.roggeland.co.za). The accolades keep rolling in for this family-run inn, which somehow manages to combine good service, outstanding food (see p.197) and informality. The homestead is an eighteenth-century masterpiece of Cape Dutch architecture, with bedrooms in outbuildings. The rate includes dinner with wine tasting, and is a third cheaper in May to July. ❻

The Town and around

Unlike Stellenbosch, which is ideal for wandering, all you're likely to get from strolling around Paarl is a tired pair of legs for relatively little return. The most rewarding sightseeing in the centre can be had by driving down the two oak-lined kilometres of **Main Street**, which has the best-preserved historical frontage in town.

The history of Afrikaans

Afrikaans is South Africa's third mother tongue, spoken by fifteen percent of the population and outstripped only by Zulu and Xhosa. English, by contrast, is the mother tongue of only nine percent of South Africans, and ranks fifth in the league of the eleven official languages.

Signs of the emergence of a new southern African dialect appeared as early as 1685, when H.A. van Rheede, a Dutch East India Company official from the Netherlands, complained about a "distorted and incomprehensible" version of Dutch being spoken in the Drakenstein Valley around modern-day Paarl. By absorbing English, French, German, Malay and indigenous words and expressions, the language continued to diverge from mainstream Dutch, and by the nineteenth century was widely used in the Cape by both white and coloured speakers, but was regarded by the elite as an inferior creole, unsuitable for literary or official communication. Even the first attempts by dominee **Stephanus du Toit** and the Genootskap van Regte Afrikaners (League of True Afrikaners) to have Afrikaans recognized as a separate language from Dutch, and their launching in 1875 of *Die Patriot*, the first white Afrikaans **newspaper**, made little impact outside Paarl.

Ironically, it was the British defeat of the Afrikaner republics in the second Anglo-Boer War at the turn of the twentieth century that provided the catalyst for a mass white Afrikaans movement. The scorched-earth policy of the British had driven many Boers from the lands and produced a demoralized and semi-literate Boer underclass, while the official British policy of anglicizing South Africa helped to unite the white Afrikaner proletariat and elite against the common English enemy.

In 1905, **Gustav Preller**, a young journalist from a working-class Boer background set about reinventing Afrikaans as a "white man's language". He aimed to eradicate the stigma of its "coloured" ties by substituting Dutch words for those with non-European origins. Preller began publishing the first of a series of populist magazines written in Afrikaans and glorifying Boer history and culture. Through this **Second Language Movement**, whites took spiritual control over Afrikaans and the pressure grew for its recognition as an official language, which came in 1925.

When the National Party took power in 1948, its apartheid policy went hand in hand with promoting the interests of its Afrikaans-speaking supporters and a concerted programme of the **upliftment of poor whites** began. Afrikaners were installed throughout the civil service and filled most posts in the public utilities. Despite the fact that there were more coloured than white Afrikaans speakers, the language quickly became associated with the **apartheid** establishment. This had electrifying consequences in the Seventies, when the government attempted to enforce Afrikaans as the sole medium of instruction in African schools, leading directly to the **Soweto uprising** in 1976, which marked the beginning of the end for Afrikaner hegemony in South Africa. The repressive period throughout the Seventies and Eighties and the forced removals under the Group Areas Act led many coloured Afrikaans speakers to adopt English in preference to their mother tongue, which they felt was tainted by apartheid.

There are few signs that Afrikaans will die out. Under the new constitution, existing **language rights** can't be diminished, which effectively means that Afrikaans will continue to be almost as widely used as before. It is now as much with coloured as white people that the future of the *taal* (language) rests.

It's here you'll find the **Paarl Museum**, 303 Main St (Mon–Fri 10am–5pm, Sat 9am–1pm; R5), in a handsome, thatched Cape Dutch building with one of the earliest surviving gables (1787) in the "new style", characterized by triangular caps. The contents don't quite match up to the exterior, but include some reasonably enlightening panels on the architecture of the town, and several eccentric glass display cases of Victorian bric-a-brac. A token "Road to Reconciliation" exhibit displays press cuttings covering Paarl during the apartheid years – amongst these you'll find passing mention of the fact that Nelson Mandela spent some time here as a "guest" of the town – his last years in jail, in fact.

Heading east down Main Street away from the museum, a left turn into Van der Lingen Street and then right into Pastorie Street brings you to the **Afrikaans Taal Museum** (☎021 872 3441, Mon–Fri 8am–5pm; R5), which chronicles a white Nationalist version of the development of the Afrikaans language (see box on p.193). Located in the house of Gideon Malherbe (1833–1921), one of the founders of the League of True Afrikaners, the museum's displays are in Afrikaans, and a leaflet available from the reception desk gives an English summary of exhibits. Some brief material gives an alternative history of Afrikaans, placing new emphasis on the role of slaves and coloured South Africans in its evolution.

On the east side of town, on Jan van Riebeeck Street, is **Clementina van der Walt Ceramic Studio** (Mon–Fri 9am–5pm, Sat 9am–4pm, Sun 10am–4pm; ☎021 872 3420), one of the best craft shops in the Winelands, selling tableware from the studio of Clementina van der Walt, who has created a mock-ethnic style with mass appeal. The shop also stocks hand-selected items of cutlery, wonderful fabrics from South Africa and the rest of the continent, and wooden bowls – all well-priced and of superior quality.

The only other sight of any interest in Paarl itself is the grandiose **Taal Monument** (daily 9am–5pm; free), the controversial memorial to the Afrikaans language, standing just outside the centre on the top of Paarl Mountain. To get there, drive south along Main Street past the head office of the KWV, and follow the signs to your right up the slope of the mountain. The monument is as important a place of pilgrimage for Afrikaners as the Voortrekker Monument in Pretoria, although when it was erected in 1973 critics joked that monuments were usually erected to the dead. From the coffee and curio shop you can admire a truly magnificent panorama across to the Peninsula and False Bay in one direction and the Winelands ranges in the other.

Groot Drakenstein (Victor Verster) Prison

Roughly 9km south of the N1 as it cuts through Paarl, along the R303, the southern extension of Jan van Riebeeck Street, stands the **Victor Verster Prison**, renamed **Groot Drakenstein** in 2000, Nelson Mandela's last place of incarceration. It was through the gates at Victor Verster (not Pollsmoor in Cape Town or Robben Island as many people believe) that Mandela walked to his freedom on February 11, 1990, and was here that the first images of him in 27 years were bounced around the world – under the Prisons Act not even old pictures of him could be published for his 27 years of incarceration. The working jail looks rather like a boys' school fronted by rugby fields beneath hazy mountains, and there's something bizarre about seeing a prison sign nonchalantly slipped in among all the vineyard and wine route pointers. Since you can't go inside, the usual tourist thing is to have yourself snapped standing in front the of the gates, though raising a clenched fist and shouting "Amandla!" is strictly optional.

The wineries

Retracing your route to town, and turning left into Langenhoven Street and left again into Main Street, will bring you to the entrance of **Laborie**, Taillefert St (Mon–Sun 9am–5pm; ☎021 807 3390; R8), one of the most impressive Paarl wineries, all the more remarkable for being right in town. The beautiful

△ Goat Tower, Fairview Estate

manor is fronted by a rose garden, acres of close-cropped lawns, historic buildings and oak trees – all towered over by the Taal Monument. There's a truly wonderful tasting room balcony, jettying out over the vineyards trailing up Paarl Mountain. Try the Chardonnay, Sauvignon Blanc, and the Pineau de Laborie, the world's first pot-stilled eau de vie made entirely from Pinotage grapes – delicious and well-priced. They also produce a nice Cap Classique, a champagne-style sparkling wine. Across the road, at the Laborie Wine House (Tues–Sun noon-3pm, ☎021 807 3095) you can get a set traditional Cape meal, or chose from the extensive, seasonal a la carte menu.

Back towards the centre along Jan Philips Drive (the main drag), a dirt track takes a detour along the hillside past **Paarl Mountain Nature Reserve**, emerging 11km later at the north end of town to rejoin Main Street. If you take a left turn from Jan Philips, after nearly 2km you'll reach **Rhebokskloof** (Mon–Sun 9am-5pm; tasting R7 which includes a cellar tour; ☎021 863 8386), a highly photogenic wine estate, overlooking a shallow *kloof* that borders on the mountain nature reserve. The Cabernet Sauvignon, Pinotage and Merlot are well worth sampling, while the estate's renowned restaurant (see opposite) overlooks an artificial lake with swans.

Back on the southern fringes of town, **Fairview** (Mon–Fri 8.30am–5pm, Sat 8.30am–1pm; R10; ☎021 863 2450) promises the most fun of all the Paarl estates, with much more than just wine tasting on offer. To get there, take the R101 (the southwest extension of Main Road) out of town, turning right at the sign and continuing for about 2.5km down a minor road to the estate entrance. Your arrival is marked by the emblem of the estate, a spiral tower which the estate's famous goats climb. A deli sells sausages and cold meats for picnics on the lawn, and you can also sample and buy the goat's, sheep's and cow's cheeses made on the estate. As far as wine tasting goes, Fairview is an innovative, family-run place, but it can get a bit hectic when the tour buses roll in, so try to phone ahead to find out when they're expected. The first-rate wines here include Shiraz-Merlot, Merlot and Chardonnay – all good value.

From here the **Backsberg Estate** (Mon–Fri 8.30am–5pm, Sat 9am–1pm; R10; ☎021 875 5141), south of the R101 along the very minor WR1, can be reached easily by backtracking from Fairview, turning right into the R101, and continuing a short way before turning left. After passing the Simonsvlei winery, go a short way till you strike a T-junction at the WR1, where you turn left and almost immediately get to the winery entrance. Outdoor seating with views of the rose garden and vineyard makes this busy estate a nice place to while away some time. Their wines are of a high standard, while the Cabernet Sauvignon, Merlot, Shiraz and Pinotage represent good value. For something unusual, sample the Malbec and, if you're into spirits, their international-award-winning brandy.

Eating and drinking

Paarl isn't a gourmet centre, but it does boast one of South Africa's top **restaurants**, as well as a couple of outstanding places in the surrounding countryside, where you can enjoy good food accompanied by great views of the vineyards and mountains. Along the main street you'll also find several coffee shops and little restaurants.

Bosman's Restaurant *Grande Roche Hotel,* Plantasie Street ☎021 863 2727. One of the best and most expensive restaurants in the country, winning accolades year after year, including Relais Gourmand status, *Bosman's* offers haute cuisine with outstanding service, in a gracious manor house with a rather formal atmosphere. Open daily for breakfast, lunch and dinner; light lunches are served all afternoon and can be eaten alfresco.
I Campanelli 62 Breda St ☎021 872 4397. A

low-key Italian restaurant, popular with locals. Closed Sun.

Kostinrichting Coffee Shop 19 Pastorie St. Conveniently close to the museums, this is a good spot for tea, cakes, toasted sandwiches and salads.

Laborie Restaurant & Wine House Taillefert Street ☎021 808 7429. *Laborie* offers seasonal à la carte and traditional Cape set-menu lunches every day and dinners. Closed Mon & Sun.

Rhebokskloof Restaurant Rhebokskloof Minor Road ☎021 863 8606. Intimate Victorian eatery overlooking a lake, with a shaded terrace for summer lunches, offering gourmet meals with thrilling combinations of flavours, both Cape and interna-

tional. It's also a good place for morning or afternoon teas. Open daily, closed Tue and Wed eves.

Roggeland Country House Roggeland Road, Dal Jospehat Valley ☎021 868 2501. The imaginative set menu here is inspired by the regional produce of Paarl, using vegetables and herbs grown in Roggeland's own gardens. Beautifully prepared dishes are accompanied by a selected wine, each of which you are talked through. Booking essential.

Wagon Wheels Steakhouse 57 Lady Grey St ☎021 872 5265. Out-of-the-ordinary steakhouse with surprisingly tasty sauces and seafood alternatives; the pepper steak flamed in brandy and doused with cream is a hit. Tues–Sat, closed Sat lunch.

Franschhoek

It's only relatively recently that **FRANSCHHOEK**, 33km from Stellenbosch and 29km from Paarl, has emerged from being the dowdy *dorp* of the Winelands to become the culinary capital of the Western Cape. Its late Victorian architecture and bland modern bungalows can't match the elegance of Stellenbosch, but the terrific setting, hemmed in on three sides by mountains, the vineyards down every other backstreet, and some vigorous myth-making, have created a place fashion-conscious urbanites from Cape Town drive out to just for Sunday lunch. And, while Capetonians dine here, Jo'burg designers, investors and bankers are buying up the place.

Some history

Between 1688 and 1700 about two hundred **French Huguenots**, desperate to escape religious persecution in France, accepted a Dutch East India Company offer of passage to the Cape and the grant of lands. They made contact with the area's earliest settlers, groups of **Khoi herders**. Conflict between the French newcomers and the Khoi followed familiar lines, with the white settlers gradually dispossessing the herdsmen, forcing them either further into the hinterland

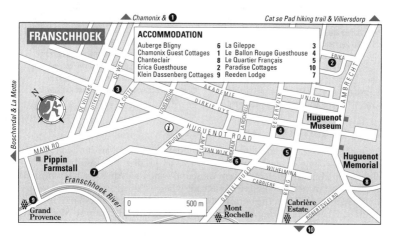

FRANSCHHOEK

ACCOMMODATION

Auberge Bligny	6	La Gileppe	3
Chamonix Guest Cottages	1	Le Ballon Rouge Guesthouse	4
Chanteclair	8	Le Quartier Français	5
Erica Guesthouse	2	Paradise Cottages	10
Klein Dassenberg Cottages	9	Reeden Lodge	7

Chamonix & ❶

Cat se Pad hiking trail & Villiersdorp

Boschendal & La Motte

Huguenot Museum

Pippin Farmstall ❼

Huguenot Memorial

Franschhoek River

0   500 m

Grand Provence ❾

Mont Rochelle

Cabrière Estate

or into servitude on their farms. The establishment of white hegemony was swift and by 1713 the area was known as *de france hoek*, but because of explicit Company policy, French-speaking died out within a generation. However, many of the estates are still known by their original French names. The town itself occupies parts of the original farms of La Cotte and Cabrière and is relatively young, having been established around a church built in 1833.

Arrival, information and accommodation

There's no public transport to Franschhoek or in the town itself; the only way to get here is in your own **car**. The **tourist information** bureau (summer daily 8.30am–6pm; winter Mon–Fri 8.30am–5pm, Sat & Sun 10am–1pm; ⊤ & ⓕ021 876 3603) is in Main Road, just north of the junction with Kruger Street, and can provide information about places to stay in the area and a few hiking maps. Guesthouse accommodation tends to be a bit pricey, but the rooms are high quality; Franschhoek is a place where you'll eat and sleep well.

Accommodation

Auberge Bligny 28 Van Wijk St ⊤021 876 3767, ⓔbligny@mweb.co.za. A centrally located Victorian house furnished in country style and with a nice guest lounge. ❹

Chamonix Guest Cottages Uitkyk Street ⊤021 876 2498, ⓦwww.chamonix.co.za. Fully equipped, self-catering cottages surrounded by vineyards on a wine farm. ❷

Chanteclair Signposted just west of the Huguenot Monument along Lambrecht Road ⊤ & ⓕ021 876 3685, ⓔchanteclair@mweb.co.za. The best thing about this guesthouse, which stands on a massive property, is that you feel you're in the country, yet are only minutes from town. It offers unfussy rooms in English country style, and breakfast outside on the verandah looking out onto a lovely garden and orchard. ❺

Klein Dassenberg Cottages Off Main Road ⊤ & ⓕ021 876 2107 or ⊤082 442 3278, ⓔkleindassenberg@kingsley.co.za. Four self-catering cottages in a peaceful and beautiful setting; two of the cottages are ideal for a couple, while the others sleep four and can accommodate families. ❷

La Gileppe Corner of Huguenot Road and De Wet Street ⊤021 876 2146, ⓦwww.lagileppe.co.za. A high-quality B&B, walkable from the centre, in a restored and immaculately maintained Victorian house with pure cotton linen, freshly squeezed

orange juice for breakfast and pretty garden spaces for each room. ❸–❹

Le Ballon Rouge Guest House 7 Reservoir Rd ⊤021 876 2651, ⓦwww.ballon-rouge.co.za. A small B&B offering rooms leading onto a side-street-facing verandah, in a Victorian town house with brass bedsteads and floral fabrics. ❹

Le Quartier Français On the corner of Berg and Wilhelmina streets ⊤021 876 2151, ⓦwww.lequartier.co.za. The most luxurious place to stay in Franschhoek, with two suites (one with its own pool) and fifteen huge rooms decorated with sunny fabrics, thick duvets and fireplaces for winter, all arranged around herb and flower gardens and the swimming pool. Child-friendly, and pricey, but worth it for a special occasion; there's also a fine restaurant (see p.201). ❼

Paradise Cottages Roberstsvlei Road ⊤ & ⓕ021 876 2160. Some of the valley's cheapest rooms in two small, basic self-catering cottages on a working farm, 5km from the centre. ❶

Reeden Lodge Off Cabrière Street ⊤ & ⓕ021 876 3174, ⓔreeden@telkomsa.net. Four lovely self-catering cottages on a farm, set along a river and within walking distance of town. Very reasonably priced, with a minimum charge based on three people staying, and winter discounts available. ❷

The Town and its wineries

Away from the wining and dining, Franschhoek's attractions are limited to hiking, horse-riding or cycling in the valley, or visiting the institutionalized Huguenot Monument and adjacent museum, which together occupy a prime position at the head of Huguenot Road, where it forms a T-junction with Lambrecht Street. The **Huguenot Monument** consists of three skinny, interlocking arches symbolizing the Holy Trinity, while the **Huguenot Museum**

(Mon–Fri 9am–5pm, Sat 9am–1pm & 2–5pm, Sun 2–5pm; R4 entrance) gives comprehensive coverage of Huguenot history, culture and of their contribution to modern South Africa.

The best **hike** in the vicinity is the Cat se Pad (Cat's Path), which starts on your left just under a kilometre from the museum as you head out of town up the Franschhoek Pass. The walk leads into fynbos with proteas, and gives instant access to the mountains surrounding the valley, with good views. The first two-kilometre section gets you to the top of the pass and you can keep going for another 10km in the direction of Villiersdorp (though you don't actually reach it). To return, simply retrace your steps.

The wineries

Franschhoek's **wineries** are small enough and sufficiently close together to make it a breeze to visit two or three on foot, by mountain bike or even on horseback. Heading north through town from the Huguenot Monument, you'll find virtually all the wineries along branches that are signposted off Huguenot Road and its extension, Main Road.

Close to the Monument, **Cabrière Estate**, on Berg Road (Mon–Fri 8.30am–5pm, Sat 11am–1pm; cellar tours Mon–Fri 11am & 3pm, Sat 11am; ☎021 876 2630), is reached through groves of fruit trees leading up to the homestead and tasting room. The winery is notable for its Pinot Noirs and colourful wine-maker Achim von Arnim, whose presence on Saturdays guarantees an eventful visit; try to catch him when he slices off the upper neck of a bubbly bottle with a sabre, sending flying the neatly detached cork encased in the severed top ring of glass. Next door, **Mont Rochelle**, on Daniel Hugo Road (Mon–Sat 10am–4pm, plus Jan–April & Sept–Dec Sun 11am–1pm; cellar tours Mon–Sat 11am, 12.30pm & 3pm; ☎021 876 3000), has one of the most stunning settings in Franschhoek and an unusual cellar in a converted nineteenth-century fruit-packing shed, edged by eaves decorated with fretwork, stained-glass windows and chandeliers. Look out for the promising new wines under their premium Mont Rochelle label – the first South African wines to be bottled by an all-woman team.

Back on Huguenot Road, keep heading north and turn right into Uitkyk Street to get to **Chamonix** (daily 9.30am–4pm; ☎021 876 2498), which holds its tastings in the cosy Blacksmith's Cottage (where you can also get a light meal). The estate's most consistent wines are their Cabernet Sauvignon and Chardonnay, but they also produce Chamonix schnapps from pear, peach, plum, apple and nectarine, and for teetotallers, Eau de Chamonix. There's a good restaurant here too (see "Eating and drinking", p.201).

Retrace your route back to Huguenot Road, and a left turn just after the Pippin Farm Stall, where the road merges with Main Road, will bring you to **Grand Provence** (daily 10am–6pm; ☎021 876 3195), across the train tracks, which produces Agusta wines. This is one of the most casual and friendly estates, where you can sit in comfy armchairs in a tasting room with a traditional *rietdak* (cane and mud ceiling). The estate is best known for "Angels' Tears", a fruity blend of Chenin Blanc and Muscat d'Alexandrie grapes, whose name derives from the legend of a French village where angels came at night to taste the new vintage and wept for joy at its brilliance. In contrast to Grand Provence's genial ambience, **La Motte Estate** (Mon–Fri 9am–4.30pm, Sat 9am–noon; ☎021 876 3119), further along Main Road (here called the R45), presents a supremely cool front, with a superb designer tasting room looking into the cellar through a sheer wall of glass. This was the estate that put to rest once and for all the long-held notion that Franschhoek was a poor region for producing red wines: La Motte offers a good Shiraz and Cabernet Sauvignon and a stunning blend known as Millennium, which sells out quickly.

If you have time for only one estate around here, **Boschendal** (summer Mon–Sat 8.30am–4.30pm; winter Mon–Fri 8.30am–4.30pm, Sat 8.30am–12.30pm; ☎021 874 1031) is the obvious choice. Equidistant between Franschhoek and Stellenbosch at the junction of the R45 and R310, it is geared to the busloads of tourists who lap up its impressive Cape Dutch buildings, tree-lined avenues, choice of restaurants and cafés (see "Eating and drinking" below), and of course its wines. Boschendal is one of the world's longest-established New World wine estates, dating back to 1685, when its lands were granted to Huguenot settler Jean Le Long. The Cape Dutch manor was built in 1812 by Paul de Villiers and his wife, whose initials appear on the front gable. Wine tasting takes place at the Taphuis, where you can sit indoors or sip under shady trees. Of its Reserve range, look out for the Merlot, and Shiraz; and from its extensive regular range, try the Sauvignon Blanc, Chardonnay and the Boschendal brut bubbly.

A great way to experience wine tasting is to get on a **horse** and ride to three different wine farms, through Mont Rochelle Equestrian Centre (☎083 300 4368) Their three-cellar ride (about two-and-a-half hours) costs roughly R150, which takes in Clos Cabrière and Grand Provence, at each of which you taste one wine, and ends at Mont Rochelle, where you get to try their whole range. Longer rides, or just plain scenic rides can be arranged.

Eating and drinking

Eating and drinking is what Franschhoek is all about, so there's little point in making the effort to get here without sampling at least one or two of its excellent **restaurants**, some of which number among the Cape's best. Restaurants in town are concentrated along Huguenot Road, but there are a number of excellent alternatives in the more rustic environment of the surrounding wine estates. **Booking** is essential. Franschhoek's cuisine tends to be French-inspired, but includes salmon trout as a local speciality. For coffee or a sandwich, head for one of the many **cafés** in town, or book a **picnic** hamper at one of the wineries and eat alfresco within sipping distance of the vineyards.

Restaurants

Boschendal On the junction of the R45 and R310 to Stellenbosch ☎021 874 1252. Boschendal is legendary for its pricey but exhaustive daily buffet lunch, which will set you up for the rest of day – you can eat as much as you can from the spread of soup, oysters, calamari, roasts, casseroles, salads, Cape specialities, cheeseboard and desserts.
Bread & Wine Môreson Farm, Happy Valley Road, signposted off the R45 ☎021 876 3692. A friendly venue beside a fountain in a courtyard surrounded by orchards and vineyards, serving excellent Mediterranean farmhouse lunches accompanied by the estate's own wines. Open daily during summer months for lunch; out of season, ring beforehand to check opening times.
Chez Michel Huguenot Road, just north of *Le Quartier Français* and opposite the post office ☎021 876 2671. Franschhoek's oldest eating

place is a congenial bistro patronized by locals, in a Victorian house. The mid-range menu has a continental emphasis, incorporating steaks, seafood and excellent homemade gateaux. Open Tues–Sun for lunch, Tues–Sat for dinner.
Haute Cabrière Franschhoek Pass ☎021 876 3688. A bunker-like venue with an interesting mix-and-match menu planned around Cabrière wines, available by the glass or bottle. There are no starters or main courses, but you can order half-portions from a menu including salmon trout, lamb, ratatouille, wonderful desserts and homemade chocolates. There's a helipad on the roof should you wish to fly in. Lunch daily, dinner summer only.
La Maison de Chamonix Uitkyk Street ☎021 876 2393. You can eat inside or outdoors here on the Chamonix Estate, surrounded by views of the

valley. The French-based menu includes oysters and smoked salmon trout. Open daily for lunch and dinner except Mondays.

Le Ballon Rouge 12 Reservoir St ☎021 876 2651. A Victorian house with a brasserie, cocktail bar and outside area. If you want to eat exotically, try the smoked salmon trout sandwiched between rosti and garnished with chive-horseradish cream; if you're feeling less adventurous, you can go for pasta and grills. Breakfast, lunch and dinner daily.

Le Quartier Français 16 Huguenot Rd ☎021 876 2151. The place that made Franschhoek synonymous with food, offering excellent formal evening meals, or informal and imaginative lunches with a local flavour. There's always a vegetarian option and delicious desserts. In winter you can sit by the fire inside, while on fine days there are pavement tables for lunch. Book ahead.

Polfyntjies Country Restaurant Main Road ☎021 876 3217. Situated in an 1860s farm-house, *Polfyntjies* serves gourmet versions of South African favourites including *boerewors*, *bredie* and *bobotie*, as well as local salmon trout, cold soups and salads. The wine list offers among the best drinking value in Franschhoek. Closed Tues.

Light meals, delis and picnics

Boschendal On the junction of R45 and R310 to Stellenbosch ☎021 874 1252. *Le Café* does light, sit-down lunches, while *Le Pique Nique* offers deluxe picnic hampers daily under the shady pines. Booking for both is essential, and children get a special picnic wrapped in a cloth and tied to a stick, Dick Whittington style.

Frandeli Co-op Building, Huguenot Road ☎021 876 3054. A licensed deli serving delicious filled focaccias and bagels accompanied by beer or wine, to eat in or take away. Picnic baskets are supplied.

Gideon's Famous Pancake House 50 Huguenot Rd ☎021 876 2227. *Gideon's* offers tasty savoury or sweet pancakes with a touch of Cape Muslim flavours, and also sandwiches and salads served on pavement tables.

Mont Rochelle Off Main Road ☎021 876 3000. Picnic baskets are on offer every day at one of Franschhoek's most scenic wineries, but they must be ordered the day before.

Pippin Farm Stall Main Road. Includes Franschhoek trout among its delicious foods, which you can use to make up your own budget picnic.

Ralf's Country Restaurant & Village Pub 3 Main Rd ☎021 876 3360. A relaxed and inexpensive bistro with a good pub and beer garden, serving pizzas, trout and other house specialities.

Route 62

One of the most rewarding journeys in the Western Cape is an inland counterpart to the Garden Route (see p.244) – the **mountain route** from Cape Town to Port Elizabeth along the R62. Nowhere near as well known as the coastal journey, this trip will take you through some of the most dramatic passes and *poorts* (valley routes) in the country and crosses a frontier of *dorps* and drylands.

Beyond the Paarl and Stellenbosch winelands, a vast hinterland fans out away from Cape Town. Just outside Paarl, the Huguenot Tunnel punches through the Dutoitsberg mountain range to emerge in the fruit-growing and wine-making country of the **Breede River Valley**, where mountains give way to a jigsaw of valleys, each quite distinct in character. It's here rather than the more developed Winelands proper that so many calendar shots are taken of isolated white-washed homesteads dwarfed by vine-covered hills.

Although the Breede River Valley is part of a through route to the Eastern Cape via Oudtshoorn, its towns also make convenient excursions from Cape Town. **Worcester**, the large functional hub of the region, is only 110km from Cape Town, while to its north, **Tulbagh**, a more promising destination, with a perfectly restored provincial Cape Dutch street, is an easy 130km from the city. South from Worcester, the R60 shadows the groove cut by the Breede River and provides access to the rather dull little town of **Robertson**, centre of yet

Passes and poorts of the Little Karoo

The **Little Karoo** is hemmed in to the north by the Langeberg range and to the south the Outeniqua (the range separating it from the Garden Route). In between lies a gauntlet of mountains and valleys that for centuries made this area virtually impassable for wheeled transport. In the nineteenth century, the British began to tackle the problem and dozens of **passes** were built through the Cape's mountains, 34 of which were engineered by the brilliant road-builder Andrew Geddes Bain and his son Thomas. In 1878, Anthony Trollope commented that the **Outeniqua Pass**, just north of George on the way to Oudtshoorn, equalled "some of the mountain roads through the Pyrenees", a description which just as easily applies today to any number of other Little Karoo passes. In fact, whatever the Little Karoo lacks in museums and art galleries is amply compensated for by the towering drama of these Victorian masterpieces.

In **Afrikaans** there are two words for pass: *pas*, meaning "a route over the mountains" and *poort*, meaning "a valley route", often following a river. Most passes are narrow, winding and steep, and frequently untarred, so they need to be driven slowly. In any case, you won't want to rush past such fantastic views, so it's worth bringing along food and drink to enjoy at the numerous picnic spots along the way. Below, we've listed a selection of some of the best of the passes and *poorts*:

Cogman's Kloof Pass, between Ashton and Montagu. A five-kilometre route that is at its most dramatic as it cuts through a rock face into the Montagu Valley (see p.208).

Du Toit's Kloof Pass, between Paarl and Worcester. The more exciting alternative to the Huguenot Toll Tunnel, with 1:9 gradients (see "Worcester" on p.203).

Gamkaskloof Pass, a.k.a. Die Hel (The Hell), reached from the summit of the Swartberg Pass. Arguably the most awesome of all the passes leading into a dramatic and lonely valley. You have to return the same way, as there's no circular route (see p.216).

Meiringspoort, just north of De Rust. A tarred road through a gorge in the

Swartberg, which keeps crossing a light-brown river, while huge slabs of folded and zigzagging rock rise up on either side. There's a picnic spot at each fording place and a waterfall at Ford 17 (they're all numbered). You can walk from here for 12km into the mountains (see p.217).

Prince Alfred's Pass, between the N2 just east of Knysna and Avontuur on the R62. A dramatic dirt road twisting through mountains, past a few isolated apple farms.

Swartberg Pass, between Oudtshoorn and Prince Alfred. Over-the-Swartberg counterpart of Meiringspoort, with 1:7 gradients on narrow untarred roads characterized by precipitous hairpins. Not recommended in poor weather or if you suffer from vertigo (see p.217).

another wine route. Some 19km south lies **McGregor**, a small, laid-back town with a rural feel, and an excellent choice for a weekend stay. Nearby, and a similar distance from the Cape Peninsula, the pleasant historic spa town of **Montagu** is towered over by precipitous red-streaked cliffs that attract serious mountaineers from all over the country.

Continuing east from Montagu, the R62 meanders into the Garden Route's backyard, the **Little Karoo** (or Klein Karoo), a vast and brittle khaki-coloured hinterland (the name is a Khoi word meaning "hard and dry"). The Little Karoo provides the easiest access to the semi-desert covering one-third of South Africa's surface. Open treeless plains, sporadically vegetated with low, wiry scrub, and dotted with flat-topped hills, dissolve eventually into the Great Karoo, which extends into the southern Free State and well into the Eastern and Northern Cape provinces. The Great Karoo is the harsh frontier which a succession of South Africans occupied by turns: San hunters, Khoi herders, Griqua (coloured) farmers and Afrikaner trekkers. Today Afrikaans is the dominant language, used by white and coloured speakers, the latter having absorbed what remained of the Khoi.

The unsung surprise along the way is **Calitzdorp**, a rustic little *dorp*, five to six hours' solid driving from Cape Town, down whose backstreets a few unassuming wine farms produce some of South Africa's best port. Around here you'll find neglected valleys where some of the old Karoo clings on tenuously in an almost feudal relationship between farmsteads and faded scatterings of coloured workers' cottages. By contrast, the well-trumpeted attractions of **Oudtshoorn**, half an hour further on, are the ostrich farms and the massive **Cango Caves**, one of the country's biggest tourist draws. Less than 70km from the coast, with good transport connections, Oudtshoorn marks the convergence of the mountain and coastal roads and is usually treated as a leisurely day-trip away from the Garden Route.

Slicing up through the northernmost third of the Klein Karoo, on its way to Johannesburg, the N1 slips past **Matjiesfontein**, a wonderfully preserved Victorian railway town, and the mountainous **Karoo National Park**, both just off the main road and definitely worth breaking a trip for.

Worcester

The fastest way to cross the mountains from Paarl into the Breede River Valley is via the **Huguenot Toll Tunnel**, which burrows straight through to the other side, but misses the wonderful scenery of driving over the **Du Toit's Kloof Pass**. Much slower but far more interesting, the pass works its way through a series of wonderful mountain ranges with views onto distant farms and villages in the valleys.

WORCESTER, 31km from Paarl through the tunnel, is a relatively large town for this part of the world, and features some attractive historic frontage down Church Street, but not enough to demand much of your time. An agricultural centre with a number of factories, it's at the centre of a wine-making region, consisting mostly of co-operatives producing bulk plonk that makes up about one-fifth of national output. There isn't much reason to dally here, apart from visiting the **Kleinplasie Living Open Air Museum** (Mon–Sat 9am–4.30pm, Sun 10.30am–4.30pm; R12), which depicts the life on the Karoo frontier between 1690 and 1900. Made up of about two dozen reconstructed buildings, with staff in old-style workshops engaged in crafts and home industries, the museum is fairly absorbing. Keep a lookout in particular for the corbelled shepherd's hut, which represents a vernacular style unique to the Karoo, using domed stone roofs rather than beam and lintel construction – a response to the dearth of timber in the treeless expanse. There's a **restaurant** and **café** on site, and next door a wine shop selling a good selection from the Worcester wineries. The museum is just outside the centre of town – to get there, head east along High Street and turn right onto the road to Robertson.

Tulbagh

The most rewarding destination in the northern section of the Breede River Valley is **TULBAGH**, easily visited in a day from Cape Town. You could drive into town, down Van der Stel Street and out the other end, and assume from this unexceptional main street that Tulbagh was just another humdrum *dorp*. But one block west, on **Church Street**, is the most perfectly restored eighteenth- and nineteenth-century streetscape. Only a fraction of what you see here is the original frontage (the town was flattened in 1969 by an earthquake), yet this is no Disneyland – the facades aren't original but they're unquestionably authentic and undoubtedly beautiful.

There's no public transport to Tulbagh; the only way you'll make it here is by **car**, taking either the **R43** from Worcester or the **R301** from Paarl. One of the highlights of the drive is crossing the beautiful **Bain's Kloof Pass** connecting these two routes. The town's **tourist information** bureau, 14 Church St (Mon–Fri 9am–5pm, Sat 10am–4pm, Sun 11am–4pm; ℡023 230 1348, ⓦwww.tulbagh.com), can give advice on activities and accommodation in the area.

Accommodation

There's a good range of accommodation in Tulbagh from budget rooms in the museum in Church Street and family cottages on surrounding farms to luxury tents at a bushcamp.

De Oude Herberg 6 Church St ℡023 230 0260, ⓔoudeherberg@hotmail.com. A well-positioned inn offering comfortable rooms with French doors opening onto the communal verandah. ❸

Hunter's Retreat Roughly 1.5km north of town along the main road ℡023 230 0582, ⓦwww.lando.co.za. Airy B&B rooms and spacious two-storey thatched cottages with lounges, on a working farm rearing cattle, ostriches and sheep. ❸

Kleinfontein 13km north of town ℡023 230 0731 or 083 235 7832. Low-key accommodation run by former opera singer Michael Kenny, on a farm in the mountains on the outskirts of Tulbagh. The two rooms adjoin the farmhouse; the *Kliphuisie*, a comfortable but basic self-contained fully equipped cottage with views of the Winterhoek Mountains; and the *Berghut*, a very rustic mountain hut with matresses on the floor. Accommodation is available on a self-catering or B&B basis, and the "singing chef" can serve up meals in the Kleinfontein restaurant. ❶

Kliprivier Park Holiday Resort ℡023 230 0506. The cheapest place to stay, in one of the nicest municipal caravan parks in the country, with campsites and very basic chalets, some of which are on the edge of a dam and have excellent mountain views. ❷

Oude Kerk Kombuis Next to the tourist information bureau ℡023 230 0428. These two rooms inside a house museum are a real curiosity. During museum opening hours you may have people drifting through "your" lounge, but after the doors close you have the whole joint to yourself. ❶

Waterval Country Lodge and Bushcamp Off the R46 to Wolseley ℡023 230 0807, ⓦwww.waterval.co.za. The most luxurious of Tulbagh's accommodation, in a restored lodge on a huge pine plantation on the southern outskirts of town. The five en-suite B&B rooms have their own verandah; you can also stay in luxury en-suite tents or log cabins on a B&B or self-catering basis. ❷–❸

Wild Olive Farm 6km south of town, heading towards Wolseley; a signposted turn-off leads you 2km down a dirt track ℡023 230 1160. Family-oriented farm accommodation is offered in five fully equipped self-catering cottages with mountain views. Guests are given milk and eggs, and you can swim in a mountain-stream dam or explore the large property on a free mountain bike. ❶

The Town

The best way to enjoy Tulbagh is to stroll up **Church Street** and take in the houses, gardens and gables that are an essential element of Cape Dutch architecture. After the 1969 earthquake, the **restoration** of the buildings used salvaged materials from the ruins, following photographic and hand-drawn records. At least six different styles can be distinguished just along this short road. At no. 23, **Paddagang** (frog passage) was originally a *taphuis* (wine house); today it's a restaurant with a wine house attached (see p.205), recommended for its wonderful labels all featuring comical frogs rather than for the liquor itself. Although the gabled Old Church, built in 1743, is of some interest, you won't miss much if you don't spend long over the collection of bric-a-brac inside that constitutes the **Oude Kerk Volksmuseum**, 2 Church St

(Mon–Fri 9am–5pm; R10). The museum has three annexes (Mon–Fri 9am–1pm & 2–5pm; all included in entry fee) at nos. 4, 14 and 22, which won't keep you busy for too long, either. No. 4 has photographs of old houses in Tulbagh before the earthquake and traces the histories of the families who lived in them.

Outside town, **De Oude Drostdy Museum** (Mon–Sat 10am–12.50pm & 2–4.30pm, Sun 2.30–4.50pm), 4km to the north on the extension of Van der Stel Street, is an impressive Cape Dutch spectacle designed by the French architect Louis-Michel Thibault. Apart from some very nice pieces of furniture and a pleasantly relaxed atmosphere, the museum's main draw is the startling view of the mountains and farmlands confronting you as you step out through the front doors.

Eating and drinking

De Oude Herberg 6 Church St. Traditional curries and country cuisine inside or on the terrace. Daily except Monday for breakfast, lunch, tea and dinner.
Le Midi *Witzenberg Country Inn*, 13 Piet Retief Street. Light meals from Monday to Saturday.
Paddagang Restaurant and Wine House 23 Church St ☏ 023 230 0242. Tulbagh's biggest attraction, apart from its historic streetscape. Established in 1821 as one of the first taverns in the Cape, it serves moderately priced traditional regional cooking and locally produced wines and has lovely gardens, where you can sit outside under vines. The restaurant is open for breakfast, lunch and tea daily.
Readers 12 Church St ☏ 023 230 0087. Small but elegant eating place and art gallery in the eighteenth-century cottage used by the church's sick comforter or "reader". The lunch and dinner menu consists of country cuisine with a touch of sophistication, so you'll find lamb cooked with citrus and served with roasted garlic or gazpacho with avocado sorbet. Closed Tues.

Robertson and McGregor

ROBERTSON, 77km off the N2, is the largest town in the physically attractive stretch of the Breede River Valley connecting Worcester to Oudtshoorn. Its size, however, does nothing to mitigate the fact that Robertson is, unfortunately, a big yawn that dies completely over weekends. The only conceivable reason for visiting this fruit-picking town is the **Robertson Winery** (Mon–Thurs 8am–5pm, Fri 8am–4.30pm, Sat 9am–1pm) just off the R60, which produces some good-value and fairly quaffable Chardonnays and Colombards that are cheaper here than in the shops. The Robertson Valley has its own **wine route**, which extends to McGregor and Bonnievale in the south (see box on p.206).

If you're not stocking up on wine, press straight on to **MCGREGOR**, fifteen minutes to the south, at the end of a minor road signposted off the R60. Although it's been described as South Africa's best-preserved Victorian Karoo village, you shouldn't expect anything like a quaint English hamlet – a description that might just about apply to Greyton on the well-watered side of the mountains (see p.223). Still, dry as it is, McGregor is an attractive enough place, with whitewashed cottages glaring in the summer daylight amid the low rusty steel-wool scrub, and a quiet, relaxed atmosphere that has attracted a small population of spiritual seekers and alternative types. In the shadow of the Dutch Reformed church down the high street, you'll find the **Temenos Retreat Centre** (see p.207) and a Waldorf school. The time to pull out your camera is in the late afternoon, when the sinking sun suffuses the landscape with deeply saturated colours.

Robertson Valley wineries: the pick of the bunch

The Robertson Valley is responsible for some ten percent of South Africa's vineyards. Its soils have an ideal acidity level for growing grapes, but because it's hot and dry, intense irrigation is necessary. Its best wines tend to be Chenin Blancs and Colombards and it can conjure up some good Muscadels. We've picked out the best of its roughly two dozen wineries.

Along the R317 from Robertson to Bonnievale

Bon Courage About 8km southeast of Robertson, on the right-hand side of the road (Mon–Fri 8.30am–5pm, Sat 9.30am–1pm; free; ☎023 626 4178). Its tasting room is in a beautiful old homestead along the Breede River; the vineyard is notable for its sweet whites, especially Muscadel.

Van Loveren Roughly 8km south of Bon Courage, on the right-hand side of the road (Mon–Fri 8.30–5pm, Sat 9.30am–1pm; free; ☎023 615 1505). Wine tasting in a lovely garden at a friendly estate known for its great-value wines, especially the River Red, a delicious and consistent blended wine with a budget price tag.

De Wetshof 500m south of Van Loveren on the left of the road (Mon–Fri 8.30am–4.30pm, Sat 9.30am–12.30pm; free; ☎023 615 1853). A top-notch estate with photogenic mountain and vineyard views, producing several excellent whites including their flagship Bateleur Chardonnay, a Rhine Riesling and a great Finesse.

Along the R60 from Robertson to Worcester

Graham Beck About 7km north of Robertson (Mon–Fri 9am–5pm, Sat 10am–3pm; free; ☎023 626 1214). A high-flying estate determined to make an international splash – and succeeding big-time with orders from the British supermarket giants, including Tesco and Marks and Spencer. Daringly modern tasting room where you can sample their vast range of reds and whites, many of them in the top rank.

Nuy Turn off 53km north of Robertson (Mon–Fri 8.30am–4.30pm, Sat 8.30am–12.30pm; free; ☎023 347 0272). Not strictly on the Robertson Valley wine route, but one of South Africa's most successful wine-making co-operatives and one that can easily be taken in as part of it. As well as visiting the winery, you can buy, but not taste their bargain-priced wines from the Pitkos Wyne stall, about 32km from Robertson and just beyond the Nuy turn-off. Their lovely Colombard is excellent value and the romantically named Chant de Nuit is a pleasant curiosity because its ingredients include unusual Ferdinand de Lesseps grapes.

McGregor gained modest prosperity in the nineteenth century by becoming a centre of the whipstock industry, supplying wagoners and transport riders with long bamboo sticks for goading oxen. There aren't too many ox-drawn wagons today and, apart from farming, tourism (which is still quite limited) is beginning to develop. Residents are being urged to build in harmony with existing style and thus maintain the town's character.

Apart from its spare beauty – and it's worth taking a late-afternoon stroll down one of the dirt roads out of town – the main reason people come here is to walk the **Boesmanskloof Traverse** (see p.224), which crosses to Greyton on the other side of the mountain.

Voortrekker Street is McGregor's main thoroughfare, where you'll find a small, clearly signposted **tourist information** bureau (Mon–Sat 9am–4pm, Sun 9am–3pm; ☎023 625 1954, ⓦwww.mcgregor.org.za).

Accommodation

All the central **accommodation** is in Voortrekker Street, or clearly indicated off it and there are also a couple of nice places in the atmospheric Karoo semi-desert outside town, including *Whipstock Farm*, which is a good base on this side of the hills if you're hiking the Boesmanskloof Traverse from Greyton.

Dove Cottage Rhebokskraal Farm, 2km south of town ☎023 625 1951, ©villagersmc@hotmail.com or enquire at *Villagers Art and Coffee Shop* on Voortrekker Street. A restored cottage on a beautiful fruit and grape farm, it's secluded and cosy, with views of mountains and the Karoo, and offers good walking opportunities. Ask for precise directions when you book, as you can't just turn up at the farm. ❷

Green Gables Country Inn Voortrekker Street ☎023 625 1626, ©grgables@telcomsa.net. Hospitable accommodation with six tastefully furnished rooms all with entrances onto a well-established Frenchified English country garden. Done out with 1930s opulence, the inn offers very good value and has a pub and highly rated restaurant. ❸

McGregor Country Cottages Voortrekker Street ☎023 625 1816, ©countrycottages@lando.co.za. Tranquil self-catering in a complex of eight workers' dwellings with traditional reed ceilings, surrounded by gardens, orchards and vegetable patches with a pool. ❷

McGregor Country House B&B Voortrekker Street ☎023 625 1656, ℻023 625 1617. Friendly guesthouse with three attractive en-suite B&B rooms, one of which can be rented on a self-catering basis, also offering substantial continental or cooked country breakfasts. ❸

Mr Oosthuizen ☎023 625 1735. A budget option for walkers doing the Boesmanskloof Traverse in basic semi-equipped huts rented out at the McGregor side of the hike. Bring your own sleeping bag, towels and supplies. ❶

Old Mill Lodge On the southern outskirts of town, at the end of Voortrekker Street ☎023 625 1841, ©mcgregor@lando.co.za. A set of cottages surrounded by vineyards and gardens with a swimming pool; it also has a good restaurant. B&B ❸, half-board ❹

Temenos Retreat Centre On the corner of Voortrekker and Bree streets ☎023 625 1871, ©temenos@lando.co.za. The least expensive accommodation in town, at a totally non-sectarian retreat centre which has ten two-person cottages open to anyone, whether on retreat or not, although the place is intended for people wanting to be quiet. Two meditations are held each day. There's a library as well as a swimming pool and two lakes in lovely gardens. ❷

Whipstock Farm 8km from the centre on the southerly continuation of Voortrekker Street ☎ & ℻023 625 1733. Restored cottages on an old citrus, almond and grape farm in the mountains. *Whipstock* is 5km from the McGregor side of the Boesmanskloof Traverse (see p.224), and the owners will pick you up from the trail for free. Swimming, bikes and canoes are available free to guests, and there's reasonably priced horse-riding too. Full-board ❸

Eating and drinking

Café Temenos (Wed–Sun 9am–5pm) in Voortrekker St, run by two Hollanders, is a delightful place for its excellent coffee, biscuits and Mediterranean-style baguettes. *Malmani Craft Shop*, in the same street, keeps similar hours and does teas, coffees and toasted sandwiches, while *Villagers*, also in Voortrekker Street, has the advantage of being open daily and is good for daytime snacks and teas with a verandah to watch the passing scene. Light lunches are on offer at the *Old Mill Lodge* (see above), where you can also splash out on a four-course set evening meal – though if you want to indulge in the latter, you'll need to have made an advance reservation by lunchtime. Best place of all for delicious and well-priced three-course dinners is *Green Gables Country Inn*, where co-owner, Jill, cooks comfort food, such as roast lamb with Mediterranean vegetables.

On Friday and Saturday nights till 10pm the hottest **drinking** place in town – literally, as it's invariably packed to its capacity of fifteen people – is the extremely popular Irish-themed *Overdraught Pub*, down the main drag. Hosted by the owner of the *McGregor Country House B&B*, it serves draught Guinness and Caffrey's imported from the Emerald Isle, as well as a range of bitters shipped in from England.

Montagu

The ultimate Breede River Valley destination is **MONTAGU** – approaching from the south through Cogman's Kloof Gorge numbers among the most dramatic arrivals in the country. A short five-kilometre winding road cuts through a rock face into a narrow valley dramatically opening out to Montagu, which is small enough to capture in one glance. Soaring mountains rise up in vast arches of twisted strata that display reds and ochres, and from September to October the gentler tints of peach and apricot blossoms flood the valley. Not only is Montagu very pleasing, with sufficient Victorian architecture to create an historic character, but there's enough to do here to more than justify an overnight stay.

The town was named in 1851 after **John Montagu**, the visionary British Secretary of the Cape, who realized that the colony would never develop without decent communications and was responsible for commissioning the first mountain passes connecting remote areas to Cape Town. The grateful farmers of Agter Cogman's Kloof (Behind Cogman's Kloof) leapt at the chance of a snappier name for their village and called it after him.

Montagu activities

To most people, Montagu is best known for its **hot springs**, but serious **rock climbers** come for its cliff faces, which are regarded as among the country's most challenging. You can also explore the mountains on a couple of trails or, easiest of all, on a tractor ride onto one of the peaks offering stunning panoramas. Montagu is also conveniently positioned for excursions along both the Robertson and Little Karoo **wine routes** (see p.206).

Three **hikes** begin from the *Old Mill* at the north end of Tanner Street, where there's also a small park at the foot of cliffs; **maps** for the hikes are available from Montagu's tourist information bureau. Shortest is the Lover's Walk, a just over two-kilometre stroll through Bath Kloof (or Badkloof) that follows the Keisie River to the hot springs and is open between 7am and 6pm. More substantial is the twelve-kilometre Cogman's Kloof Hiking Trail, which can be completed in three to six hours; only the first 2km are steep, after which it's an easy walk with nice views of Montagu, the ravines and mountains. Most ambitious is the Bloupunt Hiking Trail, at around 15.5km, which gets you up to an altitude of over 1000m and can be completed in six to nine hours. The walk passes through terrain with ravines, mountain streams, craggy cliffs and rock formations and from the summit of Bloupunt you can see as far as McGregor and Robertson. Throughout the year, you will see dassies and klip-springers as well as a large variety of wild flowers because of the presence of perennial streams. The fynbos vegetation includes proteas, ericas, aloes, lilies, watsonias and wild orchids. Carry a waterbottle to fill up at a waterpoint about halfway up the mountain.

If you don't feel like walking up the Langeberg Mountains, you can still get to the top on a highly recommended three-hour **tractor ride** (Wed 10am, Sat 9.30am & 2pm; book at the Montagu tourist information bureau), from Protea Farm, which is 29km along the Koo/Touws River road (R318). Remember to take warm clothes.

Arrival, information and accommodation

Intercity **bus** service to Montagu is restricted to Munniks (☎021 637 1850) service from Cape Town (a 2hr journey), departing on Wednesday, Friday, Saturday and Sunday from Belville, and stopping by request in the centre of Montagu at the OK shop. Montagu's **tourist information** bureau, 24 Bath St (Mon–Fri 8.45am–4.45pm, Sat 9am–5pm, Sun 9.30am-12.30pm & 2-5pm; ☎023 614 2471), is useful for picking up information about local attractions.

Accommodation

Even if you're here for the springs, it is far nicer to find somewhere to **stay** in town rather than at the spa, which amounts to little more than a large crowded resort, especially at weekends and school holidays. If you do get stuck, the tourist information bureau can help.

Avalon Springs Hotel ☎023 614 1150, ⓦwww.avalonsprings.co.za. One of two options at Montagu Springs, this tacky pink hotel offers B&B rooms and cheaper self-catering flats. ❺

Cynthia's 3 Krom St ☎023 614 2760, Ⓔcyncots@lando.co.za. Nine self-catering cottages dotted around the west side of town, all in old houses, with gardens and braai areas, and near the starting point for hiking trails. ❶

John Montagu Victorian Guest House 30 Joubert St ☎023 614 1331, ⓦwww.johnmontagu.co.za. En-suite rooms at this guesthouse two streets up from Bath Street, with enough period furniture and knick-knacks to create an historic ambience without being oppressive. ❸

Kingna Lodge 11 Bath St ☎023 614 1066, ⓦwww.kingnalodge.co.za. Nelson Mandela's choice when he came here in 1995, this large period house delivers a Victorian atmosphere in its three rooms with slight variations in their degree of luxury. The emphasis is on good food and excellent service, and there's a verandah for tea and a swimming pool and Jacuzzi at the back. ❹–❺

Mimosa Lodge Church Street ☎023 614 2351, ⓦwww.mimosa.co.za. A handsome Edwardian double-storey house just off Bath Street, with an emphasis on food using local ingredients. Rooms are en suite, with either shower or bath – the best are upstairs, with a balcony. Half-board ❺

Montagu Caravan Park At the west end of Bath Street, across the Keisie River ☎023 614 2675. A friendly municipal park, with nice personal touches such as fresh flowers everywhere, offering campsites and basic timber cabins sleeping four. The units have cookers and fridges, but ablution facilities are shared; you can rent bedding, but you'll need to bring your own towels. ❶

Montagu Rose Guest House 19 Kohler St ☎023 614 2681, Ⓔbenvr@lantic.net. Well-run guesthouse in a modern home, with very personalized service and a hallway plastered with thank-you notes and cards. All rooms have baths and mountain views. ❸

Montagu Springs ☎023 614 1050, Ⓕ023 614 2235. The resort has 120 fully equipped self-catering chalets, some more luxurious than others, that sleep four and are substantially cheaper from Monday to Thursday, Sunday and outside school holidays. Mon–Thurs & Sun ❶–❸, Fri & Sat ❸–❹.

Seven Church Street ☎023 614 1186, Ⓔmwjones@yebo.co.za. A lovely central Victorian house, offering the town's most romantic stay. Embroidered pure cotton linen, ball and claw baths, gorgeous garden, sundeck. ❹

Squirrel's Corner On the corner of Bloem and Jouberts streets ☎ & Ⓕ023 614 1081. One of the most affordable B&Bs in town, with four comfortable, spotless en-suite rooms in a friendly family house, two blocks from the main road. ❷–❸

The Town and around

Highly photogenic, Montagu is ideal for seeing on foot, taking in the interesting buildings or simply enjoying the setting, with its mountains, valleys and farms. There are also a couple of museums, neither of which is outstanding. The best thing about the **Montagu Museum**, 41 Long St (Mon–Fri 9am–1pm & 2–5pm, Sat & Sun 10.00am–12.30pm; R3) housed in a pleasant old church, is its herbal project, which traces traditional Khoisan knowledge about the medicinal properties of local plants. Work is being done in conjunction with the Pharmacology Department at the University of Cape Town and you can buy their booklet *Herbal Remedies: Montagu Museum*, which details some of the findings. The herbs themselves are also on sale, some of them grown in the gardens of the **Joubert House Museum** (Mon–Fri 9.30am–1pm & 2–5pm, Sat 10am–noon, Sun 10am–midnight), one block west at 25 Long St. Built in 1853, this was one of the first houses standing in a vast plot which was originally a town farm, and has peach-pip floors fixed with beeswax, characteristic of the area and period furniture on display in each of the rooms.

Montagu's main draw is the **Montagu Springs Resort** (daily 8am–11pm; R23), about 3km northwest of town on the R318 (or reached on foot, by following the Keisie River which flows along the north edge of town). Several chlorinated open-air pools of different temperatures and a couple of Jacuzzis are spectacularly situated at the foot of cliffs – an effect slightly spoilt by the neon lights of a hotel complex and fast-food restaurant. It's a fabulous place to take kids, but the weekends become a mass of splashing bodies. If you want a quiet time, go first thing in the morning or last thing at night; when the outside air is cooler, the steaming waters provide a wonderfully relaxing alcohol-free nightcap. The springs are popular with coloured and Indian families, who were previously barred under apartheid; this has driven some rednecks to establish a racially exclusive spring on a farm outside town, where only members are allowed.

Eating and drinking

When it comes to **eating**, Montagu has a number of good places dotted around the town centre.

Airlie's Tea Garden & Guest House 38 Bath St ☎ 023 614 2943. A pleasant daytime venue where you can have tea and scones with rose jam in a beautiful garden.

Four Oaks 46 Long St ☎ 023 614 2778. A top-quality restaurant run by two German cooks who specialize in Italian food. You can sample dishes like homemade gnocchi, Tuscan-styled rabbit, ostrich and stuffed figs in a lovely shaded courtyard. Lunch and dinner daily except Mondays.

Jessica's 28 Bath St ☎ 023 614 1805. Small friendly eatery, named after the proprietors' boxer dog and decorated with period dog prints. Here you'll get cosmopolitan bistro-type dishes and a top selection of Robertson wines; the cajun-roasted baby chicken on wild rice with peri-peri cream is recommended. Open every evening for dinner.

Kingna Lodge 11 Bath St ☎ 023 614 1066. For a formal night out, try their set-menu five-course meal (with vegetarian options), served with silver cutlery and candles. You'll need to book by lunchtime.

Montagu Dry Fruit Farmstall Bath Street. Good place to pick up snacks and supplies if you're self-catering. Sells dried fruit, *biltong*, *boerewors*, bread, milk and cheese. Mon–Fri 7am–6pm, Sat 8am–2pm, Sun 7am–1pm.

Preston's Restaurant & Thomas Bain Pub Bath Street ☎ 023 614 1633. A small, intimate nightspot that remains open till late every night and is recommended for its sole and oxtail.

Romano's Continental Restaurant Church Street. Open at lunchtime and evenings for reasonably priced pasta and pizza dishes. Closed Sun.

Oudtshoorn and around

OUDTSHOORN has been called the "ostrich capital of the world"; the town's surrounds are indeed crammed with ostrich farms, several of which you can visit, and the local souvenir shops keep busy dreaming up 1001 tacky ways to recycle ostrich parts as comestibles and souvenirs. But Oudtshoorn has two other big draws: it's the best base for visiting the nearby **Cango Caves** (see p.213), and the town is known for its sunshine and pleasant climate. Only 63km of tar separate Oudtshoorn from Wilderness on the coast, yet the weather couldn't be more different; this is especially good news in winter, when a cold downpour along the Garden Route can give the lie to the idea of "sunny South Africa".

Some 50km west of Oudtshoorn, **Calitzdorp** is a delightfully unassuming Victorian village that can be seen as part of a circular excursion incorporating the scenic **Groenfontein Valley**. Alternatively, its wineries and one or two tea shops offer the chance of a breather if you're travelling on the R62 mountain route through the Little Karoo. **De Rust**, a town with similar origins to Calitzdorp but 35km in the opposite direction, has benefited greatly from lying on the national road connecting the N1 to the Garden Route, but is little more than a pleasant pit stop on a journey north.

Some history

Oudtshoorn started out as a small village named in honour of Geesje Ernestina Johanna van Oudtshoorn, wife of the first civil commissioner for George. By the 1860s, **ostriches**, which live in the wild in Africa, were being raised under the ideal conditions of the Oudtshoorn Valley, where the warm climate and loamy soils enabled lucerne, the favourite diet of the flightless birds, to be grown. The quirky Victorian fashion for large feathers had turned the ostriches into a source of serious wealth, and by the 1880s hundreds of thousands of kilogrammes of feathers were being exported, and birds were changing hands for up to £1000 a pair – an unimaginable sum in those days. On the back of this boom, sharp businessmen made their fortunes, ignorant farmers were ripped off, and labourers drew the shortest straw of all. The latter were mostly coloured descendants of the Outeniqua and Attaqua Khoikhoi and trekboers, who received derisory wages supplemented by rations of food, wine, spirits and tobacco – a practice that still continues on some farms. In the early twentieth century, the most successful farmers and traders built themselves the "feather palaces", ostentatious sandstone Edwardian buildings that have become the defining feature of Oudtshoorn.

Arrival and information

Of the **intercity buses**, Intercape pulls in at Stanmar Motors, 187 Langenhoven Rd, and Translux at Queens Riverside Mall, off Voortrekker Street. If you're travelling on the Baz Bus or the Outeniqua Choo-Tjoe to George (see p.215) and heading for *Backpackers Paradise* in Oudtshoorn, you can arrange for a free pickup from them (although you pay to cover the route in the other direction). Oudtshoorn's **tourist information** bureau (Sept–April: Mon–Fri 8am–6pm, Sat 9am–1pm & 2–6pm, Sun 10am–1pm & 2–6pm; slightly earlier closing May–Aug; ☎044 279 2532, ⓦwww.oudtshoorn.com), next to the *Queens Hotel*, Baron van Reede Street, is good for information about the caves, ostrich farms and local accommodation. *Backpackers Paradise* rents out **bikes**, whether you're staying with them or not and also arranges spectacular **adventurous cycling trips** down the Swartberg Pass, chaperoned with motor vehicle backup. Oudtshoorn has several **internet cafés**, the most convenient of which is *Internet@café* 150 Baron van Reede St, adjacent to *Backpackers Paradise* (☎044 279 3025, ⓔnetcafe@mweb.co.za).

Accommodation

Oudtshoorn has a number of large hotels catering mainly to tour buses, plenty of good-quality B&Bs and guesthouses, a centrally located campsite with chalets, and one of the country's best-run backpacker lodges. Accommodation is varied and plentiful, and prices fall dramatically during the winter months following the arts festival. Prices below are summer rates outside December/January. The tourist information bureau offers a free accommodation booking service.

Adley House 209 Jan van Riebeeck Rd ☎044 272 4533, ⓕ044 272 4554, ⓦwww.adleyhouse.co.za. A 1905 sandstone home built during the ostrich boom with twelve en-suite rooms (all with TV), a swimming pool and garden. ❹

Backpackers Paradise 148 Baron van Reede St ☎044 272 3436, ⓕ044 272 0877, ⓔjubilee@pixie.co.za. A friendly and well-run two-storey hostel along the main drag, which makes an effort to go the extra few centimetres with three-quarter beds, en-suite doubles and family rooms as well as eighteen dorm beds – and a portion of ostrich egg on the house for breakfast in season. ❶

Bedstop 69 van der Riet St ☎044 272 4746, ⓕ044 272 2528, ⓔbedstop@mail.com. B&B in modest rooms, with gardens where you can sit outside, and a braai. It's slightly cheaper if you don't have breakfast. ❶

Bisibee 171 Church St ☎ 044 272 4784, ℱ 044 279 2373, ⓦ www.africasa.net/oudtshoorn/bisibee. A decent B&B a few blocks from the centre, run by a very welcoming owner, with five good-value rooms in a colonial-style home with verandahs, a large garden, swimming pool and braai area. ❷

De Oude Meul Signposted off the R328 to Cango Caves, 18km north of Oudtshoorn ☎ & ℱ 044 272 7190, ⓔ deoudemeul@mweb.co.za. A row of pleasant rooms and some family units facing onto a small lake and hills in Schoemanspoort, on a nursery ostrich farm. B&B and self-catering are available, plus very good dinners. ❸

Kannaland Lodge 126 St John St ☎ 044 279 2685, ℱ 044 279 2686. Reliable if predictable modern hotel-style rooms conveniently located in the centre. You can buy meat packs and braai in the garden, and also use the kitchen. ❷

Kleinplaas Holiday Resort 171 Baron van Reede St ☎ 044 272 5811, ℱ 044 279 2019, ⓔ pls@mweb.co.za. The resort offers shady camping and fully equipped brick chalets sleeping four, conveniently close to town, with a swimming pool and laundrette. ❶

Old Parsonage 141 High St ☎ & ℱ 044 279 1751, ⓔ gvs74@xsinet.co.za. Very inexpensive bedrooms with en-suite or shared bathrooms in a fabulous, centrally located, sandstone, double-storey Dutch Reformed Church parsonage that's still in use and has a very pleasant garden. ❷

Que Werf Signposted off the R328 to Cango Caves, 15km north of Oudtshoorn ☎ & ℱ 044 272 8712, ⓔ ouewerf@mweb.co.za. A farmhouse B&B in an old Schoemanshoek Valley farmstead, with good walks, bird-watching and a swimming pool. A good option if you're visiting the caves and want to stay in the country. ❷

Queen's Hotel Baron van Reede Street ☎ 044 272 2101, ℱ 044 272 2104, queens@xsinet.co.za. Nicest of the smart hotels in Oudtshoorn, with all the facilities and right in the centre, next to the museum. *Queen's* offers style and cool relief in the summer, with marble floors, a fountain, swimming pool and the expensive *Colony* restaurant with an upstairs terrace and ostrich on the menu. ❺

Rosenhof Country Lodge 264 Baron van Reede St ☎ 044 272 2232, ℱ 044 272 3021, ⓔ rosenehof@xsinet.co.za. The most elegant place to stay in Oudtshoorn; twelve white cottages arranged around a restored Victorian house on the edge of town, set in a beautiful rose garden filled with herbs, manicured lawns, a fountain and swimming pool. The lodge has a good though expensive restaurant serving *cordon bleu* food, using local ingredients. ❺

The Town and the ostrich farms

Oudtshoorn's town centre is a pretty straightforward place to negotiate, and has little more than a couple of museums worth checking out if you've time to kill. The town's main interest lies in its Victorian and Edwardian sandstone buildings, some of which are unusually grand and elegant for a Karoo *dorp*.

The **C.P. Nel Museum** (Mon–Sat 8am–5pm, Sat 9am–5pm; R8), on the corner of Baron van Reede Street and Voortrekker Road, is a good place to start your explorations. A handsome sandstone building, it was built in 1906 as a boys' school, but now houses an eccentric collection of items relating to ostriches. Nearby, **Le Roux Town House**, on the corner of Loop and High streets (Mon–Fri 9am–1pm & 2–5pm), is a perfectly preserved family town house, and the only way to get a glimpse inside one of the much-vaunted feather palaces. The beautifully preserved furnishings were all imported from Europe between 1900 and 1920, and there is plenty to stroll around and admire here.

Many people come to Oudtshoorn to see, or even ride, **ostriches**. You don't actually have to visit one of the ostrich farms to view Africa's biggest bird, as you're bound to see flocks of them as you drive past farms in the vicinity or past truckloads of them on their way to the butcher (feathers being no longer fashionable, these days ostriches are raised for their low-cholesterol flesh). A number of show farms offer **tours** (45–90min) costing around R20 a person, which include a commentary, the chance to sit on an ostrich and the spectacle of jockeys racing the birds. Best of the bunch is *Cango Ostrich and Butterfly Farm* (☎ 044 272 4623, ℱ 044 272 8241), on the main road between Oudtshoorn and the Cango Caves, which takes only one group of visitors (or individuals) at a time.

Eating and drinking

Oudtshoorn has a choice of several places to eat, mostly strung out along Baron van Reede Street and catering to the tourist trade with the obligatory ostrich dish.

Bernard se Taphuis Baron van Reede Street ☎044 272 3208. Opposite the tourist information bureau, this is a large, central restaurant with a pleasant outdoor terrace upstairs. A good place to sample ostrich, game dishes, steaks and Afrikaner specialities at a medium price. Eves, closed Sun.

Fijne Keuken Restaurant Baron van Reede Street ☎044 272 6403. In a house converted into a cosy restaurant with tables in several rooms as well as on the verandah, this is the nicest spot in town for a drink or for a reasonably priced meal with enormous salads, pasta and ostrich dishes. Mon–Sat noon–10pm.

Godfather Restaurant 61 Voortrekker Rd ☎044 272 5404. A popular eating place with a huge menu, but noted for its medium-priced pizzas, venison and ostrich steaks. It's an excellent spot in winter with its roaring fire; it's also a good place for just a drink. Closed Sun.

Friedl's Baron van Reede Street, opposite the museum ☎044 272 6244. A central coffee shop that does nice salads, *taremezzini*, burgers, pitta pockets and decent coffee. Daily 8.30am–10pm.

Headlines Baron van Reede Street, on the corner of St John's Street ☎044 272 3434. A good-value coffee shop and restaurant, serving decent sandwiches, ostrich kebabs and steakhouse-style food and fish. A good place to come for a quick lunch.

Jemima's 94 Baron Reede St ☎044 272 0808. Indisputably the best place to eat in town, with an imaginative and good-value menu ranging from deep-fried potato skins seasoned with paprika and served with a sour-cream dip and chilli jam; pasta with coarse olive tapenade; *boerewors* ravioli; and chocolate pecan nut torte. Lunch and dinner; closed Sun eve and all day Mon.

The Rock Art Café Baron van Reede St ☎044 279 1927. The only place in town consistently open after midnight, where they have four TVs blaring and serve a reasonably priced and varied menu with meat and vegetarian options, as well as local specialities including venison pie, *bobotie* and ostrich potjie and coffee spiked with liquor. Mon–Sat 11am–2am, Sun 6pm–2am.

Cango Caves

The **Cango Caves** number among South Africa's ten most popular attractions, drawing a quarter of a million visitors each year to gasp at their fantastic cavernous spaces, dripping rocks and rising columns of calcite. In the two centuries since they became known to the public, the caves have been seriously battered by human intervention, but they still represent a stunning landscape growing inside the Swartberg foothills. Don't go expecting a serene and contemplative experience, though: the only way of getting inside the caves is on a guided tour accompanied by a commentary.

Cango is a Khoi word meaning "a wet place" – accurate enough, given that the caves' awesome formations are the work of water constantly percolating through rock and dissolving limestone on the way. The solution drips from the roof of the cave and down the walls, depositing calcium carbonate which gradually builds up. Although the caves are many millions of years old, the calcite formations that you see today are geological youngsters, dating back a mere 100,000 years.

Some history

San hunter-gatherers sheltered in the entrance caves for millennia before white settlers arrived, but it's unlikely that they ever made it to the lightless underground chambers. **Jacobus van Zyl**, a Karoo farmer, was probably the first person to penetrate beneath the surface, when he slid down on a rope into the darkness in July 1780, armed with a lamp.

Over the next couple of centuries the caves were visited and pillaged by growing numbers of callers, some of whom were photographed cheerfully carting off wagonloads of limestone columns. In the Sixties and Seventies the caves were made accessible to mass consumption when a restaurant and curio complex was built, the rock-strewn floor was evened out with concrete, ladders and walkways were installed and the caverns were turned into a kitsch extravaganza with coloured lights, piped music and an indecipherable commentary that drew hundreds of thousands of visitors each year. Even apartheid put its hefty boot in: under the premiership of Dr Hendrik Verwoerd, the arch-ideologue of racial segregation, a separate "non-whites" entrance was hacked through one wall, resulting in a disastrous through-draft that began dehydrating the caves. Fortunately, the worst excesses have now ended; concerts are no longer allowed inside the chambers, and the coloured lights have been removed.

Practicalities

To **drive** here from Oudtshoorn, head north along Baron van Reede Street, and continue on the R328 for 32km to the caves. The visitors' complex includes the decent *Marimba* **restaurant** with nice views of the mountains and valley, and a souvenir shop, a curio shop, an interpretive centre with quite interesting displays about geology, people and wildlife connected with the caves, as well as a video presentation. Below the complex you'll find shady picnic sites at the edge of a river that cuts its way into the mountains and along which there are hiking trails. The nearest **accommodation** is set beautifully on the river, at Cango Mountain Resort (☎044 272 4506; ❷), signposted off the R328, 27km north of Oudtshoorn, 3km off the main road en route to the caves. This is the best self-catering accommodation in the area around Cango, with especially nice timber chalets, and a small shop on site sells basics. *Wilgewandel*, a cheap place to eat after seeing the caves, has the draw of camel rides on the property. It's 2km from the caves on the road back to Oudtshoorn and offers burgers, steak and sandwiches.

Three **tours** leave every hour (daily 9am–4pm). The half-hour Scenic Tour (on the half hour; R16.50) takes in the two largest and most spectacular caves, but is too short to give you a decent idea of the whole system. Most people join the one-hour Standard Tour (on the hour; R33), which gets you through the first six chambers. If you're an adrenaline junkie, the ninety-minute Adventure Tour (on the half hour; R44) is a must; this takes you into the deepest sections open to the public, where the openings become smaller and smaller. Squeezing through tight openings with names like Lumbago Walk, Devil's Chimney and The Letterbox is not recommended for the overweight, fainthearted or the claustrophobic, and you should wear oldish clothes and shoes with grip to negotiate the slippery floors.

Calitzdorp and the Groenfontein Valley

Just 50km west of Oudtshoorn, the tiny Karoo village of **CALITZDORP** hangs in a torpor of midday stillness. After the bustle of the "ostrich capital", it comes as a welcome surprise, with its attractive, unpretentious Victorian streets and a handful of wineries. There's nothing much to do here, apart from have tea, taste some wine and wander through the streets.

The low-key **tourist information** bureau (☎044 213 3312), JS Motors in Voortekker Street, has some first-class brochures about the village and its surroundings, as well as information about the wineries and accommodation. Some of South Africa's best ports are produced at the three modest wineries signposted down sideroads, a few hundred metres from the centre. The most highly recommended is Die Krans Estate (Mon–Fri 8am–5pm, Sat 9am–3pm; ☎044 213 3314; free), where you can sample their wines and ports (their vintage reserve port is reckoned to be among the country's top three), and stretch your legs on a thirty-minute vineyard walk in lovely countryside. Boplaas Estate (Mon–Fri 8am–5pm, Sat 9am–3pm; free tasting; ☎044 213 3326, ℱ044 213 3750) also produces some fine ports and is worth a quick look to see their massive reed-ceiling tasting room that feels like a cantina that fell off the set of a spaghetti western. If you've time, head for the Calitzdorp Wine Cellar (Mon–Fri 8am–1pm & 2–5pm, Sat 8am–noon; free; ☎044 213 3301, ℱ044 213 3110), where the main attraction is the stunning view from the tasting room into the Gamka River Valley.

Places to stay include airy B&B rooms with verandahs at the reasonably priced *Die Dorpshuis* (☎044 213 3453, ℯdorphuis@mweb.co.za; ❷), which is centrally located at 4 Van Riebeeck St, opposite the church. The best guest-house in town, but twice the price is the very friendly *Port-Wine Guest House* (☎044 213 3131, ℯportwine@mweb.co.za; ❹), in a renovated early nine-teenth-century homestead on the corner of Queen and Station streets and overlooking the Boplaas Estate. There's also the comfortable, country-style *Welgevonden Guest House* (☎ & ℱ044 213 3642; ❷), St Helena Rd, 300m from the main road, on a small Chardonnay farm; St Helena Rd is about 300m west of Queen St, across the river and accessible down Voortrekker St. *Die Dorpshuis* is also a good place to **eat**, serving reasonably priced sandwich-es, teas, light meals and heavier traditional Karoo food, such as stews and lamb. Closed for meals on Sun unless prior booking.

The Groenfontein Valley

Heading east out of town, you can return to Oudtshoorn on the tarred R62, but it would be a pity to miss out on the more circuitous minor route that diverts just outside Calitzdorp and drops into the highly scenic **Groenfontein Valley**. The narrow dirt road twists through the Swartberg foothills, past whitewashed Karoo cottages and farms and across brooks, eventually joining the R328 which goes to Oudtshoorn. An excellent reason to take this back route is to spend a couple of nights at *The Retreat Guest House* (☎ and ℱ044 213 3880; ❸), 20km from Calitzdorp and 59km from Oudtshoorn, an isolat-ed Victorian colonial farmstead on a farm that borders on the 2300 square kilo-metre Swartberg Nature Reserve, an outstandingly beautiful area of gorges, rivers and dirt tracks. Accommodation is in five comfortable en-suite rooms, each with its own fireplace (necessary on winter nights). Reasonably priced lunches and dinners – recommended since there's nowhere else to eat – are available by prior request, and vegetarians are well catered for. The exception-ally friendly hosts can also advise on simple, self-catering accommodation in the valley and on walks in the area.

De Rust

Hemmed in by mountains, **DE RUST**, 35km northeast of Oudtshoorn, is a drive-through town on the N12 cutting between the Garden Route and the N1 to Johannesburg. This accounts for the fact that most of the buildings along the town's small main road seem to be selling something: teas, crafts, *biltong* and ostrich products galore. You'll need to reach for your phrase book (or consult our language glossary on p.915) in this very Afrikaans village, which has a safe, calm atmosphere with gardens that make a bright contrast with the surround-ing stony, dry hills. De Rust is a nice enough place to stop to stretch your legs and have a drink, but there's little reason to spend the night here. In case you do, the **tourism office**, 29 Schoeman Street (Mon–Fri 8.30am–5.30pm, Sat

8.30am–12.30pm, closed Sun; ☎044 241 2109), can supply details of accommodation on surrounding farms and in town.

Translux intercity **buses** from Gauteng stop off on their way to Knysna at the *De Rust Hotel*, while Intercape pulls in at the Shell Garage – both central locations. *Avondrust B&B* (1 Vrede St ☎044 241 2459; ❷) has five en-suite **rooms** in a double-storied house a couple of streets back from the main road, as well as a self-catering flat in the garden at the back. *Oulap Country House*, some 15km east of town off the R341 to Uniondale (☎044 241 2250, ⓔoulap@mweb.co.za; half-board ❺), is an unusual place to stay, a Karoo farm in the Swartberg Mountains run by Jans Rautenbach, film producer and storyteller, and his wife. Rooms are eclectically furnished with antiques, *objets d'art* and South African paintings, each of them worth a story over an excellent dinner with the host.

For outdoor **eating**, there are two tea shops in the main road, both with gardens: *Herries*, marked by a purple elephant outside, has pleasant seating under shady trees; and *Mulberry Inn*, an acceptable tea garden. For fresh bread, rusks, cakes, indoor **teas** and light meals, *Die Groen Bliktrommel*, on the same road, is recommended.

Prince Albert and around

Isolation and poverty have left intact the traditional rural architecture of **PRINCE ALBERT**, an attractive little town 70km north of Oudtshoorn, across the loops and razorbacks of the Swartberg Pass. Although firmly in the thirstlands of the South African interior, on the cusp between the Little and Great Karoo, Prince Albert is all the more striking for its perennial spring, whose water trickles down furrows along its streets – a gift that propagates fruit trees and gardens.

Supremely old-fashioned displays make window-shopping as much fun as the interior of any country museum, but the essence of Prince Albert is in the fleeting impressions that give the flavour of a Karoo *dorp* like nowhere else: the silver steeple of the Dutch Reformed church puncturing a deep-blue sky, residents sauntering along or progressing slowly down the main street on squeaky

Go to Hell

Prince Albert is one of the best places to begin a trip into **Die Hel** (also known as Hell, The Hell or Gamkaskloof). Die Hel is not on the way to anywhere and, although it doesn't look very far on the map, by car you'll need to allow for two and a half hours in either direction to make this spectacular but tortuous expedition into the valley. Although the journey is on a dirt road, you won't need a 4WD vehicle, but you should definitely not attempt the drive in the killing heat of December or January. On foot, this makes a thrilling trip of two or three days. Reasonably priced **guided hikes** are operated by the owners of the *Saxe-Coburg Lodge* in Prince Albert (see opposite), but note that they only take parties of a minimum of four people. **Accommodation** can be arranged through the lodge in primitive self-catering huts (❷). There's no electricity in the valley, and you'll have to heat water using a wood-fired boiler; there are also no shops or any other facilities, so stock up on food and supplies before heading off.

bikes. Visitors mostly come to Prince Albert for the drive through its two southerly gateways – the **Swartberg Pass** and **Meiringspoort** – generally driving in one way, spending the night in town, and driving out the other. The town is also an excellent base for thrilling walks and drives in the mountains – the ultimate being a journey into **Die Hel** (see box on p.216).

Accommodation

Most people get to Prince Albert through the mountains by **car**, but you can get off the Cape Town–Johannesburg **train** at Prince Albert Road station, 45km from the hamlet, and arrange to be collected by *Onse Rus* B&B. Once there, the place is easily covered on foot. A number of moderately priced B&Bs, self-catering places and a good and relatively inexpensive hotel make finding accommodation here a breeze.

Bijlia Cana Wellness Centre De Beer Street ⓣ & ⓕ 023 541 1872. An excellent-value Karoo retreat with three en-suite bedrooms; the hosts pamper you with aromatherapy, reiki and reflexology, and also take guests on walks and outings to local points of interest. Although vegetarians can be catered for, meals do include meat and the menu includes healthy continental breakfasts, homemade bread and Karoo lamb. Full-board ❹

Collins House 63 Church St ⓣ 023 541 1786. The town's top place to stay consists of three air-conditioned en-suite guest rooms in a two-storey Victorian house with a swimming pool. ❸

Dennehof Guest House off Christina de Wit Street, on the outskirts of town ⓣ 023 541 1227 or 082 412 6505, ⓦ www.home.intekom.com/dennehof. Three self-contained cottages and suites in a National Monument homestead. Self-catering and B&B. ❷

Hoogenoeg Holiday Houses ⓣ 023 541 1455. The cheapest accommodation in town is run by Tannie (aunt) Alta, who rents out a number of

sparsely furnished but perfectly adequate old houses in Prince Albert at rock-bottom rates. ❶

Onse Rus 47 Church St ⓣ 023 541 1380, ⓔ lisass@intekom.co.za. Cool, thatched B&B rooms attached to a restored Cape Dutch house. Tours to Gamkaskloof and into the Swartberg range are also offered, and children are welcome. ❷

Saxe-Coburg Lodge 60 Church St ⓣ & ⓕ 023 541 1267, ⓦ www.saxecoburg.co.za. A good bet if you're hiking in the area, as the owners hike regularly in the Swartberg range and organize trips to Die Hel (see box opposite). The B&B rooms are in their house, with the best ones opening onto the back garden and duck pond. ❷

Swartberg Hotel 77 Church St ⓣ 023 541 1332, ⓕ 023 541 1383. A Victorian two-storey National Monument, that has been fully refurbished following a fire in 2001. Traditional Karoo dinners are served in an atmospheric dining room, and there's a swimming pool. ❹

Eating

Cannibal's 109 Church St ⓣ 083 674 3365. Dubiously named eating place that opens for lunch every day except Wednesday and does lamb shank, game dishes and other Karoo specialities.

CJ's Church Street, a few doors down from the *Swartberg Hotel*. Good value for no-nonsense food, including lamb chops, fish and chips and other deep-fried delights, served with a singular lack of flair.

Die Ou Kelder 5km out of town on a farm ⓣ 023 541 1908. Traditional Afrikaans catering, including

braaivleis and cold buffet, for a minimum of six people by prior arrangement in a hundred-year-old barn.

Karoo Kombui (Karoo Kitchen), 18 Droedrift St. A recommended evenings-only spot that serves traditional fare from this part of the country. Closed Sun.

Sampie se Plaasstal At the south end of the main road. A great place for snacks, with excellent dried fruit and rusks, as well as local olives which are among the best in South Africa. Open for breakfast, tea and light lunches.

The N1 from Worcester to Beaufort West

The **N1** is the main highway between Cape Town and Johannesburg, and with the majority of flights still arriving in Johannesburg it's common for visitors to arrive there and drive down to the coast. This account, however, assumes you'll be starting your journey in Cape Town and heading north. While this route isn't particularly inspiring, and won't take you through the diversity of the country, it does lead you into the Karoo, the huge semi-desert filling the centre-west of South Africa. The various towns along the way have a couple of interesting historic buildings and some of the flavour of the isolated Karoo in their street scenes – enough to fill an hour if you're looking for a break from the long journey. The most compelling places are undoubtedly the Victorian village of **Matjiesfontein** and **the Karoo National Park** just outside Beaufort West, both of which are destinations in their own right.

Matjiesfontein

One of the quirkier manifestations of Victorian colonialism lies 54km east of Touwsrivier at the historic village of **MATJIESFONTEIN** (pronounced "Mikey's-fontayn"). Little more than two dusty streets beside a train track, the village resembles a film set rather than a Karoo *dorp*: every building, including the grand railway station, is a classic period piece, with tin roofs, pastel walls, well-tended gardens and Victorian frills. At the eastern end of the main street is the centrepiece, the *Lord Milner*, a hotel decked out with turrets and balconies and fountains by the entrance. If you're passing by, make sure you stop at least for a look around, and at less than three hours' drive from Cape Town the village is worth considering as a two-day trip of its own.

The origins of this curious place lie in the enterprise of a young Scottish entrepreneur, Jimmy Logan, who came to Cape Town to work on the railways and obtained the concession to sell refreshments to passengers all the way along the line from Cape Town to Bulawayo. He built Matjiesfontein as a health resort – making much play on the clean Karoo air – and it became a gathering point for the wealthy and influential around the turn of the century.

Today the village is doing brisk trade as a treasured relic. You can still come here in the classical manner on the mainline **train** from Cape Town to Jo'burg/Pretoria (although it's a leisurely rather than direct journey), and **stay**

Capetown to Johannesburg on the N1

For practical driving purposes, the journey along the **N1** between **Cape Town and Johannesburg**, via Bloemfontein, is just over 1400km – about fifteen to twenty hours' driving time. The halfway point is marked by the small village of **Hanover**, with nearby **Colesburg** offering a wide range of reasonably pleasant places to stay. An alternative route branches off west just north of Three Sisters onto the **N12**, via **Kimberley**, adding an insignificant 20km on the journey. There is very little by way of halfway stops on the N12, although Kimberley (see p.307) certainly merits a stop on this route. If you're taking the journey slowly, Beaufort West is approximately one-third of the way from Cape Town, with Bloemfontein and Kimberley both about two-thirds of the way. All three main intercity **bus** companies, Greyhound, Intercape and Translux, ply the N1 route (18hr), with the latter two also going along the N12.

at the *Lord Milner* (℡023 551 3011, Ⓦwww.matjiesfontein.com; ❸), either in one of the grand, antique-filled rooms in the hotel itself, or in one of the annexes in the surrounding houses. Inside the hotel there are huge portraits on the wall, polished brass fittings and, perhaps taking the theme a touch too far, rather surly service from waitresses dressed in black and white, with doilies on their heads. For **eating and drinking**, the hotel has a dimly lit dining room and a wonderfully aged and creaking bar. Along the main street, you'll find a tea room, souvenir shop and post office, all in attractive Victorian houses.

Laingsburg and Leeu-Gamka

There's little incentive to stop at **LAINGSBURG**, a town only 27km further along the N1 that marks the start of the long, lonely spaces of the Karoo. A service station lies on the road as it pulls around the Buffels River, and there are a couple of nondescript hotels and a cosy **caravan park** just up behind the service station, with tiny rondavels (❶). As you drive through town, look out for the sign on the central reservation showing the water level during the catastrophic flood here in 1981 – it's level with (if not higher than) the roof of your car. Just outside Laingsburg, beside the road, is an Anglo-Boer War **blockhouse**, still largely intact on the outside and one of the best surviving examples. These were built by the British at frequent intervals along the railway line to protect their main supply route; in all they built some eight thousand blockhouses (at £16 each), prompting Boer General Christiaan de Wet to pass comment on the British "blockhead" system.

One of the longest empty stretches is along the next 124km until you reach **LEEU-GAMKA**, with a filling station and a tiny Anglo-Boer War cemetery that just about has room for the grave of Private Schultz, the tallest man in the British army. Both barrels of the name Leeu-Gamka mean "lion", the first of which is Afrikaans, the second Khoi. But the acquaintanceship of the hamlet with its namesake ended some time ago through the barrel of a gun.

Beaufort West

For over 100km on either side of **BEAUFORT WEST**, the scenery from the N1 is far away and hazy, so the appearance of the Nieuwveld Mountains, which rise up behind town, give the place a certain distinction. Beyond that, however, Beaufort West is not a pretty place, with the N1 traffic trundling through its centre (watch out for speed traps and remember to stop at traffic lights), and it devotes most of its attention to servicing road-weary travellers.

As befits a town which is the oldest municipality in South Africa, most of the old buildings have a very municipal stolidity to them. Principal among these is the town's **museum**, 87 Donkin St (℡023 415 2308; Mon–Fri 8.30am–12.45pm & 1.45–4.45pm, Sat 9–noon; entry R5), in the old town hall, which houses an exhibition honouring the glamorous life and achievements of Beaufort West's Professor Christiaan Barnard, who performed the world's first human heart transplant operation at Groote Schuur Hospital in Cape Town in 1967 and died in 2001. His burial place, in the garden of the Parsonage, is part of the museum.

Practicalities

The intercity **buses** all pull into the *Oasis Hotel* in Donkin Street. The town's helpful **tourist information** bureau at 63 Donkin St (Mon–Fri 8am–4.45pm; ℡023 415 1160), is one block along from the museum.

Accommodation

Beaufort West has no shortage of **accommodation**, though much of it is fairly characterless. There's a municipal camping and caravan park under some trees on the right as you come into the main part of town on Donkin Street, but as with other camping options along the N1, it's a bit scruffy and unappealing. If you want to **camp**, you're better off going to the Karoo National Park, just a few kilometres out of town (see opposite).

Donkin House 14 Donkin St ☏ 023 414 4287. Ideal for backpackers, this is more of a simple guesthouse than a hostel, with en-suite rooms with TVs and fridges, a swimming pool and some communal space to hang out in. ❶

Hotel Formula 1 144 Donkin St ☏ 023 415 2421, ⓦ www.hotelformula1.co.za. Part of a chain that delivers slick, ultra-modern budget rooms that resemble a ship's cabin. ❶

Matoppo Inn On the corner of Bird and Meintjies streets ☏ 023 415 1055, ⓔ matoppoinn@telkom-sa.net. Elegant accommodation, which has "antique" as well as standard and luxury rooms in the town's old *drostdy*, or magistrate's house. ❸–❹

The Wagon Wheel Country Lodge Off the N1 on the northern fringe of town, ☏ 023 414 2145, ⓦ www.wagonwheel.co.za. Clean en-suite motel rooms. ❷

Eating

When it comes to eating, you could do worse than the breakfasts and lunches in the coffee shop next to the craft gallery at Clyde House on Donkin Street, though the best breakfasts are to be had at the *Matoppo Inn*, which is open to non-guests from 7–9am. They also do four-course, set menu Karoo-style dinners, if pre-booked earlier in the day. Otherwise evening meals come down to *Mac Young's*, an upmarket, Scottish-themed restaurant nestled behind a Caltex service station. Popular with Afrikaners, anyone with Scottish ancestry will find the cringe factor rather high. Opposite the *Formula 1* hotel is the predictable but reliable *Saddles Steak House*.

Karoo National Park

Unassuming and undervalued, the **Karoo National Park** (daily 5am–10pm; R10) has emerged in recent years as a reserve with much more to offer than first meets the eye. Although it doesn't immediately feel very Karoo-like (there are too many mountains), the themes of the semi-desert are undoubtedly here, and after a night gazing at the dazzling sky, or a hot day learning about the unexpectedly intricate flora of the region, you'll start to appreciate this park's special value. Many of the slightly graceless facilities are recognizable from national parks elsewhere in South Africa, but here you do get the sense that the management are working hard to help people enjoy the place.

Much of the experience here is in the landscape and the serene atmosphere: despite the recent introduction of some **black rhino**, big game is limited, although there are some impressive raptors, including the **black eagle**. The designated drives around a limited section of the 600-square-kilometre park aren't terribly exciting; however, a recent innovation is a wider-ranging 4WD trail, with the opportunity to overnight out in the *veld* in a remote mountain hut, for around R200 per person. For bookings, contact South African National Parks (see p.221).

Near the main restcamp there is an environmental **education centre**, along with three **trails**: an eleven-kilometre day-walk; a short but informative tree trail; and a very imaginative fossil trail (designed to accommodate wheelchairs and incorporating Braille boards), which tells the fascinating 250-million-year-old geological history of the area and shows fossils of the unusual animals that lived here in the times when the Karoo was a vast inland sea. Information about these is available at camp reception.

Practicalities

The entrance gate to Karoo National Park is right on the N1, 2km south of Beaufort West. The **reception and restcamp** are a couple of kilometres into the park, hidden among the appealing flat-topped mountains in a way that makes you feel as though you're a million miles from the town and the highway. At reception there's a shop selling basic foodstuffs, a **restaurant** (Mon–Sat 8am–8.30pm, Sun 8am–7pm), and a pool nearby. Accommodation is in fully equipped **bungalows** that sleep three people (❷), strung out on either side of the main complex; the rate is for a minimum of two people and includes breakfast in the restaurant. The **campsite** is hidden away over a rise. If you're intending to overnight in Beaufort West during a long trip, it's well worth considering coming out to the park instead of staying in town. For more **information** about the park, phone ☎023 415 2828. For accommodation **bookings** contact South African National Parks in Pretoria (☎012 343 1991, ℮reservations@parks-sa.co.za).

The Overberg interior and the Whale Coast

East of the Winelands lies a vaguely defined region known as the **Overberg** (Afrikaans for "over the mountain"). In the seventeenth century, when even Stellenbosch, Franschhoek and Paarl were remote outposts, everywhere beyond them was to the Dutch settlers a fuzzy hinterland drifting off into the arid sands of the Karoo. These days it extends to an imprecise point between Arniston and Mossel Bay on the coast and somewhere east of Swellendam in the interior.

Of the two main routes through the Overberg, the **N2** strikes out across the less interesting interior, a four- to five-hour stretch most people endure rather than enjoy to get to the Garden Route – but you can make it less of a chore with a couple of well-chosen stops along the way. North of the N2 is **Greyton**, a pleasant village used by Capetonians as a relaxing weekend retreat, and the starting point of the **Boesmanskloof Traverse** – a terrific one-day trail across the mountains into the Karoo. The historic Moravian mission station of **Genadendal**, five minutes down the road from Greyton, has a strange Afro-Germanic ambience that offers a couple of hours' pleasant strolling. Along the N2 itself, the only places that justify a restorative stop are **Caledon**, for its thermal springs, and **Swellendam**, for its well-preserved streetscape as well as one of South Africa's best country museums.

The real draw of the area is the **Whale Coast**, close enough for an easy outing from Cape Town, yet surprisingly undeveloped. The exception is popular **Hermanus**, which owes its fame to its status as the whale-watching capital of South Africa. The whole of this southern Cape coast, in fact, is prime territory for land-based whale-watching. Also along this section of coast is **Cape**

Agulhas, the southernmost place on the continent, which sadly fails to deliver the drama its location promises. Nearby, and far more worthwhile, is **Arniston**, one of the best-preserved fishing villages in the country, and a little to its east the **De Hoop Nature Reserve**, an exciting wilderness of bleached dunes, craggy coast and more whales.

② Caledon

The first impression of **CALEDON** is of the huge, cathedral-like grain silos that dwarf its church spires. A low-key farming town some 111km east of Cape Town, Caledon built its former prosperity on the wheat, barley and malt trade. Now the town is gambling on making its fortune through a casino and family entertainment complex, built around the town's one natural asset, its thermal springs.

Caledon Spa (daily 6am–midnight; Mon & Wed–Sun R50, Tues R25) is the best spa in South Africa. Use of the springs predates by centuries the Victorians, who built a wrought-iron structure around the main rectangular pool in the nineteenth century (replaced in 2001 by a timber one that retains the feel of the original). When the Dutch arrived here in the eighteenth century, Khoi people were already wallowing in steaming holes dug in the ground – a practice imitated by the settlers.

Today, the spa offers a gamut of physical indulgences in, for South Africa, an unusually tasteful setting. The so-called Khoi-San spa consists of a waterfall tumbling down the mountainside into a series of rocky pools – the hottest being one at the top that clocks 40° C – getting progressively cooler as they approach the foot of the hill. Use of the saunas, a steam room, frigidarium (icy pool) and gym are all included in the price. Towels are provided and robes can be rented. A **treatment centre** offers a huge variety of expensive massages and beauty treatments, from aromatherapy massage to thalassotherapy (seaweed therapy).

The **casino** forms part of a small mall with a couple of family restaurants and a few shops. If you fancy a flutter, you can try your luck at one of the scores of slot-machines lined up inside the large gambling hall which also has a number of gaming tables. Day visitors to both the spa and the casino have to park in the hotel grounds (R10 per vehicle).

Apart from the spa and casino, Caledon has a couple of other decent attractions. The **House Museum** (Mon–Fri 8am–1pm & 2–5pm, Sat 9am–1pm; R2) at 11 Constitution St, consists of displays of mainly domestic items in a house faithfully restored to "Victorian Caledon style" (1837–1901). The most enjoyable way to see the collections is on a recommended **guided tour** led by curator Tizzie Mangiagalli (book though tourist information; R10), whose well-informed commentary makes connections between seemingly trivial household items and the broader tapestry of history – you can also arrange agricultural tours through him. A photographic display – also part of the museum – is housed with the information bureau at the old town hall.

Caledon's outdoor attraction is the **Wildflower Garden and Nature Reserve**, where you can wander through fynbos, aloes and succulents on a lovely long amble along a rocky, wooded *kloof* into the mountains, or head out on the ten-kilometre Meiring Trail, which goes deep into the nature reserve.

Practicalities

You can reach Caledon with only a minor detour from the N2: to get to the spa, follow the sign displaying the hotel and spa symbols, which if you're coming from Cape Town is a little way beyond the town centre indicator.

All intercity **buses** stop off at the *Alexandra Hotel* on Market Square in the centre of town. Caledon's **tourist information** bureau, in the old town hall, 22 Plein St (Mon–Fri 8am–1pm & 2–5pm, Sat 9am–1pm; ☎028 212 1511), with an attached crafts and home industries shop, has literature about the area as well as details of places to stay.

Accommodation

Caledon Hotel Signposted 1km east of the centre ☎028 214 1271, ℱ028 214 1270, ⓦwww.caledoncasino.co.za. The most luxurious accommodation in town caters to weekenders and the conference market and has comfortable rooms with nice views of the town across wheatfields and mountains. Half-board ❹

Libanon 21 Krige St ☎028 214 1096, ℱ028 214 1166. The smartest B&B in town; situated in a quiet neighbourhood in a historic house that sleeps five; there's also a small garden. ❸

Oom Barrie se Huisie Clearly signposted off the R406 on the way to Greyton ☎028 214 1080 or 028 214 8903. An extremely rural cottage that sleeps six, set in rolling wheatlands with a double room and space for four in the attic. The house has no electricity or phone, although there is hot and cold running water and a fully equipped kitchen, and linen is available on request. The rate more than doubles at the weekend, but it still represents good value, especially for four or more people. ❶

The Painted Lady 3 Donkin St ☎083 468 8192. The cheapest beds in town in two Victorian self-catering cottages and a cheap B&B; *Painted Lady* has five bedrooms; while *Nana Cottage*, 41 Meul St, has two; and *Kelkiewyn*, 22 Prince Alfred St, is an inexpensive B&B with five bedrooms. ❶

Eating

Caledon Hotel 1km east of the centre ☎028 214 1271. The smartest place to eat has an a la carte menu for substantial meals and also does snacks.

Museum Shop 22 Plein St. For self-catering, a good place to buy home-baked products, including fresh bread, every Friday.

Ounooi se Kuierplek Cathcart Street. Casual eating place that serves similar fare to the *Venster*. Mon–Fri 10am–5pm.

Venster Restaurant Wildflower Garden. Snacks and traditional Afrikaner fare, such as *bobotie* and *bredie* during the day.

Greyton and the Boesmanskloof Traverse

The best things about **GREYTON**, a small holiday and retirement village 46km north of Caledon, based around a core of Georgian and Victorian buildings, are the unploughed Riviersonderend (Endless River) Mountains, which set it off from the cultivated landscape typical of most of the Western Cape. There's no industry here and the only modern developments are the repro Georgian houses along its streets. The calm, bucolic atmosphere created by the shady oaks hides a real tension in the town, between the folk who want to retain the sleepy ambience and keep out economic activity, and those who see a need to create jobs for the 500-strong coloured community who don't have the privilege of living here in golden retirement or on holiday.

Apart from estate agents selling the rural dream to city dwellers who come to set up businesses, so little money changes hands here that there isn't even a bank. The town's big attraction is the superb **Boesmanskloof Traverse** hike (see box on p.224), which crosses the mountains to McGregor. Apart from that – and some shorter walks – there's very little to do but stroll down the streets and potter about in the handful of antique and tea shops.

Practicalities

As there's no public transport to Greyton, the only way to get here is by **car**, the best route being just west of Caledon on the R406, which is tarred all the way. Don't attempt to tackle the untarred route from Riviersonderend, which will hammer your suspension. The **tourist information** bureau, 32 Main St

The Boesmanskloof Traverse

One of the best reasons to come to Greyton is to walk the fourteen-kilometre **Boesmanskloof Traverse**, taking you from the gentle, oak-lined streets of **Greyton** across the Riviersonderend mountain range to the glaring Karoo scrubland around the town of **McGregor**. The stark contrast over so short a distance is staggering, made all the more so by the fact that no direct roads connect the two towns; to drive from one to the other involves a circuitous two hours on the road.

The classic way to cover the Traverse is to walk from Greyton to **Die Galg** (14km from McGregor), where people commonly spend the night, returning the same way to Greyton the following day. The route rises and falls a fair bit, so you'll have to contend with some uphill walking, but the whole way can easily be completed in a day if you're reasonably fit. If you don't want to go all the way, you can still have a rewarding outing by venturing part of the way and returning to Greyton for the evening. A decent day's walk takes you to **Oak Falls**, 9km from Greyton, the highlight of the route. Composed of a series of cascades, its most impressive feature is a large dark pool, where you can rest and swim in the tannin-coloured water.

The walk takes you through over fifty species of wonderful montane fynbos, and if you come at the right time of year you can find yourself walking through magnificent groves of flowering proteas. Mammals include small antelope, caracals, baboons and dassies, but it's unlikely you'll see many of them, so go for the scenery, with the rugged Riviersonderend Mountains, *kloofs*, streams, waterfalls and pools.

Trail practicalities

You're free to walk the first 5km of the trail and back, but if you want to complete the whole thing from Greyton to Die Galg you will need a **permit**, which limits numbers to fifty people per day. Over weekends, the trail gets extremely full and permits must be arranged in advance through the Manager, Vrolijkheid Nature Reserve, Private Bag X614, 6705 Robertson (℡023 625 1621). During the week you can buy a permit (one day R32 per person; two days R50) on the day of your hike from the Greyton Municipal Offices, Ds Botha St (Mon–Fri 8.15am–1pm & 2–3.30pm; ℡028 254 9620). You'll get a **map** when you buy the permit, although you don't strictly need one as the Traverse is very clearly marked out. A booklet is available to accompany the interpretation trail, covering the McGregor half of the route. This is keyed to numbered points along the way and helps you to get more out of the walk by drawing your attention to what's around you. The walk isn't particularly strenuous, but you should wear good shoes. It's also worth noting that this is a winter rainfall area, and can be wet at that time of year. Summers are hot and dry.

Accommodation on the McGregor side presents two possibilities: staying at the overnight hiking dorms (℡023 625 1735, ask for Mr Oosthuizen, ❶), equipped with a fridge, cooker and beds (but no bedding) at Die Galg, the other end of trail; or *Whipstock Farm* (see p.207), 4km beyond Die Galg, from where the farm owners will collect you free of charge.

(Mon–Sat 10am–4pm, Sun 10am–1pm; ℡ & ℻028 254 9414, ⓦwww.greyton.net) is along the main road as you come into town. and also runs an accommodation agency.

Accommodation

Winters can be cold in this mountainous country; it's worth getting a place with a fireplace if you're here at that time of the year. A brief caution: Greyton municipality renumbered many properties in 1997, but not all. Don't despair if the street numbering appears to obey its own random rules: it's just that some houses may not have corrected their signs yet.

Bullocks Main Road ☎028 254 9948. A self-contained section of the owners' house, with two bedrooms and its own bathroom and kitchen. One night ❶ ; 2 nights or more R400 for unit.

Greyton Lodge 46 Main Rd ☎028 254 9876, ⓕ028 254 9672. The smartest place in town, and an excellent choice if money is no object, with plush standard rooms and a "royal suite" with its own lounge and a four-poster bed. ❹–❺

Greyton Nurseries 1 Main Rd ☎028 254 9998. Two-bedroom apartment that sleeps four, attached to a house, with the use of a courtyard; it's one of the few places in Greyton that welcomes children. ❶

Guinea Fowl Ds Botha St ☎028 254 9550. Inexpensive and friendly guesthouse which has six well-priced en-suite rooms and where you'll get a full English breakfast. ❸

High Hopes 89 Main Rd ☎ & ⓕ028 254 9898.

One of the best B&Bs in a beautiful country-style home with an en-suite bedroom, two luxury suites and a self-contained unit with a kitchen, which can be taken on a B&B or self-catering basis. The house is set in magnificent gardens with a huge ornamental pond and a swimming pool. Afternoon tea and biscuits as well as delicious non-bacon and eggs breakfasts are included in the price. ❸

Municipal campsite 2.5km out of town and signposted off Main Road ☎028 254 9620. Lovely setting on the banks of the Riviersonderend, with amenities limited to an ablution block with hot and cold water.

Post House Main Road ☎028 254 9995, ⓕ028 254 9920, ⓦwww.posthouse.co.za. En-suite rooms, each named after a Beatrix Potter character, furnished with Edwardian and country furniture. Mon–Fri ❸ , Sat & Sun ❹

Eating and drinking

Blue Mountain 21 Ds Botha Street ☎028 254 9325. An eating place that's principally a sports bar; it opens its pub to non-diners at 9.30pm, closing at 2am. Food daily noon–3pm & 6–10pm except Mon lunch.

Greyton Lodge 46 Main Rd ☎028 254 9876. The smartest restaurant in the village, offering country cuisine with attitude; it's the place to go for candle-lit four-course dinners, as well as breakfasts and lunches.

Oak and Vigne Café Ds Botha Street ☎028 254 9037. Highly popular, situated in an old cottage with an oak-shaded terrace where you can

savour reasonably priced Mediterranean-influenced country breakfasts, teas and lunches daily, such as ham and cheese croissants and lasagne dishes.

Post House Main Road. Non-residents can tipple here up to 7pm.

Rosie's On the hill in High Street, off Main Road ☎028 254 9640. A good choice for steaks, pastas and pizzas.

The Terrace 14 Main Rd ☎028 254 9164. Open daily in summer (except Monday) for good homemade pastas and burgers as well as fresh fish and steaks.

Genadendal

GENADENDAL, whose name means "valley of grace", was established in 1737 and is South Africa's oldest mission station, founded by Moravians (some of the ochre and earthy-pink architecture hints at Central-European influences). The village is essentially an excursion from Greyton, 6km to its west, as accommodation is limited.

Genadendal's focus is around **Church Square**, dominated by a very Germanic church building dating back to 1891. The old bell outside dates back to the eighteenth century, when it became the centre of a flaming row between the local farmers and the mission station. The scrap broke out when missionary Georg Schmidt annoyed the local white farmers by forming a small Christian congregation with impoverished Khoi – who were on the threshold of extinction – and giving refuge to maltreated labourers from local farms. What really got the farmers' goat was the fact that while they, white Christians, were illiterate, Schmidt was teaching blacks, whom they considered uncivilized, to read and write. The Dutch Reformed Church, under the control of the Dutch East India Company, waded in when Schmidt began baptizing converts, and prohibited the mission from ringing the bell which called the faithful to prayer.

At one stage during the eighteenth century, Genadendal was the largest settlement in southern Africa after Cape Town. Although it never became more than a village, Genadendal experienced a golden age in the nineteenth century, with a flourishing economy based on home industries. In 1838 it established the first teacher training college in the country, which the government closed in 1926, on the grounds that coloured people didn't need tertiary education and should be employed as workers on local farms – a policy that effectively ground the community into poverty. In 1995, in recognition of the mission's role, Nelson Mandela renamed his official residence in Cape Town "Genadendal".

Today, the population of this principally coloured town numbers around four thousand people, adhering to a variety of Christian sects – no longer just Moravianism. The **Mission Museum** (Mon–Thurs 9am–1pm & 2–5pm, Fri 9am–3.30pm, Sat 9am–noon; R7), adjacent to Church Square, is moderately interesting and provides some clues as to why Moravians came here. You should allow up to two hours to explore the museum and wander through the town, down to the rural graveyard, spiked with tombstones dating back to the early nineteenth century. Genadendal offers few visitor facilities, but there is a tea room, just off Church Square, where you can get refreshments.

Practicalities

The Genadendal **tourism information** bureau (Mon–Thurs 8.30am–5pm, Fri 8.30am–4pm, Sat 10am–2pm; ☎028 251 8291) is on Church Square in the centre of the mission. Basic budget **accommodation** aimed principally at hikers doing the Genadendal Trail is available at the Hester Dorothea Conference Centre (☎028 251 8346; ❶), on the square, in dormitories and a few private rooms all of which share ablution and kitchen facilities.

The Genadendal Trail

While you're here, you can venture a short way from the village into the surrounding countryside along the **Genadendal Trail**. The full twenty-five-kilometre, two-day circular trail requires a high level of fitness, particularly for the first 2km of the second day. But much of the rest is fairly easy-going, passing through montane fynbos inhabited by a variety of small antelope, caracals and the odd leopard. Only 24 people are allowed on the two-day trail at one time, so reservations are essential. **Bookings and permits** (R49) are arranged by post through Vrolijkheid Nature Reserve, Private Bag X614, Robertson 6705 (☎023 625 1621); phone before sending off your application (with a cheque or postal order made out to Vrolijkheid Nature Conservation) to check availability.

Overnight **accommodation** can be arranged in a self-catering hikers' cottage on *De Hoek*, a flower farm, halfway along the trail (☎023 626 2176; ❶). The farm is home to antelope and a wide variety of birds, and you can swim in the farm dam. Book in advance through the owners, Mr and Mrs Okes.

Swellendam

SWELLENDAM, 97km east of Caledon, is an attractive historic town at the foot of the Langeberg. It has one of the best country museums in South Africa, which makes it a congenial halfway stop along the N2 between Cape Town and the Garden Route. And because of its ample supply of good accommodation and its position – poised between the significant regional highlights of the coastal De Hoop Nature Reserve to the south and the mountains around Montagu to the north – it's a suitable base for spending a few days exploring this part of the Overberg.

South Africa's third-oldest white settlement, Swellendam was established in 1745 by Baron Gustav van Imhoff, a visiting Dutch East India Company bigwig, who was deeply concerned about the "moral degeneration" of burghers who were trekking further and further from Cape Town and out of Company control. Of no less concern to the Baron was the loss of revenue from these "vagabonds", who were neglecting to pay the Company for the right to hold land and were fiddling their annual tax returns. Following a brief hiccup in 1795, when burghers declared a "free republic" (quickly extinguished when Britain occupied the Cape), the town grew into a prosperous rural centre known for its wagon-making, and for being the last "civilized" port of call for trekboers heading out into the interior.

The income generated from this helped build Swellendam's gracious homes, many of which went up in smoke in the fire of 1865, which razed much of the town centre. In 1950, transport planners widened the main road by ripping out many of the oaks that had survived the blaze. Nevertheless, Swellendam survived with enough charm to lure you off the national road.

The Town

The only building in the centre to survive the town's ravages is the Cape Dutch-style **Oefeningshuis**, 36 Voortrek St, which now houses the tourist information bureau. Built in 1838, it was first used as a place for religious activity, and then as a school for freed slaves, and has surreal-looking clocks with frozen hands carved into either gable end, below which there's a real clock above the entrance. Diagonally opposite and slightly east at no. 11, the **Dutch Reformed Church**, dating from 1910, incorporates Gothic windows, a Baroque spire, Renaissance portico elements and Cape Dutch gables into a wedding cake of a building that, against the odds, agreeably holds its own.

On the east side of town, a short way from the centre, is the excellent **Drostdy Museum**, 18 Swellegrebel St (Mon–Fri 9am–4.45pm, Sat & Sun 10am–3.45pm; R10). One of the finest country museums in South Africa, it's actually a collection of historic buildings arranged around large grounds and a lovely nineteenth-century Cape garden. The centrepiece is the **Drostdy** itself, built in 1747 as the seat of the *landdrost*, a magistrate-cum-commissioner sent out by the Dutch East India Company to control the outer reaches of its territory. The building conforms to the beautiful limewashed, thatched and shuttered Cape Dutch style of the eighteenth century, but the furnishings are of nineteenth-century vintage. From the rear garden of the Drostdy you can stroll along a path and across Drostdy St to **Mayville**, a middle-class Victorian homestead from the mid-nineteenth century with an old rose garden. Also part of the complex are the **Old Gaol**, the **jailer's cottage**, and an interesting display of eighteenth- and nineteenth-century farm implements and tools. Look out, too, for the old dung circular threshing floor in a low-walled enclosure, into which horses were driven to tramp the wheat.

Practicalities

The Greyhound, Intercape and Translux intercity **buses** travelling between Cape Town and Port Elizabeth all pull in diagonally opposite the *Swellengrebel Hotel*, 91 Voortrek St, in the centre of town, while the Baz Bus will drop you off at any of the central accommodation. Swellendam has a very switched-on **tourist information** bureau, 36 Voortrek St (Mon–Fri 8am–1pm & 2–5pm, Sat 9am–12.30pm; ☎ & ☏028 514 2770, ✉infoswd@sdm.dorea.co.za, which provides frank and helpful advice about local attractions and will book accommodation. You can easily cover the town centre on foot – there's no other way of getting around without your own transport.

Two Feathers Horse Trails (☏ & ☏028 514 3797 or ☏082 494 8279, ⓦwww.twofeathers.co.za) offers Western-style and English **horse-riding** by the hour, or you can do a full-day outing with lunch included. They also offer **cattle mustering** and **five-day wilderness trails** with accommodation in Native American-style tepees or self-catering log cabins. The landscape is varied and ranges from forest tracks past waterfalls and mountain streams to riverside trails, meandering country roads and open grass plains.

Accommodation

Anyone who enjoys the atmosphere of historic houses will be spoilt for choice in Swellendam where Cape Dutch and Georgian houses are ten a penny and prices tend to be pretty reasonable.

Braeside B&B 13 van Oudtshoorn Way ☏028 514 3325 or 083 261 1923, ☏028 514 1899, ⓦwww.braeside4u.homestead.com. A large and reasonably priced, comfortable, child-friendly Edwardian home with four en-suite rooms with separate entrances. The house has a verandah with views of the mountains, and also a swimming pool. ❷

The Coachman 14 Drostdy St ☏028 514 2294, ☏028 514 3349, ⓦwww.coachman.co.za. An old coach house close to the Drostdy Museum, offering three comfortable en-suite bedrooms with private entrances off a courtyard and two new and pricier luxury thatched cottages in the garden. ❸–❺

Cypress Cottage 3 Voortrek St ☏028 514 3296. One of the least expensive B&Bs in town, offering a central location and good value in five modest rooms in the back garden of a grand house (one of the oldest in town). ❷

Eenuurkop Huisie 8km from town ☏ & ☏028 514 1447. Two self-catering cottages, one with three and one with one bedroom, in a stunning setting with access to mountain walks. ❷

Hermitage Huisies 3km from town on R60 to Ashton ☏ & ☏028 514 2308. Two wonderful self-catering cottages, one with one bedroom the other with two rooms, on a smallholding with a duck pond and grazing sheep. ❷

Klippe Rivier Homestead Off the western end of Voortrek Street, just outside the centre ☏028 514 3341, ☏028 514 3337, ☺krh@sdm.dorea.co.za. Swellendam's most formal and luxurious accommodation in a beautiful 1825 mansion with six opulent bedrooms, a secluded cottage and saltwater swimming pool. No under-10's. ❻

Moolmanshof 217 Voortrek St ☏028 514 3258, ☏028 514 2384, ☺hhmodels@intekom.co.za. Three en-suite bedrooms in a comfortable country-style Cape Dutch homestead on the edge of town, dating back to 1798. There's a large garden and swimming pool, and children are welcome. ❷

The Old Mill 241–243 Voortrek St ☏028 514 2790. Four picturesque B&B cottages, one of them in the old mill, and all of which were refurbished and upgraded in 2001, set in the grounds of a small restaurant. ❷

Roosje Van De Kaap 5 Drostdy St ☏028 514 3001, ☺roosje@dorea.co.za. A popular B&B in a beautiful house; service is first-rate, but some of the rooms are small. ❷

Swellendam Backpackers 5 Lichtenstein St ☏028 514 2648, ☺backpack@dorea.co.za. Swellendam's only hostel is a friendly place with camping, dorms and doubles; staff can also arrange activities including horse-riding, mountain biking and canoeing. ❶

Eating

There's no shortage of decent places to eat in Swellendam – ranging from snack bars to formal restaurants where you can enjoy a romantic candle-lit dinner – many of them in delightful old buildings.

The Connection 132 Voortrek St ☏028 514 1988. A lunch and dinner restaurant in an eighteenth-century town house that does tasty light meals such as toasted sandwiches and main courses including game fowl and venison. Tues–Thurs.

La Belle Alliance Swellengrebel Street ☏028 514 2252. A restaurant that does sandwiches and light meals near the museum in a spectacular old

church, with lovely outdoor seating under trees along a river. Daily daytime.

The Old Mill 241–243 Voortrek St ☏028 514 2790. A nice inexpensive outdoor spot with ducks and chickens wandering about, where you can get tea, coffee and light meals. Open daily during the day.

Roosje Van De Kaap 5 Drostdy St ☏028 514 3001. A highly rated restaurant offering traditional

Cape food, with a great wine list – a good choice for a romantic candle-lit dinner. Tues–Sun 7–11pm.

Zanddrift Swellengebel Street ⓣ028 514 1789. A daytime venue in a reconstructed traditional farmhouse that attracts tour buses for its interesting dishes such as wild mushrooms garnered from local mountains and venison. Daily.

Bontebok National Park

Just 6km south of Swellendam along the Breede River, the **Bontebok National Park** (Oct–April 8am–7pm, May–Sep 8am–6pm; ⓣ028 514 2735; day visitors R12, overnight visitors free) is a compact 28-square kilometre reserve at the foot of the Langeberg range that makes a relaxing overnight stop between Cape Town and the Garden Route. The park was established in 1931 to save the Cape's dwindling population of bontebok, an attractive antelope with distinctive cappuccino, chocolate-brown and white markings on its forehead and hindquarters. By 1930, hunting had reduced the animal's number to a mere 30 individuals. Their survival has happily been secured and there are now 300 of them in the park, as well as populations in other game and nature reserves in the province. There are no big cats here, but **mammals** you might encounter are rare Cape mountain zebra, red hartebeest and grey rhebok, as well as 126 **bird species**. It's also a rich environment for **fynbos**, with nearly 500 species here, including erica, gladioli and proteas. Apart from game viewing, **activities** include **swimming** in the Breede River; **walking** along a couple of short nature trails and **fishing**.

Practicalities

Self-catering **accommodation** is available in inexpensive six-berth caravans (❶) with timber anterooms along the river; basic kitchen equipment, bedding, towels and soap are provided and there are communal ablution facilities. You can also **camp** in your own tent. **Booking** should be arranged through SA National Parks central reservations in Pretoria (ⓣ012 343 1991, ⓕ012 343 0905, ⓦwww.parks-sa.co.za). For day visitors, there are **picnic sites** with braai stands and communal ablution facilities. A **shop** at the park entrance sells basic commodities such as meat and booze, while fresh fruit and vegetables are available in Swellendam, and petrol is available in the park.

The Strand to Cape Hangklip

The main reason you'd take the coastal route that skirts the eastern shore of False Bay is to get to Hermanus, but scenically the drive has much to recommend it, especially once you get past the commuter settlements close to Cape Town. Leaving the N2 from Cape Town at Somerset West, the first coastal settlement you hit is **STRAND**, a massive industrial centre on the edge of Cape Town. Although it has a good beach, this isn't sufficient reason to stop off and the R44 quickly takes you to the ongoing commuter development of **Gordon's Bay**, your last chance for a decent sea swim for some distance. After here, the mountains bear down on the sea and the road winds its way around the folding mountainside, with the sea crashing against the rocks below – without a tree in sight, the barren landscape has a raw dramatic quality. **Cape Hangklip**, the tip of False Bay, earned its name from the fact that Hangklip frequently fooled Portuguese mariners into thinking they were rounding the Cape of Good Hope. A dirt road takes you down to **HANGKLIP** itself, where a succession of dwellers have made their homes since humans left stone axes here over 20,000 years ago. In the nineteenth century, outlaws lived in Hangklip's remote caves, but were flushed out in 1852, leaving the area to its present population of baboons.

Betty's Bay and around

Cape Hangklip roughly marks the point at which the commuters become holidaymakers. Just around the corner to the west, **BETTY'S BAY** was developed as a seaside retreat for Capetonians wanting to get away from the city. Prosaically named after Betty Youlden, daughter of the director of the first company to try to develop the area, this rather boring collection of holiday cottages hosts a colony of **African (jackass) penguins**. The best time to see the birds is in the morning or evening between April and June. African penguins mate for life and return to the same nest every year, but here are suffering from interference with their turf by perlemoen (abalone) poachers. Residents urge you to tell local shopkeepers if you see poaching taking place.

Betty's Bay is not geared up to visitors, though you can **eat** at the Harold Porter Botanical Garden (see below).

Harold Porter National Botanical Garden

Creeping up the mountains just above Betty's Bay, **Harold Porter National Botanical Garden** (daily 8am–6pm; R10) is a wild sanctuary of coastal and montane fynbos that makes a good stop along the R44, if only to picnic or have tea at its outdoor **café**. Once here, you'll probably get lured at least some of the way up the *kloof* that runs through the reserve, by both its beauty and the views of the sea you get as you move higher. The relatively compact botanical garden extends over two square kilometres from the mountains, through marshland down to coastal dunes. As you get higher up, you are treated to sea views in one direction and rugged mountains in the other.

Although wildlife in the form of small **antelope**, **baboons** and **leopards** are present, they are rarely sighted and it's more worthwhile to look out instead for the birds and blooms. In January you can see brilliant red disas in all their glory, while the nerine lilies flower in March. Keep an eye open for colourful, nectar-loving sunbirds and scores of other bird **species** that occur here. Four **trails** of between one and three hours meander through the gardens, but you can just as easily take yourself off on an impromptu stroll, up and across the red-stained waters (caused by phenols and tannins leaching from the fynbos) running through Disa Kloof.

Kleinmond

Because of its isolation, **KLEINMOND**, roughly 12km northeast of Betty's Bay, was an outlaws' stronghold for some two hundred years. In the twentieth century, however, relatively easy access turned the town into a holiday spot for Capetonians and for farmers from the surrounding areas. An impressive confluence of sea, dune, tidal estuary and mountain waterfalls combines with a ten-kilometre crescent **beach** curving across the Bot River Mouth to Mudge Point, a promontory that completes the vista as you look east. Swimming is safest close to the *Beach House Hotel*, but take care not to venture beyond where you see other bathers. A newish strip of craft and coffee shops that includes a deli, sports bar and an Abalone Hatchery, which is open to the public (R8), is reached down the road signposted "Harbour" off the main coastal road.

The cheapest **accommodation** is at the couple of caravan parks, signposted from the main road, where you can **camp**. The better of the two is the *Palmiet* (☏028 271 4050), which is quieter and closer to the safely swimmable river. The most luxurious place is *Beach House*, Beach Rd (☏028 271 3130, ℱ028 271 4022; ❺), a small **hotel** whose spacious rooms have king-size beds, white wicker furniture and tastefully understated floral fabrics. Here you can look out over Sandown Bay, the lagoon and mountains and enjoy the sound of the endlessly pounding surf; if you are going to fork out to stay here, you may as well stay in one of the luxury sea-facing rooms. *Beach House* is also the best place for eating, with its expensive formal **restaurant**, *Tides*, which serves seafood and meat dishes.

Hermanus, Walker Bay and around

On the edge of rocky cliffs and backed by mountains, **HERMANUS**, 112km east of Cape Town, sits at the northernmost end of Walker Bay, an inlet whose protective curve attracts calving whales as it slides south to the promontory of Danger Point. The town trumpets itself as the **whale capital** of South Africa and, to prove it, has an official whale crier (apparently the world's only one) who struts around armed with a mobile phone and a dried kelp horn through which he yells the latest sightings. There is still the barest trace of a once-quiet cliff-edge fishing village around the historic harbour and in some understated seaside cottages, but for the most part Hermanus has gorged itself on its whale-generated income that has produced modern shopping malls, supermarkets and craft shops.

Ignoring the hype, **Walker Bay** does provide some of the finest shore-based whale-watching in the world and, even if there are better spots nearby, Hermanus is the best geared-up place in the country to exploit it. From about July, southern right whales (see p.236) start appearing in the warmer sheltered bays of the Western Cape. Whales aside, Hermanus has good swimming and walking **beaches**, some excellent **wineries** you can visit and makes a good base for exploring the rest of the area.

Due east of Walker Bay, the inland hamlet of **Stanford** on the banks of the Klein River has managed to retain its historic villagey feel. If you're here for the whales, it's close enough to Hermanus to make it an alternative base. Southeast down the bay from Hermanus, the unprepossessing town of **De Kelders** outshines its smarter neighbour as a whale-watching spot, but at nothing much else; and just inland of it, the wonderful and very upmarket **Grootbos Nature Reserve** is one of the best places in the country to learn about fynbos. Heading further down the bay, you hit the fishing town of **Gansbaai** (Afrikaans for Goose Bay), which these days is far better known for its shark-cage diving than its waterfowl. Curving back to Hermanus, Danger Point is the promontory that indicates Walker Bay's southern extent, and marks the spot where HMS *Birkenhead* literally went down in history (see p.240).

An easy excursion from Hermanus takes you through attractive and relatively untrammelled farming country to **Bredasdorp**, a junction town on the R316 that gives you the choice of branching out to Africa's disappointing southern tip at **Cape Agulhas**; the well-preserved Moravian mission town of **Elim**; or the fishing village of **Arniston**, which is the least-developed and nicest town along the Whale Coast.

Arrival and information

Scant public transport passes through Hermanus, the exception being the **Splash bus** (☎082 658 5375, ⓔsplash@hermanus.co.za), which runs at least once daily between anywhere in Hermanus and Cape Town train station. The **Baz Bus** drops people off at Bot River, 28km to the north on the N2, from where you can arrange to be collected by a shuttle operated by *Hermanus*

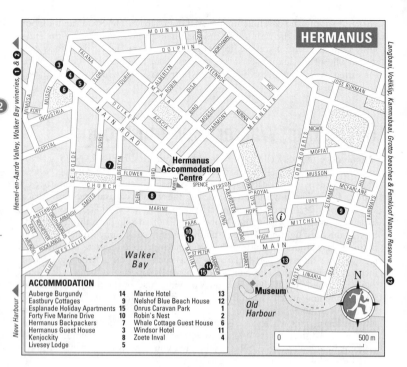

Langbaai, Voëlklip, Kammabaai, Grotto beaches & Femkloof Nature Reserve

Hemel-en-Aarde Valley, Walker Bay wineries, ❶ & ❷

New Harbour

HERMANUS

Walker Bay

ACCOMMODATION

Auberge Burgundy	14	Marine Hotel	13
Eastbury Cottages	9	Nelshof Blue Beach House	12
Esplanade Holiday Apartments	15	Onrus Caravan Park	1
Forty Five Marine Drive	10	Robin's Nest	2
Hermanus Backpackers	7	Whale Cottage Guest House	6
Hermanus Guest House	3	Windsor Hotel	11
Kenjockity	8	Zoete Inval	4
Livesey Lodge	5		

Museum

Old Harbour

N

0   500 m

Backpackers (see opposite) – booking is recommended, but the Baz carries a mobile phone and can call ahead while you're en route. Most people come to Hermanus by **car**, which takes about ninety minutes from Cape Town along the N2, or two hours via Gordon's Bay. Travelling along the N2 and striking south onto the R43 at Bot River is the more direct of the two main routes, but the winding road that hugs the coast from Strand, leaving the N2 just before Sir Lowrie's Pass, is the more scenic.

There's a helpful **tourist information** bureau (Mon–Sat 9am–5pm; ☎028 312 2629, ℱ028 313 0305, ⒲www.hermanus.co.za/info) at the old station building in Mitchell Street, with maps, useful brochures about the area and an internet café as well. The bureau also operates a free accommodation-finding service and can take bookings for boat-based and aerial whale-watching as well as shark-cage diving trips.

Accommodation

The prime spot for accommodation in Hermanus – especially in the whale season – is along the cliffs or at the edge of one of the beaches. Unsurprisingly, **B&Bs**, **hotels** and **self-catering apartments** on the shore are in high demand and tend to be more expensive than ones set back. If there are more than two of you, the best option may be to rent a whole house or apartment through Hermanus Accommodation Centre, on the corner of Church and Myrtle lanes (☎028 313 0004 or 083 651 0001, ℱ028 313 0005, ⒲www .adept.co.za/hermanus).

Auberge Burgundy 16 Harbour Rd ☏028 313 1201, ℻028 313 1204, ⓦwww.auberge.co.za. An imitation-Provençal country house in the town centre, projecting a stylish Mediterranean feel, with imported French fabrics and a lavender garden. Breakfast is served across the road at the *Burgundy* restaurant, under the same ownership. ❺

Eastbury Cottages 36 Luyt St ☏082 658 4945 (contact Jenny Bowes Meyer). Two very reasonably priced, fully equipped self-catering cottages on the same site close to the *Marine Hotel*. One has two bedrooms (R200 for two people, R250 for four) and the other one bedroom (R150 for the cottage).

Forty Five Marine Drive 45 Marine Drive ☏028 312 3610, ℻028 313 1125, ⓦwww.windsor-hotel.com. Cliffside self-catering luxury apartments next to the *Windsor Hotel*, with two bedrooms, two bathrooms, a kitchen and terrific views across the bay. R600 per apartment.

Hermanus Backpackers 26 Flower St ☏028 312 4293 or 082 890 1485, ℻028 313 2727, ⓦwww.hermanus.com. Professionally run, clean and brightly decorated two-storey house two blocks back from the shore, with dorms and doubles. There's a big pool, a bar and garden to relax in, and they serve breakfasts as well as evening meals. Activities such as shark-cage diving and boat-based whale-watching can be booked here, and the hostel also runs a shuttle to Bot River to meet the Baz bus (booking recommended). ❶

Hermanus Guest House 8 Mountain Drive ☏028 313 0212, ℻028 313 0224, ⓦwheretostay.idws.com/wc/ow/17/hermanusguesthouse. Self-catering unit that sleeps four (R250 for the unit), as well as two comfortable and very reasonably priced B&B rooms in a suburban bungalow, some way back from the shore with lots of little extras such as towelling robes, complimentary drinks and a laundry service. ❷

Kenjockity 15 Church St ☏ & ℻028 312 1772. A centrally located and friendly B&B, where you can't see the sea but you can hear the whales at night in season. The best rooms are en suite and have their own private sitting rooms, while there are also smaller, cheaper rooms with shared bathrooms. ❶–❸

Livesey Lodge 13 Main Rd ☏&℻028 313 0026, ⓦwww.liveseylodge.co.za. A welcoming and simply furnished B&B with a variety of en-suite rooms mostly arranged around a lovely courtyard garden with a large swimming pool. ❸

Marine Hotel Marine Drive ☏028 313 1000, ℻028 313 0160, ⓦwww.marine-hermanus.co.za. A grand seafront hotel with a rather formal ambience, but unquestionably Hermanus's best and easily up to the standard of the top establishments in the country. If you're shelling out, you may as well book early and pay extra for a sea-facing room. There's a Jacuzzi and an indoor swimming pool. Mountain-facing ❻–❽

Nelshof Blue Beach House 37 Tenth St ☏028 314 0201. Situated right on Voëlklip Beach in a renovated Victorian house, this is the only B&B in Hermanus where you have a choice of lying in bed or lounging in the Jacuzzi to watch whales. Accommodation is comfortable and stylish, the service is highly personalized with outstanding breakfasts on the verandah. ❹–❺

Robin's Nest Meadow Avenue ☏082 893 9911 (contact Trixie Krum) ℻028 313 2139, ⓔrobin-snest@hermanus.co.za. Three fully equipped, self-catering studio flats in the gardens of what was once Rheezicht Farm, 4km west of the centre. Reached through the Hemel-en-Aarde shopping village, these purpose-built, two-storey flats sleep two people and open onto a communal courtyard, offering a semi-rural alternative to staying in town. R250 per flat.

Whale Cottage Guest House 20 Main Rd ☏028 313 0929, ℻028 313 0912, ⓦwww.whalecot.co.za. Simple, pleasantly furnished guesthouse offering five rooms (some larger) decorated with marine themes. The only drawback is that it's away from the sea. ❹

Windsor Hotel Marine Drive ☏028 312 3727, ℻028 312 2181, ⓦwww.windsor-hotel.com. The town's second hotel has the best location in town – right on the edge of the cliffs – but otherwise isn't a patch on the *Marine*. Booking is essential, and it's worth paying a little extra for a sea-facing room. ❹–❺

Zoete Inval 23 Main Rd ☏ & ℻028 312 1242, ⓦwww.zoeteinval.co.za. An excellent-value friendly establishment, offering B&B rooms, some with their own bathrooms, as well as backpacker dorms and doubles. Run by the enthusiastic Marilyn van der Velden (a registered Satour tour guide and keen ecologist), it has huge amounts of carefully prepared information on activities in the area for guests. The owners can arrange a taxi to pick you up from the Baz Bus and are happy to advise guests on other transport options. ❶–❷

The Town and around

Main Road, the continuation of the R43, meanders through Hermanus, briefly becoming Seventh Street before again resuming its persona as the national road. **Market Square**, just above the old harbour and to the south of Main Street, is the closest thing to a centre, and here you'll find the heaviest concentration of restaurants, craft shops and flea markets – the principal forms of entertainment in town when the whales are taking time out.

Just below Market Square is the **Old Harbour Museum** (Mon–Sat 9am–1pm & 2–5pm, Sun noon–4pm; R2), whose only real attraction is its live transmission of whale calls from a hydrophone anchored in the bay to its audio room (replaced by recordings out of season). Among the other uncompelling displays, you'll find lots of fishing tackle and some sharks' jaws. Outside the museum, a few colourful boats, used by local fishermen from the mid-eighteenth to mid-nineteenth centuries, create a photogenic vignette in the tiny harbour.

An almost continuous five-kilometre cliff path through coastal fynbos hugs the rocky coastline from the old harbour to Grotto Beach in the eastern suburbs. For one short stretch the path heads away from the coast and follows Main Street before returning to the shore. East of the Old Harbour, just below the *Marine Hotel*, a beautiful tidal pool offers the only **sea swimming** around the town centre's craggy coast; it's big enough to do laps. For **beaches**, you have to head out east across the Mossel River to the suburbs, where you'll find a decent choice, starting with secluded **Langbaai**, closest to town, a cove beneath cliffs at the bottom of Sixth Avenue that has a narrow strip of beach and is excellent for swimming. **Voëlklip**, at the bottom of Eighth Avenue, has grassed terraces, toilets, a nearby café for tea and is great for picnics if you prefer your sandwiches unseasoned with sand. Adjacent is **Kammabaai**, with the best surfing break around Hermanus, and 1km further east, **Grotto Beach**, which despite its name – and unlike all the other Hermanus beaches – is not a rocky cove and marks the start of a twelve-kilometre curve of dazzlingly white sand that stretches all the way to De Kelders.

Also on the east side of town, the **Fernkloof Nature Reserve** (dawn to dusk; free), encompasses fifteen square kilometres of mountainous terrain and offers sweeping views of Walker Bay. This highly recommended wilderness area is more than just another nature reserve on the edge of town and has some forty kilometres of **waymarked footpaths** for strolls or longer walks, including a 4.5–kilometre circular nature trail. This is an excellent way to get close to the astonishing variety of delicate montane coastal fynbos (over a thousand species have been identified in the reserve), much of it flowering species that attract scores of birds, including the brightly coloured sunbirds and sugarbirds endemic to the area.

A couple of kilometres west of town along Westcliff, the **New Harbour** is a working fishing harbour, dramatically surrounded by steep cliffs, projecting a gutsy counterpoint to the more manicured central area. The whales sometimes enter the harbour – and there's nowhere better to watch them than from the *Harbour Rock* (see p.237).

Hemel-en-Aarde Valley: the Walker Bay wineries

On the eastern edge of Hermanus, **Rotary Way** is a fantastic ten-kilometre drive that follows the mountain spine through beautiful montane fynbos offering sweeping views of the town, the Hemel-en-Aarde Valley (Heaven and Earth Valley) and Walker Bay from Kleinmond to Danger Point. To get there from town, turn right just after the sports ground, and take a track straddled by

△ Whale-watching, Hermanus

a pair of white gateposts labelled "Rotary Way". The road is tarred for part of the way, then becomes a dirt track, eventually petering out altogether, which means you have to return the same way.

Some of South Africa's top wines come from the adjacent **Hemel-en-Aarde Valley**, about fifteen minutes by car west of Hermanus. Vineyards in the area date back to the early nineteenth century, when the Klein Hemel-en-Aarde Vineyard was part of a Moravian mission station, but winemaking has been established here for little over a decade. Three small **wineries** are dotted along a few gravel kilometres of the R320 to Caledon, which branches off the main road to Cape Town

Whale-watching

The Southern Cape, including Cape Town, provides some of the easiest and best places in the world for **whale-watching**. You don't need to rent a boat or take a pricey tour to get out to sea; if you come at the right time of year, whales are often visible from the shore, although a good pair of binoculars will come in useful for when they are far out.

All nine of the great whale species of the southern hemisphere pass by South Africa's shores, but the most commonly seen off Cape Town are **southern right whales** (their name derives from being the "right" one to kill because of their high oil and bone yields and the fact that, conveniently, they float when dead). Southern right whales are black and easily recognized from their pale, brownish **callosities** (rock gardens). These unappealing patches of raised, roughened skin on their snouts and heads have a distinct pattern on each animal, which helps scientists keep track of them.

Female whales come inshore for calving in sheltered bays, and stay to nurse their young for up to three months. The period from **August to October** is the best time to see them, although they start appearing in June and some stay around until December. When the calves are big enough, the whales head off south again, to colder, stormy waters where they feed on enormous quantities of plankton, making up for the nursing months when the females don't eat at all. Though you're most likely to see females and young, you may see **males** early in the season boisterously flopping about the females, though they neither help rear the calves or form lasting bonds with females.

What gives away the presence of a whale is the blow or spout, a tall smoky plume which disperses after a few seconds and is actually the whale breathing out before it surfaces. If luck is on your side, you may see whales breaching – the movement when they thrust high out of the water and fall back with a great splash.

The Overberg's hottest whale spots

In **Hermanus** itself, the best vantage points are from the concrete cliff paths, which ring the rocky shore from New Harbour to Grotto Beach. There are interpretation boards at three of the popular vantage points (Gearing's Point, Die Gang and Bientang's Cave). At their worst, you'll find the paths two or three deep with people. Although Hermanus is best known and most geared up for whale-watching, it's also the most congested venue during the whale season and there are equally good – if not better – spots elsewhere along the Walker Bay coast. Aficionados claim that **De Kelders** (see p.239), some 39km east of Hermanus, is even better, while **De Hoop Nature Reserve** (see p.243), east of Arniston, is reckoned by some to be the ultimate place along the entire southern African coast for whale-watching, with far greater numbers of southern rights breaching here than anywhere else.

Dial M for marine mammals

During the season, the Whale Information Hotline (☏083 212 1074) can tell you where the latest sightings have been.

2km west of Hermanus, and are worth popping into for their intimate tasting rooms and first-class wines, with views of the stark scrubby mountains just inland.

Closest to town of the Hemel-en-Aarde wineries, **WhaleHaven Winery** (Mon–Fri 9.30am–5pm, Sat 10.30am–1pm; free; ☎028 312 1585, ✉wh-wines@itec.co.za), a couple of hundred metres after the Caledon turn-off, released its first vintage in 1995 and its reputation has been growing since. Among the several excellent wines to look out for are the Oak Valley Pinot Noir, which scores top marks, and their Oak Matured Chardonnay, which is almost as highly rated.

Across the road from WhaleHaven in the Hemel-en-Aarde Village, the **Wine Village** (Mon–Sat 9am–7pm & Sun 10am–6pm), is possibly the best wine shop in South Africa, with a staggering selection of labels from all the country's various wine-producing districts, covering a vast price range.

The longest established of the Walker Bay wineries, **Hamilton Russell** (Mon–Fri 9am–5pm, Sat 9am–1pm; free; ☎028 312 3595, ✉hrv@her-manus.co.za) is noted for its exceptionally good Chardonnays and Pinot Noirs – among South Africa's priciest wines. If you're set on sampling a particular wine, be sure to phone ahead, as some vintages sell out fast. Hamilton Russell also bottles a range of wines under the very collectable Southern Right label, which can't be bought at the estate but are available at the Wine Village at the foot of the hill or in town liquor stores, where they quickly sell out as souvenirs.

Adjacent to Hamilton Russell, towards Caledon, **Bouchard Finlayson** (Mon–Fri 9am–5pm, Sat 10.30am–12.30pm; ☎028 312 3515, ⓦwww.bouchardfinlayson.co.za) is another establishment with a formidable reputation, and a wider range of wines than its neighbour. It consistently scores highly with its Pinot Noirs and Chardonnays.

Furthest from town and newest of the wineries is **Cape Bay** (Mon–Fri 9am–4pm & summer only Sun 9am–noon), just under 7km from the Hemel-en-Aarde turn-off and about half a kilometre after the tar ends. They produce a notable Cabernet Sauvignon, Pinotage, Chardonnay and Sauvignon Blanc under their heavyweight Newton Johnson label as well as some decent quaffers under their Cape Bay and Sandown Bay labels.

Eating and drinking

Although **seafood** is the obvious thing to eat in Hermanus – and you'll find plenty of good restaurants serving it – there's a wide range of cuisine available here including some of the best steaks around and African fare.

Restaurants

B's Steakhouse Hemel-en-Aarde Village ☎028 316 3625. A friendly and fun, buzzing steakhouse – the real thing, not part of a chain – serving brilliantly prepared, mid-priced, slabs of real beef (they hasten to tell punters they don't do burgers). Has a formidable wine list and is child-friendly. Dinner Tues–Sun, lunch Fri & Sun.

The Burgundy Marine Drive ☎028 312 2800. A fairly expensive Mediterranean-influenced restaurant above the old harbour, offering a seafood-dominated menu in one of the town's oldest buildings, with indoor as well as shady outdoor seating. Teas, lunch and dinner daily.

Fisherman's Cottage Lemms Corner ☎028 312 3642. An excellent spot for drinks – but not that hot an eating place – in an old cottage off Market Square, with verandah seating. Tues–Sat 11am–11pm, Sun lunch only.

The Greek's Coffee Shop & Restaurant Royal Street ☎028 312 3707. A tiny fisherman's cottage where you can eat genuine Greek taverna fare, including dolmades, calamari and spit-roast lamb, finishing with homemade yoghurt and honey. Breakfast and lunch daily, dinner Sat.

Harbour Rock Seagrill & Bar New Harbour ☎028 312 2920. An excellent and easy-going place for sundowners or reasonably priced fish and chips and other seafood dishes, with an outdoor deck offering stunning views from the cliffs. Daily for breakfast, lunch & dinner.

Marimba Café 108d Main Rd ☎028 312 2148.

Lively evening joint with a constantly changing mid-price menu from across Africa. Past dishes have included Ethiopian roast lamb seasoned with cardamom and ginger, and *yassa* – Senegalese-style chicken. Dinner daily – booking essential.

Milkwood Restaurant Atlantic Drive, Onrus ⊕028 316 1516. A nice outdoor family venue, a 15min drive west of Hermanus. *Milkwood* is especially recommended for its deck in an unsurpassed setting on a seaside lagoon, and does medium-priced steaks and excellent freshly caught fish.

Mogg's Country Cookhouse Hemel-en-Aarde Valley, 12km from Hermanus along the R320 to Caledon ⊕028 312 4321. A most unlikely location for one of Hermanus's most successful restaurants – on a working farm in the back country – with superb views across the valley. Mogg's is an intimate, mid-priced place that's always full and unfailingly excellent, serving whatever country-cooking surprises take the fancy of chefs Jenny Mogg and her daughter Julia, but there's always a choice of three starters, main courses and desserts. Open Wed–Sun lunch and Fri & Sat evening (booking essential).

Rossi's Italian Restaurant 10 High St ⊕028 312 2848. A cheap and child-friendly joint serving reliable pastas and furnace-baked pizzas seven nights a week.

Self-catering and take-away

There's no nicer way to eat on a beautiful day in Hermanus than to do a bit of self-catering or buy some fish and chips and eat them on the wall of the old harbour. The town has a number of farm stalls and deli-style foodshops, and grub features large at the market held every Saturday morning on Market Square, where you'll find excellent homemade cheeses from Bot River as well as homemade pasta, pesto, marinated cheeses, muffins, houmous and baked goods.

Chi Deli Shopping Centre, Main Road, Onrus. A cross between a wholefood shop and an Italian deli, selling pasta, imported luxury comestibles such as chocolates, sushi, ready-made foods, vegetarian take-away meals and snacks. Closed Tues.

Ethne's Epicure Copes Centre, Long Street. A tiny café best known for its tasty packaged meals ready to microwave at home (with good vegetarian options), sandwiches on homemade bread as well as take-away coffees.

Hemel-en-Aarde Food Corner Broad and Mitchell streets. One of the best places to stock up on goodies such as cheeses, delicious breads, cakes and organic produce.

Hermanus Fish Shoppe Market Square. Inexpensive take-away fish and chips – the best in town – as well as seafood salads and fresh seafood to cook yourself.

Pick'n'Pay Family Supermarket 81 Main St. A well-stocked shop from South Africa's premier supermarket chain.

Listings

Emergencies Ambulance ⊕10177; Fire ⊕361 0000; Police (enquiries) ⊕028 312 2626.
Hospital Hermanus Private Hospital, Hospital Street, off Main Road (⊕028 313 0168), has a 24hr casualty service.
Pharmacy Hermanus, 145 Main Rd (⊕028 312 4039 or 312 233) is open Mon–Fri 8am–6.30pm, Sat 8am–1pm and Sun 10am–noon & 6.30–7.30pm.
Taxis Bernardus shuttle service (⊕028 316 1093) runs buses to and from Cape Town (R135 per person one way), and can get you around town.

Stanford

East of Hermanus the R43 takes a detour inland around the Klein River Lagoon, past the pretty riverside hamlet of **STANFORD**. Despite its proximity to hyped-up Hermanus, the historic village (established in 1857) has become something of a refuge for arty types seeking a tranquil escape from the urban rat race. To keep visitors racing around their town they've created an **arts and crafts route** that takes in over a dozen artists' studios. But apart from the town's excellent micro-brewery, Stanford's principal attraction is its travel-brochure streetscape of simple Victorian architecture that includes limewashed houses and sandstone cottages – as well as an Anglican church – with thatched roofs that glow under the late afternoon sun. Although the **Birkenhead Brewery** (tasting daily 11am–5pm, pub lunches daily 11am–3pm, free tours Mon–Fri 11am & hourly 1–4pm) just across the R43 from the village, bills itself as a "craft brewery estate", the gleaming stainless steel pipes and equipment inside soon dispel any images of bloodshot hillbillies knocking up a bit of moonshine on the quiet. This is a very slick operation and a great place to go for a pub lunch with mountain views or to sample and buy their excellent beers that put SAB, South Africa's big brewing near-monopoly, in its place.

Practicalities

The **tourism information** bureau, next to the library and opposite the Spar mini-supermarket in the middle of the village (Mon–Fri 8am–4pm & Sat 10am–noon; ☎ & ⓕ028 341 0340), has brochures about Stanford and can help with finding **accommodation**. The top place to stay is *Stanford House*, on the corner of Queen Victoria and Church streets (☎028 341 0300; ❾), which has twenty en-suite double rooms housed in Victorian cottages. The nicest of the self-catering places is the very reasonably priced *B's Cottage*, Morton Street (☎028 341 0430, ⓔmilkwood@hermanus.co.za), a small open-plan thatched house in an English country garden that sleeps two adults. When it comes to **eating**, Stanford has several good restaurants including the small *Marianne's Bistro and Home Deli*, Du Toit Street (Fri–Sun 9am–4pm; ☎028 341 0272) in a Victorian cottage, good enough to draw Cape Town gourmands out for the day and recommended for its cream teas, homemade fare and carefully prepared and delicious lunches. Another excellent place is *Paprika*, Shortmarket Street (☎028 341 0662), which does delicious Mediterranean-style dinners from Tuesday to Saturday and Sunday lunches in a cottage with a convivial atmosphere in the evenings.

Grootbos and De Kelders

A unique place – and not just in hyperbole – is the private **Grootbos Nature Reserve** (☎028 384 0381, ⓦwww.grootbos.com; minimum stay two nights; half-board including all activities ❽), a highlight of the area, and 33km from Hermanus. Rolling across undulating, fynbos-covered country, this luxury reserve has superb middle-distance views of the coast, and is promoted as a "fynbos lodge", where experts guide you through the Western Cape's unique and richly varied plant kingdom. Outings are available in 4WD vehicles, on foot or on horseback. **Accommodation** is in self-contained stone cottages with ethnic-chic furnishings, polished granite kitchen surfaces, imported fittings, temperature-controlled showers, multiple sundecks and views of the mountain from one side and the sea from the other. The rate includes a three-course dinner served in the main lodge, breakfast in your own cottage and a choice of activities, including guided horse-rides, walks or drives through the fynbos and conducted beach hikes.

The nearest coast is a couple of kilometres to the east at **DE KELDERS**, a haphazard and treeless hamlet that stares from bleak cliffs across Walker Bay to Hermanus. Despite surpassing fashionable Hermanus as a whale-watching venue and having a marvellous, long, sandy beach, De Kelders has somehow escaped the hype, and this small aggregation of holiday homes remains a backwater, devoid of facilities apart from a few rentable **rooms**. Best value of these is *Liesje's Lodge* 77, Main Rd, (☎028 384 1277 or 072 222 0885),where there are self-catering units (❶) which can also be taken as B&B rooms (❷), some with sea views. The friendly owner Liesje van Voorkom takes guests whale-watching and can advise you about the local **shark-cage diving** operations (see also Gansbaai on p.240).

At the end of Cliff Road, you'll reach a car park from which you can clamber down to the **Klipgat Strandloper Caves**, excavated in the early 1990s, which unearthed evidence of modern human habitation from 80,000 years ago. They became unoccupied for a few thousand years after which it was used again by Khoisan people, 20,000 years ago. Shells, middens, tools and bones were uncovered, and some of these are now displayed in the South African Museum in Cape Town (see p.161).

Gansbaai and Danger Point

From the Klipgat Caves, the waymarked **Duiwelsgats Hiking Trail** goes east for 7km as far as Gansbaai and is a good way to explore this beautiful coastline. **GANSBAAI** itself is a workaday place, economically dependent on its fishing industry and the seafood canning factory at the harbour. This gives the place a more gutsy feel than the surrounding holidaylands, but there's little reason to spend time here unless you want to engage in **great white shark safaris**, Gansbaai's other major industry, an appropriately competitive and cutthroat business with at least four operators at last count engaged in a blind feeding frenzy to attract punters. Boats set out from Gansbaai to Dyer Island (see box below), east of Danger Point, where great white sharks come to feed on the resident colony of seals. Sharks are baited, but while you do stand a chance of seeing one, sightings are certainly not guaranteed, especially over December and January when the abundance of seal pups keeps the sharks well fed and less inclined to show up for tourists. Even if a shark does appear, it may not stay long enough for all the people on the boat to get into the cage for a viewing (only two can fit in at a time). For more information, contact the Gansbaai **tourist information** bureau (Mon–Fri 9am–4pm & Sat 9am–noon; ☎028 384 1439).

Danger Point, the southernmost point of Walker Bay, is where British naval history was allegedly made. True to its name, the Point lured the ill-fated HMS *Birkenhead* onto its hidden rocks on February 26, 1852. As was the custom, the captain of the troopship gave the order: "Every man for himself." Displaying true British pluck, the soldiers are said to have lined up in their ranks on deck where they stood stock-still, knowing that if one man broke ranks it would lead to a rush that might overwhelm the lifeboats carrying women and children to safety. The precedent of "women and children first", which became known as the **Birkenhead Drill**, was thus established, even though 445 lives were lost in the disaster.

Dyer Island and Shark Alley

How a black American came to be living on an island off South Africa in the early nineteenth century is something of a mystery. But according to records, **Samson Dyer** arrived here in 1806 and made a living collecting guano on the island that subsequently took his name. Dyer Island is home to substantial **African (jackass) penguin** and **seal breeding colonies**, both of which are prized morsels among great white sharks.

So shark-infested is the channel between the island and the mainland at some times of year that it is known as **Shark Alley**, and these waters are used extensively by operators of great white viewing trips. In 1996, a group of West African castaways washed up here having been put out to sea by the unscrupulous skipper of a Taiwanese merchant vessel whom they had paid to take them to the Far East, where they hoped to find work. One of them drowned in the process, but the rest (amazingly) survived five days at sea, including a stint down Shark Alley, clinging to pieces of timber and barrels.

Cape Agulhas

Along the east flank of the Danger Point promontory, the rocky and shallow coastline with heavy swells and strong currents makes this one of South Africa's most treacherous stretches of coast – one that has claimed over 250 wrecks and around 2500 lives. Its rocky terrain also accounts for the lack of a coastal road from Gansbaai and Danger Point to **Cape Agulhas**, the southernmost tip of Africa.

The plain around the southern tip has been declared the **Agulhas National Park** to conserve its estimated 2000 species of indigenous plant and marine and intertidal life as well as a cultural heritage, which includes shipwrecks, archeological sites – stone hearths, pottery and shell middens have been discovered. There are no facilities, apart from a basic **tea shop** inside the terrific **Agulhas Lighthouse** (Tues–Sat 9.30am–4.45pm, Sun 10am–3.30pm; R2), commissioned in 1849. Apart from the thrill of climbing the precipitous winding stairway to the top, from which you get vertiginous views, there are also some interesting exhibits about lighthouses around South Africa and the world.

Three-hour **tours** taking in the coast, fynbos as well as history and archeology of the area are operated by the well-informed Riaan Pienaar of Coastal Safaris (☎028 435 7148 or 082 331 6819, ⓦmembers.ncbi.com/coastalsafaris).

Practicalities

L'AGULHAS, the rather windblown settlement associated with the southern tip, consists of a small collection of houses and a few shops. When it comes to **eating**, the options are the guesthouse or the good fish-and-chip shop in the village. **To get to L'Agulhas** from Hermanus, you have to go inland and take the R316 to Bredasdorp, where the road splits and you take the west branch for 43km to Agulhas or the east one for 24km to Arniston.

Accommodation

Agulhas Guest House Main Road ☎028 435 7650, ⓦwww.agulhas.de. The smartest accommodation in town in a relatively grand stone building perched halfway up a hillside. The eight rooms vary in level of luxury from ones with just showers to sea facing suites with large rooms and huge baths One of the main reasons to stay here is for the excellent seafood dinners. ❹–❺
Oupos 258 Main Road ☎028 435 6132. A house with guest rooms facing the sea, run by a friendly elderly Afrikaner couple who adore children. ❸

Sea House B&B Van Breda Street ☎028 435 6542, ⓔpfm@isat.co.za. A formal place bang in front of the tidal pool, with three rooms in a thatched two-storey house. ❸
The Southernmost On the corner of Van Breda and Lighthouse streets ☎028 435 6565, ⓔcowper@isat.co.za. As its name implies, this place has the most southerly beds for rent in Africa, with B&B rooms and backpacker accommodation, but doesn't welcome kids, mobile phones or pets. ❶–❷

Elim

A good reason to venture along the network of dirt roads that crisscrosses the **Whale Coast interior** is to visit **ELIM**, a Moravian mission station 40km northwest of Agulhas, founded in 1824. The whole village is a National Monument of streets lined with thatched, whitewashed houses and fig trees. There's nothing twee about this very undeveloped and untouristy place – there isn't even a bottle store, and facilities amount to a couple of tiny stores where coloured kids play video games.

The **tourist information** bureau near the church in Church Street (Mon–Sat 9am–12.30pm & 1.30–5pm; ☎028 482 1806) provides brochures about the area and can advise visitors about **accommodation** at the guesthouse (due for completion in early 2002), as well as arranging for you to have a cup of tea or a **snack** at the *Old Mill Tea Room* (booking essential). **Tours** of the village start at the tourist information bureau and take in the oldest house in the settlement, the church, and the restored old water mill where wheat is still ground into flour. There's also a memorial commemorating the **emancipation of slaves** in 1834, the only such monument in South Africa; its presence reflects the fact that numerous freed slaves found refuge in mission stations like Elim.

Arniston

After the cool deep blues of the Atlantic to the west, the tepid azure of the Indian Ocean at **ARNISTON** is truly startling, made all the more dazzling by the white dunes interspersed with rocky ledges. This is one of the best places to stay in the Overberg and is refreshingly under-developed compared to Hermanus and places closer to Cape Town. The village is known to locals by its Afrikaans name, Waenhuiskrans (Wagon-house Cliff), after a huge cave 1.5km south of town, which trekboers reckoned was spacious enough for a wagon and span of oxen (the largest thing they could think of). The English name derives from a British Ship, the *Arniston*, which hit the rocks here in 1815.

Conversely, the shallow seas so treacherous for vessels provide Arniston with the safest swimming waters along the Whale Coast. Apart from sea bathing, **Kassiesbaai**, a collection of starkly beautiful limewashed cottages, now declared a National Monument, is the principal attraction of this unspoilt hamlet. Its beautifully simple dwellings invariably show up in coffee-table books whenever picturesque fishing villages are called for. But as the home to the coloured fishing families that have for generations made their living here, Kassiesbaai sits a little uneasily as a living community, as it's a bit of a theme park for visitors stalking the streets with their cameras. You can't stay in the cottages; all the holiday accommodation is in the adjacent new section of town, which has managed to blend in with the spirit of the old village.

The only regular entertainment here is wandering down to the harbour at high tide to watch the fishing boats being shoved down the slipway by a tractor that ends up half submerged. Otherwise, swimming and beach walks offer a break from the supreme languor. You can swim next to the slipway or at **Roman Beach**, the main swimming beach, just along the coast as you head south from the harbour. In season, you should also keep your eyes open for the **southern right whales** that return here every year to calve.

Heading north through Kassiesbaai, at low tide, you can walk 5km along an unspoilt beach unmarred by buildings until you reach an unassuming fence – resist the temptation to climb over this, as it marks the boundary of the local testing range for military materiel and missiles. Heading south of the harbour for 1.5km along spectacular cliffs and the road, you'll reach the vast **cave**, after which the town is named; this is a walk worth doing simply for the fynbos-covered dunes you'll cross on the way. From the car park right by the cave, it's a short signposted walk down to the dunes and the cave, which can only be reached at low tide. The rocks can be slippery and have sharp sections, so be sure to wear shoes with tough soles and a good grip. **Dune tours** in a 4WD vehicle are operated by John Midgely of *Southwinds B&B* (see opposite) and can be booked through them.

Practicalities

As there's no public transport to Arniston, your only option is to **drive** here. Of the village's **restaurants**, all of which serve fresh fish caught locally, the *Waenhuis* on Du Preez St (a continuation of the national road), is the least expensive, and is decorated to resemble a fishermen's tavern. The other two eating spots are at the hotel, whose one bar does pub lunches and you can get more formal and expensive dinners in the dining room. You can buy fresh fish from the fishermen at the slipway near the hotel.

Accommodation

Accommodation is limited to one hotel, some self-catering cottages and a handful of B&Bs, which get snapped up quickly during school holidays and over weekends.

Arniston Hotel ☎ 028 445 9000, ⓦ www.arnistonhotel.com. A luxurious and well-run hotel in a central position along the seafront. Guests are offered extras, such as massage, and this is the only place to stay in the village with sea views from some rooms. ❺

Arniston Seaside Cottages Well-signposted from the national road, along the street behind the hotel ☎ 028 445 9772, ⓔ cottages@arniston-online.co.za. Limewashed self-catering mock-Arniston cottages that come fully equipped. Out of season they're charged per person; in season (Jan, Easter school holidays & Dec) you pay for the total number of beds in the unit. ❸

Southwinds Huxham Street, just behind the hotel, ☎ 028 445 9303, ⓔ southwinds@kingsley.co.za. Three double B&B suites looking onto a courtyard garden. ❸

Waenhuis Caravan Park Along the main road into Arniston ☎ 028 445 9620. You can either pitch your own tent or stay in small, four-bed en-suite bungalows, which have no sea views, but are only a couple of minutes' walk to the beach. Cooking equipment is available at a small charge, but you'll need to bring your own bedding and towels.

De Hoop Nature Reserve

It's surprising that a reserve with as much going for it as **De Hoop** (daily 7am–6pm; R13) has the humble status of a nature reserve, when it's probably the wilderness highlight of the Western Cape. Although the reserve makes a relatively easy day-trip from Hermanus, you'll find it far more rewarding to come here for a night or more.

The breathtaking coastline is edged by bleached sand dunes standing 90m high in places, and rocky formations that at one point open to the sea in a massive craggy arch. The flora and fauna are impressive too, encompassing 86 species of mammal, 260 different birds, 1500 varieties of plants, and it's reckoned to be the ultimate place in South Africa (surpassing even Hermanus and De Kelders) to see **southern right whales**. If you're here for a couple of days in season, chances are you'll be lucky – occasionally dozens of whales are in evidence at one time. July to September is the best time, but you stand a very good chance of a sighting right through June to November. Inland, rare **Cape mountain zebra**, **bontebok** and other **antelope** congregate on a plain near the reserve accommodation. Apart from swimming and strolling along the length of white sandy beach, there are hiking and mountain-biking trails, but you'll need to bring your own bike as there's nowhere here to rent one. In 2001 a seventy–kilometre trail was opened in the reserve consisting of three days' hiking along the coast and two days along the Potberg Mountains. Overnight huts are provided along the way and numbers are limited to twelve people; book through De Hoop (see p.244).

Practicalities

De Hoop is along a signposted dirt road that spurs off the R319 as it heads out of Bredasdorp, 50km to its west. Accommodation is limited to a **campsite** and two-bedroomed **self-catering cottages** (❷) which come with a cooker, fridge and kitchen utensils but you'll need to bring your own bedding, or rent some from the office. The choicest places to stay are the three luxury thatched cottages (❸) on the lip of the estuary, also with two bedrooms, but with more privacy and a large comfortable living room. Booking should be made through the Manager, De Hoop Nature Reserve, Private Bag X16, 7280 Bredasdorp (☎028 542 1126, ☏028 542 1679). Overnight visitors must report to the reserve office, about 4km into the reserve, by 4pm. Be sure to stock up on supplies before you come – the nearest shop is 15km away, in the hamlet of Ouplaas. De Hoop is very popular and usually booked up at weekends, but there's good **private B&B accommodation** just outside the entrance gate at *Buchu Bushcamp* (☎028 542 1602, ✉bushcamp@sdm.dorea.co.za; ❸) in six open-plan timber and thatch chalets as well as a restaurant where guests can get meals. The owner is an environmental conservationist who is extremely knowledgeable about the local flora and fauna and takes tours.

The Garden Route

The **Garden Route**, a slender stretch of coastal plain between Mossel Bay and Storms River Mouth, bears a legendary status as South Africa's paradise – reflected in local names such as **Garden of Eden** and **Wilderness**. This soft, green, forested swath of nearly 200km is cut by rivers from the mountains to the north, tumbling down to its southern rocky shores and sandy beaches.

The **Khoi** herders who lived off its natural bounty considered the area a paradise, calling it Outeniqua ("the man laden with honey"). This Eden was quickly destroyed in the eighteenth century with the arrival of Dutch **woodcutters**, who had exhausted the forests around Cape Town and set about doing the same in Outeniqua, killing or dispersing the Khoi and San in the process. Birds and animals suffered too from the encroachment of Europeans. In the 1850s, the Swedish naturalist Johan Victorin shot and feasted on the species he had come to study, some of which, including the endangered narina trogon, he noted were both "beautiful and good to eat".

Despite the dense appearance of the area, what you see today are only the remnants of one of Africa's great **forests**; much of the indigenous hardwoods have been replaced by exotic pine plantations, and the only milk and honey you'll find now is in the many shops servicing the Garden Route coastal resorts. **Conservation** may have halted the wholesale destruction of the indigenous woodlands, but a huge growth in tourism and the influx of urbanites seeking a quiet life in the relatively crime-free Garden Route towns threatens to rob the area of its remaining tranquillity.

Most visitors take the Garden Route as a **journey** between Cape Town and Port Elizabeth, dallying for little more than a day or two for shopping or sightseeing. The rapid passage cut by the excellent N2 makes it all too easy to have

Garden Route transport

The **Garden Route**, is probably the best-served stretch of South Africa for **transport**. The excellent N2 makes **driving** along here an absolute breeze, and if you take it straight you'd have to try pretty hard to get lost.

Most user-friendly among the public transport options is the **Baz Bus** (daily Cape Town–Port Elizabeth; ☏021 439 2323, ☏021 439 2343, ⊛www.bazbus.co.za), which picks up passengers daily from accommodation (7.15am–8.30am), recommended if you're exploring the Garden Route and want the freedom to get on and off at will. It provides a door-to-door service within the central districts of all the towns along the way, and has the advantage over the large intercity lines that it will happily carry outdoor gear, such as surfboards or mountain bikes. Although the buses take standby passengers if there's space available, you should book ahead if you want to secure your seat.

Intercape, Greyhound and Translux **intercity buses** from Cape Town and Port Elizabeth are better for more direct journeys, stopping only at Mossel Bay, George, Wilderness, Sedgefield, Knysna and Storms River (the village, but not the Mouth, which is some distance away), but often don't go into town, letting passengers off at filling stations on the highway instead.

More of a day out than serious transport, the Outeniqua Choo-Tjoe is a **goods train** with passenger carriages attached, running the 30km between George and Knysna twice daily (Mon–Sat) in both directions. And finally, if time is tight, you may want to go by **air** to George at the west end of the Garden Route, with scheduled services from Cape Town, Johannesburg, Durban and Port Elizabeth. The only other centre served by regular flights is Plettenberg Bay, which is connected to Cape Town and Johannesburg.

a fast scenic drive – and end up disappointed because you don't see that much from the road. To make the journey worthwhile, you'll need to slow down, take some detours off the highway and explore a little to find secluded coves, walks in the forests or **mountain passes** in the Karoo.

The Garden Route coast is dominated by three inlets – Mossel Bay, the Knysna Lagoon and Plettenberg Bay – each with its own town. Oldest of these and closest to Cape Town is **Mossel Bay**, an industrial centre of some charm, which marks the official start of the Garden Route. **Knysna**, though younger, exudes a well-rooted urban character and is the nicest of the coastal towns, with one major drawback – unlike **Plettenberg Bay**, its eastern neighbour, it has no beach of its own. A major draw, though, is the **Knysna Forest**, the awe-inspiring remnants of the once vast ancient woodlands that still cover some of the hilly country around Knysna.

Between the coastal towns are some ugly modern holiday developments, but also some wonderful empty beaches and tiny coves, such as **Victoria Bay**, **Buffels Bay** and **Nature's Valley**. Best of all is the **Tsitsikamma National Park**, which has it all – indigenous forest, dramatic coastline, the pumping **Storms River Mouth** and South Africa's most popular hike, the **Otter Trail** (see p.279).

Mossel Bay

MOSSEL BAY, 397km east of Cape Town, gets an undeservedly bad press from most South Africans, mainly because of the huge industrial facade it presents to the N2. Don't panic – the historic centre is a thoroughly pleasant con-

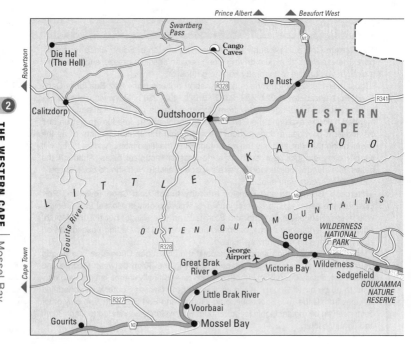

trast, set on a hill overlooking the small working harbour and bay, with one of the best **swimming** beaches along the southern Cape coast and an interesting museum. The town takes on a strong Afrikaans flavour over Christmas, when Karoo farmers and their families descend in droves to occupy its caravan parks and chalets. While Mossel Bay's modest attractions are unlikely to hold you for more than a night, it has some decent accommodation and a first-class restaurant, which make it a good place to pause before launching out along the Garden Route.

Some history

Mossel Bay bears poignant **historical significance** as the place where indigenous Khoi cattle herders encountered the Europeans in a bloody spat that symbolically set the tone for five hundred years of race relations on the subcontinent. A group of Portuguese mariners under captain **Bartholomeu Dias** set sail from Portugal in August 1487 in search of a sea route to the riches of India, and months later rounded the Cape of Good Hope. In February 1488, they became the first Europeans to make landfall along the South African coast, when they pulled in for water to the safety of an inlet they called Aguado de São Bras (Watering Place of St Blaize), now Mossel Bay.

The **Khoikhoi** were organized into distinct groups, each under its own chief and each with territorial rights over pastures and water sources. The Portuguese, who were flouting local customs, saw it as "bad manners" when the Khoikhoi tried to drive them off the spring. In a mutual babble of incomprehension the Khoi began stoning the Portuguese, who retaliated with crossbow fire that left one of the herders dead.

Arrival and information

The N2 bypasses Mossel Bay and, of all the buses, only the **Baz Bus** comes right into town, dropping you off anywhere on request. The large **intercity buses** all stop at Shell Voorbaai Service Station, 7km from the centre, at the junction of the national highway and the road into town. The town itself is small enough to negotiate on foot, but should you need transport, Jordaan runs a **taxi** service (☎044 691 1191).

The busy **tourist information** bureau (Mon–Fri 9am–5pm, Sat 9am–1pm; ☎044 691 2202, ℻044 690 3077, ⓦwww.gardenroute.net/mby), bang in the centre on the corner of Church and Market streets, has shelves of brochures about Mossel Bay and the rest of the Garden Route, and a small but very adequate **map** of the town.

Accommodation

Mossel Bay has a broad range of **accommodation**, including a number of reasonable B&Bs that can be booked through the tourist information bureau should our recommendations be full.

Allemans Dorpshuis 94 Montagu St ☎044 690 3621. A comfortable B&B in a nineteenth-century house with Victorian furnishings, on a hill three blocks south of the tourist bureau. ❹
Barnacles Econo Lodge 112 High St ☎044 690 4584 or 082 670 5259, ⓔbismos@mweb.co.za. A sparkling backpacker hostel that's a cut above the

average with an excellent kitchen, dorms and doubles and a helpful adventure desk that can book activities in the area. ❶
De Bakke George Road ☎044 691 2915. Rock-bottom-priced camping at the municipal site just back from the beach, with sea views. Good self-catering chalets sleeping four are also available. ❶

Edward Charles 1 Sixth Ave ☎044 691 2152 or 082 441 7242, ℱ044 691 1759. A comfortable guesthouse with fifteen rooms, a heated pool, mini gym and Jacuzzi. ❸

Huijs te Marquette 1 Marsh St ☎ & ℱ044 691 3182, ℮marquette@pixie.co.za. A pleasant, if rather fussily furnished B&B close to the Point, with no views but a lovely courtyard ideal for sundowners. ❹

Mossel Bay Backpackers 1 Marsh St ☎044 691 3182, ℮marquette@pixie.co.za. Among the cheapest rooms in town, in a small suburban house attached to *Huijs te Marquette*, conveniently located between the centre and the Point. Dorms, doubles with or without bath ❶

Mossel Bay Guest House 61 Bruns Rd ☎044 691 2000, ℱ044 690 4900. Comfortable rooms in a suburban home. ❸

Old Post Office Tree Manor Bartholomeu Dias Museum Complex, Market Street ☎044 691 3738, ℗www.oldposttree.co.za. Opposite the tourist bureau and close to Santos Beach and the museums, in an old Cape Dutch manor house, this stylish place is by far the best guesthouse in town, with breakfast served at *Café Gannet*, Mossel Bay's nicest restaurant. ❺

Point Caravan Park Bland Street ☎044 690 3501. Along the rocky Point, this is not as nice as the bay's main beach for swimming, but it's close to the start of the St Blaize hiking trail. ❶

Santos Beach Protea Hotel Santos Road ☎044 690 7103, ℗www.proteahotels.com. The priciest option in town, in a great location overlooking the beach, although some rooms don't face the sea. The rate doesn't include breakfast, but weekend specials are available. ❸–❺

Garden Route adventures: the highlights

The Garden Route is fast losing its reputation as the place to go for sun-soaking idleness or to commune with nature. Adrenaline and adventure are elbowing out these passive pursuits and now thrill-junkies go expressly to throw themselves off bridges, to gape into the jaws of great white sharks and to freewheel down scary mountain passes. The choice is broad – and widely spread across the entire length of the Garden Route. To help you plan, here are some highlights:

Bungee jumping Leap into the abyss of the world's highest commercial jump at Bloukrans Bridge near The Crags (see p.274). Try bungee swinging, a jump with a twist at Gouritz River Bridge near Mossel Bay (see p.250).

Cycling Tear down the hair-raising Swartberg Pass, starting out from Oudtshoorn (see p.210), or pedal your way in a slightly calmer fashion round the Homtini Trail in the Knysna Forest (see p.267).

Hiking Set out on South Africa's oldest and most celebrated hiking route along the long-distance Otter Trail, which starts at Storms River Mouth (see p.277). Alternatively, there's a terrific circular one-day hike along the edge of the Robberg Peninsula (see p.271), with a chance of seeing whales, dolphins and seals. Or take it easy and stroll along the waymarked trails in the Goudveld State or Diepwalle forests near Knysna (see p.265 and p.267).

Horse-riding Sit cowboy-style in a deep saddle and camp out in the forest, or try a short excursion, at *Southern Comfort Western Horse Ranch*, between Knysna and Plettenberg Bay (see p.261). Or head out with an English saddle through African countryside near Plettenberg Bay, for fynbos and forest trails.

Scenic excursions Catch the Outeniqua Choo-Tjoe steam train across Knysna Lagoon through beautiful back-country to George (see p.251). If you've got your own transport, try taking the old road just east of The Crags, winding your way down the fantastically scenic route to Nature's Valley (see p.276).

Whale-watching Go on a boat-based whale-watching trip from Plettenberg Bay with one of South Africa's leading marine biologists (see p.271).

Wildlife Take to the water on a well-informed eco-tour that could encounter a variety of whales and dolphins at Plettenberg Bay (see p.271), or enter a shark cage for a first-hand encounter with Jaws at Mossel Bay (see p.250). Back on dry land, there's family fun in the forest, looking for apes from around the world at Monkeyland (see p.274).

Santos Express Santos Beach ℡044 691 1995. A stationary train with a great location – on the beach, just metres from the surf. Accommodation is in four-person train compartments, but you'll have one to yourself if you're a couple or a family. Morning coffee and continental breakfast included. ❶

The Point Point Road ℡044 691 3512, ⊛www.pointhotel.co.za. The best hotel in town, in a superb location on the rocks overlooking the crashing ocean, is graded – and priced – as a three-star establishment but offers four-star luxury, making it excellent value. The fifty spacious rooms in this privately owned establishment all face seawards, with state of the art fixtures including electrical sockets for most foreign plugs as well as modem jacks for internet access. A great deal of thought has been given to making it wheelchair-friendly, with chair lifts and extremely wide corridors. The rate excludes breakfast. ❹

Valhalla Guest House 86 Montague St ℡044 691 1075 or 082 658 2532, ⒺSymbol cranbar@yebo.co.za. An inexpensive B&B with six rooms set back from the shore, but with sea views owing to its elevation on the hillside. ❷

The Town

Mossel Bay's main urban attraction is the **Bartholomeu Dias Museum Complex**, housed in a collection of historic buildings well-integrated into the small town centre, all near the tourist bureau and within a couple of minutes' walk of each other. The highlight is the **Maritime Museum** (Mon–Fri 9am–4.45pm, Sat & Sun 10am–4pm; R3 or R10 including entrance to caravel), a spiral gallery with displays on the history of European, principally Portuguese, seafaring, arranged around a full-size replica of Dias' original caravel. The ship was built in Portugal and sailed from Lisbon to Mossel Bay in 1987 to celebrate the 500th anniversary of Dias' historic journey. You can't fail to be awed by the idea of the original mariners setting out on the high seas into terra incognita on such a small vessel – particularly as the crew were accommodated above deck with only a sailcloth for protection against the elements.

The one Mossel Bay attraction that most South Africans have heard of is the **Post Office Tree**, just outside the Maritime Museum. Sixteenth-century mariners used to leave messages for passing ships in an old boot under a milkwood tree somewhere around here, and the plaque claims that "this may well" be the same tree. You can post mail here in a large, boot-shaped letterbox and have it stamped with a special postmark.

Of the remaining exhibitions, the **Shell Museum and Aquarium** (Mon–Fri 9am–4.45pm, Sat & Sun 10am–4pm; donation) next to the Post Office Tree is the only one worth taking time to visit. This is your chance to see some of the beautiful shells found off the South African coast, as well as specimens from around the world. The fascinating displays of living shellfish include cowries with their inhabitants still at home.

A short walk north down the hill from the Maritime Museum gets you to **Santos Beach**, the main town strand, and purportedly the only north-facing beach in South Africa – which gives it exceptionally long sunny afternoons. Adjacent to the small town harbour, the beach provides some of the finest swimming along the Garden Route, with uncharacteristically gentle surf, small waves and a perfect depth for practising your crawl.

East of the harbour, the coast bulges south towards the **Point**, which has several restaurants and a popular bar/restaurant (see p.251) with a deck at the ocean's edge, from which you may see dolphins cruising past, as well as a surreal five-hundred-metre rocky channel known as the aquarium, which is used as a natural **tidal pool**. Adjacent to this, the Department of Marine and Coastal Management has installed an **Aquarium** (Mon–Fri 9am–1pm & 2–4.30pm, Sat & Sun 9am–1pm; donation) under *Tidals* pub, which showcases local lobsters, crabs and fish found off this coast in a handful of small tanks, as well as a pair of Amazon piranhas.

A couple of hundred metres to the south at the top of some cliffs, the **St Blaize Lighthouse**, built in 1864, is still in use as a beacon to ships. Below it, the **Cape St Blaize Cave**, is both a marvellous lookout point and a significant archeological site. A boardwalk leads through the cave past three information panels describing the history of the interpretation of the cave as well as the modern understanding of it. In 1801 Sir John Barrow insisted that shells found at the site had been brought by seagulls, while others argued that they were relics of human habitation. It turned out that Barrow's opponents were right, but it wasn't till 1888 that excavations uncovered stone tools and showed that people had been using the cave for something close on a 100,000 years. The path leading up to the cave continues onto the Cape St Blaize Trail (see below).

Activities

Given that the seals of **Seal Island**, about 10km northwest of Santos Beach, are a popular delicacy for great white sharks, you'd be forgiven for wondering why scuba diving remains so popular off Mossel Bay. In 1990, the unfortunate Monique Price became the first fully kitted scuba diver to die in a great white attack just off the island, and divers are warned to avoid its immediate environs. There are, however, several rewarding **diving and snorkelling** spots around Mossel Bay, and full facilities, including open water certification courses (Padi R1400; Naui R1100) and one-off dives, are available from Electro Dive (T & F044 698 1976 or T082 561 1259), at the *Santos Protea Hotel*, Santos Rd. Electro Dive rents out gear (R100 per day), and provides shore-based and boat-based dives (R60–130). These aren't tropical seas, so don't expect clear warm waters (although temperatures tend to be warmer than at other Garden Route resorts), but with visibility usually between 4 and 10m you stand a good chance of seeing octopus, squid, sea stars, soft corals, pyjama sharks and butterfly fish.

If you want to see **great white sharks** face to face, there are a couple of outfits offering cage dives. The best months for sightings are March to November, and the worst January and February, but at no time are encounters guaranteed. One of the better operations in the country is Infante Shark Cage Diving, located on the corner of Upper Cross and Kloof streets (T044 691 3796 or 082 455 2438); you can either observe from a boat (R300) or go underwater in a cage for R750, with the assurance that if the sharks don't show you get half your money back. If you're unlucky the first time and choose to try again on another day, you'll only be charged the amount you were refunded.

Cruises around Seal Island to see the African (jackass) penguin and seal colonies can be taken on the *Romonza* (T & F044 690 3101) a medium-sized yacht that launches from the yacht marina in the harbour. On the mainland you can check out the coast on the **St Blaize Hiking Trail**, an easy-going fifteen-kilometre walk (roughly 4hr each way) along the southern shore of Mossel Bay. The route starts from the Cape St Blaize Cave, just below the lighthouse at the Point, and heads west as far as Dana Bay, taking in magnificent coastal views of cliffs, rocks, bays and coves. A **map** is available from the tourist information bureau (see "Arrival and information" on p.247).

If jumping off bridges is your bag, **bungee jumping** at the old Gouritz River Bridge, about 40km west of Mossel Bay along the N2, offers a considerably cheaper alternative to the Bloukrans Bridge (see p.274) near Nature's Valley. The major drawback of Gouritz is the fact that you won't be able to boast that you did the highest commercial bungee jump in the world, hence its bargain-basement price of R150. Gouritz offers the option of a bungee swing (single R100, tandem R120) in which the bungee is attached to the back of the same bridge causing you to swing down and under. For further information contact Gouritz Bungy at the bridge (℡044 697 7161), or their head office in Cape Town, Face Adrenalin, 156 Long St (℡021 424 8114).

Eating and drinking

With the notable exception of the *Gannet*, the **Point** is the nicest place for food and drinks, mainly because of the large stretch of undisturbed sea frontage it offers – one that has seen an upsurge of development over the past few years. The small Point Village shopping development at the north end has a couple of inexpensive to mid-priced family restaurants, opening daily from the morning until 11pm-ish.

Annie's Kitchen 25 Marsh Street. Sandwiches and a cheap hot lunches in the town centre.

Café Baruch Liberty Centre, Bland Street. A good place for toasted sandwiches, salads and decent coffee near the museums.

Café Gannet Market Street ℡044 691 1885. Mossel Bay's top restaurant, close to the Bartholomew Dias Museum Complex, with moderately priced seafood lunches and dinners, served daily with considerable flair in a stylish garden with glimpses across the dusk-washed harbour.

Delfino's Point Village ℡044 690 5247. Italian food with a view.

King Fisher Point Village ℡044 690 6390. A friendly and relaxed joint above *Delfino's*, specializing in seafood and offering good views.

Tidals Waterfront Tavern & Pub The south side of the Point. Mossel Bay's liveliest drinking spot buzzes until the early hours on Fridays and Saturdays, in a stunning seaside location overlooking cliffs and the open sea.

George, Victoria Bay and Wilderness

There's little reason to visit **GEORGE**, 66km northeast of Mossel Bay, unless you're starting or finishing a trip on the Outeniqua Choo-Tjoe. This large inland working town, surrounded by mountains, is a five-kilometre detour northwest off the N2, and 9km from the nearest stretch of ocean at Victoria Bay. Sadly, all that's left of the forests and quaint character that moved Anthony Trollope, during a visit in 1877, to describe it as the "prettiest village on the face of the earth", are some historic buildings, of which the beautiful **Dutch Reformed Church**, in Davidson Street at the top end of Meade Street, is the most notable. Completed in the early 1840s, the church is definitely worth a stop if you happen to be passing through, with its elegantly simple classical façade, Greek-cross plan with an impressive centrally placed pulpit and wonderful domed ceiling, panelled with glowing yellowwood. **St Mark's Cathedral**, in Cathedral Street, consecrated in 1850, is also worth seeing, but unlike the Dutch Reformed Church which is open to the public, it can only be visited by appointment. Other than that, George's claim to recent fame (or notoriety) is the fact that it was the parliamentary seat of former State President **P.W. Botha** (see box on p.253), the last of South Africa's apartheid hardliners and the immediate predecessor of F.W. De Klerk, who negotiated the demise of minority rule. The George Museum once housed the P.W. Botha collection, an exercise in blind adulation for one of the most ruthless proponents of apartheid. The collection was regarded as unsuitable for a museum in the "New South Africa" and was removed in the 1990s, but if you look hard you can still spot the odd fragment lingering here and there that the authorities failed to fully expunge.

Practicalities

Arriving in George by **air**, you'll land at the small George airport, 10km west of town on the N2. There's no public transport from here into town; most tourists flying in rent a car from one of the rental companies here and set off down the Garden Route. By **train**, Outeniqua Choo-Tjoe services arrive at the Outeniqua Railway Museum, 2 Mission Road, just off Knysna Road (☎044 801 8202). Intercape, Translux and Greyhound **intercity buses** pull in at George station, adjacent to the railway museum. The **Baz Bus** drops off at the *George Backpacker Hostel*. George's excellent **tourist information** bureau, 124 York St (Mon–Fri 8am–4.30pm, Sat 9am–noon; ☎044 801 9295, ⓕ044 873 5228, ⓦwww.georgetourism.co.za), can provide town **maps** and help with **accommodation bookings** (ⓔreservations@georgetourism.co.za).

Accommodation

10 Caledon St ☎044 873 4983, ⓕ044 874 6503, ⓦwww.10caledon.co.za. The pick of the mid-priced B&Bs, in a spotless guesthouse in a quiet street around the corner from the museum, featuring balconies with mountain views and a garden. ❸

Arbour Lodge On the corner of Davidson and Arbour roads ☎044 874 7592 or 082 412 4114, ⓦwww.ashmole.com. A modern suburban home with three large en-suite B&B rooms with kitchenettes, close to the centre on the busy road to Oudtshoorn. It's hosted by an extremely friendly and obliging couple, who also welcome children. ❷

George Backpacker Hostel 29 York St, 1km south of the town centre ☎044 874 7807. Dorms and doubles in an annexe in the garden. ❶

George Tourist Resort York St ☎044 874 5205, ⓕ044 874 4255. Camping and en-suite chalets in well-kept pleasant gardens, with a swimming pool, a shop and laundry facilities; its playground makes the resort ideal for families with children. ❶

King George Protea Hotel King George Drive ☎044 874 7659, ⓕ044 874 7664, ⓦwww.protea-hotels.co.za. Slightly out of the centre to the west of town in a quiet setting, offering comfortable rooms, each with its own verandah. ❹

Eating and drinking

Copper Pot 12 Montagu St ☎044 870 7378. One of George's best restaurants, an intimate and formal place on the west side of town that draws its culinary inspiration from all corners of the globe. Daily noon–2.30pm & 6.30pm–late.

Fong Ling Taiwanese On the corner of York and Fichat streets ☎044 884 0088. Quick mid-priced authentic Chinese lunches or evening marathons, using fresh local produce and imported ingredients. Daily.

Herman's Pub and Grill Next to the museum, in two old railway carriages, serving an inexpensive daily special such as a mixed grill or spare ribs

and chips. It's also a good central place for a drink, with some outdoor seating overlooking the busy main drag. Daily for lunch and supper.

King Fisher 1 Courtenay St ☎044 873 3127. A recommended seafood restaurant on the corner of the N12, opposite the Outeniqua High School sports fields.

Red Rock Café Red River Centre, Arbour Road. Excellent value, a few blocks from the centre, at a lively evening venue which is also open for lunch during summer and serves pizzas, seafood, ribs and a number of vegetarian options. Its lawn and small playground makes it great for kids.

Victoria Bay

Some 9km south of George and 3km off the N2 lies **VICTORIA BAY**, one of the gems of the Garden Route. The bay contains a small sandy beach wedged into a cove between cliffs, with a grassy sunbathing area, safe swimming and a tidal pool. During the December holidays it's filled with day-trippers, and also rates as one of the top **surfing** spots in South Africa. Best of all, because of the cliffs there's only a single row of houses along the beachfront, with some of the most dreamily positioned guesthouses along the coast.

There's no public **transport** to Victoria Bay, although many people **hitch** the

President Botha: the King Canute of apartheid

Pieter Willem Botha is credited with setting up an autocratic "Imperial Presidency" in South Africa, but in retrospect he was actually the King Canute of apartheid, closing his eyes to the incoming tide of democracy and believing that by wagging his finger (his favoured gesture of intimidation) he could turn it back.

A National Party hack from the age of 20, Botha worked his way up through the ranks, getting elected an MP in 1948 when the first apartheid government took power. He became leader of the **National Party** in the **Cape Province** and was promoted through various cabinet posts until he became **Minister of Defence**, a position he used to launch a palace coup in 1978 against his colleague, Prime Minister John Vorster. Botha immediately set about modernizing apartheid, modifying his own role from that of a British-style prime minister, answerable to parliament, to one of an executive president taking vital decisions in the secrecy of a President's Council heavily weighted with army top brass.

Informed by the army that the battle to preserve the apartheid status quo was unwinnable purely by force, Botha embarked on his **Total Strategy**, which involved reforms to peripheral aspects of apartheid and the fostering of a black middle class as a buffer against the ANC, while pumping vast sums of money into building an enormous military machine that crossed South Africa's borders to bully or crush neighbouring countries into submission. South African refugees in Botswana and Zimbabwe were bombed, Angola was invaded, and arms were run to anti-government rebels in Mozambique, reducing it to ruins – a policy that has returned to haunt South Africa with those same weapons now returning across the border and finding their way into the hands of criminals. Inside South Africa, security forces enjoyed a free hand to murder, maim and torture **opponents of apartheid** on a scale that only fully emerged between 1996 and 1998, under the investigations of the Truth and Reconciliation Commission.

Botha's intransigence led to his greatest blunder in 1985, when he responded to international calls for change by hinting that he would announce significant reforms at his party congress that would irreversibly jettison apartheid. In the event, the so-called **Rubicon speech** was a disaster, as Botha proved to have insufficient steel to resist pressure from white right-wing extremists. The speech shrank away from meaningful concessions to black South Africans, the immediate result of which was a flight of capital from the country and intensified sanctions. Perhaps worst of all for the apartheid regime, the **Chase Manhattan Bank** refused to roll over its massive loan to South Africa, leaving the country an uncreditworthy pariah.

Botha blustered and wagged his finger at the opposition through the late 1980s, while his bloated military sucked the state coffers dry as it prosecuted its dirty wars. Even National Party stalwarts realized that his policies were leading to ruin, and in 1989, when he suffered a stroke, the party was quick to replace him with **F.W. de Klerk**, who immediately proceeded to announce the reforms the world had expected four years earlier from Botha's Rubicon speech.

Botha lives out his retirement near George where, it is reported, he still harbours deep resentments against his National Party colleagues, whom he believes betrayed him. He has declined to apologize for any of the brutal actions taken under his presidency to bolster apartheid and, despite being subpoenaed, he refused to testify before the **Truth and Reconciliation Commission**, which led in 1998 to him being prosecuted and fined for contempt. In 1999, his appeal against this judgement was successful.

few kilometres from the N2. Arriving by **car**, you'll encounter a metal barrier as you drop down the hill to the bay, and you'll have to try and park in a car park that's frequently full (especially in summer). If you're staying at one of the B&Bs, leave your car at the barrier and collect the key from your lodgings to gain access to the private beach road. The only place to buy **food** is a small beachside kiosk selling light refreshments and unexciting snacks. However, the resort's B&Bs are served by Mr Delivery, a service that will collect from about ten fast-food joints in George and will also fetch your groceries and even a video.

Accommodation

Land's End Guest House Beach Road ⓣ 044 889 0123, ⓕ 044 889 0141, ⓦ www.vicbay.com. Two wonderful self-catering studio apartments at the end of the road, sleeping two with views out to sea from the bed, and also two B&B flats. ❹
Sea Breeze Holiday Resort Along the main road into the settlement ⓣ 044 889 0098, ⓕ 044 889 0104. A variety of budget self-catering units, including modern two-storey holiday cabanas and wooden chalets, sleeping from two to six people. The cabanas have no sea views, but it's an easy stroll to the beach. ❶
Sea Shells Beach Road ⓣ 044 889 0051. Upstairs and downstairs en-suite flats overlooking the sea, just 6m from the high-water mark. ❸–❹
Victoria Bay Caravan Park On the left as you approach the beach ⓣ 044 889 0081. Magnificently located camping on the clifftop overlooking the beach.
The Waves Beach Road ⓣ & ⓕ 044 889 0166. Two front suites, just metres from the sea, in a high-ceilinged Victorian house in an unbeatable location overlooking the water. In addition, there's also a suite in the adjacent *Tidals B&B*, and also the neighbouring self-catering *Palm Cottage*, both of which are similarly priced to *The Waves*. Dec–Easter ❺, rest of year ❸

Wilderness

East of Victoria Bay, across the Kaaimans River, the beach at **WILDERNESS** is so close to the N2 that you can pull over for a quick dip and barely interrupt your journey. Unfortunately, the position of the national road leaves the village and lakes stranded inland. Tradition has it that Wilderness village earned its name after a young man called Van den Berg bought the property in 1830 for £183 as a blind lot at a Cape Town auction. When he got engaged, his fiancée insisted that their first year of marriage should be spent out of town in the wilderness, so he romantically (or perhaps opportunistically) named his property Wilderness and built a hut on it.

If the hut still exists, you'll struggle to find it among the sprawl of retirement homes, holiday houses and thousands of beds for rent in the vicinity. Take your life in your hands and cross the N2 to get to the beach, which is renowned for its long stretch of sand, backed by tall dunes, rudely blighted by holiday houses competing to outdo each other. Once in the water, stay close to the shoreline: this part of the coast is notorious for its unpredictable currents.

Practicalities

The tiny **village centre**, on the north side of the N2, has a filling station, a few shops, restaurants and a **tourist information** bureau in Leila's Lane (Oct–April Mon–Fri 8am–6pm, Sat 8am–1pm, Sun 3–5pm; May–Sept Mon–Fri 8am–5pm, Sat 9am–1pm; ⓣ 044 877 0045, ⓦ www.wildernessinfo.co.za).

Accommodation

Fairy Knowe Backpackers ⓣ & ⓕ 044 877 1285, ⓔ fairybp@mweb.co.za. A hostel with dorms and doubles, set in woodlands near the Touws River, but nowhere near the sea. The Baz bus will drop off here. ❶
Fairy Knowe Hotel On Dumbleton Road, follow the signposts from the N2 ⓣ 044 877 1100, ⓦ www.fairyknowe.co.za. An old-fashioned and reasonably priced establishment away from the beach; the best B&B rooms face onto the Touws River, while cheaper ones face the garden. ❹
Island Lake Holiday Resort Lakes Road, 2km from the Hoekwil/Island Lake turn-off on the N2 ⓣ & ⓕ 044 877 1194. Camping and self-catering

bungalows that sleep four, on one of the quietest and prettiest spots on the lakes. ❶

Mes-Amis Homestead Buxton Close, signposted off the N2 on the coastal side of the road, directly opposite the national park turn-off ☎044 877 1928, ⒻⒻ044 877 1830, ⒺEmesamis@mweb.co.za. Nine double rooms, each of which has its own terrace and sliding doors, offering some of the best views in Wilderness. ❸

The Tops Hunts Lane, about 500m from the tourist information bureau, set on top of a hill ☎ & ⒻⒻ044 877 0187 or ☎083 631 2339. Four airy en-suite bedrooms three of which have elevated sea views and have French doors open onto a deck. ❸

Trails End Holiday Resort On Swartvlei Lake ☎044 343 1914, ⒻⒻ044 343 2006. Pricey camping and budget, fully equipped, timber chalets with good swimming. ❶

Eating

King Fisher George Road ☎044 877 0288. For seafood, this mid-price restaurant in the village centre is the place to go; they also serve spare ribs and ostrich dinners and lunches daily.

Palms At the *Palms Wilderness Guest House*, Owen Grant Road ☎044 877 1420. The resort's best and most expensive restaurant, Swiss-owned *Palms* combines middle-European and local

flavours. Opens daily for dinner (closed June & July); booking is essential.

Reel 'n Rustic Wilderness Grille George Road ☎044 877 0808. An informal restaurant open daily for breakfasts, lunches and dinners that include smoked salmon omelette, pizzas and steaks, served outside under umbrellas or indoors by the fire.

Wilderness National Park

Stretching east from Wilderness village is the **Wilderness National Park** (reception daily Feb–Nov 8am–1pm & 2–5pm; Dec & Jan 7am–8pm; ☎044 877 1197, ⒻⒻ044 877 0366; accommodation booking through South African National Parks Pretoria ☎012 343 1991, ⒻⒻ012 343 0905, ⓌⓌwww.parks-sa.co.za; day entry R12), the least aptly named national park in South Africa, as it never feels very far from the rumbling N2. Although the park takes in beach frontage, it's the **forests** you should come for, as well as the 16km of inland waterways; the variety of habitats here include coastal and montane fynbos and wetlands, attracting 250 species of **birds** – as well as many holidaymakers.

There are two **restcamps**, both on the west side of the park and clearly signposted off the N2. *Ebb and Flow North* (❶), right on the river, is cheap, old-fashioned and away from the hustle. It offers camping, fully equipped two-person bungalows with their own showers, and slightly cheaper huts with communal washing and toilet facilities. *Ebb and Flow South* (❶–❷), signposted close by, offers camping and modern accommodation in spacious log cabins on stilts and brick bungalows which, although dearer than *North* camp, represent good value if there are more than two of you (you pay for a minimum of four people). The fully equipped, self-contained family brick bungalows go for R400 and the log cabins on stilts R420. There are also cheaper en-suite forest huts with communal kitchens for two people and cheaper still, huts with shared ablution facilities. Apart from the forest huts and camping, **seasonal discounts** of twenty percent are offered on accommodation from mid-January to mid-March and from May to November. There is a **shop** selling milk, bread and basic groceries at reception, a coin-operated **laundry**, and a small **children's playground**.

Activities

To take advantage of all the water, you can rent **canoes** and **pedaloes** from reception. There are also several waymarked **walking trails** lasting from one to four hours, all well worth doing to get a feeling of the indigenous vegetation and escape the N2 and holiday homes – the reception issues trail **maps**. The **Giant Kingfisher Trail** is an easy seven–kilometre walk that starts at *Ebb and Flow North* camp and passes through the forest along the eastern bank of the Touw River to some rock pools with their minature seaworld teeming with little sea creatures, returning along the same route, taking three hours for the round trip. Another hike of about three hours is the six kilometre **Cape Dune Molerat Trail**, a circuit along the dunes separating Rondevlei and Swartvlei lakes, with good views onto both. It offers excellent birding opportunities and you'll see wildflowers during winter and spring. To get there, take the N2 east towards Sedgefield for 16km, taking the Swartvlei turn-off and continuing down a dirt road; after 2.8km turn right and continue for just over a kilometre to the conservation station and trail starting point.

Sedgefield and the Goukamma Reserve

The drive between Wilderness and Sedgefield gives glimpses on your left of dark-coloured lakes which eventually surge out to sea, 21km later, through a wide lagoon at **SEDGEFIELD**, a lacklustre holiday village a few kilometres off the road, with a safe swimming **beach** that makes a refreshing pit stop. Sedgefield's unpromising appearance of shops, restaurants and B&Bs lining the highway until recently hid a gloriously undeveloped beachfront. But with the dawn of the new millennium, the resort's authorities have woken up to the economic potential of development, and turned parts of the beachfront into a building site.

Sedgefield could be used as a base from which to explore **Goukamma Nature and Marine Reserve** and the western extent of **Groenvlei**, a freshwater lake that falls within the reserve's boundaries. An unassuming sanctuary of around 220 square kilometres, Goukamma ranges west as far as the small seaside resort of Buffels Bay to absorb 14km of beach frontage, some of the highest vegetated dunes in the country, and walking country covered with coastal fynbos and dense thickets of milkwood, yellowwood and candlewood trees.

The area has long been popular with anglers for Groenvlei's six **fish** species. Away from the water, you stand a small chance of spotting one of the area's **mammals**, including bushbuck, grysbok, mongoose, vervet monkeys, caracals and otters. Because of the diversity of coastal and wetland habitats, this is also good avifauna territory, with over 220 different kinds of **birds** recorded, including fish eagles, Knysna louries, kingfishers, and very rare African black oystercatchers. Off the shore, southern right **whales** often make an appearance during their August to December breeding season, and bottlenose and common **dolphins** can show up at any time of year.

Apart from angling and bird-watching, the Goukamma offers a number of self-guided activities, including safe **swimming** in Groenvlei. There are several day-long hiking **trails** that enable you to explore different habitats – if you plan on hiking you should pick up the Cape Nature Conservation **map** from the *Lake Pleasant Hotel*. A beach walk, which takes around four hours one way, traverses the full 14km of crumbling cliffs and sands between the Platbank car park on the western side and the Rowwehoek one at the other. A slightly longer trek across the dunes also takes you from one end of the reserve to the other, but via an inland route. A shorter circular walk starts at the reserve office and goes through a milkwood forest.

Two roads off the N2 provide **access** to the reserve. At the westernmost side, a dirt road that runs down to Platbank Beach takes you past the tiny settlement of Lake Pleasant on the south bank of Groenvlei, which consists of little more than a hotel and holiday resort. On the eastern side, access is via the Buffels Bay road, along which the Goukamma office is reached about halfway. There are no public roads within the reserve.

Practicalities

Among the forest of holiday homes in **Sedgefield**, you'll find some decent **accommodation** away from the N2 for visitors. Among the least expensive is *Landfall Resort* (T & F044 343 1804; ❶), a low-key and old-fashioned place which allows **camping** and rents out on-site **caravans** with attached kitchens, toilets and showers. The resort also rents out more spacious two-bedroom fully equipped **cottages** that sleep six.

Accommodation in **Goukamma Nature Reserve** should be booked well in advance through the Manager, Goukamma Nature and Marine Reserve, PO Box 331, Knysna 6570 (T044 383 0042, Wwww.capenature.co.za). The choice is a basic **bushcamp** (Mon–Fri R240; Sat & Sun R440) that sleeps eight on the southern shore of the lake, reached by a road past the hotel turn-off; and on the Buffels Bay side; or three thatched **rondavels** and a **river lodge** (Mon–Fri R200; Sat & Sun R300) overlooking the Goukamma River. All have fully equipped kitchens, but you must bring your own bedding. At **Lake Pleasant**, on the western edge of the reserve, you have the choice of the *Lake Pleasant Hotel* (T044 343 1313, F044 343 2040, Wwww.lakepleasanthotel.com; ❼), which has country-style public spaces, a lovely garden and simple **rooms** overlooking thick reed-beds around the lake, disturbed by the constant rumble of the N2; the hotel's *Swan Pub* does reasonably priced pub lunches. Within walking distance from here, and good for budget anglers and families, there's the *Lake Pleasant Chalets & Lodges* (T & F044 343 1985, Wwww.lake-pleasant.co.za), which has shady **campsites**, three-person self-catering **chalets** (❷) and slightly smaller (and cheaper) **lodges**. There's an a la carte **restaurant**, a pub, a store selling basics, and an exceptionally well-stocked anglers' shop. The resort also rents out **mountain bikes**, rowing **boats** and **canoes**.

Another possibility is to stay at **Buffels Bay**, 10km down a turn-off 13km east of Sedgefield along the N2, a haphazard little development at the east of the reserve. Cheapest is the *Buffels Bay Caravan Park* at the Point (T044 383 0045; ❶), while *Wild Side Backpackers*, Buffels Bay, 15km west of Knysna (T & F044 383 0609 or T082 871 9458; ❶) is a popular hostel with dorms and doubles set on the dunes, with free use of body and surf boards, that offers whale-and dolphin-watching and can arrange other adventure activities. A couple of notches up, the spacious, fully equipped *Buffalo Bay Apartments*, 160 Walker Drive (T044 383 0218, Ebuffalobay@xsinet.co.za, ❶-❷) overlooking the bay offers some of the best accommodation in the resort.

Knysna

South Africa's 1990s tourist boom rudely shook **KNYSNA** (pronounced "Nize-na") from its gentle backwoods drowse, which for decades made this the hippy and craftwork capital and quiet retirement village of the country. The town, 102km east of Mossel Bay, now stands at the hub of the Garden Route; its lack of ocean beaches is compensated by its hilly setting around the lagoon, and some hot marketing. The lagoon's narrow mouth is guarded by a pair of steep rocky promontories called **The Heads**, the western side being a private nature reserve and the eastern one an exclusive residential area along dramatic cliffs above the Indian Ocean.

Knysna's distinctive atmosphere derives from its small historic core of Georgian and Victorian buildings, which gives it a character absent from most of the Garden Route holiday towns. Coffee shops, craft galleries, street traders and a

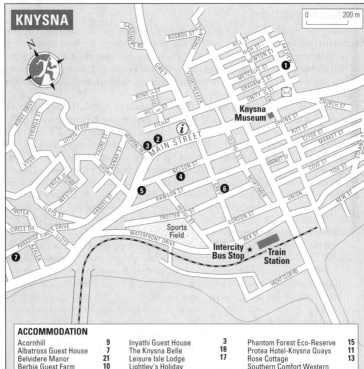

ACCOMMODATION

Acornhill	9	Inyathi Guest House	3	Phantom Forest Eco-Reserve	15
Albatross Guest House	7	The Knysna Belle	18	Protea Hotel-Knysna Quays	11
Belvidere Manor	21	Leisure Isle Lodge	17	Rose Cottage	13
Berbia Guest Farm	10	Lightley's Holiday		Southern Comfort Western	
Brenton-on-Sea Hotel	22	Houseboats	16	Horse Ranch	14
Caboose	6	Mike's Guest House	5	The Tree House	19
Forest Edge Cottages	8	Narnia Farm Guest House	12	Under Milk Wood	20
Highfields Backpackers'		Overlander's Lodge	4	Wayside Inn	2
Guest House	1				

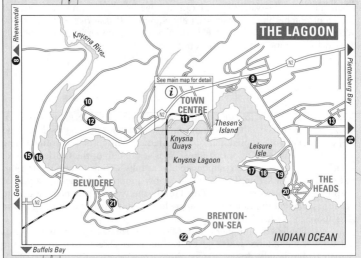

modest nightlife add to the attractions, and you may find yourself tempted to stay longer than just one night. That the town has outgrown itself is evident from the cars and tour buses which, especially in December and January, clog Main Street, the constricted artery that merges with the N2 as it enters the town.

Some history

At the beginning of the nineteenth century, the only white settlements outside Cape Town were a handful of villages that would have considered themselves lucky to have even one horse. Knysna, an undeveloped backwater hidden in the forest, was no exception. The name comes from a Khoi word meaning "hard to reach", and this remained its defining character well into the twentieth century. One important figure was not deterred by the distance – **George Rex**, a colourful colonial administrator, who had placed himself beyond the pale of decent colonial society by taking on a coloured mistress. Shunned by his peers in Britain, he headed for Knysna at the turn of the nineteenth century in the hope of making a killing shipping out hardwood from the Knysna Lagoon.

By the time of Rex's death in 1839, Knysna had become a major **timber centre**, attracting white labourers who felled trees with primitive tools for miserly payments, and looked set eventually to destroy the forest. In 1872, **Prince Alfred**, on his visit to the Cape, made his small royal contribution to this wanton destruction when he made a special detour here to come elephant hunting. The forest only narrowly escaped devastation by far-sighted and effective conservation policies introduced in the 1880s.

By the turn of the twentieth century, Knysna was still remote; and its forests were inhabited by isolated and inbred communities made up of the impoverished descendants of the woodcutters. As late as 1914, if you travelled from Knysna to George you would have to open and close 58 gates along the 75-kilometre track. Fifteen years on, the passes in the region proved too much for **George Bernard Shaw**, who did some impromptu off-road driving and crashed into a bush, forcing Mrs Shaw to spend a couple of weeks in bed at Knysna's *Royal Hotel* with a broken leg.

Arrival and information

Greyhound and Intercape **intercity buses** drop passengers off at Bern's Service Station in Main Street, right in the centre of town, while Translux pulls into the train station in Remembrance Avenue opposite Knysna Quays; the **Baz Bus** will drop passengers off at any of the town's accommodation. The **Outeniqua Choo-Tjoe**, South Africa's last scheduled mixed goods and passenger steam train, which is more of a jaunt than a means of transport, runs between George and Knysna train station (via Goukamma, Sedgefield and Wilderness) twice daily in summer from Monday to Saturday; less frequently during winter; the journey which takes about 2hr 45min costs R50 single, R60 return; ☎044 382 1361. For local transport, there are a couple of **taxi** services (see p.264).

Knysna Tourism, the **tourist information** bureau, at 40 Main St (Mon–Fri 8am–5pm, Sat 9am–1pm; slightly longer hours during the season; ☎044 382 5510, ⓕ044 382 1646, ⓦwww.knysna-info.co.za), Gray St, can provide maps and information about the town and area. From the same office, they also run a free **accommodation** booking desk (☎044 382 6960, ⓕ044 382 1609, ⓔbooking@mweb.co.za) and one for booking **adventure activities** around Knysna, from abseiling down The Heads to bungee jumping from the Gouritz River Bridge.

Accommodation

Knysna caters well for backpackers, but is short on budget B&Bs. The best places to stay are away from the main road, with views of The Heads or the lagoon; out of town there are some excellent and very reasonably priced self-catering cottages right in the forest, where you can get well away from the town buzz. For something different, you can rent a houseboat and meander around the lagoon. Knysna Toursim (see p.259) runs a busy accommodation office, whose knowledgable staff can arrange **bookings**.

Town centre and Knysna Quays

Albatross Guest House On the corner of Albatross Road and Paradise Circle (☎ & ⓕ044 382 4498, ⓦwww.123.co.za/knysna/albatross). The reasonably priced en-suite cottage-style rooms lead onto a garden with a swimming pool, one block up from the lagoon and main road in a quiet wooded area. For scuba divers, an added plus is the clued-up owner who can advise on diving and help organize dives in the vicinity. ②

Caboose On the corner of Gray and Trotter streets ☎044 382 5850, ⓕ044 382 5224, caboose.kny@pixie.co.za. Dead-cheap sleepers in spotless but cramped train-style compartments – part of a huge modern timber complex with pleasant open spaces, including a shared lounge, indoor dining areas, a swimming pool and sun deck. Have no illusions, though – even though you have your own shower, you'll be using it directly over the toilet. ①

Highfields Backpacker Guest House 2 Graham St ☎044 382 6266, ⓕ044 382 5799. The best of the backpacker lodges, with stylish decor, friendly atmosphere, swimming pool and sun deck. Dorms and double rooms are available, and reasonably priced excursions can be arranged to The Heads, Mitchell's Brewery and Brenton.

Inyathi Guest Lodges 52 Main Rd ☎ & ⓕ044 382 7768, ⓦwww.inyathi-sa.com. The most imaginative accommodation in the town centre has ten self-contained en-suite timber lodges arranged around a beautiful indigenous courtyard garden, creating a magically quiet realm in the middle of the main drag. Each of the quirky lodges is individually designed and has its own entrance and a deck overlooking the garden; one lodge has a view of the lagoon from the bathroom. The feel is J.R.R. Tolkien meets safari lodge and, despite being compact, the interiors have luxurious touches such as large Victorian-style bathtubs and pure cotton sheets. Highly recommended. ③

Mike's Guest House 67 Main Rd ☎ & ⓕ044 382 1728 or ☎082 784 4599, ⓔdolphins @mweb.co.za. One of the least expensive stays in Knysna – apart from the backpacker hostels – is an unpretentious converted suburban bungalow

with four en-suite bedrooms facing a small garden, and two garden cottages. A friendly and popular place. ②

Overlander's Lodge 11 Nelson St ☎ & ⓕ044 382 5920, ⓔinfo@gardenroute.co.za. This popular backpacker lodge achieves a delicate balance between being organized and relaxed. Camping is available, and there are clean eighteen-bed dorms and double rooms inside the house, while outside there's a bar and a fire pit. The lodge can arrange a whole array of outings, from hikes to mountain biking and adventure activities. ①

Protea Hotel – Knysna Quays Waterfront Drive ☎044 382 5005, ⓕ 044 382 5006, ⓔknysnaq@mweb.co.za. A luxury hotel on the waterfront, where most rooms have views of the lagoon and the yacht basin. ⑤

Wayside Inn Pledge Square ☎ & ⓕ044 382 6011. A clean and smart place done out with white linen on black wrought-iron bedsteads and sisal matting. Right in the centre, it makes a pleasing enough night stop, but with no communal areas it's not somewhere to spend your holiday. A continental breakfast is served in your room on a wicker tray. ④

Eastern suburbs, Leisure Isle and The Heads

Acornhill 26 Heron Way ☎ & ⓕ044 382 6054 or ☎082 770 1729, ⓦwww.knysna.co.za/acornhill. A row of four inexpensive, pleasant and well-maintained self-catering units of different sizes, in a garden not far from the main road into town. ①

The Knysna Belle 75 Bayswater Drive, Leisure Isle ☎044 384 0511, ⓕ044 384 0881, ⓦwww.knysnabelle.co.za. A well-positioned luxury guesthouse with four double bedrooms and a family unit on the edge of the lagoon with excellent views of The Heads and the Outeniqua Mountains. ④

Leisure Isle Lodge 87 Bayswater Drive, Leisure Isle ☎044 384 0462, ⓕ044 384 1027, ⓦwww.leisureislelodge.co.za. One of Knysna's top guesthouses, right on the edge of the lagoon at a good swimming spot, with a quiet and restful atmosphere. The lodge offers a heated outdoor pool, nine spacious rooms and under-carpet heating, with a choice of back rooms or more expensive lagoon-facing units. ❺

Rose Cottage 34 Wilson St ☎ 044 384 0255, Ⓕ 044 382 7075, rosecottage@mtco.co.za. A small but immaculate en-suite room; and a large, pleasant and good-value self-catering cottage suitable for two adults and a child, with a patio, use of swimming pool, and a garden. ❶

The Tree House 37 Cearn Drive, Leisure Isle ☎ & Ⓕ 044 384 0777 or ☎ 082 432 5180, Ⓔ saltdog@mweb.co.za). A lovely self-catering cottage on the lagoon near an excellent swimming spot, with two bedrooms, two bathrooms, TV, video and a large sun deck screened by a huge tree. ❷

Under Milk Wood George Rex Drive, The Heads ☎ 044 384 0745, Ⓕ 044 384 0156, Ⓦ www.milkwood.co.za). Luxury self-catering accommodation on the lagoon at the foot of The Heads with its own private beach – safe for swimming – and terrific views of the mountains and water. Sixteen two-bedroom self-catering units with their own sun decks are surrounded by milkwood trees; rates vary depending on whether the unit is on the lagoon, the hillside or between. There are also three B&B rooms. ❸–❺

West of town

Berbia Guest Farm Welbedacht Lane, 6km from Knysna off the N2 towards George ☎ & Ⓕ 044 382 5429. Four en-suite rooms, attractively furnished in warm colours, leading onto a swimming pool, from which you can see the lagoon and The Heads. Braai stands provide the only catering facilities. ❸

Lightleys Holiday Houseboats Moored at the Belvidere turn-off from the N2 ☎ 044 386 0007, Ⓕ 044 386 0018, Ⓦ www.knysna.co.za/lightleys. Four-berth fully equipped houseboats; the interiors resemble those of caravans, giving you the freedom to explore the lagoon's 20km of navigable water. R695 per day.

Narnia Farm Guest House off Welbedacht Lane, 3km from Knysna ☎ 044 382 1334, Ⓕ 044 382 2881, Ⓦ www.narnia.co.za. An imaginative, beautiful and immensely fun stone and rough-hewn timber farmhouse in a glorious garden set among 100 acres of protea plantations on a hillside with views of the lagoon. Two en-suite B&B rooms upstairs have their own balconies and swinging chairs and are decorated with enormous flair in a rustic-chic style, as is a comfortable semi-detached two bedroom cottage downstairs which has a lounge, fireplace and kitchenette for self-catering. Walks on the property include one down to a small lake; mountain bikes are available and there's a delight-

ful treehouse and children's play area next to a hen run. Self-catering ❸, B&B ❹

Phantom Forest Eco-Reserve Phantom Pass Road, off the N2 ☎ 044 386 0046, Ⓦ www.phantomforest.com. Expensive but breathtaking forest lodge set on a hill in indigenous forest with fabulous lagoon views. The extensive use of timber and glass gives the feeling you're in the trees, maintaining a supreme sense of privacy, while timber boardwalks wind through the forest to connect the suites to the main buildings, which include a safari-style dining room, an open-air hot tub, a massage suite and a Jacuzzi. The decor and soft furnishings convey a sense of unbridled luxury with African fabrics and pure cotton linen, helping to create a pervasive atmosphere of tranquillity. A swimming pool teeters on the edge of the hill, cocooned by vegetation as vervet monkeys frolic in the forest canopy. Half-board ❽

The forest

Forest Edge Cottages Rheenendal ☎ 044 388 4704 or 082 965 5765, Ⓕ 044 388 4778, Ⓔ forest.edge@knysna.co.za. Ideal if you want to be close to the forest itself, these traditional tin-roofed two-bedroomed cottages have verandahs built in the local vernacular style; self-contained, fully equipped and serviced, they sleep four. Forest walks and cycling trails start from the cottage, and you can also rent mountain bikes. ❷

Southern Comfort Western Horse Ranch 3km along the Fisanthoek road, 17km east of Knysna en route to Plettenberg Bay ☎ 044 532 7885. Budget accommodation is offered in double rooms with bunk beds, on a farm adjacent to the eastern section of the Knysna Forest. Meals are provided or you can self-cater. The ranch can pick up from the N2. Western-style riding is also available, from one-hour outings (R60) to overnight trails in the forest, sleeping in tepees (full-board R350). Doubles ❶

Belvidere and Brenton-on-Sea

Belvidere Manor Duthie Drive, Belvidere Estate ☎ 044 387 1055, Ⓕ 044 387 1059, Ⓦ www.belvidere.co.za. Thirty-four tin-roofed repro Victorian cottages set in extensive grounds with lawns sloping down to the lagoon, where you can go boating. Although spacious and smart, the furnishings are repro rather than genuine antiques, and the feel is of Laura Ashley let loose in a Holiday Inn. However, the grounds are exceptional, as are the cottages' position on the water's edge. ❺

Brenton-on-Sea Hotel C.R. Swart Drive, Brenton beachfront ☎ 044 381 0081, Ⓕ 044 381 0026,

@ www.brentononsea.co.za. The only seaside hotel in the area, overlooking the long curve of Brenton Beach, which swings round to Buffels Bay. All cabins have sea views; the cheaper ones are in the old section of the hotel, while the newer ones are larger and come with their own spa baths and balconies. There are also self-catering chalets sleeping six (R800). **❹–❺**

The Town and around

Knysna wraps around the lagoon, with its oldest part – the town centre – on the northern side. Along the eastern shore the exclusive suburbs include **Leisure Isle**, connected to the shore by a narrow causeway, and **The Heads**, a network of roads winding up to the heights overlooking the craggy coast and a wild Indian Ocean.

Main Street is the hub of the city centre, and its principal attraction is the collection of craft and woodwork shops lining the road. The **Knysna Museum** (Mon–Fri 9.30am–4.30pm, Sat 9.30am–noon; entry by donation, includes Angling Museum) on the corner of Queen and Main streets contains a complex of minor exhibits that can comfortably occupy an undemanding half-hour. Attractions here include South Africa's first **Angling Museum**, an extensive collection of antique nets and rods, tracing the changing technology of the activity. Look out for the preserved coelacanth, one of several specimens in the country of a fish long thought to have been extinct, until one turned up in a fishing net in 1939 (see p.378).

About 500m south of Knysna Tourism, at the end of Grey Street lies the **Knysna Quays**, the town's waterfront complex and yacht basin. Built at the end of the 1990s, this elegant two-storey steel structure with timber board-walks resembles a tiny version of Cape Town's V&A Waterfront – but probably owes its inspiration as much to New England or Seattle, and blows away Knysna's hippy cobwebs with a breath of upmarket supercool. Here you'll find the luxury *Protea Hotel*, some clothes and knickknack shops and a couple of good eating places, including a stunning deli-style bistro with outdoor decks, from which you can watch yachts drift past.

A short way from the centre in the industrial area, **Mitchell's Brewery**, Arend Rd, off George Rex Drive via Vigilance and Sandpiper roads, offers thirty-minute tours (Mon–Fri 10.30am), where for next to nothing you get to sample their beers, including Foresters Draught, a Pilsner-type lager, and Bosun's Bitter, an ale modelled on Yorkshire bitter. The brewery is too far to reach on foot, so take a taxi if you don't have your own transport, or stay in town and sample the beers at one of the pubs.

The main reasons to head for **Leisure Isle** are the excellent swimming in the lagoon and the views out to sea through the gap between The Heads. The best bathing spots are along the southern shore of the island, particularly the western section along Bayswater Drive; but check a tide table, as the swimming is only good around high tide (and then only in summer).

Continuing south along George Rex Drive brings you to the web of roads winding through the small suburban areas of The Heads and Coney Glen to the top of the **eastern Head**. Around *Paquitas* restaurant (see opposite) are fantastic views out to sea; for an even better viewpoint, head along the short walk-way starting outside the restaurant, taking you along the cliff edge.

The beaches

Don't come to Knysna for a beach holiday: apart from the lagoon's edge, the closest sands are 20km away, around the western edge of the lagoon at **Brenton-on-Sea**. On the shores of the beautifully sandy Buffels Bay, this is a

Cruises

One of the obligatory excursions around Knysna is a **cruise** across the lagoon to
The Heads. Knysna Waterfront Ferries (☏044 382 5520 or 082 555 7902) runs several 75-minute trips a day from Knysna Quays to The Heads (R50) and up the river
(R30) through bird-rich forests. They also run a ninety-minute catamaran trip through
The Heads into the sea (R50) as well as a 2hr 30min sunset cruise (R150) through
The Heads that includes champagne, oysters and other snacks. Another option is
the double-decker MV *John Benn*, which has a bar on board and is the only way to
reach the private Featherbed Nature Reserve on the western side of the Heads. The
entire MV *John Benn* trip costs R60, takes four hours and includes a 4WD shuttle to
the top of the western Head; there's also the option of walking the 2km back downhill to enjoy spectacular views and see the local flora and fauna, including Knysna
louries. **Bookings** are essential (☏044 382 1693 or 382 1697), and can be made at
the kiosk on the north side of Knysna Quays; **departures** are from the John Benn
Jetty, Remembrance Avenue (400m west of the Quays and station).

tiny settlement with an unexceptional hotel situated on a quite exceptional
beach. A few kilometres inland is the quaint and very upmarket settlement of
Belvidere, through which visitors are prohibited from driving (but you can
walk around). Although **Buffels Bay** (see p.257 for accommodation), the next
beach to the west, is along the same continuous stretch of sand as Brenton-on-
Sea, there's no direct route there; you have to return to the N2 and proceed
from there. In the opposite direction from Knysna things are little better, with
the closest patch of sand lying to the east at **Noetzie**, a town known more for
its eccentric holiday homes built to look like castles than for its seaside.

Eating, drinking and nightlife

Knysna has a livelier atmosphere than you might expect from a Garden Route
town, buzzing at night to the strains of decent **music** at *Tin Roof Blues*. As far
as food goes, oysters are an obvious choice, with the Knysna Oyster Company
here being one of the world's largest oyster farms, but you'll also find a lot of
good **restaurants** catering to other palates and one or two excellent **coffee
shops**. With so many forests, waterways and beaches, you may be tempted to
have a **picnic**, and there's no shortage of tempting deli food in town.
Farmhouse Picnics (see below) provides ready-prepared gourmet picnic baskets delivered to your door.

34° South Knysna Quays ☏044 382 7331. An
outstanding fine food deli and eating place, with
imported groceries, homemade food and fresh
seafood; from here you can watch the drawbridge
open to let yachts sail through. Daily 9am–6pm.
The Anchorage Garden Route Shopping Centre,
Main Street ☏044 382 2230. A city-centre seafood
and steak restaurant, where you are guaranteed
fresh fish every day. Lunch Mon–Fri & dinner daily.
Changes Pledge Square, 48 Main St ☏044 382
0456. A reasonably priced gay-run restaurant that
plugs itself as "your pink triangle on the square,"
with an imaginatively eclectic menu including
seafood and vegetable tempura, duck and cherry
pie as well as seafood, steak and vegetarian main
courses. Tues–Sat from 7pm.

Coffee Connection Main Road. Offers great coffee, with a wide choice of blends – including
flavoured beans – as well as snacks.
The Drydock Food Co Knysna Quays ☏044 382
7310. A good mid-priced seafood place where
starters include coastal oysters and local salmon
trout and main courses prawns and East Coast
sole. Daily lunch and dinner.
Farmhouse Picnics ☏044 356 2707 or 083 448
1616, ☏044 356 2710, ✉farmhouse@dodeca.co.za.
Offers picnic baskets for two delivered anywhere
in Wilderness, Sedgefield or Knysna for R100. A
choice of menus include oysters, smoked chicken
and vegetable kebabs, basil and lime couscous
with grilled vegetables, pecan pie and comes with
local beer or wine. The baskets contain crockery,

cutlery and table linen and you're even given suggestions for picnic sites. Twelve hours' notice is
required.
La Loerie 57 Main St ☎044 382 1616. Knysna's
top restaurant, a consistently excellent and intimate place where you can eat fresh lagoon oysters and some of the best fish along the Garden
Route. Mon–Sat eves.
Ocean Basket Memorial Square. A successful
family seafood restaurant chain with everything
from freshly caught fish to hake and chips.
The Oyster Tavern Thesen's Jetty, Thesen's
Island ☎044 382 6941. A tasting tavern at the
Knysna Oyster Company, where you can feast on
mussels or cultivated oysters served with bread
and a choice of sauces. Pickled hake, snoek and
angel pate are on offer, as well as take-away oysters by the dozen. Mon–Thurs 8am–5pm, Fri
8am–4pm, Sat & Sun 9am–3pm.
Paquitas Knysna Heads ☎044 384 0408. A

restaurant situated in a fabulous location right on
the rocks beneath The Heads where kids can run
onto the beach. The standard mid-priced family
fare such as burgers, ribs, pizzas is like a honey-
pot to local teenagers. Daily lunch and dinner.
Persello Pizzeria Main Road ☎044 382 2665. An
Italian family-run restaurant, offering excellent pizzas to eat in or take away.
Phantom Forest Eco-Reserve Phantom Pass
Road ☎044 386 0046. Eating is secondary to
being in one of the most beautiful places in South
Africa, in a forest with views of the whole estuary.
The expensive Pan-African set menu offers multiple choices such as ostrich medallions marinated
in orange and ginger, forest mushrooms with garlic
rocket and Knysna cheese, and tempting desserts
such as brandy snap baskets. Dinner daily.
Tin Roof Blues On the corner of St George's and
Main roads. Good live music performed by local
and visiting bands from across the country.

Listings

Car rental Avis 68 Main Rd ☎044 382 2222,
℗044 382 0222.
Emergencies Ambulance ☎10177; Fire ☎82
5066; Police ☎10111.
Hospitals and doctors Knysna Private Hospital,
Hunters Drive ☎044 382 7165, ℗044 382 7280
is well-run with a casualty department open to visitors. For malaria prophylaxis and vaccinations, go
to the SAA Netcare Travel Clinic, Unit 5 Quayside
Office Park, corner Gordon and Hedge streets
(Mon–Thurs 8am–4.30pm & Fri 8am–4pm; ☎044
382 6366 or 083 416 3048), which is geared to
travellers, and operates an affordable drop-in service and up-to-date information service.

Laundry The Knysna Wash Tub, 20 Gray St
(Mon–Fri 7.30am–5.30pm, Sat 7.30am–1pm); and
The Laundry Bin, 12 Main St (Mon–Fri
7.30am–5.30pm, Sat 8am–1pm).
Pharmacy Marine Pharmacy, on the corner of
Main and Grey streets ☎044 382 5614 (Mon–Fri
8am–9pm, Sat 8am–1pm & 5–9pm, Sun
9.30am–1pm & 5–9pm); and Village Pharmacy,
Spar Centre, 41 Main St (Mon–Fri 8am–6pm, Sat &
Sun 8am–2pm).
Taxis Glory's Cab ☎044 382 4223 or 083 226
4720 and Benwill Shuttle ☎083 728 5181 (after
hours ☎044 384 0103) are handy for transport
around town, but take care to agree your fare
before getting inside.

Knysna Forest

The best reason to come to Knysna is for its **forests**, although these are only the
shreds of a once magnificent woodland that was home to **Khoi** clans and harboured a thrilling variety of wildlife, including elephant herds. The forests attracted European explorers and naturalists, and in their wake woodcutters, businessmen like George Rex and gold-diggers, all bent on making their fortunes here.

The French explorer Francois Le Vaillant was one of the first **Europeans** to
sample the delights of these forests. He travelled through in the eighteenth century with Khoi trackers, who shot and cooked an elephant; the explorer found
the animal's feet so "delicious" that he wagered that "never can our modern
epicures have such a dainty at their tables". Two hundred years later, all that's
left of the Khoi people are some names of local places. The legendary Knysna
elephants have hardly fared better and are teetering on certain extinction.

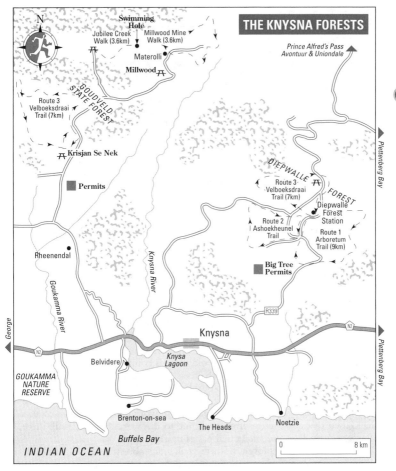

THE KNYSNA FORESTS

N

Swimming
Hole
Jubilee Creek   Millwood Mine
Walk (3.6km)   Walk (3.6km)

Materolli

Millwood

*Prince Alfred's Pass
Avontuur & Uniondale*

GOUDVELD STATE FOREST

Route 3
Velboeksdraai
Trail (7km)

Krisjan Se Nek

Permits

DIEPWALLE FOREST

Route 3
Velboeksdraai
Trail (7km)

Diepwalle
Forest
Station

Route 2
Ashoekheunel
Trail

Route 1
Arboretum
Trail (9km)

Big Tree
Permits

Rheenendal

Plettenberg Bay

Knysna River

R339

N2

Knysna

Goukamma River

George

*Knysa
Lagoon*

N2

Belvidere

GOUKAMMA
NATURE
RESERVE

Plettenberg Bay

Brenton-on-sea

The Heads

Noetzie

Buffels Bay

INDIAN OCEAN

0   8 km

Eleventh-hour **conservation** has ensured that some of the handsome hard-woods have survived to maturity in reserves of woodland that can still take your breath away. A number of walks have been laid out in several of the forests – yet the effects of the nineteenth-century timber industry means that all these reserves are some distance from Knysna itself and require transport to get to.

Goudveld State Forest

The beautiful **Goudveld State Forest** (daily sunrise to sunset; R4 if attendant is present, otherwise by self-issued free permit), just over 30km northwest of Knysna, is a mixture of plantation and indigenous woodland. It takes its name from the gold boom (*goudveld* is Afrikaans for goldfields) that brought hundreds of prospectors to the mining town of **Millwood** in the 1880s. The six hundred small-time diggers who were here by 1886, scouring out the hillsides and panning Jubilee Creek for alluvial gold, were rapidly followed by larger syndicates,

The Knysna elephants

Traffic signs warning motorists about elephants along the N2 between Knysna and Plettenberg Bay are rather optimistic: it seems that by 1995, there were only two indigenous pachyderms left, a number that may well still hold true. But such is the mystique attached to the **Knysna elephants** that locals tend to be a little cagey about just how few they number. By 1860, the thousands that had formerly wandered the once vast forests were down to five hundred, and by 1920 (twelve years after they were protected by law), there were only twenty animals left. Loss of habitat and consequent malnutrition seem to have been the principal cause rather than full-scale hunting.

An attempt was made in 1995 to create a breeding herd by introducing three young cows from the Kruger National Park, who it was hoped would breed with the forest's lone bull. The "bull" turned out to also be a cow and fled in terror when confronted with the three teenagers. In the chase that followed, one young elephant died from pneumonia, brought on by stress. By 1997, the two surviving aliens had moved east and were causing destruction to farmland near Plettenberg Bay. South African National Parks, working with local wildlife organizations, decided to relocate them to Shamwari Game Reserve (see p.362), some 300km to the east near Port Elizabeth, where they are doing well.

and a flourishing little town quickly sprang up, with six hotels, three newspapers and a music hall.

However, the singing and dancing was shortlived and bust followed boom in 1890 after most of the mining companies went to the wall. The ever-hopeful diggers took off for the newly discovered Johannesburg goldfields, and Millwood was left a deserted **ghost town**. Over the years, its buildings were demolished or relocated, leaving an old store known as Materolli as the only original building standing. Today, the old town is completely overgrown, apart from signs indicating where the old streets stood. In **Jubilee Creek**, which provides a lovely shady walk along a burbling stream, the holes scraped or blasted out of the hillside are still clearly visible. Some of the old mine works have been restored, as have the original **reduction works** around the co-co pan track, used to carry the ore from the mine to the works, which is still there after a century. The Outeniqua trail passes nearby.

The forest itself is still lovely, featuring tall, indigenous trees, a delightful valley with a stream, and plenty of swimming holes and picnic sites. To **get there** from Knysna, follow the N2 west toward George, turning right onto the Rheenendal road just after the Knysna River, and continue for about 25km, following the Goudveld signposts.

Hiking in the Goudveld

A number of clearly **waymarked hikes** traverse the Goudveld. The most rewarding (and easy going) is along **Jubilee Creek**, which traces the progress of a burbling brook for 3.5km through giant woodland to a gorgeous, deep rock-pool – ideal for cooling off after your effort. It's also an excellent place to encounter **Knysna louries**; keep an eye focused on the branches above for the crimson flash of their flight feathers as they forage for berries, and listen out for their harsh call above the gentler chorus provided by the wide variety of other birdlife here. You can pick up a **map** directing you to the creek from the entrance gate to the reserve (even if there's no one in attendance); note that the waymarked trail is linear, so you have to return via the same route. There's a pleasant **picnic site** along the banks of the stream at the start of the walk.

A more strenuous option is the circular **Woodcutter Walk**, though you can choose either the three- or the nine-kilometre version. Starting at **Krisjan se Nek**, another picnic site not far past the Goudveld entrance gate, it meanders downhill through dense forest, passing through stands of tree ferns and returns uphill to the starting point. The picnic site is also where the nineteen-kilometre **Homtini Cycle Route** starts, taking you through forest and fynbos and offering wonderful mountain views. Be warned though; you really have to work hard at this, with one particular section climbing over 300m in just 3km.

One of the nicest ways to explore are the excellent **guided walk**s led by Judith Hopley (☎044 389 0102; 7–9am & 6–9pm; R35). Balancing information with anecdote, Hopley uncovers the forest by identifying the trees and understanding the ecology of the whole system, and passes on Goudveld lore learned from foresters and forest guards. She also does a tour of a furniture factory that works with Knysna hardwoods. To join one of these two-hour walks, turn up at the Rheenendal Post Office on Wednesdays or Thursdays at 10am. To get to the meeting point from Knysna, take the N2 west toward George and turn right onto the Rheenendal road just after the Knysna River. If you want to strike out by yourself, Hopley's *On Foot in the Garden Route*, available from Kynsna's tourist information bureau (see p.259) and various Garden Route outlets, is a useful guide to fifty relatively easy hikes in the area.

Diepwalle Forest

The only elephants you can expect to see in the **Diepwalle Forest** (daily 6am–6pm; small entry fee), just over 20km northeast of Knysna, are on the painted markers indicating the three main hikes through these woodlands, which are the last haunt of Knysna's almost extinct elephant population. However, if you're quiet and alert, you do stand a chance of seeing vervet monkeys, bushbuck and blue duiker.

Diepwalle (deep walls) is one of the highlights of the Knysna area and is renowned for its impressive density of huge trees, especially yellowwoods. Once the budget timber of South Africa, **yellowwood** was considered an inferior local substitute in place of imported pine, and found its way into the structure, floorboards, window frames and doors of thousands of often quite modest nineteenth-century houses in the Western and Eastern Cape. Today, its deep golden grain is so sought-after that it commands premium prices at the annual auctions.

The **three main hiking routes** cover between 7km and 9km of terrain, and pass through flat to gently undulating country covered by indigenous forest and montane fynbos. If you're moderately fit, the hikes should take two to two-and-a-half hours. All trails begin at the Forest Station, which also provides a map of them. **To get there** from Knysna, follow the N2 east towards Plettenberg Bay, after 7km turning left onto the R339, which you should take for about 16km in the direction of Avontuur and Uniondale. The Forest Station is 10.5km after the tar gives way to gravel.

The nine-kilometre **Arboretum Trail**, marked by black elephants, starts a short way back along the road you drove in on, and descends to a stream edged with tree ferns. Across the stream you'll come to the much-photographed **Big Tree**, a 600-year-old Goliath. The easy-going nine-kilometre **Ashoekheuwel Trail**, marked by white elephants, crosses the Gouna River, where there's a large pool allegedly used by real pachyderms. Most difficult of the three hikes is the rewarding seven-kilometre **Velboeksdraai Trail**, marked by red elephants, which passes along the foothills of the Outeniquas. Take care here to stick to the elephant markers, as they overlap with a series of painted footprints marking the Outeniqua Trail. Just before the Veldboeksdraai picnic site stands another mighty yellowwood regarded by some as the most beautiful in the forest.

Plettenberg Bay

Over the Christmas holidays, 40,000 residents from Johannesburg's wealthy northern suburbs decamp to **PLETTENBERG BAY** (usually called Plett), 33km east of Knysna, and the flashiest of the Garden Route's seaside towns. It's wise to give it a miss at Christmas, when prices double, accommodation becomes impossible to find and everything gets very crowded. Yet, during low season, sipping champagne and sucking oysters while watching the sunset from a bar can be wonderful – the banal urban development on the surrounding hills somehow doesn't seem so bad because the bay views really are stupendous. The deep-blue **Tsitsikamma Mountains** drop sharply to the inlet and its large estuary, providing the constant vista to the town and its suburbs. The bay generously curves over several kilometres of white sands, separated from the mountains by forest, which makes this a green and temperate location receiving rainfall throughout the year.

   Southern right whales appear every winter, and are a seriously underrated attraction, while **dolphins** can be seen throughout the year, hunting or riding the surf, often in substantial numbers. **Swimming** is safe, and though the waters are never tropically warm they reach a comfortable temperature between November and April. River and rock **fishing** are rewarding all year long, and one of the Garden Route's best short **hikes** covers a circuit round the Robberg Peninsula – a great tongue of headland that contains the western edge of the bay.

Arrival, information and accommodation

SA Airlink (☎044 533 9041) **flights** from Johannesburg, George and Cape Town arrive daily at Plettenberg Bay airport. There's no transport from the airport into town, so make arrangements to be picked up by your accommodation. Intercape and Greyhound **intercity buses** stop at the Shell Ultra City service station, just off the N2 in Marine Way, 2km from the town centre; again, prearrange transport. The **Baz Bus** drops passengers off at accommodation in town. Plett's **tourist information** bureau, Victoria Cottage, Kloof St (Mon–Fri 8.30am–5pm, Sat 9am–1pm; ☎044 533 4065, ℱ044 533 4066, ⓦwww.plettenbergbay.co.za), has maps of the town and can help with finding accommodation.

Accommodation

Because of the hilly terrain, much of the **accommodation** in Plettenberg Bay has views of the sea and mountains, though you're likely to have to put up with views of holiday developments as well. Surprisingly for such an unapologetically upmarket resort, Plett has a number of backpacker lodges, camping and some cheaper accommodation, with additional self-catering available at **Keurbooms**, just across the river. Rates are sky-high at Christmas and Easter, and several places have two rates throughout the year, depending on the quality of the room. July and August are the cheapest months.

Guesthouses, B&Bs and hotels

Hunter's Country House Off the N2, 10km west of Plett on the way to Knysna ☎044 532 7818, ℱ044 532 7878, ⓦwww.hunterhotels.co.za. Set in a woodland area, this is the best upmarket place to stay on the Garden Route, with an emphasis on country comfort rather than seaside glitz, at half the price of the much-vaunted *Plettenberg*. Accommodation is in thatched cottages set in well-established gardens, each with an open fireplace and private patio. ⑧

Little Sanctuary 14 Formosa St ☎044 533 1344 or 083 741 6259, ℮phroan@mweb.co.za. A B&B

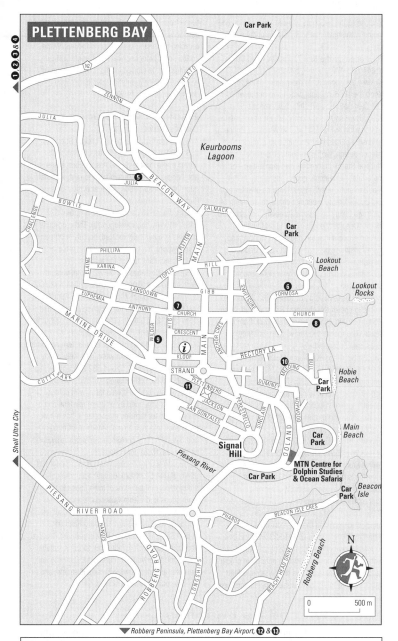

PLETTENBERG BAY

Car Park

Keurbooms
Lagoon

Car Park

Lookout
Beach

Lookout
Rocks

Hobie
Beach

Car
Park

Main
Beach

Car
Park

Beacon
Isle

Signal
Hill

MTN Centre for
Dolphin Studies
& Ocean Safaris

Car Park

Piesang River

Robberg Beach

N

0   500 m

Shell Ultra City

▼ Robberg Peninsula, Plettenberg Bay Airport, ⓬ & ⓭

ACCOMMODATION

Albergo for Backpackers	7	Little Sanctuary	6	Nothando Backpackers	9	Robberg Holiday Resort	12
Bright Water	11	The Lodge on the Bay	13	Pat's Place	10	Room with a View	5
Coral Tree Cottages	1	Masescha Self-Catering		The Plettenberg	8	Weldon's Kaya	4
Hunter's Country House	2	Cottages	3				

as close to the beach as you can get, offering bedrooms with showers and private verandahs overlooking the sea. **❹**

The Lodge on the Bay 77 Beachy Head Drive ☎044 533 4724, ℱ044 533 2681, ⓦwww.thelodge.co.za. The hippest place to stay along the Garden Route, voted one of the world's 101 best hotels by Britain's *Tatler* magazine in 2001. The *Lodge* is the embodiment of cool style and comfort, with wonderful views of the Robberg Peninsula across the sea, meticulous minimalist interior design, highly personlized service. The Philippe Starck bathrooms and inspired use of materials – limestone, quartz and maple in the vast Zen suite, which comes with its own terrace and pool – create a distinct character for each of the three luxury suites and three smaller standard rooms. Despite the initial feeling that you've walked straight into the pages of a design mag, the atmosphere is anything but stuffy and total relaxation is encouraged, with a massage room and sauna. A hot choice for your honeymoon. Standard rooms **❺**, suites **❼**

Pat's Place 4 Meeding St ☎044 533 3180. Two rooms in one of the cheapest B&Bs in Plett, in an old timber and iron house a 3min walk from Hobie Beach. The rooms don't have bath, but they're pleasantly decorated. **❷**

The Plettenberg 40 Church St, Lookout Rocks ☎044 533 2030, ℱ044 533 2074, ⓦwww.plettenberg.com. Plett's prestige establishment is a large luxury hotel offering unbeatable views straight onto the ocean. But be warned – despite the sky-high room rates, you could still end up overlooking the car park. **❼**–**❽**

Room with a View 5 Julia Ave ☎044 533 1836 or 083 261 7587, ℱ044 533 4208 ⓦwww.roomwithaview. A luxury home, set back from the beach, but with good views, offering four upmarket B&B rooms with TV, video and a champagne breakfast served on your own private deck. Standard rooms **❹**, executive suite **❺**

Weldon Kaya Along the N2, 1km west of Shell Ultra City filling station ☎044 533 2437, ℱ044 533 4364, ⓦwww.weldonkaya.co.za. Award-winning traditional accommodation on a huge property, this is the funkiest place to stay around Plett, although with the disadvantage of being some distance from the beach. Rooms are in "African magical" style, constructed using rock, brick, straw and recycled materials, such as car windows. White cotton linen, bleached walls and bright soft furnishings create vibrant interiors. The restaurant has an excellent reputation and there's also a pub and a swimming pool. **❹**

Backpacker lodges and self-catering

Albergo for Backpackers 8 Church St ☎044 533 4434. A lodge in the centre of town, with dorms and a couple of doubles. Canoes, bikes, surf and boogie boards are available to rent, and staff offer lots of information about activities around Plett. **❶**

Bright Water 15 Jackson St ☎ & ℱ044 533 0467, ⓦwww.brightwater.co.za). Three en-suite doubles in a centrally located, homely suburban house where you can rent the whole place or just a room, including use of the kitchen. **❷**

Coral Tree Cottages Off the N2, 11km west of Plettenberg Bay ☎044 532 7822, ℱ044 532 7668, ⓦwww.coraltree.net. High-quality, well-furnished and spacious self-catering thatched cottages that sleep up to four, though unfortunately the roar of the N2 is never absent. R350 per cottage.

Masescha Self-Catering Cottages 1km north off the N2, signposted 12km west from Plettenberg Bay ☎044 532 7647, ℱ044 532 7645. Three reasonably priced, self-catering whitewashed cottages, plainly furnished on a farm, with outdoor sitting areas surrounded by pleasant gardens and a forest. Good for families or couples, it has a swimming pool, and also an indigenous plant nursery and natural history bookshop. Breakfast is available as an extra. R220 per cottage.

Nothando Backpackers 3 Wilder St ☎044 533 0541, ℱ044 533 0220. Budget accommodation in a bungalow in the centre of town, close to the main shops and within walking distance of Lookout and Main beaches. Dorms and doubles **❶**

Robberg Holiday Resort Robberg Road ☎ & ℱ044 533 2571. Close to Robberg Nature Reserve and Robberg Beach, this budget option is suitable only if you have your own transport. Camping and self-catering bungalows without bathrooms, and en-suite bungalows are offered. **❶**

The Town and its beaches

Plett's town **centre**, at the top of the hill, consists of a conglomeration of supermarkets, swimwear shops, estate agents and restaurants aimed largely at the holiday trade. But the town also has the distinction of being home to the **MTN Centre for Dolphin Studies** at 26 Main St. Under the direction of Dr Vic Cockroft, one of the world's leading scientific authorities on marine mammal conservation, it includes a community environmental centre, a whale and dolphin information centre, a reference and video library and a shop. Working in association with Ocean Safaris, the centre is also the most successful operator of boat-based whale-watching excursions in the country (see p.272).

Visitors principally come for Plett's **beaches** – and there's a fair choice. Southeast of the town centre on a rocky promontory is **Beacon Island**, dominated by a 1970s hotel, an eyesore blighting a fabulous location. Beacon Island Beach, or **Main Beach**, right at the central shore of the bay, is where the fishing boats and seacats anchor a little out to sea. The small waves here make for calm swimming, and this is an ideal family spot. To the east is **Lookout Rocks**, attracting surfers to the break off a needle of rocks known as the Point and the predictable surf of **Lookout Beach**, to its east, which is also one of the nicest stretches of sand for bathers, body-surfers or sun lizards. Lookout Beach has the added attraction of a marvellously located restaurant (see p.273), from which you can often catch sight of **dolphins** cruising into the bay. From here you can walk several kilometres down the beach towards Keurbooms and the **Keurbooms Lagoon**.

Robberg Marine and Nature Reserve

One of the Garden Route's nicest walks is the four-hour, nine-kilometre circular route around the spectacular rocky peninsula of **Robberg**, 8km southeast of Plett's town centre. Here you can completely escape Plett's development and experience the coast in its wildest state, with its enormous horizons and lovely vegetation. Much of the walk takes you along high cliffs, from where you can often look down on seals surfacing near the rocks, dolphins arching through the water and, in winter, whales further out in the bay. If you don't have time for the **full circular walk**, there is a **shorter two-hour hike** and a **thirty-minute ramble**. A **map** indicating these is available at the reserve gate when you pay to enter (daily: Feb–Nov 7am–5pm; Dec–Jan 7am–8pm; R14). You'll need sturdy walking shoes, as the terrain is rocky and steep in parts, and the walk involves some serious rock-hopping on the west side. Don't forget to bring a hat and a bottle of water, as there's no drinking water for much of the way and no tea rooms. There's no public transport to the reserve; if you're staying at a backpacker lodge, ask about their **transfers**, which are generally reasonably priced. To get there **by car**, take Strand Street towards Beacon Isle, turn right into Piesangs Valley Road, and 200m further on, turn left into Robberg Road. Follow the airport signs, continuing for 3.5km and then turning left toward *Robberg Holiday Resort*; you'll find the gate to the reserve 500m beyond the resort.

Whale-and dolphin-watching

Elevated ocean panoramas give Plettenberg Bay outstanding vantages for watching **southern right whales** during their breeding season between June and October. Phone the **Whale Hotline** (☎044 533 3743) at the Whale Shop, Boekenhout Centre, Piesangs Valley Road, for information about their current whereabouts. An especially good watching point is the area between the wreck of the *Athene* at the southern end of Lookout Beach and the Keurbooms River. The Robberg Peninsula is also excellent, looming protectively over this whale nursery and giving a grandstand view of the bay. Other good town watching points are from Beachy Head Road at Robberg Beach; Signal Hill in San Gonzales Street past the post office and police station; the *Beacon Isle Hotel*; and the deck of the *Lookout* restaurant on Lookout Beach. Outside Plett, the

Whaling and gnashing of teeth

For conservationists, the monumental 1970s eyesore of the Beacon Island Hotel may not be such a bad thing, especially when you consider that previously the island was the site of a whale-processing factory established in 1806 – one of some half-dozen such plants erected along the Western Cape coast that year. Whaling continued at Plettenberg Bay until 1916. Southern right whales were the favoured species, yielding more oil and whalebone – an essential component of Victorian corsets – than any other. In the nineteenth century, a southern right would net around three times as much as a humpback caught along the Western Cape coast, leading to a rapid decline in the southern right population by the middle of the nineteenth century.

The years between the establishment and the closing of the Plettenberg Bay factory saw worldwide whaling transformed by the inventions of the industrial revolution. In 1852, the explosive harpoon was introduced, followed by the use of steam-powered ships five years later, making them swifter and safer for the crew. In 1863, Norwegian captain Sven Foyn built the first modern whale-catching vessel, which the inventive Foyn followed up in 1868 with the cannon-mounted harpoon. In 1913 Plettenberg Bay was one of seventeen shore-based and some dozen floating factories, between West Africa and Mozambique on the continent's east coast, which that year between them took about 10,000 whales.

Inevitably, a rapid decline in humpback populations began; by 1918, all but four of the shore-based factories had closed due to lack of prey. The remaining whalers now turned their attention to fin and blue whales. When the South African fin whale population became depleted by the mid-1960s to twenty percent of its former size, they turned to sei and sperm whales. When these populations declined, the frustrated whalers started hunting minke whales, which at 9m in length, are too small to be a viable catch. By the 1970s, the South African whaling industry was in its death throes and was finally put out of its misery in 1979, when the government harpooned it by banning all activity surrounding whaling.

Kranshoek viewpoint and hiking trail offers wonderful whale-watching points along the route. To get there, head for Knysna, taking the Harkerville turn-off, and continue for 7km. It's also possible to view the occasional pair (mother and calf) at Nature's Valley, 20km from Plett on the R102, and from Storms River Mouth. For more information about whales, see Hermanus on p.231.

Boat-based viewing

For **guided whale-watching** the MTN Centre for Dolphin Studies (Mon–Fri 9am–4pm & Sat 9am–1pm; ☎044 533 6185 or 082 784 5729, Ⓦwww.dolphinstudies.co.za), at 26 Main Street, in association with Ocean Safaris, runs boat-based trips to see whales, dolphins and other marine mammals, with a scientifically grounded commentary. You can also arrange tailor-made cruises with marine biologists Dr Vic Cockroft and Dr Debbie Young, who are directors of the centre. Apart from southern rights, trips run into common, bottlenose, Indo-Pacific and humpback **dolphins**, as well as **Bryde's** and **humpback whales** – and the occasional **minke** and **killer whale**. The advantage over shore-based watching is that you stand a chance of encounters throughout the year, including species that you'd be unlikely to spot from land.

Eating, drinking and nightlife

Plett has a respectable supply of good restaurants and some pleasant beachside pubs with terrific views. Locally caught fresh fish is the thing to look out for.

Blue Bay Café Lookout Centre, Main Street
T 044 533 1390. A good place to eat throughout
the day in a courtyard tucked away under trees
but overlooking both the main drag and the sea.
Their mid-priced fare includes a poached egg
breakfast with salmon on croissant, Thai prawn
dishes and ostrich fillet with mango. Breakfast to
dinner daily.

The Blue Chilli On the corner of Marine Way and
High Street T 044 533 5104. A reasonably priced
bistro with a select but superb Mexican menu.
Beware of their "hot" dishes, which positively sizzle;
meals can be washed down with a glass of tequila,
with or without worm. Mon–Sat lunch and dinner.

The Boardwalk Yellowwood Centre, on the corner
of Main and Crescent streets T 044 533 1420. A
cosy, eclectic restaurant serving moderately
priced, tasty seafood, steaks and baked potatoes.
Daily breakfast, lunch and dinner.

Brothers Restaurant and Terrace Melville's
Corner, Main and Marine streets T 044 533 5056.
Medium-priced English cooking with an edge, at a
stunning location with views of the ocean and
passing trade. It's their teas that really sing – try
their cake of the day, espresso with muffins, or
pancake dripping with blueberry sauce. Daily
breakfast and dinner.

The Cave In the *Arches* hotel, Marine Drive, off the
N2 T 044 533 2118. A young crowd lives it up at
this club, especially at weekends and in the
December holidays. Phone to check dates and
opening hours.

Cornuti al Mare Shop 1, Seaview Properties,
Perestrella Street T 044 533 1277. Terrific pizzas
– the best along the Garden Route – and also
great pasta dishes that won't break the bank. Daily
noon–11pm.

Islander Eating Place On the N2 between Plett
and Knysna T 044 532 7776. A popular, high-
quality seafood restaurant with a South Sea
theme. Eat as much as you like for a set price
from a seafood buffet to blow you away. Booking
essential. Daily breakfast, tea and lunch.

Lavender and Limes Coffee Bistro Hutchinson
House, Hill Street T 044 533 2899. A compact
bistro offering a small but select menu including
pasta and quiches. Breakfast, tea and lunch.

The Lookout Lookout Beach T 044 533 1379. A
casual restaurant-cum-pub right on the beach,
with marvellous bay views. Here you can eat reasonably priced fresh fish, or more expensive crayfish and, if you're lucky, watch whales and dolphins rollicking in the surf. Daily 9.30am–late.

Moby Dick's Seafood Bistro Main Beach T 044
533 3682. A pleasant place for a drink or tea, particularly out of season – in summer it draws a lively boogie-board crowd. A wooden deck upstairs
gives great views of Central Beach. Daily
9am–late.

Ralth's on the Bitou On the Bitou River, just off
the N2 between Plettenberg Bay and Keurbooms
T 044 535 9445. Reasonably priced meals are
served at this pleasant pub with outdoor seating
on the edge of the calm lagoon. Their fresh fish
and chips are especially recommended. Daily
11am–10pm.

Redbourne Lodge On the corner of Piesang
Valley and Country roads T 044 533 5037. An
exceptional and stylish family-run restaurant with
an eclectic menu including Mediterranean-style
seafood dishes, oven-charred sole and butternut
risotto cakes served with smoked ostrich. Daily
breakfast, dinner and lunch. Closed June. Booking
essential.

Keurboomstrand and around

Some 14km east of Plettenberg Bay, across the Keurbooms River, is the unclut-
tered resort of **KEURBOOMSTRAND** (Keurbooms for short), which shares
the same bay and has equally wonderful beaches, but is less safe for swimming.
The safest place for swimming is at **Arch Rock**, in front of the caravan park,
though **Picnic Rock Beach** is also pretty good. A calm and attractive place,
Keurbooms has few facilities, and if you're intending to stay here you should
stock up in Plettenberg Bay beforehand.

   If you can tear yourself away from the beach, **canoeing** up the Keurbooms
River gives an alternative perspective on the area. Nature Conservation (T 044
533 2125), on the east side of the Keurbooms River Bridge along the N2, rents
out fairly basic craft for R70 per day for a two-person canoe. The forest comes
right down to the river edge, and as the gorge narrows and you go higher the
journey gets better, because you leave behind the pleasure boats and water-

skiers who are restricted to an area near the caravan park. Don't be put off by the river's Coca-Cola colour (which comes from harmless oxides in the water): it's quite fresh, and wonderful to swim in during the summer. If you're renting a boat, you can stop and **picnic** at any of the little beaches upriver. While you're here, keep an eye out for the pink-flowering Keurboom trees that give their name to the river and resort.

The only place in Keurbooms for **eating and drinking** is the reasonably priced *Rafiki's*, which has an unbeatable location right on the beach and makes a great whale- and dolphin-spotting venue.

Accommodation

Abalone Beach House About a kilometre beyond *Dune Park* – follow the Ifafi/El Remo sign ☎044 535 9602, ✉beachhouse@global.co.za. Set between the forest and the sea, this backpacker hostel has dorms, doubles and triples in a large relaxed house on a hillock run like someone's home. The uncrowded beach is literally at the bottom of the lawn and you can rent boogie boards, paddle skis and fishing rods. ❶

Arch Rock Chalets and Caravan Park, On the beach ☎044 535 9409. A shady campsite with some old "standard" self-catering chalets (for which you must supply your own bedlinen and towels), and recently built fully equipped and serviced "luxury" units (minimum two nights) right on the seashore. It gets packed with families in the summer. ❷–❸

Dune Park Keurbooms Strand Road, the road leading off the N2 and running along the shore to Keurbooms ☎044 535 9606, ⊛www.dunepark.co.za. Four luxury self-catering timber chalets on the beach and ten budget ones without sea views behind the dunes, just a short walk to the sea. ❷–❺

Keurbooms Aventura 6km east of Plett and signposted off the N2 ☎044 535 9309, ⊛www.aventura.co.za. One of the country's best family-oriented resorts where you can choose between campsites on the shady banks of the river (but away from the sea) or self-catering chalets sleeping two adults and two children. Canoes and motorboats are available to rent, and there's a swimming pool. Family chalets R450.

The Crags, Monkeyland and Bloukrans River bungee jumping

Little more than a satellite of Plettenberg Bay, **The Crags**, 16km to its east, comprises a collection of smallholdings along the N2, a bottle store and a few other shops on the forest edge. At The Crags (look out for the BP filling station), take the Kurland Village/Forest Hall turn-off for 2km to reach the signposted **Monkeyland** (daily 8am–6pm; entrance to viewing deck free, safaris into the forest R60; ☎044 534 8906, ℉044 534 8907, ⊛www.monkeyland.co.za), a primate sanctuary with apes and monkeys from several continents. The animals are free to move around the reserve, looking for food and interacting with each other and their environment in as natural a way as is possible. Visitors are taken on guided walking "**safaris**" with well-informed guides in which they come across water holes, experience a living indigenous forest and have chance encounters with different primates, including lemurs from Madagascar and squirrel monkeys from South America. Whilst entertaining, the safaris are accompanied by a scientifically grounded commentary that covers issues such as the differences between monkeys and apes, primate communication and social systems. One of the highlights is crossing the Indiana Jonesesque **118-metre rope bridge** (purportedly the longest such bridge in the southern hemisphere) spanning a canyon to pass through the upper reaches of the forest canopy, where a number of species spend their entire lives. There are now plans to rescue a viable population of gorilla families, which are threatened with extinction in central Africa, and to bring them to the sanctuary where they can reproduce in safety. The day lodge has a restaurant with a forest deck, where you can get refreshments and more substantial meals. It's a child-friendly place with baby-sitting and changing facilities.

If you want to try your hand at swinging through the air, then pull in at the **Tsitsikamma Forest Village**, 20km east of The Crags and the Monkeyland turn-off along the N2, where the registration office for the world's highest commercial **bungee jump** is based. The jump takes place off the 216-metre **Bloukrans River Bridge**, 2km beyond the Village down a signposted road that also brings you to a viewpoint. There's no need to book ahead for the jump, which will cost you R500 (including video) for the seven-second descent. For further information, contact Bloukrans Bungy (a.k.a. Kiwi Extreme) at the bridge (daily 9am–5pm; ☏042 281 1458) or through their head office in Cape Town: Face Adrenalin, 156 Long St (☏021 424 8114). The Forest Village isn't a village at all, but a collection of touristy shops, an uninspiring restaurant and some offices arranged around an enormous traffic circle-cum-car park. The **tourist information** bureau (daily 9am–5pm) provides brochures about the Garden Route.

Accommodation

Should you wish to spend the night near the jump site, you could do a lot worse, as all the accommodation is in the midst of verdant indigenous forest. There's a well-maintained **caravan park** halfway down the road to the bridge with camping and, at the end of the road, a new, well-equipped log-cabin **backpacker lodge**, with two eight-bed dorms and four doubles (❶), a couple of hundred metres from the jump site. There are also some **self-catering chalets** sleeping four (R360). All the accommodation can be booked through the Tsitsikamma Forest Village Trust, whose office lies a couple of shops away from the tourist information bureau (daily 8am–4.30pm). The Baz **bus** pulls into the village and will usually take passengers as far as the backpacker lodge and jump site, but if they can't, due to time pressure, the Trust will always be willing to do so.

Rather swisher is *Hog Hollow Country Lodge*, 18km east of Plettenberg Bay in Askop Rd, then east off the N2 for 1.3km (☏044 534 8879, ⓦwww.hog-hollow.com; ❻), set in a private nature reserve and recommended for its superb food. Each of the twelve ethnic-styled chalets, done out in earthy colours and spiced up with African artefacts, has a bath or shower and its own wooden deck with vistas across the forest and Tsitsikamma Mountains. From here you could hike for a couple of hours through forest to Keurbooms Beach, or drive there in fifteen minutes.

Tsitsikamma National Park

The **Tsitsikamma National Park** (daily 7am–9.30pm; R18 per person; ☏042 281 1607), roughly midway between Plettenberg Bay and Port Elizabeth, is the highlight of any Garden Route trip. You'd be crazy to pass up its main attraction, the **Storm's River Mouth**, the most dramatic estuary on this exhilarating stretch of coast, and where South Africa's ultimate hike, the five-day **Otter Trail**, begins.

Starting from just beyond Keurboomstrand in the west, the national park extends for 68km into the Eastern Cape along a narrow belt of coast, with dramatic foamy surges of rocky coast, deep river gorges and ancient hardwood forests clinging to the edge of tangled, green cliffs. Established in 1964, Tsitsikamma was South Africa's first marine reserve, stretching 5.5km out to sea, with an **underwater trail** open to snorkellers and licensed scuba divers.

Tsitsikamma has two sections: **De Vasselot** in the west and **Storms River Mouth** in the east. Both sections can only be reached down a winding tarred road from the N2 (there's no way of getting from one to the other through the park itself). De Vasselot incorporates **Nature's Valley**, the only resort in the park, and the most low-key settlement on the Garden Route, with a fabulous sandy beach stretching for 3km.

De Vasselot and Nature's Valley

The **De Vasselot** section, at the western end of Tsitsikamma, extends inland into a rugged and hilly interior incised with narrow valleys and traversed by a series of footpaths. In fact De Vasselot is not a name that trips readily off South African tongues – most people know the section for **Nature's Valley**, the only village inside the national park. The main activity here is **walking**, and the area is covered with waymarked routes of varying lengths, including the highly popular Otter Trail (see box on p.278). Nature's Valley is a pleasingly old-fashioned settlement on the Groot River Lagoon with 20km of beach. Bypassed by the N2, and by the intercity buses, tour parties and most motorists (who can't be bothered with the slow winding road to get here), Nature's Valley is the place to go if you're after a quiet time along the Garden Route.

There are plenty of good **walks** at Nature's Valley, many starting from the De Vasselot campsite, 1km north of the village, where you can pick up maps and information about birds and trees. One of the loveliest places to head for is **Salt River Mouth**, 3km to the west of Nature's Valley, where you can swim and picnic – though you'll need to ford the tannin-dark river at low tide. This walk starts and ends at the café at Nature's Valley. Also recommended is the circular six-kilometre **Kalanderkloof Trail**, which starts at the De Vasselot campsite, ascends to a lookout point, and descends via a narrow river gorge graced with a profusion of huge Outeniqua yellowwood trees and Cape wild bananas.

Practicalities

Public transport to Nature's Valley is limited to the **Baz Bus**, which deposits passengers at the De Vasselot restcamp or the backpacker lodges. The village centre is little more than an all-in-one restaurant, pub and small trading store that acts as an informal, but excellent, **information bureau** (☎044 531 6835, ⓦwww.cyberperk.co.za/naturesvalley) which can help you find the limited **accommodation** available.

If you're **self-catering**, stock up on supplies before you get to Nature's Valley. The only place to buy a meal is at the **restaurant**, on the corner of Forest and St Michael streets, which serves seafood, steaks, burgers and toasted sandwiches, and provides the only nightlife apart from gazing at the stars.

Accommodation

Apart from the places listed below, self-catering accommodation can be rented through Clare Carr in Plettenberg Bay (☎ & ⓕ044 533 0743) who handles around eight or nine cottages (R300–500 per cottage) in and around Nature's Valley – most of which sleep between six and eight people. Arrangements in Nature's Valley for these cottages are handled by her father, Ken Corbitt (☎044 531 6725).

De Vasselot rest camp 1km to the north of the village. For bookings contact South African National Parks in Pretoria ☏ 012 343 1991, ⓦ www.parks-sa.co.za or, if you're already in Nature's Valley, the camp supervisor ☏ 044 531 6700. There are campsites tucked into indigenous forest, and basic two-person forest huts without kitchens and with communal ablution facilities. ①

Froggy Pond Contact Tish or Beefy ☏ 044 531 6835, ⓦ www.cyberperk.co.za/naturesvalley. Self-catering in a two-storey timber and brick cottage, with a self-contained flatlet downstairs with a double bedroom and living area that can sleep two adults and two children; upstairs there are two private double rooms with en-suite showers. ①

Nature's Valley Guest House & Hikers' Haven ☏ 044 531 6805, ⓔ patbond@mweb.co.za. A well-located hostel just 200m from the sea and the lagoon, offering backpacker and B&B accommodation. Choose between a fourteen-bed backpacker dorm, three doubles sharing a bathroom, two very reasonably priced en-suite rooms – one

of which is a family unit – and probably the least expensive honeymoon suite in the country, under thatch and with its own balcony and a sunken bath surrounded by mirrors. Breakfast is extra, whichever accommodation you choose. The backpacker section has a self-catering kitchen, and there's a snooker table, TV lounge and a payphone. Bikes, a canoe, rowing boat, surfboard and windsurfer are available for guests, and you can set out from the guesthouse on two- to six-hour hikes along the beaches or through the forests. ①–②

Paljas ☏ 044 531 6867, ⓔ paljas@yebo.co.za. A comfortable self-contained two-bedroom family apartment nestling in indigenous woodland that attracts wildlife such as bushpigs. The flat can be taken on a B&B or self-catering basis, and is charged per person rather than for the whole place, as are two other nearby and similarly priced cottages that the owners rent out. ②

Utopia Backpackers Retrea, 280 Forest Drive ☏ & ⓕ 044 531 6683. A well-run hostel catering to a young clientele, with dorms and doubles. ①

Storms River Mouth

In contrast to the languid lagoon and long soft sands of Nature's Valley, **Storms River Mouth**, 55km from Plettenberg Bay, presents the elemental face of the Garden Route, with the dark Storms River surging through a gorge to battle with the surf. **Storms River Mouth Restcamp**, sited on tended lawns, is poised between a craggy shoreline of black rocks pounded by foamy white surf and steeply raking forested cliffs, and is without a doubt the ultimate location along the southern Cape coast. Don't confuse this with **Storms River Village** just off the N2, which is nowhere near the sea.

Walking is the main activity at the Mouth, and at the visitors' office at the restcamp you can get **maps** of short, waymarked coastal trails that leave from here. These include steep walks up the forested cliffs, where you can see 800-year-old yellowwood trees with views onto a wide stretch of ocean. Most rewarding is the **three-kilometre hike** west from the restcamp along the start of the Otter Trail to a fantastic **waterfall** pool at the base of fifty-metre-high falls where you can swim right on the edge of the shore. Less demanding is the kilometre-long **boardwalk stroll** from the restaurant to the suspension bridge to see the river mouth. On your way to the bridge, don't miss the dank *strandloper* (beachcomber) **cave**. Hunter-gatherers frequented this area between 5000 and 2000 years ago, living off seafood in wave-cut caves near the river mouth. A modest display shows an excavated midden, with clear layers of little bones and shells.

If you're desperate to walk the **Otter Trail** (see box on p.278), which begins at Storms River, and have been told that it is full, don't despair. As a single person or a couple, you stand a chance of getting in on the back of a last-minute cancellation, so it may be worth hanging out at the Mouth for a night or two. Since the trail is booked long in advance, there's often a chance that someone won't turn up.

Swimming at the Mouth is restricted to a safe and pristine little sandy bay below the restaurant which can be icy in summer if there are easterly winds and cold upwellings of deep water from the continental shelf, only 25 nautical miles off the coast.

Major Garden Route hikes

If you're keen on walking and the outdoors, and want to schedule in at least one long walk somewhere in the country during your holiday, the Garden Route provides some fine possibilities. Indeed, walking is the only way to really experience the Garden Route's forests and coast and escape the clutter of holiday homes and the noisy N2.

The waymarked **hikes** listed below are two to five days long. You'll need to carry all your food, a sleeping bag for use in the communal hiking huts (mattresses are provided), lightweight cooking utensils and stove, and waterproofs. You should also wear proper worn-in hiking boots. For day-hikes and walks lasting only a couple of hours, consult Judith Hopley's *On Foot in the Garden Route*, available from Knysna's tourist information bureau (see p.259) and several other outlets on the Garden Route.

Harkerville Coast Hiking Trail
Start and end: Harkerville Forestry Station, 12km west of Plettenberg Bay, signposted off the N2
Distance: 26.5km
Duration: two days
Permit: Department of Forestry and Water Affairs, Kynsna (℡382 5466)
Cost: R30 per person
Features: Magnificent rocky coastline, indigenous forest and fynbos. Lots of rock scrambling and some exposed, narrow ledges above the sea. Don't attempt this hike if you're unfit or scared of heights. Monkeys, baboons and fish eagles are common, and you may also spot dolphins or whales. Closer to the roads, this trail doesn't feel as remote as the Otter Trail, but is a good second-best.

Outeniqua Hiking Trail
Wilderness
Start: Beervlei (old Forest Station – eight overnight huts)
End: Harkerville Forestry Station
Distance: 108km
Duration: seven days (shorter versions possible)
Permit: Department of Forestry and Water Affairs, Knysna (℡382 5466)
Cost: R15 per person per day

Practicalities

Storms River Mouth lies 18km south of Storms River Bridge, where most people stop to gaze into the deep river gorge and fill up at the most beautifully located filling and service station in the country. Even if your time is limited and you can't spend the night at Storms River Mouth, it's still worth nipping down for a meal, a restorative walk or a swim in the summer. You'll need your own wheels though, as there's no public transport to the Mouth.

A wide variety of **accommodation** is available at **Storms River Mouth Restcamp** (℡042 281 1607; ❶–❸), all with sea views, including superb campsites just metres from where the surf breaks on the rocks; incredibly good-value two-person cabins, which provide bedding and towels, share ablutions and have no catering facilities; comfortable one-bedroom self-catering log cottages, including breakfast; oceanette mini-apartments close to the sea, also including breakfast; and family oceanettes and cottages for a minimum of four people. All are heavily subscribed in season, but are discounted by ten percent from May to the end of August. For **bookings**, contact South African National Parks (Pretoria ℡012 343 1991, ⓦwww.parks-sa.co.za).

Features: Indigenous forest, including giant yellowwood trees, pine plantations and gold-mining remains at Millwood.

Otter Trail

Tsitsikamma National Park
Start: Storms River Mouth
End: Nature's Valley
Distance: 42km
Duration: five days
Permit: South African National Parks (Pretoria ☎012 343 1991, ℻012 343 0905, 🌐www.parks-sa.co.za). Bookings are taken up to twelve months in advance. The maximum number of people on the trail is twelve.
Cost: R275 per person.
Features: South Africa's first established hiking trail is a coastal walk crossing rivers, tidal pools and indigenous forest. You may see dolphins, whales and seals, and the spoor of the Cape clawless otter – although virtually impossible to spot, they're certainly around. Short daily stretches between log-hut nightstops gives plenty of time to walk slowly, and enjoy the vegetation and birds. Some parts of the hike are steep, so you need to be fit. The Bloukrans River has to be crossed by wading or swimming: go at low tide and waterproof your backpack.

Tsitsikamma Trail

Tsitsikamma
Start: Nature's Valley Caravan Park
End: Storm's River Bridge
Distance: 64km
Duration: five days, shorter versions possible
Permit: Safcol (Pretoria ☎012 481 3615)
Cost: R47 per person per night
Features: Not to be confused with Otter Trail, this is an inland walk through indigenous forest, long stretches of open fynbos and the Tsitsikamma mountain range. Five overnight huts accommodate thirty people. It's not a difficult hike, and you won't cover more than 17km in a day – although after heavy rains the rivers can be hard to cross.

The only **eating** place is the restcamp restaurant, serving breakfasts and a la carte meals which, alas, are less memorable than the startling views. **Activities**, include cruises, blackwater tubing, scuba diving, snorkelling and river gorge cruises in the national park (see p.280).

Storms River Village

STORMS RIVER VILLAGE lies about a kilometre south of the national road. It offers a number of places to stay, a couple of general dealers selling basics, a liquor store, a fish-and-chips shop and an adventure centre offering activities in the area. A tranquil place criss-crossed by a handful of dirt roads and with about forty houses, it enjoys mountain vistas but requires transport to get to Storms River Mouth and the national park.

Accommodation

The Armagh Fynbos Avenue ☎042 281 1512, ℻042 281 1510, 🌐www.thearmagh.com. The top place to stay and eat in the village, the *Armagh* is a thoroughly hospitable and quirky seven-room guesthouse in a beautiful garden that drifts off into the fynbos. The rooms include a luxurious honeymoon suite; four slightly less expensive standard rooms, all of which lead onto the garden; and the comfortable en-suite Africa and small Candlewood lofts, which are cheaper principally because they have no direct garden access. ❶–❹

Ploughman's Rest 31 Formosa St ☎ & ℱ 042 541 1726. A reasonably priced farm-style B&B, with five en-suite rooms with their own garden entrances. ❷

Stormsriver Rainbow Lodge Along the road into the village – turn right at the T-junction ☎ 042 281 1530, ℮ rainbow@lantic.net. A backpacker lodge-cum-B&B, aimed at more mature travellers and families. There are two dorms, three backpacker doubles, two en-suite rondavels, and a timber cottage in the garden; there's also a two-room family suite in the house with its own lounge and bathroom. Breakfast costs an extra R25. ❶

Tsitsikamma Lodge A couple of kilometres east of town along the N2, and 8km east of the Storms River Bridge ☎ 042 280 3802, ⓦ www.tsitsikam-ma.com. Thirty cosy A-frame cabins with their own decks and connected by boardwalks that traverse the beautifully kept gardens. Most cabins have their own Jacuzzi, and there are a number of forest walks including their famous nudist hiking trail along the river. A restaurant serves South African cuisine. ❺

Tube 'n Axe On the corner of Darnell and Saffron streets ☎ 042 281 1757, ℮ angus@thepub.co.za. A wacky place that works hard to compete with the bright lights of Knysna and Plett by offering backpackers a fun time. It offers a paint-ball field and three-day packages for R360 that include day-trips to Storms River Mouth, 4WD excursions into the Tsitsikamma Mountains with a 17km hike tagged on, and a visit to a local fernery and cheese farms. They offer camping, have three four-bed dorms and a twin room, but such is their popularity that they're currently expanding. ❶

Activities

Storms River Adventures (☎ 042 281 1836, ⓦ www.stormsriver.com), which has its main office next to the post office and another next to reception at the Storms River Mouth section of the Tsitsikamma National Park, has helped put the village on the map with its range of activities. The best known of these is **Blackwater Tubing** (R295) down the Storms River Canyon through the Tsitsikamma National Park to the sea, ending at the suspension bridge. Although generally regarded as a "soft adventure," it's not without its dangers – in a horrific but isolated incident in March 2000, several participants died in a freak accident when the river unexpectedly flooded. The price for a half-day-trip includes all your gear, transfers to and from the adventure centre and lunch.

Alternatively, you can experience the otherwise inaccessible gorge on one of the company's half-hour **river cruises** (daily 10am–4pm; every 45min; R35) from the jetty near the suspension bridge at the river mouth. Also recommended is their **Woodcutters Journey** (on request; R105) down the old Storms River Pass through the forest depths in a specially designed trailer drawn by a tractor down to the river where a light lunch is served. Other activities include **abseiling** (R120 for two goes) 35m into the Storms River gorge and two-and-a-half-hour **mountain-bike trails** (unguided R75, guided with lunch R170) in the Tsitsikamma Forest. They also offer **scuba diving** in the national park's marine reserve, where you can see corals and some fifty species of fish; visibility ranges from 5 to 12m, but don't expect the fluorescent colours you get in tropical waters. A four-day PADI open water diving course costs R1250; day rental of full diving kit with a guided dive is R230 with extra dives costing R80 (including your air fill). If you don't want to do the whole Jacques Cousteau thing you could settle for **snorkelling**, which costs R85 for gear and you should add an extra R25 if you want a guide to go with you.

The West Coast and the Cederberg

The **west coast** of South Africa – remote, windswept and bordered by the cold Atlantic ocean demands a special appreciation. For many years the black sheep of Western Cape tourism (a fact borne out by the prominence of industries such as fishing, and the iron-ore terminal at Saldanha Bay), it has been set upon by developers who seem all too ready to spoil the bleached, salty emptiness which many people had just begun to value. This is a region roughly cut by nature, with sandy soil and dunes harbouring a distinctive **coastal fynbos** vegetation, a coastline almost devoid of natural inlets or safe harbours, with fierce southeasterly summer winds, dank winter fogs, and the ever-miraculous **wild flowers** appearing in the *veld* in spring.

The southern West Coast region has many links to Namaqualand to the north – not least in the flowers – although this 200km or so of coastline is by far the most densely populated part of the coast and the **Swartland** region immediately inland is unusually fertile. North of Swartland lies the impressive **Cederberg mountain range**, an area of distinctive beauty, and a striking feature on the N7 highway, the main West Coast artery between Cape Town and Namibia. North from **Clanwilliam**, the attractive town at the northern end of the Cederberg, the N7 connects with Vanrhynsdorp, strictly within the Western Cape but for practical purposes linked to the flower routes of Namaqualand in the Northern Cape (see p.331).

Outside the flower months of August and September, the West Coast has a wide range of attractions, particularly during summer when the lure of the sea and the cooler coast is strong. The area is noted for its **seafood**, which is always fresh, plentiful and much cheaper than in Cape Town. It's also well-known for a wide range of activities, most popularly hiking and horse-riding along the coast or in the mountains, various types of watersports, whale-spotting and some excellent bird-watching.

Swartland

While early morning fogs often smother the coastal plain inland from Melkbosstrand on the northern edge of Table Bay, the N7 highway north from Cape Town leads quickly into the pleasing and fertile **Swartland** landscape. *Swartland* means "black country", but while the rolling countryside takes on some attractive hues at different times of year, it's never really black. The accepted theory is that before the area was cultivated the predominant vegetation was a grey-coloured bush called *renosterbos* (rhinoceros bush) which, seen from the surrounding ranges of hills, gave the area a complexion sufficiently dark to justify the name.

Bordered to the west by the less fertile coastal *strandveld* and to the east by the tall mountain range running from the Boland Mountains by Wellington to the Cederberg, Swartland is known best as a wheat-growing area, although it also

West Coast flowers

During August and September, you'll find displays of **wild flowers** across the West Coast region, with significant displays starting as far south as the inland town of Darling, just 80km north of Cape Town off the main R27 coastal route. Excellent displays are also found in the West Coast National Park and the hazy coastal landscapes around Cape Columbine and Lambert's Bay, while inland Clanwilliam is the centre of some good routes. An incredible 4000 flower species are found in the region, most of them members of the daisy and mesembryanthemum groups. For up-to-date advice and guidance, contact the helpful local information centres in Darling, Saldanha and Clanwilliam (see p.294) For further tips on flower-viewing, see p.332.

supports dairy farms, horse studs, tobacco crops and vineyards famous for earthy red wines.

The N7 skirts a series of towns on its way north, including the largest in the region, **Malmesbury**. If you're travelling south towards Cape Town, look out for some unusual views of Table Mountain, and also for tortoises, which you should take care to avoid as they cross the road.

Darling and around

The small country town of **DARLING** lies caught between Swartland and the West Coast; it's famous both for its rolling countryside and dairy products, and also for its displays of wild flowers in spring. Easily reached from Cape Town by the coastal R27 route, Darling boasts some handsome old buildings and has developed recently as an **artists' colony**. One of South Africa's best-loved comedians, Pieter Dirk-Uys, has established his most famous character, **Evita Bezuidenhout** (South Africa's answer to Dame Edna Everidge), as the hostess of a weekend cabaret show at *Evita se Perron*, the tiny **old railway station** in the centre of town (for details of shows, bookings and dinner reservations, phone ℡022 492 2831, ⓦwww.evita.co.za). Local painters are displayed at the well-cared-for **Darling Museum** (daily 9am–1pm & 2–4pm; small entry fee) on the corner of Pastorie and Hill streets, and an "Art Walk" to the homes and studios of local artists, photographers and jewellers is organized on the first weekend of every month (details from the museum).

Just under 20km to the south of Darling at **Mamre**, near the coloured commuter town of Atlantis, an old Moravian **mission station** stands on the northern edge of town. Still active, it includes a series of old thatched mission cottages, a huge church and a working water mill, and remains one of the finest examples in the Western Cape of these pragmatic but bold early nineteenth-century outposts. If you're interested in specialized **tours** of the Mamre mission, contact them on ℡021 576 1134 or 576 1579.

Practicalities

Darling's **tourist information** bureau is located inside the museum (daily 9am–1pm & 2–4pm; ℡022 492 3361). Although Darling is well within the scope of a day-trip from Cape Town, it's also a good spot for a short **stay**. *Darling Guest House*, 22 Pastorie Street (℡022 492 3062 or 072 195 6912, ⓦwww.bedandbreakfast.co.za/darling), is an old Cape cottage with a lush garden and three en-suite rooms. As well as *Evita se Perron* (see above), good **places to eat** include *Zum Schatzi*, a German restaurant on Long Street (℡022 492 3095; closed Mon) or, for pub lunches, *Bistro 7* on Main Road.

Riebeek West

To the northeast of Malmesbury lies an impressive island of hills, **Kasteelberg** (castle mountain), on the far side of which lie two small settlements, **Riebeek Kasteel** and **RIEBEEK WEST**. Roughly 3km north of Riebeek West on the road towards Moorreesburg lies a turning to a PPC Cement works. Within the site, rather incongruously set among rumbling conveyor belts and grey dirt heaps, is the whitewashed cottage where **Jan Smuts**, the South African statesman and soldier, was born in 1870. There isn't a great deal to see other than a simple old house with wooden floors and some contemporary artefacts inside but, if you can ignore the fact that it has been all but gobbled up by an industrial site, there are some pleasant lawns, flowerbeds and a handful of outbuildings to wander around – one of which displays an interesting series of storyboards about the eventful life and times of the man (see box below).

Accommodation in Riebeek West is available in a Victorian house, *Carollanns* (☏ 022 461 2245; ❷), visible from the main road, while good **meals** and rooms can also be found in the renovated *Royal Hotel*, 33 Main St (☏ 022 448 1378; ❸), in neighbouring Riebeek Kasteel.

Groot Winterhoek

Situated within the often hazy, fortress-like line of mountains on the eastern fringe of Swartland is the three-hundred-square-kilometre **Groot Winterhoek Wilderness Area**, an excellent place for lonely hiking and camping, with sparkling swimming pools, typical Cape mountain fauna such as klipspringer, rhebok and elusive felines, distinctive fynbos vegetation and – as

---

Jan Smuts

The life of **Jan Christiaan Smuts**, one of South Africa's greatest figures, perhaps embodies more than any other this country's strained relationship with itself in the first half of the twentieth century. Born to an Afrikaner farming family, Smuts spoke English with the distinctive linguistic burr of Swartland and excelled as a scholar at Stellenbosch and then Cambridge universities. During the Anglo-Boer War he waged a wide-ranging and ultimately undefeated guerrilla campaign as the leader of a Boer commando. However, he came to believe in a unified South Africa under a British flag, and was appointed commander-in-chief of imperial forces in East Africa during World War I, attending meetings of the British War Cabinet in the final phases of the war.

Smuts served as **prime minister** of South Africa between 1919 and 1924, and again between 1939 and 1948, when he led South Africa into World War II on the British side but, rather like his fellow leader and statesman Winston Churchill, he failed to hold together support at home and lost the postwar general election in 1948 to the hardline Afrikaner D.F. Malan who, coincidentally, grew up on the farm Allesvlooren, a few kilometres from Smuts' birthplace.

Smuts spent much of his career in domestic politics trying to hold together disparate political and social moralities among English and moderate Afrikaans-speaking whites. He is remembered by South Africans as a wily, tainted politician rather than as a great humanitarian. Yet he was, like very few South Africans before or since, a man of global vision and influence who as a 76-year-old played an important role in drafting the United Nations charter in 1946. He also published a philosophical treatise and was known for his love of nature and the outdoors, in particular Table Mountain in Cape Town – one of the popular routes up the mountain carries his name.

the name suggests – rather formidable winter conditions. It is also an area well worth exploring if you're a mountain biker or paraglider.

As this is a wilderness area, you're free to walk and camp where you wish, although there are a number of suggested trails varying in length from a few hours to a few days, and you must carry a **permit** (R14 entrance fee plus R20 per day). For details and **bookings**, contact the Cape Nature Conservation Office in Porterville (Mon–Fri 7.30am–4pm; ☎022 931 2900).

Langebaan Lagoon

To the west of rural Swartland and immediately north of Cape Town's fast-developing northern coastal suburbs of Bloubergstrand and Table View, the west coast of South Africa starts off much as it continues for many hundreds of kilometres north: isolated fishing settlements and windswept dune vegetation of bleak but alluring beauty. Other than river mouths, the only sea inlet and protected deep-water harbour on the entire South African Atlantic seaboard is at **Saldanha Bay**, some 100km north of Cape Town; the bay is connected to Langebaan Lagoon, the attractive centrepiece to the small but precious **West Coast National Park**.

While the holiday town of **Langebaan**, just to the north of the park on the eastern shore of the lagoon, has managed to keep its focus relatively frivolous and beach-oriented, industrial development has muscled into the northern part of the bay. This has brought in its wake a causeway stretching for 1.5km, an iron-ore railway terminal and a fast-rising steel and concrete works, which come as an ugly intrusion after the delicate simplicity of the national park. They also mean that the town of **Saldanha**, once a sturdy fishing port with historic naval and military ties, is now grim, sullied and eminently avoidable.

West Coast National Park

The **West Coast National Park** (Oct–Mar daily 6am–8pm, R16; April–Sept 7am–7pm, R8; ☎022 772 2144) is one of the best places to savour the simple, unspoilt charm of the West Coast. The park protects over 40 percent of South Africa's remaining pristine *strandveld* and 35 percent of the country's salt marshes, and incorporates both the majority of Langebaan Lagoon and a Y-shaped area of land immediately around and below it.

Much of the park's appeal lies in uplifting views over the still lagoon to an olive-coloured, rocky hillside; the sharp, saline air; the calling gulls and Atlantic mists vanishing in the harsh sunlight. This isn't a game park – a few larger antelope are located in the Postberg section of the park, an area open only during the spring flower season – but there are huge numbers of **birds**, including some 70,000 migrating waders. A number of well-organized interpretive walking trails lead through the dunes to the long, smooth, wave-beaten Atlantic coastline, offering plenty of opportunity to learn about the hardy fynbos vegetation which so defines the look and feel of the West Coast region.

On the southern tip of the lagoon is a large old farmhouse and steading called **Geelbeck**, where there's an information centre, tea room and accommodation (see p.285). There are also a number of bird hides nearby, and all the main **trails** (up to a total of 30km) start from here. If you continue from Geelbeck up the peninsula on the western side of the lagoon you'll come to **Churchhaven**, a tiny village where there are some simple private cottages and where you can swim in the still, relatively warm water of the lagoon.

A little further on is the demarcated **Postberg area**, open only during flower season (see box on p.282), but worth visiting at that time to see **zebra**, **gems-**

bok and **wildebeest** wandering through fields of wild flowers. The tip of the peninsula overlooking the mouth of Saldanha Bay is owned by the South African National Defence Force and remains inaccessible. The reserve also includes a number of islands around the mouth of the bay, home to gannets, penguins, seals and, on one, a colony of albino rabbits.

Practicalities

There are two **entrance gates** to the park: one on the R27, roughly 10km north of the turning to Yzerfontein, and the other south of the town of Langebaan. The park isn't huge; if you're driving you'll cover the extent of the roads in a couple of hours. You can see a good chunk if you enter at one gate and come out at the other – but it's worth taking the roads slowly to enjoy the views, and a visit to the **tea room** (Mon & Thurs–Sun 8am–4pm) at Geelbeck will allow you to appreciate a bit more of what you're seeing. There are also some nice **picnic** spots around the park. Overnight **accommodation** is available here in dormitories (book through West Coast National Park ☎022 772 2144; ➊) set attractively near the edge of the lagoon, principally for school groups and those walking the two-day trail, but there's nothing to stop you simply booking in. There's also a houseboat on the lagoon that sleeps four adults and two children (book through South African National Parks in Pretoria (☎012 343 1991, ✉reservations@parks-sa.co.za; R600) and a slightly more expensive guest cottage at Bossieskraal that sleeps up to eight.

The best time to visit the park is in spring, when the sun is shining and the flowers are out, although this is, inevitably, also the busiest period. Like much of the West Coast, the national park is chilly and wet in winter, and hot and wind-blasted in summer.

Langebaan

Once the home to the largest whaling station in the southern hemisphere, and for a while Cape Town's long-haul passenger flight terminus (when seaplanes from Europe touched down on the lagoon during World War II), **LANGEBAAN** is in some respects the gateway to the West Coast National Park. However, the town appears to have given itself almost entirely to sun, fun, watersports and a motley collection of what only real estate agents (of whom there's no shortage) could dare to call desirable seafront holiday homes. In summer and at weekends the holiday crowds are out in force, and neon swimsuits, ice creams and speedboats dominate. If you're into **windsurfing** and have been wondering how to harness the big southeasterly summer winds, Langebaan could be just your thing. Right off the beach the water is flat, the sailing winds – as the ragged flags above the centre testify – anywhere from fresh to fearsome, and unless you catch a fast-running tide out towards the Atlantic, it's all reasonably safe. Outside summer, the town falls deathly quiet.

Practicalities

Tourist information is available in the same building as the South African National Parks Board (Mon–Fri 9am–1pm & 2–5pm, Sat 9am–12.30pm, Sun 9am–noon; ☎022 772 1515) at the far end of Main Street. **Accommodation** is plentiful – it's what the town exists on. The municipal **caravan park** is a couple of blocks from the beach on Suffrens Street, and though it claims not to allow tents without permission, you probably won't need to ask when you arrive. Halfway between Langebaan and Saldanha is *Olifantskop* (☎022 772 2326; ➋), a **guesthouse** that has both rooms and self-contained cottages, with a restaurant, bar, pool and equestrian centre. On the bay beside this is a burgeoning Greek-village-style **holiday development** called *Club Mykonos* (☎0800 22 6770; Mon–Thurs & Sun ❹, Fri & Sat ❺), offering one-, two- and three-bedroom units, the place to go if you feel you're missing a Costa del Cape flavour in your holiday. Langebaan's most upmarket option is *The Farmhouse* (☎022 772 2062; ❹), a luxury **guesthouse** with a good restaurant, set on a hill among some new houses at the southern end of town.

As with accommodation, there's a wide selection of **places to eat** in town. *Die Strandloper* (☎022 772 2490 or 083 227 7195; booking essential), on the beach just beyond the Cape Windsurf Centre on the road to Saldanha, is a good example of the West Coast's famous open-air seafood restaurants (see box on p.291). On the main beach in town, *Pearly's* is a crowded eating, drinking and ogling spot in a prime location, while *La Taverna* (closed Mon), on the corner of Bree and Oostewal streets, serves better food and some mighty, diet-destroying cakes.

If you want to try your hand at any of the watersports on offer here, the Cape Windsurf Centre (daily: summer 9am–7pm; winter 10am–6pm; ☎022 772 1114), on the beach on the northern edge of town, rents out all levels of equipment, including the latest gear. Its main line of business is **windsurfing** and **kite surfing** tuition and equipment rental, but they also rent out **mountain bikes** and paddle skis.

Saldanha

SALDANHA is known chiefly for its links to the military (a military academy is sited here) and for the controversial iron-ore loading terminal built here in the 1970s. The iron ore arrives from Sishen in the Northern Cape, 861km away along a purpose-built railway line. The scheme has never been the success it was hoped for, and the latest attempt to paper over the cracks involved building a steel plant beside the terminal. This comes with the added bonus of a concrete works, being built to utilize the waste material from the steel plant, which will require a ten-kilometre-long conveyor belt to be constructed between it and the coast north of Saldanha. You get the sense that it's in for a penny, in for a pound, leaving the country's environmentalists – the precious ecosystems and bird habitats of the West Coast National Park are only a few kilometres away – with their heads buried in their hands.

The town, situated on the northwestern hook of the bay, regards itself as a holiday place, but visitors may well remain unconvinced – the fact that industrial effluent finds its way into the water doesn't enhance any claims to its being a beach resort. If you do spend time here, though, it's worth taking advantage of the availability of the good **fresh seafood** arriving daily from the fishing fleet. Interspersed with numerous fish-and-chip shops and fast-food chains along the cliff-edge seafront, you'll find some decent places to eat including the *Meresteijn*, Main Street, which is open for lunch and dinner daily and offers seafood, meat and pizzas. For breakfast, lunch and dinner, the *Slipway* on the main harbour is a popular spot for mussels and prawn pate and the *Blue Bay Lodge*, Kamp Street, is known for its French-influenced seafood.

There's a fair amount of **accommodation** in the town, but the two nicest places are along the shore with views of the steelworks, whose lights give a twinkly display at night. The smaller of the pair is the stylishly comfortable *Jane's* 8 Beach Rd, (☎022 714 3605, ℻022 714 1522, ✉janegh@mweb.co.za; ❸–❹), which has airy en-suite sea-facing rooms with cotton sheets and a cheaper non-sea-facing unit. It doubles up as a coffee shop serving breakfasts and light lunches indoors or on the sea-facing terrace during the day. Larger and equally comfortable, *The Blue Bay Lodge* Kamp Street, (☏022 714 1177, ☏022 714 2400, ⓔwww.blouwaterbaai.com ❸–❹), has sixteen en-suite sea-facing and non-sea-facing rooms. Its location in the *Blouwaterbaai Holiday Resort* complex, makes it an ideal place for kids, with a trampoline, swimming pool and (slightly old-fashioned) rides and things to climb.

Just under 4km north of town, but quickly returning back into the West Coast feel, is *Oranjevlei* (☏022 714 2261; ❶–❷), which has ten en-suite garden rooms on one of the oldest farms in the area, with plenty of character. A budget room is offered on a B&B basis, while breakfast is not included with the others. *Oranjevlei* also provides home-cooked lunches on request, consisting of a roast, seafood and *potjie*.

For **information**, the West Coast Publicity Association is run from an old cottage called Oorlogsvlei on Van Riebeeck Street (Mon–Fri 8.30am–4.30pm; ☏022 714 2088, ⓔbureau@kingsley.co.za). The helpful staff will assist you with information about accommodation or flowers in the region.

Around Cape Columbine

The coastline north of Vredenburg is classical West Coast territory: isolated fishing settlements with small, whitewashed cottages and a salty haze over the lazy, glinting ocean. However, despite the quaint image, most of the settlements possess alarmingly expanding holiday developments, offering (naturally) white-washed cottages in classical West Coast style. Although you can still find the odd lonely coastline and some genuine character in the old villages and their coloured inhabitants, the area feels as though it has reached that sad moment of changing from "best-kept secret" to an over-subscribed building site.

Vredenburg and the West Coast Fossil Park

North of Saldanha lies a sizeable inland farming centre, **VREDENBURG**, an unremarkable town in a featureless setting. If you're self-catering, Vredenburg's well-stocked supermarkets make it an excellent place for buying supplies. If you're driving, it's also a good idea to buy fuel here, as many of the surrounding smaller towns don't have filling stations.

About 10km southeast of Vredenburg, the **West Coast Fossil Park** (Mon–Fri 9am–4pm, Sat & Sun 9am–1pm, R5; guided tours of museum and dig Mon–Fri 11.30am, Sat & Sun 10am, R15; ☏022 766 1606), was founded in 1998 on the site of a decommissioned phosphate mine. In the process of being developed, it's still a relatively small and low-key affair, but interesting nevertheless. Displays include thousands of fossils and modern animal bones, and also information panels about the extinct species from about five million years ago found on site. Finds include fossils from lion-sized sabre-toothed cats, two species of extinct elephant and sivatheres – long-horned, short-necked giraffe-like browsers. Perhaps strangest of all are the extinct giant bears, *Agriotherium africanum*, that weighed in at 750kg (compared to 150kg for a large lion), making them the heftiest predators – and the only known bears – to have roamed sub-Saharan Africa in the past 65 million years.

Budget **accommodation** is available on the adjacent property at *Windstone Backpackers* (☏022 766 1645 or 083 477 1756, ☏083 766 1038, ⓦwww

.windstone.co.za; ❶), just past the main crossroads of the R45 from Vredenburg and the R27 from Cape Town. The lodge consists of a house with five four- and six-bedded **dorms** and **one private room** suitable for families. *Windstone* makes a friendly base for exploring the region and also has a **horse-riding centre**, run by owners Andy and Brenda Winder, the latter of whom is a qual-ified riding instructor and will take on novices as well as organizing horse trails along the coast or up in the Cederberg. They also provide mountain bikes and transport to Langebaan for about R25. The lodge is on the route of the daily Elwierda bus (☎021 418 4673), which goes from Cape Town to Saldanha.

Paternoster

The best of the coast is to be found 20km northwest of Vredenburg around the village of **PATERNOSTER** (whose name comes from the prayers uttered by Portuguese sailors crawling ashore from a shipwreck in the adjacent bay). Small-scale angling and crayfish netting is the principal economic activity of the village, and most of the fishermen live in the whitewashed cottages of the coloured district to the west of the hotel. When they're not out at sea, their small, brightly painted boats lie beached at the water's edge.

Just east of the district, you'll find **accommodation** at the rather old-fash-ioned (and a touch overpriced) *Paternoster Hotel* in the main drag, St Augustine's Road (☎022 752 2703, ⓕ022 752 2750; ❷). The hotel lies at the approximate centre of the village, which consists of little more than a couple of parallel streets tracing the shoreline. For something more homely, in the cen-tre try the *Ahoy Guest House* (☎022 752 2725 or 083 731 6703; ❷), about 100m east of the hotel, which has four rooms, one with a sea view. If you want to be close to the beach, a good bet is the *Mosselbank B&B* on the corner of Trappiesklip and Mosselbank streets (☎ & ⓕ022 752 2632, Ⓦwww.weskus.com; ❸), in a new suburban development about 1km east of the hotel. This very hos-pitable B&B has three en-suite rooms with sea views and also a self-contained two-bedroom flat rented out on a self-catering basis for R350.

Eating and seafood are virtually synonymous in Paternoster. Here you'll find probably the best fish (braaied) and chips along the West Coast, and crayfish in season, at the informal *Vissermans Kombuis* (daily noon–3pm, Wed, Fri & Sat evenings) just east of the hotel in the old general dealer's store building. Spectacularly sited on the beach, the *Voorstrand* (daily 10am–10pm) in a cor-rugated iron building at the bottom of Malgas Road, serves similar fare.

An adventure highlight of Paternoster is **sea kayaking** with former game ranger Hannes Kleynhans of West Coast Guided Trails (☎082 926 2267, Ⓦwww.kayaktrails.co.za). Trips last from two hours (R100 per person) to sev-eral days (two nights costs R650 per person, including meals) and are as much about observing and learning about birds, whales, dolphins and seals as about paddling. Kleyhhans also operates kayak trips from a yacht moored off Dassen Island and leads hiking trails. His brother, André (same contact details), a pro-fessional diver and licensed divemaster, leads **scuba trips** through multi-coloured kelp forests.

Columbine Nature Reserve

If you get as far as Paternoster, be sure not to miss the **Columbine Nature Reserve** (daily sunrise to sunset; R8), 3km to its west. A small area set aside to conserve the indigenous sandveld-fynbos heathland indigenous to the region, it makes a stunning change from the salty flats that typify the West Coast. Large vegetated dunes sweep down to a shoreline of massive pink granite boulders and little coves, with beaches that are blue-tinged, a result of oyster shells being washed up and finely crushed into the sands.

There are some excellent coastal **hiking trails** through these reserves, including two long day-trails (details from West Coast Publicity Association, see p.287). There are also some very basic but highly attractive **campsites** along the beach (❶).

Along the road from Paternoster to the reserve, you'll pass the **Cape Columbine lighthouse** (not open to the public), built in 1936 on Castle Rock. Usually the first lighthouse to be sighted by ships from Europe rounding Africa, it emits a single white flash every fifteen seconds.

St Helena Bay

St Helena Bay was the point where **Vasco da Gama** set foot in what is now South Africa during his epic voyage around the Cape and through to India in 1497. He wasn't the first European to round the Cape of Good Hope, nor the first to land, but his voyage did open up the route to the East, which was to give the Cape its strategic importance for four centuries. Three granite lumps on the shore between the fishing villages of St Helena Bay and Stompneus Bay serve as a memorial to his landing, and a no-expenses-spared **Da Gama Museum** (daily 8.30am–4.30pm; free) has also been established within the largest of the new housing developments in the area at **Shelley Point**. The museum is more a rainy-day affair than a must-see, but does include some well-devised storyboards, a collection of model ships and some early navigation devices.

Throbbing away in the background of the granite memorial is a **lobster factory**, where you can usually buy fresh or frozen specimens if you enquire at reception. It's illegal to buy the lobsters if they're offered to you on the street, although in season you can obtain a permit, available from post offices, to catch them for personal consumption. Strangely enough, fishermen once thought the lobster that got entangled in their net a pest, and during the nineteenth century sold wagonloads of them to farmers to be ground up and used as fertilizer.

Velddrif

At the northern end of the R27 from Cape Town and 15km east of St Helena Bay is **VELDDRIF**, a fishing town situated at the point where the Great Berg River meets the sea. Each year the Berg River **canoe marathon** (which starts near Ceres, 49km north of Worcester) ends here at a marina development called Port Owen. During the last few years, the town has outgrown its fishing industry origins and is now dominated by a modern suburbia of brick bungalows. The town's setting on the meandering Berg River and the surrounding wetlands – as well as the vision of some locals, who have managed to stay the eager hand of the demolition crews – has resulted in Velddrif retaining a little of its historic character.

In the quieter backwaters near the Velddrif bridge, you can still see individual fishermen in small boats landing catches of mullet or horse mackerel. The fish are then dried and salted to make *bokkoms*, called by some a delicacy, but essentially a staple form of cheap protein for fishermen and farm workers on the West Coast. To see the rickety wooden jetties where the boats tie up and the frames and sheds by the shore where *bokkoms* are strung up to dry, turn right at the roundabout just over the bridge coming into town on the R27, and after a kilometre or so take the first right-hand turn down to the riverside.

The town's best **accommodation** is at the reasonably priced *Drift Water*

Guest House 18 River Rd, (☎022 783 1756, ⓕ022 783 1771, ⓦwww.driftwater.co.za; ❷), on the banks of the Berg River. It provides six en-suite rooms and a swimming pool, and guests can take rowing boats from the guesthouse's private jetty. There are two pleasant **self-catering cottages** and rooms in the farmhouse on the historic farm of *Langrietvlei* (☎ & ⓕ022 783 0856; ❶), halfway between Velddrif and Hopefield, which also offers walking trails.

The town has no shortage of waterside **restaurants**; one of the most charming is the low-key *Vishuis*, about 3km west along the atmospheric riverside dirt road from the Velddrif bridge. Housed in a restored traditional fish-drying factory, it serves extremely well-priced English breakfasts and excellent fish-and-chips lunches, while its outdoor seating has views across the wetlands. Near the harbour (signposted from Voortrekker Road, the main artery through the town), you'll find the beachfront *Boardwalk Bistro by die See*, which does good seafood and steaks and the *Laaiplek Hotel*, which is a relaxed place for a drink in an industrial setting of large boats, fish factories and cranes.

In town, straight on at the roundabout onto Church Street and then right up a dirt driveway is the **West Coast Gallery** (Mon–Sat 9am–5pm; free), one of the best of its type in the area. Run by a local artist and essentially a shop, it displays a wide selection of art and crafts, including some interesting driftwood collages. You can also have a cup of coffee here, and explore the reed maze or have a game of petanque (boules) in the grounds. Look out for the selection of sea-salt products, including flavoured salts, seaweeds and bath salts, produced on a small pan by the coast nearby.

A pleasant way to get into the wetlands is on a **boat trip** with well-informed birder and boatman Dan Ahlers (☎022 783 0698 or 082 951 0447), who takes excursions up the Berg River, where there is a wealth of **birdlife**, including pelicans and flamingoes. A two-hour trip costs R50 per person. He also takes cruises in the bay, where you stand a chance of seeing marine mammals, including Heaviside's dolphins, which are distinguished from their commoner bottlenosed cousins by their stocky bodies and short beaks.

Lambert's Bay

The only settlement of any note between Velddrif and Port Nolloth, almost at the Namibian border, is **LAMBERT'S BAY**, 75km north of Velddrif (by indirect dirt road) and 70km due west of Clanwilliam (by tarred road). This is an important **fishing port**, although by the sights and sounds of the harbour you soon become aware that even the fishermen have to stand aside for the impressive colony of **gannets** on Bird Island in the centre of the bay. You can walk out to the island on the causeway which encloses the fishing-boat harbour for a closer look at the tightly packed, ear-piercing mass of petulant gannets, along with a few disapproving-looking penguins and cormorants.

Lambert's Bay itself is rather short on charm; the fish-processing plant sits on the edge of the harbour, right in the town centre, giving you the feeling you're in a seat behind a pillar at the theatre. Nevertheless, its isolation means that there's some deserted coastline and nature nearby. During the breeding season (July–Jan), the bay plays host to a resident pod of around seven **humpback whales**. This is also the southernmost range of **Heaviside's dolphins** – small, friendly mammals with wedge-shaped beaks (rather than the longer ones more commonly associated with dolphins), with a white, striped patterning reminiscent of killer whales. You can view the cavorting mammals on trips from the fishing port.

Practicalities

Tourist information at Lambert's Bay is available from the Sandveld Museum in Kerk Street (Mon–Fri 9am–1pm & 2–5pm, Sat 9am–12.30pm; ☎027 432 1000). There are a couple of **caravan parks** at either end of town, and no shortage of self-catering apartments, but nothing much by way of charm or character. If you need a proper bed for the night, head for Voortrekker Street in the centre of town, where the neat *Lamberts Bay Hotel* (☎027 432 1126, @marinelb@kingsley.co.za; ❹) offers comfortable **hotel** rooms with breakfast.

Eating is one of Lambert's Bay's specialities. *Bosduifklip* (☎027 432 2735), an open-air restaurant set inland among some big rock formations 6km out of town along the R364, is a reasonable option, while the original West Coast open-air restaurant, *Muisboskerm* (☎027 432 1017), scores on location – right on the edge of the ocean, 5km south of the town. For a more conventional seafood restaurant, try *Kreefhuis* (☎027 432 2235; closed Sun) at the entrance to the harbour on Strand Street. Right on the harbour, *Isabel's Coffee Shop* does the whole gamut from light meals to prawns, but is renowned for its blowout "West Coast breakfast".

Cederberg

A bold and jagged outcrop of the Western Cape fold escarpment, the Cederberg mountain range is one of the most magical wilderness areas in the Western Cape. Rising with a striking presence on the eastern side of the Olifants River Valley, around 200km north of Cape Town, these high sandstone mountains and long, dry valleys manage to combine accessibility with remote harshness, offering something for hikers, campers, naturalists, rock climbers and even astronomers. In a number of places, the pink-hued sandstone (which can glow with heartbreaking beauty in the light of a low sun) has been weathered into grotesque, gargoyle-like shapes and a number of memorable natural features – including the huge **Wolfberg Arch** and a thirty-metre-high free-standing pillar shaped like (and known as) the **Maltese Cross**. Throughout the area there are numerous **San rock-art** sites, an active array of Cape mountain fauna, from baboon and small antelope to leopard, caracal and aardwolf, and some notable montane fynbos flora, including the gnarled and tenacious Clanwilliam cedar and the rare snow protea.

The Cederberg is easily reached from Cape Town by way of the N7: the towns of **Citrusdal** and **Clanwilliam** lie just off the highway near, respec-

---

Open-air restaurants

A highlight of a number of West Coast towns is the casual but sumptuous seafood feast served in **open-air restaurants**, with little more than a canvas shelter held up with driftwood and lengths of fishing twine or a simple wind-cheating brush fence as props. Organized in the style of a beach braai, the idea is to serve up endless courses of West Coast delicacies right by the ocean. The atmosphere is informal – you eat with your fingers and stand or perch on a rock – and you're likely to hear the waves crashing on the strand a few metres away and feel the sea air rolling in after sundown. A typical menu includes several different kinds of fish cooked in different ways, *bokkoms*, mussels, lobster, paella, *waterblommetjiebredie* (waterlily stew) and homemade breads with jams. Such a meal, without drinks, will cost around R80. For open-air restaurants listed in the text, it's essential that you **book** in advance.

tively, the southern and northern tips of the mountain range. Both make attractive bases from which to explore the area, particularly during spring flower season, although you can find simple accommodation right in the mountains themselves. From Clanwilliam, set beside a man-made dam, there are worthwhile routes out to Lambert's Bay on the coast (see p.290) and over a spectacular mountain pass to the remote and unique mission at **Wuppertal**.

Citrusdal

Heading north from Piketberg on the N7, a long, flat plain reaches out to the line of Olifantsrivierberg Mountains, which the highway crosses by way of the impressive **Piekenierskloof Pass**, forged in 1857 by the indomitable road engineer Thomas Bain. Coming down the northern side of the pass, the humdrum town of **CITRUSDAL** appears in the rolling countryside of the Olifants River Valley, with the dramatic mountainscape of the Cederberg behind. Strange as it may seem now, early Dutch explorers saw huge herds of elephants here as they travelled north towards Namaqualand, hence the river's name.

There are no roads from Citrusdal into the heart of the Cederberg Wilderness Area – you have to carry on up the N7 to the Algeria turn-off – although there are various routes leading into the foothills, which are justifiably popular with mountain bikers. You can get a **map** outlining these at the town's upbeat **information centre** at 39 Voortrekker, the town's wide main street (Oct–July Mon–Fri 9am–5pm, Sat 8am–1pm; Aug–Sept flower season Mon–Sat 8am–5pm, Sun 9am–1pm; ☎022 921 3210, ⓦ www.citrusdaltourism.co.za). The staff here can provide useful information about self-catering cottages and guesthouses in the area. Of the Cederberg towns, Citrusdal is not the most enticing, although there is some inspiring mountain-backed countryside just outside town and it's here you should look for accommodation if you decide to stop for the night. Having said that, if you choose to stay in town, there's a pleasant **campsite** with a pool (☎022 921 3145), on the left-hand side as you come in over the bridge from the N7, and the garishly coloured *Cederberg Lodge* (☎022 921 2221; ❶–❷) on Voortrekker Street has 26 very inexpensive en-suite **rooms**. The lodge has the family-friendly *Tangelo's* **restaurant**, serving Afrikaner farm-style food in a garden setting, and a little further along the road at number 66 you can get light meals at the distinctive yellow and purple *Uitspan Coffee Shop*. If you're making a lunch stop along the N7, the obligatory port of call is *Craig-Royston* (☎022 921 2963), a good eating place on a working orange farm serving unpretentious meals and snacks in a former trading store, post office and hotel from the 1860s (predating Citrusdal by about forty years). The hugely atmospheric rural Victorian building still functions as a general store, but also sells a large selection of wines from the Olifants River Valley as well as local liqueurs and spirits. The shop/restaurant is signposted off the N7, about 500m south of the Citrusdal turn-off.

Citrusdal hot springs

Surrounding Citrusdal is some attractive countryside and farmland, including, as the town's name suggests, plenty of citrus groves. One of the principal attractions of this area is *The Baths* (☎022 921 3609; ❶–❷), to the south. This pleasantly old-fashioned, if rather rule-bound, mineral **spa resort** is set in a beautiful wooded glen with campsites, chalets and self-catering rooms in some large old stone buildings. There's one large hot pool (40°C), a cold pool and several large indoor Jacuzzis. The place has retained its simplicity and is a good spot to relax, particularly if you've been hauling over mountain and rock for a few days. To get there, turn right off the road leading into Citrusdal from the N7 and drive 16km down a good tarred road past the airfield – incidentally, one of the best places in the Western Cape for parachuting.

Along the same road, but 6km closer to Citrusdal, the smaller and more upmarket *Elephant Leisure Resort* (☎022 921 2884, ⓦwww.elephantleisure .co.za; ❹) is a complex of four two-bedroom and six one-bedroom self-catering chalets in a beautiful valley festooned with fynbos and arranged around a little artificial lake. Each of the chalets is finished to a high standard with air conditioning, TV and its own Jacuzzi. Meals and drinks are available at the reception complex where there's also a heated swimming pool.

The Cederberg Wilderness Area

The 710-square-kilometre **Cederberg Wilderness Area** is reached by a dirt road 28km north of Citrusdal which leads east off the N7 to the forest station at **Algeria**. The **permit** system for the area allows a certain number of people to be in each of three separate parts of the wilderness area, but you have to arrange permits in advance through the Cape Nature Conservation Office in Algeria (☎027 482 2812, ⓦwww.capenature.org.za; R14); you can hike or camp where you like within the areas you hold a permit for. There are many designated **trails**, including routes to the main rock features and the two main peaks, **Sneeuberg** and **Tafelberg**.

Camping is available at a pretty riverside site at Algeria, where there are also seven unsophisticated but fully equipped **self-catering chalets** (R320) that sleep four people; the stone cottages are the nicest. Cheaper ones 4km away at the bottom of Uitkyk Pass are unequipped and you must bring your own bedding and cooking utensils; contact the Cape Nature Conservation Office in Algeria for bookings and information.

Apart from the Cape Nature Conservation accommodation, there are several **private places to stay** south of Algeria on farms in the reserve reached along the single main road passing through this section of the Cederberg. *Sanddrif* (☎ & ⓕ027 482 2825, ⓔsandrif@mweb.co.za; ❶), about 26km south of Algeria, offers fully equipped chalets with one to three rooms (though you'll need to bring your own bedding). The farm has very nice natural river pools and good walks. At Dwarsrivier, about 6km from *Sanddrif*, there's an amateur observatory, which on summer weekend evenings occasionally features an outdoor slide show and high-powered telescopes for a closer look at the heavens. At *Kromrivier* (☎027 482 2807; ❶), about 50km south of Algeria, there are thirteen fully equipped chalets, some with their own baths and cheaper ones without, that sleep four, with bedding available for a small charge. Further south along the road on Grootrivier Farm is *Mount Ceder* (☎023 317 0113, ⓦwww .mountceder.co.za; ❷–❹), the most luxurious place to stay in the conservancy set along a perennial river, with B&B rooms in the lodge and six self-catering cottages. Although Mount Ceder can be reached from the north, if you're coming from Cape Town it's better to approach via Worcester (see p.203), 95km to its south, passing through Ceres and Prince Alfred Hamlet as this entails a shorter section of dirt road.

Weather conditions are often extreme in the Cederberg, with frost and snow during winter, and blistering heat in summer. However, a number of rivers are safe for **swimming**.

Clanwilliam and the Boskloof

Also on the N7, but at the northern end of the Cederberg, **CLANWILLIAM** is an attractive and assured town. It carries off with some aplomb its various roles, as a base for the majestic Cederberg Wilderness Area behind it; as a centre for spring flowers; as a holiday resort focused on the neighbouring dam, and as a service centre for the lower part of the fertile irrigation schemes of the Olifants River Valley to the north. Established in the last years of the eighteenth century, this is one of the older settlements north of Cape Town, and features a number of historic buildings around town, including an **information centre** (Mon–Fri 8.30am–5pm, Sat 8.30am–12.30pm, flower season mid-Aug to mid-Sep daily 8am–6pm; ☏027 482 2024, ⓦwww.capewestcoast.org) and **museum** (Mon–Sat 8am–1pm; R5) situated in the old jail at the far end of Main Street. There are some genuinely interesting attractions in town, including **Kunshuis**, a good commercial art gallery on Main Street; a traditional leather **shoemaking factory** on Ou Kaapseweg; and the country's main **rooibos tea-processing factory** next door (videos Mon–Fri 10am, 11.30am, 2pm, 3.30pm; (see box opposite), which also has a window through which you can peer at the activity on the factory floor. Just to the south of town is **Ramskop**, a wild-flower reserve set on a hillside inside the entrance to the dam resort.

The *Clanwilliam Dam Resort* (see below) is the only public access point to the **dam** – one of the country's top water-skiing venues – which in summer and at weekends is often monopolized by speedboat louts. If you want to join in the **watersports**, there isn't any local rental, unless you're a resident at the *Olifants Dam Motel*, which has boats available.

Accommodation

Blommenberg Guest House Along the village's main road ☏027 482 1851. A mid-range guesthouse with thirteen self-catering rooms arranged around a swimming pool. ❸

Clanwilliam Dam Resort ☏027 482 2133. Camping on the edge of the dam, and also a collection of plain but fully equipped chalets. ❶

St du Barrys On the way out of town on the Pakhuis road ☏027 482 1537. A country guest-

house with an upmarket feel, five antique-filled rooms and thatched roofs. ❹

Strassberger's Clanwilliam Hotel On the town's main street ☏027 482 1101. A famous South African institution, dignified and well-run; the hotel has an open-air pool and an excellent restaurant, *Reinhold's*; there's also a tea room and separate chalets. ❸

Eating

Reinhold's (see above) has the best reputation in town as a place to eat, but for something more casual head for *Olifantshuis Pizzeria* (closed Sun), on the corner as you turn into Main Road off Augsburg Drive. For daytime meals and **snacks**, try the tea room at *Strassberger's Clanwilliam Hotel*, or *Nancy's Tea Room* (daily 9am–4pm) opposite.

The Boskloof

About a kilometre east of town along the Pakhuis Pass road, a good dirt road heads south and drops into the **Boskloof**, through which the Jan Dissels River traces its course. Although less than 10km from the town, the valley feels a hundred miles from anywhere and is a relaxed spot where you can spend time lolling about along the riverbank, swimming in its natural pools or just walk along the dirt road which twists through the mountains. If you're up for something more energetic, you can go on two-hour or two-day horse-riding expeditions at Karukareb farm (☏027 482 1675), or head into the Cederberg on

Rooibos tea

Few things in South Africa create such devotion, derision, hype and, among visitors, bemused suspicion as **rooibos** (literally, "red bush") **tea**. Still sown and harvested by hand on many farms, rooibos is a type of fynbos plant grown only in the mountainous regions around Clanwilliam and Nieuwoudtville. The caffeine-free, tan-coloured tea brewed from its leaves has been a traditional South African drink ever since it was developed by Asian slaves two centuries ago, but it is only in the last twenty years that it has broken free from its health-food-shop earnestness and established mainstream credibility. In homes and tea rooms throughout South Africa you'll find rooibos firmly entrenched alongside regular tea and coffee. It can be drunk with milk and sugar, or just with a slice of lemon and a teaspoon of honey.

the **Krakadouw Hiking Trail**, which starts at *Krakadouw* cottages in the valley (permits available through Cape Nature Conservation Office at Algeria ☎027 482 2812, ⓦ www.capenature,org.za; R18 entrance fee plus R18 per day; or via *Krakadouw* cottages if you're staying there – see below). You can also do shorter day or half-day hikes along a section of the trail.

There are a number of good **places to stay** along the quiet road terminating in a dead-end in the valley. *Klein Boschkkloof Chalets*, 9km from Clanwilliam (☎027 482 2441; ❶), is a very reasonably priced collection of 250-year-old Cape Dutch farm buildings converted into guest cottages. The thatched chalets stand in the middle of fragrant citrus groves, and are finished to a high standard, with cooking gear, bedlinen and towels. Breakfast and dinner can be provided by prior arrangement. Some 4km further down the valley, *Krakadouw* (☎027 482 2507; ❷) has three fully equipped secluded cottages; it's also the starting point for the Krakadouw Hiking Trail, although you can do shorter walks on the property too. Finally, at the end of the road, where the valley drifts off into mountain wilderness, 13km from Clanwilliam, *Karukareb* (☎027 482 1675; B&B ❺) offers a luxury bushcamp and guest lodge along the river as well as a refurbished claybrick farmhouse with reed ceilings and country-style furniture with five en-suite rooms. There's also some self-catering accommodation and a swimming pool. Best known for their reputable horse eco-safaris, the Besters have trails for either novice or experienced riders along the river and into the mountains, in one of the loveliest and wildest valleys in the Western Cape, though you needn't be a rider to stay at their farmhouse. Some secluded, self-catering stone cottages are also planned, each with a private river beach.

Pakhuis Pass to Wuppertal and rock-art sites

Leaving Clanwilliam to the northeast, the untarred R364 winds through the northern Cederberg over the **Pakhuis Pass**, a drive worth taking for its lonely roadside scenery and inspiring views. A couple of places on the R364 north of Clanwilliam, about two kilometres before the turn-off to the historic **Wuppertal** mission station, offer excellent access to ancient San **rock art**. You'll also find more rock paintings 48km north of Clanwilliam at the inspiringly isolated country retreat of **Oudrif**. If you keep straight along the R364 for another 100km or so beyond the Wuppertal turn-off, it leads though some remote and beautiful landscapes, renowned for their spectacular **wild flowers** in spring, to Soetwater, on the R27 between Nieuwoudtville and Calvinia.

Traveller's Rest and Bushman's Kloof

Good-value **budget accommodation** is available at *Traveller's Rest* 36km north of Clanwilliam (T & F 027 482 1824, E travrest@cybertrade.co.za; ①). Situated on a farm, *Traveller's Rest* offers various self-catering cottages and the well-regarded *Khoisan Restaurant*, which serves South African farmstyle home cooking. The main attraction, apart from its Cederberg setting, is the four-kilometre **Sevilla Bushman Painting Trail**, starting right beside the farm. The trail takes in nine separate rock-art sites, and provides an easy and varied introduction to rock art; if you're pushed for time, you can restrict yourself to the first six, which are the best. Enquire at the farm house or restaurant for **permits** (R15) to walk the trail; a leaflet and book covering the trail are also available here.

About a kilometre beyond *Traveller's Rest* is *Bushman's Kloof* (T 027 482 2627; bookings T 021 797 0990, F 021 761 5551, W www.bushmanskloof.co.za; ⑧), a **luxury lodge** set in a wilderness area. The focus here is on rock art, with over 125 recorded sites on the property; the rangers here are trained in both wildlife guiding and rock-art interpretation. The rate includes all meals, game drives and guided rock-art trails.

Wuppertal

Two kilometres beyond *Bushman's Kloof*, a turn-off from the road after it drops into the Doring River Valley takes you to **WUPPERTAL**. Set deep in the tunefully named Tra-tra Valley, the Moravian mission station is one of the oldest in the Western Cape; with its tiny collection of thatched cottages, it remains one of the most untouched settlements in South Africa. The mission is famous for making *velskoene* (literally "hide shoes"), the suede footwear commonly known as *vellies* and part of Afrikaner national dress. You can see the shoes being made and, of course, buy them.

Oudrif

Oudrif (T 027 482 2397, W www.oudrif.co.za; full-board rate weekdays ④, weekends ⑤), an exeptional retreat lodge in the Cederberg backcountry, lies 48km from Clanwilliam, some of it along rough dirt roads. It occupies inspiring countryside in the transitional zone between the foothills of the mountains and the dry Karoo, with redstone gorges and a wide valley incised by the Doring River. You can pick up early marine fossils on nearby hills, from the days when the area was flooded by an inland sea. More recently, the area was once inhabited by San hunter-gatherers, who left their mark on a number of painted rock-faces in the area. Although there are wonderful walks through **fynbos** to **rock art**, this is as much a place where you just chill out – the only rule enforced by the co-owner and manager Bill Mitchell is that there are no rules. The multi-talented Mitchell is also a qualified chef and does all the cooking at this full-board establishment (he's a vegetarian, but will prepare meat dishes). The river has beaches for sunbathing and there are some fine spots for cooling off in its flow on hot days; as a former river-rafting guide, Mitchell can take you onto the water in a boat.

Accommodation is in five straw-bale houses, with stylish retro furniture, built on the edge of the gorge that falls away to the Doring River. (Straw-bale construction is a traditional North American method in which the bales are sandwiched between solid facings – in this case concrete.) The earth-red chalets have an uneven hewn quality that befits their isolation on the rock-strewn hillside, and each has a double and a three-quarter bed; the power for lighting is provided by solar panels and showers are heated.

If you want some more sustained adrenaline, the best **whitewater rafting trips** in the Western Cape set out a short walk downstream from *Oudrif* (mid-July to mid-September) on the Doring River. Weekend trips with River Rafters (℡021 712 5094, ⓦ www.riverrafters.co.za) include one night sleeping under an overhang, and cost around R700 per person.

Travel details

Most public transport in the Western Cape originates in Cape Town, and the main services are outlined in the "Travel details" at the end of Chapter One.

Trains

The most useful **trains** in the Western Cape are the two Metrorail services connecting Cape Town with Stellenbosch and Paarl (all a 1hr journey). Outside peak morning and evening hours, trains are irregular, but run at approximately two-hour intervals. Phone the station to confirm times.

Intercity buses

In addition to the major points of departure listed below, the **intercity buses** stop at a number of intermediate points. Principal routes are Cape Town–Port Elizabeth along the N2 coastal route, with an inland alternative along the Little Karoo mountain route; Cape Town–Johannesburg/ Pretoria along the N1; and Knysna–Johannesburg/ Pretoria via Mossel Bay and the N12.

George to: Cape Town (6–7 daily; 6hr); Durban (1 daily; 18hr); Johannesburg (1–2 daily; 15hr); Knysna (6–7 daily; 1hr); Mossel Bay (6–7 daily; 45min); Oudtshoorn (3–4 daily; 1hr 30min); Plettenberg Bay (6–7 daily; 1hr 30min); Port Elizabeth (6–7 daily; 4hr 30min); Pretoria (1–2 daily; 16hr).
Knysna to: Cape Town (6–7 daily; 7hr); Durban (1 daily; 17hr); George (6–7 daily; 1hr); Johannesburg (1–2 daily; 16hr); Mossel Bay (6–7 daily; 1hr 15min); Oudtshoorn (1–2 daily; 2hr); Plettenberg Bay (6–7 daily; 1hr 30min); Port Elizabeth (6–7 daily; 4hr 30min); Pretoria (1–2 daily; 17hr).
Mossel Bay to: Cape Town (6–7 daily; 5hr 30min); Durban (1 daily; 18hr 30min); George (6–7 daily; 45min); Johannesburg (1–2 daily; 14hr); Knysna (6–7 daily; 1hr 15min); Oudtshoorn (1–2 daily; 1hr

15min); Plettenberg Bay (6–7 daily; 2hr 15min); Port Elizabeth (6–7 daily; 4hr 30min); Pretoria (1–2 daily; 15hr).
Oudtshoorn to: George (3–4 daily; 1hr 30min); Johannesburg (1–2 daily; 13hr 30min); Knysna (1–2 daily; 2hr); Mossel Bay (1–2 daily; 45min); Pretoria (1–2 daily; 14hr 30min).
Paarl to: Beaufort West (4–5 daily; 5hr); Durban (2 daily; 18hr); East London (daily; 11hr 30min); Johannesburg (4–5 daily; 14hr); Pretoria (4–5 daily; 15hr).
Plettenberg Bay to: Cape Town (6–7 daily; 7hr 30min); Durban (1 daily; 16hr); George (6–7 daily; 1hr 30min); Knysna (6–7 daily; 1hr 30min); Mossel Bay (6–7 daily; 2hr 15min); Port Elizabeth (6–7 daily; 2hr 30min).

Backpacker buses

The Baz Bus (℡021 439 2323) travels once daily (in both directions) along the N2 between Cape Town and Port Elizabeth. You can be let off anywhere along the national road, and the bus pulls into all the major destinations along the way (with the notable exception of Storms River Mouth).

Cape Town to: Bot River (daily; 1hr 30min); George (daily; 7hr); Hermanus (daily*); Jeffrey's Bay (daily; 12hr 15min); Knysna (daily; 8hr 30min); Mossel Bay (daily; 6hr); Nature's Valley (daily; 10hr); Oudtshoorn (daily*); Plettenberg Bay (daily;

9hr 30min); Port Elizabeth (daily; 13hr 30min); Storms River (daily; 10hr 30min); Swellendam (daily; 3hr); Wilderness (daily; 7hr 30 min).
*Note: shuttle buses connect with the Baz at Bot River for Hermanus; and at George for Oudtshoorn.

Flights

George to: Cape Town (2–4 daily; 1hr); Durban (daily; 2hr 15min); Johannesburg (2 daily; 1hr 30min); Port Elizabeth (3 weekly; 1hr).

Plettenberg Bay to: Johannesburg (1 daily; 2hr 15min).

The Northern Cape

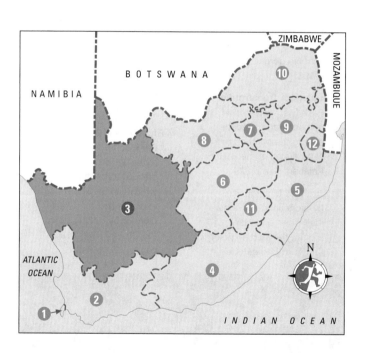

CHAPTER 3 Highlights

✱ Kimberley Diamond Tour
Head 1km underground
on a working mine then
visit the hand-diggings
on the Vaal River, in the
steps of Cecil Rhodes
and the pioneer diamond
hunters. **See p.312**

✱ Augrabies Falls Africa's
second-biggest water-
fall, where the Orange
River thunders into an
echoing gorge. **See
p.323**

**✱ Kgalagadi Transfrontier
Park** Discover lion,
gemsbok and suricate
among the parched red
sand dunes of the
Kalahari. **See p.325**

✱ Kuruman Mission Built
by pioneering missionar-
ies Robert and Mary
Moffat, the starting point
for David Livingstone's
exploration into the interior, and still a venerable
and tranquil spot. **See
p.330**

✱ Namaqualand flowers In
August and September
the *veld* hosts a superb
natural floral display. **See
p.331**

✱ Pella Mission One of the
country's most improba-
ble sights, a towering
yellow cathedral built in
the middle of a tiny,
dusty mission village.
See p.341

**✱ Richtersveld National
Park** South Africa's only
mountain desert, a hot,
dry and forbidding place
which can only be
explored by four-wheel-
drive or by drifting down
the Orange River in a
canoe. **See p.343**

3

The Northern Cape

T he vast **Northern Cape**, the largest and most disseminated of South Africa's provinces, is not an easy region to tackle as a visitor. From the lonely **Atlantic West Coast** to **Kimberley**, the provincial capital on its eastern border with the Free State, it covers over one-third of the nation's landmass – an area dominated by heat, aridity, empty spaces and huge travelling distances. The miracles of the desert are the main attraction – improbable swaths of flowers, diamonds dug from the dirt and wild animals roaming the dunes.

The most significant of these surprises is the **Orange River**, flowing from the Highlands of Lesotho to the Atlantic, where it marks South Africa's northern border with Namibia. The river, often with parched land stretching for hundreds of kilometres on either side, separates the **Kalahari** and **Great Karoo** – the two sparsely populated semi-desert ecosystems that fill the interior of the Northern Cape. It was by the Orange that **diamonds** were first discovered in the 1860s, although it was in the Vaal River's alluvial deposits and the nearby dry diggings around Kimberley that the story of diamonds would unfold in its most compelling detail.

Large **irrigation schemes** have created a stretch of incongruous green along the course of the Orange, principally around the isolated northern centre of **Upington**, the main town in the Kalahari region. A small but important town, Upington acts as a major gateway to the magnificent **Kgalagadi Transfrontier Park**, one of the finest game-viewing parks in South Africa, and the smaller **Augrabies Falls National Park**, where the Orange plunges dramatically into a large granite gorge.

In **Namaqualand**, on the western side of the province, the presence of the Atlantic Ocean means that the land, while still harsh and dry, is subject to different influences. The brief winter rains here produce one of nature's truly glorious transformations, when in August and September the land is carpeted by a magnificent display of **wild flowers**.

Despite these impressive natural attractions, the most commonly visited part of the Northern Cape is its southeastern corner. This is where both of the two main routes between Johannesburg and Cape Town, the **N1** and the **N12**, pass before meeting just northeast of Beaufort West in the Great Karoo. While the N12 provides a good opportunity to spend a day or so in Kimberley, neither route offers particularly inspiring scenery or sights; anyone hoping to see a cross-section of South Africa by driving between Johannesburg and Cape Town will find themselves hot, tired and rather disappointed.

A less obvious but more attractive option is to take the **N14** from Johannesburg through Upington, passing the atmospheric old mission station

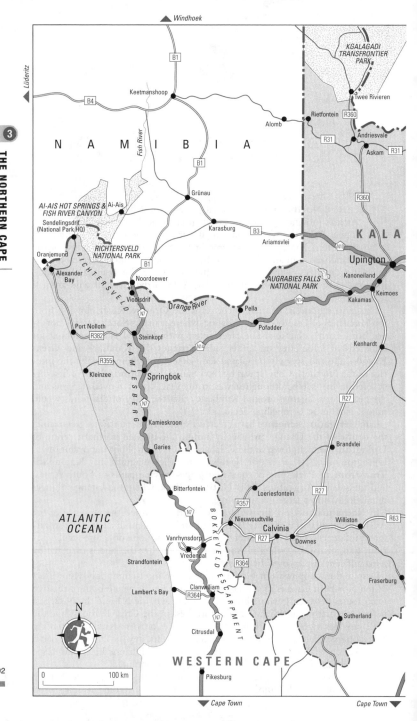

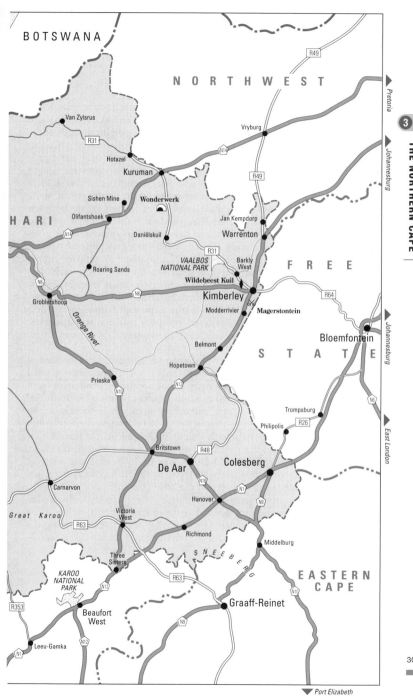

BOTSWANA

NORTHWEST

Van Zylsrus

R49

Pretoria

Johannesburg

Vryburg

R31

N14

Hotazel

R49

Kuruman

Sishen Mine **Wonderwerk**

Jan Kempdorp

Olifantshoek

N14

Daniëlskuil

Warrenton

HARI

R31

VAALBOS NATIONAL PARK

Barkly West

FREE

Roaring Sands

N8

Wildebeest Kuil

Kimberley

R64

N8

Groblershoop

N8

Modderrivier **Magerstontein**

Johannesburg

Bloemfontein

Belmont

STATE

Orange River

Hopetown

N12

Prieska

N10

N12

Trompsburg

N6

Philipolis

R26

East London

Britstown

R48

Colesberg

De Aar

N10

N1

Carnarvon

Hanover

N9

Great Karoo

R63

Victoria West

Richmond

Middelburg

Three Sisters

SNEEBERG

R63

EASTERN CAPE

KAROO NATIONAL PARK

N12

N10

R353

Graaff-Reinet

N1

Beaufort West

N9

Leeu-Gamka

N12

N1

Port Elizabeth

at **Kuruman,** and on to **Springbok** and the main West Coast route (the N7) to Cape Town. This route is only 400km longer than the N1 or N12 and, while it doesn't offer respite from long, empty landscapes, the sights on the way are more interesting; it also puts both the Kgalagadi Transfrontier Park and little-visited **Richtersveld National Park** within striking distance.

Some history

The history of the Northern Cape area is intimately linked to the **San,** South Africa's first people whose hunter-gatherer lifestyle and remarkable adaptations to desert life exert a powerful fascination. Although no genuine vestiges of the San way of life can be found in South Africa (only tiny pockets remain in Namibian and Botswanan sections of the Kalahari desert), their heritage is most visible in the countless examples of **rock art** across the province, and to a lesser extent in their ancient legends and place names. The movement of Africans from the north and east, and Europeans from the southwest, drove the San from their hunting grounds and eventually to extinction; yet for both sets of newcomers, the semi-desert of the Karoo and the Kalahari at first appeared to offer little more than hopelessness and heartbreaking horizons. What it did provide – wealth under the dusty ground – the Europeans pursued without restraint, beginning with an expedition into Namaqualand to mine for copper led by **Governor Simon van der Stel** soon after the Dutch first established their settlement in the Cape. The other Europeans who made an early impression on the province were **trekboers,** Dutch burghers freed from the employment of the Dutch East India Company in the Cape who wanted to find new lands to farm away from the authoritarian company rule, and **missionaries,** who established a framework of settlement and communication used by all who came after.

Within a few years of the discovery of **diamonds** in the area, a settlement of unprecedented size had grown up around Kimberley. The town soon boasted more trappings of civilization than most of the southern hemisphere, with public libraries and tramways, as well as South Africa's first urban "location" for Africans and coloureds. The British authorities in the Cape were quick to annex the new diamond fields – a move which didn't endear them to either the Orange Free State or the mainly coloured **Griqua** people (see box on p.566), who both claimed this ill-defined region. It was no surprise, therefore, that at the outbreak of the **Anglo–Boer War** in 1899, rich and strategic Kimberley was one of the first towns besieged by the Boer armies, and many reminders of the war can still be seen in the area.

At the beginning of the twenty-first century, the harsh land has relented little and, in some ways, the province has changed little. Kimberley is still the largest town, farming is still tempered by the lack of water, wealth is still gathered greedily from the ground and anyone travelling into the interior is regarded as adventurous.

△ Windmill over wheatfields

Kimberley and around

The **N12** highway, running from Johannesburg through **Kimberley** and then down to meet the N1 link to Cape Town, is the main reason most visitors find themselves in this area. Although the term might suggest a wonderland of romance and riches, the surrounds of Kimberley and its **Diamond Fields** are mostly dry and uninspiring, and the city will never again know the importance and glamour it had for two heady decades at the end of the nineteenth century.

A short history of the Diamond Fields

The area now known as the **Diamond Fields** was once unpromising farmland, marked by occasional *koppies* inhabited by pioneer farmers and the Griquas, an independent people of mixed race (see p.566). In 1866 this changed forever, when a 15-year-old boy noticed a shiny white pebble on the banks of the Orange River near Hopetown, about 120km southwest of Kimberley. Just as word of that discovery was spreading, another Hopetown resident, Schalk van Niekerk, acquired from a Griqua shepherd a massive 83.5-carat diamond. It is common practice for significant diamonds to be given a name, and these two became known, respectively, as "Eureka" and "The Star of South Africa". The latter – with some justification – was described at the time by the British Colonial Secretary as the "rock on which the future success of South Africa will be built". Certainly in the short term, the discoveries provoked wild optimism; thousands of prospectors made the gruelling trek across the Karoo to sift through the alluvial deposits along the banks of the Orange and Vaal rivers, and by 1873 there were an estimated fifty thousand people living in the area.

Although plenty of diamonds were found in the rivers, prospectors also began scratching around in the dry land between them, encouraged by tales of diamonds found in farmhouse bricks made from local earth. Two of the most promising "dry diggings" were on a farm owned by two brothers, **Johannes** and **Diederick de Beer**. In 1871 the brothers sold the farm, which they had bought a few years previously for £50, to prospectors for the sum of £6300. The two sites subsequently became the **Kimberley Mine**, or Big Hole, and the **De Beers Mine**, situated on either side of the city centre of Kimberley. The Big Hole was the focus of the most frenetic mining activity of the early years, and the shantytown that grew up around it, New Rush, was the origin of the present city.

Kimberley in those days was a heady, rugged place to live, with little authority or structure, but with prizes rich enough to attract bold men with big ideas. Of these, two very different, if equally ambitious, men rose to prominence in the new settlement. **Barney Barnato**, a flamboyant cockney, established his power base at the Kimberley Mine, while **Cecil Rhodes** (see p.309), a parson's son who had come out to join his brother in South Africa to improve his health, gradually took over control of the De Beers Mine. The power struggle between the two men was intense, culminating in the formation in 1888 of the De Beers Consolidated Mines Limited, an agreement involving the transfer of over £5 million, an astronomical sum in those days, from Rhodes to Barnato.

This consolidation laid the foundation for De Beers' monopoly of the diamond industry in South Africa, which has remained intact ever since. The rise of the gold fields on the Witwatersrand soon overshadowed Kimberley's importance, and although three of the five large mines in the area still produce diamonds, and the alluvial claims along the Vaal are still worked, the firm hand of De Beers has stifled the enterprise which initially gave the area its character.

For those passing through, however, there is enough in the area to justify spending a day here, especially if you're interested in the complex history of South Africa. The biggest draw is Kimberley itself, but trips to the nearby **Anglo-Boer War battlefields** and the **alluvial diamond diggings** around the Vaal River are well worth the effort.

Despite being the provincial capital, Kimberley does not really act as a gateway to the Northern Cape – it's far nearer to Bloemfontein and the Free State. The obvious route to the Kalahari and Namaqualand from Johannesburg is along the N14 through Upington, and from Cape Town up the N7 to Springbok.

Kimberley

Despite being a provincial capital and the centre of production of one of the world's most valuable materials, **KIMBERLEY** itself is neither large nor glamorous. During the diamond rush, it was the fastest-growing city in the southern hemisphere and **Cecil Rhodes** held in his grip not only the fabulously wealthy diamond industry, but the heart and mind of the British Empire – yet status and sophistication have been draining from Kimberley ever since. Even the all-controlling **De Beers Group** (sometimes called the "grandfather" of Kimberley for the number of people it directly and indirectly employs) is largely controlled from Johannesburg, and the city lives in the chilly shadow of the day when the diamonds finally dry up.

However, Kimberley's legacy gives it an historic flavour few other cities in South Africa can match. It's worth spending a few hours seeking out some of the many old buildings, not forgetting to peer into the depths of the **Big Hole**, the remarkable, hand-dug chasm taking up almost as much land area as the city's central business district (CBD). With a little more time, an **underground tour** of a working diamond mine, or a visit to the diamond miners who make a living on the Vaal River's alluvial diamond diggings, are fascinating opportunities to experience some of the grit and excitement which made the city famous.

Arrival, information and orientation

Kimberley's **airport** (℡053 838 3337), serving domestic flights only, lies 7km south of the city centre. Arriving by **train** (℡053 838 2631), you're within easy walking distance of the town centre, though be warned that the daily service from Cape Town pulls in here at 2am, while trains from Johannesburg arrive at 4.30am and 9pm. All the main **intercity buses** terminate at the tourist information bureau; a desk inside sells tickets and provides information on timetables and fares. If you're arriving by **car**, you'll find plenty of parking space outside the tourist information bureau.

Kimberley's helpful **tourist information** bureau is in the City Civic Complex on Bulfontein Road (Mon–Fri 8am–5pm, Sat 8.30–noon; ℡053 832 7298; for information on **tours** of the town, see p.312). The fact that the best-known sight, the Big Hole, is underground doesn't make orientation immediately easy – although the tell-tale mounds of dead earth lying immediately to the west of the CBD indicate its location. Another useful landmark is the stern-looking **Harry Oppenheimer House**, often just referred to as HOH, one of the town's few skyscrapers, near the tourist information office.

ACCOMMODATION

Big Hole Caravan Park	2
Carrington Lodge	11
Cecil John Rhodes	6
Guest House	4
Diamond Protea Lodge	9
Edgerton House	7
Estate Private Hotel	5
Gum Tree Lodge	5
Kimberley Club	3
Milner House	10
Savoy Hotel	1
Stay-a-day	8

5, C & Bloemfontein ▲

De Beers Mine

Train Station

◀ Galeshewe & Barkly West

◀ Johannesburg N12

Kimberley Tram Line

The Big Hole

Kimberley Mine Museum

De Beers Head Office

City Hall/ Market Square

Tram terminus

Africana Library

Kimberley Club

Rhodes Statue

Sister Henriette Stockdale Statue

Medi-Clinic

William Humphries Art Gallery

Oppenheimer Memorial Gardens & Diggers' Fountain

Harry Oppenheimer House

Library

City Civic Complex

Sol Plaatje House

McGregor Museum

▲ N8 Upington

◀ N12 Cape Town

▶ Bultfontein & Du Toitspan Mines

▶ 11, Honoured Dead Memorial & Airport

N

0   300 m

RESTAURANTS & PUBS

Barnato's	F
Halfway House Pub	G
Keg & Falcon	E
Mario's	D
Old Digger's Restaurant	C
Star of the West Pub	A
Tiffany's	B

KIMBERLEY

Cecil John Rhodes

When **Cecil Rhodes** first arrived in the Kimberley Diamond Fields he was a sickly 18-year-old, sent out to join his brother for the sake of his health. Soon making money buying up claims, he returned to Britain to attend Oxford University, where his illnesses returned and he was given six months to live. He came back out to South Africa, where he was able to improve both his health and his business standing, allowing him to return to Oxford and graduate in 1881, by which time he had already founded the **De Beers Mining Company** and been elected an MP in the Cape Parliament.

Within a decade, Rhodes controlled ninety percent of the world's diamond production and was champing at the bit to expand his mining interests north into Africa, with the British Empire in tow. With much cajoling, bullying, brinkmanship and obfuscation in his dealing with imperial governments and African chiefs alike, Rhodes brought the regions north of the Limpopo under the control of his South African Company. This territory – now Zimbabwe and Zambia – became known as Rhodesia in 1895, the same year as a Rhodes-backed invasion of the Transvaal Republic, the Jameson Raid, failed humiliatingly. Rhodes was forced to resign as prime minister of the Cape Colony, a post he had assumed in 1890 at the age of 37, while the Boers and the British slid towards war. He spent the first part of the war in besieged Kimberley, trying to organize the defences and bickering publicly with the British commander. A year after the end of the war, aged only 49 and unmarried, Rhodes died at Muizenberg near Cape Town and was buried in the Matopos Hills near Bulawayo in Zimbabwe.

City transport

Kimberley is poorly served by public transport, and beyond the walkable city centre, getting around without a car isn't easy. Note that all the city's **car rental** firms are located at the airport: these include Avis (T053 851 1082), Budget (T053 851 1182) and Imperial (T053 851 1131). There are a couple of **taxi** companies in town, Rikki's (T082 461 8818) and AA Taxis (T053 861 4015). Unusually for South Africa, Kimberley has a restored **tram** service, but its only function is to transport visitors to the Big Hole. Trams depart regularly from Market Square in the centre.

Accommodation

Kimberley's **accommodation** is targeted mainly at through-traffic and business travellers. However, there are a handful of pleasant guesthouses in historic buildings, and because the city isn't regarded as a main centre, prices are generally reasonable. While most hotels are within walking distance of the centre, some guesthouses and both campsites are over 2km away, and the backpackers' lodge is too far to consider walking if you're carrying luggage. If you're stuck, the tourist information office (see p.307) can provide an accommodation list and help you find somewhere to stay.

Hotels and guesthouses

Carrington Lodge On the edge of Belgravia, on the corner of Carrington and Oliver roads T053 831 6448, www.carringtonlodge.co.za. A friendly and reasonable eight-room guesthouse, with a pool and pleasant garden. ❸

Cecil John Rhodes Guest House 138 Du Toitspan Rd T053 831 8318, www.ceciljohn-rhodes.co.za. The most central of the historically themed guesthouses, with airy rooms and some elegant furnishings, as well as a shady tea garden by the main road. ❸

Diamond Protea Lodge 124 Du Toitspan Rd T053 831 1281, www.proteahotels.com. Rather overshadowed by the six-storey *Holiday Inn* next door, the *Diamond* is a little more intimate, but still aimed primarily at business travellers. Room only ❸

Edgerton House 5 Egerton Rd ☏053 831 1150, ⓔedgerton@kimberley.co.za. An elegant guesthouse in a National Monument, situated in an historic Belgravia suburb, with thirteen rooms, a pool and a tea room; it also offers expensive dinners. ❹

Estate Private Hotel 7 Lodge Rd ☏053 832 2668. Situated in a National Monument, the former home of the Oppenheimer family (they moved to Johannesburg in 1915). The historical theme predominates, but the guesthouse has all mod cons, including a pool. ❸

Kimberley Club 70–72 Du Toitspan Rd ☏053 832 4224. Filled with portraits of Cecil Rhodes, and run along the lines of a London club. The bedrooms fail to match the grandeur of the rest of the building (see p.311). ❸

Milner House 31 Milner St ☏053 831 6405, ⓔfires@kimnet.co.za. One of the most pleasant guesthouses in Kimberley: comfortable, well-run and down-to-earth, in attractive Belgravia surroundings. ❸

Savoy Hotel 19 De Beers Rd ☏053 832 6211, savoy@icon.co.za. Not in the best part of town, and very plain from the outside, but the 45-room *Savoy*'s interior retains an old-fashioned charm. ❷

Campsites and budget lodging

Big Hole Caravan Park West Circular Road ☏053 830 6322. Best of the campsites in the city, located among the old mine heaps just beside Big Hole. Lush, neat and relatively quiet, with a pool, although the shade from the young trees isn't generous. The office is open 6am–8pm.

Gum Tree Lodge Bloemfontein Road ☏053 832 8577. Kimberley's only backpackers' lodge, inconveniently located 5km out of town, but it's pleasantly shady and has a swimming pool. Dorms and more comfortable self-catering units are available, and there's an inexpensive restaurant, *Old Diggers*, next door. ❶

Stay-a-day 72 Lawson St ☏053 832 7239. Very central basic dorms and stark but clean double rooms, including a couple of self-catering flats, run as a revenue earner by a Dutch Reformed Church orphanage. ❶

The City

Many of Kimberley's main sights lie on or near **Du Toitspan Road**, which slices diagonally across the city centre and becomes one of the main arteries out of town to the southeast. The must-see **Big Hole** lies just west of the centre, while the more open central business district (CBD) lies to the south of Lennox Road.

Kimberley's Big Hole

Where there is now a gaping five-hundred-metre-wide cavity was once a small hill on a typically dry, Northern Cape farm, which belonged to the brothers Johannes Nicolaas and Diederick Arnoldus de Beer. In the early 1870s, with diamonds known to be in the area, various work parties scratched around in the hope of a lucky find. One such group, known as the Red Cap Party, worked at the base of **Colesberg koppie** in July 1871. The story goes that they sent one of their cooks to the top of the hill as a punishment for being drunk, telling him, with a laugh and a clip round the ear, not to return until he'd found a diamond. The unnamed servant duly came back with a peace offering, and within two years there were over fifty thousand people in the area frantically turning Colesberg *koppie* inside out.

By 1914, when **De Beers** closed the mine, some 22.6 million tonnes of earth had been removed, yielding over 14.5 million carats of diamonds. Incredibly, the hole was dug to a depth of 240m entirely by pick and shovel, and remains the largest man-made excavation in the world. In its heyday, tens of thousands of miners swarmed over the mine to work their ten-square-metre claim, and a network of ropes and pipes criss-crossed the surface; each day saw lives lost and fortunes either discovered or squandered. Once the mining could go no further from the surface, a shaft was dug to allow further excavations beneath it to a depth of over 800m.

The Big Hole: Kimberley Mine Museum

Although the **Big Hole**, just west of the city centre, is neither the only nor even the biggest hole in Kimberley, it remains the principal attraction of the city. The only official way to see it is from inside the **Kimberley Mine Museum** (daily 8am–6pm; R15), spread out along the western side of the hole. To get there, drive to West Circular Road, or take a tram from the City Hall (hourly at quarter past the hour 9.15am–4.15pm; R4 one way). The museum has two viewing platforms, from which you can peer down into nothingness, where once mountains were moved in the quest for wealth. On the opposite side of the crater, the now diminutive outline of the city is almost swallowed up by the size and silence of the hollow below.

The rest of the museum comprises a large collection of **historic buildings**, many of them originating from the days of Rhodes and Barnato; they were moved here from the city centre when development and demolition threatened. With old shops, churches, bars, banks and sundry other period institutions, including Barney Barnato's Boxing Academy and a skittle alley, there's enough here to create a fairly complete settlement, and most of the fixtures, fittings and artefacts are genuine. You can walk down these old Kimberley streets, peer into shop windows and wander through a couple of the buildings, but for a "living museum", the atmosphere is somewhat soporific. One of the more engaging features is an area where you can buy a bucket of alluvial river diggings and sift through it on old sorting tables, in the hope of finding one of the mock diamonds planted among the gravel. Your chances of striking lucky are about one in five – much better odds than the original miners faced.

Market Square and around

At the heart of the city centre is **Market Square**, dominated by the white, Corinthian-style **City Hall**. During the early diamond days, the square was the hub of buying and selling. It was also the scene of two occasions significant in South Africa's history: the public crushing of gold-bearing rock from the Witwatersrand that persuaded Rhodes, Barnato and others to further their investments in gold-mining; and the departure in 1890 of the Pioneer Column, which effectively established "white" Rhodesia by pursuing Rhodes' expansionist claims to the territory north of the Limpopo. Around the square, the sense of movement and commerce is perpetuated by a large taxi rank and an assortment of scruffy but colourful stalls and traders.

One block west of Market Square along the tramline, at 36 Stockdale St, lies the head office of **De Beers**, a dignified but unremarkable old building rather swallowed up by the city around it. You can read the brass plates by the door, but the building is not open to the public.

The Kimberley Club and around

Not far southwest of Market Square, on Du Toitspan Road, is the two-storey **Kimberley Club**, founded in 1881 by the new settlement's movers and shakers. The club was modelled on gentlemen's clubs in London, but its colourful, enterprising members made the place dynamic rather than stuffy. It was claimed that there were more millionaires to the square foot here than any other place in the world, and acceptance within the club was allegedly a significant carrot in Rhodes' wooing of Barnato in 1888 – together with a cheque for £5 million. Although the present building is the third on the site, it was completed in 1896 and would have been known by Rhodes, whose presence dominates even today, with countless portraits, busts and other memorabilia of

De Beers' diamond mines

If you join an **underground tour** of two of De Beers' working diamond mines – **Bultfontein** and **Dutoitspan**, both on the outskirts of the city – instead of being whisked around a sanitized visitor centre, you get right to the working heart of the mine, amid the noise of turbines and engines, the dust, the mud, the heat and thick air. After an introductory video and safety talk, visitors are kitted out with overalls, hard hats, torches and emergency oxygen packs – the same gear as the miners wear – and then taken down (in groups of about twelve) by the shaft lift to a depth of 825m. Once down, you'll be shown around caves where kimberlite is loosened by explosions, dragged out into trolleys, crushed and then taken to the surface for cleaning and sifting. In the event you spot a diamond while underground, De Beers will give you twenty percent of its value, more (they claim) than it would fetch on the black market. Don't get too excited, though; mostly all you'll see is grey clay dirt. Tours last three and a half hours (Mon–Fri 8am, except Wed 9.15am; ☎053 842 1321; R75), and you have to book beforehand. They're not a good idea for the timid or claustrophobic, and De Beers won't allow anyone under the age of 16 to go underground, but **surface tours** of the same mines (Mon–Fri 9am & 11am; 90min) are also available.

Ghost tours

As the light fades in early evening and the city centre empties, the many restless spirits produced by over a century of surreptitious diamond wheeling and dealing begin to make their presence felt. If you're brave enough to hear the stories, or simply like the idea of poking around some of Kimberley's most interesting buildings after hours, join a **Ghost tour** in the company of Dr Le Sueur, the city's resident ghost expert, who will show you scenes of strange encounters such as the Africana Library, the Regimental headquarters and the spooky Bungalow in Belgravia. Tours begin just before sunset at the Honoured Dead Memorial and last three to four hours. For details contact the tourist information office.

Township tours

Kimberley was the first settlement in South Africa to establish "locations" on its fringes to house the African and coloured labourers working in the mines. A tour of **Galeshewe** offers an insight into a typical modern South African township with its mix of shacks, simple government houses and the more ostentatious homes of locals-made-good. In contrast to townships attached to places like Jo'burg and Cape Town, Galeshewe has a very unintimidating atmosphere, allowing an easy introduction to township life, including spaza shops, African restaurants and *she-beens*. The tour also takes in some alternative historic sights – including the grave of Sol Plaatje and the house where Robert Sobukwe (see p.391), founder of the Pan-African Congress (PAC), lived after his release from Robben Island.

The tour can be extended to take in Platfontein, a San rock art site and base for the crafts workshops of the !Xûn and Khwe San communities (see p.316). For details on these tours contact Dirk Potgieter of Diamond Tours Unlimited (☎053 843 0017 or 083 265 4795, ⊛www.kimberley.co.za/diamondtours), or the tourist office.

Tours in the Kimberley Area

Other organized tours around Kimberley include visits to the controlled area on the banks of the Vaal River where **alluvial diamond digging** takes place (see p.316), the Anglo-Boer War battlefield at **Magersfontein** (see p.317, and a series of **archeo-logical** and **San rock art sites** in the local area (contact the McGregor Museum on ☎053 842 0099 for details).

the man in all parts of the building. As well as leather armchairs in the smoking lounge and marble in the hallway, there are plenty of fine antiques and a few quirky pieces, such as a weighing chair presented to the club by Lord Randolph Churchill, Winston Churchill's father. It's possible to look around or go for a drink in the **bar**, though you'll get a much less chilly reception if you introduce yourself at reception and pay due respect to the club's rules, which include no jeans or T-shirts, and no women in the bar – though this might be waived if a senior member gives permission. It's also possible to spend a night at the club (see p.310).

Across the road is the small but engrossing **Africana Library** (Mon–Fri 8am–12.45pm & 1.30–4.30pm), specializing in historical material relevant to Kimberley and the Northern Cape. Opened in 1887, it retains many original features, and one of the librarians will show you around if you ask nicely. The excellent Kimberley Ghost Tour (see opposite) visits the library; although you don't enter the building, you'll hear about the restless spirit of its first librarian.

The CBD

At the junction of Du Toitspan and Lennox roads stands a statue of **Cecil Rhodes**. He is portrayed astride a horse, and the tributes around the plinth are rich with the swagger common to most Rhodes memorials. Across the road in the grounds of St Cyprian's Cathedral, and a little more humble in tone, stands what is reputed to be the only statue of a nun in the world, depicting **Sister Henriette Stockdale**, a pioneer of nursing in South Africa.

Moving south of Lennox into the CBD area, you'll come to the **Oppenheimer Memorial Gardens**, which contain a bust of mining magnate Sir Ernest Oppenheimer and the **Diggers Fountain**. The combination maintains a balance of respect which Kimberley, to its credit, perpetuates between those who got dirt beneath their fingernails and those who made the money. The fountain depicts five miners holding aloft a massive sieve, and looks particularly impressive when floodlit after dusk. The tall building overlooking the gardens is **Harry Oppenheimer House** (HOH), the offices of De Beers' DTC (Diamond Trading Company), on the upper floors of which all of the company's South African-mined diamonds are assessed for caratage, colour, clarity and shape. To allow this to take place in the best natural light, the building faces south, with special windows to eliminate glare. Not surprisingly, it's closed to the public.

On the opposite side of the gardens to HOH lies an unexpected gem: the **William Humphreys Art Gallery** (Mon–Sat 10am–1pm & 2–5pm, Sun 2–5pm; free entry Wed, small fee at other times), South Africa's only Grade One art gallery. Although dominated by European Old Masters when it opened in 1952, the collection has always moved with the times and now houses an impressively well-balanced representation of South African art, with traditional and contemporary work, including some excellent modern sculpture. The gallery was one of the first places in the world to display **San rock paintings** as works of art rather than museum pieces. At the back of the gallery is a very pleasant **tea room**, *The Palette*, which serves breakfasts, light lunches and snacks on a terrace beside a small garden.

On the other side of the City Civic Complex on Angel Street stands **Sol Plaatje House** (Mon–Fri 8am–4pm; R2), a small two-room museum in the former home of the author and activist. Born near Barkly West, Plaatje was the first black South African to publish a novel in English; he's also known for the diary he kept during the siege of Mafikeng in the Anglo-Boer War, describing a very different experience to that popularized by British hero Sir Robert Baden-Powell (see p.658). Plaatje returned to Kimberley in 1910, editing newspapers and helping to establish the South African Native National Congress, a forerunner of the ANC (African National Congress).

Just south of the CBD, in the middle of a roundabout where Dalham and Memorial roads meet, is the **Honoured Dead Memorial**, a monument to the victims of the Kimberley siege during the Anglo-Boer War. Beside the memorial is the British gun used in the siege known as **Long Cecil** – built in the De Beers' workshops to respond to the Boer's Long Tom cannon.

Belgravia

About 1km southeast of the CBD, along Du Toitspan Road, lies **Belgravia**, the residential suburb where most of Kimberley's wealthy families lived. A stroll around these streets is a good way to get a feel for the more refined side of the diamond age. The focus of the area is at the junction of Du Toitspan and Egerton roads, where you'll find the historic **Halfway House** pub. The pub takes its name from its location halfway between the De Beers and Bultfontein mines, and gained fame as a drive-in (or, in those days, ride-in) pub frequented by the celebrities of the pioneer days. The sign outside shows a badly drawn Cecil Rhodes on his horse, holding a glass of beer – though presumably not just "The Half" the inscription hints at (Cecil not being one to do things in part measures). Happily, the pub has not fallen victim to tourist kitsch, and remains a popular local drinking hole.

Next door is **Edgerton House** (Mon–Sat 10am–4pm), a National Monument built in 1901; it has been converted into an upmarket guesthouse, with a tea room in the internal courtyard (see p.310). Across the road is the famous **McGregor Museum** (Mon–Sat 9am–5pm, Sun 2–5pm; small entry fee), housed in a magnificent Victorian mansion and named after an early mayor of Kimberley. The highlight of the museum is its **Ancestors Display**, which draws on archeological evidence to piece together an absorbing and – unusual still in South Africa – well-balanced exhibition on the various ancestral roots of today's inhabitants of the Northern Cape, going right back to evidence of the earliest hominoids millions of years ago. There's also an evocative section on the siege of Kimberley, including the two rooms with period furniture where Cecil Rhodes stayed during the siege. The McGregor Museum is highly respected in South Africa for its dedicated conservation work and research throughout the Northern Cape, with satellite museums at places such as Magersfontein battlefield (see p.317) and Wonderwerk Cave (see p.317).

Still in Belgravia, you can visit a couple of restored houses, both on Lodge Road: **The Bungalow**, the mansion of mining magnate H.P. Rudd; and **Dunluce**, an elegant Edwardian home. To see inside either house, you must make arrangements with the museum. You can also walk past over thirty other historic homes and points of interest on a self-guided **walking tour** of Belgravia, details of which can be obtained from the tourist information office (see p.307).

Adjacent to the McGregor Museum on Egerton Road is the **Duggan-Cronin Gallery** (Mon–Sat 9am–5pm, Sun 2–5pm; small entry fee), which includes a large collection of endearingly unsophisticated photographs. These were taken by Alfred Duggan-Cronin, a night watchman for De Beers, and portray the lifestyles of the indigenous people of South Africa.

Eating, drinking and nightlife

Beyond the familiar range of franchised steakhouses, Kimberley offers a reasonable selection of locally run, mid-priced **restaurants**. Apart from a handful of historic **pubs**, which can be entertaining for their atmosphere and clientele, there's little in the way of **nightlife**.

Barnato's 6 Dalham Rd, close to the information office ☏053 833 4110. A friendly local restaurant with a predictable historic theme, serving decent mid-priced steaks and fish.

Halfway House Pub On the corner of Du Toitspan and Egerton roads. Cecil Rhodes' old refreshment stop, known as "the Half" and still a popular, unpretentious local. Pub lunches are available, although *Umberto's* restaurant next door is perhaps better for a slap-up meal.

Keg & Falcon On the corner of Du Toitspan and Memorial roads. This traditional English theme pub promises more than it delivers, but it's inexpensive and very popular with locals.

Mario's 159 Du Toitspan Rd ☏053 831 1738. In a small house across the road and just along from the *Holiday Inn*, this medium-priced Italian restaurant is one of the most popular eating places in town, with friendly staff and a big menu. You can also eat outside, although it fronts a main road. Mon–Fri 11.30am–2pm & 6–10.30pm, Sat 6–10.30pm.

Old Diggers Restaurant Bloemfontein Road, next to *Gum Tree Lodge*. Serves cheap, wholesome meals at all hours of the day, principally for residents of the backpackers' lodge; takeaways are available, and there's also a bar.

Star of the West Near the Big Hole, on the corner of West and North Circular roads. A good place to drink, Kimberley's oldest pub still serves beer to diggers after the diamond markets on Saturdays. The decent cheap pub lunches here are a better option than the Mine Museum's tea room.

Tiffany's In the *Savoy Hotel*, 19 De Beers Rd ☏053 832 6211. A meal at Kimberley's most formal restaurant doesn't come cheap, and the atmosphere can be a bit intimidating – but the food is good.

Umberto's On the corner of Du Toitspan and Egerton roads, next door to the *Halfway House Pub*, this regular Italian restaurant, with red-checked tablecloths, serves decent pizza and pasta. The rest of the menu is slightly pricier. Closed Sun.

Listings

Airlines South African Express Airways is situated at the airport ☏053 838 3337.

Bus information Details of all intercity bus services are available at the desk (☏053 832 6040) in the tourist information centre.

Emergencies Ambulance ☏831 1954; Fire ☏832 4211; Police ☏10111.

Hospitals The best hospital for visitors is the 24hr Medi-Clinic, 177 Du Toitspan Rd ☏053 838 1111 or 053 831 1453.

Internet café Small World Net Café, 42 Sidney St, near the tourist office opposite the library ☏053 831 3484, info@smallworld.co.za.

Pharmacy Piet Muller Pharmacy, 52 Market Square ☏053 831 1787. Open daily until 9pm.

Swimming Karen Muir Pool (open-air) in Queen's Park, off Regiment Way. Open Sept–April.

Taxi AA Taxis ☏053 861 4015 or Rikki's ☏083 342 2533.

Train information ☏053 838 2631.

Around Kimberley

The handful of interesting places around Kimberley include **Barkly West**, the town where some of the first diamond camps sprung up in the 1860s, Vaalbos National Park and some fascinating San rock art at **Wildebeest Kuil** and Wonderwerk Cave. All these lie on or near the **R31**, which runs northwest out of Kimberley in the direction of Kuruman. Roadsigns warn you not to exceed 60kph because of the very real danger of kudu leaping out of the bushes by the side of the road – sometimes they try to jump over the beam of headlights, often with fatal results for both kudu and driver.

The mostly unremarkable landscape around **Magersfontein,** lying to the south of Kimberley along the N12, was the setting for one of the most dramatic campaigns of the Anglo-Boer War.

Wildebeest Kuil

Some 15km along the road towards Barkly West out of Kimberley, and due to open in 2002, is **Wildebeest Kuil**. This small *koppie* of ancient andesite rock is an important **rock art** site, unusual both in that the images are engraved (rather than painted) on the stone and that they are found on loosely scattered rocks and small boulders, rather than cave walls or overhangs. There are more than 400 engravings, showing elephant, rhino, dancing human figures and, most common of all, the eland, a central religious metaphor in San art. A number of boardwalks have been built to allow access without disturbing the engravings and, under the auspices of the McGregor Museum, trained **guides** from the local community are on hand to show you around. The **visitor centre** at the base of the *koppie* provides an introductory display and shows a short video documentary.

Under South Africa's programme of land restitution, Wildebeest Kuil is now owned by the **!Xûn & Khwe San communities**. Originally from Angola and Namibia, they were recruited as trackers by the South African Defence Force during the war fought in those countries during the 1970s and 80s. When Namibia became independent in 1990, 370 of these soldiers and their families chose to relocate to South Africa. Largely ignored and forgotten thereafter, and subsisting on meagre military pensions, they established various projects to generate income. The most successful of these have been **art projects**: some vivid and attractively designed ceramics and art work, mostly drawing on traditional San images and motifs, are on sale in a shop beside the visitor centre and tea room.

Barkly West

Thirty-five kilometres northwest of Kimberley lies the small town of **BARKLY WEST**, originally a convenient crossing point of the Vaal River known as Klipdrif. It was the first important focus of the diamond rush, out of which rose the short-lived **Klipdrif Republic**, proclaimed by militant miners when British, Boer and Griqua authorities squabbled about who was to control the area. Later, political representation came in the form of Cecil Rhodes, who was the MP for the town up to and including his time as prime minister of the Cape Colony.

Visibly poor, Barkly West is in a fairly sorry state today, although the alluvial beds along the river on the fringes of town are still being worked, and on Saturday mornings diggers come to sell their week's findings to licensed buyers at the **Diamond Market**. Some of the older diggers still prospect by hand, finding perhaps just five good stones in a year and always hopeful of one "big one". If you want to investigate further – and it can't be denied that a rough romance still surrounds the whole business – snooping around on your own is inadvisable. The best way to explore is to join one of the fascinating insider **tours** of the alluvial diggings with Dirk Potgieter of Diamond Tours Unlimited (see "Kimberley tours" on p.312). He will take you on half-day (around R250) and full-day tours (around R500, including lunch) to meet both the old hand-prospectors and the more modern operators – something you won't be able to do on your own.

For a bit more about the diamond-digging history of the area, Barkly West

Diamonds are forever

Diamonds originate near the centre of the earth as particles of carbon in the earth's mantle which are subjected to such high pressure and temperature that they crystallize to form diamonds. Millions of years ago the molten rock, or magma, in the mantle burst through weak points in the earth's crust as volcanoes, and it is in the pipe of cooled magma – called **kimberlite**, after Kimberley – that diamonds are found. Finding kimberlite, however, isn't necessarily a licence to print money – in every one hundred tonnes there will be about twenty carats (4g) of diamonds.

The word "carat" comes from the carob bean – dried beans were used as a measure of weight, now standardized as 0.2g. (Carat has a different meaning in the context of gold, where it is a measure of purity.) De Beers estimates that fifty million pieces of diamond jewellery are bought each year, which represents a lot of marriage proposals.

has a **small museum** (daily 9am–5pm; R5) located in the old toll house for the bridge built over the Vaal River in 1884. To get there, turn right towards the town's campsite/resort just after crossing the new bridge over the Vaal as you approach Barkly West from Kimberley.

Vaalbos National Park

Further along the Vaal River, about 20km from Barkly West on the R31, **Vaalbos National Park** (summer 5.30am–6.30pm; winter 6am–5.30pm; R10) is an 18,000-hectare reserve opened to the public in 1994 to protect a unique confluence of vegetation types. While it's fairly unremarkable compared to many of the country's national parks, and the facilities are limited, it features some very African-looking camelthorn plains which look particularly attractive at sunrise or sunset. You have a good chance of seeing game, such as buffalo, giraffe, zebra and plenty of buck – though the resident rhino, which include some rare desert black rhino, are seldom seen from the single road through the park which is open to the public. Near the entrance are three pleasant self-catering chalets, each sleeping four to six (☎012 343 1991, ⓦwww.parks-sa.co.za; ❷).

Wonderwerk Cave

Further along the R31 towards Kuruman is the intriguing **Wonderwerk** (Miracle) **Cave**, a major archeological site which has produced important evidence of human occupation in various eras dating back nearly one million years, including fossils, animal teeth, artefacts and San rock art. There is a small visitor centre on the site, run by the McGregor Museum in Kimberley, and a **campsite** and self-catering **chalet** run by the local farmer (☎053 384 0680; ❷). Sometimes there are archeologists working in the cave; if there's no one around, you'll have to ask at the farm for the gate to be unlocked. A small admission fee is charged.

Magersfontein

Just over 30km south of Kimberley along the N12, the Anglo-Boer War battlefield 4 at **Magersfontein** provides a poignant reminder of the area's bloodspattered past. This is where Boer forces put trench warfare into effect against British troops, with devastating results (see box on p.318). Signposts point the way to a recently spruced-up **visitor centre** (daily 8am–5pm; R5) with a tea

The Kimberley campaign

At the outbreak of the **Anglo-Boer War**, the Boer forces identified diamond-rich Kimberley as an important strategic base, and quickly besieged the city, trapping its residents, including Cecil Rhodes, inside. In response, the British deployed an army under **Lord Methuen** to relieve the city. The army was compelled, by its size and lack of knowledge of the terrain, to advance from the coast along the line of the railway so that a supply of troops, water, food and equipment could be ensured.

Methuen first encountered Boer forces at Belmont, just across the Orange River. This was followed by further battles at Graspan and the Modder River, from which the Boers made a tactical withdrawal to Magersfontein, a range of hills 30km south of Kimberley. Here, rather than defending the top of the ridge of hills, as was their usual tactic, the Boer generals, under the leadership of General Cronjé but the tactical direction of **Koos de la Rey**, decided to dig a line of **trenches** along the bottom of the *koppie*.

In the early hours of December 11, 1899, the British, led by the Highland Regiment fresh from campaigns in North Africa and India, and considered the elite of the British army, advanced on Magersfontein, fully expecting the enemy to be lined along the ridge. Just before dawn, as they fanned out into attack formation, four thousand Boers in the trenches just a few hundred metres away opened fire. The use of trenches was, at that point, a rare tactic in modern warfare, and the element of surprise caused devastation in the ranks of Highlanders. Those not killed or wounded in the first volleys were pinned down by snipers for the rest of the day, unable to move in the coverless *veld* and suffering appallingly under the hot sun. The next day the British withdrew to the Modder River, and the relief of Kimberley was delayed for two months. The defeat was one in a series of three the British suffered within what became known as "Black Week", news of which sent shock waves through the British public expecting their forces to overrun the "crude farmers" before Christmas.

room and a small museum, which has some vivid but sensitive and balanced exhibits about the battle. You can also hike up to various monuments situated on the western end of the line of hills. Out on the battlefield itself, now open *veld* with springbok grazing and the occasional car throwing up a plume of dust along the dirt road, the lines of **trenches** can still be seen, along with other memorials, including a pair of granite crosses marking the graves of Scandinavian soldiers who fought on the Boer side.

One of the most enjoyable ways of finding out more about the history is to book a one-day **battlefield tour** with Steve Lunderstedt (☎053 831 4006 or 083 732 3189), a highly entertaining and well-informed military historian. The tours provide a vivid picture of the campaign, with trips to battlefields, fortifications and gun positions, and walks to get a sense of the terrain and look for old shells and other evidence of the fighting.

If you want to stay in the area instead of heading back to Kimberley, a good option is *Langberg Guest Farm*, 21km south of Kimberley on the N12 (☎053 832 1001, ⊛www.langberg.co.za; ❷), a very hospitable B&B on a historic farm at the western end of the Magersfontein battlefield, set in several Cape Dutch horse stables. Dinner is also available – the food here is excellent, and the rooms good value.

The Kalahari

While the Northern Cape has no shortage of dry, endless expanses, the most emotive by far is the **Kalahari**. The very name holds a resonance of sun-bleached, faraway spaces and the unknown vastness of the African interior, both harsh and magical. The name derives from the word *kgalagadi* (thirsty land), and describes the semi-desert stretching north from the Orange River to the Okavango Delta in northern Botswana, west into Namibia and east until the bushveld begins to dominate in the catchment areas of the Vaal and Limpopo rivers.

The Kalahari in the Northen Cape is characterized by surprisingly high, thinly vegetated red or orange sand dunes scored with dry river beds and large, shimmering saltpans. Like most deserts (although this is strictly semi-desert), daytime temperatures are searingly hot in summer and numbingly cold at night in winter. North from the Orange, South Africa's largest river which flows defiantly through the parched regions, the land is populated by tough, hard-working farmers and communities largely descended from the indigenous San hunter-gatherers and nomadic Khoi herders. For many land-users, there is an increasing realization that **eco-tourism**, rather than being a First World luxury, may be the only viable option on huge areas of land where stock farming and hunting provide at best a marginal living.

Upington, the main town in the area, stands on the northern bank of the Orange, at the heart of an irrigated corridor of intensive wheat, cotton and, most prominently, grape farms. At the far end of the farming belt, about an hour east, the Orange picks up speed, and froths and tumbles into a huge granite gorge at **Augrabies Falls**, the focus of one of the area's two national parks.

The other is the undoubted highlight of this area, the **Kagalagadi Transfrontier Park**, incorporating South Africa's Kalahari-Gemsbok National Park and Botswana's Gemsbok National Park. A vast desert sanctuary rich in game and boasting a magnificent landscape of red dunes and hardy vegetation, it's well worth the long trek to get there. The options if you're coming to it directly from Johannesburg along the N14 highway are either to turn off at **Kuruman**, site of a famous nineteenth-century **mission station** established by Robert and Mary Moffat, along the R31 (a long, bleak dirt road which should only be tackled in a sturdy vehicle), or to travel on to Upington, the established gateway for the park, from where the road is tarred for all but the last 50km.

Upington and around

As an inevitable focus of trips heading to the Kgalagadi and Augrabies national parks, as well as those to and from Namaqualand and Namibia, **UPINGTON** is a good place to stop to gather supplies, organize a park tour or onward accommodation, or simply draw breath. Situated on the banks of the Orange River, it can also be a mellow spot, although its savage summer temperatures mean you probably won't want to linger. The climate doesn't necessarily improve once you leave, but at least you're on your way to something interesting.

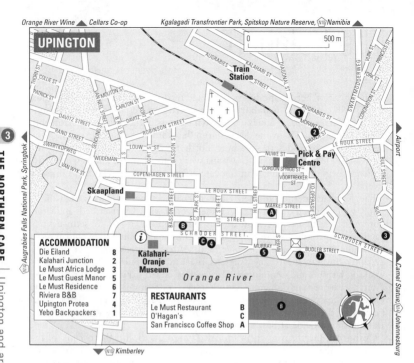

Orange River Wine ▲ Cellars Co-op   Kgalagadi Transfrontier Park, Spitskop Nature Reserve, Namibia ▲

UPINGTON

0   500 m

Train Station

Pick & Pay Centre

Skaapland

Orange River

ACCOMMODATION

Die Eiland	8
Kalahari Junction	2
Le Must Africa Lodge	3
Le Must Guest Manor	5
Le Must Residence	6
Riviera B&B	7
Upington Protea	4
Yebo Backpackers	1

Kalahari-Oranje Museum

RESTAURANTS

Le Must Restaurant	B
O'Hagan's	C
San Francisco Coffee Shop	A

Kimberley ▼

Arrival and information

Arriving by **car**, you'll quickly find yourself in or near the centre of town; parking is easy, although it's worth hunting for a bit of shade. Intercape **buses** (☎054 332 6091, ⍵www.intercape.co.za) will take you to their office beside the *Protea* hotels, right in the heart of town, while **minibus taxis** tend to arrive at the train station, a ten-minute walk away. A daily SA Airlink service from both Cape Town and Johannesburg flies into Upington's **airport** (☎054 337 7900), 7km northeast of town on Diedericks Road.

Central Upington is compact and easy to get around, with most of the activity on the three main streets running parallel to the river. The helpful **tourist information** office is located in the Kalahari Oranje Museum complex on Schröder Street (Mon–Fri 8am–5.30pm, Sat 9am–noon, ⍵www.green-kalahari, ☎054 332 6064). If you want to **book a tour** from Upington to either of the national parks, see the box opposite. You can rent **4WD vehicles** from Walker's Midas, 53 Market St (☎054 332 4441), who offer good deals with unlimited mileage (they also rent out standard cars at decent rates), or from Kalahari 4x4 Hire (☎054 332 3099 or 082 570 5218). Avis **car rental** (☎054 332 4746) is based at the airport, and there are other car rental agencies in town, including Tempest (☎054 331 2268) and Imperial (☎054 332 2383).

Accommodation

While there are enough **places to stay** in Upington, many guesthouses – with the exception of the various *Le Must* houses – are still largely geared to South

Kalahari tours from Upington

To save yourself driving the vast distances of the Kalahari region – and to take advantage of specialized knowledge of the region's distinctive flora, fauna, landscapes and climate – it's worth considering joining a guided tour. Most of these incorporate a visit to the Augrabies Falls and the Kgalagadi Transfrontier Park, although some operators can customize tours to suit your requirements. For details and prices, which vary depending on how many people are on the tour, phone the companies directly.

Kalahari Adventure Centre ☏ & ℻054 451 0177, ⓦwww.kalahari.co.za. An energetic backpacker outfit located near Augrabies Falls, offering a budget four-day Kalahari Backroads Safari, with two nights in the Kgalagadi Transfrontier Park and one in the rarely explored Riemvasmaak area. They also offer multi-day canoe and rafting trails on the Orange River.

Kalahari Tours and Travel ☏054 338 0375 or 082 493 5041, ⓦwww.kalahari-tours .co.za. Very well-organized, adaptable, mid-priced tours, including two-day tours to Kgalagadi Transfrontier Park and desert camping experiences. Longer trips to other parts of the Kalahari and canoeing on the Orange are also available.

Diamond Tours Unlimited ☏053 843 0017 or 083 265 4795, ⓦwww.kimberley.co .za/diamondtours. A knowledgeable and enthusiastic Northern Cape specialist offering a range of flexible tours in the mid- to upper-price range to the Transfrontier Park and the wider Kalahari region.

African holidaymakers, and the tastes of international travellers are not always catered for or even understood.

Die Eiland On an island in the river immediately opposite the town centre ☏054 334 0286. This huge, busy holiday resort has a pleasant campsite and self-catering chalets, the best of which are right by the river and sleep four. ❷

Kalahari Junction 3 Oranje St ☏054 332 7874. One of two backpacker hostels in town – this one is busier and more compact. Camping and doubles are both available, with some odd triple-storey bunk beds and outside beds for the hot summer nights. This hostel is a useful stop-over if you're making your way to the Kalahari Adventure Centre near Augrabies (see p.324). ❶

Le Must Guest Manor 12 Murray Ave ☏054 332 3971, ⓦwww.lemust.co.za. The *Manor* comprises two Cape Dutch houses on the riverbank with elegantly comfortable rooms, minimalist design and large gardens, offering tasteful luxury and sophistication rarely encountered in the Northern Cape, let alone Upington. A few hundred yards away, the

Residence has some stunning antique-filled rooms. Also run by *Le Must*, the *Africa Lodge* has less-expensive rooms but in many ways a more relaxed ambience further from the centre at 26 Bult St. *Africa Lodge* ❷, *Guest Manor* & *Residence* ❸–❹.

Riviera B&B 16 Budler St ☏054 332 6554. Homely B&B in a large guesthouse with a lush garden running down to the river bank. ❷

Upington Protea 24 Schröder St ☏054 332 4414. The more characterful of the town's two *Protea* hotels, with decent but unexceptional rooms, a few of which look out onto the river. There's a *Spur Steak Ranch* downstairs. ❸

Yebo! Backpackers & Guest House 21 Morant St, just up the road from *Kalahari Junction* ☏054 331 2496, ℯteuns@intekom.co.za. A pleasant house with spacious double rooms, and a dorm with single beds. It's fairly quiet and relaxing, with a braai area and a pool. ❶

The Town

Unfortunately you can see very little of the Orange River from Upington's town centre. The best place to glimpse it is from the grounds of the **Kalahari–Oranje Museum** (Mon–Fri 9am–12.15pm & 2–5pm; free), at the southern end of Schröder Street. The museum itself is based in the 1875 mission church which was the origin of the settlement here, and tells a fairly predictable history of isolated missionaries, hardy pioneer farmers and less-than-perfect race relations. The grounds are pleasant enough, and contain a quirky sculpture of a donkey. A couple of kilometres away, at the other end of Schröder Street, is an equally bizarre **statue of a camel**; this commemorates Upington's days as a frontier station, when the police – often mounted on camels – patrolled large tracts of the wider Kalahari area, dealing with Griqua rebels, recalcitrant San bands and hostile German forces based in Namibian territory.

Thanks to irrigation schemes, Upington is surrounded by vineyards, producing ten percent of the country's grapes – mostly table grapes and dried fruit, but wine is also produced. Wine tasting is available at the **Orange River Wine Cellars Co-op** (Mon–Fri 8am–12.45pm & 2–5pm; free) in the industrial estate west of the town centre off Dakota Road. Factory tours are also offered during the harvest season (approximately Nov–March). Meanwhile, the **South African Dried Fruit Co-op** has a shop selling various locally grown products, including raisins (the biggest export crop) in a building beside the tourist information office and museum. Consumables of another kind entirely can be found at the remarkable **Skaapland** ("Sheepland", in English), a huge modern butchery which stands testimony to the devotion locals have for red meat. Located on the corner of Brug and Le Roux streets, it's worth a visit for all but the most devout vegetarian simply to see this vast, bright and spotless emporium selling everything from whole lamb carcasses (which can be cut up to your specific requirements at a special bay) to *biltong* which hangs in dark forests in one corner of the shop.

Spitskop Nature Reserve

About 13km north of town along the R360, **Spitskop Nature Reserve** (dawn to dusk; ☎054 332 1336; R12) offers an accessible taste of the semi-desert, although with its limited array of rather skittish zebra and large antelope such as gemsbok, the experience lacks the fullness you'll get further afield. The name Spitskop refers to a small rocky hill with decent views of the surrounding plains. At its base is a quiet **campsite**, with simple **chalets** sleeping four – worth considering if you want some peace and quiet away from town (❶). There are hiking and mountain-bike trails throughout the reserve (staff will talk you through routes), and you can take game-viewing drives in your own car.

Eating and drinking

As the only large centre for hundreds of kilometres, Upington seems like culinary heaven compared to the towns you pass through to get here. If ever conditions were right for you to appreciate a franchised **steakhouse**, this is it and, sure enough, they are lined up in anticipation in the town centre. However, it's hard to ignore the draw of *Le Must* **restaurant** at 11 Schröder St (☎054 332 3971); this venue stands comparison with the better restaurants in Cape Town and Johannesburg. Moderately priced and open for lunch and dinner, it serves very imaginative modern South African meat and fish dishes as well as delicious salads and lighter meals.

For **coffee** or a snack, head for the *San Francisco* coffee shop, located in the mall bordered by Market and Hill streets, or one of the chain outlets in the Pick 'n Pay shopping centre at the end of River Street. Decent places to down a **beer** include *Scotty's Bar* in the *Upington Protea*, 24 Schröder St, and *O'Hagan's*, a few doors away.

Augrabies Falls National Park

From Upington, you're well-positioned to head the 100 or so kilometres to **Augrabies Falls National Park**, one of South Africa's most dramatic natural spectacles. The falls are easily visited as a day-trip from Upington, although there's plenty of reasonable accommodation both in the park itself and nearby. The route from Upington is west along the **N14**, following the Orange River and its rich fringe of vineyards, orchards and alfalfa fields.

Some 39km southwest of Upington, the road passes through **KEIMOES**, where, if you have time, it's worth driving to the top of **Tierberg Reserve**, a small *koppie* at the eastern end of town commanding impressive views over the riverine farming strip and the harsh semi-desert beyond.

The falls

Roaring out of the barren semi-desert just over 100km west of Upington, and sending great plumes of spray up above the brown horizon, is the most spectacular moment in the two-thousand-kilometre progress of the Orange River. The mighty waterfall is still known by its Khoikhoi name, Aukoerebis, "the place of great noise".

At peak flow, the huge volume of water plunging through a narrow channel at the head of a deep granite gorge actually compares with the more docile periods at Victoria Falls and Niagara, although **Augrabies** lacks both the height and the soul-wrenching grandeur of its larger rivals. However, it is free of rampant commercialization, and in its eerie desert setting under an azure evening sky, the falls provide a moving and absorbing experience.

To **view** the falls, walk across the smooth granite domes beside the main restcamp to the fence along the edge of the gorge. The sides of the canyon are shaped like a smooth parabola, and there are many tales of curious visitors going too far in their quest to peer at the falls and sliding helplessly into the seething maelstrom below. Despite the odd miraculous survival – most famously a Scandinavian who was stripped of all his clothes by the force of the water before he was plucked out – over twenty people have died here since the national park was created in 1966. There is now a large fence, but ever since the suspension bridge across the gorge washed away there is no one spot where

---

Activities at Augrabies Falls

Apart from viewing the waterfall and driving around Moon Rock, various adventure activities are promoted within the park, though none really matches the adrenaline surge of the falls themselves. The half-day **3-in-1 Gariep Trail** combines a short canoeing trip in the gorge with a cycle ride and walk back to the restcamp. The **Dassie Trail** is a single-day hike out from the main restcamp, while the **Klipspringer Trail** involves an overnight stop at a simple hut. Details for all these are available from the park reception.

Rather more exciting is the "**Augrabies Rush**", a half-day trip on small rafts down 8km of increasingly swift river immediately above the falls, run by the Kalahari Adventure Centre (℡054 451 0177, ⊛www.kalahari.co.za; around R225). The Adventure Centre also runs four-day canoe trails taking you deep into the empty country downriver of the falls, while another two-day trip surges down the exciting rapids of the Oneepkans Gorge near Pella. Khamkirri Private Game Reserve (see p.324) also offers a range of activities including gentle canoe trips and horse-riding.

you can get a clear view of the main event, and the temptation to edge closer and closer to the edge of the gorge for a better look is strong.

The atmosphere, always noisy and awesome, is at its best near **sunset**, when the softer sun shines straight into the west-facing gorge. To see more of the gorge, walk the short distance from the restcamp to **Arrow Point** or drive on the link roads round to **Ararat** or **Echo Corner**.

The rest of the park

The rest of the park covers an extensive 184 square kilometres on both sides of the river. The land is dry and harsh, with sparse plants typical of arid areas such as *kokerboom* (quiver tree), camelthorn and Namaqua fig. There are various striking rock formations, notably **potholes** scoured out by the river when it ran a different course to its present one, and **Moon Rock**, a huge dome of smooth, flaking granite rising out of the flat plains. If you drive on the (untarred) roads in the park you'll probably spot some of the resident fauna, notably **eland, klipspringer** and other small antelope. On foot around the falls and the camp, you're likely to see the smaller animals, including dassie, mongoose and lizards.

Practicalities

The best time to visit Augrabies (daily: April–Sept 6.30am–10pm; Oct–March 6am–10pm; around R30) is from March to May, when the temperatures are slightly cooler and the river is at its maximum flow after summer rainfall up in the Lesotho catchment areas. Most of the Kalahari **tours** out of Upington (see box on p.321) incorporate a visit to the falls, but note that if you're coming independently, you'll have difficulty getting here without your own car as there's no public transport.

The **entrance gate** is 30km from the N14 along a good, tarred road; the **reception** (daily 7am–7pm; ℡054 451 5000) is a little way inside, and has some displays on the park. Facilities in the main camp include swimming pools, self-catering **chalets** and **cottages**, and a large **camping** and caravan area. Bookings are advised during school holidays (℡012 343 1991, Ⓦwww.parks-sa.co.za; ❶–❹). Alongside the reception area is a shop, a self-service snack bar and a **restaurant** with views towards the gorge.

Accommodation outside the park

The town of **KAKAMAS**, 40km on from Keimos, offers a few options for somewhere to **stay** near the park. Along Voortrekker, the shady main street, is the large *Kalahari Gateway Hotel* (℡054 431 0838; ❷) and, a couple of blocks further, the friendly *Lapa-side* guesthouse (℡083 332 5127; ❷). The best of the lot is *Vergelegen* (℡054 431 0976, Ⓦwww.augrabiesfalls.co.za; ❷) by the main road about 3km before you reach Kakamas; it offers a number of neat, tasteful rooms, a decent restaurant and a small farm shop and information centre.

Closest to the park, around 30km from Kakamas but only a couple of kilometres from the main gate, *The Falls Guesthouse* (℡082 928 7938, Ⓦwww .augrabiesthefalls.com; ❸), is a renovated farmhouse with big, cool rooms, nice furnishings and a verandah overlooking rows of vines. There's also pleasant backpacker accommodation, with both dorms and doubles at the *Kalahari Adventure Centre* (℡ & ℻054 451 0177, Ⓦwww.kalahari.co.za; ❶) in Augrabies village, 10km before the park gate. For activities run from here, see p.321.

Also nearby, on the north bank of the Orange (you have to take a turn-off near Kakamas) is **Khamkirri Private Game Reserve** (℡054 451 0325,

@ www.khamkirri.co.za; ❶–❷). This 7500-hectare reserve offers a flavour of the dry, unirrigated, rocky landscape which fringes most of the Orange River. Here there's a campsite and a number of semi-permanent safari-style tents on the edge of the river, with game drives, horse-riding and gentle river-rafting trips all available.

Kgalagadi Transfrontier Park

The result of the formalization of a long-standing joint management arrangement between South Africa's **Kalahari–Gemsbok National Park** and Botswana's neighbouring **Gemsbok National Park** was the creation in 1999 of Africa's first official transfrontier park, named **Kgalagadi Transfrontier Park** after the ancient San name for the area. The enlarged park is run as a single ecological unit and gate receipts are shared, although the tourist facilities in the two separate areas are still run autonomously. Almost all visitors to the park will, however, encounter only the South African section, where all the established tourist facilities are found. The old names won't die away immediately, so expect to find the new park referred to by its former names for a few years yet.

In another recent development, the park entered into an agreement with the local **Mier** and **San** communities, under South Africa's programme of restitution of land rights to communities which had lost land under the apartheid regime. The Mier and San communities have in turn agreed that their land be jointly managed by themselves and South African National Parks, so the land remains part of the wildlife sanctuary. The agreement also states that tourism opportunities for the local community will be explored. While these cover obvious areas such as jobs within the park and the sale of local crafts, locals have also been employed as trackers on a lion-monitoring project and to work on dune rehabilitation and alien plant eradication.

The new park covers an area of over 38,000 square kilometres – nearly twice the size of Kruger National Park – and although the South African side is by far the smaller section, it still covers a vast 9500 square kilometres, bounded on its western side by the Namibian border, and to the south by the dry Auob River and a strip of land running parallel to this. The national boundary with Botswana is along the dry Nossob River bed, along which one of the few roads in the park runs, but no fences exist along this line, allowing game to move freely along the ancient **migration routes** that are so necessary for survival in the desert.

The best time to visit the park is between **March** and **May**, when there is still some greenery left from the summer rain and the sun is not so intense. Winter can be very cold at nights, while spring, though dry, is a pleasant time before the searing heat of summer. The only entrance to the park is at **Twee Rivieren**, and opening hours vary from month to month, roughly following first and last light. If you arrive any time between 7.30am and 6pm, you'll find the gates open. Unlike other national parks in South Africa where a single entrance charge is made, here you pay a fee (R25) for each day you are in the park. The park's airstrip is here, as is the **visitor centre** (☎054 561 2000), with exhibitions and slide shows worth checking out. All the roads in the park are sand, but they're in good condition, and a normal car will be perfectly adequate given that you're likely to be driving much slower than the 50kph speed limit to give yourself a chance to spot some game. **Fuel** is available at all three restcamps (see p.327).

Getting to the park

The journey to **Kgalagadi Transfrontier Park** is, whichever way you travel, a long, hot and weary one. You'll see plenty of the classic **red dunes** of the Kalahari, and every so often a huge, crazily paved grey saltpan, but the vegetation has been largely denuded, and the landscape is filled with desolate images,

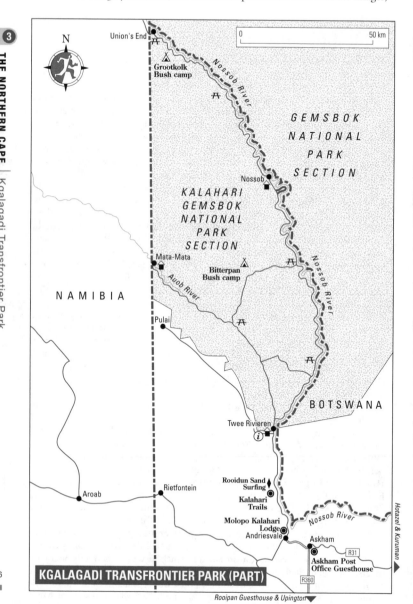

N

Union's End

Grootkolk
Bush camp

Nossob River

GEMSBOK
NATIONAL
PARK
SECTION

0   50 km

Nossob

KALAHARI
GEMSBOK
NATIONAL
PARK
SECTION

Mata-Mata

Auob River

Bitterpan
Bush camp

Nossob River

NAMIBIA

Pulai

BOTSWANA

Twee Rivieren

Aroab

Rietfontein

Rooidun Sand
Surfing

Kalahari
Trails

Nossob River

Molopo Kalahari
Lodge
Andriesvale

Askham

R31

Askham Post
Office Guesthouse

Hotazel & Kuruman

KGALAGADI TRANSFRONTIER PARK (PART)

R360

Rooipan Guesthouse & Upington

such as broken windmills and rusting frames of motor cars, drowning in the desert sand.

From Upington, the R360 is tarred all the way to Andriesvale, about 210km, after which it becomes a sand road for the 50km to the park entrance at Twee Rivieren. The longer approach via the R31 is tarred only between Kuruman and Hotazel. Drive carefully when you're on dirt (sand) roads, be extra alert at corners (where deep sand can build up), and beware of dust clouds when you pass another vehicle. It's also a good idea to reduce the pressure in your tyres by about half a bar before setting off. If you're just visiting the park, there's no need to go to the extra expense of renting a 4WD; a normal, reasonably strong car will do fine, but bear in mind that the higher the clearance the better – a car packed with four adults might struggle.

The two alternatives to making the long drive to Kgalagadi are to go on a **package tour** (see p.321) or to **fly** by private charter plane to the main camp at Twee Rivieren (contact Walkers Fly-In Safaris; ☏082 820 5394), from where you can pick up a car by prior arrangement with Avis in Upington (see p.320).

Accommodation outside the park

On the long approach road to Kgalagadi there are a number of **places to stay** – useful if the park's accommodation is fully booked or you want to stop within easy reach of the main gate. Remember, however, that the park's best **game viewing** is in the morning, so stopping en route isn't really an option if you're on a tight schedule. Roughly halfway between Upington and the park, not far off the R360, *Rooipan* (☏082 415 1579; ❸), is a hospitable farmhouse offering full-board. Much closer to the park, at **ANDRIESVALE**, the *Molopo Kalahari Lodge* (☏054 511 0008, ⓦwww.molopo.co.za; ❶–❷) is a smart, well-run place with over twenty comfortable rondavels arranged around a very enticing pool, as well as camping sites and a decent **restaurant**, which is open to non-residents. Andriesvale also has a **filling station** and a small shop. Alternatively, at the nearby settlement of **ASKHAM**, *Askham Post Office Guest House* (☏054 511 0040; ❷) offers B&B in three simple, pleasant rooms on the site of the old post office, though nothing much of its original function can be seen

The closest accommodation to the park entrance is at *Kalahari Trails* (☏054902 916 341, Ⓔkalahari-trails@freemail.absa.co.za; ❶), 35km from Twee Rivieren, where you can stay in the main guesthouse or camp. Here you can arrange a **guided walk** over the dunes, learning about the desert plant and animal life. A few kilometres closer to the park at *Rooidun* ("Red dune"), one of the local community projects offers **sand-surfing** – a bit like snow-sledging, sitting on a strip of plastic – down the face of one of the large nearby dunes.

Accommodation inside the park

It's important to **book your accommodation** (☏012 343 1991 or 021 422 2810, ⓦwww.parks-sa.co.za) as far ahead as possible – the park is becoming increasingly popular and, especially during school holidays, it can be impossible to find space. For safety reasons you'll be given a **permit** on arrival, and you have to sign in and out whenever you are leaving or arriving at a restcamp.

Twee Rivieren, the first (and most developed) of the three **restcamps**, is right by the entrance and offers functional but pleasant self-catering chalets with thatched roofs and nice patio areas. Also here is a sizeable **campsite**, the park's only swimming pool, a mediocre **restaurant**, a takeaway and a shop selling souvenirs and simple foodstuffs (❶–❺). The other two camps are at **Mata**

Mata, 120km away at the end of the road which follows the course of the Auob River, and at **Nossob**, 160km along the Nossob River road. Both are far more basic than Twee Rivieren, but they hold so much of the raw flavour of the desert that it's worth making the effort to get to one or the other. If your time is limited, the shorter distance to Mata Mata makes more sense, but Nossob is better for atmosphere and game viewing: as well as hearing the lions roaring at night, you'll probably have your best chance of seeing them in this area. At Mata Mata you'll find fully equipped family cottages, comfortable two-person bungalows and campsites (❶–❺), while Nossob has cottages, simpler huts (❷) and camping. There's also a **visitor centre** at Nossob with photos and background information on the park's predators. Both camps have a **water hole** which is lit up at night.

The only accommodation outside the restcamps is at two simple, unfenced **bush camps**, offering a much starker experience of the Kalahari. One is located near the centre of the park and accessible only by 4WD, the other at Grootkolk near Union's End at the very northern tip of the South African section. You must bring all your own food and bedding to stay here – further details are available from central reservations. Camping is also possible on a 4WD-only route on the **Botswana side**. The Botswana Department of Wildlife & National Parks has an office just over the border at Twee Rivieren, but arrangements have to be made in advance through the Parks and Reserves Reservations Office in Gaborone, Botswana (☎09267/580774, ✉dwnpbots@global.bw).

The park

Following the long slog to get to Twee Rivieren, be prepared to clock up even more mileage inside the park – the shortest circular game drive is over 100km long, not far short of the distance to Mata Mata restcamp. The main roads follow the **river beds**, and this is where the game – and their predators – are most likely to be. Water flows very rarely in the two rivers, but frequent **boreholes** have been drilled to provide water for the game. Larger **trees** such as camelthorn and *witgat* (shepherd's tree) offer a degree of shade and nutrition, and desert-adapted plants, including types of melon and cucumber, are a source of moisture for the animals. Both the outlying restcamps are located along the main roads which follow the river beds, so by making your way to them you're going through the best game-viewing areas.

Much of the park is dominated by **red sand dunes** which, when seen from the air, lie strung out in long, wave-like bands. From your car, the perspective is different, as you are in the valley of the river bed, but this doesn't prevent the path from offering one of the finest **game-viewing** experiences in South Africa – not only for the animals, but for the setting, with its broad landscapes, the crisp light of morning and the huge open skies. The clear viewing and wonderful light are ideal for **photography**, as shown by the exhibition at the visitor centre at Twee Rivieren camp or in any number of glossy coffee-table wildlife books.

The focus in Kgalagadi Transfrontier Park is on self-guided **game drives**; there aren't many alternative activities on offer. However, both day walks and night drives are sometimes offered by rangers at Twee Rivieren and Nossob – look out for details posted at the restcamp offices about what's happening on any given day.

Seeing the animals

The game-viewing highlights in Kgalagadi Transfrontier Park are, inevitably, the predators, headed by the **Kalahari lion** and, enjoying rare status alongside the Big Five, **gemsbok**, the large, lolloping antelope with classically straight, V-shaped horns. You won't find buffalo, elephant or rhino, but the other animals more than compensate. Of the remaining Big Five, the **leopards**, as elsewhere, are not uncommon, but remain elusive. Kalahari lions commonly have much darker manes than those found in the bushveld, and studies have shown their behavioural and eating patterns to be distinctively well-adapted to the semi-desert conditions here. Beyond the Big Five, there are various species of **antelope**, **hyena**, **jackal**, **bat-eared fox**, **cheetah**, and some extravagant **birdlife**, including vultures, eagles, the dramatic bateleur (which takes it's name from the French word for an acrobatic tumbler), bustards and ostrich. There's also a good chance you'll see family groups of **suricate**, a relative of the mongoose and squirrel, striking their characteristic pose of standing tall on their hind legs, looking round nervously for signs of danger.

The best time to take your game drives is as early as possible in the **morning**, when you're more likely to see animals out in the open. Drives normally take at least four to five hours, so an early start means you can avoid the desert sun at its zenith. The last couple of hours of light in the afternoon are also a good time for game (and for taking photographs), but it's a lot more relaxing to go out for a little foray from your base than to be en route for a new camp, destined to arrive just as it's getting dark. The middle of the day, especially during summer, is a necessarily inactive time for both animals and humans, so don't plan too full a programme.

Kuruman and around

Lying near the border between the Northern Cape and Northwest Province, the historic settlement of **KURUMAN** is an important landmark along the main N14 route to or from Gauteng. The settlement grew up around **The Eye**, a natural spring which, since time immemorial and through drought and flood, has consistently delivered twenty million litres a day of crystal-clear water. The Eye was the focal point for a rather unsettled Tswana clan called the **Batlhaping**, whose chief, Mothibi, first invited missionaries to live among his people in the early nineteenth century, a decision that led to the building of the famous **Mission Station** by Robert Moffat, and the establishment of Kuruman as the "Gateway to the Interior" of darkest Africa.

In addition to the historical charm of the mission and the natural beauty of the Kalahari, the area around Kuruman is important for its minerals, with iron, manganese and asbestos **mines** in the region. The associated infrastructure includes a single-track railway line running from **Sishen**, a vast open-cast iron-ore mine just to the east of Kuruman, all the way to Saldanha on the west coast, some 850 very lonely kilometres away.

The town centre of Kuruman itself is pretty scruffy, dominated by cut-price chain stores, faceless bulk-buying supermarkets and litter-strewn minibus taxi ranks. The only sight of interest is The Eye ("Die Oog" in Afrikaans), just along from the information office, but there's not much to look at: a moss-covered slab of rock dribbling water and a lily-covered pond surrounded by a high green fence, which you'll be charged a nominal sum to get past.

Moffat Mission Station

Of far greater interest than Kuruman itself is the **Moffat Mission Station** (Mon–Sat 8am–5pm, Sun 3–5pm; R5), a collection of old stone-and-red-clay buildings on the outskirts of town just over 4km from the N14 along the R31 to Hotazel. It was here that a large, often gruff, energetic Scot, **Robert Moffat**, and his demure but equally determined wife, **Mary**, established a mission station (see box below) where they lived for fifty years. During this time they produced and printed the first Tswana Bible, and saw their eldest daughter, also called Mary, married to the missionary/explorer **David Livingstone**.

The Mission is a pleasant place to spend a few hours wandering around. Charmingly overgrown and shaded by tall acacia and camelthorn trees, the old village includes the Moffat homestead, with furniture and exhibits inside, the schoolroom housing the Tswana printing press, and the large rough-stone church, with rows of pews standing on an uneven dried-dung floor, huge rafters holding up a thatched roof and shafts of sunlight angling in through the small windows and split wooden door. In front of the homestead is the furrow that carried water from The Eye, and beyond that, in Mary Moffat's garden, is the stump of the almond tree (destroyed by lightning) under which David Livingstone proposed to his future wife. Livingstone used Kuruman as an initial stepping stone for his first explorations of the interior, later becoming one of the greatest explorers of his age.

Practicalities

When you arrive in Kuruman, ignore misleading street signs for the **tourist information** office (Mon–Fri 8am–4.30pm, Sat 8am–12.30pm; ☏053 712 1001); the building you want is on Main Road (N14), between the main junction with Voortrekker (R31) and The Eye. The office is located in the old

---

The Moffats and their mission

Robert and Mary Moffat, newly married and envoys of the London Missionary Society, arrived in the Kuruman area in 1820, initially at a place rather charmingly mistranslated by early explorers as Lattakoo, about 14km from Kuruman. As a former market gardener, however, Moffat soon saw the advantages of irrigating the flow of The Eye of Kuruman, and began to build his mission on the closest land wide and flat enough to plough.

Moffat didn't clock up too many converts – by the time he had built his 800-seater church he had just nine – but the challenge of preaching and establishing a school inspired him not only to learn the local language, which he did by living for a period in a remote Tswana village, but also to attempt the daunting task of **translating the Bible** into Tswana, which he then published on an imported iron printing press, now on display in the old mission schoolroom.

The late nineteenth century was a time when the popular imagination of Victorian Britain about "Darkest Africa" was at its height, and the most famous of the missionaries had the status of movie stars today. The Moffats may have lived for fifty years in a remote outpost of Africa, but they were treated as celebrities when they retired back to Britain in 1870, not least because of the continuing exploits of their son-in-law, David Livingstone. The Mission at Kuruman, meanwhile, carried on until the passing of the Group Areas Act of 1950, which brought about the end of the school and the church as a functioning place of (multiracial) worship. The old Mission, neglected and forgotten, was revived in the 1980s as an interdenominational trust; a retreat and educational centre has been built behind the old village, under the supervision of a permanent director and volunteer staff.

drostdy (magistrate's house), which also has a pleasant tea room inside. After hours, there is a board outside with various accommodation options displayed.

The cheapest **rooms** in town are at the Moffat Mission (℡053 712 1352; ❶), in the conference centre just behind the old homestead. Bear in mind, however, that this a quiet retreat, not a lively hostel. Self-catering facilities are provided, although meals can be arranged in advance. Slightly more expensive are the brightly coloured *Janke Guest House*, 16 Chapman St (℡053 712 0949 or 083 310 0209; ❷), a large house obvious from the road as you head out towards the Mission, and the *Riverfield Guest House*, 12 Seodin St (℡053 712 0003; ❷), a functional and welcoming rest-stop not far from the centre. You can **camp** at *Kuruman Caravan Park* (℡053 712 1479; ❶), 500m from Main Road on the Kimberley road, although *Red Sands Country Lodge* (℡053 712 0033, ℮red-sands@spg.co.za; ❶–❸), a **resort** set among hills 15km along the N14 towards Upington, is a much more pleasant option if you avoid noisy weekends and school holidays. *Red Sands* also has chalets and a restaurant.

The best of a very limited choice of **eating** places in Kuruman is *Over-de-Voor* restaurant, on Main Road, in a small white building with a green roof, across from The Eye. *Die Oog Bistro* by the entrance gate to The Eye is a tiny bar serving snacks, while the restaurant at *Red Sands Country Lodge* serves reasonable food if you don't mind driving out of town.

On to Tswalu Kalahari Reserve

Some 60km north of Kuruman on the R31 is **Hotazel**, a tiny settlement rivalling Pofadder as the epitome of dead-end, deserted *dorps* in the Northern Cape. With its soaring temperatures, the town's name (the only reason to visit Hotazel) describes it admirably.

The one other reason you might be out on this road is to get to the upmarket **Tswalu Kalahari Reserve** (℡053 781 9311, ⓦwww.tswalu.com; ❾), an impeccably stylish and ultra-expensive game lodge tucked under the 1500m Korannaberg Mountains, not far from the tiny settlement of Sonstraal. The largest privately owned game reserve in South Africa, Tswalu was created by an English businessman, the late Steven Boler, who spent R50 million bringing over nine thousand head of game to this desert setting, including some highly endangered **desert black rhino**, sable, roan antelope and cheetah. Now owned by the Oppenheimer family, it remains part rich-man's dream, part dedicated wildlife protection project, and part glamorous safari experience. Along with the wide desert panoramas, serious luxury and sumptuous meals, game viewing on foot or on horseback is also offered

Namaqualand

Namaqualand is another Northern Cape region with a name that conjures a blend of desolation and magic. According to an oft-quoted saying about the area, in Namaqualand you weep twice: once when you first arrive and once when you have to leave. It is the land of the **Nama** people, Khoikhoi herders who were divided between the Little Nama, who lived south of the **Orange**

River, and the Great Nama, who lived north of the river in what is now Namibia. Still sparsely populated, the region stretches south from the Orange to the empty **Knersvlakte** plains around Vanrhynsdorp, and from the **Atlantic coast** east to the winter rainfall area beyond **Pofadder** in Bushmanland. Above all, Namaqualand is synonymous with the incredible annual display of brightly coloured **wild flowers** which carpet the landscape in August and September, one of South Africa's most compelling spectacles. Even outside the flower season, swaths of orange, purple and white daisies emerge, and there is a tenacious beauty about the dry, empty landscape, with mountain deserts, mineral-bearing granite hills, and drought-defiant succulents.

Viewing the flowers of Namaqualand

The seeds of the multicoloured daisies, mesembryanthemums (*vygies*), aloes, gladioli and lilies, which make up the spectacular **flowers of Namaqualand**, lie dormant under the soil through the harshest droughts of summer, waiting for the rain that sometimes takes years to fall. Because different species – about four thousand are found in the area – react to different conditions, in any given place the flowers will come at different times each year, and attempting to predict where the best displays will occur is fraught with uncertainty.

One of the clues is **winter rainfall**, unusual in semi-desert ecosystems, which is why the flowers appear only in August and September; they follow the rainfall, so early in the season they will be out near the coast, moving steadily inland. The other factor is **temperature** – flowers rarely open before 10am and on cool or cloudy days the displays are muted. In simple terms, the flowers stay closed to protect their pollen from being blown away by the wind, which they assume is blowing if the temperature is below 16°C.

The tourist information offices in the area can offer guidance and help organize accommodation. Decide whether you'd rather stay on a farm or in one of the main centres, such as Calvinia or Springbok, from where you can follow a wider range of routes. You can also contact the central Whale & Flower Hotline in Cape Town (late July to early October; ☏083 910 1028) for updates on the best flower displays and a weather forecast.

Flower tactics

• Day by day, plan your route before heading out. Speak to your hosts, who often have inside information about the best spots on a particular day, or talk to the tourist information offices or Flower Hotline. Be warned, however, that their information is more public and you sometimes get "gold rush" situations, with everyone flocking to certain places.

• Remember the flowers open up around 10am and close between 3pm and 4pm, which gives you plenty of time for a good breakfast and to get yourself where you want to be. Because the flowers orientate themselves to face the sun, it's best to drive westwards in the morning, eastwards in afternoon, and generally from south to north.

• Get out of your car! All the most dedicated flower-watchers have muddy patches on their knees.

• Although it goes without saying, don't pick the flowers. Take pictures, or buy a book such as the *Garden of the Gods* by Freeman Patterson.

• Pack warm clothes, as it gets chilly at night.

• If it's rainy or dull, drive down to the coast, go for a walk in the mountains, or brush up on your Voortrekker history in the museums in places such as Vanrhynsdorp, Calvinia or Springbok.

The area is reached by the **N7** highway which runs north from Cape Town. While flowers occur as far south as Darling, the town of **Vanrhynsdorp** marks the start of the northern section of the flower area, with the region's capital, **Springbok**, well-placed right at its heart. To the east of Vanrhynsdorp, the intriguing settlements of **Nieuwoudtville** and **Calvinia** offer a slightly alternative flower-viewing experience within relatively easy reach of Cape Town and the south. Beyond the crossroads of Springbok, however, much of the territory is remote: roads lead north to the Orange River and Namibia, west to the coast at **Port Nolloth** and the harsh but spectacular **Richtersveld National Park**, and east along the N14 to Upington, passing the fascinating cathedral-village of **Pella**.

Northern Cape flower routes

Flower-viewing anywhere in Namaqualand means you spend a lot of time in your **car**, simply because the distances in this region are so great and flowers can never be guaranteed – you may spend some time tracking them down (see box opposite). If you don't have a car your options are limited. Walking among the flowers is a highly recommended way of seeing them, but you have to get to them in the first place, and **bus tours** tend to be inflexible. **Cycling** is an option, although with accommodation at a premium in the flower season you'd need to organize your itinerary carefully – it becomes a frustrating business when you're told that the best displays are 20km away.

The flower areas of Namaqualand are most commonly approached from Cape Town. While coming this far north involves a lot more time and effort than making one- or two-day trips out of Cape Town, the rewards are found in the variety of landscapes and flowers, and in experiencing the sheer geographical scope of this remarkable phenomenon.

Vanrhynsdorp to Springbok

Although not strictly part of Namaqualand and still within Western Cape province, the town of **Vanrhynsdorp** is really the gateway to the Northern Cape flower routes. It marks the crossroads between the N7 (the main road north) and the R27, which connects with **Calvinia** and ultimately Upington, on the northern fringe of the Great Karoo. The stretch of N7 between Vanrhynsdorp and **Springbok** eventually becomes attractive among the **Kamiesberg Mountains** between Garies and Springbok, although the 100km of **Knersvlakte** plains immediately north of Vanrhynsdorp can seem bleak and grey, particularly out of flower season.

Vanrhynsdorp and around

The main street in **VANRHYNSDORP** is Van Riebeeck, dominated by a tall church steeple at its far end. The town's **museum** is here (Mon–Fri 8am–4pm & 2–4.30pm; also Sat & Sun during flower season; free), featuring a collection of old domestic and military pieces. Also in town is the quirky **Latsky Radio Museum** on Church Street (open by appointment; ☎027 219 1032), a private collection of some 200 valve radios dating back to the 1920s.

If you travel to the outskirts of town on Voortrekker Street, which runs parallel to and south of Van Riebeeck, you'll soon reach a **nursery** (☎027 219 1062) specializing in the succulents that grow in such profusion in the area. Around a third of the succulent species found in the world grow in this region, many of them endemic. You can buy plants at the nursery or, more practically for overseas visitors, obtain a permit for the three-kilometre-long **succulent**

trail, situated 25km north of town off the N7 and a worthwhile diversion if you're travelling on that way. As well as displaying a fascinating range of succulents, the walk introduces you to the unusual **Knersvlakte**, the bleak plains to the north of Vanrhynsdorp covered in small white pebbles. *Knersvlakte* means "plains of the gnashing teeth", referring to the sound made by wagon wheels toiling across the harsh terrain.

Practicalities

The first thing you come to after turning off the highway into town are two service stations, open 24 hours a day for fuel and food. The Shell garage is also the stop for **intercity buses** and **minibus taxis** departing for Cape Town, Springbok or Upington. There's a simple and friendly **tourist information** office (Mon–Fri 8am–1pm & 2–4.30pm; ☎ & ℱ 027 219 1552, ⓦ www.vanrhynsdorp.org.za) in the museum, on the right as you approach the church. Right beside this is the town's old gaol, which has a small tea room and, making use of the old cells, various small crafts stalls displaying the woodwork and needlework of older members of the local Afrikaner population. For a decent light **meal** or snack, head for the friendly *Rock Art Café* next to the Shell garage.

If you're planning on **staying** more than one night, you're probably best off looking for somewhere on a farm or in the nearby mountains. The *Namaqualand Country Lodge*, Voortrekker Street (☎027 219 1633, ⓔ info@namaqualodge.co.za; ❷) is the town's rather gloomy and plain **hotel**. The best of the **guesthouses** in town is *Van Rhyn's*, Van Riebeeck Street (☎027 219 1429, ⓔ virons@marques.co.za; ❷), which offers reasonable rooms in converted outbuildings. On the outskirts of town, the *Vanrhynsdorp Caravan Park*, Gifberg Road (☎027 219 1287; ❶), is reasonably quiet out of season and has a cheap **campsite** and basic self-catering **chalets**.

More interesting accommodation is found in the surrounding district. Some 29km south of town, on the plateau of the dramatic Gifberg Mountain, *Gifberg Farm* (☎ & ℱ 027 219 1555, ⓦ www.gifberg.co.za; ❶–❷) has various self-catering cottages to rent, as well as rooms in a large farmhouse. From the farm there is a network of paths and trails leading to San rock paintings and swimming holes. A good base for finding flowers is the friendly *Aties Farm Guesthouse* (☎027 219 1534, ⓔ aties@freemail.co.za; ❸) which provides dinner, bed and breakfast. It's 9km south of town along the N7, then signposted a further 5km along a dirt road.

Garies and Kamieskroon

North from Vanrhynsdorp, the N7 crosses the Knersvlakte before passing **GARIES**, the first town inside the boundary of the Northern Cape. A sleepy *dorp* for much of the year, Garies comes to life during the flower season, when the **Town Hall** is used as a flower information centre and casual market. There are a couple of **hotels**, of which the *Garies* (☎027 652 1042; ❷) is reasonable, with a simple restaurant attached to the hotel. Further along Main Street, a left-hand turn if you're coming in from the N7 leads to a pleasant caravan park (☎027 652 1014) with space for **camping** and some nice views up the Green Valley.

About 50km north of Garies, the village of **KAMIESKROON** is set among the Kamiesberg Mountains, beneath the rocky peak – or *kroon* – from which it takes its name. There isn't much to the village other than a pretty setting, the crisp air of the mountains and, in flower season, a sense of being at the heart of the garden of the gods. As you come off the highway the village is to the

Kamieskroon photographic workshops

If you're in Namaqualand for the flowers, it's likely you'll take a few photos – yet capturing the immensity and spectacle of the landscapes on film is no easy task. One way of improving your technique is to book a place on one of the popular **photography workshops** at the *Kamieskroon Hotel*. Here you'll also learn more about the inspiring landscape and flora of Namaqualand, and hear the odd epiphany about the meaning of life. The residential courses last a week, and involve lectures, tuition and field work under the instruction of the dynamic Colla Swart (whose family runs the hotel) and the internationally renowned Canadian photographer **Freeman Patterson**, whose coffee-table book on the flowers of Namaqualand, *The Garden of the Gods*, is a classic portrait of the region. Although flowers are the principal focus, workshops are also held in the autumn (March–May), when field work takes place around the dunes on the Atlantic coast near Hondeklip Bay. The workshops are often fully booked, so contact the hotel as far in advance as you can (T027 672 1614, Wwww.agape.co.za; full-board & tuition from around R3500).

right, while to the left is the *Kamieskroon* (T027 672 1614, F027 672 1675, Ekamieshotel@kingsley.co.za; ❹), seemingly an inauspicious wayside **hotel**, but in fact a vibrant and creative place. The hotel has become famous for running photographic workshops during the flower season (see box above), and is the centre for a growing number of activities in the surrounding Kamiesberg. The hotel also has a **camping** area, a much better option than the caravan park in the village.

Deeper into the mountains, at places east of Kamieskroon such as **Nourivier** and the old Moravian mission station of **Lelifontein**, the land is owned and farmed as a community project by the local Nama people. In places you'll see families living in traditional *matjieshuis* (reed huts); these settlements, many of which are still based around a mission, are connected by dirt roads, and so make good flower-viewing routes. A place worth going to in flower season, even if you're just passing through on the highway, is the **Skilpad section** of the **Namaqua National Park** (flower season only 8am–5pm; R10), 17km to the west of Kamieskroon. The displays here tend to be more reliable than elsewhere, with great swaths of orange colour. There is a circular drive around the reserve, but only a few facilities, including toilets and a farm stall offering light meals. Some sections of the reserve have been given over to experiments on the effect ploughing and grazing animals have on the natural flower displays.

Vanrhynsdorp to Calvinia

Heading **east from Vanrhynsdorp towards Calvinia** on the R27, you have a very clear impression of the sudden elevation of the land from the plains up to the Bokkeveld escarpment, which the road tackles by way of **Van Rhyn's Pass**, complete with a couple of neck-achingly tight hairpins near the top. There's an excellent viewpoint, signposted soon after you reach the plateau overlooking the plains. You'll notice (as the early settlers did, much to their relief, after hauling their ox wagons up the escarpment) that the vegetation on top of the plateau is suddenly more fertile.

Halfway between **Nieuwoudtville** and Calvinia, the R27 is joined by the **R364**, a dirt road connecting with **Clanwilliam** via the inspiring **Botterkloof** and **Pakhuis passes**. This is one of the more spectacular remote drives in the Western Cape area, particularly with flowers at the roadsides.

Nieuwoudtville

Ten kilometres on from the top of Van Rhyn's Pass, the R27 passes just to the north of attractive **NIEUWOUDTVILLE**, with its appealing collection of tin-roofed, honey-coloured sandstone buildings. For such a small place, the town is full of character and history, from the sombre **ruins** of early settler homesteads on the outskirts of the settlement, to its designation as "the bulb capital of the world" – the soil here has the highest concentration of **bulb** species on earth. Although most of the flowering species appear in August and September, a time of spectacular colourful display, you're likely to find something in flower here any time between March and October.

On your left as you drive through on Voortrekker Road (the only tarred road), look out for a grand **church** set in a large plot of attractively unkempt ground. An **information centre** (℡027 218 1336) operates out of the house in the church grounds during flower season only and is a reliable source of local advice; year-round **information** is best obtained at the *Smidswinkel* restaurant on Neethling Street. The flower season here is also notable for the highly recommended **tours** run by **Neil MacGregor**, one of the gurus of Namaqualand flowers, on his farm, Glenlyon (see box below).

For an atmospheric **place to stay** in Nieuwoudtville itself, contact the *Van Zijl* guesthouses at the *Smidswinkel* restaurant (℡027 218 1535 or 082 829 6855, ℮nieuvz@interkom.co.za; ❷). These include various restored properties around the village with yellowwood floors, internal shutters and characterful old furniture. Just over 1km outside town is a pleasant **campsite**; book through the municipality office (℡027 218 1316). Alternatively, some of the farms around Nieuwoudtville offer accommodation in classic, old, thatched Karoo cottages, ranging from typically hearty farmhouse B&B to more basic self-catering rooms. *Kliprivier* (℡027 218 1204; ❷) and *Papkuilsfontein*, which has some charming stone cottages (℡027 218 1246; ❷), are recommended. For somewhere to **eat**, head for the excellent *Smidswinkel* (open for lunch, afternoon tea and pre-booked dinners), or *Rooi Dakhuis*, a restaurant and guesthouse at the far end of the village on Voortrekker Street (℡027 218 1125; ❷).

Around Nieuwoudtville

Some 2km east of Nieuwoudtville on the R27 is the town's **wild flower reserve**. Due to its location at the edge of the escarpment, the area receives

---

Glenlyon

The old Bedford bus, called Flora, is one of the great characters of Nieuwoudtville. Behind the wheel is another, **Neil MacGregor**, a man whose love and knowledge of the botany of the land he has farmed all his life has won him admiration not just in Namaqualand, but around the world. The visitors' book at **Glenlyon**, Neil and Neva MacGregor's farm just outside town, includes such names as David Attenborough, who came with the BBC Wildlife team to film *The Private World of Plants*, and Sir Ghilleam Prance, director of Kew Gardens in London.

Each flower season, during August and September, Neil and Flora take tours around the farm, a 65-square-kilometre property where he breeds pure merino sheep and has been striving for three decades to prove that farming and the spectacular natural flora can flourish successfully alongside one another. The house special at Glenlyon are orange bulbinellas, but Neil's enthusiasm and expertise soon have you down on your hands and knees examining all kinds of fascinating flowers. Tours lasts for two and a half hours and depart each day during season at 2pm (℡027 218 1200, ⊛http://glenlyon.4dw.com).

unusually high rainfall, and consequently boasts over three hundred different species of flower. Seven kilometres north from town, towards the settlement of Loeriesfontein, is **Bokkeveld Nature Reserve** and its ninety-metre waterfall which, when the Doring River is flowing between April and October, tumbles down into an impressive gorge where large raptors can sometimes be seen soaring around the tall cliffs. A few kilometres north of this on the R357 a dirt road leading towards Gannabos will take you to another of the area's botanical oddities, an extensive **aloe forest**, containing some of the tallest specimens of the succulent *aloe diechotoma*, also known as the *kokerboom*, found in South Africa.

Worthwhile for those who have a bit of time in the area, especially out of flower season, is a hike or visit to **Oorlogskloof Nature Reserve** (Mon–Fri 8am–4pm), which has various hiking and mountain-bike trails and natural swimming pools. The reserve is perched on the edge of the escarpment south of Nieuwoudtville; the entrance is off the N27 near the top of the Van Rhyn's Pass, but you must contact the conservator at the information and booking office on Goedehoop Street (℡027 218 1159, after 4pm ℡027 218 1010), where you can also get maps.

Calvinia

Despite its stern name, bestowed by an early dominee, **CALVINIA** has quite an appealing setting beneath the Hantam Mountains. The town acts as a service centre for a large area, but it isn't a place you'll want to spend a lot of time in, unless you are here for the flowers in the surrounding area. Outside flower season, the **climate** can make the area fairly unwelcoming, with temperatures climbing towards 40°C during summer and dipping below freezing in winter, when snow is sometimes seen on the mountains.

The centre of Calvinia is dominated by the **Dutch Reformed church**, although it now has to vie for your attention with a cylindrical water storage tank dressed up as a huge red **postbox**, just along on Hope Street. The idea behind this was to create a tourist attraction, and however crass the concept it does turn heads; letters and postcards posted in the box will be stamped with a special postmark. Immediately opposite the postbox is a more serious attraction, **Hantam Huis** (Mon–Sat 7.30am–5pm, also Sun during flower season), the oldest building in Calvinia, which has won various awards for its restoration. Inside it's principally a tea room (see p.338) and gift shop.

The large **Calvinia Museum** (Mon–Fri 8am–1pm & 2–5pm, Sat 8am–noon; R3) is housed in a 1920s Art Deco synagogue on Church Street, a link to the sizeable Jewish community which once lived in town but has since melted away (one of its more famous sons is the Shakespearean actor Antony Sher, born in nearby Middlepost). Inside are some extensive displays on settler life, including old wooden flour mills, printing presses, huge forge bellows and no fewer than six pianos. There are also some bizarre exhibits, which include a black wedding dress and a display of *dagga* (marijuana) pipes. Predictably, a display cabinet displaying the memorabilia of the town's two **rugby Springboks** is as large as that showing San artefacts.

Practicalities

Despite its isolation, Calvinia lies on a main cross-country route. Intercape **buses** and **minibus taxis** travelling between Upington, Vanrhynsdorp and Cape Town stop at Trokkies Service Station at the western entrance to town. Tickets for the Intercape services are available in, of all places, the butcher's shop on Hope Street (☎027 341 1073). You'll find the **tourist information** office (Mon–Fri 8am–1pm & 2–5pm, Sat 8am–noon; ☎027 341 1712) in the museum, where staff can provide details of the **flower routes** in the Hantam district.

The **accommodation** with the most character here is a collection of old **town houses** operated by Hantam Huis (☎027 341 1606, Ⓦwww.calvinia.co.za; ➌). The houses have wooden floors, lace curtains and quirky antique furnishings; some have self-catering facilities, and dinner is available every night to guests. Opposite Hantam Huis, another nineteenth-century building, 35 Water St, houses *Pionierslot Guesthouse* (☎027 341 1263; ➋); the most pleasant rooms here are in the side annexe. The **camping and caravan park** (☎027 341 1011) is on the corner of Station and Hofmeyr streets, on the way through town towards the Upington road. *Hantam Huis* is the place to head for traditional **food** during the day, while *Die Blou Nartjie* restaurant (closed Sat lunch & all day Sun; ☎027 341 1263) is a rather grander affair within *Pionierslot Guesthouse*. The *Paladium* café on Stigling Street serves good **ice cream**. Remember that the word for ice cream in Afrikaans is *roomys*, which, when writ large on a shop front, can cause some confusion if you're crawling around town looking for accommodation.

Into the Great Karoo

Just beyond Calvinia the road splits, with the R27 going north through **Brandvlei** and **Kenhardt** towards Upington, while the R63 goes east through **Williston** and **Carnarvon** to Victoria West and the main N12 route between Cape Town and Johannesburg via Kimberley. Other than their sheer isolation, these **Karoo settlements** offer the odd interesting feature, such as ancient fossil remains and corbelled houses – whitewashed, beehive-like constructions, built because of the lack of timber available for roofs.

Springbok and around

SPRINGBOK is the main commercial and administrative centre of Namaqualand, and an important staging post on the N7. It lies around 550km from Cape Town, just over 100km south of the border with Namibia, and marks the junction with the **N14**, which runs east from here right across the Northern Cape through Upington and ultimately on to Johannesburg.

The Great Karoo

Strange though it may seem, the **Great Karoo**, the vast, dry, empty interior of South Africa was, some 250 million years ago, an equally vast inland lake. It was populated by tiny marine creatures and, around its fringes, dinosaur-like amphibians, some of which left footprints in the mud that have been preserved as fossils. The contrast now could hardly be greater, with slow creaking windmills struggling to bring water to the surface and the baked, brown-red earth roamed only by small herds of antelope or tough merino sheep.

Farmers here talk about the terrain in terms of hectares per sheep rather than sheep per hectare. The summer heat is fierce, the winter biting cold, the rain elusive, and the soil all but barren. Yet the Karoo has a special place for many South Africans, who take an almost perverse joy in the crisp air, the colours of the scattered *koppies* at sunset, the vastness of the pale sky, the depth of the darkness at night and the jostling galaxies of stars.

Hemmed in by hills, the main action in town is centred on a mound of granite boulders called Klipkoppie (Rocky Hill), the site of a British fort blown up by General Jan Smuts' commando during the Anglo-Boer War. A short walk up Monument Street brings you to the town's **museum** (Mon, Wed & Fri 8.30am–3.30pm; R3) in an old synagogue. A little way along from this at the back of town a gash in the hillside marks the **Blue Mine**, the first commercial copper mine in South Africa, sunk in 1852. Recent activity here has been in search of gemstones – previously ignored in the search for copper ore – for the Far East market.

Following the R355 past Springbok airport to the southwest of town for around 10km takes you to **Goegap Nature Reserve** (daily 8am–6pm; R10), an area described as "Namaqualand in miniature". The reserve incorporates the **Hester Malan Wild Flower Garden**, and offers two-day hiking trails, mountain-bike trails and 4WD routes; the visitor centre (8am–4pm; ☎027 712 1880) can provide details.

Practicalities

Flights from Cape Town arrive at Springbok's **airport** (☎027 712 2380), 5km out of town along the R355 road to Goegap Nature Reserve. Intercape **buses** stop in front of the *Springbok Lodge*, while the **minibus taxis** line up by Klipkoppie; VIP Taxis (☎027 851 8780) serve Port Nolloth, Upington and Kimberley. For **car rental** try Jowell's, Voortrekker Road (☎027 712 2061), or for 4WD Richtersveld Challenge, Jurie Kotze Road (☎027 712 1905). Springbok's **tourist information** centre (Mon–Fri 7.30am–4.15pm, open later and on Saturday during flower season; ☎027 712 2011) is in the little Anglican church beside the post office on Namakwa Street. Another source of local wisdom and decent, inexpensive **food** is the *Springbok Lodge & Restaurant* on the corner or Voortrekker and Keerom roads – a hub for travellers, information-swapping and local chitchat. You could also try *Melkboskuil*, a brightly painted converted town house on Voortrekker Street which offers a restaurant/café serving meals, drinks and coffees, and a curio shop incorporating an internet café and basic information centre (Mon–Fri 8am–5pm, Sat 8am–1pm).

Cat Nap Accommodation Beside the Shell filling station on Voortrekker Street ☎027 718 1905, ✉richtersveld.challen@kingsley.co.za. Offers rudimentary but adequate bunkhouse accommodation in the garage behind the house – there's even room for you to park your 4WD or motorbike beside your bed – and four good-quality guesthouse rooms in the main house. ❶–❷

Goegap Nature Reserve (see above). If you don't want to be in Springbok itself, the reserve has self-catering accommodation in a couple of large chalets. ❷

Mountain View Guest House 2 Overberg Ave ☎027 712 1438, ✉mountview@worldonline.co.za. Tasteful, African-themed B&B rooms in a pleasant situation on the fringe of the town, right by a short trail offering views over Springbok and the surrounding countryside. ❸

Naries Guest House 27km west of Springbok ☎027 712 2462. A homely, comfortable place to stay on a remote farm – perfect for the flower season, although you'll have to book well in advance to secure a room. ❹

Springbok Caravan Park 2km out of town along the R355 to Goegap ☎027 718 1584. The easiest place to camp near Springbok, with limited facilities which do include a swimming pool, although it lies near the noisy highway. ❶

Springbok Lodge & Restaurant Voortrekker Street ☎027 712 1321, ✉sblodge@interkom.co.za. Encompasses a variety of nearby houses, mostly painted in white and yellow, offering plain but reasonable rooms, including some self-catering apartments; make arrangements in the restaurant. ❶–❷

North to the Namibian border

Lying 8km north of Springbok on the N7 is the slightly scruffy little town of **OKIEP**, which took over from Springbok as the copper-mining centre of Namaqualand in the 1880s. Miners and engineers from the tin mines in Cornwall arrived to help establish the mines, and you can still visit both the easily identified **smokestack** and **Cornish beam pump** beside it. Visits are arranged through the *Okiep Country Hotel* (☎027 744 1000, ⓦwww.okiep.co.za; ❷–❸), under the palm trees on the main street. The hotel itself is pleasant enough, with rooms in the main building or in an annexe.

Some 40km further north, **Steinkopf** marks the junction of the N7 with the R382 to Port Nolloth and the Richtersveld National Park. An otherwise nondescript little settlement, Steinkopf is a good example of how community tourism initiatives are trying to take root in South Africa. The **Kookfontein Information Centre** (daily 8am–5pm; ☎027 721 8162, ⓦwww.south-north.co.za), 500m north of the turn-off on the N7, can provide details of the local sights, which include lookout points, a succulent nursery and Kinderlê, a mass grave of local Nama children massacred by the San two centuries ago. To make the project viable, the centre will organize a local guide to accompany you to these sights. Self-catering accommodation is also available at the centre (❶), and traditional Nama meals can be provided.

For 50km north of Steinkopf, the N7 crosses some fairly bleak Namaqualand plains, before descending through a band of rocky hills, burnt black and ochre in the heat, and into a haunting pass with the Scrabble-winning name of **Vwfmylpoort**. The road then breaks through into the green floodplain of the **Orange River**, which marks South Africa's northern border with Namibia. The gathering of buildings on the South African side of the river is called **Vioolsdrif**; there isn't much here apart from a filling station, a dusty store and a high-fenced government building.

A turning here along a dirt road traces the south bank of the Orange, 10km along which is a **campsite** right on the edge of the river, called *Fiddlers Creek* (☎027 761 8953, ⓔhome@kingsley.co.za). It acts as a base for one of the companies offering canoe trips down the Orange (see box on p.343). A further 10km downstream is a more luxurious campsite, *Peace of Paradise* (☎027 761 8968, ⓦwww.peaceofparadise.co.za), offering camping on lush green grass, the meandering river to swim or canoe in and a bar serving ice-cold beer.

If you're going on into Namibia from Vioolsdrif you have to clear immigration and customs on both sides of the bridge; the border is open twenty-four hours a day. The town on the Namibian side, **Noordoewer**, has several service stations and *Orange River Lodge* (☎09264/63 297 133; ❷), which offers simple rooms, camping, a bar and restaurant.

Springbok to Upington

After leaving the mountains around Springbok, the **N14** from Springbok to Upington is long, flat and empty, with telegraph-poles stretching off to a shimmering horizon. The scarcity of trees means that a number of the poles have been adopted as hosts for huge brown **sociable weaver nests**, a distinctive feature of these arid northern regions. There's almost no sign of human habitation for hundreds of kilometres along this road, which is one of the reasons why the tiny town of Pofadder has a reputation in South Africa for being a little way past the back of beyond. While Pofadder has little going for it, the (relatively) nearby mission station of Pella is a delightful discovery, with its towering cathedral and reed-walled coffee shop.

Pella

Roughly 150km from Springbok is a turning to **PELLA**, an intriguing settlement established around a mission station. After the turning off the N14, take the right-hand fork after 3km and follow the dirt road for another 10km towards the range of mountains which follow the course of the Orange River. Pella is a simple gathering of shacks, sandy roads and a few stone or brick buildings, in the midst of which a striking yellow **cathedral** stands in an open, dusty -white plot surrounded by stately date palm trees. The cathedral was built by a group of French missionaries in the 1880s who, lacking an experienced cathedral-builder in their group, used the *Encyclopédie des Arts et Métiers* for guidance. The surrounding attractive mission buildings are still home to a community of nuns, and the cathedral itself is in continual use. The two small **museums** among the mission buildings are of some interest; if they're not open, ask at the mission office.

On the corner where the road into Pella swings left to pass the mission you'll find the *Kultuur Koffie Kroeg*, a **coffee shop** run from a flimsy-looking reed house by a local woman and her daughters. With *kokerboom* trunks for stools and coffee brewing on an open fire in the back yard, it's a triumph of local enterprise appreciated by the few visitors who make it this far. Very basic but relatively authentic **accommodation** is available at the back of the *Koffie Kroeg* in *matjieshuis*, the traditional domed reed huts of the Nama people (☎054 971 0040; ❶). Evening meals, normally a *potjie* stew, will be rustled up if you're staying. The only real alternative is a decent **guesthouse** at Klein Pella (☎054 972 9712; ❸), by the banks of the Orange 24km away.

Pofadder

Back on the N14, and about 15km further on, the famously hot and remote town of **POFADDER** won't delay you for long, except perhaps to take a photo to prove you've been there. The name, much ridiculed by South Africans (it's Afrikaans for "puff adder", a highly venomous snake found around the country), in fact refers to a nineteenth-century bandit called Klaas Pofadder, who spent most of his time on an island in the Orange River near Upington but had a hideout here. There is a **hotel** in town, the *Pofadder*, Voortrekker Street (☎054 933 0063; ❷), and a triangle of grass at the caravan park a couple of blocks away if you want to pitch a **tent** (☎054 933 0056).

The West Coast

North from St Helena Bay, the hook of land 100km north of Cape Town, the long, lonely **west coast** of South Africa has two simple components: the cold, grey Atlantic Ocean, and the dominant sandveld vegetation, hardy but infertile. There isn't much more to the region: between the mouth of the Olifants River at Papendorp, parallel to Vanrhynsdorp, and the Orange River over 400km to the north, there is just one tarred road connecting the N7 highway to the coast, which leads to the only settlement of any significance, **Port Nolloth**.

Access to much of the coast is restricted due to **diamond-mining**, which has in many cases involved disturbance on a huge scale to the sandveld and coastal dunes. The first diamonds were discovered in Namaqualand in 1925, which confirmed that diamonds could be carried the length of the Orange, washed out into the ocean, and then dispersed by currents and the processes of longshore drift. Although initial prospecting was carried out along the course of the Orange and in the coastal dunes, the diamonds lying offshore on the sea bed are now the more eagerly chased, mostly by boats operating with huge underwater "vacuum cleaners" and divers working in often dangerous conditions.

During the flower season, the rains fall first on the coastal areas, and you can often see displays beginning about 20km inland, making the few roads down to the coast from the N7 worthwhile options for day routes. The dirt road through the **Spektakel Pass** between Springbok and Kleinzee is one of the most spectacular drives in Namaqualand, and the **Anenous Pass** on the tarred R382 between Steinkopf on the N7 and Port Nolloth is also impressive. Along this road you'll also see wandering herds of goats belonging to the pastoral **Nama** people living in the area, as well as the peaks and valleys of the Richtersveld, the mountain desert occupying the area immediately south of the Orange River.

Port Nolloth

PORT NOLLOTH is an odd but delightful place. In the hazy, windblown sunshine the horizons are never quite in focus, while the heavy fogs of the mornings shroud the town in a quiet eeriness. Populated by an eclectic mix of races and professions, including fishermen, diamond-boat-owners, fortune-seeking commercial divers, diver-seeking girls and a significant Portuguese community, Port Nolloth is a place with a whiff of mystery and excitement, and tales are thick about "IDB" (illegal diamond buying).

Attractions in town are limited, but a stroll to the **harbour** is always interesting. There's also a small **museum** (Mon–Fri 9am–5pm) on the corner of the main road and Beach Road, where you can view an adhoc collection of flotsam, jetsam, artefacts, photographs and newspaper articles about Port Nolloth, as well as find out about some of the local plant and sea life.

A **minibus** to and from Springbok is run by VIP Taxis (℡027 851 8780). The best sources of local **information** are the museum and, immediately next door, *Bedrock Lodge* (℡027 851 8865, ℮bedrock@icon.co.za; ❶–❷), also a wonderful **place to stay**, in a stylish old beach house with wooden floors, old furniture and laid-back staff

If you're looking for something to eat, the *Bedrock Tea Garden*, in the back garden of the Bedrock Lodge, is normally open during the daytime. Alternatively, the *Port Nolloth Fish Shop*, along from the Royal Pub, has a tiny restaurant attached. More formal meals can be found in cosy *Anita's Tavern*, offering plain fish, meat and pasta dishes in a garage-type building opposite the *Scotia Inn*. There's also an **espresso bar**, *Mar-e-sol*, on the main road.

North of Port Nolloth

Diamond activity is also much in evidence if you drive **north from Port Nolloth** towards the diamond town of **ALEXANDER BAY**, the most westerly point of South Africa, at the mouth of the Orange River. The town is run by the mining company Alexkor and has recently opened to visitors, who can take a diamond mine tour (Thurs only) or walking trails around town and to the mouth of the river, noted for its birdlife. Local guides can also show you to a **lichen "forest"** which boasts 29 different species, or accompany you on a **desert walk** through the barren-looking landscape which surrounds the town. For details, contact the **tourist information** centre (Mon–Fri 8.30am–4.30pm; ℡027 831 1330, ℗www.diamondcoast.co.za).

The road is en route to the Richtersveld National Park, and for those looking for a base either side of their visit to the park there's a very pleasant **place to stay** at *Brandkaros*, 27km from Alexander Bay (℡027 831 1856; ❷), a farm with chalets and a **campsite** 400m from the river.

Richtersveld National Park

The area of northwestern Namaqualand known as the **Richtersveld** covers an area roughly bounded by the Orange River to the north, the N7 to the east, the R382 to Port Nolloth to the south and the Atlantic Ocean on its western side. The **Richtersveld National Park**, created in 1991, covers 1600 square kilometres of the most dramatic parts of the region, tucked into an omega-shaped loop in the Orange. The landscape is fierce and rugged; names such as Hellskloof, Skeleton Gorge, Devil's Tooth and Gorgon's Head indicate the austerity of the inhospitable brown mountainscape, tempered only by a broad range of hardy succulents, mighty rock formations, the magnificence of the light cast at dawn and dusk, and the glittering canopy of stars at night. There's little fauna in the park other than lizards and klipspringers, although along the Orange you'll find surprisingly rich birdlife. The rainfall in parts of the park is as low as 50mm per annum, making this the only true desert – and mountain desert at that – in South Africa. In summer the daytime heat can be unbearable – recorded at over 50°C – while on winter nights temperatures drop below freezing.

The wider Richtersveld area outside the park is largely inhabited by Nama people living simple lives herding sheep and goats. As part of a community development programme, some of the settlements, including **Eksteenfontein** and **Rooiberg**, provide rudimentary accommodation available for travellers, but as with the rest of the area you're only likely to venture this far in a 4WD vehicle.

Practicalities

Facilities at Richtersveld are extremely limited – this is not the place for a casual visit. Normal (saloon) cars are not allowed inside the park; the only way to explore is in a **4WD** or a pick-up with a high enough clearance to handle the sandy river beds and rough mountain passes between the designated campsites. On arrival, visitors must report to the park headquarters, **Sendelingsdrift** (℡027 831 1506; daily 8am–4pm; R30), 94km from Alexander Bay. The most

---

Canoeing trips on the Orange River

One way to enjoy the majesty of the mountain-desert landscape of the Richtersveld is to take a **canoe down the Orange River**. This is not, as sometimes portrayed, whitewater rafting – by the time it reaches northern Namaqualand the river is broad and easy-paced, so the few rapids you encounter tend to rouse you from slumber rather than quicken the pulse. More exciting grade 3 and 4 rapids are found on another stretch of the Orange, in the Onseepkans Gorge closer to Augrabies Falls (see p.323). On the Richtersveld trip, popular with South African families and groups, the highlights of the trip are the dramatic rock formations and varied birdlife – but above all relaxation is the key. Trips from Noordoewer or nearby last two to six days, with camps set up by the riverbank en route, from around R250 a day. For more details, contact Felix Unite – pronounced "Unit" – (℡021 683 6433, ⊚www.felixunite.co.za), River Rafters (℡021 712 5094, ⊚www.riverrafters.co.za), both based in Cape Town, or Bushwhacked (℡027 761 8953 or 082 509 4552), based at *Fiddler's Creek* campsite on the south bank of the river itself.

popular time to visit is during the cool winter months; avoid coming here in the extreme summer heat. No driving is allowed at night, and the only fuel available is at the park headquarters. It's recommended that you travel in groups of two vehicles.

Accommodation is in three **chalets** at Sendelingsdrift (❷) or at the designated **campsites** around the park, which have no shelter or facilities. Water is scarce, and only very limited stores are available at the park headquarters. It's possible to **hike** with a guide in the park between April and September along designated trails of one, two or three nights' duration. For **bookings** and information contact the National Parks Board (℡012 343 1991, ⓦwww.parkssa.co.za).

Possibly the best way of seeing Richtersveld is as part of a guided **4WD tour**. The most experienced operation is Richtersveld Challenge (℡027 712 1905, ⒺRichtersveld.challen@kingsley.co.za), based in Springbok. Expeditions of varying lengths into the park and surrounding areas can include hiking or canoeing on the Orange if requested. You can rent 4WD vehicles from the same company, although prices aren't much cheaper than the full guided tour, travelling in a party of less than two vehicles isn't allowed in the park, and you have to make sure you are fully equipped. Also operating out of Springbok is Southern Cross Adventures (℡027 712 2624, ⓦwww.scadventures.co.za), who organize 4WD expeditions into Namibia as well as Richtersveld National Park and the surrounding areas of Namaqualand.

Travel details

Trains

Kimberley to: Bloemfontein (daily except Sat; 2hr 50min); Cape Town (1 daily; 16hr 55min); Durban (Tues; 19hr 45min); Johannesburg (2 daily; 8hr); Pretoria (2 daily; 10hr).

Buses

Calvinia to: Cape Town (4 weekly; 5hr 45min); Upington (4 weekly; 4hr 45min).
Kimberley to: Cape Town (1 daily; 11hr 40min); Johannesburg (1 daily; 5hr 15min); Knysna (Thurs & Sun; 11hr 5min); Pretoria (1 daily; 6hr 15min).
Kuruman to: Johannesburg (4 weekly; 6hr); Upington (4 weekly; 3hr).
Springbok to: Cape Town (4 weekly; 6hr 30min); Pretoria (4 weekly; 7hr).
Upington to: Calvinia (4 weekly; 4hr 45min); Cape Town (4 weekly; 10hr 30min); Johannesburg (4 weekly; 9hr); Pretoria (4 weekly; 10hr).

Flights

Kimberley to: Cape Town (2 daily Mon–Fri, 1 daily Sun; 2hr 10min); Johannesburg (1 daily; 1hr 15min).
Springbok to: Cape Town (1 daily Mon–Fri; 1hr 20min).
Upington to: Cape Town (1 daily; 1hr 50min); Johannesburg (1 daily; 1hr 50min).

The Eastern Cape

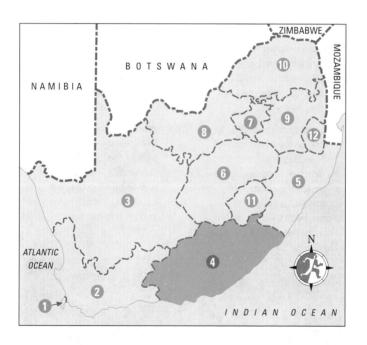

CHAPTER 4

Highlights

✳ **Port Elizabeth township tour** Several guides run very accessible tours into the African areas of the province's largest city. See p.354

✳ **Addo Elephant National Park** The best game reserve in the malaria-free southern half of the country. See p.360

✳ **Grahamstown Festival** Africa's largest arts festival wakes up this pretty colonial university town. See p.374

✳ **Karoo farmstays** Stay at one of the farms around Nieu Bethesda and Graaff-Reinet, and experience the sharp light and panoramic landscape of the Karoo semi-desert that sweeps across South Africa's interior. See p.388

✳ **Fort Hare art gallery** A superb collection of black South African art buried in the remote university that educated many of the country's leaders, including Nelson Mandela. See p.405

✳ **Wild Coast family hotels** Stay at one of the terrific full-board hotels occupying isolated spots along ravishing subtropical coastline. See p.417

✳ **Amadiba Horse Trail** Excursions led by members of the local Pondo community – the best way to travel in unspoilt areas where there is no vehicle access. See p.420

The Eastern Cape

Sandwiched between the Western Cape and KwaZulu-Natal, South Africa's two most popular coastal provinces, the **Eastern Cape** tends to be bypassed by visitors – and for all the wrong reasons. The relative neglect it has suffered as a tourist destination and at the hands of the government is precisely where its charm lies. You can still find traditional African villages, and the region's one thousand kilometres of undeveloped **coastline** alone justify a visit, sweeping back inland in immense undulations of vegetated dunefields. For anyone wanting to get off the beaten track, the province is, in fact, one of the most rewarding regions in South Africa.

Port Elizabeth is the province's commercial centre and transport hub, principally used to start or end a trip along the Garden Route. **Jeffrey's Bay**, 75km to the west, has a fabled reputation among surfers for its perfect waves. East of the city, the **R72** coastal road, a great rolling journey, provides easy access to a series of unassuming resorts, all gloriously sited on euphorbia-clad hillsides at the mouths of lazy rivers. Around an hour's drive inland are some of the province's most significant game reserves, the only places in the southern half of the country providing serious game viewing: **Addo Elephant Park**, where sightings of elephants are virtually guaranteed; and some private reserves including the seriously upmarket **Shamwari**. These are the only game reserves in South Africa that are malaria-free throughout the year. The hinterland to the north takes in areas appropriated by English immigrants shipped out in the 1820s as ballast for a new British colony. Here, **Grahamstown**, a pretty university town, glories in its twin roles as the spiritual home of English-speaking South Africa and host to Africa's biggest arts festival. Close by, the giraffe, antelope and hippo country of the **Great Fish River Reserve Complex** comprises stony hills vegetated by monumental candelabra-like succulents and river courses lined with thorn trees.

The northwest is dominated by the sparse beauty of the **Karoo**, the thorny, semi-desert stretching across much of central South Africa. The rugged **Mountain Zebra National Park**, 200km north of Port Elizabeth, is a terrific place to watch herbivorous game in a stirring landscape of flat-topped mountains and arid plains stretching for hundreds of kilometres. A short step to the west, **Graaff-Reinet** is the quintessential eighteenth-century Cape Dutch Karoo town, with its serene whitewashed streetscape.

The eastern part of the province, largely the former Transkei, is by far the least developed, with rural Xhosa villages predominating. **East London**, the province's only other centre of any size, sits on the cusp of the former "white" South Africa and the African "homelands", and also serves well as a springboard for heading north into the central region, where the principal interest derives from political and cultural connections. **Steve Biko** was born here, and you can visit his grave in **King William's Town**. To the west is **Alice**, though it's less well known than its university, **Fort Hare**, which educated many contemporary African leaders, including Nelson Mandela. The only established resorts in this section are in the **Amatola Mountains**, where indigenous forests and mossy coolness provide relief from the dry scrublands below. Tucked

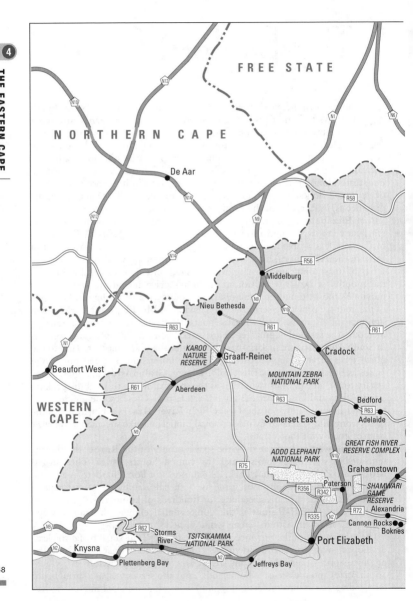

into the northeastern corner of the province, the **Drakensberg range**, more commonly associated with KwaZulu-Natal, makes a steep ascent out of the Karoo and offers trout-fishing, skiing in winter and ancient San rock art. The focus of the area is the remote, lovely village of **Rhodes**, a long journey down a rough road, which rewards you with absolute tranquillity and exceptional views.

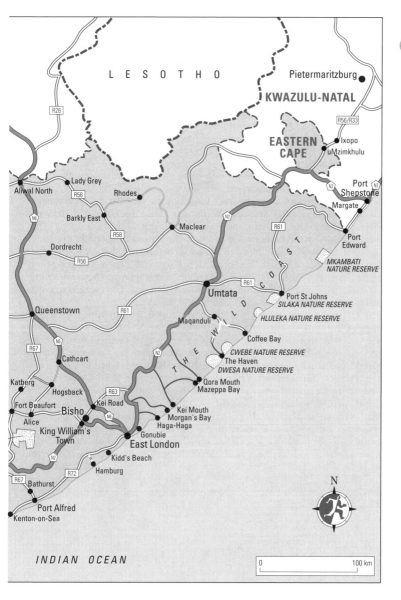

Further east, the **Wild Coast region** remains one of the least developed and most exciting regions in the country. It's also the poorest part of the poorest province, a fact reflecting its historic role as a dumping ground for black South Africans. Despite this, the region is blessed with fabulously beautiful sub-tropical coast. From here, all the way to the KwaZulu-Natal border, dirt roads trundle down to the coast from the N2 to dozens of remote and indolent hillside resorts, of which **Port St Johns** is the biggest and best known. West of Port St Johns, the **Wild Coast Hotel Meander**, an organized walking trail, takes in a deserted stretch of cliffs and sands with convenient stops at small family resort hotels. Along the coast to the east of town, you can explore beaches and rural villages on horseback as part of the community-run **Amadiba Trail**, which starts near the KwaZulu-Natal border. In the rugged goat-chewed landscape inland, Xhosa-speakers live in mud-and-tin homesteads, scraping a living herding stock and growing crops. Most visitors pass as quickly as possible through **Umtata**, the ugly former capital of the Transkei – but if you're following in the footsteps of Nelson Mandela, the **Nelson Mandela Museum** in the centre of Umtata and **Qunu**, his birthplace west of the town, are obvious ports of call.

Some history

The Eastern Cape was carved up into black and white territories in a more consolidated way than anywhere else in the country. The stark contrasts between **wealth and poverty** were forged in the nineteenth century when the **British** drew the Cape colonial frontier along the Great Fish River, a thousand kilometres east of Cape Town, and fought over half a dozen campaigns (known as the Frontier Wars) to keep the **Xhosa** at bay on its east bank. In the 1820s, the British shipped in thousands of settlers to bolster white numbers and reinforce the line. West of the Kei River you'll encounter fenced-off white farms, pretty historic towns and industrial development. Across the river, the scourges of imperialism and apartheid have left little but overgrazed communal lands dotted with traditional huts and skinny cattle.

Even for a country where everything is suffused with politics, the Eastern Cape's identity is excessively **political**. South Africa's black trade unions have deep roots in its soil, which also produced many anti-apartheid African leaders, including former president **Nelson Mandela**, his successor **Thabo Mbeki**, and Black Consciousness leader **Steve Biko**, who died in 1977 at the hands of Port Elizabeth security police. The Transkei or **Wild Coast** region, wedged between the Kei and KwaZulu-Natal, was the testing ground for grand apartheid when it became the prototype in 1963 for the *bantustan* system of racial segregation. In 1976 the South African government gave it notional "independence", under the puppet leadership of the Matanzima brothers, in the hope that several million Xhosa-speaking South Africans, who were surplus to industry's needs, could be dumped in the territory and thereby become foreigners in "white South Africa". When the Transkei was reincorporated into South Africa in 1994, it became part of the new Eastern Cape province, which is now struggling for economic survival under the weight of its apartheid-era legacy.

Port Elizabeth and the western region

A city of flyovers and sprawling townships, **Port Elizabeth** is the industrial centre of the Eastern Cape, where African shanty dwellers scrape a living on the dusty fringes of well-tended middle-class suburbs. In 1820, it was the arrival point for four thousand British settlers, who doubled the English-speaking population of South Africa. Today, their descendants risk the hellish national roads from Gauteng every Christmas to speed down to the "Friendly City" and holiday along the institutionalized beachfront, with its burger bars and performing dolphins.

The main reason most people wash up here is to start or finish a tour of the **Garden Route** – Port Elizabeth is the largest city in the province and the prime transport nexus, with an airport, good road links to the rest of the country and car rental facilities. The port's industrial feel is mitigated by some outstanding city beaches, and should you end up killing time here (and you could certainly do worse), you'll find diversion in beautiful **coastal walks** a few kilometres from town and in the small **historical centre**. There are also a couple of excellent township tours, which offer valuable insight into apartheid and the new South Africa and are a welcome contrast to the Garden Route's beach focus. With time in hand, **Addo Elephant Park** is a recommended day's excursion out of the city.

To the east of Port Elizabeth, a handful of **resorts** are found along the **R72 East London coast road**, where the roaring surf meets enormously wide sandy beaches, backed by mountainous dunes. The inland route to East London deviates away from the coast to pass through **Grahamstown**, a handsome university town, worth at least a night (more if you're interested in English settler history and the frontier conflicts with the Xhosa). Nearby, pretty settler villages trace the spread of the **1820 Settlers** into the interior.

A couple of hundred kilometres north from Port Elizabeth, an area of flat-topped hills and treeless plains opens out to extend across a third of South Africa. Its name, the **Karoo**, means "hard and dry" in the tongue of the Khoikhoi pastoralists, the region's original inhabitants, who were exterminated by Dutch frontiersmen. The oldest and best known of the settlements here is the picture-postcard town of **Graaff–Reinet**, a solid fixture on bus tours. Just a few kilometres away is the awesome **Valley of Desolation**, and the village of **Nieu Bethesda**, best known for its eccentric Owl House museum. Nearly as pretty as Graaff-Reinet, though not as architecturally rich, the town of **Cradock**, to its east, has the added attractions of mineral baths and the rugged **Mountain Zebra National Park**. Some of the best places to stay in the *platteland*, or interior, are on sheep farms or in historically listed guesthouses.

Port Elizabeth

PORT ELIZABETH, commonly known as **PE**, is not a place to visit if you're looking for cosmopolitan urban culture or beautiful buildings. The smokestacks along the N2 bear testimony to the fact that the Eastern Cape's

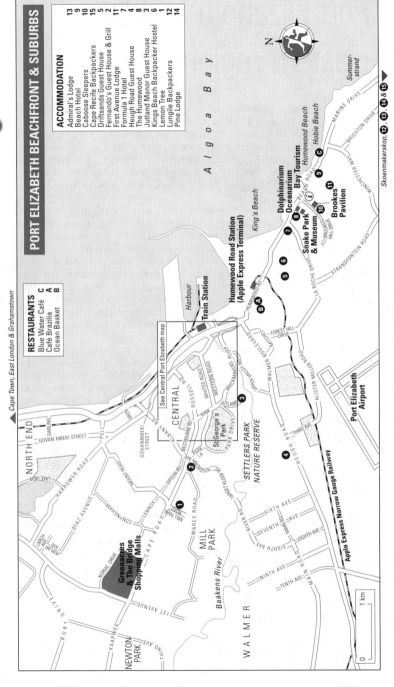

PORT ELIZABETH BEACHFRONT & SUBURBS

ACCOMMODATION

Admiral's Lodge	13
Beach Hotel	9
Caboose Sleepers	10
Cape Recife Backpackers	15
Driftsands Guest House	5
Fernando's Guest House & Grill	2
First Avenue Lodge	11
Formula 1 Hotel	4
Heugh Road Guest House	7
The Humewood	8
Jutland Manor Guest House	3
Kings Beach Backpacker Hostel	6
Lemon Tree	1
Lungile Backpackers	12
Pine Lodge	14

RESTAURANTS

Blue Water Café	C
Café Brazilia	A
Ocean Basket	B

largest centre has thrived on heavy industry and cheap African labour, which accounts for it's deep-rooted trade unionism and strong tradition of African nationalism. So it may come as a surprise that this has long been a popular holiday destination for white Gauteng families – but then the town beachfront, stretching for several kilometres along Humewood Road, has some of the nicest, safest and cleanest **city beaches** in the country, thoroughly geared up with waterslides, performing dolphins and snakes to keep the kids occupied.

As a city, PE is pretty functional. There's enough reason to linger for a couple of days, however, and the city has some terrific accommodation and good restaurants in a relatively crime-free environment. Although the town has been ravaged by industrialization and thoughtless modernization, one or two buildings do stand out in an otherwise featureless **city centre**, and a couple of classically pretty rows of Victorian terraces still remain in the suburb of **Central**. There are also some excellent **tours** around PE and into the townships.

For practical purposes, PE is one of the easiest entry points into South Africa. Its small **airport** lies just ten minutes from the compact and manageable city centre, which is itself the **transport hub** of the Eastern Cape, well served by flights, trains, buses and car rental companies. It's a useful springboard, not just for exploring the Eastern Cape, but for launching out into the rest of South Africa.

Arrival and information

Port Elizabeth airport (☏041 581 2984 or 041 507 7319) is conveniently situated on the edge of Walmer suburb, 4km south from the city centre. From here, the reasonably priced Supercab Shuttle **minibus** (☏041 457 5590) will get you into town, stopping at all the main hotels, and making unscheduled stops on request. A metered **taxi** from the airport will cost you twice as much.

Trains arrive at the centrally located station (☏041 507 1400), from where you need to catch a bus or taxi to your accommodation. The **Baz Bus** (☏021 439 2323, ☏021 439 2343, ⓦ www.bazbus.com) will drop you off at any central location or accommodation. Arriving by **intercity bus**, alight at Greenacres shopping mall in Newton Park suburb, 3km from the centre, or continue to the terminals of each of the lines (far more convenient if you're going to stay in the suburb of Central): Translux (☏041 392 1333) at the train station; Greyhound (☏041 363 4555) nearby in Fleming Street; and Intercape (☏041 586 0055) at 107 Govan Mbeki Ave. Of the **regional bus services**, Leopard Express (☏041 484 1057) runs a weekend service to and from Grahamstown (1 daily Fri–Sun), stopping at PE airport.

Information

The extremely helpful **Tourism Port Elizabeth** (Mon–Fri 8am–4.30pm, Sat & Sun 9.30am–3.30pm; ☏041 585 8884, ☏041 585 2564, ⓦ www.ibhayi.com), has an office in the Donkin Lighthouse Building (itself a National Monument with a good view from the top) on the Donkin Reserve in Belmont Terrace, Central suburb. It also has a satellite office, **Bay Tourism** (☏041 585 5427), on the corner of Brookes Hill Drive and Beach Road. Both offices offer a drop-in accommodation booking service for R40.

If you're spending any length of time in the city, **Braby's Map Book** of Port Elizabeth is invaluable. It's often out of stock at CNA newsagents, so you may need to go to the suburbs (see p.358) and try Fogarty's Bookshop or Exclusive Books at Walmer Park Shopping Centre. The Automobile Association also has a good selection of maps available from 14 Albany Rd (☏041 585 6716).

City transport and tours

If you're staying in Central, exploring the city **on foot** is a realistic possibility – try the self-guided **Heritage Walk** (map available at Tourism Port Elizabeth). However, for any serious exploration of PE, or for getting to and from the beachfront, **renting a car** is your best option, as the city's transit system leaves much to be desired (see "Listings", p.360). **Buses** operated by the municipal service Algoa Bus Company (⊤041 451 4241) are inexpensive but infrequent, running from the Market Square bus depot to the suburbs, the beaches and Greenacres shopping mall. The fifteen-seater Sunshine Passenger Service (⊤042 293 1911 or 082 956 2687) offers a 24-hour door-to-door **shuttle bus** from PE to Jeffrey's Bay, Cape St Francis and Addo (note that it charges for a minimum of two passengers). PE's **minibus taxis** run from town to the beachfront on a regular basis, but are the least recommended way to travel. **Metered taxis** are reliable but more expensive (see "Listings", p.360). They don't have ranks so you'll need to phone for service; if you're going to the airport or the bus or train stations, it's advisable to book ahead.

Tours

The best way to see Port Elizabeth is on one of the several excellent **bus tours** run by operators whose perspective on the culture and history of the city does not begin and end with the 1820 English Settlers. The following are highly recommended, offering a range of day- and night-trips around the city and the townships, longer jaunts to game parks, rock-painting excursions and eco-trails. For an insight into African Port Elizabeth, Gqebera Tours (⊤041 581 7085 or 082 970 4037) goes to Walmer Township; they also run golf tours to greens between Port Elizabeth and Cape Town. Calabash Tours (⊤041 585 6162 or 083 303 7553, ⊛www.axxess.web.za/calabash) offers a well-researched, well-presented "Real City Tour". Fundani Cultural Tours (⊤041 454 2064/66 or 082 964 6563, ⊛www.satours.co.za) includes an historic battlefields excursion, while Pembury Tours (⊤041 581 2581, ⊛www.pembury-tours.com) runs some wonderful big-game getaways to local reserves and explorer-type trips further afield.

Accommodation

The obvious, if most expensive, **place to stay** is at the **beachfront**, where hotels with a curious 1930s fusion of Art Deco and colonial style vie with more functional apartment blocks. Beachfront B&Bs have boomed over the last couple of years, so there's a great deal of choice. Cheaper, but away from the sea, the well-preserved Victorian suburb of **Central** makes a pleasant alternative, with B&B accommodation, a few backpacker lodges, and plenty of restaurants. There are a couple of excellent places in the less convenient (but greener) outlying suburbs of **Mill Park** and **Walmer**, plus a chance to stay with a family in an **African township** (see box below).

During the December and January peak holiday period, the beachfront becomes the focus for most of the city's action, while February and March are much quieter yet still offer perfect beach weather. Note that PE is subject to **strong winds**; when these sweep across town the beachfront becomes a sandblaster, and you'd be better off booking into Central for the night – Algoa Leasing (⊤ & ℱ041 363 0404 or ⊤083 394 2307) is a central **booking agency** for the area.

If you fancy a slice of **African township life**, Fundani Lodge (⊤041 454 2064/6 or 082 964 6563 ⊛www.satours.co.za; ❷) offers a unique and very reasonably priced opportunity to enjoy football matches, traditional ceremonies and good African cooking, while staying with a family in the New Brighton, Zwide or Motherwell townships.

Beachfront

Admiral's Lodge 47 Admiralty Way, Summerstrand ☏041 583 1894 or 083 455 2072, ⓔadmiralslodge@mweb.co.za. Spacious and stylish rooms at a good B&B, close to the sea but at the far end of Summerstrand, so you'll need a car. There's a braai area, communal lounge and pool, and airport transfers are available. ❷

Beach Hotel Marine Drive, Humewood ☏ & ⓕ041 583 2161, ⓔreservation@pehotels.co.za. Once the epitome of 1930s-style elegance, this hotel still retains some of that glamour with lots of plush and varnish, and an occasional piano player. Across the road from popular Hobie Beach, and sited at the centre of the beachside action, the hotel has a great patio bar overlooking the sea, offering snacks, cocktails and cold beer and *The Bell*, a very decent a la carte restaurant. Recent renovations have included a sundeck and pool. Ask about the weekend specials. Breakfast extra. ❹

Caboose Sleepers Brookes Hill Drive, Humewood ☏041 586 0088, ⓕ041 586 0087. Attractive, inexpensive place to stay a step away from PE's youthful action, in a wooden lodge that is very popular with tourists and South Africans. Most rooms are tiny, but can sleep up to three people, and you might just manage to swing a cat in the larger two-bed suite, which is a bit more expensive and comes with a TV. The cramped sleepers are offset by a roomy, stylish lounge, sun deck and good self-catering facilities. ❶

Driftsands Guest House 2 Marshall Rd, Humewood ☏041 586 0459, ⓕ041 585 6513, ⓦwww.driftsands.co.za. Recommended cosy and friendly B&B, close to the beach. All rooms are ensuite, and some have private lounges and sea views. Secure off-street parking, and airport transfers are available. ❷

First Avenue Lodge 3 First Ave, Summerstrand ☏041 583 5173, ⓕ041 583 5176. Fourteen ensuite rooms close to the beach with their own entrances, offered on a B&B or self-catering basis, in a popular and pleasant establishment with a pool and entertainment area. A favourite with foreign visitors and South Africans. Airport transfers are available. ❸

Formula 1 Hotel On the corner of Beach Road and Laroche Drive ☏041 585 6380, ⓕ041 585 6383, ⓔbetteri@zipisp.co.za. Budget rooms with baths in a clean but rather impersonal hotel. Perfectly adequate as a last resort, and well placed to hit the hot-spots. ❶

The Humewood 33 Beach Rd, Humewood ☏041 585 8961, ⓕ041 585 1740, ⓦwww.sunsetcoast.co.za/humewood. A family hotel that has resisted modernization but offers really good service. Lovely rooms, a good bar and a nice sun deck. Airport transfers. ❸

King's Beach Backpacker Hostel 41 Windermere Rd, Humewood ☏041 585 8113, ⓕ041 585 1693, ⓦwww.backpack.co.za. Spotless, well-established hostel, a block away from the beach, with outside bar and braai area. Although principally for self-catering, it lays on tea, coffee, bread and jams in the morning. There's also a helpful travel desk which can book township, game park and other tours. Camping, dorms and doubles. ❶

Lungile Backpackers 12 La Roche Drive, Summerstrand ☏041 582 2042, ⓕ041 456 2108, ⓔlungile@netactive.co.za. Large and popular beachfront hostel where you can stay indoors and party, or step out the front door into the heart of PE's beachfront nightlife strip. Perched on a hill, it has a large lawn to relax on, sea views, a pool table, bar and swimming pool. Self-catering only. Camping, dorms and doubles. ❶

Pine Lodge Resorts & Cape Recife Backpackers off Marine Drive, Humewood ☏041 583 4004, ⓕ041 583 3839, ⓦwww.pinelodge.co.za. Right on the beach at the Cape Recife Nature Reserve, near the wonderful historic lighthouse. Offers log cabins sleeping up to six people and backpacker dorms with a nice kitchen. Owls, mongooses and antelope make their appearance, and there's a swimming pool, games room, a trampoline, popular bar and restaurant. ❶–❷

Central

Calabash Lodge 8 Dollery St ☏041 585 6162 or 083 303 7553, ⓦwww.axxess.web.za/calabash. Cool simplicity, with cotton sheets and a touch of the ethnic in a stylish, well-located house, offering bargain budget rooms with or without bath. This beats the rest of the town's budget accommodation hands down; it can also provide airport transfers. ❷

Jikeleza Lodge 44 Cuyler St ☏041 586 3721, ⓕ041 585 6686, ⓔwinteam@hinet.co.za. Port Elizabeth's best backpacker lodge, with dorms, doubles and a family room. Friendly, and a good source of local information. ❶

Jutland Manor Guest House Jutland Crescent ☏041 585 6064, ⓦwww.jutlandmanor.mrinfo.co.za.

New, upmarket B&B in one of PE's remarkable old mansions, on a cliff-top setting with an awesome view. The price includes continental breakfast; dinners on request, room service, airport transfers and trips to Addo and Shamwari. Highly recommended. ❸

Millbrook House 2 Havelock Square, Havelock Street ☎ 041 585 3080, ℻ 041 582 3774 ⓦ www.atyourleisure.com/site/millbrookhouse. Charming B&B in a Victorian house along Central's prettiest street, offering a chance to appreciate some British colonial architecture. Plunge pool, braai area and airport transfers. ❸

Port Elizabeth Backpackers 7 Prospect Hill, Central ☎ 041 586 0697 or 041 585 2032, ⓦ welcome.to/pebakpak. Conveniently close to the intercity bus stops, with dorms sleeping six or eight as well as doubles, this quiet hostel tends to attract slightly older travellers. Delicious quality breakfasts and evening meals available for an extra charge. Offers an extensive travel information and booking service. ❶

The suburbs

Fernando's Guest House & Grill 102 Cape Rd, Mill Park ☎ 041 373 2823, ℻ 041 374 5228, ⓦ www.wheretostay.co.za/find/fernandos.htm. A popular string of Victorian houses, with the office at the above address, offering either self-catering or full-board. There's a restaurant on the premises. The drawback is that they're on Cape Road, one the city's busiest traffic arteries. ❸

Heugh Road Guest House 55 Heugh Rd, Walmer ☎ 041 581 1007, ℻ 041 581 4468. Luxurious accommodation close to the airport; quite pricey, and breakfast is extra, but the guesthouse is tranquil and rather pretty. Rooms are built around a courtyard, each with its own private entrance and bath. ❹

Lemon Tree 14 Mill Park Rd, Mill Park ☎ 041 373 4103, ℮ lemon@intekom.co.za. Lovely B&B with choice of English and continental breakfasts included in the price. Consistently (and deservedly) wins accommodation awards, but somewhat off the beaten track. ❸

The City

Port Elizabeth's **city centre** is marred by a network of freeways that cuts a swath across the south of town, blocking off the city from the harbour. The city's white population retreated to the suburbs some time ago, taking the big department stores with them, and leaving the centre to African traders and township shoppers, who are slowly resuscitating its commercial spirit.

City Hall and Central

The city's main street, which runs parallel to the freeway as it sweeps into town, has been renamed **Govan Mbeki Avenue** in honour of the veteran activist (father of Thabo, South Africa's president), who did time with Nelson Mandela and died in 2001. This is one of the few pockets of PE that retains its historic texture, with lovely old office buildings remaining intact save for their gaudy shop fronts. African traders dealing a pretty standard line in crochet tat and leather goods line up along the pavements giving the precinct a livelier feel than the dreary suburban malls. Unfortunately, it's not very safe after dark.

Down Govan Mbeki, the symbolic heart of town is the **City Hall**, standing in **Market Square**, a large empty space surrounded by some striking mid-Victorian buildings, adjacent to the train and bus stations on the edge of the harbour. But the dejection of the quarter, under the grimy shadow of a flyover, conspires against it ever pumping any real life into the district. Nevertheless, the **City Library**, on the corner of Whites Road and Govan Mbeki Avenue, is a real attraction, especially the second floor, with its beautiful stained-glass dome and windows and magical little balconies of bookshelves.

Heading west up hilly **Donkin Street**, past its exceptionally well-preserved Victorian street frontage, you'll come upon a curious stone pyramid commemorating the city's namesake, **Elizabeth Donkin**. Elizabeth was the young wife of the Cape's acting governor in 1820, Sir Rufane Donkin; she died of fever in India in 1818.

West from here through **Central**, you cross Lawrence Street, which has some

CENTRAL PORT ELIZABETH

ACCOMMODATION
Calabash Lodge	1
Global Backpackers	2
Jikeleza Lodge	5
Millbrook House	3
Port Elizabeth Backpackers	4

RESTAURANTS
Aviemore	D
Natti's Thai Kitchen	F
Ranch House of Steaks	C
Rome	B
Royal Delhi	A
Zorba's	E

4

THE EASTERN CAPE | Port Elizabeth

browsable antiques and collectables shops. Along Parliament Street (the continuation of Donkin) the succeeding two blocks as far as Rink Street form a packed strip of secondhand book shops, a fun retro-furniture store and several first-rate restaurants. South into Rink Street, you reach St George's Park and the **King George VI Art Gallery**, 1 Park Drive (Mon–Fri 8.30am–5pm, Sat 9am–4.30pm, Sun 2–4.30pm; free), which has a collection of contemporary local work, visiting exhibitions and a small but decent gallery shop selling postcards and local arts and crafts. **St George's Park** itself is a huge circular green, dominated by the St George's Cricket Ground. It contains a public swimming pool, and the tiny, beautiful iron and glass **Pearson Conservatory**, an elegantly bulbous Victorian hothouse. The components of the conservatory were shipped out from Scotland and erected in Port Elizabeth in 1882. Across Park Drive, at the junction of Rink and Cape roads, stands the **Horse Memorial**, commemorating the gallant horses who fell during the Anglo-Boer South African War. Below a larger-than-life British soldier kneeling to feed a horse, the quintessentially English inscription reads: "The greatness of a nation lies not so much in the number of its people or the extent of its territory but in the extent and justice of its compassion."

The beachfront and around

Just southeast of the harbour, on Humewood Road, **Humewood Road station** is the starting point for the **Apple Express**, a beautifully restored steam train that usually runs on Sundays and occasional Saturdays during holidays (leaving at 9.30am) to Thornhill Village and other destinations, stopping on Van Staden's River Bridge, the highest narrow-gauge railway bridge in the world. After a leisurely lunch at Thornhill, the train trundles back to Humewood, arriving at 4pm. Tickets (R60) can be booked through Spoornet (ⓣ041 507 2333) or Tourism Port Elizabeth (see p.353).

Diving around PE

Although the Indian Ocean around PE isn't tropically clear and warm, **diving** here is good, especially for soft corals. For dive courses, try the five-star Pro Dive, at the Red Windmill, Beach Road, Summerstrand (℡041 583 5316, ℻041 583 5434, ⓦwww.prodive.co.za), which is highly competitive at around R700 (excluding gear rental) for a three- to five-day course leading to an internationally recognized PADI certificate. Pro Dive also offers caged dives with sharks at the Oceanarium, and its shop at Walmer Park Mall sells diving gear

PE's wonderful **beaches** are its main attraction. The protection provided by Algoa Bay makes them safe for swimming and clean enough to make **beach-combing** a pleasure. The beachfront strip, divided from the harbour by a large wall, starts about 2km south of the city centre at **King's Beach**, a built-up curve of strand with a children's paddling pool. The best place to swim and sunbathe, it only gets really crowded at Christmas and on New Year's Day.

To its east lies **Humewood Beach**, and across the road from that is a complex housing the **Port Elizabeth Museum & Snake Park** (daily 9am–1pm & 2–4.30pm; R10), which has a surprisingly good display on Xhosa culture. The **Oceanarium** (daily 9am–1pm & 2–4.30pm; dolphin shows 11am & 3pm; R17) has performing seals and dolphins, who bring huge pleasure to hordes of excited children during the December holidays, and an equal measure of displeasure to environmentalists. Next door, **Brookes Pavilion** is a complex of restaurants, pubs and clubs with great views. Close by, and not much to chose between the two, **Dolphin's Leap** offers much the same experience. Beyond that, to the south, **Hobie Beach** and **Summerstrand** are great for walking and sunbathing. Summerstrand's spanking new **Boardwalk Casino Complex** has some pleasing shops, including a smashing deli, a cinema complex and some reasonable eating places with outside tables dotted around an artificial lake.

Marine Drive continues down the coast as far as the suburb of **Schoenmakerskop**, along impressive coastline that alternates between rocky shores and sandy beaches. From Schoenmakerskop you can walk the eight-kilometre **Sacramento Trail**, a shoreline path that leads to the huge-duned **Sardinia Bay**, the wildest and most dramatic stretch of coast in the area. To get there by road, turn right at the Schoenmakerskop intersection and follow the road until it signals left to Sardinia Bay.

The suburbs

PE's **suburbs** offer little to draw you away from the beachfront, unless you're a shopaholic, in which case you should make a beeline for **Newton Park**, 5km west of the centre and home to **Greenacres** and **The Bridge**, vast shopping malls to which all the city-centre department stores have relocated en masse. So strong is their status as the consumerist heart of Port Elizabeth that bus companies use Newton Park as an alternative terminus for travellers wishing to avoid the city centre.

Two kilometres southwest of the centre, near the airport, tranquil and leafy **Walmer** suburb sits complacently between two irreconcilable landscapes. To its left, on the city side, is **Settlers' Park Nature Reserve**, with entrances on Park Drive and Third Avenue, which follows the Baakens River Valley from Valley Road, south of Main Street, to Newton Park, and has 54 square kilometres of indigenous growth and impressive cliffs. To its right lies **Walmer Township**, a dilapidated jumble of houses and shacks, divided from the mansions of Walmer's millionaires by a single strip of wasteland. Despite some small post-apartheid improvements, conditions here are generally appalling. The area is home to many of the domestic workers serving the suburban surrounds, and it's not unusual to find township cattle grazing on the wide grassy pavements which line Walmer's wealthy streets. A highly worthwhile **tour** (see p.354) can take you into the area.

Eating, drinking and nightlife

Port Elizabeth has no great culinary reputation, but there are some decent **eating places** to suit most budgets, especially along the beachfront, and in Central, where there tends to be a greater proportion of multiracial options. Apart from the hotel bars mentioned in the accommodation section, there are a few other passable joints for a drink, and a couple of **nightclubs**.

Restaurants

Aviemore 12 Whitlock St, Central ☎041 585 1125. Highly recommended (and expensive) restaurant in the centre, serving regional specialities, including springbok salad and seafood melange. Mon–Sat 6.30–10.30pm.

Blue Water Café Hobie Beach ☎041 583 4110. Great sea views, good pasta and light snacks at this pleasant eating place. Open daily.

Café Brazilia Humerail Centre, Humewood. Portuguese-inspired menu at a beachfront coffee shop and eating place with nice decor. Friendly service and a lovely view. Daily from 10am.

Le Med 66a Parliament St, Central ☎041 585 8711. Medium to expensive eating and a lively atmosphere. Choose from fish dishes and unusual specialities, such as *tagine*, a Middle Eastern stew cooked in an earthenware pot. Booking essential.

Natti's Thai Kitchen 21 Clyde St, Central ☎041 585 4301. Booking is essential at this excellent restaurant specializing in authentic hot'n'spicy Thai cuisine magicked up by Natti. Lovely, laid-back ambience. Evenings only.

Ocean Basket Humewood Shopping Centre. Pleasant, busy fish place with a stunning harbour view. Part of a national chain of family-friendly

eating places. No reservations. Closed Sun evenings.

Ranch House of Steaks Russell and Rose streets, Central ☎041 585 9684. A popular family-oriented dinner and lunchtime spot for juicy slabs of beef, seafood and Greek-style offerings. Voted the best steakhouse in the province in the 2000 Steakhouse of the Year Contest. Despite the carnivorous emphasis, vegetarians are well catered for. Closed for lunch on Sat & Sun.

Rome 63 Campbell St, off Russell Road, Central ☎041 586 2731. Mouthwatering pizza made in a wood-burning oven plus lots of specials. Decent prices and a pleasant, buzzy vibe. Open Mon–Sun for lunch and dinner.

Royal Delhi 10 Burgess St ☎041 373 8216. Pleasant eating place and bar, with lamb, chicken, oxtail and prawn curries on the menu, plus some outstanding Indian starters. Closed Sat lunch & Sun.

Zorba's 68 Parliament St, Central ☎041 585 2553. Varied, mid-priced menu, including tiger fish, stuffed squid and kebabs. The attached bar stays open well after the restaurant has closed. Mon–Sat lunch & dinner.

Bars and nightlife

There's some lively local **music** in town, with talented garage and hip-hop bands and a plethora of DJs playing at bars, clubs and tapas joints, plus a decent jazz club. Your best bet of catching something live is visiting the **bars** listed below, most of which stay open late if there are enough customers. The hub of the pub and club universe is Brookes Pavilion. Information on techno raves is generally found on flyers at main music venues and shops.

The daily *Eastern Province Herald* lists PE's Opera House's occasional **concerts** and the odd **cabaret** at other venues, particularly Centrestage at the Boardwalk (☎041 581 2245). **Cinema** includes a good selection of current and art films showing at the Kine Park Cinema, 3 Rink St, Central (☎041 582 3311), and the usual Hollywood fare at the Nu Metro, Walmer Park Shopping Centre, Walmer (☎041 367 1102), Ster Kinekor (☎041 363 0577) in The Bridge shopping complex and Cinema Starz (☎041 583 2000) at the Boardwalk Casino Complex – check the *Herald* for programme details.

Bourbon Street Brookes Pavilion, Marine Drive ☎041 586 1078. Raucous nightclub specializing in 1980s music, foam parties and the like. Open Wed, Fri & Sat.

Lizard Lounge 1st floor, Conning House, 72 Westbourne Rd ☎083 722 9157. Simply the best music venue. An eclectic mix of hip-hop, rock, *kwaito* and cool samba, both live and spun; laid-back, with a great cross-cultural vibe. Closed Mon.

Razzmatazz 4th floor, Central House, Grace Street, Central ☎041 585 9012 or 082 576 1811. PE's greatest jazz venue, suitably dark and smoky. Hosts some of SA's best musicians, as well as sessions with young locals. Sat only.

Tapas Al Sol and **Easy Street** Brookes Pavilion, Marine Drive ☎041 586 2159. Adjacent venues sharing a great deck with wonderful views. *Tapas* is a restaurant/bar specializing in live SA rock music, and *Easy Street* has plentiful pool tables and a bar.

Tarantino's 76 Parliament St ☎041 585 0321. Popular licensed late-night chill-out café with lots of delicious snacks and delectable cakes, hot chocolates and coffees. Daily 8am till late.

Viper Room 123 Parliament St ☎041 585 1121. Groove lounge and nightclub with guest and resident DJs, fireshows and cocktails, and extensive food menu. Wed & Fri.

Listings

Airlines SAA ☎041 507 1111.

Car rental Companies at the airport are: Avis ☎041 501 7200, toll-free ☎0800 02 1111; Budget ☎041 581 4242; Hertz ☎041 581 6550, toll-free ☎0800 60 0136; Imperial ☎041 581 1268, toll-free ☎0800 13 1000; and Tempest ☎041 581 1256.

Consulates British Consulate, First Bowring House, Ring Road, Greenacres (Mon–Fri 9am–12.30pm; ☎041 363 8841, ☏041 363 8842).

Emergencies Ambulance ☎10177; Fire ☎585 1555; Police ☎10111.

Hospitals St George's (private), Park Drive, Settlers Park ☎041 392 6111; Provincial (state),

Gibson Road, Central ☎041 392 3911.

Laundries Automat, 6a Parliament St, Central; Rub & Tub, Rink House, 70d Clyde St, Central.

Pharmacy Mount Road Medicine Depot, 13 Lower Mount Rd ☎041 484 3838. Daily until 10.30pm.

Post office Brookes Pavilion, Humewood. Mon–Fri 9am–3.30pm & Sat 8.30–11am.

Taxis Good firms include Eagle ☎041 582 4439; Hurters Taxis ☎041 585 5500; and Mr Cab ☎041 374 5856.

Travel agents Atkinsons, 50a Pickering St, Newton Park ☎041 365 2344, ☏041 365 2345; Pentravel, Walmer Park Shopping Centre, Walmer ☎041 368 6151, ☏041 368 6162.

Addo Elephant Park and the private game reserves

Port Elizabeth is the nearest large centre to **Addo Elephant Park**, the most significant game reserve in the southern half of the country. Also within easy striking distance are several other small private game reserves. These include **Shamwari**, a luxury establishment boasting the "Big Five" (elephant, lion, leopard, buffalo and rhino). Cheaper and less ambitious alternatives in the vicinity are **Schotia** and **Amakhala**. At present, none is a substitute for serious game viewing in KwaZulu-Natal or the Kruger National Park, but plans are underway to make Addo one of South Africa's three largest game reserves. The big attraction of these reserves is that – unlike the country's major game parks – the entire Eastern Cape region is totally **malaria free** throughout the year. They also tag conveniently onto the end (or start) of a tour along the Garden Route (see p.244).

Addo Elephant National Park

Addo Elephant National Park (daily 7am–7pm; R12), 73km northeast of Port Elizabeth, should be your first choice for a day-trip from Port Elizabeth.

It also makes for a rewarding and peaceful overnight stop. The Addo bush is thick, dry and prickly, making it difficult sometimes to spot any of the 200–300 elephants; when you do, though, it's often thrillingly close up. The best strategy is to ask at the park's reception where the elephants have last been seen, and also to head for the elevated viewing platform to scan the bush for large grey backs quietly moving about. **Night drives** with a National Parks ranger, which cost R60, can be booked at reception if you're staying in the park (see below). Other animals to watch out for include **eland**, **kudu**, **buffalo** and **red hartebeest**.

A good break from waiting at water holes or scouring the bush is to walk the six-kilometre, circular **Spekboom Trail**, taking you through the indigenous spekboom *veld* which predominates in the park. The walking area is fenced off from the elephants, and gives you a real feel of the landscape.

In the late 1990s, Addo began acquiring land with the aim of becoming the third-largest conservation area in South Africa – the **Greater Addo National Park**. It will also be the most diverse, with six of South Africa's seven biomes within its boundaries, and will take in the Alexandria coastal dunefield, two small islands, and a large tract of marine reserve. In addition to its famous **elephants**, the park has other mega-herbivores such as **rhinos** and **hippos**, large predators including **lions** and **cheetahs**, the largest colony of African (jackass) **penguins** in the world, 400 species of birds, and an impressive array of indigenous plant species including cycads. Apart from harbouring the Big Five, visitors to the reserve can also see **dolphins** throughout the year and **southern right whales** during the South African winter.

Practicalities

To **get to Addo Park** from Port Elizabeth, take the N2 towards Grahamstown for 15km, branching off at the Addo signpost onto the R355 through Addo village. The network of roads within the park is untarred, but is in good condition. **Maps** of the park are available at reception and indicate the location of **picnic** and braai sites. A good **restaurant** (6am–8pm) offers three meals a day, while the shop is well-stocked with food and drink.

Addo's main restcamp provides comfortable **national park accommodation**, a range of thatched, fully equipped self-catering cottages (❸), less expensive bungalows with communal kitchens (❷) and budget forest huts (❶). The park's rapid expansion means the list of accommodation choices is growing, so enquire on booking. **Reservations** are essential, and can be made through SA National Park's central 24-hour booking service (☏012 343 1991 ℱ041 343 0905, ⊛www.parks-sa.co.za) or, less than 72 hours in advance, directly with Addo (☏042 233 0556, ℱ041 233 0196).

Outside the park, several private B&Bs and guesthouses are springing up around Addo, especially among the citrus groves of the Sunday's River Valley. These include:

The Elephant House 5km north of Addo village on the R335 ☏ & ℱ042 233 2462 or ☏083 799 5671, ⊛www.elephanthouse.co.za. One of the Eastern Cape's top stays is a stunning thatch-roofed lodge on a stud farm just minutes from Addo Elephant Park, filled with Persian rugs and antique furniture. The five bedrooms, two of which are in garden cottages, open onto a lawned courtyard. Candlelit dinners available. The hosts can arrange tours into the surrounding areas including game reserves. ❹

Happy Lands 11km from Addo on the R335 ☏ & ℱ042 234 0422, ℮nitataylersmith@hotmail.com. Secluded B&B cottage with a large garden and a river bank ideal for bird-watching. Hostess Nita's knowledge of local history is a bonus, and she's happy to arrange trips into the national park. Horse-riding and swimming also available. ❸

Valleyview 300m outside Addo village ☏ & ℱ042 233 0349, ⊛www.valleyview.co.za. Situated on a former farm, a pair of comfortable cottages that sleep two, with the option of additional sleeper couches. Swimming pool, braai area and splendid river frontage. ❸

Woodall About 1km from the park entrance ☎ & ℗ 042 233 1028, ⓦ www.woodall-addo.co.za. Luxury B&B noted for its hospitality on a working citrus farm, with a swimming pool, a garden cottage and rooms inside the beautiful homestead. A lovely sundowner deck overlooks a small dam full of swans and other birds. Three-course dinners are available for R90. ❹

The private game reserves

If the national park is full, or you want to see lions (absent at Addo), you may decide to stay at one of the private game reserves – especially if you just want to be pampered. For luxury, **Shamwari** is unbeatable, but you pay well over the odds for the privilege. **Amakhala** offers the "colonial" experience of staying on an African farm and seeing game, while **Schotia**, with its free-ranging lions, provides exciting night drives.

Shamwari Game Reserve

Shamwari Game Reserve, 65km north of Port Elizabeth on the N2 (☎ 042 203 1111, ℗ 042 235 1224, ⓦ www.shamwari.com) is cultivating an image as a jetsetter destination. While it certainly excels at delivering luxury, it's questionable whether this relatively small tract really delivers the kind of wilderness experience you'll find in the game reserves in the northern half of the country.

Accommodation is the colonial-style Long Lee Manor and a number of attractive lodges, dotted around the reserve. Prices start at a hefty R2600 per person at Long Lee, and rise to R3100 at Lobengula Lodge with all the service and luxury one would expect at those prices. If that seems a bit steep, you can opt for the **Shamwari Day Experience**, which starts at around R600 per person. The day starts with a visit to the Born Free Animal Rescue and Education Centre; after lunch, you'll be taken to Khaya Lendaba, where Xhosa traditions are enacted and explained. This is followed by a game drive accompanied by rangers, where you can look out for the big five from the back of an open 4WD vehicle.

Amakhala Game Reserve

Two kilometres north of the Shamwari turn-off from the N2, **Amakhala Game Reserve** (☎ 042 235 1608 or 082 966 5696 ⓦ www.amakhala.com /home.html) is the brainchild of several farming families. Removing the fences between their farms, they have stocked the area with a variety of game, and either built or used existing farm buildings, including farmhouses, for guest accommodation.

Giraffe, zebra, and several species of antelope stroll around the reserve, as well as black-backed jackals, bat-eared foxes, dassies, otters, vervet monkeys, fish eagles, guinea fowl, kingfishers and buzzards. The absence of predators means you aren't confined to game drives, and paths make hiking among the aloes and other beautiful indigenous flora a great way to get close to the landscape.

The Bushman's River meanders through the reserve and there are plans to provide boat rides. For an additional charge, most of the hosts offer **game drives** on the property in open 4WD vehicles. If you want to see elephants you'll have to head out to Addo, and for lions you must visit the other nearby private reserves.

Accommodation

Although Amakhala is a consolidated game reserve, each of the members runs their own guesthouse, lodge or B&B individually. You'll find a variety of accommodation, all of it very comfortable, some in historic farmhouses and some decorated in a more conventional safari style. Book through central reservations, who will give you directions on how to reach the farms. (see p.361).

Carnarvon Dale A two-bedroom farmhouse built in 1857 on Amakhala's northern boundary. Guests have access to the home farm, and the opportunity for game and bird watching walks along the Bushman's River. Dinner is available on request. ❹

Eliweni Lodge Thatched lodge with an airy deck perched high above a treed *kloof*, offering panoramic views into a valley where the looping Bushman's River cuts through dense bush. The lodge sleeps five people. ❹

Leeuwenbosch Country House Elegant and supremely comfortable late Victorian farmhouse, with a classic wraparound verandah. Spacious bedrooms and a fully equipped kitchen. Dinner

available on request. ❹

Reed Valley Cottage Quaint private cottage on the western boundary of the reserve, with two large bedrooms in a stunning ethnic-cool style, each with a separate entrance. The cottage is on the same property as the Reed Valley Crocodile Farm, which offers a guided tour. Dinner and breakfast are optional extras. ❹

Woodbury Lodge Set in a spectacular ravine above the river valley, two tastefully furnished two-bedroom stone chalets under thatch with wooden decks, served by a separate dining lodge. Can be taken on a self-catering, B&B or full-board basis. ❹

Schotia Private Game Reserve

Schotia Private Game Reserve (☎042 235 1436, ℻042 235 1368, ⓔschotia @intekom.co.za) is the smallest of the private reserves. It compensates by running thrilling night outings to see its three resident **lions** as well as other denizens of the night, including zebra and twelve species of antelope. The night excursions are full of shining eyes caught by powerful lamps, and are followed by a meal cooked on an open fire in a thatched *lapa*. **Accommodation** is in a two-person cottage (❷), a large lodge sleeping eight (❹) and a wilderness camp (❷) deep in the bush. Schotia provides a pick-up service for visitors from a depot 2km up the N10 to Cradock after it turns off the N2.

West of Port Elizabeth to Storms River

Among the few reasons to turn off the N2 as it stretches for 186km from Port Elizabeth to Storms River are the resorts of **Jeffrey's Bay** and **St Francis Bay**. Of the two, Jeffreys is the more famous, at least if you happen to be a surfer; more than anywhere in the country, it has dedicated itself to having fun and making money from its pumping surf. Although St Francis Bay has some fine surfing breaks, its tranquil atmosphere and beauty have made it a popular spot with upcountry South Africans. For travellers heading along the coast, it's a good place to break a journey.

Jeffrey's Bay (J Bay)

Some 75km west of Port Elizabeth, off the N2, **J Bay**, as it's known locally, is said by some to be one of the top three surfing spots in the world. Architecturally, the town is grim, the product of a series of recent building booms. Mansions dot the town's hill, but there's little grace and beauty here. In the holiday seasons it's jammed, as thousands of visitors throng the beaches, surfing shops and fast-food outlets, giving the place a real seaside resort feel.

For **surfing aficionados**, however, these are trifling details, given the possibility of the perfect wave (see box p.365). If you've come to surf, head for the break at **Super Tubes**, east of the main bathing beach, which produces an impressive and consistent swirling tube of white water, attracting surfers from all over the world throughout the year. Riding inside the vortex of a wave is considered the ultimate experience by surf buffs, but should only be attempted if you're an expert. Other key spots are at Kitchen Windows, Magna Tubes, the Point and Albatross. Surfing gear, including wet-suits, can be rented from the multitude of surfing shops along Da Gama Road, while Derek at South Coast Surf School (☎082 576 4259) will show you the finer points of both surfing and sand-boarding. **Dolphins** regularly surf the waves here, and **whales** can sometimes be seen between June and October. The main **bathing areas** are Main Beach (in town), and Kabeljous-on-Sea (a few kilometres north), with some wonderful seashells to be found between Main and Surfer's Point. **Rock fishing** is very popular, as is **scuba diving**; for the latter, contact Baydive (☎042 293 2444 or 082 659 2541). If you want a bit more than surf and sun, Paul and Sharon at A1 Eco-Tours (☎042 296 1845) will show you some sites rich in **Khoisan history** and can take you up the dazzling Gamtoos River Valley, noted for its bird life. Some 10km out of town, Papiesfontein Farm (☎082 574 9396) offers both guided and free-range **horse-riding** along 6km of beautiful beach.

Practicalities

Getting to Jeffrey's Bay from PE without a car is straightforward. The **Baz Bus** stops at J Bay on its daily trek in either direction between Cape Town and Port Elizabeth. The Sunshine Passenger Service (☎042 293 2221 or 082 956 2687) will take you here from PE (R60 per person, minimum two passengers). The **tourist information** office (Mon–Fri 8.30am–5pm, Sat 9am–noon; ☎042 293 2588, ℱ042 293 2227, ⓦwww.jeffreysbaytourism.com is on the corner of Da Gama and Dromedaris roads. Booking is essential in December, January, Easter and July.

Accommodation

The tourist information office publishes a wide-ranging list of **places to stay** With half a dozen hostels to choose from, JBay is definitely backpacker territory – but if communal living isn't your scene, you're still in luck, as there are numerous good and inexpensive B&Bs and some self-catering places in town. There's also camping right near the beach at the municipal caravan parks, *Kabbeljous* (☎ & ℱ042 29 33330) and *Jeffrey's Bay* (☎042 200 2214) in Da Gama Road, but the price is barely cheaper than a backpacker dorm.

A1 Knyaston 23 Chestnut Ave ☎042 296 1845, ℱ042 293 2650. Self-contained flat or bedrooms in the main house with great views, mega-breakfasts and a warm ambience. Hosts Paul and Sharon run A1 Eco-Tours; they know the Jeffreys Bay area well and can suggest places to visit. ❷

Island Vibe 10 Dageraad St ☎ & ℱ042 293 1625, ℮ivibe@lantic.co.za. Backpacker lodge built on a dune with a wooden walkway onto the beach. Offers camping, dorms, doubles, with spectacular views; also a lounge, bar, pool table and self-catering facilities. Breakfasts are available. ❶

Jeffrey's Bay Backpackers 12 Jeffrey St ☎ & ℱ042 293 1379, ℮backpack@netactive.co.za. Two blocks away from the beach, this functional establishment has been going for some time and offers guests the use of bar, lounge and swimming pool as well as board rental. No breakfast is served but there are good self-catering facilities. Dorms and doubles. ❶

Lazee Bay 25 Mimosa St ☎ & ℱ042 296 2090, ⓦwww.lantic.co.za/~lazeebay. Light and airy B&B with panoramic views and lots of marine murals indoors. An informal place, it has a spacious communal lounge, comfortable kitchen available to guests, and airy ethnic decor. There's also a swimming pool and sundeck. ❷

Mount Joy Guest House 31 Mimosa St ☎ & ℱ042 296 1932. B&B with five beautiful en-suite bedrooms. The fabulous view demands you take breakfast on the terrace. Access is up a narrow precipitous pathway. ❸

Sandkasteel 3 Diaz St ☎042 293 1585 or 082 657 4564. An unusually designed self-catering and B&B establishment on the beach, with loft sleeping quarters, nice kitchens and a braai area in each flat. Potentially raucous during the holiday season, but off-season it's a quiet, quirky and inexpensive place to stay. ❷

Surfing etiquette

Jeffrey's Bay's legendary reputation with international surfers was built on the Sixties cult movie *Endless Summer*, featuring surfer Bruce Brown trotting the globe in search of perpetual sunshine and the perfect wave. Although J Bay is by no means the best place to surf in South Africa – there are hundreds of good breaks up and down the coast between Cape Town and Durban – it is probably the place most single-mindedly devoted to the sport.

If you come here to surf, paddle-ski or boogie-board (aka "shark biscuit"), you should take care to observe the fundamentals of **surfing etiquette**. On arriving at a new spot, always hang around the margins sussing out the scene, never intruding on someone else's patch and always remembering that you are a visitor. Surfers are highly territorial and there are clearly defined rules governing who takes precedence in the water. These often come down to proficiency. In the surfing pecking order, the rising stars are "grommets" or "surf rats", 16- or 17-year-olds who challenge the "old bullets" – the 20- or 30-somethings whom they consider to be over the hill. Half-crazed rodeo-riders of the swell, who take on seven-metre waves, are known as "hell men", while at the other end of the spectrum you'll find "doormats", "spongers" and "tea bags", who take to the sea on boogie- or knee-boards, and receive only marginally less contempt from surfers than paddle-skiers, who are termed "egg whippers" or "deckchairs". If you observe these conventions, the chances are you'll find South African surfers exceptionally friendly, ready to talk and happy to offer tips. And beginners will find it easy to locate someone willing to get them started for a small fee.

Eating

For **eating**, J Bay has the usual collection of pizza, burger and steak bars, and lots of takeaway joints. The resort's top restaurant is *The Walskipper*, on the beach in Marina Martinique Harbour; here you can eat luxurious and expensive seafood lunches and dinners in an alfresco setting, with lovely homemade bread, pates and jams, while your main courses are cooked on an outside fire. Other local favourites include: *Le Grotto* on Da Gama Road, famous for its cheap 1kg steaks; *Breakers*, a popular eating place on Diaz Road specializing in fish and game and offering a good wine list; and *The Sunflower*, 20 Da Gama Rd, with nice decor and breakfasts and interesting pastas and salads for lunch.

St Francis Bay

Endless Summer may have put J Bay on the surfing map, but the break named after Bruce Brown (Bruce's Beauties) is, in fact, in **St Francis Bay**. Surfing is not the only reason to visit this beautiful part of the coast, which runs from the Kromme River to Cape St Francis. The resort has none of the brassy swagger of J Bay; instead, fifty percent of the town is built around an attractive artificial network of canals leading to the river. Houses in this part of town are white-washed and thatched, and there are some fine B&Bs among them. Further towards Cape St Francis, the houses are Mediterranean-influenced, as is the new Port St Francis harbour, both holiday resort and haven for the fleet of *chokka* (squid) boats. The town is ringed by a series of small nature reserves, offering beautiful **walks**, some of which are trails through the fynbos. During the holiday season the town bustles with thousands of upcountry South Africans who own holiday homes here, but at other times, peace and tranquillity reign. The commanding **lighthouse**, now a National Monument, was once described as the loneliest in Africa.

Arrival and information

St Francis Bay is easily reached **by car** along the N2, turning south at Humansdorp and continuing for 15km to the coast. The **Sunshine Bus** travels here on request. The **tourist information** bureau (Mon–Fri 8.30am–4.30pm & Sat 9am–12.30pm, ☎042 294 0076, ⍟www.stfrancistourism.com) at the Village Centre can help find accommodation.

Accommodation

Accommodation at Port St Francis ranges from modern chic at the resorts along the harbour to thatched rural cosiness on the canals.

Cape St Francis Resort ☎042 298 0054, ⍟www.capestfrancis.co.za. B&B and self-catering thatched cottages, with a pub and a restaurant on site. This pleasant resort also offers excursions, such as a 4WD visit to archeological sights in the Shark Point Nature Reserve, a ten-kilometre cruise up the Jurassic Kromme River, a canal trip, and a sunset cruise around the bay. ❷

Port St Francis Resort ☎042 294 1223, ⍟www .portstfrancis.co.za. A Mediterranean-style complex at the harbour with self-catering apartments. Some of these face the ocean, with panoramic views of the bay in front and the marina to the rear; beautifully decorated, with stunning patios, some have

their own plunge pools. From R200 per unit.

Seal Point Backpackers ☎042 298 00284, ⍟www.capestfrancis.co.za On Da Gama Road, about 20m from the beach. A good bet if you're on a budget; the double rooms have a self-catering kitchen unit attached, as well as a TV and duvets; there's also a restaurant and bar, *The Full Stop*. ❶

Waterways ☎042 294 0282. Of the many B&Bs under thatch, *Waterways* is recommended for its friendliness as well as its situation at the confluence of the canals and river, with a beautiful beach nearby. There are two en-suite bedrooms with their own outdoor living areas and spectacular views; cruises can also be arranged. ❸

Eating

For **eating**, there are a few pubs, coffee shops and restaurants dotted around the village and marina; calamari has to be pick of the menu. On the quayside, *The Chokka Block* and *Quayside Café* are recommended.

Port Elizabeth to Port Alfred

One of South Africa's most undeveloped stretches of **coast**, with wide beaches and exhilarating surf, stretches east from **Port Elizabeth** for a sandy 150km to **Port Alfred**. The sea temperature here is several degrees higher than around Cape Town (though not as warm as KwaZulu-Natal, and never tropically clear), and the beaches are a walker's paradise, with shells, birds and rock pools. The only problem is the summer **wind**, which often affects the whole Eastern Cape coast – particularly in the afternoon, so set out as early as you can. The weather is at its calmest from April to September, and while it's not hot enough to tan, you'll certainly be comfortable picnicking or walking along the beaches. April to July is the optimum season for scuba diving, with the water at its clearest.

The beaches can be deserted out of season, apart from the occasional growl of **4WD vehicles** embossing their heavy tread into the sands. The question of vehicles on beaches bitterly divides South Africans, and vehicles are banned on some parts of the coast.

The resort of **Kenton-on-Sea** is one of the most arresting spots along this coast, with two rivers dotted with boats, rocky coves and fabulous beaches for swimming and walking. Most of the houses are holiday homes, unoccupied much of the year, belonging to white South Africans, but there is a fair bit of **accommodation** – good B&Bs in beautiful locations, at much lower prices than along the sometimes overrated Garden Route.

Alexandria State Forest and Diaz Cross

A fifty-kilometre tract of Eastern Cape beachfront is protected by the **Alexandria State Forest** and can be walked on the circular two-day **Alexandria Hiking Trail**, one of South Africa's finest **coastal hikes**, which winds through indigenous forest and crosses a desert landscape of great hulking sand dunes, all the way to the ocean.

The 35-kilometre trail starts at the Alexandria Forestry Station, 8km from the R72. The signposted turn-off is on the right, just before you reach Alexandria, 86km from Port Elizabeth. There's an **overnight hut** (❶) at the station, for use at the beginning or end of the trail, and another at Woody Cape, both with mattresses and drinking water, but no cooking facilities. You'll need to drive to the starting point, as there's no public transport. The hike is quite tough going, especially along the windy dunes – the markers in the sand can get blown over, obscuring the route – but in fine weather the isolated beaches are magnificent. You'll need to **book** one of the limited places on the trail through the Woody Cape Nature Reserve (PO Box 50, Alexandria 6185; Mon–Fri 8am–1pm & 2–4pm; ☎046 653 0601, ⓕ046 653 0302; R25) especially at weekends, when the trail tends to be full. The **forest** itself, with yellowwood trees trailing lichen, is accessible on a seven-kilometre day-walk from the forestry station, with a nice picnic and braai place.

ALEXANDRIA, a pineapple- and chicory-growing centre with a strip of shops and an imposing Dutch Reformed Church, is the closest town to the reserve. If you want a more comfortable night than the Alexandria hut can provide, *Heritage Lodge*, along the main street (☎046 653 0024, ⓕ046 653 0735, ⓔgordons@imaginet.co.za; ❷), is one of the few **places to stay**, and although its reasonably priced rooms are nothing special, the **restaurant** (closed Sun evenings) has a good reputation for lunches and dinners. Better still, you can stay at the recommended *Quins Sculpture Garden and B&B* at 5 Suid St (☎046 653 0121 or 082 770 8000, ⓔquin@intekom.co.za; ❷). Animal sculptures peep through the foliage and in a section of the main house there's a lovely, two-bedroomed apartment linked by a sitting room.

From Alexandria, a good dirt road takes you 18km through the State Forest and farmland to the coast at Boknes. This tiny resort is the start of an hour-long beach walk eastwards to the monument of **Diaz Cross**, commemorating the Portuguese adventurer and explorer, Bartholomeu Diaz, who rounded the South African coast in 1487 in search of a profitable new sea route between Europe and the East. The first European to make recorded contact with the Khoikhoi, Diaz was also the first to kill one of them. The cross, on a rocky promontory, marks the spot where he was forced by his crew to turn back to Cape Town, rather than face the journey eastwards.

Accommodation along this stretch of coast is in short supply: the only place to stay is at **CANNON ROCKS**, 2km west of Boknes and 135km east of Port Elizabeth, where you'll find the thoroughly family-oriented *Cannon Rocks Holiday Resort* (☎046 654 0043, ⓕ046 654 0095). You can pitch a tent (❶) and rent a two-bedroom chalet (❷) or luxury flat (❸). The resort is protected from the wind by trees, and is a five-minute walk to the beach. Although there's a small shop, you're best off buying **supplies** from Alexandria, linked to Cannon Rocks by a tarred road. *Sandon B&B*, 187 Alice Rd(☎046 654 0217 or 082 5944699, ⓔtindal@intekom.co.za; ❷), a large, modern house right on the beach, has two en-suite bedrooms inside the house, and a separate flat with two double bedrooms where you can also self-cater.

Kenton-on-Sea

Some 26km west of Alexandria, along two river valleys, lies the resort of **KENTON-ON-SEA**, perfect for a short beach holiday. A modest conglomeration of holiday houses served by a few shops and places to eat, Kenton is a good choice if you want to be somewhere undemanding and very beautiful. There's little to do here except enjoy the surf, sandy beaches and dunes, wallow in big shallow tidal pools, and swim in the rivers. The area doesn't see many foreign visitors and South Africans pack in principally during the school holidays, so the rest of the year, especially during the week, you're assured of a quiet time. Note that while **swimming** in the rivers is great, you should avoid getting close to the entrance to the sea, as strong riptides are frequent. Swimming off the sea beaches is fine.

If you want to spend time on Bushman's River, you can rent small **motor boats** from Kenton Marina (from R60 per hour; ☎ & ℻046 648 1223), well signposted off the R72, 300m up the R343 to Grahamstown. The marina also rents out two-person beaver **canoes**, for paddling the 15km upriver from here that constitute the **Bushman's River Trail**. The trip passes through countryside lined with cycads and euphorbias, filled with chattering birdlife. It takes between two and five hours, depending on your fitness, the direction of the tide, and weather conditions. At the end of the trail, there's a **hut** (book at the marina; ❶) that sleeps sixteen in bunks. Mattresses, cooking utensils, braai facilities and outdoor cold showers are provided, but you must bring your own sleeping bag and food as there are no shops or any other facilities here. It tends to be full at weekends, but at other times booking should be easy.

Practicalities

Kenton is a very small place, but facilities include a couple of restaurants, mini-supermarkets, a bank and cash machine, post office and a filling station – all along the main street, Kenton Road. However, many people do their shopping fifteen minutes' drive away in Port Alfred, which has much better-stocked supermarkets. The **tourist information** bureau, signposted on the main road, is run by the very able Erica McNulty (☎046 648 2418 or 082 772 5069). Erica also runs **Kenton township tours**, which include lunch in someone's home, and she is also the co-ordinator of an interesting sustainable community project, Masithandane, run by Xhosa women in Grahamstown.

Accommodation

Accommodation consists of reasonably priced self-catering cottages and B&Bs, most of which provide breakfast as an extra. The nicest places to stay are close to the river.

Berribridge B&B 28 Oxford St ☎046 648 1048. In a fine location, five minutes' walk from the Kariega River, this family home has three doubles sharing two bathrooms, set apart from the main house. ❷

Burke's Nest 38 Van der Stel Rd ☎046 648 1894 or 082 577 2142. Garden cottage and a flatlet connected to a family home away from the beach, a short amble from the Kariega River. ❶

Bushman's River Caravan Park 2 Loerie Rd, ☎046 648 1227. A few minutes' drive west of Kenton – follow the signs from the turn-off to Bushman's from the R72. You can camp at this

well-kept caravan park right in the centre of Bushman's River Mouth, a resort that's effectively an extension of Kenton. ❶

Lime Tree House 96 Westbourne Rd ☎082 568 0432, ✉jann@imaginet.co.za. Four tastefully furnished bedrooms where you can self-cater or have breakfast in a house overlooking the Bushman's River, with a courtyard, fountain, and large garden. ❷

Woodlands Country House and Tea Garden 2km from the centre along the R343 to Grahamstown ☎ & ℻046 648 2867 or ☎082 808 5976, ✉woodlands@compuscan.co.za. Twelve acres of garden and bush down to the

Bushman's River, with little cottages dotted along pathways cut through the vegetation. Birdlife thrives here and it's a very relaxing place to have teas or meals at the small restaurant. ②

Eating and drinking

The best-located **eating and drinking** place in Kenton is *Homewoods*, 1 Eastbourne Rd, a restaurant and pub at the mouth of the Kariega River. It has two decks and grand views, but is not noted either for service or food; the run-of-the-mill fare includes steaks, fish and burgers. In the village centre, *The Local*, a pub and grill joint, is the only place for reliable evening meals (closed Sunday evenings), while during the day you can usually get coffee, teas and cake at *Allies Coffee Shop*. Outside town, 2km along the R67 Grahamstown Road, *Woodlands Tea Garden* is the best place for teas and light lunches, serving good cheesecake, apple pie, quiches and fish and chips; you can eat outside in a beautiful garden setting. A kilometre further on along the same road, the child-friendly *Stanley's* (Mon–Sun for lunch and dinner, Sat dinner only; ☏046 648 1332) offers well-cooked English-style roasts and veggies, fish, steaks and ribs in an unpretentious farmhouse; you can eat on the deck, while taking in views of the Kariega River. Booking is essential, especially during holiday season and on Sundays. Upstream along the Bushman's River is *The Sandbar Restaurant* (☏046 648 2192), a modest pontoon that doubles as a pub, serving hamburgers, chips and calamari. The views of the steep cliffs, thick with euphorbia, amply compensate for any lack of flair. To get there, head out on the R67, taking the Riversbend turn-off west of Bushman's River Mouth.

Port Alfred

Of all the settlements between Port Elizabeth and East London, only **PORT ALFRED**, midway between the two, can make any claims to a town life outside the holiday season, when for a few weeks the small centre is transformed into a hectic bustle of cars and people. For the rest of the year, the town's population is swelled every weekend by wet-suited surfers and partying students from Rhodes University in Grahamstown, less than an hour away. Besides beach walking and swimming, it's an excellent place to do some **canoeing**: the Kowie Canoe Trail is an overnight jaunt up the Kowie River, or you can paddle for a day up the Lynedoch River to the east of Port Alfred.

Although it started life as a port for settler enterprises in the 1840s, Port Alfred was never quite suitable (the river kept silting up) and it quickly faded away into a resort. No large ships navigate the Kowie River, but plenty of **fishing boats** brave its turbulent mouth every day, watched by fascinated bystanders on the end of the pier. Nicknamed "Kowie" by locals, after the river, Port Alfred was named in honour of the second son of Queen Victoria, although he never actually made it here. The prince, who visited the Cape in 1870, cancelled a trip to Port Alfred at the last minute, because the prospect of an elephant hunt seemed more appealing.

Arrival, information and orientation

The Minilux **bus service**, connecting Port Elizabeth to East London via Grahamstown, pulls into the *Halyards Hotel*, off the main coastal road on the east side of the Kowie River on Tuesdays and Thursdays. The **Baz Bus** stops daily at the backpackers' hostel close to *Halyards*, as well as at *Beaver's Restaurant*, on the west bank which is good for getting to the self-catering places in Salt Vlei. From *Halyards*, it's about ten minutes' walk to the helpful **tourist information** bureau and *Mama Temba* tea shop, on the riverfront as you cross the bridge into Main Street (Mon–Sat 10.30am–4.30pm; ☏046 624 1235). **Main**

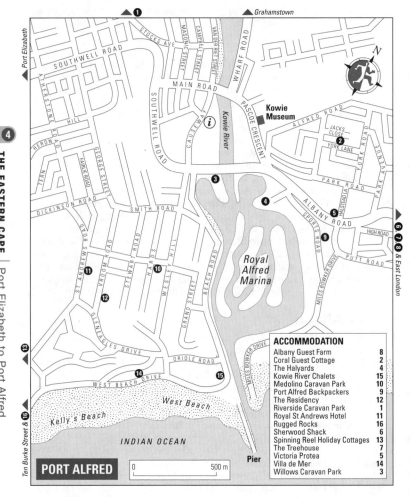

ACCOMMODATION

Albany Guest Farm	8
Coral Guest Cottage	2
The Halyards	4
Kowie River Chalets	15
Medolino Caravan Park	10
Port Alfred Backpackers	9
The Residency	12
Riverside Caravan Park	1
Royal St Andrews Hotel	11
Rugged Rocks	16
Sherwood Shack	6
Spinning Reel Holiday Cottages	13
The Treehouse	7
Victoria Protea	5
Villa de Mer	14
Willows Caravan Park	3

PORT ALFRED 0 — 500 m

Street, the town centre, is lined with banks and small shops, while the biggest supermarket, Spar, is in a small mall at the end of Main Road.

The **Kowie River** slices through Port Alfred, creating an **east** and **west bank**, with the town and most popular swimming **beaches** to the west, and the less-developed dunes stretching east. The river is traversed by two bridges: a concrete bowstring-arch bridge that has become Port Alfred's symbol, and an older one, which leads straight into Main Street. Sadly, the natural lagoon was blasted away in the 1980s and replaced by a marina, floating with dozens of boats and artificial islands dotted with Toytown holiday homes. The *Halyards Hotel* and a pub constitute the town's ersatz caged-in waterfront. Far more authentic, the river frontage on **Wharf Street**, next to the old bridge, has been revamped and the row of Victorian buildings spruced up. At #20, the **Coelacanth Brewing Company**, the Eastern Cape's only micro brewery, ferments the very drinkable Old Four Legs Lager. The fish shop a couple of doors along is the place to buy fresh fish and seafood.

Accommodation

Outside school holidays, you should have no problem finding a **place to stay**. The tourist information bureau (see p.369) publishes a useful accommodation list, including B&Bs and self-catering cottages. The priciest and most sought-after places are on **West Beach**, while you'll find more affordable options back from the seafront and particularly in the older and slightly more characterful areas on the hill on the east side of town. Most B&Bs are indicated from the main roads with official brown signs, making them relatively easy to find. If you're on a budget and value seclusion, one of the several self-catering cottages at **Salt Vlei** is an option worth considering.

Hotels, guesthouses and B&Bs

Coral Guest Cottage Jack's Close ☎ & ⓕ046 624 2849. Reasonably priced B&B on one of the East Bank hills, a 20min walk from East Beach. Comfortable rooms with bath in a restored corrugated-iron settler cottage, though the walls are not at all soundproof. You can expect to be pampered by the ebullient owner. ❷

The Halyards Royal Alfred Marina, Albany Road ☎046 624 2410, ⓕ046 624 2466. The smartest hotel in town, with marine-themed decor, swimming pool and wooden deck area. From here it's a 10–15min walk to East Beach, or to the centre of town. ❹

The Residency 11 Vroom Rd, ☎046 624 5382 or 083 260 0334, ⓦ www.theresidency.co.za. Spacious, beautifully restored Victorian house on the West Bank with views across the dunes to the sea. It has lemon yellowwood panelling, large comfortable beds, fine attention to detail and breakfast served on the verandah making this one of the most stylish places to stay in town. ❸

Royal St Andrews 19 St Andrews Rd ☎046 624 1379, ⓕ046 624 2080, ⓦ www.compushop.co.za /standrew. The Tudor-style exterior and conservative image cunningly disguise thoroughly modern refurbished interiors. Besides hotel rooms, there are larger apartments which offer the town's best self-catering. Outside, the pool has a wooden deck and terraced seating under trees. The hotel is across the road from the golf course, a 10min walk from Kelly's Beach. ❸

Victoria Protea corner of Albany Road and Halstead Lane, just up the hill from the marina ☎046 624 1133, ⓕ046 624 1134. Reliable and comfortable mid-range hotel that won't deliver any surprises. Ask about discounts for two-night stays during quiet periods. ❹

Villa de Mer 22 West Beach Drive ☎ & ⓕ046 624 2315 or ☎ 082 833 0634, ⓔ villademer

@intekom.co.za. Ostentatious guesthouse in the best location in town, right across the road from the beach. Five en-suite rooms, including a family unit, a courtyard swimming pool and huge windows. ❸

Camping, budget and self-catering

Albany Guest Farm ☎046 675 1170, ⓦ www .imaginet.co.za. An outstanding trio of remote cottages on a farm east of Port Alfred, a 20min drive towards East London. The cottages have fabulous views of the Kap Nature Reserve, where you can canoe or hike. Bush Cottage (❷), has paraffin lamps, a wooden deck and an open rock fireplace, while the luxurious Tudor House (❸) has a sauna and Jacuzzi.

Kowie River Chalets West Beach ☎ & ⓕ046 624 4182. Port Alfred's most luxurious self-catering units, sleeping two to six, in timeshare timber chalets on stilts with terrific views. Close to the river mouth and a stone's throw from the sea. ❷

Medolino Caravan Park Prince's Avenue, Kowie West ☎046 624 1651, ⓕ046 624 2514, ⓦ www.caravanparks.co.za/medolino. A very efficiently run place, in shady grounds behind the dunes, protected from the wind by its trees. A 10min walk from Kelly's Beach. Good camping facilities, excellent wooden self-catering chalets and swimming pool. ❷

Port Alfred Backpackers 29 Sports Rd ☎046 624 4011 or 082 784 4028, ⓔ bapack@imaginet .co.za. Well-located hostel near East Beach, on the Baz Bus stop. Three bright, clean dorms and one double. Quietish as hostels go. ❶

Riverside Caravan Park Mentone Road ☎046 624 2230. Small caravan park where you can rent two-bedroomed chalets (no camping). Peacefully set next to the river (but 3km from the town and beach), it faces onto a wetland; you can rent boats to explore the waterways. Bed linen can also be hired, but you must bring your own towels. ❶

Rugged Rocks Salt Vlei ☎046 624 3112 or 082 781 4682, ⊛www.ruggedrocks.co.za. A ten-acre beachside property, 4km from the town centre. Six cottages, either tucked in the coastal bush or with sea views, come fully equipped with linen provided, and offer greatly discounted rates for week-long stays out of school holidays. ❶

Sherwood Shack Seafield Road, 22km east of Port Alfred, signposted off the R72, on the Baz Bus route ☎046 675 1090, ⓕ046 624 2272, ⓔback-pack@border.co.za. Large dorms and two self-catering doubles on a farm, away from the coast. Emphasis is on getting to know the local area, with pineapple "safaris", trips to collect shellfish for feasts, and jaunts to Kleinemonde Beach or the Fish River wetland. They also offer drives on a nearby game farm. ❶

Spinning Reel Holiday Cottages and B&B Freshwater Road, Salt Vlei, 3km west of West Beach ☎046 624 4281, ⓕ046 624 4062, ⊛www.imaginet.co.za/spinreel. Relaxed beach cottages where you can spend the day in your swimming gear, or more expensive en-suite B&B rooms with sea views. ❶–❷

Willows Caravan Park Riverside, off the R72, by the bow-arch bridge ☎046 624 5201. Camping at the most central (but not the nicest) of the caravan parks, alongside Children's Beach, a 5min walk from West Beach. ❶

The Town and its beaches

Port Alfred's attractions are firmly rooted in its **beaches** and the **Kowie River**. The town itself has little else to offer, apart from functional shopping in its one main street and a couple of open-air shopping malls. Of passing interest is the tiny **Kowie Museum**, in Pascoe Crescent (Tues–Sat 9.30am–12.30pm; free), on the east side of the old bridge, featuring sepia photographs of Port Alfred before the marina and its mansions gobbled up the magnificent lagoon.

Beach life is focused on popular **West Beach**, where the river is sucked out to sea and the breakers pound in. From the café and stone pier you can watch the surfers and see fishing boats make dramatic entries into the river from the open ocean. Fifteen minutes' walk west along the beach lies **Kelly's Beach**, where you can swim safely in a gentle bay. **East Beach**, reached from the signposted road next to *Halyards Hotel*, is the nicest beach for walking, with a backdrop of hilly dunes stretching to the horizon. For toddlers, the safest and most popular spot is **Children's Beach**, a stretch of sand close to the town centre along a shallow section of river, reached from Beach Road, a few hundred metres from the arched bridge.

Port Alfred is home to the reputable **Keryn's Dive School** (☎082 692 6189 or 046 624 4432), based next to the *Halyards*. Boats go out to Fountain Rocks, and to a couple of nearby wrecks. Don't expect to see crystal waters and fluorescent fish (the Indian Ocean isn't tropical here), but the slightly murky water contains colourful underwater denizens, as well as beautiful corals and sponges. You can qualify here in a week for an internationally recognized **diving certificate**.

When the weather is blowy (or should you want to swim laps or join a water aerobics class), head for the heated **indoor swimming pool** next to *Halyards Hotel* (daily from 7.30am for laps and aerobics, otherwise 9.30am–7pm; ☎046 624 1945; R5). There's a small pool for toddlers, and a takeaway kiosk selling canned drinks and basic burgerish meals.

Eating

Port Alfred offers **fresh fish** galore, but the real surprise and the biggest treat in town is the *Ying Thai Restaurant* (see opposite), a private house serving authentic **Thai food**.

Buck & Hunter Main St, close to First National Bank ☎046 624 5960. Reliable and fairly lively pub and grub place. Mon–Sat.

Butlers 25 Van der Riet St ☎046 624 3464. The town's swankiest restaurant enjoys a lovely riverside setting and is good for fish. Open for lunch and dinner from 11am Tues till Sun lunchtime.

Activities around Port Alfred

The two-day **Kowie Canoe Trail**, a 21-kilometre paddle up the Kowie River, is a much-sought-after trip and one of the few self-guided canoeing and hiking trails in South Africa (elsewhere you're accompanied by a nature conservation officer). Much of its charm is the colourful birdlife, and the landscape – hills of dense, dry bush that slope down to the river. You **stay overnight** in a hut in the **Horseshoe Bend Nature Reserve**, from where you can explore the forest on foot, and climb up the steep escarpment to get an impressive view over the horseshoe. The biggest difficulty on this trip is the tide – make sure you check the tide table in the local *Kowie Announcer*, and paddle with the flow, going up the river when the tide is coming in, and back to Port Alfred when the river is flowing out. If it's windy, stay close to the shore and ensure your gear is in waterproof bags. **Booking** is essential (℡046 624 2230) and, while weekends are almost always full, weekdays out of school holidays are easy to book, and cost R65 per person, including accommodation and a double canoe.

If the trail is full, you can get a taste of the landscape **on foot** by driving to the reserve and taking the two-hour circular walk that traces its way through thick bush to the Kowie River and along its banks. Look out for primeval **cycads**, some as much as a thousand years old, in the riverine woodland. It's not unusual to see tortoises, monkeys, bushbuck and duikers. The main access point is 3km before you reach Bathurst, on a dirt road signposted "Waters Meeting", which takes you to the top of the escarpment for a postcard view of the horseshoe. If you're feeling energetic, you can walk down through the forest to the river to get a real feel of the landscape.

Another alternative is the **Kayak Camp Canoe Trail** (℡046 675 1060 or 046 624 2881), which can be done as a day-trip for R30, or overnight for R50. The canoe trail goes up Lynedoch River at Kleinemond, with a camp set up under trees, with enough sleeping space for eight people. The exciting birdlife includes African fish eagles, kingfishers and colourful Knysna loeries. After paddling through bushveld to riverine thicket and forest, you can take a **two-hour walk** through pristine forest to a tree house built into a yellowwood tree overhanging a river pool, a possible overnight stop. There is no vehicle access, giving a real feeling of remoteness.

Port Alfred has three horse-riding establishments. Glenhope Riding, off the Bathurst Road (T046 625 0866), is based on a pineapple farm and has first-rate horses and fabulous views to the sea. The Three Sisters Horse Trail, signposted 14km east of Port Alfred off the R72 towards East London road (booking essential T046 675 1269 or 082 645 6345) has access to one of the loveliest stretches of the coast in the region, and is recommended for children. Rufane's River Horseback, 5km east of town, also has mountain-bike trails on their farm (℡ 046 624 1469 or 082 697 1297).

Guido's on the Beach Main Beach ℡046 624 5264. Pizzas, pasta and booze at a young, atmospheric place on the beachfront, with an upstairs deck. Service isn't their strong point. Daily.
Papa Charlie's Main Street, close to the R72. The best-value takeaway in town is their freshly fried fish and chips (while you wait) which comes with a small helping of salad.

Ying Thai Restaurant 6 York Rd ℡046 624 1647. The best food in Port Alfred: outstanding, authentic Thai cuisine served in a front room of a private home on the east side of town. Booking essential. Fri & Sat evening only, but open every night during Dec and Jan.

Grahamstown

Just over 50km inland from Port Alfred, but worlds apart in terms of ambience, **GRAHAMSTOWN** projects an image of a cultured, historic town, quintessentially English, Protestant and refined. Dominated by its cathedral, university and public schools, this is a thoroughly pleasant place to wander through, with well-maintained colonial **Georgian** and **Victorian buildings** lining the streets, and pretty suburban gardens. Every July, the town hosts an **arts festival**, the largest of its kind in Africa, and purportedly the second largest in the world (after Edinburgh).

As elsewhere in South Africa, there are reminders of conquest and dispossession. Climb up Gunfire Hill, where the fortress-like 1820 **Settlers Monument** celebrates the achievement of South Africa's English-speaking immigrants, and you'll be able to see Makanaskop, the hill from which the **Xhosa** made their last stand against the British invaders. Their descendants live in desperately poor ghettos here, in a town almost devoid of industry. Marking the gap are the Kowie Ditches (which you'll cross if you take the old East London Road out of town), a waterway that ran red with Xhosa blood in the 1819 battle of Grahamstown.

Despite all this, and the constant reminders of poverty, Grahamstown makes a good stopover, and is the perfect base for excursions: a number of **historic villages** are within easy reach, some **game parks** are convenient for a day or

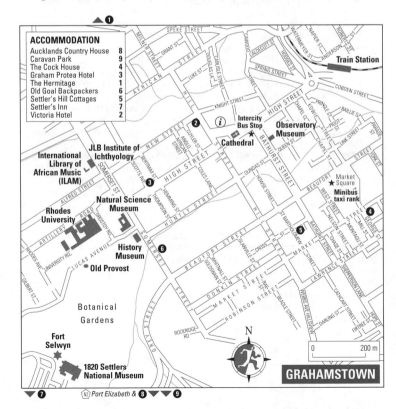

THE EASTERN CAPE | Grahamstown

weekend visit and, best of all, kilometres of **coast** are just 45 minutes' drive away. Cupped in a valley surrounded by hills, Grahamstown itself is compact; you'll only need a car to get out of town.

Some history

Grahamstown's sedate prettiness belies its beginnings as a **military outpost** in 1811. **Colonel Graham** made his name here (and gave it to the town), driving the Xhosa out of the Zuurveld, an area between the Bushman's and Fish rivers. The Fish River, 60km east of Grahamstown, marked the eastern boundary of the frontier, with Grahamstown as the capital. The ruthless expulsion of the Xhosa sparked off a series of nineteenth-century **Frontier Wars**.

A line of **forts** was built to defend the frontier, subsequently developing into the settlements, which now include Fort Beaufort, Fort Hare and Peddie, but these alone were not enough to hold the line, and the British decided to reinforce the frontier with a human barrier. With the promise of free land, they lured the dispossessed from a depressed Britain to occupy the lands west of the Fish River. In the migration mythology of English-speaking whites, these much-celebrated **1820 Settlers** came to take on a larger-than-life status as ancestors to whom many trace back their origins. However, far from the hoped-for paradise, the ill-equipped settlers found themselves in a nightmare. The plots given them were unsuitable for crops and too small for cattle in the harsh Eastern Cape; drought, floods and disease were a constant problem, and the threat of Xhosa attack was never far away.

Not surprisingly, many settlers abandoned their lands and headed to Grahamstown in the early 1820s. This brought prosperity and growth to the town, which enjoyed a boom in the 1840s, when it developed into the emporium of the frontier. Xhosa traders came to barter ivory and hides for beads, buttons and brass wire, while some colonists, who had persisted with farming in the surrounding district, traded **wool** from Spanish merino sheep which thrived in the Eastern Cape.

Arrival and information

Grahamstown is on the N2, 127km inland from Port Elizabeth, roughly an equidistant twelve hours by bus from Cape Town, Johannesburg and Durban. Translux, Intercape and Greyhound **buses** stop outside the Conference Centre on the corner of Bathurst and High streets. The Minilux **minibus**, which connects Grahamstown with the airport at Port Elizabeth, and goes on to Port Alfred and East London on Tuesdays and Thursdays, stops at the petrol station opposite the Shoprite supermarket in Beaufort Street.

The **train station** is at the bottom of High Street, but sees only one train a day, a branch-line service connecting to the Johannesburg–Port Elizabeth line. Grahamstown is easily covered **on foot**, and the central accommodation and tourist information office are easily and safely reachable, but if you want a **taxi** use the reliable Beeline (☏082 651 6646), the only licensed company in town. Their main trade is zipping up and down to Port Elizabeth airport. The helpful **tourist information** bureau (Mon–Fri 8.30am–5pm, Fri 8.30am–4pm, Sat 8.30am–noon; ☏046 622 3241, ℻046 622 3266) on the High Street, next to the City Hall, has information on accommodation. **Internet facilities** are available at The Office Shop (Mon–Fri 9am–7pm, Sat 9–1pm) in the Pepper Grove Mall, African Street.

Accommodation

The only time you may have difficulty finding **accommodation** is during the festival in July, when you'd be well-advised to book as early as March. If you've just arrived from the Garden Route or one of the more popular tourist areas of South Africa, prices will seem very reasonable. Grahamstown has the distinction of hosting the only backpackers' lodge in the country in an historic gaol, where you sleep in a cell. Other than that, the most notable and choicest places to stay are in historic houses, and there's a good selection of hotels. You also have the opportunity to stay in an **African home** in the townships (see box below).

Aucklands Country House 8km outside Grahamstown along the N2 to Port Elizabeth. ☎046 622 2401, ℱ046 622 5682, ⊛www.aucklands.co.za. A fabulous stone-and-thatch country lodge, on three square kilometres of indigenous bush where you can walk and see resident herds of blesbok. The emphasis here is on style and gourmet food. ❹

Caravan Park On the right of the N2 as you come into town from Port Elizabeth ☎046 622 9112. Nicely located next to wooded hills, and an easy walk to town. Besides camping, there are basic rondavels with bunks and modest self-catering chalets sleeping five (bring your own linen). ❶

The Cock House 10 Market St ☎046 636 1295, ℱ046 636 1287, ⊛www.imaginet.co.za/cockhouse. Plush rooms in a beautiful Victorian house, considered the town's top place to stay. Satisfied guests have included Nelson Mandela. ❹

Graham Protea Hotel 123 High St ☎046 622 2324, ℱ046 622 2424, ⊛grahotel@intekom.co.za. The most central of Grahamstown's hotels, across the road from the University. Overpriced, given its impersonal ambience. Ask about low-period discounts, especially Dec and Jan. ❹

The Hermitage 14 Henry St ☎ & ℱ046 636 1503. The best-value B&B in town, with bed and sitting room suites in a luxurious and stylish historic house, which would be well over twice the price in Cape Town. The owners are exceedingly obliging, but there are only two rooms, so book ahead. ❷

Old Gaol Backpackers Somerset Street ☎046 636 1001 or 083 982 5966, ⊛gsapelt@yebo.co.za. Dorms and doubles in the dark cells of an old jail built in 1824. A truly atmospheric experience that may well encourage good behaviour in the hope of an early release. ❶

Settlers Hill Cottages 8 Bartholomew St & 1 Sheblon Lane, off Cross Street ☎046 622 9720 or 082 809 3395, ℱ046 622 9720, ⊛www.geocities.com/thetropics/cabana/5593. Reasonably priced settler cottages (both National Monuments) in the old part of town, with yellow-wood floors. ❷

Settlers' Inn Hotel Just out of town off the N2, next to the 1820 Settlers Monument ☎046 622 7313, ⊛settlersinn@intekom.co.za. A motel feel in peaceful surroundings, with a nice garden and pool. Great for kids. ❸

Victoria Hotel 8 New St ☎ & ℱ046 622 7261, ⊛www.imaginet.co.za/hotelvictoria. Decent, reasonably priced central hotel. There's also an excellent self-catering flat with three simple but clean and freshly painted bedrooms. B&B. ❶–❷

Grahamstown East homestays

Under apartheid, there were no B&Bs in the "African areas" of South Africa, and today they are still a rarity. However, this is slowly changing. Spending even a little time in one of the **townships** will give you a different perspective on the country. Grahamstown provides the ideal opportunity to do this conveniently without having to traipse too far – the townships are less than ten minutes' drive from the centre. Mrs Habana (☎046 637 0776) co-ordinates the B&Bs and can place you with a hospitable Xhosa family in Grahamstown East. The accommodation is in brick homes, some with en-suite rooms, and all have secure off-street parking. Expect to pay around R80 per person per night for B&B.

The Town

Reminders of the **colonial past** are everywhere in central Grahamstown, not just in the architecture, but also in streets named after Cape governors and soldiers: Cradock, Meyer, Somerset, Stockenstrom and Cuyler. The University itself, of course, is named after Cecil John Rhodes (see p.309). While the High Street has most of the shops you'd need, many businesses have relocated, or opened up in a recently developed shopping mall, **Pepper Grove**, five minutes' walk north of High Street, with entrances in African and Allen streets. Pepper Grove also has the town's best-stocked supermarket, a chemist, cinemas, doctor, cafés, internet facilities, and a natural food store selling herbal remedies.

High Street

Virtually all the shops and banks you'll need are down **High Street**, Grahamstown's major shopping axis, with terraces of nineteenth-century buildings lending it a graceful air. Running from the station at its seedier east end, High Street continues past the cathedral at the junction of Hill Street, terminating at the 150-year-old Drostdy Arch, the whitewashed entrance gate to Rhodes University. Hawkers on the pavements sell small bags of fruit and vegetables, and you may see young Xhosa men in new caps and jackets, with red clay on their faces, signifying that their initiation period is over. At the centre of the street is the **Cathedral of St Michael and St George**, opened in 1830; like many churches in the area, this became a refuge for women and children during the Frontier Wars. Inside, on the right as you come in, is a quietly ironic memorial tablet to Colonel John Graham, who commanded the frontier.

Rhodes University and the museums

Strung along Somerset Street, which runs at right angles to the top (west end) of High Street, is **Rhodes University** and a succession of modest museums – all are covered by a convenient multi-entry ticket, and can take up a pleasant morning's visit.

If you've time for only one, head for the **Natural Science Museum** (Mon–Fri 9.30am–1pm & 2–5pm, Sat 9.30am–1pm; R5), just south of the university entrance on the same side of the street. The display of Eastern Cape fauna and flora from 250 million years ago is excellent, with intriguing plant fossils and the bones of dinosaurs which once roamed these parts. Also worth a look is the **gallery** of the curator who worked for 48 years at the museum, containing his personal collection of objects in beautiful old teak display cases. The **History Museum** next door houses a dusty collection of 1820 Settler memorabilia, nineteenth-century paintings and antique firearms.

Beyond the Drostdy Arch, tucked behind some buildings at the corner of Somerset and Prince Alfred streets, is **ILAM**, the International Library of African Music (Mon–Fri 8.30am–12.45pm & 2.15–4.45pm; free; ☎046 603 8557, ⓔilam@ru.ac.za). The library is an absolute treasure trove of recordings of **traditional African music** from southern Africa, as well as Zaire, Rwanda, Uganda and Tanzania. It also sells cassettes on request, and there's a collection of over 200 traditional instruments on view and for sale. Phone beforehand to be shown around (from R80), and to get a demonstration and also the chance to play some instruments with African music expert Andrew Tracey. Reasonably priced instruments, handmade using high-quality timber, can be bought from their **workshop** in Froud Street at the opposite side of town. This is *the* place in South Africa to buy an authentic instrument to take home. Their reasonably priced thumb pianos (*mbiras*) are beautifully made and easily portable.

On the same side of the road as ILAM, the **JLB Smith Institute of Ichthyology** (Mon–Fri 8.30am–1pm & 2–5pm; free) is named after the Rhodes University scientist who shot to fame in 1939 after identifying the coelacanth, a "missing link" fish, caught off the East London coast and thought to have been extinct for fifty million years. In the foyer are two huge stuffed specimens, with fins that look like budding arms and legs. Far from being extinct, plenty of coelacanths have now been spotted by deep-sea divers; their preferred dwelling is in the pressurized, pitch-dark depths of the Indian Ocean.

Heading back down High Street and right onto Bathurst Street brings you to the **Observatory Museum** (Mon–Fri 9.30am–1pm & 2–5pm; Sat 9.30am–1pm; R8), a fun display in a restored building that was the home and shop of a notable watchmaker and jeweller during the mid-1850s. Also well worth a visit is the rooftop Victorian **camera obscura**, which projects onto a wall magnified images of the streets below. It's best seen on a clear day, when the reflections are crisp and clear.

The Old Provost, Monument and Botanical Gardens

One of Grahamstown's rewarding short walks starts at the **Old Provost** in Lucas Avenue, on the edge of the Botanical Gardens and University, and heads up through the gardens to the 1820 Settlers Monument, on the hill above. Built as a prison in the nineteenth century, the whitewashed stone Provost is now a craft shop. Next to it are some graves of British soldiers, killed by Xhosa warriors.

Looming on Gunfire Hill, the **1820 Settlers Monument**, built in 1974 to commemorate the British settlers, is an ugly fortress-like building, supposedly fashioned to look like a ship. The best reason to trudge up here is for the panoramic views, or for a performance at the Monument Theatre (see p.379). Avoid wandering around the gardens alone, especially in the evenings, as there has been the occasional mugging.

Xhosa Grahamstown

Xhosa Grahamstown starts buzzing around **Market Square**, off Beaufort Street, where you'll see hawkers by the dozen and a busy minibus-taxi rank. In the late 1820s, the square was the trading venue for ivory, hides, wool and farm produce. If you're in the area, it's worth walking west of Market Square to see the restored **1820 Settlers cottages** in Cross and Bartholomew streets, some flat-roofed and two-storeyed, others with pitched tin roofs.

Beaufort Street, the main road for traffic passing through, leads up the hill towards the townships on the eastern side of town. At the top, the road cuts through a hill of white clay, where Xhosa people scratch out pigment for face markings. From this cutting, looking into the valley, well away from the squatters' shacks, you'll see some roughly made traditional huts, used during the seclusion period, when young men, **amakweta**, are initiated. All over the Eastern Cape, it's not unusual to see *amakweta* on the roadside wearing very little and smeared in white clay, which signifies they've just been circumcised and initiated into manhood (Nelson Mandela went through the same ordeal).

Beyond the cutting lies the treeless **Kings Flats** township, where the **Umthathi Self-help Project** teaches people how to grow vegetables and raise chickens. Umthathi's office in Grahamstown train station (☎046 622 4450) can arrange **township tours** that include a traditional Xhosa lunch in a township house with a local African family. The money goes to the family, and it's a great way to experience authentic black South Africa in safety.

Eating, drinking and entertainment

Eating prospects in Grahamstown are far from exciting, but there's at least one good pub, a decent coffee shop and a couple of restaurants with pleasant settings. If you're **self-catering**, the Home Industries shop at the Pepper Grove Mall is great for homemade pies, seasonal fruit and vegetables, and venison and ostrich eggs for gigantic omelettes (all produce comes from local farms).

137 High Street. Close to the Drosty Arch, in a Georgian building with an outdoor courtyard. The best coffee and cheesecake in town. Daytime only from 7.30am; closed Saturday afternoons and Sunday.

The Blue Room 127a High St. You may find yourself accidentally sitting in on a tutorial at this thoroughly convivial upstairs venue frequented by university staff and students. Excellent for light meals, interesting sandwiches, bottomless cups of coffee and the birds-eye view down High Street.

Cecil John's 63 New St. Student hangout more commonly known as CJ's, with a dance floor, pool table and lively bar. Open from 9pm.

The Cock House Corner of Market and George streets ☎ 046 636 1295. Grahamstown's best restaurant, serving Provençal country cuisine; their speciality is local lamb shank, braised and marinated. There's home-baked bread, and after dinner rum and chocolate truffles. Open for lunch and dinner Mon–Sat, closed Sunday lunch, Sun eves set menu R85. Booking advised.

La Galleria 13 New St ☎ 046 622 2345. Recommended, moderately priced Italian restaurant with tempting starters and desserts, run by an Italian. Open Mon–Sat 7pm–midnight.

Pop Art Café New Street, opposite *La Galleria*. Grahamstown's most self-consciously stylish pub, where art students pose and cocktails are *de rigeur*. A juke box with a decent selection of modern and retro sounds is an added attraction.

The Rat & Parrot 59a New St. Jekyll and Hyde venue that's a lively student bar and restaurant by day, but can become yobbish by night. Decent food, notably the dishes cooked and served in individual pots, or *potjies* (the seafood *potjie* is outstanding). Open from noon daily; closed Sunday.

Redwood Spur 97 High St, near the cathedral. Reliable American-style food, mainly burgers and beef, with big salads and late-night bottomless coffee, served with a smile by clean-cut young waiters. One of the few places in town open daily till late including Sunday.

Settler's Inn Just behind the Monument, off the PE road. Grahamstown's best outdoor venue, in large gardens around a pool and duck pond, affording views across the roofs of the town. Just about passable steaks, fish and other standard cheap- to medium-priced fare, this is the best place for a bite if you've got kids. You can get here by walking up through the Botanical Gardens.

Entertainment

Despite being the home of the country's premier **arts festival** (see box on p.380), and dominated by Rhodes University, Grahamstown's nightlife, culture and entertainment is far less exciting than you might expect. Outside the hectic festival fortnight in July, the town relies on the **cinema** at the Pepper Grove Mall to deliver its only regular evening entertainment. However, because of the university connection, the town is periodically treated to a better selection of events than you'd be likely to find in the average Karoo *dorp*. You may stumble into town when something exceptional is going on, so keep your eyes peeled. The two main venues for **live performances** are the Monument Theatre, and the Rhodes University Theatre, where the Drama Department puts on productions from time to time. Well worth catching is anything staged by solo-artist **Andrew Buckland**, a local actor with an international reputation in physical theatre.

The university's Music Department also puts on eclectic and fairly regular classical **music concerts**. Black musicians also sometimes hit town, performing at the town hall or venues in the African townships. To find out **what's on**, check the flyposters down High Street and also look in *Grocott's Mail*, the local rag, which comes out on Tuesday and Friday afternoons. Another source of information is *GOG* – *Good Old Grahamstown*, a monthly booklet available from the tourist information bureau.

The Grahamstown Festival

Every July, Grahamstown bursts to overflowing, with visitors descending for the annual National Arts Festival – usually called the **Grahamstown Festival**, or more simply The Festival. The hub of the event is the 1820 Settlers Monument, which hosts not only big drama, dance and operatic productions in its theatres, but also art exhibitions and free early evening concerts. Grahamstown's festival proper began in 1974 when the Monument building was opened; today, it's the largest arts festival in Africa, and even has its own fringe festival. For eleven days, the town's population doubles to 200,000, with seemingly every home transformed into a B&B and the streets alive with colourful food stalls. Church halls, parks and sports fields become flea markets and several hundred shows are staged, spanning every conceivable type of performance.

The published festival programme is bulky, but absolutely essential – it's worth planning your time carefully to avoid walking the potentially very cold July streets, snooping around the markets and seeing nothing of the festival proper. The programme includes jazz, classical music, drama, dance, cabaret, opera, visual arts, crafts, films and a book fair. While work by African performers and artists is well represented, and is perhaps the more interesting aspect of the festival for tourists, festival-goers and performers are still predominantly white. If you don't feel like taking in a show, the free art exhibitions at the museums, Monument and other smaller venues are always worth a look.

For more **information and bookings**, contact the Grahamstown Foundation, PO Box 304, Grahamstown 6140 ☎046 622 7115, ℻046 622 3082, ⊛www.sbfest.co.za.

Around Grahamstown

From Grahamstown, it's a short journey to the **coast**: Port Alfred and Kenton-on-Sea are both less than an hour by car (see p.366), and each has a historic settler village en route – **Bathurst** and **Salem** respectively. A bit further afield, you can meander down dirt roads, pausing at old settler churches and graves, and end up at the **Great Fish River Wetland Reserve** (see p.396), which has a magnificent beach and river frontage.

Grahamstown is also close to a couple of fine **wildlife reserves**, especially good for experiencing the striking, dry bush particular to this area and the animals that little over a century ago roamed the land freely. The highlight is the **Great Fish River Reserve Complex** (distinct from the wetland reserve), a rambling wilderness slaked by the Great Fish and its tributary, the Kap. Its appeal lies in its backwoods feel and the beauty of its landscape, offering a different experience to that found in the well-organized **Addo Elephant Park** (see p.360) or the upmarket **Shamwari Game Reserve** (see p.362), both of which are more usually reached from Port Elizabeth but are actually a tad closer to Grahamstown.

Bathurst and around

A significant centre in the nineteenth century, **BATHURST**, 45km south of Grahamstown, is today little more than a picturesque straggle of houses, gardens and curiosity shops. The *Pig and Whistle Hotel*, on the corner of the Grahamstown road as you drive into Bathurst, started life as a smithy in 1821, with an inn attached a few years later; they can provide maps and directions to historical sites. A pleasant two-kilometre walk from the *Pig and Whistle,* the water-powered **Bradshaw's Wool Mill** marks the spot where South Africa's wool industry started.

The setup at **Summerhill Farm** (see below) should keep kids occupied for a while, with an outsized yellow-and-green plastic pineapple museum plonked in the middle of a field full of the genuine article, as well as a pool, playground and mini-farm.

Accommodation

All the accommodation in Bathurst is strung along the main road between Grahamstown and Port Alfred (the R67) that runs through the hamlet. The range is broad from budget self-catering to luxury rooms on a farm on the outskirts of town.

Cosy Corner Hill St ⓣ & ⓕ046 625 0955. Two reasonably priced B&B cottages with a pool and braai facilities, also available as fully equipped self-catering units. ❶
Hayhurst Midway through Bathurst on the Port Alfred road ⓣ046 625 0856, ⓔhayhurst@intekom.co.za. Self-catering accommodation in two converted railway buses, with kitchens and baths, in a garden with a pool. ❶
Pig and Whistle ⓣ046 625 0673. Historic colonial Victorian village inn; particularly recommended are the old rooms upstairs, furnished with period pieces. ❷

Summerhill Estate Along the main Port Alfred road (the R67), landmarked by its enormous plastic pineapple ⓣ046 625 0833, ⓔsummerhill@albanyhotels.co.za. The town's most luxurious and spacious accommodation; best here are the en-suite B&B units in the original farmstead, overlooking pineapple plantations, with double beds, sitting areas and bunks for kids. There's a pool and you're free to explore the farm; it's also very child-friendly. ❸
Terrace House B&B 96 Donkin Terrace, just off the R67 ⓣ046 625 0906. En-suite rooms in a Victorian house. ❷

Eating and drinking

When it comes to **eating and drinking**, the atmospheric *Pig and Whistle* is a favourite weekend spot for locals downing a beer or five. Across the road, the *Bathurst Arms* serves pub lunches, and has a few tables in the garden. *Summerhill Farm* offers a bar and a mid-priced restaurant, open daily for lunches and dinners, including English-style fish, chicken and meat, plus veggie meals. On Sundays they do a self-service carvery (booking essential, see above).

Thomas Baines, Salem and Kariega Game Park

Grahamstown's closest nature reserve, **Thomas Baines Nature Reserve** (daily dawn–dusk; free), is a hilly area 15km south of town on the road to Kenton-on-Sea. The main attraction here is **Settler's Dam**, good for picnics, *braais* and wandering around the vicinity of the dam. Walking elsewhere isn't permitted, as rhino and buffalo live in the thick, prickly bush. During late afternoons, you're very likely to see antelope grazing on open spaces.

SALEM, 20km southwest of Grahamstown along the same road, comprises a scrawny collection of settler homesteads dating back to 1822, surrounded by khaki scrub and arranged around a village green, on Sundays sometimes dotted with the bleached whites of local cricket teams. Salem's centrepiece is a little whitewashed church, now a National Monument and worth a brief visit, though there's nowhere to get anything to eat or drink in Salem. Inside, a plaque commemorates the Quaker Richard Gush, whose descendants still live in the hamlet. During the Sixth Frontier War, local settlers took refuge in a stone church, where they were confronted by Xhosa raiders. Fed up with the ceaseless conflict, Gush stepped out unarmed to confront the Xhosa about their grievances. On being told they were driven by hunger, he went inside and, to the irritation of his fellows, returned with armloads of food. The town was subsequently left in peace. A different picture altogether is painted by J.M. Coetzee in his Booker Prize-winning novel *Shame* – a thoroughly disturbing book largely set in the hamlet during the present post-apartheid era, its landscape infused with menace rather than reconciliation.

Just 14km from the coast, upmarket **Kariega Park** (℡046 636 7904, Ⓦwww.kariega.co.za), is a delightful privately run game reserve set in the bush. Its balconied lodges feature three or four bedrooms, rented out on a fully inclusive basis that includes all meals and game drives (Ⓕ), or as B&B (Ⓔ) or self-catering units (Ⓓ). The main activity is walking through the reserve looking for its varied range of herbivores including giraffes, and going on game drives or evening river booze cruises. You can also swim in the river or the park's pool. It's worth coming as a day visitor (R220) if you want to get close to zebras and grazing antelope, as they are very tame and used to cars. The entrance fee includes lunch, a game drive and river cruise.

The Great Fish River Reserve Complex

Thirty-four kilometres north of Grahamstown on the Fort Beaufort Road (the R67), lies the huge **Great Fish River Reserve Complex** (office daily 8am–5pm, gate open 24hr; R20 per vehicle plus R6 per person). It forms an amalgamation of three separate reserves covering 430 square kilometres. Provided you're ready to rough it, Great Fish is the Eastern Cape's most rewarding wildlife destination after Addo (see p.360), despite the notable absence of lions. A far cry from the well-tended game parks of Mpumalanga or KwaZulu-Natal, it has no shops or restaurants and the roads are often horrible, but it's wild and beautiful. Along the banks of the Fish and Kat rivers, stands of thorn trees afford welcome shade during the summer heat, while in the parched areas away from the rivers, the striking landscape of cliffs and dense valleys is overgrown with scrubby bush, thick with succulents, euphorbias and aloes.

The varied terrain supports an abundant range of **game** (although not in large numbers) including black-backed jackals, hyenas and rarely seen leopards. Among the trees and bushes are several species of browsers and grazers, from blesbok to nyala, including numerous white rhinos, a handful of elephants, and warthogs by the dozen. A few snorting hippos while away their days in the rivers, and along the banks you may see waterbuck; look out for vervets in the trees.

Arrival

Self-driving is the only way to visit the Complex, most easily reached from the tarred R67, which connects Grahamstown to Fort Beaufort and provides **access** to the two entrances on the western flank: **Kamadolo Gate** in the south and **Sam Knott Gate** in the north. The R345 runs through the eastern section of the reserve, connecting the N2, at a point around 70km east of Grahamstown (just beyond the town of Peddie) with Alice (see p.406); this reasonable dirt road takes you to **Charles Tinley Gate**, the park headquarters, though the gate is often unattended. The Great Fish River and its tributary, the Kat, flow in a series of sinuous oxbows to segment the reserve into three, so you can't always count on getting from one section to another in an ordinary vehicle, particularly when the river levels rise to flood the fords. If you do intend driving through the reserve, either enquire at headquarters about conditions before leaving or take a direct route to your destination. Roads in the

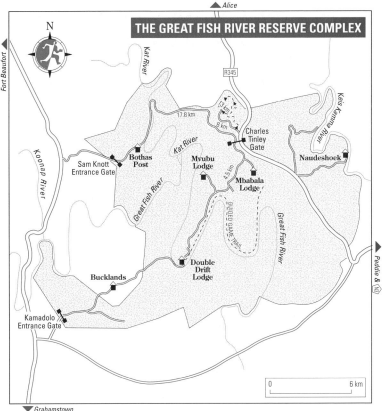

reserve are dirt tracks and are frequently poor, so you'll have to drive carefully and slowly.

Accommodation

A limited selection of **lodges** and **cabins** serves each of the reserve's three sections. Staff are on hand at the lodges to cook for guests (included in the price) and you pay a minimum charge based on a group of four, with the exception of Botha's Post, where it's two. All bookings (except Bucklands) are through the Eastern Cape Tourism Board in Bisho (℡040 635 2115, ℻046 636 4019).

In the **eastern section** (east of the Fish River), *Mbabala Lodge* (❷), 2km south of Charles Tinley Gate, offers five doubles and is charged out to a single party at a time. Thirteen kilometres southeast of the gate, on the banks of the Keiskamma River, *Naudeshoek* has a single log cabin sleeping six (❶). At Mvubu, 9km southwest of the gate, four twin-bedded chalets (❶) share a communal kitchen, dining area and plunge pool. Another six rustic maisonette-style family chalets (❷), each sleeping two adults and two children, sit on the banks of the Great Fish.

In the **southwestern section** (the closest to Grahamstown), *Double Drift Lodge* (❶), 16km northeast of Kamadolo Gate, is a basic place with five doubles, perched on the north bank of the Great Fish. Also accessible through

Kamadolo Gate is the privately owned *Bucklands Farm* (☎ & ℱ046 622 8055, ℯbuck@imaginet.co.za), in a small salient with 17km of its own river frontage, technically outside the reserve. There's a large modern prefab house (❶) in the farmyard for rent with single beds and bunks, which is equipped for self-catering.

Finally, in the **northwestern section**, 3km inside the reserve from Sam Knott Gate, at *Botha's Post,* you'll find four self-catering cabins (❶) that sleep four, each with en-suite shower, toilet and kitchenette.

Game viewing and activities

Most people coming to the reserve want to see **hippos**, a relatively rare sight in the Eastern Cape. To do so, report to Charles Tinley Gate and ask for an armed ranger to take you on the **guided game trail**, which runs along the northern bank of the Great Fish from *Double Drift Lodge*. Despite their cumbersome appearance, hippos – with a top speed of 30kmh and the ability to turn on a sixpence – can easily outmanoeuvre a human, and can be extremely dangerous if they feel threatened. If you're staying at *Bucklands Farm*, you can arrange a similar outing through the owner, Lynne Philips. *Bucklands* also lay on excellent guided day- and night-time **game drives**.

If you're **self-driving**, your best bet is to make for the **Nyathi** loop, in the northeastern section of the reserve, where game tends to concentrate. The best time to see the wildlife is early morning and late afternoon; at midday the animals duck into the deep shade of trees and bushes, where you won't see them. This is your cue to head for the terrific picnic spot near Double Drift, on the south bank of the Great Fish, under the shade of huge acacia trees.

Inland to the Karoo fringes

Travelling between Grahamstown and the towns of Cradock and Graaff-Reinet (the Eastern Cape's two most-visited Karoo towns), you'll be heading into **sheep farming country**, with the occasional *dorp* rising against the horizon, offering the experience of an archetypal Eastern Cape one-horse outposts. The roads through this vast emptiness are quiet, and lined with rhythmically spaced telephone poles. Dun-coloured sheep, angora goats and the occasional springbok graze on brown stubble, and you'll often see groups of charcoal-and-grey ostriches in the *veld*, once farmed to satisfy an Edwardian feather fetish, and now reared to cater for a fashion for lean and healthy meat.

Bedford and Somerset East

In the foothills of the Kaga Mountains, 87km north of Grahamstown, lies **BEDFORD**, the former realm of Xhosa Chief Phato. It became one of the little "English" towns Cape governor Sir Harry Smith promised to create in the nineteenth century. Now a drive-through place as you come off the road from Grahamstown, Bedford nevertheless has some attractive settler buildings. In the mountainous backdrop you'll find some **farmstays**, most notably *Cavers*, 16km north of Bedford (☎ & ℱ046 685 0619; ℯckross@intekom.co.za; ❹), a working settler dairy farm tucked away in the mountains in a pretty valley. It has an 1850 refurbished two-storey stone manor house with four en-suite bedrooms, and a thatched two-bedroom cottage with its own garden, and the use of a swimming pool and tennis courts; walks on the property give you the chance to see antelope and myriad birds. You need to book in advance, and the owners will give you directions.

Just under 60km west of Bedford lies **SOMERSET EAST**, a town that gets chewing during its *biltong* festival in June, and where Afrikaans matrons with tight perms, cardigans and plump brown arms stroll the main street. The historical part of the town merits a visit; down Beaufort Street, on an axis with the white-spired Dutch Reformed Church, is the **Somerset East Museum** Mon–Fri 8am–5pm; donation). The building was once the home of a Victorian pastor. One block from the museum is Somerset East's second attraction, the **Walter Battiss Art Gallery** (Mon–Fri 9am–1pm & 2–4pm, Sat & Sun by arrangement through the museum), in a handsome two-storey house on the corner of Beaufort and Poulet streets. Inside, you'll find a very uneven collection of drawings and paintings by one of South Africa's most well-known modern artists (his best work hangs in galleries elsewhere). It's worth a visit though; Battiss is noted for his sense of humour, which shines out even in this collection.

Cradock and around

CRADOCK, 240km north of Port Elizabeth, lies in the Karoo proper, the semi-desert heartland of South Africa, with knee-high bush, clear dry air and an enormous sense of open space. It makes a great stopover on the Port Elizabeth to Johannesburg run, not least because of the excellence of its accommodation in historical houses, and also for the **Mountain Zebra National Park**, one of the country's most beautiful game parks.

On the surrounding sheep farms, the silvery **windmills** have become an unofficial symbol of Cradock. Xhosa hawkers (often kids) stand along the main road around the city limits, selling intricately crafted wire model windmills, their blades spinning in the breeze.

Poverty has overshadowed Cradock since the Frontier Wars of the nineteenth century and the subjugation of the Xhosa people that continued right up to the 1990s. Against this history of conquest, the town has provided fertile grounds for **resistance**: some members of the ANC were based in and around the town, and almost single-handedly kept the organization alive during the 1930s. In 1985, Cradock hit the headlines when anti-apartheid activist **Matthew Goniwe** and three of his colleagues were murdered (see box on p.387).

Political controversy is also the theme at Cradock's biggest attraction, **Schreiner House**, 9 Cross St (Mon–Fri 8am–4.30pm; donation). The house is dedicated to the life of the writer Olive Schreiner, best known for her ground-breaking novel *The Story of an African Farm* (1883). It was remarkable enough for a woman from the conservative backwoods of nineteenth-century Eastern Cape to write a novel (it was published under the pseudonym Ralph Iron), but even more amazing that she espoused ideas considered dangerously radical even a century later. While in London looking for a publisher, Schreiner mixed with the likes of Havelock Ellis and Eleanor Marx, returning to South Africa at the turn of the century to campaign for universal franchise for men and women irrespective of race. After a life of campaigning, Schreiner died in Cape Town in 1921 and is buried near Cradock on the Buffelskop peak, overlooking the Great Fish River Valley. Her **burial site** has become something of a place of pilgrimage and details of how to get there are available from

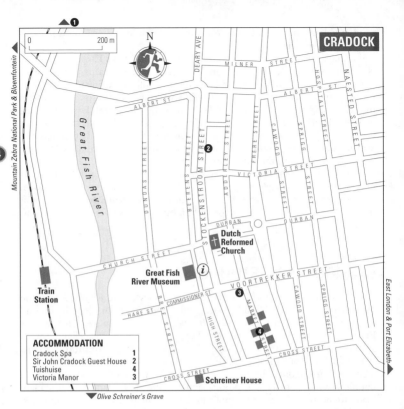

Mountain Zebra National Park & Bloemfontein

East London & Port Elizabeth

CRADOCK

0 — 200 m

N

Train Station

Great Fish River Museum

Dutch Reformed Church

ACCOMMODATION
Cradock Spa 1
Sir John Cradock Guest House 2
Tuishuise 4
Victoria Manor 3

Schreiner House

Olive Schreiner's Grave

Schreiner House, along with a photocopied Ordnance Survey map. You'll need a car to get to the starting point, and you should allow a good half-day for the trip, which involves a very stiff climb.

Cradock's other points of interest include the **Dutch Reformed Church** at the upper end of Church Street, based on London's St Martin's in the Field and completed in 1868, and a hot sulphur spring-fed **swimming pool**, at the Cradock Spa on Marlow Road, 4.5km from town (daily 7am–6pm; R11), which has indoor and open-air pools, and is a great place to relax after a long journey. The **Great Fish River Museum** behind the Town Hall (Tues–Fri 8am–1pm, Sat 8am–noon) is housed in an 1849 Dutch Reformed Church parsonage and depicts the early history of Eastern Cape pioneers.

Arrival and information

Daily **trains** (℡041 507 2400 or 041 507 2647) from Port Elizabeth to Johannesburg arrive at Cradock station at the south end of Church Street at 7pm in the evening, and far less conveniently at 4.30am going the other way. Translux and Intercape **buses** pull in daily at *Struwig Café* (℡048 881 2787) on Voortrekker Street, where you can buy tickets and get information for onward travel to Cape Town, East London, Port Elizabeth and Johannesburg.

Cradock is small and easily covered **on foot**, but you'll need your own transport to get to the sulphur spring pool or Mountain Zebra National Park. The very helpful but desperately overworked one-person **tourist information**

Matthew Goniwe and the murder of the Cradock Four

Even by apartheid standards, 1985 was a dark year for South Africa. In July, the hawkish President P.W. Botha declared a state of emergency in response to a nationwide wave of popular resistance; by the end of the year, over 500 people had been killed in police action. In this maelstrom of repression, **Matthew Goniwe** and three other Eastern Cape leaders from Cradock died in "mysterious" circumstances.

Goniwe was a prominent member and rural organizer for the United Democratic Front (UDF), a proxy organization for the then-banned ANC. Early on June 27, 1985, he left Vergenoeg township on the outskirts of Cradock, heading for a UDF meeting in Port Elizabeth. He was accompanied by **Fort Calata**, **Sparrow Mkhonto** and **Sicelo Mhlauli**. The four were never to return. On their way home, they were ambushed, murdered and their bodies burnt and spread several kilometres apart. The nature of the murder indicated considerable planning and resources. A highly publicized inquest in 1989 could not find the evidence necessary to incriminate apartheid government forces. In May 1992, a chilling document leaked to the anti-apartheid *New Nation* newspaper revealed that a signal had been sent by Commandant du Plessis to General van Rensberg calling for Matthew Goniwe to be "permanently removed from society".

Although there was now proof that the Port Elizabeth security police were responsible, the identities of the men were protected. It wasn't until 1997, during the **Truth and Reconciliation Commission** hearings, that the whole sickening story came out, including the identities of the five security police officers who confessed to the killings. The policemen were granted amnesty, despite the bitterness this caused.

bureau in Stockenstroom Street (Mon–Fri 8.30am–12.30pm & 2–4pm; ☎048 881 2383, ⊛www.cradock.co.za) can supply maps, accommodation lists and information on farmstays.

Accommodation

For a small town, Cradock offers some delightful accommodation; the *Tuishuise*, in particular, is recommended if you want to taste some Karoo country style.

Cradock Spa 4.5km north of town on the road to the signposted Mountain Zebra National Park ☎048 881 2709. The best bet for budget accommodation, with self-catering, fully equipped chalets sleeping two to four. ❶

Sir John Cradock Guest House Stockenstroom Street ☎048 881 1443. Inexpensive accommodation in nicely furnished rooms, with a small garden and lock-up garages; unfortunately, there's also considerable noise from the truck stop next door. ❶

Tuishuise Market Street ☎048 881 1322, ⊛www.tuishuise.co.za. A street of comfortable and very stylish one- to four-bedroomed Victorian houses. Each party has the sole use of a cottage; you can either self-cater, or eat at the *Victoria Manor*, where you also collect keys and pay. ❸

Victoria Manor 36 Market St ☎048 881 1650, ☏048 881 5388. Old, but restored and characterful hotel with nineteen decent en-suite rooms that are cheaper but smaller than those at the *Tuishuise*. ❷

Eating

When it comes to **eating**, the *Schreiner Tea Room* (Mon–Sat 10.30am–5pm) next to the *Victoria Manor* in Market Street is the nicest place for tea and sandwiches. The manor itself does lunches and dinners, including favourites like Karoo lamb and *malva* pudding, and is open for teas on Sundays. The *1814* (☎048 881 5390), with a distinctive sloping red roof standing out on Main Road, offers tasty breakfasts, lunches and teas with an Afrikaans bias. A good bet for steaks is *Fiddler's Grill* (☎048 881 1497), a favourite with local families, in the Total filling station complex on Voortrekker Street.

Mountain Zebra National Park

When the **Mountain Zebra National Park** (daily: May–Sept 7am–6pm; Oct–April 7am–7pm) was created in 1937, there were only five Cape **mountain zebras** left on its 65 square kilometres. If that wasn't bad enough, four of them were males. At the time, environmental issues were far from being vote-winners; indeed, one cabinet minister dismissed the threatened animals as "a lot of donkeys in football jerseys". Miraculously, conservationists managed to cobble together a breeding herd from the few survivors on surrounding farms, and the park now supports several hundred, while also translocating healthy numbers to various corners of South Africa.

For **game viewing**, the park has a couple of good part-tar, part-gravel loop roads forming a rough figure of eight. Most rewarding is the northernmost route, 14.5km long, which circuits the Rooiplaat section where the plains game tend to congregate. As well as zebra, keep an eye out for **springbok**, **blesbok** and **black wildebeest**. The introduction of **buffalo** in 1998 and plans to bring in **cheetahs** and **rhinos**, adds to the wildlife interest, but has ended hiking in the park, one of its previous highlights. Unlike docile Asian water buffalo, their African cousins have a reputation for extreme aggression and rancour, which instils justified fear in even hardened hunters. Apart from two short **waymarked walks** near the camp, you're no longer allowed to wander around on your own.

Practicalities

Mountain Zebra National Park is 26km west of Cradock. To get there by **car**, head north out of Cradock on the N10, turning west after about 6km onto the Graaff-Reinet Road. After a further 5km, turn left at the National Park sign onto a good gravel road, which reaches the park gate after a further 16km.

The park has **accommodation** in twenty comfortable two-bedroomed cottages (❷), all of which have outstanding mountain views and their own kitchens and bathrooms. The price includes breakfast in the camp restaurant. There's also a good **campsite**, but the unrivalled highlight of the park's lodgings is the self-catering **Doornhoek Guest House** (❹, minimum four people), a beautifully restored Victorian homestead set in splendid isolation with great Karoo views across a small lake to the surrounding chain of scrubby hills. Extremely comfortable, it sleeps six people in three en-suite bedrooms furnished with antiques. For **bookings** contact South African National Parks (Pretoria ☎012 343 1991, ℻012 343 0905, ✉reservations@parks-sa.co.za). A twenty-percent discount on accommodation and camping is available from June to September, excluding school holidays (when the park is always booked out).

A small **shop** at reception sells basics, souvenirs, alcohol and soft drinks, but if you're staying for a few days you should stock up in Cradock. There's a reasonable licensed **restaurant**, a post office, a filling station and a lovely swimming pool set among huge rocks, all near reception.

Graaff-Reinet and around

It's little wonder that the tour buses pull in to **GRAAFF-REINET** in their numbers; this is a beautiful town, and one of the few places in the Eastern Cape where you'd want to wander freely day and night, taking in historical buildings and the occasional little museum, have a meal or a drink before strolling back to your accommodation. All the sights are accessible on foot.

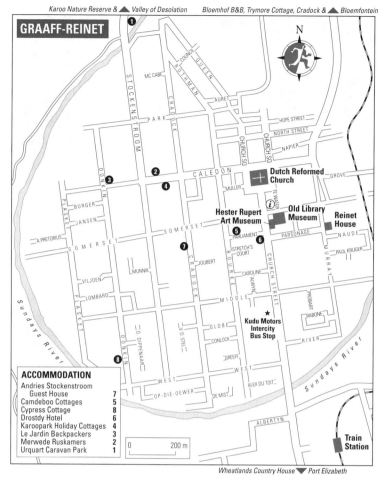

ACCOMMODATION

Andries Stockenstroom Guest House	7
Camdeboo Cottages	5
Cypress Cottage	8
Drostdy Hotel	6
Karoopark Holiday Cottages	4
Le Jardin Backpackers	3
Merwede Ruskamers	2
Urquart Caravan Park	1

Wheatlands Country House ▼ *Port Elizabeth*

Established in 1786, Graaff-Reinet is one of the oldest towns in South Africa, and much of its historical centre is intact. Exploring its charms takes at least a day and many people stop over en route from Johannesburg to the Garden Route. December is the busiest month, and you should definitely book well ahead if you want to stay over. Graaff-Reinet has a large population of Afrikaans-speaking coloured people, mostly living on the south side of town, some of slave origin, others the descendants of indigenous Khoi and San who were forced to work on frontier farms. The dry mountains surrounding the town are part of the **Karoo Nature Reserve**, whose main attraction is the **Valley of Desolation**, a B-movie name for an impressive site. The rocky canyon, echoing bird call and expansive skies of the valley, shouldn't be missed.

Some history

By the late eighteenth century, Dutch burghers had extended the Cape frontier northwards into the Sneeuwberg Mountains, traditionally the stomping

△ Church exterior, Graaff-Reinet

ground of Khoi pastoralists and San hunter-gathers. Little more than brigands, the settlers raided Khoi cattle and attacked groups of San, killing the men and abducting women and children to use as farm and domestic labourers. Friction escalated when the Khoi and San retaliated and, in 1786, the Cape authorities sent out a *landdrost* (magistrate) to establish **Graaff-Reinet**, administer the surrounding area and pacify the frontier.

Nine years later, *landdrost* Honoratus Maynier, following orders to stop vigilante rule by white settlers and to curb the maltreatment of Khoi and San servants, was forced out of town at gunpoint by a group of burghers, bandying catchphrases from the recent French revolution. Declaring South Africa's **first Boer republic**, they complained that Maynier was "protecting the Hottentots and Kafirs against the Boers".

In 1800 Maynier was again put in charge of Graaff-Reinet, and colonial control over the district was slowly consolidated, with vast tracts turned over to grazing sheep. The **wool boom** of the 1850s brought prosperity to the town and established a pattern of farming and land ownership which continues to this day.

Arrival and information

Translux **buses** between Johannesburg and Port Elizabeth, and Intercape buses connecting Jo'burg with the Garden Route towns, pull in daily at Kudu Motors, 84 Church St, a stone's throw south from the historical centre. However, for tickets and timetables you need to go to the **tourist information**

Robert Sobukwe and the Africanists

One of Graaff-Reinet's most brilliant but often-forgotten sons is **Robert Managaliso Sobukwe**, founder of the Pan Africanist Congress (PAC). Born in 1923, Sobukwe won a scholarship to Healdtown, a boarding school near Fort Beaufort, going on to Fort Hare University (see p.405), where he joined the African National Congress Youth League. After graduating in 1947, he became a schoolteacher and then a lecturer at the University of the Witwatersrand. A charismatic member of the Africanist wing of the ANC – even the ultra-apartheid prime minister B.J. Vorster acknowledged him as "a man of magnetic personality" – Sobukwe questioned the organization's strategy of co-operating with whites, and formed the breakaway PAC in 1959. The following year he launched the nationwide **anti-pass protests**, which ended in the Sharpeville massacre and his imprisonment on Robben Island for nine years. In 1969, Sobukwe was released under a banning order to Kimberley, where he died in 1978. Five thousand people attended his funeral in Graaff-Reinet. Unlike some followers of the PAC, who have not always held back from anti-white rhetoric, Sobukwe maintained that whites were capable, in time, of becoming genuine Africans.

You can visit the Sobukwe home and grave on a **township tour** with Xolile Speelman (℡049 892 2924, ℡049 892 4661), who also accompanies people to traditional events, with music and the chance to meet members of Graaff-Reinet's African community.

bureau at 13 Church Street (Mon–Fri 8am–12.30pm & 2–5pm, Sat & Sun 9am–noon; ℡049 892 4248, ⊛www.graaffreinet.co.za). This is also the place for **maps** and details on accommodation, including a list of more than a dozen people running B&Bs from their homes. Umasizakhe **township tours** are a recommended way to experience the other side of Graaff-Reinet; contact Xolile Speelman (see box above).

Accommodation

Graaff-Reinet has plenty of decent **places to stay** in the centre; the nicest are in listed historic buildings. There's a well-maintained **campsite** on the edge of town, with good-value chalets, and a cheap rooming house closer to the centre. Staying in a private home can work out less expensive than a guesthouse, and many have pools, braai facilities and welcome kids, though you'll have less privacy. The tourist bureau provides a list and map (see above) – as in some other South African towns, private houses offering B&B are not allowed to put up notices, so it's pointless strolling around looking for accommodation. If the Karoo landscape grabs you, you might want to head for one of the **farmstays** around Nieu Bethesda and Graaff-Reinet, and witness some of the country's most dazzling night skies and spacious landscape.

Andries Stockenstroom Guest House
100 Cradock St, a couple of streets back from the
Drostdy Hotel ℡ & ℡049 892 4575, ⊛www
.stockenstroom.co.za. A handsome listed house
with five air-conditioned rooms that has several
times won the Automobile Association award for
the best guesthouse in South Africa. It's worth
staying just for the evening meals (only for guests)
– outstanding French-Karoo cuisine with imaginative game and mutton dishes and scrumptious
desserts. You're unlikely to eat better anywhere in

the Karoo. Half-board ❺
Camdeboo Cottages 16 Parliament St ℡049 892
3180, ℡049 891 0919, ℡sunnykaroo@worldon-
line.co.za. Bang in the historical centre, these eight
fully equipped nineteenth-century self-catering
cottages built around a courtyard are smallish but
pleasant (hot-water bottles in winter). ❶
Cypress Cottage 80 Donkin St ℡049 892 3965
or 083 456 1795, ⊛www.cypresscottage.co.za. A
restored Karoo cottage with three double en-suite
rooms and a communal lounge and dining room,

all furnished with antiques. You have the place to yourself, whatever size your party. Families are welcome and the garden makes it good for kids. ⓷

Drostdy Hotel 30 Church St ☎049 892 2161, ⓕ049 892 4582, ⓔdrostdy@intekom.co.za. Elegant Cape Dutch landmark in a prime location, with a candle-lit dining room, shady gardens and fountains. The rooms, in terraced artisan cottages behind the hotel, are comfortable but small; larger rooms are pricier. ⓸

Karoopark Holiday Cottages 81 Caledon St ☎049 892 2557, ⓕ049 892 5730, ⓔinfo @karoopark.co.za. Complex of self-catering cottages set in a garden with a pool, plus dinky B&B units that are adequate for an overnight stay. ⓶

Le Jardin Backpackers 103 Caledon St/Donkin Street ☎049 892 3326 or 082 644 4938. Three well-priced air-conditioned rooms in a pleasant eighteenth-century home, with a big garden and communal kitchen. The hostel will collect people free from the intercity buses, and lockup parking is available. ⓵

Merwede Ruskamers 100 Caledon St ☎049 892 3749. The least expensive rooms in town, offering doubles and mini-dorms. Perfectly clean but a trifle dingy, and there are no cooking facilities. B&B dorms and doubles. ⓵

Urquhart Caravan Park on the outskirts of town, at the extension of Stockenstroom Street, next to the Karoo Nature Reserve ☎ & ⓕ049 892 2136. Large, well-maintained park with campsites and good-value rondavels, chalets and bungalows, next to the Sundays River. The bungalows are more roomy than the stuffy rondavels and have linen, but you must bring your own towels. ⓵

Farmstays

Bloemhof Bed & Breakfast 27km north of Graaff-Reinet on the N9, and 5km down a good gravel road ☎ & ⓕ049 840 0203, ⓔmurray-bloemhof@yebo.co.za. Grand, turn-of-the-century homestead built on ostrich-feather money, on a large sheep and game farm. Mid-priced Karoo lamb dinners available, and children welcome. ⓷

Trymore Cottage Wellwood Farm, off the N9, on the road to Nieu Bethesda, 31km north of Graaff-Reinet ☎ & ⓕ049 840 0302 or 082 379 0131, ⓔwellwood@yebo.co.za. Self-catering four-bedroomed cottage on a farm famous for its private collection of Karoo reptile fossils, merino sheep stud and orange grove. Braai packs are available on request as are evening dinners, with Karoo lamb or venison on the menu. The stunning fossil collection is not open to the public, but you may view it if you're staying here, and non-guests can write for permission to see it (PO Box 204, Graaff-Reinet 6280). Half-board and self-catering. ⓶

Wheatlands Country House 42km south of town, and 8km on a gravel road, off the R75 to Jansenville and Port Elizabeth ☎ & ⓕ049 891 0422 or 082 414 6503. A real gem: two en-suite bedrooms and a family unit in a spacious 1912 manor house filled with antiques on a wool and mohair farm, with large gardens. Book ahead for dinner. ⓷

The Town

Graaff-Reinet centres around the imposing 1886 **Dutch Reformed Church**, with its pointy steeple and cake-icing decoration. The main thoroughfare, **Church Street**, splits at either side of the church, heading northwest to the Valley of Desolation and northeast to Nieu Bethesda, Middelburg and eventually Johannesburg. On either side of Church Street, little roads fan out, lined with whitewashed Cape Dutch, Georgian and Victorian buildings – it's in these parts that you'll find the town's museums, restaurants and most attractive buildings.

Church Street itself bustles with antique shops and businesses with Karoo-inspired names, such as Merino Pharmacy and Kudu Motors. One block south of the church is the **Old Library Museum** (Mon–Fri 8am–12.30 & 2–5pm, Sat & Sun 9am–noon). The only attraction here is the excellent collection of **fossil skulls** and skeletons of reptiles that populated the marshes, lakes and pools of prehistoric Karoo, some 230 million years ago. These Karoo dinosaurs were entombed in mud, and their bones became embedded in the present-day Karoo shale; the fossils were collected from the hills and river channels in the surrounding area. There's an even better collection on Wellwood Farm (see *Trymore Cottage* above), but you'll need to write for permission to see it.

Next door, in a restored 1821 mission church with Dutch gables, is the

Hester Rupert Art Museum (Mon–Fri 8am–5pm, Sat 8am–1pm; 50c), which features a representative selection of work by South African artists (primarily white) active in the mid-1960s. Much of it is dreary and derivative of European art, but a few pieces stand out. Look out in particular for Cecil Skotnes's woodcuts, the strong expressionistic work of Johannes Meintjies, and Irma Stern's very appealing paintings.

Opposite the Art Museum stands the graceful, whitewashed **Drostdy Hotel**, a historical building in its own right, as the former residence of the *landdrost*. Most of the hotel guests are housed behind the main building, in Stretch's Court, a cobbled lane of nineteenth-century cottages with brightly coloured shutters. It hasn't always been so twee: Drostdy's slaves lived here, and after slavery ended in 1838 their descendants stayed on until they were kicked out under the 1950 Group Areas Act (when the area was zoned for whites only).

From the front steps of the Drostdy, you can look down Pastorie Street, lined with Cape Dutch buildings, to **Reinet House** (Mon–Fri 8am–1pm & 2–5pm, Sat 8am–1pm; R5), Graaff-Reinet's finest museum. Formerly a parsonage, it was built in 1812 in the traditional Cape Dutch H-plan, with six gables and a spiral stairway leading to the garden. Essentially a period house museum with wooden floors and airy rooms, it's filled with covetable furniture and intriguing household objects. Strangely enough, the museum is the only place allowed to distil an illicit home-brewed spirit called "Withond" (white dog), which has an exceptionally sharp bite. Little bottles of the clear liquor, labelled with a picture of a bull terrier, are sold at the front desk.

Eating and drinking

You'll find a fair number of centrally located **restaurants** and **tea shops** catering for Graaff-Reinet's many visitors, though the town is pretty dead on Sundays. The culinary highlight is unquestionably the *Andries Stockenstroom Guest House* (see "Accommodation" on p.391), but you need to be staying there to enjoy its cooking, which attracts gourmets from across the country.

Coral Tree 3 Church Square. Best place for light lunches such as pitta pockets, venison pies and open sandwiches, and for evening meals it's a good place to sample local meats such as Karoo lamb, pork loin or springbok steaks. Mon–Sat 10am–2.30pm & 6pm till late.
Drostdy Hotel 30 Church St. Unrivalled garden setting for drinks or tea. Rather formal dinners are served in the grand dining room, with a pricey English-style set menu and the odd Afrikaans speciality thrown in. Their buffet lunches and breakfasts are better value. Open daily.
Iets Anders 3 Parsonage St. Daytime café/bar serving reasonably priced Afrikaans specialities,

such as *bobotie* and rice, tomato *bredie* done in a *potjie* (a three-legged pot), hearty breakfasts, sandwiches, hamburgers, homemade ginger beer and cakes including syrupy *koeksisters* and *melktert*. Closed Sundays.
Kliphuis 46 Bourke St. Open during the day only for tea and sandwiches or a light lunch at pavement tables. Closed Sundays.
Number 8 Pub & Grub 8 Church Square. Primarily a family restaurant and pub with a pleasant atmosphere serving steaks, burgers and fish and chips. Daytime and evenings with a big screen for sports viewing. Closed Sundays.

Karoo Nature Reserve and the Valley of Desolation

The low-lying **Karoo Nature Reserve** (open daily dawn–dusk; free) totally surrounds the town, with its entrance 5km north of Graaff-Reinet's centre, off the Murraysburg Road. Its indisputable highlight is the strikingly deep **Valley of Desolation**. To get there by car, follow the narrow tarred road from the reserve's entrance, ascending the bush-flecked mountainside, passing a series of viewpoints up to the cliffs overlooking the valley. Late afternoon is the best time to enjoy the scenery, when the sun saturates the ochres and reds of the rock towers soaring from the valley floor. The views from the lip of the canyon, beyond the rocks and into the plains of Camdeboo, are truly thrilling, and even better if you tune into the echoing bird calls, especially when black eagles circle the dolomite towers, scanning the crevices for prey. There's a 45-minute looped **walk** along the canyon lip, well marked with a lizard emblem. For longer trails, and **staying overnight** in a hiker's hut (with a braai area), you'll need to book at the Department of Nature Conservation, Bourke Street (℡049 892 3453), where you can also pick up detailed **maps**.

Nieu Bethesda

There's a mystique about the Karoo being at the unfathomable heart of South Africa, and if you want to get a sense of its dry timelessness, **NIEU BETHESDA** is the place to do it. Winding into the mountains 50km north of Graaff-Reinet, much of the Karoo's attraction lies in its spareness, set against expansive skies. Nieu Bethesda is drier and dustier than you might wish, however, especially in midsummer when it boils with harsh, bright light. There are no streetlamps, and on winter nights temperatures plummet to zero, the sky filled with icy stars.

Most people come to Nieu Bethesda to marvel – or shudder – at the **Owl House** on River Street (daily 8am–6pm; R9; ℡049 841 1603, ⊛www.owl-house.co.za), once the home of Helen Martins, a reclusive artist who expressed her disturbing and fascinating inner world through her work. Every corner of the house and garden has been transformed to meet her vision, the interior walls glittering with crushed glass. At the back of the house, trapped by a stone wall and high chicken wire, are hundreds of glass and cement sculptures: camels, lambs, sphinxes and human figures, while owls with large eyes gaze from her tin-roofed verandah. Martins never exhibited her work or courted publicity, though since her death in 1976 many have visited the museum and pondered on her life in this Karoo backwater. South African playwright Athol Fugard, who loves the Karoo and has a house in Nieu Bethesda, used her life and creative toil as inspiration for his celebrated play *The Road to Mecca*.

Owl House aside, the whitewashed **village** has plenty of charm. It's a tranquil place, accessible on a good gravel road, with the sound of spring water flowing down furrows into the little windmilled allotments. Once an archetypal conservative Karoo *dorp*, the town has reinvented itself as an artists' colony of about fifty white people, attracting a growing number of visitors. Nearby, a few hundred coloured residents somehow manage to eke out a living in this harsh environment. Making the most of the creative forces and lack of distractions, the **Ibis Gallery** on the main road (℡049 841 1623, ⊛www.ibisartcentre.co.za; free) hosts first-rate exhibitions of contemporary South African art, some of it made locally. It also sells artwork, notably ceramics, wire bathroom accessories, candles and dolls. The Nieu Bethesda Community Art Group's gallery, opposite the police station, also exhibits local artwork.

The **Compassberg Mountain**, one of the highest peaks in the Eastern Cape and part of the Sneeuberg range, dominates the Nieu Bethesda skyline. Ibis Gallery can arrange permits to climb the mountain, and gives advice on other local activities. It's also worth contacting Idil Sheard for details of **trails** (℡049 842 2418), all operated from private farms.

Practicalities

Nieu Bethesda is 23km off the N9 between Graaff-Reinet and Middelburg. There's a **village shop** and butcher on the main road, but if you're self-catering you should stock up elsewhere, especially for fresh fruit and vegetables, which are scarce in the Karoo. No petrol is available in Nieu Bethesda, so fill up in Graaff-Reinet. Luxury is not absent in this *dorp,* though – it's a good place to have an aromatherapy massage; book through Ibis Gallery (see p.394).

Given how tiny Nieu Bethesda is, it's surprising to find any **restaurants** at all, but you actually have a choice. You can pop into *The Waenhuis*, on the main road, for pub fare and drinks every evening except Sunday; their satellite aerial caters to the village's sport junkies. A couple of blocks from the Owl House in New Street, *The Barn* (Wed, Fri & Sat nights & Sun lunchtime), offers pizzas and pasta. The *Ibis Café* at the gallery is open daily (closed Sat afternoons) and serves decent coffee, a range of tea and local ginger beer and country comestibles such as ice cream with prickly pear sauce. During the day you can eat at the *Village Inn*, along from the Owl House in New Street. The food is nothing special, but the owner, Egbert, is a mine of **information** about the area.

Accommodation

There's an excellent selection of cheap **places to stay**: the Ibis Gallery (℡049 841 1623, ⊛www.ibisartcentre.co.za/aba) in the main road runs an accommodation agency. Accommodation is primarily in **self-catering** cottages, with one party per house, at under R100 per person. Secluded on a hillside at the edge of town is *Pepper Tree Cottage* (❷), with reed ceilings. *Beaumont Cottage* (❷), the town's smartest, is a tastefully renovated Karoo cottage in farmland with brilliant views of the Compassberg. *Huis Nommer Een*, Murray St (book through Suzette Pienaar ℡049 841 1700; ❷), with three spacious rooms furnished in South African country style, a farm-style kitchen, and a handsome verandah, is another great option.

The only **B&B** is *Stokkiesdraai Guest House*, Murray Street (℡049 841 1658; ❷) in a two-bedroomed Karoo cottage. The hamlet's only **backpacker lodge**, *Owl House*, Martin Street (℡049 841 1642; ℮owlhouse@global.co.za; ❶) is an old house with a nice garden and six-bed dorm, plus a garden cottage with shower for a couple or a double room in the main house. If you want to stay on a **farmhouse**, head for *Weltevreden Farm* (booking through Ibis; ❶), 13km north of the village, in the Sneeuberg Mountains, which has two self-catering cottages, hiking and riding. Alternatively, try the friendly *Doornberg Farm* (℡ & ℗049 841 1401; ❶), which has a pub and serves evening meals, or you can self-cater; there's also a trampoline, pool, riding and hiking.

East London and the central region

Between Port Alfred and East London lies some of the Eastern Cape's least-developed **coastline**, saved from the hands of developers because it fell into the neglected Xhosa *bantustan* of the Ciskei. **East London**, wedged uncomfortably between two ex-*bantustans*, is the largest city in the central region of the province, with excellent beaches for surfing and swimming and good transport links to Johannesburg and along the coast. Heading inland, **Fort Hare University** near Alice has educated political leaders across the subcontinent, including Nelson Mandela, and has the country's finest collection of contemporary black South African art.

Sweeping up from Fort Hare's valley, the gentle, wooded **Amatola Mountains** yield to the dramatic landscapes of the **Eastern Cape Drakensberg**, which offer hiking, horse-riding and even skiing opportunities. Before white settlers (or even the Xhosa) arrived, these towering formations were dominated by **San hunter–gatherers**, who decorated the rock-faces with thousands of ritual **paintings**, many of which remain surprisingly vivid.

The coast: Fish River Mouth to East London

Heading 38km east of Port Alfred, along the R72, you'll come to the **Great Fish River**, the boundary across which the British drove the Xhosa in the Fourth Frontier War of 1811–12. It's a major landmark, cutting through a steep-sided valley shrouded in thick prickly bush. During apartheid, the river became the frontier of the notionally independent Ciskei *bantustan*, whose multi-million-rand border post on the east bank of the river stood unused until the 1990s, when it became a rather pleasant roadside tea room.

The **Great Fish River Wetland Reserve** between the R72 and the river mouth is noted for its beautiful plants and prolific birdlife. There's nowhere to stay in the reserve, but just across the Great Fish is the luxurious *Fish River Sun Hotel* (✆040 676 1102, or central reservations ✆011 780 7800, ⓦwww.sun-international.com; ❹). Conforming to the bizarre logic of apartheid, this is where Eastern Cape whites could nip over the border to the *bantustan* to the South African-owned **hotel** and enjoy a spot of gambling, which was banned in "White South Africa". The *Sun* has arguably the best **golf** course in the country (open to non-residents) with stunning views of the river and beach. A few kilometres further east, the *Mpekweni Sun Marine Resort* (✆040 676 1026, or central reservations ✆011 780 7800, ⓦwww.sun-international.com; ❸) is very comfortable, but not as glitzy. Its position couldn't be better, though, with rooms close to the beautiful lagoon and beach, which the hotel has managed to nab for its own exclusive use.

Hamburg

One of the few resorts along the Pineapple Coast that feels like real Africa is **HAMBURG**, a low-key village on a good dirt road, 14km off the R72. The route passes through **Xhosa settlements** and shanties, where you'll see traditionally decorated thatch-and-mud huts. Look out for animals wandering perilously into your way and strolling around Hamburg itself, lending the town a truly rural feel. Hamburg is renowned for **fishing**, and the muddy-bottomed Keiskamma River is excellent for catching prawns. The sea offers a good beach break for **surfers**. Apart from that, there's not much to do except laze on the beach, go for walks and birdwatch.

There are a couple of **places to stay**, both with views over the wide, brown Keiskamma River and high olive hills, but a three-kilometre walk to the beach. There's nothing at the beach except a car park, broken-down toilets and miles of sand and sea. Mr Vorster rents out a self-catering flat (℡ & ℻ 040 678 1000; ❶) in the lower section of his timber house. The flat sleeps six people and has a sundeck and braai area. *Sampie's Landing* (℡ 040 678 1032; ❷) rents out rooms, and the owner takes guests fishing. There's a little shop, but no restaurants.

East London and around

EAST LONDON, the second-largest city in the Eastern Cape, is the obvious jumping-off point for exploring the Transkei or the coast west to Port Elizabeth. It has good **connections** to the rest of the country by air, rail and bus, and you don't need a car to enjoy the beach life. But without fine, warm weather, the city can be dreary. What does happen takes place along the beachfront, where there's a plethora of places to stay, eat and drink. **Nahoon Beach** is a great **surfing spot**, and the town has a dedicated and lively surfing scene. It's also gradually becoming a place for black holidaymakers – a post-apartheid phenomenon. The beaches to the east of town are very beautiful, with long stretches of sand, high dunes, estuaries and luxuriant vegetation, and good swimming. Although definitely not a fashionable city, it's small and easy to drive around, with some excellent restaurants and good accommodation. All in all, you could have a fine time for a night or two.

Away from the holiday strip, East London is dominated by an industrial centre served by **Mdantsane**, a huge African township 20km from the city towards King William's Town. Apart from the active river port, there are several large factories, including Mercedes-Benz, whose workers presented Nelson Mandela with a bright red, top-of-the-range Mercedes as a coming-out-of-prison present.

Some history

East London began life as a permanent British settlement during the nineteenth-century **Frontier Wars**, when it was used as a beachhead to land military supplies needed to push back the Xhosa. Taken by its strategic possibilities as a port, the British governor Sir Harry Smith optimistically called it **London** in 1848, after the capital of the Empire. Later it was changed to the Port of East London, not after London's East End, but because the port was on the east side of the Buffalo River. British connections are still obvious, though: East London's main thoroughfare is called Oxford Street and there's a Fleet Street and even a Belgravia suburb.

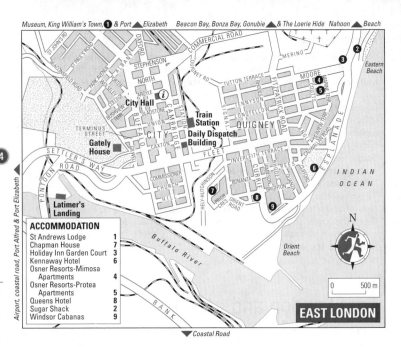

ACCOMMODATION

St Andrews Lodge	1
Chapman House	7
Holiday Inn Garden Court	3
Kennaway Hotel	6
Osner Resorts-Mimosa Apartments	4
Osner Resorts-Protea Apartments	5
Queens Hotel	8
Sugar Shack	2
Windsor Cabanas	9

EAST LONDON

▼ Coastal Road

Before the British, and even the Xhosa, this was home to the **Khoikhoi** people, who called it Place of the Buffaloes. The Buffalo River once teemed with game, but the animals were gradually killed off with the arrival of British hunters.

Arrival, information and orientation

East London's small **airport** (☎043 706 0211), a few kilometres west of the centre on the R72, connects the city to all major centres. The **airport shuttle** (☎082 663 3087, after hours ☎082 925 2475) meets all flights and drops off at the *Holiday Inn* near the beachfront. Coming in **by train** from Johannesburg, you'll arrive at the station on the eastern edge of East London's small business and shopping district. All three of the **intercity buses** – Translux from Durban, Intercape from Port Elizabeth, and Greyhound from Johannesburg – take you to the beachfront, dropping off at the coach terminal at Windmill Park on Moore Street. From the train station, it's a thirty-minute walk to the backpacker hostel at Eastern Beach, and a slightly shorter stroll to Orient Beach. Buses are scarce, but there are metered **taxis** (see p.402) outside the station.

Like many South African cities, central East London is gridded; with uncongested roads and easy parking, it's far more orientated to **driving** than walking. **Public transport** connects the African townships to the centre, via speeding minibus taxis, and buses link the city's two hubs, the **city centre** and **beachfront**.

Maps and a comprehensive list of B&Bs are available from the helpful **tourist information** bureau, 35 Argyle St (Mon–Fri 8.30am–4.30pm, Sat 9am–noon; ☎043 722 6015, 043 743 5091, eltour@mweb.co.za), behind the City Hall. Amatola Tours (☎043 743 0472, info@amatour.co.za) conducts **tours** of the city centre and townships, including a visit to the Khaya Labantu Cultural Village (☎043 851 1011; visits by prior arrangement), 30km east of town, where there's a storyteller, Xhosa dancing and traditional food.

Accommodation

To get the best out of East London, **stay** either at the beachfront, or up the hilly and wooded east coast, towards Gonubie. There are also a couple of convenient places near the airport. East London fills up over the Christmas period, when prices rise sharply. For **backpackers**, the best lodge is *Sugar Shack*, at Eastern Beach, spectacularly situated in a former lifeguard's lookout.

Beachfront

East London's **beachfront** sports graceless blocks of holiday apartments and functional hotels, redeemed only by their fabulous views of the Indian Ocean. The really cheap hotels are mostly filled with long-term residents, and are often rough drinking hangouts – best avoided.

Holiday Inn Garden Court Beachfront ☎043 722 7260, ℗043 743 7360, ⊛www.sixcontinentshotels.com. Close to Eastern Beach, and no surprises here in terms of price or decor. ❹

Kennaway Hotel Beachfront ☎ & ℗043 722 5531, ⊛www.osner-resorts.co.za/snooze.html. Comfortable rooms in a reliable hotel with exceptional views. The sea-facing rooms are a bit more expensive, but definitely worth it. ❸

Osner Resorts ☎043 743 3433, ⊛www.osner-resorts.co.za/snooze.html. Decent, dependable and outstanding-value self-catering units with phones and TVs in beachfront apartment blocks. All have family rooms, and continental breakfast is provided. ❶

Sugar Shack Eastern Beach ☎ & ℗043 722 8240, ⊛www.backpackafrica.co.za/accommod /eastcape/sugarshk.html. Brilliantly located, right on the beach, with terrific views. Bright dorms and outdoor relaxation area. Expect a lively surfing and partying crowd. Free pick-up is available from town or the station. ❶

Windsor Cabanas George Walker Parade, Beachfront ☎043 743 2225, ⊛www.osner-resorts .co.za/snooze.html. Spanish-style block, with B&B pads near Orient Beach, offering great views, terraces, cane furniture and tiled floors. Also fully equipped for self-catering. ❸

Eastern suburbs and resorts

If the urban nature of the main beachfront doesn't appeal, your best bet is to head for the mostly white suburbs of **Beacon Bay**, **Bonza Bay** or **Gonubie**, close to the river and sea. Besides a couple of old-fashioned hotels, these areas have a good selection of smart **B&Bs** in private houses. You'll need your own transport to get there, unless you arrange to be picked up beforehand or take a taxi. East London's **campsites** are out this way too, near the water. There are also places to stay in the suburb of Selborne, an easy drive from the beach but close to the centre, near the Vincent Park Mall.

Blue Lagoon Hotel Blue Bend Place, Beacon Bay ☎043 748 4821, ℗043 748 2037, ℮blhotel @iafrica.com. Very pleasant accommodation surrounded by palm trees and close to the beach. Rooms are quiet and spacious with balconies looking onto the river, which you can reach via a short path that also leads to the beach. ❹

Dolphin Hotel 85 Harewood Drive, Nahoon ☎043 735 1435, ℗043 735 4639, ⊛196.7.177.40 /dolphin/default.htm. A plain, 1950s suburban hotel: the prim style gives no hint of the lush vegetation and wonderful beach just a 15min walk away. ❸

Gonubie Resort & Caravan Park 19km east of town off the N2 ☎043 740 2021. The best camping place in East London, which is well-maintained, neat and clean, and has sheltered camping spots, near the beach and lovely estuary, which are safe for swimming. There are also wooden, fully equipped self-catering chalets. ❶

Habitat 2 Cane St, Gonubie, one block away from Gonubie Beach ☎043 740 3703. Two self-catering units with private entrances, one in the garden, the other on the ground floor of the main house. Run by a tourist guide who is also an organic gardener. No children. ❶

The Loerie Hide B&B 2B Sheerness Rd, off Beach Road, Nahoon ☎043 735 3206, ℱ043 735 4957, ✆www.eastlondonsa.com/bnbs/loerie. Two reasonably priced cottages in the vicinity of Nahoon Beach, decorated in ethnic African and English country-cottage style, at the bottom of a garden that gives way to indigenous bushland. ❸
Meander Inn 8 Claredon Rd, Selborne ☎043 743 6181, ℱ043 743 6188, ℮meross@iafrica.com. Five spacious rooms tastefully furnished with timber beds, white linen and ceiling fans in a luxurious yet relaxed two-storey house set in a manicured garden, and hosted by a friendly young couple. Swimming pool, patio and bar. Often used as the starting or finishing point of the Wild Coast Meander (see p.420). ❸

Nahoon Caravan Park Beach Road, Nahoon ☎043 705 2129, ℱ043 743 4120. At the Nahoon estuary, the secure camping area nestles among riverine trees with plenty of grassy sites. A short walk to the river and a bit further to the open beach. ❶
Selborne B&B 9 Salisbury Rd, off Frere Road, Selborne ☎043 726 9666. Near the Vincent Park Centre. A clean, friendly and reliable no-frills B&B with wooden beds. ❶
St Andrews Lodge 14 St Andrews Rd, Selborne ☎043 743 5131 or 082 474 8698, ℱ043 721 0960, ℮sandrews@iafrica.com. Four well-priced en-suite B&B units with separate entrances and TV inside a suburban house, as well as a garden cottage with cooking facilities. Swimming pool. ❷

The City

East London's drab city centre is dominated by **Oxford Street**, once the main shopping precinct, parallel to Station Street and the train station. Although a major traffic thoroughfare, it is largely deserted at night, when you shouldn't wander around alone. White East Londoners have abandoned the centre, preferring to shop at the **Vincent Park Centre** on Devreux Avenue, 5km north of the city centre (leave the centre on Oxford Street, and turn right into Devreux just beyond the museum), in the midst of the salubrious suburbs of Vincent and Stirling. This is the best place for shopping, or to find anything practical such as banks and the post office.

Apart from a couple of handsome buildings, East London's Victorian heart has progressively been demolished. From the station you can walk a few blocks north up Cambridge Street to the city centre's principal landmark, the splendid terracotta and lace-white **City Hall**, opened in 1899. Its tall, colourful clock tower amongst the otherwise dreary modernish buildings is a useful orientation point. Over the road is a rather lifeless statue of martyred Black Consciousness leader **Steve Biko** (see p.405), a minor point of pilgrimage for visitors, unveiled by Nelson Mandela in 1997. Staying with the Biko theme, the **Daily Dispatch Building**, dressed in a surrounding colonial-style verandah, is also worth taking in, at the corner of Caxton Street and Cambridge Road. The newspaper, founded in 1879, made national headlines in the 1970s, when its editor Donald Woods earned the wrath of the apartheid government for being involved with Biko, who contributed to the newspaper under a pseudonym. After endless police harassment, Woods fled the country dramatically, a story told in the book and 1987 movie *Cry Freedom*. Woods died of cancer in 2001.

One street north of here, Terminus Street leads to the Victorian **Gately House** (Tues–Thurs 10am–1pm & 2–5pm, Fri 10am–1pm, Sat & Sun 3–5pm; entry by donation). This was the home of the city's first mayor, John Gately, and contains some fine period furniture. You can also enter Gately House via **Queen's Park & Zoo** (daily 9am–5pm; R8), a good spot to take children, with its farmyard, reptiles and birds, as well as a playground and refreshment kiosk. At weekends there are pony rides (10am–4pm) and a little train runs all day at the weekend and at 11am and 2.30pm on weekdays. On the east side of the railway line, is **Quigney**, a racially mixed area of small colonial-style Victorian houses, some nicely restored with verandahs and corrugated-iron roofs, others run-down. Quigney slopes downhill to the **Esplanade** and **Orient Beach**, the safest place to swim and most easily reached along Currie Street, off Fleet Street. The city's best curio outlet, stocking handmade **African crafts**, is Umzi Wethu Curio Shop, 110 Moore St, up the hill from the *Holiday Inn*. African Culture, 46 Station St, has ceramics, sculpture, drawings, batiks and tie-dyed products made on the premises; nearest the beach is the consistently reliable Africa Curio Shop in Lock Street Gaol, Fleet Street which sells curios, leather and woodwork.

Two kilometres uphill from the centre is **Latimer's Landing**, the working dockland waterfront on the Buffalo River. Never the success it was hoped to be, it appears a little deserted, and business is slow – but there's still a pub, and it's good for a wander around to see the boats. To get there, head west along Fleet Street towards the airport, and just before crossing the Buffalo Bridge head steeply down Pontoon Road. **Boat trips** from here head through the Buffalo harbour out to sea and along the beachfront shore. Yacht Miscky (☎043 735 2232) offers trips by arrangement.

A few kilometres north of the city centre, the **East London Museum**, Upper Oxford Street (Mon–Fri 9.30am–5pm, Sat 2–5pm, Sun 11am–4pm; R5) has a stunning collection of South Nguni beadwork, and contemporary wire sculpture, including an inventive wire car made by Mdantsane resident Phillip Ntliziywana. The museum's pride and joy, however, is its stuffed coelacanth (see p.378), caught off the coast in the 1950s.

The beaches

East London's **Esplanade** loops from Orient Pier in a wide and beautiful sweep of rocks, beach and sand dunes to Eastern Beach, marred only by the motley assortment of holiday apartments, hotels and restaurants lining the beachfront. It's about thirty minutes' walk from the city centre; buses here are sporadic, but it's easy enough to stroll from one end to the other

Tucked in next to Orient Pier, with dockland cranes poking their necks above the water, **Orient Beach** is a wonderful place to swim, though it looks a bit grim and industrial. The waves are gentle, and the water and sandy beach are clean. Red-hatted lifeguards lend a sense of security, and there are changing rooms, and a couple of little pools for kids. You pay a small fee to enter the beach area during the day, but it's free after 5pm.

From Orient Beach, the sea-walled Esplanade continues northeast, along sand and black rocks, to **Eastern Beach**, with its high, bush-capped sand dunes. Although far more attractive, Eastern Beach is not really safe for swimming, and muggings have been reported. Don't leave your belongings unattended, and give the beach a wide berth at night.

Heading northeast beyond Bat's Cave – a distinctive chunk of rock jutting out to sea – is popular **Nahoon Beach**, a long stretch of sand, backed by dunes. This wonderful natural setting is superb for swimming and surfing, with some of the best waves in the country. Public transport is scant, but there are three **buses** a day from the Esplanade, or you can walk the 5km from the centre if you're feeling energetic. East of the Nahoon River, 10km from the centre, the coast curves into **Bonza Bay**, with kilometres of beach walks and a lazy lagoon at the mouth of the Quinera River. The closest campsite to the city centre is the *Nahoon* (see p.400), nestling in the riverine trees. Further on, **Gonubie Beach**, 25km northeast of the centre, at the Gonubie River Mouth, is still close enough to be considered part of East London, with some good accommodation, a beautiful beach and walks.

Eating, drinking and nightlife

East London has several surprisingly good restaurants and a couple of very decent places serving **fresh fish** in an outdoor setting. **Drinking** spots abound, from beachfront sleaze at lowlife hotels to lively surfers' hangouts or swanky places overlooking the ocean. Some of the pubs double up as **live music** venues, as well as offering a bite to eat.

Bellami's 18 Marine Terrace, Beachfront, opposite the *Osner Hotel* ☏ 043 743 2145. A family of chefs produces imaginative and delicious global dishes such as lemon, ginger and chilli calamari with creme fraiche, North African spiced line fish with chilli-cucumber yoghurt and venison fillet on smoked root vegetables. Dinner Mon–Sat.

Buccaneer's Pub Eastern Beach, next to *Sugar Shack*. Lively bar that buzzes till the early hours, with occasional live music (Wed, Fri & Sat). During the day there are fantastic views of the rodeo riders of the surf. Good pub fare includes fish and chips and, best of all, chicken schnitzel.

Ernst Chalet Suisse upstairs at the paying entrance to Orient Beach ☏ 043 722 1840. One of East London's top restaurants; its outstanding Swiss chef cooks up a seafood storm and delectable desserts. Smart, but reasonably priced. Open daily except Sat for lunch and daily except Sun for dinner.

Le Petit 54 Beach Road Shopping Centre, Nahoon ☏ 043 735 3685. Reputed eating place serving rich food with an emphasis on game, seafood and veal. The decor is dark wood panelling and red plush. Mon–Sat (dinner only on Sat).

Nao Faz Mal *Windsor Cabanas*, behind Orient Beach ☏ 043 743 2225. Courtyard tables with umbrellas, and an exotic palm-tree setting for an excellent and very reasonably priced blow-out buffet of Mozambican Portuguese food. At least ten cold and hot starters with a strong emphasis on fish, salads and vegetables, seafood and meaty main courses and a huge array of desserts. Relaxed atmosphere, attentive service and child-friendly. Booking essential for the flat-rate meal. Closed Sun eves.

O'Hagan's Esplanade, midway along, next to the Aquarium. Pub restaurant with spectacular setting on a terrace jutting out over the waves. Even when the weather is bad you can watch the surfers through huge picture windows, although the food is unexciting. Open daily.

Quarterdeck Orient Beach, overlooking the paddling pool ☏ 043 743 5312. The informal part of the *Chalet Suisse*, served by the same kitchen. It's one of the best beachside places for a quiet drink, with reasonably priced catch of the day served daily. Closed all day Sun and Sat lunchtime.

Tug & Ferry Latimer's Landing ☏ 043 743 1187. Great for its location next to a functioning river port, this English-themed pub has a deck for watching the low-key bustle. Pub grub includes a good beer-and-steak pie as well as fresh line fish. There's a large selection of draught beers on tap and fires indoors for chilly winter days. Lunch and eves.

Listings

Car rental Avis ☏ 043 736 2250, Imperial ☏ 043 736 2230.

Emergencies Ambulance ☏ 10177; Fire ☏ 722 1212; Police (Flying Squad) ☏ 10111.

Garages Stirling Motors, 8 Old Transkei Rd, does repairs and is open 24hr.

Hospitals Frere Hospital (state), Amalinda Drive ☏ 043 709 1111; St Dominics (private), 45 St Mark's Rd ☏ 043 743 4303.

Internet access Cyberlink ☏ 083 375 9040 has facilities at several places in town including their main branch at Cyber Lounge, 58 Beach Rd, Nahoon (Mon–Fri 3–9pm, Sat & Sun 9am–9pm) and in the centre at Almega College, 151 Oxford St.

Laundries Washing Well, Currie Street, or Laundromat (coin-operated washing machines and ironing) at the Edcott Centre, Oxford Street.

Pharmacies John Forbes, 205a Oxford St (☏ 043 722 2062; till 10pm) and Berea Pharmacy, Pearce Street (☏ 043 721 3000; Mon–Sat 8am–10pm, Sun 9am–1pm & 2–9pm).

Taxis Springbok ☏ 043 722 4400.

Train information Station ☏ 043 700 2118; Johannesburg passenger enquiries ☏ 043 740 2020.

Travel agents Rennies Travel, 33 Chamberlain Rd, Berea ☏ 043 726 0698; and Let's Travel, Kennaway Building, Esplanade ☏ 043 743 2983.

Around East London

Several worthwhile excursions detailed below are within an hour's drive from East London. If you don't have your own wheels, this ground is covered by Amatola Tours (℡043 743 0472, ⓦwww.touringsa.co.za), who offer half-day trips from R350 per person, and full days from R650. Amatola Tours also takes trips further afield to King William's Town.

Inkwenkwezi Game Reserve

Inkwenkwezi Game Reserve lies 23km from East London (book in advance for a safari ℡ & ⓕ043 734 3234). This small private game reserve is set in an appealing landscape, encompassing bushveld, grassland, forest and two rivers, with views of the Indian Ocean. Wildlife, including rhino, giraffe, zebra, wildebeest, various antelope and some rare birds, is viewed on early-morning or afternoon/evening game drives in one of the reserve's 4WD vehicles. The centrepiece is a magnificently sited, thatched lapa with spacious decks where you eat and drink. To get there, drive out of East London towards Umtata along the N2, taking the Brakfontein off-ramp onto the East Coast Resorts Road; then travel east for about 20km, until you reach the Inkwenkwezi Entrance Gate on your left.

Xhosa and township cultural tours

Khaya La Buntu, near Mooiplaas, 30km east of East London, signposted off the N2 (booking essential: ℡043 851 1011), is a real **Xhosa village** which sees only twenty or thirty tours a year, so it's not one of the dressed-up villages deemed suitable for tourists. It's best visited for a traditional lunch, in a group, so there's enough atmosphere for dancing and storytelling. It's possible to have a more casual **lunch** at the *Emzini Traditional Food Restaurant*, 14 Station St, Berlin, 45km northwest of East London. Follow the N2 in the direction of King William's Town, take exit 19 and turn right at the stop sign towards Border Technikon which brings you to the little town of Berlin. At the four-way stop, turn right into Immigrant Road, then right into Station Street.

The Amatola Mountains

Most visitors drive quickly through the scrubby, dry impoverished area between East London and the **Amatola Mountains** proper, to reach the cool forests and holiday lands at the **Hogsback**. However, it's worth deviating en route, to see the marvellous collection of African art at Fort Hare University, close to the little town of Alice, and to visit apartheid martyr Steve Biko's grave in **King William's Town**. King, as it's usually called, has a couple of worthwhile museums which help you absorb some of East Cape's settler history and Xhosa culture.

One of South Africa's least-explored game reserves, **Mpofu**, lies in this region, with hiking trails and cheap self-catering accommodation. If you want to do the reserve in style, stay in a fabulous, settler farmhouse on a working farm at Waylands, 40km north of **Fort Beaufort,** the region's farming centre.

King William's Town

KING WILLIAM'S TOWN, more commonly known simply as **King**, lies 56km northeast of East London. It started life as a military frontier and missionary outpost, and today has a large population drawn from the former Ciskei. There's enough historical interest here to satisfy at least half a day's visit. To get a feel for **Xhosa history**, head for the **Amatola Museum** (Mon–Fri 9am–1pm & 1.45–4.30pm, Sat 10am–3pm; R5) in Alexandra Road; the Xhosa Gallery has unusually good displays, including full accounts of the British tactics and campaigns which crushed the Xhosa. Traditional culture is well represented, with contemporary exhibitions on current building styles. Don't miss Phillip Ntliziywana's imaginative bus and car sculptures made from wire and discarded bits and pieces.

Two blocks north of the museum, off Albert Road, is the nineteenth-century **Edward Street Cemetery**, notable for the story it tells of the conflicts in the area. Besides a memorial to those killed in the innumerable Frontier Wars against the Xhosa, there is an open piece of ground on the far side of the cemetery which marks a mass grave. This is where hundreds of Xhosa were buried; they died of starvation as a result of the disastrous 1857 **Cattle Killing**, when many Xhosa people destroyed their cattle at the behest of the false prophetess Nongqawuse (see p.423).

About fifteen minutes' walk north of the Kaffrarian, the **Missionary Museum** in Berkeley Street (Mon–Fri 9am–1pm & 1.45–4.30pm; R5) is mainly of interest for the glimpse it gives into early educational institutions in the Eastern Cape. South Africa's first black professionals were schooled here, including many of the new nation's heavyweights such as Nelson Mandela.

King's only other attraction of note is **Steve Biko's grave** in the Ginsberg Cemetery. It's a moving place, and the grave is much humbler than you'd expect for such an important figure in black politics. The polished, charcoal-coloured tombstone sits midway through the graveyard, among the large patch of paupers' graves. To get there, take Cathcart Street south out of town (towards Grahamstown), turning left onto a road signposted to the cemetery, after the bridge (just before the turn-off to your right to Alice).

Rob Speirs of the Keiskamma Ecotourism Network (☎043 642 2571, ✉printl@his.co.za) offers affordable **battlefield tours** around King William's Town, visiting various forts and battle sites from the Frontier Wars and grave sites of Xhosa chiefs. King is also the place to set out on all or part of **the Amatola Hiking Trail**, which starts from Maiden Dam, just outside town, and continues as a five-night/six-day hike into the mountains (see p.408).

Practicalities

Alexandra Road is the town's main drag, where you'll find a 24-hour filling station and signs for King's **tourist information** bureau (Mon–Fri 8.30am–5.30pm, Sat 8.30am–1pm; ☎043 642 3391), which is in the public library opposite the Kaffrarian Museum, and can provide an accommodation list. The **minibus taxis** rank is in Cathcart Street, with connections to East London and the rest of the Eastern Cape. For **eating and drinking**, *Archie's Pub & Pizzeria* in Taylor Street is popular, while *Guido's* on Alexandra Road serves good steaks and has a salad bar. *Nando's*, which offers spicy grilled chicken and *Steers*, which does burgers, are handy fast-food joints on Alexandra Road, where you can eat in or take away.

Accommodation in King William's Town is principally geared to business travellers; at weekends, you'll find a greater choice and often discounted rates.

Dreamers Guest House 29 Gordon St ☎ & ☎043 642 3012, ✉dreamers@imaginet.co.za. Pleasant five-bedroom B&B in a centrally located Victorian house with a lovely garden, pool and real log fires in winter. **②**

Grosvenor Lodge and Grosvenor Guest House Taylor Street ☎043 642 1440, near the Kaffrarian Museum. The best hotel in town, with all the

Steve Biko and Black Consciousness

Steve Biko's brutal interrogation and death while in police custody triggered international outrage and turned opinion further against the apartheid regime. His death was followed by the banning of the Black Consciousness organizations, and was a major factor in the imposition of a mandatory arms embargo against South Africa by the United Nations Security Council.

Steven Bantu Biko was born in 1946 in **King William's Town**. His political ascent was swift, due in no small part to his eloquence, charisma and focused vision. While still a medical student at Natal University during the late Sixties, he was elected president of the exclusively black South African Students' Organization (SASO) and started publishing articles in their journal, fiercely attacking white liberalism. In an atmosphere of repression – both ANC and PAC leaders were serving hefty sentences at the time – Biko's brand of Black Consciousness immediately caught on. He called for blacks to take destiny into their own hands, to unify and rid themselves of the "shackles that bind them to perpetual servitude". He became honorary president of the Black Peoples' Convention, an umbrella organization which attracted mainly young intellectuals and professionals. From 1973 onwards, Biko suffered banning, detention and other harassment at the hands of the state. In 1974, he defended himself in court, presenting his case so brilliantly that his profile in the international press soared.

Barred from leaving King William's Town, Biko continued working and writing, frequently escaping his confinement. In 1976, black outrage burst into the open with the **Soweto riots**, when school pupils took to the streets in protest against the imposition of Afrikaans as the language of instruction in their schools. The police response was brutal: hundreds of people were killed and imprisoned, and the search for "agitators" led to Biko's hundred-and-one day detention. In August the following year, he was stopped at a roadblock near Grahamstown (outside his restricted area), taken to Port Elizabeth, intensively interrogated and tortured. On September 12, 1977, Biko died from a brain haemorrhage, sustained at the hands of security police. No one was held accountable. Diplomats from thirteen Western countries joined the thousands of mourners at his funeral in King William's Town.

---

extras you'd expect from a business hotel, including air conditioning and cable TV (**❸**); they also run a cheaper, less luxurious guesthouse around the corner **❷**
Hemingway's Guest House 16 Beaumont Rd ☎ & ℱ043 643 3544. Pleasant, well-laid-out and reasonably priced accommodation in 25 rooms in a converted old house. **❸**

Keiskamma Ecotourism Network 9 Chamberlain St ☎ & ℱ043 642 2571. The cheapest accommodation in King. Two rooms with bunk beds in converted outhouses, available to hikers embarking on the Amatola Trail (see p.408) or backpackers overnighting in town. A swimming pool is available to guests. **❶**

Fort Hare

Despite decades of deliberate neglect and relegation after 1959 to a "tribal" **university** under apartheid, **FORT HARE**, 64km west of King William's Town, is assured a place in South African history. Established in 1916 as a multiracial college by missionaries, it became the first institution in South Africa to deliver tertiary education to blacks. Many prominent African leaders, including Zimbabwe's president Robert Mugabe and Tanzania's former president, Julius Nyerere, came here for their tertiary education. The most famous former student is **Nelson Mandela** (see p.434), making this an essential port of call if you're following his footsteps. Sadly, though, the Wesley Residence from whose window the young Mandela reputedly used to climb to go ballroom dancing, has been pulled down. The spot it occupied is now the lawn just to your right as you enter through the main gate. **Freedom Square**, at the centre of the campus, was the scene of many protests at the university – this is the spot where several members of the present government cut their teeth politically.

It's possible to visit **Beda Residence** where Mugabe studied, though the dormitory where he stayed has been converted into single rooms. This is one of the pleasanter old residences; some of the others are pretty dilapidated owing to underfunding during the apartheid years. Virtually all students live on campus as Alice, the adjacent town, is too undeveloped to offer much in the way of digs.

If you have even the slightest interest in African art, Fort Hare's **De Beers Art Gallery** (Mon–Fri 8am–4.30pm; free) is well worth a visit. From the outside, the cylindrical gallery resembles a high-security bank vault. Once inside, you're faced with a treasure trove of contemporary black southern **African art** – one of the most significant and least publicized collections anywhere. The gallery also houses Fort Hare's **ethnographic collection** – a major museum of traditional crafts and artefacts, with many rare and valuable pieces.

Pioneers of black painting, including Gerard Sekoto and George Pemba, are represented, and you should look out for the lively oils of Dan Rakgoate. There are some stunning sculptures: Uneas Sithole's elongated *Is my Friend the Chameleon Hiding?*, Percy Konqobe's *Ntsikana and his Cow*, and Sydney Kumalo's *Robot Man*. Also unmissable is the sequence of fifteen woodcuts by Lucky Sibiya called *Umabatha*, the Zulu adaptation of *Macbeth*. The best way to see the gallery is to take a **free tour** with the gallery's erudite curator, Reggie Letsatse (℡040 602 6442).

The **ANC's archives** (Mon–Fri 8am–4.30pm; ⊛www.ufh.ac.za), which include historic documents and photographs, are housed in the university's library and are open to the public. For tours contact Mrs Soul on ℡040 602 2275.

Practicalities

Fort Hare, a couple of kilometres east of Alice on the R63, is most easily reached with your own transport – although from King William's Town there are **minibus taxis** to Alice (see below) that drop off passengers at the university gates. Visits can be done as a day-trip from Grahamstown or East London, or as part of an excursion to the Hogsback. With the virtual absence of **accommodation** in Alice, you're better off staying either in Fort Beaufort or Hogsback – the choice of many of the university's lecturers. **Tours** of the university and art gallery should be arranged beforehand through the university's public relations department (Mon–Fri 9am–5pm; ℡040 602 2239; free).

Alice

A handful of photogenically decaying colonial houses with peeling corrugated-iron roofs and balconies smothered in creepers, constitute the main interest in **ALICE**. It's the closest town to the university, but can in no way be called a university town. The lengthy decay of the town reflects the second-class status accorded the university under Afrikaner Nationalist rule. There's one hopelessly tiny bookshop, a depressing reflection of local poverty and the high cost of books in South Africa, which puts them beyond the reach of the majority of the population. Alice's two **hotels** are little more than run-down carousing joints. Of the two, the *Amatola* is favoured for drinking by university staff and students.

Just 1km east of the town centre is **Lovedale College**, older than Fort Hare, and no less significant in educating Africans. Built in 1842 as a Presbyterian mission station, it was soon educating the country's first black professionals, and became an important publishing centre. The Xhosa language was first transcribed here, and one of Lovedale's students, J. Tengo Jabavu, was the founder of South Africa's first weekly African-language paper, *Zabantsundu*. With the passing of the Bantu Education Act under the apartheid government, Lovedale was closed. Now the college is in use again as a high school, you can drive in and look at the Victorian buildings. The actual site doesn't have any displays or information – for that, visit the Missionary Museum in King William's Town (see p.404).

Hogsback

Made sweeter by the contrast with the hot valleys below, the village of **HOGSBACK** in the Amatola Mountains, 32km north of Alice and 145km from East London, offers cool relief after hauling through prickly, overgrazed country. This village in the Amatola Mountains represents a corner of England, a fantasy fed by mists, pine plantations and exotic trees such as oak, walnut and azaleas, and guaranteed snowfalls each winter. In fact, the real attraction of the place is the **Afro-montane cloud forest**, singing with bird calls and gauzy waterfalls, and populated by the odd troop of **samango monkeys**, which survive on the steep slopes above the pine plantations. Winding your way up the mountains on the road from Alice, you'll have a good view of the forest, dense with yellowwood, stinkwood and Cape chestnut.

Hogsback is a great place to spend a relaxing couple of days, with plenty of walks and good air amongst the flowers, grasslands and forests, and there are many places to stay. The name "Hogsback" applies to the area as much as to the village, and comes from the high rocky ridge (actually three peaks) resembling a bushpig's spine, which runs above the settlement. Hogsback can be wet and cold, even in summer, so bring a warm pullover, sturdy shoes and rain gear all year round.

The hamlet itself is strung out along 3km of gravel road, with lanes branching out on either side to hotels and cottages. The closest thing to a **centre** is the small conglomeration of a general store, post office, filling station and some nearby craft shops. Hogsback has its own **indigenous craft** found nowhere else in the country: prepare to be pestered by Xhosa kids selling the characteristic unfired clay horses and hogs with white markings. Storm Haven Crafts on the main road has some nice stuff, and doubles up as Hogsback's tourist information bureau (see p.408).

Hogsback is prime **rambling** country with short, relatively easy trails indicated by hogs painted onto trees. For a rewarding taste of indigenous forest, the Contour Path above the campsite makes an easy, one-hour walk. From this path, a route goes steeply up **Tor Doone**, which overlooks the settlement, and is the easiest summit to climb. One of the most rewarding waterfall trails is the one-hour steep downhill walk to the lovely **Madonna and Child Waterfall**. A number of short and long routes, including the Amatola Trail and Zingcuka Loop (see box on p.408), are detailed in inexpensive **guidebooks** available at the village shops.

Practicalities

It's worth spending a couple of nights in Hogsback, but you'll need a car, as no public transport serves the village. A cheap shuttle (☎043 722 8240) connects *Sugar Shack* in East London and Cintsa three days a week; the *Away With The*

The Amatola Trail and Zingcuka Loop

Ranked among South Africa's best forested mountain walks, the **Amatola Trail** is a tough but fabulously beautiful five-night trail. Starting at Maiden Dam in the Pirie Forest, some 21km north of King William's Town, it stretches 105km to end at Hogsback. There are huts with mattresses and braai facilities at each designated nightstop along the way – some have showers.

The main attraction of this walk is the dense, high forest, and the numerous water-falls, rivers and bathing pools. There are also a number of shortened versions of the trail, but these can only be done outside school holidays, or at short notice if the huts are not filled. Best of the shortened trails is the 36-kilometre **Zingcuka Loop** from Hogsback, which scales the Hogsback itself, and follows streams much of the way, past idyllic waterfalls and pools. Right in the forest at the base of a cliff, the overnight hut has the luxury of a primitive shower, and firewood.

To go on one of these trails, you'll need well-broken-in boots, plus waterproofs, and warm clothes – you could get rained on between October and March. **Book** through the Keiskamma Ecotourism Network, 9 Chamberlain St, King William's Town 5600 (T & F 043 642 2571, W www.skyboom.com/amatola). The complete trail costs around R200.

Fairies hostel (see below) can make arrangements – you needn't stay there. On the main road, Storm Haven Crafts is also the town's **tourist information** bureau (T & F 045 962 1050, E rshep@global.co.za), and can supply accommodation details, **hiking maps**, and information on activities like mountain bike trails. One 21-kilometre trail has shorter family routes, but you'll need to bring your own bike, unless you rent one from the backpacker hostel. Cathy Ash Riders (T 045 962 1148) offers excellent **horse trails** for experienced riders and also has some old cart horses for beginners.

Hogsback has a general **shop** selling basic supplies. For **eating**, it's down to the King's Lodge's *Purple Cameleon* or the *Hogsback Inn*, which is much better for drinks than it is for food. Cream teas are served at *Walden House* (see below), which has a deck in the garden.

Places to stay are plentiful, but the village tends to fill up during holidays and weekends, when you'll need to book ahead.

The Amatola T & F 045 962 1059. Signposted on the main road. A hikers' and backpacker dorm, and individual rondavels. ❶

Away With The Fairies Hydrangea Lane T 045 962 1031. Down the first turning on your right and signposted as you drive into Hogsback. Unequivocally geared to the backpacker scene, it's a large converted house on a sizeable property, with fabulous views of the Tyumi Valley. Small dorms sleep three to eight guests, and there's a double in the house and one in a garden cottage. Mountain bikes are available to rent, horse-riding can be arranged, and the owners offer free guided hikes in the forests and mountains. One of the nicest features of the hostel is a platform in a tree for drinks and hanging out. Dorms and doubles. ❶

The Edge T & F 045 962 1159 or T 082 603

5246, W www.besc.co.za/hogsback.htm. The best of the self-catering accommodation: five cottages in separate locations a couple of kilometres off the main road. Superb valley and forest views, and a herb patch to garnish your meals – the owners grow 25 kinds of lavender on the property. They also have space for twenty tents. Booking is essential for the cottages, which range in price from R175 to R400, sleeping two to four people.

King's Lodge Signposted along the main road T 045 962 1024, F 045 962 1058. The best of the hotels, with wood-panelled interiors and two self-catering units. Also the best food and bar. ❷–❹

Walden House Wolfridge Road, T 045 962 1022 or 082 649 1669, E waldenhouse@intekom.co.za. Thatched guesthouse with three en-suite rooms on a large property. ❷

Fort Beaufort

A farming town at the heart of a citrus and wool district, **FORT BEAU-FORT**, 80km northwest of King William's Town, is nothing to get excited about. The most likely reason for a close encounter is because you're passing through on your way from Grahamstown or East London to Katberg or Mpofu Game Reserve. Having said that, Fort Beaufort does have a reputation throughout the Eastern Cape for its lusciously sweet **oranges**; should you find yourself here in winter, look out for African traders selling them by the sackful for a song, at the main crossroads out of town.

Founded as a link in the chain of forts built along the eastern frontier to form a buffer against the Xhosa, Fort Beaufort's moment in history came in 1845, when Tsili, a Xhosa man, stole an axe from a shop here, precipitating the bloody **War of the Axe** – the Seventh Frontier War. The theft provided a pretext for the British to act on a growing and expedient belief among whites that Xhosa land would be put to better use in their own hands. In 1847, after literally bringing the Xhosa chiefs to their knees (forcing them at bayonet point to kiss his boots), Governor Harry Smith told the vanquished that their land would be divided into counties, towns and villages bearing English names. "You may no longer be naked and wicked barbarians," he informed them, "which you will ever be unless you labour and become industrious."

The axe shop is still here, as is the 1830 officer's mess, now the highly eccentric **Fort Beaufort Museum**, which doubles as a tourist office and resembles a bric-a-brac shop. Interesting items include a painting by the Victorian documentary oil colourist, Thomas Baines. There's also a proclamation by Sir Harry Smith, inviting anyone with a gun to take pot-shots at the Xhosa, with the incentive that they could keep any cattle they rustled. The other notable historical building is a **Martello Tower**, still intact and exactly the same as those built two hundred years ago along the British coastline to keep out the French. The underworked tourist office will direct you there and fill you in on local history.

Practicalities

The **tourist office** in Fort Beaufort Museum (T046 645 1555) can provide lists of places to stay. For **accommodation** in town, head for Durban Street, where you'll find the unexceptional *Savoy Hotel* (T046 645 1146, F046 645 2082; ❷), not far west of the museum on the other side of the road, with a couple of reasonable **B&Bs** nearby. The pick of the bunch is the *De Villa Guest House,* 13 Henrietta St (T046 645 1071; ❷), run by the *Savoy's* chef, which has five rooms in a late Victorian house with a front and back garden.

The best **eating** place in town is *Helena's,* opposite the *Savoy* in Campbell Street, a daytime venue serving light meals and sandwiches. The *Country Club*, outside town on the R67 north to Queenstown, is a farmers' hangout that does good steaks and pizzas and also has a bar. Outdoor seating overlooks a golf course, with views of the surrounding hills. The only place for evening meals is the acceptable *Savoy*.

Mpofu Game Reserve and Katberg

If you want somewhere like the Hogsback, but even less developed, you'll find it in the mountainscapes of **Mpofu** and **Katberg**. Both are within spitting distance of Fort Beaufort, yet less than an hour's drive transports you dramatically from parched scrubby lowlands into high country, broken with cliffs and draped with indigenous forests. Facilities are fairly basic, but the plus is that the area draws far fewer visitors than the Hogsback and feels far more pristine.

Mpofu Game Reserve

Mpofu Game Reserve, 21km northwest of Fort Beaufort, is a 75-square-kilometre tract of land with spectacular views over the Katberg Mountains. The steep terrain and changing rainfall generates a varied habitat, supporting a respectable cross-section of **wildlife;** this includes white rhino, giraffe, waterbuck, warthog, plus a wealth of antelope such as springbok, kudu, eland, reedbuck and lechwe. Baboons, vervet monkeys, black-backed jackals, caracals and ostriches are also found. A number of **trails**, from ninety minutes to a full day, allow you to experience the countryside on foot. To get there, take the Lower Blinkwater/Post Retief turn-off to the left, 13km from Fort Beaufort, and continue for a further 8km to the entrance gate.

There is **accommodation** at two houses in the game reserve: *Mpofu* in the north, a six-bedroom house (minimum charge for four people R580), and in the south, the four-bedroom *Ntloni* (minimum charge for four people R550). These should be booked through the Eastern Cape Tourism Board in Bisho (℡040 635 2115, ℗040 636 4019).

Outside the reserve, *Waylands Farm* (℡046 684 0151 or 072 289 8468, ℗046 684 0881, ℮waylands@procomp.co.za) is a large, working organic stock-farm on a north-facing slope of the Katberg, 40km north of Fort Beaufort. It has budget self-catering accommodation in the original 1850s homestead (❶); in the nearby Art Nouveau farmhouse – a historic monument – are some very upmarket **guest suites** with four-poster beds, yellowwood floors and period furniture (full-board ❺).

The farm arranges **hikes** and **game drives** in Mpofu, guided horse trails and mountain biking on its grounds, occasional art and music workshops, and has resident natural health practitioners. It's possible to arrange work experience on the farm.

If you're driving, continue for 30km from the entrance through the game reserve; at the T-junction, turn right towards Post Retief and drive for about 10km to Post Retief Country Club. From here take the right fork and continue for another 10km and you'll see *Waylands* signposted to your left. Alternatively, the farm can pick you up by prior arrangement from Adelaide or Fort Beaufort.

Katberg

KATBERG, an area of mountains and indigenous forest west of Hogsback, is a sort of poor relation of that same village, since it fell into the former Ciskei and never developed into a residential area. To get there, take the R67 from Fort Beaufort towards Queenstown; after 40km, follow the dirt road signposted to the *Katberg Protea* for 13km. It's essentially a weekending spot, with only one **place to stay** – the *Katberg Protea* itself (℡040 864 1010, ℗040 864 1014, ℮phkatberg@mweb.co.za; during school terms half-board ❸, during school holidays full-board ❹), a mountain resort that's great for families, offering walking trails, horse-riding, tennis and pleasant, shady gardens. Maps and information are available from the hotel, which is also worth visiting for **tea** or a **meal** – it has a good reputation for food.

East London to Aliwal North

Besides the mountainous scenery of the Amatolas, there's little to encourage a stop along the N6 highway from East London en route to Johannesburg until you reach the inviting **hot springs** of **Aliwal North**. The road traverses a region which was once home to **German settlers**. Between 1857 and 1859, over four thousand Germans arrived in the Eastern Cape, initially drawn from a German regiment fighting for the British in the Crimea, and brought in by the Cape Governor to act as a buffer against the Xhosa. The once-cohesive German-speaking community has long been diluted, and the last settler farms were abandoned in the 1980s when the area came under the auspices of the Ciskei government.

Queenstown and around

There's no reason at all to pause in **QUEENSTOWN**, 190km north of East London, a sizeable workaday shopping and administrative centre serving a large and poor black rural community and white stock-farmers. However, if you're here for the night on a cross-country journey, the **Lawrence de Lange** and **Longhill nature reserves**, just out of town in the mountains, are worth a visit. From Cathcart Road, the main street, head out of town on Kingsway and Hangklip roads, and look out for signs to the reserve.

The **tourist information** centre, Pick'n'Pay Mall, Cathcart Road (Mon–Fri 9am–5pm; ☎045 839 2265), represents the surrounding Stormberg region, and can help with finding accommodation and posts up an emergency B&B list after hours. The best **places to stay** are in the middle-class suburbs above the railway line, where you'll find some excellent B&Bs. *Carthews Corner*, 1 Park Ave, Blue Rise (☎ & ☎045 838 1885 or ☎082 492 7547; ❷) has garden cottages, a pool and braai facilities, and secure off-street parking.

Recommended **places to eat**, particularly for steaks, include the *Spur* in Cathcart Road and *The Parlour and Grill* (☎045 838 1483) in Ebden Street right in the centre, which also serves pasta and bar meals, and opens daily except Sunday evenings. The *Acropolis Restaurant* (☎045 839 6997) in a railway carriage in the Sandringham Sports Club, opposite the Pick'n'Pay Mall in Cathcart Road is a good choice for an evening meal with a bit of Greek food and steaks. It's open daily (except Monday) for dinner and lunch.

Dramatic scenery surrounds Queenstown, with tawny grass-covered mountains and rocky outcrops. *Carnarvon Estates* (☎ & ☎045 856 0011, ⓔcarnarvon@worldonline.co.za; half-board ❹), 50km north of town on the N6, is the longest-established of several **game farms** in the area. Here you can go on botanical walks and view 17 species of antelope and 250 bird varieties. You'll find accommodation in a luxury farmhouse lodge with seven en-suite bedrooms, or a garden cottage suitable for a couple. There is also the plus of seeing Bushmen paintings on the farm.

Aliwal North

ALIWAL NORTH, 158km north of Queenstown, on the Orange River, borders Free State province and has a distinctly Afrikaner flavour. The town's name celebrates the smashing of the Sikhs at Aliwal in India in 1846 by the governor of the Cape Colony, Sir Harry Smith. (Aliwal South was the former name of Mossel Bay in the Western Cape.) More relevant to its Afrikaans character is the town's role in the Second Anglo-Boer War, when the Boers under General Olivier occupied the town and declared the Republic of

Oliviersfontein in 1900. What remains of the short-lived republic is a sobering memorial to the Boers who died in concentration camps set up by the British. Historic interest aside, the main reason to come to Aliwal North is for its curative **mineral springs**, 3km from the centre, which merit a restorative stop-off.

The town is effectively divided into two: the central area dominated by the N6 traffic, and the area built up around the spa which, although ugly, has the best places to stay, shop and eat. The **Spa** (8am–10pm; R11), signposted off the N6 and R58, centres around an Olympic-sized outdoor pool with palm trees and green lawns – perfect for swimming and relaxation. The indoor pools are much warmer, but not quite hot enough in winter. Admission also gives you access to the modest gym and tennis courts, but you'll need your own racquet and balls.

At the southern edge of town, signposted off the N6, is a **Boer War Concentration Camp Memorial**. On the site of two camp cemeteries, the memorial looks from the outside like a prison or crematorium. Inside, the walls are plastered with handmade gravestones of the 716 people (many of them Afrikaner children) who died as a result of the terrible conditions in the tented camps set up by the British.

Practicalities

Translux and Greyhound **buses** between Port Elizabeth/East London and Johannesburg pull in daily at the *Balmoral Hotel* in Somerset Street; **tickets** for Translux buses can be bought at Dampier Motors (℡051 633 2488) in the same street, while Greyhound must be booked through their East London office (℡043 743 9284). The **tourist information** office, 97 Somerset St (Mon–Fri 8am–4.30pm; ℡051 633 3567), can supply **maps** and lists of places to stay in the North Eastern Cape and over the river in the Eastern Free State mountains.

Opposite the spa entrance, adjoining the *Spa Hotel* in Dan Pienaar Avenue, the smart *Pink Lady Steakhouse* serves reasonably priced fish and steak main courses (closed Sundays). Back in the centre, the nicest place is *Between Us*, opposite the Pick'n'Pay Mall in Somerset Street, serving good teas and light lunches.

Most of the town's **accommodation** is clustered around the spa, and prices are modest since the springs are essentially for a local, rather than foreign market.

Aliwal Spa De Wet Drive ℡051 633 2951, ℻051634 1307. Municipal outfit with a huge caravan park, camping and run-down bungalows. Set on a lake 8km beyond the campsite are *Islands*, spanking new two-bedroom self-catering cottages. When booking, ask specifically for these timber cottages – they're the best place to stay in Aliwal North. ❶

Buffelsbron Chalets 35 Dan Pienaar Ave ℡ & ℻051 633 3129. Fully equipped and spotlessly clean self-catering brick chalets sleeping four to six people. ❶

Spa Hotel 14 Dan Pienaar Ave ℡051 634 2189, ℻051 634 2008, ✉bjp@cybertrade.co.za. Over the road from the spa, offering the best-value hotel rooms in town with a fair bit of comfort, including electric blankets in winter, M-Net television and tea-making facilities in the en-suite rooms. ❷

Umtali Motel Dan Pienaar Ave ℡ & ℻051 633 2400. At the end of the avenue, this is the smartest hotel, but it's a bit characterless and it's a long walk to get to the spa from here. ❷

The Eastern Cape Drakensberg

The **Eastern Cape Drakensberg** is the most southerly section of southern Africa's highest and most extensive mountain chain, stretching east across Lesotho and up the west flank of KwaZulu-Natal into Mpumalanga. Although known misleadingly as South Africa's "little Switzerland" in tourist brochures, they are wonderful African mountains, full of **San rock paintings**, sandstone **caves** and craggy sheep farms. **Rhodes**, one of the country's best-preserved and prettiest Victorian villages, is the obvious goal in the region; it makes a good base for riding, walking, skiing and trout fishing. While it's very cold, dry and sunny in the winter, summer is idyllically green, with river pools to swim in. There are some appealing cottages for rent on farms, and a number of **hiking trails**, many of which offer the opportunity to see rock paintings and sleep in enormous caves. Since there is no national park in the Eastern Cape Drakensberg, activities are all done through private farms. For **bird-watchers**, the region is especially good for raptors (notably the rare lammergeier and Cape vulture), as well as orange-breasted rock jumpers and ground woodpeckers.

From Aliwal North to Rhodes

LADY GREY, 50km east of Aliwal North and 5km off the R58, is the only place worth a stop en route to Rhodes. It has one **hotel**, the *Mountain View Country Inn*, signposted from Botha Street (T051 603 0421, F051 603 0114; ❸), which has nice old-fashioned rooms with great views. The staff keep a list of **walks** to help you explore the surrounding peaks, and the owners can organize **fly-fishing**. The town offers a tiny **museum** at the Dutch Reformed church, dominated by a Victorian horse-drawn hearse and more like a curiosity shop under dust covers than anything else. It is open by arrangement only, through the hotel. The first minister of the Dutch Reformed church was a Scot, **David Ross**, who used to preach both in Afrikaans and English. His anti-imperialist views got him imprisoned by the British during the Anglo-Boer War, after which he is said to have never spoken his native tongue again.

Some 79km southeast of Lady Grey, **BARKLY EAST** serves a large surrounding farming community. If your destination is Rhodes, it's the last place to get money and fill up your car. Don't expect much help from the **tourist information** bureau, which doubles as the manual telephone exchange in the municipal offices. There's nothing at all to do in the town, so unless night is falling, push on for another ninety minutes to Rhodes. The sixty-kilometre dirt road to Rhodes is tortuous and rough with sheer, unfenced drops – definitely not recommended in the dark or mist. The very comfortable *Elanli Guest House*, 33 Cole St (T045 971 0185; ❷), in a Victorian house on the signposted road to Elliot, provides the best **accommodation** in Barkly East. There's also a little-used **campsite** 100m off to the right as you hit town from Lady Grey.

Rhodes and around

Some 60km northeast of Barkly East, **RHODES** is almost too good to be true – a remote and beautiful village girdled by the Eastern Cape Drakensberg. Few people actually live here: like other villages in this region, Rhodes was progressively deserted as residents gravitated to the cities to make a living, leaving its Victorian tin-roofed architecture stuck in a very pleasing time warp. Today,

Tiffendell Ski Resort

Tiffendell, South Africa's only **ski resort**, promotes itself as a little Switzerland, with Alpine ski lodges and European instructors on the slopes. However, it's essentially a venue for fun-loving South Africans, most of whom are conspicuous consumers in search of a nonstop party (packages tend to include free booze from lunch to midnight). The resort is enormously successful, and for foreign visitors it provides, if nothing else, a quirky experience of Africa.

Skiing at Tiffendell is on **artificial snow** (despite regular winter falls, the real snow melts too quickly to provide a reliable piste). You can rent everything you need at the resort at about R250 per day, slightly cheaper out of school holidays. A four-hour beginner's lesson costs R155. Three-night, fully inclusive packages, including on-site accommodation, work out at around R1600–2500 per person, much less out of school holidays. Day visitors need to book, as there is a maximum of 180 people on the slopes per day. The season runs from May 30 to August 31. **Book** through Tiffendell, Shop 34, Randburg Waterfront ☎011 787 9090, ℻011 886 9443, ⓦwww.snow.co.za.

The only on-site **accommodation** is at the lodge, which is usually full. Rooms are small and functional, with shared washing facilities, though the higher-priced packages are for en-suite rooms. Many people stay at Rhodes village, one hour's 4WD across mountain passes, or on guest farms in the area. Of these, one of the nicest is *Burnbrae Guest Farm*, PO Box 123, Barkly East 9786 (☎045 971 9092 or 083 308 5172; ❷), 15km from Tiffendell, which also offers self-catering (❶). There are rock paintings and caves on the farm you can hike to and, in the summer, trout fishing and riding. *Fetcani Glen*, PO Box 88, Barkly East (☎04542, ask for 7412; ❶) offers similar attractions with a rambling five-bedroomed farmhouse for rent and a beautiful river cutting through a sandstone gorge on the property. The closest farm to Tiffendell is *Bidstone* (☎04542 ask for 8003, Di or Leon Istead; ❷) with a couple of stone cottages for rent, good food, a pub and pool table. The shortest route for **getting to Tiffendell** is via Rhodes, but the road is steep and needs 4WD at all times. The alternative starts 23km north of Barkly East, and if the road is wet or snowy needs a 4WD vehicle for the last 19km. If you don't have the right transport, both the *Rhodes Hotel* and Henri Reeders (☎04542, ask for 9120) provide daily transfers to the resort from Rhodes.

Out of the ski season, Tiffendell runs as a **summer holiday** location, with trout fishing, mountain biking, grass skiing, horse-riding and hiking. Bookings for summer holidays are done locally (☎045 974 9005), and cost R185 per person per day for half-board.

its *raison d'être* is as a low-key holiday place for people who appreciate its isolation, wood stoves and restored cottages. Although electricity reached the village a few years ago, very few establishments have it, and paraffin lamps and candles are the norm.

Given that Rhodes is not on the way to anywhere (on some maps it doesn't even appear), it is a place to go to for a few days, rather than an overnight stop. While nights are cool even in summer, in winter they are freezing, and there's no central heating, so pack warm clothes. The village itself is not much more than a few crisscrossing gravel roads lined with pine trees. The trees were donated in the 1890s, so the story goes, after a group of scheming townsfolk hoped to extract a large donation from **Cecil Rhodes**, by changing the village's name in his honour. All they got from the astute entrepreneur was a sackful of seeds. At the heart of the village is the *Rhodes Hotel*, a general shop and a garage; there's also a post office and payphone, but no banking facilities and no public transport in or out of the village.

Rhodes is busiest in the winter, when **skiers** use it as a base for the Tiffendell slopes (see box opposite), an hour's 4WD drive into the highest peaks of the Eastern Cape Drakensberg. December to May are the best months for swimming, trout fishing and hiking, all of which are easy to do using the village as a base. This is one of the best places in the country for **fly-fishing**, with all the solitude and glorious landscape you could hope for: the rivers jump with rainbow and brown trout, stocked in the 1920s. The *Rhodes Hotel* can give advice about where to fish; better still, you can go out for a day or longer with Dave Walker of *Walkabout* (see p.416), who can organize permits giving you access to 150km of river, but you'll need all your own gear. Dave also runs **Highlands Information**, a service which can be used to book any sort of holiday in the area and arrange transport if you fly into East London.

Rock-art sites

Rhodes is a good base for exploring millennia-old **San rock paintings**, the majority of which are on surrounding private farms which can be visited with the farmers' permission (some farms also take guests). The South African Heritage Resources Agency (☎021 462 4502, ☏021 462 4509) in Cape Town has a comprehensive list, and Rhodes locals can point you to local farms, such as Buttermead and Hillbury, which have their own paintings. Sue Tonkin in Maclear (☎082 686 4468) does fully guided **rock-art tours**.

Close to Rhodes, **Martin's Hoek** farm, 16km from the village, is worth a visit, not just for the well-preserved, photogenic paintings, but for the lovely, lonely valley you have to drive though to get there. Make an appointment with Russie or Lookie Schmidt (☎04542, ask for 7003) to see them. The signposted turn-off to Martin's Hoek is 8km from Rhodes on the road to Barkly East. From the turn-off it's another 8km to the site, with parking and a couple of picnic tables. The paintings, which are fenced off, are on the cliff face opposite the parking area. It's a ten-minute uphill scramble, much easier than it first appears, with views out onto the rough and streaky sandstone peaks. Local farmer Vasie Murray (☎04542, ask for 7012) does **tours** of the Martin's Hoek site. A second site, at **Denorben Farm**, 32km from Barkly East, offers the longest series of San paintings in the country. It's only 1km to the farm from the main road, and the long, painted panel is behind the house, at the bottom of the garden. A nominal entry fee is charged and there's a helpful information sheet on the images, many of which are confusing. Don't miss the impressive (unpainted) cave in the farm yard – it's common practice for farmers in the area to use overhangs as cosy sheep pens and sheds.

Rock art had an essentially religious purpose, usually recording experiences of trance states. Shamans' visions often included powerful animals like the eland, which you can see depicted at both Denorben and Martin's Hoek, and whose power shamans were able to access for healing. A dying eland is a metaphor for the shaman who enters a **trance** and takes on aspects of an animal. At Denorben there's a half-animal, half-human figure, an image of transformation during the trance state. Also at Denorben are painted figures dancing, clapping and singing, in the process of inducing trance.

Accommodation

Gateshead Lodges ☎045 971 0233. Several farmhouses and excellent cottages on huge properties in marvellously remote and rugged territory, all within a large radius of Rhodes. Some cater specifically for fly-fishing, river swimming, hiking, riding or bird-watching, while a few have caves

and rock paintings on the property. All are clearly detailed in a brochure available from PO Box 267, Barkly East 5580. ❶

Rhodes Hotel Main Road ☎04542, ask for Rhodes 21. Decorative exterior and charming Victorian furnishings. Quiet horses are available for hire, there are tennis courts and the owner is a trout-fishing guide. Full-board ❸

Rubicon Flats PO Box 5, Rhodes ☎04542, ask for 9002. The best-value, and the warmest, place in town, this handsome old schoolhouse has been converted into self-catering rooms, each with an anthracite burner, and simple dorms. The owner, Mrs Reeders, also rents out self-catering cottages in the village and provides meals, but you need to book ahead for dinner. ❶

Walkabout Country Retreat signposted off the main road ☎04542, ask for 9203 or ☎082 892 6998, ✉dave@lesoff.co.za. Relaxed house with six en-suite guest rooms, slightly cheaper than the hotel. The friendly owner, Dave Walker, knows a good deal about the area and can organize almost any activity, including fly-fishing and horse-riding. Half-board ❸

Eating and drinking

For **eating**, your best choice is *Walkabout*, which does home-cooked meals, with two wood-burning pizza ovens on site and, if booked in advance, vegetarian food. Cheapest of all are the ready-cooked meals, such as curry and rice, from local farmer's wife Marian Henning (☎04542, ask for 9013), who'll deliver to your door. For **drinking**, the hotel bar is one of the most atmospheric pubs in the country. It's decorated with the horns of Wydeman, the lead ox of the supply wagon from Barkly East, who dropped dead outside the hotel in 1896, while smoky relics of the days when this was a frontier town of gamblers, cattle rustlers and bar-room shoot-outs also line the walls.

Naude's Nek and the route south

The most exhilarating drive out of Rhodes is along **Naude's Nek**, the highest mountain-pass road in South Africa, connecting Rhodes with **Maclear** to the south, in a series of snaking hairpin bends and huge views. If you're chiefly looking for scenery, it's not essential to do the whole route to Maclear. Many people go from Rhodes to the top of the pass and back as a half-day trip, during which you can make a call from the highest phone (with a crank handle) in the country, in a corrugated-iron booth in the middle of a sheep pen at the top of the pass.

While it's only 30km from Rhodes, the journey can take a couple of hours to the Nek because so many changing vistas en route demand stops. You don't need a 4WD, but if you feel precious about your car don't attempt this route, as the road is harsh. The surface deteriorates from the top of the pass to Maclear, with sharp stones and a hump down the centre of the road, which may scrape the bottom of your vehicle, and is definitely impassable after snow. If you're wanting to use this route into the Transkei and KwaZulu-Natal, check with the *Rhodes Hotel* as to the current state of the road (see p.415), and take two spare tyres.

If you're not aiming for the Transkei, you can loop west from Maclear, at the bottom of the escarpment, and take the tarred R56 towards **Dordrecht** and the N6. The string of small towns along the R56 from Maclear to Dordrecht are unmemorable trading centres, with nowhere to stay. All along the route though, the high Drakensberg march along, providing a dramatic backdrop to the journey. **Sheep farming** is the mainstay of white farmers in the region, though rampant stock theft is putting many out of business. One farmer has employed armed San ex-trackers from a defunct unit of the South African army to patrol his farm.

The R56 gives access to a couple of **hiking trails** with farm cottages for rent in the southern part of the Cape Drakensberg, notably **Woodcliffe** near Maclear, and **Kranskop** near Dordrecht, both of which have caves and rock paintings (see box on p.417).

The **North Eastern Cape** is prime **walking** country, with expansive skies and long views across the mountains. There is no national park, so all walks have to be done (and booked) on private property, but are very reasonably priced. Three of the best trails are listed below.

Ben Macdhui Hiking Trail. A three-day circular trail along a 51-kilometre route, involving about eight hours' walking each day. It begins and ends at Rhodes village, and takes in magnificent mountain scenery, wild flowers and waterfalls, and the chance to see rare mountain birds (such as the bearded vulture) and climb Ben Macdhui, the highest mountain (3000m) in the Eastern Cape. Accommodation is in an old farmhouse and a mountain hut, both equipped with beds, mattresses, drinking water, long-drop toilets, a gas stove, kettle, pans, basin and a coal stove for heating. Rhodes village makes a convenient place to stay at the start and finish of this hike. Book through Gideon van Zyl, PO Box 299, 5580 Barkly East ☎045 971 0446.

Woodcliffe Farm. A variety of one- to four-day trails on a farm, 22km north of Maclear, on the Naude's Nek Road. The trails include stunning Drakensberg scenery, rock art, dinosaur footprints on the Pot River and 185 bird species. Accommodation, in a self-catering cottage, can be used as a base for day-walks or at the start of a longer hike, while cave overhangs can be used on longer hikes. Maps are provided and planning advice is offered for a route matching your fitness and time available. Book through Phyll Sephton, PO Box 65, Maclear 5480 ☎ & ℱ045 932 1550.

Kranskop Hiking Trail. One- to two-day hike on a farm, 33km north of Dordrecht, on the Barkly East Road. Highlights include some beautiful *kloofs*, sleeping overnight in a sandstone cave, and seeing some San rock art. Accommodation at the start or finish of the trail is in a comfortable rustic farm cottage sleeping twelve. Beds, mattresses, pillows, hot water, stove, fridge, lamps, candles and a coal stove are provided. Farm milk and meat are also available. Book through Frans Slabbert, PO Box 85, Dordrecht 5435 ☎045 944 1014.

The Wild Coast region

The **Wild Coast region** is aptly named: this is one of South Africa's most unspoilt areas, a vast stretch of undulating hills, lush forest and spectacular beaches skirting a section of the Indian Ocean. Its undeveloped sandy beaches stretch for miles and miles, punctuated by rivers and several wonderful, reasonably priced hotels geared to family seaside holidays. The wildness goes beyond the landscape, for this is the former **Transkei** homeland, a desperately poor region that during apartheid was disenfranchised and turned into a dumping ground for Africans too old or too young for South African industry to make use of.

Few whites live in the Wild Coast region; nearly everyone is Xhosa, and those in rural areas live mostly in traditional rondavels dotting the landscape for as far as the eye can see. This neglect lives on in the negative image most white South Africans still have of the Transkei. Unless they have actually visited the area and

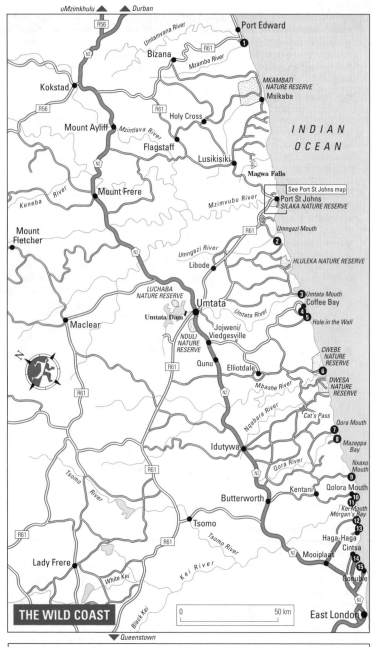

ACCOMMODATION

Anchorage	**3**	Haga Haga	**13**	Kob Inn	**7**	Ocean View	**4**
Buccaneers	**14**	The Haven	**6**	Mazeppa Bay	**8**	Seagulls	**11**
Gonubie Mouth	**15**	Hole in the Wall	**5**	Morgan's Bay	**12**	Trennery's	**10**

Umngazi River Bungalows	**2**
Wavecrest	**9**
Wild Coast Sun Hotel	**1**

come to appreciate it, most people have an exaggerated image of its dangers: legendary (and wildly overstated) tales of crime, hostile locals (quite untrue), and shocking roads (these are being upgraded).

Also in the Transkei's favour, this is the "Africa" completely missed by those who restrict their holiday to Cape Town and the Garden Route. One or two of the hotels – and most of the backpacker lodges – offer a chance to experience traditional Xhosa life, with **village visits to healers** or overnight stays with a Xhosa family. In all of South Africa, this is the best and easiest place to experience authentic African rural life as a tourist.

Despite the obvious hardship, it's refreshing – at least for visitors – to find that rural areas are still communally owned rather than parcelled up into private farms. Instead of the fenced-off spaces edged by squatter camps found in most of rural South Africa, here the land is unfenced and fully inhabited.

The **N2** highway runs through the middle of the region, passing through the old Transkei capital of **Umtata** and a host of scruffy, busy little towns along the way. Northwest of the N2, towards the Lesotho border and the Drakensberg Mountains, you'll find beautiful mountainous country and endless little villages, but the lack of accommodation and poor roads make travelling here difficult.

Far more accessible is the **coastal region**, which runs from just north of East London to the mouth of the **Mtamvuna River**. With its succession of great beaches, hidden reefs, patches of subtropical forest, rural Xhosa settlements and the attractive little towns of **Coffee Bay** and **Port St Johns** (both popular with backpackers), this region, along with northern KwaZulu-Natal, offers the most deserted and undeveloped beaches in the country. While there are some beautiful, state-run **nature reserves** along the coast, they are totally underfunded and poorly run, with inefficient booking systems. **Mkambati Nature Reserve**, however, has a good system operating, and is nothing short of totally fabulous, with outstanding beaches, lagoons and wildlife, though some of the accommodation is very shabby. A good way to see it is on the **Amadiba Horse Trails**, which finish at the reserve.

Practicalities

The Wild Coast, unlike the Western Cape Garden Route, is not a stretch that you can easily tour by car; there's no coastal road, and no direct route between one seaside resort and the next. Yet in this **remoteness** lies the region's charm. Resorts are isolated down long, winding gravel roads off the N2, which sticks to the high inland plateau. Choose one or two places, and stay put for a relaxing few days.

Most roads in the Wild Coast region are **untarred** and, while generally passable in an ordinary car, they invariably take their mechanical toll. Always carry a tool kit, a spare tyre, and take the roads slowly. When you choose a resort, phone to ask for the best road route, as road conditions change. Watch out for livestock on all Wild Coast roads, including the N2, and avoid driving in rainy weather and at night. **Public transport** in minibuses links villages throughout the region – easiest from Umtata to Port St Johns and Coffee Bay along the tarred roads. The Baz Bus stops in Umtata; you can arrange to be met by hostels in Port St Johns and Coffee Bay, or in Butterworth for Mazeppa.

Car theft at night, or the removal of tyres or wheels, even in remote areas, is the biggest crime problem in the Transkei. All the hotels are surrounded by fences and lock up their gates at night to counter this problem.

The **hotels** here have playgrounds, pools and large gardens. Based along old-fashioned, colonial lines, meals and tea are at specific times, and many offer the services of experienced **Xhosa nannies** who can be employed for the whole day or for short stretches while you take a break to go the beach or have a meal. Some hotels even have separate meal times for children, and recommend that children stay with their nannies during adult meal times. Apart from Port St Johns, none of the places on the coast has a **bank** or ATM, so be sure to organize money in East London or Umtata. As for **self-catering**, you'll also need to buy groceries at a big centre on the N2. Most of the hotels offer full-

A walk, gallop or drive on the Wild Coast

The inaccessibility and beauty of the Wild Coast make joining a tour once you're there a sensible option. Since there's no coastal road, this is effectively the only way of exploring sections of its highly explorable coastline. Choose between walking, horse-riding or 4WD vehicle.

Wild Coast Hotel Meander

The popular **Wild Coast Hotel Meander** from Qora Mouth to Morgan Bay covers a 55-kilometre section of the coast over an easy-going five days (six nights). Despite being packaged, this is still an adventurous excursion with some moderate challenges such as river crossings and hiking over headlands, though it poses no great difficulties to anyone of average fitness. **Accommodation** is at hotels along the route (*Kob Inn*, *Mazeppa Bay*, *Wavecrest*, *Trennery's* or *Seagulls* and *Morgan Bay*), where you eat breakfast and dinner. They will also provide a picnic lunch for each day's walk and, together with your personal effects, this is all you have to carry. **Bookings and cost**: Wild Coast Holiday Reservations ℡043 743 6181, ℻043 743 6188, ℮meross@iafrica.com. The whole deal, including transfers between East London airport and the Wild Coast, five nights' accommodation, all meals and the services of guides, costs around R2200 per person for a minimum of four, but less if there are more participants.

Amadiba Horse Trail

A Wild Coast highlight, the **Amadiba Horse Trail** is a fifty-kilometre, four- to six-day excursion run entirely by members of the local Pondo community. It's probably the best way to spend time with Xhosa speakers and travel in unspoilt areas with no vehicle access. The easy-going trail uses well-schooled horses and is suitable for beginners – distances aren't long between the magical **tented camps** on the banks of the Kwanyana and Mtentu rivers. From these bases you while away gentle days exploring the coast, rivers and inland, sometimes visiting villages on horseback, on foot or in canoes with your Pondo guides. The trail runs from the *Wild Coast Sun* casino and hotel to the exquisitely beautiful Mkambati Nature Reserve (with plans to extend the trip as far as Port St Johns). There are regular shuttle buses from Durban to the *Sun*. **Bookings and cost**: Amadiba Adventures ℡031 205 5180, ℮cropeddy@iafrica .com. Fully inclusive trips cost R1100 per person for four days and R1380 for six days. Maximum group size is ten.

4WD Mobile Coastal Safaris

If walking or horse-riding sounds too much like hard work, there's always the more luxurious alternative of one of the **coastal safaris** offered by African Coastal Adventures. They do a fabulous five-night trip from East London to Coffee Bay, travelling along the (roadless) coast on old sleigh paths, visiting culturally interesting sights, fording rivers, walking on beaches, bird-watching, snorkelling, fishing and staying at reputable hotels dotted along the coast. All age groups are catered for. **Bookings and cost**: African Coastal Adventures ℡043 748 4550 or 082 650 1427, ℗www.africoast.co.za. The cost is approximately R850 per person per night.

board – outside Port St Johns, there are no restaurants besides those provided by the accommodation establishments.

There a number of good backpacker lodges along the coast, and plenty of campsites. Although security is no longer the worry it once was, **camping in rural areas** is not advisable, even if a beach looks idyllically deserted. If you want to stay among the rural Xhosa, the safest way to do so is with a guide.

It's wise to book accommodation in advance: the Umtata-based Wild Coast Reservations (see p.431) is useful if you are planning to stay in several places on your journey. Even better is the superbly well-informed and efficient **Wild Coast Holiday Reservations** (℡043 743 6181, ℻043 743 6188, ℮meross@iafrica.com), based in East London which, apart from being able to arrange places to stay, is unsurpassed when it comes to organizing **activities** in the region, including hiking.

The hotels themselves offer a variety of activities, from canoeing to horse riding. To visit the region's **nature reserves** you'll usually need to book in advance. However, a word of caution: the post-apartheid reorganization in the Wild Coast, combined with a bankrupt provincial administration and a disintegrating civil service, can make it exceedingly difficult to make arrangements. Provided you are resourceful, you should overcome these bureaucratic obstacles – an effort worth making, as the region's wildernesses are exceedingly beautiful. We have provided the most up-to-date booking information available at the time of writing for each reserve.

For some people, one attraction of the Wild Coast region, especially the Port St Johns area, is the ready availability of high-quality **cannabis** (*insango* in Xhosa). Be warned, though, that cannabis is as illegal here as anywhere else in South Africa, and that the former Transkei police are trying to prove their worth to the national force with regular busts.

Cintsa, Haga-Haga and Morgan's Bay

Of the smattering of resorts between East London and the Kei River, the best are at Cintsa and Morgan's Bay, where endless sandy beaches back up into forested dunes sliced through by lagoons and rivers. Cintsa is actually two places with distinct characters, Cintsa East and Cintsa West, divided by a river.

CINTSA EAST, 15km off the N2 on a tarred road and 45km from East London, is an upmarket holiday village of some 200 houses. For **accommodation**, *Cintsa East B&B* (℡043 738 5021; ❷) offers two modestly priced rooms in the owners' two-storey house with sea views, a five-minute walk from the glorious eight-kilometre-long sandy beach; while *The Gables* (℡043 738 5353 or 083 676 0213, ❹), facing inland onto a valley, is an upmarket, luxurious country lodge with five en-suite bedrooms, which also does dinner. Of the handful of **eating** places, the fancy *Michaelas* restaurant (℡043 738 5139; daily except Tues 10.30am until late) is set on top of a dune with spectacular views. You can take a funicular up or stroll along the boardwalk from the restaurant's car park. More modest fare is served at the popular and friendly *Fred's Pub & Grub* in Cintsa Drive (open for lunch and supper daily except Mon). Takeaways are available from the shop next door. **To get to Cintsa East**, take the N2 for about 30km out of East London, turning off at the East Coast Resorts Road. After 8km, turn left at the sign to Cefane Mouth and *Michaelas Restaurant,* and continue for another 7km.

Across the river, on the Baz Bus route, **CINTSA WEST** is home to *Buccaneer's* (℡043 734 3012, ℻043 734 3749, ⓦwww.cintsa.com), one of South Africa's most popular hostels. *Buccaneer's* has built its reputation on the excellence of its **backpacker accommodation** in eight cottages of varying sizes, with fantastic sea and lagoon views, unspoilt beaches, and a plethora of activities such as hiking, surfing (free boards) and horse-riding. You can self-cater, or eat inexpensive breakfasts and dinners in the café and pub. It also lays on trips to a local African school and township, and its Adventure Company will take you for surfing lessons, out kloofing, or for day-trips deeper into the Wild Coast. Game drives in neighbouring Inkwenkwezi Nature Reserve cost R75.

Just northeast of Cintsa, **HAGA-HAGA** (72km from East London, 27km of this along a dirt road off the N2) is dominated by the box-like but perfectly positioned *Haga-Haga Resort* (T & F 043 841 1670, E hagahaga@intekom.co .za; ❸). It offers a very reasonable half-board rate in fifteen hotel rooms (❸), and self-catering in fourteen other flatlets sleeping two or four people (❷). A tidal swimming pool is sculpted into the rocky shoreline in front of the hotel; to reach a sandy beach, take the two-kilometre path to Pullens Bay, which is ideal for swimming among the breakers. A four-kilometre walk takes you to Bead Beach, where you can fossick for beads made from carnelian gemstones and bits of pottery.

MORGAN'S BAY, 90km from East London (50km of this also along a dirt road off the N2), lies magnificently in an estuary at the convergence of two rivers carving their passage through forested dunes. The *Morgan's Bay* (T & F 043 841 1062, E mb.hotel@mweb.co.za; full-board ❹), is a friendly, well-run **hotel** overlooking a gorgeous beach. It's one of the best hotels along the Wild Coast, particularly for family holidays, and offers good food and fresh, airy rooms with beachside motifs and furnished with limewashed furniture. Cheaper rooms have shared bathrooms, and there's also **camping**. A hike from the hotel leads over some grassy knolls to the fifty-metre Morbay Cliffs, an excellent vantage point for spotting dolphins and, in season, whales. The bay is pounded by massive breakers, but the estuary provides a safe and tranquil place for toddlers to paddle.

Qolora Mouth

From Morgan's Bay, it's a short, rough drive to the village of **Kei Mouth** (it's not signposted, so get directions from **Morgan's Bay Hotel**). You can take your car on a ropey-looking pontoon across the Kei River, before driving on to *Trennery's Hotel* at Qolora Mouth. The roads are shocking, so go slowly. While there are some self-catering places in Kei Mouth itself, which is a proper village with a post office and small shops, Morgan's Bay and *Trennery's* on either side are both so outstanding there's little point dallying.

From Kei Mouth, a six-kilometre walk along the beach or an hour by car (including the ferry crossing) leads to beautiful **QOLORA MOUTH** (roughly pronounced "kalocha" – the 'r' in Xhosa is like the 'ch' in loch). The resort is dominated by the marvellous and reasonably priced family **hotel** *Trennery's* (T 047 498 0004, F 047 498 0011; full-board ❹), an old-fashioned place founded in 1928 and with its heart still somewhere in the 1950s or 1960s. While the self-contained en-suite thatched bungalows feel slightly worn, the seamless organization and attentive service make up for the lack of modernization. Uniformed nannies are on hand to accompany children around the playground and the separate children's dining room, where the little darlings need neither be seen nor heard by their parents. The English-style food is wholesome and well-cooked, if unrevelatory. A verandah in front of the hotel

The great cattle killing

The 1850s were a low point for the Xhosa nation: most of their land had been seized by the British, drought had withered their crops, and cattle-sickness had decimated their precious herds. In 1856, a young woman called **Nongqawuse**, whose uncle Mhlakaza was a prophet, claimed to have seen and heard ancestral spirits in a pool on the Gxara River. The spirits told her the Xhosa must kill all their remaining cattle and destroy their remaining crops; if they did this, new cattle and crops would arise, along with new people who would drive the whites into the sea.

As news of her **prophecy** spread, opinion was sharply divided amongst the Xhosa. Those whose herds had been badly affected by cattle-sickness were most inclined to believe her. A turning point came when the Gcaleka paramount chief Sarili visited Nongqawuse, became convinced she was telling the truth and ordered his subjects to start the killing. Thousands of cattle were killed, but when the "new people" failed to materialize on the expected day, the unbelievers who had not killed their herds were blamed. By February 1857, the next date for the appearance of the new people, over 200,000 cattle had been slaughtered, their corpses left decomposing everywhere. When the new people failed once more to materialize, it was too late for many Xhosa. By July there was **widespread starvation**; 30,000 of an estimated population of 90,000 died of hunger.

The British administration saw the famine as a perfect way to force the destitute Xhosa into working on white settlers' farms. To speed up the process, the Cape governor Sir George Grey closed down the feeding stations established by missionaries and laid the blame for the disaster on the Xhosa chiefs, imprisoning many of them on Robben Island.

Not surprisingly, the 1856 cattle killing is often used by whites as evidence of the folly of black superstition. The Xhosa, however, have a different interpretation: "*Intombi kaMhlakaza yathetha ubuxoke*" goes the song – "Mhlakaza's girl told lies".

overlooks the swimming pool and sunbeds, while the spectacular beach is a steep walk from the hotel through luxuriant vegetation. Canoes and rowing boats are available for outings on the lagoon.

Although Trennery's dominates Qolora Mouth, a cheaper and more modest hotel, Seagulls (T047 498 0044, www.seagulls.co.za; 3) has the advantage of being right on the beach, and does half- rather than full-board. Both offer seven-night specials, and are a bit cheaper outside school holidays.

A recommended excursion (bookable through reception from either hotel) is **Trevor's Trail**, run by local resident Trevor Wigley every morning. This three-hour walking and boating trip to the "The Gates" – the short corridor of rock-face towering above the Qolora River – gives you the chance to walk in the bush. Other trails run by Trevor include: an exploration of the enormously varied shell life of the seashore and some of the coastline's many **shipwrecks**; a visit to a local *igqirha*, or **traditional healer**, who enacts a typical consultation; an historical trip to the **Gxara River**, where the prophetess Nongqawuse's disastrous visions induced the Xhosa to kill their cattle (see box above); and a visit to the major **battlefields** of the last Frontier War between the Xhosa and the British in 1878. These trails involve a 4WD vehicle, so are more expensive than the daily jaunt.

The easiest way **to get to Qolora Mouth** is to cross the Kei River on a small pontoon (which you can take your car on) that operates from 6am to 6pm in summer and from 7am to 5.30pm in winter. After disembarking, continue for another 17km to *Trennery's*, which is signposted. The road is shocking, so go very slowly.

Nxaxo Mouth and Wavecrest Hotel

NXAXO MOUTH, just north of Qolora, is a tranquil location with mangrove swamps teeming with wildlife. It's an ideal place for hiking, shoreline fishing and general relaxation, as well as the more strenuous **activities** of canoeing, water-skiing and deep-sea fishing. All of this can be arranged through the resort's only **accommodation**, the *Wavecrest* (☎047 498 0022, ⓦwww.wildcoast.co.za; ❹), a cluster of pleasant bungalows and family rooms – arguably the most beautifully positioned of all the Wild Coast hotels.

To get there, follow the 34km of tarred road to Kentani from the N2 at Butterworth. At Kentani, take the signposted road (to the left) to Nxaxo for 8km, then the road to *Wavecrest* (on the right) for 24km. This road is in poor condition, so go slowly.

Mazeppa Bay, Qora Mouth and Kob Inn

Two good **fishing** and general chill-out spots on the Wild Coast, **MAZEPPA BAY** and **QORA MOUTH**, lie northeast of Nxaxo. Mazeppa Bay, a lovely spot surrounded by dunes and coastal forest, is reached along the signposted road from Kentani (34km of tarred surface from Butterworth, and about 45km further of dirt road). Since there are two routes for getting there, it's advisable to contact the hotel when you're about to travel for advice about road conditions. The slightly downmarket *Mazeppa Bay* (☎047 498 0033, ⓕ047 498 0034, ⓦwww.wildcoast.co.za; ❹) offers full-board **accommodation** in comfortable cabanas or family rooms in the hotel, 39 steps up from the beach. It has the added attraction of its own island (reached along a bridge), on which there's an unexcavated Khoisan midden. Swimming in the bay is safe, and surfing is good. *Mazeppa Bay Backpackers* (☎082 956 8037; ❶) offers decent accommodation, including en-suite doubles, in a large house at the beach with great sea views. They have seafood evenings, with free mussels and oysters in the bar, and organize cultural trips to a traditional healer, or ones where you stay overnight in a Xhosa village. Ring the hostel for a pickup from the Baz Bus stop in Butterworth.

Just northeast of Mazeppa, **QORA MOUTH** is the site of the *Kob Inn* (☎ & ⓕ047 499 0011, ⓔkobinn@iafrica.com; ❹), set away from the beach on a rocky shore close to the wide Mbashe River. The hotel has well-kept thatched bungalows, a good bar with views of the sea, and a breathtaking swimming pool built into the tidal rocks. Staff can arrange a boat and fishing tackle, or equip you for canoeing, water-skiing and boardsailing. A small ferry traverses the mouth and takes you to some good hiking trails along the coast, through grassland and into nearby forest patches. To get to Qora Mouth, take the signposted dirt road heading south for 64km from Idutywa (see opposite), passing through grassy rolling hills and Xhosa villages.

Butterworth and Idutywa

Butterworth, 110km from East London on the N2, and **Idutywa**, 35km further on, are places you pass through rather than visit. Both are busy centres, barely distinguishable from each other, although Butterworth is the larger. They serve the vast rural communities on either side of the N2 and each has a reasonable hotel – useful if you find yourself stranded at nightfall.

Butterworth

BUTTERWORTH, the oldest town in the Transkei, is located near the site of the Gcaleka chief Hintsa's Great Place, and was founded by Methodist missionaries in 1827. The town, known to Xhosa as Gcuwa (after the river running through it), derives its English name from the then-treasurer of the Wesleyan Mission Society, Reverend Butterworth. It was selected as the focal point of Transkeian industrial development in the 1970s, with its new industries drawing thousands of workers from the surrounding countryside. Most of the industries have now closed, but the people are still living in sprawling townships and squatter camps around the town, where unemployment is worryingly high.

While Butterworth itself is unattractive and a bit chaotic, with tatty department stores and supermarkets, the nearby **Bawa Falls** on the Qolora River, which have a sheer drop of nearly 100m, are spectacular and worth a visit if you're not pressed for time. The poorly maintained twenty-kilometre dirt track leading to them is just west of town past the Shell filling station, but numerous twists and turns make the falls quite hard to find, so you will need to ask directions.

The well-signposted road to Kentani and the Wild Coast is at the eastern end of Butterworth, past the Gcuwa Bridge, and winds through the sprawling Zitulele Industrial Township, where the tar stops and gives way to a potholed dirt road. Butterworth's **bus** station is at the western end of town, next to the Shell garage, from which numerous buses and increasing numbers of **minibus taxis** run to East London, Umtata and Kentani. Daily Greyhound and Translux **buses** stop off the main road on Merriman Street, which is just before the Gcuwa Bridge.

The N2 highway runs through Butterworth and is lined with **takeaways**, beer halls and filling stations. The only decent **accommodation** in town is the *Wayside Protea* (☎047 491 4615, ℻047 491 0440, ℮wayside@cybertrade.co.za; ❸), reached by turning right down King Street off the main road, and taking the first right into Sauer Street, where you'll see the hotel on your left. The rooms are comfortable and a fair bit cheaper over weekends. The hotel has safe underground parking, and a good **restaurant** serving lunchtime buffets and a la carte evening meals. The one drawback is that it's right next to a busy taxi rank swarming with people until late into the evening.

Idutywa

The small town of **IDUTYWA**, 35km north of Butterworth on the N2, is only a place to head for if you are short of fuel, or very hungry and tired. On the main road going through town you'll find a passable *KFC* and the unassuming hotel *Idutywa* (☎047 489 1040; room only ❷), the only good place to stay on the main road between Butterworth and Umtata. Though the mattresses are poor, the hotel is clean, and the 1950s furniture lends it a modest charm. Their restaurant, the only one in town, serves a typical South African selection of steaks and grills.

A few kilometres east of town, a right-hand turn leads to **Colleywobbles**, the name given by British soldiers to a particularly tortuous and fascinating stretch of the Mbashe River about 10km down an exceedingly difficult dirt track. The river reaches the sea 50km further east, disgorging between the **Cwebe** and **Dwesa** nature reserves, but the best way for you to reach these two beautiful places is by continuing for another 60km or so along the N2 until **Jojweni** (sometimes still called by its former name of Viedgesville), and turning right down the Coffee Bay road.

Dwesa Nature Reserve

North of Qora Mouth, 73km from the N2, the **Dwesa Nature Reserve** (daily 6am–6pm) has for years been in the throes of a protracted dispute over land ownership, rendering its future uncertain. The reserve is still very much visitable and safe, but its facilities and trails have fallen into disrepair. This is a shame, because Dwesa *should* be one of the best places to stay on the coast, with rare animals such as tree dassies and samango monkeys, pristine forest, grassland and coastline, and well-sited (though run-down) self-catering wooden chalets

Some Xhosa traditions

The Wild Coast region is largely populated by **rural Xhosa**, who still practise traditions and customs that have faded in more urban areas. Many people, for example, still believe that the sea is inhabited by strange people who do not always welcome visitors, which explains the relative scarcity of the activities you would normally find thriving among seashore-dwelling people, such as fishing and diving.

Initiation for teenage boys and young men is still common. Young men usually leave their homes to stay in "circumcision lodges", dress in distinctive white paint and costumes and learn the customs of their clan. At the circumcision ceremony the young men are expected to make no sound while their foreskin is cut off (with no anaesthetic) with a single slice of a knife. After the ceremony, they wash off the paint and wrap themselves in new blankets, and all their possessions are thrown into a hut and set alight – they must turn away from this and not look back. There follows a feast to celebrate the beginning of manhood and the start of a year-long intermediary period during which they wear ochre-coloured clay on their faces. After this, they are counted as men. Boys who have gone through the experience of initiation together are supposed to remain bonded at a deep level for the rest of their lives.

Like other African peoples, although they believe in one God, uThixo, or uNhkulukhulu (the great one), many Xhosa also believe that their **ancestors** play an active role in their lives. However, the ancestors' messages are often too obscure to be understood without the aid of specialists, or *amagqira*.

The Xhosa are patriarchal by tradition, with women's subordinate status symbolized by *lobola*, the **dowry** payment in cattle and cash that a prospective husband must make to her parents before he can marry her. If the woman is not a virgin, the man pays less. Married Xhosa women have the same right as men to smoke tobacco in **pipes**, and can often be seen doing so, the pipes' long stems designed to prevent ash falling on babies suckling at their breasts. Pipes are shared, but each person must have their own stem, not just for matters of hygiene but also to prevent witchcraft: bits of the body make the most effective poisonous medicines against people, and that includes hair, skin and spittle.

The Xhosa did not wear cloth until it was introduced by Europeans, when it was quickly adopted. Today, what is now seen as traditional **Xhosa cloth** is almost always worn by women, mostly in the form of long skirts, beautifully embroidered with horizontal black stripes placed at varying intervals, which are displayed to subtle effect when the wearer is walking. Bags in matching colours with long shoulder straps are popular accessories, especially at weddings, when people put cash gifts inside them. The breasts of unmarried women were traditionally uncovered, while those of married women were usually covered with beads or matching cloth. These days, most women wear T-shirts, though almost all women still cover their heads with scarves intricately tied to form two peaks above the forehead. The **traditional colours** of the Thembu and Bomvana clans are red or orange, while the colour of the Pondo and the Mpondomise clans is light blue. In practice, these traditions are not always observed, and married women from a number of clans often wear white instead.

(❶). There's also a campsite. To **stay** at Dwesa you should ideally book ahead, but the system is rather haphazard and not entirely reliable. You could try just turning up, but either way make sure you have enough time to drive on to another resort if necessary. To get to the reserve, turn south off the N2 at Idutywa towards the coast; the road forks right to *Kob Inn* and left to Dwesa.

Cwebe Nature Reserve

North of the Mbashe River from Dwesa, the **Cwebe Nature Reserve** (daily 6am–6pm) makes up for its lack of big game with dense subtropical forest, brimming with flora and fauna. Stinkwood and samango monkeys, both of which have all but disappeared from most of southern Africa's east coast, are to be found here along a poorly maintained network of trails. Thankfully, the trail to the beautiful **Mbanyana Waterfall** is in good shape, easily walkable from the *Haven* (see below) if the ground is dry. The remaining section of the reserve comprises rolling grassland and a long stretch of wonderful dune-filled shoreline lying in the shadow of the Mbashe lighthouse.

Exploring this area is the best reason to stay at the privately owned *Haven* (☎047 576 006 or 083 494 5575, ☎047 576 0008, ✉thehaven@wildcoast.com; ❸–❹). Its **bungalows** are dotted fairly close together on the fringes of a small golf course regularly grazed by **wildebeest** and **zebra**, only a short walk through milkwood groves to the sea. The swimming pool has sea views, as does the main hotel building.

To get to **Cwebe**, take the Coffee Bay turn-off from the N2 at Jojweni, turn right 27km later at Gogoswayo Trading Store, following the tarred road another 17km to the small hamlet of **Elliotdale**, the main administrative centre in the communal lands of the Bomvana people. From here it's 47km of generally good-quality dirt road to the *Haven*. Avoid the route off the N2 at Qunu to Elliotdale, as this section requires a high-clearance vehicle.

Hole in the Wall

The village of **HOLE IN THE WALL** has grown up on the shoreline near the large cliff that juts out of the sea a short distance from the Mpako River Mouth, from which it gets its name. The cliff has a tunnel at its base through which huge waves pound during heavy seas, making a great crashing sound that has led the Xhosa to call it esiKhaleni (the place of sound). As well as good fishing, safe swimming and snorkelling, there are several spectacular hikes, including a coastal walk to Coffee Bay. A recently built nine-kilometre gravel road – a **scenic drive** through traditional villages and along cliffs with sea views – links Coffee Bay with Hole in the Wall, a trip definitely worth making if you're based at Coffee Bay. Its a very pleasant one-kilometre walk from the village to **the hole**, a lovely spot ideal for picnics or just relaxing.

A **hotel**, the *Hole in the Wall* (☎ & ☎043 575 2001; half-board ❹), situated on a small sandy bay, is a conglomeration of white thatched rondavels surrounded by green lawns, with a pool, bar and playground, dominating the tiny settlement. While the hotel doesn't have a great reputation for food, accommodation or organization, it does offer the possibility of self-catering – rare for a Wild Coast hotel – but buy all your supplies in Umtata. The well-equipped self-catering units (❷) sleep two to six people, while more basic bedsit units are cheaper (❶). A **hostel** on the same site, the quiet *Hole in the Wall Backpackers* (☎083 317 8786, ☎047 575 0010, shuttle bus ☎083 996 7855; ❶), is owned by the hotel, and allows guests to use hotel facilities. It has five dorms, and three tiny doubles. There isn't the same social scene here as at the Coffee Bay hostels, but you can get free **surfing lessons**, and there are reasonably priced day excursions to hard-to-reach and spectacular spots along the coast, such as Umdumbi. If you give the owners advance notice, they will pick you up in Umtata at the Shell Ultra City, where the Baz Bus stops. Otherwise, make your own way on a minibus taxi from Umtata to Coffee Bay, then walk or hitch the rest of the way.

Coffee Bay

The densely populated, gentle hills of **COFFEE BAY**, known to the Xhosa as Tshontini after a dense wood that grows there, mark the traditional boundary between the Bomvana and Pondo clans of the Xhosa nation. Coffee Bay, with its laid-back, relaxed atmosphere, draws a growing number of visitors – yet retains its feeling of idyllic obscurity. It has easy access on a tarred surface all the way from the N2, and nearby attractions like the Hole in the Wall (see p.427).

The **landscape** at Coffee Bay contrasts with the grasslands, forested sand dunes and lagoons further south, dramatic high cliffs dropping to sandy beaches speckled with black pebbles. The main attraction here is the **coastal hikes**; the walk to Hole in the Wall is particularly outstanding. To start the trail, head south along the track from Coffee Bay, and turn left at a small sign just past the Telkom tower, from where it's another 5km along the coast.

The **huts** here are also very distinctive; many are thatched with a topknot made from a tyre, coloured glass or even an aloe plant – said to discourage owls, harbingers of ill-omen, from roosting on roofs. An excellent community-run **village tour** can be organized through the impressive ANC Women's League veteran, Betty Madlalisa (☎083 341 0041, or contact her through the *Ocean View Hotel*). Apart from visiting homesteads, the outing takes in the **Masizame Women's Project** (daily 8am–5pm), housed in a colourful building opposite the Bayview Store, 5km out of Coffee Bay on the Umtata Road. If you're not taking the tour, it's still definitely worth visiting the project – it's one of the very few outlets in South Africa where you can buy traditional Xhosa craftwork, including beaded bags and belts, traditional clothing, baskets, mats and blankets. With advance notice, they also offer **Xhosa meals** – based mostly around meat stews, maize meal, and homegrown vegetables like spinach and pumpkin, washed down with traditional beer.

Practicalities

The smartest **accommodation** is the full-board **hotel**, the *Ocean View* (☎ & ⑤047 575 2005 or ☎047 575 2006, ⓔoceanview@coffeebay.co.za; ❹), right on the sandy bay. It's an exceptionally friendly and well-run place, with bright rooms decorated in floral motifs, terraced gardens, a pool area, and a trampoline and playground right next the beach. The restaurant and bar are open to day visitors, and the food is good with seafood splurges on Saturday nights and bar snacks including fresh oysters. Of the **backpacker lodges**, the best is *Coffee Shack* (☎047 575 2048 or 083 236 9251, ⓔcoffeeshack@wildcoast.com; ❶), well located on the Bomvu River. It offers seafood suppers and day-trips, and activities including surfing (with lessons and free boards), hiking, canoeing and abseiling. Its shuttle bus plies the route between Umtata and Coffee Bay, meeting the Baz Bus on request. They have four dorms, a double room and camping. One bay west of Coffee Bay, and set high above the water on dramatic cliffs, *Davy Jones' Locker* (☎047 575 0008; ❷) has six **self-catering** double rooms with shared bathrooms in the house of the owner, Dave Pringle. The location couldn't be better, with gorgeous views. You can see whales, literally a stone's throw away in the bay below, between August and November, and dolphins all year round. No one else lives on this bay, so you have it all to yourself. Dave cooks plain meals, with seafood in season.

There are no grocery **shops**, **banks** or **ATMs** in Coffee Bay, so make sure you come prepared. Petrol is available at the hotel, and food basics can be purchased at the Bayview Trading Store, 5km out of Coffee Bay towards Port St Johns.

Umtata River Mouth

The **Umtata River** disgorges 6km north of Coffee Bay into another soothing lagoon. This is the site of a **hotel**, the *Anchorage* (℡047 534 1671; head office & ℻047 534 0061, ✉anchorage@wildcoast.co.za), 70km from the N2, offering old-fashioned bungalow accommodation with half-board (**❹**), self-catering (**❶**), or camping. You step from your room onto the lawn and then onto the sandy beach. The *Anchorage* has a **general dealer's** and liquor store, where you can buy bread, milk, eggs and braai packs. While the *Anchorage* is no great shakes as a resort-style hotel – there are better for the same price – it's worth considering for its self-catering and camping facilities, as the area itself is lovely. Set between two rivers, the hotel is a three-kilometre walk along the beach to the Umtata River Mouth, and another 3km to the Mdumbi River Mouth, with good fishing at both. An excellent way to see the surrounding area's gentle hills, coastal forest and shoreline is on **horseback**, which the hotel can arrange.

The best route to the *Anchorage* is the tarred Coffee Bay road from the N2, 14km south of Umtata's Shell Ultra City; 6km before you reach Coffee Bay, turn left at the *Anchorage* signboard, and drive another 14km on an extremely rough dirt road.

Hluleka Nature Reserve

One of the loveliest of the Wild Coast nature reserves, **Hluleka Nature Reserve** (daily 6am–6pm; R5), consists of coastal forest whose coral trees flower scarlet in July and August, a strip of grassland and outstanding sandy beaches interspersed with rocky outcrops tattooed with extraordinary wind-shaped rock formations. Although Hluleka's trails are poorly maintained and frequently dead ends, the reserve is sufficiently small to make getting lost for a while no great disaster. In the grassland strip, you're likely to encounter wildebeest, zebra and blesbok.

Accommodation is in two sets of chalets which sleep up to six people, one on stilts overlooking the sea (R300), the other further up the hill in the forest (R200). Both are spacious but poorly equipped and subject to electricity curfews, so bring candles. You'll also need all your own food, though you may be able to buy fish from local fishermen if you tell the reserve's staff, who will tip them off. **Fishing permits** should be arranged via the Nature Conservation Office in Umtata (see p.431), where bookings for Hluleka must be made.

You can reach Hluleka along the difficult coastal road from Coffee Bay. After heading back on the Umtata road from Coffee Bay for a short distance, take the Mdumbi turn on the right, and continue for some 30km, when signs to Hluleka appear. Alternatively – and more easily – take the Hluleka turn on your right, 30km along the R61 from Umtata to Port St Johns, and continue for another 57km to the coast.

Umtata and around

Straddling the Umtata River and the N2 highway 235km from East London, the fractious, shambolic town of **UMTATA** is the former capital of the Transkei and is the Wild Coast region's largest town. Unfortunately, it's a pretty ugly place, its litter-strewn streets lined with nondescript 1970s office buildings and crowded with people. However, the town is useful for stocking up and drawing money, all of which can be done at the Spar Centre or Shell Ultra City on the edge of town. The best reason to venture into the town centre is to visit the **Nelson Mandela Museum**.

The Umtata River was traditionally the boundary between the Thembu and Pondo clans of the Xhosa nation, with the Thembu to the south and the Pondo to the north. Whites farmed by the river from the 1860s, and when Britain acquired Thembuland in 1875, Umtata was established as the site of one of its four magistracies. From 1976 until 1994, Umtata was the capital of the Transkei homeland, with a smattering of showcase large buildings and a reputation for some of the most corrupt officialdom in South Africa.

Arrival and information

The small **Umtata airport** (☎047 536 0023) lies 10km west of town on the Queenstown Road. There is no public transport from the airport, but you can rent a car here (see p.434). The **Baz Bus** stops at the Shell Ultra City.

Given the crowds, traffic and fear of crime in Umtata, most motorists, and backpackers on the Baz Bus, orientate from **Shell Ultra City**, 6km from the centre, on the N2 towards East London side. This is where the Greyhound and Translux **buses** pull in. It's a convenient place to stop, refuel, **eat** at the reasonably pleasant *Whistle Stop Restaurant* and buy basic groceries – milk, bread,

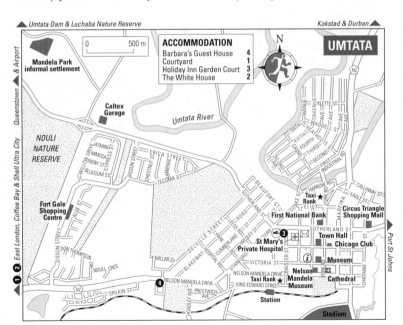

cheese, chicken and soup – from the Select Shop. A bank ATM takes Cirrus, Maestro, Mastercard and the major South African cards; a little **Eastern Cape Tourism Board caravan** in the car park provides maps and basic information. If you're self-catering along the coast, two-and-a-half kilometres away towards town on the N2, the **Spar Centre** (daily 7am–9pm) is the best place to stock up with groceries. The Spar is far better stocked than the shop at the Shell Ultra City, with a surprisingly good selection of fresh produce and luxury food items; you'll also find an ATM, and a *Wimpy* burger restaurant here.

Umtata's **tourist information** bureau (Mon–Fri 8am–4.30pm; ☎047 531 5290) at 64 Owen St in the town centre has useful **maps** and knowledgeable staff. The **Nature Conservation Office** (Mon–Fri 8am–4.30pm; ☎047 531 1191) on the corner of York and Victoria, is the place to book accommodation in Silaka and Hluleka nature reserves, both reached by heading south out of town on the R61. Here you can also pick up **maps** of the areas you want to visit and buy a helpful booklet about the whole coastal strip. **Wild Coast Reservations**, 3 Beaufort St (daily 8am–6pm; ☎047 532 5344), can arrange accommodation at resorts and hotels throughout the region.

Accommodation

Umtata is not somewhere you'd chose to spend a night, but there's some decent (not cheap) **accommodation** catering mostly to people on business, predominately on the quieter fringes of the city. Weekend nights are always less expensive. The cheapest B&B, half an hour out of the centre, is in Qunu at the Cultural Centre (see p.433).

Barbara's Guest House 55 Nelson Mandela Drive, near the centre ☎047 531 1751, ℉047 531 1754, ℮barbp@cybertrade. Decent establishment in a nice garden, with thirty mostly en-suite rooms with TVs, a swimming pool and a bar with a pool table, where you can have good pub lunches. Half-board ❹, B&B ❸

Courtyard On the corner of Sutherland Street and Savoy Terrace ☎ & ℉047 531 0791 or ☎082 556 3988. Part of the *Savoy Hotel*, with smart, refurbished and reasonably priced rooms in the centre. The *Courtyard's* rooms are better than those of the *Savoy* itself. ❷

Holiday Inn Garden Court along the N2 ☎047 537 0181. Large 1970s building on the way out of Umtata, with a stylish pool, slot machines, a chic cocktail bar and restaurant. The rooms are unre-

markable and all the singles face the car park. ❹

Travel Inn Adjoining the Shell Ultra City (see p.430) ☎047 537 0761. A totally impersonal place set behind gates and fences with no public spaces or meals; it's suitable only for a stopover, but the en-suite family rooms are comfortable and clean, and its very much cheaper over weekends. ❸

The White House 5 Mhlobo St, South Ridge Park ☎047 537 0580 or 083 458 9810, ℮whitehouse@intekom.co.za. Seventeen clean rooms, with eight decent en-suites in two adjoining suburban houses in a quiet area just off the N2, opposite the Shell Ultra City. Cheaper rooms share bathrooms. An evening meal can be provided if booked beforehand, and there is a communal lounge and pool table. ❸

The Town and around

Central Umtata comprises a small grid of crowded streets lined with dull office buildings, interspersed with the odd older architectural gem. One of these is the elegant **town hall** on Leeds Street, with a fine clock stuck at nearly 6pm, which looks down onto a war memorial and pleasant gardens. One block south, opposite the tourist office, stands the town's small and neglected **museum** (Mon–Fri 8am–4.30pm; free), which has fairly informative displays of traditional Xhosa costume, local geology and an exhibit on the ANC that stops before the 1994 elections.

Continue further south to the corner of Owen and Nelson Mandela Drive

△ The Nelson Mandela Museum, Umtata

for the new **Nelson Mandela Museum** (Mon–Fri 8am–4.30pm, Sat 9am–1pm; free), housed in the old **parliament**, or *bungha*, built in 1927. The museum is divided into three sections; the most interesting of these is the central section, "The Long Walk to Freedom", which traces the great man's life with photos and other visual material. The other two rooms house the extraordinary number of gifts given to Mandela from all over the world. The museum also offers free guided trips to **Qunu** and **Mveso** (see below), Mandela's birthplace. Contact the museum, or the tour co-ordinator Miss Tetani (☎082 933 6264).

One block east of the museum, on the corner of Alexandra and York streets, is an elegant sandstone Anglican **cathedral**, sadly permanently closed. A major taxi rank straggles along the opposite side of Alexandra Street, and behind it is the small **stadium** used by the Umtata Bucks soccer team. If you are in town for a few days and the weather is good, head for the pleasant open-air **swimming pool** (daily 9am–12.30pm & 2–4.45pm) at the western end of Sutherland Street, near the junction with Stanford Terrace.

Qunu and Mveso

Thirty kilometres west of Umtata are the scattered dwellings of **Qunu**, where Mandela grew up (see box on p.434). The N2 thunders through it, but his large and rather plain mansion, which you may photograph but not enter, is clearly visible, planted on the roadside, 28km from Shell Ultra City in Umtata, on your left, or 52km from Idutywa if you're coming from the south, on your right. A tunnel under the N2 connects his house with the village, built so that visiting children could cross the road in safety. You can also visit the remains of Mandela's primary school, the rock where he used to slide down with friends, and the graveyard where his parents, son and daughter are buried. The best way to appreciate Qunu is to take one of the free **guided tours** run by the Mandela museum.

Seven kilometres west of Mandela's house, the **Jonopo Cultural Village** (daily 8am–5pm; R5) has **B&B accommodation** in rondavels (❶) and makes a fun stopover. If you book in advance, a Xhosa dinner will be cooked for you. There are also good crafts for sale and some exhibitions of rural life.

Mandela spent his first two years at **Mveso**, an hour south of Umtata. The **open-air museum** here contains the remains of the rondavels where he was born and raised, and a photographic exhibition with photos such as Mandela burning his pass – the infamous identity documents Africans were forced to carry under apartheid.

Eating

As well as the hotel restaurants (see p.431), there are a limited number of good **places to eat** in Umtata. *La Piazza* (☎047 531 0795), in Delville Road at the Country Club, does varied and tasty Italian-based food, with a good range of salads, in a friendly, family-oriented setting. The *Country Club Restaurant* (☎047 531 0795) at the same address is open to non-members (closed Sunday) and serves food and drinks on a thatch-covered deck overlooking the golf course, and is a pleasant place to spend the evening. Of the **fast-food** chains, *Nando's*, 85 York Rd, opposite the town hall, is the best, serving up the usual tasty grilled chicken meals. If you're just passing through and want a bite before pressing on, the *Whistle Stop* at the Shell Ultra City filling station complex is good for quick meals and to freshen up. Umtata has a thriving **nightlife**, with bars and *shebeens*, but exploring it without a local escort isn't recommended.

Nelson Mandela and the Qunu connection

Nelson Rolihlahla Mandela was born near tiny **Qunu** in the even tinier village of Mveso on July 18, 1918. His father was a member of the Xhosa royal house and a custodian of Xhosa history – he was also chief of Mveso, until he crossed swords with the local white magistrate over a minor dispute concerning an ox. After his sacking, the family moved to a small *kraal* in Qunu, which Mandela remembers as consisting of several hundred poor households.

Mandela is often called **Madiba** – the name of his family's subclan of the Thembu clan. The name Nelson was given to him by a schoolteacher, and Rolihlahla means "pulling the branch of a tree" or, more colloquially, "troublemaker". Mandela has said that at home he was never allowed to ask any questions, but was expected to learn by observation. Later in life, he was shocked to visit the homes of whites and hear children firing questions at their parents and expecting replies.

Shortly after his father died, Mandela was summoned from Qunu to the royal palace at Mqhakeweni, where he sat in on disputes in court and learnt more about Xhosa culture. At 16 he was **initiated** – and burnt with shame for a long time afterwards over the cry he let slip out when circumcised. He enrolled in Clarkebury, a college for the Thembu elite, then the Wesleyan college of Healdtown at Fort Beaufort, and finally the celebrated **Fort Hare** in Alice (see p.405), which had educated generations of African leaders. Mandela was expelled from Fort Hare after clashing with the authorities, and returned to Mqhakeweni. In 1941, faced with the prospect of an arranged marriage, he ran away to Johannesburg and there immersed himself in politics.

It was only in 1990 (at the age of 72) when released from prison that Mandela was able to return to Qunu, visiting first the grave of his mother, who had died in his absence. He noted that the place seemed poorer than he remembered it, and that the children were now singing songs about AK47s and the armed struggle. However, he was relieved to find that none of the old spirit and warmth had left the community, and he arranged for a palace (or "country house" as he called it) to be built there. This palace has become the venue for Mandela's holidays and family reunions and has a floor-plan identical to that of the house in Victor Verster prison where Mandela spent the last few years of his captivity. In his autobiography he writes:

The Victor Verster house was the first spacious and comfortable home I ever stayed in, and I liked it very much. I was familiar with its dimensions, so at Qunu I would not have to wander at night looking for the kitchen.

Listings

Banks First National Bank, corner of Sutherland Street and York Road; Standard Bank, corner of York Road and Leeds Street. Expect large queues – it's better to use the ATMs at the Spar Centre or at Shell Ultra City, both on the East London side of the N2.
Car rental Avis ☎047 536 0066, at Umtata airport.
Emergencies Ambulance ☎10177 or 047 532 2222; Police ☎531 2333.

Garages Fort Gale Motors ☎047 532 3882, on Queenstown Road.
Hospital St Mary's Private Hospital, 30 Durham St ☎047 531 2911.
Nature Conservation Office Corner of York Road and Victoria Street ☎047 531 1191.
Pharmacy Triangle Pharmacy ☎047 531 0215 Circus Triangle Centre, Port St Johns Road.
Travel agents Sure Travel Centre ☎047 531 2011 Metropolitan Place, Leeds Street.

Port St Johns and around

The sixty-kilometre drive to **PORT ST JOHNS** from Umtata is one of the best journeys on the Wild Coast. After passing tiny **Libode**, with its small hotel and restaurant, you start the dramatic descent to the coast, past craggy ravines and epic vistas of forest and rondavel-spotted grassland. The road runs alongside the Mzimvubu River for the last few kilometres, giving you a perfect view of the Gates of St John, before reaching the town square and taxi rank. The big surprise, coming from the sparse hillsides around Umtata, is how dramatic, hilly, lush and steamy it all is.

Port St Johns is a favoured destination for backpackers, drawn by its stunning location at the mouth of the Mzimvubu River, dominated by Mount Thesiger on the west bank and Mount Sullivan on the east. A further attraction for some visitors is the strong cannabis grown in the area, and the town's famously laid-back atmosphere may tempt you to stay for longer than you intended. Port St Johns also has good fishing and swimming beaches, a wider choice of accommodation than anywhere else on the Wild Coast, and a good tarred road all the way into town.

Some history

The origins of Port St Johns' name is something of a mystery but may derive from the sixteenth-century Portuguese ship, *São João*, which was wrecked nearby, leaving around four hundred survivors to complete a seven-hundred-kilometre walk to Mozambique. Only eight survived, and one of those was shipwrecked again near the Umtata River Mouth two years later. He reportedly died of despair, unable to face the trek to Mozambique once more.

In 1878, in an effort to reduce gun-running from the harbour, a representative of the Cape governor bought a fifteen-kilometre stretch of the river from the shore inland, and the land on the western side from the Pondo for R2000. While he was waiting for the money, an armed force arrived from Natal and annexed the eastern side of the river. A compromise was found by making Port St Johns a crown colony in its own right, though this was rescinded when the whole of Pondoland was annexed by Britain in 1895.

The area was then known for its **tobacco**, which was exported from Durban and East London. During the negotiations for the Act of Union, the Transvaal demanded the cessation of the trade to allow its white tobacco growers to expand their business without competition. The Cape Colony obliged and in 1906 stopped exporting tobacco. Local farmers responded by switching to **cannabis** (*insango*), supplying the growing numbers of men from the area working in the Gauteng mines. Today, the cultivation and trade are as strong as ever, which may explain the presence of so many white South African hippies in the town.

Arrival and information

The Baz Bus drops off at Shell Ultra City (a filling station-cum-restaurant and shopping complex) in Umtata. Book in advance to be met here by one of the hostels. Port St Johns is also easily reached by **minibus taxi** from Umtata: plenty run from the *Steer's* restaurant at the Circus Triangle Mall.

If you're travelling **from KwaZulu-Natal** to Port St Johns by public transport, an alternative route is via the *Wild Coast Sun* (see p.439), Bizana and Lusikisiki on the R61. This journey is most easily done by catching the Grimboys bus from Durban, which runs daily directly to Port St Johns.

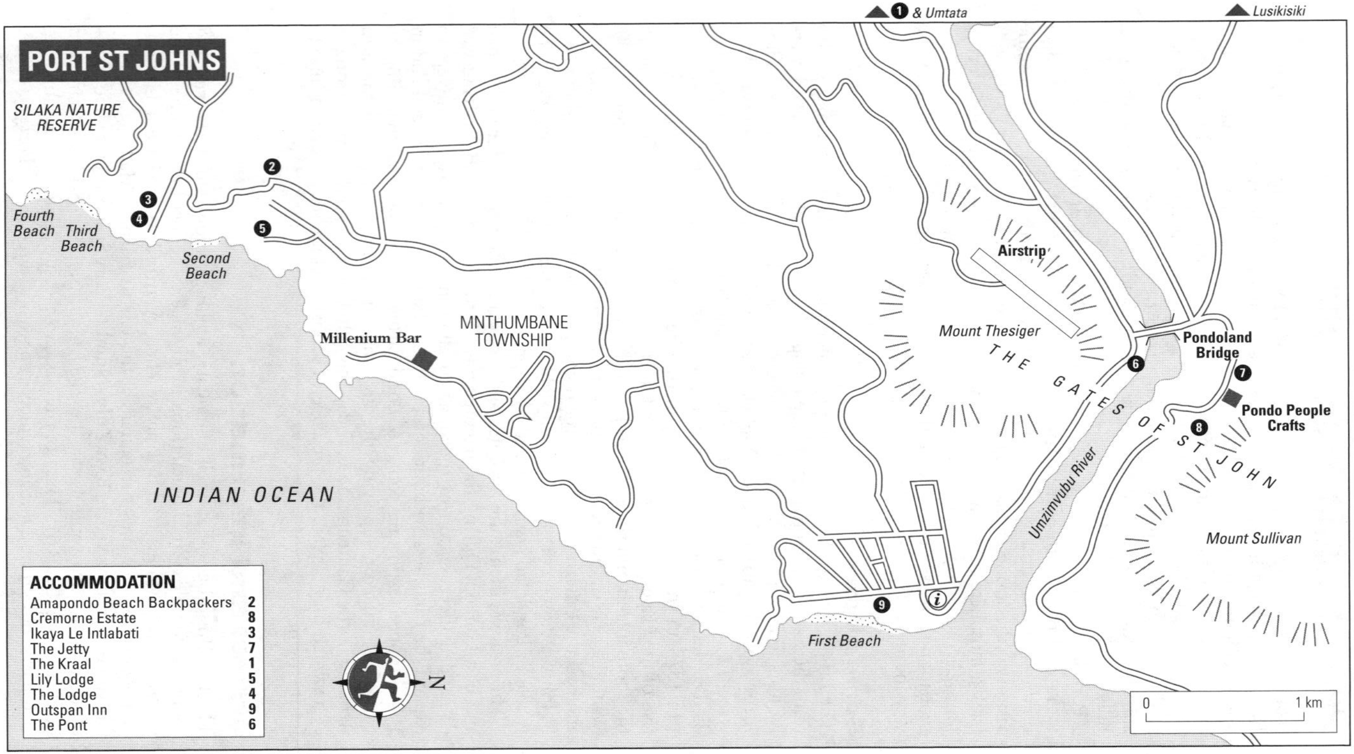

PORT ST JOHNS

SILAKA NATURE
RESERVE

Fourth
Beach

Third Beach

Second
Beach

Millenium Bar

MNTHUMBANE
TOWNSHIP

First Beach

Airstrip

Mount Thesiger

THE GATES

Pondoland
Bridge

Pondo People
Crafts

THE GATES OF ST JOHN

Mount Sullivan

Umzimvubu River

Lusikisiki

& Umtata

INDIAN OCEAN

N

0   1 km

ACCOMMODATION

Amapondo Beach Backpackers	2
Cremorne Estate	8
Ikaya Le Intlabati	3
The Jetty	7
The Kraal	1
Lily Lodge	5
The Lodge	4
Outspan Inn	9
The Pont	6

Driving from Durban, you should follow the same route, continuing along the coast after Port Shepstone to Port Edward, rather than striking inland on the N2. Sticking to the R61 is by far the most direct route and is tarred all the way, bar the final eighteen-kilometre stretch from Lusikisiki.

There's a **tourist information** bureau (Mon–Fri 8.30am–5pm, Sat 9am–noon) in an obvious building at the roundabout as you enter town. As well as maps, they provide information about local Xhosa homestays. Jimmy Gila from the tourist office (☎082 507 2256) runs **tours** in the area. Also in the centre you'll find a post office, a bank with an ATM and a Boxer Supermarket.

Accommodation

Port St Johns has the best selection of **accommodation** on the Wild Coast, with a healthy number of backpacker lodges, B&Bs and resort complexes. Neither of the hostels in Port St Johns itself is in a particularly exciting location, although there are some other well-positioned budget options. For a **hostel** offering a beach and rural experience, head for Mpande, some way out of town.

Amapondo Beach Backpackers Second Beach ☎047 564 1582 or 082 630 7905, ⊛www.portstjohns.org.za/amapondo. Lively hostel situated on a hilltop with a sea view, but some way from Second Beach. A free shuttle heads into the centre each morning, 5km away, and the hostel liaises daily with the Baz Bus to collect passengers. The hostel, which has internet facilities and can provide evening meals, has two dorms, doubles, and permanent tents mounted on decks. Trips can be arranged to walk in Silaka Nature Reserve, or to spend the night in a rural village and meet a traditional healer. ❶

Cremorne Estate 5km from the centre on the Umzimvubu River, signposted from the Pondoland Bridge ☎ & ⒻF047 564 1113, ⊛www.cremorne.co.za. Port St John's only upmarket place, offering smart, self-catering timber cottages on stilts set on tidy lawns running down to the Umzimvubu River, with views of Mount Thesiger's red-slabbed cliffs. The cottages have two en-suite bedrooms, making it very affordable for a party of three or four. A less expensive row of small, clean B&B doubles shares the view; cheaper still are some tiny cabins equipped with double bunks, where you can also camp. There's a restaurant, bar and a relaxing swimming pool area. ❶–❹

Ikaya Le Intlabati The last driveway on the right along the Second Beach Road ☎ & ⒻF047 564 1266, ⒺE riverz@intekom.co.za. A secluded, delightfully homely cottage with two doubles sharing a bath and another en-suite, plus two self-contained flats in the garden of friendly, artistic owners with children and dogs. The cheapest doubles in town, outside the hostels. The beach, conveniently at the

bottom of the sub-tropical garden, is reached via a jungly walkway. Self-catering only. ❷

The Jetty ☎047 564 1072. Tranquil, reasonably priced lodge, on the Umzimvubu's eastern bank. A short distance from the Pondoland Bridge and Lusikisiki Road, 5km from the centre of town. Mainly self-catering (though meals are available), it offers five en-suite rooms in an old house, three of them with beds for children. There's an extensive garden with lawns and spreading trees, where you can sometimes see flocks of rare Cape parrots feeding on the pecan nut, avocado and lychee trees, and a deck and verandah with views onto the river. Cooking is in a communal, well-equipped kitchen, but there's no bar. It's a casual place with an emphasis on fishing; you can rent boats here for fishing trips or river cruises. Self-catering ❶, B&B ❷

The Kraal Near Mpandi, bookings ☎043 683 2384, ⒻF043 683 2098, ⒺE thekraal@hotmail.com. Four traditional huts, each sleeping four people, on community land well off the beaten track. Efficiently run and wonderfully set right on the beach, it has no electricity or flushing toilets (enviroloos are used), and showers and washing facilities are in reed huts. Meals are available and you can often get crayfish, oysters and mussels; activities include beach hikes, snorkelling, surfing, and dolphin-watching (also whale-watching in season). A hostel bus connects with the Baz Bus at Shell Ultra City in Umtata (book in advance by phone); by car, turn off at Tombo Stores, 70km from Umtata on the Port St Johns Road, and travel another 30min to the little village of Mpandi.

Lily Lodge signposted off Second Beach Road ☎ & ⒻF047 564 1229 or ☎082 926 0077,

@ lilys@wildcoast.co.za. A row of comfortable brick cottages set in a luxuriant subtropical garden, very close to Second Beach, but not especially cheap. Best known for its seafood restaurant. ❸

The Lodge Second Beach Road ☎047 564 1171 or 082 977 6989. The best setting in Port St Johns, at the end of Second Beach Road. A charming and secluded thatched house with three tastefully simple twin bedrooms, wooden floors, lovely views of the beach from the verandah, and the best wine and cooking in town. Booking is essential for the restaurant, which only operates if you have pre-booked. B&B ❷

Outspan Inn In the centre, past the town hall on the road to First Beach ☎ & ℗047 564 1057 or ☎047 564 1345, ⊛www.wildcoast.com/outspan. Two-storey, ochre B&B with twelve rooms set in an appealing large garden with ethnically decorated en-suite rooms, some with high beds that give a view of nearby First Beach. The restaurant and pub is open daily and there's a swimming pool. Frequently used by aid workers and business people, it's cheaper at weekends. ❸

The Pont 5km out of town, signposted at Pondoland Bridge ☎047 465 11324, @pont@wildcoast.com. A good place to camp on extensive, sunny lawns

going down to the Umzimvubu River, but the bamboo huts are grotty. ❶

Port St Johns Backpackers Berea Road, first right off the main road after the post office ☎047 564 1517, @psjbackpackers@wildcoast.com. Although this converted house near the centre doesn't have a reputation as a happening hostel, it's actually quite adequate. It can arrange guided trips into the villages and overnight visits to a traditional healer as well as drive you to the Silaka Nature Reserve. Camping, dorms & doubles. ❶

Umngazi River Bungalows Umngazi River mouth, west of Port St Johns ☎ & ℗047 564 1115 or ☎043 701 6881. Unsurpassed as a Wild Coast holiday resort, Umngazi delivers probably the best beachside family holiday in the country. It's frequently fully booked, especially during school holidays, so book as far in advance as possible. The beach and pool are inviting and the lunchtime buffet spread is particularly good. It's signposted off the R61, about 10km before you reach Port St Johns from Umtata; from the sign, continue another 11km along a pot-holed road. Alternatively, guests can fly into Port St Johns and get picked up. Full-board ❹

The Town and around

Although there is nothing much to see in town, Port St Johns is still a nice place to take a leisurely stroll, particularly in the early evening, when many residents are doing the same. Initially the town is quite confusing – it meanders into three distinct localities, some kilometres apart. **First Beach**, where the river meets the sea, is along the main road from the post office and offers good fishing, but is unsafe for swimming. Close to First Beach is the town centre, where you'll find shops and minibus taxis. **Second Beach**, 5km along a tarred road off a right turn past the post office, is a fabulous swimming beach with a lagoon; it has a couple of nice places to stay close by, and a number of alternative folk living locally.

Other accommodation popular with anglers can be found along the river, near the **Pondoland Bridge**, 4km before you enter town. Most people rarely go anywhere else, though the rocky coastline into the **Silaka Nature Reserve** (see p.439) and as far as the **Umngazi River Mouth** provides wonderful walks, as do the endless stretches of pristine beach east of the Mzimvubu River. The Mzimvubu is muddy in summer, disgorging topsoil washed down the Drakensberg from Lesotho, but cleans up dramatically in winter, when it is clear and good for fishing.

Both the mountains of the **Gates of St John** merit a stiff climb to the top, from where you get a superb view of the lush surrounding landscape. The Gates are two sentinel-like mountainous outcrops on either side of the Mzimvubu River, marking the point where it flows out to the Indian Ocean. By car, drive up to the aircraft landing strip at the top of Mount Thesiger. Look out for the birds of prey, making use of the updrafts.

For **crafts**, check out Pondo People on the east side of the Mzimvubu River across the Pondoland Bridge, easily the best craft shop on the Wild Coast, with wooden sculptures, baskets, carved wooden animals, and immaculate bead jewellery and clothing – all at affordable prices. Jakotz, next to *The Lodge* on Second Beach, sells African printed clothes.

Silaka Nature Reserve

Just south of town, the **Silaka Nature Reserve** (daily 6am–6pm; R5) is a small reserve with a dramatic coastline, and comprises the idyllic Third Beach, dense and beautiful tropical-forest areas with huge trees – through which there are good **trails** – and a handful of animals, including zebra and wildebeest. **Accommodation** is in spacious self-catering chalets surrounded by grassland, sleeping four (❶); book through Nature Conservation in Umtata. To get to the reserve, travel down the Second Beach road from Port St Johns and then up the treacherously steep dirt road to the reserve's office. Some of the backpacker lodges will drop you in the reserve, and you can walk back along the coast.

Eating and drinking

There are a couple of decent places to **eat** and **drink** in Port St Johns. If you're self-catering, tempting local fruits are sold by the roadside, and you can sometimes buy fresh fish. Boxer Supermarket in the centre has most foodstuffs you'll need, while Green Foods is the place for vegetables.

Cremorne Umzimvubu River; follow the signs from the Pondoland Bridge ☎047 564 1113. Port St John's poshest eating place – in fact, the only conventional restaurant. Very good fish, steaks and puddings, a pizza oven, pub, and seating both indoors and out. Open daily for lunch and dinner.

Delicious Monster Second Beach. A couple of tables in the owner's garden, off Second Beach, where you can get breakfast, lunches with fresh herbs from the garden, and homebaked goodies for tea. There's a little craft shop too, in a caravan with nice postcards.

Hippo's On the main road, very near the Second Beach turn-off. Popular with locals, and serves inexpensive traditional dishes such as *samp* and bean stews.

The Island Signposted off First Beach ☎047 564 1958 or 082 813 611. Funky, fun place where you sit Japanese style, and eat anything from toasted sandwiches to Thai vegetable stir fry. The food is reasonably priced, well-cooked and well-presented. You can watch videos on a giant screen in one room while large speakers blast out in another.

Takeaways and deliveries possible. Daily noon–midnight, except Tues.

Lily's Restaurant *Lily Lodge*, signposted left off Second Beach Road ☎047 564 1229. Set menu that often includes reasonably priced seafood, either marvellous or disappointing. In any event, enjoy the perfect view from the sun deck across the palms to the sea. Closed Mon.

The Lodge Second Beach Road ☎047 564 1171. Tiny B&B restaurant at Second Beach serving good seafood and European meals, with fine wines to wash it all down. Booking essential.

Millennium Bar Mthubane township, between the town and Second Beach. Great sea views from an outside deck and a friendly atmosphere, with chickens and kids running about.

Outspan Inn In the centre of the village, past the town hall on the road to First Beach. The restaurant is a great place for blow-out breakfasts, and has an interesting and inexpensive lunch and dinner menu, but enjoys surprisingly little custom. Closed Sun evening.

The northern Wild Coast and the KwaZulu-Natal enclave

For many visitors to the northern part of the Wild Coast, the main draw is the **Wild Coast Sun**, a hotel and casino on the border of KwaZulu-Natal. However, the stretch of coast from Port St Johns to the Mzamba River by the

Sun is outstandingly beautiful, with three of only five waterfalls in the world that fall over 100m directly into the sea, as well as countless deserted beaches and cosy bays. The best way to see it is to walk though you can drive, with some difficulty, to the **Mkambati Nature Reserve**, which contains a good portion of this coast.

The **Lusikisiki** road from Port St Johns to the *Wild Coast Sun* via Bizana makes an interesting alternative to the N2 for getting from the Eastern Cape to KwaZulu-Natal. Inland, the road through the Eastern Cape enclave in KwaZulu-Natal takes you into the rolling hills of **Ixopo**, made famous by Alan Paton's novel, *Cry the Beloved Country.*

Mkambati Nature Reserve

The largest of the Wild Coast reserves, **Mkambati Nature Reserve** (daily 6am–6pm; book through Keval Travel, Kokstad ☏039 727 3124, ⓔwendyr.kevaltravel@galileosa.co.za) covers eighty square kilometres. It consists almost entirely of grassland, flanked by the forested ravines of the Msikaba and Mtentu rivers, and a **ravishing coastline** of rocky promontories and deserted beaches. The park has **plenty of game**: you're likely to see eland, hartebeest, wildebeest and blesbok, as well as Cape vultures. The highlight, though, is the Mkambati River itself, which cuts through the middle of the reserve down a series of striking waterfalls, of which the **Horseshoe Falls** near the sea are the most spectacular. **Horse-riding** is on offer and there's plenty of fine walking. Although the road to the reserve restcamp is fine, **driving** anywhere in the park except to the beach requires a high-clearance vehicle to negotiate the crumbling roads. The beach road itself is poor, and passable in an ordinary car only with considerable care in good weather and when the road is dry. Fortunately, the footpath to the beach through tropical forest is not too long.

Swimming is idyllic: a warm sheltered lagoon is flanked by steep dunes down which you can slide into the water; trees offer some shade along the wide, clear river, and there's the rolling surf itself. There are no facilities at the beach, so bring whatever you need for a picnic, including drinking water.

Accommodation – all of it **self-catering** – in a variety of locations, is a bit run down, but cheap. Bring all you need, as there are no shops. The prime place to stay is *The Lodge*, built as the doctor's stone house when the restcamp was a sanatorium some years ago. It has a verandah set on a hilltop overlooking the sea and its own swimming pool. Paths slither through thick vegetation, down to the lagoon, river and sea. With several bedrooms, it's ideal for a family or group and costs R440 per night. Around reception, there are some basic **self-catering cottages** (❶), the best of which are the two stone houses with a couple of bedrooms each – try for one of these when you book, rather than the one-bedroomed cottages which are pretty tatty, but given their bargain price tag you can't really complain. All this accommodation is fully equipped with electricity. At the beach, in another dreamy location, is a three-bedroom thatched house, **The Point**, the only place on the beach for miles. There is no electricity here, just solar power and gas lamps.

To get to Mkambati, turn towards the coast at the Mkambati signpost, at Flagstaff on the tarred R61. From Flagstaff, it's 70km on dirt road, which is very variable in quality. While its normally fine, if slow, in a normal car, when it has been raining hard you'll need a 4WD vehicle. From Port St Johns, count on two to three hours for the trip.

North to the Wild Coast Sun

The road from Port St Johns to the small, unremarkable town of **LUSIKISI-KI** is untarred and hard to negotiate in wet weather for the first 16km, but is tarred for the rest of the way to the *Wild Coast Sun*. Beyond Lusikisiki, the hills of Pondoland seem to stretch for miles, punctuated 50km later by the small village of **Flagstaff**. Roughly 30km further on, a junction leads back to the N2, and 20km beyond that through heavily populated hillsides is the busy town of **BIZANA**, 60km from the coast in an area where both **Oliver Tambo** and **Winnie Madikizela-Mandela** were born. The *Bizana Hotel* on the left side of the main road has a quiet **restaurant** serving good-value steaks and curries, but is not recommended as a place to stay.

Some 60km further along is the glitzy *Wild Coast Sun* (℡039 305 9111, ℻039 305 1012, ⑩www.suninternational.co.za; ➍) in a well-chosen location by the Mzamba River Mouth. Despite its tacky Pacific island-themed decor, some of the hotel complex is quite pleasant. Most people are here to gamble, but an impressive games arcade, ten-pin bowling, pony rides and minigolf are also on offer. **Accommodation** is in small, well-equipped rooms, with some suites looking onto the sea. You can **eat** tasty (if overpriced) fish steaks at the *Driftwood Terrace*, which has a fantastic sea view.

Opposite the complex is the **Mzamba Crafts Market**, arranged in a circle to resemble a traditional *kraal*. The central shop sells authentic crafts from all over southern Africa for reasonable prices, with local ones the cheapest, particularly the grasswork. Reject goods are on sale in the outlying huts for even better prices. **Taxis** and **buses** stop outside the market on their way to Bizana and **Port Edward** in KwaZulu-Natal.

The hotel also marks the start of the **Amadiba Horse Trail** (see p. 420) down the coast to Mkambati Nature Reserve. A **daily shuttle** run by Utours (℡031 561 5896) **from Durban beachfront** to the *Wild Coast Sun*, makes it easy to reach this area from Durban without a car – a two-hour journey.

Towards KwaZulu-Natal

The quickest and busiest way from the Eastern Cape to KwaZulu-Natal is on the **N2**, passing by the scraggy towns of Mount Frere and Mount Ayliff, before reaching Kokstad and the provincial boundary. From the road you'll see hillsides dotted with densely packed dwellings. Closer inspection reveals that the hillsides are not coping well with the strain, as there are massive *dongas* (eroded gullies) creating scar-like craters in many places where huge volumes of topsoil have simply been washed away. **Mount Frere** is about 100km from Umtata, and is called kwaBhaca in Xhosa, meaning "the place of the Bhaca" – for many of those fleeing south from the Zulu king Shaka settled here, earning themselves name *amaBhaca*, "the people who hide". Today, Mount Frere is a fairly rough town and you'd be wise to pass swiftly through.

The Eastern Cape enclave

The **Eastern Cape enclave in KwaZulu-Natal** for many years sat uncomfortably with the crass ethnic categorizations of past regimes, and the legacy of this lives on today. The people living in the enclave, whose main town is uMzimkhulu, are a mixture of Zulu, Pondo, Bhaca and Griqua, economically tied in the main to Pietermaritzburg and Durban. The apartheid regime yoked them with the Transkei, ostensibly on the grounds that most were Pondo, and thus part of the Xhosa nation, but in fact to tap them as a cheap labour reserve.

Controversially, the area was included in the Eastern Cape when the boundaries were redrawn after the 1994 elections, in part because many in the area support the ANC and did not want to be part of a province ruled by the Zulu nationalist Inkhata Freedom Party.

The enclave is reached by turning off the N2 onto the R56 at the Stafford's Post junction towards **Ixopo**. It's scenic and pleasant enough to pass through, though not a good place to travel around – there's nowhere to stay or any infrastructure for tourists, and it's desperately poor. **uMzimkhulu** is a busy transport centre, with a large taxi rank by its Shell garage and plenty of fast-food outlets to feed hungry passengers, most of whom are going to and from **Pietermaritzburg** and **Durban**. After passing the remnants of a small border post just east of the town, you will find yourself back in KwaZulu-Natal, a short distance from Ixopo.

Travel details

All major **transport** in the Eastern Cape runs between Port Elizabeth and East London – the two hubs of the province – or from these centres to other major cities: Johannesburg, Cape Town and Durban. In addition to train, intercity bus and air services, there are backpacker buses and scheduled minibuses making additional connections to one or two smaller centres. Failing these, the option remains of cheap and frequent (though unscheduled and less comfortable or safe) minibus taxis.

Trains

Two mainline **trains**, the Amatola from East London, and the Algoa from Port Elizabeth, connect the Eastern Cape with Johannesburg and Pretoria, both stopping along the way.

East London to: Bloemfontein (daily; 13hr); Johannesburg (daily; 20hr); Pretoria (daily; 21hr 30min); Queenstown (daily; 4hr 30min).

Port Elizabeth to: Bloemfontein (daily; 11hr 30min); Cradock (daily; 4hr 30min); Johannesburg (daily; 18hr); Pretoria (daily; 19hr 30min).

Intercity buses

The main **bus routes** run from Port Elizabeth (up the N10) and East London (up the N6) to join the N1 via Bloemfontein to Johannesburg and Pretoria; and along the coast to Cape Town in the west and Durban in the east. An alternative route goes inland through the Little Karoo to Cape Town.

East London to: Alexandria (5 weekly; 3hr 15min); Aliwal North (daily; 5hr); Bloemfontein (daily; 7hr 30min); Cape Town (1–2 daily; 14hr); Durban (2 daily; 9hr); Grahamstown (2 daily; 2hr); Johannesburg (daily; 13hr); Kenton-on-Sea (5 weekly; 3hr); King William's Town (2–3 daily; 45min); Knysna (1–2 daily; 7hr 30min); Mossel Bay (1–2 daily; 9hr); Paarl (5 weekly; 14hr 30min); Plettenberg Bay (1–2 daily; 7hr); Port Alfred (3 daily; 2hr 30min); Port Elizabeth (3 daily; 4hr); Port Shepstone (2 daily; 8hr); Pretoria (daily; 14hr); Sedgefield (1–2 daily; 8hr); Storms River (1–2 daily; 6hr); Swellendam (1–2 daily; 11hr) Umtata (2 daily; 3hr 30min); Wilderness (1–2 daily; 8hr 30min).

Port Elizabeth to: Alexandria (5 weekly; 1hr); Bloemfontein (1–2 daily; 10hr); Cape Town (6–7 daily; 11hr); Durban (2 daily; 13hr 30min); East

London (3 daily; 4hr); George (6–7 daily; 4hr 30min); Graaff-Reinet (5 weekly; 3hr 30min); Grahamstown (2 daily; 1hr 30min); Jeffrey's Bay (2 daily; 45min); Johannesburg (3–4 daily; 16hr); Kenton-on-Sea (5 weekly; 1hr 30min); Knysna (6–7 daily; 3hr 30min); Mossel Bay (6–7 daily; 4hr 30min); Paarl (4 weekly; 10hr); Plettenberg Bay (6–7 daily; 3hr); Port Alfred (5 weekly; 1hr 45min); Port Shepstone (2 daily; 12hr); Pretoria (1–2 daily; 17hr); Sedgefield (6–7 daily; 3hr 30min); Stellenbosch (6 weekly; 10hr); Storms River (6–7 daily; 2hr); Umtata (2 daily; 7hr 30min); Wilderness (4 daily; 3hr 30min).

Umtata to: Cape Town (1–3 daily; 17hr 30min); Durban (3 daily; 5hr 50min); East London (1–2 daily; 3hr); Johannesburg (2 daily; 12hr 45min); Port Elizabeth (daily; 5hr 40min); Pretoria (daily; 13hr 45min).

Backpacker bus

The **Baz Bus** plies the coastal route daily between Port Elizabeth and Cape Town. It also goes all the way through to Durban four times a week.

Port Elizabeth to: Durban (5 weekly; 15hr 30min); East London (1–2 daily; 2hr 30min); George (daily; 7hr 45min); Jeffrey's Bay (daily; 1hr 45min); Knysna (daily; 6hr 30min); Mossel Bay (daily; 10hr 15min); Nature's Valley (daily; 4hr 30min); Oudtshoorn (daily; 9hr); Plettenberg Bay (daily; 5hr 30min); Port Alfred (4 weekly; 2hr 15min); Port Shepstone (4 weekly; 14hr); Umtata (4 weekly; 8hr 30min); Wilderness (daily; 7hr 15min).

Flights

East London to: Cape Town (2–3 daily; 2hr); Durban (2–3 daily; 1hr); Johannesburg (5–6 daily; 1hr 20min); Port Elizabeth (2–4 daily; 45min). **Port Elizabeth** to: Bloemfontein (1 daily Mon–Fri & Sun; 1hr 20min); Cape Town (3–4 daily; 1hr 15min); Durban (4 daily; 1hr 10min); East London (1–4 daily; 45min); George (1 weekly; 1hr); Johannesburg (6 daily; 1hr 30min). **Umtata** to Johannesburg (2 daily; 1hr 30min).

KwaZulu-Natal

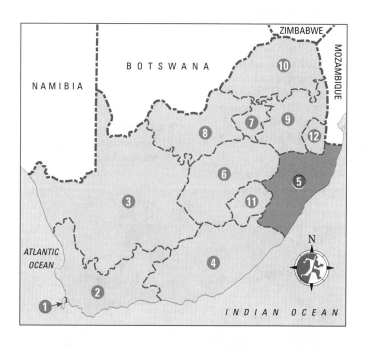

CHAPTER 5   # Highlights

✳ **Indian culture** The Hindu temples and tangy food of KwaZulu-Natal's second-largest ethnic group add spice to a very African province. See p.468

✳ **Kayak the Umkomaas** Learn the art of paddling with nine-times world champion Oscar Chalupsky. See p.475

✳ **Drakensberg range** Towering peaks and ancient San (Bushman) rock paintings in one of KwaZulu-Natal's two World Heritage Sites. See p.499

✳ **Walking safaris** Some of the country's finest wilderness trails are

found in the Umfolozi Game Reserve. See p.516

✳ **Rhinos** Hluhluwe-Umfolozi and Mkhuze game reserves are the best places in the world to see this endangered species. See p.519 & p.528

✳ **Zulu baskets** The Vukani Collection in Eshowe includes some of South Africa's most beautiful woven artefacts. See p.542

✳ **Battlefield tours** Experience the drama of the Anglo-Zulu wars with inspirational storyteller and guide David Rattray. See p.545

KwaZulu-Natal

KwaZulu-Natal, South Africa's most African province, has everything the continent is known for – beaches, wildlife, mountains and accessible ethnic culture. South Africans are well-acquainted with KwaZulu-Natal's attractions; it's the leading province for domestic tourism, although foreign visitors haven't quite cottoned onto the incredible amount packed into this compact and beautiful region.

Among white South Africans, KwaZulu-Natal is well-known for its subtropical **coastline**, which offers a temperate climate even in the winter, when the Cape can be showered by an icy downpour. This is where you'll find Africa's most developed beaches, in a 250-kilometre ribbon of holiday homes stretching along the shore from the Eastern Cape border in the south to the Tugela River in the north.

At the ribbon's centre lies **Durban**, the industrial hub of the province and the country's principal harbour. Apart from Cape Town, Durban is the only major city in South Africa that warrants a visit in its own right. British in origin, its heady mixture of cultural flavours derives from its Zulu, Indian and white communities. You'll find palm trees fanning Victorian buildings, African squatters living precariously on truncated flyovers, high-rise offices towering over temples and curry houses, overdeveloped beachfronts, and everywhere an irrepressible fecundity.

Paradoxically, while the coasts immediately on either side of Durban – known as the **North and South coasts** – are South Africa's busiest and least enticing, north of the Tugela River are some of the most remote and pristine shores in the country. Here, **Maputaland**, a patchwork of wetlands, freshwater lakes, wilderness and Zulu villages, meets the sea at a virtually seamless stretch of sand that begins at the St Lucia Estuary and slips across the Mozambique border at **Kosi Bay**. Apart from southern **Lake St Lucia**, which is fairly developed in a low-key fashion, Maputaland is one of the most isolated regions in the country, traversed only by dirt roads. The reward at the end of one such track is **Rocktail Bay**, a dreamscape of tropical vegetation, tepid water and soft sands stretching as far as you can see in either direction. South Africa's best snorkelling and scuba diving is found just south of here, along the coral reefs off **Sodwana Bay**.

KwaZulu-Natal's marine life is matched on land by its **game reserves**, some of which are beaten only by the Kruger National Park, and easily surpass the latter as the best place in the continent to see both black and white rhinos. Concentrated in the north, just west of Maputaland, the reserves tend to be compact and beautiful places with some of the most stylish game-lodge accommodation in the country. Most famous and largest of the reserves is the

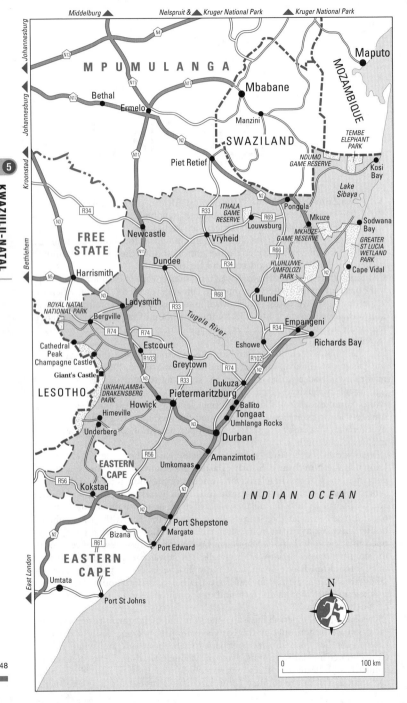

Hluhluwe–Umfolozi Park, trampled by a respectable cross-section of wildlife that includes all of the Big Five. The low-key **Mkuzi** and **Ndumo** game reserves are two of South Africa's best destinations for bird-watching, while near the northern provincial border, most surprising of all is the little-known **Itala Game Reserve**, a mountainous delight that year after year wins awards for its top-class accommodation.

The interior, north of the Tugela River, marks the **KwaZulu-Natal Battlefields**. This heartland of the nineteenth-century Zulu kingdom saw gruesome battles between Boers and Zulus, British and Zulus, and finally Boers and British. Today, the area can be explored through Battlefield tours, a memorable way of taking in some of South Africa's most turbulent history.

Since the nineteenth century, when missionaries were homing in on KwaZulu-Natal, the **Zulus** have captured the popular imagination of the West and remain one of the province's major pulls for tourists, despite the fact that you're more likely to encounter a Zulu dressed in jeans in Jo'burg than someone in traditional garb in KwaZulu-Natal. You'll find constant reminders of the old Zulu kingdom and its founder Shaka, including an excellent reconstruction of the beehive-hutted capital at **Ondini** and the more touristy **Shakaland**, near Eshowe.

The area south of the Tugela, designated "white man's country" in the mid-nineteenth century and consolidated a century later under apartheid, represents the most English area of South Africa. It's the least compelling section of the province, though it is known for some fabulous accommodation in country houses. The **Midlands**' rolling green sugar estates, polo clubs and rather contrived arts and crafts routes pale by comparison with the drama of the rest of the province, but it is extremely pretty.

From the Midlands, South Africa's highest peaks sweep west into the soaring **Drakensberg** range, known to the Zulus as the "Barrier of Spears" and protected by a chain of KwaZulu-Natal Wildlife reserves. The area's restcamps are ideal bases for walking in the mountains or heading out for ambitious hikes in the High Berg; with relatively little effort, you can experience crystal rivers tumbling into marbled rock pools, peaks and rock faces enriched by ancient San paintings. The most elemental area of all KwaZulu-Natal, the Berg sees dramatic thunderstorms in summer, with lightning flashing across huge charcoal skies.

KwaZulu-Natal experiences considerable variations in **climate**, from the occasional heavy winter snowstorms of the Drakensberg to the mellow, sunny days and pleasant sea temperatures a couple of hundred kilometres away along the coast. This makes the region a popular winter getaway, but in midsummer (January, February & December) the low-lying areas, including Durban, the coastal belt and the game reserves, can experience an uncomfortably high humidity.

5

KWAZULU-NATAL

KwaZulu-Natal Wildlife

KwaZulu-Natal, particularly Maputaland, incorporates a wealth of game parks, designated wetlands and wilderness areas. All the public resorts described in this chapter fall under the auspices of **KwaZulu-Natal Wildlife** (also known as KZN Wildlife or KwaZulu-Natal Conservation Services) and, unless otherwise stated, **hutted accommodation** at these should be booked in advance through KwaZulu-Natal Wildlife, PO Box 13069, Cascades, Pietermaritzburg 3202 (℡033 845 1000, ⓦwww.kznwildlife.com), or in person at Tourist Junction, Old Station Building, 160 Pine St, Durban (℡031 304 4934). **Camping** reservations and **late bookings** for hutted accommodation must be made through the relevant camp.

The province is also the country's most turbulent region, wracked by political violence that has divided its Zulu majority in a low-key but deadly war of attrition and vendetta – one you're unlikely to encounter, as it takes place in remote rural villages.

Durban

Until the 1970s, **DURBAN** was regarded as white South Africa's quintessential seaside playground – a status fostered by its tropical colours, oversized vegetation and an itinerant population of surfers, hedonists and holidaying Jo'burg families. Then, in the 1980s, the collapse of apartheid population-influx controls saw a growing stream of Africans flood in from rural KwaZulu-Natal – and even from as far afield as Zaire – to stake their claims in the city centre, with shantytowns and cardboard hovels revealing the reality of one of the most unmistakably African conurbations in the country.

South Africa's third-largest city is a thriving industrial centre and the largest port in Africa; its **harbour** remains a photogenic place for meandering or eating and drinking at the dockside. Another unmistakable feature of Durban is a legacy of the city's **Indian population** (its second-largest group): mosques, bazaars and temples, festooned with wildly coloured deities, stand juxtaposed with the Victorian buildings marking out the colonial centre.

The city's main interest lies not in its seaside, but its gritty urbanity, a seemingly endless struggle to reconcile competing Indian, African and English cultures and to keep the rampant vegetation at bay. There's enough here to keep you busy for a few days, looking at mosques, exploring the Indian area around Grey Street, or passing by the Dalton Road Zulu Market. However, most people come to Durban because it provides a logical springboard for the KwaZulu-Natal game parks, the Drakensberg and the Battlefields. Durban is well-connected to the rest of South Africa by air and through intercity buses and trains, and some international flights call here.

Some history

Less than two hundred years ago, Durban was known to Europeans as **Port Natal**, a lagoon thick with mangroves, eyed by white adventurers who saw business opportunities in its ivory and hides. In 1824, a British party led by **Francis Farewell** persuaded the Zulu king, **Shaka**, to give them some land. Not long after, the British went on to rename the settlement **Durban** after Sir Benjamin D'Urban, governor of the Cape Colony, whose support, they believed, might not come amiss later.

Britain's tenuous colonial toehold looked threatened in 1839, when **Boers** trundled over the Drakensberg in their ox waggons and declared their Republic of Natalia nearby. The threat was compounded the following year, when a large force of now-hostile Zulus descended on the settlement and razed it, forcing the British residents to take refuge at sea in the brig *Comet*. Capitalizing on the British absence, a group of Boers annexed Durban, later laying siege to a British detachment. This provided the cue for a much-cele-

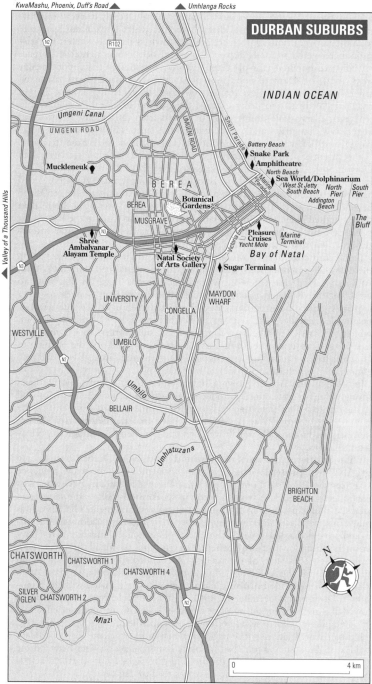

KwaMashu, Phoenix, Duff's Road ▲   ▲ Umhlanga Rocks

DURBAN SUBURBS

N2

R102

INDIAN OCEAN

Umgeni Canal

UMGENI ROAD

UMGENI ROAD

Snell Parade

Battery Beach
Snake Park
Amphitheatre

Muckleneuk

B E R E A

North Beach
Sea World/Dolphinarium
West St Jetty North South
Marine South Beach Pier Pier
Parade
Addington
Beach

BEREA

Botanical
Gardens

BEREA

The
Bluff

MUSGRAVE

Valley of a Thousand Hills

N3

Shree
Ambalvanar
Alayam Temple

Natal Society
of Arts Gallery

Pleasure
Cruises
Yacht Mole

Victoria Embankment

Marine
Terminal

Bay of Natal

N3

Sugar Terminal

UNIVERSITY

MAYDON
WHARF

CONGELLA

WESTVILLE

N2

UMBILO

Umbilo

BELLAIR

Umhlatuzana

BRIGHTON
BEACH

N

CHATSWORTH CHATSWORTH 1

CHATSWORTH 4

SILVER
GLEN CHATSWORTH 2

N2

Mlazi

0   4 km

▼ Durban International Airport & Port Edward

brated piece of Victorian melodrama, familiar until recently to every English-speaking school child in South Africa – when teenager **Dick King** heroically rode the 1000km from Durban to Grahamstown in ten days to alert the garrison there, which promptly dispatched a rescue detachment to relieve Durban.

While two-hundred-year-old Cape Town was becoming a cosmopolitan centre by the 1840s, Durban's population of barely one thousand lived a basic existence in a near wilderness roamed by lions, leopards and hyenas. Things changed after Britain formally annexed the **Colony of Natal** in 1843; within ten years, a large-scale immigration of settlers from the mother country had begun. Over the next couple of decades all the niceties of English life – horse racing, postal deliveries, two-storey houses and newspapers – started to appear.

The promise of the industrial age, heralded in 1852 with the arrival in Durban of the first steamship, the *Sir Robert Peel*, actually pointed to the settlement's Achilles heel: the sand bar across the harbour mouth which prevented large vessels from entering. Work to clear it continued through the 1850s and beyond, while in 1860 the first railway tracks in town were laid. More than three hundred indentured **Indian labourers** arrived to work in the KwaZulu-Natal cane fields, planting the seeds for South Africa's lucrative **sugar industry** and the city's now substantial Indian community.

The British **conquest of the Zulus** in 1879, and the imposition of taxes on the defeated warrior nation, paved the way for their enforced entry into South Africa's growing cash economy. Many Zulus headed north in the 1890s to work on the Gauteng goldfields, while others were drawn south to enter Durban's expanding economy. In 1895, the completion of the railway connecting Johannesburg and Durban accelerated the process of migrant labour, which still carries hundreds of thousands of Zulu workers to Johannesburg every year. This link to South Africa's industrial heartland, and the opening of Durban's harbour mouth to large ships in 1904, ensured the city's eventual preeminence as South Africa's principal harbour.

In 1922, in the face of growing Indian and African populations, Durban's strongly English city council introduced **legislation** to restrict the sale of land in the city to whites, predating Afrikaner-led apartheid by 26 years. During the boom years of World War II, Africans flooded into the city in even greater numbers, leading to calls, which were ignored, for their recognition as permanent residents.

With the strict enforcement of **apartheid** in the 1950s, Durban saw a decade of ANC-led **protests**. These started with the country-wide Defiance Campaign in 1952 (see Contexts, p.834), and reached a peak in 1959 when *shebeen* queens (the African women who ran speakeasies) took to the streets and attacked municipal beer halls in protest at police harassment. The ANC was quick to seize this localized momentum, steering it towards nationwide marches and protests that led to nearly three years of turmoil, culminating in the government clampdown of 1961, when the authorities swamped the streets with troops, declared a state of emergency, and banned the ANC. Left with no peaceful option, the ANC formed its armed wing, Umkhonto we Sizwe, with plans for a nationwide **bombing campaign** that was initiated with an explosion in Durban on December 15, 1961. In the comprehensive swoop that followed, the government put most of the ANC's activists behind bars, effectively paving the way for a decade of unopposed apartheid.

Durban scored another first in 1973, when workers in the city initiated a wildcat strike, despite a total ban on black industrial action. This heralded the rebirth of South Africa's **trade unions** and reawakened anti-apartheid activity, sparking the final phase of the country's road to democracy.

By the 1980s, Durban had become the busiest port in Africa. Today, it's reputedly the fastest-expanding city in the southern hemisphere, with thousands of people forced to live in rude shacks in any open space or live rough in the city centre.

Arrival

As a major industrial city and gateway to the country's densest ribbon of holiday beaches, along the North and South coasts, Durban is served by international and domestic flights, intercity buses, backpacker buses, trains, and the ubiquitous informal minibus taxis.

By air

Durban International airport (☎031 451 6667), 14km south of the centre on the Southern Freeway, handles flights from Singapore and Mauritius, as well as neighbouring countries and all the main centres inside South Africa. The domestic and international terminals are in the same building. Bus services leave every hour (7am–9pm; ☎031 465 1660; R25) from outside the domestic terminal and go to the SAA building on Aliwal Street, corner of Smith Street, in the city centre (a 20min journey). The bus will also take you on request to any of the central or beachfront hotels, and it's a better option than the rather rickety taxis waiting outside the terminal exits. A bank and ATM at the international terminal opens from 7am to 8pm.

By train

The Trans-Natal service from Johannesburg (a 13hr journey), and the interminable Trans-Oranje from Cape Town via the Free State (36hr), both arrive at the grim **New Durban station** (☎031 361 7609), off NMR Avenue, just

---

Useful bus routes from the city centre

To North/South Beach (daily to South Beach: every 10min 6am–11pm; daily to North Beach: every 10min 6.10am–10.15pm). Mynah buses leave from St Andrews Street, on the north side of Albert Park, which stretches down to the Victoria Embankment at the western edge of the city centre (an inner-city strip of high-rise apartments best avoided at night, especially if you're carrying luggage or cameras). From here they turn north into Russell Street, before running all the way east along West Street to Marine Parade, where they either strike north as far as Battery Beach, or south as far as Addington Beach. Boards on the front of the bus indicate whether they're bound for North or South Beach. On their return trip, buses head through the centre along Smith instead of West Street.

To the Berea – "Musgrave–Mitchell Park Circle" (Mon–Fri every 10min, Sat slightly less frequent, Sun hourly 6.30am–7pm). Mynah buses leave from the Pine Street bus depot, heading west down Smith Street to the Berea, taking in Florida Road (a restaurant strip) and Musgrave Road (Musgrave Centre), before returning to the city centre via Berea Road.

To Natal Society of Arts Gallery Aqualine buses (route 86/87) leave from the Pine Street bus depot and go to Glenmore, via Bulwer Road, for the NSA Gallery (Mon–Fri every 15min 6.50–8.35am, every 30min 8.35am–5pm; Sat less frequently; Sun 3 daily 7am–5.30pm).

For more information, call ☎031 309 4126.

north of the main commercial centre. The best option from here is to take one of the metered taxis that rank inside the station complex, for around R25 to the beachfront.

By bus

Two of the main country-wide **bus operators**, Greyhound (☎031 309 7830) and Translux (☎031 361 8333), end their runs at the **Motorcoach Terminal** attached to the New Durban station complex. The Margate Mini Coach (☎039 312 1406) from the South Coast pulls in here and also outside domestic departures at Durban airport.

Two **minibus shuttles**, Rollercoaster Taxi (☎031 464 5858 or 072 101 7353) and Rasool's (☎031 208 0803), each run a door-to-door service twice a day (pickup 5–6.30am & 5–6.30pm; a 6–7hr journey) in each direction between Johannesburg and Durban and will drop you anywhere in Durban. A number of other small companies operating limited routes within the province use other arrival points: the Cheetah Coach (☎033 342 2673), from Pietermaritzburg, lets passengers off at the airport and outside the Local History Museum on Aliwal Street; the Umhlanga Express (☎082 268 0651), from Umhlanga Rocks, drops off at a number of points in Durban, the most central of which is opposite Tourist Junction (see "Information" below). The Umhlanga Express will also taxi you as far north as Ballito or anywhere else, by prior arrangement. The Baz Bus (☎031 304 9099, ⊕www.bazbus.com), from Port Elizabeth, and from Johannesburg via either Swaziland and Zululand, or the Northern Drakensberg, stops at most of the Durban backpackers' lodges.

By minibus taxi

Long-distance **minibus taxis** from Gauteng arrive opposite the Umgeni Road entrance to the train station, while those from the South Coast and Transkei terminate at Berea Road in the Warwick Triangle area at the west of the city centre. Both are very busy points, rife with pickpockets, so take care of your baggage – and bear in mind that the city-centre and beachfront accommodation are a fairly brisk walk away. If you're planning on staying in the Berea, catch a Mynah bus to Smith Street and the main bus depot, from where you'll be able to get another Mynah bus connection.

Information and city transport

The obvious first port of call for information is the central **Tourist Junction** at Old Station Building, 160 Pine St (Mon–Fri 8am–5pm, Sat 9am–2pm; ☎031 304 4934, ⊕www.durbanexperience.co.za), which houses Durban Africa (the city's tourist bureau) and Tourism KwaZulu-Natal (the province's tourist bureau, third floor), the KwaZulu-Natal Wildlife (see p.449) and the South African National Parks booking offices, accommodation agents, and a couple of travel agents who can book intercity coaches and **tours**.

Durban Africa and Tourism KwaZulu-Natal can provide brochures and free maps of the city centre; however, if you're planning on staying a while, it's worth investing in one of the several street **map books** covering the city and suburbs in detail. MapStudio produces a range of maps, from mid-priced foldout plans of the city to pricier charts that include the surrounding area. The best selection is at Adams Bookshop, 341 West St (☎031 304 8571), in the centre, or at Exclusive Books, Lower Level, Pavilion Shopping Centre in the suburb of Westville (℡031 265 0454). You can also pick up maps at any branch of the CNA chain.

While **buses** cover the centre, beachfront and the Berea, it's more difficult to get **public transport** to the suburbs. If you're **driving**, you'll find Durban fairly easy to negotiate, although traffic on the freeways can be fast and aggressive.

Buses

Durban's most useful urban transport is the cheap and regular **bus** system operated by Mynah and Aqualine (℡031 309 5942), who cover the central districts, including the city centre, the beachfront and the Berea. If you want to get to the more far-flung suburbs, Durban Transport Municipal Buses (℡031 309 4126), are quite functional, although slightly the worse for wear and not as frequent. For quick and easy reference to **times and routes**, pop into the Pine Street bus depot, which is adjacent to The Workshop mall and is the starting point for local bus services.

Licensed taxis

More convenient (and more expensive) than buses, several reputable taxi companies in central Durban will take you almost anywhere. Some, like Mozzies (℡031 263 0467), have minibuses which can take up to fifteen people and work out cheaper the more of you there are in a group; they also have a novelty London taxi for special occasions.

Minibus taxis

Minibus taxis can be hailed along any busy road. Although they bear no obvious identification, you can usually recognize them by the frighteningly loud music blaring from their sound systems; they also have a high accident rate. To get to town or the beachfront from any of the suburbs, stand along the sidewalk and signal assertively with an index finger. Minibuses follow set paths (you can get off at any point by asking the driver); once in the city centre, they follow West Street to the beachfront, but turn south into Marine Parade as far as Addington Beach.

Car and bike rental

The easiest way to explore Durban is by **car**. The city's freeways are well-signposted, and careful map-reading makes getting around straightforward. You need to plan ahead, though, as Durbanites drive fast and there's no time to dither at lane changes and junctions. **Cycling** is safe along the beachfront, but hazardous on any major road. There are several car and bicycle **rental companies** in Durban; to find out who's currently operating and where to get the best deal, either pick up one of the brochures at Tourist Junction or look in the *Yellow Pages*. We've recommended some larger operators in "Listings" (see p.477).

Durban tours

One of the safest and easiest ways to get under the skin of ethnic Durban is to take a **guided tour**, which can get you into African and Indian areas or out-of-the-way places. Standard three-hour tours cost around R150 per person.

Amatikulu Tours 38 Rapson Rd ☎039 973 2534, ⓦwww.amatikulu.com. Based at Umkomaas, close to the outstanding Aliwal Shoal scuba-diving site, this top-notch tour company offers provincial tours, including ones in and around the city of Durban, diving tours, and excursions further afield to the game reserves and the Drakensberg.

Cycle Tours De Durban ☎031 564 0730. Four relaxed two-wheeled tours around the city, including a trip to the Hindu temple and museums.

Ekukhanyeni Travel & Tours ☎083 756 3695. Ekukhanyeni offers township tours and visits to less accessible parts of the city.

Strelitzia Tours Suite 21/22, Multichoice Centre, Westville Rd, Westville ☎031 266 9480, ⓕ031 266 9404. Strelitzia runs daily minibus trips around the major sights, the centre and the Berea, as well as trips further afield to the game parks, the Battlefields and up Sani Pass in the Drakensberg.

Tekweni Eco Tours 169 Ninth Ave, Greyville ☎031 303 1199, ⓦwww.tekwenieco-tours.co.za. Drive and walk into the heart of the city and through informal settlements, before joining locals for a Zulu meal and beer at the *shebeen*, or into local nature reserves and the Valley of a Thousand Hills. Tekweni also runs camping safaris into the Drakensberg, with river tubing and horse trails. Tours go on Tues, Thurs and Sat from noon till 6 or 7pm and cost around R220 per person.

Tourist Junction (see p.454). The staff here can arrange a number of excellent outings, including walking tours of the Grey Street area, city centre and historical tours.

Tours of Remembrance ☎031 337 7879 or 083 560 9999. A community-based tour company that can take you to parts many other companies can't – or don't care to – reach and include historical and cultural sites such as the Gandhi settlement, Hindu temples and the African areas. Their day tour costs R360 per person.

Accommodation

Durban's **accommodation** is concentrated along the **beachfront**, where sleek towers of chain hotels with sea views and swimming pools offer comfortable but pricey places to stay. Far more affordable are the scores of self-catering **apartments** (some with sea views, others a block or two back, and thus in less salubrious areas), which can offer exceptional value for several people sharing. Staying at the beachfront ensures you're close to the action and only a few minutes from the central business district, and the area is well-served with buses and taxis. Accommodation tends to be scarce during school holidays, and much more expensive in the peak holiday month of December.

While the **city centre** is a convenient location to stay, it's not great at night, when the deserted streets are potentially menacing; taking private taxis to your doorstep is recommended after dark. An alternative to the city centre and beachfront is the cool and leafy **Berea** residential area, ten minutes west of the centre and with excellent restaurants and cafés. Adjoining the Berea is **Morningside**, a hip and happening area wall-to-wall with restaurants, pubs and tattoo parlours You'll find the best backpackers' lodges here and in the Berea, as well as a couple of other budget guesthouses and B&Bs where you can smell the frangipani and tropical scents on balmy nights.

Beachfront

The Balmoral 125 Marine Parade ☎ 031 368 5940, ⓔ balmoral@icon.co.za

ⓦ www.raya_hotels.com. Dark timbers and historical photographs of Durban create a serious, colonial atmosphere; the verandah is magnificent for sipping drinks on balmy summer nights while watching the buzz along the Marine Parade and the ocean beyond. Large gracious rooms, with remote-control TV, air conditioning, and classy fittings, most with glorious sea views. Also internet facilities available in the more expensive rooms and suites. ❺

The Beach Hotel 107 Marine Parade ☎ 031 337 5511, ⓕ 031 368 2322. While the bland but spacious rooms provide great views, the major drawcard here is the lively verandah buzzing with punters from the hotel's pubs and restaurants. ❹

The Blue Waters Hotel 175 Snell Parade ☎ 031 332 4272, ⓕ 031 337 5817. A delightful 1950s Durban landmark opposite Battery Beach, with mangroves on the pavement and plush furnishing inside, while the leisure lounge has great views onto the oceanfront. ❹

The Edward On the corner of Marine Parade and Seaview Road ☎ 031 337 3681, ⓦ www.proteahotels.com. Crystal chandeliers, dense colonial-style ambience, sea-view balconies and a ladies' bar leading onto a cool verandah make this Art Deco mansion the *grande dame* of the beachfront. Breakfast not included. ❹–❺

Golden Sands Holiday Apartments 95 Snell Parade ☎ 031 368 2995, ⓕ 031 337 1825. Functional self-catering apartments saved entirely by the (more expensive) rooms with magnificent sea views. Conveniently opposite North Beach and the Amphitheatre, the rooms are great-value outside the December holiday season, when the rates double. ❶

Holiday Inn Garden Court – Marine Parade 167 Marine Parade ☎ 031 337 2231, ⓦ www.southernsun.com. Crisp mirage with a cool through-breeze and tropical vegetation offering respite against the summer heat. While all the rooms face the sea, those on the top floors are best, and the view from the 30th-floor swimming pool is fabulous. A back entrance across from Victoria Park also provides handy access to the city centre. ❸

Impala Holiday Flats 40 Gillespie St ☎ 031 332 3232. Large family apartments and bachelor units sleeping two to six people, one block back from South Beach, close to the Wheel Shopping Centre. ❶

Palace Protea Hotel 211 Marine Parade ☎ 031 332 8351, ⓦ www.optimabreak.com. Opposite the Durban Fun Fair, this modern Art Deco landmark on Durban's Golden Mile offers self-catering apartments and good access to the city centre. ❸

Protea Hotel Landmark Lodge – Durban On the corner of West and Point roads ☎ 031 337 3601, ⓦ www.proteahotels.com. Three-star hotel rooms and cheaper self-catering holiday apartments sleeping up to four, equidistant between the beach and town, in a tall block offering east-facing sea views and B&B. ❸–❹

Silversands 16 Erskine Terrace, South Beach ☎ 031 332 7391, ⓔ silversands@worldonline.co.za. Along the far end of Addington Beach, near the Addington Hospital, these clean, comfortable and spacious apartments sleep two to eight people (cheaper for more sharing). ❷

City centre

Albany Hotel 225 Smith St ☎ 031 304 4381, ⓦ www.albanyhotel.co.za. A stone's throw from the harbour, this centrally situated budget hotel, with comfortable if slightly old-fashioned rooms, is right next to the Playhouse Theatre Complex, across the road from the Natural Science Museum and Durban Art Gallery. ❷

Banana Backpackers 61 Pine St, 1st floor, Ambassador House ☎ 031 368 4062, ⓔ aroutes@iafrica.com. Recently renovated dorms and doubles in an old Durban building with a congenial courtyard, in the heart of the city, very close to the beach, Tourist Junction and the bus terminal. ❶

Hotel Formula 1 On the corner of NMR Avenue and Jeff Taylor Street ☎ 031 301 1551, ⓦ www.hotelformula1.co.za. No frills at this clean, budget hotel right next to the train station; a flat room-rate makes it only slightly pricier than a backpackers' hostel, if there are two or three of you. ❶

The Royal Hotel 267 Smith St ☎ 031 333 6000, ⓦ www.theroyal.co.za. Durban's finest hotel, and a local institution in the city centre. Used mainly by business visitors, it's worth considering if you can afford five-star splendour and fancy the liveried service and its legendary *Ulundi* Indian restaurant. Special discounts are often available. ❻

The Berea and Morningside

The Benjamin 141 Florida Rd, Morningside ☎ 031 303 4233, ⓕ 031 303 4288, ⓦ www.benjamin.co.za. A swish boutique hotel aimed at business travellers, in the heart of a vibrant area and with 45 luxurious rooms. ❺

Big J's Backpackers 47 Essenwood Rd, Berea

☎ 031 202 3023, ✉ bjbackpack@hotmail.com. This funky spot in a prime area offers camping, dorms and doubles, with the fourth night free to Baz Bus passengers. There's also a swimming pool, bar, sundeck, herb garden, skateboards and bodyboards for use by guests. *Big J's* pride themselves on being the first accommodation in Durban to stock Rizlas. ❶

Brown Sugar Kinnord House, 6 Kinnord Place, 607 Essenwood Rd ☎ 031 209 8528, ✉ brownsugar2000@hotmail.com. Set in a beautiful old mansion high on the ridge built more than a century ago, the lodge has glorious grounds, free breakfasts and ultra-cheap evening meals. However, it verges on spartan inside; the cavernous dorm has mattresses (no beds). ❶

The Elephant House 745 Ridge Rd, Berea ☎ 031 208 9580, ✉ elephanthouse@mweb.co.za. A B&B in Durban's oldest house, built in 1850 as a hunting lodge, in the tranquil part of the ridge where the vegetation has won the day. The very hospitable owners have a good collection of African literature and love showing travellers around. ❸

Hippo Hide Lodge and Backpackers 2 Jesmond Rd, Berea ☎ 031 207 4366, ⓦ www.hippohide.co.za. A stunning, imaginative and cosy lodge in a beautiful indigenous garden with a rock pool and great hosts. It's clean and quiet, with a guesthouse feel, and conveniently located on the bus route to the centre (10min). Some of the doubles are en suite, and there are also log cabins. ❶

Hotel California 170 Florida Rd, Morningside ☎ 031 303 1146. Genteel architecture and several restaurants above *Butcher Boys Restaurant* and *Bonkers* club, in the heart of the Florida Road nightlife strip. ❸

Laletsa Lodge 21/25 South Ridge Rd, Berea ☎ 031 201 0785, ⓦ www.laletsa.co.za. A beautifully restored upmarket old home with good views and African-flavoured decor, within walking distance of upmarket Musgrave shopping mall, and a 10min bus ride to town. There's also a saltwater

pool, barbecue facilities, halal buffet breakfasts and air-conditioned luxury rooms with TVs and phones. ❸

Meg's B&B 12 Nutall Gardens, Morningside ☎ 031 312 9045 ✉ maasdyk@mweb.co.za. *Meg's* offers dignified opulence in a quiet part of Durban, with rich colours, generous bedding and original South African artwork. ❹

Napier House 31 Napier Rd ☎ 031 207 6779. A stone's throw from the scenic Botanic Gardens, you'll find charming clean rooms with the ambience of a country estate and an expansive view over the city; their curries are excellent. ❸

Nomad's Backpackers 70 Essenwood Rd, Berea ☎ 031 202 9709 or 082 920 5882, ⓦ www.zing.co.za/nomads. One of Durban's best hostels (two houses next door to each other), *Nomad's* is a short walk from the upmarket Musgrave shopping centre, on a main bus route (a 10min ride from the beach and Golden Mile). A black-bottomed swimming pool, a pool table, the *Bambooza Pub*, and friendly hosts who cook up a mean Durban curry, all add to the attractions of this highly recommended establishment. ❶

Tekweni Backpackers 169 9th Ave, Morningside ☎ 031 303 1433, ⓦ www.tekweniecotours.co.za. A favourite and buzzing Durban backpacker spot in three neighbouring houses, well situated just off Florida Road. The atmosphere is chilled-out, and the bar serves drinks on a shady, cool verandah. Guests have the use of the kitchen, pool room, swimming pool and leisure lounge; there's also an excellent travel/information centre on the premises. ❶

Traveller's International Lodge (central) 743 Currie Rd (off Florida Road), Morningside ☎ & ⓕ 031 303 1064. A friendly double-storey building in a leafy suburb, one house away from Florida Road's clubs, nightlife and eating places. It's a seven-minute bus ride to the city and a thirty-minute walk to the beach. No pool, but there's a comfy leisure lounge and your hosts can arrange pick-ups and tours. ❶

The City

Durban's **city centre**, confined by the Bay of Natal to its south and the beaches of the Indian Ocean to its east, grew around the arrival point of the first white settlers. The remains of the historical heart, some monumental Victorian and Edwardian buildings, including the City Hall, are concentrated around **Francis Farewell Square**, five minutes' walk north of the bay. The central business area, studded with high-rise buildings, is full of traffic and one-way street systems; without any views of the ocean, it gives no hint you're in a sea-side city.

On the western side of the city centre, around Grey and Victoria streets, lies Durban's most fascinating area, the **Indian district**. This is where you'll find a pulsing warren of bazaars, alleyways, the Juma mosque and Victoria Street market, as well as Zulu traders selling *umuthi* (traditional herbal medicines). Although the laws enforcing the divide between the white-dominated business centre and the Indian district have now gone, each area still has a distinct feel. Further west and deeper downtown, situated in the hub of taxi ranks and bus depots, the **Warwick Triangle** seethes with ceaseless activity; the *shebeens* do a brisk trade while the poorest of the poor spend the nights on their market stalls under plastic and cardboard.

Durban's **beachfront**, or Golden Mile, on the eastern edge of the centre, is the magnet that pulls thousands upon thousands of white Jo'burgers down to "Durbs" every year. Although the beachfront's growing reputation for crime has sent many middle-class families scurrying out to safer beaches up the North and South coasts, you'll still find one of the city's greatest and busiest concentrations of restaurants and a surfeit of tacky family entertainment here.

South of the centre, skirting the north of the bay, lies **Victoria Embankment**, historically one of Durban's most desirable residential areas but now witnessing a decline as former residents attempt to escape its city-rim apartment blocks. The Embankment provides access to the northern side of the **harbour**; despite its handful of trendy pubs and restaurants, this compelling industrial marinescape is still the real economic hub of the city. Protruding south from the southern corner of the city centre and the beachfront to enclose the northern half of the harbour, the **Point**, a seedy red-light peninsula, is slowly transforming itself. The bottom end has now been restored, and a couple of decent pubs and clubs have moved in as well as some excellent restaurants – and it has the best view of the city across the water.

Rising above the flat city centre and harbour is the **Berea**, a desirable residential district on a cooler ridge which, despite its proximity to the centre, has luxuriant gardens alive with the sounds of birds, and fashionable restaurants, cinemas and shopping malls. Further afield lie the **western suburbs**, including Pinetown, Westville, Kloof, Gillitts and Hillcrest, while further still are the apartheid **ghettos** of KwaMashu, Inanda and Clermont to the northwest, and Umlazi to the southwest – dormitory towns for blacks who commute vast distances to work every day. **Cato Manor**, the closest township to the city, provides an easily accessible vignette of South Africa's growing urban contradictions.

The centre

Francis Farewell Square, a sultry palm-fringed garden overlooked by some fine old buildings, stands at the heart of colonial Durban. Hemmed in by the centre's two main thoroughfares, West Street to its north and Smith Street to its south, it was here that the British adventurers Francis Farewell and Henry Fynn set up Durban's first white encampment to trade ivory with the Zulus. Today, down-and-outs enjoy its lawns, dotted with statues of city fathers, while the yellows and blues of the **Cenotaph**, a marvellous Art Deco monument to the fallen of World War I, creates an eye-catching focus for the square. The granite obelisk is decorated with ceramics depicting angels delivering the soul of a dead soldier. Regarded initially by Durban's prim citizens as improperly

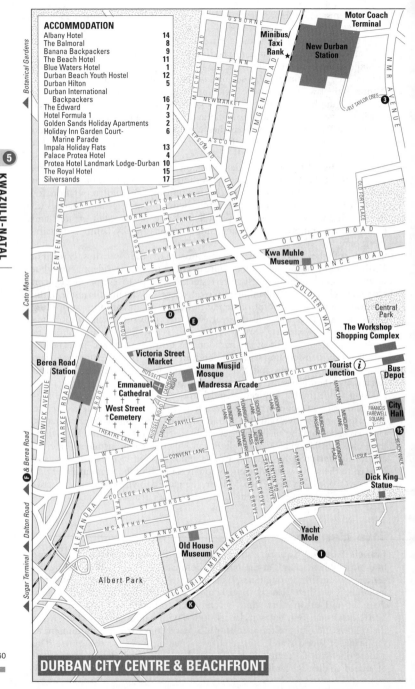

ACCOMMODATION

Albany Hotel	14
The Balmoral	8
Banana Backpackers	9
The Beach Hotel	11
Blue Waters Hotel	1
Durban Beach Youth Hostel	12
Durban Hilton	5
Durban International Backpackers	16
The Edward	7
Hotel Formula 1	3
Golden Sands Holiday Apartments	2
Holiday Inn Garden Court-Marine Parade	6
Impala Holiday Flats	13
Palace Protea Hotel	4
Protea Hotel Landmark Lodge-Durban	10
The Royal Hotel	15
Silversands	17

DURBAN CITY CENTRE & BEACHFRONT

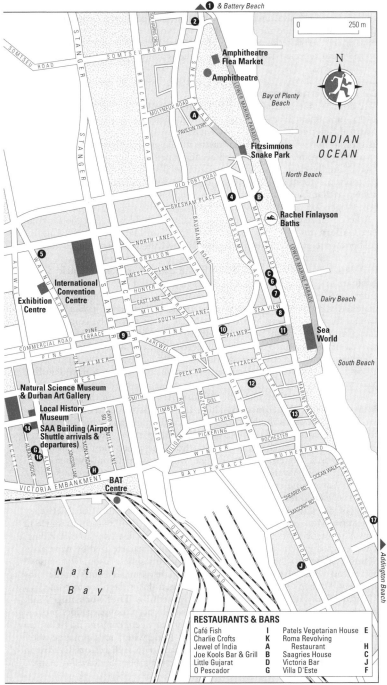

& Battery Beach

Amphitheatre
Flea Market

Amphitheatre

Bay of Plenty
Beach

INDIAN
OCEAN

Fitzsimmons
Snake Park

North Beach

Rachel Finlayson
Baths

International
Convention
Centre

Exhibition
Centre

Dairy Beach

Sea
World

South Beach

Natural Science Museum
& Durban Art Gallery

Local History
Museum

SAA Building (Airport
Shuttle arrivals &
departures)

BAT
Centre

Addington Beach

Natal
Bay

RESTAURANTS & BARS

Café Fish	**I**	Patels Vegetarian House	**E**
Charlie Crofts	**K**	Roma Revolving	
Jewel of India	**A**	Restaurant	**H**
Joe Kools Bar & Grill	**B**	Saagries House	**C J**
Little Gujarat	**D**	Victoria Bar	**J**
O Pescador	**G**	Villa D'Este	**F**

The Point

vibrant, it clearly also offended an anti-apartheid activist, who bombed it in 1984 – but today the monument is intact. North of Farewell Square at 160 Pine St are the pathetic remnants of the **Natal Great Railway Station**, built in 1894 and recycled a century later as shops and the Tourist Junction information centre.

City Hall and around

East of the cenotaph, the imposing neo-Baroque **City Hall**, erected in 1910, is the monumental centrepiece of the city-centre area. It now houses the **Natural Science Museum** (Mon–Sat 8.30am–4pm, Sun 11am–4pm; free) on its ground floor. Along with an array of stuffed animals (useful if you want to brush up on your mammals before heading north to the game reserves), is the "KwaNunu" section, featuring oversized insects such as cockroaches – all a little too close to home for anyone living in Durban, where such creatures, known as "Durban prawns", are an ongoing menace and a constant topic for urban legends.

A far better reason to cross the City Hall's threshold is to visit the **Durban Art Gallery** upstairs (Mon–Sat 8.30am–4pm, Sun 11am–4pm; free). This fine collection includes Art Nouveau glassware by Lalique, bronzes by Rodin and Victorian paintings, but is most notable for its pioneering vision back in the 1970s in becoming the first gallery in the country to collect **black South African art**. This approach has since been expanded into the recognition of indigenous craft as an art form of equal status with painting or sculpture, which is why the gallery has an outstanding collection of *hlabisa* baskets, a refined form indigenous to KwaZulu-Natal. In no way to be confused with cheap souvenirs bought at roadside stalls, the traditional craft of *hlabisa* was revived in the province around two decades ago, and is now highly sought-after by galleries and collectors worldwide. Although usually a woman's activity, one of the most highly regarded proponents of *hlabisa* is a man, **Reuben Ndwandwe**.

Northwest of the City Hall, the **African Art Centre** on the first floor of Tourist Junction, Old Station Building, 160 Pine St (Mon–Fri 8.30am–5pm, Sat 9am–1pm; free), is the heart of Durban's artistic life, and where many rural artists sell their work. Primarily a gallery and shop, the centre is also involved in work to move rural craftsmen away from the production of curios and towards artistic expression. Tito Zungu, who draws pen-and-ink aeroplanes and boats; Bheki Myeni, who sculpts wooden insects; and Mzwakhe Mbatha, originally an airline cook, who now carves wooden aircraft, are a few artists who have gained recognition through this centre.

East of the City Hall, on the corner of Smith Street, the **Local History Museum** (Mon–Sat 8.30am–4pm, Sun 11am–4pm; free), with its entrance in Aliwal Street, occupies the Old Courthouse. Durban's first two-storey building, it was erected in 1866 in the Natal Verandah style, characterized by wide eaves to throw off heavy subtropical downpours. The atmosphere is somewhat austere but, if you want to see a reconstruction of Henry Francis Fynn's wattle-and-daub hut, Durban's first European structure, then this is the place to come.

North of Aliwal Street's Local History Museum is **The Workshop Mall**, which sounds more interesting than it proves to be, although it does provide parking and every type of shop you're likely to need, conveniently close to Tourist Junction. On its north side, **Central Park**, with a lovely mosaic water fountain as its focus, offers a large green space. The **Exhibition Centre** in nearby Walnut Road, to the east, is the venue for a busy Sunday flea market, where you can pick up trinkets, authentic didgeridoos and (a hot tip if you need footwear) handmade leather shoes and hiking boots from the Ground Cover workshop in the KwaZulu-Natal Midlands. The market's popularity is paradoxically its drawback, and you'll need to shop quickly to avoid getting smeared by *boerewors* rolls or getting crushed.

Kwa Muhle Museum

North of the Exhibition Centre, at 130 Ordnance Rd, is Durban's newest and most fascinating museum, the **Kwa Muhle** (daily 8am–4pm; free), also known as the "Apartheid Museum." It's one of the few museums in the country devoted to South Africa's twentieth-century urban social history, and should not be missed if you have the slightest interest in understanding modern South Africa. Permanent exhibitions include one on the Durban System, which enabled the city council to finance the administration of African affairs without ever spending a penny of white ratepayers' money. It achieved this by granting itself a monopoly on the brewing of sorghum (a type of grain) beer, which it sold through vast, African-only municipal beer halls. The resulting revenue was used to ensure that blacks lived in an "orderly" way. The exhibit also illustrates the Pass System, one of the most hated aspects of apartheid, through which constant tabs could be kept on Africans and their influx into the urban areas. Look out, too, for photographs of life in the single-sex, artificially tribalized worker hostels, which deliberately sowed divisions among blacks by creating separations and divisions, and so played its part in much of the current violence in South Africa.

Grey Street and around

Moving west to where **Grey Street** draws a north–south line across the city, the pace accelerates perceptibly, and you leave behind the formal city centre for the densely packed warren of shops and living quarters of Durban's central **Indian district**, the best place in town to sample local spicy food (see p.470). Post-1910 Union-style architecture is well-preserved here and, along with minarets and steeples, it punctuates the skyline with an eclectic roofscape. Down at street level, the rich cultural blend includes African sidewalk vendors selling herbs, fruit and trinkets outside the Indian general dealers and spice merchants.

On the corner of Grey and Queen streets stands the **Juma Musjid Mosque** and its gilt-domed minarets, completed in 1927. It's the largest mosque in the southern hemisphere, and the area's focal point, although Muslims are a minority among Durban's predominantly Hindu Indian population. You're welcome to enter the mosque, but make sure you leave your shoes at the door. The colonnaded verandahs give way to the alley of the bazaar-like **Madressa Arcade** next door, which provides tantalizing glimpses through mountains of coloured plastic bowls and draped bolts of cloth into general dealers cluttered with aluminium pots and kettles, and Indian traders peddling kerosene lamps, tailor-made outfits and beads. The arcade emerges with a start into Cathedral Street, dominated by the **Emmanuel Cathedral**, built in 1902 in the Gothic-revival style.

North across Queen Street, the **Victoria Street Market** is a bright building with purple minarets, where traders sell curios and spices with labels that include "mother-in-law exterminator". The hectic fish market downstairs can provide drama, particularly on Saturdays when the stall holders compete to sell their stocks before the Sunday close-down.

Moving west, towards the end of town (where it hits the railway tracks), African hawkers unable to afford official stalls gather on **Russell Street**, where they scrape an existence trading *umuthi*, used goods or anything that might raise a few bucks. Extreme poverty dictates that they spend nights on their market pitches in plastic and cardboard hovels: the minibus taxi fare to any of the township areas would cost an entire day's takings. West of Russell Street and jammed between the railway tracks and the N3 freeway into town, **West Street Cemetery** is zoned according to religion, with many of the city's colonial big names buried here, such as Durban's first mayor, George Cato, and the Victorian documentary painter, Thomas Baines. In the Muslim section some tombstones are inscribed "*hagee*" or "*hafez*", the former indicating someone who has been to Mecca and the latter an individual who managed to memorize the entire Koran.

If the crowds feel too intimidating – there is always the risk of mugging – you can explore this area on one of the reasonably priced daily **walking tours** from Tourist Junction (see box on p.456).

Warwick Triangle

In an Africanized *Bladerunner* setting west of Grey Street, concrete freeways run overhead chaotic roadways and minibus taxi ranks; here you'll find Durban's real urban heart of hawkers, shacks and *shebeens*. You'll need to be bold to explore the **Warwick Triangle**, which lies between Berea Road, Brooke Street and Cannongate – police advise tourists to always go in a group, to leave cameras behind and to wear nothing easily snatched.

The gateway to the triangle is across Brooke Street – known until 1988 as Slaughterhouse Road, because butchers slaughtered livestock here – and then through the Berea station concourse and across the Market Road footbridge to the market area between Market Road and Warwick Avenue. The station concourse, which services most of the African townships, pumps with reggae and the music of popular South African musicians such as Lucky Dube, while hawkers sell baseball caps, patent leather shoes and tortoise shells. As you move across the footbridge, take a look at the truncated flyover alongside the station, going nowhere, but now the site for shacks. On a buttress at the end of the flyover, an eight-metre mural of the African goddess Nomkhubulwana stretches out her arms in a gesture of greeting and protection.

Durban's major fruit, vegetable and flower **market** lies between Warwick Avenue and Market Road, extending well beyond its walls in a dense mass of vendors. Operating in the early morning only, the shopping is frenetic; take your own basket and load up with the cheapest produce in town, from aubergines and jackfruit to betelnut leaf for red-stained lips and a two-minute rush.

Victoria Embankment and the harbour vicinity

The **Victoria Embankment**, or the Esplanade, running along the harbour edge south of the city, is Durban's palm-lined city avenue, connecting Point Road in the east to Maydon Wharf Road (which leads to the container terminal piers and the dry dock off Bay Road) in the west. The Embankment was the prime residential area during the city's early development in the nineteenth century, and it's here, one block north at the east end of the road, that the **Old House Museum**, 31 St Andrews St (Mon–Sat 8.30am–4pm, Sun 11–4pm; donation optional), is sited. Once the home of Sir John Robinson, who became Natal's first prime minister in 1893, the renovated settler house serves as a reminder of Durban's colonial heritage.

About 500m east along the Embankment is the entrance to the **Yacht Mole**, a slender breakwater jutting into the bay and home to the Point and Royal Natal Yacht clubs, with an amazing variety of craft. Here you'll also find the upmarket *Café Fish* bar and restaurant, which specializes in great seafood (see p.471). A walk along here provides both a photogenic view of Durban from across the water and a breather from the city traffic. A little further east along the dockside, a statue of **Dick King** celebrates his heroic ride to save Durban (see p.452), and if you keep going in the same direction along the Embankment you'll reach the **BAT (Bartle Arts Trust) Centre**, a focal point for arts in the city. This industrial-chic arts development and community venue right on the dockside offers a concert hall, practical visual art workshops, classes and exhibition galleries while the *Molweni Restaurant* upstairs (9am until very late) provides a magnificent lookout for watching the passing harbour scene. Regular drum circles as well as jazz and *maskanda* performances are also staged here (see p.473).

Back on the Esplanade, heading east towards the Stanger Street intersection, enter the Harbour at Port Entrance no. 3 and follow the signs to the **Ocean Terminal Building**, which harks back to the romantic days of sea travel and is one of Durban's architectural masterpieces. Formerly the harbour reception building, this is now the headquarters for Portnet, the public utility that maintains South Africa's harbours. Although you can't enter the building, the view from outside it at night, looking back onto the city, is spectacular.

Striking south from the city centre and Winder Street, the eastern extension of Victoria Embankment, **Point Road**, known in its heyday in the early 1900s as Africa's most exciting thoroughfare and Durban's hottest red-light district, cuts down the **Point**, the northernmost of the two arms that enclose the Bay of Natal to contain Durban's harbour. At the city end of the road are cheap and tawdry hotels renting out rooms by the hour, late-night takeaways, loud drunks, lurking pickpockets, drug dealers, and scantily clad women lingering by the roadside. At the end of 2001 a huge R400-million deal was signed for the construction here of uShaka Island, a massive marine theme park development. Due to be completed in 2003, it will incorporate the existing aquarium/dolphinarium and oceanographic research centre from the beachfront, as well as dozens of new restaurants, shops and children's water parks, themed around a giant simulated shipwreck.

Maydon Wharf wraps around the harbour's western edge in a photogenic complex of functional industrial architecture, most notable of which are the three dramatic sugar silos at the **Sugar Terminal**, 57 Maydon Wharf Rd, used to store Durban's white gold (one of the city's biggest revenue-earners) and whose design has been patented and used internationally.

Inland from the Sugar Terminal, across the Southern Freeway, the Dalton Road area clings closer to the city centre than any other African residential area. Craftsmen toil in the dingy hive of activity that constitutes **Dalton Road Market**, turning out traditional Zulu costume and regalia including *amabheshu* (leather aprons), shields, *izimboko* (staffs), dancing sticks and beadwork. Every Saturday night, the *Dalton Road Men's Hostel* comes alive with *isicatamiya* concerts (see p.472), which start around midnight and continue into the small hours, with competing groups singing in unaccompanied harmony. This genuine Durban experience, not aimed at tourists, would be worth catching, but it's inadvisable to come to this ropy part of town at night (doors open around 11.30pm) unless you know someone involved.

The beachfront

Durban's **beachfront**, a high-energy holiday strip just east of the city centre, is South Africa's most developed seaside, and one to avoid unless you enjoy unabashed kitsch and garish amusement parks. This six-kilometre stretch from the Umgeni River in the north to the Point in the south was traditionally called the **Golden Mile**, but it's rapidly becoming known as Mugger's Mile, which is why so many middle-class Gauteng families are breaking the habit of generations and deserting the beachfront for the safer (white, middle-class) sands north and south of Durban.

Addington Beach, the southernmost swimming strand and a favourite spot for apprentice surfers, with a smaller swell, draws Durban families to its wide expanse of sand and lawns for sunbathing. Just north lies **South Beach**, the busiest beach in South Africa, which packs tight at peak times, and nets visitors with the start of the beachfront tourist tack: a refreshment and shopping complex and the dubious attraction of Sea World Durban (daily 9am–5pm; dolphin shows 10.15am, 11.45am & 2.30pm; shark feeding daily at 12.30pm; R40), with its tropical aquaria, tanks of sharks, and performing dolphins, seals and penguins.

Further along Marine Parade, you'll find paddling pools, fountains, stepping stones, bridges, an aerial cableway and amusement rides. The only redeeming feature along here is the saltwater **Rachel Finlayson Baths** (Mon–Fri 6am–8.30pm, Sat & Sun 6am–5.30pm; R6; ☏031 337 2721), which offer sheltered swimming and sunbathing. Next is **Dairy Beach**, so called because of the milking factory that once stood here; now regarded as one of the country's best surfing beaches, it's also home to the Oceans Entertainment Centre, whose bars and restaurants are popular with the surfer-groupie crowd.

Dairy Beach adjoins **North Beach** and the adjacent **Bay of Plenty**, both of which make up the venue for the international professional surfing contest held every July. North Beach is Durban's prime angling, bathing and surfing beach, made even more popular by the presence of hip bars and restaurants. Between Snell Parade and the pedestrian walkway at the Bay of Plenty is the **Amphitheatre**, the venue for Sunday flea markets. Here, local hawkers are joined by travelling merchants from Zimbabwe, Malawi and as far afield as Kenya, who trundle down the continent to sell their wares, trading for two weeks, before returning to restock. Any surplus goods are sold at cost to the Zulu traders who line the whole Marine Parade. Rickshaws also gather here, with their ornate carriages pulled by elaborately decorated Zulus decked out in beads and streamers.

Just north of the Bay of Plenty, on the corner of Snell Parade and Old Fort Road, is the **Fitzsimons Snake Park** (daily 9am–4.30pm; R12), which offers the chance to gawp at reptiles in cramped glass boxes. Continuing north, the beachfront hype steadily diminishes with the less frenetic **Battery Beach**, which has good swimming and fewer crowds.

Beachfront safety

Durban's **beaches** are notorious hunting grounds for sharks – though not of the piscean variety. **Muggings** are common, though frequently avoidable if you take sensible precautions. Despite repeated warnings, tourists continue to venture onto beaches wearing expensive watches and jewellery and carrying large wads of cash. On the beachfront, you should stay in a group, and at night never go out alone, no matter how enticing the seafront seems on a balmy evening. Street children are an occupational hazard in most South African cities and they positively thrive on the rich pickings of Durban's beachfront. No matter how small they look, make no mistake – many are skilful pickpockets and accomplished bag-snatchers.

The Berea

West of the city centre, high on a ridge that cuts north–south, the **Berea** is Durban's oldest and most desirable residential district, where mansions and apartment blocks enjoy airy views to the harbour and the sea. Its palmy avenues provide an alternative to the torrid atmosphere of the city centre and beachfront for accommodation, eating and entertainment.

Undulating **Ridge Road** cuts a six-kilometre axis through the Berea from the Umgeni River in the north to the University of Natal. South of the N3, which passes through the Berea to the city, and east of Ridge Road, in Bulwer Road, the **Natal Society of Arts Gallery** (Tues–Fri 11am–5pm, Sat 10am–4pm & Sun 11am–3pm; free), or NSA, adjacent to Bulwer Park, provides a breezy venue for taking in fortnightly exhibitions by local artists and for relaxing in a great coffee shop (the coffee shop has longer hours). Designed for the local climate, the 1990s building is a mass of interlinked spaces, divided by a timber screen that forms a verandah. The gallery shop has a good collection of original art pieces and cheaper, jazzy creations.

Keep going northwards along Bulwer Road, still on the **Upper Berea**, and you'll come to the **Botanical Gardens** (daily: mid-April to mid-Sept 7.30am-5.15pm; mid-Sept to mid-April 7.30am-5.45pm) on the corner of Edith Benson and St Thomas roads. These offer a pleasantly shady break from the surrounding urban torpor, with cool paths, excellent picnic spots, a lovely tea house and a magnificent orchid collection. Established in 1849, the gardens are famous for their cycad collection, which includes *Encephalartos woodii*, one of the rarest specimens in the world. A notice board outside the entrance advertises forthcoming functions, including the regular Natal Philharmonic Orchestra **concerts**.

Heading north for several blocks up Musgrave Road and west into Marriott Road, on the corner of Essenwood Road you'll find another magnificent garden at **Muckleneuk** (by appointment only ☎031 207 3432, ✉harkness@kcc.und.co.za; tours R15), the turn-of-the-century Cape Dutch-revival former homestead of sugar baron Sir Marshal Campbell and home to the outstanding Campbell collections. This is Durban's premier museum, with one of the finest private collections of Africana in the country, including material relating to KwaZulu-Natal's ethnic heritage. The **Killie Campbell Africana Library** is well-known for its comprehensive collection of books, manuscripts and photographs, while the **William Campbell collections** comprise artworks and excellent examples of Cape Dutch furniture. The **Mashu Museum of Ethnology**, also on site, consists of a superb collection of Zulu crafts, including tools, weapons, beadwork and pottery.

Cato Manor

A short drive west of the city centre takes you through **Cato Manor**, a graphic cross-section of Durban's twentieth-century history, where you can see the juxtaposition of African squatter camps, Hindu temples and entropic vegetation mingling in the heart of the city's middle-class suburbs. A large area in a valley below the Berea, Cato Manor was named after Durban's first mayor, **George Cato**, who arrived here in 1839. During the first half of this century, the district was home to much of Durban's Indian community, who built temples on its hills. They were later joined by Africans, who were forced into crowded slums because of the shortage of housing. In 1949, an incident in which an Indian trader assaulted a Zulu man flared up into Durban's worst **riot**, with thousands of Africans attacking Indian stores and houses, leaving 142 people dead.

Some quintessential Durban experiences rarely make it into the pages of tourist brochures; however, with a little effort and some courage you can get a glimpse of KwaMashu township, visit the place where Gandhi dreamed up passive resistance, witness the epic religious ceremonies of the Zulu-Christian Shembe sect and walk among the serene buildings of Inanda – a nineteenth-century seminary for Zulu girls.

A word of **warning** before you leave: self-driving through some of the areas covered here carries a certain risk, and you're advised to go with someone familiar with the road and local customs. Be particularly aware here of the national penchant for car-jacking, and check with Tourist Junction (see p.454) for the best **maps** to use. Alternatively, avoid the risk and take one of the tours on offer; the following tour guides (see box on p.456) are all affiliates of the Inanda Community Tourism Bureau: Ekukhanyeni Travel & Tours, Tours of Remembrance, and Strelitzia Tours.

Heading out of town towards the North Coast, take the M19 along Umgeni Road past the Durban City Dump. Once along the M19 West, take the North Coast R102 turn-off leading to KwaMashu/Phoenix/Duff's Road. As the Duff's Road turn-off approaches, look up to the prominent hillside for Dookie Ramdaari's **Aeroplane House**. An affluent Indian bus builder with a taste for the unconventional, Ramdaari was a voracious traveller, a passion reflected in his first home built in the form of a ship, sailing east out of Duff's Road Indian township. Poised for take off, his current abode, the Aeroplane House, has wings, an undercarriage, a television room with row seats in the tail and a superb lounge in the cockpit.

Further on to Inanda, you'll pass the African township of **KwaMashu** on your left, separated by the Phoenix Industrial Park buffer strip from Phoenix itself, established in the late 1950s to house the forced-removal residents of Cato Manor. It displays all the unimaginative planning typical of such low-cost housing schemes, as does Umlazi, its counterpart to the south of Durban. The area is a sea of hills, vegetation and colour, which makes it tempting to romanticize the tropical poverty of the locality.

A turn-off to the right indicates "Bhambayi" (the Zulu approximation of Bombay), denoting Gandhi's **Phoenix Settlement** on the eastern edge of the vast Inanda squatter camp. Phoenix is the site of a self-help scheme established by Mohandas Gandhi soon after his arrival in Durban in 1903. It was from here that he began to forge his philosophy of passive resistance and it's a sad irony that violence brought it to ruin in 1985 when squatters from the adjacent camp spilled over and looted and razed the settlement. Of Gandhi's house, **Sarvodaya** ("a place for the upliftment for all"), only the foundations remain, although the printing press still stands, albeit in ruins, a melancholic reminder of the spirit and community of the area. The area now hums with traders along the roadside selling anything from water to hair makeovers or "Durban poison" – a highly sought-after type of *dagga* (marijuana).

The M25 continues to **Ekupakumeni** ("the elated place"), where two "stars" are

Because Cato Manor was right in the middle of white suburbs, the apartheid government began enforcing the Group Areas Act in the 1960s, moving Africans north to KwaMashu and Indians south to Chatsworth, leaving a derelict wasteland guarded only by the handful of Hindu temples left standing. The vacuum was filled again in the late 1980s, when Africans pouring into Durban built the closely packed tin shacks that line Bellair Road, winding its way through Cato Manor's valley.

Along this interesting, but not altogether safe, drive (carjackers are a potential hazard), it's well worth stopping to visit the **Shree Ambalvanar Alayam Second River Hindu Temple**, a National Monument in Bellair Road, something you can safely do on a tour (see p.456) The temple has no number, but if you're coming from town it's on your right (just before the Edwin Swales laid in stone in the hilly landscape marking the spots where meteorites from the 1906 Halley's Comet struck the earth. This is also the site of the **Shembe settlement**, established by the Holy Church of Nazareth as a refuge for Africans dispossessed as a result of the Land Act of 1913. According to the founding history of the church, its prophet, Isaya Shembe was "called" in 1910 to the summit of a mountain outside Durban where he vowed before God to bring the Gospel to the Zulus. The church drew membership from rural people whose lives had been devastated by colonization and who were eager to embrace Christianity, but were unwilling to give up traditional customs. Shembe brought about a rich religious synthesis that rejected drinking, smoking and cults, while encouraging a work ethic that centred around crafts, leading to a sect that now has tens of thousands of adherents.

Continuing to the Inanda police station at the top of the hill, turn left to descend into the valley and cross the Umhlanga River bridge. At the next intersection, take the dirt road to the left, past the sports field, and turn left again to view **Ebuhleni**, where every July, devotees of the Holy Church of Nazareth gather for a month of worship. Ignoring the dirt road turn-off, head straight on to reach the Inanda Dam. The deep gorge to your left is the **Inanda Falls**, where the Shembe have baptismal ceremonies, which visitors are welcome to attend.

At the entrance gates to the settlement, rows of tables display what appear to be religious knick-knacks for sale to tourists, but to the converted of Shembe are actually revered religious artifacts. These include holographic images of Isaya Shembe, and key rings with religious icons embedded in perspex. A range of traditional outfits are sold in the village, from men's ceremonial skirts to the magnificent headdresses of the women. The settlement resembles an emerging medieval city, replete with winding pathways negotiating the narrow spaces between buildings. Many homes are owned by believers who come to Ebuhleni only at festival times, timeshare Zulu-style. On these occasions, the men and women live on different sides of the village, and the unmarried maidens live in a separate enclosure.

From Ebuhleni, make your way back to the M25, and continue to the **Inanda Seminary** along a well-indicated route. It's strongly recommended that you visit Inanda's heritage sites in the company of a guide who knows the area well. The oldest secondary school for African girls in southern Africa, the seminary was established in 1869 by Daniel Lindley, an American missionary and pastor of the Voortrekkers; it also played a pioneering role in the liberation of Zulu women. Dignified old buildings give the place an air of serenity. Staff members have always been drawn from all race groups, which is why the school received no funding from the apartheid educational authorities after 1957. The story of Inanda between 1869 and 1969 is recounted in a book by Agnes Wood, *Shine Where You Are*.

To return to Durban, simply turn tail and head east along the M25.

freeway). The building is a 1947 reconstruction of the first Hindu temple in Africa, built in 1875 on the banks of the Umbilo River and subsequently destroyed by floods. The facade is adorned with a pantheon of wonderfully garish Hindu deities and the beautifully carved entrance doors are the originals salvaged from the flood. Around Easter every year the temple hosts a **firewalking festival** in which unshod devotees emerge unscathed after walking across red-hot coals. Visitors are welcome to join the melee of thousands of worshippers who come to honour the goddess Draudpadi. To get there, leave the city centre on the M13, take the Brickfield Road exit and then turn left into the M10; this becomes Bellair Road.

Eating

Eating out is a favourite pastime in Durban, whether you're a suburbanite rel-ishing the seafood of a swanky restaurant, or an African worker shelling out a few rand for a filling Indian takeaway. Although all types of cooking are found here, **Indian** food is what Durban excels at – hardly surprising for a city with one of the largest Indian populations outside Asia. Perhaps less obviously, Durban also has some fine **Portuguese** restaurants, serving cuisine often imported from Mozambique, including highly spiced *peri-peri* dishes, of which chicken is the most common variety and prawns the tastiest. And of course, in this port city, **seafood** is excellent.

For a city that prides itself on its dedication to hedonism, Durban turns in disappointingly early; **closing time** for most restaurants is around 10.30pm. A notable exception is *Legends* in the Musgrave Shopping Centre (see opposite), which stays open past midnight. The best areas for restaurants are the city cen-tre, along the beachfront and the Berea district. Prices are generally very rea-sonable, though you'll pay more for seafood. For Indian food, the best selec-tion is in the Grey Street area; for fish, visit the industrial marine landscape of the harbour. It's a good idea to **phone** before you set out, as opening hours change frequently.

Durban's big contribution to the national fast-food scene is *bunny chow*, a cheap and filling half-loaf of bread scooped-out and traditionally stuffed with curried beans, but now available with an array of mutton, vegetable, beef or even tinned fish curries. Similar are the curries wrapped in *roti* (a traditional Indian pancake). *Shisanyama* outlets at the African markets and around the taxi ranks offer hunks of meat cooked over an open fire.

If you're **self-catering**, you can buy groceries at any of the supermarket chains found in shopping malls. **Tropical fruit** such as mangoes, papayas, bananas, lychees, pineapples, guavas and granadillas are available in season from supermarkets and street traders, and also at the Indian market off Warwick Avenue. In summer, try masala pineapple – cubes of the skewered fruit sprin-kled with red-hot spices.

Restaurants

Beachfront

The Brasserie Smorgasbord *The Edward*, 149 Marine Parade ☎031 337 3681. Delicious break-fasts on the terrace and very good smorgasbord lunches at this beachfront hotel, where you'll find a magnificent and reasonably priced spread of seafoods, including crayfish, oysters and calamari. Open daily.

Jewel of India *Holiday Inn Durban*, 63 Snell Parade ☎031 362 1300. A plush venue with authentic Eastern decor and an adjoining informal lounge, where you can recline on cushions at low tables. Varied with a superb section for vegetari-ans. Lunch Tues–Sun; dinner daily.

Joe Kool's Bar & Grill 137 Lower Marine Parade ☎031 332 9697. A trendy, ultra-clean eating place and pub right on the beach, with pool tables and first-class live music. Mon–Thurs 10am–late, Fri–Sun 8.30am–late.

Saagries House of Curries *Holiday Inn Garden Court*, Marine Parade ☎031 332 7922. This grand upmarket Durban landmark offers some ultra-tangy curries and side dishes. Lunch Mon, Wed–Fri & Sun; dinner daily except Tues.

City centre

Little Gujarat 107 Prince Edward St ☎031 306 2272. Cheap, delectable and excellent-value sit-down or takeaway meals, including vegetarian *bunny chows*, *rotis* and a regular special of the day. Mon–Fri 7am–5pm, Sat 7am–2pm.

O Pescador 52 Albany Grove ☎031 304 4138. As the name suggests, seafood is the speciality at this moderately priced Portuguese restaurant, which serves outstanding crab, complete with nutcracker and bib. The starters and crab curries are recom-mended, as are the mussels in onion and tomato sauce. Mon–Sat noon–3pm & 6–10pm, Sun 6–9pm.

Patel's Vegetarian House Rama House, Grey Street ☏ 031 306 1774. One of the few places where Indians go to buy sweetmeats, and one of the original homes of *bunny chow*. Mon–Fri 6am–4.45pm, Sat 6am–2pm.

Villa D'Este On the corner of Davenport and Bulwer roads ☏ 031 202 7920. One of the oldest and best places in town for fresh fish and seafood, offering Italian charm and a fairly expensive menu. Lunch Tues–Fri & Sun; dinner Tues–Sun.

Victoria Embankment and the harbour

Café Fish Yacht Mole, Victoria Embankment ☏ 031 305 5062. A beautiful and moderately priced restaurant looking out onto the harbour, which specializes in great seafood – eating the catch of the day is *de rigueur*. Daily lunch and dinner.

Charlie Crofts Wharfside Diner 18 Boatsman Rd, Maydon Wharf ☏ 031 307 2935. Right by a slipway in the industrial section of the harbour, the spicy calamari grill is first-class, as is the *eisbein*. Daily noon–10pm.

The Famous Fish Co North Pier, end of Point Road ☏ 031 368 1060. Perfectly positioned at the port entrance, this seafood restaurant is recommended for the wonderful views of ships navigating the harbour mouth. Daily lunch and dinner.

Roma Revolving Restaurant John Ross House, Victoria Embankment ☏ 031 337 6707. No visitor to Durban should miss the view from the *Roma* as it revolves above the city. The international menu includes great mussel starters and Italian specialties, like gnocchi and veal dishes. Mon–Sat lunch and dinner.

The Berea and Morningside

Baan Thai 138 Florida Rd, Morningside ☏ 031 303 4270. The unfailingly excellent Thai food here includes *tom yum* soup and steamed mussels, outshone only by their honeyed duck, at surprisingly moderate prices.

Bean Bag Bohemia 18 Windermere Rd, Greyville ☏ 031 309 6019. A trendy young eating place in a two-storey house, with an informal bar/bistro downstairs and a more formal restaurant above. The reasonably priced duck dishes are particularly recommended. Daily lunch and dinner, Sun breakfast.

Blue Zoo Café 6 Nimmo Rd, Berea ☏ 031 303 2265. A varied and unusual menu features delicious Cajun chicken, lamb shank in a port wine sauce, steaks, fish and salads with mango and chilli dressings. Beautifully located in Mitchell Park Gardens, with moderate prices. Closed Mon. Tues–Sat lunch; Tues–Sun dinner.

Café 1999 Silvervause Centre, Silverton Road, Berea ☏ 031 202 3406. An excellent fusion restaurant which is also good for late night coffees. Mon–Fri 12.30–2.30pm & 6.30–10.30pm, Sat 6.30–11pm.

El Turko 413 Windemere Rd, Morningside ☏ 031 312 7893. A cosy, moderately priced restaurant with pavement seating and a recommended *meze* platter with fiery olives. "Turkish Tigers" (vodka, condensed milk, cream and cinnamon) are also worth trying. Closed Sat lunch & all day Sun.

Gulzar 71 Stamford Hill Rd, Morningside ☏ 031 309 6379. Durban's classiest Indian restaurant, serving magnificent curries and tandooris amid Moorish decor and tasteful Oriental carpets. Daily lunch and dinner.

Legends Café Musgrave Centre ☏ 031 201 0733. A long-standing comfortable restaurant with Thai and Mexican influences, as well as seafood dishes such as seafood crepes and tangy grilled calamari. It also offers terrific prawn curry and the best breadrolls in town. Daily till late.

Marco's 45 Windermere Rd, Greyville ☏ 031 303 3078. A classy trattoria, with fresh pasta made daily and delectable pizzas. Lunch Mon–Fri; dinner Mon–Sat.

Palki 225 Musgrave Rd ☏ 031 201 0019. The South African representative of a chain of restaurants based in the Far East, this authentic Indian eating place has mouthwatering North and South Indian foods, created by chefs shipped in from other branches. Vegetarians are well catered for, and it's very reasonably priced. Lunch Tues–Sun; dinner daily.

Vintage 20 Windermere Rd, Greyville ☏ 031 309 1328. Less formal than some of the other Indian restaurants in town, *Vintage* offers both North and South Indian fare and some unusual dishes. There's a great range of inexpensive starters and a comprehensive vegetarian selection. The stuffed chicken legs are good, and their "Bombay crush", a traditional Indian milkshake invented for "cooling the palate" is a must after a fiery curry. Daily lunch and dinner.

Coffee and snack shops

Boa Vista 463 Innes Rd, Morningside ☏ 031 312 3456. Opposite Mitchell Park gardens, this deli and coffee shop allows you to make up your own platter and pay by weight. Mon–Fri 8am–6pm, Sat &

Sun 8am–3pm.

Delicious Delicatessen and Coffee Shop Windermere Centre, Windermere Road ☏ 031 312 8699. Seriously delicious noodle salads and breadrolls, with excellent coffees. Mon–Fri 8am–6pm, Sat 7am–2pm.

Franko's 300 Smith St. An unpretentious coffee shop in the centre, offering great pepper steak and light snacks. Mon–Fri 7am–3.30pm, Sat 8am–12.30pm.

Fressh 141 Musgrave Rd, next to Musgrave Centre. A great bagel and coffee shop, popular with the Berea's upper crust. Mon–Sat 7.30am–5pm, Sun 8am–3pm.

Loafers Bakery & Coffee Shop 514 Windermere Rd ☎031 312 2100. A light and airy venue, popular with Durbanites for Sunday breakfast; budget prices, but still offering a first-class full English breakfast. Mon–Sat 6.30am–6pm, Sun 6.30am–5pm.

Takeaways

Charlie Croft's Wharfside Diner 18 Boatsman Rd, Maydon Wharf ☎031 307 2935. Delicious seafood and meat takeaways from an eating place with one of the best settings in Durban.

Delicious Delicatessen Windermere Centre, Windermere Road. Delicious and healthy takeaways such as green Thai chicken bagels, pasta salads, including tomato pesto and feta; spinach and basil; and smoked chicken with sesame seeds and honey mustard dressing.

Sunrise Chip 'n' Ranch 89 Sparks Rd, Overport. The fastest and tastiest curries and *bunny chows* in town, 24 hours a day to take away, at rock-bottom prices.

Victory Lounge On the corner of Grey and Victoria streets. Hot and spicy *bunny chow* to take away, in the Indian quarter of the city centre.

Nightlife and entertainment

You'll find plenty of live **indie music** on offer in Durban, much of it derivative of European or North American trends. More interesting, but less accessible, are some of the **Zulu forms** such as *isicathamiya* and *maskanda*. On the **jazz** scene, the city's most indigenous offering is a spicy combination of American mixed with township jazz and Zulu forms. Talented Durban musician Sipho Gumede delivers outstanding African jazz fairly regularly at the BAT Centre (see p.465), while Jimmy Dludlu, another hot favourite, performs his more American-styled jazz. Also listen out for good jazz from Darius Brubeck (son of Dave), while *Rivets Bar* at the *Hilton Hotel* in Walnut Road has established itself as the top jazz club, with gigs every Thursday night (free), from 8pm till late.

The best place to hear **classical concerts** by the Natal Philharmonic Orchestra – more for the tropical ambience than the quality of performance – is at a sundowner concert held in the Botanical Gardens or the Kingsmead Cricket Grounds. Check for listings and adverts in the press, or on the notice board in the Gardens.

For details of **what's on**, the *Mercury* is the better of Durban's two English-language dailies, while the *Sunday Tribune* has a thorough and comprehensive section on forthcoming events in its *SM* magazine. The Johannesburg-based weekly *Mail & Guardian* also covers Durban nightlife in its *What's On* supplement.

Bars

Billy The Bums 504 Windermere Rd, Greyville. Acrobatic barmen juggle bottles while mixing highly imaginative cocktails at a popular singles' watering hole, which also does good food. Mon–Sat noon–midnight.

Cool Runnings 39 Milne St. A brilliant rasta/reggae hangout. Daily noon–6am.

Jack Rabbits 1 McCarthy Centre, North Ridge Road, Morningside. Sports bar with a wonderful outside deck to watch passing traffic, inexpensive meals and nightly happy hours with cheap booze. Daily 10am–late.

Monkey Bar 263 Florida Rd, Morningside. A fun place to hang out, with a good mix of contempo-

rary music, house and Afro-jazz. Closed Sun.
Thirsty's King's Battery Development. Worth visiting for the harbour view alone, *Thirsty's* serves scampi baskets and also has a beer garden with a variety of imported beers. Mon–Fri 7am till last person leaves, Sat 7am–1am & Sun 7am–11pm.
Victoria Bar Point Road. A seedy but highly popular Portuguese venue, good for boozing and watching sport on TV. *Catembe* (cola and wine) is a house speciality, as is the excellent prawn curry

and *peri-peri* chicken. Bar: Mon–Sat 10.30am–11pm; restaurant: Mon–Sat 12.30pm–3pm & 6.30–10pm.
Wonder Bar Windermere Road, Greyville (next to *Billy The Bums*). An increasingly popular bar/club, with hi-tech stainless steel decor, lava lamps and a good vibe. Front bar: daily 6pm; inside area: Tues,Thurs, Fri & Sat 2.30pm–2.30am. Cover charge Fri between 10pm and midnight: women R5, men R10.

Clubs

100 on Point A newish club in the burgeoning Point Road area, with three dance floors and live musicians. Friday nights are more geared to over-25s, with jazz and old R&B. Fri & Sat from 9pm; R20.
80s Absa Stadium off Walter Gilbert Road. Hugely popular, particularly on Wednesday nights, when local students are on the loose. *80s* offers a large dance floor, several bars, pool tables and an outdoor area, and has top DJs hosting. Wed, Fri & Sat 8pm–4am; Wed & Fri R10, Sat R15.
Club 330 Point Road. Durban's definitive techno-

rave club; the dress code is high fashion, accessories are body piercing, spring water and tiger balm ointment. Sat only, from 10pm. R20 before, R40 after 11pm.
Night Fever 123 Argyle Rd, Greyville. A popular under-30s hangout with normal and shooter bars, and large dance floor, led by top DJs. Tues & Thurs–Sat 8pm–4am; R10.
Skybar Silver Avenue, off Stamford Hill Road. A sophisticated and upmarket joint specializing in house music, with a fabulous outside deck. Open Sat & Sun 8pm–4am; R30.

Gay spots

Durban has a fairly well-established and lively **gay scene**, with a handful of excellent nightclubs where heteros are also welcome.

Axis Gillespie Street, beachfront. Durban's premier gay nightclub grooves to the sounds of disco classics. Wed, Fri & Sat 9.30pm–5am.
Bean Bag Bohemia 18 Windermere Rd, Morningside. Also a restaurant (see p.471), *Bean Bag Bohemia* has a great bar downstairs and is very gay-friendly. Frequented by young beautiful things of both sexes, it's one of the best places in town to meet new friends. Last drinks daily 2.30am; restaurant: Mon–Sat till 1am, Sun till midnight.

Roman Lounge 202 Florida Rd, Morningside. An upmarket gay bar open seven days a week. No meals are served, but *La Mafia Italian* restaurant nearby will deliver your orders. Mon, Tues & Thurs 4pm–late, Wed & Fri–Sun 2pm–late.
Shaftsbury's Overport Drive, Berea. A decent pub downstairs, with what is commonly known as the "black hole" – a sex room – upstairs. Daily from 5pm.

Jazz

BAT (Bartle Arts Trust) Centre Small Craft Harbour, entrance opposite Hermitage Lane, off Victoria Embankment. Probably the best jazz venue in Durban; don't miss sundowner time here on Friday evenings, when local musicians hold alternating jazz/*maskanda* sessions (5–7pm; free). There's also a drum circle by top local drummers,

performing in the *Bat Café* most Tuesdays (7.30–9.30pm; cover charge R10).
The Rainbow 23 Stanfield Lane, Pinetown ☎031 702 9161. From Afro-fusion to jazz, on occasional Sunday lunchtimes; check the press for programme details.

Theatre and cinema

There are two major **theatres** in town: the Playhouse Drama Theatre, 231 Smith St (☎031 260 2296), a mock-Tudor building that tends to host middle-of-the-road productions, but also sees performances by the resident progressive Playhouse Dance Company; and the Elizabeth Sneddon Theatre, at the University of Natal, on South Ridge Road (☎031 260 2296), a modern venue for university and visiting productions, which also hosts Monday lunchtime concerts, including Zulu traditional *maskanda* and piano recitals. Also popular is Backstage at The Royal, 267 Smith St (℡031 304 0331), a supper club/cabaret venue featuring topnotch shows, which includes a first-rate three-course meal.

As far as movies go, the best and most convenient **cinemas** are the multi-screen complexes at the Musgrave Centre on Musgrave Road and The Workshop Mall in the city centre. There are no art-house cinemas in Durban, but the Musgrave occasionally screens film-festival releases.

Outdoor activities

Durban's generous climate and beachside location foster a wide variety of **outdoor activities**. Not surprisingly for a city with such a British heritage, **cricket** and **horse racing** are high on the agenda of spectator sports; the Kingsmead Cricket Ground, 2 Kingsmead Close (℡031 335 4200), is the principal cricket venue for local and international matches and is home to the KwaZulu-Natal provincial cricket team. You'll also have plenty of opportunity to watch **rugby** in season at Absa Stadium, Walter Gilbert Road, Stamford Hill (℡031 308 8400), which is the home to the local Sharks. **Horse racing** is popular: the main season runs from May to August, and centres around the course at Greyville, Avondale Road (℡031 314 1651). The annual "July at Greyville" is South Africa's premier horse-racing event, drawing bets from across the length and breadth of the country and wildly exhibitionist fashions in the spectator boxes.

Surfing

More than a pastime, **surfing** in Durban is a way of life. Night surfing competitions draw enormous crowds, as does the annual **Mr Price Pro** (formerly the Gunston 500 and the world's longest-running professional surfing competition), held here every July. During this month, the city goes surf-mad, with a large expo displaying the latest equipment and accessories.

The favourite spot for surfers is **North Beach**, while a good place to pick up gear is the Safari Surf Shop, 42 Brickhill Rd (℡031 337 2176), where Spider Murphy, South Africa's top board-shaper, will custom-make you a world-class board far cheaper than anything you'll find in Europe or North America. Island Style Surf Shop, 121 Old Fort Rd, Marine Parade (℡031 305 4505), is a good bet for accessories.

Diving and swimming

Diving is an obvious and pleasurable activity in KwaZulu-Natal's subtropical waters, but is somewhat limited immediately around Durban. The best diving sites around town are Vetches Pier, at the southern tip of Durban's beachfront, and Blood Reef at the tip of the Bluff. Further along the coast, Aliwal Shoal along the South Coast (see p.480), and Sodwana up the North Coast (p.530), are superb. **Scuba courses** can be arranged through Underwater World, 251 Point Rd (℡031 332 5820). For a full six-day internationally recognized NAUI course you pay R1500, including your main scuba equipment. Additional gear costs an extra R600. A five-day private course, including all your gear is R2500; Meridian Dive Centre, 19 Glenore Centre, Glenashley (℡031 573 2190, @www.scubadivesouthafrica) can also organize courses and charters.

If you fancy doing some laps, Durban's largest **swimming pool** is the heated King's Park Olympic Swimming Pool on NMR Avenue, between Argyle and Battery Beach roads in Stamford Hill (℡031 312 0404). Convenient for the Berea are Sutton Park Baths, Stamford Hill Rd (☎031 303 1823), while the seawater Rachel Finlayson Baths, Lower Marine Parade (☎031 337 2721), are handy if you're staying near the beachfront.

Bird-watching and hiking

Bird-watching, a major activity in the green fringes of the city, is being encouraged by the Durban Metropolitan Open Space System (DMOSS), a project linking all the city parks via narrow green corridors. Promising spots include the Manor Gardens area; the Botanic Gardens; the Berea; Burman Bush, to the north of the city; Pigeon Valley, below the University of Natal; the Umgeni River Mouth; Virginia Bush, on the road to Umhlanga Rocks; and the Havana Forest in Umhlanga, where the spotted thrush and green coucal have been seen. Also worth a visit is the **Umgeni River Bird Park**, 490 Riverside Rd, Durban North (daily 9am–5pm; ☎031 579 4600; R25), which has a fantastic free-flight bird show twice-daily (Tues–Sun), with spectacular specimens as well as a vast collection of indigenous and exotic birds, including flamingos, finches, magpies and macaws; there's also a tranquil tea garden. For organized bird-watching outings and courses, contact the **Wildlife Environment Society of South Africa**, 100 Brand Rd, Glenwood (☎031 201 3126).

You can arrange **hiking** in the relatively close **Drakensberg** through one of the several hiking clubs that organize expeditions to Injasuti, Cathedral Peak and the Southern Berg. These can be contacted through the Wildlife Environment Society of South Africa, which organizes a variety of bush outings; non-members are welcome. For equipment, head for Cape Union Mart, 306 Musgrave Centre, Musgrave Road (☎031 201 0231), or Bushwackers, 110 Pavilion Shopping Centre, Spine Road, Westville (☎031 265 0102).

Canoeing and kayaking

One of the South African adventure highlights for any outdoor enthusiast must be paddling with world-champion paddler Oscar Chalupsky, nine-time winner of the World Kayak Championship in Hawaii. Chalupsky Paddling & Adventure School, Third Floor, Pulbo House, 25 Silver Avenue (☎031 303 7336, ⓦwww.chalupsky,com) offers **kayaking and canoeing** through spectacular scenery on inland whitewater as well as at sea. Even Chalupsky's assistants are top-notch paddlers, all having represented South Africa. There's a wide range of venues near Durban and further afield throughout KwaZulu-Natal with typical trips costing $50 for two hours on the water.

Extreme sports

For awesome **rapp jumps** off local buildings (R80 a jump), **mountain boarding**, **surfing safaris**, **skydiving** (R750 for a solo and R950 for a tandem jump) and **extreme safaris** try the Vertical Group (☎083 306 9268, ⓦwww.vertical.co.za), *Legends*, Musgrave Centre, Musgrave Road.

Shopping

As one of South Africa's major cities, Durban is a good centre to pick up general supplies and local books and records. But it's for **crafts and curios** that it scores particularly highly, being the largest city in KwaZulu-Natal, home turf to the Zulus, who produce a dazzling range of handmade goods (see box on p.476). The best places to browse for crafts are in the downtown markets, the weekend flea markets and the specialist shops around the city.

Books and music

Adams & Co 341 West St ☎ 031 304 8571. In the city centre, this is Durban's oldest book store, and has an excellent selection of books on the history of Durban and KwaZulu-Natal. There's also a branch at the Musgrave Centre (☎ 031 201 5123) with a coffee bar.

Exclusive Books Lower Level, Pavilion Shopping Centre ☎ 031 265 0454. Durban's flashiest general book store, where browsers are welcome to pore over titillating coffee-table books. Closes 10pm Sat.

Ike's Books and Collectables 4th Avenue, Greyville, upstairs from *Mam Lucian's Coffee Shop* ☎ 031 303 9214. A fascinating second hand bookshop, with an interesting range of items covering KwaZulu-Natal's history and the fauna and flora of the area. Speciality areas include Africana and the Boer War, travel and exploration, and left-wing classics.

Look and Listen Lower Level, Pavilion Shopping Centre ☎ 031 265 0826. Durban's best-stocked music shop, with a comprehensive range of indigenous music from the whole continent, including local favourites such as Ladysmith Black Mambazo and Hugh Masekela.

Crafts and curios

African Art Centre 160 Pine St, Old Durban Station, 1st floor ☎ 031 304 7915. A gallery and shop well worth visiting for its traditional and modern Zulu and Xhosa beadwork, beaded dolls, wire sculptures, woodcuts and tapestries.

The Bat Shop The BAT Centre, Harbourside, off Victoria Embankment ☎ 031 332 9951. Offers contemporary works with an excellent collection by African artists, in a bright and colourful venue with masterful wireworks and robust ceramics. Closes 4pm Sat.

NSA Gallery Shop NSA Gallery, Bulwer Road, Berea. This menagerie of hand-crafted goods includes a wonderful selection of functional art, including pewter cutlery, etchings and paintings; there's also an outdoor coffee shop.

Tourist Junction Shop 160 Pine St ☎ 031 304 7915. Quality African artefacts, from Zulu basketwork to tribal masks and weaving.

The Workshop Mall On the corner of Commercial and Aliwal streets. Located in part of the old station building, this is the city centre's largest shopping mall, and a handy place to shop for gifts, souvenirs and curios.

Zulu crafts and curios

Durban's huge range of galleries, craft shops and markets make it one of the best centres in the country to pick up **Zulu crafts**. Traditional works include a range of functional items, such as woven beer strainers, grass brooms and basketry that can be extremely beautiful. Other traditional items are beadwork, pottery and Zulu regalia, of which *assegais* (spears), shields, leather kilts and drums are a few examples. However, drastic social changes in South Africa over the last century have affected the Zulus along with every other South African – black and white. The availability of cheap plastic crockery and enamelware has significantly eroded the time-consuming production of traditional ceramics and woven containers for domestic use. Instead, these personal household items are now frequently churned out en masse for sale to curio hunters who are indifferent to the authenticity or quality of what they are buying.

Fortunately, the news isn't all bad and, although urbanization has stifled the production of much traditional craft, it has thrown up creative adaptations making use of new materials, or old materials used in new ways. Among these are beautifully decorated black and white **sandals** made from recycled rubber tyres, wildly colourful **baskets** woven from telephone wire and *sjamboks* (whips) decorated with bright insulation tape. On the more frivolous side are a whole genre of affordable curios that break away from the stereotypes of tribal woodcarvings and masks, and marry industrial materials with rural life or rural materials with industrial life. Attractive tin boxes made from flattened oil cans, chickens constructed from sheet plastic, and aircraft and little 4WD vehicles carved from wood are some of the results.

If you're serious about quality, an entire movement of **master craftspeople** draws on traditional forms to produce objects of the highest quality, many of which are sought after by art collectors. Among these many excellent craftworkers are woodcarver Vuminkosi Zulu, scrap-metal car sculptor Nkosinathi Gumede and potter Nesta Nala – contact them through the Natal Society of Arts shop in the Berea (see p.467).

Fleamarkets

Essenwood Fleamarket Berea Park, Essenwood Road. Upmarket stalls in a beautiful park setting on the Berea. Sat.

Farepark Market On the corner West and Farewell streets. Permanent stalls in rustic cabins. Daily.

South Plaza Fleamarket Durban Exhibition Centre, Walnut Road. Centrally situated, this is the largest fleamarket in town. Sun 6.30am–5pm.

Thirsty's Waterfront Market King's Battery, The Point. An interesting harbour venue where you can pick up handmade clothing, spicy pineapples, marsala green mangoes, silver jewellery and African arts and curios. Sun.

Listings

Airlines British Airways/Comair ☏ 031 450 7000 and Intensive Air ☏ 011 927 5111 offer discounted fares, as does the newly established internet-based airline, ⓦ www.kulula.com; SA Airlink ☏ 031 250 1111; South African Airways ☏ 031 250 1111.

American Express Nedbank Centre, 10 Durban Place ☏ 031 301 5541. Mon–Fri 8.30am–4.30pm, Sat 8.30am–noon.

Banks First National Bank, 32 West St, Marine Parade ☏ 031 337 9464, has extended hours for changing foreign currency. Mon–Fri 9am–6pm, Sat 8.30am–6pm, Sun 10am–3pm.

Bicycle rental/tours Cycle Tours De Durban (see p.456) offers tours around the city; or phone Nick's Cycle Hire ☏ 031 564 6804 on the beachfront for bike rental.

Camera repairs Camera Clinic, Shop 4, Standard Bank Centre, 135 Musgrave Rd ☏ 031 202 5396. Repairs and services of all photographic and video equipment.

Car parks The most convenient and central are those at Pine Arcade, at the west end of Pine Street, and in The Workshop Mall, on the corner of Commercial Road and Aliwal Street.

Car rental Avis ☏ 0861 021 111 (toll-free); Berea ☏ 031 202 3333; Budget 031 304 9023; Europcar 031 469 0667; Imperial ☏ 0800 13 10 00 (toll-free); Rent & Drive ☏ 031 332 2803; Tempest 031 368 5231; and Windermere ☏ 031 312 0339. Berea also rents minibuses.

Consulates UK, 19th floor, Marine Building, 22 Gardiner St ☏ 031 305 2929; USA, Durban Bay House, 333 Smith St ☏ 031 304 4737.

Emergencies Ambulance ☏ 10177; Police (Flying Squad) ☏ 10111; Rape Crisis ☏ 031 312 2323.

Hospitals and medical centres The main state hospital is the central Addington, Erskine Terrace, South Beach (☏ 031 332 2000), which offers a cheap 24hr emergency ward, but the level of care cannot be guaranteed. A better alternative is Entabeni Private Hospital, 148 South Ridge Rd, Berea (☏ 031 204 1300), which has a casualty unit and can also treat minor conditions, but where you will have to pay a deposit on admission and settle up before leaving town. A convenient option is South Beach Medical Centre, Rutherford Street (☏ 031 332 3101), 24hr, which has a pharmacy, doctors, an optician, a dentist, a physiotherapist, as well as aromatherapy, reflexology and homeopathy. Travel Doctor at 45 Ordnance Rd, International Convention Centre (☏ 031 360 1122, ⓦ www.traveldoctor.co.za) is a clinic offering information and advice on local and international destinations, as well as on malaria and the necessary jabs for venturing into African countries to the north.

Internet access Internet Café, Shop 71, The Workshop ☏ 031 304 0915; daily until 7pm. Free email address and lots of specials such as two free print-outs with an hour's computer use, and good prices on scanning and photocopying.

Laundries Musgrave Laundromat, 2nd Level, Musgrave Centre and Econ-O-Wash, ground floor, Berea Centre, Berea Road are both convenient for the Berea. Mont Blanc Laundromat, 54 Gillespie St, is within walking distance of the beach.

Left luggage Durban station has inexpensive left-luggage facilities on the first floor (daily 6am–6pm).

Pharmacies Sparkport, corner Smith and Broad streets (Mon–Sat 7.30am–9.30pm, Sun 9am–9pm; ☏ 031 304 9767), offers a doctor on call 24 hours a day as well as a range of specialist treatments, film processing and all pharmaceutical travel requirements. Medicine Chest, 155 Berea Rd, Berea (daily 8am–midnight; ☏ 031 305 6151) offers free deliveries; Daynite Pharmacy, corner of West Street and Point Road (daily 7.30am–10.30pm; ☏ 031 368 3666), also has free deliveries; and Mediquick Pharmacy, 98 Overport Drive, outside Overport City Shopping Centre, Berea (8am–10pm; ☏ 031 209 3456) can deliver anywhere in town for a nominal charge.

Post office The main branch, on the corner of Gardiner and West streets, has a poste restante and enquiry desk. Mon–Fri 8am–4.30pm, Sat 8am–noon.

Taxis Aussies ☏ 031 337 4232; Eagle ☏ 031 368 1706; Swift ☏ 031 332 5569; Zippy ☏ 031 202 7067.

Around Durban

If you're looking for quieter beaches, the **North** or **South coasts** around Durban make an obvious and easy day-trip or weekend jaunt out of the city. The coast around Durban, with its easy access to Johannesburg, the warmest waters in the country and decidedly tropical feel, has primarily been developed for white South African families on holiday. In a country with so many spectacular landscapes and wild places to visit, the coasts around Durban can seem rather bland. Having said that, there are kilometres of uncongested sandy beaches backed by wild banana trees, and the chance to spot dolphins, especially along the North Coast.

The South Coast draws diving enthusiasts to **Aliwal Shoal**, one of the country's top dive spots near Umkomaas, and is also notable for two nature reserves in the south: Oribi Gorge, inland from Port Shepstone, where you can overnight or visit by steam train; and Umtamvuna, inland from Port Edward, which offers day-walks along the Umtamvuna River.

Unless you're travelling to or from the Eastern Cape, the North Coast is preferable to the South Coast – it's a lot less built-up and tacky. **Umhlanga Rocks**, an upmarket resort less than half an hour's drive from Durban on the N2, offers beach walks, as well as great places to have a drink or meal, and gaze at the sea, and indeed offers an alternative to staying in Durban itself. Further up the coast are a string of resorts which get more low-key the further north you go, all with sandy beaches and large tidal rock pools to swim in. Inland is sugar cane country, with a couple of upmarket guesthouses reflecting the colonial-style grandeur of the early sugar barons. The old road north, the **R102**, which takes an inland route, is far more interesting than the coastal road, giving access to visiting Indian temples at **Tongaat**, the grave of one of the ANC's best-loved leaders, Albert Luthuli, at **Groutville**, and the Shaka memorial and museum, as well as the bustling Indian and African markets, at **Dukuza**.

Heading 80km northwest from Durban is **Pietermaritzburg**, the provincial capital, with an excellent art gallery and some interesting red-brick Victorian architecture combining with a vibrant mix of Zulu and Indian culture. Sampling Pietermaritzburg can be combined with the all-time favourite day-trip out of Durban, the **Valley of a Thousand Hills**, which can be visited by driving along the Old Main Road (R103) towards Pietermaritzburg; you can combine great scenery with doing a bit of Zulu craft shopping.

Beyond Pietermaritzburg, and definitely more of a weekend stay than a day-trip, are the Natal **Midlands**, with appealing scenery in the Drakensberg foothills, trout fishing, numerous craft shops, and a number of hotels, guesthouses and cottages catering especially for the weekend trade. Although it's very pretty, the area is probably best experienced through the windows of your vehicle, as you head towards the real reward of the region, the stunningly beautiful Drakensberg Mountains.

The South Coast

The South Coast, the 160-kilometre seaboard from Durban to Port Edward on the Eastern Cape border, is a ribbon of seaside suburbs where thousands of upcountry families have built holiday homes along what is the closest stretch

The sardine run

Once a year, the South Coast is witness to the extraordinary annual migration of millions of **sardines**, moving northwards along the coast in massive shoals. Around June or July, the shoals leave their feeding ground off the Southern Cape coast, and move up the coast towards Mozambique. They are followed by about 23,000 dolphins, 100,000 Cape gannets and thousands of sharks and game fish, attracting fishermen from all over the province to join in the jamboree.

The shoals appear as dark patches of turbulence in the water, and when they are cornered and driven ashore by game fish, hundreds of people rush into the water to either scoop them out with their hands or to net them.

of sand to Johannesburg. Although in wilderness terms the area is unexciting, it does have some lovely beaches and ample accommodation, and it wins hands down in the winter months, when it's much warmer and sunnier along this stretch than on any of the beaches between here and Cape Town.

South Coast beaches are sandy and backed by luxuriant wild banana trees wedged between the holiday developments. Many shelve steeply into the powerful surf, so only swim where it's indicated as safe. Away from the sea, the land is very hilly and green, dotted with sugar cane fields, banana plantations and palm and pecan nut trees. Gardens are bright with exuberant flowering trees and shrubs, and in some places alive with monkeys.

Transport from Durban and Johannesburg to the South Coast is good (see p.480) and there are plenty of caravan parks next to the beaches, a couple of backpacker lodges and a number of mid-priced places to stay. **Margate**, 133km from Durban, is the transport and holiday hub of the area, with plenty of resorts lying to the east and west of it. **Port Shepstone**, 117km south of Durban, is the grim industrial and administrative centre along the coast, while **Oribi Gorge Nature Reserve**, just 21km inland from Port Shepstone, has lovely forest hikes, breathtaking views and good-value accommodation.

Amanzimtoti, Warner Beach and Umkomaas

Some 27km south of Durban and just minutes from Durban airport, **AMANZIMTOTI** (Zulu for "sweet waters") earned its name, according to tradition, because it was here that King Shaka slaked his thirst, in the river that took the same name. Toti, as the resort is known to locals, is the largest town along the upper South Coast, yet feels more like a beachside suburb than a place in its own right. Outside weekends and school holidays – when its highrise holiday developments are full to bursting point – it's worth coming here for a day's swimming and lounging on Nyoni Rocks Beach.

If you're looking for somewhere to **stay**, however, **WARNER BEACH**, 3km further south, is the place to head for. Far less developed than Amanzimtoti, Warner Beach offers some excellent surfing spots, as well as good swimming and a large tidal pool that's safe for children. Overlooking the beach, the supremely relaxed *Angle Rock Backpackers*, 5 Ellcock Rd (⊕031 916 7007, ⓦwww.anglerock.co.za; ❶), is a cut above the average **hostel**, with a swimming pool, four dorms and three doubles – one of which is en suite with a marble bathtub. The lodge offers free use of surfboards and canoes. Warner Beach has a handful of decent pubs and restaurants.

Roughly 16km further down the coast, **UMKOMAAS**, a faded town of buildings with corrugated-iron roofs, exudes an atmosphere that is more laidback still. Perched on a headland with outstanding views across the sea, this is

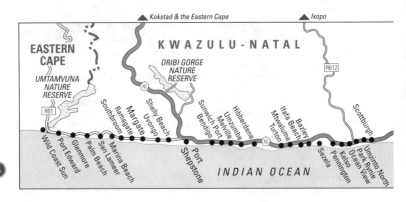

essentially a retirement village with beaches that are periodically discoloured by effluent washing down the Mkomazi River from the Saiccor cellulose mill, just upriver. For diving enthusiasts, Umkomaas is the perfect point to set out for **Aliwal Shoal**, a scattered reef quite close to the shore and one of southern Africa's top dive sites. On the beachfront, *Umkomaas Lodge Dive Centre*, Roland Norris Drive (☏039 973 2542, ℮umkomaas@netactive.co.za; ❶), offers a wide range of **diving activities** with self-catering **accommodation**, from dorms to luxury en-suite rooms. Their four-day Open Water diving course leads to an internationally recognized PADI certificate and costs around R1200 with own mask and fins or R1400 if they provide the gear. The best time to dive is between June and October, when visibility is at its best. Amatikulu Tours (☏039 973 2534, ℻039 973 2438, ⓦwww.amtikulutours .com) offers a four-day PADI open water diving course for R1500 (includes all equipment and accommodation at their backpacking lodge). Rewards for experienced divers include sightings of whale sharks, ragged-tooth sharks, potato bass, manta rays and eels, as well as shoals of tropical fish, corals and anemones; enthusiasts can also go wreck-diving to three stunning sites.

South Coast transport

By car, head for the N2, which runs south from Durban as far as Port Shepstone, before heading inland to Kokstad. From Port Shepstone to Southbroom, the South Coast Toll Road is even faster and less traffic-clogged. **By air**, daily direct flights (90min) from Johannesburg on SA Airlink (central reservations ☏031 312 1017) go to Margate airport (☏039 312 0560).

If you're travelling to the South Coast **by intercity bus**, you have two choices. Luxliner (☏039 315 7206 or 039 315 7306) operates daily from Pretoria, running through Pietermaritzburg and Durban and passing through most of the South Coast towns of Amanzimtoti, Scottburgh, Hibberdene, Port Shepstone, Shelly Beach and Margate. It's recommended that you phone to check their schedule, as their timetable is seasonal. Margate Mini Coach, Gird Mowat Building, Marine Drive, Margate (☏039 312 1406), has a daily service from Durban station (Translux terminal) via Durban (*Royal Hotel*), Durban airport (domestic arrivals), Amanzimtoti (prebooked only), Hibberdene (prebooked only), Hibberdene (Super Tube), Port Shepstone (LSC Motors) and Margate (Dennisons Funworld). The **Baz Bus** (☏031 304 9099) runs from Port Elizabeth to Durban and back three times a week, pulling in at major South Coast resorts, although you can ask to be put off at intermediate destinations.

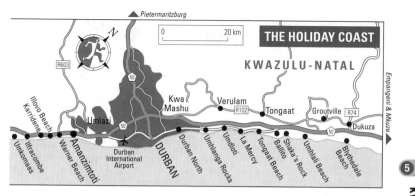

Scottburgh to Port Shepstone

A further 9km south brings you to **SCOTTBURGH**, the oldest town along the South Coast and one of the most appealing because of its sheltered and lawn-covered beach fringes. The *Cutty Sark*, on the beachfront (☏039 976 1230, ⓦwww.cuttysark.co.za; ❹), offers reasonable hotel **accommodation** as well as some discount specials out of the peak Christmas and Easter seasons, while camping and self-catering in six-bed cottages are available at the nearby *Scottburgh Caravan Park* (☏039 976 0291, ⓕ039 976 2148; ❶), on the seafront and a short walk from the shops. The park is huge, and during school breaks you're likely to be swamped by family holidaymakers, but outside these periods it's less hectic.

Some 100km south of Durban along the N2, turn off at Hibberdene and continue south on the R102 for a couple of kilometres till you reach Umzumbe Station Road, along which you'll find *Mantis and Moon Backpackers* (☏039 684 6256, ⓔtravelsa@saol.com). A friendly and laid-back place, it's just two minutes' walk from the beach and you'll be able to see dolphins frolicking most mornings, or you can bask in an outdoor Jacuzzi or relax on the rooftop deck. Activities offered include making necklaces, didgeridoos or rain sticks, whale-watching in season, abseiling at Oribi and free surfing lessons; the hosts Murray and Brad are also famous for their mouthwatering fish braais.

About 15km south along the R102 from *Mantis and Moon*, you'll come to **Umtentweni**, where there's another **backpacker lodge**, *The Spot*, 23 Ambleside Rd (☏039 695 1318, ⓔspotbackpackers@netactive.co.za; ❶), right on the beach. The lodge has a dorm sleeping fifteen, plus doubles, or you can camp. Amenities include a bar and pool table and you have free use of surfboards and boogie boards. Nearby, you can charter boats to take you **dolphin -** and (from March to September) **whale-watching**, and can arrange **abseiling** or **whitewater rafting** at nearby Oribi Gorge. The lodge also organizes cheap diving packages.

From here, one resort after another follows the shoreline to gritty, sprawling **PORT SHEPSTONE**, a dismal place where you won't want to linger for long, although there are a couple of reasonable beaches just south of the town centre, and it's the gateway to the nearby Oribi Gorge Nature Reserve (see p.482). The town is also the place to hop on one of the Banana Express steam train journeys (see box on p.482).

The Banana Express

A diesel train, the **Banana Express**, Princess Elizabeth Drive, Port Shepstone (☎039 682 1507 or 039 682 2455), chugs south from Port Shepstone to either the hamlet of Paddock or Izotsha along a scenic narrow-gauge railway twice a week on Tuesdays and Saturdays out of season. It's an outing in its own right rather than transport to the nature reserve. During December and January there are additional services (phone for details). The longer Paddock return trip leaves at 10am and takes six hours, meandering along the coastline and then inland through hilly country covered with banana and sugar-cane plantations, and costs R100. The trip includes a visit to the Zakhele Homecraft Training Centre and a ninety-minute stop for a DIY braai lunch on the lawns of the Paddock stationmaster's garden. The stationmaster's wife sells braai packs with salad for R30.

The shorter Izotsha return trip leaves at 11am and takes about two hours and costs R40 (first class recommended) or R30 tourist class (a bit windy, as the coaches have no glass in the windows).

Oribi Gorge Nature Reserve

The South Coast's most compelling attraction is the **Oribi Gorge Nature Reserve** (daily 8am–4.30pm; ☎039 679 1644, ⓦwww.kznwildlife.com; R10), about 21km inland (west) from Port Shepstone. A highly scenic area with cliffs rising from vast chasms and jungly forest, it's traversed by the fast-flowing Umzimkulu and Umzimkulwana rivers. There are numerous other idyllic picnic spots on the riverbanks (avoid swimming here, as bilharzia parasites are present in the water) and waymarked **hikes** ranging from thirty-minute to day-long excursions leading to dizzying look-out points or through the forest. A fine one-hour **walk** starts from the Umzimkulu car park and picnic site, crosses the river and heads immediately up some steps into the forest. You can hear the river through the dense vegetation, but you'll only see it when it opens out quite dramatically to reveal **Samango Falls** and a perfect little rock-bounded sandy beach.

Wildlife in the reserve includes bushbuck, common reedbuck, blue and grey duiker, but not oribi, which have left for the succulent shoots of the surrounding sugar cane plantations. You're more likely to hear than to see the shy samango monkeys, hiding in the high canopy of the forest, and although leopards are present it's probable that they'll see you before you catch sight of them.

Practicalities

Travelling by car to Durban from the Eastern Cape along the N2, you'll find the reserve just a few hundred metres signposted off the main road. You can also get here by train from Port Shepstone on the Banana Express (see box above), though this is more of an excursion than a convenient means of transport.

The nicest accommodation is in the KZN Wildlife huts (❷) in the **restcamp** at the head of the Umzinkulwana Gorge, peering into the chasm of Oribi Gorge itself. There's a swimming pool here, and all crockery, cutlery and bedding is provided. Booking ahead is recommended (contact KZN Wildlife ☎033 845 1002). Alternatively, you can stay in the old-fashioned, colonial-style *Oribi Gorge Hotel* (☎039 687 0253, ⓔoribigorge@worldonline.co.za; ❸), some 16km from the restcamp, off the Oribi Flats road, which has spectacular views, including the famous overhanging rock and offers spacious good-value rooms, meals to suit most budgets and a pleasant outdoor tea area. They also accommodate backpackers in a separate cottage (❶). From here, you can arrange to tackle one of the world's highest commercial abseils (110m), white-water rafting, scuba diving, deep-sea fishing, plane trips through the gorge, hiking trails, and bird-watching. Abseiling costs around R140 and rafting around R260 per person.

The Hibiscus Coast

The 44km of coast from Port Shepstone to Port Edward has been dubbed the Hibiscus Coast because of its luscious, bright gardens, luxury suburbs, beach-side developments and attractive caravan parks. It's also known as the Golf Coast: there are seven top courses on this short stretch of coastline, and many people come specifically to the area for its golfing opportunities. Although the whole area, the centre of which is at Margate, is built-up, the Hibiscus Coast gets nicer the further south you go, escaping the development.

Uvongo

Some 12km south of Port Shepstone, the Vungu River narrows into a gorge and crashes down a **waterfall** before opening out onto a broad sandy beach at **UVONGO**. The waterfall is definitely the town's biggest attraction; elsewhere, tatty cliff-top developments have destroyed much of the natural vegetation. To see the falls, take the path from the bottom of the cliffs to the rear of the beach and follow the steps in the corner away from the river, following the path through some undergrowth until you reach the viewpoint on a ledge. Uvongo's pleasant beach is the site of a daily market, where Zulu women sell fruit, crafts and good-quality basketwork.

One of the most comfortable **places to stay** is *Glyndale Guest Lodge*, just east of the beach (℡039 315 0918; ❷), with a good full-board rate outside school holidays and nice gardens, a swimming pool and an excellent sea view. Nearby, the *Uvongo Beach Lodge*, Pioneer Road (℡039 315 0013, ℻039 315 5194; full board ❸), is a bit old-fashioned, but it's only a three-minute stroll from the beach. If you want something smarter, the very appealing thatched *Shaka's Inhlaba Lodge*, Riviera Crescent (℡039 315 5171, ✉shakas@adventurenet.co.za; ❹) to the west of *Uvongo Beach Lodge*, offers B&B rooms and excellent, inexpensive home-cooked pub lunches and dinners. Even if you're not staying, the pub is recommended. If you're after a cottage for a weekend or short break, contact the Shelly Beach Information Centre (℡039 315 0265) which can help you find accommodation in Uvongo itself and also all the way down to Ramsgate.

The best **places to eat** are the *Pavilion*, a restaurant right on the beach with a curving glazed frontage looking out to sea, and the *Edelweiss* in town, which serves excellent food at reasonable prices.

Margate

The brash, built-up holiday town of **MARGATE**, 2km south of Uvongo, is the South Coast's undisputed tourism hub. Connected by daily direct SAA **flights** with Johannesburg and by buses with Gauteng and Durban (see p.480), Margate is as far as you'll get down the South Coast using public transport. With its high-rise apartments, fast-food outlets, and ice-cream parlours, Margate offers little in the way of undiscovered coves or hidden beaches. However, its big plus point is the wide choice of good-value places to stay, especially out of season (see p.484).

It's worth making use of Margate's **tourist information** bureau on the beachfront (Mon–Fri 8.30am–4pm, Sat 9–11am; ℡039 312 2322), which can provide details of accommodation and general information about the whole South Coast area.

Five minutes south of Margate, across the lagoon in Ramsgate, it's worth stopping off at the Gaze Gallery (9am–5.30pm; free), which displays some reputable work by local artists, and sampling the best waffles in the province at the attached waterside *Waffle House*.

Accommodation

The Courthouse 2079 Buck Drive, ☎ & ℉039 314 4046. Four beautiful upmarket self-catering apartments along the water, all with four-poster beds and some with Jacuzzis, a couple of kilometres south of Margate in the adjacent town of Ramsgate. ❸–❹

De Wet Caravan Park St Andrews Avenue, along the beachfront ☎039 312 1022. Fully equipped four-berth caravans, park homes and grassy campsites. ❶

Margate Backpackers 14 Collis St, Manaba Beach ☎039 312 2176, ℮ulrike@adventurenet.co.za. Dorms, doubles and camping are offered at a hostel that is almost on the beach and only 200m from a great tidal pool. The hostel has a big self-catering kitchen, as well as a pool table; shark diving and deep-sea fishing can also be arranged. ❶

Margate Hotel Marine Drive ☎039 312 1410, ℉039 317 3318. Very comfortable accommodation near the centre of town, right on the beach, with discounts offered out of season. ❸

Skipper's Lagoon Road ☎039 315 1223, ⓦwww.mrinfo.co.za. An old-fashioned, but clean and well-maintained boarding house close to the centre. Popular with South African families, it overlooks the beach amusement park. ❷

Suntide Resort and Cabanas Duke Road ☎039 317 4010. Excellent-value, comfortable and modern self-catering apartments in a quiet stretch right on the beach. The only drawback is that most doubles face onto the car park; you're better off paying a little extra and, even if there are only two of you, taking a larger, sea-facing four-bed apartment. ❷–❸

Southbroom, Palm Beach and Port Edward

Some 7km beyond Margate, **SOUTHBROOM** is known disparagingly as "Houghton-by-Sea" after Johannesburg's wealthiest suburb, which allegedly relocates here en masse in December. The town is predominantly a sumptuous development of large holiday houses set in expansive gardens; out of season, it can feel quite deserted. Huge dunes covered by lush vegetation sweep down to the sea, and there are good long walks along the shore – although heading out alone isn't advisable along this coastline for safety reasons. The best place for swimming is **Marina Beach**, 3km south of Southbroom Beach. Southbroom is home to the area's most upmarket **hotel**, the tranquil *Country Lodge*, signposted off the R61 to Port Edward (☎039 316 8380, ⓦwww.countrylodge.co.za; half board ❺), a romantically secluded place surrounded by forest, away from the beachfront buzz. Champagne breakfast and light meals are served at the marvellous *Treehouse Restaurant* on the premises. You can also eat at the *Cycad Restaurant*, adjoining the Lodge building, with a menu that includes delicacies like curried kudu and saffron and sweet potato gnocchi.

On the R61 at the sign for *Country Lodge*, S'khumba Crafts is a recommended stopoff where you can have a coffee in soothing forest surrounds and look at the finely crafted leather footwear. Besides *Country Lodge*, other **places to eat** are the *Riptide Restaurant*, which is highly rated for its excellent wellpriced seafood; the *Trattoria*, which, no surprises here, serves Italian food; or *The Bistro*, known for its Beef Wellington. For **pubs**, the *Pistols Saloon,* adjoining the *Old Bavaria* restaurant on the road to Port Edward is notable for its resident pet pig, Bandit, with a penchant for crisps and beer.

Heading closer to Port Edward, which marks the border with the Eastern Cape, you'll soon get to **Palm Beach**, a rocky beach bordered with banana palms with a tidal pool for swimming, and one of the quietest spots along the South Coast.

The main attraction of **PORT EDWARD**, 9km further on, is its proximity to the Umtamvuna Nature Reserve (see below). Nevertheless, it's a fairly relaxed and pleasant resort, with some nice sandy beaches. There are some good **places to stay** near the beach. *Windwood Lodge*, adjoining *Sleepers' Restaurant*, Owen Ellis Drive (℡039 313 2169, ✉woodldg@iafrica.com; ➋), is a smart, family-oriented guesthouse some 500m from the seafront. Right next door, if you can handle the institutionalized flavour, the *Port Edward Holiday Resort* (℡039 313 2333, ✉peresort@venturenet.co.za), is mainly used by the South African Police Service for rest and recreation for their staff, has a perfect setting along the seafront and is close to the swimming beach, with cheap caravans, camping and older rondavels (➊) as well as more modern chalets (➋) ideal for families. Facilities are available for disabled visitors.

Moving west from Port Edward, the only public transport is the minibus taxis that form a lively rank on the R61 just outside town, collecting passengers for the Eastern Cape, many heading across the old Transkei border to gamble at the *Wild Coast Sun* casino (see p.439).

Umtamvuna Nature Reserve

Some of the best nature walks in the whole of KwaZulu-Natal are to be found at the **Umtamvuna Nature Reserve** (daily: April–Aug 7am–5pm; Sept–March 6am–6pm; R5), about 8km north of Port Edward. Extending 19km upriver along the tropical Umtamvuna River and the forested cliffs rising above it, the reserve is well known for its spring flowers, and the sunbirds and sugar birds feeding on the nectar. It's home to three hundred species of birds, including a famous colony of rare Cape **vultures**, though to see where they nest you'll have to be prepared for a whole day's walk. Waymarked paths are dotted throughout the reserve.

Umtamvuna is off the R61 to Izingolweni, signposted near Port Edward. If you want to **stay overnight**, head for one of the pleasant options nearby. *Umtamvuna River Lodge*, Old Pont Rd (℡039 313 2313, ⊛www.riverlodge .co.za; ➋), has ten good B&B rooms in tranquil forested surroundings on the banks of the river inside the reserve. Canoeing and water-skiing are available, and there are also nature trails. *Old Pont Holiday Resort*, Old Pont Rd, Banners Rest ℡039 313 2211, ℻039 313 2033; ➊–➋), is also on the banks of the river, has a swimming pool and is a good spot for fishing, with jetskis for rent. Six- and four-berth caravans and camping are available, as well as six-person rondavels and three-bedroom park homes. There's a useful shop selling basics.

A few hundred metres along the same road, turn right to the highly recommended *Vuna Valley Backpackers* (℡083 992 6999, ✉vunavalley@hotmail.com; ➊), which has four attractive dorms and a double. Meals can be provided on request, although the emphasis is on self-catering, and horse-riding, hiking, canoeing, surfing and dolphin-watching can be arranged.

North of Durban: the Dolphin Coast

The Dolphin Coast is the appealing name given to the eighty-kilometre stretch along the coast north of Durban, from Umhlanga Rocks to the mouth of the Tugela River. This narrow, continental shelf combines with warm, shallow waters to create ideal conditions for attracting bottle-nosed dolphins all year round to feed. Though the chances of sighting a cetacean are fairly high, you'd be unwise to base a visit solely around the possibility.

Less tacky and developed than the South Coast, the North Coast attracts an upmarket breed of holidaymaker, especially to the main resorts of **Ballito** and **Salt Rock**. If you're after an easy beachside holiday close to Durban, **Umhlanga Rocks**, less than half an hour's drive from the centre of the city, and served by public transport, is the best choice. The beaches here are long, steep and sandy, backed by banana palms, with warm strong surf, and shark nets to protect swimmers.

Rolling in from the coast are hills of sugar cane plantations, the main industry of the area (it was barons who established the first holiday retreats along the coastline). Driving along the roads here you'll be competing with long transport trucks, which litter the tarmac with dry stalks and strands of cane. While the Dolphin Coast is still pretty well dominated by whites, the inland towns of **Verulam**, **Tongaat** and **Dukuza** have substantial Zulu and Indian populations, but lack of facilities for travellers.

Umhlanga Rocks

UMHLANGA ROCKS, 20km from the centre of Durban, is a substantial settlement with a permanent population of around 50,000, which merges with the suburb of Durban North, and makes a good day out from the city if you're after a beach walk, swim and a meal, or even an alternative place to stay.

The town's main attraction is as a swish resort offering hotel-based holidays. The pleasant, sandy beach dominated by a red-and-white lighthouse, while the town's shopping area along Chartwell Drive has a collection of smart, well-stocked malls as well as the monster Gateway Mall at Umhlanga Ridge, a massive shopping complex with 400 shops and 14 cinemas. To find it, follow the N2 from Durban and take the Umhlanga/Mt Edgecombe offramp, following the signs.

Nearby, also a couple of kilometres north of Umhlanga's centre, signposted off the N2, the **Natal Sharks Board**, 1a Herrwood Drive (☎031 566 0400; R12), shows a multiscreen audiovisual about sharks and conducts a dissection of a recently caught shark (Tues, Wed & Thurs 9am & 2pm, Sun 2pm), which disabuses any notions of sharks as the hooligans of the oceans and plugs the work of the Board in maintaining Natal's shark nets. Although these nets protect swimmers all along the coast, they are controversial: endangered turtles and dolphins also die in them, and by killing sharks, the natural balance of the inshore ecosystem is affected. The Sharks Board is now investigating an electronic shark barrier that might improve the situation, while still ensuring safe swimming. If you take an early-morning **boat trip** on a Sharks Board skiboat (when staff service the shark nets off the beaches), look out for dolphins and whales. Bookings for this two-hour trip are done by phone (☎082 403 9206, 4–5pm daily). Trips cost R100 per person, depart at 6am, and a minimum of eleven passengers are needed for the trip to run. Without your own transport, the best way to get to the Sharks Board is by minibus taxi or shuttle, outside the Umhlanga Publicity Association.

Practicalities

The Sugar Coast Tourism Association, Chartwell Drive (Mon–Fri 8am–4.30pm, Sat 9am–noon; ☎031 561 4257), is a useful source for **maps and information** about attractions up the coast. Outside, you'll find the departure point for the Umhlanga Express minibus service (☎082 268 0651), which runs trips on request to the Musgrave Centre in Berea and to Durban city centre.

Accommodation

Beverly Hills Sun Lighthouse Road ☎031 561 2211, ⓦwww.southernsun.com. The flashest place to stay in Umhlanga, but you'll get better value at half the price at the more characterful *Oyster Box*. **❼**
Honey Pot Cottage 11 Hilken Drive, north of the M4 ☎031 561 3795, ⓔsugarfld@iafrica.com. Five B&B units that sleep two, set in gardens with a swimming pool. **❸**
Jessica's B&B 35 Portland Drive ☎ & ⓕ031 561 3369. Two self-contained flats accommodating four people in each. **❹**

Oyster Box Lighthouse Road ☎031 561 2233, ⓔoysterbox@iafrica.com. The oldest hotel on the Dolphin Coast oozes established elegance with a choice of rooms. The *Box* is also a great place for tea or drinks on the outside terrace overlooking the ocean. **❹–❺**
Sylvan Grove 49 Sylvan Grove ☎031 561 5137, ⓔsylvangrove@mweb.co.za. Four rooms in a sea facing guesthouse in a tropical garden, offering great breakfasts and also convenient transfers from Durban airport. **❹**

Eating

Ambrosia Chartwell Drive. A recommended Greek eating place, with exceptionally friendly staff.
Cottonfields 2 Lagoon Drive. A popular local bistro and bar whose menu features *potjiekos* served in a small three-legged cast-iron pots. Daily noon till late.
Ming Bow Hillcon Centre, Chartwell Drive. The prawn omelette and tasty crab dishes are recommended at this Cantonese restaurant. Daily 5.30–10pm.
Oyster Box Grill Room At the *Oyster Box Hotel*, Lighthouse Road. First-class curries and great seafood at one of the few eating places around offering dancing on a Saturday night. Daily

noon–3am.
Razzmatazz At the *Cabana Beach Hotel*, Lagoon Drive. If you can afford to splash out, look no further. The restaurant has a great outdoor deck overlooking the ocean, and a big reputation for its eclectic cuisine, which ranges from springbok fillets to Indonesian-style langoustines, with an emphasis on seafood and game dishes. Daily lunch and dinner.
Sailor's La Lucia Mall. A family restaurant offering a wide selection of seafood, steaks and Mediterranean-style specials. Tues–Sun 10.30am–10.30pm.

Umdloti, La Mercy and Tongaat

North of Umhlanga, the blur of development unexpectedly opens out into sugar cane hills and subtropical coastal vegetation. **UMDLOTI**, just 6km north of Umhlanga, has a safe swimming beach, as well as a fabulous natural rock pool, great for swimming or snorkelling on the calm inside of the shallow reef. A couple of kilometres further along at **LA MERCY** is a highly recommended **restaurant** – the long-established *Sea Bell*, a slightly tatty curry house under a dingy hotel, which is noted for its piquant prawns (there's also a vegetarian alternative).

Three kilometres north of the restaurant, you'll come to **Causarina Beach**, the location of *Beachbums Backpackers Lodge*, 65 Causarina Drive (☎032 943 1401 or 082 4458 951, ⓔbsbeach@iafrica.com; **❶**), which lies literally right on the beach. This is the only **backpacker lodge** in the area, and conveniently on the Baz Bus route. The two-storey home is famed for its pizza and has three double rooms and eleven dorm beds; there's also space to camp. It's a good place to chill out, with two sundecks overlooking the ocean; the lodge can also provide free surfboards and bodyboards. Five minutes away lies **Westbrook Beach**, good for swimming and with a popular surfing break.

TONGAAT lies a few kilometres inland from here across the N2 highway, a barrier between the coastal resorts and the industrial workings of Natal's sugar industry. Arriving in town, you're confronted by a massive sugar mill pumping pungent white smoke from its towering chimneys, and people walking down the road chewing sticks of sugar cane. The town, fronted by neglected imitation Cape Dutch cottages, has long associations with South Africa's Indian community and boasts a handful of garish temples. The most distinguished of these is the small but awesome **Shri Jugganath Puri Temple**, off the main road, on the corner of Catherine and Plane streets. A whitewashed, phallic building tipped by deities on each corner, and surrounded by mango trees, the temple is dedicated to Vishnu and is a National Monument, built at the turn of the century by the Sanskrit scholar Pandit Shrikishan Maharaj who came to Natal in 1895. To get to the temple, take the R102 towards Durban, turn right into Ganie Street at the first traffic lights after the police station, then left into Plane Street and left again into Catherine Street.

Ballito

There's nothing very African about **BALLITO**, a Mediterranean-style resort 43km up the coast from Durban, with a splurge of time-shares, high-rise holiday apartments and shopping malls by the sea. Nevertheless, it's a pleasant enough place, with a beach offering safe swimming and full-time lifeguards, and a couple of natural rock pools for bathing – one at Ballito itself, and the other at the far northern end of Ballito Beach, near the Santorini development. The area is also well-known for its luxury guesthouses on wealthy sugar estates, set back from the coast and all signposted from the N1.

The excellent Dolphin Coast Publicity Association (Mon–Fri 8.30am–4.30pm; ☎ & ℱ 032 946 1997), just before the BP service station as you enter town, has an up-to-date list of B&Bs and can supply **information** about the surrounding area.

Even if the accommodation (see below) is beyond your budget, it's worth stopping off here for a meal in the *Zimbali Lodge's* **restaurant**, a cup of tea or, best of all, a sundowner in the bar, which is raised on stilts overlooking the fourteenth fairway of the golf course, and rewards you with soaring views across the Indian Ocean. In Ballito itself, the best place to eat is *Mariner's*, Ballito Shopping Centre, Compensation Beach Road, which serves pricey but outstanding seafood.

Accommodation

Dolphin Holiday Resort On the corner of Compensation Beach Road and Hillary Drive ☎ 032 946 2187, ⓦ www.dolphinholidayresort.co.za. A well-shaded campsite and collection of self-catering cottages; there's no sea view, but it's only a five-minute walk from the beach. ❶
Shorten's Country House Compensation Beach Road ☎ 032 947 1140, ⓦ www.threecities.co.za. Elegant accommodation in a historic colonial homestead, with fourteen luxury rooms surrounded by wonderful gardens. ❺

Zimbali Lodge 1km south of Ballito ☎ 032 538 1007, ⓦ www.sun-international.com. The swishest establishment in the vicinity is set in lush subtropical coastal forest in the heart of a network of wetlands. Antelope are frequently seen, and the butterflies, such as the citrus swallowtail, are larger than life, and the birdlife is prolific – you might even see the rare spotted narina trogon. Accommodation is in luxury suites attended by private butlers, and you can avail yourself of clay-pigeon shooting, beach or forest walks, steam-rooms, massages, and pedicures. ❼

Shaka's Rock

Some 49km north of Durban, the rather tame coastal resort of **SHAKA'S ROCK** feels at odds with the name of Shaka, whose warrior reputation reverberated across southern Africa in the nineteenth century. More or less a continuation of Ballito, Shaka's Rock is dominated by the *Salt Rock*, Basil Hulett Drive (☎032 525 5025; ❹), a **hotel** built and still run by the Huletts, one of the region's biggest sugar dynasties. The beach here is good for swimming, and guests can go on daily excursions diving with the dolphins. Adjoining the hotel is its **caravan park** (❶), situated on grassy terraces. Two tidal pools, great for swimming, are built into the rocks below the hotel; this is where Zulu women are reputed to have collected salt in King Shaka's day. There's an even better tidal rock pool at Thompson's Bay, built on an elevated rocky platform with changing rooms and big enough for anyone wanting to swim serious lengths. To get to Thompson's Bay, simply walk back along the beach towards Ballito, about 2km from the *Salt Rock Hotel*.

Dukuza and Groutville

You'll get far more of a sense of Shaka's legendary status as founder of the Zulu state by heading inland along the R102 to **DUKUZA** (still widely known by it's pre-1994 election name, Stanger), which has a special place in the cosmology of Zulu nationalists. Roughly 70km north of Durban, KwaDukuza is the site of the Zulu king's last *kraal* and the place where he was treacherously stabbed to death in 1828 by his half-brother Dingane, who succeeded him. Shaka used his exceptional military talents to build up the Zulu state into the greatest power in southeast Africa by the mid-1820s – creating disquiet even among the British with their mighty army. The warrior-king is said to have been buried upright in a grain pit, and is commemorated by a small park and memorial in Couper Street, right in the centre of town. Near the memorial is a rock with a groove worn into it – supposedly where Shaka sharpened his spears. These days, the park is the venue for a semi-religious pilgrimage by modern-day **Zulu warriors** from all over the country – members of the fiercely Zulu nationalist Inkatha Freedom Party (IFP), which controls the province. Every year, on September 24, formerly Shaka's Day, now Heroes' Day, they gather here to be addressed by their leader, **Chief Mangosuthu Buthelezi**, a mercurial figure who started his political life as an ANC member, but later fell out with the organization. Those attending Buthelezi's speech are often colourfully clad in traditional Zulu garb and armed with traditional weapons.

At the rear of the memorial park, the **Dukuza Interpretative Centre** (Mon–Fri 8am–4pm, Sat & Sun 9am–4pm; free) has a small display on Shaka and a very good fifteen-minute audiovisual display; you can also see craftspeople at work and sample traditional meals in an attached café. Nearby, the lively **Dukuza Market** in Market Road, off King George Road, is where Zulu and Indian traders sell fresh spices, herbs, fruit and vegetables, not for the benefit of tourists (you're unlikely to meet any here), but simply for local consumption.

Some 8km south of Dukuza on the R102, just across a rusty bridge over the Mvoti River, tiny **GROUTVILLE** is remarkable mainly for the grave of **Albert Luthuli**, one of South Africa's greatest political leaders. A teacher and chief of the Zulus in Groutville, Luthuli became President General of the ANC in 1952. Advocating a non-violent struggle against apartheid, Luthuli was awarded the Nobel Peace Prize in 1960, which at home earned him a succession of banning orders restricting him to the Dukuza area. In 1967, he died in mysterious circumstances in KwaDukuza, apparently knocked down by a train. He is buried next to a whitewashed, nineteenth-century corrugated-iron mission church. Luthuli's life is recounted in a moving autobiography, *Let My People Go*.

Blythedale

The closest stretch of sand to Dukuza is at **BLYTHEDALE**, some 8km away, where a ban on high-rise construction has preserved the deserted appearance of its endless beach and kept buildings screened behind the curtain of thick coastal vegetation. Swimming here is possible; shark nets are in place between December and April, and lifeguards are on duty in season. As with many spots along the KwaZulu-Natal coast, you're likely to see local fishermen trying their luck for shad, garrick, kingfish and barracuda.

Accommodation

Baroque B&B 14 Dolphin Crescent ☎ 032 551 5272. Attractive and reasonably priced rooms with en-suite showers, 150m from the beach. ❷

Bush and Beach 71 Umvoti Drive ☎ 032 551 1496, ℗ 032 551 1546. Pleasant cottages located in a nice setting. ❷–❸

La Mouette Caravan Park 1 Umvoti Drive ☎ 032 551 2547. Camping and a small self-catering log cabin are offered, just back from the beach. ❶

Mini Villas Just across the road from the caravan park ☎ 032 551 1277, ℗ 032 551 1628. Budget cottages to rent. ❶

Palm Dunes Umvoti Drive ☎ 032 552 1588, ℮ palmdunes@maggie.co.za. Self-catering or B&B at an upmarket resort and conference centre, chalet or a double room. The resort also offers jet-skis, canoes, a theatre (in season), and can arrange guided hiking and mountain biking in the nearby forests. ❸–❹

Harold Johnson Nature Reserve

Abutting the Tugela River is the KwaZulu-Natal Wildlife **Harold Johnson Nature Reserve** (daily dawn–dusk; R10), signposted 24km north of Dukuza off the N2 (take the Zinkwazi turn-off and turn left at Darnall). With its well-preserved coastal bush, steep cliffs and gullies, this is a fine place to come for a day's visit or to camp overnight (☎ 032 486 1574); it's possible to simply turn up, but there are no shops or facilities, so be sure to stock up in Dukuza beforehand. At the main picnic site and parking area, you'll find a cultural museum housed in huts and featuring good displays of Zulu beadwork and aspects of Zulu society. You can follow the two-kilometre "Remedies and Rituals" **trail**, which starts from the picnic site and takes you through plants whose medicinal uses you can read about. Alternatively, pick up the Thukela Trail booklet and follow a walk which highlights various historical sites in the reserve, most of them connected to the Anglo-Zulu War of 1879 and Ultimatum Tree. This wild fig tree, all but demolished in a cyclone in 1987, was where the British issued their ultimatum to King Cetshwayo in 1878, part of which required the Zulus to demobilize their standing army. The British used his non-compliance as an excuse to attack the Zulus and crush their independence. The remains of Fort Pearson, from which the British launched their invasion of Zululand, are also on the trail.

Valley of a Thousand Hills

The evocatively named **Valley of a Thousand Hills**, 45km from Durban, makes for a picturesque drive along the edge of densely folded hills where Zulu people still live in traditional homesteads, and which visitors rarely venture into. The spectacular landscape goes some way to soothing any misgivings you might have about ethnographic "game viewing", but it's only worth a special effort if you're not exploring the KwaZulu-Natal interior, where scenes like this occur in abundance.

The trip to the valley and back can be done in half a day, but there are sufficient attractions laid on along the route to extend it to a full day's outing. Of the several good places to stay, *The Rob Roy Hotel*, Rob Roy Crescent, Botha's Hill (℡031 777 1305, ⓦwww.robroyhotel.co.za; ❹), is the most appealing, with magnificent views over the valley; it's a good stop for tea or lunch, with curio shops and an animal farmyard for kids.

While the valley is best suited to touring in your own car, there are **daily tours** from Durban offered by Tekweni Eco Tours (see p.456) which take in the highlights. Alternatively, if you're in Durban on the last Sunday of the month, take a **vintage train trip** with Umgeni Steam Railways (℡082 353 6003; R45; trains leave at 8:45am and 12:30pm), which boasts one of the largest collections of historic locomotives and coaches in the southern hemisphere.

If you're self-driving, head inland from Durban along the N3, following the Pinetown signs. At the Hillcrest/Old Main Road turn-off, turn right over the freeway onto the Old Main Road (R103) and continue along here following the Thousand Hills Experience Route sign. Within a kilometre you'll pass the thriving Victorian-styled **Heritage Market**, with craft shops, restaurants and jewellery stores. Continue for several kilometres, past the Fainting Goat, a small shopping centre, and a selection of interesting shops, including the Swazi Candle Shop and the appealing *Pot & Kettle* restaurant and gallery, which offers unparalleled views of the Thousand Hills. Just around the bend is **Phezulu Safari Park** (daily 8.30am–4.30pm; R40), which brings you close to deadly serpents – though they're tucked away in cramped little glass boxes – crocodiles, and other penned animals. Give it a miss if you're heading onto the real game reserves, just a few hours, unless you want to see the reconstruction of a pre-colonial Zulu village, where you can watch tourist-orientated – but nonetheless spirited – displays of **Zulu dancing**, set against the dramatic horizon of the valley (daily 10am, 11.30am, 2pm & 3.30pm; price included in R40 entrance fee).

Pietermaritzburg

Although **PIETERMARITZBURG** (often called Maritzburg) sells itself as the best-preserved Victorian city in South Africa, with strong British connections, little of its colonial heritage remains, and it's actually a very South African city. Zulus make up the largest community, with people of **Indian** descent coming second, and those of **British** extraction a minority – albeit a high-profile one. This multiculturalism, together with a substantial student population, adds up to a fairly lively city that's also relatively safe and small enough to explore on foot.

Only 80km inland from Durban along the fast N3 freeway, Pietermaritzburg is an easy day's outing from the coastal city, and one you can do taking in the Valley of a Thousand Hills (see opposite) along the way. Maritzburg is also well positioned for an overnight stop on your way to the Drakensberg (see p.499) or the Battlefields in the Ladysmith (see p.549) vicinity.

Some history

Pietermaritzburg's Afrikaner origins are reflected in its name; after slaughtering three thousand Zulus at the Battle of Blood River, the Voortrekkers established the fledgling Republic of Natalia in 1839, naming their capital in honour of the Boer leaders Piet Retief and Gerrit Maritz. The republic's inde-

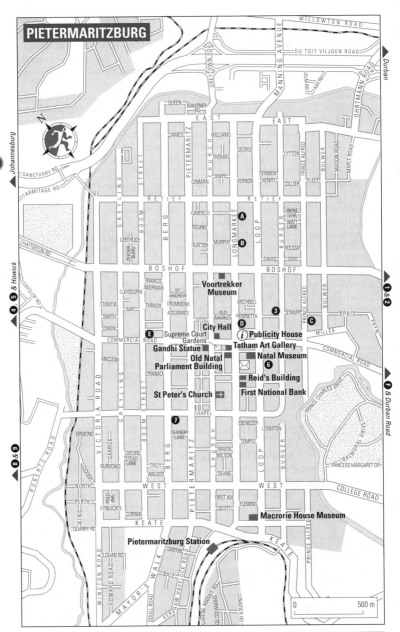

PIETERMARITZBURG

WILLOWTON ROAD
DU TOIT VILJOEN ROAD
Durban
GREYTOWN ROAD
MANNING AVENUE
OHRTMANN ROAD

Johannesburg
SANCTUARY RD
ARMITAGE RD

QUEEN
CHUTNEY RD
EAST
EAST
JAMES
WILLIAMS
CHURCH STREET
THOMAS
GEORGE
PIETERMARITZ STREET
KNIPE
DERWENT
VERNON
HENRY
GINMAN
COLLIER
LYTTON
PRINCE ALFRED
FLEET
BULWER
MASON ROAD
MAPLE ROAD

RETIEF
RETIEF
GARFIELD
A
LOOP
IRENE TERR
WATT LANE
GREYLING
BOOM STREET
BERG
BOURKE
LONGMARKET
BURGER
SLATTER
MURPHY
B
HOLIDAY
GERTRUDE
ZIEBR-BURG
DAVIS
DOIG

CHATTERTON RD
BOSHOF
BOSHOF

4 5 & Howick
HYSLOP RD
FRANCIS
AKERMAN
CLAYBOURNE
ST ANDREW
DRUMMOND
Voortrekker Museum
ARCHBELL
PRINCE ALFRED
BULWER
BRAID
STANTIAL
SMITH
MAY
THRASH
ASSURANCE
HENRIETTA
3
STRAPP
C
PAYN
OWEN
OTTO
OLD MARKET
MILLER
COMMERCIAL ROAD
City Hall
D
i **Publicity House**
COMMERCIAL ROAD
MACLEAN
E
Supreme Court Gardens
Tatham Art Gallery
Gandhi Statue
Old Natal Parliament Building
Natal Museum
6
STRANACK
St Peter's Church
Reid's Building
First National Bank
CHAPEL

VICTORIA ROAD
GREYLING STREET
BOOM STREET
DEANERY LANE
7
PIETERMARITZ STREET
CHURCH STREET
EBENEZER
TEMPLE
LEIGHTON
LOOP
BURGER
PRINCE CHARLES DRIVE
ORMOND
GARRICK
OXFORD STEAD LANE
BURROWS
TROY LANE
WALKER
RAVEN-WILSON
DEANE
BALMORAL DRIVE
PRINCESS MARGARET DR

1 & 2

F & Durban Road

COMMERCIAL ROAD

PRINCE CHARLES DRIVE

8 & 9
ROBERTS ROAD
KING
NORTH
PERTH
PECOU AVE
SYNDICATE
CURRAN
QUARRY RD
WEST
WEST
FIRST AVE
SCOTT
FLEMING
KEATE
Macrorie House Museum
COLLEGE ROAD
PRINCE ALFRED

WINSTON ROAD
HOWARD ROAD
LOGAN RD
Pietermaritzburg Station
GRIFFIN
BALE
KEATE
MAYOR'S WALK
DOULL ROAD
KAW HAVELOCK ROAD
EUGENE MARAIS RD
DOCKWERS
NAPIER RD

0   500 m

ACCOMMODATION

African Dreamz	8	Duvet & Crumpets	9
Ascot Inn	1	Imperial Hotel	6
Briar Ghyll Lodge	5	Rehoboth Cottages	2
City Royal Hotel	3	Sunduzi Backpacker Lodge	7
Crossways Country Inn	4		

RESTAURANTS

Café du Midi	E	Restaurant da Vinci	F
Characters	C	Tropicana	A
Els Amics	B	Upper Crust	D

pendence was short-lived; only four years later, Britain annexed it and spent the rest of the century transforming Pietermaritzburg into an English town stamped with all the grandeur and pomposity of empire. Even as the Afrikaners trekked north to escape the irksome British, English settlers were arriving from the south to swell the city's population, and during the closing decade of the nineteenth century, Maritzburg was the most important centre in the colony of Natal with a population of nearly 10,000 (more than Durban at that time).

Indians arrived at the turn of the twentieth century, mostly as indentured labourers, but also as traders. Among their number was a young, little-known lawyer called Mohandas Gandhi, who went on to change the history of India. He later traced the embryo of his devastatingly successful tactic of passive resistance to an incident in 1893, when as a non-white he was thrown out of a first-class train compartment at Pietermaritzburg station.

Pietermaritzburg is the provincial capital of KwaZulu-Natal, but its exact status is ambiguous, as Ulundi, in the former KwaZulu *bantustan*, is currently striving for recognition as the political centre of the province.

Arrival and information

Daily flights from Johannesburg, used mainly by business travellers, arrive at the city's **Oribi airport** (☏033 386 9577), about 6km south of the town centre. The only means of getting from here to town is by taxi. It's far easier to fly into Durban airport (see p.453), which is connected twice daily to Pietermaritzburg by the Cheetah intercity shuttle bus (☏033 342 0266). The journey takes about 75 minutes and the bus drops off outside the *Imperial Hotel*, 224 Loop St. The Cheetah also picks up passengers in the centre of Durban, outside the Local History Museum in Aliwal Street and Durban Station at the motorcoach terminal. Intercape **intercity buses** pull in at the bus terminal on the north side of the information bureau, on the corner of Longmarket Street and Commercial Road. From here, you can walk to the most central of the city hotels or take a taxi, which is also your best option to get to the suburban B&Bs. Greyhound buses also stop nearby, at *MacDonald's* in Burger Street, while Translux pulls in at the Premier Caltex garage on the corner of Commercial and Burger streets. If you're staying at the backpacker lodge, you can arrange for staff to pick you up; alternatively, the **Baz Bus** drops off at any of the central places to stay.

Arriving **by train**, the station (☏033 897 2350) lies at the unsavoury southwest end of Longmarket Street, one of the main city thoroughfares. The station's down-at-heel environs make it advisable to arrange beforehand to be collected, particularly at night.

The **tourist information** bureau at Publicity House, on the corner of Longmarket Street and Commercial Road (Mon–Fri 8am–5pm, Sat 8am–3pm; ☏033 345 1348), stocks an excellent selection of books and accommodation leaflets; you can buy tickets for Translux and Greyhound buses in the same building. If you intend to stay any length of time and plan to travel into the suburbs, a fold-out map of the whole city will come in handy. The best place to find these is at Shuter & Shooter, 230 Church St, which also sells travel guides, natural history field guides and books covering Natal history.

The hectic **minibus taxi rank** lies outside the tourist information bureau, and stretches from the bus terminus right down the block (destinations are posted outside the taxis). Metered taxis should be booked in advance (see "Listings", p.497), and in this compact city are unlikely to break the bank.

Accommodation

Maritzburg has the whole gamut of accommodation, ranging from a good backpacker lodge – conveniently located for the station and the central nightspots – to self-catering places and cheap B&Bs around the university on the south side of town, and more comfortable B&Bs in the lush northern suburbs – ideal if you're in a car. You'll also find a handful of good-value hotels in the city centre; or try Pietermaritzburg B&B Network (℡082 897 4453).

African Dreamz 30 Taunton Rd, Wembley ℡ & ℗033 394 5141. One mini-suite in a family home on a large property 2km from the centre, where you can self-cater or get breakfast. Guests have use of the garden beside a stream, as well as the tennis court and swimming pool. ➊

Ascot Inn 210 Woodhouse Rd, Scottsville; about 4km east of the city centre ℡033 386 2226, ⓦwww.ascot-inn.co.za. A complex of comfortable mock-colonial cottages with a swimming pool, set on a large lawned property next to Scottsville race course and the N3. You can self-cater or eat in their dining room. ➋

Brevisbrook 28 Waverleydale Rd, Boughton ℡033 344 1402. Four en-suite rooms with private entrances, set in a large garden. There's a swimming pool and braai area, and breakfast can be served on the patio. ➌

Briar Ghyll Lodge George MacFarlane Lane, off Howick Road, Town Hill ℡033 342 2664, ⓦwww.bglodge.co.za. A magnificent Victorian homestead, 5km northwest of the city centre, on rolling lawns, with a tennis court and swimming pool. You can choose between spacious suites within the main homestead or two self-contained cottages. ➍

City Royal Hotel 301 Burger St, City Centre ℡033 394 7072, ⓦwww.cityroyalhotel.co.za. Pietermaritzburg's only four-star hotel is in a fully modernized 1930s building and caters mainly to business travellers. It's worth asking about their substantial discounts, offered over weekends and during school holidays. ➎

Crossways Country Inn Old Howick Road, Hilton ℡033 343 3267, ℗033 343 3273, ⓦwww.futurenet.co.za. Roughly 9km north of Pietermaritzburg, *Crossways* is a fine choice if you want to stay out of town. Modelled on an English country pub, with nice old furniture, it's also a good place to stop off for teas and lunches. ➍

Duvet and Crumpets 1 Freelands Place, Wembley, 2km north of the centre ℡ & ℗033 394 4133, ⓔdesrayb@lantic.net. Self-catering or B&B are offered in a simple but pleasantly furnished mini-apartment in a 1930s family home. ➊

Imperial Protea Hotel 224 Loop St, City Centre ℡033 342 6551, ⓔimperial@iafrica.com. Popular with business travellers, this grand red-brick hotel is looking a bit past its prime, with a huge entrance foyer, large rooms and heavy staircases. ➏

Rehoboth Cottages 276 Murray Rd, Hayfields ℡033 396 2312, ⓦwww.safarinow.com. Bright and cheerful mock-Victorian self-catering cottages, set in large gardens 6km south of the centre. A full English breakfast can be served as an extra. ➎

Sunduzi Backpacker Lodge 140 Berg St, City Centre ℡033 394 0072, ⓔsunduzi@hotmail.com. You'll find a party atmosphere at this centrally located lodge close to all the town nightspots. Choose from the family house, where bedrooms have been turned into dorms, or camping in the garden. Cheap meals (vegetarians catered for) are available, as are free pick-ups from the train or bus station, while the friendly staff can help you arrange trips around the country. ➊

The City

Most places of interest in Pietermaritzburg are within easy walking distance of the centre's heart, which is crossed by the junction of **Commercial Road** and **Longmarket Street**, cutting across it from the train station in the southwest. The inevitable old apartheid divisions are marked out by roads and railways, with the African majority crammed into townships south of the station, as they used to be excluded from the city centre. By contrast, Indians were allowed to bring their business into the city fringes, but only as far as Boshoff Street, northeast of Commercial Road. Around here, and in the nearby Asian suburbs of Woodlands, Mountain Rise and Willowton, you'll find the greatest concentration of shops selling cheap spicy snacks like *rotis* and *bunny chows*, as well as the city centre's mosques and Hindu temples. On the hills, northwest of the centre, the predominantly white and affluent suburbs of Wembley, Athlone and Montrose look down from their heights at the sweaty buzz in the valley below, while south of the centre, the **University of Natal-Pietermaritzburg campus** in Scottsville attracts large numbers of students to set up digs in the suburban houses.

City Hall, Tatham Art Gallery and around

The City Hall, on the corner of Commercial Road and Church Street, once achieved international fame when it was recognized by Ripley's *Believe it or Not* as the "largest work-laden brick building south of the equator". It's certainly a great example of late Victorian red-brick civic architecture, self-assuredly holding the prime spot in town, with wonderful detailing and an impressive fifteen-metre clock tower.

Across Commercial Road, the **Tatham Art Gallery** (Tues–Sun 10am-6pm; donation), another fine brick edifice, is the highlight of Pietermaritzburg's formal attractions, housing one of the country's best collections of international and local art. Completed in 1871 as the Supreme Court of the Colony of Natal, the building formed the central complex of the capital's defences when an invasion was feared during the Zulu War of 1879. In 1990, the building became home to the Tatham collection and the Zulus finally made it inside, with artworks by black South Africans exhibited alongside those by Pablo Picasso, Graham Sutherland, Edgar Degas, David Hockney and Henri Matisse.

Adjacent to the Tatham, firmly rooted on the corner of Longmarket and Commercial streets, the **Old Natal Parliament Building** represents a typical piece of imperial architecture. Started in 1889 for Queen Victoria's Jubilee, it borrows the grand language of columns and pediments from the Roman Empire. Standing amid the formal front gardens is a statue of the unamused "Queen Empress" wielding a distinctly Freudian combination of a sceptre and orb. From here, heading down Longmarket Street as far as Chapel Street, you'll pass a series of attractive period buildings, most notable of which are: the **post office**, a solid dressed stone pile built in 1903; the three-storey **Reid's Building**, a little further along and considered a daringly tall skyscraper in its day; and the **First National Bank**, even further along, which dates from 1903 and had its facade chosen from an Edwardian catalogue and shipped out from the mother country. Between this section of Longmarket and Church streets is the tightly gridded warren of alleyways known as **the Lanes**, a mostly pedestrianized quarter of lawyers' offices, takeaways, shops and an inordinate number of hairdressers. The area, which was the financial hub of Natal from 1888 to 1931 and housed four separate stock exchanges, is enjoyable to explore during the day, but is a notorious stamping ground of pickpockets, so stay alert and don't come here after dark. Any of the Lanes will bring you through to Church Street, which is worth wandering along back to Commercial Road to take in some more period buildings.

On the corner of Chapel Street, **St Peter's Church**, completed in 1857, was the base for Bishop John Colenso after he was kicked out of the Church of England for his liberal theological ideas and his role in championing the Zulu cause against the British. As you head up Church Street, back toward the City Hall, you can't miss the **Gandhi Statue**, unveiled on June 6, 1993, on the centenary of his ejection from a first-class train carriage at Pietermaritzburg station because he wasn't white. Adjacent to Gandhi, the **Supreme Court Gardens** on the corner of Commercial Road and Church Street, are filled with monuments to Britons who died fighting against the Zulus, the Boers and other European powers in two world wars.

On the corner of Longmarket and Boshoff streets, the **Voortrekker Museum** (Mon–Fri 9am–4pm, Sat 9am–1pm; R3), centres on the original Church of the Vow, built in 1838 by Boers in honour of their victory over the Zulus three years earlier at the Battle of Blood River. The church was their part of a bargain allegedly struck with God (see p.548). The museum connects with the Voortrekker roots of Pietermaritzburg and is worth a fleeting visit to gain some insight into life on trek. The most interesting items are the homemade children's toys and beautifully embroidered *kappies* (hats) which the women used to shield themselves from the sun. New additions include a replica of a Hindu Shiva temple and a Zulu hut, as well as a display relating to the French Prince Imperial, who died during the Zulu War of 1879. Across the lovely courtyard garden is the reconstructed house of **Andries Pretorius**, leader of the Voortrekkers at Blood River and the driving force behind the establishment of the Boer Republic of Natalia. The thatched house, originally built in 1846, is appealing for its sheer simplicity, which stands in contrast to fussy Victorian fashion.

Less inspiring is the **Natal Museum**, 237 Loop St (Mon–Fri 9am–4.30pm, Sat 10am–4pm, Sun 11am–3pm; R4), one block east of the Old Natal Parliament, with a collection of stuffed animals, dioramas, a small dinosaur display and a reconstruction of a late Victorian Maritzburg street. The best reason to visit is for the display of African sculpture, crafts and masks from across the continent, the highlight of which is a golden stool taken by British invaders as booty from the Asante people of Ghana. The museum also boasts the third largest butterfly collection in the world.

Continuing down Loop Street for about 1km, you'll reach Pine Street, on the corner of which is the **Macrorie House Museum** (Mon 11am–4pm Tues–Fri 9am–1pm; R5), a beautiful two-storey Victorian house with intricate wrought-iron detailing. The house, which contains furniture and relics of early British settlers, was built in 1862 and became the home of Bishop Macrorie from 1869 to 1891, after he arrived to take over from Bishop Colenso.

Striking northwest up Pine Street brings you to the classically Victorian **train station** at the end of Church Street. Although a little neglected in this now seedy part of town, the station remains notable for its alternating courses of red-brick and stone facings and for its fine wrought-iron lacework dripping from the forecourt eaves. As you enter the concourse, a small plaque on your

Alan Paton

Writer, teacher and politician **Alan Paton** was born in Pietermaritzburg in 1903. *Cry, the Beloved Country*, his visionary first novel, focusing international attention on the plight of black South Africans, was published in 1948 – the same year the National Party assumed power and began to establish apartheid. Despite selling millions of copies worldwide, Paton's book coincided with a rising tide of repression inside the country and he entered politics to become a founder-member of the non-racial and fiercely anti-apartheid Liberal Party. He was president of the party from 1960 until 1968, when it was forced to disband by repressive legislation forbidding multiracial political organizations.

Paton died in Durban in 1988, having published a number of works, including two biographies and his own autobiography. The following year, the Alan Paton Centre was established at the University of Natal's archives building at 165 King Edward Ave (visits by appointment, ☎033 260 5926). The Centre includes Paton's re-created study, personal memorabilia and documents.

left, just before the platform, records (yet again) that this was where Gandhi was thrown off the train.

Eating, drinking and nightlife

Pietermaritzburg has a fairly good choice of restaurants, as well as a handful of decent nightclubs and pubs, particularly along Commercial Road. Nightlife in the town centre is mostly white-dominated.

The two **cinema** complexes – the Nu Metro, in the Cascades Centre, McCarthy Drive, in the northern suburbs, and Ster-Kinekor, 50 Durban Rd, in Scottsville – show mainstream releases. The university's Hexagon and Churchill theatres host occasional productions – check the *Natal Witness* newspaper for details.

Restaurants and cafés

Café du Midi 262 Boom St ☎033 394 5444. Mediterranean-style food in an old house, which is also good for outdoor coffee during the day.

Characters 266 Prince Alfred St ☎033 345 5084. A pricey restaurant with haute cuisine; closed Sun.

Els Amics 380 Longmarket St ☎033 345 6524. Set in a colonial house, Maritzburg's oldest restaurant is a popular place with a pleasant atmosphere, good prices and varied menu. Closed Mon & Sun.

Kara Nichha's 470 Church St ☎033 342 8015. An excellent, very cheap Indian takeaway, particularly good for filled *rotis* and Indian sweets.

Restaurant da Vinci 117 Commercial Rd ☎033 345 6632. A rowdy American-Italian place, offering cheap pasta dishes.

Stagecoach 44 Durban Rd ☎033 394 7727. Close to the university, this popular eating place offers good pub lunches, with live music on Wednesday nights.

Tatham Art Gallery Coffee Shop Commercial Road. The best place in town for coffee and light lunches, located in the old Supreme Court, right in the centre, opposite the tourist information bureau. Closed Mon.

Tropicana 418 Longmarket St ☎033 345 0051. Popular with Indian families, *Tropicana* serves cheap curries and an extensive menu of burger and steak grills with chips.

Turtle Bay 7 Wembley Terrace, Wembley, just off the N3 circle ☎033 394 5390. A decent but pricey seafood restaurant in the northern suburbs. Closed Sun.

Upper Crust Longmarket Street, opposite the taxi rank ☎033 342 7625. Good for a range of breads and imported foods, such as olive oil and Swiss chocolate, with home-baked pastries and pies. Open until 9pm daily.

Bars and nightclubs

80s Fever 91 Commercial Rd. A huge place that pulsates with students, particularly on Thursday nights, when they usually have top DJs guesting. Thurs–Sat 8pm until very late.

Crowded House 124 Balhambra Way & Commercial Road. Pleasant indoor and outdoor bars which attract a late-20s crowd. Wed, Fri & Sat; R15.

The Elephant 80 Commercial Rd. Offers cheap pub meals popular with a racially mixed crowd of students and townsfolk.

McGinty's Irish Pub 50 Durban Rd, Scottsville. A fairly smart pub with occasional live Irish music.

Listings

Emergencies Ambulance ☎10177; Police (Flying Squad): ☎10111; Rape Crisis ☎033 394 4444.
Hospital For medical emergencies, contact Med 24, Payn Street ☎033 342 7023 or 033 342 7024.
Laundry The Wash Tub, Shop 2, Park Lane Centre, Commercial Road ☎033 345 7458; daily 7am–6pm, Sat 8am–4pm, Sun 8am–3pm.

Pharmacy PMB Medicine Depot, 33 Commercial Rd ☎033 342 4581; Mon–Fri 9am–8pm, Sat 9am–5pm, Sun 10am–1pm & 3–9.30pm.
Taxis Junior Taxi Service, Echo Garage, Echo Road ☎033 394 5454; Unique Taxis, 524 Khans Rd ☎033 391 1238.

The Midlands

For most travellers, the verdant farmland that makes up the **Midlands** is picture-postcard terrain, whizzed through on the two-hour journey from Durban or Pietermaritzburg to the Drakensberg. There's little reason to dally here, unless you've time to kill, money to spend and fancy taking in the region's quaint, English-style country inns, tea shops and craft shops. From 1842 to 1897, battalion after battalion of British troops marched through the Midlands during a succession of wars to pacify first the Zulus and later the Boers. The region plays up its British connections, with trout-fishing clubs, polo clubs (over eighty percent of the country's clubs are based here), posh boarding schools and old-fashioned country hotels. The cosy image is deceptive: security fences erected around most farms indicate deep levels of black resentment, with theft common and the murder of white landowners not unusual.

Public relations consultants in the Midlands have been working overtime and have dreamt up the **Midlands Meander**, a route that takes in a number of dispersed craft stalls, hotels and other minor attractions along a series of very attractive back routes. The scenery and little stopoffs are more appealing than any of the Midlands towns, which you can comfortably bypass in the certainty that you're not missing much. A number of upmarket country hotels offer plush accommodation, and there are B&Bs and self-catering cottages for cheaper stays. A free **map** outlining the attractions on this trip is available from most information bureaus throughout the vicinity.

The Midlands has an interesting historical footnote. Heading north out of Pietermaritzburg on the N3 through the Midlands, you're roughly tracing **Nelson Mandela's last journey** as a free man before being arrested in 1962 and imprisoned for 27 years. **Howick**, 18km northwest of Pietermaritzburg, is recorded as the place where his historic detention began. The actual spot is on the R103, 2km north of a sideroad heading to the Tweedie junction. On the run from the police, Mandela had been continuing his political activities, often travelling in disguise – a practice that earned him the nickname of the "Black Pimpernel". On this occasion, he was masquerading as the chauffeur of a white friend, when their car was stopped on the old Howick road, apparently because of a tip-off. A memorial unveiled by Mandela himself in 1996 marks the unassuming spot, along farmland between a railway line and the road.

Practicalities

For self-catering accommodation in the Midlands, try KwaZulu-Natal Wildlife (see p.449), or contact Selected Ministays (☎033 330 3343, ⓦwww.ministays .co.za), an agency renting out a wide range of accommodation.

Nottingham Road, a hamlet 25km north of Howick along the R103, makes a good orientation point for the Midlands, and has a couple of excellent country hotels. In the town centre, the *Nottingham Road*, 26 Nottingham Rd (☎033 263 6151, ⓕ033 263 6167; ❸), purportedly has the oldest pub in the province, dating back to 1854. The hotel has retained the character of a coaching inn and features hand-coloured portraits of British officers from the Zulu Wars. Just south of town, *Rawdon's*, Old Main Rd (☎033 263 6044, ⓦwww.rawdons.co.za; ❹), is a gracious, thatched, English-style country estate looking onto its own trout lake, with welcoming log fires for cool misty days and airy verandahs for the hot summer. Although this is a pricey place to stay, it's also highly tranquil, and has an atmospheric pub with an on-site brewery and a pleasant tea room – both of which are open to passers-by. For something more remote, head 22km west of Nottingham Road on the signposted Loteni road, and turn off after 17km onto the D544. This will take you to rustic *Bramleigh Manor* (☎033 263 6903; ❸–❹), a large, thatched B&B guesthouse facing onto its own yellowwood and blackwood forests, which offers trout fishing, bird-watching, horse-riding, boating and sailboarding, and has two splendidly isolated cottages which can be taken on a B&B or self-catering basis.

For eating and drinking, *Rawdon's* (see p.498) is excellent, as is the *Rose & Pig*, a pleasant pub with indoor and outdoor seating in the tiny hamlet of Rosetta, 6km north of Nottingham Road on the R103.

The Drakensberg

Proclaimed a World Heritage Site in 2000, South Africa's premier mountain wilderness hugs the border with Lesotho and is mostly a vast national park, officially now renamed as the **uKhMweni Valleyahlamba-Drakensberg Park**. The highest range in southern Africa, the "Dragon Mountains" (or, in Zulu, the "barrier of spears") reach their highest peaks along the border with Lesotho. The mountain range is actually an escarpment separating a high interior plateau from the coastal lowlands of Natal, and is the source of many streams and rivers which flow out to the sea. Although this is a continuation of the same escarpment that divides the Mpumalanga highveld from the game-rich lowveld of the Kruger National Park, and continues into the northern section of the Eastern Cape, when people talk of the Berg, they invariably mean the range in KwaZulu-Natal.

For elating scenery – massive spires, rock buttresses, wide grasslands, glorious waterfalls, rivers, pools and fern-carpeted forests – the Drakensberg is unrivalled. Wild and unpopulated, it's a paradise for **hiking** or **fly-fishing**; angling at Lotheni, Kamberg, Cobham or Giant's Castle costs R50 per day by permit only from KwaZulu-Natal Wildlife (see p.449), with a bag limit of three trout per day. You'll need to bring all your own gear.

The Drakensberg is one of the richest **San rock-art** repositories in the world. More than six hundred sites have been recorded, featuring more than 22,000 individual paintings by the original inhabitants of these mountains. You won't see anything like this number, as they are hidden all over the mountains, but there are three easily accessible caves at **Giant's Castle**, **Injisuthi** and **Kamberg**. One of the best and most up-to-date introductions to rock art is the slim booklet by David Lewis-Williams, *Rock Paintings of the Natal Drakensberg*, published by the University of Natal Press and available from most decent bookshops.

There are no towns close to the mountains; instead the park is hemmed in by rural African areas – former "homeland" territory, unsignposted and unnamed on many maps, but interesting to drive through and take in a slice of traditional **Zulu life**, complete with beehive-shaped huts.

In terms of **weather**, summers are warm but wet, with some cracking thunderstorms and misty days that block out the views. Winters tend to be dry, sunny and chilly, and you can expect freezing nights and, on the high peaks, occasional snow. The best times for hiking are probably the transitional periods of spring and autumn.

Getting to the Drakensberg

There is no connecting road system through the Drakensberg, so it's not possible to drive from one end to the other. Besides **Sani Pass** in the south, which takes you into Lesotho on a hairpin dirt road requiring preferably a 4WD vehicle, roads to the mountains branch off westwards from the N3, between

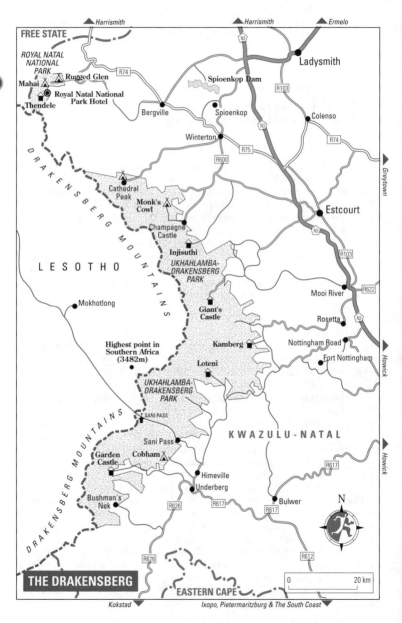

Pietermaritzburg and **Ladysmith**, and come to a halt at various KwaZulu-Natal Wildlife camps. There is no public transport to any of these.

The most practical way of **visiting the Drakensberg** is to base yourself in the northern, central or southern section of the mountains, staying either in the self-catering and camping options provided by KwaZulu-Natal Wildlife, or in one of several hotels that offer full-board rates. Without your own car, you'll have to go for the hotel or backpacker lodge option. Nearly all hotels in this area offer transfers from the Greyhound or Translux **intercity bus terminals** in Estcourt or Ladysmith. The **Baz Bus** drops off at Mooi River; their Durban–Jo'burg route goes via Winterton for the Northern Drakensberg; or Mooi River and Estcourt for the Central Berg. The Sani Pass Carriers (☎033 701 1017) **shuttle service** connects Maritzburg at least twice a day with Underberg and can also transport visitors around the Southern Berg. The highest concentration of hotels and resorts is in the Central Berg area, midway between Johannesburg and Durban.

The nearest commercial centres lie on or just off the arterial N3, and are useful for stocking up on supplies, filling up your car or arranging transport into the mountains. Largest and least appealing of these is **ESTCOURT**, 88km north of Pietermaritzburg, home to a cold-meat factory that processes bacon which, when the wind blows, perfumes the town with the smell of an all-day fry up. It's worth stopping off here to see the superb little museum housed at **Fort Durnford**, Cemps Road, off the R103 (daily 8am–noon, 1pm–4pm; donation). The museum recreates an old Estcourt street, complete with pawn shop, blacksmith, wholesale merchant and even railway ticket office, and has some displays on local military history as well as an impressive collection of wild bird eggs.

WINTERTON, 43km north of Estcourt along the R74 as it deviates west off the N3, is a tiny hamlet with some interesting little shops and eating places, filling stations and banks. The **museum** (Mon–Fri 9am–3pm, Sat 9am–noon; donation), signposted from Colenso Road, the main drag next to the municipal offices, justifies a stop for its excellent displays on San rock art and coverage of the Boer War Battlefields in this vicinity, notably Spioenkop and Vaalkrans.

If you get stuck around here and need a place to stay, Winterton's pleasant *Purple House B&B* (☎036 488 1025; ❷), on Springfield Road, the main drag as you drive into the town, is a good option. It has its own coffee and arts and crafts shop, and the accommodation consists of small cottages. *Ukuthula Bush Camp* at Rolling M Ranch (☎082 773 9914), a working farm outside town on the banks of the Tugela, is another appealing choice. Accommodation consists of a huge, single self-catering cabin sleeping fourteen and divided into cubicles (❶); two self-catering cottages up at the homestead, one sleeping eight to twelve and the other two to four (❶); and B&B rooms in the farmhouse itself (❷). The camp organizes walks up the river and into the mountains, plus, as they're on the Battlefields route, they also trail to Spioenkop and Buller's Cross monuments. Other activities include riding, whitewater canoeing, tubing and fishing. To get there, take the R23 to Ladysmith, then turn right at the signposted Skietdrift road; the camp is around 20km down this route; alternatively, backpackers can be collected from Winterton.

BERGVILLE, 23km north of Winterton, is another tiny and rather ugly village, notable only for being the last place to stock up before heading on to the Royal Natal National Park. Apart from the helpful Drakensberg Tourism Association (Mon–Fri 9am–5.30pm, Sat 9am–1pm; ☎036 448 1557, ℉036 448 1088) in Tatham Road, there's not much to keep you here.

The San and their rock paintings

Southern Africa's earliest inhabitants and the most direct descendants of the late Stone Age, the San, or Bushmen, lived in the caves and shelters of the Drakensberg for thousands of years before the arrival of the Nguni people and later the white farmers. There is still some disagreement over what to call these early hunter-gatherers. Many liberal writers use the word "Bushmen" in a strictly non-pejorative sense – though the word was originally deeply insulting. Several historians and anthropologists have plumped for "San" but, as the term refers to a language group and not a culture, this isn't strictly accurate either. Since there is no agreed term, you'll find both words used in this book.

The San hunted and gathered on the subcontinent for a considerable period – paintings in Namibia date back 25,000 years. In the last two thousand years, the southward migration of Bantu-speaking farmers forced change on the San, but there is evidence that the two groups were able to live side by side. However, serious tensions arose when the white settlers began to annex lands for hunting and farming. As the San started to take cattle from farmers, whites came to regard these people as vermin, and felt free to hunt them in genocidal campaigns in the Cape, and later in other areas, including the Drakensberg, until they were literally wiped off the South African map.

San **artists** were also **shamans**, and painted trance-induced images, mostly depicting their spiritual beliefs. Interpreting their paintings of hunting, dancing and animals as realistic narratives of everyday life in the Drakensberg is thus a pointless exercise. However, it's easy and rewarding to pick out some of the most significant elements in San paintings. The **medicine** or **trance dance** – journeying into the spiritual world in order to harness healing power – was the Bushmen's most important religious ritual and is depicted in much of their art. Look out for the postures which the shamans adopted during the dance, including arms outstretched behind them, bending forward, kneeling, or pointing fingers. Dots along the spine often relate to the sensation of energy boiling upwards, while lines on faces or coming out of the nose usually depict nosebleeds – a common side effect of the trance state. Other feelings experienced in trance, such as elongation, attenuation or the sensation of flight, are expressed by feathers or streamers.

To enter the spirit world, shamans often tapped into the spiritual power of certain **animals**. You'll see the spiral-horned **eland** depicted in every cave – not because these antelope were prolific in the Berg, but because they were considered to have more power than any other animal. Sometimes the elands are painted in layers to increase their spiritual potency. In the caves open to the public, you can see depictions of human-like figures in the process of transforming into their power animal. Besides antelope, other animals associated with trance are honeybees, felines, snakes and sometimes elephants and rhinos.

It's difficult to **date** the paintings in the Drakensberg with accuracy, but the oldest are likely to be at least eight hundred years old (although Bushmen lived in the area for thousands of years before that) and the most recent are believed to have been painted after the arrival of the whites towards the end of the nineteenth century. The depictions of horses, cattle and white settlers, particularly in the Southern Berg, mark the end of the traditional way of life for the Drakensberg Bushmen, and it is possible that the settlers were painted by shamans as a supernatural technique to try to ward off their all-too-real bullets.

Paintings weather and fade, many have been vandalized, and well-meaning people dabbing water on them to make them clearer, or touching them, has also caused them to disappear – so never be tempted.

Hiking in the Drakensberg

Whether you choose to take your time on easy walks or embark on a challenging three- or four-day trip into the mountains, **hiking** in the Drakensberg remains one of South Africa's top wilderness experiences. The marvel of setting out on foot in these mountains is that you're unlikely to encounter vehicles, settlements, or even other people, and the scenery is sublime.

The Drakensberg is divided into the High Berg and Little Berg, according to altitude. In the **High Berg**, you're in the land of spires and great rock buttresses, where the only places to sleep are in caves or, in some areas, huts. You'll need to be totally self-sufficient and obey wilderness rules, taking a trowel and loo paper with you and not fouling natural water with anything − which means carrying water away from the streams to wash in. Both mountaineers' huts and caves must be booked with the KwaZulu-Natal Wildlife office you start out from, and you'll also need to write down your route details in the mountain register. Slogging up the passes to the top of the mountains requires a high degree of fitness, some hiking experience and a companion or guide who knows the terrain.

If you're not bothered about reaching the high peaks, the **Little Berg**, with its gentler summits, rivers, rock paintings, valleys and forests, is equally remote and beautiful. It's also safer, and easy enough to explore if you're of average fitness. If you don't want to carry a backpack and sleep in caves or huts, it's feasible to base yourself at one of the **KZN Wildlife camps** and set out on dayhikes, of which there are endless choices. It's also possible to do a two-day walk from one of the camps, spending one night in a cave. Two highly recommended bases for walking are **Injisuthi** in the Giant's Castle Game Reserve (see p.508), or **Thendele** in the Royal Natal National Park (see p.511). If you want the added luxury of spending your nights in a hotel, base yourself in the **Cathedral Peak** area at the *Cathedral Peak Hotel* (see p.510).

Each of the KZN Wildlife offices sells books on Drakensberg walks, as well as *Slingsby* **maps** (1:150,000), though some of the paths indicated have now disappeared. If you want to hike up to the **High Berg** but don't feel confident to tackle the terrain, or are alone, Stef Steyn (☎033 330 4293, ⓦwww.kzn-tours.co.za) specializes in **guided hiking tours** across the Drakensberg, as well as scenic tours all over the province. If he's not available, try Drakensberg Spectacular Tours (☎036 631 0011).

The **weather** can change rapidly at any time of year, so always take sufficient clothing and food. Use tried and tested, well-worn hiking boots, and don't forget a hat − the sun is fierce and bright, even in winter.

The Southern Berg

Although for the most part the Southern Berg, the closest mountains to Durban and Pietermaritzburg, lacks the drama and varied landscape found further north, its outstanding highlight is the hair-raising **Sani Pass**, a precipitous series of hairpins that twist to the top of the escarpment up to the highest point in southern Africa reachable on wheels. The Southern Berg, with its extensive grasslands, is also the terrain of the highly recommended **Giant's Cup Hiking Trail** (see p.505), the only organized trail in the Drakensberg and an exhilarating introduction to the mountains.

Although Sani Pass is the Southern Berg's most popular destination, further north KZN Wildlife offers campsites and cottages at Cobham, **Lotheni** and

△ Mweni Valley, Drakensberg

Giant's Cup Hiking Trail

The sixty-kilometre, five-day **Giant's Cup Hiking Trail** is the only laid-out trail in the Drakensberg and makes an excellent introduction to the mountains. The trail starts at the Sani Pass road, leading through the foothills of the Southern Drakensberg and winding past eroded sandstone formations, overhangs with San paintings, grassy plains, and beautiful valleys with river pools to swim in. No single day's hike is longer than 14km and, although there are some steep sections, this is not a difficult trail – you need to be fit to enjoy it, but not an athlete. The trail is restricted to thirty people per day and tends to get booked out during holiday periods; **booking** should be made through the KwaZulu-Natal Wildlife (see p.449), who provide a map and a trail booklet. The trail costs R48 per person per night, which includes a one-off entrance fee of R15.

The **mountain huts** at the four overnight stops have running water, toilets, tables and benches, and bunks with mattresses. It's essential to bring a camping stove, food and a sleeping bag. The trail can be shortened by missing the first day and starting out at Pholela Hut, an old farmhouse where you spend the night, then terminating one day earlier at Swiman Hut, close to the KZN Wildlife office at Garden Castle. You can also lengthen the trail by spending an extra night at Bushmen's Nek Hut, in an area with numerous caves and rock-art sites.

Giant's Cup Trail is linear, so you'll need to arrange **transport** at the end of the hike to get back to where you parked. This should be arranged through Sani Pass Carriers (☎033 701 1017), who can pick you up at Himeville or Underberg, or move and store your car if you're driving.

Kamberg, and plenty of opportunity for trout fishing. Despite its isolation, even without transport the Pass is accessible via transport links and has a couple of hostels.

Underberg and Himeville

The main access into this part of the Drakensberg is along the R617, which strikes out west off the N3 north of Pietermaritzburg (take the Bulwer/Underberg exit). **UNDERBERG** on the R617, is the main gateway, with a good supermarket for stocking up and some emergency services should you run into difficulties in the mountains. It also has a selection of good craft shops and attractive pubs. At the *Underberg Hotel* a few metres from the supermarket is the Major Adventure offices (☎033 701 1628), where you can book overnight, three-and five-day **tours to Lesotho**. There's also a **pharmacy**, the Sani (☎033 701 1034, after hours ☎033 701 1955) and a **private hospital**, the Riverview (☎033 701 1331) for 24-hour emergencies. The Automobile Association offers a 24-hour breakdown service (☎033 701 1430 or 082 417 8897).

HIMEVILLE, 4km north of Underberg, is the last village you'll find before heading up Sani Pass. At the centre of the village, Sani Saunter Publicity (Mon–Fri 8am–4pm; ☎033 702 1902) is the best place to get **information** about the region, being the official representative of the whole Southern Drakensberg region. The town also has a supermarket, and opposite Sani Saunter Publicity is the decent *Himeville Arms* (☎033 702 1305; ❸), a country **inn** which makes a good stopover before the final haul to the mountains. They also accommodate backpackers in two-and four-bed rooms (❶) and offer 4WD trips, horse-riding, tennis and golf. There's a plethora of **B&Bs** along this road, one of the nicest being *Yellowwood Cottage* (☎ & ☎033 702 1065; ❷); set in a spectacular garden with wonderful Berg views, it has three double bedrooms with private bathrooms and fully equipped and serviced kitchenette.

Sani Pass

Sani Pass, the only road from KwaZulu-Natal into neighbouring Lesotho, connects South Africa to the tiny highland outpost of **Mokhotlong** in Lesotho (see p.775), once known as the "loneliest settlement in Africa" and still no great metropolis. But it's the pass itself, which zigzags into the clouds, that draws increasing numbers into the High Berg. Sani Pass is the only place in the KwaZulu-Natal Drakensberg range where you actually can drive up the mountains – though it's preferable to use a 4WD vehicle to negotiate the road and you'll need a passport to cross the **Lesotho border** (daily 8am–4pm). If you don't have your own transport, consider booking a tour with one of the handful of operators (see below) running journeys to the "roof of Africa".

Access and information

For all its isolation, Sani Pass is fairly straightforward to get to. Transport is available on Sani Pass Carriers **buses** (☎ & ℱ 033 701 1017, after hours ☎ 033 701 1030, ℮ sanipasscarriers@wandata.com), based in Underberg, which runs a service between Pietermaritzburg and Underberg (Mon, Wed & Fri 2 daily; Tues, Thurs & Sat 1 daily; R90 one way, R160 return) timed to connect with the Cheetah Coach and other intercity bus schedules. They will also shuttle passengers to any of the accommodation in the Southern Berg subject to demand (charge depends on destination with minimum fee for two people). Thaba Tours (☎ 033 701 2888) offers several **tours**, including a daily jaunt into Lesotho, where they take you by 4WD to the highest point on the Sani/Mokhotlong Road to visit shepherds and learn about their lifestyle; they also organize horse-riding trails and walking trips to see rock art. It's also possible to do Sani Pass as a worthwhile, though very long, day-trip from Durban, with Strelitzia Tours (☎ 031 266 9480, ⓦ www.strelitziatours.com), which includes a visit to a Lesotho village, where you get to taste homemade sorghum beer and lunch at the *Sani Top Chalets*. For **information** about the area contact the Southern Drakensberg Sani Saunter (☎ 033 701 1471, ⓦ www.sanisaunter.com).

Accommodation

You'll find most accommodation at the foot of the mountains, just before the pass hairpins its way up to the top. Closest to the start of the pass is *Mkomazana Lodge*, while the highest is *Sani Top Chalets*.

Mkomazana Lodge 25km northwest of Underberg along the Sani Pass road ☎ 033 702 0340, ℮ wendy@mkomazana.co.za. Self-catering in four- and six-bed dorms, a huge thirty-bed dorm, doubles with shared toilets and washing facilities, plus two fully equipped houses sleeping eight. The lodge is also near the start of Giant's Cup Hiking Trail (see box on p.505), and you can safely leave your car here before setting out on the trek. Less ambitious walks into the mountains begin on the property, which has its own river and waterfall, and a private dam with trout. ❶

Sani Lodge Backpackers Hostel 19km north-west of Underberg along the Sani Pass road ☎ 033 702 0330, ⓦ www.sani-lodge.co.za. Dorms and doubles at a lodge with pleasant verandahs and lawns where meals are served all day, and a mean reputation for chocolate cake. It's a good base for walking to waterfalls and rock paintings – they can supply packed lunches – and there's horse-riding and mountain biking. Tours up Sani Pass and into Lesotho are also on offer, and you can stay in a nearby homestead to experience ordinary Zulu life. ❶

Sani Pass Hotel A little beyond *Sani Lodge Backpackers* ☎ 033 702 1320, ℮ sanipasshotel @futurenet.co.za. A comfortable, conservative hotel offering full-board and plenty of extras, including horse-riding and tennis facilities. ❺

Sani Top Chalets ☎ 033 702 1158. Double rooms as well as backpacking facilities at the top of Sani Pass, just inside Lesotho. Recommended if you're after a serious hiking vibe, but with a relaxed atmosphere, spectacular views and the highest pub in Africa; meals and teas are also available. ❶

North of Sani Pass: Lotheni and Kamberg

Well off the beaten track, along dirt roads and seldom explored by foreign visitors, the two KZN Wildlife camps at **Lotheni** and **Kamberg** (both daily: April–Sept 6am–6pm; Oct–March 5am–7pm; R15) are worth venturing into for their isolated wilderness, good trout fishing and, at Kamberg, some exquisite San rock paintings. Booking is through KZN Wildlife central bookings (see p.449).

In a valley in the foothills of the Berg, **LOTHENI** is tranquil and beautiful, with waterfalls, grasslands and the lure of fishing in the Lotheni River, which flows through the reserve and is stocked with brown trout. The **Settler Museum** is worth a quick look; it's housed in the original stone buildings belonging to the Root family who left Britain in the nineteenth century and farmed here for two generations before the area was proclaimed a reserve, and Arnold Root became the first warden. Displays include wagons, farm tools and period furniture, re-creating early settler life.

It's possible **to get there** by car via either Nottingham Road, 76km to its northeast, or from Himeville 74km to the southeast. You'll need to bring all your own supplies, or visit the trading store, 10km before you reach the restcamp (☎033 702 0540). There are twelve cheap but comfortable self-catering chalets (❷), eight of which sleep two people, and four of which have three beds, and all with their own well-equipped kitchen and bathroom; and a small campsite (❶). Best of all here is *Simes Cottage* (❷), a stone farmhouse with a majestic outlook, its own trout lake and grounds traversed by bushbuck and eland. The cottage sleeps ten, and there's a minimum charge for six people.

The best reason to visit **KAMBERG**, 42km west of Rosetta, apart from the superb fishing, is for the rock art at one of the three caves in the Drakensberg open to the public. At **Shelter Cave** (also known as Game Pass Cave), images of stylized figures in trance states and large, polychrome eland dance across the wall. The paintings can only be visited with a guide; arrange this beforehand, or join one of the guided tours departing daily from the restcamp (R35) at 9am. The walk there and back takes around three hours, following a contour path through grasslands. There are other less distinct paintings (free), which you can visit at will, near the waterfall. There's also a brand new **rock-art centre** due to open in 2002.

Kamberg's **restcamp** (☎033 263 7251; ❶–❷) consists of chalets, huts, sharing a communal kitchen, and a rustic cottage. There's a basic supply store just before you reach the reserve, and as the nearest major supplies are at Rosetta, you'll need to bring all your own food and drink. Walks from here are undemanding and very scenic, and there's a four-kilometre trail with handrails for wheelchair-users and the visually impaired. There's no camping here.

The Central Drakensberg

The **Central Drakensberg** incorporates four distinct areas, all clearly signposted from the N3 and the R615. **Giant's Castle**, the site of a beautiful game reserve, is where you'll find the popular Lammergeyer bird hide and access to important San rock paintings. More San art is at **Injisuthi** to the north, principally a hiking destination and the place to head for if you're after complete wilderness. Far more accessible and tourist-trammelled is **Champagne Valley**, which offers a healthy number of full-board hotels with ample sporting facilities, while to the north, and out on a limb, the hotel at **Cathedral Peak** is the best place to base yourself for some serious walking.

Giant's Castle Game Reserve

Giant's Castle Game Reserve (daily: April–Sept 6am–6pm; Oct–March 5am–7pm; R20) was created to protect the dwindling numbers of **eland**, which occurred in great numbers in the Drakensberg before the arrival of colonialists. The reserve is also home to antelope of the montane zone: oribi, grey rhebok, mountain reedbuck and bushbuck. Despite its four dozen mammal species and around 160 bird species, this is not a traditional game park – the way to see the wildlife here is by walking or hiking through the terrain, not by driving around in a car. There are no roads inside the reserve apart from access routes, which terminate at the two main KZN Wildlife accommodation areas – **Giant's Castle** and **Injisuthi**. The reserve is bordered to the west by three of the four highest peaks in South Africa: Mafadi (the highest at 3410m); Popple Peak (3325m) and the bulky ramparts of Giant's Castle itself (3314 m).

One of the big attractions at Giant's Head is the thrilling **Lammergeyer Hide** (May–Sept), where you can see the rare lammergeier, Cape vulture, black eagle, jackal buzzard and lanner falcon, attracted by the carcasses of animals put out by rangers during the winter. The lammergeyer, a giant, black and golden bird with massive wings and a diamond-shaped tail, was thought to be extinct in southern Africa until only two decades ago. Today, the bird is found only in mountainous areas such as the Himalayan foothills, and in South Africa only in the Drakensberg and Maluti mountains. The lammergeyer, a scavenger, is an evolutionary link between eagles and vultures. To visit the hide (R100 per person, minimum charge three people), you'll have to **book** as much as a year in advance through Giant's Castle Game Reserve, PO Box X7055, Estcourt 3310 (☏036 353 3718).

Giant's Castle has one of the three major **rock-art sites** open to the public in the Drakensberg, with more than five hundred paintings at **Main Caves**, about a half-hour's easy walk up the Bushman's River Valley. There's a R15 entry fee to the fenced-in caves, and self-guided tours with some interpretative materials on site.

If the KZN Wildlife accommodation is full, you'll have to head for the one **hotel** that gives access to the reserve: *White Mountain Lodge*, along the road to Giant's Castle hutted camp (☏036 353 8644, ℻036 353 8437; ❶–❷), 34km on a tarred road from Estcourt and 32km from the reserve. The hotel offers full-board accommodation and self-catering cottages, and is in the foothills and close to Zulu villages and farmlands, so while the area is pretty, it's neither grand nor remote. The only option for backpackers, and rather a wonderful one, is *Mount Lebanon Park* (☏033 263 2214, ✉lebanonpark@freemail.absa.co; ❶) a great **backpacker lodge** on a 500-acre farm with a trout dam. The lodge runs three-hour to three-day horse treks into the area, as well as trails to Bushman caves and paintings. On the farm are lots of antelope and baboons as well as lammergeyer. The lodge offers pick-ups from Mooi River, or if you're driving, take the Giant's Castle Road from Mooi River for 40km. It's another 29km to the reserve. There are extremely inexpensive family cottages which sleep ten (minimum charge R360) and double rooms.

Giant's Castle

The most comfortable of the reserve's **accommodation**, *Giant's Castle Lodge* (bookings through KZN Wildlife; see box on p.449) has self-contained and revamped chalets (❹), with wonderful picture windows looking out to the peaks, and cosy open fireplaces. They vary in size, sleeping from two to eight people and are self-catering, though you can eat at the newly built *Izimbali* buffet-style **restaurant**. A curio **shop** at the reception area also sells frozen meat for braais and some tinned food and beers, but it's preferable to stock up before getting here. The reserve's only **filling station** is here, at the main entrance.

There are fabulous **hiking trails** from the camp, with some of the best-located and equipped hiking **huts** (❶) in the Berg at Meander Hut, Giant's Hut and Bannerman's Hut. The only drawback is that there is no campsite at *Giant's Castle Lodge*, so if you're planning an overnight hike in the mountains, you'll need to book into one of their bungalows for the first or last night of your trail.

Injisuthi

Some 50km from both Winterton and Estcourt, **INJISUTHI** – previously spelled Injasuti – (April–Sept 7am–6pm; Oct–March 6am–7pm; R15 entrance fee) is a hikers' dream. You can walk straight out into the mountains (there are ten different day hikes, lasting from one to seven hours), swim in the rivers or look at rock art. One of the best day walks is up Van Heyningen's Pass to the **View Point** – the friendly staff at reception will direct you. It's also supremely relaxing and beautiful. To get there, take the indicated turning off the R615, which takes you along 30km of dirt road, passing through **Zulu villages** with traditional beehive huts along roads that are frequently blocked by groups of Nguni cattle.

If you have even a passing interest in rock art, don't miss the paintings at **Battle Cave** so named because of a series of paintings that apparently depict an armed conflict between two groups of Bushmen. There are more than 750 beautifully painted figures of people and animals in this extensive cave, though many are faded. They're also fenced off, and can be visited only in the company of a KZN Wildlife guide, who sets out most days at 8.30am on the three- to four-hour walk (bookings a day in advance through the Injisuthi office ☎036 431 7848; R35 per person; minimum four people). Once at the cave, the guide will play a recorded commentary on the paintings. Lewis-Williams has argued that, contrary to popular belief, the battle scene is unlikely to depict a territorial conflict, because there is no evidence that such conflicts ever took place in a society that was very loosely organized and unterritorial. Instead, he claims, the paintings are about the San spiritual experience and shamanic trance, the battles taking place in the spiritual realm where marauding evil shamans shoot arrows of "sickness", while good shamans attempt to fight them off. A **fossil trail** is also planned in the vicinity to open up some valuable fossil finds made in 2001.

Most people come here with the express purpose of taking to the hills and camping in one of the designated **caves**, which have absolutely no facilities and must be booked at reception; or you can use your own tent.

Champagne Castle and Champagne Valley

Champagne Castle, the second-highest peak in South Africa, provides the most popular view in the Drakensberg, with scores of resorts in the valley cashing in on the soaring backdrop. The name, so the story goes, derives from an incident in 1861, when a Major Grantham made the first recorded ascent of the peak accompanied by his batman, who inadvertently dropped the bottle of bubbly and christened the mountainside.

These days, champagne tends to be enjoyed within the confines of the hotels down in the **Champagne Valley** by cityslickers who refuse to follow in the major's footsteps, preferring to enjoy their tipple in comfortable surroundings. This overcivilized but extremely pretty area, which lies outside the KwaZulu-Natal Wildlife reserve, is best avoided if you want to hike from your doorstep

– you'll have to drive along the R600 through the valley to **Monk's Cowl** (R15 entrance fee), from where plenty of hikes set off into the mountains. The valley is an easy 32km all the way from Winterton, and has facilities absent in other parts of the Drakensberg, such as a supermarket, liquor store, greengrocer, laundry and a couple of restaurants, all indicated along the route.

The **Ardmore Ceramic Art Studio** (daily 9am–4.30pm; ☎036 468 1314, ⊛www.ardmore.co.za), 5km down off the R600, indicated between the *Nest Hotel* and the *Drakensberg Sun*, is one of the highlights of the valley. The studio was started in the 1980s by fine-arts graduate **Fée Halsted–Berning** with trainee **Bonnie Ntshalintshali**, a young Zulu girl suffering from polio. By 1990 they had collected a clutch of awards for their distinctive ceramic works, and the studio now has around forty people creating beautiful sculpture and crockery with wildly colourful and often impossibly irrational motifs that have included rhinos dressed as preachers, administering the sacrament to a congregation of wild animals. Bonnie has since died of AIDS, as have at least eight others of the artists from the studio, but the distinctive style she pioneered has been continued by other artists at the studio, and the works here are well worth seeing and buying. There's also a less pricey local **curio shop** on the premises, with works by other local artists on sale.

Accommodation

You shouldn't have any problem finding a **place to stay** in Champagne Valley, as numerous hotels, family resorts and B&Bs are signposted off the R600. There are no KZN Wildlife chalets, only a campsite at **Monk's Cowl** (☎036 468 1103).

Ardmore Guest Farm Signposted off the R600, midway between Winterton and Monk's Cowl ☎ & ℗036 468 1314. A thoroughly hospitable B&B on a farm, with accommodation in en-suite rondavels or inside the main house, attached to the Ardmore Ceramic Studio (see above); guests eat together from marvellous hand-crafted crockery made on the farm. *Ardmore* can also arrange horse trails into Spioenkop Game Reserve through the Battlefields. ❷–❸

Champagne Castle Along the R600 ☎036 468 1063, ℗036 468 1306. One of the nicest hotels in the area, and also the closest to the hiking trails beginning at Monk's Cowl. Recently refurbished, it has comfortable en-suite chalets set in lovely gar-

dens with a swimming pool, and a rate that includes three meals a day. ❺

Graceland Cottage Signposted off the R600 ☎ & ℗036 468 1091. A three-bedroomed self-catering cottage with TV and fireplace (R500 per night), as well as a larger cottage, the *Homestead* (R600 per night), perched right on the edge of a mountain with spectacular views.

Inkosana Lodge Halfway along the R600 from Winterton to Monk's Cowl ☎ & ℗036 468 1202. Backpacker and B&B accommodation in unpretentious, ethnic-style rooms, with beautiful indigenous gardens and a retreat-centre feel. Self-catering is available, and the lodge can provide free transfers from Winterton and up to the Berg trailheads. ❶–❷

Cathedral Peak

North of Monk's Cowl and the Champagne Valley resorts is the Mlambonja River Valley and *Cathedral Peak Hotel* (☎036 488 1888, ⊛www.cathedral-peak.co.za; ❺), the closest hotel in the Drakensberg to the mountains, and within the KZN Wildlife protected area. There are no other hotels in the vicinity, so the views are perfect and the rooms in thatched two-storey wings are comfortably furnished with pine and country-style floral fabrics. The *Cathedral Peak* is well-signposted, 44km from either Winterton or Bergville.

Hiking trails start right from the hotel, which provides maps and books. One of the most popular day walks is to the beautiful **Rainbow Gorge**. This eleven-kilometre round trip takes four to five hours, and follows the Ndumeni

River with pools, rapids, falls, lichens, mosses and ferns to detain you. The hike can be wet, so wear proper walking boots. The hotel also operates guided trips up **Cathedral Peak** itself, a freestanding pinnacle sticking out of the five-kilo-metre-long basalt Cathedral Ridge. You should expect the ten-kilometre round trip to take nine hours, which includes plenty of time at the top to revel in the views. It's a very steep climb, and the final section beyond Orange Peel Gap should only be tackled by experienced climbers – you'll probably be quite sat-isfied to stop at this point. The peak looks nothing like a cathedral (its Zulu name, Mponjwane, means "the horn on a heifer's head").

The only other place to stay is the small KZN Wildlife campsite (☎036 488 1880), opposite the Mike's Pass guardhouse, about 4km before the hotel, although a major new camp, **Didima**, should be open by 2003. Didima is an upmarket hutted camp, with San rock-art as its major theme; a sound-and-light interpretation centre as well as a restaurant and campsite are also planned. For the latest **information and reservations**, contact KZN Wildlife (see box on p.449).

The guardhouse itself is the place to buy a permit to drive up **Mike's Pass** (R15 per person, R35 per vehicle), a ten-kilometre twisting forestry road which takes you to a car park from where, on a clear day, you'll get outstand-ing views of the entire region. There's a scale model on top to help identify the peaks. An ordinary car will make the journey when the weather is dry and the road is hard, but you'll need a 4WD when it's wet.

The Northern Drakensberg

The dramatically beautiful **Northern Drakensberg** consists mainly of the **Royal Natal National Park**, with a few resorts scattered around the fringes and Zulu villages pressing around the borders. The Tugela River and its bouldered gorge offer some of the most awe-inspiring scenery in the area, while the Amphitheatre, the main geographical feature, is a striking, five-kilometre rock wall over which the Tugela plunges. With a complete cross-section of accom-modation, the Northern Berg is a very desirable area to visit. The best place to get a real feeling of these pristine mountains and valleys is at **Thendele**, the main KwaZulu-Natal Wildlife camp, with chalets but oddly enough no camping.

Royal Natal National Park

The **Royal Natal National Park** (daily 24hr; R15), 46km west of Bergville, is famed for its views of the **Amphitheatre**, a crescent-shaped rock edge of the escarpment that virtually encloses the park, and probably appears on more posters and postcards and in more books than any other single feature of the Drakensberg. Almost everyone does the **Tugela Gorge walk**, a fabulous six-hour round trip from Thendele, which gives close-up views of the Amphitheatre and the **Tugela Falls** plummeting over the 500-metre rock wall.

The park itself is at the northern end of the High Drakensberg, tucked in between Lesotho to the west and Free State province to the north, and is the closest section of the Berg to Johannesburg. The three defining peaks are the Sentinel (3165m), the Eastern Buttress (3048m) and the Mont Aux Sources (3282m), which is also where five rivers rise – hence its name, given by French missionaries in 1878. The park was established in 1916 but only earned its royal sobriquet in 1947, when the Windsors paid a visit.

Access and information

The best way to get into the Royal Natal is with your own transport; the route comprises tarred roads all the way. Coming from Durban along the N3, take the Winterton/Berg resorts turn-off and follow the clear signposts through the village of **Bergville** to the park entrance, some 46km away. Several of the resorts offer transfers from Bergville or the N3 if you book ahead and notify them, but they tend to be expensive. Although there are plenty of **Zulu** settlements en route, Bergville is the nearest place to stock up on supplies.

Accommodation

KZN Wildlife accommodation consists of two campsites and the hutted camp. **Bookings** for chalets should be made through the KZN Wildlife offices (see p.449), while camping should be arranged locally. Outside the park, just before you reach the entry gate, from Bergville, a well-signposted dirt road heading north is the location for the handful of resort-style hotels in the area.

Inside the park

Mahai Campsite ☎036 438 6303, ⊕036 438 6231. Adjacent to the Royal Natal, this huge campsite set along the river caters for up to four hundred campers, attracting hordes of South Africans over school holidays and weekends. From here you can strike straight into the mountains for some of the best walks in the Berg.

Rugged Glen Campsite Signposted 4km from Mahai ☎036 438 6303, ⊕036 438 6231. This campsite is smaller and quieter than *Mahai*, but the views and walks aren't as good; the *Mont-Aux-Sources Hotel* is an easy walk away – handy if you want a substantial meal. ❶

Thendele Hutted Camp ☎033 845 1000, ⊕033 845 1001. At the end of the road, right in the mountains, this is one of the most-sought-after places to stay in South Africa, with splendid views of the Amphitheatre and excellent walks right from your front door. Accommodation is in 29 comfortable two-, four- or six-bed en-suite units, the cheapest of which have hotplates, fridges, kettles, toasters and eating utensils. If you opt for the more luxurious cottages or lodge, chefs are on hand to cook for you, though you need to bring the food. There's a good curio and supply shop, but you might also want to stock up beforehand. ❸–❹

Outside the park

The Cavern ☎036 438 6270, ⊛www.cavern-berg.com. Off the R74 on the way to the resort, about 20km from the Royal Natal. The most tucked-away of the hotels, the *Cavern* is family run, has an old-fashioned feel with adequate rooms, and is very much a South African weekend getaway with a swimming pool, horse-riding, Saturday night dances and a TV room; the rate is full-board, and cheaper during the week. Transfers from the Durban/Johannesburg buses at the N3 cost R220 per return trip and must be booked beforehand. ❹

Hlalanathi Berg Resort ☎036 438 6308, ⊕036 438 6852. Some 10km from the Royal Natal, this family resort offers camping and self-catering thatched chalets, which sleep from two to six people. There's also a swimming pool, trampolines, a TV room as well as a sit-down and take-away restaurant serving cheap burgers, sandwiches and more substantial meals. ❶–❷

Mont-Aux-Sources Hotel ☎036 438 6230, ⊛www.orion-hotels.com. Roughly 4km from the park, this smart but impersonal hotel has views of the Amphitheatre behind scrawny villages and cattle-chewed hillsides. ❺

The Zululand Coast and
game reserves

In startling contrast to the intensely developed 250-kilometre ribbon of the
Holiday Coast, which runs north and south of Durban, the seaboard to the
north of the Dolphin Coast drifts off into some of the wildest and most breathtaking sea frontage in South Africa – an imprecisely defined area known as
Maputaland. Roughly speaking, Maputaland is the funnel-shaped slab
wedged into the corner formed by Swaziland and Mozambique in the north,
and confined to its east and west between the N2 and the coast.

If you've travelled along the Garden Route and wondered where stereotypical Africa was, the answer is right here in this tight patchwork of wilderness

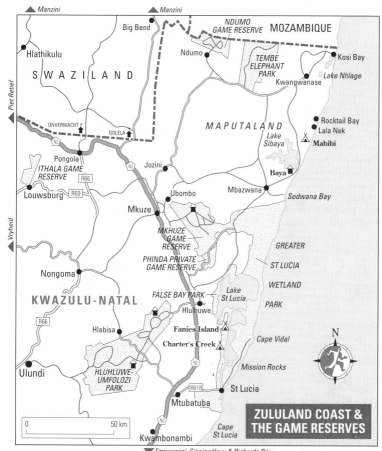

and **ancestral African lands**. The figures speak for themselves: Maputaland has more *nyangas* and *sangomas* (traditional healers and spirit mediums) per head than anywhere else in the country. With one healer for every 550 people – compared with one Western-style doctor to 18,000 people – **traditional life** continues in this forgotten corner of sub-Saharan Africa's most industrialized country.

It's only since the 1960s that **navigable tracks** have twisted their way through Maputaland's grasslands and tangled forests, and even today there's no tarred road leading all the way from the N2 to its 200km of virtually uninterrupted beachfront, most of which is still only accessible with a 4WD vehicle – although this will probably change in the next few years.

Driving for less than three hours on the N2 north from Durban gets you into the **big game country** of Hluhluwe-Umfolozi, which rivals even the Kruger National Park in beauty and a sense of the wild. Drive the same distance, but turn right instead of left at the Mtubatuba junction, and you'll hit the southernmost extent of South Africa's most satisfyingly "tropical" **coast**, protected all the way up to Mozambique by wetland reserve and marine sanctuaries, all falling under the umbrella of the Greater St Lucia Wetland Reserve, declared a UNESCO World Heritage Site in 1999. The coast gets remoter and more exhilarating the further north you head, with two of South Africa's best upmarket beachside stays at **Rocktail Bay** and **Kosi Forest Lodge** – both near Mozambique, where fewer than two dozen fortunate guests have kilometres of rolling dunes and coastal forest to themselves.

So far, the only major development blighting the area is the large modern industrial port of **Richards Bay**, 185km north of Durban, nudging the southern edge of Maputaland. But with the possibility of a continuous strip of resorts all the way from Durban to the Mozambique border, there are real fears for the whole of this fragile ecosystem. Conservation and poverty sit uncomfortably here; for **indigenous people** struggling to sustain a livelihood, the sight of visitors in their air-conditioned vehicles raising dust in their backyard leaves a bitter taste. In the past, African farmers were banned from planting crops in the wetlands, traditional fishermen were arrested for casting their nets on waters they believed to be theirs, and cattle herders had their livestock confiscated if they wandered into certain areas. It's not surprising that for some local people, eco-tourism equals dispossession. This has understandably led to resentment, but a number of locals have responded positively to the influx of visitors, and Zululand is one of the best areas to buy **crafts**. Even on remote roads, you'll come across stalls with beautiful carvings, often suspended like windchimes from their roofs or from trees. Objects include platters, sticks or, in a more contemporary vein, models of little 4WD vehicles. More positive still is the growth of eco-tourism projects in the vicinity that involve partnership with the community. An example of this is **Phinda Private Game Reserve**, a seriously upmarket park near Mkhuze Game Reserve that has brought tangible benefits to the local community and suggests a way in which business, communities and the environment can gain mutual benefit from tourism.

Note that the northern KwaZulu-Natal coastal region is **malarial**. For details on necessary precautions, see "Health" on p.22.

Richards Bay to Hluhluwe

There's no reason to spend time in either **Empangeni**, 173km north of Durban, or **RICHARDS BAY**, 12km east, on the coast. Two modern industrial sprawls that are the only centres of any size in the vicinity, they are completely at odds with the remote and pristine coast to the north and are best passed through quickly, even if you're making **transport** connections here. Given that you can avoid these towns on the **Baz Bus**, which links up with transport to points along the Maputaland coast and to Hluhluwe-Umfolozi Park, you only need come here if you're **flying** into Richards Bay and plan on renting a car to make a quick getaway. SA Express (☏035 786 0301) flies three times daily from Johannesburg and touches down at **Richards Bay airport** (☏035 786 0301), 6km north of the town centre. **Car rental**, including 4WD, can be arranged from the airport through Avis (☏0861 021 111) and Imperial (☏0800 131 000). The only way to get to Richards Bay from Durban is on one of the bus services, or by car. Greyhound **intercity buses** arrive at the *Steers* restaurant, next to the Total filling station in Anglers Rod Street and the *Richards Bay Hotel*. Greyhound (☏031 309 7830) runs from Durban, and Translux (Johannesburg ☏011 774 3333) goes to Durban from Johannesburg/Pretoria. If you're stuck here for the night, the **Richards Bay Tourist Information** (Mon–Fri 8am–4pm, Sat & Sun 10am–2pm; ☏035 788 0039, ⓦwww.futurenet.co.za/richards), at the Small Craft Harbour, off John Ross Parkway, can help you find accommodation.

Kwambonambi and Mtubatuba

Some 26km north of Richards Bay, the tiny village of **KWAMBONAMBI** (known locally as Kwambo) lies on the Baz **bus** route. The predominantly African hamlet is safe and friendly and makes a preferable base to the less appealing village of Hluhluwe for exploring St Lucia and the Hluhluwe-Umfolozi game reserve. Kwambo has a small supermarket, a bottle store, post office and filling station and an excellent **backpacker lodge**, the congenial *Cuckoo's Nest*, 28 Alibizia St (☏035 580 1001, ⓔcuckoos@mweb.co.za; ❶), which has A-frame doubles, teepees, camping, some dorms, plus a great treehouse. The lodge can organize diving at Sodwana and overnight trips to the Hluhluwe-Umfolozi Game Reserve, boat tours on the St Lucia Estuary, and visits to a traditional Zulu village.

Another 25km further north, **MTUBATUBA** (pronounced mmm-too-ba-too-ba, often shortened to Mtuba), is a thriving centre for the local sugar cane industry – both large commercial farms and small-scale African growers – whose economy focuses on the sugar mill. An interesting place, with lots of herbalists, traditional healers and a Zulu market, it's situated at the crossroads of the R618 with the N2, and offers the enticing choice of heading west for Hluhluwe-Umfolozi Game Reserve or east to the St Lucia Estuary – both an easy twenty minutes away. Among its basic facilities, the hamlet has some banks, chemists, supermarkets and filling stations. There are also a couple of good **places to stay**: *Wendy's Country Lodge*, 3 Riverview Drive (☏035 550 0407 or 083 628 1601, ⓦwww.Wendybnb.co.za; ❸), has six luxurious rooms in a house set in an acre of tropical gardens with a swimming pool. They offer advice on touring the area. *The Circle*, 92 Umkuhla Crescent (☏035 550 0660, ⓕ5501 209; ❸) is a tranquil place with two two-bedroom cottages, one of which is self-catering, as well as four double rooms and two single rooms. From here you can go on forest walks and an array of wildlife activities organized by the host, who's fluent in Zulu and has excellent local knowledge.

Some 35km north of Mtubatuba there's another good accommodation option, the *Emdoneni Lodge and Game Farm* (☏035 562 2256 or 083 654 1161, ⓦwww.emdonenilodge.com; ❸–❹), a family-friendly place with a swimming pool and some big cats in enclosures. There's also a **restaurant** and bar serving home-cooked meals. Their **accommodation** consists of B&B and self-catering in four two-bed en-suite rooms as well as six cottages. To get there, take the **Bushlands turn-off** on the east side of the N2; from here turn left, then immediately right over the motorway bridge and continue for another kilometre.

Hluhluwe village

Nearly 60km north of Mtuba, just off the N2 is the straggling village of **HLUHLUWE**, a much less attractive place than either Kwambo or Mtuba. A few shops service the surrounding game farms and there's a friendly **tourist information** office at the Engen filling station, Main St (Mon–Fri 8.30am–5pm, Sat 9am–1pm & Sun 10am–noon; ☎035 562 0353, ⓦwww.hluhluwe.org), which can provide details of numerous lodges and game farms in the vicinity. Definitely worth checking out here is *Ilala Weavers and Savanna Restaurant*, five minutes' drive from Hluhluwe, a hub of community projects that sells well-priced traditional **crafts** in a cheerful atmosphere. The restaurant does decent breakfasts, lunches and dinners and serves cold beers. If you want to visit a Zulu theme park, **Dumazulu Traditional Village**, 14km south of Hluhluwe, has displays of energetic Zulu dancing, beer brewing, spear and basket making.

Accommodation

Dumazulu Kraal and Lodge 1km north of *Isinkwe Backpackers* ☎035 652 2260, dumazulu@iafrica .com.Comfortable en-suite cottages on a farm done out with ethnic African decor. The lodge has an a la carte restaurant and bar, and next door is a Zulu traditional village and a snake park. Half board ⑤
Hluhluwe Guest House In the residential area behind the Engen garage ☎035 562 1462 or 082 629 1462, ⓔhluguest@iafrica.com. B&B accommodation in six comfortable en-suite double rooms, with a pool and small bar and meals on request; the guesthouse can also arrange trips into the Hluhluwe-Umfolozi Game Reserve and Sodwana Bay. ❸
Isinkwe Backpackers Wetlands Lodge 14km

south of Hluhluwe near the Dumazulu Traditional Village ☎035 562 2258, ⓦwww.africasafari.co.za /isinkwe. Rustic hostel with plenty of birds and monkeys living on its 22 hectares of indigenous bush. Dorms, wooden cabins and camping are offered, as well as more comfortable doubles in the lodge and a traditional Zulu-style beehive hut dorm; there's also very reasonably priced meals, or you can self-cater and eat in the massive *boma*. The lodge does tours in open-topped 4WD vehicles to Hluhluwe-Umfolozi and Mkhuze, as well as to Cape Vidal and the St Lucia Wetlands; they can arrange reasonably priced transfers on Wednesdays, Fridays and Sundays to and from Sodwana Bay. ❶

Hluhluwe-Umfolozi Park

Hluhluwe-Umfolozi (daily: April–Sept 6am–6pm; Oct–March 5am–7pm; R30 per vehicle, R15 per person) is KwaZulu-Natal's most outstanding game reserve, considered by some even better than the Kruger. While it certainly can't match Kruger's sheer scale (Hluhluwe is a twentieth of the size) or its teeming game populations, its relatively compact 960 square kilometres have a wilder ambience. This has something to do with the fact that, besides **Hilltop** – an elegant hotel-style restcamp in the northern half of the park – none of the other restcamps are fenced off, and wild animals are free to wander through. The vegetation, with subtropical jungly forest in places and Tarzan-like monkey ropes dangling over the rivers, adds to the sense of adventure. The park also offers the best **wildlife wilderness trails** in the country.

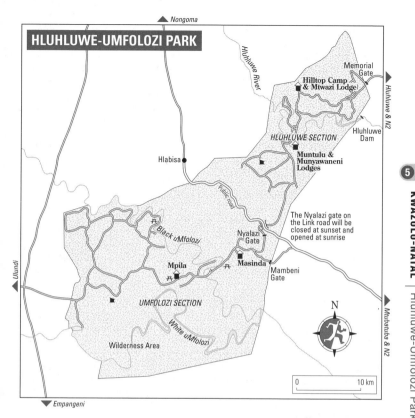

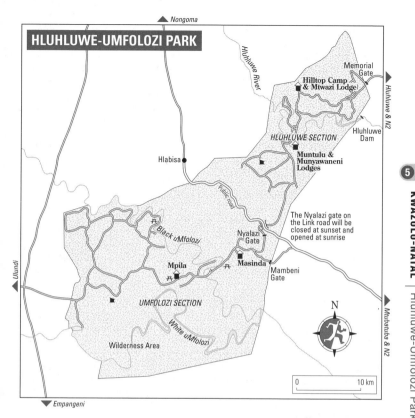

Until recently, the park was two distinct entities – hence its tongue-twisting double-barrelled name (pronounced something like shla-shloo-wee-oom-fa-low-zee) – and the two sections retain their separate characters, reinforced by a public road slicing between them. The southern or **Umfolozi section** takes its name from a corruption of *mfulawozi*, a Zulu word that refers to the fibrous bushes that grow along its rivers. The topography here is characterized by wide, deep valleys incised by the Black and White Umfolozi rivers, with altitudes varying between 60 and 650 metres. Luxuriant riverine vegetation gives way in drier areas to a variety of woodland, savannah, thickets and grassy plains.

The notable feature of the northern **Hluhluwe section** is its river of the same name, so called because of the dangling monkey ropes that hang from the canopy of the riparian forest. A slender, slithering waterway, punctuated by elongated pools, the Hluhluwe rises in the mountains north of the park and passes along sandbanks, rock beds and steep cliffs in the game reserve before seeping away into the St Lucia Wetlands to the east. The higher ground is covered by *veld* and dense thicket, while the well-watered ridges support the softer cover of ferns, lichens, mosses and orchid.

Some history

The sense of pristine wilderness you get at Hluhluwe-Umfolozi is entirely illusory – the result of careful **management** since the 1950s. Despite being the oldest proclaimed national park in Africa (it was created in 1895), Hluhluwe-

517

Umfolozi's future as a game refuge has hung by a thread on several occasions in the last two hundred years. In the nineteenth century, the park lay at the very centre of the **Zulu kingdom** and Umfolozi was the private hunting preserve of the Zulu king, Shaka. During Shaka's reign between 1818 and 1828 the area saw the most sustained campaign of hunting in Zulu history, but this was nothing compared to the destruction caused by white men in the twentieth century, when the park was twice de-proclaimed under pressure from neighbouring farmers whose cattle were being infected by **nagana**, a disease transmitted by tsetse flies from wild to domestic stock. Between 1929 and 1950, a crusade of game **extermination** was launched to wipe out the disease and saw 100,000 head of game from sixteen species fall to the gun, with rhinos alone spared.

It was only in 1952, when the park was handed over to the newly formed organization now known as **KwaZulu-Natal Wildlife**, that the slow process of resuscitation to the threadbare game reserve began. This was done with considerable flair and has been topped by the brilliant success of re-establishing its white rhino population from twenty animals at the start of the twentieth century to nearly two thousand today. In 1994, the **white rhino** became the first species to be removed from the World Conservation Union's endangered list; their survival is down mostly to efforts by conservationists in the Hluhluwe-Umfolozi Park, which has become the world's breeding bank for these animals.

Access and information

There is no public transport into Hluhluwe-Umfolozi. The only way of getting there without your own car is on one of the tours, such as those operated by the Durban operators listed on p.456. Access to the park is via one of three **gates**, two from the east along one of the two tarred roads leading straight off the N2 into the park, and the other from Ulundi in the west. The R618, which begins 23km north of Kwambonambi, reaches **Mambeni Gate** after 27km, providing access to the southern section of the park. Some 46km beyond the R618, an unclassified but signposted and tarred road takes you via **Memorial Gate** into the northernmost section of the park. A third gate, **Cengeni**, is accessible along a thirty-kilometre dirt road from Ulundi to the west. You cannot enter the park from the public road connecting Hlabisa and Mtubatuba, which slices through its centre. Maps and information, including details of guided walks, are available at the receptions of *Hilltop* and *Mpila* camps.

Accommodation

Accommodation is available in both the Umfolozi and Hluhluwe sections of the game reserve. Umfolozi is the less developed of the two sections and you need to bring all your own food, while Hluhluwe's *Hilltop* has a pleasant **restaurant**, the *Mpunyane*, and the *Uzavolo Bar Lounge*, both attached to the central block. **Bookings** for accommodation should be made through KwaZulu-Natal Wildlife (see box on p.449), while camping should be arranged locally.

Umfolozi section (southern)

There are no fences around the Umfolozi camps, so take care when walking around, particularly at night. If there are four or more of you, and you're looking for a thrilling bush experience, one of the **exclusive lodges** – *Gqoyeni*, *Hlatikulu* and *Nselweni*, which come with a cook and a field ranger – offer outstanding value.

Masinda Near the Mambeni Gate, this secluded lodge sleeps eight people in four bedrooms, two of which are en suite. The services of a cook are included in the tariff, with a minimum charge for four people. ❹

Mpila In the centre of the section. *Mpila* offers excellent views of the surrounding wilderness in twelve one-roomed huts with four beds each and communal ablutions (❸); two self-contained three-bedroom cottages for seven people (minimum charge for three people; ❹); and six self-catering chalets that accommodate five people (minimum charge for three people; ❸). There is also a safari camp with seven tents with two beds, and two with four (❸).

Hluhluwe section (northern)

Hluhluwe's *Hilltop* is probably the best publicly run safari camp in South Africa, while the northern section also has some wonderful exclusive lodges.

Hilltop Excellent accommodation set high on the edge of a slope, with sweeping views across the park's hills and valleys. *Hilltop* is surrounded by an electric fence, which keeps out most animals. You may, however, come across nyala, zebra and other herbivores grazing around the chalets – remember that all wild animals are potentially dangerous and should be treated with respect. The camp has modern, comfortable and varied accommodation, with 20 budget two-bed rondavels that share communal ablutions and kitchen facilities; 27 en-suite chalets with bar-fridges, tea- and coffee-making facilities, and some with kitchenettes; and 20 en-suite chalets without kitchens. ❸–❺

Mtwazi Lodge Near *Hilltop.* A comfortable exclusive lodge in a secluded private garden that sleeps nine people. Minimum charge for four people self-catering. ❸

Muntulu and Munyaweneni Four bedrooms with secluded verandahs at each of two upmarket and totally private bush lodges overlooking the Hluhluwe River, rented out to single groups. A cook is on hand to cater and a field ranger is available to take guests on walks. Minimum charge for five people. ❺

Game viewing and activities

Despite its compact size, Hluhluwe-Umfolozi is home to 84 mammal species and close on 350 varieties of birds. The Big Five are all here, and it's no exaggeration to say that this is the best place in the world to see **rhinos** both black and white. **Lions** had become extinct in Umfolozi until 1958, when a black-maned male made an appearance, apparently having traversed the 400km from Mozambique. Females were later introduced, and today there are around seventy of the big cats in the reserve, although they're not easy to see and their future hangs in the balance.

Other **predators** present are cheetah, leopard, spotted hyena and wild dog. **Herbivores** include blue wildebeest, buffalo, giraffe, hippo, impala, kudu, nyala and zebra. When it comes to **birds**, there are over a dozen species of **eagle**, as well as other **raptors** including hawks, goshawks and honey buzzards. Other larger birds include ground hornbills, vultures, owls and herons, and there are hundreds of other beautiful species to look out for. **Reptiles** number in the sixties, including crocodiles and several types of venomous snake, none of which you're likely to see. Along the Hluhluwe River, keep an eye open for the harmless monitor lizards, which resemble miniature dragons.

Where Hluhluwe-Umfolozi really scores over the Kruger is in the variety of activities on offer. Apart from **self-driving** around the park, there are also **self-guided walks** near several of the restcamps, **guided trails** in the company of an armed field ranger, and guided **night drives**. South Africa's first **wilderness trail** started in Umfolozi, and the reserve has remained the best place in South Africa for these. Four-night trails, on which gear is carried by pack donkeys, leave from the base camp – you sleep under canvas for the next two nights, returning on the fourth to base. These all-inclusive trails, which must be booked through the KwaZulu-Natal Wildlife (see p.449), run from March to the end of October and cost around R1800 per person. You are accompanied by an armed ranger and all your gear – including linen and food, but excluding alcohol – is included in the price. Shorter weekend trails, giving you two nights in the bush, run over the same period for about half the price.

The Greater St Lucia Wetland Park

Five distinct ecosystems make up the **Greater St Lucia Wetland Park**, a 2750-square-kilometre patchwork of separate pieces locking together the St Lucia Reserve, St Lucia Park, False Bay Park, St Lucia Marine Reserve, Sodwana Bay National Park, Cape Vidal State Forest, Mkhuze Game Reserve, and other interlinking areas. Planned developments will make this the third-largest protected area in the country – it's already one of the most fascinating. The Wetland Park's origins as several separate reserves is readily apparent in the fact that few internal roads link one area to another, and each section is reached by a separate road that spurs off the N2.

The most striking feature is the 360-square-kilometre **Lake St Lucia**, South Africa's largest inland body of water, formed 25,000 years ago when the oceans receded. The lake is flanked by mountainous **dunes** covered by forest and grassland, whose peaks soar to an astonishing 200m above the beach to form a slender rampart against the Indian Ocean. Aside from the lake and dune ecosystems, the reserve protects a **marine zone** of warm tropical seas, coral reefs and endless sandy beaches; the **papyrus and reed wetland** of the Mkuze Swamps, on the north of the lake; and on the western shore dry **savannah** and **thornveld**. Any one of these would justify conservation, but their confluence around the lake makes this a world-class wilderness – a fact recognized in 1999, when it was declared a UNESCO World Heritage Site.

St Lucia

Once a rough and out-of-the-way anglers' hangout, **ST LUCIA**, which lies at the mouth of the **St Lucia Estuary** in the extreme south of the park, is in the process of reinventing itself as a well-organized eco-destination. Reached after 32km at the end of the R618, east of Mtubatuba, the town can become pretty hectic in midsummer when the **angling** fanatics descend on the town for the school holidays; you can't miss the plethora of tackle and bait shops, seafood restaurants and vehicles buzzing up and down the main street bristling with fishing rods, beers and men. A spin-off is that out of season, when the hordes of anglers have left, there's plenty of accommodation across a broad range of budgets.

The town takes its name from the estuary, whose mouth was reached by Portuguese explorers in 1576, and which they named Santa Lucia. During the second half of the eighteenth century, landlocked Boers made attempts to claim the mouth as a port, but were pipped at the post by the British, who sent HMS *Goshawk* in 1884 to annex the whole area, which then developed as a fishing resort. In the 1920s, the town got its first hotel, and in the 1950s, it was connected to the mainland by a bridge.

St Lucia's best feature is the **estuary**, hidden behind the buildings along the main drag, and easy to miss if you drive quickly through. The main reason to come here, however, is to get to **Cape Vidal** (see p.523), the real prize of the area, inside the **Greater St Lucia Wetland Park**, where strictly limited accommodation may necessitate basing yourself in St Lucia town.

Arrival, information and orientation

The **Baz Bus** comes into town several times a week and drops passengers off anywhere in town. The main drag is MacKenzie Street, where at no. 57 you'll find the official St Lucia **Tourism and Information Centre** (Mon–Fri 8am–5pm, Sat & Sun 8am–1pm, ☎035 590 1075, ⊛www.stlucia .co.za), as well as some filling stations, two well-stocked supermarkets, an ATM, two banks (Mon, Wed & Fri 9am–3.30pm) and a string of eating places. For information about the Wetland National Park, your best bet is the KwaZulu-Natal Wildlife office (daily 8am–4.30pm; ☎035 590 1340), at the south end of Pelican Road, which runs parallel to MacKenzie, but is two blocks to its east.

Accommodation

Out of season, reasonably priced accommodation isn't hard to find in St Lucia, but during December/January and around Easter, expect to pay double. KwaZulu-Natal Wildlife (see p.449) has three excellent camping grounds: Eden Park, on the banks of the estuary, across the road from the KwaZulu-Natal Wildlife office; Sugarloaf, a sizeable camp on the best site in St Lucia, also along the estuary and a few hundred metres north of Eden Park in the same road; and Iphiva, the quietest and most rustic of the camps, reached off MacKenzie Street, north of the R618. Book through the KwaZulu-Natal Wildlife office in St Lucia.

Bib's International Backpackers 310 Mackenzie St ☎035 590 1056, ⊛www.bibs.co.za. Firmly on the Baz Bus route, this decent thatched lodge offers camping, dorms, doubles and self-catering en-suite private rooms, and facilities such as internet access, microwaves, laundry and pool tables. They also offer a range of tours and day-trips, including boat trips, cultural visits and overnight trails and drives. ❶

Boma Hotel Mackenzie Street ☎035 590 1330. Twenty luxury self-catering cabanas that sleep six people, and four that sleep four, some of which have balconies with wonderful views of the estuary, plus there's a pool, wooden sundecks and braai stands. ❷

iGwalagwala Guest House 91 Pelican St ☎035 590 1069, ⊛igwala@mweb.co.za. Five spacious en-suite rooms in a house in a quiet part of town, with a large garden and swimming pool. ❸

Jo a Lize Mackenzie Street ☎035 590 1085, ⊛joalizelodge@futurenet.co.za. Self-contained, self-catering flats and tiny but clean en-suite B&B units. ❷–❸

Kingfisher Lodge Mackenzie Street ☎035 590 1015, ⊛stluciakingfisherlodge@mweb.co.za. The most comfortable B&B in town has one of the few views of the estuary, with seven African-themed chalets, which may mean a stuffed buffalo head glaring down at you from the walls. ❹

Pumula Lodge 25 Pelican St ☎ & ⊕035 590 1328. Clean B&B doubles in a family house and a self-catering lakeside chalet. ❷–❸

St Lucia Wetlands Guest House 20 Kingfisher St ☎035 590 1098, ⊛www.stluciawetlands.com. Five large en-suite rooms with queen-size beds in an owner-run guesthouse, offering exceptional service and comfort. ❸

The Town

There's not much to do in St Lucia itself, but it does provide an excellent base for a number of activities (see box on p.522). This aside, other than eating, drinking and fishing, the main way of killing time in the village is at the **St Lucia Crocodile Centre** (daily 8am–4.30pm, crocodile feeding Sat 3pm; R20), at the park gate about 2km north of town on the road to Cape Vidal. This isn't another of the exploitative wildlife freak-shows common throughout South Africa, but a serious educative spin-off of KwaZulu-Natal Wildlife's crocodile conservation campaign. Up until the end of the 1960s, "flat dogs" or "travelling handbags" were regarded as pests, and this led to a hunting free-for-all that saw them facing extinction in the area. Just in time, it was realized that crocs have an important role in the ecological cycle, and the KZN Wildlife began a successful **breeding programme**, returning the crocs to the wild to

Activities around St Lucia

Small as it is, St Lucia is the biggest settlement around the Greater St Lucia Wetland Park, and it is the best place to link up with the activities on offer that can really enhance your visit. You can book most activities through the operators themselves, or through one of the agents such as Leisure Eco Tours (☎035 590 1467) in Mackenzie Street.

African village visits
Trips to an authentic Zulu community (not a constructed "cultural village"), where you can visit the local church, *shebeen* and a *sangoma* or traditional healer. Tours operated by Khula Village Tours (☎082 765 2021) depart at 9am and 1pm from St Lucia and cost R100 per person, including a meal.

Ecotours
An outstanding range of tours in the wetland led by a qualified zoologist and marine biologist, including the full-day St Lucia World Heritage Tour; the Turtle Tour (Nov–March) to watch the annual turtle egg-laying migration; and the interesting and unusual Chameleon Night Drive, which goes out in search of the sixteen chameleon species of the St Lucia region (a staggering fourteen of which are endemic). Tours operated by Shaka Barker Tours (☎035 590 1162, ✉shakabarker@futurenet.co.za) cost from R200 to R400, depending on length, and usually include a meal.

Fishing
Eco-friendly river fishing trips for novices and seasoned anglers with a skipper, guide, experienced fisherman and tackle supplied. Suitable fish will be tagged and released in your name as part of the oceanographic fish-tagging programme. The approximately five-hour trip run by Fish on Line (☎035 590 1536 or 082 765 2448, ✉fishonline@worldonline.co.za) costs R250 for the first person and R100 for the second, and includes refreshments and a light meal.

Hiking
There are a number of short and longer hikes under the authority of KwaZulu-Natal Wildlife in the St Lucia/Cape Vidal area. A guided full-day Wetland Walk costs R35

bolster numbers. The Crocodile Centre aims to rehabilitate the reputation of these maligned creatures, with informative displays and an astonishing cross-section of species (although only the Nile crocodile occurs in the wild in South Africa) lounging around enclosed pools. There's also an impressive collection of snakes and a very good **bookshop** at the centre, with items on natural history and cheap but informative booklets about the local coastal and wetland ecology, as well as the *Zulu & I* restaurant (see below).

Eating

For **eating**, the best place is the *North Coast Restaurant,* Mackenzie Street, which serves good, reasonably priced seafood. Another option is the *Zulu & I Restaurant and Tea Garden* at the St Lucia Crocodile Centre (daily till about 9pm), a family restaurant where you can eat reasonably priced sandwiches, pasta, pizzas, chicken and meaty dishes while watching birds, crocs and 25 species of snake (not on the menu). The *Boat House Gallery Fish Grill*, at the ski-boat club at the end of Pelican Street has an interesting and affordable menu and pleasant views of the estuary. If you want to enter the spirit of the place and catch your own fish, head for the Bait and Tackle Shop, also in Mackenzie Street, which sells rods, tackle and (should you fail to hook anything) fresh fish, as well as all the spices and condiments you'll need for a fish braai.

and there are several overnight trails. The four-night/five-day Emoyeni Trail costs R35 per person per night; the two-night/three-day Mziki Trail costs R45 per person per night; while the fully catered and portered four-night Wilderness Trail works out at R1300 per person. For further information contact KwaZulu-Natal Wildlife Central Bookings in Maritzburg (℡033 845 1000, ⍾www.kznwildlife.com) or the St Lucia office (℡035 590 9002 or 035 590 1340).

Horse-riding

Zululand Horse Trails (℡035 562 0701 or 083 591 2119) offers rides on the western shore of the lake system from the gate of the False Bay Park (see p.526).

Kayaking

Kayaking in the lake system gives an unparallelled experience of the wetland. St Lucia Kayak Safaris (℡083 448 6466) runs half- and full-day outings which cost R175–200 including all gear, transfers to the launch site, a light lunch and refreshments.

Lake cruises

If you spend any time in St Lucia, it's well worth going on a one-and-a-half-hour guided lake cruise on KwaZulu-Natal Wildlife's *Santa Lucia* (R65). From the deck, you stand a good chance of seeing crocodiles and one of the eight hundred hippos wallowing and snorting in Lake St Lucia, as well as pelicans, fish eagles, kingfishers and storks. Cruises leave daily from the launch site next to the bridge on the west side of the estuary at 8.30am, 10.30am & 2.30pm; and on Friday and Saturday at 4pm there's a **sunset cruise. Bookings** are essential in peak season and can be made though the KwaZulu-Natal Wildlife office (℡035 590 9002 or 035 590 1340).

Whale-watching

Humpback whales cruise along the wetland's shore, and in season (June–Oct) you can join a two-hour boat excursion to look for them. Trips on the *Aurora* leave at 9am and 2pm and cost R230 for a minimum of six people. Book through Leisure Eco Tours (℡035 590 1467).

Cape Vidal

Another popular fishing spot, **Cape Vidal** (daily: April–Sept 6am–6pm; Oct–March 5am–7pm; R25 per vehicle, R20 per person) has the edge over St Lucia in that numbers are limited to just one hundred day-visitors' vehicles, while accommodation for overnight stays is limited to KwaZulu-Natal Wildlife's facilities. The only way of getting there is via St Lucia, from where you take a rough dirt road (tarring began in 2001) north for 32km, navigating a narrow bridge of land between the lake on the west and the Indian Ocean on the east. The journey passes through pine plantations, open grassland and wetland areas.

Even if you aren't a keen angler, there's enough stunning wilderness at Cape Vidal to keep you chilling out for several days. The sea is only minutes from the KZN Wildlife accommodation, and an offshore reef shelters the coast from the high seas, making it safe for **swimming**. If you're keen on **snorkelling**, an underwater extravaganza of hard and soft corals and colourful fish awaits. Burly anglers who use the rocks for casting their lines into the wide ocean may look at you in disbelief if you go looking into the tiny water worlds of the **rock pools**, but you'll be rewarded with sightings of seaweeds, snails, crabs, sea cucumbers, anemones, urchins and small fish.

Large mammals and fish move just offshore in the open seas beyond the reef. Cape Vidal is an excellent place for shore sightings of **humpback whales**, which breed off Mozambique, not far to the north, in winter. In October they move south, drifting on the warm Agulhas current with their calves. If you're lucky you may see these and other whales from the vantage of the dunes, but without binoculars they'll just look like specks on the horizon. A **whale-watching tower**, reached through the dune forest south of the restcamp, provides an even higher viewpoint. Eighteen-metre plankton-feeding whale sharks, the largest and gentlest of the sharks, have been sighted off this coast in schools of up to seventy at a time, and manta rays and dolphins are also common in these waters.

Practicalities

If you're planning to stay overnight, and this is highly recommended, prebook your **accommodation** before trawling out. There are eighteen five-bed chalets (minimum charge for three people; ❸); twelve eight-bed Swiss-style log cabins (minimum charge for four people; ❸), all of which are en suite and fully equipped at the service camp – all you need to bring is your own food and drink; and an eight-bed bush lodge (❸). Cabins are serviced and cleaned every morning by camp staff. There's also a campsite with space for fifty tents, in the dune forest near the beach, with ablution facilities; there are also four cabins for large groups. On **arrival** at Cape Vidal, report to the Conservation Services office (daily 8am–12.30pm & 2–4.30pm).

Reservations for cabins and chalets should be made through KwaZulu-Natal Wildlife (see box on p.449). **Bookings for the campsite** are vital during school holidays and over long weekends, and can be made in writing up to one year in advance through the Officer-in-Charge, Cape Vidal, Private Bag X01, St Lucia Estuary 3936 (☎035 590 9012; note that the phone lines can be erratic). Although **petrol** and firewood can be bought at Cape Vidal, for all other **supplies** the nearest place to stock up is St Lucia.

The western shore

The **western shore** of Lake St Lucia marks the old seashore, harking back for aeons to a time when the ocean level was 2m higher than it is today. Decayed matter from marine animals has created a rich soil that once supported an extensive array of animal life, and although the Big Five were shot out ages ago there are still **birds** and over a hundred species of **butterfly** flitting about. Among the **herbivores** are suni, Africa's smallest antelope, as well as nyala and red duiker. With no dangerous predators apart from **crocodiles** (take care along the shore), the inland bushveld and woodlands are safe for walking without a guide.

The main activities along the western shore, which is accessible only in your own vehicle, are **fishing** and **bird-watching**. Most camps also have **waymarked trails** that make a thoroughly enjoyable way, if you're moderately energetic, to explore the lakeside vegetation and birds. You should also keep an eye open for game, especially the water-loving reedbuck that take refuge in the swamps.

The most luxurious place to stay in the Greater St Lucia Wetland Park – and indeed the only **privately run accommodation** in this World Heritage Site – is the seriously upmarket *Makakatana Bay Lodge* (☎035 550 4189, ⓦwww.makakatana.co.za; ❸) near the Charter's Creek KZN Wildlife camp. The lodge's five luxury suites on the lake's edge or in tangled forest are connected by wooden walkways, are air-conditioned and have indoor bath facilities as well as outdoor showers. The fully inclusive price takes in all meals and activities – canoe safaris, boat trips, beach safaris and game drives.

Charter's Creek

Primarily an anglers' retreat, **CHARTER'S CREEK** (daily: April–Sept 6am–8pm; Oct–March 5am–8pm; R20), which lies at the southern end of the lake, is also excellent for **bird-watching** and has two half-day **trails**. The major attraction here is the camp, situated on a cliff edge with views across the lake. From here you can spot waterfowl and flamingos – even pelicans make an appearance – while permanent residents include hippos and crocodiles. The seven-kilometre **Isikhova Trail** and the five-kilometre **Umkhumbe Trail** both leave from the camp and shouldn't take more than two to three hours to complete. The trails take in typical western-shore coastal forest and provide the opportunity to spot small **game**, including the tiny red duiker, with its short, backward-pointing horns. Other species occasionally encountered include mongooses, bushbuck, jackals, bushbabies and, commonest of all, vervet monkeys.

To **get there**, turn off the N2, some 20km north of Mtubatuba and follow the signs all the way to Charter's Creek, via the Nyalazi River halt. **Accommodation** is in a choice of a seven-bedded cottage (minimum charge for four people; ❷), and chalets (❷) – ten four-bedded, fourteen three-bedded and one two-bedded – all of which are fully equipped. There are also fourteen camp sites. Servicing is done by camp staff, and you must bring your own food as there are no restaurants, shops or other facilities. Although you can't swim in the lake, there's a pool at the camp for cooling off in. **Bookings** should be made through the KwaZulu-Natal Wildlife office (see box on p.449).

Fanies Island

Not an island at all but part of the western shore, approximately 20km north of Charter's Creek as the crow flies, **Fanies Island** (daily: April–Sept 6am–8pm; Oct–March 5am–8pm; R20) looks out onto reeded islands between networks of waterlogged paths worn away by hippos. The views are magnificent across the reed beds to the grasslands, forests and misty hill-like dunes of Cape Vidal on the coast; however, the large croc population here makes bathing or paddling out of the question. Like all the western shore camps, Fanies Island is much favoured by anglers, but this is one of the most secluded, and attractively positioned.

Even if you're not fishing, it's a tranquil enough place to spend time, with a couple of walking trails to help you explore. The five-kilometre **Umkhiwane Trail** can be completed in two hours and goes through forest, open grassveld and swamp forest, and is highly recommended for bird-watching. Hippos, vervet monkeys, bushbuck, warthog, reedbuck and waterbuck are among the common mammals you stand a good chance of seeing. The **Umboma Trail** is shorter, wending its way through forest and back to camp along the lake shore.

To **get there**, follow the instructions for Charter's Creek, but 20km north of Mtubatuba, take the undesignated tarred road that runs east from the N2. Eleven kilometres from the N2, the route splits into two dirt roads; take the northernmost one for 14km to reach Fanies Island. The route is well signposted. **Accommodation** is in a seven-bedded cottage (minimum charge for four people; ❷); and twelve fully equipped two-bedded rondavels (❷) with their own fridges, but sharing an ablution block and a self-catering kitchen. There are twenty shaded **campsites**, for which **reservations** should be made through the Camp Manager, Fanies Island, PO Box 1259, Mtubabtuba 3935 (☎035 550 9035). All other accommodation should be booked through the KwaZulu-Natal Wildlife office (see box on p.449). **Fuel** is available at the camp, as is a limited range of basic foods, but you're far better off stocking up in Hluhluwe or Mtubatuba before you come. You can arrange two-hour boat trips (R65 per person) on the lake with Imvubu Launch Tours through the KwaZulu-Natal Wildlife office.

False Bay Park

Situated about 20km north of Fanies Island, **False Bay Park** (daily: April–Sept 6am–8pm; Oct–March 5am–8pm; R20) perches on the west shore of a small, lozenge-shaped waterway connected to Lake St Lucia by a narrow steep-sided channel known colourfully as "Hell's Gates". Excellent for bird-watching, it's a quiet place, which doesn't see many tourists or even anglers despite offering opportunities to fish for both freshwater and marine species, as well as Cape salmon. The park gives an excellent, low-key experience of the lake, which you can get onto with **launch tours**. If you want to get out into the bush, the eight-kilometre **Dugandlovu Trail** and the ten-kilometre circular **Mpophomeni Trail** will easily keep you busy for a couple of days. Both are clearly waymarked, pass through a variety of terrain and offer the opportunity of seeing birds and a decent variety of antelope and other small mammals such as jackals, mongooses, servals, genets, warthogs and vervet monkeys. If you're not so energetic, there's the shorter six-kilometre **Ingwe Trail**, which runs alongside the lake.

To **get there**, turn off the N2 towards Hluhluwe 49km north of the Mtubatuba turn-off, and continue east for 4km until you reach Hluhluwe. Continue through the village to a T-junction at the end of the road and follow the signposts for 15km to the False Bay Gate. There's a **campsite** at Lister's Point about midway down the west shore of False Bay, which has communal ablutions, but you must supply everything else. About 8km to the south, *Dugandlovu* **hutted camp** has four basic, four-bed chalets (❶) with cold showers, toilets, gas cookers and paraffin lamps. If you want hot water, the camp has big, fat, three-legged pots which you can put on the fire to heat water, then lug into the shower. You must bring all your own gear, including linen and sleeping bags. **Bookings** for both camps must be made through the Officer-in-Charge, False Bay Park, PO Box 222, Hluhluwe 3960 (☎035 562 0425).

Mkhuze Game Reserve

Mkhuze Game Reserve (daily: April–Sept 6am–6pm; Oct–March 5am–7pm; R35 per vehicle, R30 per person) is a major part of the Greater St Lucia Wetland Park, connected to the coastal plain by a slender corridor through which the Mkuze River flows before emptying itself in Lake St Lucia. Reached across the Lebombo Mountains, 28km from Mkuze village on the N2, the reserve has no lions, but a rich cross-section of mammals covering 78 species inhabits its confines. It's for its varied and highly beautiful countryside and the avifauna that the reserve really rates – this is among the top spots for bird-watching in the country, with an impressive 430 species on record. Some of the prizes include Pels fishing owl and Rudd's apalis, a small insect-eating bird with a very restricted distribution. Even if you know nothing about birds, you're likely to appreciate one of Africa's most colourful here – the lilac-breasted roller.

Defined to the west by the Lebombo Mountains, Mkhuze marks the final haul of the coastal plain stretching down the east of the continent from Kenya. The landscape varies from wetlands consisting of seasonal flood plains floating with waterlilies, reed beds and swamps, to savanna covered with grass. Elsewhere you'll come across stands of acacias (thorn trees) and in the south across the Mkuzi River you can wander through the cathedral-like fig forest that echoes to the shriek of trumpeter hornbills.

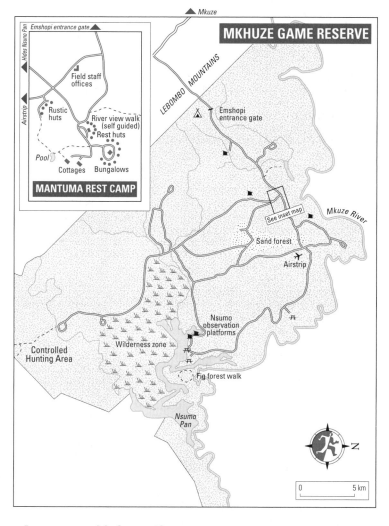

MKHUZE GAME RESERVE

LEBOMBO MOUNTAINS

Emshopi entrance gate

See inset map

Mkuze River

Sand forest

Airstrip

Nsumo observation platforms

Wilderness zone

Controlled Hunting Area

Fig forest walk

Nsumo Pan

0   5 km

Inset map — MANTUMA REST CAMP:

Emshopi entrance gate ▲

Hides Nsumo Pan ◄

Airstrip ◄

Field staff offices

Rustic huts

River view walk (self guided)

Rest huts

Pool

Cottages   Bungalows

MANTUMA REST CAMP

KWAZULU-NATAL | The Greater St Lucia Wetland Park

Access and information

There's no public **transport** into Mkuze, and if you don't have your own vehicle you'll need to join one of the **tours** that start in **Mkuze**. The village has a few shops for supplies, a garage for petrol and repairs and the very pleasant *Ghost Mountain Inn* (℡035 573 1025, ❀www.ghostmountaininn.co.za; ❺) signposted off the N2, which is great for a drink or meal and a dunk in their pool, even if you aren't staying. Tribe Africa which operates from the hotel, runs four-hour day and night **game drives** in Mkuze (R120 per person; minimum three people; ℡035 573 1474).

If you're **self-driving**, the easiest way to get to the reserve is to leave the N2 at Mkuze and follow the signs along a good dirt road for 28km to **Emshopi Gate**. An alternative route, which leaves the N2 further south, 35km north of

Hluhluwe village, involves a lot more driving on dirt and doesn't knock off that much distance. For navigating your way around the park, the **reception office** (☏035 573 9004) provides a clear map that shows all routes and distances and gives general information about the park.

Accommodation

A **campsite** is situated right at Emshopi Gate, while **Mantuma**, the main public restcamp, 9km into the park in the northern section, has a range of **accommodation**. Cheapest are the three-bedded rest huts with shared ablution facilities and a kitchen (❷). There are also larger chalets that sleep three (❸), five (minimum charge for three people; ❸) and seven (minimum charge for four people; ❹). The most enticing units are the large two- or four-person traditional walk-in en-suite safari tents, each with its own roofed, but open-sided kitchen across the way (❸). All units are fully equipped and you need only bring food and drink. **Reservations** for camping should be made through the Camp Superintendent, Mkuze Game Reserve, PO Box X550, Mkuze 3965 (☏035 573 9004); all other accommodation must be booked through the KwaZulu-Natal Wildlife (see box on p.449).

There's a **fuel pump** at the entrance gate where you can fill up your car, and a **shop** that sells basic supplies and books at the camp reception, but you should really stock up in Mkuze village before heading out here.

Game viewing and activities

Of the predators, **cheetah** and **leopard** are present but rarely glimpsed; you stand a better chance of seeing fox-like black-backed **jackals**. The obvious draw-card of Mkuze, however, are its black and white **rhinos**. The **impala** antelope will also be hard to miss, and you should catch sight of the large, spiral-horned **eland** and **kudu**. **Baboons** and **vervet monkeys** are generally found rustling around in the trees and making a nuisance of themselves on the ground, while at night you could be treated to the eerie call of the thick-tailed **bushbaby** from the canopy.

Some 84km of road traverse Mkuze, but one of the best ways to see game is to stay put and wait for the animals to come to you. As a result, several **hides** (marked on the map given out at reception) have been erected at artificial waterholes and on the edge of pans. All animals have to drink at some time, particularly in the drier months when naturally occurring water is scarcer, so you're bound to have a relaxed and interesting time at a hide if you chill out with a pair of binoculars and a good field guide.

The two hides at **Nsumo Pan**, in the southern section of the park, apart from overlooking a very beautiful natural waterway, are superbly placed for observing waterfowl. The picnic site at Nsumo is one of the few places in the game reserve where you may leave your car, and it makes a great place to stop and eat. Between July and September, if conditions are right, you can catch up to five hundred **birds** on the water at one time. Flocks of pelicans and flamingos make their appearance, as do kingfishers, fish eagles, waders, ducks, geese and countless other species.

KZN Wildlife offers a number of activities, including their recommended **night drives** from Mantuma (R60). During the day, you can explore Mkuze on foot on a two-hour **conducted walk** (R45) with a field ranger. Many of the older rangers speak very little English, and their main function is to protect you; current KZN Wildlife policy, however, is to employ younger guides who speak English well and have a knowledge of the environment, so check out the situation when you book your walk at the restcamp reception. One of the areas you can explore with a guide is the three-kilometre **Mkhuze Fig Forest Trail** – another highlight of the reserve. **Sycamore fig forest** is one of the rarest types of woodland in South Africa, and the stands of massive trees give the forest a gentle green glow. Look out for the flashing red flight feathers of fruit-eating **birds** like the purple-crested lourie or green pigeons, and listen for the tap-tap of golden-tailed woodpeckers on the trees. **Monkeys** and **baboons**, which pass through from time to time pose no threat, except to steal your food, but you should keep alert to the possibility of encountering **black rhinos** or **hippos**.

The small **Crafts Centre**, marked on the map you pick up at reception, offers some excellent and inexpensive Zulu crafts made by local people.

Phinda Private Game Reserve

Although it's not one of the great South African game-viewing destinations, **Phinda Private Game Reserve**, on a 150-square-kilometre ranch at the southern end of the Mkhuze reserve, is certainly a contender for the most stylish. The reserve offers a good chance of seeing **lion**, **cheetah** and both varieties of **rhino** on your game drives, but you can't help feeling it's all a bit too well-managed. At the moment the property is too small to sustain a self-regulating wildlife ecology, but if, as is hoped, it becomes integrated with surrounding parks (as has happened around the Kruger National Park) this could change dramatically.

Phinda is interesting, however, as an **eco-tourism** experiment based on the philosophy that to conserve wildlife in Africa it is necessary to bring tangible benefits to local communities. Not only has degraded farmland been returned to wilderness (*phinda* means "return" in Zulu), but more people now work providing services to tourists than were employed when it was ranchland.

Whatever Phinda may lack as a wildlife destination is made up for abundantly by the sheer panache with which it provides fine-tuned luxury and hospitality to its upmarket clientele. **Accommodation** is at four lodges, with *Mountain Lodge* providing vistas of the Lebombo range and the nearby St Lucia coastal plain; *Rock Lodge* embracing a more intimate experience, with just six glass chalets chiselled into rock; *Forest Lodge* offering stunning Afro-Japanese-style timber houses on stilts, each tucked away discreetly among bush and trees; and *Phinda Vlei Lodge*, in a sand forest on the edge of a pan system, with highly polished timber and glass chalets. The **food**, described as "eclectic pan-African", is excellent. All game drives or walks are accompanied by well-informed expert guides, who are as good as any you'll find in South Africa.

Bookings should be made through Conservation Corporation Africa in Johannesburg, Private Bag X27, Benmore 2010 (☎011 809 4300, ⓦwww.ccafrica.com), or through one of the specialist travel agents listed in Basics. Unlike public parks, Phinda's wilderness is only open to its resident guests and you'll be given detailed instructions on **how to get there** when you make your booking. **Prices** (❾) include all meals and game activities.

Northern Maputaland

Northern Maputaland, roughly the region north of Mkhuze Game Reserve, is the remotest tract of South Africa, mostly accessible only along dirt roads that work their tortuous way to the coast. For much of this area, a 4WD vehicle is essential and it's best to travel in two vehicles as there's nowhere to get repairs done and facilities are poor. It's also essential to carry an inflated spare tyre, jack and wheel spanner and spare water. Watch out for unattended stray animals and school children wandering onto the roads; never resort to speeding on dirt roads to make up time, and watch out for potholes on all roads.

Some 11km north of **Mkuze** village, the longest tarred road in Maputaland snakes north and then east for 133km, before stopping abruptly at the busy, run-down settlement of **Kwangwanase** (Manguzi on some maps), 24km short of the coast. As it turns toward the sea, the road brushes past a short track that leads to **Ndumo Game Reserve** and 8km later the entrance gate to Tembe Elephant Park, both reaching down from the Mozambique border. The latter is a very underdeveloped conservation area, to which only the dedicated go, as only five, private 4WD vehicles are admitted per day. It's far easier to see elephants elsewhere, such as the Kruger Park (see p.693). From Kwangwanase, 26km beyond Tembe, a road heads for Kosi Bay and the Mozambique border.

To the south of Tembe, roads branch off this tarred spine, leading to **Mbazwana**, a tiny settlement that gains some status from being poised between **Sodwana Bay** to the south and **Lake Sibaya** to the north. Mbazwana can be reached by striking south off the tar at **Jozini**, a small, dog-eared town that will seem like a thriving metropolis next to anything you'll encounter beyond.

Sodwana Bay

A tiny scoop in the Zululand Coast, **SODWANA BAY** (daily 24hr; R20), 19km south of Mbazwana along an unexpected interlude of tar, is the only breach in an almost flawless length of strand extending 170km from St Lucia to Kosi Bay. It's the fortuitous convergence of the bay (which makes it easy to launch boats) with the world's southernmost coral reefs that makes Sodwana the most popular base in the country for **scuba diving** and the most popular KwaZulu-Natal Wildlife resort. Because the continental shelf comes extremely close to shore with near-vertical drops less than 1km away, it offers very deep waters, much loved by anglers, who gather here to launch out for some of South Africa's best deep-sea **game fishing**, mostly tag and release. The abundance of game fish also makes for some of the best surf fly-fishing in the country.

When there's no one around, Sodwana Bay is paradise: a truly magnificent place with tepid waters (21–27°C), terrific sandy beaches, relaxed diving or snorkelling and plenty of cheap and basic accommodation. Over weekends and during school holidays, however, the picture changes, with fashion-conscious Jo'burgers tearing down in their late-model 4WDs trailing boats to show off their designer wet-suits, while thick-set anglers from Gauteng, Free State and Mpumalanga kick up some sand with their heavy tread, drink themselves into a stupor and turn the beach into a massive 4WD car park. A gentler presence from mid-November to February are the leatherback and loggerhead **turtles**, who make their way onto Sodwana's beaches to reproduce, as they've been doing for the last 60,000 years (see box on p.534).

Access and orientation

There is no public **transport** to Sodwana, although some of the local dive operators will meet the **Baz Bus**, when it pulls into the village of Hluhluwe on its four-times-a-week run from Durban. This tends to be changeable, so check when you book. Alternatively, **taxi** operator Themba Nkosi (☎035 571 0177 or 083 742 4520) can arrange transfers from Hluhluwe or from *Isinkwe Backpackers*, 14km south of Hluhluwe (see p.516). Some of the Johannesburg-based dive outfits also provide transport from the city to Sodwana (check when booking). **Hitching** is possible, but even if you succeed in thumbing a lift there, the place is so spread out that getting around on foot is a major hassle. The park takes in the bay itself, while the desultory collection of shops and an upmarket lodge that pass for the **town** are 8km to the west, back along the Mbazwana road. The KwaZulu-Natal Wildlife office, park entry gate, campsites, chalets and three of the dive lodges are up the hill past the "town". Here you'll also find a small shop selling **food** (but no liquor) and other camping basics. It closes at around 5pm, so don't leave your purchases until you return from the beach. **Petrol** is available from 6am till 6pm. There is no ATM, but the shop may be prepared to help you draw cash if you have a recognized credit card. Some public phones next to the shop take coins or cards.

Accommodation

Most **accommodation** at Sodwana lies inside the KZN Wildlife conservation area along the bay's beaches but the most luxurious place to stay, *Sodwana Bay Lodge*, is outside.

Inside the park

If you're staying at any of the *Coral Divers* or *Sandton Scuba* you must pay a R35 daily camping fee directly to KZN Wildlife at their office. This buys you a paper disc that gives you entrance to the campsite. *Mseni* includes the fee in their rate. The camping fee is additional to the R20 park entrance fee that everyone pays.

Coral Divers ☏ 035 571 0290, ⊛ www.coraldiver.co.za. The largest dive outfit at Sodwana is an inexpensive, relaxed and friendly place, with a variety of two-bedded safari tents, two-bedded cabins with shared ablutions, and two-bedded cabins with en-suite showers and toilets available on a half-board or self-catering basis. A large dining area next to the bar overlooks the pool and sundeck; takeaways are available throughout the day, and there's also satellite TV. PADI-certified scuba courses range from a one-day "discovering scuba" to open water certification and up to instructor level. *Coral Divers* supplies all your equipment for training and subsequent dives, and also rents out scuba gear. Transport is supplied to and from the beach to coincide with dives and meal times. ❶–❹

KZN Wildlife campsites ☏ 035 571 0051, ℻ 035 571 0115. There are a staggering 413 campsites, with a minimum fee of R140 per site during public and school holidays as well as Friday and Saturday nights; the seasonal population explosion allegedly gives Sodwana the largest campsite in the southern hemisphere.

KZN Wildlife chalets ☏ 033 845 1000. Ten five-bedded (minimum charge for three people) and ten eight-bedded (minimum charge for four people) fully equipped log cabins. ❷

Mseni Lodge ☏ 035 571 0284, ⊛ www.msenilodge.com. A comfortable lodge with twenty en-suite log cabins spread out between thick coastal forest, providing bedding and linen, but no cooking facilities; half-board includes KZN Wildlife daily fee. Dinner and breakfast are served in the a la carte restaurant, and there's also a bar, satellite TV, a swimming pool and email facilities. The lodge has a full-time registered dive operation and qualified dive masters and skippers. A variety of dive packages are offered, some only for divers who already hold a recognized qualification. Land excursions include 4WD day trips to lakes Sibaya and Bangazi (in the park's wilderness area) and lower Mkhuze; and trips to secluded beaches for snorkelling, fishing or plain fun. ❺

Sandton Scuba ☏ 082 560 7303 or 082 253 3714; bookings Johannesburg ☏ 011 463 2201. Budget self-catering accommodation is offered in two-bedded tents with mattresses. Plates, crockery, pots, pans and gas stoves are provided, but you have to bring your own linen. PADI diving courses from open water to instructor are offered, with experienced and qualified instructors and skippers. The price does not include the KZN wildlife fee of R35. ❶

Outside the park

Sodwana Bay Lodge In the village, 8km from the bay ☏ 035 571 0095, central booking ☏ 0861 000 333, ⊛ www.sodwanadivelodge.co.za. An upmar-ket hotel-style lodge, with en-suite two-bedded B&B chalets and six- or eight-bedded self-catering cottages. The reasonably priced *Leatherback*

Restaurant and Bar offers decent food, including the best pizzas around and a carvery most evenings. A groovers' bar downstairs has pool tables, music, a swimming pool and a sundeck that attracts both visitors and locals. The full-time registered dive operation here offers diving instruction from open water to instructor level, and rents out scuba equipment and they can arrange horse trails through the area and down to Mngobolezeni Lake. R440 per person.

Visagie's Camp 500m beyond _Sodwana Bay Lodge_ towards the bay ☏ 035 571 0104 or 082 440 4141, ℮ visa1234@iafrica.com. Basic accommodation in cabins sleeping from two to eight people, with a restaurant and bar on site. Half-board. ❸

Diving

Unless you're a keen angler, the principal reason to come to Sodwana is for the diving off its coral reefs. More commonly found further north, **coral reefs** and bright tropical fish thrive here in the warm waters carried down the coast by the Agulhas current. Both soft and hard corals cover the rocks with their convolutions and delicate formations and their range of textures, shades and colours. The waters are clear, silt-free and perfect for spotting some of the 1200 varieties of **fish** that inhabit the waters off northern KwaZulu-Natal, making it second only to the Great Barrier Reef in its richness.

The closest to the bay and consequently the most visited, is **Two Mile Reef**, which is 2km long and 900m wide, reaches depths of between 9m and 34m and offers excellent dives. Among the others is **Five Mile Reef**, which is further north and is known for its miniature staghorn corals, while beyond that, **Seven Mile Reef** is inhabited by large anemone communities and offers protection to turtles and rays, which may be found resting here.

Snorkelling, turtle tours and the Mngobolezeni Trail

If you don't want to go the whole hog with diving, you can still enjoy excellent **snorkelling** at Jesser Point, a tiny promontory at the southern end of the bay. Just off here is **Quarter Mile Reef**, which attracts a wide variety of fish, including moray eels and rays. Low tide is the best time to venture out – a sign on the beach indicates daily tide times. You can buy competitively priced snorkels and masks from the **dive shop** at _Sodwana Bay Lodge_ (see p.531), and they may be prepared to rent these as well as wet-suits during off-peak periods.

During December and January, when loggerhead and leatherback turtles (see box on p.534) come to nest and lay their eggs on the beach, you can join one of the guided **turtle tours** from Sodwana. As a limited number of licences are issued each year for these, the operators change from year to year, so enquire locally.

The starting point for the five-kilometre circular **Mngobolezeni Trail** is just across from the park reception and winds its way through a variety of habitats, including woodland, to the coastal lake that gives the hike its name. Arrows and signs indicate the way – but take care not to get sidetracked down one of the many game paths that crisscross it. The walk takes around three hours and there's no drinkable water along the way, so you should take refreshment. **Crocodiles** live in the lake, as do hippos, who leave the water to feed, usually at dusk. If you encounter a hippo on land, treat it with the utmost respect: hippos are responsible for more human deaths than any other African mammal. Avoid getting between a hippo and its line of retreat, which will generally be the most direct route to the safety of the water. If you do disturb one, find a tree to hide behind or, even better, to climb.

Apart from hippos, you may be lucky enough to see some of the other animals that inhabit the dune forest and its surrounds, among them bushbuck, duiker (red and common), reedbuck and Tonga squirrels. An informative booklet, *Mngobolezeni Trail*, interprets points of interest along the way, and is available from the park reception.

Lake Sibaya and Baya Camp

On a windless day, **Lake Sibaya**, 10km due north of Sodwana, appears glassy, azure and flat; the waters are so transparent that when the KZN Wildlife takes a hippo census they just fly over and count the dark blobs clearly visible from the air. South Africa's largest natural freshwater lake covers 77 square kilometres, and is fringed by white sandy beaches disappearing into dense forest. From the margins, timid crocodiles cut the lake surface, exchanging the warmth of the sun for the safety of the water. This is not an unpopulated wilderness: the lake fringes are dotted with traditional African lands and villages.

The only **accommodation** on the lake is at *Baya Camp* (daily: April–Sept 6am–8pm; Oct–March 5am–8pm; R20 per person, R15 per vehicle; accommodation extra), on its western shore, 16km north of Mbazwana along a dirt track that traverses thick sand in places; although you won't need a 4WD vehicle to get here, because of the thick sand elsewhere you'll need one to explore the forest areas around the lake. Three four-bedded and four two-bedded huts (❷), connected by boardwalks, are each equipped with a handbasin with cold running water. The lounge, dining, kitchen and ablution facilities (with hot water if there's been enough sun to power the solar panels) are all shared. **Reservations** can be made up to six months in advance through the KwaZulu-Natal Wildlife central office (see box on p.449). Don't just turn up expecting to find a vacant chalet, because if they're full you have to drive to the nearest hotel in Mkuze, some 111km away. There are no **facilities** apart from those already mentioned; the nearest shops and fuel are in Mbazwana, but you'd be better off stocking up at a larger centre, such as Mkuze or Jozini.

Boredom is a potential hazard in staying at Lake Sibaya, so consider coming here only if you're in a contemplative frame of mind as there's little to do apart from watch the hippos and crocs on the lake, survey the birdlife or embark on an exceptionally easy-going three-kilometre **circular walk** that starts from the viewing platform behind the camp. Nearby are two hides, and **bird-watching** can be rewarding with close on three hundred species present. Needless to say, with crocs and hippos lolling about, swimming in the lake is most unwise.

Mabibi

On the west side of Sibaya, **MABIBI** (daily: April–Sept 6am–8pm; Oct–March 5am–8pm; R20 per person, R15 per vehicle) is probably the most remote and idyllic campsite in South Africa, made all the more appealing by the difficulty of getting there. Situated in luxuriant subtropical forest, about 20km from Sodwana up the coast towards Mozambique, the ten **campsites** perch on a plateau at the top of monumental dunes that descend sharply to the sea. Booking is through KwaZulu-Natal Wildlife's Manzengwenya office (☎035 592 0142, ℻035 574 8017). The camp is protected from the winds by the dune forest and a boardwalk leads down the duneside to the **sea** – a walk that takes about ten minutes. This is one of the most undisturbed sections of coast in KwaZulu-Natal, and outside school holidays you stand a fair chance of having a perfect tropical beach all to yourself. You won't get the frenetic activity of outboard motors and 4WD vehicles found at Sodwana and other spots to the south – they're banned within the Maputaland Coastal Forest Reserve, which Mabibi falls under.

The sea here is excellent for **surf angling** and the **snorkelling** matches that at Sodwana, with a rich tropical marine life thriving on the coral reefs offshore. A number of mammals live in the forest, but most of them – bushbabies, large-spotted genets and porcupines – only come out after dark, while others like suni and samango monkeys tend to be shy. Vervet monkeys, on the other hand, are fairly bold and you're bound to encounter a troop if you stay for more than a day.

The best **access** to the camp is along the tarred Kwangwanase (also called Manguzi) road from the N2, some 11km north of Mkuze. At the Manzengwenya intersection, turn right and follow the Mabibi signboards. Because this final 45km from the junction is along gravel and thick sand tracks, a 4WD vehicle, or at least one with high clearance such as a *bakkie* (pick-up truck), is essential. You can also reach Mabibi on the coastal forest link road between Mbazwana and the Jozini-Kwanganase/Manguzi tar road; turn right at the Manzengwenya road and follow the signs. The closest **shops and fuel** are at Mbazwana, 60km to the south. The campsites can be **booked** up to six months in advance through the KwaZulu-Natal Wildlife Manzengwenya office (see p.533).

Rocktail Bay

South Africa's most sublime beachstay lies about 40km north of Mabibi along the coast at **ROCKTAIL BAY**, an even less accessible stretch of sand and sea that is restricted to guests who are prepared to pay for the undeniable privilege of staying at the upmarket *Rocktail Bay Lodge* (book through Wilderness Safaris, PO Box 78573, Sandton 2146 (☎011 883 0747 or 011 257 5015, ⓦwww.wilderness-safaris.com; full-board ❼). **Accommodation** is in ten

Maputaland's turtles

The whole of the Maputaland coast is excellent for spotting **loggerhead** and **leatherback turtles** when they come ashore every year between October and February to breed, but Rocktail Bay is probably the best spot of all. Turtles from as far afield as Malindi in Kenya (3500km to the north) and Cape Agulhas (2000km west along the South African coastline) converge on the beaches of Maputaland to lay their eggs. Sea turtles have survived virtually unchanged for almost a hundred million years and it's reckoned that loggerheads have been using Maputaland's beaches to lay their eggs for 60,000 years.

When the female turtle's eggs are ripe, she heads for the beach to lay them. It is believed that the turtles are lured onto the beach by a hormone that oozes from the beach, a scent that they follow. The scent is believed to have been programmed into their subconscious while they were in their eggs. The myopic turtle, whose eyes are adapted to underwater vision, pulls herself along the beach in the dark until she encounters an obstruction such as a bank or a log, where she begins digging a pit using her front flippers until she has scooped out a nest big enough to hold her own volume. She then digs a flask-shaped hole about 50cm deep and lays her eggs into this, a process which takes about ten minutes.

The female turtle fills the hole and covers it with sand using her front flippers, disguising the place where the eggs are stored, and returns to the sea. After about two months the eggs hatch, and when the temperature drops below 28°C the entire clutch of hatched turtles will simultaneously race down the beach to the ocean. Only one in five hundred will survive to return. Once in the ocean, the hatchlings swim out to sea where they are either carried away by the Agulhas current into the Atlantic or along the Indian Ocean coast.

As the turtles are easily disturbed, only a few operators with permits are allowed on the beaches at night, escorting groups of visitors to watch the turtles.

reed-and-thatched chalets with private toilets and showers raised on stilts into the forest canopy, each with its own wooden deck. This is the ideal place to get away: there's no phone, limited solar electricity (about 3hr per day), and the last few kilometres are so heavy-going that you leave your vehicle at the Coastal Forest Reserve office and have to be ferried in by 4WD.

Few parts of the South African coastline are as unspoilt as the beaches around here, and although there's no big game to pull in the punters, there's excellent **scuba diving** offshore and a dive centre with a qualified PADI instructor, a boat and skipper. You can also go **snorkelling** in the bay at low tide (fins and snorkels are available to guests). The **bird-watching** here is also excellent, and you could see a number of rare and sought-after species, among them the green twinspot, green coucal, grey waxbill, purple-crested and Livingstone's louries as well as the Natal robin and emerald cuckoo; a particularly rare and prized bird to spot is the palmnut vulture.

Supreme idleness is one of the big attractions of the place, but if you're feeling perky you can walk in the coastal forest, join an excursion to Black Rock or Lake Sibaya and go onto the beach to watch turtles during the summer egg-laying season. **Surf fishing** for shad, springer, kingfish, bonefish, stumpnose, barracuda and blacktail is another possibility.

Ndumo Game Reserve

One of the most beautiful of the KwaZulu-Natal reserves, **Ndumo** (daily dawn–dusk; R30 per vehicle, R10 per person) looks across the flood plain into Mozambique to the north and up to the Lebombo Mountains in the south. Its northern extent hugs the **Usutu River**, which rises in Swaziland and defines South Africa's border with Mozambique. The turn-off to the reserve is 56km along the tar north of Jozini, with the final 15km along a rough gravel track.

No great volume of animals trammel the reserve, but the beauty, solitude and prolific birdlife here make this a good place to head for if you're not simply into the game of ticking off your list of **mammals**. That's not to underplay the 62 species here (including buffalo, jackal, wildebeest, giraffe, hippo, hyena, zebra and both species of rhino), but they may be more difficult to see than elsewhere. For bird-watchers, however, Ndumo is in the premier league, ranking among the country's **bird-watching** top spots. The staggering 420 different varieties recorded here include the African broadbill, pink-throated twinspot, Pels fishing owl, gorgeous bushshrike, cuckoo hawk, southern banded snake eagle and the palmnut vulture.

As in other public game reserves, you can **self-drive** around some areas, one of the highlights being the trip to **Redcliffs**, where there's a picnic site with a towering vantage point offering soaring views across the Usutu River into both Swaziland and Mozambique. KwaZulu-Natal Wildlife offers open-topped 4WD outings in the mornings and evenings to the lovely **Inyamiti pan**, which is inhabited by hippos and crocodiles and receives visits from an array of waterfowl; guided **walking trails** are also available.

The small **public restcamp** is sited on a hill and has a number of camping sites and seven old, but well-maintained, two-bedded **huts** (➋), each with a fridge and handbasin with cold water and shared ablutions. A shop near the entrance gate sells basic **supplies**, but you're better off stocking up en route in Mkuze village. **Bookings** should be made through KwaZulu-Natal Wildlife central office (see box on p.449) or, if at the last minute, through the local office (☏035 591 0032).

The private **Ndumo Wilderness Lodge** (book through Wilderness Safaris, PO Box 78573, Sandton 2146 ☏011 883 0747 or 011 257 5015,

@www.wilderness-safaris.com; ❼) consists of a series of luxury en-suite safari tents on decks overlooking a beautiful pan in an area of the reserve closed to the general public. The units are connected by boardwalks on stilts above the flood level of the pan. The lounge area is an open-sided deck that jetties out towards the water, offering fabulous views of its crocodile-infested waters and the perfect vantage from which to watch water birds with a pair of binoculars. The lodge also provides **game drives** and informative **guided walks**, including to Inyamiti pan; prices are inclusive of all meals and game activities.

Kosi Bay

The northernmost place along the KwaZulu-Natal coast, **KOSI BAY** (daily: April–Sept 6am–8pm; Oct–March 5am–8pm; R15 per vehicle, R20 per person) is at the centre of an enthralling area of waterways fringed by forest. Despite the name, this is not a bay at all, but a system of four lakes connected by narrow reed channels which eventually empty into the sea at Kosi Mouth. You will only be able to get to the mouth itself if you have a 4WD and are extremely intrepid.

One of the most striking images of Kosi Bay is of mazes of reed fences in the estuary and other parts of the lake system. These are **fish kraals**, or traps, built by local Tonga people, a practice that has been going on for hundreds of years. Custom has made the method of harvesting sustainable, because trap numbers are strictly controlled; they are passed down from father to son and designed to only capture four percent of the fish that pass through.

△ Kosi Bay fisherman

Staying at Kosi Bay, you're likely to feel frustratingly land-locked; you won't so much as glimpse the coast unless you sign up for the four-day **Amanzimnyama Trail**, one of the few ways the general public can see South Africa's northernmost section of the Indian Ocean. The circular hike begins at the base camp on the west shore of Nhlange and passes through beautiful coastal forest, along the beach, through cycad and giant raffia palm groves. In summer, there's the chance of seeing turtles on the beach. Beds, pots, cookers, ablution facilities and limited water are available at night stops along the route, but there's no electricity or refrigeration, and you must bring your own eating utensils, food, bedding, torches and snorkelling gear. Mosquito repellent is recommended, and this is one of the few parts of the country where it's advisable to use water purification tablets. **Bookings** for the trail, which costs R250 per person, should be made through KwaZulu-Natal Wildlife central office (see p.449).

A highly recommended alternative way to explore the area is on a **tour** guided by members of the local community, who can show you the lakes and the fish traps. Trips start just outside the restcamp from the reserve **office** (☎035 592 0236), where you can gather more **information**.

Accommodation

Kosi Bay Lodge 500m from the lake, a little back from the "bay" itself. Central bookings ☎031 266 4172 or 082 7714857. Private accommodation outside the KZN Wildlife reserve is offered in spartan A-frame huts with communal ablutions or two-bedded en-suite reed chalets. There's a bar with a viewing deck, and a restaurant serving run-of-the-mill fare. The lodge also runs trips across the lake to the eastern shore with a 5km hike to wonderful unspoilt beaches. A-frame ❶, B&B ❹, half-board including boat trip on lakes ❺

Kosi Forest Lodge Inside the reserve ☎035 474 1504, ⓦ www.zulu.net.co.za. Arguably the most dreamy place to stay in KwaZulu-Natal, in eight reed-and-thatch suites in a landscape of palms, sand forest, lakes, river mouth, bleached white beaches and tepid sea. The lodge is so isolated that there is no electricity or tar and you have to be collected from the Kwanganase police station and taken by 4WD along sandy tracks to the lodge. Activities include guided canoe trips, reef snorkelling and forest walks, and there's a good chance you'll see hippos, crocodiles and marine turtles. The rate is fully inclusive of all meals and activities. May–Aug ❼, Sept–April ❽

Kwazulu-Natal Wildlife restcamp Inside the reserve, on the west shore of Nhlange, the largest of the lakes. Two-bed, five-bed (minimum charge for three people) and six-bed chalets (minimum charge for four people). There's a small campsite nearby and a private lodge is in the pipeline. Book through KZN Central Office. ❸

Ithala Game Reserve

West of Maputaland and close to the Swaziland border, the small **Ithala Game Reserve** (daily: April–Sept 6am–6pm; Oct–March 5am–7pm; R30 per vehicle, R30 per person) is little-known, despite being one of the country's most spectacularly scenic places to watch wildlife. The reserve's relative youth (it was only proclaimed in 1972) may be why it is frequently bypassed by visitors, who rush for the big names such as Kruger and Hluhluwe-Umfolozi. This could soon change, especially as Ithala's main camp, **Ntshondwe**, is one of the best game-reserve restcamps in South Africa. Ithala is largely mountainous, and the terrain extremely varied; contained within a protective basin are numerous cliffs and rock-faces.

If you're obsessed with seeing the Big Five, Ithala is not the place to visit – the king of the beasts is notably absent here, even though the other four make periodic appearances. Come instead for the most relaxed, uncrowded and beautifully set game viewing you'll get in southern Africa. Like the rest of the

KwaZulu-Natal game reserves, Ithala is excellent for white **rhinos** and there's plenty of **plains game**, including zebras and giraffes. Of the **predators**, you could, if you're very lucky, encounter brown hyenas, cheetahs and leopards. But the best idea is to throw away your mammal check list and take a slow drive around the mountains into the valleys and along the watercourses. Because there are no lions, the game is relaxed, and on a quiet weekday watching **animal behaviour** can be fascinating. Slow down, keep your eyes open, and you may see a rhino male defending his territory, or two young giraffes testing their strength with neck wrestling. One of the most rewarding **drives** is along Ngubhu Loop, with a detour to Ngubhu picnic site. You can get information and maps from the reception at *Ntshondwe* chalets.

There are some **self-guided trails** into the wooded mountainside above *Ntshondwe*, which give the chance to stretch your legs if you've spent a morning driving around. **Day and night drives** in open vehicles can be booked through *Ntshondwe* reception at a cost of R70 per person.

Practicalities

There's no public **transport** into the park, or even near to it, so self-driving is your only option. The main restcamp, **Ntshondwe**, 7km beyond the entrance gate, is ingeniously camouflaged against a high plateau with views at the foot of huge cliffs. There are no lawns or gardens; each chalet is surrounded by indigenous bush through which paved walkways weave their way around granite rocks and trees to the main reception area, which has a small shop, a restaurant, and bar with a deck overlooking a waterhole.

If you're happy to shell out, eat in *Ntshondwe's* a la carte **restaurant**, which serves a surprisingly varied range of foods from *escargots* to steaks. Don't bother with self-catering unless you're a vegetarian (meat-free meals aren't always on the menu), as you'll need to get **supplies** before you come – the camp shop is poorly stocked with fresh foods and specializes in frozen meats and beers. **Louwsburg** has a very small general dealer that's a little better, but you'd be wise to pick up supplies at Vryheid, Pongola, Mkuze or one of the larger villages en route. A cosy **bar** also has a sundeck overlooking the waterhole and out across the valleys.

Accommodation

All accommodation in Ithala is run by KwaZulu-Natal Wildlife and bookings should be made through their central office (see box on p.449); for camping, contact the Officer-in-Charge, PO Box 98, Louwsburg 3150 (℡034 907 5105).

Mbizo Campsite If you want an extremely pared-down bush experience, you won't beat the marvellous tiny campsite (space for just twenty people), shaded by thorn trees and ilala palms, on the banks of the Mbizo River. Expect no frills here – it's cold showers in reed enclosures and cooking over wood fires, the only concession to civilization being a flushing toilet.

Mhlangeni, Mbizo and Thalu bush camps A wonderful choice if you want something a bit wilder. The three bush camps are all in beautiful secluded settings and cater for four to ten people, and there's no minimum charge. Camps come with an attendant and you can make arrangements to have a field ranger to take you on walks. ❸

Ntshondwe Rest Camp One of the best game reserve restcamps in the country has 25 extremely comfortable two-bed self-catering chalets with fully equipped kitchens, lounge areas and verandahs, and 28 non-self-catering ones as well as a few larger units. ❹

Central Zululand and the Battlefields

Central Zululand – the Zulu heartland – radiates out from the unlovely modern town of **Ulundi**, some 30km west of the Hluhluwe-Umfolozi Park. At the height of its influence in the 1820s and 1830s, under King Shaka, the core of the Zulu state lay between the **Black Mfolozi River** in the north, and in the south, the **Tugela**, which discharges into the Indian Ocean, roughly 100km north of Durban.

Despite being a beautiful area of dry thornveld, large hills and impressive views, Central Zululand tends to be visited as a series of routes taking in museums and **Battlefield sites**. The Zulu heartland, where you'll find **museums** relating to local history and culture, is concentrated just to the west of the Hluhluwe-Umfolozi Park, King Shaka's personal hunting preserve. The heartland can be taken as a side-trip from a visit to Hluhluwe-Umfolozi or Ithala Game Reserve, which lies about 150km north of Ulundi.

Contained in a relatively small area to the west of the heartland are a series of battle sites from wars fought in the nineteenth century, first between Zulus and Boers, then Zulus and the British and finally between the Boers and Brits. Don't attempt to visit this area on your own: all you'll see is empty *veld* with a few memorials. Far better is to join a tour with one of the several excellent guides who make it their business to bring the region's dramatic history alive (see p.545).

The Zulu heartland

Don't expect to see "tribal" people who conform to the Zulu myth outside theme parks such as Shakaland. Traditional dress and the **traditional lifestyle** are largely a nineteenth-century phenomenon, deliberately smashed by the British a century ago, when they imposed a poll tax that had to be paid in cash – thus ending Zulu self-sufficiency, generating urbanization and forcing the Africans into the modern industrial economy, where they were needed as workers.

You will find beautiful Zulu crafts, the best examples being in museums such as the little-known but outstanding **Vukani Collection** in Eshowe. Also worth checking out is the reconstructed royal enclosure of Cetshwayo, the last king of the independent Zulu, at **Ondini**, near Ulundi.

Some history

The truth behind the Zulus is difficult to separate from the mythology, which was fed by both the Zulus themselves as well as white settlers. Accounts of the Zulu kingdom in the 1820s rely heavily on the diaries of the two adventurers **Henry Fynn** and **Nathaniel Isaacs**, who portrayed King Shaka as a mercurial and bloodthirsty tyrant who killed his subjects willy-nilly for a bit of fun. Despite their attempts to cover up their profligate disregard for the truth, a letter from Isaacs to Fynn was uncovered in the 1940s. In it he encourages his

5

THE ZULU HEARTLAND
& THE BATTLEFIELDS

0   25 km

FREE
STATE

INDIAN OCEAN

HLUHLUWE-
UMFOLOZI PARK

ITHALA GAME
RESERVE

Black Mfolozi River

Tugela River

SPIOENKOP NATURE
RESERVE

UKHAHLAMBA-
DRAKENSBURG
PARK

Mtubatuba
Empangeni
Shakaland
Battle of
Gingindlovu
1879
Nkwalini
Eshowe
Gingindlovu
Melmoth
Ondini
Battle of
Ulundi
1879
Ulundi
Nongoma
Louwsburg
Vryheid
Babanango
Battle of
Blood River
1838
Nqutu
Battle of Isandlwana
1879
Battle of
Rorke's Drift
1879
Battle of
Talana
1899
Utrecht
Dundee
Glencoe
Newcastle
Siege of Ladysmith
1899-1900
Ladysmith
Colenso
Weenen
Capture of
Winston Churchill
1899
Chievely
Estcourt
Greytown
Winterton
Spioenkop
Battle of
Spioenkop
1900
Bergville
Cathedral
Peak
Champagne
Castle

Hluhluwe
Pongola
Piet Retief
Ermelo
Harrismith
Harrismith
Stanger
Pietermaritzburg
Pietermaritzburg

N2
R618
R66
R618
R66
R34
R66
R34
R69
R33
R34
R33
R33
R34
R68
R602
N11
N11
R74
N3
R74
R600
R103
N2

friend, who was en route to London to publish his memoirs, to depict the Zulu kings as "bloodthirsty as you can, and describe frivolous crimes people lose their lives for. It all tends to swell up the work and make it interesting."

A current debate divides historians about the real extent of the **Zulu empire** during the nineteenth century. Some now question the conventional wisdom that Shaka was the "African Napoleon", a military genius who transformed the politics of nineteenth-century South Africa. What we do know is that in the 1820s Shaka consolidated a state that was one of the most powerful political forces in the subcontinent, and that internal dissent to his rule culminated in his assassination by his half-brother **Dingane** in 1828.

In the 1830s, pressure from whites exacerbated internal tensions in the Zulu state and reached a climax when a relatively small party of Boers defeated Dingane's army at **Blood River**, leading to a split in the Zulu state, with one half following **King Mpande**. Collapse threatened when Mpande's sons Mbuyazi and Cetshwayo led opposing forces in a pitched battle for the succession. **Cetshwayo** emerged victorious and successfully set about rebuilding the state, but too late. Britain had already determined that its own interest would best be served by a confederated South Africa under its own control and a powerful Zulu state wasn't going to be allowed to stand in the way. On the banks of the Tugela River, the high commissioner, Sir Bartle Frere, delivered a Hobson's choice of an **ultimatum** that Cetshwayo should dismantle his polity or face invasion.

In January 1879, the British army crossed the Tugela, and suffered a humiliating disaster at **Isandlwana** – the British army's worst defeat ever at the hands of native armies. However, the tide turned against the Zulus after just over a hundred British soldiers, many of them sick, repulsed a force of between 3000 and 4000 Zulus at Rorke's Drift. By the end of July, Zulu independence had been snuffed, when the British lured the reluctant (and effectively already broken) Zulus, who were now eager for peace, into battle at Ulundi. The British set alight Cetshwayo's capital at Ondini – a fire which blazed for four days – and the king was taken prisoner and held in the Castle in Cape Town.

Gingindlovu

At **GINGINDLOVU** (shortened to Ging by local whites) the Zulus attacked a British relief column on April 2, 1879, as it was marching on Eshowe to relieve a siege. In one of the decisive battles of the Anglo-Zulu War, the colonial invaders delivered a crushing defeat to the Zulus that destroyed their morale, with the loss of only thirteen British lives. The following day, the British column continued its advance, and successfully raised the Eshowe siege.

There's nothing much to see in Gingindlovu, which is 50km north of Dukuza along the R102, but it makes as good a base as any to explore the Zulu heartland and the Battlefields, and has the advantage of being a mere 15km from the coast.

The Baz Bus pulls in and can drop you off at either of the two excellent **places to stay**, the cheaper being the eccentric and thoroughly entertaining *Inyezane Backpackers* (☏035 337 1326, ⓦwww.inyezane.lodge.tc; ❶), on a sugar farm just outside town; phone ahead for directions. Accommodation consists of a series of eclectically decorated rondavels, with dorms, doubles and camping available. The hostel is well-known for its mud-baths, and you can also learn to make your own curios out of elephant dung, or play traditional musical instruments. Also on a sugar estate, but at the opposite extreme with its old-fashioned elegance, in a grand homestead resembling something out of *Gone with the Wind*, is *Mine Own Country House* (☏035 337 1262, ⓔremark@netac-

5

tive.co.za; **➍**), 4km north of Gingindlovu on the R102. It's fifteen minutes' drive from the beach and offers a golf course, en-suite rooms, well-tended gardens, a swimming pool and tennis courts.

Eshowe

Visitors generally give **ESHOWE** a miss on their way to the more obvious drama of the old Zulu capital at Ondini and the Battlefields; however, the place deserves more than a passing glance as it offers a gentle introduction to the **Zulu heartland**. Apart from its attractively organic setting, interlacing with the **Dlinza Forest**, this town, 22km inland from Gingindlovu, is home to one of the finest historical and contemporary collections of Zulu crafts as well as southern Africa's only aerial forest boardwalk. It also has a half-decent museum and offers exceptional tours that take you under the skin of a modern KwaZulu-Natal country town. Eshowe's name has an onomatopoeic Zulu derivation evoked by the sound of the wind blowing through the trees.

Graham Chennels, former mayor and current proprietor of the *George Hotel* in Main Street (see p.543), leads enthusiastic **tours** of Eshowe, taking in the white, coloured and African areas as well as the rural surrounds. This is one of the best and easiest ways of understanding exactly how segregation worked under apartheid, and one of the most optimistic views of South Africa's future you'll find.

The Vukani Collection and Zululand Historical museums

One very good reason for coming to Eshowe is for the brilliant **Vukani Collection Museum**, the largest and among the best collections of traditional **Zulu arts and crafts** in the world, containing more than 3000 pieces. The museum is housed in a purpose-built structure in the grounds of Fort Nongqayi on Nongqayi Road, which itself houses the Zululand Historical Museum, signposted and a five-to-ten minute walk from the city centre (Mon–Thurs & Sun 9am–4pm, Fri 9am–3pm; closed Sat; R10; ☎035 474 5274). The best way to see the museum is to arrange a 45-minute guided tour, which is included in the price. On display is a huge range of **baskets**, something Zulu culture excels at (and examples of which are held in many major international art collections), each made for a specific purpose. There are also carvings, clothing, beadwork, tapestries and some outstanding ceramics, including works by **Nesta Nala**, one of the leading contemporary proponents of the form. After seeing the bench-mark examples here, you'll have a good idea about the quality of basketry and crafts you'll see for sale as you work your way around Zululand. There are plans to run an artist-in-residence scheme in which craftworkers will live and practise their skill in the grounds of Vukani. The **Vukani shop** on Main Road, near the *George Hotel*, sells examples of contemporary Zulu craftwork.

Also inside Fort Nongqayi is the **Zululand Historical Museum** (daily 7.30am–4pm; R10), a collection that is eccentric and informative by turns, but never dull. Among the displays is furniture belonging to **John Dunn**, the only white man to become a Zulu chief and, incidentally, also to take 49 wives, so becoming the progenitor of Eshowe's coloured community, many of whom still carry his last name. You can also see Zulu household artefacts, the replica of a silver beer mug given by Queen Victoria in London to Cetshwayo, the last king of the free Zulus in 1882, and displays on Zulu history. One of these covers the **Bambatha Rebellion**, in which Fort Nongqayi saw action, when Natal's colonial forces put down the last armed resistance by Africans till the formation of the ANC's armed wing in the 1960s. Also on site are the *Adams Outpost Restaurant* and the **Zululand Missionary Museum** in the fort's chapel.

Dlinza Forest and the aerial boardwalk

A must for bird-watchers, **Dlinza Forest** is also a great place for picnics or trekking along South Africa's only aerial boardwalk. The impressive **Dlinza Forest Aerial Boardwalk** (Sept–April 6am–6pm, May–Aug 8am–5pm; R20) off Kangella Street, on the southwestern side of Eshowe and accessed from the museums complex at Fort Nongqayi, spans 125 metres and is raised ten metres into the air just under the forest canopy, giving visitors a chance to experience a section of the woodland normally restricted to birds. The wheelchair-friendly boardwalk leads to a 20-metre-high stainless-steel **observation tower**, offering stunning panoramas across the treetops to the Indian Ocean shimmering in the distance. There is also a **visitor information** centre (same opening times as the boardwalk) at the foot of the boardwalk, which provides information about the forest ecology. Among the birds you could see are black sparrowhawks, crowned eagles and green coucals, while seventy species of butterfly have also been recorded in the forest.

Practicalities

The Translux **intercity bus** stops in front of the City Hall on its three-times-a-week haul between Pretoria/Johannesburg and Richards Bay, and the **Baz Bus** also passes through town on its Durban–Johannesburg route.

The cheapest **accommodation** in town is at *Zululand Backpackers* (part of the *George Hotel*), 38 Main St (☎035 474 4919, ⦿www.eshowe.com; ❶), which has camping, dorms and doubles in a beautifully maintained hostel. Outside, there's a big fig tree under which you can have meals and chill out. The hostel offers cultural encounters where you can meet rural Zulus at traditional wedding ceremonies and sangoma (diviner) rituals. There's also rapp jumping, abseiling, mountain biking, canoeing, hiking, waterfalling and rock sliding, plus there's a large swimming pool. The *George Hotel* itself (☎035 474 4919; ❷) offers good value, with comfortable en-suite rooms with TVs, while *Amble Inn*, 116 Main St (☎035 474 1300, ⓔambleinn@corpdial.co.za; ❷), has eleven rooms and its own **restaurant**, serving English-style meals.

Shakaland and Simunye

North of Eshowe, the winding R66 leaves behind the softer vistas of the Dlinza Forest, the citrus groves and green seas of cane plantations and looks across huge views of the valleys that figure in the creation mythology of the Zulu nation. In no time you're into thornveld (acacias, rocky *kopjes* and aloes) and **theme park** country. Most accessible of these "Zulu-village hotels" is **Shakaland**, Norman Hurst Farm, Nkwalini (☎035 460 0912, ⓕ035 460 0842, ⦿www.shakaland.com), 14km north of Eshowe off the R68, which just about manages to remain on the acceptable side of exploiting ethnic culture, but isn't quite as "authentic" as its publicity materials claim.

Built in 1984 as the set for the wildly romanticized TV series *Shaka Zulu*, Shakaland's management was taken over in 1988 by the Protea hotel chain. What the brochures don't tell you is that the village is a reconstruction of a nineteenth-century Zulu kraal (homestead) and is quite unrepresentative of how people live today. Howeve r, Shakaland does offer the chance to sample **Zulu food** in a spectacular dining area. **Tours** for day visitors (daily 11am & 12.30pm; R137) begin with an audiovisual about the origin of the Zulus, followed by a guided walk around the huts, an explanation of traditional social organization, a beer-drinking ceremony and a buffet lunch with traditional food (including vegetarian), before concluding with some energetic **dancing**. You also get to see a Zulu courting ritual, stick fighting and spear throwing; all activities are included in the price. **Accommodation** is available in comfortable traditional beehive huts (❻), with untraditional luxuries such as electricity and en-suite bathrooms.

In a different league, **Simunye**, along the D256, off the R34, and 6km from Melmoth, offers a far more authentic experience of Zulu culture, introducing guests to contemporary ways of life as well as traditional customs. Visitors are conveyed to the camp by horse, ox-wagon or 4WD, and while there you'll get to see dancing, visit a working *kraal* and meet local people. Full-board **accommodation** (☏035 450 3111, ℻035 450 2534; ❻), is offered in stone-and-thatched huts at the main camp, overlooking the Mfule River, or at a kraal in a beehive hut or rondavels (for those who need mod-cons, five of the rooms have electricity).

Ulundi and Ondini

Some 83km north of Eshowe on the R66, **ULUNDI** is the former capital of the KwaZulu *bantustan* and lies at the centre of the **Makhosini Valley** (Valley of the Kings). The latter holds a semi-religious status among Zulu nationalists as the birthplace of the Zulu state and the area where several of its founding fathers lived and are now buried. Now that KwaZulu has been reintegrated with Natal, this rather unattractive modern town is tussling with Pietermaritzburg for pre-eminence in the province, but for the moment the two are joint capitals – a fact that brings joy to no one except the airlines that have to ferry provincial legislators from one centre to the other. There's nothing in Ulundi itself worth stopping for, apart from its historical connections.

The **Battle of Ulundi Memorial**, just outside town on the untarred road to the Cengeni Gate of the Hluhluwe-Umfolozi Park, is the poignant spot marking the final defeat of the Zulus. An understated small stone structure with a silver dome houses a series of plaques listing all the regiments on both sides involved in the last stand of the Zulus on July 4, 1879. The rectangular park around the memorial marks the site of the hollow infantry square adopted by the British and supported to devastating effect by seven- and nine-pounder guns.

By far the most interesting sight around here is the **Ondini Historical Reserve** (Mon–Fri 8am–4pm, Sat & Sun 9am–4pm; R8), a few kilometres further along the road, which houses the reconstruction of the royal residence of **King Cetshwayo**, a site museum and a cultural museum. After the decisive Battle of Ulundi, the royal residence at Ondini was razed to the ground and Cetshwayo was captured. Still puzzled by Britain's actions, Cetshwayo wrote to the British governor in 1881 from his exile at the Castle in Cape Town: "I have done you no wrong, therefore you must have some other object in view in invading my land." The *isigodlo*, or **royal enclosure**, has been partially reconstructed with traditional Zulu beehive huts, which you can wander round, while the site museum has a model showing the full original arrangement. Among the items in the **Cultural Museum** is a major bead collection.

A **picnic site** has been provided in the extensive grounds of the reserve and there's camping and **accommodation** in the traditional *umuzi* (homestead) in a group of beehive huts (❶–❷) inside a stockade with beds and communal kitchens, with ablution facilities outside. Bookings for these should be made through the Amafa-Heritage KZN, PO Box 523, Ulundi 3838 (☏035 870 2050, ✉amafahq@mweb.co.za).

The Battlefields

Most of the major KwaZulu-Natal Battlefields lie in the northwestern corner of the province, where first the Boers came out of the mountains from the northeast into Zulu territory and inflicted a severe defeat on the Zulus at **Blood River** in 1838, 13km southeast of the tiny town of Utrecht. Some four decades later, the British spoiled for war and marched north to fight a series of

Going into battle

Visiting the **Battlefields** with a qualified guide will infinitely enhance your experience. Our recommended guides specialize in different battle sites, usually those closest to their base. Most guides have an informal price agreement and you should expect to pay in the region of R400 for a day-trip. You are usually expected to provide your own transport.

Battlefield and Zulu heartland guides

Elisabeth Durham 39 Tatham St, Dundee ☎034 212 1014. Informative French and English tours of Rorke's Drift, Isandlwana and the route followed by the French Prince Imperial, who fell at Nqutu. Tours cost R500–800.

Evan Jones PMB Heritage Tours, PO Box 1380, Cascades 3203 ☎ & ☏033 344 3260, ✉heritage.battlefield@futurenet.co.za. Extensive tours of the Battlefields are conducted by a guide with a vast repository of knowledge, who breathes life into the battles and their theatre of activity. A two-day trip for four costs R1320 each and includes accommodation at the fabulous *Lennox Guest Cottage* (see p.548), meals, transport, entrance fees and transfers to and from Pietermaritzburg.

Pam McFadden Box 1852, Dundee ☎082 541 4832. The curator of the excellent Talana Museum in Dundee offers tours of all of the Battlefields. R400 per day.

David Rattray PO Box 3016, Rorke's Drift ☎ & ☏034 642 1843. A consummate storyteller, who infuses his accounts of Rorke's Drift and Isandlwana with emotion more than anyone else. In 1997, Britain's Prince Charles was fortunate enough to be taken around by Rattray, who grew up around Isandlwana and has a prodigious knowledge of the area. The Isandlwana and Rorke's Drift combined tour costs R395 per person, and could easily be the best live performance you attend in South Africa. Rattray has problems with his voice, which means you may get another guide, but it's worth making an effort to ensure that he's leading the tour on the day you go.

John Turner PO Box 10, Babanango ☎035 835 0062, ☏035 835 0160. Highly qualified as a natural scientist, with a degree in animal behaviour, Dr Turner is able to combine tours of Hluhluwe-Umfolozi Game Reserve and ecological topics, including birding and basic tree identification, with Zulu historical sites and the Anglo-Zulu Battlefield. Full-day tours cost around R275 per person per day, excluding transport, but including lunch and all entrance fees. Vehicles available for rental at R720 per vehicle per day.

Foy Vermaak PO Box 1358, Dundee 3000 ☎ & ☏034 642 1925. Based close to Isandlwana and Rorke's Drift sites, in which he specializes; he also covers Helpmekaar and Fugitive's Drift. The rate is R400 per party, irrespective of size; you pay for the entrance fees, your own packed lunch (which he can provide for R35), and he travels in your car.

Do-it-yourself tours

If you can't afford a guide, the next best thing is to buy an audiotape to listen to in your car. These are available from reception at the Talana Museum (see p.548). David Rattray's excellent set of tapes/CDs *The Day of the Dead Moon*, covering Rorke's Drift and Isandlwana, is available from Exclusive Books or directly from Rattray (see above). One of the most authoritative books about the Anglo-Boer War is the highly entertaining *Boer War* by Thomas Pakenham (see p.887).

battles against the Zulus, the most notable being at **Isandlwana** and **Rorke's Drift**, southeast of Dundee.

Twenty years on, Britain again provoked war, this time against the **Boers** of the South African Republic and the Orange Free State to the north and west. The Second Anglo-Boer War (also known as the South African War) was fought over control of the Gauteng goldfields. British troops were landed at Durban, in the British colony of Natal, and boldly marched north. Britain believed the campaign would be quick, cheap and over by Christmas. But in the early stages of the war, the huge but lumbering British machine proved no match for the mobile Boers who fought a guerrilla campaign that checked the British advance in northern KwaZulu-Natal.

At **Ladysmith**, the British endured months of an embarrassing siege, while nearby at **Spioenkop**, bungling British leadership snatched defeat from the jaws of victory. Although the Empire successfully struck back, it took three years to subdue the South African Republic and the Orange Free State, two of the smallest states in the world, after committing half a million troops to the field in an operation that was the costliest campaign since the Napoleonic Wars nearly a century earlier.

Isandlwana and Rorke's Drift

On January 22, 1879, the British suffered the most humiliating defeat in their colonial history when virtually their entire force of 1200 men at **Isandlwana** was obliterated by warriors armed with spears. That same evening, honour was restored when a group of British veterans and sick successfully defended the field hospital at **Rorke's Drift**, just across the Buffalo River from the site of the earlier disaster, against four advancing Zulu regiments with a combined strength of 3000 to 4000, a sequence of events romanticized in the 1960s film *Zulu*, which made the reputation of an ever-grateful Michael Caine and led him to "thank God for the Zulus."

If you're only planning to take in one Battlefield site, then Isandlwana should be that one, and once you're making the effort you really should take in Rorke's Drift as well to complete the day. Isandlwana is just over 130km northwest of **Eshowe**, but the closest town of any size is **Dundee,** about 70km to its west. Both Isandlwana and Rorke's Drift are eerily beautiful places, which you can visit and walk around on your own, but a guide is highly recommended (see box on p.545).

For somewhere to stay in the vicinity, you could do worse than the blink-and-you've-missed-it village of **BABANANGO**, 92km northwest of Eshowe, which consists of a shop or two and the *Babanango Hotel*, 16 Justice St (☎035 835 0029, ℻035 835 0322; ❸), a small atmospheric country **hotel** whose rate includes dinner, bed and breakfast. Backpackers are also accommodated at a bargain rate (❶) that includes breakfast, though it remains a mystery as to how its tiny, renowned *Stan's Pub* manages to cram in its drinking clientele. The hotel has a 4WD vehicle to take guests to the Battlefields and game reserves, or to a bush camp where you can go on trails and rough it among the thorn trees. A quieter option is *Babanango Valley Lodge* (☎035 835 0062, ⓦwww.babanangovalley.com; half-board ❺), situated on a Natural Heritage Site and signposted 4km west of Babanango on the R68, deep in a beautiful valley, where you can be taken on walks to explore the *veld*, rocks and river. **Accommodation** is in pleasant en-suite rooms set in the garden, and there's a swimming pool. Under the same ownership is the luxury tented *Rockpools Bush Camp*, which consists of nine units along the edge of a stream each with

5

its own private patio and rock pool (❹). The proprietor, Dr John Turner, is a registered guide (see p.545).

If you prefer to stay in the surrounding beautiful countryside, a couple of good alternatives exist. Near the minuscule settlement of **HELPMEKAAR**, along the R33 south of the Rorke's Drift Battlefield and 30km south of Dundee, *Penny Farthing* (☎ & ℻034 642 1925; ❹) is an historic pioneer farm still furnished with a lot of original objects and generations of hunting trophies, set in an area of big open grasslands and hills, criss-crossed with hiking trails. The host Foy Vermaak is a Battlefields guide (see p.545) who enjoys fireside chats on the subject, and has a personal collection of memorabilia.

The ultimate Battlefields place to stay, however, is at *Fugitives' Drift Lodge* (☎ & ℻034 642 1843, ✉fugdrift@trustnet.co.za; full-board ❻), 9km north of Rorke's Drift, where you're hosted by David Rattray (see box on p.545). Located on a huge game farm, the lodge overlooks the drift where the few British survivors of Isandlwana fled across the Buffalo River. Rooms are in individual cottages that open onto lawns and gardens, and guests eat together in a central dining room.

Isandlwana

Dominated by an eerie hill, the **ISANDLWANA** Battlefield, off the R68 between Nqutu and Babanango (daily 8am–5pm; R8), remains unspoilt and unchanged apart from some small homesteads and the graves of those who fell. A small **interpretation centre** houses artefacts and mementos.

The monumental bungling and the scale of the Zulu victory over the British sent shock waves back to London. Following the British ultimatum to the Zulus, three colonial columns were sent to invade Zululand. King Cetshwayo responded by sending a force against each of these. On January 21, 1879, Zulu troops encamped 6km from Isandlwana Hill, where one of the British columns had set up camp. Unaware of the Zulus over the brow, the British commander took a large detachment to support another British force, leaving the men at Isandlwana undefended and unfortified.

Meanwhile, a British scouting party rode to the brow of a hill and were stunned to find the valley filled with some 25,000 Zulu warriors sitting in utter silence. Because of a superstition surrounding the phase of the moon, the Zulus were waiting for a more propitious moment to attack. On being discovered, they rose up and converged on the British encampment using the classic Zulu "horns of the bull" formation to outflank the unprotected British who they completely overran. Few of the 1200 British forces survived.

The British press at the time demonized the Zulus for disembowelling the dead. In fact, the practice had a religious significance for the Zulus, who believed that it released the spirit of the dead. The custom also had a less spiritual significance; a Zulu warrior was required to "wash his spear" (ie kill an enemy) before he was allowed to marry.

Rorke's Drift

RORKE'S DRIFT is the most rewarding Battlefield to visit on your own, thanks to its excellent **field museum** and interpretation centre (Mon–Fri 8am–4pm, Sat & Sun 9am–4pm; R8). A new road connects it with Isandlwana, 15km to the east.

Despite Cetshwayo's express orders to his men not to attack Rorke's Drift, several thousand hot-headed young men, part of a reserve force, were so fired up by the victory at Isandlwana and eager, since they had not yet seen action, to "wash their spears" that they launched an assault on the hospital. For twelve hours spanning January 22 and 23, 1879, just over a hundred British soldiers (many of whom were ill) repulsed repeated attacks by four thousand Zulus, thus saving tattered British honour and earning eleven Victoria Crosses – the largest number ever awarded in one battle.

While you're here, it's also worth taking in the **Rorke's Drift ELC Craft Centre** (Mon–Fri 8am–4.30pm, Sat 10am–3pm), which is known for its hand-printed fabrics and tapestries depicting rural scenes.

Dundee and the Talana Museum

Some 32km west of the Rorke's Drift turn-off, along the R68, **DUNDEE** is a one-trick coal-mining town you can safely miss because its single draw-card, the **Talana Museum** (Mon–Fri 8am–4pm, Sat & Sun 10am–4pm; R10), is 2km outside town on the R33 to Vryheid. The museum itself is excellent, consisting of ten historic buildings still standing from the time of the Battle of Talana Hill – the first engagement of the Anglo-Boer War, in 1899, and a landmark for the British army, which wore khaki for the first time.

The museum is scattered around the grounds in a series of whitewashed buildings under shady blue gums, the most interesting being **Talana House**, which gives information about northern KwaZulu-Natal conflicts, including Anglo-Zulu, Zulu-Boer and Anglo-Boer wars. The displays include weapons and uniforms, but most evocative are the photographs, which really personalize the wars, and provide fascinating details such as the POW camps Boers were exiled to in far-flung parts of the Empire, including St Helena and the Far East. Often-neglected aspects of the Anglo-Boer War, including the roles of Africans and Indians, also get some coverage. In a photograph of Indian stretcher-bearers, you may be able to spot the youthful Mohandas Gandhi, who carried wounded British soldiers off the Spioenkop and Colenso Battlefields. Arrangements can be made with the curator for guided tours of the museum and surrounding Battlefields (☎034 212 2654). The museum also has the lovely *Miners Rest Tea Shop*, a nicer place for a drink and a snack than anywhere in town.

If you're looking for **accommodation** in the vicinity, try the excellent *Lennox Guest Cottage* (☎ & ℗034 218 2201 or ☎082 574 3032 ℮lennoxc @xsinet.co.za; half board; ❹), by the museum and at the foot of Talana Hill. Run by former rugby Springbok Dirk Froneman and his wife, Salome, the B&B is unpretentious and comfortable, with great cooking. An alternative is *Chez Nous* at 39 Tatham St (☎034 212 1014; ❶–❷), where charming French hostess and Battlefields guide Elisabeth Durham (see box on p.545) offers B&B and self-catering cottages. Backpackers get a good deal at the *Battlefields Country Lodge Backpackers* (☎034 218 1641, ⓦwww.battlefieldslodge.co.za; ❶); overlooking Talana Hill and close to the Battlefields, it offers bungalows and camping. By day, you can take a tour with guides organized by the hostel; in the evenings, chill out at the lovely Zulu-style *Lapa Ukhamba* and enjoy traditional Zulu beer and good food.

Blood River and Vryheid

You can't fail to be amazed by the monument at the **Blood River Battlefield** (daily 8am–5pm; R10), 48km from Dundee on the way to Vryheid off the R33. Of all the Afrikaner quasi-religious shrines across the country, this definitely takes the biscuit. A replica *laager* of 64 life-size bronze waggons stands on the site where on December 16, 1838 the Boers defeated a Zulu army. During the apartheid years, this date was celebrated by Afrikaners as the **Day**

The unknown soldiers

Africans are rarely mentioned in the context of the Anglo-Boer war, a confrontation fought in a theatre where eighty percent of the population was black. Although both sides denied that Africans served on their side, the British employed around 100,000 both as labourers and under arms, while the Boers had at least 10,000 blacks on their side – often press-ganged into service. After the war, the British denied recognition to Africans who had seen service with them, to the extent that Sir George Leuchars, Natal Minister for Native Affairs, blocked them from receiving their campaign medals on the grounds that it would "irritate" the Boers – to whom the British were now nuzzling up.

of the Vow, a public holiday honouring a supposed covenant made by the Boers with God himself that if he granted them victory, they would hold the day sacred. Afrikaners still visit the monument on this day, but under the new government the public holiday has been recycled as the **Day of Reconciliation**.

Back on the R33, it's 56km east to **VRYHEID** (Freedom), one-time capital of the Nieuwe Republiek (New Republic), which for many whites, who refuse to fly the new South African flag, still represents some kind of Boer stronghold. Unless you're stopping for the night at the highly recommended *Villa Prince Imperial*, 201 Deputation St (℡034 983 2610, ⓦwww.etictours.net; ❸), clearly signposted from the main street, there's little reason to dally. The villa is a breath of French air in the heart of redneck country, offering thirteen en-suite rooms with baths or (less expensively) showers, a swimming pool, billiard room and bar. The owner, Alain Delvilani, is a knowledgeable (and Satour-registered) Battlefield guide. There is also a **Zulu art gallery** on the premises, with the only display in northern KwaZulu-Natal of authentic and very beautiful antique Zulu beadwork, as well as works by young Zulu artists.

Ladysmith and around

LADYSMITH, 61km south of Dundee on the N11, owes its modest fame to one of the worst sieges in British military history nearly a century ago, and more recently to **Ladysmith Black Mambazo**, the local vocal group that helped Paul Simon revive a flagging career in the mid-1980s. Now one of South Africa's best-known black groups, Mambazo are rarely at home, but the new Cultural Centre and Museum honours their status as local heroes, and a Mambazo trail has been created around the town. The longer-established reason to hang out here is to explore the Anglo-Boer War in the Ladysmith Siege Museum, monuments and the surrounding Battlefields. Some 40km south of Ladysmith, near **Chievely**, is the spot where an armoured train carrying **Winston Churchill** was blown up by Boers.

Some history

"[Ladysmith] is famous to the uttermost ends of the earth: centre of the world's attention, the scene of famous deeds", wrote Winston Churchill as a young, gung-ho journalist covering the Anglo-Boer War for the *London Morning Post*. The siege began on November 2, 1899 and lasted 118 days, with 12,000 British troops suffering the indignity of being pinned down by undisciplined farmers. It was one of three sieges (the others being at Kimberley and Mafikeng) that began the early phase of the war; it also shocked a British establishment fully expecting to thrash the Boers by Christmas.

Arrival and information

Of the **intercity buses**, Greyhound (☎036 637 4181) pulls into Ted's Service Station on its Johannesburg–Durban route, and Translux (☎036 637 1111) breaks its Bloemfontein–Durban run at the **train station** (☎036 637 7273), 500m east of the town hall. Daily trains arrive from Johannesburg and Durban, but arrival and departure times make the train an unrealistic option unless you're pressed. There's no public transport, but it's easy to walk around Ladysmith's small centre. The **tourist information** bureau, Siege Museum, Murchison Street (Mon–Fri 9am–4pm, Sat 9am–1pm; ☎036 637 2992), has a good selection of literature on the Battlefields. They can put you in touch with their recommended **tour guide** Liz Spiret (☎036 637 7702 or 072 248 8929), who charges R450 for up to four people (must provide own transport).

Accommodation

There are plenty of **places to stay** in Ladysmith, some of them plugging right into the Battlefields scene, with proprietors offering themselves as "Battlefields hosts."

The Aloes Game Farm and B&B 33km from Ladysmith, signposted a further 6km south of Colenso on the R103 ☎036 422 2834, ℗036 422 2592. A farmstay in a thatched cottage, sleeping five, with fishing, and mountain biking, close to a small game reserve and the Drakensberg. Breakfast costs extra. ❶

Battlefields B&B 25 Cove Crescent ☎ & ℗036 631 2585. A gracious home in a quiet and peaceful neighbourhood. ❷

Bullers Rest Lodge 61 Cove Crescent ☎036 637 6154, ℮bullers@worldonline.co.za. A smart thatched establishment on a ridge overlooking town. ❹

Hunters' Lodge 6 Hunter St ☎036 637 2359 or 083 627 8480, ℗036 631 3144. A lovely old home in a peaceful neighbourhood, with three single and three double rooms, all en suite. ❷

Mac's Nest Heronmere Farm, 5km from town on Windsor Dam Road, off the R103 to Harrismith ☎036 635 4093 or 082 802 1645. A homely B&B on a smallholding with scenic sunsets, first-rate cooking and a small brass foundry; there's also prolific birdlife and small antelope. ❷

Mambasa Hutted Camp Adjoining Spioenkop Nature Reserve, off the R600, 35km west of Ladysmith ☎036 488 1003, ℗036 488 1116. The least expensive accommodation in the Ladysmith Battlefields area, in traditional Zulu beehive huts on the banks of the Tugela River. Furnished only with beds and mattresses, there are paraffin lamps, open fires for cooking meals, a deep freeze, hot and cold running water and flush toilets in a communal ablution block; canoes and rubber tubes are available for use on the river. ❶

Royal Hotel 140 Murchison St ☎ & ℗036 637 2176, ℗www.royalhotel.com. In the heart of town, the original hotel that harboured the town's most privileged during the siege – and regularly shelled by the Boers – is now a three-star establishment catering mainly to travelling reps. It's full during the week, which makes booking essential at any time of year. ❹

Spioenkop Game & Safari Lodge Adjacent to the Spioenkop Nature Reserve, 35km west of Ladysmith ☎036 488 1404, ℗www.spionkop.co.za. A choice of self-catering or B&B rooms in two cottages, with guided tours of Spioenkop Battlefield, sunset cruises, fishing, canoeing, birding and game viewing also on offer. ❹–❻

Tugela Game Ranch Bush Camp 33km south of Ladysmith ☎036 422 2592, ℗036 422 2532. Fully equipped rondavels overlooking a bass dam with game drives, game viewing, nature walks, fishing and bird-watching. ❶

The Town

Along Murchison Street, the main artery running through Ladysmith, you'll find banks, the post office and shops as well as the main tourist attractions. Of these, the **Ladysmith Siege Museum** (Mon–Fri 9am–4pm, Sat 9am–1pm; R2), next to the Town Hall, on the corner of Queen and Murchison streets, is the obvious starting point for any tour of the Anglo-Boer Battlefields. This compelling little museum tells the story of the war through text and photographs, conveying the appalling conditions during the siege as well as key points in a war that helped shape twentieth-century South Africa, paving the way for its unification. The museum is also a good source of books about the war, written from both the British and Boer points of view. The neighbouring **Town Hall**, where the British were to "thank God we kept the flag flying" after the siege, is also worth a peek for its collection of photographs depicting the town's history up to the present.

Right behind the Town Hall and Siege Museum stands the **Cultural Centre and Museum**, 25 Keate St (Mon–Fri 9am–4pm; R2), housed in a lovely classic Victorian colonial house. Opened in 1997, when Ladysmith Black Mambazo were granted the freedom of the town, life-size cut-outs of the group dominate a mock stage in the Ladysmith Black Mambazo Hall – the first room to the left of the foyer, which is filled with the strains of their stirring choral music. Other rooms display artefacts from the town's various cultures, tributes to local high-fliers – such as world boxing champion Sugarboy Malinga – and work by local artists. For kids, the Jungle/Discovery room offers an adventure into a tropical world with bugs and all, where they are encouraged to touch the exhibits.

Back on Murchison Street, 600m southwest of the Town Hall, is **All Saints** Anglican church, a Victorian Gothic edifice, built from chiselled shale in 1882 after the contemporary English style, with extensions carried out in 1902 as a memorial to those who died during the siege. Take a step inside to see a plethora of military memorials and some nice stained-glass windows.

Retrace your steps to the Town Hall, and diagonally opposite stands the **Royal Hotel**, where the more privileged of the besieged passed their time, including Leander Starr Jameson and Frank Rhodes (brother of the more famous Cecil), who routinely lunched there. In 1895, both had been involved in the Jameson Raid, an attempt to overthrow the Boer government, which was why some believed that the Boers regularly shelled the hotel around lunchtime.

Head down Queen Street away from the *Royal Hotel* to Forbes Street, where a **statue of Gandhi** stands in front of the unprepossessing Vishnu Temple. Although the monument depicts Gandhi in his later role as the saintly Mahatma, his associations with Ladysmith go back to the Boer War, when he enrolled in the British army as a stretcher-bearer and trained members of Ladysmith's Indian community to do likewise. Gandhi, still at an early stage of his political education, believed that by showing the British that Indians were loyal subjects, they would grant independence to India.

Around the **Forbes and Lyell streets** areas, near the temple, Ladysmith presents an altogether more African face. Here you'll find people thronging the taxi ranks and informal market stalls on empty plots dotted between run-down Indian shopping malls, while people jive to the rhythm of backstreet music bars and mothers shop with babies strapped to their backs.

The Muslim side of Ladysmith is represented by the **Soofie Mosque**, across the Klip River in Mosque Road, in the Indian suburb of Rose Park, said (most notably by the Publicity Association) to be the most beautiful mosque in the southern hemisphere.

Eating

The siege is over and horse is off the menu, but the *Royal Hotel*, with its three restaurants, is still the best place to eat in town. Less formal is the *Guinea Fowl Steakhouse* on Alfred Street, noted for its spare ribs; *Wimpy*, 7 Murchison St, is the only fast-food place, staying open until 8pm.

Spioenkop

Spioenkop Battlefield lies 35km west of Ladysmith and is set in the **Spioenkop Nature Reserve** (daily: April–Sept 6am–6pm; Oct–March 6am–7pm; R9). The bloodiest of all the Boer War battles, Spioenkop took more British lives than any other and taught the British command that wars fought by means of set-piece battles were no longer viable. After this, the guerrilla-style tactics of modern warfare were increasingly adopted.

Some 1700 British troops took the hill under cover of a mist without firing a shot, but were able to dig only shallow trenches because the surface was so hard. When the mist lifted they discovered that they had misjudged the crest of the hill, but their real failure was one of flawed command and desperately poor intelligence. Had the British reconnoitred properly, they might have discovered that they were facing a motley collection of fewer than 500 Boers with only seven pieces of artillery, and they could have called in their 1600 reserves to relieve them. Despite holding lower ground, the Boers were able to keep the British, crammed eight men per metre into their trenches, pinned down for an entire sweltering midsummer day. Around six hundred British troops perished and were buried where they fell on the so-called "acre of massacre".

Meanwhile the Boers, who were aware of the 1600 British reinforcements at the base of the hill, had gradually been drifting off, and by the end of the day, unbeknownst to the British, there were only 350 Boers left. In the evening the British withdrew, leaving the hill to the enemy.

Travel details

As the economic centre of KwaZulu–Natal, Durban is also its transport hub, with the majority of links into the province beginning or ending here. For travellers, the most useful mode of transport are the **backpacker buses**, which provide access to interesting destinations not on other regular routes.

Trains

Durban to: Johannesburg (1 daily; 15hr); Pietermaritzburg (1 daily; 2hr 10min).

Buses

The main **bus lines** serving the principal routes from Durban to Johannesburg or Cape Town are Translux (☏ 031 361 8333) and Greyhound (☏ 031 309 7830). Supplementary services are offered daily down the South Coast as far as Margate by Margate Mini Coach (☏ 039 312 1406).

Durban to: Ballito (2 daily; 35min); Bloemfontein (3 daily; 10–12hr); Cape Town (4 daily; 20hr); East London (2 daily; 9hr); Empangeni (1 daily; 2–3hr); Dukuza (6 weekly; 1hr); Grahamstown (2 daily; 12hr); Harrismith (4 daily; 4hr 30min); Johannesburg (8 daily; 11hr 30min); Knysna (2 daily; 15hr); Ladysmith (2 daily; 3hr 30min); Margate (2 daily; 2hr); Melmoth (1 daily; 4hr); Pietermaritzburg (10 daily; 2hr 15min); Plettenberg Bay (2 daily; 14hr 30min); Port Elizabeth (2 daily; 13hr 30min); Port Shepstone (2 daily; 1hr 30min); Pretoria (5 daily; 9hr); Richards Bay (1 daily; 2hr 30min); Sedgefield (2 daily; 15hr); Umhlanga Rocks (1 daily; 15min); Umtata (2 daily; 6hr); Vryheid (2 daily; 6hr).

Margate to: Durban (1–2 daily; 2hr); Johannesburg (5 weekly; 8hr 30min); Pretoria (5 weekly; 10hr).

Pietermaritzburg to: Bloemfontein (2–3 daily; 8hr 30min); Cape Town (4 daily; 19hr); Durban (9 daily; 2hr 15min); Johannesburg (6–7 daily; 7hr); Kimberley (3 weekly; 10hr); Ladysmith (2 daily; 2hr); Pretoria (6–7 daily; 8hr).

Richards Bay to: Durban (2–3 daily; 2hr 30min); Johannesburg (6 weekly; 9hr 30min); Pretoria (6 weekly; 10hr).

Backpacker buses

The **Baz Bus** (☏ 031 304 9099, ⓦ www.bazbus.com) follows routes specifically designed to take in places of interest that link in with hostels. From Durban the Baz follows three routes. Its route **to Port Elizabeth** goes along the KwaZulu-Natal South Coast, through the Transkei (giving access to the Wild Coast) and on to East London and finally Port Elizabeth passing en route through Warner Beach, Port Shepstone, Kokstad, Umtata, Cintsa, East London and Port Alfred. In Port Elizabeth you can connect with another Baz the following day to continue on to Cape Town via the Garden Route. The **bus to Swaziland** travels principally along the N2 up the KwaZulu-Natal North Coast, passing through Ballito, Gingindlovu, Eshowe, Empangeni, Kwambonambi, St Lucia, Hluhluwe (which gives access to Sodwana Bay), Mkuzi and in Swaziland, Manzini and Mlilwane. The following day the same bus continues on to Johannesburg/Pretoria via Nelspruit (which provides access to the Kruger National Park); from there it completes the leg in a single day and passes along the west side of the province, giving access to the Drakensberg and passing through Pietermaritzburg, Howick, Mooi River and Harrismith. The direct bus **to Johannesburg/Pretoria** skirts the Drakensberg taking in Durban, Pietermaritzburg, Mooi River (Sani Pass & Southern Drakensberg), Winterton (Central Drakensberg), Amphitheatre (Northern Drakensberg) and Ficksburg.

Durban to: Amphitheatre (3 weekly; 5hr); Ballito (3 weekly; 45min); Cintsa (5 weekly; 6hr 30min); East London (5 weekly; 9hr 45min); Eshowe (4 weekly; 2hr); Gingindlovu (4 weekly; 1hr 30min); Hamburg (5 weekly; 10hr 45min); Harrismith (4 weekly; 7hr); Hluhluwe (4 weekly; 7hr 15min); Howick (4 weekly; 2hr 30min); Johannesburg (4 weekly; 9hr); Kenton-on-Sea (5 weekly; 11hr 30min); Kokstad (5 weekly; 3hr 40min); Kwambonambi (4 weekly; 4hr); Manzini (4 weekly; 10hr 30min); Mkuzi (4 weekly; 8hr); Mlilwane (4 weekly; 10hr 30min); Mooi River (4 weekly; 3hr); Pietermaritzburg (4 weekly; 2hr); Port Alfred (5 weekly; 11hr 45 min); Port Elizabeth (5 weekly; 13hr 30min); Port Shepstone (5 weekly; 1hr 30min); Pretoria (4 weekly; 10hr); Richards Bay (4 weekly; 3hr); St Lucia (4 weekly; 5hr); Umtata (5 weekly; 5hr 45min); Warner Beach (5 weekly; 30min); Winterton (3 weekly; 4hr).

Minibus shuttles

Two **minibus shuttles**, **Rollercoaster Taxi** (☏ 031 464 5858) and **Rasool's** (☏ 031 208 0803), run a door-to-door service twice a day (Rollercoaster pick-up 6–7am & 4–5pm. Rasool's pick-up 5–6am and 5–6pm) in each direction between Jo'burg and Durban (6–7hrs). Apart from a halfway break in Harrismith to stretch your legs, there are no intermediate stops.

Flights

Durban to: Bloemfontein (12 weekly; 1hr 20min); Cape Town (12 daily; 2hr 15min); George (7 weekly; 3hr); Johannesburg (32 daily; 1hr 10min); Pietermaritzburg (10 weekly; 25min); Plettenberg Bay (3 weekly; 2hr 50min); Port Elizabeth (5 daily; 1hr 20min); Ulundi (10 weekly; 40min).

Margate to: Johannesburg (1 daily; 1hr 30min).
Pietermaritzburg to: Durban (2 daily; 25min); Johannesburg (7 daily; 2hr 15min); Ulundi (2 daily; 1hr 30min).
Richards Bay to: Johannesburg (1 daily; 1hr 20min).

Free State

CHAPTER 6

Highlights

* **Highlands Route** A scenic drive past massive rock formations, cherry orchards and sandstone farming towns. **See p.568**

* **Basotho vernacular architecture** See the decorative adobe huts typical of the Eastern Free State and Lesotho at the Basotho Cultural Village. **See p.569**

* **Golden Gate Highlands National Park** A stunning reserve dominated by the beautiful Maluti Mountains with their stripy red sandstone outcrops. **See p.571**

* **Street Café Restaurant** Sample one of 107 varieties of beer, sitting outdoors in the delightful town of Clarens. **See p.573**

* **Rustler's Valley Easter Festival** A legendary festival in a beautiful valley, which draws hordes of young South Africans to listen to music, get down and chill out. **See p.574**

6

Free State

T he Highlands Route, one of South Africa's most scenic drives, skirts the mountainous eastern flank of the **Free State**, the traditional heartland of conservative **Afrikanerdom**, which lies landlocked at the centre of the country. If you're driving from Johannesburg to Port Elizabeth or Cape Town, **the Eastern Highlands**, which sweep up to the subcontinent's highest peaks in the Lesotho Drakensberg, are worth the detour off the more humdrum N6. The eastern Free State is also the **gateway to Lesotho**, with border posts close to each of the small towns on the South African side. **Bloemfontein**, the capital, is only worth visiting if you driving on the N6 to reach the Cape, rather than taking the Highlands Route, but once there you'll find very good guesthouses, restaurants and museums. The highlight of the Eastern Highlands is the **Golden Gate National Park**, designated a national park not for its wildlife, but because of the beauty of the Maluti Mountains with their stripy red sandstone outcrops. It's an easy three- to four-hour drive from Johannesburg, and from here it's possible to do a round trip of the Highlands, taking in Lesotho as well.

Southeast of Golden Gate you can drive to the **Sentinel car park** via the interesting **Basotho Cultural Village** and **Phuthadijhaba**. It's possible to hike up to the highest plateaus of the **Drakensberg** – easier than starting from a much lower altitude in the Royal Natal National Park. West of the park is **Clarens**, by far the nicest of the string of towns running along the Lesotho border. It has a distinctly arty feel, good guesthouses and outdoor cafés, and some of the country's best horse-riding, taking in Bushmen cave paintings as well. For young travellers, party-goers and ageing hippies, the real focus of the region is **Rustler's Valley**, west of Clarens, where you can ride, hike in the hills, party or simply hang out on a truly magnificent farm.

In the rest of the province, flat farmlands roll away into miles of bright-yellow sunflowers and mauve- and pink-petalled cosmos, with maize and wheat fields glowing under immense blue skies. Nelson Mandela described this area as gladdening his heart, "no matter what my mood. When I am here I feel that nothing can shut me in, that my thoughts can roam as far as the horizons."

Some history

Intriguing though it sounds, the name "Free State" applies to former redneck country. For nearly 150 years, the only free people in the Free State were its **white settlers**, who in 1854 were granted independence from Britain in a territory between the Orange and Vaal rivers, where they created a Boer Republic called the **Orange Free State**. The "Orange" part of the name came from the Orange River, which in its turn was named in 1777 by Colonel

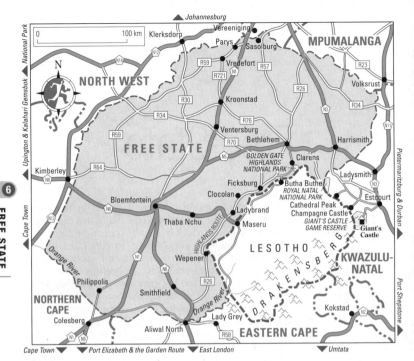

Robert Gordon, commander of the British garrison at the Cape, after the royal Dutch House of Orange.

The system of government in the republic, inspired by the US Constitution, was highly democratic – if you were white and male. Women couldn't vote, while Africans had no rights at all, and were even forbidden from owning land.

Two expansionist military campaigns were launched in 1858 and 1865 to drive out independent **Basotho** people from fertile lands along the Caledon River, which had been their home since the sixteenth century. Although many Basotho under the paramount chief **Moshoeshoe** retreated to strongholds in the Drakensberg (see p.748), the thousands who remained were reduced to squatters, sharecroppers and labourers facing poor wages on the 15,000 thinly distributed white farms.

A century later, the Orange Free State was a bastion of apartheid, being the only province to ban anyone of Asian descent from remaining within its borders for longer than 24 hours. Africans fared little better; in 1970, under the grand apartheid scheme, a tiny barren enclave wedged between Lesotho, KwaZulu-Natal and the Free State became **QwaQwa**, a "homeland" for Southern Sotho people. As a result of forced clearances from white-designated areas, in the two decades after 1970 its population swelled from 24,000 to nearly half a million, creating one of the worst rural slums in the country. Many men were forced to seek work as migrant labourers in the Gauteng gold mines. Another tiny area around Thaba Nchu, 63km east of Bloemfontein, was part of Bophutatswana, the Tswana *bantustan*, which became nominally independent from South Africa in 1977, but was never more than a series of disconnected fragments scattered all over the country, the capital at Mmabatho, in another shard of land in Northwest Province.

The *bantustans* have since been reincorporated into South Africa, and after an ANC landslide in Free State province in the 1994 elections, the "Orange" part of the name, with its Dutch Calvinist associations, was dropped.

Bloemfontein and around

BLOEMFONTEIN, the only centre of any size in the province, is unlikely to feature on anyone's list of must-see destinations. However, its location at the crossroads of South Africa means that many travellers break their journey across the country here. There's enough diversion for a day or two in Bloemfontein's surprisingly fine **Oliewenhuis Art Gallery**, set in beautiful gardens, and in the unmistakably provincial **President Brand Street**, lined with handsome, sandstone public buildings.

As an overnight stop, the city offers good accommodation at reasonable prices, including *Hobbit House,* often voted the best guesthouse in South Africa. People home in from all over the Free State for hospital treatment, for the university (highly regarded for its medical school) and several boarding schools. It's also the seat of the provincial parliament and the judicial capital of the country – a sop tossed out to draw it into the Union when South Africa federated in 1910.

Bloemfontein's urban origins go back to 1846, when **Major Henry Warden** was dispatched to establish a fort and residency here to enforce British control over the unruly Boers, Griquas and Basotho, who were in a constant state of conflict. Knocking their heads together proved fruitless; the frustrated Warden was withdrawn eight years later and the territory left to the Boers, who set up the capital of their new republic here.

Gauteng to Bloemfontein: some route tips

Taking the **N1** from Johannesburg to Bloemfontein is the fastest way of covering the distance – and there's a lot to be said for getting the journey over with as quickly as possible. This is no scenic route, especially the Gauteng section and the northern Free State area, which is full of ugly industrial towns. Toll booths are strategically positioned at intervals along the N1, but the charge hardly makes it worth taking free detours. **Kroonstad**, 207km south of Johannesburg, is the biggest town along the N1 before you get to Bloemfontein. The Kroon Park, a large and popular resort beside a river, with a swimming pool, offers a pit stop if you want to cool off or get something to eat.

The alternative route from just south of the provincial border to Kroonstad goes via **Parys**, first along the R59 and turning onto the R721 at Vredefort, 13km south of Parys. But while Parys is quite green and pleasant, you're likely to get stuck behind slow traffic, whereas the N1 at this point is still straight, smooth and wide.

The further south you go, the flatter the Free State becomes. There's an exceptionally long, dull stretch with no services between **Ventersburg** and Bloemfontein.

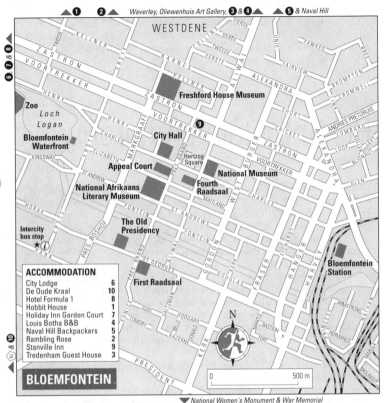

WESTDENE

Freshford House Museum

Zoo
Loch
Logan

Bloemfontein Waterfront

KINGSWAY

City Hall

❾

Hertzog Square

Appeal Court

National Afrikaans Literary Museum

Fourth Raadsaal

National Museum

The Old Presidency

Intercity bus stop
★ ⓘ

Bloemfontein Station

ACCOMMODATION

City Lodge	6
De Oude Kraal	10
Hotel Formula 1	8
Hobbit House	1
Holiday Inn Garden Court	7
Louis Botha B&B	4
Naval Hill Backpackers	5
Rambling Rose	2
Stanville Inn	9
Tredenham Guest House	3

First Raadsaal

N

BLOEMFONTEIN

0   500 m

▼ *National Women's Monument & War Memorial*

Arrival and information

Translux (☎051 408 3242), Intercape (☎051 447 1435) and Greyhound (☎051 447 1558) **buses** pull in at the central bus terminal in the tourist complex at the east end of Park Avenue, opposite the swimming pool. There's also a **tourist information** bureau (Mon–Fri 8am–4.15pm, Sat 8am–noon; ☎051 405 8490, ⊕051 447 3859, ⊛www.bloemfontein.co.za), which provides **maps** of the city.

Few travellers fly into **Bloemfontein airport** (☎051 433 2901), 10km east of town on the N8, although there are scheduled flights between here and the major cities. There are no shuttle buses from the airport into town, so your only choice is to phone for a fairly expensive **taxi**, or **rent a car** (see "Listings" on p.566 for details of both). By **train**, you arrive at Bloemfontein station (☎051 408 4843, after hours ☎051 408 2262) in Harvey Road at the east end of Maitland Street. By minibus taxi, you'll be dropped off at the rank in Hanger Street, one block west of the station. The area around the station and the minibus taxi rank is regarded by some residents as the dodgiest in the city centre, but there have been few actual incidents. Stay alert, and avoid the area at night. Fortunately, metered taxis usually rank outside the train and at the bus station; alternatively, you can phone for one (see p.566).

Accommodation

Bloemfontein's *Hobbit House* is regularly voted South Africa's best guesthouse. Also here is some of the cheapest overnight **accommodation** in South Africa, mainly concentrated around the hospitals, in Universitas suburb to the west of the city centre, and around Oranjesig to its south. However, you're better off heading for the nicer and more central suburbs of **Westdene** and **Waverley**, both north of the centre and easily reached on foot.

City Lodge On the corner of Zastron Street and Parfitt Avenue, Westdene, and well situated for lively Second Street ☎051 444 2974, ⨍051 447 5669, ⓔcl/bloem@citylodge.co.za. A fully revamped hotel offering good value, with cheaper rates at weekends. Serves excellent breakfasts. ❹

De Oude Kraal 35km south of Bloemfontein on the N1, off the Riversford exit ☎051 564 0636, ⨍051 564 0635, ⓦwww.deoudekraal.co.za. A restored original farmhouse, famed for its splendid Afrikaner meals. The en-suite rooms have their own fireplace. ❹

Hobbit House 19 President Steyn Ave, Westdene ☎ & ⨍051 447 0663, ⓔhobbit@intekom.co.za. The best place to stay in Bloemfontein, *Hobbit House* is a luxurious establishment filled with beautiful and comfortable antique furniture, with teddy bears tucked into every bed under handmade quilts. With only five rooms, you'll need to book well in advance. Excellent three-course dinners are available for guests (phone by lunchtime). ❹

Holiday Inn Garden Court Bloemfontein On the corner of Zastron and Melville streets, Westdene ☎051 444 1253, ⨍051 444 0671. The best of the posh hotels, with large rooms, a nice swimming pool, and weekend discounts. ❹

Hotel Formula One Zastron Street ☎051 444 3523. No frills, thrills or surprises at this basic, but predictably clean and reliable chain budget hotel. ❶

Louis Botha B&B 18 Louis Botha St, Waverley ☎ & ⨍051 436 4533, ⓔmwctrade@mweb.co.za. Reasonably priced rooms in a suburban house, situated in a pleasant street with a large garden, a 15min walk from the centre. ❶

Naval Hill Backpackers Delville Road, as you turn into the old waterpump station ☎051 447 4413 or 082 579 6509, ⨍051 444 6065. Four clean dorms and two private rooms (linen available) in a nicely done-up late nineteenth-century pumping station, with washed orange and silver walls. The hostel offers internet facilities as well as bar and restaurant; it can arrange transport to Lesotho and free pick-ups from the station, and provides excellent information on Bloemfontein's nightlife. ❶

Rambling Rose 77 President Reitz St, Westdene ☎051 447 1634, ⨍051 430 5713, ⓔpretorius1@worldonline.co.za. Bright, comfortable garden B&B rooms attached to a suburban house with swimming pool. ❷

Stanville Inn 85 Zastron St ☎051 447 7471, ⨍051 447 7514. Tiny, well-maintained rooms in a five-storey apartment block on a busy road. Excellent value, and reasonably priced breakfasts are also available. ❶

Tredenham Guest House Off Eeufees Road, just north of town ☎ & ⨍051 433 1285. Colonial English farmhouse built in 1925, now Afrikaner-owned and furnished in period style, offering good meals and a relaxing rural atmosphere. ❹

The City

For a city with a countrywide reputation as the bumpkin capital of South Africa, Bloemfontein is actually quite agreeable. Its slightly unreal character results from many of its late nineteenth- and early twentieth-century **public buildings** paying a pick'n'mix homage to Mediterranean, British, Renaissance and Classical influences. The lack of public transport is no obstacle to getting around, as the central area can easily be crossed on foot in ten minutes.

In common with other South African cities, the white population has begun to desert the city centre. Instead, the suburb of **Westdene**, just to the north of the city centre, has become the place to shop and hang out; the large four-storied Mimosa Mall in Kellner Street provides all you'd need, from coffee shops and chain restaurants to banks and bookshops. Westdene's Second Avenue has burgeoned with restaurants and nightspots, and is safe to stroll about at night, as is the **Waterfront** on Loch Logan, three blocks west of the City Hall – all conveniently near most of the accommodation. The city centre is nevertheless still worth exploring for its architecture.

City Hall and around

For a rewarding stroll in the centre, head down **President Brand Street**, starting at the **City Hall** at the north end on the corner of Charles Street. Built in 1934, the hall was designed in the "new tradition style" by Gordon Leith, a former employee of Sir Herbert Baker. On the opposite side of President Brand Street, **Hertzog Square** honours the dubious achievements of the Boer general, high court judge and Afrikaner nationalist **J.B.M. Hertzog**, who founded the National Party in 1914 and went on to become prime minister of the Union of South Africa in 1924. Herzog was also responsible for harsh segregationist legislation, including the stripping of voting rights from Africans in the Cape in 1936. Across the square at 36 Aliwal St, the **National Museum** (Mon–Sat 8am–5pm, Sun 12–5.30pm; R5) is worth visiting for its rather good dinosaur fossil collection, an actual beehive, cut away to reveal the workings within, and an outstanding reconstruction of a turn-of-the-century Bloemfontein street. The latter features a general dealer, pharmacy, doctor's consulting rooms and a family scene capturing in frozen diorama a father telling off his son under a stern portrait of President Steyn, who looks on approvingly at the father's strictness. The museum also has a tea room.

Returning to President Brand Street, south of the City Hall stands the highest court in the country, the Roman-style **Supreme Court of Appeal of South Africa**, built in 1929. Staring at it from across the road is the **Fourth Raadsaal**, the last parliament building of the independent Orange Free State republic (it's now the provincial legislature). Built in 1890 – and still regarded as the province's "architectural jewel" – the Raadsaal is an imposing sandstone and red-brick construction, typical of Free State buildings of the period, and brilliantly merging Greek, Roman and Renaissance elements.

National Afrikaans Literary Museum

One block south of the Appeal Court in the Old Government Building, on the corner of President Brand and Maitland streets is the **National Afrikaans Literary Museum** (Mon–Fri 8am–noon & 1–3.45pm, Sat 9am–noon; free). Inside, a corridor of offices has been reconstructed as the studies of luminaries of Afrikaans writing; name plates on the doors make you feel rude for not knocking before entering. Look out for the display on **Eugene Marais**, a remarkable polymath active around the turn of the century. A lawyer, poet and journalist, Marais contributed articles to the *Observer* and *The Times* in London and to the Reuter news agency – his works also include a couple of trail-blazing natural histories on termites and baboons. Also represented are the "Sestigers" (generation of the Sixties), such as novelist **André Brink**, a vociferous critic of apartheid, and poet **Breyten Breytenbach**, who went into exile in Paris in 1961. Breytenbach returned to South Africa under cover in 1975 to gain support for Okhela, a largely white section of the ANC, and was captured by the South African authorities and imprisoned for seven years, leading to the publication after his release of *The True Confessions of an Albino Terrorist*.

Towards the end of the museum, a couple of rooms are devoted to displays of Afrikaans as a language of oppression. One of the leading lights of coloured Afrikaans (which has its own distinct flavour) is the poet **Adam Small**; in one display, he describes the predicament of being a member of an oppressed community, while at the same time being a speaker of Afrikaans – regarded as the language of white persecutors during the uprisings of the Seventies. "I grew up with Afrikaans. Afrikaans is part of my culture," he is quoted as saying, "and when people said to you that Afrikaans was the language of the oppressor it was very painful, because it was also the language you got from your parents, it was your mother tongue and it was beautiful and full of humanity."

The Waterfront and Zoo

Following the huge success of the Victoria and Alfred Waterfront in Cape Town, every city in the country, landlocked or not, seems eager to jump on the bandwagon. Bloemfontein is no exception; its **Waterfront**, opened in 1998 on Loch Logan in King's Park, is a couple of blocks west of the National Afrikaans Literary Museum. A refreshing addition to the city, the waterfront has movie houses, pubs and restaurants. Also in King's Park, **Bloemfontein Zoo** (daily: summer 8am–6pm; winter 8am–5pm; R15) is a reasonable place to catch African wildlife, but obviously offers no serious competition to the game reserve.

The Supreme Court of Appeal, Old Presidency and First Raadsaal

Carrying on south down President Brand Street to the corner of Selborne Street, opposite the Fire Station, is the **Supreme Court of Appeal**, completed in 1906. It stands on the site of the home of the Fischers, a prominent Orange Free State Afrikaner family, whose heir, lawyer Bram Fischer, betrayed his Afrikaner tribal roots to defend Nelson Mandela during the 1963 Rivonia Trial (see p.836). After Mandela was found guilty and handed a life sentence, it was discovered that all the time Fischer had secretly been the leader of the proscribed Communist Party, and he too was jailed for life, later being released to die at home of cancer.

The **Old Presidency** (Tues–Fri 10am–noon & 1–4pm, Sat & Sun 2–5pm; free), on the opposite side was built on the site of the home of Major Henry Warden, the founder of Bloemfontein. Built in 1861 in "Scottish baronial style" as the official seat of the head of the republic, the Presidency is surprisingly plain, due as much to the nineteenth-century state's lack of funds as to the severe Calvinism characterizing the Boer republics. Although you can go inside, it's difficult to get an idea of how the president lived because virtually none of the original furnishings remain.

Turning east after the Old Presidency into St George's Street, you'll come to the **First Raadsaal** (Mon–Fri 10.15am–3pm, Sat & Sun 2–5pm; free), the oldest-surviving building in Bloemfontein. Built in 1849 by Major Warden as a school, the building was later used as a Dutch Reformed church and venue for public meetings. At independence in 1854 it became a meeting chamber for Free State Volksraad ("people's assembly"), before reverting to a schoolhouse and church.

National Women's Monument and War Museum

Just over 2km south of the centre, along Monument Street, across the train tracks in an ugly industrial part of town, a sandstone needle pointing skywards marks the **National Women's Monument and War Museum** (Mon–Fri 9am–4.30pm, Sat 9am–5pm, Sun 2–5pm; R5). This stands as a memorial to the 26,370 Afrikaner women and children who died in British concentration camps during the second Anglo-Boer War. It is impossible to overestimate the scars left on the Afrikaner psyche by the concentration camps – probably still the single most divisive issue between English and Afrikaans-speaking white

J.R.R. Tolkien

Bloemfontein's biggest surprise is that it's the birthplace of **John Ronald Reuel Tolkien**, author of *Lord of the Rings* and *The Hobbit*, a fact the city seems curiously reluctant to publicize.

Tolkien's father, Arthur, left his native Birmingham to work in the colonies, eventually becoming manager of the Bank of Africa in Bloemfontein. J.R.R. was born in 1892, in a house standing on the corner of West Burger and Maitland streets, a couple of blocks east of President Brand Street. When Arthur Tolkien died in 1895, his wife returned to England with her two infant sons; their house was later torn down to make way for a Bradlow's showroom, part of a cheap, nationwide furniture chain.

Despite wild claims that Tolkien's experience of the South African landscape inspired him to create the world of Bilbo Baggins, in fact, the flatness of the Free State and the down-to-earth Calvinism of its farming community could hardly be further from *The Hobbit*'s fantastical realm of mountains, forests and supernatural beings. Some accounts claim Tolkien was inspired by the Natal Drakensberg, or the Amatola Mountains around Hogsback. While both these areas do seem to possess an otherworldly magic, it should also be noted that Tolkien left South Africa for good when he was 3 years old, never having set foot outside Bloemfontein prior to his departure.

South Africans. At the foot of the monument lies buried **Emily Hobhouse**, a British woman who energetically campaigned on behalf of the Boer internees.

The interest of the adjacent **museum** lies principally in its status as a record of apartheid propaganda. The suffering depicted isn't an exaggeration, but it's a little heavy-handed in its unrelenting dioramas of dignified Boers suffering at the hands of faceless British bastards. Two cursory panels on concentration camps for Africans (never widely publicized in South Africa in the old days), are a post-apartheid afterthought that at least provides a partial record of the more than 14,000 black South Africans who died incarcerated.

A room near the entrance of the museum is lined with brilliant ceramic-tile tableaux, depicting scenes from the Anglo-Boer War. The tiles were brought here in 1969 after being uncovered when wallpaper was stripped off the walls of the Transvalia Theatre in Rotterdam, the Netherlands – an indication of how the war rallied the popular imagination in Europe on the side of the Boers.

Oliewenhuis Art Gallery and Freshford House Museum

The best of Bloemfontein's museums is the **Oliewenhuis Art Gallery** on Harry Smith Street (Mon–Fri 8am–5pm, Sat 10am–5pm, Sun 1–5pm; free), about five minutes north of the centre by car. The collection is housed in the former residency of South African presidents, a beautifully light neo-Cape Dutch manor set in large, attractive gardens, surrounded by wild bush traversed by short walking trails. The gallery contains a surprisingly good range of **South African sculpture** and **painting**. Particularly satisfying is the landscape collection, which includes a Van Gogh-esque interpretation of one of the city churches by **Bertha Everard**, and a **Thomas Baines** painting of Bloemfontein as a tiny settlement in 1850. Even if you're not interested in the gallery, it's still worth having tea at the **café** on the lawn – its trees and fountain make it the most harmonious location in town.

Also to the north of the city centre, **Freshford House Museum**, 31 Kellner St (Mon–Fri 10am–1pm, Sat & Sun 2–5pm; R2), makes a lightweight but enjoyable visit. This is especially true if you're interested in **interiors**, as it has been refurbished impeccably in Victorian and Edwardian style. One highlight is a room authentically decorated in daring lime green, with three distinct William Morris wallpapers.

Eating and drinking

While Bloemfontein is no culinary capital and there are no regional specialities to sample, you can still have a good and inexpensive **meal** out here, mostly around Second Avenue. You'll also find the usual steakhouse chains scattered around the centre and in the shopping malls. For gluttonous **breakfasts**, the *City Lodge* and *Holiday Inn Garden Court* hotels (see p.561) are always good bets.

Acropolis C.R. Swart Building, Elizabeth Street ☎051 447 0464. Bloemfontein's most stylish eating place, a revolving 24th-floor restaurant with soaring city views and decor based on London's *River Café*. Best at night, it serves wholesome Greekstyle food. Closed Sat lunch and Sun evening.

Barbas Café On Second Avenue, near the university ☎051 430 2542. Barbas serves good Greek food, a range of cocktails and the best coffee in town; its starkly fashionable decor also helps attract the young and trendy. Parties every Saturday night. Open Tues–Sun 10am until late.

Beef Baron 22 Second Ave ☎051 447 4290. True to its name, this is the place to come for beef, where your mug-shot could join those of other carnivores who downed 1.5kg steaks and survived. It also has tempting seafood and an excellent wine cellar. Closed Sat & Mon lunch and Sun evening.

Café Oliewenhuis Harry Smith Street, signposted off the R700. Tables in the formal gardens at the back of the gallery, leading onto a nature reserve, make this Bloemfontein's nicest place for a relaxing outdoor tea or lunch. Though the food itself is generally nothing to write home about, this is definitely *the* place for Sunday afternoon tea and cake.

Café Rossini Mimosa Mall, Kellner Street ☎051 444 6222. Gourmet sandwiches, salads and baked potatoes in relaxing surroundings. A handy stop if you're doing a bit of mall shopping. Open daily 8.30am–9.30pm.

Jazz Time Waterfront ☎051 430 5727. No live jazz here, but a lively atmosphere and background music; there's also a wooden deck from which you can survey passing pedestrians. Good cocktail menu, burgers and Middle Eastern food. Open daily 8am–midnight.

Mystic Boer 84 Kellner St. If you have only a night in Bloemfontein, spend it here. Knowingly kitsch, this alternative and trendy Afrikaner venue offers live performances; you can also enjoy a drink and choose pizzas and vegetarian meals from their reasonable pub menu.

Oude Kraal 35km south of town on the N1 ☎051 564 0636. Six-course blow-out evening meals of rich, fattening Afrikaner-style food in lovely surroundings on a historic farm. Booking essential.

Roma Coffee Bar 24 West Burger St. Daytimeonly venue for good filter coffee and their legendary two-tone chocolate cake, baked by a schoolgirl who won't divulge the recipe.

Upstairs at Grill Kellner Street and Second Avenue, Westdene ☎051 430 07050. Possibly the best restaurant in town, with well-priced dishes like rump steak rolled in black pepper, garlic, rosemary and lemon, then flamed in brandy, or tequilaand lime-marinated prawns. Flavours are Mediterranean, Oriental and Cajun, and the choice of local wines is dazzling. Mon–Fri & Sun 11am–11pm, Sat 5.30pm–late.

Nightlife and entertainment

Finding out what's going on in Bloemfontein can be a problem for visitors, as there's no English-language newspaper, though *Naval Hill Backpackers* (see "Accommodation", p.561) is always a good source of information on drinking spots and clubs. For something quite different that you won't catch anywhere else in the country, the *Mystic Boer* has local bands playing on a regular basis plus dancing in the back. A handful of bars down Second Street are worth checking out; *Barba's Café* (see above) is a lively place for a drink. The excellent *Moods and Flavours* (☎051 432 2864) in Heidedal – the coloured quarter – has live jazz from all over the country, though only on four nights a month; people dress up for a really good time here.

Bloemfontein's handful of **theatres** include the Observatory, inside a real observatory north of the centre on the crest of Naval Hill. It's situated in the city's nature reserve, which supports a few giraffe and some antelope. The most prestigious theatre is the Sand du Plessis, on the corner of Markgraaff and St Andrew streets. Bloemfontein has several **cinemas**, mostly in suburban shopping malls; the Mimosa Mall in Westdene contains seven screens, and the Waterfront has five, all showing mainstream movies.

Listings

Airlines South African Airways, St Andrew's Street ☎051 447 3811.

Car rental Avis (☎051 433 2331), Budget (☎051 433 1178), Hertz (☎051 433 4018) and Imperial (☎051 433 3511) are all found at the airport.

Emergencies Ambulance ☎10177; Fire ☎10178; Police (Flying Squad ☎10111) Rape Crisis ☎447 6678.

Hospitals The main state hospital is Universitas, offering a free 24hr emergency ward, but you may wait hours and the level of care is variable. Far better, if you can afford it or have travel insurance, is one of the private hospitals: Hydromed, Kellner

Street ☎051 404 6666, and Rosepark, Fichmed Centre, Gustav Crescent ☎051 422 6761.

Pharmacies Medirex Pharmacy, Southern Life Building, Maitland Street ☎051 447 5822 (daily 8am–10.30pm).

Post office Main branch, corner of East Burger and Maitland streets (Mon, Tues, Thurs & Fri 8am–4.30pm, Wed 8.30am–4.30pm, Sat 8am–noon).

Taxis Silverleaf ☎051 430 2005 is recommended.

Train information Spoornet ☎051 408 4843, after hours ☎ 051 2262.

South from Bloemfontein

Two major routes splay out and head south from Bloemfontein, the **N6** to the Eastern Cape via Aliwal North and the **N1** to the Western Cape via Colesberg. There's nothing much along either route apart from a couple of quirky small towns. **SMITHFIELD**, a tiny *dorp* 145km south of Bloemfontein, makes a good place to break a journey along the N6, if only to stay at the pleasant *Artists Colony Guest House* (☎ & ℱ051 683 1138, ℮colony@global.co.za), or the more luxurious *Smithfield House* in Brand Street (☎051 683 0071, ℮smithfieldho @icon.co.za; ❸), a restored Victorian house with three en-suite rooms, its own pool and tennis court, and a seven-acre garden on the outskirts of town

The Griquas

In the early nineteenth century, roving bands of cattle-herders and raiders with a reputation for horsemanship and fierce independence appeared on the eastern edge of the Cape Colony around the Orange River. They called themselves, with some pride, "Bastaards", being mixed descendants of European, Khoikhoi, Asian and African people. Missionaries persuaded them to establish settlements at places such as Griquatown, Campbell and Philippolis, but took exception to their name, which was changed to **Griqua**. Though Griqualand West was still theoretically independent, clashes with the Boers and squabbles over land ownership when diamonds were found in their territory saw the Griquas turning to the British for protection, faith which was all too hastily swallowed up by the gorging Cape Colony.

In 1861, three thousand Griquas from Philippolis under their leader Adam Kok III trekked across the Drakensberg to southern Natal to found a pocket of land known as **Griqualand East**. The settlement failed, and slowly the Griquas dispersed and became assimilated into the wider coloured community, although there are still odd pockets of their descendants living in various places around the Northern, Western and Eastern Cape provinces.

Laurens van der Post

Laurens van der Post achieved world renown as an explorer, writer, soldier and philosopher. He became fascinated by the stories and legends of the "Bushman", the San people dispossessed of their traditional homes by the advance of African and European settlers and forced into the northern deserts. "What drew me so strongly to the Bushman was that he appeared to belong to my native land as no other human being has ever belonged," wrote van der Post, referring to the Bushman's self-sufficient yet intensely spiritual and aesthetic way of life. It prompted him to take a famous journey in search of the last remnants of the San, one he recorded in his book (later a film) *The Lost World of the Kalahari*. This narrative, along with its sequel *The Heart of the Hunter*, was one of the first literary works to prick the Western conscience with the idea that such a primitive "tribe" had anything to teach it.

Van der Post was also a Japanese prisoner of war during World War II. His book about these experiences, *The Seed and the Sower*, was made into the film *Merry Christmas, Mr Lawrence*. He lived in both London and South Africa, and died in 1996, aged 90.

where kids are welcome to run about. The English restaurant *Colony Room* (℡051 683 0021), along the N6, off Juana Square, opens daily from morning till night for pub lunches, including genuine pork bangers and mash and puddings such as "Death by Chocolate."

PHILIPPOLIS, 168km south of Bloemfontein along a slight detour (tarred) off the N1 between Trompsberg and Colesberg, is where **Sir Laurens van der Post** (see box above) grew up. It's also a good place to see the mighty **Orange River** – it's easier to stop and contemplate the river on a quiet country road than flashing over it at 120kph as you do on the highway. There isn't much to the town itself, although it was one of the first settlements north of the Orange River, established in the 1830s and named in honour of **Dr John Philip**, a British cleric who set up a mission station here. Way ahead of his time, Philip actively campaigned for the full integration of former slaves, Africans and coloured people into the white economic and social system.

Today, many of the tourists passing through Philippolis are disaffected city people in search of a rural idyll. Besides the van der Post connection, 75 of the town's houses have been declared National Heritage sites – a mixture of simple, flat-roofed Karoo and Cape Dutch gabled houses and Victorian buildings with characteristic wrought-iron decorative flourishes. Among the attractive old buildings lining the few streets is the house of **Adam Kok III**, leader of the Griqua (see opposite). This small, white, flat-roofed house lies just before the post office on Voortrekker Street, the main thoroughfare running through the village.

Signposted along the main road, an **information** bureau (Mon–Fri 8am–4pm; ℡051 773 0209) can direct you to **accommodation** and informal tours of the town. For self-catering, the *Philippolis Old Gaol* in Justisie Street (℡082 550 4421; ❶), two streets off the main road, is cheap, clean and more attractive than it sounds, with two beds to a cell. *Oppie Stoep*, run by Mrs Britz (℡051 773 0390; ❷), is a Victorian bungalow with verandahs front and back, with six B&B rooms, or try the inexpensive *Philipollis Lodge* on Kok Street (℡051 773 0422; ❷), a guesthouse and restaurant (closed Sundays). For **eating**, apart from *Philipollis Lodge*, the *Kokkewiet Café* in the heart of town is the town's meeting place; on Sundays, churchgoers sit at plastic tables and chairs to gossip and drink tea.

The old **van der Post family home** (see box above) on Colin Fraser Street, is privately owned, but if you contact the owners you may be allowed to look around it. Laurens, the thirteenth of fifteen children, was born on a farm outside town in 1906 and moved here when he was still very young. His ashes are in the Sir Laurens van der Post Memorial Garden, unmissable as you drive into town from Bloemfontein. The garden has been built round the old pathway linking the white side of town with the black township, and there are plans to create a van der Post museum and writers' retreat in the little house next door.

At the end of Voortrekker Street stands the large **Dutch Reformed Church**, built on the site of the original Griqua mission station. It's worth visiting on Sundays to sample local Afrikaans culture.

The Highlands Route

Hugging the Lesotho border for 280km from **Phuthadijhaba** (Witsieshoek) in the north to Wepener, beyond Ladybrand in the south, the tarred **Highlands Route** offers one of South Africa's most scenic drives. It takes you past massive rock formations streaked with red and ochre, cherry orchards and sandstone farming towns. Wedged into a corner between Lesotho and northern KwaZulu-Natal, Phuthadijhaba is the gateway to **the Sentinel**, the easiest route onto the **Drakensberg Escarpment**, the roof of southern Africa. Not far to the west is the highlight of the region, the **Golden Gate Highlands National Park**, encompassing wide open mountain country. The park is an easy three- to four-hour drive from Johannesburg, which means you could use

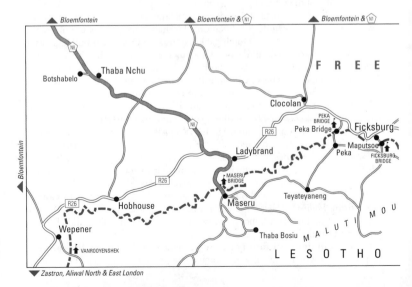

it as a first- or last-night stop if you're arriving or leaving from Johannesburg and don't want to spend the night in the city. Nearby, the **Basotho Cultural Village** is worth visiting to gain some insight into Basotho traditions. The closest village to the Golden Gate is **Clarens**, a centre for arts and crafts and the most attractive of all the villages along the route.

Basotho Cultural Village

The **Basotho Cultural Village** (Mon–Fri 9am–4pm, Sat & Sun 9am–5pm; entrance and guided tour R15; ☎ & ☎ 058 721 0300, ✉ basotho@dorea.co.za) is 20km east of Golden Gate National Park and signposted from the main road, in the QwaQwa National Park (next to Golden Gate). It offers a sanitized view of the traditional lives of the **Basotho** people, who have lived in the vicinity for centuries and have a close affinity to the people living just across the border in Lesotho. The main display in the village is a courtyard of beautiful **Basotho huts**, from organic circular sixteenth-century constructions to square huts with tin roofs and bright interior decor influenced by Boer scissorwork. Outside the huts are people in traditional dress; visitors get to meet the chief and sample traditional beer, hear musicians play and see a traditional healer throwing the bones. Although the whole setup is contrived, the half-hour tour can be good fun. Also interesting is the *litema*, or external decoration on houses, put on by women and still visible in rural Lesotho and Free State. The decoration varies from repeat patterns scratched into the mud-coloured plasterwork to vivid, modern motifs. While you're here, you can also book to go on the intriguing two-hour **Matlakeng Herbal Trail**, guided by a traditional healer who gives an informed introduction to *veld* herbs. The tour also takes in a well-preserved **rock painting**.

There's a limited amount of very reasonably priced **accommodation** available in a couple of thatched, stone huts (❶) with external toilets and washing facilities. A two-plate electric cooker and kettle are provided, along with basic utensils, and linen, blankets and towels. The views from the shuttered windows across the QwaQwa National Park are awesome, and this is a great place to

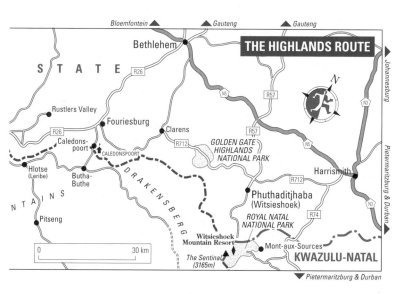

stay, with an endless choice of walks. Don't expect to be looked after though, and be warned that the village is largely deserted at night, when the workers head back to contemporary urban Sotho life in Phuthadijhaba. A **curio shop** sells some quality local crafts (look out for raffia mats and baskets and the conical straw hats unique to this area and Lesotho), and an open-air **restaurant** serves teas and traditional food.

Phuthadijhaba and around

The only reason you're likely to drive through **PHUTHADIJHABA** (sometimes called Witsieshoek), roughly 2km off the R712 and east of Golden Gate, is to reach the Witsieshoek Mountain Resort and the Sentinel car park, the easiest hiking access onto the High Drakensberg Escarpment. Phuthadijhaba itself is rather bleak and functional, home to light industry and brick matchbox houses. In contrast to the emptiness of the landscape around Golden Gate, in Phuthadijhaba you'll see minibus taxis zipping around, and people and animals walking on the roadsides past shacks, their tin roofs weighted down against the wind with stones. Phuthadijhaba was the artificially created capital of the former **QwaQwa** *bantustan*, and references to that miserable episode are still found in road signs and around town.

Signposted from here, the road to **Witsieshoek Mountain Inn** about 15km from the town, in a fork, one branch of which ends at the inn and the other

Hiking up the Drakensberg Escarpment

South Africa's most spectacular mountain views are from the **Drakensberg Escarpment** – the broad area right at the top of the major peaks, and the top of the **Amphitheatre**, the grand sweep of mountains dominating the Royal Natal National Park. Both of these require a high level of fitness if approached from KwaZulu-Natal (see p.503). However, they can be achieved relatively easily via the Free State from the Sentinel car park to a chain ladder, which gets you to the bottom of the final short onslaught on **Mont aux Sources**, the highest peak on the escarpment (3278m). The ladder is reached after a tough ten-hour climb from the *Mahai* campsite in the Royal Natal National Park, or a 2.5-hour walk from the Sentinel car park (8km from Witsieshoek Mountain Inn) in the Free State. Set out early so you have the whole day for the excursion onto the escarpment. A three-kilometre walk from the car park brings you to the foot of the thirty-metre-high chain ladder; from the top, you can climb to the summit of Mont aux Sources. The downside of this short cut is the litter around the ladder, although no more than one hundred people are allowed up per day. Don't be lulled by your apparently easy conquest: it's the Berg's prerogative to have the last word. Always tackle the magic ladder with enough food, water, clothes and a tent in which to sit out violent storms.

If the mountain bug has bitten, some serious **hikes** are available, including a two-week trek along the escarpment plateau to Sani Pass in the southern Drakensberg. You can also take in the most dramatic parts of the Berg on a five-day, 62-kilometre escarpment traverse, sleeping in caves, from the Sentinel car park to Cathedral Peak in the Natal Drakensberg Park, roughly 40km to the southwest. For any hikes of this nature you'll need a map and the excellent *Drakensberg Walks* by David Bristow (see p.894), available in most bookshops. There's accommodation in a mountain hut at the Sentinel car park, where 24-hour security protects vehicles. The hut has no hot water or electricity, so you may be better off at the more comfortable *Witsieshoek Mountain Inn* (see p.571). To book for the car park hut and one of the hundred places a day allocated to climb the chain ladder, contact the Basotho Cultural Village (see p.569).

at the **Sentinel car park**. The road is tarred until the final few kilometres. On maps, it looks as if the Royal Natal National Park and Witsieshoek are adjoining. They are, but only via footpaths up and down mountains – by road, the journey is about 100km, into KwaZulu-Natal and around the high peaks.

Witsieshoek Mountain Inn (☎058 713 6361 or 058 713 6362, ℱ058 713 5274; half-board ➍) is one of the great lost opportunities of South African architecture; it has the most spectacular setting of any mountain resort in the country, but possibly the worst planning. **Accommodation** has been placed just below the brow of a plateau, thus denying guests one of the best views in the entire Drakensberg. Still, you can always walk in the mountains to take in the views, and the functionality of the rooms is made up for by friendly service. The more expensive rooms have excellent views of the Sentinel Mountain. There is an overnight hikers' hostel in the hotel grounds (➊), which sleeps twelve and has electricity and hot water – but you need your own sleeping bag.

Golden Gate Highlands National Park

Roughly 300km northeast of Bloemfontein on the R712, **Golden Gate Highlands National Park** (open daily; free) is Free State's only national park. It was designated for its outstanding beauty rather than its wildlife; although **eland**, **zebra**, **mountain reedbuck** and **black wildebeest** roam the hillsides, the real attraction here is the unfettered space, eroded sandstone bastions and seamless blue skies. These rocks, grassy plateaus and incised valleys belong to the Drakensberg range, characterized here by spectacular yellow-and-red cliffs and overhangs.

A number of roughly one-hour **rambles** into the sandstone ravines start from a direction board near the footbridge at the *Glen Reenen* campsite. There aren't many medium-length hikes in the park, the only exception being a half-day walk up **Wodehouse Kop**, which offers great views and is more physically challenging than any of the short rambles. The most strenuous hike is the two-day circular Rhebok Trail, which reaches the highest and lowest points of the park. Because the trail is so demanding you'll need to make an early start, after staying the previous night at *Glen Reenen*, where the trail begins (see "Practicalities" below). The Rhebok mountain hut on the trail provides basic accommodation for hikers; bookings for the trail and hut must be made through South African National Parks. **Horse-riding** is also on offer, and can be booked through either restcamp, while in the summer you can **swim** in a natural waterfall pool close to *Glen Reenen* campsite.

Practicalities

Golden Gate is almost equidistant from Bloemfontein or Johannesburg (320km to the north on good, tarred roads); it's easily reached from either city. There are no entry gates to the park, which is open all the time. **Accommodation** is at two restcamps, close to one another and both right on the R712, a fact which, combined with the ease of access, deprives them of any sense of being wilderness retreats, although both have lush settings amidst the sandstone bastions. The cheaper of the two is *Glen Reenen*, with a **campsite**, which at peak holiday times becomes little more than a car park jammed with Afrikaner families and their caravans, and closely packed en-suite rondavels with kitchenettes (➊). *Brandwag*, the more upmarket, though mundane-looking camp about a kilometre away offers well-equipped self-catering chalets and comfortable hotel rooms (➌) with bath, phones and TV. For **bookings**, contact South African National Parks (Pretoria ☎012 343 1991, ℯreservations@parks-sa.co.za).

If the accommodation is full, or you want somewhere cheaper to stay with more solitude, consider the basic but highly atmospheric huts at the Basotho Cultural Village (see p.569). Or head to nearby Clarens (see below), for a wider range of guesthouse options.

Fuel is available at *Glen Reenen*, which also has a provisions store selling basics, as well as frozen braai packs, firewood and alcohol. Your only choice for eating out here is at the unexceptional restaurant at *Brandwag* – otherwise, drive to Clarens.

Clarens

Some 20km west of Golden Gate Highlands National Park lies the tree-fringed village of **CLARENS**, the most appealing of the settlements along the Highlands Route. Founded in 1912, Clarens is especially remarkable for its dressed stone architecture, which glows under the sandstone massif of the **Rooiberge** (Red Mountains) and the **Malutis** to the southeast. The best time to see the village is spring, when the fruit trees blossom, or in autumn, when the poplar leaves turn golden russet. But at any time of year, Clarens's relaxed air makes it a rare phenomenon in the Free State – a *dorp* you'd actually want to explore, or sip a sidewalk lager and simply hang out in.

Clarens was named after the Swiss town where **Paul Kruger**, president of the South African Republic, ended his days in 1904 after the Boers' defeat in the second Anglo-Boer War (see p.829) Clarens today is an **arts and crafts centre**, with a number of studios and shops peppering the streets. If you arrive

---

Farmstays and horse-riding around Clarens

Horse-riding is big along the Eastern Highlands. A couple of **farms** near Clarens – both excellent family destinations – provide outstanding riding onto the Drakensberg Escarpment, from where you can gaze across into Lesotho and view southern Africa's highest peaks.

One of the most interesting farms is friendly **Bokpoort** (℡058 256 1181, ℻058 256 1048, ✉bokpoort@clarenstourism.co.za; ❶–❷), set in brilliant hiking country, but more notable for its riding. The B&B accommodation in farmhouse outbuildings is pretty basic, with brunch served in a converted shearing shed. There are also a couple of self-contained, self-catering, en-suite "mountain" huts with basic cooking facilities, as well as dorms in an old sandstone barn and space for camping, with a pleasant communal cooking and eating place. Reasonably priced meals can be ordered from the farmhouse kitchen, while a small shop sells basics.

Bokpoort's big draw is the memorable **Western-style riding** in deep, comfortable cowboy saddles on sure-footed horses. Short rides from the farmhouse (R95 for 2hr) take in San rock paintings, swimmable river-pools, and the chance of seeing eland, zebra and springbok on the adjoining game farm. Two-day riding trails into the mountains on the Lesotho border cost R600, while three-day trails are R900. You carry your own bedroll and waterbottle on your horse and sleep on your saddle blanket in a remote mountain hut. A packhorse brings the food, and you ride about six hours a day.

Riding is also available at **Schaaplaats Cottage & Ashgar Connemara Stud** (℡058 256 1176, ℻058 256 1258; ❶), right in the mountains, 6km south of Clarens off the R711 to Fouriesburg). An establishment with a more English flavour, this turn-of-the-century farm has two sandstone cottages (❷) and a cheap shepherd's hut above the homestead (❶). From here you can go on terrific mountain hikes, visit Boer War graves and San rock paintings and, of course, ride horses (R75 for 2hr). There's also a chance to brush up your equestrian skills, as the owner is a qualified riding teacher. Moreover, there is some game on the farm (zebra and antelope) which adds zest to any ride.

around lunchtime on a weekend, there's a chance you'll catch some local live music at one of the streetside cafés on **President Square**, effectively the town centre in the middle of Main Street.

The several **galleries** along Main Street and around President Square are worth a visit if you're after gifts or souvenirs; look out for the local Basotho tapestries, baskets and traditional hats. A real treat is the Di Mezza & De Jager Trading Store; to get there, follow the main road northwest to Bethlehem, before taking the *Maluti Lodge* turn-off. This is one of the few places in South Africa outside a museum where you're likely to catch an old-time general dealer's. The shop is crammed with provisions, lamps, bicycle parts, sweets and colourful blankets. The latter are traditionally worn like cloaks by Basotho people, and make outstanding souvenirs.

Accommodation

There's plenty of **accommodation**, both in the village (all signposted off Main Street and easily walkable) and on surrounding farms.

Clarens Inn Van Reenen Street ℡ 058 256 1542 or 082 3773621. The cheapest place to stay, with the choice between a functional dorm with a communal kitchen or a self-catering unit sleeping six in two bedrooms. ❶
Cottage Pie 89 Malherbe St ℡ 058 256 1214 or 082 853 5947, ⓦ www.suedafrika.net/cottagepie. One of the town's best B&Bs, with a garden chalet and two rooms inside the main house, offering breakfast on the patio and views onto a stream

and the dramatic cliffs surrounding the village. ❸
Maluti Mountain Lodge Signposted just off the R712 on the edge of town ℡ 058 256 1422. The most expensive place to stay, in pleasant rondavels in the garden; prices include dinner. ❹
Village Square Guest House Right in the centre ℡ & ⓕ 058 256 1064 or ℡ 083 635 8667, ⓔ villagehouse@isat.co.za). Two family suites as well as two en-suite bedrooms, with breakfast at the owners' *Street Café Restaurant*.

Eating and drinking

Of the half-dozen or so **eating and drinking** places in Clarens, the *Street Café Restaurant* on Main Street is the busiest, due to its reasonably priced pizzas, snacks, steaks and salads, and the 107 (at last count) varieties of local and imported beers on offer. *The Highland Brasserie* (℡ 058 256 1534) on the town square offers similar prices, with an indoor fire in winter and outdoor tables and chairs when the weather is fine. Best for breakfasts and cheesecake and coffee (Tues–Sun daytime, Wed & Fri nights).

Fouriesburg and around

The funny little town of **FOURIESBURG**, 36km south east from Clarens on the R711, earned its name from the high density of people named Fourie who farmed in the district. The hamlet hit the big time briefly in 1900; when Bloemfontein fell to the British in the Anglo-Boer War, Fouriesburg was proclaimed capital of the Orange Free State. Nothing much seems to have happened since, and a century later they still haven't got round to rescinding the proclamation – so technically it's still the provincial capital. Overshadowed by the **Maluti Mountains** and the **Witteberge** (White Mountains), Fouriesburg serves as a decent overnight stop.

There's some good **accommodation**; the nicest place to stay is the *Fouriesburg*, 17 Reitz St (℡ 058 223 0207, ⓕ 223 0257, ⓔ fburginn@worldonline.co.za; ❷). This small, wonderfully antiquated hotel has a green, low-slung corrugated-iron roof and comfortable rooms leading off the street-facing verandah. The owners let you rummage through the wine cellar to pick a bottle for dinner. Just under 2km out of town and signposted from the centre, the

Meiringskloof Nature Reserve (☎ & ℱ058 223 0067; ❶) offers one of the few places worth **camping** along the Highlands Route, and also a few self-catering stone chalets. Set in a sandstone *kloof* with plenty of trees, a swimming pool and a small grocery shop, the reserve is best avoided during holidays, when it gets packed. It's the starting point for a number of short **hikes**.

Rustler's Valley

In contrast to the conservatism of Fouriesburg, **Rustler's Valley** (☎ & ℱ051 933 3939, ℱ051 933 3286, ⓦwww.rustlers.co.za; ❶–❷), 27km to its south and well signposted off the R26, has set itself up as the New Age epicentre of South Africa. Located in a very beautiful valley in the foothills of the Maluti Mountains, it brings together a mixture of rave culture, Gaia philosophy and plain old-fashioned hippiedom. In this alternative getaway you need to be ready to submit to the wound-down atmosphere, in which everything is slow and haphazard, including the service. It's a good place to spend a couple of days, to get into the way of life, relax and meet people. Scheduled events take place about once a month (a calendar is available via the website), and there's horse-riding, hikes, swimming in the dam, and bass and trout fishing. The biggest crowd-puller is the **Easter Festival**, which draws in hordes of young South Africans to listen to music, dance and chill out, and the New Year's Eve parties are legendary.

Accommodation ranges from camping, backpacker dorms and en-suite doubles, to thatched rondavels with baths set among peach trees and decorated with goblins and fairies. A kitchen is available for guests in the dorms; everyone else must rely on the bar and **restaurant**, which serves good vegetarian food for a range of budgets. **Getting there** without your own transport entails finding your way to Ficksburg (see below), from where staff at Rustler's can pick you up. When you phone to book your accommodation, ask for the best way to get to Ficksburg. If you're driving, enquire about the variable condition of the dirt road.

Ficksburg

FICKSBURG, 48km south of Fouriesburg, is the closest town to Rustler's Valley. It's also the centre of South Africa's cherry and asparagus farming. The town's sandstone architecture gives it a pleasant ambience, and it's a good place to make a stop halfway down the Highlands Route. An annual **Cherry Festival** in the third week of November is the highlight of Fickburg's calendar; it features a marathon, floats, stalls, a "cherry queen" competition and a popular beer festival.

The cheapest way to stay here is **camping** at *Thom Park* (☎051 933 4141), a caravan park bang in the centre of town, on the corner of Bloem and McCabe streets. Nearby, *Bella Rosa*, 21 Bloem St (☎ & ℱ051 933 2623; ❸) is a hugely popular and well-priced pair of Victorian sandstone houses with ten nicely furnished **rooms**, all with baths, telephones and TVs. Dinner is available but must be booked, and tea is served on the very pleasant verandah. An alternative is *Green Acorn*, 7 Fontein St (☎051 933 2746; ❸), which has decent rooms with baths inside the house and in the garden. The best options for **eating** are the *Bella Rosa* (Mon–Fri till 10pm), which is licensed and serves above-average English-style food, and the family-oriented *Bottling Co*, corner of Piet Retief and Erwee streets (☎051 933 2404, closed Sun), which also serves booze and does steaks, pastas, chicken, fish and a good lobster bisque.

Clocolan and around

CLOCOLAN, 33km south of Ficksburg, is a tiny farming town dominated by enormous grain silos. It has little to offer travellers apart from a visit to the **Lethoteng Weavers**, in a house on the main road. The weavers are Southern Sotho women who use angora rabbit and wool to produce lively tapestries based on traditional geometric motifs and imaginative illustrations of everyday life. To get to the main point of interest around here, you need to head some 9km out of town to the **Tandjiesberg rock paintings** at Tripolatania Farm (☎051 924 2475). Here you'll find some of the best San art in the Free State, with panel after panel of rock paintings overpainted with animal, human and supernatural motifs. These are also interpreted in an excellent monograph available from the Bloemfontein Museum (see p.562) and sometimes from the farmer, from whom you have to collect keys and pay a small fee to get to the paintings.

If you're simply passing through, Clocolan's best overnight **accommodation** is at *Makoadi B&B* (☎ & ⓕ051 943 0273; ❷) on Makoadi Farm, clearly signposted 1km southwest of town along the R26. Its three spacious rooms off a verandah are furnished with antique farm items, ball-and-claw baths, and have original mud-and-dung floors. Rooms are available for the same price on a B&B or self-catering basis. For longer stays, try the outstanding *Evening Star Cottage* (☎051 943 7147 or 083 305 0658; ❷), 13km west from Clocolan on the R703. This romantically secluded self-catering thatched cottage is tucked into a rocky outcrop, its French doors opening onto a balcony with views of farmlands and mountains. While cooking is done on a fire outside in a beautiful rocky sitting area, a breakfast basket is sent up to the cottage, so you needn't move. The farm serves **tea** (Mon–Sat 9am–5pm, Sun 10am–1pm) in a converted monastery with an overgrown garden, where the owner sells her own pottery. There's also a good **hiking trail**.

Ladybrand

LADYBRAND lies on the main route into Lesotho, just over 40km south of Clocolan. The town gets its name from the mother of Johannes Brand, President of the Orange Free State four times after 1864. It's one of the only towns in the Free State which is expanding, with a huge turnover of foreign currency in the local bank; this is due not to tourism, but to the Highlands Water Project across the nearby border in Lesotho (see p.778).

Many of the foreign engineers and technicians working on the Highlands Water Project in Lesotho stay in Ladybrand, so **accommodation** is in high demand, and doesn't come cheap. The only budget option is *Leliehoek Resort* (☎051 924 0260; ❶), 2km south of the town hall, a rather run-down park with camping and dubious self-catering chalets. As for B&Bs, nothing along the Highlands Route can touch *Cranberry Cottage*, 37 Beeton St (☎051 924 2290, ⓕ051 924 1168, ⓔcrancott@lesoff.co.za; B&B ❹), which offers comfortable country-style rooms and excellent dinners, with vegetarians well catered for. Under the same ownership, and a touch less expensive, are the equally imaginative self-catering units at the *Railway Station* (room only ❸) quirkily located in the refurbished ticket office, stationmaster's office and waiting rooms on the Ladybrand Station platform, which no longer serves passengers but occasionally sees goods trains trundling by. The owners act as an unofficial tourist information centre and are able to give guests **information** on pony trekking and rock-art sites.

It's certainly fine riding country, and Greenock Riding (☎051 924 2961,

@ www.greenockriding.com; **2**), situated in a beautiful valley just north of town, offers superlative guided riding in isolated mountains. Accommodation is in self-catering log cabins, or you can take plain, well-cooked meals with the friendly hosts (and their pets) for a very reasonable amount.

When it comes to **eating**, Ladybrand shapes up well for a *dorp*, offering pasta, pizza and good Irish coffee from an Italian chef at *Imperio Romano*, on Church Street. For light meals, teas and coffees, *Zabi's Coffee Shop* (Mon–Sat 7am–6pm) also on Church Street, is the best daytime place in town. Housed in the now-defunct museum, *Zabi's* quirky charm derives from the fact that it houses a lot of the museum's former displays. It serves sandwiches made with bread baked on the premises in clay ovens – the spinach delight and delicious cakes are recommended. *Cranberry Cottage*, 37 Beeton St (open daily to non-residents), does excellent breakfasts and four-course dinners.

Travel details

Trains

Bloemfontein to: Cape Town (Fri; 20hr 45min); Durban (Mon; 16hr); East London (daily; 14hr 15min); Johannesburg (daily except Sat; 13hr); Port Elizabeth (daily; 12hr 15min); Pretoria (daily except Sat; 15hr 45min).

Buses

Bloemfontein to: Cape Town (4 daily; 11hr); Durban (2–3 daily; 9hr); East London (daily; 7hr 10min); Graaff-Reinet (5 weekly; 7hr); Grahamstown (daily; 7hr 30min); Johannesburg (4–5 daily; 6hr); Knysna (5 weekly; 11hr); Mossel Bay (5 weekly; 9hr 30min); Oudtshoorn (5 weekly; 8hr); Pietermaritzburg (2–3 daily; 8hr); Port Elizabeth (1–2 daily; 9hr); Pretoria (4–5 daily; 7hr).

Bloemfontein is not served by the Baz Bus.

Flights

Bloemfontein to: Cape Town (3–4 daily; 1hr 20min; Durban (2–3 daily; 1hr 15min); Johannesburg (9 daily Mon–Fri, 3 daily Sat & Sun; 1hr 10min); Port Elizabeth (1–2 daily; 1hr 20min).

Gauteng

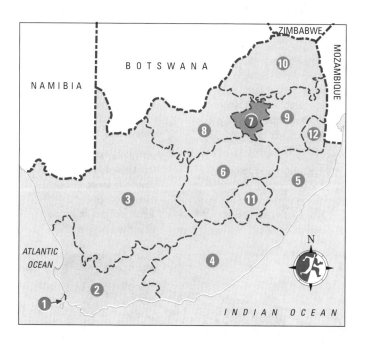

CHAPTER 7

Highlights

✳ **Downtown Johannesburg**
Experience a true pan-
African urban buzz at the
heart of the continent's
richest city. **See p.595**

✳ **Melville** Hang out with
Johannesburg's arty set,
in one of the few places
in the city where trendy
cafés and decent restau-
rants line the street. **See
p.604**

✳ **Township tour** Many
tours run to Soweto, the
world's most famous
township, while a few go
to Alexandra, offering a
much richer township
vibe. **See p.608**

✳ **Jazz at Kippies** Jo'burg's
finest jazz joint attracts
mixed crowds and South
Africa's top musicians.
See p.613

✳ **The big match** Whether
it's Chiefs v Pirates at
FNB or the Springboks v
All Blacks at Ellis Park,
sport in Jo'burg is always
big news. **See p.618**

✳ **Cradle of Humankind** A
series of caves on the
fringe of Johannesburg
provides vital fossilized
evidence of human
ancestry. **See p.620**

✳ **Church Square**, **Pretoria**
Sip an espresso at *Café
Riche* or sit in the shade
of Paul Kruger's statue
and admire the grand
architecture. **See p.630**

✳ **Voortrekker Monument**
This icon of Afrikanerdom
offers a fascinating insight
into the people who
dominated South Africa
for a century. **See p.635**

Gauteng

Gauteng means "Place of Gold" in Sotho, and no wonder: South Africa's smallest region comprises less than five percent of its landmass, yet contributes around forty percent of the GDP. Home to at least eight million people, the flavour of Gauteng is almost entirely urbanized. While the province encompasses a section of the Magaliesberg Mountains to the east and the gold-rich Witwatersrand to the south and west, the area is dominated by the huge conurbation incorporating Johannesburg, Pretoria and a host of grim satellite industrial towns and townships which surround them.

Although lacking the spectacular attractions of the Cape Province or Mpumalanga, Gauteng has a subtle character all of its own. Startling outcrops of rock known as *koppies*, with intriguing and often lucrative geology, are found in the sprawling suburbs and grassy plains of deep-red earth that fringe the cities. The usually mild climate is broken occasionally by spectacular summer lightning storms, which can unleash torrents of water over the Transvaal plains within seconds. The area is also prone to drought, and water supplies remain a constant and worsening problem. Yet the light, particularly at dawn and dusk, is a photographer's dream, rendering serene even the starkest of industrial landscapes.

Gauteng is dominated by **Johannesburg**, whose origins lie in the exploitation of **gold**. Although it has grown rapidly in just over a century to become the largest and richest city in Africa, it has somehow held onto its tough mining origins and is a hectic, sometimes dangerous city, home to extreme contrasts of wealth and poverty. It has a reputation among both visitors and South Africans as a place to avoid, but those who acquire a taste for Jo'burg – something you can do in just a few days – are seduced by its energy and vibrancy, unmatched by any other city in South Africa. A highly cosmopolitan city and the most Africanized in the country, Jo'burg has South Africa's most famous and liveliest townships, its most active and diverse cultural life, some of its best restaurants and most progressive nightlife.

Some 50km north lies dignified **Pretoria**, the country's administrative capital. Historically an Afrikaner stronghold, today it is a fast-changing place full of civil servants and students from South Africa and around the world. Very different to Johannesburg in looks and atmosphere, Pretoria is an important and attractive destination in its own right, with its range of interesting museums and historic buildings. Many visitors, however, see it simply as a safer and less intimidating alternative to its larger rival.

Less than an hour's travel from the centre of Jo'burg, the section of the **Magaliesberg Mountains** which creeps into Gauteng is a magnet for

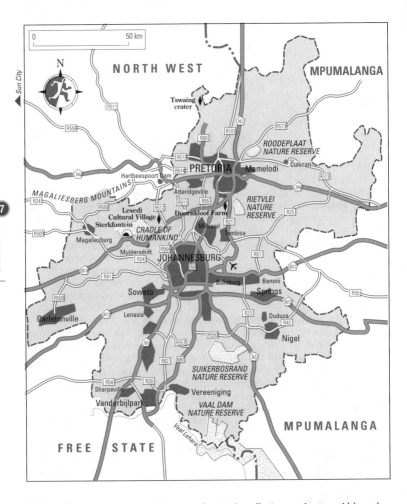

Johannesburgers desperate to escape the city's pollution and stress. Although the hills can hardly be described as remote and untamed, you'll find ample opportunities for nature trailing and hiking. Like much of Gauteng, however, the important part lies underground, with a series of caves, underground passages and archeological sites making up the **Cradle of Humankind** World Heritage Site. Most famous of these sites are the **Sterkfontein Caves**, where some of the world's most important discoveries of pre-human primate fossils have been found.

Johannesburg and around

Fast-paced, frenetic **JOHANNESBURG** has had a reputation for immorality, greed and violence ever since its first plot auction in December 1886. Despite its status as the largest and richest city in the country, it has never been the seat of government or national political power, allowing it to concentrate fully on what it has always done best: make money and get ahead. Those priorities have, over the years, cut across political and racial lines: only in Jo'burg would ambitious black Africans like Nelson Mandela have been able to train in a white law firm; only in Jo'burg would creative hotspots like Sophiatown and Alexandra exist at all; and only in Jo'burg would white liberalism have been given any intellectual recognition in the dark days of apartheid.

Even so, the divisions of the old South Africa are as apparent here as anywhere else. Ridiculously opulent white mansions in leafy **suburbs** are protected by high walls and razor wire, only a mile or two from sprawling **shanty towns** housing millions of intensely poor blacks. As the new political dispensation sees formerly white areas administratively yoked with the black townships, so the city struggles to cope with massive pressures on housing, services and law and order. Nowhere is the new tension more in evidence than in the previously all-white central business district, where an influx of poor blacks, and a soaring crime rate, has caused a mass exodus of shops and restaurants to the northern suburbs.

As the centre readjusts, so the fringes expand: there will be a continuous ribbon of development between Johannesburg and Pretoria, originally 50km apart, within a decade. Meanwhile, the black middle class, much more evident in Johannesburg than anywhere else in South Africa, is moving from township to suburb, while tens of thousands of immigrants from elsewhere in Africa flood into inner-city suburbs like Hillbrow and townships like Alexandra.

There are very few conventional tourist sights in Johannesburg, and some visitors fall into the trap of retreating to their hotel room, too intimidated by the city's reputation to explore, venturing out only to the bland, safe, covered shopping malls of the northern suburbs while making hasty plans to move on. However, once you've found a convenient way of getting around, either by car or in the company of a tour guide, the history, diversity and stimulating energy of the city can quickly become compelling. Johannesburg offers fascinating **museums**, most notably the Museum Africa in Newtown, as well as excellent art galleries. A number of suburbs have a thriving **café culture**, which by the evening transforms to a lively restaurant scene. There are shops with excellent contemporary African art and design, striking buildings, and of course the **townships**, most easily explored on a tour but, in some places, somewhere you can get to under your own steam. Johannesburg is also a great place to watch **sport**: Ellis Park was the scene of South Africa's emotional victory in the 1995 Rugby World Cup, the IAAF World Cup was held at the neighbouring athletics stadium in 1999, and the massive FNB soccer stadium on the edge of Soweto, which fills to capacity for local derbies or international fixtures, remains the principal venue for the country's most popular sport.

Some history

Johannesburg dates back to 1886, when Australian prospector **George Harrison** found the main Witwatersrand gold-bearing reef. Almost immedi-

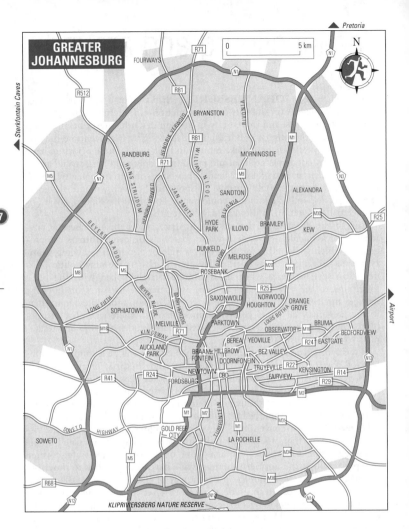

ately, this quiet area of the Transvaal became swamped with diggers from near and far, and a tented city sprang up around the site. The Pretoria authorities were forced to proclaim a township nearby: they chose a useless triangle of land called the Randjeslaagte, which had been left unclaimed by local farmers. **Johan Rissik**, the surveyor, called it Johannesburg, either after himself, Christiaan Johannes Joubert, the chief of mining or ZAR president Paul Johannes Kruger.

Mining magnates such as Cecil Rhodes and Barney Barnato possessed the capital necessary to exploit the world's richest gold reef, and their **Chamber of Mines** (a self-regulatory body for mine owners, founded in 1889), attempted to bring some order to the digging frenzy, with common policies on recruitment, wages and working conditions. In 1893, due partly to pressure from white workers, and with the approval of the ZAR government, the chamber introduced the **colour bar**, which excluded black workers from all but manual labour.

By 1895, Johannesburg's population had soared to over 100,000, many of whom were not remotely Boer and had no interest in the ZAR's independence. Kruger and the burghers regarded these *uitlanders* (foreigners) as a potential threat to their political supremacy, and denied them the vote, despite the income they generated for the state's coffers. Legislation was also passed to control the influx of blacks to Johannesburg, and Indians were forcibly moved out of the city into a western location. Before long, large shantytowns filled with blacks and Indians were springing up on the outskirts of Johannesburg.

In 1900, during the Anglo-Boer War, Johannesburg fell to the British, who had attempted to annex the gold-rich area for some time. The High Commissioner Sir Alfred Milner imported whiz kids fresh out of Oxford and Cambridge to modernize the city. They lived in Parktown, and commissioned their houses from the celebrated English architect, **Sir Herbert Baker** (see p.602). At the same time, more black townships were established, including **Sophiatown** (1903) in an area previously used for dumping sewage, and **Alexandra** (1905). Bubonic plague erupted on the northern fringes of the city in 1904, providing justification for the authorities to burn several Indian and African locations, including **Newtown**, just west of the centre.

Meanwhile, white mine workers were becoming unionized, and outbreaks of fighting over pay and working hours were a frequent occurrence. Their poorly paid black counterparts were also mobilizing; their main grievance was the ruling that skilled jobs were the preserve of white workers. Resentments came to a head in the **Rand Revolt** of 1922, after the Chamber of Mines, anxious to cut costs, decided to allow blacks into the skilled jobs previously held only by whites. White workers were furious: street battles broke out and lasted for four days. Government troops were called in to restore order and over 200 men were killed. Alarmed at the scale of white discontent, Prime Minister Jan Smuts ruled that the colour bar be maintained, and throughout the 1920s, the government passed laws restricting the movement of blacks.

During the Thirties, the township of **Orlando** became established southwest of the city, with accommodation for 80,000 blacks; this was the nucleus around which **Soweto** evolved. By 1945, 400,000 blacks were living in and around Johannesburg – an increase of 100 percent in a decade. In August 1946, 70,000 African Mineworkers Union members went on strike over working conditions. The government sent police in, and twelve miners were killed and over 1000 injured. In the same year, informal settlers on municipal land attempted a rent boycott, proclaiming "Asinamali!" ("We have no money!"). They were ignored, and non-rent-payers were evicted.

Forced removals of black residents from Johannesburg's inner suburbs, particularly from Sophiatown, began in 1955. Thousands were dumped far from the city centre, in the new township of Meadowlands, next to Orlando, and Sophiatown was crassly renamed Triomf (triumph). The **ANC** (see p.832) established itself as the most important black protest organization during this period, proclaiming the **Freedom Charter** in Kliptown, Soweto, that year.

During the 1950s, *kwela*, a black urban culture unique to Johannesburg, began to emerge in the townships, and the new *marabi* jazz was played in illegal drinking houses called *shebeens*. This was also the era of *Drum Magazine*, which revealed a sophisticated black Johannesburg culture, and introduced a host of talented journalists, like Can Temba and Casey "Kid" Motsisi, to the city and the world. *Mbaqanga* music emerged, with its heavy basslines and sensuous melodies capturing the bittersweet essence of life in the old townships.

The formation in 1972 of the **Black Consciousness Movement** (BCM) rekindled political activism, particularly among Soweto students. On June 16, 1976, student riots erupted in the township, and the unrest spread nationwide (see p.609). The youth's war against the State escalated in the 1980s, resulting in regular "**states of emergency**", during which the armed forces had permission to do anything they liked to contain revolt. Towards the end of the decade, the government relaxed "petty" apartheid, turning a blind eye to the growth of "grey" areas like Hillbrow – white suburbs where blacks were moving in.

The three years after **Nelson Mandela**'s release in 1990 saw widespread political violence in Gauteng right up until the day before elections. However, as elsewhere in South Africa, the election on April 27, 1994 went off peacefully. The ANC won comfortably in Gauteng and, as expected, consolidated their hold on power in 1999, albeit to the sound of grumbling from some elements of their constituency about corruption, unemployment and crime.

Just as new faces populate the corridors of political power, so blacks are also making steady inroads into positions of influence in business, finance and industry, where the true power of the province lies. Signs of such changes can be seen almost daily on the pages of the country's business newspapers, and public-private partnerships are now initiating some bold plans for the province, notably the controversial Gautrain Rapid Rail Link, a high-speed train planned for completion in 2006 and designed to link Johannesburg airport, Johannesburg city centre, Sandton and Pretoria.

Arrival and information

Johannesburg's large **international airport** (flight information ☎011 975 9963), once known as Jan Smuts, lies 20km east of the city. There's a range of options for getting from the airport into the city or suburbs. Of the scheduled **bus services**, Impala (every 45min 6.15am–10pm; 30min) will take you to Park station in the city for around R50. If your destination is the northern suburbs, you'll find it easier to take the Magic Bus (every 30min 5.30am–9.30pm; 30min), which costs about R75. Get tickets for both services at the companies' desks in the Parkade building, just outside the domestic arrivals foyer.

The more expensive hotels often provide **courtesy buses**, while most backpackers' hostels and some smaller guesthouses or B&Bs arrange **pick-ups**. Depending on your length of stay, these may be free; otherwise they tend to cost no more than the scheduled bus service. Touting at the airport by backpackers' hostels has been aggressive at times recently – sidestep the mayhem by booking in advance.

Taking a **taxi** from the airport is convenient and safe, but be sure to take a metered Johannesburg airport taxi or a reputable tour/transfer operator and make certain the driver knows where you're going before you set off. Plenty of taxi touts hang around the airport – you can usually discuss a price quite civilly with them. The desk in the centre of the international arrivals terminal can give you some advice if you're uncertain about the options. Be prepared to pay at least R150 per person for most destinations. If you want to prearrange a taxi, Airport Link (☎011 792 2017) charges around R165 for the first person and R45 for each additional passenger.

Greyhound (☎011 830 1301), Intercape (☎012 654 4114) and Translux (☎011 774 3333) **buses** and **intercity trains** (☎086 000 8888) arrive at Park station in the centre of town. Once notoriously unsafe, Park station has been

585

△ Ponte City Tower, Hillbrow

significantly improved in recent years, and the main concourse is big, open and safe, with information desks for all the bus companies and various fast-food outlets. From Park station, you're best off – and safest – taking a taxi to your final destination or arranging a pick-up with your accommodation. While buses and minibuses run from the station to virtually everywhere, finding out about them can be confusing, and waiting around outside the station – especially surrounded by luggage – can be risky.

Information

Like many parts of South Africa, tourist information in Johannesburg isn't all that reliable. Not only do the organizations running tourism information services seem to arrive and disappear with bewildering frequency, but even-handed and well-informed tourist information is hard to come by. **Gauteng Tourism** (daily 8.30am–5pm; ℡011 340 9000, ⓦwww.gauteng.net), situated in the Upper Level of the Rosebank Mall in Rosebank, runs the show in Johannesburg; their most useful outlet is a **kiosk** (Tues–Sun 8.30am–4.30pm) attached to the African Craft Market in Rosebank. The international arrivals hall of the airport has a **tourist information office** (daily 7am–9pm; ℡011 970 1669), offering brochures on Johannesburg and other parts of South Africa; the staff are keen, but the office is a little disorganized and the information supplied can be patchy.

Free **maps** are available in various forms from the information offices, but they normally only cover the CBD and parts of the northern suburbs. To get around other parts, particularly if you're driving around the city, you'll need a detailed street guide; the hefty *Witwatersrand Street Guide* is best, available from CNA newsagents or Exclusive Books bookshops.

City transport

Johannesburg's **public transport system** leaves much to be desired: it's slow and unreliable, and practically nonexistent after commuting hours. **Cars** are very much the order of the day, and without one, Jo'burg can seem a much larger and more daunting place. If you're not driving, though, don't despair entirely: with patience and a bit of stamina, it's possible to negotiate your way around the city using the **buses**, including the city's sightseeing bus, and some areas are easily explored **on foot**. Avoid the city's **train** system, which has a poor reputation and very limited services.

Cars and private taxis

By far the best way to explore Johannesburg is in your own **car**. Although road signs can be poor, the local drivers pushy, and the lack of landmarks confusing, familiarity with a few key roads and careful map reading before you set out makes getting around relatively straightforward.

The **M1** connects the centre to the northern suburbs, crossing above Newtown on a flyover, through Braamfontein and Parktown, and heading into Houghton and Sandton, eventually turning into the N1 for Pretoria. Heading south, the M1 is one of the best routes to Soweto. The next artery west of the M1, also useful for heading north, is **Oxford Road**, which starts off in Parktown, and becomes Rivonia Road once it enters Sandton. West again is **Jan Smuts Avenue**, which passes through Rosebank and Dunkeld,

Safety and crime in Johannesburg

With its extremes of poverty and wealth and its brash, get-ahead culture, it's hardly surprising that Johannesburg can be a dangerous place. The city has an unenviable reputation, although in many cases intimidation is a bigger problem than crime itself. As in all major cities, taking sensible precautions is likely to see you through safely, although the presence of illegal firearms makes taking extra care especially important.

If you're wandering around on foot, the crime you are most at risk from is **mugging** (sometimes violent). Certain areas carry a much higher risk than others; be particularly alert when exploring the central business district (CBD), Braamfontein and Newtown, and only walk the streets here during office hours. Joubert Park, Hillbrow and Berea are regarded at present as no-go zones, and although Yeoville and Observatory are a little safer, these are places for those who are particularly confident or have someone to show them around. You are very unlikely to be mugged on the streets in Melville, Parktown or Rosebank.

In high-risk areas, try not to look like a tourist. Ideally, travel in a small group. Study maps beforehand (not on street corners), avoid asking for directions from passersby, and don't walk around with luggage. Try to look into the crowds coming your way, to see if there are any groups of young men (the main offenders) moving as a block. If you're carrying valuables, leave a portion of them easily available, so that muggers are likely to be quickly satisfied and not investigate you further. Never resist muggers; running like hell can work, but some have guns, which you won't know about until too late. You're unlikely to be mugged on **public transport** but, as always, it's wise to stay alert, especially around busy spots such as Park station and bus stations or taxi ranks. Waiting for buses in the northern suburbs is generally safe.

Don't expect too much from the **police**. Police on the street are rare, and normally have other distractions than keeping an eye out for tourists. In the city centre and Rosebank you can make use of **City Ambassadors**, identified by their yellow caps and bibs. These are people hired by a partnership between local government and local shops and businesses to provide an anti-crime presence on the street. Some are better trained than others to help tourists, but you can always approach them for directions, or if you think you're being followed.

If you're driving around, there is a small risk of **car-jacking**, and thieves have also been known to reach into open windows or break side windows to snatch jewellery or valuables left on passenger seats. It's a good idea to keep all car doors locked and windows up – never wait in an unlocked car while a friend goes into a shop. Leaving or returning to your car are the most dangerous times, so keep a good lookout, seek out secure and preferably guarded parking, and don't dawdle. Although local urban legends suggest you should never stop at traffic lights at night, you're more likely to increase your risk of injury doing this – statistics show more people get injured in car accidents than become crime victims. If you stop at traffic lights in suspicious areas, keep a good distance between you and the car in front and stay aware of people moving around the car.

However, it's important to retain a sense of proportion about potential risks in Johannesburg. Most importantly, don't let paranoia ruin your stay in the city – remember that most Jo'burgers have no intention of doing you any harm at all. The most sensible course is to do as they do: juggle your fear and your bravado, without letting one swamp the other.

before hitting Sandton. In the city centre, the grid system, though beset by one-way streets and pedestrian precincts, does make navigation relatively logical.

The city is relatively well-served for **car rental** (see "Listings" p.619), and you'll often find that backpacker lodges and some guesthouses can arrange the best deals. For longer stays, **buying a car** is a practical option; the weekly *Junk*

Mail has a large selection of private sales – expect to pay upwards of R20,000 for a decent vehicle. You can resell through *Junk Mail*, too, if you have a contact telephone number.

For short journeys around the city, use **private taxis**, which must always be telephoned in advance (see "Listings" p.620). This is an expensive option, however, as a simple journey to the CBD from the northern suburbs will cost at least R120.

Buses

Johannesburg's **buses**, many of which are double-deckers, offer the safest and cheapest public transport during weekdays. Most bus routes start and end at the main terminus (☎011 430 4300) in the newly spruced up Ghandi Square, off Eloff Street, in the city centre; this is also where you can pick up timetables and route maps.

Buses only run between the suburbs and the centre, so are useless for getting from one suburb to another, unless they both lie on the same route to town. Most buses stop by 6.30pm, though a small number keep going until 9.30pm. Weekend services are poor, with very few routes, and waits of at least one hour between buses.

Though under-utilized and much-maligned by locals, the **City Slicker sightseeing bus** is a great boon if you don't have a car and feel daunted by the regular buses. The open-topped double-decker bus sets off five times a day from Sandton, passing Randburg Waterfront, Rosebank, Melville, the CBD, Gold Reef City and Soweto. It runs from 9am to 9pm and a hop-on-hop-off day ticket costs R70 (☎011 957 0034).

Minibus taxis

Even cheaper than buses, **minibus taxis** cover a far wider area, and can be picked up at ranks, or hailed mid-route by either raising your forefinger (if you're heading into town), pointing downwards (if you want to go uptown) or pointing towards yourself (if you want Park station). The drawbacks, however, are worth bearing in mind: cramped cars, hair-raising driving, frequent accidents and petty criminals working the major taxi ranks have combined to deter most white Jo'burgers from using this mode of transport. If you do want to try one out, you'd be wise to wait at a smaller taxi rank, or wave one down en route – but never with bulky baggage. Most backpacker lodges know nearby useful routes and pick-up points and can give you a few tips.

Accommodation

Accommodation in Johannesburg is fairly easy to find, as the city is well-equipped to cope with large numbers of business travellers and tourists. Where you decide to stay depends less on availability than on budget, the length of your visit and how concerned you are about safety. As a basic rule of thumb, the further from the city centre you are, the safer but more soulless the suburb. With the exception of the suburb of Melville, where you can walk safely to a great range of nearby cafés and restaurants, it's hard to get out and about in the city without a car – regardless of where your accommodation is located.

There's little point in planning to stay in the **CBD**, most hotels having joined the exodus to the northern suburbs, though if you do want to be close to town, **Observatory** has a couple of pleasant options in a safer area. The east of the city is really worth considering only if you need easy access to the airport:

Eastgate and **Bruma Lake** are self-contained around their vast eponymous shopping centres, while plain and suburban **Bedfordview** is easily reached from the motorway.

There's plenty of accommodation to be found in the affluent, predominantly white **northern suburbs**, which with various artery roads leading out from the centre are also the easiest place to stay if you have to rely on public transport. **Melville** and its neighbour Auckland Park offer something many visitors don't expect to find in Johannesburg: a characterful, tight-knit community with hip cafés, restaurants and bars within walking distance from most of the guesthouses. **Rosebank** is well-located at the heart of the northern suburbs, and has a number of popular shopping malls with a decent selection of places to eat out or shop. Further north, **Sandton** is almost the Monte Carlo of Johannesburg, with a wealth of pricey chain hotels aimed at business executives, as well as some lovely large private homes with huge gardens which offer bed and breakfast. West of Sandton, **Randburg** is less expensive, but a bit isolated from the best parts of the city.

It is possible to stay in the **townships**, though there are no established guesthouses; the most rewarding option is to stay with locals, something best arranged through an experienced tour operator (see p.608).

Backpacker and budget accommodation

Less numerous and more changeable than the backpacker lodges in Cape Town or Durban, Jo'burg's **backpacker hostels** have by and large moved out of the city centre and settled in the safer, but more isolated, northern suburbs. While most lodges go to some lengths to promote the city, particularly its nightlife, Jo'burg is still primarily a transitory place – most lodges offer free-pick ups from the airport, and a few are located within twenty minutes drive of the airport itself.

Central suburbs

Brown Sugar 75 Observatory Ave, Observatory Extension ☎011 648 7397 or 0800 004 951, ⓔbrownsugar2000@hotmail.com. A notorious backpackers' hostel located in a bizarre ex-drug baron's mansion on Observatory Ridge, and the only hostel left near Yeoville's Rockey Street (see p.600). It's not for the faint of heart – come here for a fast-track introduction to Jo'burg's hedonistic nightlife rather than comfort or chilled-out vibes. ❶

Northern suburbs

Backpackers' Ritz 1A North Rd (off Jan Smuts Avenue), Dunkeld West ☎011 327 7125, ⓔritz@iafrica.com. A well-known and busy lodge in a large suburban house halfway between Rosebank and Sandton, with a pool, gardens and a good bar. It remains popular with overlanders, and camping is allowed in the grounds. ❶

Pension iDube 11 Walton Ave, Auckland Park ☎011 482 4055 or 082 682 3799, ⓔidube@mail.com. Not a backpacker's lodge; more (in its own words) an "economy-class" B&B, with tastefully decorated doubles and a friendly, easy-going atmosphere, only a few blocks from Melville's cafés and nightlife. It also has a pool,

and breakfast is included in the price, although you have to prepare it yourself. ❷

Rockey's of Fourways 22 Campbell Rd, Craigavon, Fourways ☎011 465 4219 or 082 342 5109, ⓦbacpacrs.www.icon.co.za. Run by folk long-established in the Jo'burg backpacking scene, this is a great place if you don't mind staying 20km from town in a newly built suburb. It's certainly a relaxing place, with a pool and big shady garden; there are also malls within easy walking distance and lots of organized tours. ❶

Zoo Lodge 233A Jan Smuts Ave, Parktown North ☎011 788 5182, ⓦwww.zoolodge.co.za. One of the most central lodges, with Rosebank nearby and good transport links along busy Jan Smuts Avenue. A medium-sized hostel, it's well-run and the staff are knowledgeable both about Jo'burg and travelling to other parts of southern Africa. ❶

Eastern suburbs

Airport Backpackers 3 Mohawk St, Rhodesfield, Kempton Park ☎011 394 0485 or 083 758 4344, ⓦwww.home.mweb.co.za/ai/airbackp/. Handily placed for the airport and Caesar's, one of Jo'burg's new casino/shopping centres, this small but respectable backpacker hostel can also provide useful travel information. ❶

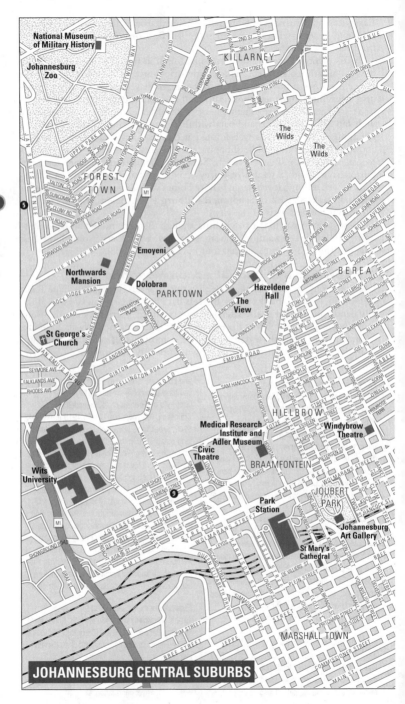

National Museum
of Military History

Johannesburg
Zoo

KILLARNEY

The Wilds

The Wilds

FOREST
TOWN

M1

BEREA

Emoyeni

Northwards
Mansion

Dolobran

PARKTOWN

Hazeldene
Hall

The
View

St George's
Church

HIELBBROW

Medical Research
Institute and
Adler Museum

Windybrow
Theatre

Civic
Theatre

BRAAMFONTEIN

Wits
University

M1

JOUBERT
PARK

Park
Station

Johannesburg
Art Gallery

St Mary's
Cathedral

MARSHALL TOWN

JOHANNESBURG CENTRAL SUBURBS

RESTAURANTS

Benkei	**A**
Cento	**F**
The Congolese Restaurant	**D**
Moyo	**B**
Sechuan Garden	**C**
Senor Prego	**E**

ACCOMMODATION

Ah Ha Guest House	6
Airport Backpackers	7
The Bedford View	8
Brown Sugar	1
The Cottages	4
Devonshire Hotel	9
Eastgate Backpackers	2
Fountain Head Guest House	3
The Westcliff	5

GAUTENG

7

591

Eastgate Backpackers 41 Hans Pirow St, Bruma ⓣ011 616 2741, ⓔeatebp@netactive.co.za. Located on a suburban street near Eastgate and Bruma shopping complexes, this often busy and lively lodge has dorms and doubles, a swimming pool and a small bar with a pool table. It also provides easy links to the airport, and runs personalized tours of Soweto and other happening parts of Jo'burg. ❶

Gemini Backpackers Lodge 1 Van Gelder St, Crystal Gardens ⓣ011 882 6845 or 082 574 4270, ⓦwww.geminibackpackers.com. Rambling suburban property near Kew with dorms, doubles and all kinds of extras such as a full-sized snooker table, tennis court, pool and a rudimentary gym tucked away in an assortment of outbuildings. You'll need a car or the local bus service to get to decent shops and bars, although meals are served here daily. ❶

Hotels, guesthouses and B&Bs

Despite Jo'burg's corporate, business-oriented atmosphere, it's possible to find some very comfortable and characterful **guesthouses** and **bed & breakfast** establishments, particularly in the central and northern suburbs. In the upmarket range there are some wonderfully opulent **hotels**, though Johannesburg is peppered with large multinational **chain hotels** such as Holiday Inn (central reservations ⓣ0800 117 7711, ⓦwww.southernsun.com), Protea Hotels (central reservations ⓣ0800 111 9000, ⓦwww.proteahotels.com), City Lodges (ⓣ011 884 9500, ⓦwww.citylodge.co.za) and Formula 1 (ⓣ011 887 5555 or central reservations ⓣ011 440 1001). All of these offer reasonable – if predictably characterless rooms – and are often well-located; many can offer good deals. Also available are short-stay **self-catering apartments**: Don Apartments (ⓣ0800 115 446, ⓦwww.don.co.za; ❹) has various apartment blocks around the city, including some in Rosebank and Sandton; all are secure, tastefully furnished and well-equipped.

Central suburbs

The Cottages 30 Gill St, Observatory ⓣ011 487 2829, ⓔmckenna@iafrica.com. Thirteen comfortable, characterful cottages perched on the Observatory ridge, with a large rock pool and paths through the lush two-acre plot opening out to great views from the top of the *koppie*. Self-catering or B&B are offered, with evening meals available on request. A safe, relaxing and welcoming place. ❸
Devonshire Hotel On the corner of Melle and Jorissen streets ⓣ011 339 5611, ⓕ011 403 2495. A decent choice if you have to be near the downtown area, this smart executives' hotel offers the best views in Braamfontein, from rooms equipped with several bars and restaurants. ❹
Fountain Head Guest House 52 Urania St, Observatory ⓣ011 487 3564, ⓕ011 648 8009. Large, decent rooms and wide balconies in a stunning Italian-style villa in a safe area in Observatory, with immaculate gardens and fountains from which to admire them. ❹

Northern suburbs

Ant Hill 124 Second Ave, Melville ⓣ011 726 4197. An alternative guesthouse with two doubles, one single and a koi pond. Owned by a local restaurateur and artist, *Ant Hill* contrives to convey Zen-like minimalism and be a tad scruffy at the same time. ❸

Coopers' Croft 26 Cross St, Randburg ⓣ011 787 2679, ⓕ011 886 7611, ⓔcooperscroft@global.co.za. A homely, no-frills B&B with a gentle, friendly atmosphere. The rooms are in the main house located on a suburban street near the Randburg Waterfront; there's also a pool and tennis courts. ❷
Die Agterplaas 66 Sixth Ave, Melville ⓣ011 726 8452 or 082 902 5799, ⓔagterplass@icon.co.za. Just a short walk from the heart of Melville's restaurants and cafés, this neat, tasteful seven-room guesthouse provides views over the Melville koppies from various pleasant balconies. ❸–❹
The Grace in Rosebank 54 Bath Ave, Rosebank ⓣ011 280 7200, ⓦwww.grace.co.za. One of the most luxurious and individual hotels in town, used mainly by upmarket business travellers. ❼
Liliesleaf Rivonia ⓣ011 803 3787, ⓦwww.liliesleaf.com. If not the most luxurious bed & breakfast in Jo'burg (it certainly comes close), this is surely the most historic, as the farmhouse was used by Nelson Mandela while in hiding in the early 1960s, and is the place where many of his fellow Rivonia Trialists were arrested. ❼
Melrose Place 12A North St, Melrose ⓣ011 442 5231 or 083 457 4021, ⓔsuetruter@global.co.za. A friendly, well-run family guesthouse located close to Rosebank and the Wanderers cricket stadium, offering self-catering cottages and double rooms filled with African artefacts. ❹

The Melville House 59 4th Ave, Melville ⓣ011 726 3503, ⓕ011 726 5990, ⓦwww.melville-house.co.za. The pick of the Melville guesthouses, only a few hundred yards from Melville's cafés and restaurants. It's a lively, sociable place, genuinely involved with what's going on in Jo'burg. The main house has a pleasant little garden and tastefully decorated rooms. ❹

Melville Turret Guesthouse 118 Second Ave, Melville ⓣ011 482 7197, ⓔturret@totem.co.za. Although the rooms are quite small, this pleasant and well-presented guesthouse in trendy Melville has designer decor and an airy patio. ❹

Oxford Lodge 28a Oxford Ave, Sandhurst ⓣ011 884 5240, ⓔoxlodge@mweb.co.za. A large thatched home not far from Sandton City, with three top-notch cottages, each with a separate entrance and a lounge, either attached to the house or tucked away in the large, verdant garden which has a pool and lush lawns. ❹

A Room with a View 1 Tolip St, Melville ⓣ011 482 5435, ⓣ082 567 9328, ⓔroomview@pixie.co.za. A grand two-storey Italian-style villa, laid out and decorated in exuberant style. Balconies, skylights and, of course, the view make it light and bright, a relief given the opulent flavour of some of the antique furniture and artwork. The villa has seven double rooms and provides a smart, efficient service. ❺

Sans Souci Hotel 10 Guild Rd, Parktown West ⓣ011 726 6393, ⓕ011 480 5983. A wonderful old building on the Parktown ridge, with well-stocked bars, good-value buffet and restaurant lunches, swimming pool and relaxing garden. The rooms are in a Sixties extension, but are pleasant enough. ❸

Ten Bompas 10 Bompas Rd, Dunkeld West ⓣ011 327 0650, ⓦwww.tenbompas.co.za. One of Jo'burg's most stylish small hotels, with each of its ten rooms decorated by a different interior designer. Quiet, intimate and expensive. ❼

Under the Stairs 114 Putney Rd, Auckland Ridge ⓣ011 837 6683 or 082 222 3074, ⓔmeer-cat@54.co.za. Three simple but pleasant rooms with wooden floors and unfussy decor in a 1906 house right by the SABC tower, not far from Melville. There's also a pool and small garden. ❸

The Westcliff 67 Smuts Ave, Westcliff ⓣ011 646 2400, ⓦwww.westcliff.orient-express.com. The *grande dame* of Jo'burg upmarket hotels, painted pink and the size of a small village on an east-facing Parktown ridge. The cocktails are recommended; from the bar, you can watch the elephants in the nearby zoo. ❼

Eastern suburbs

Ah Ha Guest House 17a Talisman Ave, Bedfordview ⓣ011 616 3702 or 083 266 0047, ⓦwww.ahhalux.co.za. A pleasant if unglamorous family-run guesthouse, located near various shopping malls halfway between the airport and city centre, offering comfortable double rooms, self-catering suites and a decent swimming pool. ❹

The Bedford View 26 Douglas Rd, Bedfordview ⓣ011 455 1055, or 082 576 4999, ⓔbview@global.co.za. A fairly typical but neat suburban guesthouse with five rooms, two of which are in self-catering units, a nice garden and pool, within easy reach of various local shopping centres. ❹

The City

Johannesburg is large, sprawling and poorly planned, with few conventional sights and a bewildering number of districts. The **central business district (CBD)** is the Manhattan of Africa with tall crowded office blocks crowded together and lively street life. Nearby, the **Newtown Cultural Precinct** is the place to head for jazz bars, theatre and the highly informative Museum Africa. The inner-city districts of **Berea** and **Hillbrow** are packed with migrants from all over the continent, and are generally no-go areas for visitors. This label is now also being given to **Yeoville**, once the city's trendiest and most integrated suburb.

The city's seemingly endless **northern suburbs**, the preserve of white, middle-class Johannesburg, dominate the northern half of the city. Despite the lack of real sights, they do offer a few pleasant surprises, notably **Parktown**, the original home of Johannesburg's richest residents, leafy **Melville**, with its trendy street cafés and lively nightlife, and **Rosebank**, an easy-going suburb

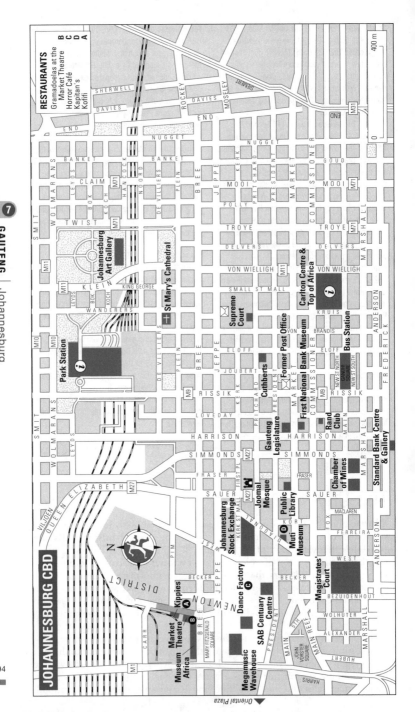

JOHANNESBURG CBD

RESTAURANTS
Gramadoelas at the
Market Theatre   B
Horror Café   C
Kapitan's   D
Kofifi   A

0   400 m

▲ Oriental Plaza

Megamusic Wavehouse
SAB Centuary Centre
Museum Africa
Market Theatre
Kippies
Dance Factory
Johannesburg Stock Exchange
Joomal Mosque
Muti Museum
Public Library
Park Station
Johannesburg Art Gallery
St Mary's Cathedral
Supreme Court
Former Post Office
First National Bank Museum
Cuthberts
Gauteng Legislature
Rand Club
Chamber of Mines
Standard Bank Centre & Gallery
Magistrates' Court
Carlton Centre & Top of Africa
Bus Station

with some decent galleries and craft markets. The archetypal northern suburb is opulent **Sandton**, full of brand new offices and mind-boggling shopping malls. Strangely enough, only the highway separates Sandton from one of Jo'burg's poorest areas, the vibrant but risky **Alexandra** township. Southwest of the centre lies the city's most famous township, **Soweto**, the single most popular tourist destination in Johannesburg, with its evocative memories of the struggle against apartheid and poor but lively neighbourhoods.

The CBD

Johannesburg's **central business district**, the grid of streets and tightly packed skyscrapers just to the south of the Witwatersrand ridge, is the most recognizable and feared part of the city. From the time of the first mining camp, located on what is today Commissioner Street, and for nearly a century, it was the core of Jo'burg's buzzy commercial and financial life. Then, in the 1980s and 90s it became riddled with crime, precipitating a mass evacuation by businesses, shoppers, restaurants and tourists. When the Jo'burg Stock Exchange moved out in 1999 in favour of safe, opulent Sandton, the city centre was all but written off. However, determined efforts over the last few years to clean up the streets, make them safe, and reopen some of the neglected buildings have been surprisingly successful (see box below). With upgrading now going on precinct by precinct, and yellow-bibbed "city ambassadors" a common sight on street corners, many parts of the CBD are now not only safe, but they are drawing businesses and tourists back. Though the prospect would still horrify most white Jo'burgers, a visit to the CBD offers a rare chance to get a feel for the real Jo'burg. Refreshingly multiracial, the mix of office workers, shoppers and street traders probably comes closer to reflecting the overall demographic mix of white, black and coloured South Africa than anywhere else in the country. Here you can see people going about their everyday business, observe buildings and institutions with a fascinating history, and get a taste for the bustle, sounds and thrill of a genuinely African city.

If you're coming into the city centre by car, **park** either in the Carlton

Revitalizing the City

For a decade and more, downtown Johannesburg has been synonymous with crime and lack of safety. In a city with an unenviable reputation, it was the ultimate no-go area. But no city lives for long without a healthy heart and these days much is being done to inject vitality back into the downtown area. The task of making the streets safe again has been taken up by the Central Johannesburg Partnership (CJP), who deployed the first yellow-bibbed City Ambassadors to keep an eye out for crime, pick up litter and, if asked, help out tourists wanting to find some of the local sights. Real investment has followed: streets are being pedestrianized and adorned with public works of art, Vanderbijl bus station was changed into Gandhi Square, and Mary Fitzgerald Square in Newtown upgraded.

Even now it is safer to walk downtown, and a handful of tourists can be seen checking out the buildings and getting a sense of the buzz of the city centre. There is talk of boutique hotels moving in. In the next few years, projects such as the building of a new constitutional court in Braamfontein and the massive Nelson Mandela Bridge from Braamfontein to Newtown will be well under way. Perhaps it won't be long till downtown Jo'burg transforms from a no-go to a must-go place for locals and tourists.

For information on the latest developments, including the status of a planned Tourist Orientation Centre, call the CJP on ☏011 688 7800 or go to ⊛www.cjp.co.za.

Centre or underneath Gandhi Square. Scheduled city **buses** from the northern suburbs terminate at Gandhi Square, while the **City Slicker** tour bus comes right into the city, stopping at the Carlton Centre and Newtown. Another good way to see the city centre is to see it in the company of a **guide**: Dumela Africa (℡083 659 9928, ⓦwww.dumelaafrica-res.co.za) offers expert and interesting walking tours of the downtown area as well as Jo'burg as a whole.

Central CBD

The **Carlton Centre**, roughly halfway down Commissioner Street, is a good place to start explorations. There's a tourist office on the ground floor, and lots of shops and fast-food outlets, but the main attraction of this fifty-storey building is its top-floor **Top of Africa** lookout point (daily 9am–7pm; R7.50), which offers breathtaking views of the centre of Johannesburg, with a chance to see the way the mine dumps, reef and city concrete exist cheek-by-jowl.

From the Carlton Centre, head west for about three blocks along Commissioner or pedestrianized Fox Street, then turn south to **Gandhi Square**, site of the bus station. A good example of the city's regeneration, this was formerly Vanderbijl Square, full of grim bus shelters and gangsters. As the former location of the Magistrate's Court where Gandhi spent so much of his time working in the city, the square was named in his honour and spruced up with some attractive brickwork. Still the main bus terminal in the city, it's now a clean and safe place to orientate yourself.

A couple of blocks to the northwest, on Loveday Street, the grandiose Rand Club (visits by prior arrangement only, ℡011 834 8311) is where mining magnates have come to dine and unwind for nearly a century. Completed in 1904, the building is actually the fourth to occupy the site, as each successive club was replaced to reflect the owners' growing wealth.

Four blocks south, going down Simmonds Street, on the corner of Frederick Street, lies the superb **Standard Bank Art Gallery** (Mon–Fri 8am–4.30pm, Sat 9am–1pm; free), a large and imposing round building with sweeping staircases where changing exhibitions consistently show off some the best contemporary African art in South Africa. Just across the road in Standard Bank's head office at 5 Simmonds St, you can take a lift from the main concourse down to **Ferreira's Stope** (Mon–Fri 8.30am–5pm; free), an old mine tunnel discovered when the building was being constructed in 1986. As a modern office, it's unusual to stand beside the plain rock face (still with pick-axe scars) on which it's built, but the simple display is a fascinating way to put the history of Johannesburg in context. Look out also for the old sepia photographs of the mine and early Jo'burg.

Among the city's skyscrapers, imperious mining halls and boarded-up office blocks stand numerous interesting buildings, quirky facades and architectural features. North of Commissioner Street, look out for the recently revamped **Gauteng Legislature**, formerly the City Hall, on the corner of Harrison Street, while the former **Post Office** is one block east on the corner of Rissik Street. When this was completed in 1897, it was the tallest building in the city, and is still impressive, despite being dwarfed by later additions to the skyline. Whilst basically neo-Baroque in style, it has quirky Dutch touches, primarily in its gabling. The fourth floor and clock tower are later additions, timed to coincide with the accession of the British king, Edward VII, in 1902. Elsewhere, on Pritchard Street stands **Cuthberts**, a department store which opened as a shoe shop in 1904, and **Markham's**, built in 1886. The **Rand Supreme Court**, two blocks further east on Pritchard Street, was once a hated

Gandhi in Johannesburg

Although **Mohandas Gandhi** has many strong links with Durban, the South African city he arrived at in 1893, it was the ten years he spent in Johannesburg between 1903 and 1913 that first tested the philosophies for which he is famous. As a qualified advocate, he frequently appeared in the Transvaal Law Courts (now demolished), which stood in what has recently been renamed Gandhi Square in downtown Jo'burg (see opposite). Defending mainly South African Indians accused of breaking the restrictive and racist registration laws, Gandhi began to see practical applications for his concept of **Satyagraha**, soul force, or passive resistance, as a means of defying immoral state oppression.

Gandhi himself was twice imprisoned along with other passive resisters in the Fort in Braamfontein; on one of these occasions he was taken from his cell to the office of General Jan Smuts to negotiate the prisoners' release, but finding himself at liberty, had to borrow the railway fare home from the general's secretary.

Gandhi's ideas found resonance in the non-violent ideals of the founders of the **African National Congress** in 1912. Forty years later, only a few years after Gandhi's successful use of Satyagraha to end the British Raj in India, the start of the ANC's Defiance Campaign against the pass laws in 1952 owed much to Gandhi's principles. Museum Africa (see below) contains displays on Gandhi's time in Johannesburg.

symbol of oppression, but has been making a new and better name for itself since 1994, with landmark rulings on the new constitution. There are plans to move the Supreme Court to a custom-built building in Braamfontein.

Diagonal Street

Moving west from Simmonds Street in the vicinity of Pritchard and Jeppe streets, look out for the rather forbidding **Bank City**, home of a number of banks, but also with the kind of arcades and plazas found in a continental European capital. West of this is **Diagonal Street**, heart of one of the most fascinating areas in the CBD. In the shadow of various concrete and glass behemoths, including the former Johannesburg Stock Exchange, are streets of old two-storey buildings, some of which date back to the 1890s; the lines of washing on the upstairs balconies show that they are still residential. On the streets are a jumble of street traders and shops, with traditional medicines (*umuthi*), Sotho blankets and paraffin stoves sold alongside mobile phones. Though it might not feel it at first, the area is fairly safe, and with businessmen mingling with hawkers it has a very African buzz.

If you're feeling brave, take a look at the rather spooky **KwaZulu Muti Museum of Man and Science** at 14 Diagonal St, a shop selling all kinds of traditional medicines, often manufactured from the dried animal skins hanging from the ceiling. You might also find yourself brushing against dangling ostrich feet or a pair of monkey skulls.

Newtown

On the western edge of the CBD Between Diagonal Street and the M1 motorway flyover, **Newtown** is an area of redevelopment where some of Johannesburg's most vibrant cultural hot-spots are found alongside derelict factories and areas of wasteland. The main draw is its **Cultural Precinct**, where a lot of money is being spent to ensure it's a safe place to visit both by day and at night, when the various music and theatre venues are in full swing.

At its heart is the excellent **Museum Africa** at 121 Bree St (Tues–Sun 9am–5pm; R5), which overlooks Mary Fitzgerald Square. Housed in the city's huge former fruit and vegetable market, the sheer size of the museum can make it seem a bit sparse and empty, but in fact the four permanent exhibitions and numerous temporary displays are well worth seeing. Most successful is **Johannesburg Transformations**, which tells the story of the city from early days of gold prospecting to the 1994 elections. Among the imaginative exhibits are recreations of shacks and *shebeens* playing well-selected soundtracks from musical giants of the past, such as *kwela* maestro Spokes Mashiane. In a side room, look out for **Tried for Treason**, a exhibition dedicated to the Treason Trial of the 1950s, when 156 people, including Nelson Mandela and many well-known ANC activists of all races, were accused of plotting against the state.

On the upper floor, and rather less engaging, is the **Bensusan Museum of Photography**, which grandly aspires to be a "newseum of the present and future" but adds up to little more than a collection of cameras, holograms and CD ROMs. On the lower floors, the **Museum of South African Rock Art** has few original paintings, as most of them are still on rocks scattered around South Africa, but there are some convincing replicas – which are as close as you'll get to the real thing without a hike up country. A useful text gives background on the artists and their work.

At the eastern end of the same building is the entrance to the famous **Market Theatre** (see p.616), a reliable source of stimulating and often ground-breaking dramatic output over the last 25 years or so. Outside, there's a worthwhile collection of shops, places to eat and drink, and *Kippies*, a former public toilet which is now South Africa's most famous jazz venue (see p.614). The cultural centre continues south of Jeppe Street, with a live music venue (*Megamusic*), a dance rehearsal and performing space called the **Dance Factory**, and the **Electric Workshop**, which is used for the annual Arts Alive Festival (see box on p.616). One of the city's better **flea markets** takes place every Saturday outside the theatre and on Mary Fitzgerald Square (see "Shopping" on p.617).

On the corner of President and Bezuidenhout streets is the **South African Breweries (SAB) Centenary Centre** (Tues–Sat 10am–6pm; R10). A ninety-minute tour takes you through 6000 years of brewing history, which begs the question why SAB's ubiquitous end product, the anaemic, fizzy Castle lager, is so disappointing. Still, the reconstructed gold-rush pubs and Sixties *shebeen* are fun, along with the greenhouse where sample crops of barley and hops grow, and from the balcony of the *Tap Room* bar you can watch the city rush by.

Moving southwest, over President and Main streets, you'll come to the infamous **John Vorster Square**, site of the Johannesburg police headquarters, where anti-apartheid activists were detained and tortured, and some fell to their deaths having "jumped" from the tenth floor. After this, it's a pleasant relief to find the remains of the old Indian neighbourhood just further west, where Jeppe Street turns into Minnaar Street. A busy commercial street ends up at the **Oriental Plaza**, an Indian-owned shopping complex, selling everything from suitcases and bric-a-brac to fabrics and spices. This is just about all that remains of Newtown's once-thriving Indian community, most of whom were forcibly removed in 1904 to make way for whites.

Braamfontein

The only time you're likely to visit the district of **Braamfontein**, which starts at the main train station and extends north as far as Empire Road, is for its transport facilities at Park station. The only other attractions marginally worth a visit are the **Civic Theatre** in Rissik Street, which hosts some of

Johannesburg's best theatrical, musical and dance productions (see p.616), and the **University of the Witwatersrand**, otherwise known as "Wits", which lies in Braamfontein's northwest corner, on the corner of Jorissen Street and Jan Smuts Avenue. The university has played an important role in the country's history, educating many future leaders, and acting as a site of major intellectual and political struggles. The large attractive campus contains a number of impressive Classical buildings and some lovely terraced gardens, a far cry from the bustling streets nearby. On the ground floor of Senate House (best accessed from Jorissen Street), is the **Gertrude Posel Gallery** (Mon–Fri 10am–4pm; free), which houses an extensive collection of traditional and contemporary African art.

Joubert Park

On the eastern side of Park station, **Joubert Park**, named after General Piet Joubert (who lost the South African Republic general election to Paul Kruger in 1893), is largely regarded as a no-go area. The one sight you can visit, the **Johannesburg Art Gallery** (Tues–Sun 10am–5pm; free), is located in the only inner-city green space, the park itself. If you're planning to walk there, it's probably best to find a City Ambassador willing to escort you; otherwise get a taxi to drop you off at the main entrance on Klein Street or make use of the gallery's secure parking. An elegant, predominantly nineteenth-century building and one of the most progressive galleries in the country, the regular exhibits include vast wooden sculptures by the visionary Venda artist Jackson Hlungwani that tower up to the gallery's ceilings. Elsewhere, the gallery shows a very South African mixture of African artworks and artefacts from the ceremonial to the purely decorative, and a range of European paintings, including some minor Dutch Masters. The special exhibitions are usually good, too; consult the *Mail & Guardian* newspaper for details.

The central suburbs

Grouped around the CBD are various suburbs which, with Johannesburg's itinerant population and fast-changing demography, seem to be in a state of constant change. Some, particularly **Hillbrow**, **Berea** and **Yeoville**, were once the "grey areas" of Johannesburg, where apartheid first started to break down in the Eighties. The police turned a blind eye as large numbers of blacks started moving into these previously all-white areas from the townships. Today, most whites have left, and migrants from all over the continent, but especially Nigeria and the Congo Republic, have flooded in. All three suburbs have their moments of architectural excellence, though their hectic street life and fearsome reputation will probably leave you disinclined to savour them at leisure.

Hillbrow and Berea

Smit Street, running north of Joubert Park, marks the boundary with infamous and densely populated **Hillbrow**, dominated by multistorey apartment buildings, all crammed with people. Traditionally, Hillbrow attracts the city's new immigrants. Immediately after World War II, the typical immigrant was English, Italian or East European. These days, Africans from all over the continent are arriving in numbers, lending the area a uniquely pan-African atmosphere, with music from Lagos to Kinshasa pumping from the bars and clubs. Along the many side streets, the scene is distinctly seedy, with drug pushers loitering outside gaudy strip joints. The main thoroughfares, with their markets, clubs and bars, teem with activity, but the suburb is widely recognized as a **no-go area** for tourists; your best chance to experience it is to visit one of the better-known nightclubs or bars in a group, accompanied by a knowledgeable local.

If you're in the area, keep an eye out for Hillbrow's most famous apartment building, the **Ponti** or "le petit Kinshasa", the round tower visible from miles around that is home to many of the suburb's Congolese immigrants. Also worth a look is the lovely mock-Tudor **Windybrow Theatre**, tucked away on the corner of Nugget and Pietersen streets.

Berea is mostly residential, dominated by tower blocks crammed with people. Its streets are increasingly monopolized by drug dealers and prostitutes, and most people who can afford to move away are doing so.

Yeoville and Observatory

Lying east across the Harrow Road from Berea, **Yeoville**, and in particular its main drag **Rockey Street**, was long a melting pot where bohemian whites and progressive blacks mixed in Johannesburg's most vibrant and creative area. Thousands of blacks, rich enough to avoid Hillbrow, but too poor for the northern suburbs, arrived here from the townships, but in recent years the crime and drug-dealing of Hillbrow have moved in too, driving all but the most die-hard whites and backpackers from the area.

At the other end of Rockey Street lies **Observatory**, whose leafy, residential streets are still home to affluent whites, though as elsewhere in the city, most live behind high walls in streets cordoned off by security barriers.

The eastern suburbs

Amongst the oldest of the city's suburbs, and home for years to Johannesburg's Jewish and Portuguese communities, the suburbs of **Kensington** and **Bezuidenhout Valley** (better known as Bez Valley), immediately east of the CBD, have also changed dramatically in recent years, with whites moving out of much of the old housing to make way for township and immigrant blacks. Exuding a very different flavour, **Cyrildene**, to the east of Observatory, has become the city's new Chinatown, with a fascinating collection of Chinese supermarkets, businesses and authentic restaurants along Derrick Avenue near its junction with Marcia Street.

Most visitors to this area, however, come to **Bruma Lake**, an artificial stretch of water which has proved a disappointing attraction save for its popular and lively **Flea Market** (Tues–Sun 9am–5pm), one of the best places in Johannesburg to find inexpensive curios, as long as you don't mind pseudo-traditional dance troupes entertaining you while you browse. Nearby is one of central Johannesburg's more accessible green spaces, **Gillooly's Farm**, a park set around a dam and a safe place for walkers, joggers and picnickers.

The northern suburbs

Safe, prosperous and packed with shops and restaurants, the **northern suburbs** seem a world apart from the CBD and its surrounds. The name is actually a catch-all term for the seemingly endless urban sprawl running over 30km from Parktown, beyond the N1 ring-road and into an area known as Mid Rand which is itself creeping toward the southern edge of Pretoria. With the notable exception of Alexandra, this is a moneyed area, where plush shopping malls and well-tended parks are often the only communal meeting points, and most streets have a fortress-like appearance with high walls, iron gates and barbed wire used by the majority of home-owners to advertise how security-conscious a life they lead. Despite the often numbing sheen of affluence, however,

NORTHERN SUBURBS

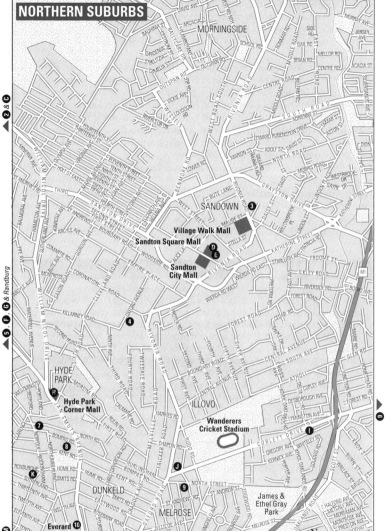

MORNINGSIDE

SANDOWN ③

Village Walk Mall
Sandton Square Mall
D
E
Sandton
City Mall

④

HYDE
PARK
Hyde Park
Corner Mall

ILLOVO

Wanderers
Cricket Stadium

DUNKELD

MELROSE

James &
Ethel Gray
Park

Everard ⑩
Read Gallery
PARKTOWN
NORTH
ROSEBANK ⑪
⑫
N
Rosebank Mall
& Rooftop Market
Goodman Gallery

N

0   1 km

RESTAURANTS

2 Thai 4	**I**	Cranks	**N**
Anno Domini	**L**	Fruits & Roots	**A**
Broughtons	**D**	Ile de France	**C**
The Carnivore	**F**	Jimmy's Killer Prawns	**G**
The Codfather	**B**	Mamas	**O**

Montego Bay	**E**
Osteria Tre Nonni	**K**
Plaka	**J**
The Red Chamber	**H**
Ruby Grapefruit	**M**

ACCOMMODATION

Backpackers' Ritz	**7**	The Grace in	Oxford Lodge **4**
Cooper's Croft	**5**	Rosebank **11**	Rockey's of
Don Apartments	**3&12**	Lilliesleaf **1**	Fourways **2**
Gemini Backpackers	**6**	Melrose Place **9**	Ten Bompas **8**
			Zoo Lodge **10**

interesting pockets do exist, such as the centres of the suburbs of Melville, Rosebank and Parkhurst. As most of the suburbs are close to major arterial roads, they're best explored by car.

Parktown

The first elite residential area in Johannesburg, **Parktown** has retained its exclusive tag despite its proximity to Hillbrow, which lies just northwest on the other side of Empire Road. The first people to settle here were Sir Lionel Philips, president of the Chamber of Mines, and his wife Lady Florence. In 1892, seeking a residence that looked onto the Magaliesberg rather than the mine dumps, they had a house built on what was then the Braamfontein farm. The rest of the farm was planted with eucalyptus trees and became known as the Sachsenwald Forest, some of which was given over to the Johannesburg Zoo a few years later. The remaining land was cleared in 1925 to make way for more residential developments.

Parktown's main attraction lies in its distinctive **architecture**, largely the legacy of Sir Herbert Baker (see below). Baker's arrival in 1902 heralded a style particular to this district, which is still evident today in the opulent mansions lining the streets. Parktown & Westcliff Heritage Trust (office open Mon–Fri

---

Sir Herbert Baker

South Africa's most famous architect, **Sir Herbert Baker** was born in Kent, England, in 1862. Apprenticed to his architect uncle in London at the age of 17, Baker attended classes at the Royal Academy and Architectural Association, where he took care to make the contacts he would use so skilfully in later life. By the time he left for the Cape in 1892, Baker was already a convert to the new so-called **Free Style**, which advocated an often bizarre, but roughly historical eclecticism. The young architect's favourite influences, which would crop up again and again in his work, were Renaissance Italian and medieval Kentish.

Once in the Cape, Baker met **Cecil Rhodes**, and this connection, assiduously cultivated, established him as a major architectural player. The second Anglo-Boer War began in 1899 and Rhodes, assuming eventual British victory, sent Baker off to study the Classical architecture of Italy and Greece, hoping that he would return fully equipped to create a British imperial architecture in South Africa. Baker returned to South Africa deeply influenced by what he had seen, and was summoned by **Lord Alfred Milner**, the administrator of the defeated Transvaal, to fulfil Rhodes' hopes. Baker took up the challenge enthusiastically, beginning with the homes of the so-called "kindergarten", the young men, mostly Oxford- and Cambridge-educated, whom Milner had imported to bring British-style "good governance" to the defeated territory. The result was the **Parktown mansions**, the opulent houses lining the roads of Johannesburg's wealthiest suburb. In adherence to the architectural creeds he had learnt in England, Baker trained local craftsmen and used local materials for these mansions. He also pioneered the use of local *koppie* stone, lending a dramatic aspect even to unadventurous designs.

Baker's major public commissions were the **St George's Cathedral** in Cape Town, the **South African Institute for Medical Research** in Johannesburg, and the sober, assertive **Union Buildings** in Pretoria, which more than any other building express the British imperial dream – obsessed with Classical precedent, and in a location chosen because of its similarity to the site of the Acropolis in Athens.

Baker left South Africa in 1913 to design the Secretariat in New Delhi, India. He returned to England on its completion, where he worked on South Africa House in Trafalgar Square, London, and was knighted in 1923. He died in 1946, and is buried in Westminster Abbey.

9am–1pm; ☎011 482 3349) runs **walking or bus tours** most Saturday afternoons; these follow themes such as "Johannesburg Gold" or "Edwardian Elegance" and often involve knowledgeable guides decked out in full Edwardian costume who will show you through some of the lavish mansions and their grounds. Tours cost between R40 and R80, and can be booked directly through Computicket (☎011 340 8000, ⊛www.computicket.com). The Trust also publishes an inexpensive walking tour guide, so you can walk or drive the routes covered by the tours unguided, but without access to the houses.

For your own tour, a good place to start is **Ridge Road**, just north of the Randjeslaagte beacon, which marks the northern point of old Johannesburg. To get there, turn north off Louis Botha at Boundary Road (a small road that is easily missed), and take the second left. The best of the houses on this street are **The View** at no. 18, built in 1897, with carved wooden verandahs and an elegant red-brick exterior. Next door, **Hazeldene Hall** was built in 1902 and features cast-iron verandahs imported from Glasgow. Turning north into **York Road** takes you past **Sunnyside Hotel**, a massive complex which Lord Alfred Milner used as his governor's residence from 1900. The road curves to the left into Jubilee Road, with several palaces on its northern side; the neo-Queen-Anne-style **Emoyeni**, at no.15, built in 1905, is especially striking. At the corner of Jubilee Road and Victoria Avenue stands **Dolobran**, a weird and impressive house, also built in 1905, with a perfect verandah, wonderful red-brick chimneys, red Marseilles roof tiles and hallucinatory stained glass.

Crossing the busy M1 onto **Rock Ridge Road**, you'll reach the **Northwards Mansion**, home of the Parktown Trust, and built by Sir Herbert Baker in 1904. Unfortunately, there's no access along the road to Baker's own residence at no. 5. On parallel Eton Road you can see Baker's attractive **St George's Church** and its rectory, which mix Kentish and Italian features and were built in local rock.

Zoo Lake and Houghton

Roughly 2km north of Parktown, off Jan Smuts Avenue, **Johannesburg Zoo** (daily 8.30am–5.30pm; R15), is home to over three thousand species, including polar bears. Despite recent attempts at revitalization, a sad air pervades the zoo, making this a good place for a melancholic wander, but not much else. A few years ago, it hit the headlines when a criminal tried to avoid pursuing policemen by hopping over the wall into the zoo. Unfortunately, he jumped straight into the cage of Max the gorilla; the indignant Max suffered a gunshot wound from the encounter, while the criminal was hospitalized with serious bites.

Next door, and of greater interest, is the **National Museum of Military History** (daily 9am–4.30pm; R5), where amongst the tanks, guns and uniforms you'll find a display on **Umkhonto we Sizwe (MK)**, the armed wing of the ANC, although the other liberation armies are conspicuous by their absence. The display focuses on the wing's commander, Joe Modise, who became Minister of Defence in the ANC government. Opposite the zoo, on the west side of Jan Smuts Avenue, is the artificial but pleasant **Zoo Lake**. The park here is a popular and safe walking and picnic spot and occasionally hosts outdoor performances, including an all-day music event every September during the Arts Alive festival (see p.616).

East of the zoo is the suburb of **Houghton**, one of Johannesburg's wealthiest and greenest suburbs. This is where Nelson Mandela lives, in a large white mansion dubbed Casa Graça after his third wife, Graça Machel. Interestingly, it was the country's only constituency to return an anti-apartheid MP, Helen Suzman, between 1961 and 1974.

Melville

The most relaxed, unintimidating and appealing of the northern suburbs, **Melville** lies west of Parktown between the two main road arteries of Barry Hertzog and Beyers Naude (formerly D.F. Malan). The suburb's villagey atmosphere has proved highly attractive to the stressed ranks of Johannesburg's upwardly mobile, who are steadily buying up property here. When so many shops and restaurants in Jo'burg are tucked away in soulless malls, it's refreshing to find streets with busy shops and pavement cafés. The suburb's most interesting shops lie around the junction of 7th Street and 4th Avenue, where you can linger in the inviting coffee shops, trendy restaurants, secondhand bookshops and quirky antique dealers. There's plenty going on here at night, too, when it's still safe to walk on the main streets.

The **Melville Koppies Nature Reserve** (℡011 788 7571, Ⓦwww.veld .org.za) to the north of the suburb is a pleasant hillside reserve containing hundreds of species of indigenous flora and fauna, as well as archeological remains of both Stone and Iron Age settlements. There are two parts to the reserve: the **Louw Geldenhuys View Site**, reached from Zambesi Road or any of the roads running north from 7th Avenue, offers great views over Jo'burg and has open access at all times; to the west, the larger **central section** has a number of good walking trails, but is open only on the first three Sundays of every month. On the northern side of the reserve lies Jan van Riebeeck Park, a large spread of green parkland running north and west for several kilometres, which contains the **Johannesburg Botanic Garden** in its northeast corner. Beside Emmarentia Dam, a popular spot for paddling and rowing, the garden is noted for its wide open spaces and safe routes for joggers and walkers rather than for its botanical exuberance – although in the northeast corner there are some attractive formal herb and rose gardens. The tiny Shakespeare Garden is often used for plays or small concerts, which are advertised in the local press.

Sophiatown

East of Melville lies the suburb of **Sophiatown**, architecturally unremarkable but significant in the history of apartheid – it was here that **Archbishop Trevor Huddleston**, the English cleric who established the Anti-Apartheid Movement, worked in the Fifties. For many years, Sophiatown was one of the few places within the city where blacks owned property, and as a result it became a melting pot of music, dance, culture and liberal thinking on issues of politics and race. In the 1960s, the suburb was designated a white area by the government, who sent in the bulldozers, scattering the inhabitants to Soweto regardless of their claim to the land and, with a degree of irony, if not fatalism, renamed the suburb Triomf, a name that remains on many maps and signboards. Although the name Sophiatown has now been reinstated, nothing of the original suburb remains apart from one house and **Christ the King** Anglican church, from where Trevor Huddleston conducted his ministry. When he died in 1998, his ashes were brought from London to be scattered in Sophiatown.

Rosebank and Parkhurst

The small suburb of **Rosebank**, northwest of Houghton and a couple of kilometres north of the zoo, is dominated by a collection of **shopping malls**. There is also the **African Craft Market** (Tues–Sun 9am–5pm), a two-storey ochre building in a hip adobe style which houses a collection of stalls selling reasonable-quality African arts and crafts. It's not the cheapest place to buy crafts in the city, but prices are still much lower than the upmarket galleries nearby, and you are able to bargain. Sundays are the busiest day for crafts, when a large **flea market** selling everything from drums to cheese takes over a floor of the car park adjoining the Rosebank Mall.

Also in and around Rosebank are a number of galleries where you can view (and often purchase) traditional and contemporary African art, often of a very high standard. The Everard Read Gallery (Mon–Fri 9am–6pm, Sat 9am–5pm; free) at 6 Jellicoe Ave has varied exhibitions, often featuring South Africa's leading painters and sculptors. The Goodman Art Gallery (Tues–Fri 9.30am–5.30pm, Sat 9.30am–4pm; ⓦwww.goodman-gallery.com) at 163 Jan Smuts Ave is smaller and more avant garde, while at 153 Jan Smuts Ave, the Kim Sacks Art Gallery specializes in traditional arts and crafts from around Africa, with most items on display for sale.

Not far to the west of Rosebank lies **Parkhurst**. This suburb, along with Melville, is one of the few places in the northern suburbs where there's an element of street life – particularly on and around 4th Avenue. It's safe to walk around here, checking out the antique and interior design shops, as well as the smattering of trendy cafés and restaurants.

Sandton and Randburg

Some 20km north of the CBD, **Sandton** is the archetypal northern suburb. It is outrageously rich, with plush shopping centres and endless rows of lavish houses protected by high walls and sophisticated security systems. In recent years, it has become the retreat of choice for banks and large corporations fleeing the CBD; however overpowering the office blocks seem, there is little doubt that they will be humbled by those which will rise from the various building sites at work now. A stroll through the linked **Sandton City** and **Sandton Square** shopping centres, complete with a pseudo-Italian piazza and attendant restaurants and cafés, may make you shudder at the vulgarity of such an ostentatious display of wealth, but it's also one of the best ways to appreciate this suburb and its inhabitants.

North of Sandton, the suburbs roll on for 15km and more. Here you'll find large domestic plots interspersed with lush country clubs, shopping centres and, increasingly, the new phenomenom of "clusters", little developments of upmarket, newly built houses behind an imposing perimeter wall and equipped with every available security device. Whether such levels of paranoia are altogether necessary in keeping crime at bay is not a subject you'll find open to debate among locals, but there is little doubt that the tone it sets dominates the northern suburbs.

Among the few points of interest here is the **Waterfront** on Republic Road in the suburb of **Randburg**. Themed restaurants, bars, amusement arcades and shops, along with cinemas and a flea market, have been built around an artificial lake in a crude attempt to cash in on the success of the Cape Town Waterfront. The most recent attempt to brighten things up is a tame spectacle called **Liquid Fireworks** (nightly 7.30 & 8.30pm), which involves a series of fountains illuminated by multicoloured lights. Further north, beyond the N1 highway on William Nicol Drive, Jo'burg's latest foray into OTT shopping malls is **Monte Casino**, from the outside a huge mock-Italian palazzo and on the inside a replica of a Tuscan village, filled with cobbled streets, cast-iron street lamps and red-tiled buildings housing chain shops such as Diesel and Next. Alongside are restaurants, cinemas, a theatre, a casino and banks of gaming machines – again, this is a place to visit if only to marvel at the imagination the South Africans continue to invest in retail escapism.

Alexandra

The contrast between **Alexandra** (just east of the M1) and its surrounding suburbs could hardly be greater. This intensely crowded, desperately poor, black township was, when it was founded, one of the few places where blacks could own property, and this sense of ownership and independence helped Alex, as it is commonly known, to avoid the forced removals of former governments. Despite the simple grid design its map suggests, the township is actually a bewildering maze of smashed-up streets, filled to bursting point with people, with overcrowded housing and a woeful lack of basic services such as sewage and water. Today, half a million people live in an area of less than eight square kilometres.

"Exhilarating and precarious" was how Nelson Mandela described Alex when he lived here in the early 1940s after running away from the Eastern Cape to find work in Jo'burg as an articled law clerk. In those days, the township was well-known for gangster gangs as well as its developing political militancy, which saw **bus boycotts** preventing bus companies from raising their fares, one of the first examples of mass action by blacks achieving political results. Alexandra has long been an ANC stronghold, and paid dearly for it until the collapse of apartheid, with on-going warfare between Zulus and the ANC in the Eighties leading to one section of Alex being dubbed "Beirut".

While the old spirit of Alex lives on in the bustling streets on the western side of the polluted Jukskei River, the eastern bank is now lined with **new houses**, some built by government funding and others by middle-class blacks looking to improve their quality of life but still wanting to remain in the township. Here you can also see the athletes' village built when the 1999 All African Games were held in Johannesburg; named "Tsutsumane" (Shangaan for "runner"), this section has also been turned into housing for locals. Not far from here a patch of land has been turned into a **cricket oval**; if there's a match going on, you can observe the incongruous sight of this most colonial of games being played against a backdrop of densely packed township shacks, with the skyscrapers of opulent Sandton peaking over the horizon behind.

As part of Alex's renewal programme, it's possible to take a **tour** of the township in the company of a guide. Much less formalized and certainly less touristy than Soweto tours, this is a great way to get close to the raw energy and spontaneity of township life: Abbey Sechoaro of Bosele Township Experience (℡011 882 1142 or ℡083 553 5688) runs excellent tours and also works for the Alexandra Tourism Association (℡011 882 3899), who can put you in touch with other guides. If you can't visit in person, tuning into Alex FM, the township's entertaining community **radio** station (see p.615), will at least give you a feel of this lively, though poverty-stricken suburb.

South of the CBD

The suburbs immediately **south of the city centre** were traditionally the preserve of the white working class, but since the repeal of the Group Areas Act in 1990, blacks have started moving in; unusually in contemporary South Africa, many are wealthier than the original residents. Aside from **Gold Reef City**, the only attraction of this area is the sizeable **Klipriviersberg** Nature Reserve, just south of the N12, in Winchester Hills. Few Jo'burgers know about this undeveloped, unspoilt parkland, which provides wonderful views of the city to the north. To get there, take the N1 heading south, turn left into Columbine Avenue (M68), and then right a kilometre or two further, at Ormonde Street.

Gold Reef City

Gold Reef City (Tues–Sun 9am–5pm; R50), 15km south of the city centre, is where old Johannesburg meets Disneyland: a large, gaudy entertainment complex built around the old no. 14 shaft of the Crown Mines. If you can take the tackiness and piped ragtime music, there are some points of interest at what is essentially a theme park, notably the **old gold mine** itself, which you can descend 200m into and get at least an inkling of how it is to work underground. Keep an eye out, too, for the tribal dancing that happens five times a day; the dancers are excellent, even if their routines bear little resemblance to the real thing.

You are encouraged to wander round the streets filled with period houses, shops and museums, though most are generally disappointing, with the possible exception of those dedicated to early Johannesburg, such as Olthaver and Nourse House. Otherwise, the most enjoyable thing to do in Gold Reef City are the **thrill rides** (all included in the entrance ticket), which include the Raging Rapids water ride and the terrifying Anaconda roller coaster. In the unlikely event that you want to stay the night, the *Gold Reef City Hotel* (☎011 248 5200; ❺) offers Victorian-themed decor, complete with a saloon, mock-oil lamps and four-poster beds. Various restaurants serve decent though pricey food, but the main focus of this section of Gold Reef City is the vast casino, complete with hundreds of slot machines and various gaming tables.

To get to Gold Reef City, take the M1 heading south, and turn off at the Xavier Street exit. Otherwise, join one of the many tours that go there, which advertise in nearly every hotel lobby.

Soweto

South Africa's most famous township, **SOWETO** (short for South West Townships) is a place of extreme contrasts. The area has the only street in the world where two Nobel Peace Prize winners once lived, yet suffers one of the highest rates of murder and rape in the world; it is the richest township in South Africa, but has some of the most desperate poverty; it is the most political township, yet has the most nihilistic youth.

Soweto is huge, stretching as far as the eye can see, with estimates of its population ranging between three and four million. Like any city of that size, it is divided into a number of different **suburbs**, with palpably middle- and upper-class neighbourhoods among them. At first sight, it appears an endless jumble of houses and shacks, overshadowed by palls of smoke. Once inside, parts of it have a villagey feel, especially if you are exploring on foot, and unlike anywhere else in Jo'burg, Sowetans will often stop to greet you or to chat, regardless of your colour.

Most of Soweto's **tourist highlights** are famous for historical reasons and are physically unimpressive. That history, however, is enthralling, not least because here it is told with a perspective and context rarely found in the rest of South Africa. For visitors it means an insight not just into a place famous from 1980s news bulletins for funerals and fighting, but into a way of life most Westerners have rarely, if ever, encountered.

A visit to Soweto with one of the many **tours** (see box on p.608) is the single most popular attraction in Johannesburg. Where once these had a whiff of daring and originality, a well-trodden tourist trail has developed, and unless

The most common – and safest – way to **visit Soweto** is with a tour operator. By far the oldest, biggest and slickest operation is Jimmy's Face to Face Tours (☎011 331 6109, ⊛www.face2face.co.za). Jimmy pioneered tours into the township, and his operation has grown steadily over the years. Imbizo Tours (☎011 838 2667 or 083 700 9098, ⊛www.imbizo.co.za), run by the irrepressible Mandy Mankazana, provides stiff competition. Mandy is a mine of information and contacts, and her three-hour day tours and four-hour night tours of Soweto are excellent. Tours can be customized, and Imbizo also organizes evening *shebeen*-crawls lasting up to five hours, depending on your stamina. Indicate what kind of company you would like to keep, from politicians to sports fanatics, and Mandy will select an appropriate venue.

As well as the well-established operators, smaller, more flexible outfits offer imaginative **alternative tours** such as jazz outings, walking around Orlando West and Diepkloof, visits to Sowetan artists or local churches, and homestays with locals. Try Max Maximum (☎011 933 4177 or 082 770 0247) or African Prime Tours (☎011 794 4708); alternatively, the place you're staying may well have links to a reliable tour company.

Before you go to Soweto on any kind of tour, it's worth preparing yourself for the fact that as a tourist you will always stand out, and that there's a good chance you'll be in the company of at least one other group of tourists. Most outfits are keen for you to "meet the people", though they all tend to visit the same shanty towns and *shebeens*, and you'll find that resulting conversations sometimes turn to you leaving a donation, tipping casual guides or buying local craftwork. While this gets a few tourist dollars directly into the townships, it often leaves visitors feeling pressurized and vulnerable. Ask your guide about the best way to deal with this.

you're content to follow the herds of minibuses and coaches around the conventional sights, it's well worth using an operator who mixes the highlights with lesser-known sights. And where once taking yourself to Soweto would have meant a display of bravado bordering on foolhardiness, it's now possible to **drive** there, though you'll need good navigational skills (the lack of obvious landmarks amidst the mile upon mile of bungalows can be highly confusing), and to stick to the main sights – exploring less-visited areas by yourself, or going after dark, isn't recommended for safety reasons. However, your time will be your own, and you'll be able to check out the growing number of bars and eating places catering to tourists.

Taking a **minibus taxi** to Soweto is more confusing than dangerous, as it isn't always easy to ascertain which part of the township it's heading for, for which reason it's not recommended. The best place to pick up **information** about visiting on your own is from the new Soweto Tourism Centre at 49 Madlala St in Orlando East (Mon–Fri 8.30am–4.30pm; ☎011 938 4929), located very close to Soweto's one distinctive landmark, the huge cooling towers of a former electricity plant.

Orlando West and Dube

Set in the northern part of Soweto, **Orlando West** and **Dube** qualify as two of its more affluent suburbs, with a number of sights and the greatest concentration of places to eat and drink. Orlando East, across Klipspruit Valley from Orlando West, was the first part of Soweto to be established in 1932, and the area is fairly easily accessible off the Soweto Highway (M70). Here, **Hector Petersen Square**, named after the first student to be killed in the 1976 uprising (see box opposite), has a memorial to Petersen and the other students who died. Alongside, a new museum is due to be completed in 2002, showing images associated with the Soweto uprising, including those taken by famous black photographers, including Peter Magubane and Sam Nzima.

Nearby is **Vilakazi Street**, a few hundred metres to the southwest, once home to Nelson Mandela and Desmond Tutu. Mandela's bungalow is where he lived with Winnie in the late Fifties and early Sixties, before his imprisonment on Robben Island, and where Winnie lived until exiled to the Free State (from which she returned to an imposing brick house with high walls and security cameras, just down the road). On his release, Nelson insisted on returning to his old home, but its smallness and lack of security proved too much of a strain, and he moved out of Soweto. Opened up by Winnie, tours of the old bungalow, **Mandela House** (daily 10am–4.30pm, R15), mix fascinatingly mundane memorabilia and large amounts of pro-Winnie propaganda.

The Soweto uprising of 1976

The **student uprising** that began in Soweto in June 1976 was a defining moment in South African history. The revolt was sparked off by a government ruling that **Afrikaans** should be used on an equal basis with English in black secondary schools. Whilst this was feasible in some rural areas, it was quite impossible in the townships, where neither pupils nor teachers knew the language.

On June 16, student delegates from every Soweto school launched their long-planned mass protest march through the township and a rally at the Orlando football stadium. Incredibly, details of the plan were kept secret from the omnipresent *impimpis* (informers). Soon after the march started, however, the police attacked, throwing tear gas and then firing. The crowd panicked, and demonstrators started throwing stones at the police. The police fired again. Out of this bedlam came the famous photograph of Hector Petersen, bleeding at the mouth, being carried by a friend, while a young girl looks on in anguished horror.

The police retreated to Orlando East, and students rushed to collect the injured and dead, erect barricades, and destroy everything they could belonging to the municipal authority, including beer halls. The attacks heightened the antagonism between the youth and many older people who thought that class boycotts were irresponsible, given the students' already dismal employment prospects. Students responded angrily, accusing their elders of inactivity in the face of oppression, which they attributed in part to drunkenness. In a society that has traditionally regarded respect of the old by the young as sacrosanct, this was an historic departure and its effects still reverberate throughout South Africa's townships.

In the days following June 16, all Soweto schools were closed indefinitely, thousands of police were stationed throughout the township, and police brutality continued unabated. In the face of worldwide condemnation, the government insisted that there was no real problem, ascribing the violence to Communist agitation. As evidence, it cited the clenched-fist salutes of the students, though this was really an indication of their support for the Black Consciousness Movement, founded by Steve Biko (see p.405). Meanwhile, rebellion spread to other townships, particularly in Cape Town. In Soweto, schools did not reopen until 1978, by which time many students had abandoned any hope of formal education. Some had left the country to join the military wings of the ANC and PAC, while others stayed at home, forming "street committees" to politicize and police the communities. Others drifted into unemployment.

Now the armed struggle is over, the problems that face the former students of 1976 are manifold. As their parents warned, their lack of qualifications count against them in the job market, even if June 16 is now a national holiday, during which they are praised for their role in the struggle. The street committees have dissolved, but the guns remain.

Rather spoiling the scene is a new coffee shop and restaurant crudely tacked onto the outside of the house, an unsubtle attempt to milk a little more cash from the huge numbers of tourists who pass this way.

About 1.5km away, near the junction of Klipsruit Valley (the M10) and Potchefstroom (the M68) roads, is **Regina Mundi Church**, Soweto's largest Catholic church and the focus of numerous gatherings in the struggle years. Again, its impact owes more to historical aura than anything particularly notable about its features, although with so few large buildings in the township it achieves a certain presence. Inside, look out for the **art gallery** displaying and selling the work of various Sowetan artists. Regina Mundi and the thousands of churches around the township play a vital role in visitors understanding Soweto. Church services here, as in all townships, are friendly affairs, with liberal doses of fantastic music and, depending on the denomination, religious ecstasy too. Be prepared to give at least a small testimony (a brief rundown of your spiritual life to date). Services last several hours, but no one will think it a crime if you leave before the end.

Other tourist attractions will undoubtedly develop, such as **Freedom Square** – currently a combination of wasteland and taxi rank – in **Dube**, where the ANC's Freedom Charter was proclaimed to thousands in 1955. In the meantime many visitors enjoy paying a visit to the various **shebeens**, restaurants and even coffee shops that are making a big effort to attract outsiders as well as locals. We've listed the best in "Eating" on p.613.

Eating

The wealth, diversity and fast-paced social life found in Johannesburg means that the city has a huge range of places to **eat out**. You can find all sorts of styles, from ultra-chic fusion cafés to formica-tabled Chinese eating dens where there's no English menu, meat-guzzling steakhouses to wonderfully graceful Thai restaurants. Cultural interaction was obstructed for so long that a cuisine unique to the city has never emerged, but such is the cosmopolitan nature of Jo'burg that authentic French, Italian and Portuguese restaurants are all found here, and there are increasing numbers of African restaurants, not just township South African but Congolese, Moroccan and Cape Malay. **Prices** are inevitably a bit higher than elsewhere in the country outside Cape Town and the Winelands, and you can blow out in spectacular style, but an average meal out is still good value.

All of Jo'burg's **shopping malls** are well-stocked with restaurants, some housing the very top-notch venues, but more frequently they are dominated by unadventurous, bland chains. Thankfully, a number of suburbs have small, interesting eating places; the key places are 7th Street in **Melville**, the junction of Greenway and Gleneagles in **Greenside**, Grant Avenue in **Norwood** (to the east of Houghton) and, to a lesser extent, 4th Avenue in **Parkhurst**.

If you don't fancy eating out, most shopping centres have plenty of **takeaway** options, while a **delivery** service called *Mr Delivery* has come to the rescue of many a weary traveller and unwilling self-caterer. They pick up from a range of reasonable mid-market eating places: contact them on ⓦwww.mrdelivery.com or in the northern suburbs ☎011 482 4748 (Melville), ☎011 442 4411 (Rosebank) and ☎011 784 6000 (Sandton).

CBD and central suburbs

There are one or two truly original lunch options in downtown Jo'burg, but you're only likely to eat out at night in **Newtown**. Given the lack of tourist market, the choices here are all local favourites, often serving decent African food.

The Congolese Restaurant Piccadilly Centre, Rockey Street, Yeoville. Entirely appropriate for the cosmopolitan African flavour of Yeoville, this fairly simple, inexpensive restaurant serves up *saka saka*, soup made from pounded cassava leaves, and fiery Central African favourites including specially imported porcupine or crocodile meat.

Gramadoelas at the Market Theatre Wolhuter Street, Newtown ☎011 838 6960. One of the best-known spots for excellent Cape and African dishes like *sosaties*, mopane worms and *melktart*; it isn't cheap, but the visitors' book is star-studded. Closed Sun & Mon lunch.

Horror Café 15 Becker St, Newtown. An unusual two-storey bar and café between the Cultural Precinct and the SAB centre, serving decent pub grub.

Kapitan's 11a Kort St, CBD ☎011 834 8048. Located upstairs in a decrepit-looking building near Diagonal Street, and gloomy and kitschy inside, this Jo'burg classic serves delicious South African curries. It was Mandela's favourite eating place when he worked as a lawyer nearby in the Fifties – his letter from prison holds pride of place. Lunchtime only Mon–Sat.

Kofifi Newtown Cultural Precinct, Newtown. Lively bar and restaurant directly opposite the Market Theatre, serving inexpensive burgers and simple African dishes, occasionally with live music.

Greenside, Melville, Parkhurst and Rosebank

These are the **northern suburbs** with the safest street life, as well as many of the city's more original and adventurous restaurants. They're also the preserve of much of Jo'burg's fashionable café culture.

Anno Domini On the corner of 4th Ave and 13th Street, Parkhurst ☎011 447 7634. A pleasant, quiet Italian restaurant serving slightly upmarket pizza and pasta fare. The upstairs balcony is great on warm summer evenings.

Circle 141 Greenway, Greenside ☎011 646 3744. Don't be discouraged when your bread arrives in a brown paper bag – they do want you to hang around. For some it's a bit too showy and minimalist, but the fusion menu introduces all sorts of interesting flavours, and trendy Jo'burgers flock here. Closed Sun & Mon.

Cranks The Mall, Cradock Avenue, Rosebank ☎011 880 3442. *Cranks* cooks up a storm with its Bangkok go-go bar theme; the menu extends to Vietnamese and Indonesian dishes, and there's live music Friday and Saturday nights. No reservations.

El Johara 4 Main Rd, Melville ☎011 726 8352. An unassuming little Egyptian/Arabian restaurant with carpets draping the walls and ceilings, and thick coffee poured from tall brass pots; it's intimate, authentic and memorable.

Karma Gleneagles Road, Greenside ☎011 646 8555. A small but stylish modern Indian restaurant specialising in tandoori but with a few fusion dishes thrown in.

Mamas Sanlam Building, on the corner of Baker Street and Craddock Avenue, Rosebank ☎011 442 5917. One of very few restaurants in Jo'burg still plying the upmarket traditional African theme. It's a bit too touristy and predictable with its ethnic patterns and artefacts, but the buffet served in big black *potjie* pots is excellent. Closed Mon.

Pomegranate 79 3rd Ave, Melville ☎011 482 2366. *Pomegranate* offers a high-quality, innovative international menu with Thai overtones, set in a typically charming Melville house. Closed Sat lunchtime & Sun.

Ruby Grapefruit 24 4th Ave, Parkhurst. A fun and funky little sushi bar, open during the day only, with other healthy snacks and drinks also on offer.

Sam's Café 11 7th Street, Melville ☎011 726 8142. Smarter than its name implies, and comfortably sophisticated, *Sam's* serves mostly Mediterranean dishes which are reliably tasty at moderate prices (particularly the specials). Closed Sat lunchtime & Sun.

Service Station On the corner 9th Street and Rustenburg Road, Melville. One of Jo'burg's "it" places, a superbly stylish café/deli located in a converted car garage. It serves original, classy food including breakfasts, tasty sandwiches and great cakes. Daytime only.

Soi On the corner 7th Street and 3rd Ave, Melville ☎011/726 5775. With its understated but exquisite bamboo and dark wood decor, this classy and popular Thai/Vietnamese restaurant serves authentic, tasty food at reasonable prices.

Elsewhere in the northern suburbs

The eating in the northern suburbs is amongst the very best in Johannesburg, with some of the country's most ambitious upmarket restaurants and a number of places which have been around for decades. The range is still broad, from right-on vegetarian cafés to places flying in the freshest seafood.

2 Thai 4 On the corner of Cross Street and Corlett Drive, Birnam ☏ 011 440 3000. A good-quality, mainstream Thai restaurant in a friendly, easy-going setting, at decent prices and with takeaway available.

Broughton's Sandton Square, Sandton ☏ 011 884 1608. In the upper echelons of exciting, new fine-dining restaurants in Jo'burg: expect perfectly designed, vaguely French-influenced modern food combinations, superb wines and a hefty bill. Closed Sun.

The Carnivore *Misty Hills Country Hotel*, 69 Drift Boulevard, Muldersdrift ☏ 011 957 2099. Located a fair way northwest out of town, on the edge of the Magaliesberg. Join crowds of white South Africans as they devour crocodile, giraffe, ostrich and buffalo, along with more humdrum meat dishes, in this rather OTT African "experience". A no-go zone for vegetarians.

The Codfather 1 First Ave, on the corner of Rivonia Road, Morningside ☏ 011 803 2077. Select your fresh fish from the vast displays, then watch it scaled, filleted and cooked to order. Simple, but delicious and hugely popular, with a sushi bar alongside. Daily noon–10pm.

Fruits and Roots Hobart Corner Shopping Centre, Grosvenor Road, Bryanston. One of the city's top organic, health and wholefood shops, with a great sandwich bar/café alongside. Open daytime only Mon to Wed, till 8.30pm Thurs to Sat. Closed Sun.

Ile de France Cramerview Centre, 277 Main Rd, Bryanston ☏ 011 706 2837. Deep in the northern suburbs but away from the glitzy malls, this long-standing favourite serves excellent – if expensive – traditional French provincial cooking in pleasant, spacious surroundings. Closed Sat lunchtime.

Jimmy's Killer Prawns Piazza Centre, corner of Jan Smuts Avenue and Republic Road, Randburg ☏ 011 886 8844. A big noisy restaurant, with a long menu offering large helpings of seafood; the expansive views of the city lights are entirely appropriate, and much preferable to the glitz of the nearby Waterfront. Closed Sat lunchtime & Sun evening.

Montego Bay Sandton Square, Sandton ☏ 011 883 6407. Using the argument that if you're in Sandton Square you could be anywhere in the world but mid-town Jo'burg, why not make it a sun-kissed Caribbean beach? Pricey (what else?) but lip-smacking seafood (including fresh oysters) together with sleek and slick service.

Osteria Tre Nonni 9 Grafton Ave, Craighall Park ☏ 011 327 0096. Not far from Hyde Park, this is one of Jo'burg's best Italian restaurants, with a range of food from northern Italy, and a comfortable ambience. Great homemade *grappa* liqueurs round off the evening. Book ahead. Closed Sun & Mon.

Plaka 3 Corlett Drive, Melrose North ☏ 011 788 8777. A long-established, unpretentious spot if you're keen on Greek. Not surprisingly for cosmopolitan Jo'burg, there's no shortage of local custom delighted to sample the real thing.

The Red Chamber Upper Mall, Hyde Park Corner, Hyde Park ☏ 011 325 6048. If you're a little daunted by Chinatown, this is a good spot for medium-priced Chinese in rather plusher surroundings.

East of the centre

The key area in the eastern part of the city is Norwood, where **Grant Avenue** offers little else but wall-to-wall cafés and restaurants. The more adventurous can explore **Kensington** with its neighbourhood feel and **Cyrildene**, home of the city's new Chinatown.

Benkei 48 Grant Ave, Norwood ☏ 011 483 3296. A chic modern Japanese restaurant (one of a number around Jo'burg, though most are tucked away in malls) filled with pictures of fierce sumo wrestlers and serving authentic, traditional food.

Cento 100 Langerman Drive, Kensington ☏ 011 622 7272. A haven of imaginative vegetarian and seafood fare in an unexpectedly opulent atmosphere. Closed Sun evening.

Moyo 80 Grant Ave, Norwood ☏ 011 403 1246. A Moroccan-themed restaurant with a wonderful tent-like interior, and everything from the waiters to the dishes exotic and intriguing. The big menu has lots of reasonably priced spicy stews and African combos.

Sechuan Garden Derrick Avenue, Cyrildene. One of a number of truly authentic Chinese restaurants in Jo'burg's new China Town: don't expect English menus or explanations, but the food is great.

Senor Prego On the corner of 5th and Broadway, Kensington ⓣ011 614 8850. Portuguese restaurants have a special resonance in Johannesburg, thanks to the Mozambique connection. This place isn't particularly sophisticated or classy, but the flavours are genuine and spicy.

Soweto

Anyone on a **Soweto** tour can arrange to eat in a local restaurant, bar or *shebeen*, and so long as you're not amongst a huge group of tourists, it's not a bad way to meet some locals. If you're heading to Soweto under your own steam or with a local contact, any of the places below are worth checking out and will give you a warm welcome. Commonly, some kind of meat and pap is the staple dish on offer, often with locals' favourites such as tripe or ox shin as an alternative.

Palazzo Di Stella Mncube Dr, Dube. "Stella's Palace", and the lady herself presides over a great venue for pizzas, lively drinking and Sunday afternoon jazz sessions.

Shakara, Jabulani Shopping Centre, Jabulani Ext. 1, Soweto. A large, safe bar on the Shebeen Route, but generally tourist-free with a good local feel and meals available.

Shana's Place 9136 Pimville ⓣ072 127 1619. Located on Enoch Sontoga Hill overlooking Orlando, a rather classy new bar-café that has the Soweto yuppies flocking. Cappuccino, cocktails and food available, and B&B also offered, although the party goes on all night.

Vardos Place 2525 Ngalela St, Mapetla ⓣ083 260 3970. One of the most upwardly mobile *shebeens* in Soweto, a burgeoning open-plan bar and club under one of the township's few thatched roofs. Come to shoot pool, watch sport or admire the newly installed water features; guest rooms also under construction.

Wandie's Place 618 Makhalamele St, Dube ⓣ011 982 2796. Once Soweto's archetypal tourist-friendly *shebeen*, now well on the way to becoming the area's smartest eating spot. Local African food predominates, and *Wandie's* is still used by locals as a place to eat and drink.

Entertainment, nightlife and culture

Johannesburg has always offered the best **entertainment** and **nightlife** in South Africa: the city draws top performers from all over the world, and its well-integrated audiences are the most sophisticated around. The best way to find out **what's on** is to keep your ears open, listening to the local radio stations (see p.615) and keeping your eyes peeled for roadside posters and leaflets. *SA Citylife* magazine has a good blend of features and listings, but only comes out monthly; the *Mail & Guardian* newspaper publishes decent weekly listings and articles on the main events, while the daily *Star* newspaper tracks mainstream cinema and theatre. Tickets for most events can be booked from Computicket (ⓣ011 445 8000 or 083 915 8000, ⓦwww.computicket.com) or Ticketweb (ⓣ083 140 0500, ⓦwww.ticketweb.co.za).

Live music: jazz, blues and rock

Although Johannesburg dominates the South African **music scene**, the city's lack of venues means that it's not always easy to track down good live music, even at weekends. Friday and Saturday are the busiest nights, but are by no means the only times you'll find live music playing – keep an eye on the listings. The Newtown Cultural Precinct and a couple of venues in the northern suburbs are the best bets for live **jazz**, rock groups find an eager young audience in the northern suburbs, while **kwaito** bands attract enthusiastic crowds in Hillbrow and Yeoville. In Soweto, live music is infrequent due to a venue shortage, but there are hundreds of excellent clubs and all-night street parties.

A number of bars and clubs have occasional live acts, but normally feature DJs – some of these are listed in "Clubs and bars" below. Large concerts tend to happen at the Standard Bank Arena in Ellis Park or the FNB Stadium on the way to Soweto. Medium-sized acts generally play in the Newtown Cultural Precinct, especially at the *Megamusic Warehouse*.

CBD and central suburbs

Kippies Market Theatre/Newtown Cultural Precinct, on the corner of Bree and Wolhuter streets ☎011 833 3316, ⓦwww.kippies.co.za. Probably the country's most famous jazz venue, *Kippies* has for years hosted South Africa's finest jazz acts – not bad for a former municipal toilet. It's tiny, so bands are best seen during the week, although the weekend vibe is one of the city's highlights.

Megamusic Warehouse Market Theatre/Newtown Cultural Precinct, on the corner of Bree and Wolhuter streets ☎011 834 2761. At the heart of the Cultural Precinct, this mid-sized venue copes with all but the very biggest acts. The acoustics are good and the layout has room for sitting as well as standing, although the ventilation is lousy when it's busy.

Tandoor 26 Rockey St, Yeoville ☎011 614 6737. Yeoville's main live-music venue, specializing in ragga and reggae, is still lively, if a bit seamy – only come here if you're confident about being in Yeoville at night.

Northern suburbs

Bassline 7 7th St, Melville ☎011 482 6915, ⓦwww.baselinejazzclub.co.za. An intimate and unflashy local venue which has a reliable and busy line-up of southern Africa's finest jazz and blues musicians. Reasonable food is served, so if you want a good seat it's worth coming early. Otherwise, join the hip, mixed crowd who fill up the spaces at the back.

The Blues Room Village Walk Mall, Sandton ☎011 784 5527, ⓦwww.bluesroom.co.za. Here you'll find some of the best blues in town; quite smart (as you'd expect for Sandton), but also refreshingly mixed and lively.

Cornuti Cradle of Humankind ☎011 659 1622, ⓦwww.thecradle.co.za. Located far out in the rolling hills of the Magaliesberg, this excellent restaurant often hosts mellow jazz evenings.

Morgan's Cat Randburg Waterfront, Randburg ☎011 886 4408. Rock and pop bands play for free to suburban teenagers in a rather synthetic environment.

Roxy's Rhythm Bar 20 Main Rd, Melville ☎011 726 6019. A large, veteran establishment hosting local indie bands; recently it has become a raucous student favourite, so it's worth making sure you really want to see the band that's playing. The rooftop bar is great on summer nights.

Clubs and bars

Johannesburg is the country's most desegregated city, which has improved nightlife greatly. Add to that the stylish fashion sense of many Johannesburg *jollers* (good-timers), and their celebrated love of a party, and you have the main ingredients for a memorable night out. In many parts of the city, particularly the **northern suburbs**, straight drinking pubs and bars have been replaced by combination café/bar/restaurants, open most hours, and commonly located in malls and shopping centres. Avoid pretentious "cigar bars", which tend to be upmarket and artificial, but don't be surprised to find Irish theme pubs and sports bars thronged with local revellers. The adventurous can enjoy some excellent nightlife in the **CBD** and **central suburbs**, though to sample the happening clubs of Hillbrow and Yeoville you're advised to go with a knowledgeable local. For Soweto *shebeens* you can visit during the day, see "Eating" on p.613; at nighttime, only head to the townships in the company of a guide.

CBD and central suburbs

Base On the corner of Twist and Kotze streets, Hillbrow. This club has a heavy sound system and an excellent chill-out balcony overlooking the busy street. At weekends, it attracts a well-dressed, cosmopolitan crowd, and plays soul and *kwaito*, occasionally live; it's in the heart of Hillbrow, so make sure you can get there and away again safely.

Local radio

Given that a large percentage of the population can't afford to own a TV, and many Jo'burgers spend a lot of time in their car, **radio** is big in Gauteng. In fact, listening to the radio is one of the essential ways to pick up news, gossip, and the general Jo'burg vibe, and if you're in town for a few days it's worth flicking around the airwaves to sample some of the local stations. Not all are in English, of course, but don't let that put you off: the following is a selection of the current favourites:

Alex FM 89.1FM. Broadcasting out of the Alexandra township, Alex FM can be picked up in most northern and some eastern suburbs. It focuses on township issues, but avoids excessive worthiness, and plays a fine selection of soul, R&B, reggae, *kwaito* and gospel, making it one of the most musically reliable stations around.

Highveld Stereo 94.7FM. Endless classic mainstream tracks, soft-rock and Celine Dion for the white northern suburbs.

Khaya 96.9FM. For listeners who are too old and boring for YFM: a mellower mix of mainstream *mbaqanga* and jazz, with good information on what's playing live around the city. Can be picked up city-wide.

Metro 96.4FM. Metro offers a good balance of hard-hitting, up-to-the minute news and decent black-oriented music, though with a tendency to slip into schmaltzy soul.

Radio 702 702MW. A well-established local talk-radio station famed for its lively discussion programmes, excellent presenters and news coverage.

Voice of Soweto 87.6FM. Soweto's finest DJs spin some great contemporary sounds. It can only be picked up in Soweto and the adjoining suburbs.

YFM 99.2FM. The station for under-21s. A blistering introduction to the upwardly mobile young black culture of Johannesburg, with wall-to-wall *kwaito*, slick news bulletins and risqué phone-ins.

Carfax 39 Pim St, Newtown ☎011 834 9187. A seriously hip alternative venue, offering performance art, jazz bands and highly rated resident DJs.
Horror Café 15 Becker St, Newtown ☎011 838 6735. A consistent line-up of good DJs and interesting music are found here, including world music on Sat.
Radium Beer Hall 282 Louis Botha Ave, Orange Grove ☎011 728 3866. A long-established pub which draws a cultured, mixed crowd. It also serves food, and revs into action as a club playing a mostly reliable selection of grooves, including *mbaqanga* and *kwaito*. Closed Sun.
Therapy 39A Juta St, Braamfontein. A gay nightclub big on rave, house and techno. Thurs & Sat night only.

Northern suburbs

Buzz 9 On the corner of 7th Street and 3rd Avenue, Melville. A seriously stylish bar, though everyone seems to relax after one or two of the speciality cocktails, and the vibe carries on late into the night.

Calabash Benmore Gardens, Benmore Road, Sandton. A hard-core venue for serious R&B and funk, popular at weekends with a smart, young black set. The mid-week West African theme nights are worth checking out.
Catz Pyjamas 12 Main Rd, Melville. A 24hr bar and food stop; it's nothing special during daylight hours, but gets more interesting when the clubs spill out in the wee small hours.
Cool Runnings 4th Avenue, Melville. A hugely popular Jamaican-themed bar, with drumming sessions and comedy, decent food and lots of Red Stripe beer and rum.
Katzy's at the Grillhouse The Firs Shopping Centre, Oxford Road, Rosebank. A rather middle-of-the-road and very white cigar and piano lounge, with live bands belting out gruesome cover versions.
Ratz 7th Street, Melville. A slightly grungy, but ever-popular Melville bar, which spills onto the street and is usually going strong long into the night.
Sublime 130 11th St, Parkmore ☎011 884 1649, ⊛www.sublime.org.za. A smart dance venue with big name DJs playing tech-house and hip-hop.

Johannesburg festivals

Johannesburg hosts regular **festivals** in nearly every artistic field. These include:

Arts Alive Festival ☏ 011 832 2777. The city's major festival for the performing arts takes place over three weeks at various venues, mainly in the Newtown Cultural Precinct, but also in some townships. Live music dominates, but dance, cabaret and theatre are also well-represented. "Jazz on the Lake", on Zoo Lake, is a mainstay of the festival, and always features major South African artists in front of big crowds. Every Sept.

FNB Vita Dance Umbrella Wits Theatre, Braamfontein ☏ 011 442 8435, ⊛ www .artslink.co.za. Africa's largest festival of dance and choreography. Hosts international companies such as Nederlands Dans Theatre 3, but also acts as the major national platform for work by South African talent such as Robyn Orlin and Boyzie Cekwana. Lasts for three weeks during Feb & March.

Heritage Weekend run by Parktown & Westcliff Heritage Trust (office open Mon–Fri 9am–1pm; ☏ 011 482 3349). A weekend of tours and special events around the magnificent Parktown mansions of the Randlords. Second weekend in Sept.

Joy of Jazz Festival Newtown Cultural Precinct ☏ 011 726 2610, ⊛ www.tmusicman.co.za. A weekend festival in late Aug/early Sept which draws the cream of South African jazz, including Pops Mohamed and Hugh Masekela, along with international guest stars.

Classical music, theatre, dance and film

The Civic Theatre in Braamfontein and the Market Theatre in Newtown are Johannesburg's premier venues for **theatre** and **opera** productions, but there are several other good venues, and the city is blessed with some innovative companies, including the Johannesburg Youth Theatre, while South Africa's **National Symphony Orchestra** (☏ 011 714 4501) performs regularly at Linder Auditorium in Parktown. Johannesburg **dance** is going through a revival: key players are the Moving into Dance Academy, which is rearing new generations of South African choreographers, and the Dance Factory in the Newtown Cultural Precinct, with several dance companies revolving around it.

Civic Theatre Loveday Street, Braamfontein ☏ 011 403 3408. A good mix of both mainstream and more adventurous productions at this impressive, four-stage venue.

The Dance Factory Newtown Cultural Precinct, Newtown ☏ 011 716 3891. An interesting but irregular programme in downtown Jo'burg – check local papers for details.

Market Theatre Newtown Cultural Precinct, Newtown ☏ 011 832 1641. The venue for some of Johannesburg's finest stage productions and top-

grade visiting music acts, celebrated for its innovative community theatre, and the odd costly epic.

Pieter Toerien Theatre Montecasino, Fourways ☏ 011 511 0239. Theatre performing comedies, musicals and touring shows, but also some serious and heavyweight productions.

Theatre on the Square Sandton Square, Sandton ☏ 011 883 8606. One of the few theatres in the northern suburbs, playing lightweight theatre and a handful of mainstream music or cultural acts.

Film

The multi-screen Nu-Metro and Ster-Kinekor **cinemas** control the movie market and can be found all over the city, especially in shopping malls. The *Mail & Guardian* newspaper, published on Fridays, contains good listings, while independent and foreign films are screened at the following:

Hyde Park IMAX Theatre Hyde Park Mall ☏ 011 325 6182. For vast acreage of cinema screen, showing impressive but short films, mostly on nat-

ural history themes.

Northcliff On the corner of Weltevreden and Arbor streets, Blackheath ☏ 011 782 6816. Off D.F.

Malan, just before the N1 highway, showing a good selection of art-house movies.
Rosebank Cinema Nouveau Mall of Rosebank, Rosebank ☎011 880 2866. Presents itself as the *grande dame* of the avant-garde, screening a hip selection to a discerning audience.
Sandton Sandton City, on the corner of Rivonia and Sandton streets, Sandton ☎011 784 3113. A

pleasant cinema with a good programme, surrounded by over twenty other screens showing mainstream movies.
Village Walk Nu-Metro Village Walk Mall, Rivonia Road, Sandton ☎011 883 9558. One arts screen squeezed between the action movies, in a rather nondescript uptown mall.

Shopping

With its vast availability of goods, Johannesburg is a magnet for consumers from all over the subcontinent, who zoom down the highways to stock up before heading back the same day. For visitors, the city is the best place in South Africa to find **arts and crafts**, with excellent flea markets and galleries offering a plethora of goods, some of a very high quality. As the queen of **mall culture**, Johannesburg is also home to over twenty major malls (daily 8am–6pm), most of which are depressingly anonymous. A handful, however (listed below), are so plush and enormous that they merit a visit in their own right.

Malls

Hyde Park Mall Jan Smuts Avenue, Hyde Park. A trendy and upmarket mall, awash with swanky cafés and *haute couture* outlets. The excellent Exclusive Books chain has a good branch here.
Randburg Waterfront Republic Road, Randburg. Built around an artificial lake, this popular if slightly downmarket centre offers restaurants, a flea market and a cinema alongside the clothes shops and chain stores.
Mall of Rosebank On the corner of Baker and Cradock streets, Rosebank. One of the city's nicest

malls, with exclusive boutiques, craft shops and – unusually – outdoor cafés, restaurants and walkways.
Sandton City Shopping Centre On the corner of Sandton Drive and Rivonia Road, Sandton. Linked to the seriously opulent Sandton Square mall, this enormous mall is worth a visit for its sheer size and mind-boggling abundance of shops, cinemas and African art galleries; it also has some good bookshops.

Craft shops and markets

Art Africa 62 Tyrone Ave, Parkview ☎011 486 2052. A good selection of innovative and more familiar crafts, many ingeniously created out of recycled material.
Bright House Bamboo Centre, on the corner of 9th Street and Rustenburg Road ☎011 726 5657. Inspiringly stylish contemporary interior design shop, with an impressive selection of South African products, most items made locally yet with very little sign of "ethnic" influences.
Bruma Lake Flea Market Bruma Lake. A huge, permanent market of mostly African crafts and souvenirs: mainstream and fairly cheap.
M2 Highway CBD. An informal market stretching underneath this major artery, a few blocks south of Anderson Street. Most stalls specialize in *umuthi* medicine, but there are plenty of local crafts as well.
Market Africa Newtown. The city's liveliest flea market, next to the Market Theatre; rifle through

colourful blankets from Mali, Congolese masks and statues, and more. Sat 9am–4pm.
Michael Mount Organic Market Culross Road, off Main Road, Bryanston ☎011 706 3671. Right-on but interesting collection of stalls selling lovely organic food, unusual home crafts and handmade clothes. Thurs & Sat mornings.
Rosebank Rooftop Market Mall of Rosebank, 50 Bath Ave, Rosebank. An entertaining place with an impressive array of cottage-industry crafts and clothes. Sun 9am–5pm.
Rural Craft Shop 42E, Mutual Gardens, Rosebank ☎011 788 5821. A non-profit-making city outlet for various craft co-operatives around South Africa – a refreshing alternative to hard-sell pavement hawkers. Mon–Fri 10am–4pm, Sat 9am–1pm.
Visual Arts Gallery 67 4th Ave, Melville ☎011 482 2370. A fine contemporary gallery in a bright modern house in the heart of Melville.

Bookshops

Books Galore Shop 2B on Main Road, Melville (☎011 726 6502) and 66 Tyrone Ave, Parkview (☎011 486 4198). These friendly shops offer a good selection of secondhand books.
Exclusive Books South Africa's biggest and best bookshop chain, with all the latest titles. There are branches in many malls, but the best shops are in: Hyde Park Corner, Jan Smuts Avenue (☎011 325 4298); Sandton Square (☎011 748 5416); Killarney Mall, Houghton (☎011 646 0931); and The Mall of Rosebank (☎011 447 3028).
Out of Print 78 4th Avenue, Melville ☎011 482 6516. A great little antiquarian and secondhand bookseller, open till 9pm every day of the week, with a tiny internet café at the back of the shop.

Music shops

Johannesburg is a good place to pick up a wide range of **African music**; if you really want to go exploring, the CBD (especially) has dozens of small shops selling cassettes of South African and American sounds. The Musica chain of shops is the most prevalent, and concentrates on soul and rock import CDs, with small selections of local music.

Bizarre Generation On the corner of Rockey and Raymond streets, Yeoville. The best rave music shop in Johannesburg.
Cadence Tropical Calton Centre, CBD ☎011 331 3100. South Africa's finest stockist of Central and West African music, and *the* place to find out about clubs currently playing these sounds.
CD Wherehouse, Mutual Square, Rosebank and Sandton City. Best selection of CDs in Johannesburg, with all the latest local and international sounds, good deals and helpful staff.
Kohinoor 54 Market St, CBD. Excellent vinyl selection, as well as a range of tapes and CDs. The focus is on jazz, but you'll find all manner of South African styles here, ranging from gospel to *maskanda* and *mbaqanga*.

Sport in Jo'burg

Sport is big anywhere you go in South Africa, but in Johannesburg it's an obsession. Here you'll find the biggest stadiums and the biggest teams, and watching a match can be a great experience. The major **cricket** games, including five-day test matches, are played at the Wanderers Stadium, off Corlett Drive, Illovo (☎011 788 1008), though if you look carefully at the touring programme for any visiting international teams you may find fixtures scheduled to be played in Soweto or Alexandra.

The towering Ellis Park in downtown Jo'burg (☎011 402 8644) is a South African **rugby** shrine, particularly since the triumph there of the Springboks in the 1995 World Cup. As well as hosting international fixtures it's also home ground to the provincial Gauteng Lions team. The best way to get there is to make use of the park and ride system which operates for big games, with buses shuttling in from car parks outside the centre.

Despite what you'll hear from white Jo'burgers, however, the big sport is **soccer**, and like any self-respecting football-mad city there's an intense local rivalry fuelled by scandal, intrigue and mutual loathing which keeps squads of sports reporters in work. In Jo'burg (and, more particularly, Soweto), you're either a fan of Kaiser Chiefs or Orlando Pirates, and a local derby draws crowds of 50,000 either to FNB Stadium, on the NASREC road on the outskirts of Soweto, or Ellis Park, scene of a tragic crush at a Chiefs-Pirates game in 2001 in which over fifty fans died. It's perfectly possible to go to a home game of either team: tickets are cheap, the atmosphere is festive but normally trouble-free, and there is safe parking. FNB is quite easy to reach off either the M2 motorway from the eastern suburbs or the Soweto Highway from the centre of the city. Orlando Stadium, in Orlando, Soweto, also hosts major games, though it's more run-down and less safe than the FNB. Tickets for big games can be obtained from Ticket Web (☎083 1400 500).

△ Soweto township tour

Listings

Airlines Air France, Oxford Manor, 196 Oxford Rd, Illovo (☎011 770 1600); American Airlines, Hyde Park Corner, Jan Smuts Avenue (☎011 325 5777); British Airways/Comair, 195 Jan Smuts Ave, Rosebank (☎011 441 8400); KLM Royal Dutch Airlines, Sable Place, 1a Stan Rd, Morningside (☎011 881 9600); Lufthansa, 22 Girton Rd, Parktown (☎011 484 4722); Qantas, 195 Jan Smuts Ave (☎011 441 8550); SA Airlink, South African Airways & SA Express Airways Park, Jones Road, Johannesburg International airport (☎011 978 1111); Virgin Atlantic, Hyde Park (Shopping Centre), Jan Smuts Avenue (☎011 340 3400).
American Express The Zone, 177 Oxford Rd, Rosebank (☎011 880 8382); and Sandton City Shopping Centre, Sandton Dr (☎011 883 1316).
Bureau de change Foreign exchange is available 24hr at Johannesburg International airport, and in banks in all the main shopping malls.
Car rental Standard deals are available from the main companies such as Avis (☎0861 02 1111);

Budget (☎011 392 3929); EuropeCar/Imperial (toll-free ☎0800 011 344); and Tempest (toll-free ☎0800 031 666). For cheaper, local deals try Apex (☎011 402 5150), Comet (☎011 453 0188) or Swans (☎011 975 0799). It's also always worth asking your accommodation if they have any discount arrangements, or you can try ⊛www.hire-car.co.za for good deals.
Emergencies For all emergencies, call ☎10111.
Hospitals State-run hospitals with 24hr casualty departments include Johannesburg Hospital, Parktown (☎011 488 4911); Helen Joseph, Auckland Park (☎011 489 1011); Hillbrow, Hospital Road, Hillbrow (☎011 720 1121); and Baragwanath, Zone 6, Diepkloof, Soweto (☎011 933 8000). Private hospitals include Millpark Hospital, Guild Street, Parktown (☎011 480 5600); and Morningside Medi-Clinic, off Rivonia Road (☎011 282 5000), in Morningside, near Sandton.
Internet cafés Milky Way Internet Café, 206 Times Square Building, corner of Raleigh and

Fortesque streets, Yeoville (Mon–Thurs 9am–8pm, Fri 8.30am–midnight, Sat 9am–7pm; ☎011 487 1340, ⊛www.milkyway.co.za); The Net, Shop #1, 37 4th Ave, Parkhurst (☎011 442 8753, ⊛thenet@icon.co.za); there are also three terminals at the back of Out of Print bookshop, 78 4th Avenue, Melville (☎011 482 6516).

Poste restante Avoid the main poste restante post office on Jeppe Street, as it's in an unsafe part of town. Make arrangements instead with your accommodation, or use Amex.

Swimming & gyms Public swimming pools around Johannesburg are not always kept in great repair – one exception is the superb, outdoor,

Olympic-sized Ellis Park pool (Sept–March Mon–Fri 6.30am–9pm, Sat & Sun 6.30am–6pm). Also worth considering is the chain of Virgin Active gyms around the city (☎0860 200 911, www.virginactive.co.za); some hotels hold vouchers for single visits to the gyms, or there is a single visit fee of R50.

Taxis Maxi Taxis, Yeoville (☎011 648 1212), rank in Cavendish Street, and are the most reliable for almost all parts of town. Otherwise Rose Radio (☎011 403 9625 or 011 403 0000), Good Hope (☎011 725 6431) and Metro (☎011 484 7975) cover most of the city. Taxis often also wait outside the large hotels.

Around Johannesburg

Johannesburgers wanting to get away from it all tend to head northwest in the direction of the **Magaliesberg mountains**, stretching from Pretoria in the east to Rustenberg in the west. Don't expect to see a horizon of impressive peaks: much of the area is private farmland running across rolling countryside, although there are some impressive *kloofs*, as well as refreshingly wide vistas after the crowded roads and high walls of the big city.

Unprepossessing as the mountain range might be, a series of caves on their southeastern (Johannesburg) side hold some of the world's most important information about human evolution stretching back some three and a half million years. These caves, including the renowned Sterkfontein Cave, are now protected as part of the **Cradle of Humankind**, one of South Africa's first World Heritage Sites.

The Magaliesberg has a well-developed tourist network of small arts and crafts workshops, game parks, outdoor activities and places to stay. Most of these, both in the Cradle of Humankind and beyond, are part of either the **Crocodile Ramble** or the **Magalies Meander**, two tourist routes well-promoted in the area. South of the city, the **Suikerbosrand Nature Reserve**, 40km from Johannesburg, is the biggest and best nature reserve in Gauteng, offering interesting archeology and good hikes.

The Cradle of Humankind

Covering some 47,000 hectares, the Cradle of Humankind, now a World Heritage Site, is the name given to the area in which a series of dolomitic caves have in the last fifty years or so produced nearly forty per cent of the world's hominid fossil discoveries. Given its accessibility and the richness of the finds, it has now arguably overtaken Tanzania's Olduvai Gorge as Africa's (and therefore the world's) most important paleolontological site.

As yet, the tourist facilities are few: many of the caves are fragile, and jealously protected by the scientists working on them. However, you can see inside the famous **Sterkfontein Caves** and if you're particularly interested in the subject, excellent specialized paleontological tours are available (see box on p.621). Elsewhere within the Cradle are largely unrelated attractions, such as the **Rhino and Lion Nature Reserve** and the **Kromdraai Wonder Cave**.

Mrs Ples and friends

Embedded in the dolomitic rock within a dozen caves in the area now called the Cradle of Humankind are the fossilized remains of **hominids** which lived in South Africa up to 3.3 million years ago. Samples of fossilized pollen, plant material and animal bones also found in the caves indicate that the area was once a tropical rain forest inhabited by giant monkeys, long-legged hunting hyenas and sabre-toothed cats.

Quite when hominids arrived on the scene isn't certain, but scientists now believe that the human lineage split from apes in Africa around five to six million years ago. The oldest identified group of hominids is *Australopithecus*, a bipedal, small-brained form of man. The first *Australopithecus* discovery in South Africa was in 1924 when Professor Raymond Dart discovered the **Taung child** in what is now Northwest Province. In 1936, australopithecine fossils were first found in the Sterkfontein caves, and in 1947 Dr Robert Broom excavated a nearly complete skull which he first called *Plesianthropus transvaalensis* ("near-man" of the Transvaal), later confirmed as a 2.6 million-year-old *Australopithecus africanus*. Identified as a female, she was nicknamed "**Mrs Ples**", and for many years she was the closest thing the world had to what is rather confusingly dubbed "**the missing link**".

A number of even older fossils have since been discovered at Sterkfontein and nearby caves, along with evidence of several other genus and species, including *Australopithecus robustus*, dating from between one and two million years ago, and *Homo ergaster*, possibly the immediate predecesor of *Homo sapiens*, who used stone tools and fire.

If you're keen to learn more about this fascinating topic and want to visit some of the caves and dig sites not open to the general public, excellent **tours** are run by *Palaeo-Tours* (☎011 837 6660, ☎082 804 2899, ⊛www.palaeotours.com), run by Colin Menter, a palaeontologist working at the University of Witwatersrand.

It's hard to get to the Cradle of Humankind by public transport. In a **car**, travel west out of Johannesburg on the R47 (Hendrik Potgieter Road) or M5 (D.F. Malan/Beyers Naude Drive), follow the N14 until the R563 junction. A few kilometres northwest along the R563 is a right turn which will take you to the Sterkfontein Caves turn-off. The other attractions in the area are further along this road.

Sterkfontein Caves

The best-known of the Cradle of Humankind sites are the **Sterkfontein Caves** (Tues–Sun 9am–5pm; ☎011 956 6342; R12), believed to have been inhabited by pre-human primates who lived here up to 3.5 million years ago. They first came to European attention in 1896, when an Italian lime prospector, Gulgimo Martinaglia, stumbled upon them. Martinaglia was only interested in the bat droppings, and promptly stripped them out, thus destroying the caves' dolomite formation. Between 1936 and 1951, archeologist Dr Robert Broom excavated the caves and in 1947 found the skull of a female hominid (nicknamed "Mrs Ples") that was over two-and-a-half million years old. In 1995, another archeologist, Ronald Clarke, found "Little Foot", the bones of a 3,000,000-year-old walking hominid, with big toes that functioned like our thumbs do today. The latest discovery, in 1998, was of the oldest complete *Australopithecus* skeleton yet found in the world, reckoned to be 3.3 million years old.

Fairly well-informed, if rather short **guided tours** of the cave leave every hour (departing on the half-hour) and take you around the main features.

Kromdraai Wonder Cave and the Rhino and Lion Nature Reserve

The only other cave with open public access is the **Kromdraai Wonder Cave** (daily 8am–5pm; R25), located on the edge of the Rhino and Lion Nature Reserve to the northeast of Sterkfontein. Also mined for lime in the 1890s, this cave hasn't revealed any paleontological finds, and the main focus of attention are the extraordinary stalactites, stalagmites and rimstone pools to be found in a huge underground chamber. Once you've descended into the cave by a lift, carefully placed lighting and marked trails make the experience theatrical and unashamedly commercial. For a few more thrills, you can **abseil** into the cave rather than use the lift – make arrangements with Wild Cave Adventures (☎011 956 6197 or 082 632 1718). To get there, the easier route is through the Rhino & Lion Nature Reserve, although you do have to pay the normal entrance charge to the reserve; the longer route is on a rough dirt road on the left before you get to the nature reserve.

The fourteen square-kilometre **Rhino and Lion Nature Reserve** (daily 8am–5pm; R30), is really more a safari park than anything resembling a wilderness game reserve as found in other parts of South Africa, but it is the principal place in the area for seeing large mammals. The main section of the reserve has white rhino, wildebeest, hartebeest and giraffe roaming free while the Lion and Predator Camp has several large enclosures containing lions, cheetahs and wild dogs. Elsewhere, there's a vulture hide for seeing Cape vultures, a series of hippo pools and a breeding centre; it's also possible to **stay** in a self-catering chalet sleeping four if you pre-book (❷). Game drives, horse trails and mountain-bike trails are also all available – contact the Conserv Booking and Information Office (see below). They can also organize a visit to the nearby **Old Kromdraai Gold Mine**, the second-oldest mine on the Witwatersrand, where you can follow the original mining tunnel 150m into the hillside.

Practicalities

A dedicated **information centre** for the Cradle of Humankind is due to open sometime in late 2002, located on the R563 a little beyond the turn to the Sterkfontein Caves. Alternatively, useful information on tours, local adventure activities and accommodation in the area can be gathered at the Conserv Booking and Information Office (daily 8am–7pm; ☎011 957 0034) located 3km from the Sterkfontein Caves.

It is possible to **stay** in or near the Cradle of Humankind: the *Cradle Forest Camp* in the private Cradle Game Reserve (☎011 957 0242 or 083 250 2527, ⓦwww.thecradle.co.za; ❸) has self-catering two-person chalets, and the restaurant here, *Cornuti*, is renowned for its fine food, modern, minimalist decor and great views. More upmarket is *Toadbury Hall* (☎011 659 0335, ⓦwww.toadburyhall.co.za; ❺), a colonial-style country lodge, while the rather old-fashioned *Aloe Ridge Hotel* (☎011 957 2070; ❹ for dinner, bed & breakfast) has the unique attraction of a 25-inch telescope and a resident astronomer. You can come here simply for a meal, or stay in a specially erected Zulu village of grass huts (❷). Other accommodation options include the camp in the Rhino and Lion Nature Reserve (see above) and the many hotels and guesthouses advertised through the Magalies Meander and Crocodile Ramble (see opposite).

Magalies Meander and Crocodile Ramble

An increasingly popular way of promoting different localities in South Africa is to describe some kind of **route** through them; with a huge population on their doorstep, the residents of the Magaliesberg and adjoining areas have adopted this approach with enthusiasm. At the information centre on the banks of the Crocodile River in the village of **Muldersdrift**, barely beyond the suburbs of northwest Jo'burg, you can pick up a hefty brochure listing all kinds of attractions and places to visit on the **Crocodile Ramble** (T011 662 2810, Wwww.crocodileramble.co.za). You could only ever hope to visit a fraction of the places listed, and it's worth remembering that much of it is aimed at locals escaping for the weekend rather than tourists who have the chance to explore other parts of the country: highlights of the route include a number of artists' workshops, including the Swazi glass factory of Nwgenya.

Meanwhile, to the northwest of the area covered by the Crocodile Ramble, a group of local attractions known as the Magalies Meander has as its focal point Magaliesburg Village. Named after Mohali Mohale, a chief of the Po clan of the Ndebele people, the village is functional, though not wildly attractive, providing stressed city-dwellers with accommodation and facilities amid the fresh mountain air. You can pick up a map and brochure for the meander from Magaliesburg Information and Reservations (daily 9am–4pm; T014 577 1733), located in the Magaliesburg Mall on Rustenburg Road in the village.

Magaliesburg Village lies on the R24, west of Krugersdorp. For a day-trip from Johannesburg, it's sometimes possible to travel here by **train**: the Magalies Express (T011 888 1155) runs most weekends, and the fares for the three-hour return journey are quite reasonable at around R100. A more unusual mode of transport locally are the **balloon** flights run by Bill Harrop's "Original" Balloon Safaris (T011 705 3201 or 082 379 5296 Etravelsa@iafrica.com), which take off from a site between Magaliesberg Village and Hartbeespoort Dam.

Accommodation

If you're planning a jaunt up here, be sure to book **accommodation** ahead, especially at weekends. The nicest (and priciest) place to stay by far is *Mount Grace*, Rustenburg Rd (T014 577 1350, Wwww.grace.co.za; ❺–❽), a hotel magnificently located on a hilltop, and offering immaculate and stylish rooms. The restaurants here are superb, and classical concerts are held outside on the last Saturday of every month during the summer. For impressive B&B, *Out of Africa* (T014 577 1126 or 082 900 8205, Wwww.goblins.co.za; ❹) offers luxury cottages by the river, tastefully decked out with antique furniture and original art. Alternatively, you can get a better feel of the rolling, open landscapes of the countryside at *Wind in the Willows* (T014 557 3401 or 083 657 3401, Emwwitw@mweb.co.za; ❸), a well-run guesthouse set on a horse stud 15km west of the village along the R509, from which it's signposted, with good trails nearby for horse-riding or hiking.

Suikerbosrand Nature Reserve

Though hardly in the same league as the epic parks of Kruger and the like, the **Suikerbosrand Nature Reserve** (Mon–Fri 7.15am–4pm, Sat & Sun 7am–5pm; R20 per person, R10 per vehicle), south of Johannesburg, is nonetheless attractive, and easy to reach from the city. The beautiful Suikerbosrand mountain range dominates the reserve, but you'll find gentle grassland plains too, with antelope, zebra and wildebeest, and even the odd cheetah and leopard.

The **visitor centre**, at the entrance to the reserve, can supply maps and guidebooks. Next door, the **Diepkloof Farm Museum** is worth a visit, as careful renovation has ensured that the farm buildings look pretty much as they did when they were first built in 1850. The farm was worked by one Gabriel

Marais, a veteran of the Great Trek, but it was burnt by British soldiers in the Anglo-Boer War, and remained neglected until its renovation in the 1970s. Most of the exhibits are aimed at Afrikaner children, in the hope of interesting them in their rapidly disappearing rural culture. However, other brief displays dwell on the extensive sixteenth- to nineteenth-century settlements of Sotho and Tswana people excavated nearby.

You can **explore the reserve** on foot or by car, following a network of trails. Several hiking trails include overnight accommodation in camps (book at the visitor centre; ☎011 904 3933). Alternatively, you can book the very basic meditation hut, 18km from the visitors' centre; there's no electricity, but it's definitely quiet and undisturbed.

To get to the reserve and farm, take the N3 south of Johannesburg, and turn right onto the R550. The turn to the reserve is a few kilometres along the road, on your left.

Pretoria and around

Gauteng's two major cities are just 50km apart, but could hardly be more different. **PRETORIA**, or ePitoli as it is known in the townships, has throughout much of its history been the epitome of staid traditionalism, with its graceful government buildings, wide avenues of purple flowering jacarandas, and staunchly Boer farming origins. Yet, although South Africa's administrative capital was long regarded as a bastion of **Afrikanerdom**, with its notorious supreme court and massive prison, things are changing fast. Ever since the nation's re-acceptance into the international arena, Pretoria has become increasingly cosmopolitan, with a substantial diplomatic community living in Arcadia and Hatfield, east of the city centre. Furthermore, most Pretorians are not Afrikaner, but Sotho and Ndebele, and the change of government has brought many more well-educated and well-paid blacks into the ranks of civil servants living in the capital. The city's Afrikaner community is hardly monolithic, either: as well as the stereotypical khaki-shorted rednecks, there are thousands of students, an active art scene and a thriving Afrikaans gay and lesbian community.

Pretoria is close enough to Johannesburg's airport to provide a practical alternative base in Gauteng, though don't fall into the blithe assumption that Pretoria is crime-free. The main attractions are that it feels safer and less spread out than Johannesburg, there are more conventional sites, some of which are worth seeing, and the **nightlife** of Hatfield and Brooklyn is energetic and fun.

Some history

Unlike Johannesburg, Pretoria developed at a leisurely pace from its humble origins as a **Boer farming community** on the fertile land around the Apies River. When the city was founded in 1855 by **Marthinus Wessel Pretorius**, who named it after his father, Andries Pretorius, it was intended to be a unifying hub around which the new South African Republic (ZAR) would prosper. Embodying the Afrikaner conviction that the land they took was God-given, Pretoria's first building was a church. The town was then laid out in a grid of streets wide enough for teams of oxen brought in by farmers to turn corners.

In 1860, the city was proclaimed the capital of the new ZAR, the result of tireless efforts by Stephanus Schoeman to unite the squabbling statelets of the Transvaal. From this base, the settlers continued their campaigns against local African peoples, bringing thousands into service, particularly on farms. Infighting also continued amongst the settlers, and violent skirmishes between faction leaders were common. These leaders bought most of the best land, resulting in the dispossession and embitterment of many white trekkers, and also in the large-scale massacre of the wild animals of the region, particularly its elephants.

The British annexed Pretoria in 1877, and investment followed in their wake. Although the town prospered and grew, farmer **Paul Kruger**, who was determined not to be subjugated by the British again, mobilized *commandos* of Afrikaner farmers to drive them out. This resulted in the first Anglo-Boer War (1877–81). After defeat at Majuba on the Natal border, the colonial government abandoned the war and ceded **independence** in 1884. Paul Kruger became ZAR president, and ruled until 1903. However, his mission to keep the ZAR Boer was confounded by the discovery of **gold** in the Witwatersrand, which precipitated an unstoppable flood of foreigners. Kruger's policy of taxing the newcomers, while retaining the Boer monopoly on political power, worked for a while. Most of the elegant buildings of Church Square were built with mining revenues, while the Raadsaal (parliament) remained firmly in Boer hands. At the same time, the ZAR's military arsenal grew, largely thanks to imported German weapons.

ZAR independence ended with the second Anglo-Boer War (1899–02), but despite the brutality of the conflict, Pretoria remained unscathed. With the creation of the **Union of South Africa** in 1910, the city became the administrative capital of the entire country. In 1913, Sir Herbert Baker built the epic Union Buildings to house the civil service, and some ministries, including the office of the president, are still there today.

In 1928, the government laid the foundations of Pretoria's industry by establishing the **Iron and Steel Industrial Corporation** (Iscor), which rapidly generated a whole series of related and service industries. These, together with the civil service, ensured white Pretoria's quiet, insular prosperity. Meanwhile, increasing landlessness amongst blacks drove many of them into the city's burgeoning **townships**. Marabastad and Atteridgeville are the oldest, and Mamelodi is the biggest and poorest.

After the introduction of apartheid by the National Party in 1948 (see p.833), Pretoria acquired a hated reputation amongst the country's black population. Its supreme court and central prison were notorious, as the source of the laws and regulations that made their lives a nightmare.

Mandela's inauguration at the Union Buildings in 1994 was the symbolic new beginning for Pretoria's political redemption. Through the 1990s, the stages of South Africa's revolution could be seen as clearly in Pretoria as anywhere else: the gradual replacement of the diehards from institutions like the army and civil service, new faces in almost all the old government offices, the return of foreign representation, aid agencies and NGOs, the influx of students and the change in demographics of the city-centre suburbs. While the newcomers have absorbed a good deal of the sense of decorum which was always a hallmark of Pretoria, even in the apartheid years, the capital city is these days quite clearly livening up with the creativity and vibrancy they also bring.

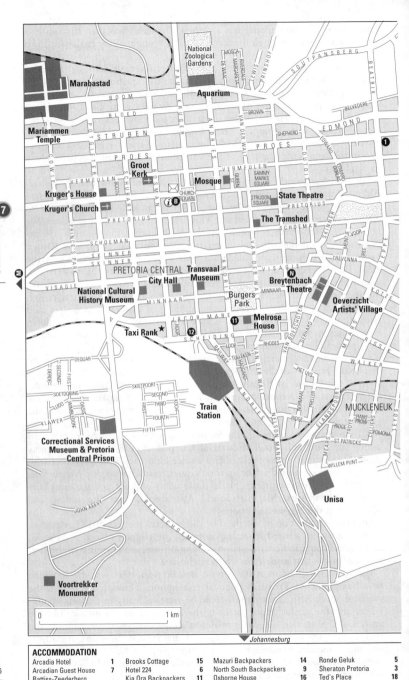

Marabastad

Mariammen
Temple

Kruger's House

Kruger's Church

National
Zoological
Gardens

Aquarium

Groot
Kerk

Mosque

State Theatre

The Tramshed

PRETORIA CENTRAL

City Hall

Transvaal
Museum

Breytenbach
Theatre

Oeverzicht
Artists' Village

National Cultural
History Museum

Burgers
Park

Melrose
House

Taxi Rank

Train
Station

MUCKLENEUK

Correctional Services
Museum & Pretoria
Central Prison

Unisa

Voortrekker
Monument

0   1 km

Johannesburg

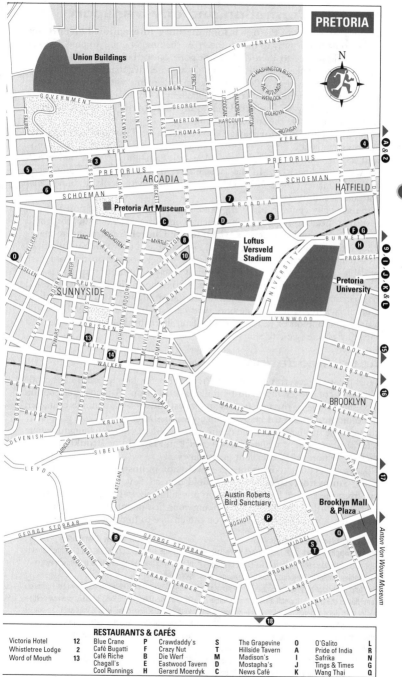

PRETORIA

N

Union Buildings

GAUTENG

Pretoria Art Museum

Loftus Versveld Stadium

Pretoria University

SUNNYSIDE

ARCADIA

HATFIELD

BROOKLYN

Austin Roberts Bird Sanctuary

Brooklyn Mall & Plaza

Anton Van Wouw Museum

		RESTAURANTS & CAFÉS					
Victoria Hotel	**12**	Blue Crane	**P**	Crawdaddy's	**S**	The Grapevine	**O**	O'Galito	**L**
Whistletree Lodge	**2**	Café Bugatti	**F**	Crazy Nut	**T**	Hillside Tavern	**A**	Pride of India	**R**
Word of Mouth	**13**	Café Riche	**B**	Die Werf	**M**	Madison's	**I**	Safrika	**N**
		Chagall's	**E**	Eastwood Tavern	**D**	Mostapha's	**J**	Tings & Times	**G**
		Cool Runnings	**H**	Gerard Moerdyk	**C**	News Café	**K**	Wang Thai	**Q**

Arrival, information and city transport

The nearest airport to Pretoria is **Johannesburg International airport** (see p.584) some 50km away to the southeast. At the time of going to press, the airport shuttle service to Pretoria had just gone out of business, but it's likely a replacement service will fill the gap. Otherwise, negotiate a taxi fare (it's unlikely to be less than R200) or make arrangements with wherever you're staying. If you're arriving by **train** you'll alight at Pretoria station (℡012 334 8470), designed by Sir Herbert Baker, to the south of the city centre; **intercity buses** stop beside the station building.

The main point of **information** for Pretoria – or **Tshwane**, as the greater metropolitan area is known – is the Tourist Information Centre on the southwest corner of Church Square (Mon–Fri 8am–4pm; ℡012 308 8909, ⓦwww.pta-online.co.za). In the same office you'll find a travel agent called Travel the Planet (℡012 337 4337), who will help with booking tours, transport and accommodation.

Pretoria's city centre is easily explored on foot, but public transport is useful if you are heading slightly further afield. For journeys to the suburbs, you'll need the municipal **bus** services, which start in **Church Square** (where there's a bus information office ℡012 308 0839), and spread outwards. You buy tickets – which are never more than a few rand – when you get on; timetables are available from Church Square, the buses themselves and from pharmacies.

The best place to catch **minibus taxis** is from the corner of Jacob Maré and Bosman streets, just north of the railway station, though you can hail them from anywhere. As in Johannesburg, you can't hail metered **taxis**, but you'll usually find one on or near Church Square; alternatively, cabs can be booked ahead by phone (see p.638).

Accommodation

With plenty of government custom, Pretoria has no shortage of soulless modern hotel complexes, most run by multinational chains. A much nicer option is to stay at one of the few **hotels** and **guesthouses** with genuine character, some of which are listed below. Unlike Johannesburg, you can feel reasonably comfortable staying close to the centre, although there isn't much nightlife here – for that, you might prefer to base yourself in **Hatfield** or **Brooklyn**, where there are a number of excellent guesthouses.

Backpackers can choose from a good selection of **hostels**, most of which are in the **Sunnyside**, **Arcadia** and **Hatfield** districts. Few, if any, offer free pick-ups from the airport, but their transfers are still likely to be the cheapest you'll find. As with Jo'burg, it's worth booking your first night before you arrive, to make transport easier and to give you the chance to find your bearings.

Backpacker lodges

Kia Ora Backpackers 257 Jacob Maré St ℡012 322 4803, ⓦwww.kia-ora.co.za. The most central backpacker hostel in Pretoria, close to Museum Mall and next door to Melrose House. While not as convivial as the others, it's still a neat, comfortable hostel with decent doubles and average dorms. Food is available from the gloomy public bar where the TV is on constantly. ❶

Mazuri Backpackers 503 Reitz St, Sunnyside ℡ & ℗012 343 7782, ⓦwww.mazuri.freeserve.com. Few frills but a friendly, easy-going hostel in the once vibey but now slightly downmarket Sunnyside suburb. Dorms and doubles are spread across two houses and various tacked-on extensions. ❶

North South Backpackers 355 Glyn St, Hatfield ℡012 362 0989 or 082 533 2837, ⓦwww.north-southbackpackers.com. Now established as one of Pretoria's best backpacker hostels, this neat, well-run place is in a good location for the lively Hatfield nightlife. It offers dorms and plenty of doubles in a large, quiet suburban house with a great garden and pool. ❶

Pretoria Backpackers 425 Farenden St, Clydesdale ☏ 012 343 9754 or 083 302 1976 ⓦ www.ptabackpackers.co.za. A more upmarket backpacker place with plenty of doubles as well as smallish dorms spread over two lovely old houses with wooden floors, original features and a relaxing garden *stoep*. Massages and beauty treatment are available, while the knowledgeable owner, François, is a great Pretoria enthusiast and runs a useful travel centre for local tours and onward travel. ❶

Word of Mouth 430 Reitz St, Sunnyside ☏ 012 343 7499, ⓦ www.wordofmouth.co.za. A colourful, welcoming but slightly downmarket hostel not far from the centre, with some wooden Wendy houses in the garden serving as doubles. ❶

Hotels, guesthouses and B&Bs

Arcadia Hotel 515 Proes St ☏ 012 326 9311, ⓦ www.arcadiahotel.co.za. A centrally located business-oriented hotel; it's a little over-priced, especially as there's no pool, but the rooms are comfortable and the restaurant reliable. ❹

Arcadian Guest House 870 Arcadia St ☏ 012 342 4588 or 082 787 5274, ⓦ www.arcadianguesthouse.co.za. A classic old house filled with antique furniture, with tip-top modern facilities such as a pool and cable TV. It's also close to Hatfield nightlife and the embassy district. ❸

Battiss-Zeederberg Guesthouse 3 Fook Island, 92 20th St, Menlo Park ☏ 012 460 7318 or 083 271 0819). Very comfortable B&B accommodation in the original home of eccentric artist Walter Battiss. Brightly painted floors, unusual decorations and a distinctly Greek feel. ❸

Brooks Cottage 283 Brooks St, Brooklyn (☏ 012 362 3150 or 082 448 3902, ebrookscottage @iafrica.com). A rather cute Cape Dutch home in the upmarket Brooklyn area with three rooms, one of which is part of a self-catering unit. ❸

Hotel 224 On the corner of Leyds and Schoeman streets ☏ 012 440 5281, ⓦ www.hotel224.com. Single and double rooms in this dated-looking but fairly characterful budget hotel near the Union Buildings, with a restaurant and bar attached and safe parking. ❷

La Maison 235 Hilda St, Hatfield ☏ 012 430 4341, ⓦ www.lamaison.co.za. A very pleasant guesthouse with lovely gardens, six Victorian-styled rooms full of antiques, and an outstanding restaurant. ❹

Osborne House 82 Anderson St, Brooklyn ☏ 012 362 2334 or 083 302 1049, ⓔ osbornehouse @worldonline.co.za. A wonderfully elegant guesthouse set in a restored Edwardian manor house with lovely furniture, big windows, wooden floors and a pleasant secluded pool. ❹

Ronde Geluk 570 Pretorius St, Arcadia ☏ 012 341 9221 or 082 965 7995. Hidden away among some ugly apartment blocks in central Pretoria, these charming self-contained thatched cottages are beautifully decorated and sleep two to four. ❷

Sheraton Pretoria 643 Church St, Arcadia ☏ 012 429 9999, ⓦ www.fourpoints.com. This fine five-star hotel boasts all the usual upmarket Sheraton touches, but most importantly has the best views of the Union Buildings. If you can't afford a room with the view, head to the *Union Gardens Lounge* beside *Tiffens Bar & Lounge* for high tea. ❻

Ted's Place 961 Wagon Wheel Ave, Wapadrand ☏ 012 807 2803, ⓦ www.teds-place.za.net. One of the nicest places to stay on the outskirts of Pretoria, this large, elegant hilltop house offers friendly B&B with great views over the city and the Magaliesberg. ❷

That's It Guest Home 5 Brecher St, Clydesdale ☏ 012 344 3404, or 082 781 7230, ⓦ www.gauteng.com/thatsit. A neat, unelaborate, reasonably priced B&B in a family home with four rooms and a relaxing garden and pool. ❷

Victoria Hotel On the corner of Scheiding and Paul Kruger streets ☏ 012 323 6052, ⓕ 012 323 0843. This historic building opposite the railway station was once the railway workers' bar; now it offers plush accommodation and is often filled with affluent travellers taking luxury trains to Cape Town. ❹

Whistletree Lodge 1267 Whistletree Drive, Queenswood ☏ 012 333 9915 or 082 446 8858, ⓦ www.whistletree.freeservers.com. A classy, upmarket designer guesthouse, with beautiful antiques, eclectic artwork and stylish furniture. The facilities include a pool, sauna and private balconies. ❺

The City

Pretoria's city centre is a compact grid of wide, busy streets, easily and comparatively safely explored on foot. Its central hub is **Church Square**, where you can see some fascinating architecture, and there are other historic buildings and museums close by around the **Museum Mall**. To the north lie the vast **Zoological Gardens**, while the Arcadia district is the site of the city's famous **Union Buildings**. Away from the centre, **Hatfield**, close to Pretoria University, is where students and yuppies throng the latest bars and restaurants, as well as being the home of Pretoria's diplomats, who live in the swankiest houses in town. On the southern fringes of the city is the remarkable **Voortrekker Monument**, as close as the Afrikaner race have to a sacred site. You need to travel 15km east out of town to find the sprawling township of **Mamelodi**; Pretoria's other major township, **Atteridgeville**, is equally far out of town to the west, off the N4, or R104, on the way to the Hartbeesport Dam and Sun City.

Church Square and the city centre

The heart of Pretoria is undoubtedly **Church Square**, surrounded by dramatic and important buildings, and a place where you can at least try to put South Africa's complex history into perspective. It was here that Boer farmers *outspanned* their oxen when they came into town for the quarterly Nagmaal (Holy Communion) of the Dutch Reformed Church, turning the square temporarily into a campsite. Today this spot continues to be a meeting point for Pretorians of all races, many of whom you'll see lounging on the grass in the sun, gathering to protest with placards and singing, or simply watching it all go on while sipping coffee at the cultured *Café Riche*.

Nearly every important white meeting, protest or takeover the city has known happened in Church Square; the ZAR Vierkleur ("four colours") flag was lowered here in 1877 to make way for the Union Jack, only to rise again in 1881, after the British eviction from the republic; the British flag flew again in 1900 but was lowered for the last time in 1910; Paul Kruger was proclaimed head of state in the square four times, and 30,000 crammed it in 1904 for his memorial service. Such historical resonances are viewed differently by Pretoria's black community, and the square's central **statue of Paul Kruger** – the work of Afrikaner sculptor Anton Van Wouw – is for many an unwanted relic of a dismal past. Van Wouw had to work fast: Kruger hated posing and the sculptor had little time with him. Nevertheless he still managed to produce this frighteningly miserable representation, set above four rugged Voortrekker archetypes; today, the pigeons which squat on his top hat provide a suitably subversive touch.

The Continental-style square is surrounded on all sides by some of the most impressive buildings in South Africa. Look out for the old **Raadsaal** (parliament) on the southwest corner of the square, built in neo-Renaissance style in 1891, and still exuding the bourgeois respectability yearned for by the parliamentarians of the ZAR. Across the narrow side-street from this is the Capitol Theatre, rarely used now as a performance space but home to Tshwane Craft Market. Next door to this is the **Netherlands Bank Building**, now home of the tourist information office. Unbelievably, it took a gathering of 10,000 people in 1975 and five years of deliberation to reverse a decision to demolish this building and its two neighbours. The Art Nouveau **Café Riche** (see p.636), on the corner of Church Street, adds a sophisticated and cultured touch to the day-to-day business of the area; it's a handy source of information, and you can buy a booklet or rent a cassette player explaining the history and architecture of the square.

On the opposite side of Church Street is the imposing **General Post Office**, beside which is a **Stamp Museum** (Mon–Fri 7.30am–4pm; free), which displays over half a million stamps, including a rare Cape Triangle of 1853. The grandiose **Palace of Justice**, on the northwest side of the square, was started in 1897 and, half-completed, was used as a hospital for British troops during the second Anglo-Boer War. After its completion in 1902, the building was home to the Transvaal Supreme Court for many years and was the location of the Rivonia Trial in 1963–64, when Nelson Mandela and other leaders of the ANC were sentenced to life imprisonment. Recent restoration work has revealed and repaired the splendid facade and balconies, although the new court is an ugly box sitting squatly in a street behind the Palace. Next to this is the **Reserve Bank** building, designed in distinctive style by Sir Herbert Baker (see p.602). Other buildings of note around the eastern and northern side of the square include the **Tudor Chambers**, built in neo-Tudor style in 1904, and the Neoclassical **Standard Bank** building on the site of the old Grand Hotel.

Sammy Marks Square and around

Moving east from Church Square, Church Street takes you towards Sammy Marks Square. Just before you get there, a left turn into Queen Street and a further left turn along a passage-way halfway down the block reveals the unexpected site of a bright white **mosque** sitting askew of its surroundings so as to face Mecca. Pretoria's Muslims, who reportedly got on well with Kruger, acquired the site in 1896, and the current building was constructed in 1927 by Cape artisans. The mosque is now hemmed in by ugly tower blocks, but is somehow all the more indomitable for that.

Garish **Sammy Marks Square** itself is named after the founder of South African Breweries (SAB), who was a patron of the city. Dominated by modern shopping malls filled with chain stores, the only thing worth checking out here is the excellent **library** (Mon–Fri 8am–5.50pm, Sat 8am–12.50pm; ☎012 313 8956), geared to adult education, with every available space decked out in Pretoria's trademark purple.

Across Church Street is **Strijdom Square**, so named because it was the location of a vast and horrific bust of the man himself, encased in a modernistic arch. Prime minister from 1954 to 1958, Strijdom strongly supported apartheid and was a firm believer in "white supremacy". Dramatically, forty years to the day after the statue was completed on 31 May, 1961, a structural fault (or divine intervention, depending on your point of view) caused it to collapse. While many would like to see it remain a symbolic pile of rubble, others say it's high time the statue was replaced by a memorial to the seven victims of the random shooting at minibus taxis here by a right-wing delinquent namesake, Barend Strijdom, in 1993.

Paul Kruger's House and around

To find **Paul Kruger's House** (Mon–Fri 8.30am–4.30pm, Sat, Sun & public holidays 9am–4.30pm; R10), head west along Church Street from Church Square, crossing Bosman and Schubart streets. Kruger's House was built in 1884 by the English-speaking Charles Clark, described by Kruger as one of his "tame Englishmen", who mixed his cement with milk instead of water. Inside, the museum is rather dull, though you may find some interest in Kruger's effects, such as his large collection of spittoons. The *stoep* (verandah) is the most famous feature of the house, for here the old president would sit and chat to any white who chose to join him. Out at the back is Kruger's private railway coach, built in 1898, which he used during the second Anglo-Boer War.

Opposite is a characteristically grim Reformed church known as **Kruger's Church**. The **Groot Kerk** (**Great Church**), on the corner of Vermeulen and Bosman streets, is more impressive; its strikingly ornate tower is one of the finest in the country.

Burgers Park and the Museum Mall

South from Church Square lies a precinct of museums and open spaces that has drawn complimentary comparisons with Washington DC's Smithsonian Institute. On Jacob Maré Street between Andries and Van der Walt streets is the restful **Burgers Park** (daily 8am–6pm; free), named after ineffective ZAR president Thomas Burgers, who ruled between 1873 and 1877. The park has a good botanic garden, a quirkily designed curator's house and a pavilion at its centre, once the preserve of brass bands and all-white tea parties, but now multiracial and a good place to relax.

Opposite the park's southern border, **Melrose House**, 275 Jacob Maré St (Tues–Sun 10am–5pm; R3), is an overdecorated Victorian house with a wonderful conservatory, interesting exhibitions and a great African arts and crafts shop. The house was built in 1884 for local businessman George Heys, who made his money running mailcoach services. Lord Kitchener used the house during the second Anglo-Boer War, and the treaty of Vereeniging that ended hostilities was signed inside. Outside, a sumptuous tea garden serves cakes and scones, light meals and, on certain days, hearty South African lunches such as *bobotie* and savoury rice.

Head west of Burger Park along Minnaar Street, and then turn right into Paul Kruger Street and past a huge whale skeleton for the grand **Transvaal Museum** (Mon–Sat 9am–5pm, Sun 11am–5pm; R8), Pretoria's oldest museum and centrepiece of the Northern Flagship Institution, the collective name for Pretoria's main museums. Dedicated to natural history, the museum has plenty of stuffed animals, models of dinosaurs and wonderful fossil remains, some over one million years old. This is a good place to come if your interest in man's origins has been stirred by the discoveries of the nearby Cradle of Humankind (see p.620): alongside a bronze bust of Robert Broom staring into the three-million-year-old eye sockets of Mrs Ples are an assortment of fossilized discoveries and various models and reconstructions of early hominid life. Nearby is a selection of stuffed animals, never particularly inspiring when many of the animals can be seen in real life in game reserves not too far away, though beside the paleontological displays, the various stuffed primates are particularly relevant. In the Austin Roberts Bird Hall, you'll find an informative exhibit on South Africa's many species of birds, while the Geoscience Museum highlights another Gauteng speciality, rocks and minerals.

Opposite the museum at the far end of a series of fountains and well-tended flower beds is the **City Hall**, with its eclectic mix of Greek and Roman architectural styles, and two rather good statues of Andries and Marthinus Pretorius immediately outside. The next large block to the west is taken up by the **National Cultural History Museum** (daily 8am–4pm; R5), formerly known as the **African Window**, accessed from Visagie Street. This large, airy exhibition space is, like many public collections, gradually feeling its way in the new South Africa. Generous room is given to temporary displays, although this tends to give the museum a rather tentative air. Meanwhile, the permanent exhibitions are interesting in themselves, but seem a bit unconnected. They include "Access to Power", which displays and explains San rock art, and "People's Choice", where groups of local people, including township women's groups and schoolchildren, have been invited to select objects from the museum's vast collection of some three million pieces. Also here is a room showing work by J.H. Pierneef (1886–1957), one of the country's most famous artists, who is known for his bushveld landscapes.

North of Church Square

North of Church Square, busy Proes and Struben streets are filled with cut-price stores, black shoppers and minibus taxis heading for the townships. While other parts of central Pretoria are fairly safe to walk around if you take the normal precautions, take extra care if you're wandering in this direction, as gangs have been known to work these streets, and a number of tourists have been mugged here.

Head across Bloed and Boom streets for the **National Zoological Gardens** (daily 8am–6pm; R20), which are spacious and surprisingly good, housing rare species of antelope, a white rhinoceros, and a wide selection of South American as well as African animals. A cableway (R8) carries you right over the zoo on both sides of the Apies River, while there are also a total of some 6km of trails, and you can even rent golf cars if you're feeling lazy (R60 per hour). It's well worth trying to book on one of the **night tours** (R40; ☎012 328 3265), starting at 6pm on Wednesdays, Fridays and Saturdays, when you'll see some of the zoo's freakiest creatures at their most active. Next door, the **Pretoria Aquarium and Reptile Park** (entrance included with Zoo entry charge) is less impressive, but nonetheless has plenty of beasts, some very weird and highly poisonous.

West of here lie the scruffy streets of **Marabastad**, the city's first "non-white" area. While you're here, don't miss the intricately decorated Hindu **Mariammen Temple**, right next to the market. The area, while fascinating, can feel quite intimidating, and you may feel more comfortable exploring here with a guide.

Arcadia and the Union Buildings

Head east along Vermeulen or Church streets, and you'll soon reach the **Arcadia** district, where Pretoria's **Union Buildings**, the headquarters of the South African government, perch majestically on the main hill. Designed by Herbert Baker in 1910, allegedly to symbolize the union of Briton and Boer, the lashings of colonnades and lavish amphitheatre seem instead to glorify British imperial self-confidence. Nelson Mandela had an office inside, and the buildings were famously the site of his inauguration in 1994. This was perhaps the first time their imperialist symbols were transformed, not least by the African praise-singers who delivered their odes from the amphitheatre, proclaiming Mandela as the latest in a long line of African heroes from Shaka to Hintsa, and beyond. You can walk around the buildings and their gardens, and if you're a particular enthusiast of Baker's work and the Union Buildings in particular, take one of the tours called The Baker's Dozen, run by the talkative Leone Jackson (around R50; ☎012 344 3197).

South of the Union Buildings, the **Pretoria Art Museum**, corner of Schoeman and Wessels streets (Tues & Thurs–Sat 10am–5pm, Wed 10am–8pm, Sun noon–5pm; R3), houses an excellent selection of South African art and Dutch Masters, as well as some black artists, including Ephraim Ngatane. There is a small gallery (same hours; free) just beyond the main entrance which is worth popping into for its contemporary exhibitions and small café.

Sunnyside and Hatfield

Southeast of the centre, desegregated **Sunnyside** is the central suburb with the strongest African feel, with a busy street life, distinctive old houses and a multitude of cafés. **Oeverzicht Artists' Village**, on the corner of Kotze and Gerard Moerdyk streets, once a lively little node of old cottages with interesting craft shops and restaurants, is quickly losing its vitality, and there's now quite a rapid turnover of business and fewer of the venues which gave the place some spark. The **Breytenbach Theatre** at 137 Gerard Moerdyk St – said to be haunted by the ghosts of those who died there when it was a hospital for Germans – hosts mainly student productions. Nearby **Esselen Street** is Sunnyside's busiest thoroughfare, brimming with bars and street hawkers.

West of Sunnyside is the huge **Loftus Versveld Stadium**, where major rugby and soccer games are played. On the other side of the railway line, **Pretoria University** has some excellent gallery and museum space, including an exhibition in the Ou Lettere (Old Arts) building (Tues–Fri 10am–4pm; free) dedicated to the remarkable archeological finds at Mapungubwe (see p.721), a hill-top fort by the Limpopo River which was the ancient capital of a major southern African kingdom. Among the artefacts on display are a gold rhinoceros made from thin gold foil, figurines, jewellery and decorated pots, all at least 700 years old. Also in the same Ou Lettere building is an art gallery with changing exhibits; the university has a fantastic permanent collection, including Dutch Masters and Chinese ceramics dating back to the Han dynasty (206 BC–221 AD), but this is viewable by appointment only (℡012 420 3100).

Beyond this is **Hatfield**, which has developed in the last few years into Pretoria's liveliest area, with the trendiest hangouts and nightlife around Park, Burnett and Hilda streets, where you'll find a plethora of studenty cafés, bars and restaurants. To visit the elegant house and museum of acclaimed Afrikaner sculptor **Anton van Wouw**, 299 Clark St (Mon–Fri 10am–4pm; free), you'll need to head southeast of the university to the wealthy suburb of **Brooklyn**. Van Wouw was responsible for most of the brooding effigies of Afrikaner public figures from the 1890s to the 1930s scattered around the country, including the Kruger statue in Pretoria's Church Square (see p.630). His most famous work is the Voortrekker Monument, further south of the city (see opposite). The museum, designed by the celebrated architect Norman Eaton in 1938, houses a collection of his smaller pieces. Van Wouw's figures tend to be placed in rural settings, but here you'll find two striking, non-rural pieces, one of a mine worker, the other an accused man standing in the dock. Keep an eye out, too, for *The Guitar Player*, a feisty-looking woman strumming away with a trace of a smile on her face.

South to the Voortrekker Monument

Travelling south towards Johannesburg on Preller Road, you can't miss the enormous and head-shakingly ugly **UNISA**, South Africa's largest university. Over 300,000 students are enrolled here – though most of them are on correspondence courses. Inside, on the fifth floor, a very good **art gallery** (Tues–Fri 10am–4pm; ℡012 429 6255; free) hosts some of Pretoria's most innovative exhibitions, as well as a permanent collection exhibiting young South African talent of all races. Telephone in advance to make sure the curator is here.

On the outskirts of Pretoria, west of UNISA, the chilling **Correctional Services Museum** (Mon–Fri 9am–3pm; free), at Pretoria Central Prison, is well worth a visit. Make for Potgieter Street, which runs vertically three blocks west of Church Square, and stay on it while it becomes the R101 to Johannesburg. You'll see the notorious prison, where many famous political prisoners were held (and many executed), on your right. Be prepared to walk past depressed-looking visiting relatives on your way in. Inside the museum you can see artworks made by prisoners, including a life-size statue of an inmate crawling towards an expressionless prison warder, who has his arms outstretched, ready to correct him. There are also exhibits of knives concealed in Bibles and shoes, files in cakes and so forth. Most alarming by far are the group photos of various forbidding-looking prison warders through the ages, which seem a strange sort of propaganda for the prison service.

Continue out on the R101 and follow the signs to view the famous **Voortrekker Monument and Museum** (daily 8am–5pm; R18). For many years an ominous symbol of Boer domination, the monument is now more generally accepted as one of South Africa's many cultural waypoints, and a visit does allow you a penetrative insight into the Afrikaner mindset. The striking, austere block of granite was built in 1940 to commemorate the Boer victory over the Zulu army at Blood River on December 16, 1838 (see p.548), and its symbolism is crushingly heavy-handed. The monument is enclosed by reliefs of ox wagons, with a large statue of a woman standing outside, shaking her fist at imaginary oppressors. Inside, a series of moving reliefs depict scenes from the Great Trek. Outside, hidden by some trees, are two pint-size replicas of the huts of Zulu kings Dingane and Cetshwayo. The monument is set within a small **nature reserve** which has various hiking and mountain-bike trails leading you to look out-points over Pretoria and the surrounding countryside; an alternative way to explore the reserve is on a pony trek – call ☏012 326 3929 for more details (booking essential).

Eating and drinking

Pretoria has plenty of good **restaurants**, particularly around the Hatfield and Brooklyn areas, where they tend to congregate around a handful of popular upmarket shopping centres. If you're prepared to explore a bit further there are some very interesting places serving South African food. **Cafés** are numerous and varied; again, Hatfield is the more stylish area, although you can still find a place to sip espresso right in the city centre.

Restaurants

Blue Crane 156 Melk St, New Muckleneuk. A fairly traditional and well-turned-out restaurant in a unique location, overlooking the dam and the Austin Roberts Bird Sanctuary. Open daily for breakfasts, afternoon teas and hearty, medium-priced main meals.

Brasserie de Paris 525 Duncan St, Hatfield ☏012 362 2247. This faithful reproduction of the classic Parisian café has a pleasant terrace, spacious and classy interior, smart service and a great menu. It's also quite expensive. Closed Sat lunchtime & Sun.

Chagall's 924 Park St, Hatfield ☏012 341 7511. A chic, expensive restaurant with excellent French-style cooking, wines to match, and a lovely setting in the heart of the diplomatic community. Closed Sat lunchtime & Sun.

Crawdaddy's Brooklyn Plaza, corner Middle and Day streets, Brooklyn. A popular and good-time Cajun-themed restaurant, serving tasty steaks and a range of decent seafood dishes.

Crazy Nut On the corner of Day and Bronkhorst streets, Brooklyn. A surprisingly large set-up incorporating a vegetarian café-restaurant and well-stocked health food store.

Die Werf Plot 66, Olympus Road, Pretoria East ☏021 991 1809. Serves up a hearty and reason-

ably priced selection of homecooked *boerkos* (farmers' food) classics, including *kerrie skaapafval* (curried tripe and trotters) and *melktart* (milk tart). Closed Sun evening & Mon.

Gerard Moerdyk 752 Park St, Arcadia ☏012 344 4856. Beautifully prepared South African cuisine served at a price amidst lavish surroundings; choose from ostrich, springbok pie and other intriguing dishes. Closed Sat lunchtime & Sun.

Hillside Tavern Rynial Building, 320 The Hillside, Lynnwood ☏012 348 1402. Moderately priced restaurant, celebrated locally for its steaks, but also serving imaginative seafood specials.

Madison's Gilles Botbyl Centre, Duncan Street, Hatfield ☏012 342 2012. The hip hangout of Pretoria's style set, with minimalist design and beautifully presented global fusion food. Closed Sat lunch & Sun.

Mostapha's 478 Duncan St, Hatfield ☏012 342 3855. The fame of Mostapha, once chef to Moroccan royalty, has spread far across Gauteng. Tasty, unusual and moderately priced.

O'Galito Hatfield Rendezvous, 367 Hilda St, Hatfield ☏012 342 6610. Rich and spicy Mozambiquan and Portuguese dishes served in suitably grand surroundings.

Pride of India Groenkloof Plaza, George Storrar Drive, Groenkloof ☏012 346 3684. Filled with exquisite, imported Indian artefacts and oozing class and confidence, this is the place in town for beautifully prepared North Indian curries. Closed Sat lunch & Sun evening.

Safrika Kutlwanong Democracy Centre, 357 Visage St. The best African restaurant in Pretoria, a small, friendly place frequented by high-powered NGO officials and civil servants. The decor is fairly plain, but the food is tasty, authentic and inexpensive. Closed Sun.

Wang Thai 281 Middel St, Brooklyn ☎ 012 346 6230. An elegant, authentic Thai restaurant in the heart of Brooklyn, complete with noble stone carvings and calm, friendly staff.

Bars and cafés

Café Bugatti Hatfield Galleries, Burnett Street, Hatfield. A popular spot for breakfasts among the Hatfield style set.

Café Riche 2 Church Square West, in the city centre. One of the finest cafés in the country, overlooking Church Square. It boasts a Continental atmosphere and a quirky events programme, including late-night philosophical discussions and

Sunday brunch on Church Square. Daily 6am–midnight.

Cool Runnings 1071 Burnett St. A massively successful reggae bar which always seems to have a party going on; it also serves hearty food.

Eastwood Tavern 391 Eastwood Rd, Arcadia. A popular, often raucous pub near Loftus Versveld rugby stadium, serving huge, inexpensive steak dishes.

The Grapevine 204 Sunnyside Galleries, Esselen Street, Sunnyside. A long-established French-style café-patisserie, with generally mellow and cheerful regulars. It's also a great bakery if you want a quick takeout.

News Café Hatfield Square, Burnett Street, Hatfield. A popular bar and café in the heart of Hatfield, serving breakfasts and brunches from 9.30am at weekends, and decent food well into the night all week.

Tings and Times Hatfield Galleries, Burnett Street, Hatfield. One of Pretoria's happening bars, popular with students, but also a wider clientele who come for the easy-going style, the vibe and great reggae.

Nightlife and entertainment

Pretoria lacks the dynamism and breadth of Johannesburg's **arts and music** scene, but with the State Theatre and the lively social scene of Hatfield there's still a fair amount going on. **Sunnyside**, once the city's most dynamic area for nightlife, is now a bit sleazy in places. Much of the scene has moved on to the Hatfield and Brooklyn area, where stylish yuppies and richer students tend to hang out. Things are very different in the township areas of Mamelodi and Atteridgeville, where plenty of small clubs play South African and soul sounds.

Theatre and cinema

Pretoria's main venue for **theatre**, **opera** and **classical concerts** is the State Theatre, Church Street (☎012 322 1665). Under the leadership of its director Hugh Masekela, the programme of jazz and black theatre is increasingly interesting. Nearby in Church Square, the Basement Theatre below *Café Riche* (☎012 328 3173) is an elegant, compact venue with a good record of adventurous productions. For lively student productions, head for the Breytenbach, 137 Gerard Moerdyk St, Sunnyside (☎012 341 3517), beside the Oeverzicht Artists' Village.

Pretoria's **cinemas** carry the typical selection of Hollywood fare, and the city is amongst the first to receive new releases. For big releases, the Nu-Metro in Menlyn Park (☎012 368 1301) is the biggest and best; there's also an IMAX screen here (☎012 368 1186). You'll find branches of Ster-Kinekor at Beatrix Street in Arcadia (☎012 341 7568), and the New Brooklyn Mall (☎012 346 7683). Back in the centre, on the corner of Schoeman and Van der Walt streets, the cinema in The Tramshed (☎012 320 4300) screens decent non-mainstream films. Also recommended for art films is the Cinema Nouveau at Brooklyn (☎012 346 3435). *The Pretoria News* is good for theatre and cinema **listings**, while the national *Mail & Guardian* covers the visual arts, theatre and major musical events. Computicket (☎083 915 8000, ⓦwww.computicket.com) and Ticket Web (☎083 1400 500, ⓦwww.ticketweb.co.za) are the big central ticket agencies for most arts and sports events, with outlets in malls and department stores.

Live music and clubs

Club @ 297 Lynnwood Rd, Lynnwood. A popular, busy club with student nights and various DJs through the week.

Crossroads Blues Bar The Tramshed (upper level), on the corner of Schoeman and Van der Walt streets ☎012 322 3263. A hip, downtown venue, in the same complex as the cinema, hosting rock and blues bands.

DNA 600 Van der Walt St. A popular Friday night club playing funk and progressive house. On Saturday night, Orange plays garage and hard house.

Tequila Sunrise Café 1141 Burnett St, Hatfield. A popular live-music venue with an eclectic line-up, ranging from acoustic sets to punk parties. Daily.

Up the Creek On the corner of Prospect and Hilda streets ☎012 362 3712. A sophisticated venue for jazz, folk and acoustic evenings, often hosting big local names.

Upstairs at Morgan's Burnett Street, Hatfield ☎012 362 6610. Live music Mon–Sat, from some of South Africa's hottest bands to run-of-the-mill fare. There are frequent party nights and promotions, and it's popular with students.

Listings

American Express 306 Brooklyn Mall, Bronkhorst Street, Brooklyn (travel section: Mon–Fri 8.30am–5pm; foreign exchange: Mon–Fri 9am–4.30pm; ☎012 346 3580, after hours ☎082 901 5910).

Banks Most banks are around Church Square and along Church Street.

Bookshops Exclusive Books at the Centurion Centre in Centurion ☎012 663 3204 is the best in the city. Protea Book House, 1067 Burnett St, Hatfield ☎012 362 5683 claims to be the largest bookshop in South Africa, with a huge range of new and secondhand books.

Camping/hiking Trappers Trading, Atterbury Value Mart, Atterbury Road ☎012 991 5585. Cape Union Mart, Brooklyn Mall, Bronkhorst Street, Brooklyn ☎012 460 5511.

Car rental Avis ☎012 325 1490; Budget ☎012 341 4650; Imperial ☎012 348 4838; Swans ☎082 658 0078; and Tempest, 186 Struben St ☎012 324 5007.

Embassies and consulates Australia, 292 Orient St, Arcadia ☎012 342 3740; Canada, 1103 Arcadia St, Hatfield ☎012 422 3000; Germany, 180 Blackwood St, Arcadia ☎012 427 8900; Ireland, Southern Life Plaza, 1059 Schoemann St, Arcadia ☎012 342 5062; Lesotho, 1 T. Edison St, Menlo Park ☎012 460 7648; Malawi, 770 Government Ave, Arcadia ☎012 342 0146; Mozambique, 199 Beckett St, Arcadia ☎012 343 7840; Namibia, 702 Church St, Arcadia ☎012 344 5992; Netherlands, 825 Arcadia St, Arcadia ☎012 344 3910; Swaziland, 715 Government Ave, Arcadia ☎012344 1910; UK, 256 Glen St, Hatfield ☎012 483 1400; USA, 877 Pretorius St, Arcadia

☎012 342 1048; Zambia, 570 Ziervogel St, Arcadia ☎012 326 1854; Zimbabwe, 798 Merton St, Arcadia ☎012 342 5125.

Emergencies AIDS helpline ☎0800 012 322; Ambulance ☎10177; Fire ☎012 310 6300; Police ☎10111; Rape helpline ☎012 786 6608.

Flea markets Hatfield Flea Market, Hatfield Plaza, every Sun, is Pretoria's best flea market, with crafts, bric-a-brac and lively banter. Irene Village Market in Smuts House holds a market of good-quality arts and crafts on the second and last Sun of the month.

Hospitals Those with 24hr casualty services include Pretoria Academical Hospital, Doctor Savage Road ☎012 354 1000; Pretoria West, Trans Oranje Road ☎012 386 5111; and the private Starcare Muelmed, 577 Pretorius St, Arcadia ☎012 440 2362.

Intercity buses Intercape ☎012 654 4114, Greyhound ☎012 323 1154 and Translux ☎012 334 8000 have their terminal and office beside the train station. North Link Transport ☎082 846 6539, runs buses to Pietersburg and the north from Bosman Street, between Church and Pretorius streets.

Internet cafés Net Café, Hatfield Square, Prospect Street, Hatfield (Mon–Sat 11am–3am; Sun 10am–2am; ⓦwww.netcafe.co.za); Odyssey, Hatfield Galleries, Burnett Street, Hatfield (daily 9am–11.30pm); May Vision, Shop 11, Pavilion Center, 92 Jeppe St, Sunnyside (daily 8am–2am).

Pharmacies Crest, Duncan Walk, Hatfield ☎012 362 0304; Station, 509 Paul Kruger St ☎012 323 1239; and in every shopping mall.

7

GAUTENG | Pretoria

637

Around Pretoria

The most absorbing sight in the immediate vicinity of Pretoria is **Doornkloof Farm**, the former home of Prime Minister Jan Smuts. Further out, to the east of Pretoria, the mining town of **Cullinan** harks back to the pioneering days of diamond prospecting a century ago, while north of the city the **Tswaing meteorite crater** and nearby **Mapoch Ndebele Village** are efforts by disadvantaged communities to create a worthwhile tourist attraction in their area. To the west, on the other hand, the **Hartbeesport Dam** and nearby **Lesedi Cultural Village** have become victims of their own popularity, and most visitors happily bypass them on their way to less crowded and more genuine attractions in the provinces beyond.

Doornkloof Farm and Rietvlei Nature Reserve

Doornkloof Farm in Irene, just south of Pretoria, was the home of **Jan Smuts** for much of his life, including his periods as prime minister of South Africa. His fairly simple wood-and-corrugated iron house is now a museum (Mon–Fri 9.30am–4.30pm, Sat & Sun 9.30am–5pm; R5), which does tend toward hagiography, but still sheds some light on one of South Africa's most enigmatic politicians (see box on p.283). The massive library reflects his intellectual range, while numerous mementos confirm his internationalism. Other displays focus on Smuts' role as one of the most successful commanders of Afrikaner forces during the Anglo-Boer wars. The surrounding farm is also part of the museum, with the pleasant 2.5-kilometre **Oubaas Trail** leading from the house to the top of a nearby *koppie*, a walk the nature-loving Smuts took every day. There's also a **tea room** next to the house, while scattered nearby are various pieces of military hardware such as cannon and armoured vehicles – a little incongrously, given the declarations of peace and tranquillity posted along the trail and elsewhere. To get to the museum, travel south from Pretoria towards Irene on the M18 or R21 for about 20km, and follow the signs to Smuts House.

The **Rietvlei Nature Reserve** (Mon–Fri 7am–6pm, Sat & Sun 6am–6pm; R15), on the other side of the R21, is unspectacular but does at least offer Burchell's zebra, rhino and antelope, and plenty of birdlife.

Cullinan

Popular with tourist coaches, **CULLINAN** lies 50km east of Pretoria. It was in the town's Premier Mine, still working today, that the world's largest diamond, the 3106-carat Star of Africa was discovered in 1905. The De Beers mine dominates the small town, but the oldest buildings, many from the turn of the century, are being used to cater to the swarms of tourists. Unless you take a **surface tour** of the mine (Mon–Fri 10am & 2.30pm, Sat & Sun 10am; R30), there isn't much to do other than wander around, though a couple of pleasant places to **eat** include the *Station Restaurant* in the old railway station and the *Lemon Tree* tea garden on Oak Avenue. You can **stay** at *The Oak House* (℡012 734 0083; ❹), Cullinan's second-oldest building, attractively set on Oak Avenue, leading up to the mine.

Tswaing Crater and Mapoch Ndebele Village

Some 40km north of Pretoria, located off the M35, **Tswaing Crater** (daily 7.30am–4pm; R7 unguided, R12 for a guided visit) is one of the youngest and best-preserved meteorite craters in the world, a five-hundred-metre-wide depression created around 220,000 years ago. Tswaing means "place of salt" in Tswana, and the rich deposits of salt and soda around the edge of the shallow crater lake have attracted people from earliest times; artefacts up to 150,000 years old have been discovered here. A simple visitors' centre marks the start of a seven-kilometre trail to the crater and back, while a shorter walk, which you can do alone or in the company of a local guide, goes to a viewpoint on the crater rim.

Ten kilometres west of Tswaing is **Mapoch Ndebele Village** (daily 10am–4pm; R10), where the houses and enclosures are painted with the colourful geometric patterns for which the Ndebele are famous, often incorporating modern aspects such as telephones and the South African flag. These, and the equally colourful beadwork, both among South Africa's most distinctive art forms, are always done by women. Unlike other Ndebele villages, Mapoch is relatively uncommercialized, and little attempt is made to cover up the less traditional parts of the village. You are expected to pay for a guide (R10–20) in addition to the admission charge.

Hartbeespoort Dam and Lesedi Cultural Village

In the Magaliesberg Mountains west of Pretoria, the man-made **Hartbeespoort Dam** has the potential to be a pleasant escape from the urban sprawl of Gauteng. Unfortunately, large numbers of Gauteng's inhabitants have already had the idea, and the dam and its surrounds have been thoroughly mauled by camping and picnic sites, animal parks, cableways, mini-resorts and endless ranks of arts-and-craft emporiums. At weekends, the mid-week jams of Sandton and Randburg are simply transferred to the countryside, and petrol-heads scream up and down the dam on jet skis in much the same way as they do the M1 in urban 4WDs.

Slightly more interesting, though hardly more inspiring, **Lesedi Cultural Village** (tours daily at 11.30am & 4.30pm; R235 for the tour plus a meal, R145 for the tour only), off the R512 south of Hartbeespoort, crams four cultural villages into one bewildering experience, with the Zulu, Pedi, Xhosa, Ndebele and Basotho all represented. Twice a day, tourists are escorted round the fairly authentic *kraals*, entertained by a lively display of colourful costumes, singing and dancing, then fed heartily with a **traditional African feast** in the vividly decorated restaurant. You can also **stay a night** in a grass hut with a Lesedi family (℡012 205 1394, ⓦwww.lesedi.com; ❻ including a full tour, dinner, bed and breakfast).

Travel details

Trains

Johannesburg to: Bloemfontein (2 daily; 13hr 20min); Cape Town (1 daily; 26hr 15min); Durban (1 daily; 13hr 30min); East London (1 daily; 19hr 45min); Kimberley (1 daily; 8hr 15min); Messina (1 daily; 15hr); Nelspruit (1 daily; 9hr 45min); Port Elizabeth (1 daily; 20hr); Pretoria (32 daily; 1hr 30min).

Pretoria to: Bloemfontein (1 daily; 14hr 50min); Cape Town (1 daily; 28hr); Johannesburg (32 daily; 1hr 30min); Kimberley (1 daily; 10hr 35min); Messina (1 daily; 14hr); Nelspruit (1 daily; 8hr 20min).

Buses

Johannesburg to: Bloemfontein (3–4 daily; 5–6hr); Cape Town (3–5 daily; 16–18hr); Durban (6 daily; 8–11hr); East London (1 daily; 11hr 30min); Kimberley (3–4 daily; 6–8hr); King William's Town (2 daily; 12hr 15min); Klerksdorp (3–5 daily; 2–4hr); Knysna (2–3 daily; 14–16hr); Kuruman (1 Tues, Thurs, Fri & Sun; 8hr 15min); Ladysmith (1 daily; 6hr 30min); Louis Trichardt (1 Tues, Thurs, Fri & Sun; 4hr 15min); Mossel Bay (1–2 daily; 14hr 30min); Nelspruit (1 daily; 5hr); Newcastle (1 daily; 4hr 45min); Oudtshoorn (1–2 daily; 13hr); Pietermaritzburg (7 daily; 6–8hr); Pietersburg (1–2 daily except Sat; 3hr 45min); Plettenberg Bay (1 Tues & Fri; 15hr 30min); Port Elizabeth (2–4 daily; 13–15hr); Potchefstroom (1–3 daily; 1hr 30min); Pretoria (over 70 daily; 1hr); Queenstown (2 daily; 10hr); Rustenburg (1 daily; 2hr); Umtata (1 Mon, Wed, Fri & Sun; 12hr 45min).

Pretoria to: Aliwal North (2 daily; 9hr); Beaufort West (3–5 daily; 12–13hr); Bloemfontein (3–4 daily; 6–7hr); Cape Town (3–5 daily; 17hr); Durban (6 daily; 9hr); East London (1 daily; 12hr 30min); Ermelo (1 daily; 4hr 20min); George (1–2 daily; 16hr); Graaff-Reinet (2 daily Mon–Sat; 11hr 45min); Harrismith (1 daily; 4hr 45min); Johannesburg (over 70 daily; 1hr); Kimberley (3–4 daily; 7hr); King William's Town (2 daily; 13hr 25min); Klerksdorp (3–5 daily; 3hr–4hr 30min); Knysna (2–3 daily; 16hr); Kuruman (1 Tues, Thurs, Fri & Sun; 9hr 15min); Ladysmith (1 daily; 7hr 30min); Louis Trichardt (1 Tues, Thurs, Fri & Sun; 5hr 15min); Mossel Bay (1–2 daily; 15hr 35min); Nelspruit (1 daily; 4hr); Newcastle (1 daily; 4hr 45min); Oudtshoorn (1–2 daily; 14hr); Pietermaritzburg (7 daily; 7hr 15min); Pietersburg (1–2 daily except Sat; 3hr); Plettenberg Bay (1 Tues & Fri; 16hr 30min); Port Elizabeth (2–4 daily; 16hr); Potchefstroom (1–3 daily; 2hr 30min); Queenstown (2 daily; 10–11hr); Umtata (1 Mon, Wed, Fri & Sun; 13hr 45min).

Flights

Johannesburg is a major international point of entry into South Africa, with flights from all around the world. The city is also an important centre of the domestic network, and you can fly to virtually anywhere in the country from here. Services include:

Johannesburg to: Bloemfontein (6 daily Mon–Fri, 3 daily Sat & Sun; 1hr 10min); Cape Town (20–26 daily; 2hr); Durban (17–22 daily; 1hr); East London (3 daily; 1hr 25min); Hoedspruit (1 daily; 1hr); Kimberley (1 daily; 1hr 15min); Manzini (4 daily Mon–Fri, 3 daily Sat & Sun; 1hr); Nelspruit (3–6 daily; 1hr 50min); Pietersburg (4 daily Mon–Fri, 1 daily Sat & Sun; 50min); Port Elizabeth (6–9 daily; 1hr 40min); Upington (1 daily; 1hr 50min).

Northwest Province

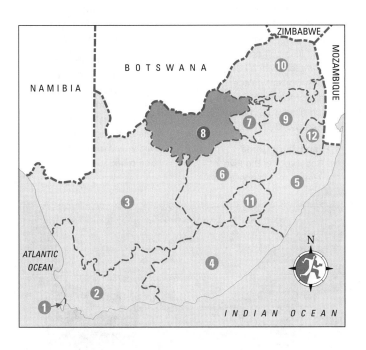

CHAPTER 8

Highlights

✳ **Magaliesberg mountains**
Rolling hills, rocky *kloofs*
and sparkling streams
on the edge of the
province, separating the
vast spaces of the
Northwest from the bus-
tle of Johannesburg. See
p.647

✳ **Sun City** A unique fanta-
sy-land of hotels, slot
machines, stage shows
and lush golf courses,
complete with a Lost
City, opulent palace,
explorable jungle and
fun-filled water park.
See p.649

✳ **Pilanesberg Game
Reserve** The Big Five
reserve most accessible
from Johannesburg and
Pretoria, with beautiful
landscapes and terrific
game viewing. See p.651

✳ **Groot Marico** One of the
most characterful of
South Africa's tiny *dorps*,
or small farming towns,
famed for its literary connections and the poten-
cy of the local fruit spirit,
mampoer. See p.653

✳ **Madikwe Game Reserve**
An often-overlooked Big
Five reserve in the cor-
ner of the province; the
limited tourist numbers
here enhance your
wilderness experience.
See p.655

Northwest Province

S outh Africa's **Northwest Province** is one of the country's most-visited but least-understood regions – renowned, among tourists at least, for the famously vulgar **Sun City** resort and Big Five **Pilanesberg Game Reserve**, but not much else. Few people venture beyond these attractions to explore this area in greater depth; consequently, it can be curiously rewarding to do so. There are myriad little *dorps* scattered throughout the region where few whites are fluent in English, and most blacks speak only Tswana. Outside the main cities, the old-fashioned hospitality you'll encounter, along with the stillness and tranquillity in the endless stretches of grassland and fields of *mielies* (sweetcorn) are a refreshing change after hectic Johannesburg.

Northwest Province extends west from Gauteng to the Botswana border and the Kalahari desert. Along the province's eastern flank, essentially dividing Northwest from Gauteng, loom the **Magaliesberg mountains**, one hundred times older than the Himalayas and these days dotted with holiday resorts for nature-starved Jo'burgers. If you're driving from Johannesburg to Cape Town and can afford a bit of meandering, try taking the **N12** through Northwest via Kimberley (in Northern Cape); the road follows the Vaal River for hundreds of miles, and once you're past uninspiring **Potchefstroom** and **Klerksdorp**, a detour to the riverbanks provides a lovely breather, particularly to **Bloemhof** for its quiet nature reserve teeming with birdlife. The province also has a healthy number of **game lodges** where, depending on your budget, you can view game from a luxurious verandah or camp under the stars in the bushveld.

The N4 from Pretoria leads you into the Magaliesberg mountains and through the main town of the northeastern part of the province, **Rustenburg**, which has a windswept **nature reserve** where you can hike high enough to gaze down onto the shimmering plains beneath. **Groot Marico**, further west, is a friendly *dorp* with powerful home-brews and laid-back people to share them with. Further on towards the Botswanan capital Gaborone, the **Madikwe Game Reserve** is one of South Africa's undiscovered wildlife gems, a massive Big Five park which sees remarkably few visitors and boasts some superb game lodges.

Relentless sun alleviated only by torrential rain makes summer in Northwest something of an endurance test: aim to come here in spring or autumn. For the more adventurous, **camping** in the quiet and timeless *veld* is especially rewarding in this part of South Africa.

Some history

San hunter-gatherers were Northwest's first inhabitants: they were displaced some one thousand years ago by Iron Age peoples from the north, who pitched their first settlements on low ground near watercourses. By the sixteenth century, these settlements had developed into stone-walled towns on hilltops; the largest, Karechuenya (near Madikwe), was estimated by a Scottish observer in

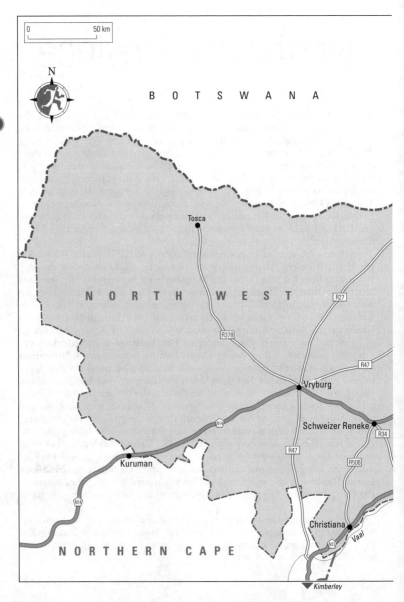

1820 to have at least 20,000 inhabitants – more than Cape Town had at that time. By the nineteenth century, the dominance of the Rolong, Taung, Tlhaping and Tlokwa clans was established. European observers classified them all as **Tswana**, but it's unclear whether these people regarded themselves as very different from people further east classified as "Sotho".

The outbreak of intense **inter-clan violence** in the early 1800s was due to

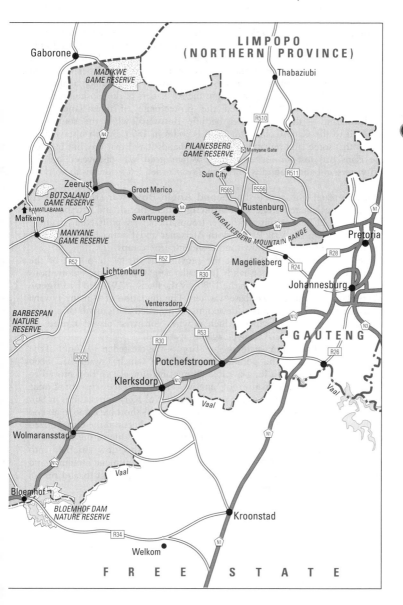

displacements caused by white settler expansion, and the growing availability of firearms. Victory went to those who made alliance with the new arrivals, whether **Griqua** from the Northern Cape, or **Afrikaners** from further south. The Tlhaping were soon driven out, eventually finding their way to Zambia. Mzilikazi's Ndebele ruled the region in the 1820s and 1830s, but they too were forced out, this time to modern Zimbabwe. The victories of the remaining clans were short-lived: their Griqua and Afrikaner allies soon evicted them from their land and forced them into service.

Potchefstroom and **Klerksdorp** were the first towns established here by the Afrikaners, and more followed, each forming the nucleus for a quarrelsome mini-state. In 1860 these mini-states amalgamated to form the **South African Republic** (ZAR), with Pretoria as its capital. The first Anglo–Boer War lasted from 1877 until British defeat in 1881, with most of the province unaffected. In 1885, the British successfully fought the Afrikaners of the Goshen republic near Mmabatho and established the protectorate of north and south Bechuanaland – the north later became Botswana, while the south was annexed to the Cape Colony by Cecil Rhodes in 1895. British intervention meant that some land remaining in Tswana hands stayed that way, but by then the clans had lost almost everything. When **gold** was discovered on the Witwatersrand and around Klerksdorp, Tswana men left in droves to work in the mines.

Of far greater impact was the **second Anglo–Boer War** (1899–1902). As well as the celebrated **siege of Mafikeng**, where British and Tswana forces held out for 217 days against Afrikaner troops, there were protracted skirmishes up and down the Vaal River. Both Afrikaner and Tswana had their lands torched, and many were thrown into concentration camps.

The Union Treaty of 1910 left the province as the western part of the Transvaal, firmly in Afrikaner hands. Its smaller *dorps* soon became synonymous with rural racism, epitomized in the 1980s by the fascistic AWB led by **Eugene Terreblanche**, whose power base was here. The migration of so many Tswana men and the lack of industrial development impeded the growth of a black working class in the province, which is why Northwest played a relatively minor role in the national struggle against apartheid.

The **Bophuthatswana** *bantustan* – or "Bop" – was created in 1977 out of the old "native reserves", the poor-quality land into which Tswana had been forced. Far from being a long-awaited "homeland" for blacks, Bop proved to be a confusing amalgamation of enclaves, ruled by the corrupt **Lucas Mangope**, who grew rich on the revenues from **Sol Kerzner**'s casinos in Sun City and the discovery of platinum. Bophuthatswana's short life came to an end with the elections of 1994, though its legacy is still evident in the disorganized provincial administration and inefficient infrastructure. One of the more evident hangovers is the former Bop capital, **Mmabatho**, now absorbed into Mafikeng, the capital of Northwest, where huge government buildings and endless civil service offices seem hopelessly out of proportion to, and out of keeping with, the wider province.

The Magaliesberg

Given that large parts of the province are empty and flat, one of Northwest's more distinctive assets is the **Magaliesberg mountain range**, which gets its name from the Tswana chief **Mogale** of the Kwena clan. Kwena people lived here from the seventeenth century until 1825, when most of them were forced out by the Ndebele chief **Mzilikazi**. Afrikaner farmers continued the process of eviction, and today the dispossession of the Kwena in the Magaliesberg is complete.

The Magaliesberg's great asset is that it's easily accessible from Johannesburg and Pretoria, with the result that great chunks have been fenced off and turned into time-shares or resorts. Nevertheless, there are oases of unspoilt nature, notably the outstanding **Pilanesberg Game Reserve**, the lesser-known **Rustenburg Nature Reserve** and the **Mountain Sanctuary Park**, all preserved in something like their previous natural state and well-stocked with wildlife. The towns dotted throughout the mountains are fairly dull, though the main town, **Rustenburg**, is useful as a first orientation point for the province. If you're in the mood for a fun-in-the-sun waterpark and some surreal tourist opulence, **Sun City** is worth checking out, if only as a stopover on your way in to Pilanesberg.

Rustenburg and around

Some 120km northwest of Johannesburg lies the mining town of **RUSTEN-BURG**. A useful service point on a busy road, the town's main appeal lies in its proximity to the **Rustenburg Nature Reserve**, and for the many pleasant country resorts which lie in the surrounding hills.

There's not much to see in Rustenburg itself, apart from the **Dutch Reformed Church** on Burger Street, and a mediocre **museum** (Mon–Fri 8.30am–4.30pm, Sat 9am–1pm, Sun 3–5pm; free), which contains a battered old ZAR flag. Paul Kruger is commemorated by a statue by French sculptor

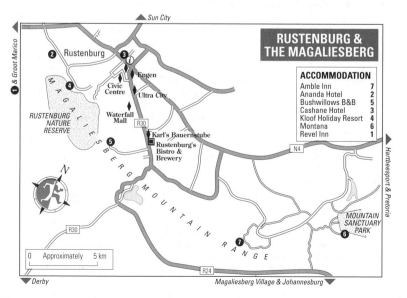

RUSTENBURG &
THE MAGALIESBERG

ACCOMMODATION

Amble Inn	7
Ananda Hotel	2
Bushwillows B&B	5
Cashane Hotel	3
Kloof Holiday Resort	4
Montana	6
Revel Inn	1

Sun City

Rustenburg

Engen

Civic
Centre

Ultra City

RUSTENBURG
NATURE
RESERVE

Waterfall
Mall

R30

Karl's Bauernstube

Rustenburg's
Bistro &
Brewery

N4

1 & Groot Marico

MAGALIESBERG

MOUNTAIN RANGE

MOUNTAIN
SANCTUARY
PARK

N

R30

0   Approximately   5 km

R24

Harbeesport & Pretoria

Derby

Magaliesberg Village & Johannesburg

Archard; located in front of the town hall, it shows the President in his last days in exile in France sitting grumpily in an armchair.

Some 4km southwest of town, **Rustenburg Nature Reserve** (March–Aug 6.30am–6pm, Sept–Feb 5.30am–7pm; R10 per vehicle plus R10 per adult; ☎014 533 2050) spans a spectacular portion of the Magaliesberg, and offers sweeping views and great hikes over terrain spotted with rock formations created by millennia of erosion. You'll find dry *veld* too, and streams coursing through the valleys that have generated a lush flora all of their own. Scattered around the reserve are aloes indigenous to the Magaliesberg, and the discreet *frithiapulchra*, a succulent with only its leaf tips exposed, flowering between November and March. Rustenburg is home to a host of **antelopes** – klipspringer, mountain reedbuck, sable and impala – and also **zebras**, and the many hilly crags are perfect for predatory birds; keep a lookout for the rare **black eagle** and **Cape vulture**, as well as parrots and paradise flycatchers.

The reserve can be explored on a day or overnight hike. For **day hikes**, head south out of town on Wolmarans Street and take the left turn into Boekenhout Street, which leads to the main reserve gate. From here, the road winds dramatically up to the mountaintop, where you'll find the **visitors' centre**, with useful maps and information on hikes and trails, as well as **camping** and braai facilities. The three-hour "Peglerae" interpretative trail takes in most of the reserve's best features, and the Parks Board provides a good booklet to go with it.

To hike **overnight** at weekends you must book in advance, but during the week, overnight huts are often available at short notice. Make for the **northern gate** by heading south out of Rustenburg on Smit Street, turning right some way down onto Wildevy Street, and then following the road to the gate. The huts have firewood and cooking utensils, but you must bring your own food. Hikes last two days and two nights, with a leisurely nine-kilometre walk on the first day and a slightly more strenuous twelve-kilometre one on the second.

Smaller than Rustenburg Nature Reserve, but a gem nonetheless, **Mountain Sanctuary Park** (March–Aug 8am–5.30pm; Sept–Feb 8am–6.30pm; R10 per vehicle plus R22 per adult; ☎014 534 0114) lies about 15km east of Rustenburg. The park has been allowed to return to a wilderness state, and is dotted with bilharzia-free streams safe for swimming, and spectacular *kloofs* and gullies. Klipspringer, rhebok and duiker wander freely, and the area supports abundant birdlife. Chalets, safari tents, caravans and camping are available for **overnight stays** (❶–❷), but bring your own bedding. There's an extraordinary **swimming pool** by the caravans, which gives the impression that you're on the edge of a precipice as you look out into the valley below. The simplest way to **get to the park** is to take the N4 as far as the Marikana turn-off, and then turn right (instead of left to Marikana). Once on this road, take the second dirt track on your left and continue for about 3km. It is worth phoning ahead before you go, even as a day visitor, as the numbers allowed in the park are limited.

Practicalities

Public transport connections to Rustenburg are poor. Apart from minibus taxis, mainly from Pretoria, the only regular **bus** is run by Protours (☎012 664 5880), which operates a daily service from Pretoria to Mafikeng via Rustenburg. You'll find Rustenburg's **tourist information** office (daily 7am–5pm; ☎014 597 0904) fairly prominent on the main road into town on the corner of Kloof and Van Staden streets.

Eating in the centre of Rustenburg is limited to a snack or grill; for anything more substantial, head for the Waterfall Mall, on the edge of town along the R30 (signposted as the Johannesburg road), where you'll find a predictable range of pizza/pasta restaurants and steakhouses. A little further out on the same road, the more individual but reasonably priced *Karl's Bauernstube* (closed Mon, Sat lunch & Sun evening) serves delicious Austrian and German food and beers. *Rustenburg's Bistro & Brewery* next door is essentially a drinking establishment, but offers reasonable meals.

Accommodation

Rustenburg has a handful of **hotels**, but you'll get the most out of this area by staying in one of the out-of-town options listed below, or in the simple chalets in either the Rustenburg Nature Reserve or Mountain Sanctuary Game Reserve (see p.648). Avoid the B&Bs advertised in the tourist office – they tend to be in the dull suburbs. There's no backpacker hostel in Rustenburg, though the laid-back *Revel In* (☎072 263 0964, ⓦwww.revelin.co.za; ❶), based at a farm around 40km west out of town in the direction of Swartruggens, offers dorms and stone bungalows and hosts regular reggae festivals.

Amble Inn ☎014 534 0608. Self-catering chalets southeast of town, in a pretty mountainside setting which, despite the owners' enormous dogs, is very restful. Follow the N4 to Pretoria, turning right at the sign for Rex and left at the Kromriver turn-off; continue for about 10km. ❷

Ananda Hotel ☎014 597 3875. Cosy accommodation in a fantastic spot, with a variety of sports, a swimming pool and a decent restaurant. Head west on Malan Road, and at the T-junction out of town turn left and follow the signs. ❸

Bushwillows B&B Waterkloof Farm, south of town off the R24 ☎ & ⓕ 014 537 2333. Attractive, well-run B&B with a pool, on a farm beside the nature reserve 10km from Rustenburg town centre. ❷

Cashane Hotel On the corner of Steen and Van Staden streets ☎014 592 8541. One of the two hotels in the centre of town, offering comfortable rooms with TV. There's a reasonable restaurant attached, but no pool. ❸

Kloof Holiday Resort ☎014 594 1037, ⓦwww.rustenburgkloof.co.za. An uninspiring housing estate layout with lots of activities such as floodlit tennis courts and putt-putt (crazy golf), made up for by the magnificent hill towering above, which is within hiking distance. The resort gets packed during school holidays. ❶

Montana ☎014 534 0113. Eight self-contained cottages sleeping two to four on a long, thin, hikeable strip of the Magaliesberg. Cottages 6 and 7 have the best views. Follow the N4 to Pretoria, turning right at the sign for Rex and left at the Kromriver turn-off, then continue for about 20km. ❸

Sun City

A surreal pocket of high-rise hotels and tinkling gaming machines in the endless bushveld, **SUN CITY** consists of four hotel/resorts tightly packed together with golf courses, a water park and various entertainment centres. Despite its enduring appeal to holidaying South African families and somewhat bemused foreign visitors, it has fallen on hard times now **gambling** is legal in South Africa. When entrepreneur Sol Kerzner began building the vast complex some twenty years ago, however, the area was part of the Bophuthatswana *bantustan* and therefore one of the few places in the country where you could throw dice legally. Thousands visited from "across the border" to sample Kerzner's blend of gambling, topless shows and over-the-top hotels. During apartheid, the resort played host to a series of high-profile rock concerts, with artists such as Elton John taking the stage despite the cultural boycott in operation at the time. These days, although the crowds have diminished, Sun City's bizarre and unique attractions haven't faded, and if you're in the area it's well worth popping in, especially if you're travelling to Pilanesberg Game Reserve.

Arrival and information

You can **fly** to Sun City's small airport (roughly 7km away), from Johannesburg on SA Airlink (℡011 978 1111). Daily Sun City **buses** drive from Johannesburg and Pretoria (book through Computicket ℡011 915 8000). If you're **driving** from Johannesburg, it's easier to take the R24 towards Rustenburg until you meet the N4, and then take the next right turn, the R565, which goes through Boshoek to Sun City. From Pretoria, follow the N4 past the Brits turn-off, and turn right onto the R556; from here it's roughly 70km to the resort. A popular option – particularly if you're not a millionaire – is to join a **day tour** here from Pretoria or Johannesburg; a large number of operators based in these cities offer trips, with prices varying depending on the target market.

Entrance to Sun City costs R40, R30 of which you get back in Sunbucks, the Sun City currency, used to pay for most things inside, including restaurant meals. Not surprisingly, however, rand can still be used everywhere inside. From the vast car park by the main gate, use the free **monorail** that runs from here to the **Welcome Centre** (℡014 557 1544; daily 8am–8pm). This is a good starting point for an exploration of Sun City (which, though it looks huge, is easily explored on foot), and can provide plenty of maps, leaflets and details of special offers. You can also book **game drives** into the Pilanesberg Game Reserve at the Safari Desk here (℡014 552 1561).

Accommodation

All accommodation should be booked through Sun International Central Reservations (℡011 780 7800).

The Cabanas ℡014 557 4227. Practical for families, this cluster of self-catering holiday chalets offers the cheapest accommodation in Sun City; moderately priced restaurants, an adventure playground and good indoor pool complete the picture. **❺**

Cascades Hotel ℡014 557 3442. After the *Palace*, this is the resort's most comfortable place to stay. Next door to the Entertainment Centre, it's a stylish high-rise, with "designer-tropical" decor, a mini rainforest and aviary, and outside lifts offering splendid views of Sun City and the surrounding hills. The inviting pool and bar are for residents only. **❼**

Palace of the Lost City ℡014 557 3133. Like something out of an Indiana Jones movie, "the Palace", as it is commonly known, is a fantastically opulent and imaginative hotel, designed as a soaring African jungle palace with towers, domes, extravagant carvings and sculptures. A stay here is bank-breakingly expensive, but unforgettable. **❽**

Sun City Hotel ℡014 557 4210. The original Sun City, housing the main casino and nightclub. If you can handle the tackiness and sound of slot machines, this hotel is worth considering for its well-furnished rooms and three decent restaurants. **❻**

The resort

The resort's showpiece is the **Lost City**, separated from the rest of Sun City by an entrance fee (R40) and the vibrating Bridge of Time. On entering, you'll encounter the **Valley of the Waves**, a gigantic pool area designed to look like a beach, complete with sand, palm trees and a wave machine producing a two-metre-high break suitable for surfing. Surrounding the valley are four excellent twisting waterchutes with names such as Scorpion and Mamba, a near-vertical waterslide called the Temple of Courage and various relaxing swimming pools. Deeper into the acres of specially planted rainforest above the valley, you'll find waterfalls, trickling streams and a network of explorable paths, all interspersed with "remains" of the lost city.

Overlooking the whole scene is the staggering *Palace of the Lost City* (see above). Despite the laughable mythology about it being part of a lost civilization, the *Palace* is breathtaking in concept and execution: a soaring, distinctively African edifice covered in elaborate woodcarvings and glowing mosaics, with beautiful, palatial interiors. You can pop in for a drink if you're not staying, or join one of the daily **Sun City tours** (2pm from the Welcome Centre; R20) for a more thorough look.

The **Entertainment Centre** is the focal point of the rest of Sun City, with rows of bleeping slot machines and arcade games. The centre's **cinema** has the best movie selection in Northwest, and the **concert hall** hosts regular beauty contests, music and sports events, which have improved since the lifting of the cultural and sports boycotts in the Nineties. If you're after something to **eat**, there's a wide choice of decent restaurants, snack bars and coffee shops dotted around the resort.

Watersports from windsailing to powerboating are offered at Waterworld, a large artificial lake near the *Cabanas* hotel, and you'll also find tennis courts, a fitness centre and three golf courses, including the internationally renowned Gary Player Country Club.

Pilanesberg Game Reserve

Immediately adjacent to Sun City and home to a huge variety of animals, the **Pilanesberg Game Reserve** (daily: April–Aug 6am–6.30pm; Sept–March 5am–7pm; R15 per car plus R20 per person) is Northwest's biggest tourist draw. Don't let the crowds put you off though: this huge, well-managed park offers game-viewing thrills aplenty, with a good chance of seeing all of the **Big Five**, along with **hippo**, **giraffe** and **cheetah**, as well as a vast range of **birdlife**. If you've only limited time in South Africa, and are based in Johannesburg, this is definitely the place to come to see some game.

Pilanesberg is the site of an earthquake that erupted some 1300 million years ago in what is now Lake Mankwe. Before the eruption, the magma's pressure cracked the earth's surface into unusual concentric circles. After the eruption, the earth's crust collapsed into the resulting underground vacuum, which squeezed the remaining magma into the cracks. The magma solidified, and now constitutes the park's many beautiful hills, which are in some ways Pilanesberg's finest feature, though often ignored by visitors more interested in scouring their slopes for wildlife. These hills were home to **Tswana** people until the Seventies, when Operation Genesis saw huge numbers of animals shipped from all over the country to fill the 55,000-hectare wildlife reserve.

You'll need at least a day to do Pilanesberg justice. If you're driving, aim to travel at under 20km per hour and allow plenty of time if you want to catch sight of the animals. An excellent **map** and **guidebook** are available at reception explaining the various habitats, enabling you to plan your journey around what you most want to see. Bear in mind that other drivers have this map too, so the areas recommended for popular animals can become congested. The most sought-after big animals are lion, elephant, white and black rhino, hippo, giraffe, buffalo, cheetah, leopard and the most recent introduction, wild dog. The majority of antelope species are here too, along with hundreds of bird species and snakes. At night, some fantastic creatures emerge, including civet, porcupine and caracal, though their dislike of the large vehicles with spotlights used for night rides means you'll be lucky to catch a glimpse of them.

Practicalities

There are four entrances to Pilanesberg: the most commonly used are the **Manyane Gate**, on the eastern edge of the reserve, and the **Bakubung Gate** just to the west of Sun City off the R565. The park's **reception** at the

Manyane Gate (daily 7am–6.30pm) provides useful maps and leaflets. In the centre of the park, the **Pilanesberg Centre**, an old Cape Dutch building left over from the days when the reserve was farm land, is due to open in 2002 as a café and shop.

Pilanesberg is easily explored in your own car, especially with the official map. The main roads in the park are tarred, and side roads are good-quality gravel, so normal sedan cars can get around easily. The various picnic spots and hides dotted around are ideal for breaking the drive – the hides in particular aren't used by many visitors and as a result can be cool, peaceful places to appreciate the natural surroundings. Alternatively, you can book **game drives** (2hr 30min; from R110) with Pilansberg Safaris, who have desks at Manyane (☎014 555 6135) and Sun City (see p.649), a good way to see the Big Five. They also operate **hiking trails** in the reserve (from R140), which give you a genuine feel for the bush and the chance to stand close to large and potentially dangerous animals, fortunately in the company of an armed warden. Also available are **night drives** (from R110) and, for a hefty R1650 per person, you can waft above the park on a four-hour **balloon safari**, which includes food and drink.

Accommodation

Pilanesberg has large numbers of day visitors – many from Sun City – but like any other decent game reserve you'll get most from it if you're able to stay a little bit longer and put yourself in pole position for the best game-viewing time, at dawn, before the day visitors arrive. Pilansberg's **accommodation** ranges from the upmarket *Kwa Maritane* and *Tshukudu* lodges to large, resort-style complexes on the fringes of the reserve; sadly, the small, simple tented camps in the heart of the park have been closed down over the last few years. **Bookings** for *Bakgatla*, *Bosele* and *Manyane* must be made through Golden Leopard Resorts (enquiries ☎014 555 6135, bookings ☎0800 601092, ⓦwww.goldenleopard.co.za), and those for *Bakubung*, *Kwa Maritane* and *Tshukudu* through Legacy Hotels (☎011 806 6888, ⓦwww.legacyhotels.co.za).

Bakgatla Resort Near the Bakgatla Gate. A large collection of self-catering chalets sleeping five and an area for caravans and camping near a large swimming pool, all set among weird-looking hillocks. ❺

Bakubung Lodge On the southern edge of the park, just west of Sun City. The highlight at this large, modern lodge is the hippo pool, a stone's throw from the restaurant. With hotel rooms and chalets, the accommodation is pleasant if bland, and guided walks and game drives are offered. ❼

Bosele Group Centre By the Manyane Gate. Inexpensive dorms with shared kitchen facilities and use of the pool, shop and restaurant at neighbouring *Manyane Resort*. ❶

Kwa Maritane Lodge In the southeast corner of the park, near Pilanesberg airport, this vast, upmarket lodge feels somehow detached from its fabulous surroundings. Full-board, good facilities, and game drives. ❼

Manyane Resort Just by the Manyane Gate. The low cost and convenience compensate for the distinctly un-bushlike atmosphere of the park's main camp. Thatched chalets with kitchen and camping are available; there's also a bar and restaurant, pool, gym and mini-golf. ❹

Tshukudu Lodge In the southern part of the park, about 8km from Bakubung Gate. Gaze out at big game from your verandah in an outstanding setting in the southwest of the park, at the most upmarket and exclusive lodge in Pilanesberg. Picturesque thatched huts offer luxury accommodation (with sunken baths and roaring log fires) for a maximum of fourteen guests; the high price includes all meals and game drives. ❾

The Central Region

Thanks to its scrawny and desolate dryness, Northwest Province's **Central Region** feels especially remote. **Mmabatho**, once the capital of Bophuthatswana and now incorporated into neighbouring **Mafikeng**, capital of Northwest, forces reluctant bureaucratic pilgrimages on people from all over the province but the linked town remains profoundly uncosmopolitan. The city's monthly *What's On* magazine invariably reveals "not much", and the same is true, only more so, of **Zeerust**, **Groot Marico** and **Lichtenburg**. The region's appeal lies elsewhere, in the brooding plains and lush river valleys of Marico and the rarely visited game reserves, including the superb **Madikwe Game Reserve** near the Botswana border. Then there are the remains of the rich but depressing history of the region, centring on the relentless dispossession of the Tswana, but also including the famed **siege of Mafikeng** during the second Anglo-Boer War, and the incredible **Lichtenburg diamond rush** of 1926. Lastly, there are the people themselves: local Tswana and Afrikaners are both short on English but long on hospitality, at least to visitors.

Groot Marico

GROOT MARICO, a tiny but characterful *dorp* resting contentedly by the banks of the Marico River, just south of the N4 and 90km west of Rustenburg, gained fame through Herman Charles Bosman's short stories based on his time as a teacher here (for a sample of his writing, see p.875). Every October, Groot Marico hosts the Herman Charles Bosman Literary Weekend, drawing fans of one of South Africa's best-loved authors from far and wide. The town's handful of attractions include the **Art Factory** on the main street (Mon–Sat 9am–5pm), where you can pick up local Tswana cultural artefacts, along with any local news about what's going on.

Also worth a visit if you're interested in the cultural history of the area are the remains of **Tshwenyane** and **Karechuenya**, two Tswana towns built in the sixteenth and seventeenth centuries. There's a display on these archeological findings at the Mafikeng Museum (see p.656). They lie 36km northwest of town, on the Orion Farm (℡018 642 3350), which is reached by taking the signposted turn-off from the Zeerust–Gaborone section of the N4, about 16km from Zeerust. Marico's information centre (see below) can help with transport details.

Although prone to stultifying heat, particularly in summer, the hills of the Marico district are good for hiking, and when it all gets too much you can make for the river for cool relief. The water of the **Marico Oog**, a spring some 20km south of town, is particularly clear and refreshing: festooned with water lilies and surrounded by beautiful dolomitic rocks, it makes a tranquil place for a picnic.

Most **minibus taxis** travelling along the N4 from Pretoria to Gaborone or Pretoria will stop at the Groot Marico turn-off on request (it's a 20min walk north of the village), but you'll find it easiest to reach Groot Marico by **car**. The town's idiosyncratic but friendly **information centre** (℡014 503 0010 or 083 272 2958, ⓦwww.marico.co.za), marked by a small signpost along the main street from the *Bosveld Hotel,* is open most hours of the day and night, but if it's closed call in at the Art Factory. The *Bosveld* has Groot Marico's only public bar, where white locals, inspired by beer, brandy and their own good humour, have been known to dance traditional Afrikaans two-steps.

For **accommodation**, go a few doors further along Paul Kruger Street to *Lavender Guest House* (℡082 822 8397; ❷), providing four rooms and a typically

Mampoer

Mampoer is the Afrikaans word for the fearsomely strong, distilled, alcohol so beloved by Marico locals for many years. Any fruit can be used to make *mampoer*, but peach is the most traditional: until 1878, much of Northwest's farmland grew peach trees solely devoted to this purpose. Things changed with the ZAR government's distilling tax, and the new licensing system introduced in 1894, and thousands of *mampoer* stills were destroyed. A few, however, escaped detection. One farmer, according to a local story, cleaned out his entire drainage system but made no attempt to conceal his fifteen barrels of *mampoer*. The inspectors found the barrels, split them open and poured the entire contents down the drain. Meanwhile, the canny farmer had his family stationed in the field where the pipe ended up with every container the household possessed, and managed to recover fourteen of the fifteen barrels.

To make *mampoer*, distillers put the fruit in a copper still and allow it to ferment until the juice is settled, at which point they light a fire under the still. A copper pipe leads from the top of the still to a drum filled with cold running water, which it coils inside. As the juice heats up, steam gathers at the top of the still and comes down the pipe, condensing when it reaches the coil in the drum. This liquid is distilled once more, this time over a slow fire. In the old days the alcohol content was measured by throwing a chunk of lard into a sample: if it floated halfway, the *mampoer* was perfect.

The drink is celebrated in Herman Charles Bosman's short story, **Willem Prinsloo's Peach Brandy**, set in the Twenties:

"... we arrived at Willem Prinsloo's house. There were so many ox-waggons drawn up on the veld that the place looked like a laager [circle of wagons]. Prinsloo met us at the door.

'Go right through, kerels,' he said. 'The dancing is in the voorhuis [barn]. The peach brandy is in the kitchen.'

Although the voorhuis was big, it was so crowded as to make it almost impossible to dance. But it was not as crowded as the kitchen. Nor was the music in the voorhuis – which was provided by a number of men with guitars and concertinas - – as loud as the music in the kitchen, where there was no band, but each man sang for himself.

We knew from these signs that the party was a success.

When I had been in the kitchen for about half an hour I decided to go into the voorhuis. It seemed a long way, now, from the kitchen to the voorhuis, and I had to lean against the wall several times to think. I passed a number of men who were also leaning against the wall like that, thinking. One man even found that he could think best by sitting on the floor with his head in his arms.

You could see that Willem Prinsloo made a pretty good peach brandy."

If you want to sample *mampoer*, either head for Pieter Roets's Vergenoeg Farm (open most days, closed evenings) a few kilometres south of Marico along the untarred main road, where you can cautiously pick up a bottle of barbed-wire-entwined, eighty-percent-proof *Doringdrood*, or to Tienie Zwart's Driefontein Farm, 2.5km beyond the Groot Marico turn-off on the N4, where you can see the stuff being made.

warm, hospitable welcome, or *Angela's Guest House* (☎014 503 0082; ❷) which is closer to the highway, but has a lovely garden and can organize massage and beauty treatments nearby. For the more adventurous, a **farmstay** can be booked through the information centre. The nicest **camping** spots around here are on the Mafikeng Road, near the centre of the village (details from the information centre), and Kleinfontein Camp Site (☎083 700 9751) where there are rondavels and guesthouse rooms (both ❶) as well as camping sites. Neither site has electricity.

Zeerust and around

The large and unprepossessing regional centre of **ZEERUST**, 40km west of Groot Marico on the N4, is essentially a supplies town, and only worth stopping at on the way to Gaborone or one of the surrounding game reserves. There's an annual **mampoer festival** (check with the Groot Marico tourist information centre for dates); otherwise, apart from the shops, there's precious little to see. Just outside town, the **Abjasterkop** is a striking, pointed hill which rewards a quick scramble or a more serious hike. You can park at the *Abjasterkop Hotel* (☎018 642 2008; ❷), 2km east on the N4, and ask the manager for directions. The hotel itself offers doubles, rondavels and camping in a magnificent hilly setting, ideal for hiking; it's also the best **place to eat** in the area, with a restaurant with an a la carte menu, and a good bar. Also near Zeerust is the **Klein Marico Resort** (☎018 646 0146), which occupies a beautiful position high above the town. As a reserve it isn't all that memorable, and apart from the views, all you're likely to see is various types of **antelope** roaming around the *veld*. The ugly brick chalets (❶), mercifully do not intrude on Klein Marico's soothing midweek tranquillity. To get to the resort head back to Groot Marico on the N4, turn off at the Total garage and continue for 4km.

Madikwe Game Reserve

Tucked up in the very north of the province near the Botswana border, **Madikwe Game Reserve** is one of the least known of South Africa's large wildlife areas. At 600 square kilometres, Madikwe, established in 1991 from reclaimed farm land and now run by Northwest Parks Board, is larger even than her sister reserve in the province, Pilanesberg, and in South Africa only Kruger National Park and the Kgalagadi Transfrontier Park cover a greater area. Thanks to **Operation Phoenix**, a massive programme of reintroduction, the largely low-lying plains of woodland and grassland of Madikwe are amply stocked with the Big Five and hundreds of other species, including spotted hyena, giraffe, cheetah and wild dog.

For such a large wilderness area run by a publicly funded organization, Madikwe enjoys very low-density tourism. There is no access for day visitors and entry to the park is limited to those booked in at one of the reserve's handful of private game lodges. All game drives are conducted in vehicles belonging to these lodges. Because access to such a vast area is limited to such a relatively small number of people, the wilderness experience is rich indeed, and the quality of the game viewing very high. Further lodges are planned, but these will take some time to establish themselves. The reserve is also making attempts to involve local communities in the benefits of tourism, with various training programmes in place and local services being used by the lodges.

Madikwe is accessed from the N4 highway running north of Zeerust towards Gaborone, the capital of Botswana, although depending on where you're staying the reserve can be approached from the east via Dwarsberg by way of gravel roads. It is also possible to fly in on a regular light-aircraft shuttle between Madikwe and Wonderboom airport by Pretoria – the lodges have information on this. As with Pilanesberg, Madikwe has the advantage of being **malaria-free**.

Accommodation

To visit Madikwe you have to book into one of the **lodges** listed overleaf. Unlike other large wilderness areas there are no restcamps with self-catering facilities and space for tents. Rates at all lodges include full-board and game drives.

Jaci's Safari Lodge ☏ 083 700 2071, ⊛ www
.madikwe.com. *Jaci's* sense of style, comfort and
laid-back luxury are hard to beat anywhere in
South Africa. Notable for its funky African designs,
wooden carvings and ragged-thatch, open-plan
constructions, the eight-room lodge overlooks a
natural waterhole on the Marico River and has a
natural rock swimming pool nearby. *Jaci's* also
welcomes children.

Madikwe Bush House ☏ 011 708 1709,
⊛ www.madikwehouse.co.za. Situated on the very
western edge of the reserve, *Madikwe Bush House*
has more of the feel of a stylish guesthouse than a
game lodge, though game drives are still part of
the full-board package. ❼

Madikwe River Lodge ☏ 011 268 0151 or 014
778 0891, ⊛ www.threecities.co.za/madikwe. An
intimate and attractively designed place on the
lush Marico River, offering luxury chalets with
wooden decks reaching out over the water. ❽

Mosetlha Bush Camp ☏ 011 802 6222,
⊛ www.thebushcamp.com. Madikwe's only budget
game lodge, offering the reserve's most intense
wilderness experience and the best-value game
viewing. Located in the centre of Madikwe,
Mosetlha has no perimeter fence and accommodation is in very simple open-sided log cabins,
with no electricity and hot outdoor showers delivered by an ingenious donkey boiler and bucket
system. What it lacks in luxury it makes up for in
atmosphere and expertise, with an emphasis
placed on game walks as much as drives. ❻

Tau Lodge ☏ 011 315 5272 or 018 365 9027,
⊛ www.taugamelodge.co.za. A larger lodge full of
fairly predictable African designs on the northern
edge of the reserve, with 30 wooden, thatched
guest cottages offering spectacular views over a
large waterhole. ❽

Mafikeng and Mmabatho

The twin towns of **Mafikeng** and **Mmabatho** offer a unique portrait of the
vision of apartheid and its deep contradictions. On the one hand, **Mafikeng** is
most famous for Baden-Powell and the Boer **siege** of 1900 (see box on p.658).
Serving a wide area of farmland, in many ways it's a typical colonial settlement;
it has a smattering of graceful buildings, with its entrenched whites living in
dull suburbs, and a centre used increasingly as a shopping and transport hub by
blacks from the surrounding area. Less than 5km away, but a world apart in
appearance, values and atmosphere, is **Mmabatho**, designated capital of the
former homeland of Bophuthatswana, and a showcase for the grandiose visions
of Bop dictator **Lucas Mangope**. The monumental constructions built by
Mangope on the back of revenues generated from Sun City, from huge government offices to the towering sports stadium, along with the wide boule-
vards that connect them, are undoubtedly worth experiencing, even if the
wiser course for finding somewhere to stay or eat and drink is to retreat to the
Mafikeng side. Although the twin cities are the capital of Northwest Province,
and despite the fact that Mmabatho's notoriety as the epitome of homeland-
hypocrisy will linger, the conurbation incorporating the two is usually referred
to these days simply as Mafikeng.

Mafikeng

Mafikeng's smattering of historic buildings make for a pleasant stroll. Starting
from Victoria Street, four blocks north of Main Street, look out for **Victoria
Hospital**, which was pounded during the siege of 1900, and the elegant **St
Joseph's Convent**. Three blocks south, on Martin Street, stands the splendid
St John's Anglican Church, designed by Sir Herbert Baker and built in
1902. Nearby is the town's main attraction, the **Mafikeng Museum** on
Martin Street (Mon–Fri 8am–4pm, Sat 10am–1pm; free), which has some
intriguing exhibits on the San, with a range of the poisons and weapons that
they hunt with, and photos of hand signals San make to each other when hunting in their customary silence. Tswana exhibits include a life-size recreation of
a traditional hut, complete with its trademark enclosed porch, and samples of
pottery and beadwork. An extensive display of herbs and medicines includes

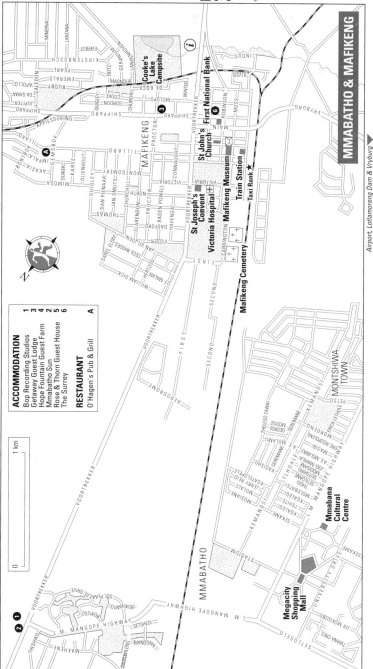

Manyane Game Reserve & Zeerust

4, **5** & Rooigrond

Airport, Lotlamoreng Dam & Vryburg

Botsalano Game Reserve, Botswana

ACCOMMODATION
Bop Recording Studios — 1
Getaway Guest Lodge — 3
Hope Fountain Guest Farm — 4
Mmabatho Sun — 2
Rose & Thorn Guest House — 5
The Surrey — 6

RESTAURANT
O'Hagen's Pub & Grill — A

1 km

0

Cooke's Lake Campsite

First National Bank

St John's Church

Mafikeng Museum

Train Station

Taxi Rank

St Joseph's Convent

Victoria Hospital

Mafikeng Cemetery

MAFIKENG

MONTSHIWA TOWN

MMABATHO

Mmabana Cultural Centre

Megacity Shopping Mall

The siege of Mafikeng

Mafikeng was **besieged** within three days of the start of the second Anglo-Boer War (1899–1902) by generals Snyman and Cronje. **Colonel Robert Baden-Powell** (founder of the Boy Scouts) had the task of defending the town. This he did for 217 days, from October 16, 1899 until May 17, 1900, when relief arrived from Rhodesia and from the south. In the process, Baden-Powell became a British household name and hero.

Strategically, Mafikeng was irrelevant to the war; Baden-Powell's real achievement was to distract the six thousand Afrikaners besieging the town from fighting elsewhere. He relied heavily on the Barolong people for defence, labour and reconnaissance, but failed to record this either in his dispatches to London or in his memoirs. The Barolong received far fewer rations than the British and over one thousand subsequently died of starvation; they received none of the £29,000 raised in Britain for the rehabilitation of Mafikeng. To add insult to injury, not one Barolong was decorated for bravery, in contrast to the plentiful medals dished out to the British regiments, and none of the promises Baden-Powell made about land grants to them was ever kept. An important legacy of the involvement of the black population was the diary of the siege kept by **Sol Plaatjie**, one of the first black writers to make an impact on English literature, who was later to become one of the founder members of the ANC.

sweet violet with five times the Vitamin C content of oranges, and a relative of the potato called the mandrake, with awesomely hallucinogenic powers. The **Mafikeng Siege** is given a room of its own, filled with classic British imperial memorabilia, including a tattered flag, ration book, diaries and a wonderful collection of photos. Extensive quotations from Peter Warwick's *Black People and the SA War 1899–1902* intersperse the exhibits, offering a subversive account of the events. The Tswana writer and activist Sol Plaatje lived in Mafikeng for many years, and wrote a diary of the siege (see box above), and he receives a full, informative display. Keep an eye out too for the fascinating exhibit on Mafikeng and the railways, which provides evidence of the connection between their spread from Cape Town and Rhodes' mission to colonize Africa.

The only other sight in Mafikeng worth a visit is the **cemetery** on Carrington Street, in the town's northwestern corner, next to the sleepy railway sidings. Dusty and unkempt, it counts amongst its headstones white iron crosses marking the graves of British soldiers. Some were casualties from the siege, and others are from the many other battles waged by the British against the Afrikaners and Tswana. Until the 1980s this was a whites-only cemetery, and still commemorates only the Europeans who died during the siege.

Mmabatho

Mmabatho was created from nothing in 1977 as the capital of the new "independent homeland" of Bophuthatswana. The city prospered fast, both from the discovery of platinum and the revenue from Sol Kerzner's gambling resort. Under the direction of Bop president Lucas Mangope, the capital became an ostentatious attempt to show off what a prosperous independent African state could become, though in practice it was a bloated and surreal quasi-state, riddled with corruption and egocentricity. Huge buildings were constructed for the burgeoning civil service; brand new casino-hotels catered to the new black elite, as well as South Africans chasing the illicit thrills denied them across the border. Money was poured into bizarre enterprises, including a sports stadium with 80,000 seats but scarcely any shade, and a state-of-the-art **recording studio**, which has been highly regarded but little-used by the world's rock and pop stars.

Practicalities

Daily Protour **buses** (☎012 664 5880) from Pretoria stop in both Mafikeng, by the train station, and Mmabatho Megacity Shopping Mall. To get here by **car**, take the R27 from Zeerust and Vryburg, or the R52 from Lichtenburg; Mafikeng is only 25km from the Ramatlabama border post with Botswana. For getting around, **minibus taxis** making the short hop from Mmabatho's Megacity Shopping Mall stop in Mafikeng at the train station, and at the corner of Warren and Shippard streets. The train station is these days serviced by a freight line only.

The **tourist information** office (Mon–Fri 8am–6pm, Sat 8.30am–noon; ☎018 381 3155), is in a thatched complex beside the entrance to *Cook's Lake Campsite*, off Voortrekker Street, on the far side of the railway track from the centre of Mafikeng.

If you're looking for something to **eat**, the most reliable options are the upmarket restaurant in the *Mmabatho Sun*, or the more casual *O'Hagan's Pub and Grill*, 1km northeast of the centre of Mafikeng, on the corner of Gemsbok and Tillard streets, not far from the Zeerust road.

Accommodation

Bop Recording Studios Voortrekker Road, Mmabatho ☎018 386 2609. The most interesting accommodation option in Mafikeng: a handful of attractive and comfortable thatched chalets beside the hi-tech but underused recording studios. The chalets are available to travellers as long as they haven't been booked up by visiting rock stars and their entourages (which isn't all that often). To get there, take the road just before the turn off to the *Mmabatho Sun*. ❹

Cooke's Lake Camping Ground Cooke's Lake. The only campsite in town, located just south of the centre off the R503. The facilities are a bit basic, and beside the road it can be quite noisy.

Getaway Guest Lodge 39 Tillard St ☎018 381 1150. Usefully located in central Mafikeng, with thirty recently upgraded rooms, a nice pool and a restaurant attached. ❸

Hope Fountain Guest Farm Rooigrond ☎018 645 0781. A pleasant option if you've got a car, with cosy chalets in semi-rural surroundings. To get there, turn off the R503 at the "*Sehuba Protea*" sign, from where it's indicated. ❷

Mmabatho Sun Voortrekker Road, Mmabatho ☎018 389 1111. On the main road which connects Mmabatho to Mafikeng; surprisingly poky for a casino-dominated Sun hotel, but its three restaurants, two bars, two swimming pools, sauna and spa are some compensation. ❺

Rose & Thorn Guest House ☎018 381 6675. A smaller and more personable guesthouse in a pleasant location on the edge of Mafikeng overlooking the small game reserve. ❷

The Surrey 32 Shippard St ☎018 381 0420. The best budget accommodation in Mafikeng, a useful central option, but quite run-down. ❶

Around Mafikeng

East of Mafikeng, 10km along the R49 to Zeerust, lies **Manyane Game Reserve** (daily 7am–6pm; R10, R5 per car). Run by the Northwest Parks Board, it's well-stocked with primarily herbivorous plains game, including **rhino** and **buffalo**, but the landscape is a bit flat and drab. There is also a separate **lion enclosure** (R5). You can **stay** in pleasant self-catering chalets (☎018 381 6020; ❷). Nearby is the **Wondergat**, a deep, water-filled cave, the bottom of which has only recently been reached; if you swim you might feel the warm stream 20m below the surface, which makes the water sparkle. On a good day, particularly in summer, this area makes a fine picnic spot. To get there, take the first right turn after Manyane, travel 4km and then take a left turn down a dirt track; continue for a further 8km and turn right.

To the north of Mafikeng lies **Botsalano Game Reserve** (daily 8am–5pm; R10, R20 per car; ☎018 386 2433), whose name means "friendship" in Tswana. **White rhino**, **giraffe** and other plains game roam the wooded grasslands, and the **birdlife** is pretty impressive, with around 140 different species. You can go as a day visitor or stay at the campsite or in a safari tent (❷), and you stand a good chance of having Botsalano to yourself. To get there, take the R503 to the Ramatlabama border post for 20km; just before the border, take the Dinakana turn-off, and continue for about 7km to a crossroads. From here, take the turn marked "Dinakana", and travel another 7km up a dirt track. The gate here should be open. If it isn't, drive a further 12km to the management gate and enter from there.

Closer to town, and to the west, the **Lotlamoreng Dam Resort** (daily 8am–8pm; R7) has two cold pools, braai stands, a tuck shop and bar that's popular with locals at weekends, but is quiet during the week. The remains of the Credo Mutwa Cultural Village can be found inside its grounds; it once featured *kraals* built in the traditional styles of South Africa's ethnic groups, and bizarre religious statues. The village was badly damaged in 1994 by members of the ANC youth wing for allegedly perpetuating tribal divisions, and while plans to rebuild the village are "in the pipeline", today only goats roam the ruins. To find Lotlamoreng, travel 5km along the R27 to Vryburg and turn right at the signs.

Lichtenburg and around

The deeply conservative *dorp* of **LICHTENBURG** lies some 65km southeast of Mmabatho on the R503, close to the N14 highway which connects the Northern Cape to Gauteng. Lichtenburg's name means "place of light"; when the town was proclaimed in 1873, it was hoped that the new settlement would bring some light to this forsaken spot. Progress was deadly slow until 1926, when a Tswana labourer on the Elandsputte farm of Jan Voorendyk discovered a **diamond**. News spread fast, and by 1927 the Lichtenburg diamond diggings were 36km long and around 1.5km wide. Incredibly, a shantytown of 150,000 people had sprung up by then, sporting over 200 diamond-buying offices. The quantity of diamonds discovered here threatened the diamond market, but De Beers bought nearly every one to maintain its monopoly and the diamonds' worth.

The shantytown was famed for its **dust**, which was alleged to waft from Lichtenburger mouths as they spoke. By 1935, the rush had petered out, but a few prospectors continued working the diggings right up until 1993. Today, only one company still works the diggings; you can watch its men in action by following the R505 north of Lichtenburg towards Zeerust, and turning left just before the Bakerville turn-off.

In De La Rey Square, the **Ampie Bosman Cultural History Museum** (Tues–Fri 10am–12.30pm & 1.30–5pm, Sat 10am–1pm; free) is worth a visit for its display on **General Koos De La Rey**, who tried and failed to capture Lichtenburg from the British in 1900. Though one of the Boer's most brilliant military strategists, De La Rey was also one of the "bitter enders", who only stopped fighting in 1902 with the greatest of reluctance. Nearby, on Melville Street South, the linked **Diggings Museum** (Mon–Fri 10am–1pm & 2–4pm; free) offers some background to the rush of 1925–35 with assorted artefacts and some lively stories from Lichtenburg's heady days as a diamond town.

Digging for diamonds

"Once you have found your first diamond, you will never give up looking."

Digger proverb

According to digger mythology, all that anyone needs to find diamonds is a claim, a pick, a shovel, a wheelbarrow, and the luck of the gods. In practice, however, extra equipment comes in pretty handy. First off, you'll need a "dummy", which is a swinging sieve in a frame that gets rid of larger stones. After this, you'll need a "washing machine", which mixes the gravel left by the dummy with muddy water, its rotating arms and teeth holding the mixture in suspension. The diamonds and heavier gravel sink to the bottom, and the lighter gravel, called "tailings", floats to the top and is poured out. Another sieve separates the tailings from the water, which is reused. After the washing machine, the remaining gravel is poured into a sluice and then a washing tub, which removes the last of the water, and grades the gravel into three sizes. These are then pored over with a knife, in the hope that this time there will be a diamond. In 1926, at the time of the Lichtenburg diggings, all this equipment cost around £600, which effectively meant you needed a diamond to pay for it.

Accommodation is limited, the only hotel being the rather grim *Elgro* (☎018 632 3051;) on Republiek Street. Far more comfortable is the *Melville*, 20 Melville St (☎018 632 3514;), a B&B with a small art gallery attached. For **eating and drinking**, you could try the *Spur* steakhouse next door to the *Elgro*, or *O'Hagan's* pub on Melville Street. Marginally better than both is *La Taverna*, 145 Melville St, offering reasonably priced steaks and desserts.

Lichtenburg Nature Reserve

The **Lichtenburg Nature Reserve** (Mon–Fri 8am–4pm, Sat & Sun 8am–6pm; R10; ☎018 632 2818;) operates as a game-breeding farm, and as a result has an unusual selection of wildlife, including an excellent vulture restaurant in its small forest. The vultures usually feed in the afternoon, but enquire at the gate for precise times if you enjoy the sight of birds devouring raw flesh. Less gory are the hundreds of birds you can watch from the hide by the lake. **To get to the reserve**, take the R505 north of the town to Ottoshoop and Zeerust, turning left 2km later at the easily missed signpost, and go under the railway bridge. The reserve is another 2km further on.

Along the N14

Lichtenburg lies just off the main N14 route between Johannesburg and Upington in the Northern Cape. This journey is worth considering as an alternative to the more direct Jo'burg to Cape Town routes through Kimberley or Bloemfontein, as it takes in a wider diversity of South Africa's landscapes and, particularly once it reaches the Northern Cape, offers a number of worthwhile diversions. The section running through Northwest Province, however, has little worth stopping off to see. The most interesting diversion is the **Barberspan Nature Reserve** (daily 6am–7pm; R10; ☎053 948 1854), not far from Delareyville, a large, natural wetland in striking contrast to the fields of *mielies*, home to tens of thousands of birds, including flamingos, herons, storks and ibis. Some 365 different species have been recorded here – one of the highest figures anywhere in South Africa. There's a simple **campsite**, or you can **stay** at the adjacent *Barberspan Hotel* (☎053 948 1930; ❷), which has a collection of A-frame wooden chalets right by the edge of the pan, as well as a bar, restaurant and swimming pool.

West of Delareyville lies Bophirima, the western section of the province, an area of huge cattle ranches, hunting concessions and little else. The main town here is **VRYBURG**, which has the usual range of chain steakhouses and stark wayfarers' hotels, but nothing beyond that to divert the passer-by. South of Vryburg, around 70km along the road to Warrenton, the small settlement of **TAUNG** is famous for the discovery in 1924 by Dr Raymond Dart of the Taung Child, the fossilized skull of an early hominid ancestor of modern man, *Australopithecus africanus*. Although it was a vital link in confirming man's evolution from apes, little more than a memorial plaque can be found at the Buxton quarry site where Dart made his famous find.

Along the Vaal River

The mighty **Vaal** (or Lekwa) was the historic boundary between the Orange Free State and the South African Republic (ZAR). Still the provincial boundary, separating Northwest from the Free State, today the Vaal runs alongside the N12 highway between Johannesburg and Kimberley. There are various towns along the route, including the historic university town of Potchefstroom and the somewhat uninspiring sprawl of Klerksdorp, though both have a handful of reasonable places to break your journey. Although a national highway, sections of the N12 aren't in the best repair, and after nightfall the busy, unlit road can be an unpleasant place to drive. The landscape is dominated by flat maize fields, and the proximity to the river provides opportunities for sorties from the beaten track. None of the towns along the way are particularly important places to visit, though you will find one or two decent options for an overnight stop.

Potchefstroom

Located just under 100km southwest of Johannesburg, **POTCHEFSTROOM** is one of the largest and oldest towns of Northwest, a classic Afrikaner settlement with main streets wide enough to turn a wagon, a large square and plenty of churches. Founded by Voortrekker leader **Andries Potgieter** on the banks of the Mooi River in 1837, Potchefstroom means "stream of chief Potgieter". Once the capital of the ZAR, today "Potch" is best known for its university, which has known some turbulence between black and Afrikaner students since blacks were admitted in the Nineties, but the presence of a large student population does give parts of town a youthful and energetic vibe.

The main highway cuts through town, leaving the central area with little of the charm you'd expect of such an old settlement. Kerk Street, at right-angles to the highway, is now an inelegant shopping arcade, although parallel Greyling Street is the site of the old *landdrost* and post office; Potchefstroom played a major role in the ZAR's postal services, and black runners were employed here to deliver mail as far away as what is now Mpumalanga province, hundreds of kilometres distant. The **Potchefstroom Museum**, Gouws Street (Mon–Fri 9am–5pm; free), houses one of the few remaining Voortrekker wagons used at the Battle of Blood River in 1838 (see p.548), when Voortrekkers defeated the Zulus.

Away from the centre and the main highway, Potch takes on a much more appealing demeanour, especially around the university area. Tom Street boasts an impressive avenue of oak trees leading all the way to the university precinct, known as "Die Bult", where you'll find attractive old buildings and functional new ones, along with the buzz of university life. It's a long walk from the centre – you'll need to drive or cycle here – and some nearby attractions include

Pretorius House (Mon–Fri 10am–1pm & 2–4pm; small entry fee), Van der Hoff Road (an extension of Kerk Street), the former home of Marthinus Pretorius, the ZAR's first president. It's a beautiful old house with whitewashed walls, green doors and a thatched roof, and is typical of nineteenth-century Afrikaner dwellings. Inside, you'll find dour photos and ornate wallpaper, minimal furnishings and a family Bible. On the opposite side of the street stands the **Totius Museum** (Mon–Fri 10am–1pm & 2–4pm; free), recreated to be as it was when the poet lived here a century ago. Totius was a key figure in the Dutch Reformed Church and Afrikaans language movement: as well as establishing the church's theological college in Potchefstroom, he was one of the first poets to publish in Afrikaans, and translated the Bible into Afrikaans between 1923 and 1933. The most striking part of the museum is the poet's tome-filled study, but look out also for paintings by the celebrated and controversial Jacob Pierneef, which were especially dedicated to Totius.

Practicalities

Potchefstroom is well served by public transport. Daily Translux, Greyhound and Intercape **buses** stop on Potgieter Street, near the tourist information centre, on their route between Cape Town and Johannesburg via Kimberley. **Trains** from Cape Town and Johannesburg terminate at the train station west of the city centre (☎018 299 3205). Like many university towns, the classic way of **getting around** in Potch is by bike – to rent one, head for Dingo Cycles in the Cachet Park Shopping Centre, Tom Street (☎018 293 2456).

The helpful **tourist office** in a new building next to the Town Hall, on the corner of Kerk and Potgieter streets (Mon–Fri 7.45am–1pm & 1.45–4.30pm; ☎018 299 5130), has maps and leaflets about the town available inside as well as posted outside if you arrive after hours. The only budget **place to stay** is *Lake Recreation Resort* (☎018 299 5474; ❶), north of the town centre on Tom Street, where you can rent a self-catering bungalow or **camp** with good facilities beside a lake. Otherwise, there's the large *Willow Garden Court* (☎018 297 6285; ❸), at the corner of Potgeiter and Mooi River streets by the Riverwalk Centre, though a better option is one of the B&Bs scattered around town – *Ou Drift* (☎018 297 4939; ❸), by the banks of the Mooi River, is comfortable and relaxing.

The best place for **eating and drinking** is the university area. At the heart of Die Bult complex is the great *Akker Coffee House* on Tom Street, open for most of the day and night, and the best place to hang out. For livelier action, the *Bourbon St Brewery*, also in Die Bult, has live music at weekends and serves pub grub, while for more conventional fare the familiar line-up of pizza/pasta restaurants and steakhouses are well represented at the Riverwalk Centre, Potch's main mall, off Potgeiter Street on the Johannesburg (east) side of the town centre.

Vredefort, a settlement 30km southeast of Potch just over the border in the Free State, near Parys, lies in the world's largest and oldest meteorite impact site, a ninety-kilometre-wide depression known as the Vredefort Dome dating back to a meteorite strike some 2000 million years ago. Nominated as a World Heritage Site, it has become a focus for outdoor sports and adventure tourism. For details of what's going on, contact the tourist office in Potch.

Klerksdorp and around

Nondescript **KLERKSDORP**, 25km down the N12 from Potchefstroom, is a busy agricultural and mining centre near some of the world's largest gold mines. The only significant attraction here is the **Klerksdorp Museum** at the

Afrikaner museums

The former Transvaal and Orange Free State are filled with museums dedicated to the preservation and propagation of **Afrikaner mythology**. Typically they include mementos from the Great Trek (waggons are particularly prized); displays of farm-life domesticity such as butter-churning and candle-making; children's toys (generally toy waggons made from bones); photos of Afrikaner generals from the Anglo-Boer Wars, with accompanying text about the "War of Liberation"; tattered Afrikaner flags, rifles and bullet belts; details of Afrikaner casualties of concentration camps; and, finally, a plaque to tell you where the town's 1938 Voortrekker centenary monument is.

Not surprisingly, given the new political dispensation, many such museums struggle to attract funding, and as a result find it hard to remain open. Some have tried widening their focus to include an element of local black African culture, although the results are often awkward or simply crass.

corner of Margaretha Prinsloo and Lombard streets (Mon–Fri 10am–1pm & 2–4.30pm, Sat 9.30am–noon, Sun 2–5pm; R2). Hardly surprising for a former prison, this is a fairly creepy place, with displays of flogging equipment, solitary confinement and the like, which effectively evokes the once-grim conditions. The courtyard has been converted into a standard Afrikaner museum, complete with waggon and candle-making displays.

Some 11km northwest of Klerksdorp, the **Faan Meintjes Nature Reserve** (daily 10am–6pm; ☏018 462 5700; R30 per vehicle plus R2 per adult; caravan stands and chalets **❶**), has few carnivores of note, but plenty of **white rhino**, **giraffe** and **antelope** wandering its bushveld terrain. To reach the reserve, head north on Van Riebeeck (R30), which is also called Church Street, south of the N12, and turn right at the signpost a few kilometres later, along Brady Lane. There are **San rock engravings** nearby on the Bosworth farm, which you can visit by appointment through the owner of the *North Hills Country House* (see below).

Practicalities

Daily Translux, Greyhound and Intercape **buses** stop on Church Street on their way from Cape Town to Johannesburg via Kimberley. The **train station** is just off Margaretha Prinsloo Street, a few blocks east of the city centre, with daily arrivals from Cape Town and Johannesburg (train information ☏018 406 2022).

Klerksdorp's **best place to stay** is unquestionably the *Fountain Villa Guest Lodge*, 21 Hendrik Potgieter Rd (☏018 464 1394 or 082 466 4001; **❷**), a National Monument house in the old town sporting elegant turrets and wooden lattice work, and featuring an outstanding **restaurant** in the converted stables, where there are also a couple more rooms. Further out, on the road to the Faan Meintjes reserve, the *North Hills Country House* (☏018 468 6416, Ⓦwww.northhills.co.za; **❷**–**❸**) provides comfortable double rooms and cosy suites with their own fireplace. Dinner and breakfast are extra, but at weekends a German restaurant with good vegetarians dishes operates. It's set on a small private nature reserve with an Arabian stud farm next door, and horse-riding can be arranged.

The road to Kimberley

Once past Klerksdorp, the N12 passes through vast stretches of maize-growing country. There are no big towns until you reach **Kimberley** in the Northern Cape; you'll pass through a succession of sleepy *dorps*, none of them particularly appealing. A string of small nature reserves on the banks of the Vaal and the excellent *Lindbergh Safari Lodge* provide the best opportunities to break up your journey.

Wolmaransstad and around

Wolmaransstad, 90km southwest of Klerksdorp on the N12, consists of little more than two or three streets with a handful of shops. There's a scraggy **campsite** off the R504 on the way to Leeudoringstad, but the nicest place to stay in these parts is the *Lindbergh Safari Lodge* (℡011 884 8923, ℮lindbergh@global.co.za; dinner, bed & breakfast ❺). Here you can get a tantalizing glimpse of how the Northwest *veld* looked before maize took over, when it was home to abundant birds and wildlife. Set in a small nature reserve, the beautiful thatched lodge looks out onto a busy watering hole, enabling indolent game viewing from an armchair. The rooms are luxurious, and there's a simple bush camp if you'd rather self-cater. The absence of predators makes it safe to wander the lodge on foot, and get close up to the giraffe, antelope and other plains game. To reach *Lindbergh*, turn right onto a dirt road, off the N12 some 20km south of Wolmaransstad, and follow the signs to Rietpan, and then to Leeufontein. The lodge is about 15km from the main road, but the roads are bad and signposting poor, so aim to travel during the day.

Further down the road, the *Buisfontein Safari Lodge* (℡018 598 6704; ❸) is a much plainer alternative, with eighteen thatched chalets and a good restaurant attached. For a taste of the scenery around the Vaal River, continue past Leeudoringstad and head east a few kilometres, avoiding the R504 to Bothaville, for the *Wolwespruit Nature Reserve* (℡018 581 9705; ❶), which has a decent **campsite** and some **stone cottages**.

Bloemhof and Christiana

Heading further down the N12, tiny **Bloemhof** is an agricultural town that also serves as a stopover for buses on the long haul between Johannesburg and Cape Town. Laid out by one James Barkly on his farm in 1866, the town was named after a garden of flowers cultivated by his daughter. Greyhound, Intercape and Translux **buses** all stop in town. Nearby is the large Bloemhof Dam; as well as a nature reserve (daily 8am–5.30pm) there is a plain camping and caravan resort, *Die Hoek* (℡053 433 0256) with chalets (❷) near the water's edge. Otherwise, the uninspiring *Bloemhof Hotel* (℡053 433 1211; ❶) is on the main street, offering rooms with TV and bath, and an adjoining windowless restaurant serving standard meaty fare.

Even smaller than Bloemhof, **Christiana** lies just over 50km further south, its few shops straggled out along the main road. **Accommodation** is limited to the tolerable *Christiana Hotel* (℡053 441 2326; ❶), on the main street, which has a **restaurant** serving grills, and two bars: one decorated and formerly for whites; the other windowless, shed-like, and formerly for blacks. There's a decent **campsite** on the banks of the Vaal, with showers, braai facilities, and incredibly noisy birds.

Travel details

Trains

Bloemhof to: Cape Town (1 daily; 19hr); Kimberley (2 daily; 2hr 40min); Johannesburg (2 daily: 6hr); Klerksdorp (2 daily; 2hr 30min); Potchefstroom (2 daily; 3hr 30min).

Klerksdorp to: Cape Town (1 daily; 22hr); Kimberley (2 daily; 5hr); Johannesburg (2 daily; 3hr 30min); Potchefstroom (2 daily; 50min).
Potchefstroom to: Cape Town (1 daily; 23hr); Kimberley (2 daily; 6hr); Johannesburg (2 daily; 2hr 20min); Klerksdorp (2 daily; 50min).

Buses

Bloemhof to: Cape Town (1 Mon, Wed & Fri–Sun; 13hr 45min); Johannesburg (2–3 daily; 3–4hr); Kimberley (2–3 daily; 2hr); Klerksdorp (2–3 daily; 2hr); Potchefstroom (2–3 daily; 2hr).
Christiana to: Cape Town (1 Tues & Sun; 12hr 15min); Kimberley (1–2 daily; 1hr 30min); Klerksdorp (1–2 daily; 2hr); Johannesburg (1–2 daily; 5hr); Potchefstroom (1–2 daily; 3hr).
Klerksdorp to: Cape Town (1–2 daily; 15hr); Johannesburg (3–4 daily; 2hr); Kimberley (2–3 daily; 4hr); Potchefstroom (3–4 daily; 45min).

Mafikeng to: Johannesburg (1 daily; 4hr); Rustenburg (1 daily; 2hr 30min).
Potchefstroom to: Cape Town (1–3 daily except Tues; 16hr); Johannesburg (3–4 daily; 2hr); Kimberley (2–3 daily; 4hr 15min); Klerksdorp (3–4 daily; 45min).
Rustenburg to: Pretoria (1 daily; 2hr); Mafikeng (1 daily; 2hr 30min).
Sun City to: Johannesburg (2–3 daily; 2hr 30min); Pretoria (1 daily; 2hr 30min).
Zeerust to: Pretoria (1 daily; 3hr 15min).

Flights

Sun City to: Johannesburg (1–3 daily; 35min).

Mpumalanga

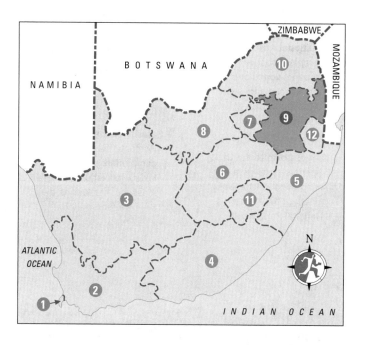

✳ Raft the Blyde River Canyon

Get an unconventional view from the bottom of a spectacular thirty-kilometre canyon. See p.678

✳ Mad Dogz

A superb craft gallery west of Hoedspruit, attached to a bistro with terrific B&B rooms. See p.680

✳ Traditional African meal

Sample crocodile, mopane worms or more conventional fare such as beef pot roast at Shangana Cultural Village. See p.688

✳ Kruger north to south

Spend several days covering the 414-kilometre length of the Kruger National Park, South Africa's premier game reserve. See p.693

✳ Night drive

Join a Kruger Park night drive and see what comes out after dark. See p.700

✳ Walking adventure

Take a hike in the wilderness on a guided walking safari in the Kruger. See p.703

✳ Spot leopards

The luxury camps in the Sabi Sands Game Reserve offer excellent opportunities to observe leopards in the wild. See p.708

✳ Safaris for the soul

Romantic *Garonga* safari camp offers sensuous luxury, relaxation and massage – as well as the Big Five. See p.709

Mpumalanga

M pumalanga, "the land of the rising sun" to its Siswati- and Zulu-speaking residents, extends east from Gauteng to Mozambique and Swaziland. To many visitors the province is synonymous with the **Kruger National Park**, the real draw of South Africa's east flank, and one of Africa's best game parks. Kruger occupies most of Mpumalanga's and Northern Province's borders with Mozambique, and covers over 20,000 square kilometres – an area the size of Wales or Massachusetts. Unashamedly populist, Kruger is the easiest African game park to drive around in on your own, staying at one of its many well-run restcamps. On its western border lie a number of **private reserves**, offering the chance to escape the Kruger crush – at a price – with well-informed rangers conducting safaris in open vehicles.

Apart from the irresistible magnet of big-game country, Mpumalanga also has some spectacular scenery in the mountainous area known as the **Escarpment**, a couple of hours' drive west of Kruger and easily tacked onto a visit to the park. With the exception of **Pilgrim's Rest**, none of the Escarpment towns merits exploration, but they make good night stops to and from Kruger, and there are some famously stunning views as you drive around, where the mountains drop to the Lowveld. The most famous viewpoints – **God's Window**, **Bourke's Luck Potholes** and **Three Rondavels** – are along the lip of the Escarpment, which can be seen on a one-day 156-kilometre drive from Sabie. The views of **Blyde River Canyon** are most famous of all and, while you can't drive into the canyon, there are some fabulous hiking and river-rafting opportunities in this area.

Jammed between the mountains and Kruger are the former African **bantustans**, created under apartheid: Lebowa for Sotho speakers and Gazankulu for Shangaan- and Tsonga-speaking people. The poverty of these artificial statelets was exacerbated in the 1980s, when hundreds of thousands of Mozambicans fled into Gazankulu to escape the civil war in their home country. Even today, with the war over, Mozambicans attempt to cross illegally into South Africa, braving lions, National Parks officials and anti-poaching units in Kruger in a quest to reach the "golden city" of Johannesburg.

For overseas visitors, the **route** is usually the other way round, starting from Johannesburg and heading through the unattractive industrial corridor traversed by the N4 as it races to **Nelspruit**, the modern capital of Mpumalanga. From here the N4 continues to the **Mozambique** border. This route gives you access to the southernmost part of Kruger; Nelspruit lies 62km from Malelane Gate and 51km from Numbi Gate. The town also connects with the road south through **Barberton** to Swaziland.

Descending the Escarpment on one of four mountain passes takes you into

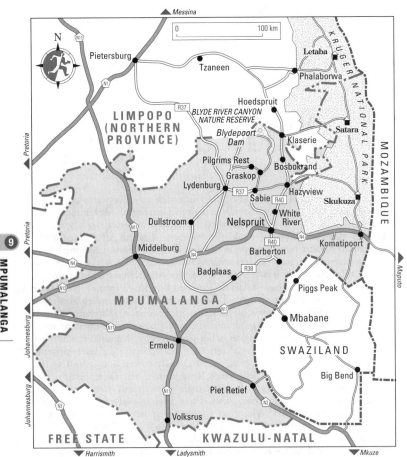

the tropical-fruit-growing and bushveld country of the Lowveld, with impressive views back towards the towering massif of the Escarpment. A number of places close to the **Blydepoort Dam** at the foot of the Blyde River Canyon can be taken in as bushveld breaks on the way to or from Kruger. In the same vicinity, around the tiny centre of **Hoedspruit**, roughly 90km via a route arching east from the Escarpment, a number of small **game farms** offer cut-price bush experiences. While these are good for a couple of nights, they lack the variety of animals and big game provided by Kruger and the pricier lodges in the Manyeleti and Timbabavati private game reserves.

The Escarpment

Four hours' drive east of Johannesburg International Airport takes you to one of the city's favoured mountain retreats: the waving grasslands and luxury guesthouses of the Mpumalanga Drakensberg, generally known as the **Escarpment**. While most travellers visit the region purely because of its proximity to the Kruger National Park, it provides some of the most dramatic views in the country, which can be enjoyed with little effort. Unlike the KwaZulu-Natal Drakensberg, this section of the range is one you can tour in your own car, stopping at one of the tourist towns for lunch and retiring to comfortable lodgings at the end of the day.

There's little reason to stop off in the functional town of **Lydenburg,** but **Dullstroom** has established itself as an upmarket fly-fishing resort. Other than this, there's no reason to dally along this route, especially since the little forestry towns of **Sabie** and **Graskop** have ample accommodation for all budgets and are convenient bases for exploring the area, but only **Pilgrim's Rest**, a reconstructed mining settlement from turn-of-the-century gold-rush days, merits a visit for itself. The main draw of the Escarpment is the **Blyde River Canyon**, whose dizzying views into one of the world's great gorges appear in countless South African tourist brochures. In addition to a number of viewpoints along the Escarpment lip, the canyon can also be seen from the **Blyderivierspoort Nature Reserve** at its foot. The five-day **Blyderivierspoort Hiking Trail**, one of South Africa's best walks, starts at **God's Window** on the lip; it takes in all the major viewpoints and gives access to the flora and (if you're quiet and lucky) fauna of the reserve, which includes zebra, hippo, kudu and the entire range of South African primates – baboons, vervet and samango monkeys and bushbabies.

Dullstroom

Some 209km east of Johannesburg, the R540 branches off the N4 at nondescript **Belfast** and heads into the hills, where the typical highveld countryside is covered by grasslands, waving tall and green in summer, but turning russet in winter.

Unless your passion is fly-fishing, chances are you'll find the tiny crossroads settlement of **DULLSTROOM**, 35km north of Belfast on the R540, as unexciting as its name suggests. However, Dullstroom can be a useful place to stop over for a night on your way to Kruger National Park; it certainly caters to the weekend trade of Johannesburg escapees looking for a rest and fine food – most of the accommodation doubles up as restaurants.

Accommodation

Critchley Hackle Lodge Teding van Berkhout Street ☎013 254 0145, ⓔ chl/wks@mweb.co.za. A gracious country-style hotel with stone and brick cottages, each with a fireplace, and also with a recommended restaurant and a tea-and-scones patio. Half-board ➏

Dullstroom Inn Teding van Berkhout Street ☎013 254 0071, ⓕ013 254 0278. A pleasantly cool Victorian country inn that is one of the least expensive places to stay in the village, with a draught beer pub which gets packed at weekends. ➌

Old Transvaal Inn 117 Hugenote St ☎013 254 0222, ✉ggg@worldonline.co.za. A quiet and friendly B&B offering good food, a fine location and cultivated quaintness of style. Recommended. ❸ The Poacher 66 Hugenote St ☎013 254 0108, ✉info@poacher.co.za. A small, friendly lodge with four rooms, plus dam, river frontage and a tackle shop, but mostly used for its restaurant and pub with Guinness on tap. ❸

Walkersons Country Manor 20km north of Dullstroom on the R540 ☎013 254 0246, ✉www .walkersons.co.za. The most luxurious of the upmarket country lodges catering to fly-fishing enthusiasts, with sixteen rooms in thatched stone buildings on a nature reserve, which provides exclusive fishing for its guests in ten dams and 2km of river frontage. The restaurant, open to the public, includes dishes like roasted beetroot salad, ostrich steak and marinated artichoke. Half-board ❼

Eating

Dullstroom's best-known restaurant, *Die Tonteldoos Bistro*, in the main street (☎013 254 0115) is a popular, busy, daytime place with big breakfasts, a kids' menu and homemade bread. The deli at the front of the restaurant stocks smoked trout and other delicacies like nougat. Also in the main street, catering for the daytime trade, is *Harrie's Pancakes,* popular for sweet as well as savoury pancakes, soups, open sandwiches and breakfasts.

Lydenburg and Long Tom Pass

Some 58km north of Dullstroom, humdrum **LYDENBURG** is the site of one of South Africa's major archeological finds, replicas of which are on display at the **Lydenburg Museum** (Mon–Fri 9am–noon & 2–4.15pm, Sat & Sun 10am–4pm; small entry fee) in the Gustav Klingbiel Nature Reserve, 3km out of town along the R37 to Sabie. The **Lydenburg Heads**, seven beautiful ceramic masks (probably ceremonial) dating back to the fifth century, are some of the first figurative sculptures in southern Africa. As well as replicas of these heads (the originals are in the South African Museum in Cape Town), there are excellent displays on human activity in the vicinity over the past million years or so.

Striking east from Lydenburg, the R37 twists its way up **Long Tom Pass**, which takes its name from the Scheider siege guns used here by the Boers during the 1899–1902 Second Anglo-Boer War against the British. Known as Long Toms because of their elongated necks, the artillery pieces were able to throw a 43kg shell a distance of 10km. You can still see the holes blasted by retreating Boers into the series of switchbacks cutting up the pass, known as the Staircase.

Sabie, Pilgrim's Rest and Graskop

Sabie, the largest of the three towns occupying the heights of the Escarpment, has its personality split between serving the surrounding agroforestry industry and trying to please the tourists who use it as a base. Of the other two, **Pilgrim's Rest** unashamedly plays to the tour buses, pushing hard with its restored gold-rush buildings and themed museums, while the relatively uninteresting timber centre of **Graskop** is trying to develop its potential in an attempt to secure those elusive tourist bucks.

Sabie and around

Lying on the R37 beyond Long Tom Pass, **SABIE** (pronounced "Saabie", like the car) is the centre of Mpumalanga's agroforestry industry. With 450 square kilometres under active cultivation, it holds the dubious distinction of lying at the heart of South Africa's largest artificial forests – the extensive pine plantations look monotonous compared to the rich, jungly variety of the remaining pockets of indigenous woodland. Before the foresters arrived, Sabie made its name as a gold centre, with a lucky strike in 1895 at the Klein Sabie Falls. Mining stopped halfway through the twentieth century, and today the gold prospectors have been replaced by escapees from hectic Johannesburg, who make a living here running restaurants, B&Bs or craft shops. Sabie's compact size, slow pace, mildly arty ambience and gentle climate make it a congenial base for exploring the Escarpment, providing you have your own transport.

Arrival and information

Public **transport** to Sabie is limited to minibus taxis plying the routes from neighbouring towns; otherwise, the only way to get here is in your own car. The official **information office** is the Panorama Information Bureau (Mon–Fri 9am–5pm, Sat 9am–2pm, Sun 9am–1pm, ☎013 764 1125, ⓦwww.sabie.com) in the Market Square mall in Main Road in the village centre; it can also arrange accommodation bookings. In the same mall, you can check your email around the corner at Playweb **cybercafé** (Mon–Sat 9am–6pm & Sun 2–5pm, ☎013 764 3483).

Accommodation

Sabie offers a good supply of reasonably priced **accommodation**, though prices can rise dramatically during South African school holidays. Avoid the rock-bottom B&Bs listed at all the information bureaus: most of them offer no privacy.

Artist's Cafe Hendriksdal, 15km south of Sabie along the R37 ☎013 764 2309. Situated in the beautifully converted colonial station buildings of Hendriksdal siding, which still has goods trains trundling along its tracks; the stationmaster's house has been converted into a first-class restaurant, and a gallery features work by local artists. It has only four rooms, so you should book well ahead. Kids are welcome. ❹

Jock of the Bushveld Off Main Road, in the centre ☎013 764 2178, ⓦwww.jock.co.za. A well-maintained, popular caravan park with backpacker dorms and self-catering, en-suite chalet rooms and a restaurant on the premises. ❶–❸

The Kranz 2km on the R537 to White River ☎013 764 1330, ⓦwww.thekranz.co.za. Friendly B&B in a deluxe cottage with a view over a cliff, as well as a slightly cheaper log cabin or garden cottage. Less expensive still are a couple of rooms in the main house with a shared bathroom. You'll need to drive the 2km to town for dinner. ❷–❸

Merry Pebbles Holiday Resort 2km west from the centre on the Old Lydenburg Road ☎013 764 2266, ⓦwww.merrypebbles.co.za. The pick of the Sabie self-catering establishments, rated the third-best caravan park in the country by the AA. The resort offers camping, self-catering and en-suite chalets, and its facilities include a heated pool and children's playground. ❶–❷

Misty Mountain Lodge 24km southwest of Sabie on Long Tom Pass ☎013 764 3377, ⓔmystymtn@iafrica.com. Pleasant, newly refurbished B&B units (with self-catering available), some with splendid views across pine plantations into the valleys. Trout fishing on the property is possible, with rods and flies for rent at a nominal rate; the lodge is also well-placed for walks into indigenous forest. ❸

Sabie River Backpackers Lodge 185 Main Rd ☎013 764 2118 or 082 349 2820, ⓔghoeks @iafrica.com. Dorms, doubles, a tree house and camping available at this well-run hostel, which also organizes adventure activities such as river tubing trips. ❶

Villa Ticino On the corner of Louis Trichardt and Second streets ☎013 764 2598, ⓦwww.villaticino.co.za. An extremely hospitable Swiss-owned B&B with a terrace looking onto the hills, and a guest lounge with a pool table. Winter discounts are available. ❸

The Town and around

Sabie is segmented by **Main Street** (the R37, which is the continuation of the Long Tom Pass from Lydenburg), which meanders into the town centre where it hits **Main Road** at right angles. At the junction of the two, the compact **St Peter's**, an English-style country church designed in 1912 by Sir Herbert Baker, hides in a verdant garden dominated by a gigantic jacaranda tree, which in early summer covers the lawn with mauve petals like confetti. Nearby at the corner of Tenth and Seventh streets, the **Safcol Forest Industry Museum** (Mon–Fri 8.30am–4pm, Sat & Sun 10am–3pm; R5) is a small, but worthwhile display on the history of forestry and the timber industry in South Africa; there's also a small section on the evolution of papermaking.

A large number of **waterfalls** drop down the slopes just outside Sabie. Just 7km from town, down the Old Lydenburg Road (which culminates in a dead end), you can visit three of the most impressive: **Bridal Veil**, **Horseshoe** and, appropriately at the end of the road, **Lone Creek Falls**. The loveliest and most accessible of the three, Lone Creek is conveniently reached down a paved, circular path that crosses a river and works its way back to the car park.

Thirteen kilometres north of Sabie along the Graskop road are the more spectacular seventy-metre-high **Mac Mac Falls** – named after the many people of Scottish descent who died looking for gold in the area and whose names appear on dozens of tombstones in the vicinity. Unfortunately, views here are restricted by a mesh fence around the viewing platform. Since these are the most visited of the falls, local craftworkers have set up a **market** in the car park. While you can't swim in the inviting waterfall pool at the base of the

---

Activities in Sabie

With its forest, massive gorge and mountains, the Escarpment offers good opportunities for adventure activities. Among the operators running a range of these is Sabie Extreme Adventures, Main Street, Sabie (☏082 507 9108), based at *Sabie Backpackers*.

Bunji Swing Big Swing (☏072 223 8155) operate a bunji swing with a 69-metre drop into the Graskop Gorge and a 150-metre swing, purportedly the longest swing in world.

Horse trails On the way to Lone Creek, Sabie Horse Trails (☏013 764 1011 ext. 205, after hours ☏013 764 3324) offers **horse-riding** outings from one hour to two days, depending on your level of experience. Fern Tree Holiday Resort (Murray ☏013 764 2215 or 082 349 1109) and Smokey Mountains Horse Trails (☏013 764 1596 or 082 899 2164) also offers horse-riding.

Mountain biking For cycling in the hills and backroads, you can rent mountain bikes from Denzil Lawrie (☏082 878 5527, ✉denzilbikedoc@xsinet.co.za), who also offers guided trails.

River rafting The Blyde River Canyon is one of the largest in the world, with river rafting on the Blyde the only way, apart from hiking, you can explore the wilderness of the canyon itself. Spectra Ventures (☏013 744 1582 or 083 409 3505 ✉bushwise@icon.co.za) and Blyde River Rafting (☏015 795 5250 or 082 572 2223, ✉catfish@mweb.co.za) run the river on their overnight trip (about R800). This covers the whitewater section – mostly grade two and grade three rapids with a couple of grade fours on the first day – overnighting at a forest camp at one of the Three Rondavel mountains, with a flatwater paddle over the Blydepoort Dam on the second day to finish off. A one-day rafting trip (about R500) takes in the whitewater section, while a two-hour trip (about R150) on the lower Blyde River goes through thick riverine forest with plenty of birds, and over some safe (but lively) rapids.

falls, there is a river pool at the Mac Mac Pools, a few kilometres further on where there is also a picnic and braai area (R5 entry) and the three-kilometre **Secretary Bird Walking Trail**. Less popular, but surpassing the Mac Mac Falls, are the **Berlin** and **Lisbon** falls. They are signposted and easily accessible off the R532 (close to God's Window), and you can get close enough to feel the spray near the vertiginous, unfenced drops.

Eating and drinking

Sabie has a couple of memorable **restaurants**, some relaxed places for light meals or drinks and one or two places you'd probably rather forget.

Artists Café Hendriksdal, 15km south of Sabie along the R37 ☎013 764 2309. A restaurant in converted station buildings, with an art-gallery setting and great atmosphere for lunch or dinner. The owners cook up a real storm – their Italian-style dishes are especially recommended. Booking essential.

The Country Kitchen Main Street. Popular dishes at this venue with outdoor seating include crocodile strips served with pumpkin and potato *rosti*, venison with peppercorn juice infused with *waterblommetjies*, ostrich and beef. Lunch Tues–Sun and dinner Tues–Sat.

Midnight Express Spar Centre. Indoor and outdoor seating, with mountain views; good for coffee

and sandwiches while doing your shopping.

Petena Pancakes Main Street. Cheap but unremarkable creperie with outdoor seating, serving pancakes with savoury mince or fish as well as sweet fillings.

The Wild Fig Tree On the corner Main and Louis Trichardt streets. South African dishes are the speciality at this family restaurant set in an attractive, lush garden.

Woodsman Restaurant On the corner of Main and Mac Mac roads. A licensed restaurant with a beer garden, serving Cypriot Greek food, including vegetarian *meze*, plus local specialities such as ostrich and trout, and delicious slow-cooked lamb. Also good for coffee and snacks too.

Pilgrim's Rest

Hiding in a valley 35km north of Sabie, **PILGRIM'S REST**, an almost too-perfectly restored gold-mining town, is an irresistible port of call for the scores of tour buses meandering daily through the Escarpment's passes. A collection of red-roofed, corrugated-iron buildings, including a period bank, a filling station with pre-1920 fuel pumps and the wonderful *Royal Hotel* brimming with Victoriana, the place is undeniably photogenic. But you can't help feeling there's little substance behind the romanticized gold-rush image, especially when the village nods off after 5pm once the day-trippers have been spirited away.

Pilgrim's Rest owes its origins to South Africa's first **gold rush**, which predates the uncovering of the great Gauteng seams. In 1873, Alex "Wheelbarrow" Patterson discovered gold in the creek; his attempts to keep his discovery secret were a total failure, and by the end of the year, Patterson had been joined by 1500 diggers frantically working 4000 claims. Far from the pristine little village of today, the **Pilgrim's Rest diggings** were the site of gruelling labour and unhygienic conditions. Many diggers arrived malnourished, suffering from dysentery and malaria after punishing treks through the Lowveld. Those who survived could expect drab lives in tents or, if they struck lucky, more permanent wattle-and-daub huts. In 1896, the diggings were bought up by the Transvaal Gold Mining Estates (TGME); in 1972 the TGME closed its Beta Mine and Pilgrim's Rest was handed over to the provincial administration. In the 1980s the whole settlement was declared an historic monument. Hidden behind the hill to the southwest of town, away from tourist eyes, mining continues, with functional buildings, cyanide-filled slime dams and great red scars hacked into the hillside, the indigenous forest having been bulldozed out of existence.

Orientation and information

Pilgrim's Rest stretches along its one main road and is divided into Uptown and Downtown. **Uptown** (or Lower Town), to the east, centres around the *Royal Hotel* and the **tourist information** centre (daily 9am–12.45pm & 1.15 –4.30pm; ☎013 768 1060, ☏013 768 1469, ☺jonstep@mweb.co.za), which can also provide details of accommodation. Commercialized Uptown has the greatest concentration of shops and restaurants and consequently draws the bulk of tourists. **Downtown**, just 1km to the west, has a more down-to-earth atmosphere, and is the better bet for exploring and finding something to eat – though many visitors slip in and out of Pilgrim's without realizing the area even exists.

Accommodation

Although Pilgrim's Rest is by far the prettiest of the Escarpment towns, it has very little **accommodation**.

Beretta's Downtown ☎013 768 1066 or 083 444 2639, ☏013 768 1222, ☺m.stuart@freemail .absa.co.za). Excellent-value B&B with eight clean and functional en-suite rooms in a former hardware store. Far nicer are the two Victorian corrugated-iron cottages, which are rented out for the exclusive use of a single group or couple for the same price as the rooms. Breakfast, included in the bargain rate, is served at the *The Vine* restaurant (see p.677). ❸

District Six Miners' Cottages Downtown ☎013 768 1211; bookings during office hours Mon–Fri only. Self-catering accommodation in authentic two-bedroomed 1920s workers houses with

verandahs overlooking the town and mountains; these are among the best places to stay on the Escarpment, and cheap. Book ahead, as there's no on-site office. ❶

Pilgrim's Rest Caravan Park Downtown ☎013 768 1427. Grassy campsite with a river running through it, as well as six erected tents furnished with two beds, chairs, table and lamp. ❶

The Royal Hotel Main Street, Uptown ☎013 768 1100, ⓦwww.royal-hotel.co.za. Atmospheric hotel that dates back to the gold-rush days and brims with luxurious Victoriana, with guests mostly accommodated in restored houses on the main road. ❺

The Town

Apart from souvenir hunting and lingering in the cafés and tea shops, the main activity in Pilgrim's is visiting its handful of **museums**. Tickets for all these must be bought in advance at the tourist information centre (see above). You can whip through the three modest town "museums" in a matter of minutes, as they amount to little more than rooms reconstructed as they were in the gold-rush days. More interesting are those out of the centre. To get a really authentic impression of the gold-mining days, head for the open-air **Diggings Site Museum** on the eastern edge of town on the Graskop Road (guided tours only, daily at 10am, 11am, noon, 2pm & 3pm; R5), where you can see demonstrations of alluvial gold-panning and get a guided tour around the bleak diggers' huts, remnants of workings and machinery from the early mining days. By contrast, if you want to see how those at the top lived, visit **Alanglade**, just west of the Downtown area (guided tours only, Mon–Sat 11am & 2pm; R20), the reconstructed home of the former general manager of the mine. The house has a wonderful collection of early twentieth-century British fashion and decorative arts and reveals a sheltered way of life far removed from either Africa or mining.

Eating and drinking

Pilgrim's Rest has plenty of restaurants and tea shops to provide for the daily influx of visitors using Graskop or Sabie as their base. Of the **places to eat** in Uptown, only the *Digger's Den*, a lively, canteen-style place attached to the

Royal (see opposite), is open all day and every evening. For lunches the choice is wider: *Chaitow's*, a small café opposite the hotel, serves pricey but tasty pastas and pizzas, as well as smoked trout fillets and pate. For something more exciting, head for *Edwin Wood's Wine Cellar*, below their wine shop on Main Street, which serves the best Cape wines with cheese platters. There are a few more daytime places along the Downtown section of the main drag, all of which have outdoor seating: *Scott's Café* (daily 9am–6pm) serves pancakes, sandwiches, salads and other light meals and has a pleasant bar; *Jubilee Potters & Coffee Shop* (daily 9am–7pm) does chicken, pies, trout and burgers; and *The Vine* has South African specialities such as *bobotie* or oxtail and *samp* on the menu and stays open till 7pm.

Graskop

Some 15km southeast of Pilgrim's Rest, **GRASKOP** owes its place on the tourist map to *Harrie's Pancake Shop*, which serves much-imitated but rarely rivalled crepes, and attracts all the tour buses doing the Escarpment viewpoints. The town itself is very ordinary, with timber trucks rumbling heavily through, and nothing much to see in the centre apart from the shops eyeing the tourist trade. Its location, however, as the closest town to the Blyde River Canyon to the north, goes some way towards compensating, and the growing number of artists, together with a small gay community, are helping to shift Graskop's lumberjack image. One of the village's new industries that stand out is its **wild African silk** factory and showroom, a couple of doors down from the tourist information bureau, which manufactures and sells a range of clothes, soft furnishing, duvets and even teddy bears from the silk of mopane silk worms (indigenous to Botswana).

Information

Panorama Information & Central Reservations (Mon–Fri 9am–5pm, Sat 9am–2pm, Sun 9am–1pm; ☏013 767 1377, ☏013 767 1975, ⓦwww .graskop.com) on Louis Trichardt Street, is the official **tourist information** bureau and can also provide details of **accommodation**.

Accommodation

Given its size, Graskop has a surprisingly large number of self-catering places, but few B&Bs, although it does have the delightful, stylish and reasonably priced *Graskop Hotel*.

Graskop Backpackers On the corner of Eeufees and Blood River streets ☏013 767 1761, ©graskop@global.co.za. A suburban two-storey house converted into dorms, as well as the property next door, where there are doubles, some en suite. Camping is allowed on the large shady lawn and bedding can be rented at a small charge. Lifts can be arranged from Hazyview, although there's no official shuttle from Nelspruit or Hazyview. ❶
Graskop Hotel On the corner of High Street and Louis Trichardt Avenue ☏013 767 1244, ⓦwww.graskophotel.co.za. From the outside it looks deceptively like a bog-standard travelling-salesman's joint, but actually has a very stylish interior of retro furniture, African baskets, fabrics and sculptures; its 34 airy rooms, some of them in garden wings, are decorated with considerable flair. Combined with its personal and relaxed atmosphere, this makes it one of the nicest places to stay on the Escarpment. The breakfasts are excellent, and the hotel is in walking distance of the town's restaurants. ❸
Graskop Log Cabin Village Oorwinning Street ☏013 767 1974, ⓦwww.logvillage.co.za. A resort right in the centre of town, with a swimming pool, and log fires for the cold winter nights, but no views. ❷
Kloofsig Chalets Just outside town on the road to Hazyview ☏013 767 1489, ©sdog@iafrica.com. This resort makes up for the fact that it's over the road, rather than right on the lip of the canyon, by offering modern and luxurious townhouse style

units, with discounts during quiet periods. ❸
Panorama Rest Camp Outside town on the
Hazyview road ☎ & ℱ013 767 1091, ⓦwww.satic
.co.za). Inexpensive accommodation in gardens

looking out over the Escarpment as well as campsites and a variety of units sleeping two to eight
people. Views aside, *Panorama* is slightly showing
its age, though renovations are taking place. ❷

Eating

For **eating**, the legendary *Harrie's* on Louis Trichardt Street serves sweet or
savoury pancakes and has a nice outdoor terrace, and an inside dining room
with a roaring log fire in winter. *The Lonely Tree*, on the corner of Louis
Trichardt and Kerk streets, works hard to compete, with pancakes, chocolate
cake, filter coffee and good service. For more substantial meals, *Leonardos
Trattoria*, Louis Trichardt Street (☎013 767 1076), with an adjoining art and
craft shop, is one of the few places open in the evening (closed Sunday) and
does good pizza and pasta lunches and dinners.

Blyde River Canyon and Blydepoort Dam

There are few places in South Africa where you can enjoy such easily accessible and dramatic scenery than the **Blyde River Canyon**. Dropping sharply
away from the Escarpment into the Lowveld, the colossal canyon is weathered
out of strata of red rock. **Blyde River Canyon Nature Reserve** (also known
as Blyderivierspoort Nature Reserve) stretches from a narrow tail near Graskop
in the south, and broadens into a great amphitheatre partially flooded by the
Blydepoort Dam about 60km to the north. The views of the canyon are
wonderful from both above and below, but the nicest way to take in the vistas
is on an easy half-day's drive along the canyon lip.

Canyon viewpoints

Some 3km north of Graskop, the road branches and the easterly R534 takes a
fifteen-kilometre loop past a series of superb viewpoints. The road winds
through pine plantations until it comes to the turn-off to the **Pinnacle**, a
gigantic quartzite column topped with trees, rising out of a ferny gorge. After
another 4km the road reaches the sheer drop and Lowveld views of **God's
Window**, one of the most famous and most developed of the viewpoints, with
toilets and specially constructed stalls for curio sellers. The looping road returns
to rejoin the R532, which from here heads north for 28km beyond the turn-
off to reach **Bourke's Luck Potholes** at the confluence of the Treur and
Blyde rivers – a collection of strange, smoothly scooped formations carved
into the rocks by water-driven pebbles. The best view of all lies 14km beyond,
at the **Three Rondavels**. The name describes only one small feature of this
cinemascope vista: three cylinders in the shape of ships with the meandering
Blyde River twisting its way hundreds of metres below. No photograph does
justice to the sheer enormity of the view, punctuated by one series of cliffs after
another buttressing into the valley.

The only **place to stay** in the nature reserve is *Aventura Blydepoort* (☎013
769 8005, ⓔaventura@iafrica.com; ❸), 5km north of the turn-off to the Three
Rondavels lookout. The resort has comfortable, self-contained and fully
equipped cottages, a swimming pool, supermarket, bottle store and filling station; the atmosphere can feel a little institutionalized, but it's a good place for
children.

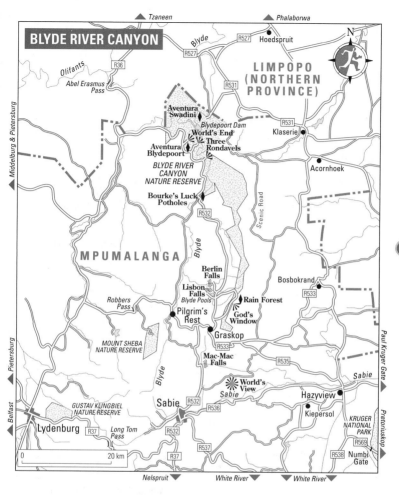

BLYDE RIVER CANYON

Three Rondavels to Blydepoort Dam

The ninety-kilometre **drive** from the Three Rondavels viewpoint to the base of the canyon provides spectacular views of the Escarpment cliffs rising out of the Lowveld and is easily incorporated into your itinerary if you're heading for Kruger. The drive winds west to join with the R36 and heads north to begin its descent through the Abel Erasmus Pass and then the J.G. Strijdom Tunnel through the mountain, with the wide Lowveld plains opening out on the other side. The road takes a wide arching trajectory to circumnavigate the canyon.

Along the R527, near its junction with the R36, the **Monsoon Gallery**, (☎015 795 5114, ⓦwww.monsoongallery.com), 29km west of Hoedspruit, makes a good place to pause on your journey to browse in their excellent shop, have a meal or spend the night. Their great African arts and crafts showroom has an absorbing selection of authentic material, including ironwork and woodcarving from Zimbabwe, superb tapestries from the Karosswerkers factory near Tzaneen, Venda pots and jewellery, as well as African music CDs and books. Next door to the gallery, a **silk shop** sells beautiful African and Indian silk garments, silk-filled duvets, cravats and scarves. Also part of the same outfit is a good **place to eat** – *Mad Dogz Café*, where breakfasts, lunches and teas are served every day. They also offer **accommodation** nearby at *Blue Cottages* (☎015 795 5425; ❸–❹), in superbly comfortable suites in a farmhouse filled with African artefacts and fabrics, set in an enticingly cool and colourful garden; more modest, but also beautiful, are the garden cottages. Breakfast is served at *Mad Dogz*; you can also have a medium-priced dinner served in your garden under candle-light.

Roughly 15km further east, the untarred Driehoek road hives off to the south past the *Aventura Swadini* resort and on to the Blydepoort Dam. Alternatively, you can continue on the R531 for a further 12km and take the tarred turn-off to the southwest, which leads straight down to the dam. At a dead end along this road, the **Blyde River Canyon Visitor Centre** (daily 7am–5pm) has interesting displays on local ecology and a useful model of the canyon that helps you get orientated. The best reason to come here though is for the views across the flooded valley below and to spend the night close to indigenous bushveld at the foot of the mountains.

Blydepoort accommodation

Reached along the same road as the visitor centre, *Aventura Swadini* (☎ & ☎015 795 5141; ❸) has 78 **chalets** that sleep up to six and a **campsite** with stunning scenic surrounds; it's great for kids, and cheap for a group, but has a similar institutional feel to its sister resort on the mountain. A number of short trails start from here and you can take cruises on the Blydepoort Dam. More intimate, and highly recommended, is the nearby *Trackers* (☎015 795 5033, ✉trackers@lantic.net; ❶–❹), a quiet and spectacular retreat abutting the canyon's cliffs 25km from Hoedspruit. It offers a variety of accommodation on a marvellous farm full of indigenous bushveld vegetation (as well as zebra and antelope): camping, a backpacker house with a dorm and six doubles, self-catering chalets and half-board. A trained botanist living on the farm runs

---

Blyderivierspoort Hiking Trail

The only way to get directly into the canyon from the Escarpment is on foot, and the five-day **Blyderivierspoort Hiking Trail** is a great way of doing this. Although the 65-kilometre route requires a fair degree of fitness, the gradients aren't generally too taxing and the walk could be undertaken by a hardy novice. The hike starts at God's Window, 5km north of Graskop, and works its way north, ending at the Blydepoort Dam in the valley, 38km from Hoedspruit. There's a diversity of plant and animal life along the way and you may be lucky enough to spot hippos, crocodiles, zebras, baboons and monkeys.

Accommodation is provided in four fully equipped huts that can sleep up to thirty people (the maximum allowed on the trail), with flush toilets, cold showers and firewood. For somewhere to stay near the start or end of the trail, see the Graskop and Blyde River Canyon accounts. As the start and finish of the trail are 150km apart by road, you'll need to have access to two vehicles or make arrangements to get back to your starting point. You must carry all your own food. Take note, too, that although the trail starts in **malaria**-free terrain, you'll be entering the Lowveld, where the disease is a potential hazard, especially in summer.

Reservations can be made through Mpumalanga Parks Board (☎013 759 5432, ✉mpbinfo@cis.co.za).

recommended **guided walks** through the indigenous vegetation. To get to
Trackers, turn south into Driehoek road (as for the *Aventura* resort), continue
for a little over 6km, then follow the "D. Rushworth" sign on your right.
Trackers can also direct you to *Candle Cottage* (❶), a **forestry bungalow** on the
edge of the canyon with views across to the Kruger National Park. From the
fully equipped cottage, which sleeps eight people in three rooms, you can set
off on trails through the forest.

The Lowveld

South Africa's **Lowveld** is wedged between the Mpumalanga section of the
Drakensberg and Mozambique. It is part of a vast sub-tropical region of savannah that stretches north through Zimbabawe and Zambia, as far north as Central
Africa. Closely associated at the turn of the century with fortune-seekers,
hunters, gold-diggers and adventurers, these days the South African Lowveld's
claim to fame is its proximity to the Kruger National Park and the adjacent private game reserves. Although several of the towns on the game park fringes are
pleasant enough, most people come here to get into big-game country.

Largest of the Lowveld towns (and the capital of Mpumalanga), **Nelspruit**
lies on the N4, five hours' drive east from Johannesburg, and accessible by air
and bus (with buses to Maputo as well), making it the transport hub of the
region. From Nelspruit, you can head south for 32km to **Barberton**, an attractive settlement in the hills with strong mining connections, or continue another
41km to **Swaziland**. East from Nelspruit, the N2 runs close to the southern
border of the Kruger, providing easy access to its Malelane and Crocodile
Bridge gates; the latter is just 12km north of Komatipoort, a humid frontier
town on the border with **Mozambique**.

Heading north from the provincial capital, the R40 passes through **White
River**, **Hazyview**, **Klaserie**, **Hoedspruit** and **Phalaborwa**, a series of small
towns which act as good bases for exploring the Kruger (see p.693). Each town
is well-supplied with accommodation, and has a Kruger entrance gate nearby;
tours are available from some. Hoedspruit and Phalaborwa actually fall within
Northern Province, but for the sake of continuity have been included in this
chapter.

Note that the Lowveld area is **malarial**. For details on necessary precautions,
see p.22.

Nelspruit

Mpumalanga's provincial capital, **NELSPRUIT**, 358km east of Johannesburg
on the N4, is a traditionally conservative Afrikaner town that is rapidly transforming itself into one of South Africa's most relaxed and racially integrated
cities. The town's importance lies in its status as the business capital of the
province, but it is also a gateway into the southern part of Kruger and has the
province's best transport connections.

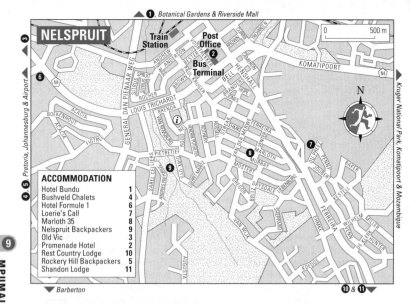

Botanical Gardens & Riverside Mall

NELSPRUIT

Train Station
Post Office **2**
Bus Terminal
KOMATIPOORT

N

0   500 m

Botanical Gardens & Riverside Mall

Pretoria, Johannesburg & Airport

Kruger National Park, Komatipoort & Mozambique

ACCOMMODATION
Hotel Bundu	1
Bushveld Chalets	4
Hotel Formule 1	6
Loerie's Call	7
Marloth 35	8
Nelspruit Backpackers	9
Old Vic	3
Promenade Hotel	2
Rest Country Lodge	10
Rockery Hill Backpackers	5
Shandon Lodge	11

Barberton   **10** & **11**

9

MPUMALANGA | Nelspruit

Arrival and information

Daily nonstop flights from Durban and Johannesburg on SA Airlink (☎013 741 3557) and three flights a week from Matshapa airport in Swaziland on Swazi Express Airlines arrive at **Nelspruit International airport** (☎013 741 3192), 12km southwest of town. This grandiosely named landing strip is served by the car rental offices of Avis (☎013 741 1087) and Budget (☎013 741 3871) – pretty handy as there's no transport into town. Greyhound (☎013 753 2100), which has its office inside the *Promenade Hotel*, as well as Intercape and Translux **intercity buses** from Johannesburg, stop in the hotel's parking area in Louis Trichardt Street. The **Baz Bus** drops off at the town lodges on its four-times-weekly trip (both directions) from Mbabane (Swaziland) and Jo'burg. The more frequent Citybug **shuttle bus** (☎013 741 4114, ✉citybug@soft.co.za) offers daily services from Jo'burg and Pretoria, and weekly from Durban, which pull into the BP garage in the Sonpark Centre, Piet Retief Street, just south of the city centre. They can arrange a taxi from here to your accommodation. **Minibus taxis** generally rank in Bester Street North, just east of the Nelspruit station, while Daily Spoornet **trains** from Johannesburg stop at **Nelspruit station** (☎080 000 8888), off Andrew Street at the north end of the town centre. Arrangements can also be made with hostels in Hazyview (see p.688) to pick you up from Nelspruit.

Lowveld Info, the town's **tourist information** bureau, on the ground floor of the Civic Centre at 1 Nel St (Mon–Fri 8am–4.30pm; ☎013 755 1988/ 1989, ⓦwww.nelspruitinfo.co.za), provides **maps** and basic information; the staff can also arrange accommodation bookings, including Kruger Park rest-camps. Lowveld Info also has a kiosk at the **Riverside Mall**, just north of the city centre on the R40 to White River and Hazyview. This upmarket shopping centre, adjacent to the casino and provincial parliament, has the best collection of shops in the province as well as the Alpha **cybercafé** (Mon–Thurs 9am–9pm, Fri & Sat 9am–11pm, Sun 10am–9pm; ⓦ www.aic.co.za); it's a good place to stock up if you're planning to self-cater in the Kruger Park; you can also make any travel arrangements here.

Accommodation

Nelspruit's **accommodation** tends to be geared to business travellers, so rooms are on the pricey side. If you're on a tight budget, head for the better-value options away from the centre or to the *Hotel Formula 1*, which offers the cheapest beds in town.

Hotel Bundu 11km from Nelspruit off the R40 towards White River ☎013 758 1221, ℮debundu@mweb.co.za. Popular, good-value family accommodation in an old-fashioned country hotel, decorated with animal hides and hunting trophies. There's camping and a swimming pool; the hotel also offers horse-riding and hiking trails to caves with rock paintings. ❸

Bushveld Chalets Kaapschehoop Road, 6km from Nelspruit, near the airport ☎013 741 5058. Small, self-catering chalets, sleeping two to four people. ❷

Hotel Formula 1 On the corner of N4 and Kaapschehoop Road ☎013 741 4490, ⓦwww.hotelformula1.co.za. The only budget option in the centre, in no-frills, en-suite boxes, making for a functional night stop. Continental breakfast is available for a small extra charge. ❷

The Loeries Call 2 Du Preez St ☎013 752 4844, ℮info@loeriescall.co.za. A modern house with pool, offering en-suite rooms with private verandahs overlooking the Crocodile River Valley. ❹

Marloth 35 35 Marloth St ☎013 752 4529. The cheapest of Nelspruit's B&Bs, featuring simple furnishings in ceramic-tiled rooms, with breakfast served outdoors under sun umbrellas. There's a swimming pool and braai facilities. ❷

Nelspruit Backpackers 9 Andries Pretorius St ☎013 755 4429. A former guesthouse close to the centre, with an easy-going party atmosphere, several dorms and one double. They also offer budget trips to Kruger and the Blyde River Canyon. ❶

Old Vic Inn 12 Impala St, 3km from town ☎013 744 0993 or 082 340 1508. Six clean, comfortable doubles and a dorm in a quiet backpacker hostel, with a pool, garden and walks in the adjoining nature reserve. Good for couples, and a family can also be accommodated. The owners arrange transport from their pub in the centre of town. ❶

Promenade Hotel Louis Trichardt Street ☎013 753 3000, ⓕ013 752 5533. Nelspruit's main hotel, aimed primarily at business people, but right in the centre of town. Room only. ❷.

The Rest Country Lodge Uitkyk Road, 10km from Nelspruit ☎013 744 9991 or 013 744 9992, ⓦwww.therest.co.za. Each luxury suite in this modern, purpose-built lodge has its own balcony with beautiful views over the Lowveld. There's also a swimming pool, sun deck and verandah. ❹

Rockery Hill Backpackers Mataffin Road, about 12.5km southwest of town along the Kaapschehoop road, just beyond the airport ☎ & ⓕ013 741 5011, ℮colorex@freemail.absa.co.za. Choose from camping, dorms lit by oil lamps, or a cottage with a communal kitchen and campfire cooking. It's a place for a quiet stay rather than for meeting other travellers. The owners can usually arrange transfers and budget Kruger tours. ❶

Shandon Lodge 1 Saturn St ☎013 744 9934, ⓕ013 744 1045, ⓦwww.shandon.co.za. Rooms with private entrances arranged around a swimming pool, in a well-established and large suburban home run by friendly hosts who provide good food and information. ❸

The Town and around

Nelspruit grew in the 1890s as a base for transport riders, farmers and prospectors, but there is little evidence left of these origins. Most of the old buildings have been ripped out and replaced by shopping malls and freeways, and the town has a bustling and mildly prosperous feel, mostly due to the fact that it is a major commercial centre, not only for the Lowveld, but also for shoppers from Swaziland and Mozambique.

The town centre, roughly six streets crisscrossed by another half dozen, could hardly be easier to get around. The N4 from Johannesburg to Komatipoort sweeps through town, briefly pausing to become **Louis Trichardt**, Nelspruit's main street, before reassuming its identity as the national highway. But as in most South African cities, much of middle-class shopping has migrated from the centre into shopping malls in the surrounding suburbs. Snazziest of these is the **Riverside Mall** complex, some 5km north of the city centre, which feels like it could have been lifted straight out of affluent northern Jo'burg suburbs, with all the same shops, including a well-stocked supermarket, some excellent coffee shops and a better-than-average bookshop. Next to the mall is a casino and, perhaps aptly, the controversial new prestigious **provincial legislature**, which cost around R600m to build and resembles a theme park. The massive price tag attached to its towering beehive domes and Queen-of-Sheba-style architecture caused a scandal in 1999 when it turned out that the legislature would have to slash its departmental budgets to pay the construction costs; meanwhile, inside the chamber, members of the legislature were hearing how some major tarred roads in the province had deteriorated into pot-holed tracks because of lack of funding.

Over the road from the Riverside Mall is Nelspruit's major attraction, the **Lowveld National Botanical Garden** (daily: May–Sept 8am–5.15pm; Oct–April 8am–6pm; R10). Set on the banks of the Crocodile River, the garden comes a close second to Cape Town's Kirstenbosch Gardens. Natural waterfalls and walks through rainforest make a pleasant break from the boiling midday heat. If you've been to Kruger, you'll have a chance to look at some of the same **trees** here, helpfully identified with labels. The plants are grouped according to habitat, and the garden specializes in **cycads** from around the world. There is also a grove of baobabs from South Africa and other African countries. A useful brochure sold at the entrance gate has a map showing the highlights of the garden and the paths through it.

Eating and drinking

Most of Nelspruit's **restaurants** are buried in shopping malls, where you'll find all the usual steakhouses and fast-food chains. *Spur*, in the Riverside Mall, is good for salads. In the same mall, *Seattle Coffee* and the *Brazilian* are both excellent for coffee and sandwiches. You'll find spicy Portuguese-style grilled chicken to eat in or take away at *Nando's* in Brown Street off Louis Trichardt. *Café Mozart*, Promenade Centre, Louis Trichardt Street, does quiches, coffee and tea. For a more expensive and imaginative meal, head for *Costa Do Sol*, in Nel City, on the corner of Kruger and Louis Trichardt streets, serving good Portuguese and Italian dishes. **Drinking** is done mostly at the restaurants or at the *Hotel Promenade* in the centre.

Listings

Emergencies Ambulance ☎013 10177; Fire ☎013 753 3331; Police ☎10111.
Hospitals Nelmed Clinic ☎013 755 2672 (open 24hr) is suitable for non-emergency treatment. For urgent cases contact Nelspruit Private Hospital ☎013 744 7150.
Laundry The Laundrette (open daily), is at the Youth Centre along the N4, next to Joshua Doore on the corner of Paul Kruger and Louis Trichardt streets.
Mozambique Embassy Brown St ☎013 752 7396, for visa applications.
Post office The main post office, in Voortrekker St, is open 8.30am–4pm.

South from Nelspruit and Swaziland via Barberton

With your own transport, **Barberton** makes a more relaxed staging post than Nelspruit for journeys between the south of the Kruger National Park and Swaziland. The closest and most beautiful route into **Swaziland** from Barberton is through the border crossing at Bulembu (8am–4pm), but the road is poor and should be avoided in the summer unless you're in a 4WD vehicle, though a sedan car can make it in the dry season. There have been rumours that a paved road will be built in the near future. In the meantime, a more practical option is to enter Swaziland via the border posts of Ngwenya/Oshoek (7am–10pm) or Jeppe's Reef/Matsamo (8am–4pm), though you pay extra using Jeppe's Reef, as the route takes you through the Kaapmuiden toll gate. There's no organized transport to Swaziland from Barberton.

Barberton

BARBERTON lies 36km south of Nelspruit and has a colonial backwater charm, a handful of historical sights, tropical vegetation and an attractive setting in a basin surrounded by mountains. The town began its urban existence after Auguste Robert ("French Bob") discovered **gold** in 1883 on a nearby farm. Despite his attempts to keep the news to himself, other diggers realized something was up when French Bob began building a canal to his claims. The following year, **Graham Barber** discovered another incredibly rich gold reef and got his name hitched to the town at a riotous christening using a bottle of gin. An influx of shopkeepers, hoteliers, barmen and prostitutes and even ministers of religion soon joined the diggers in the growing frontier town, which consisted of tents, tin, thatch and mud, with nearly every second building functioning as a boozing joint. During the fabulous **boom** of the 1880s the mines slipped out of the grasp of the small-time prospectors and came under the control of the large corporations that still own them today. This is the best place in the country to take a goldmining tour, or watch gold-panning being done.

Arrival, information and accommodation

No scheduled public **transport** comes into Barberton: the closest transport hub is Nelspruit, from where you'll need to find a minibus taxi for Barberton. The **tourist information** bureau, Crown Street (Mon–Fri 8am–1pm & 2–4.30pm, Sat 8.30am–noon; ☎013 712 2121), can help find accommodation in the area, or point you to local walks, as well as supply you with reams of brochures and maps covering the whole province. To book **mining tours**, or adventure activities such as **horse-riding**, **microlight** flights or **hot air balloon** safaris, try the efficient Origins, 20 Sheba St (Mon–Fri 8am–5pm, Sat 8am–noon, ☎013 712 5055).

Because it's a bit off the main trail, Barberton is short on **places to stay**, but the prospects get better as you head a little out of town.

Fountain Baths Guest House 48 Pilgrim St ☎013 712 2707, ☎013 712 3361. Pleasant rooms and self-catering mini-apartments for 2–4 people with a garden edging onto the hills and a swimming pool. ❷
Jock of the Bushveld Huts Nelspruit Road, 4km from town ☎013 712 4002 or 083 376 1199, ☎712 5915. Reasonably priced, thatched self-catering chalets, huts and a guesthouse, sleeping two to six, on a lychee and mango farm, with horse-riding, swimming and microlight flights on offer. ❷
Old Coach Road Guest House and Restaurant 13km north of Barberton on the R38 to Kaapmuiden

☎013 719 9755, ☎oldcoach@global.co.za. Comfortable twin and double en-suite rooms, as well as two family units, at a friendly establishment set in its own peaceful 13 acres, with a pool. The recommended licensed restaurant has a terrace looking onto spectacular mountains. A convenient stop en route to the southern Kruger rest-camps or Swaziland. ❸
The Phoenix 20 Pilgrim St ☎013 712 4211, ☎013 712 5741. Barberton's only hotel has a long corridor of standard en-suite rooms, where the noise of television can seep through doors. ❷

The Town

There are seven working **mines** around Barberton, and each has its own club and entertainment scene, which means you won't find miners packing out public bars as in the wild days of old. Neither do the mines run tours; since they are all fully operational, there's no time to humour a few visitors. However, there is one small-time prospector in Barberton (see box below) who will give you a go at gold-panning, swilling water and sand in a big dish to watch for the telltale thread of gold appearing in the dark sand, or you can take a day-long mining and geology tour.

You can explore the mining history of the town at the **Barberton Museum**, 36 Pilgrim St (Mon–Fri 8am–4pm, Sat & Sun 9am–1pm & 2–4pm), three blocks east of the tourist information bureau. In a well-designed, modern building, the museum has good displays on the gold-rush era and, if phoned in advance, staff can demonstrate gold-panning for groups.

The museum can also let you have a map of the **Victorian houses** under their supervision, which also have flamboyant gardens. A ticket to all three costs R10. Built for a wealthy middle-class family and restored to its 1904 grandeur, **Belhaven House** at 18 Lee Rd (10am–3.15pm), is a five-minute walk north from the museum. Further up Lee Road, **Fernlea House** (Mon–Fri 8am–12.30pm & 1.30–4pm) is a wood-and-iron structure, while to the east, **Stopforth House** at 18 Bowness St (10am–3.15pm), is the most interesting of the three, and a guard can take you through the house. The original wood-and-iron house and outbuildings were built by James Stopforth, a local baker and general dealer.

Eating and drinking

Barberton's best place to **eat** is the cheap and friendly *Co-Co Pan* in Crown Street, which serves straightforward hamburgers, steaks and omelettes. Your best chance to meet locals is to head downstairs to the lively **pub** below the restaurant. Next to the tourist information bureau on Crown Street is the pleasant *Victorian Tea Garden*, with a white gazebo straight out of a London park, and good tea and light snacks served outdoors. The *Old Coach Guest House* (see p.685), 13km from town, is recommended both for its good cooking and beautiful surroundings.

Gold-panning and Barberton mining tours

Unlike at Pilgrim's Rest, where you'll have to be content with merely watching how panning was done, at Barberton you can try it yourself on reasonably priced trips operated by Danny Brink (☎083 482 1803). Origins (20 Sheba Rd, ☎013 712 5055, ⊛www.origins.co.za) does a fascinating four-day trip along a disused ox-wagon track, focusing on the geology of the area and showing you meteorite deposits. The trip finishes at **Eureka City**, an 1880s mining settlement that died forty years later. Eureka hasn't been reconstructed like Pilgrim's Rest – you'll only see walls and foundations, after driving through a real mine to get there. The tour finishes with a trip to the huge excavations of Golden Quarry, once a fabulously rich mine.

To get a sense of what the old mines were like, the two-kilometre circular **Fortuna Mine Hiking Trail**, just south of town, takes you through a disused tunnel built to transport gold-bearing ore to the Fortuna Mine. The actual tunnel is 600m long and you'll need to take a torch. The trail, which starts at the car park off Crown Street to the south of town, goes through an attractive area of indigenous trees before entering the tunnel, and once you're through you get good views of Barberton and the De Kaap Valley.

East from Nelspruit: Komatipoort and the Mozambique border

Heading east from Nelspruit, the N4 roughly follows the progress of the **Crocodile River**, which traces the southern boundary of Kruger National Park on its journey to the Indian Ocean through Mozambique. For 58km to the tiny settlement of **Malelane**, the road travels within view of the Crocodile's riverine forest, passing lush, subtropical farmlands and the grey Dali-esque formations of granite *koppies*. Some 4km further on, the road turns off to Kruger's **Malelane Gate**, the most convenient entry point for *Berg-en-Dal* restcamp (see p.702). A signpost 12km east of Malelane indicates *Buhala Game Lodge* (☎013 790 4372, ☏013 790 4306, ⓦwww.buhala.co.za; ❾), a fabulous **guesthouse** on a mango, sugar cane and papaya farm, set high on the banks of the Crocodile, with views across the slow water into Kruger. Trips into the Kruger Park can be arranged from here for around R450 per person and guides take nature walks on the farm itself, where there is also horse-riding and quad-biking.

Komatipoort

Of all the towns along the Kruger fringes, **KOMATIPOORT**, 87km east of Nelspruit, owes its frontier character to the fact that it lies between one of Africa's richest countries and one of its poorest. The exotic flavour of this small, rambling town comes from its dusty streets dotted with small-time market traders selling tiny piles of tomatoes and onions, the vivid green of the surrounding cane plantations and the colourful wraps of Mozambican women. Despite a slightly seedy edge and the unshakeable whiff of wheeling and dealing in sweaty hotel bars, it's a safe and friendly place, where you can enjoy a hint of what lies in Mozambique, just across the Crocodile River.

Komatipoort's **Ressano Garcia** border post is the bottleneck through which hundreds of dispossessed **Mozambicans** attempt to squeeze their way each day to get to the "gold-paved streets" of Johannesburg. Some who get turned back will chance their lives attempting to steal in elsewhere through the wilds of Kruger, while the luckier ones who already have jobs on the mines pass through on the thrice-weekly train that takes them home to Maputo and returns this way with a fresh cargo of labour. Unless you're flying, this is the only major South African gateway into Mozambique. A favoured holiday playground for white South Africans and Rhodesians until the 1970s, when it gained majority rule, Mozambique was brought to its knees by a devastating, apartheid-sponsored war that stopped tourism for nearly two decades, but with the war thankfully now long over, travellers are delighting again in the tropical waters and plentiful, cheap seafood.

Practicalities

Greyhound, Translux and Intercape **intercity buses** all pass through town on their way between Jo'burg and Maputo (via Nelspruit), stopping at the border post outside town and there are the ubiquitous **minibus taxis** from Nelspruit. If you're planning on heading into Mozambique, contact Mozambique Tours (☎013 790 8000/8222; ask for Carl Parsons), who can advise on visas and travel.

Places to stay include *Komati Holiday Resort* (☎013 790 8040; ❷), roughly 2km east of town, which has self-catering en-suite timber cabins (each with a double and two singles) and camping, set among indigenous thorn and fever trees. To get there, take the N4 towards Nelspruit for about 200m out of town and turn right at the Shell garage, following the signs to the resort. The only upmarket place to stay is the motel-style *Border Country Inn* (☎013 790 7328, ℱ013 790 7100; ❸), 3km out of town just before the border – a convenient option if you're making an early start into Mozambique the following morning.

Komatipoort's big surprise is a humdinger of a **restaurant**: the *Tambarina* on Rissik Street. This Mozambican-style cantina captures the taste and feel of the former Portuguese colony, with vibrantly tropical decor and a courtyard shaded by mango trees.

North from Nelspruit: Kruger's western flank

The **R40** heads north from Nelspruit along the western border of the Kruger National Park, passing through prosperous tropical-fruit-growing farmlands and poverty-stricken former black "homeland" areas. Guesthouses, many of them fairly upmarket, pop up all along the way to Hazyview until you reach the densely populated former *bantustan* areas around **Bosbokrand** (also known by its English name, Bushbuck Ridge). Roadside lodgings reappear once you reach Klaserie, which lies on the border of Mpumalanga and Northern Province. Many of these are located on game farms – poor cousins to the pricier lodges inside the game reserves to the east.

North of the Mpumalanga border you'll pass little towns en route to the central section of Kruger National Park and the Manyeleti and Timbavati private game reserves. Coming down the Escarpment along the R36/R527 from the Blyde River viewpoints, after about 75km you'll encounter a fork in the road. The more northerly road leads to the towns of **Hoedspruit** and **Klaserie**, both of which lie in the heart of bushveld **game farm** country, which offers budget game viewing, but is no substitute for the big-game country of Kruger and its adjacent private reserves. Much further north and generally reached from Pietersburg on the N1, the mining town of **Phalaborwa** is unavoidable if you're heading into central Kruger through Phalaborwa Gate.

Hazyview

HAZYVIEW, 43km north of Nelspruit, is little more than a couple of large well-stocked shopping centres buzzing with minibus taxis and small market stalls selling fruit and goods to the surrounding African community. The village's only interest is the fact that it lies just 19km from the Kruger National Park's Numbi Gate, and only a little further from Paul Kruger Gate, making it perfectly positioned for access to the game-rich southern section of the game reserve. This is one of the best bases for visitors who aren't spending the night in the park itself and would prefer to return to a comfortable hotel after a hard day's game viewing. No public **transport** comes into Hazyview, but if you're staying at one of the local backpacker lodges you can arrange to be collected from Nelspruit.

The **Shangana Cultural Village** (9am–4pm; ⓦwww.shangana.co.za), about 5km west of Hazyview, just off the R535 to Graskop is also a good place to get a sense of the cultural traditions of the local Shangaan community as well as enjoy an excellent lunch (noon–2pm; R115; see p.690). Entrance is free to the reception area and its craft shop, but the village can only be visited on a guided tour (every hour on the hour; R55). The tour follows a winding path through fields and bush to the kraal where a family lives; you'll also meet a *sangoma* (healer/diviner) and learn about traditional remedies.

Accommodation

Hazyview has a wide range of **accommodation**, most of it in farmland strung along the roads radiating out to the neighbouring towns of Sabie (the R536), Graskop (the R535) and White River (the R538), as well as to the Kruger National Park's Paul Kruger Gate (the R40). For the cheapest B&B rooms in town, enquire at the *Hysterical Hornbill Restaurant* (℡013 737 8124 or 013 737 7404).

Hippo Hollow Country Estate Just south of town, along the R40 to Paul Kruger Gate ℡013 737 7752, ⊛www.hippohollow.co.za. Luxurious B&B accommodation in thatched cottages, nicely positioned on the banks of the Sabie River, and with a restaurant, reception and bar area. The self-catering units are less expensive though the facilities are not geared up for any real cooking. Trips into Kruger leave from here every morning; a full day-trip to Kruger costs around R550. ❹–❺

Idle and Wild 6km from Hazyview, on the R536 ℡013 737 8173 or 083 455 8171, ⊛www.idelandwild.co.za. This working mango farm in a lush valley on the banks of the Sabie River offers two thatched rondavels, a family unit and honeymoon suite (with its own spa bath) in the lush garden, as well as two en-suite bedrooms in the main house. All have kitchenettes, and there's a spa bath, sauna and swimming pool. ❸–❹

Kruger Park Backpackers Main Road ℡013 737 7224, ⊚krugback@mweb.co.za. A pleasantly located hostel under shady bushveld trees, offering campsites, dorms, rondavels and, nicest of all, Zulu beehive huts. There's a swimming pool and they run organized tours into Kruger from here, Jo'burg or Pretoria. ❶

Numbi Main Road ℡013 737 7301, ℻013 737 7525, ⊚hotelnumbi@worldonline.co.za. An old-fashioned but comfortable place offering camping, bungalows and hotel rooms. ❹

Rissington Inn 2km south of town, just off the R40 ℡013 737 7700, ⊛www.rissington.co.za. Hazyview's most upmarket country lodge is a relaxed and informal place (and kids are welcome), with seven plush rooms set in the gardens of a large thatched homestead with a swimming

pool and excellent food. To get there from Hazyview, take the R40 south and turn right at Kiaat Park, after the Haze Nissan garage on the left-hand side of the road. ❹

Sabi River Sun 2km from Hazyview on the R536 on the banks of the Sabie River ℡013 737 7311, ⊛www.southernsun.com. A luxury family resort along the Sabie River, landscaped around a beautiful golf course. Other activities include measured tracks for jogging or cycling, a swimming pool and kids' playground, or you can just wander down to see if there are any hippos about. The resort has a family restaurant and pub. ❺

Tembi Along the R40, just north of the Sabie River ℡013 737 7729, ℻013 737 7036, ⊚tembi@intekom.co.za. Reasonably priced en-suite B&B rooms in a farmhouse with a peaceful garden. The restaurant serves game pie, trout, seafood and steaks, and the bar opens for dinner every night except Sunday. ❸

Thika Thika Guest Farm and Backpackers 3km from Hazyview on the R536, on the banks of the Sabie River ℡013 737 8108 or 082 403 9676, ⊚thika@worldonline.co.za. Three fully equipped timber chalets sleeping up to six people, on a sweet-smelling citrus farm with lush subtropical vegetation. There's also a comfortable backpacker dorm at the main bungalow with crisp white linen. ❶–❷

Thulamela 1km down White River Road, off the R40 ℡ & ℻013 737 7171, ⊚info@thulamela.co.za. An out-of-the-ordinary guesthouse run by a dietician who serves healthy breakfasts and puts you up in en-suite timber cottages, each with its own deck, Jacuzzi and bushveld views. Weekday discounts, but no children under 16. ❺

Eating and drinking

A number of decent places to eat around Hazyview are, like the town's accommodation, mostly dotted along the main roads connecting Hazyview with neighbouring towns. In the centre, the *Hysterical Hornbill Pub and Restaurant* (℡013 737 7404), opposite the Engen filling station along the R538, is a relaxed family-friendly spot offering reasonably priced meals such as steak or fish and chips till late; they also have a buzzing pub. The informal *Rissington Inn* (see p.689) serves reasonably priced dishes such as almond chicken and caters well for vegetarians, while the *Shangana Cultural Village* (☎013 737 7000), about 5km west of Hazyview, just off the R535 to Graskop, offers delicious African dinners cooked in massive pots over an open fire by the chief's wives; the menu can include crocodile in spicy peanut sauce, beef, and honey-glazed sweet potato.

On to Klaserie

The only reason you're likely to find yourself heading along the R40 from Hazyview is to reach the private game reserves – **Sabi Sand**, **Manyeleti** or **Timbavati** – that join up with the western flank of Kruger (see p.708).

After Hazyview, the R40 passes through irrigated farmlands and low hills dotted with bushveld trees. As you approach **Bosbokrand**, 28km to the north, the corridor between the Escarpment and big-game country changes, with the sudden appearance of shantytowns, busy roads, overgrazed lands and dense settlements interspersed with the odd papaya and banana tree. Also known as Bushbuck Ridge (a direct translation from the Afrikaans), the town's name comes from the hilly finger extending east from the Escarpment – although any bushbucks that might once have wandered here have long since been displaced by the cattle and goats.

Despite the fact that maps indicate little or no habitation, the busy and sometimes hazardous road passes through the former *bantustan* of **Lebowa**, where people live crammed at a density six times greater than the provincial average. **Klaserie**, 42km north of Bosbokrand in the middle of game farms, sits poised on the border between Mpumalanga and Northern Province. Forty-five kilometres east from here lies **Orpen Gate**, which gives access to the rewarding central section of Kruger National Park.

Hoedspruit

Lurking in the undulating Lowveld, straight up the R40 from Klaserie, with the hazy blue mountains of the Escarpment visible on the distant horizon, is the small service centre of **HOEDSPRUIT**. The town lies at the heart of a concentration of **private game reserves** and lodges. There aren't any sights here; the only reason to pass through is en route to Kruger or to stay at one of the game lodges (booking essential).

It forms a good base for specialist activities, such as **horse-riding** and **rafting** on the Blyde River, **birding** on the slopes of the Escarpment, and visiting the **animal rehabilitation centres**.

Hoedspruit is a significant arrival point for air travellers heading for Kruger; it's the only Lowveld destination with daily direct flights from Cape Town. Like Nelspruit and Skukuza, it's also served by Johannesburg. Daily scheduled **flights** from Johannesburg and Cape Town arrive at Eastgate airport (☎015 793 3681), some 14km south of Hoedspruit. For **car rental**, Avis (☎015 793 2014) has an office at the airport. If you're phoning around for the cheapest deal, companies based in Nelspruit can send cars up to Hoedspruit. For transfers to game lodges from here, contact Eastgate Lodge Transfers (☎015 793 3678) though most lodges send their own vehicles to meet guests. Hoedspruit itself is a collection of gun shops, liquor stores, butchers, service stations and a good Spar supermarket, where you'll find a coffee shop and chemist in the same little shopping complex.

There's a mix of **accommodation** available within striking distance of

Hoedspruit; westwards towards the Blyde River Canyon is the wonderful Monsoon Gallery (see p.679) and there are reasonably priced game farms close to Hoedspruit, and reaching east to the fringes of Kruger itself takes you to some of South Africa's most luxurious safari camps.

Around Hoedspruit

The **Moholoholo Wildlife Rehabilitation Centre** lies on the R531 between the R40 and R527, about 3km from the tarred turn-off to the Blydepoort Dam (tours Mon–Sat 9.30am & 3pm; R40; booking essential ℡ & ℻015 795 5236). Ex-ranger Brian Jones has embarked on an individual crusade to rescue and rehabilitate injured and abandoned animals, notably raptors, but also lions, leopards and others. The centre is part of a wider reserve and both night drives and early-morning walks are offered, as well as the opportunity to touch animals and see Brian fly eagles. You can also make an easy tour of the rehabilitation cages and pens. The game-lodge-style fully catered **accommodation** (**⑤**) here includes three meals, a night drive and an early-morning walk, although there's no restaurant on site.

Along similar lines is the larger **Hoedspruit Research and Breeding Centre for Endangered Species**, more commonly called the **Cheetah Project**, 20km south of Hoedspruit on the R40 (Mon–Sun 8am–3pm; ℡015 793 1633; R40). Open vehicles depart from here every hour on the hour to take visitors around pens and cages containing cheetah, wild dog, blue crane and other endangered species such as ground hornbills. The animals are bred for purposes of protection, restocking and research; while the centre gives you an opportunity to see some of these animals at close quarters, you can't actually touch anything and it does feel a bit like a zoo. It can be tough work convincing yourself that it's all done in the name of science. A small restaurant on site serves tea, cake, sandwiches and hot dogs.

The **Nyani Shangaan Cultural Village** (℡015 793 3816 or 083 512 4865; **①**), 4km along the Guernsey Road which turns off the R40, 22km south of Hoedspruit, is a good option for lunch or overnighting with dinner and a display of traditional dancing laid on. Unlike some of the more commercialized cultural villages, this is a genuine effort developed by Axon Khosa, a local Shangaan man, who asked his grandparents what the villages were like when they were children. He hosts visits along with his extended family, taking visitors on a tour of the village and offering a **meal**, which is usually a chicken dish with butternut, gem squash (a delicious local cricket-ball sized marrow), served with wild spinach and groundnuts mixed into *mielie pap* (maize meal). You can also **stay overnight** (advance booking essential) in a hut with traditional dung floors and thatching that looks untidy by comparison with the safari lodges, but is authentically Shangaan. The walls are constructed with mud taken from termite mounds and are beautifully hand-decorated with white, orange and black motifs. You sleep on fold-up mattresses and there are cold showers and flush toilets for guests. Nyani can also be taken in as part of a tour to the Kruger operated by Trans Frontiers Safaris (see Kruger "Tours and packages" on p.699).

Hoedspruit game farms

None of the following **game farms** has direct access to Big Five game viewing, but they're worth considering as relatively inexpensive and comfortable places to stay in the bush on your way to or from Kruger. Because each camp is small, and right in the bush, you have the feeling of being in a far wilder place than when you're staying in the Kruger Park itself. All offer walks since there are no lions or elephants on the properties; a number of farms also offer specialist activities, and most take children.

Eyrie Birding Lodge 36km from Hoedspruit on the R531 ☎015 795 5775. Four doubles in a two-story house, in a fantastic elevated site on the slopes of the Escarpment. The lodge is run by Dr Peter Milstein, one of South Africa's most knowledgeable experts on birds, and chosen by him as one of the finest bird-watching spots in the country. Bring your own liquor, but no kids under 12. Full-board **⑤**

Gwala Gwala 35km south of Hoedspruit ☎015 793 3491, ⓦwww.gwala.co.za. The place to go if you're looking for tranquillity, walking and birding, with accommodation in luxury safari tents. The owners give you plenty of space and privacy, and there are no more than ten guests. Big Five game drives into a neighbouring reserve can be arranged, as can drives into Kruger itself. **⑥**

Kwa-Mbili Game Lodge 30km east of Hoedspruit ☎015 793 2773, ⓔsafaris@kwambili .com. An intimate, unpretentious owner-run lodge with African decor, bush cuisine and plenty of game in the vicinity. A maximum of ten guests are housed in chalets or luxury tents; the activities on offer include game viewing on foot or by Landrover,

and baby-sitting facilities are available. Full-board **⑦**

Off-Beat Safari Camp 13km north of Hoedspruit ☎ & ⓕ015 793 2422 or ☎082 494 1735, ⓦwww.offbeatsafaris.cp.za. A great little rustic camp on a game farm, whose appeal is its affordability, pleasant owners and the big plus of horse-riding across the farm to view giraffe, kudu, zebra and wildebeest. The chilling sound of lions roaring in the darkness is guaranteed, the roars filtering through the mosquito netting, from the lion enclosure on the adjacent property. Mountain bikes are available, and kids are welcome. **③–⑥**

Otter's Den On the R531, not far from the junction with the R521 ☎015 795 5250 or ☎082 572 2223, ⓔcatfish@mweb.co.za. A small and relaxing camp sleeping eight, on a bush-covered island in the Blyde River recommended for fishing and bird-watching. The en-suite chalets are on stilts overlooking the river, and there's a river-fed rock swimming pool. A field guide can accompany you on walks to identify trees and birds, and the owners run river rafting trips through the Blyde River Canyon. Full-board **⑤**

Phalaborwa

The most northerly access to the central section of Kruger is at **PHAL-ABORWA**, 74km north of Hoedspruit. The name means "better than the south", a cheeky sobriquet coined as the town developed on the back of its extensive mineral wealth. During the Sixties, the borders of the park near Phalaborwa suddenly developed a kink, and large copper deposits were found, miraculously, just outside the protected national park area.

The only reason to visit Phalaborwa is on your way in or out of Kruger; there's little to divert you unless you need a bed for the night. However, keen golfers shouldn't miss the chance of a round in the company of big game at the signposted **Hans Merensky Country Club** (☎015 781 5931), where its not unusual to see giraffes and elephants sauntering across the fairways. You can whet your appetite before heading into the park with a short **microlight flight** over the park (☎082 956 1502; R400 per hour), or a sundowner **boat trip** with Jumbo River Safaris (☎015 781 6168; booking essential R50), which sets out at 3pm down the Olifants River and frequently encounters game, including elephants.

You may see dust-encrusted vehicles driving around town which have long aerials with small flags attached to the top of them – this is so that they don't get squished by the big trucks manoeuvring around the mines. Also unusual is the number of Mozambiquans in town; originally having crossed over from Mozambique, only 60km away on the other side of Kruger National Park, using Phalaborwa as a navigation aid, guiding themselves by the smoke of the chimneys by day, and the lights by night.

Arrival and information

Regular SA Airlink (℡015 781 5823) flights arrive from Johannesburg at Phalaborwa **airport** (℡015 781 5823), five minutes' drive from Kruger's Phalaborwa Gate, off President Steyn Street. Phalaborwa is the least expensive destination serving Kruger. The closest rest camps from here are Letaba, 50km into the park, and Shimuwini, 52km inside. All Phalaborwa's **car rental** firms are represented at the airport: Avis (℡015 781 3169), Budget (℡015 781 5404) and Imperial (℡015 781 0376). Olifants Valley Experience (℡015 781 7041) offers transfers from the airport to game farms and lodges, as well as day-trips into the park.

Phalaborwa has a good selection of **shops**, including the well-stocked Link pharmacy, open until 8pm, in the shopping mall in Nelson Mandela Avenue.

Accommodation

Phalaborwa has plenty of **places to stay**, but prices can be steep unless you opt for the backpacker lodge or self-catering.

Elephant Walk 30 Anna Scheepers St ℡015 781 2758/5860 or 082 495 0575, ℮elephant.walk@niz.co.za. A small and friendly hostel with camping facilities and budget tours into Kruger on offer. They also have a self-contained B&B garden flat as well as two self-catering cottages at Kruger's Phalaborwa Gate, which work out cheaper than staying in the park and are handy if all the accommodation on the other side is full. They also take children. Cottages & flat ➋, other accommodation ➊

Impala Protea Inn On the corner of Essenhout and Wildevy streets ℡015 781 3681. Pretty char-acterful as Proteas go, this hotel has a pool and a pleasant pub. ➌

Matomani Lodge Essenhout Street, opposite the *Protea* ℡015 781 5681. Reasonably priced self-catering apartments in a refurbished 1960s block, with the option of breakfast as an add-on. ➋

Sefapane Lodge Copper Street ℡015 781 7041, ℮www.sefapane.co.za. Relaxed and upmarket accommodation in neat beehive huts, with a restaurant, a nice pool and a poolside bar. ➎

Steyns Cottage 67 Bosvlier St ℡015 781 0836. A fairly classy Victorian-style guesthouse, with a swimming pool, tea garden and restaurant. ➍

Eating and drinking

Phalaborwa's selection of **places to eat** are mostly linked to accommodation establishments. The restaurant at *Sefapane Lodge* five minutes' drive out of town towards the Kruger Gate, is pretty decent and its sunken **bar** beside the swimming pool is convivial. You'll find the usual steaks and fresh salads on offer at the *Yurok Spur* in the main shopping mall in Nelson Mandela Avenue.

Kruger National Park

KRUGER NATIONAL PARK is arguably the emblem of South African tourism; the place that delivers best what most visitors to Africa want to see – scores of elephants, lions and a cast of thousands of other game roaming the savannah. A narrow strip of land hugging the Mozambique border, Kruger stretches across Northern Province and Mpumalanga, an astonishing 414-kilometre drive from Pafuri Gate in the north to Malelane Gate in the south, all of it along tar, with many well-kept gravel roads looping off to provide routes for game drives.

△ Kruger resident

Kruger is designed for **self-driving** and **self-catering**, though the temptation is to drive too much and too fast, leading to fewer sightings, and rental cars tend to be low off the ground and aren't as good for game viewing as those used by lodges or tour operators. However, self-driving offers complete flexibility, and you can hop in a car knowing you'll find supplies once you arrive at most of the restcamps (though not much in the way of fruit or vegetables) – indeed it remains the only way of seeing Kruger's animals if you're travelling with children, as many lodges don't allow under-12s. The park's popularity means that not only are you likely to share animal sightings with other motorists, but that **bookings** are at a premium, particularly during South African school holidays, and that at any time of year you may have to stay in whichever camp has accommodation, rather than in your first choice. Book as far in advance as possible.

Kruger comes pretty close to fulfilling *Out of Africa* fantasies in the **private game reserves** on its western flank – where you'll get luxury accommodation and food, but more importantly (especially if this is your first safari), qualified rangers to show you the game and the bush with only a tiny group of other guests.

The ideal is to do a bit of each, perhaps spending a couple of nights in a private lodge to "get your eye in" and a further two or so exploring the public section. But whatever you choose, be sure to relax and don't get too obsessed with seeing the Big Five. Remember that wildlife doesn't imitate TV documentaries and you're most unlikely to see lion-kills (you may not see a lion at all), or huge herds of wildebeest migrating across dusty savannah. There is always an element of luck involved in what you see, and this is exactly what makes game spotting so addictive. A few **game-spotting tips** are outlined on p.699, which can make a big difference to your trip.

Walking in the wild is growing in popularity and the Kruger Park (see p.700), all of the private reserves (see p.708) and some private operators (see p.699) offer **escorted morning game walks**. There are also several three-night **wilderness trails** (see p.703) in different parts of the park, led by armed rangers – a fabulous way of getting in touch with the wilderness, but one you'll have to book months in advance.

Note that Kruger National Park is **malarial**. For details on necessary precautions, see p.22.

Some history

It's highly questionable whether Kruger National Park can be considered "a pristine wilderness", as it's frequently called, given that people have been living in or around it for thousands of years. **San hunter-gatherers** have left their mark in the form of paintings and engravings at 150 sites that have so far been discovered and there's evidence of farming cultures at many places in the park. Around 1000 to 1300 AD, centrally organized states were building stone palaces and engaging in **trade** that brought Chinese porcelain, jewellery and cloth into the area.

But it was the arrival of white **fortune seekers** in the second half of the nineteenth century that made the greatest impact on the region. The twentieth century has had an ambivalent attitude to the hunters, criminals and poachers (like the notorious ivory hunter Cecil Barnard), who made their livelihoods here decimating game populations. Barnard's exploits are admiringly recounted in the *Ivory Trail* by T.V. Bulpin, while every other episode of the still-popular yarn, *Jock of the Bushveld*, set in the area, includes accounts of hunting. In the early twentieth century, African farmers were kicked off their traditional lands to create the park.

Paul Kruger, former president of the South African Republic, is usually credited with having the foresight to set aside land for wildlife conservation. Kruger figures as a shrewd, larger-than-life figure in Afrikaner history and it was **James Stevenson-Hamilton**, the first warden of the national park, who cunningly put forward Kruger's name in order to soften up Afrikaner opposition to the creation of the park. In fact, Stevenson-Hamilton knew that Kruger was no conservationist and was actually an inveterate hunter; Kruger "never in

Mammals, birds, reptiles and insects

Among the nearly 150 species of **mammals** seen in the park are cheetah, leopard, lion, spotted hyena, wild dog, black and white rhino, blue wildebeest, buffalo, Burchell's zebra, bushbuck, eland, elephant, giraffe, hippo, impala, kudu, mountain reedbuck, nyala, oribi, reedbuck, roan antelope, sable antelope, tsessebe, warthog and waterbuck. The staggering 507 **bird species** include raptors, hefty-beaked hornbills, ostriches and countless colourful specimens.

Keep your eyes open and you'll also see a variety of **reptiles, amphibians** and **insects** – most rewardingly in the grounds of the restcamps themselves. Although the camps are fenced off from big game, there's always something to see up the trees, in the bushes or even inside your rondavel. If you spot a miniature ET-like reptile crawling upside down on the ceiling, don't be tempted to kill it; it's an insect-eating gecko and is doing you a good turn. If, however, you have a horror of insects or frogs, stay away from Kruger in the rainy season (Nov–March).

his life thought of animals except as biltong", Stevenson-Hamilton wrote in a private letter.

When to visit

Kruger is rewarding at any time of the year, though each season has its advantages and drawbacks. If you don't like the heat, avoid high **summer** (Dec–Feb), when on a bad day temperatures can nudge 45°C – though they're generally in the mid- to high thirties. Many of the camps have air conditioning or fans, and it's definitely worth considering renting an air-conditioned car. Throughout the summer (Nov–March) the heat can be tempered by short thunder showers. At this time of the year, everything becomes greener, softer and prettier, and from early November you're likely to spot cute young animals.

There's little rain during the cooler **winter** months of April to August; the vegetation withers over this period, making it easier to spot game. Although daytime temperatures rise to the mid-twenties (days are invariably bright and sunny throughout winter), the nights and early mornings can be very cold, especially in June and July, when you'll definitely need warm clothes. Rondavels in the public restcamps do have heaters in the bedrooms. A definite plus of winter is the virtual absence of mosquitoes and other insects.

Orientation and arrival

The public section of Kruger can be divided roughly into **three sections**, each with a distinct character and terrain. If your time is limited, it's best to choose just one or two areas to explore, but if you're staying for five days or more, consider driving the length of the park slowly, savouring the changes in landscape along the way. The southern, central and northern sections are sometimes referred to as "the circus", "the zoo" and "the wilderness" – sobriquets that carry more than a germ of truth.

The **southern section** has the greatest concentration of game; it attracts the highest number of visitors and is the most easily accessible part of the park if you're coming from Johannesburg, 478km away on the N4 national highway. The park headquarters (Skukuza) are here, with an airport, car rental facilities, a filling station, car repair workshop, car wash, bank, post office and doctor, as well as enough rondavels to accommodate 1000 people. The **central section** also offers good game viewing, as well as two of the most attractive camps in the park at **Olifants** and **Letaba**. The further north you go, the thinner both animal populations and visitors become, but it's the **northern section** that really conveys a sense of wilderness, reaching its zenith at the marvellously old-fashioned **Punda Maria** camp, which dates back to the 1930s.

Outside the public section, big-game country continues in several exclusive and expensive **private game reserves**, clustering on huge tracts of land to the west. The three major private reserves are **Sabi Sand** to the south and **Timbavati** and **Manyeleti**, adjoining the central section of the national park. Although they are privately owned, as far as animals are concerned the private and public areas are joined in an enormous, seamless whole. The only real difference is that private reserves are not places you drive around yourself, and they're for the exclusive use of private guests. If you do arrive here by car, you'll have to leave it at the lodge and won't see your vehicle again until you leave. In 2001, National Parks began awarding concessions to private investors to build seven new lodges within the park, which will provide stiff competition to the safari camps in the private game reserves.

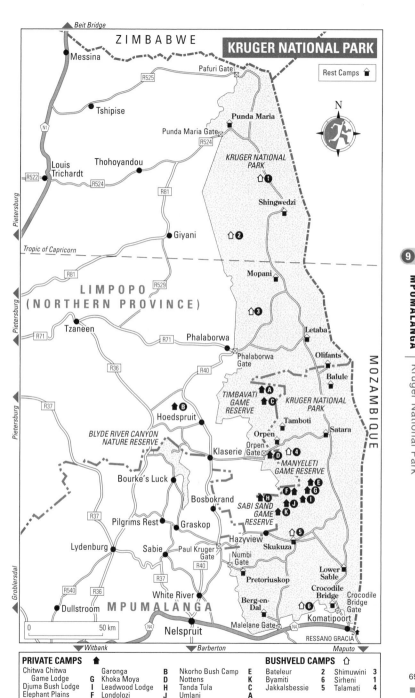

KRUGER NATIONAL PARK

Rest Camps 🏠

N

ZIMBABWE

▲ Beit Bridge

Messina

R525

Pafuri Gate ⊠

Tshipise

Punda Maria 🏠

Punda Maria Gate ⊠
R524

KRUGER NATIONAL PARK

Louis Trichardt

Thohoyandou

R522

R524

R81

🏠❶

Shingwedzi ◼

Giyani ●

🏠❷

Tropic of Capricorn

LIMPOPO (NORTHERN PROVINCE)

R81

R529

Mopani ◼

🏠❸

Tzaneen ●

R71

R71

Phalaborwa

Letaba ◼

Phalaborwa Gate ⊠

Olifants ◼

R36

R40

Balule ◼

TIMBAVATI GAME RESERVE

KRUGER NATIONAL PARK

R37

🏕 A
🏕 C

Hoedspruit

🏕 B

Tamboti ◼

Satara ◼

BLYDE RIVER CANYON NATURE RESERVE

Orpen ●

Klaserie ●

Orpen Gate ⊠
🏕 D 🏠❹

MANYELETI GAME RESERVE

Bourke's Luck ●

🏕 F 🏕 G 🏕 E

Bosbokrand ●

🏕 H

🏕 J 🏕 I

SABI SAND GAME RESERVE

🏕 K

Pilgrims Rest ●

Graskop ●

🏠❺

Lydenburg ●

Sabie ●

Paul Kruger Gate ⊠

Hazyview ●

Skukuza ◼

Numbi Gate ⊠

Lower Sable ◼

R37

Pretoriuskop ◼

Crocodile Bridge ◼

Crocodile Bridge Gate ⊠

R540 R36

White River ●

MPUMALANGA

Berg-en-Dal ◼

🏠❻

Dullstroom ●

0 ——— 50 km

Malelane Gate ⊠

Komatipoort ◼

Nelspruit ●

N4

N4

RESSANO GRACIA

▼ Witbank ▼ Barberton ▼ Maputo

MOZAMBIQUE

Pietersburg (×3)

Groblersdal

PRIVATE CAMPS 🏕		**BUSHVELD CAMPS** 🏠	
Chitwa Chitwa	Garonga **G**	Nkorho Bush Camp **E**	Bateleur **2** Shimuwini **3**
Game Lodge **G**	Khoka Moya **D**	Nottens **K**	Byamiti **6** Sirheni **1**
Djuma Bush Lodge **I**	Leadwood Lodge **H**	Tanda Tula **C**	Jakkalsbessie **5** Talamati **4**
Elephant Plains **F**	Londolozi **J**	Umlani **A**	

Access and getting around

There are four options for getting to Kruger: you can **drive** there; take one of the many **tours** on offer – some involving day-trips from points just outside the park, others involving camping inside the park; you can fly into one of the several airports around the park and **rent a car**; or you can stay in a **private reserve** and arrange to be transferred from one of the Lowveld towns served by buses or planes (see p.681). However, flights to airports servicing Kruger and car rental are expensive, and there are no special deals.

By road

There are eight **entrance gates** along the western and southern borders of Kruger; where you enter depends on where you're coming from and which camp you're heading to. **From Johannesburg**, the quickest way to get to Kruger is along the N4, which brushes along its southern boundary en route to Mozambique and quickly gets you close to the **southern gates** of Malelane, 411km away, and Crocodile Bridge, another 57km further on. These are also the closest if you're coming **from KwaZulu-Natal**, either via Barberton or Swaziland. If you've been exploring the **Blyde River Canyon** area, access is off the R538/R40 between White River and Klaserie to the **western gates** (Pretoriuskop, Paul Kruger, Orpen and Phalaborwa) leading into the southern and central sections of the park. The easiest way to get to the two **northern gates** on the west side is off the N1 from Johannesburg to Messina on South Africa's northern border, taking the R524 east at Louis Trichardt for Punda Maria Gate, or the R525, 58km further north, to Pafuri Gate (see p.704).

Remember, if you're trying to get from one part of the park to another, that although it's far more fun driving inside, the speed limit (50kph on tar, 40kph on dirt) makes it a slow journey – and you're bound to make frequent stops to watch animals.

By air

SAA (☎011 356 1111) **flies** out three times daily from **Johannesburg** to **Skukuza**, Kruger's headquarters. SA Airlink (☎0800 114 799) flies three times every weekday (less frequently over weekends) from Johannesburg to **Phalaborwa** (see p.692), which lies just outside Phalaborwa Gate, and six times every weekday (less often over weekends) to **Nelspruit**, 45 minutes' drive from either Numbi or Malelane gates. SA Airlink also flies daily **from Durban** to Nelspruit and **from Cape Town** to Hoedspruit.

Car rental

For **car rental**, Johannesburg or Pretoria are obvious centres to make your arrangements, but closer to the Kruger you can sort out a vehicle at Nelspruit International airport, 56km from Numbi Gate, through Avis (☎0861 021 111, ⓦwww.avis.co.za), Budget (☎0861 016 622, ⓦwww.budget.co.za) or Imperial (☎0861 131 000, ⓦwww.imperialcarrental.co.za). Phalaborwa airport also has branches of Avis (☎0861 021 111, ⓦwww.avis.co.za), Budget (☎0861 016 622, ⓦwww.budget.co.za) and Imperial (☎0861 131 000, ⓦwww.imperialcarrental .co.za). Europcar (☎015 793 3678, ⓦwww.europcar.co.za) serves Hoedspruit, while at Skukuza airport, inside Kruger, you'll find only Avis.

Tours and packages

An increasing number of **tours** will take you into the Kruger – your best bet, if you're not self-driving. As well as those listed below, it's also worth checking out the backpacker lodges in the vicinity, most of which either operate budget safaris or have links to operators who do. In **Hazyview** contact *Big Five Backpackers* or *Kruger Park Backpackers* (see p.689); in **Nelspruit**, *The Old Vic Inn* and *Nelspruit Backpackers* can both arrange tours (see p.683); and in **Phalaborwa** (see p.693), *Elephant Walk* does reasonably priced day-trips.

Bhejane Safaris ☎013 737 7242, ⊛www.bhejane.co.za. Run by an ex-Natal Parks Board trail guide, Bhejane offers one- to three-night walking safaris in the Hoedspruit area, staying at a rustic camp (about R800 per person per night sharing)

and more upmarket overnight walking and driving safaris in the Sabi Sands game reserve, the best place in Africa for big cats (about R2000 per person per night, reducing to about half that if there are four or more of you).

Game-viewing tips

• **Binoculars are a must** for scanning the horizon when you're out viewing. Don't try consciously to spot animals – many are well disguised. Instead, watch for any movement or something that strikes you as a bit out of place.

• **Look out for other stopped cars** – often a good indicator of a game sighting.

• **Plan your game drive carefully** and invest in a detailed map of Kruger (available at virtually every restcamp). Use the map to choose a route which includes rivers or pans where you can stop and enjoy the scenery and birdlife while you wait for game to come down to drink, especially in the late afternoon.

• **Driving really slowly** pays off, particularly if you stop often. Switch off your engine when you stop, open your window and use your senses. Being in the bush isn't just about seeing animals: there are also the smells and sounds of the wilds, which complete the picture and provide useful clues. Twigs breaking or the alarm calls of animals can hint at something afoot.

• **Don't embark on overambitious drives** from your restcamp. You'll see as much game sitting quietly in your car as you would frantically driving around all day.

• **Take food and drink** with you. You don't want to have to break off that terrific lion-sighting because you're starving and can't miss lunch. Carry plenty of water to avoid dehydration or heatstroke. If you have your own teabags and milk you can make tea at the designated picnic sites, where there is always boiling water available, tables and chairs to enjoy your picnic in the wild, and braai places powered with gas.

• **Tuning into animal behaviour** can greatly enrich your experience and provides constant interest even on days when big cats stubbornly refuse to put in an appearance. Even commonplace species such as impala become fascinating when you understand what they're doing and why. Although the widely available *Safari Companion* by Richard Estes sounds like a manual on how to treat your porters, in fact it's an accessible and engrossing guide to the behaviour of African mammals (see "Books" on p.895).

• **Take an interest in geology, trees and birds** and you need never be bored because "there's nothing going on". The excellent *Make the Most of Kruger*, available at most restcamps, is well worth investing in for the basic interpretation it provides of the park ecology and for filling in those empty moments.

• **The best times of day** for game viewing are when it's cooler, during the early morning and late afternoon. Set out as soon as the camp gates open in the morning and go out again as the temperature starts dropping in the afternoon. Take a siesta during the midday heat, just as the animals do, when they head for deep shade where you're less likely to see them.

For more information, see the spotter's guide on pp.xvii–xxxii and "Wildlife" on p.848).

Bundu Bus Tours and Safaris ☏011 675 0767 or 082 567 7041, ⊛www.bundusafaris.co.za. A range of safaris, all departing and returning to wherever you're staying in Johannesburg, Pretoria or Nelspruit. Most popular is a four-day trip (Mon, Wed & Fri) staying in three different parts of Kruger, starting in the south at Berg-en-Dal (R1750, or R3000 if you opt for the luxury tour which uses *Nkorho Lodge* in the Sabi Sands). An exciting option is a three-night Kruger Park wilderness trip, where you camp in an unfenced area and go for walks with an armed ranger (R2600). A seven-day tour takes in Kruger, Swaziland and KwaZulu-Natal (R2500), and a ten-day trip takes in Kruger and Zimbabwe (R3250).

Livingstone Trails ☏011 867 2586, ⊛www.livingstonetrails.co.za. Four-day camping trips from Johannesburg, using *Maroela* campsite or Orpen Gate in the park as a base (Mon, Wed & Sat;

R1500) include a game walk (not Wed trip). Six days costs R2000. A more upmarket three-day choice, where you stay in huts or equipped tents in land adjoining Kruger, costs R2000.

Trans Frontiers Safaris ☏015 793 3816 or 083 700 7987, ⊛www.tsafaris.co.za. Good backpacker-friendly tours, with an emphasis on game walking, run by a couple with an outstanding track record. Four-night/five-day safaris from Jo'burg hostels, overnighting at the very pleasant *Backpack Safari Lodge* before going big-game walking in the Manyeleti reserve adjoining Kruger. A drive to Satara in the park itself is included. Close to the *Safari Lodge* is the authentic *Nyani* Shangaan village, with a traditional dinner and post-prandial singing and drumming, and the owners can book you onto rafting on the Blyde River or recommended horse-riding on a game farm in the vicinity. Four days costs R1800, five days R2200.

Walks and game drives

Whether you're staying in Kruger or not, you can still join one of the daily morning (5.30–8.30am) or night (5–8pm) **game drives** organized by the national park. Not only is the viewing unsurpassed because of the height of their vehicles, at R115 it's one of the cheapest ways of accessing the park. Drives leave from every camp in the park (book at reception) and, for those staying outside the park, from the four southern gates through which bookings can also be made: **Paul Kruger** (☏013 735 5107), **Numbi** (☏013 735 5133), **Malelane** (☏013 735 6152) and **Crocodile Bridge** (☏013 735 6012). Three-hour **game walks** (R140) are conducted every morning at 5.45am from every camp in the park except *Olifants*, *Shingwedzi* and *Punda Maria*; book through reception at your camp.

Accommodation: restcamps

Note: The following pages refer to the public section of the park; for accommodation on the private reserves see p.708.

At most of Kruger's fourteen main **restcamps** the sounds of the African night tend to get drowned out by air conditioning and the merriment of braais and beer. It's not all bad news, though; at least you'll have all the facilities you could ever want on hand. Nearly all camps have electricity, public telephones, petrol stations, shops, restaurants, laundrettes and snack bars. Some also have pools and most offer night drives for viewing nocturnal animals on large trucks equipped with spotlights. The restcamps are actually very pleasant, with walks around the edges, labelled trees to help you identify what you see on drives, and plenty of birds and smaller creatures around the camps themselves. Several, including *Lower Sabie*, *Skukuza*, *Olifants* and *Letaba* have views onto rivers where, from a distance, you can see game coming to drink.

Kruger camps have a variety of accommodation. At most of them you'll find **thatched rondavels**, each with an outdoor eating area and facing communally towards each other rather than out towards the views. The best rondavels are on the camp perimeters or directly facing onto rivers. Nine of the rest-

Accommodation bookings

Kruger's rest and bushveld camps are adminstered by South African National Parks. If you're planning on staying at the park over school holidays or weekends, book well ahead. Booking in writing opens thirteen months in advance; closer to the date, you'll usually find somewhere, especially at off-peak times, if you're not too particular about where you stay in the park. For **bookings** contact South African National Parks (Pretoria ☏012 343 1991, 📠012 343 0905, @reservations@parks-sa.co.za).

Entry gate admission fees

To enter Kruger, you pay a fee per person plus a charge for the vehicle.

Adult	R30
Child (2–15)	R15
Vehicle	R24
Minibus	R97

Opening hours

Gates

Every restcamp is fenced off and has an entrance gate that's closed and opened at the times indicated below. You are required to return to your rest camp or leave the park prior to gate closing times. Except where specified, all times refer to both entrance and camp gates.

Jan	04.30am–6.30pm (camp); 5.30am–6.30pm (entry)
Feb	5.30am–6.30pm
March	5.30am–6pm
April	6am–6pm
May–Jul	6am–5.30pm
Sept	6am–6pm
Oct	5.30am–6pm
Nov & Dec	4.30am–6.30pm (camp); 5.30am–6.30pm (entry)

Reception at restcamps
8am–5.30pm

Shops
8am–half an hour after gate closing

Restaurants

Breakfast	7–9am
Lunch	noon–2pm
Supper	6–9pm

Driving

• Speed limits are: 50kph on tar, 40kph on untarred roads and 20kph in restcamps.
• Speed traps operate in some parts of the park.
• Approved roads only should be used. Don't drive on unmarked roads and never drive off-road.
• Never leave your car (it's illegal and dangerous), except at designated sites.

---

camps have a **campsite** (with shared kitchen and washing facilities), which provide the park's cheapest accommodation (R40–75 for two people). Sites for **caravans** and **camper vans** are available wherever there's camping, cost up to R70 for two people and often have a power point. Some camps have **furnished safari tents** and **huts**, in configurations usually sleeping two to four people. Most of these have fridges and air conditioning, some come with basic crockery and cutlery, and all share communal kitchens and ablutions at prices starting from R125 for two people. Huts with shared ablution facilities go for about R100–150 for two people, while **en-suite bungalows and cottages** come in several variations, ranging from those with just showers, toilets and fridges to ones fully equipped with kitchens. Prices range from around R300 to around R400 per couple, and often reflect how modern the camp is rather than the accommodation facilities. There are also larger units for groups or families that work out slightly cheaper per person if there are four or more of you.

For a more rustic (and pricier) experience, head out to one of the handful of smaller **bushveld camps**, which dispense with all the niceties of shops and restaurants and get down to basics. These camps are more exclusive, and out of bounds to anyone not booked in to stay.

Southern Kruger restcamps

The so-called "circus" is the busiest section of the Kruger, with its hub at **Skukuza**, the biggest of all the Kruger camps and **Lower Sabie**, one of the most popular. Apart from containing some of the best places for seeing large quantities of game, southern Kruger is also easily reached from Johannesburg along the N4. At peak times of year, this area buzzes with vehicles jostling to get up close to big cat sightings, which always appear to evoke poor human behaviour.

Berg-en-Dal

In the southwest corner of the park, **Berg-en-Dal** is one of the newest camps, built in the Eighties and with modern chalets that break with the Kruger tradition of thatched rondavels. Set attractively among *koppies* in a shallow grassy basin (its Afrikaans name means "hill and dale"), 12km northwest of **Malelane Gate**, the camp overlooks the Matjulu stream and dam, both of which can be reached by means of a walkway running along the perimeter fence. The modern, fully equipped chalets with terraces are widely spaced to provide privacy and are landscaped among indigenous bushveld vegetation. Facilities include a beautifully positioned swimming pool, a shop selling a good range of food, a licensed restaurant, snack bar, filling station and laundry.

Crocodile Bridge

East of *Berg-en-Dal*, **Crocodile Bridge** is the least impressive of Kruger's restcamps, and its position at the very southern edge of the park overlooking farmland does nothing to enhance your bush experience. Located at the **Crocodile Bridge Gate** on the north bank of the Crocodile River, the camp is reached via Komatipoort, 12km to its south on the Mozambique border. The main reason to spend the night here is if you're arriving late and don't have time to press on into the park. Facilities are limited to a laundry and filling station, and a shop selling the most basic of supplies. Accommodation is in en-suite huts sleeping two to three, with cooking facilities. If you're pushing north to *Lower Sabie*, it's worth taking the drive slowly, as this area, dotted with knobthorn and marula trees, is known for its herbivores, which include giraffe, kudu, steenbok, wildebeest, zebra, buffalo and waterbuck as well as ostrich, warthog and the magnificent black sable antelope. You should also keep your eyes peeled for predators such as lion, cheetah, hyena and jackal.

Lower Sabie

Some 35km north of *Crocodile Bridge*, **Lower Sabie** occupies game-rich country that places it among the top three restcamps in the Kruger for animal-spotting. The surrounding open savannah and the camp's position on the banks of

Wilderness trails

Wilderness trails in Kruger don't bring you closer to game than driving: the experience is really about getting closer to the vegetation and smaller creatures, though you have a good chance of encountering big game. Under the guidance of an experienced ranger, the two-day trails pass through areas of notable beauty with diverse plant and animal life. Groups (limited to eight people) spend three nights in four rustic, two-bed huts, served by reed-walled showers and flush toilets. Simple meals are provided. Trails cost in the region of R1100 per person fully inclusive.

The trails are closed over the Christmas school holidays and are heavily subscribed for the rest of the year. **Booking** in writing opens thirteen months in advance and is recommended if you have your heart set on a particular trail; contact South African National Parks (see p.701).

• **Bushman Trail** covers the southwestern section of the park, near *Berg-en-Dal* restcamp. The trail camp is in a secluded valley, characterized by granite hills. San paintings in many of the hill shelters are an added feature of the trail.

• **Metsimetsi Trail** operates midway between Skukuza and Satara, with the camp at the foot of a mountain and overlooking a small waterhole. Black rhino and large predators move through the undulating savannah and rocky gorges and ravines.

• **Napi Trail** sets out from a camp between *Skukuza* and *Pretoriuskop* into woodland bushveld. Undulating terrain and granite hills suit the area's resident population of white rhino, while black rhino, elephant, lion and buffalo are also often seen. Birdlife is prolific.

• **Nyalaland Trail** is based in the remote northern section of the park along the Madzaringwe Stream north of *Punda Maria*. The area is known for its fever-tree and baobab forests, prolific birdlife and spectacular views.

• **Olifants Trail** has its camp on the southern bank of the Olifants River, from which it offers a magnificent view of the river. Riverine bush and gorges characterize the terrain, and lion, buffalo and elephant are often seen.

• **Sweni Trail** camp overlooks the Sweni stream in the wilderness area near Nwanetsi and provides a view of marula and knobthorn savannah. A resident pride of lions pads about here and is frequently seen.

• **Wolhuter Trail** lies in the vicinity of *Berg-en-Dal* and *Pretoriuskop* camps in the southern section of the park, where rhinos are relatively common, as is a wide variety of other game.

the Sabie River attract game coming to drink and graze, and the terrain around here is rated among the most beautiful in the southern Kruger. Within kilometres of the entrance gate to the camp, a number of waterholes and dams populated with crocodiles and hippos make good spots to park and watch for game coming to quench their thirst. In the thorn-thicket country hard by the west of the camp, you'll find promising terrain for catching sight of elephants moving between the trees as well as white rhino grazing on the sweet grasses, which also bring herds of buffalo and, in their wake, lions. Accommodation is in huts with shared ablutions as well as more expensive en-suite units with kitchens, some with river views. There's a restaurant, a cafeteria, a shop, a filling station and a laundry.

Pretoriuskop

Due west of *Lower Sabie*, but not directly connected to it, **Pretoriuskop** is reached via **Numbi Gate**, 9km to its west. Set in an area of sourveld, characterized by granite outcrops, tall grass and sickle bush favoured by mountain reedbuck, sable and white rhino, the camp is in an area stalked by lions, wild dogs and side-striped jackals. However, given the dense bush, you're more likely to spot larger species such as kudus and giraffes poking their necks over the bushes. Accommodation consists of en-suite cottages and rondavels in addition to cheaper units with shared ablution and cooking facilities. The camp has a restaurant, a snack bar, a shop, a laundry, a swimming pool and a filling station, and also offers night drives.

Skukuza

Kruger's largest restcamp, **Skukuza** (☎013 735 4000, reservations ☎013 735 4184) lies at the centre of the best game-viewing area in the park. Its position is a mixed blessing; although you get large amounts of game, hordes of humans aren't far behind. *Skukuza* accommodates over one thousand people, and its sprawling collection of rondavels resembles a small town. It lies on the edge of the Sabie River, which is overlooked by a wide paved walkway furnished with park benches, from which you can see crocodiles floating by like driftwood on the brown water. Most people drive along the Sabie River to *Lower Sabie*, so if you want to avoid this busy route, chose another direction for your game drive.

Skukuza is the hub of Kruger, with its own airport and car rental agency. The restcamp's garage can repair your vehicle, and there's also a post office, a bank, a filling station, two **restaurants**, a **cafeteria** and a really good **library** (Mon–Fri 8.30am–4pm & 7–9pm, Sat 8.30am–12.45pm, 1.45–4pm & 7–9pm, Sun 8.30am–12.45pm & 1.45–4pm) with a collection of natural history books and exhibits. Another highlight of *Skukuza* is the **open-air cinema** showing wildlife videos every evening under the stars.

The closest entry point is through **Paul Kruger Gate**, 12km to the west, which in turn is 42km east of Hazyview. Accommodation is in a range of thatched, en-suite units, or more cheaply in some furnished East African-style tents in the caravan park, with shared ablutions and kitchens. Night drives and day drives in open vehicles can be arranged at the main complex – the night drives are excellent, since all the other vehicles are safely tucked up for the night, and you'll have the road to yourself.

Central Kruger restcamps

Game viewing can be extremely good in the "zoo", with the area between *Skukuza* and *Satara* reckoned to be one of the global hot spots for lions. At **Olifants** you'll find the Kruger's most dramatically located camp, with fantastic views into a river gorge, while **Satara** is the second-largest and one of the most popular – its placement is ideal for making sorties into fertile wildlife country.

Orpen and Maroela

Like *Crocodile Bridge*, **Orpen** is located right by an entrance gate, 45km east of Klaserie, and is recommended mainly if you're arriving late and don't have time to get further into the park before the camp gates close. *Orpen* is far preferable to its southern counterpart though, because although it's on the western periphery of Kruger, the substantial Timbavati Private Game Reserve lies to its west, so you're already well into the wilderness once you get here, and it's very good for game viewing. The camp is small, peaceful and shaded by beautiful trees; it's a lovely drive from here along a river to get to *Satara*, the nearest big camp. Facilities are pretty basic, with a filling station and a reception doubling as a rudimentary shop; none of the accommodation is en suite, and cooking is done in communal kitchens. If you want to camp, you'll need to go to the small **Maroela** satellite camping area, overlooking the Timbavati River, approximately 4km from *Orpen*. You must report to *Orpen* reception to check in before going to the campsite, which has electricity.

Tamboti

Not far from Orpen Gate into the park, Kruger's only tented camp **Tamboti** is reached by turning left 2km after *Orpen* and continuing for 1km. While it doesn't quite match up to its promise of a traditional East African safari, its position on the banks of the frequently dry Timbavati River is superb, among apple leaf trees, sycamore figs and jackalberries. You'll often see elephants from your tent just beyond the electrified fence, digging in the river bed for moisture, hence the camp's popularity (you'll have to book ahead to be sure of getting a place). Each walk-in tent has its own deck overlooking the river, but best of all are numbers 21 and 22, which enjoy the deep shade of large riverine trees, something you'll appreciate in the mid-summer heat. The tents also have fridges and electric lighting, while all kitchen, washing and toilet facilities are in two shared central blocks (bring your own cooking and eating utensils).

Satara

Forty-six kilometres due east of Orpen Gate, **Satara** ranks second only to *Skukuza* (92km to its south), in size and the excellence of its game viewing. Set in the middle of flat grasslands, the camp commands no great views, but is preferable to *Skukuza* because it avoids the feeling of suburban boxes on top of each other. Accommodation is in cottages arranged around lawned areas shaded by large trees. Facilities include a restaurant, cafeteria, shop, filling station, laundry and vehicle repair workshop. About halfway along the tarred road between *Satara* and *Skukuza*, the vicinity around Tshokwane picnic site reputedly has the highest concentration of lions in the world, hence the number of motorists here. The area around *Satara* itself is usually good for sighting grazers such as buffalo, wildebeest, zebra, kudu, impala and elephant.

Balule

On the southern bank of the Olifants River, **Balule** is 41km north of *Satara* and 87km from Phalaborwa Gate. The only electricity you'll find at this very basic satellite to *Olifants* (11km to the north) is in the fence to keep out lions. Compact *Balule* has two sections, one consisting of six spartan rondavels and another of fifteen camping and caravan sites. Each section has its own communal ablution and cooking facilities. *Balule* takes its bushveld identity seriously and luxuries are kept to a minimum – as is the price: this is one of the few restcamps where, unless you're camping, two can stay for under R100. There are iron washstands with enamel bowls, no windows and you can forget about air conditioning. Guests have to bring their own crockery, cutlery and utensils, and must report to *Olifants* at least half an hour before the gates close.

Olifants

Because of its terrific setting on cliffs overlooking the braided Olifants River, **Olifants** is reckoned by many to be the best restcamp in Kruger. It's possible to spend hours sitting on the benches on the covered look-out terrace, gazing into the valley whose airspace is crisscrossed by Bateleur eagles and yellow-billed kites cruising the thermals, while the rushing of the water below creates a hypnotic rhythm. The camp has a charmingly old-fashioned feel. Accommodation is in thatched, en-suite rondavels, with numbers 1 to 24 possessing superb views overlooking the valley; it's worth booking well in advance to get one of these. The river marks the division between rugged, rocky *veld* with ghostly fever trees growing along the riverbanks to the south, and to the north, mopane woodland which attracts the large antelope such as eland, roan, sable and tsessebe. This is also promising country for spotting elephant, giraffe, lion, hyena and cheetah, and you should look out for the tiny klipspringer, a pretty antelope that inhabits rocky terrain which it nimbly negotiates by boulder-hopping. A highlight of the area are some of the dirt roads which loop along the Olifants River. Facilities include a restaurant, a snack bar, a shop and a laundry.

Letaba

Set in mopane shrubland, **Letaba** is 34km north of *Olifants*, set beautifully on an oxbow curve along the Letaba River, a vista which, sadly, very few of the rondavels enjoy. The restaurant does have great views of the floodplain, and you can spend a day just watching herds of buffalo mooching around, elephants drifting past and a host of other plains game. The camp is old and quite large, a fact mitigated by large acacias and mopanes as well as ilala palms. *Letaba* has an interesting museum with exhibits on the life cycle of elephants, including displays on bulls with inordinately large tusks. Accommodation is in rondavels, either en-suite or with shared ablution and cooking facilities as well as large furnished tents. The camp offers all the usual restaurant, shopping and laundry facilities, as well as a vehicle repair workshop.

Northern Kruger restcamps

You won't find edge-to-edge game in the northern "wilderness", but crossing the Tropic of Capricorn after **Mopani** camp gives a symbolic boost to the idea that you're entering hot savannah country. The north is the least visited of Kruger's regions and creates the most convincing impression of African wilderness, especially once you hit **Punda Maria** camp, which feels like a real old-time outpost in the bush.

Mopani

Some 42km north of *Letaba*, **Mopani** is one of the newer camps in Kruger and overlooks the Pioneer Dam. A sprawling place in the middle of monotonous mopane scrub, its swimming pool provides cool relief after a long drive. The dam, one of the few water sources in the vicinity, attracts animals to drink and provides an outstanding lookout for a variety of wildlife including elephant, buffalo and antelope. The modern en-suite accommodation, built of rough-hewn stone and thatch, is quite spread out and designed more for driving than walking. The restaurant is above average for Kruger and the bar has a good view across to the dam. Other facilities include a shop, a laundry and filling station, and you can go on organized night drives.

Shingwedzi

A fairly large camp featuring square, brick chalets and a few older, colonial-style whitewash and thatch bungalows, **Shingwedzi**, 63km north of *Mopani*, is sited in extensive grounds shaded by pals and mopane trees. The dining room has a terrace, frequented by starlings and cheeky hornbills jostling to pounce on your food. From the terrace you get a long view down across the usually dry Shingwedzi River. Look out for the weavers' nests with their long, tube-like entrances hanging from the eaves outside reception and the cafeteria. Facilities include a restaurant, a cafeteria, a shop, a filling station and a swimming pool, and night drives are on offer.

Bushveld camps

Bushveld camps are far smaller, more remote and much more basic than the main restcamps. You won't find any shops or restaurants, but they are all within reasonable reach of larger restcamps – just in case you can't survive without a Coke. The appeal of the bushveld camps is that they get you into the wilderness, away from day-to-day trivialities and the tourist pack. Most offer game drives during the day and at night. Prices start at around R180 per person for two people sharing. Because of their exclusivity, you should book the camps as early as possible.

Bateleur

About 40km southwest of *Shingwedzi* restcamp, **Bateleur** is well off the beaten track, in the remote northern section of the park on the banks of the frequently dry Mashokwe stream. The camp has a timber viewing-deck, excellently placed for views of game coming to drink at a seasonally full waterhole. The nearby Silver Fish and Rooibosrand dams also attract game as well as birdlife in prodigious quantities. Seven family cottages can accommodate up to 34 people; each has its own kitchenette and fridge, with electricity provided by solar panels.

Biyamiti

Biyamiti lies on the banks of the Mbiyamiti River, about 41km northeast of the Malelane Gate and 26km west of Crocodile Bridge Gate. Its proximity to the latter is one of the main advantages of this very southerly camp. Another plus point is that the terrain attracts large numbers of game including lion, elephant and rhinos. Fifteen family cottages, all with fully equipped kitchens, can accommodate a maximum of seventy visitors.

Jakkalsbessie

On the bank of the Sabie River, some 7km north of *Skukuza* restcamp, near the airfield, **Jakkalsbessie** is one of the less remote bush camps and is periodically treated to the sound of aircraft taking off or landing at the *Skukuza* landing strip. Although it may be too close to the "city lights" of *Skukuza* for some, the camp is beautifully positioned, with easy access to some of the richest game country in Kruger. Eight thatched cottages with fully equipped kitchens accommodate a maximum of 32 people.

Shimuwini

Shimuwini lies on the upper reaches of the Shimuwini Dam, which is filled by the Letaba River, about 50km from the Phalaborwa Gate on the Mooiplaas Road. Situated in mopane and bushwillow country, with sycamore figs along the banks of the river, this camp is not known for its game but is a perennial favourite among birdwatchers. It's an excellent place for spotting riverine bird species, including fish eagles. Up to 71 people can be accommodated in fifteen family cottages equipped with kitchens and with verandahs.

Sirheni

Sirheni is on the bank of Sirheni Dam, roughly 54km south of *Punda Maria*. It's a fine spot for bird-watching, with some game also passing through the area. The big pull, however, is its remote bushveld atmosphere in an area that sees few visitors. The fifteen one- or two-bedroom cottages, all equipped with kitchens, can accommodate eighty visitors.

Talamiti

Lying on the banks of the usually dry Nwaswitsontso stream, about 31km south of Orpen Gate, **Talamiti**'s mixed bushwillow woodland setting attracts giraffe, kudu, wildebeest, zebra and predators like lion, hyena and jackal, as well as rhino and sable. The camp has the capacity for eighty people in its ten six-bed and five four-bed cottages.

Punda Maria and Pafuri

Kruger's northernmost camp, **Punda Maria**, 71km beyond *Shingwedzi*, is also the park's wildest and least visited. There's less concentration of game up here, but to aficionados, this is the real Kruger: a relaxed, tropical outpost near the Zimbabwe border, well away from the bustle of motorists. This isn't to say you won't see wildlife here (the Big Five all breeze through from time to time), it's simply that you have to work that much harder at game spotting amongst its woodlands and dense mopane scrubland. The real rewards of *Punda* are in its landscapes and stunningly varied vegetation types, with a remarkable nine biomes all converging here, which also makes it a paradise for bird-watchers. Some of the accommodation is in the original 1930s huts, which ought to be declared National Monuments as they're in danger of being pulled down for modernization. All units are en suite and have fridges, while some have kitchens and the rest make use of communal cooking areas. The camp has a very simple restaurant, a small shop and a filling station.

Pafuri picnic site, 46km north of Punda, should on no account be missed, as it's here that you'll experience the true richness of northern Kruger. The site is a large area under the shade of massive thorn trees, leadwoods and jack-alberry trees on the banks of the Luvuvhu River and is the ultimate place for lunch. An interpretation board gives a fascinating account of human history in the area. There are braai facilities, a constantly boiling kettle to make your own tea and the attendant can sell you ice-cold canned drinks.

Private reserves

The **private camps** follow the same basic formula of full-board, with dawn and late-afternoon game drives conducted by a ranger, assisted by a tracker, in open vehicles. Afternoon outings usually turn into night drives following sundowners in the bush. They all offer bushwalks, usually after breakfast, and most overlook waterholes or plains, so that you can look out for animals during the time you're in camp, laze around the pool, or peruse their collection of animal books. The difference in price depends on the level of luxury you're after in the camp. The Sabi Sands reserve has the reputation of being the best managed of all the game areas, and it's one of the best places in the world for seeing leopards and lions.

Private camps aren't places you can casually pop into. You'll need to **book ahead** either directly through the contact addresses given here or through a specialist travel agent (such as those listed in Basics). There are scheduled **flights from Johannesburg** to Phalaborwa (the cheapest route), Hoedspruit, Nelspruit and Skukuza; **from Cape Town** to Hoedspruit; and **from Durban** to Nelspruit (see p.712). Camps generally pick up guests from the airport. By car it will take five to six hours from Johannesburg; you'll be given detailed instructions on how to get to your camp when you book. The camps can all be accessed in an ordinary car, 4WD is not necessary.

Prices quoted are per person, per night, sharing a double unit, including all meals (where relevant) and game activities. A few places still charge below R1000 per person, but the majority start at R1300 and go upwards of R2000. On the whole, the huge price gulf between the bottom and top ends reflects the incidental extras, such as level of luxury, size of public spaces and cuisine – and often simply reputation. All are en suite and have proper beds and a swimming pool unless specified. Prices are R500–600 cheaper in the winter months

(May–August). This is a superb time to visit, not just on the grounds of price, but because there are no mosquitoes about, the daytime temperatures are in the mid-twenties (Celsius) and it's sunny most days – although game drives can be chilly.

Chitwa Chitwa Game Lodge

Sabi Sand Game Reserve, North (℡011 883 1354, ⓦwww.chitwa.co.za; ❽–❾). Beautifully set on the edge of the largest pan in the Sabi Sand, *Chitwa Chitwa* maintains its competitive edge by providing both luxury and the chance to see the big cats, but keeping its rates lower than the high-profile places like neighbouring *Mala Mala* and *Londolozi*. It has two camps on the property, *Main Lodge* and *Safari Lodge*, both with decks overlooking waterholes. *Main Lodge* accommodates eighteen guests and is much more luxurious, with grand public spaces and baroque suites, while *Safari Lodge* sleeps ten people in an attractive cluster of thatched rondavels, with a highly enthusiastic game guide. The food is the same at both camps, and both accept children, while the drivers of vehicles from the two lodges are in contact with each other to share sightings. The price difference reflects only the level of splendour.

Djuma Bush Lodge

Sabi Sand Game Reserve, North (℡013 735 5118, ⓦwww.djuma.co.za; ❾). A very relaxed lodge set in mixed woodland with eight A-frame thatched chalets decorated in simple but tastefully pared-back African style, using traditional baskets, hardwood fixtures and white linen. Each chalet has a small verandah with deck chairs. Pathways connect chalets to the two-storey communal eating area, lounge and bar. The viewing deck overlooks woodland that attracts elephants and other game, while breakfast and evening meals are taken in a *boma* under the sky. The emphasis is on good food, and *Djuma* employs a culinary consultant to dream up South African-inspired flavours. Children are welcome, and the lodge will take 3-year-olds and up on game drives – or you can leave your kids with one of the babysitters. As with all the Sabi Sand private camps, game viewing is excellent at *Djuma*.

Elephant Plains

Sabi Sands North (℡013 735 5358, ⓦwww.elephantplains.co.za; ❼). An unpretentious and well-priced camp with accommodation for twelve guests in thatched en-suite rondavels in a garden of aloes and vibrant bougainvillea. The swimming pool and deck overlook a plain dotted with leadwoods and the occasional elephant. Meals are taken outside, and this camp follows the de rigeur Sabi Sand routine of bushwalks in the morning after breakfast and game drives early morning and late afternoon.

Garonga

Makalali Conservancy, an hour's drive west of Hoedspruit (℡011 537 4620, ⓦwww.garonga.com; ❽). A spacious, very beautiful camp offering "safaris for the soul" with billowing white drapes, terracotta colours, cushioned low beds – all utterly languorous and romantic. The camp sleeps just fourteen (no children), and the emphasis is on relaxation and tuning into nature and yourself, as well as game viewing – in contrast to the usual goal-oriented list-ticking common in the Sabi Sands. Game drives allow you to view elephants and lions, but there are also contemplative nature walks, healthy and delicious meals, and massages available in a gorgeous treatment room overlooking a waterhole.

Khoka Moya

Manyeleti Game Reserve; close to Orpen Gate (☎015 793 1729, ⓦwww
.threecities.co.za/khoka.htm; ❼). An easy-going, tasteful game lodge taking
sixteen guests (children welcome), verging on the luxurious but still affordable.
Accommodation is in comfortable huts connected by boardwalks set in semi-
woodland savannah. Prices are lower for the original, unmodernized units.

They also run the *Trails Camp*, a very basic reed camp, elevated 2m in the air,
deep in the bush beside a waterhole, with a bucket shower (❺). The camp is
rented out to a single group of four to eight people, for a minimum of two
nights, with its own chef and waitress. There are no game drives, but walks with
a tracker are offered instead. An absolute steal at a price that includes meals.

Leadwood Lodge

Sabi Sand Game Reserve, South (☎011 783 2800, ⓦwww.exeterlodges.com;
❼). Operated by Exeter Safaris, *Leadwood Lodge* offers self-catering accommodation in five thatched, two-bed cottages along the banks of the Sand River
under jackalberry, leadwood and tamboti trees. The comfortably furnished air-
conditioned units come with all cooking utensils; just bring your own food
and drink. The price includes two daily game drives and a walk, and children
from 6 upwards are welcome.

Londolozi

Sabi Sand Game Reserve (☎011 809 4300, ⓦwww.londolozi.com; ❾). Leopards
are virtually synonymous with *Londolozi*; you stand an excellent chance of seeing these notoriously elusive stalkers. *Londolozi's* camps carry the imaginative
stamp of the Conservation Corporation Africa, whose hallmark is unapologetic
indulgence with a green conscience. Of South Africa's most exclusive safari
lodges, *Londolozi* wins hands down on style. The biggest of the three camps on
Londolozi's land is *Bateleur Camp*, accommodating twenty (no kids) in comfortable chalets. Best of all is the wonderful outdoor dining room surrounded
by woodland and jettying out over the Sand River basin. But once you're
spending this kind of money you may as well go the extra to stay in the more
intimate surroundings of the smaller bush camps.

Nkorho Bush Camp

Sabi Sand Game Reserve, North (☎013 735 5367, ⓕ013 735 5585, ⓔnkorho
@mweb.co.za; ❼). A small family-operated outfit, *Nkorho* is possibly the most
relaxed and child-friendly camp in the Sabi Sand. Despite being one of the
least-expensive private lodges around Kruger, you'll see exactly the same
animals that stalk the *veld* around the adjacent upmarket lodges, some of which
charge up to six times the price. Its lack of pretension and homely atmosphere
give *Nkorho* the feeling of being on a friend's farm. Set in thinly wooded grassland, the accommodation is in five, simple but comfortable, rectangular chalets
with showers, catering to a maximum of fourteen guests. The rooms are set
around communal areas consisting of an open-air lounge area, a bar with a pool
table and an African fantasy of a *boma* – constructed from gnarled tree trunks
– where evening meals are served around a large open fire. The price includes
two game drives and a bush walk and, as with all the Sabi Sand lodges, you
stand a good chance here of seeing leopards and lions – especially since *Nkorho*
maintains radio contact with its neighbours during outings.

Nottens Bush Camp

Sabi Sand Reserve (℡013 735 5105, ⓦwww.nottens.com; ❽). Over a decade old and still resisting the temptation to expand, this family-run outfit is one of the most popular and attractive small camps. Dinners are served at a communal table, with other meals on a massive deck that acts as a viewing platform for the open plain in front of the camp. Accommodation for a maximum of twelve (children over 8 welcome) is in pleasant double-bedded chalets lit by oil lamps, with tin roofs. The lack of electricity is a deliberate part of the camp's philosophy of bringing guests into contact with the bush.

Tanda Tula

Timbavati Game Reserve (℡021 794 6500, ⓦwww.tandatula.co.za; ❾). One of the longest-established and friendliest Mpumalanga bush camps offers luxurious accommodation in twelve en-suite, East African-style walk-in tents, each with its own private deck overlooking the riparian forest of the usually dry Nhlaralumi River. The thatched dining room and bar also overlook the dry river bed, to which the guests sometimes decamp for silver-service dining under the stars. A small waterhole and hide on the site offer game-viewing without you having to leave the camp, and there's a much-needed swimming pool for cooling off in the sweltering summer.

Umlani

Timbavati Game Reserve (℡012 803 4000, ⓦwww.umlani.com; ❼). One of the more reasonably priced bush camps gets down to basics with eight reed-walled huts overlooking the dry Nhlalumi River. Each has an attached open-topped bush shower, heated by a wood boiler (there's no electricity); the languid atmosphere is reinforced by hammocks hanging lazily from the trees and a plunge pool. The camp isn't fenced off, the emphasis being very much on a bush experience, and windows are covered with flimsy blinds. While it's not recommended if you're of a nervous disposition, there's barely another camp that will bring you closer to the feeling of being in the wild. Children are accepted at half-price.

Travel details

Mpumalanga is primarily a **self-drive** province. Apart from flights serving Skukuza, Hoedspruit and Phalaborwa, scheduled transport consists of a daily **train** service between Johannesburg and Nelspruit and, most practical of all, a daily Greyhound or Translux **bus** between the two cities. If you want to get to anywhere else in the province, you need to use Nelspruit as a springboard and take **minibus taxis**. The Baz Bus travels between Johannesburg and Durban via Nelspruit and Swaziland.

Trains

Nelspruit to: Johannesburg (1 daily; 10hr); Pretoria (1 daily; 8hr).

Buses

Nelspruit to: Johannesburg (3 daily; 5hr); Maputo (2 daily; 4hr); Pretoria (3 daily; 4hr).

Backpacker bus

Nelspruit to: Johannesburg (4 weekly; 4 hr);
Manzini (4 weekly; 2 hr 30min); Mbabane (4
weekly; 3hr 30min); Pretoria (4 weekly; 5 hr).

Flights

Nelspruit to: Durban (1 daily; 1hr 30min);
Johannesburg (3–6 daily; 1hr 50min); Maputo
(daily; 1hr 35min).
Hoedspruit to: Johannesburg (1 daily; 1hr); Cape
Town (1 daily; 3 hr).

Phalaborwa to: Johannesburg (1–3 daily; 1hr).
Skukuza to: Johannesburg (3 daily; 1hr 5min).

Limpopo
(Northern Province)

CHAPTER 10

Highlights

* **Archeological discoveries** Limpopo contains many of South Africa's finest archeological sites, including Mapungubwe, home of an ancient African kingdom. **See p.721**

* **Exploring the Letaba** Experience this otherworldly area of forests, sub-tropical tea plantations, misty lakes and upmarket country-house guesthouses. **See p.726**

* **Horse-riding in the Waterberg** The Waterberg mountain range offers some of South Africa's finest wilderness riding and horseback safaris. **See p.731**

* **Lapalala Wilderness** A wildlife conservation area at the heart of the Waterberg Biosphere, containing the world's only rhino museum. **See p.734**

* **Venda crafts** Explore the remote, simple villages of the mystical Venda region and discover its skilful and distinctive art, pottery and wood carvings. **See p.740**

Limpopo
(Northern Province)

impopo province (formerly known as the Northern Province) is South Africa's no-man's-land: a hot, thornbush-covered area caught between the dynamic heartland of Gauteng and, to the north, the Limpopo River, which acts as South Africa's border with Zimbabwe and, further west, Botswana. Towards the eastern side of the province is the game-rich lowveld, dominated by the seventy-kilometre-wide strip of Kruger National Park abutting the Mozambique border. This part of Limpopo is covered in the previous chapter (see p.681).

Running through the centre of this no-man's-land is the busy **N1** highway, often called here the **Great North Road**. This is South Africa's umbilical cord to the rest of Africa, and the importance of the N1 overshadows the rest of the province; indeed it's invariably the only part of the province most travellers see, with those travelling north eager to get on to Zimbabwe, and those heading south impatient to reach Johannesburg.

The principal attractions of Limpopo lie in its three wild and distinctive **mountain escarpments**. The most significant of these is the first rise of the **Drakensberg** Escarpment, on its long and often spectacular sweep through South Africa from north to south, marking the descent from highveld to

Name changes in Limpopo

Early in 2002, it was announced that the official name of the Northern Province would be changing to **Limpopo**, while the capital, Pietersburg, was to become **Polokwane**. A number of other towns with "colonial" names also announced an official name change. The most significant of these are summarized below:

Northern Province	Limpopo
Pietersburg	Polokwane
Potgietersrus	Mokopane
Warmbaths	Bela-Bela
Messina	Musina
Nylstroom	Modimolle

Other changes may well follow. While the dual names will inevitably cause travellers some confusion, it is unlikely that the old names will fall out of use all that quickly.

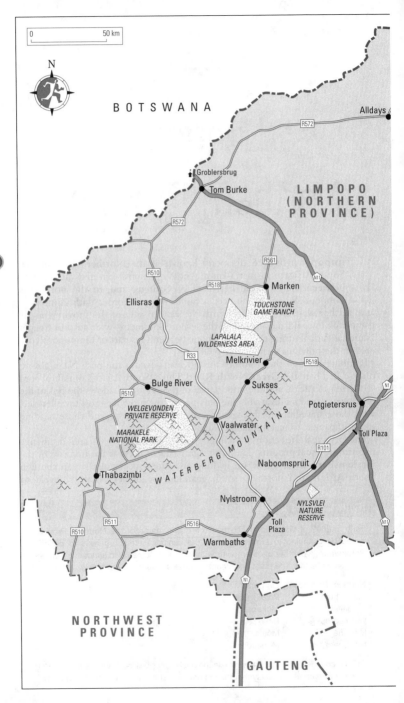

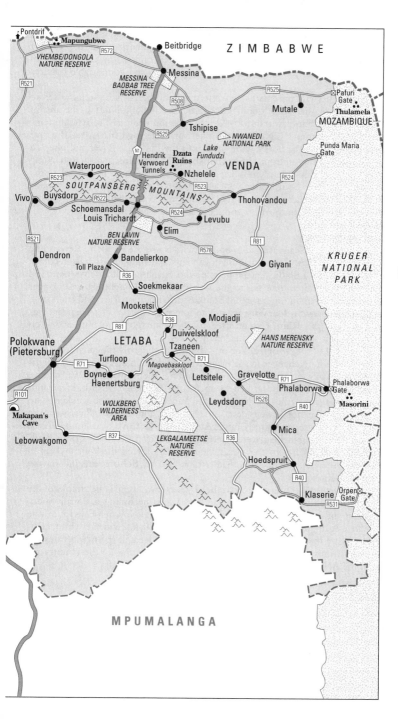

lowveld. There's a lot to see in the mountains themselves, especially in the haunting, forested slopes of the **Letaba** area immediately to the east of **Polokwane** (formerly Pietersburg), the provincial capital. This region of lakes and waterfalls also provides some excellent walking and comfortable country guesthouses.

On the otherwise unremarkable western side of the N1 lies the more sedate **Waterberg** massif. Once a domain of cattle farming and hunting, the area in the last two decades has transformed into a region dedicated to wildlife conservation, becoming a UNESCO Biosphere and offering malaria-free Big Five game viewing. In the north, lying parallel to the Limpopo River and bisected by the N1, are the subtropical **Soutpansberg Mountains**, and the intriguing and still very independently minded **Venda** region, a former homeland, to the east. North of the Soutpansberg are wide plains dominated by surreal baobab trees, much in evidence along the N1 as it leads to the only (very busy) border post between South Africa and Zimbabwe, at Beitbridge.

Some history

The first black Africans arrived in South Africa across the Limpopo River some time before 300 AD. The various movements and migrations, and of course trading, ensured a fluidity in the people who established themselves here, and the historical and cultural ties to the north are, as you might expect, stronger in this region than in other parts of South Africa. Traditional arts and crafts such as **pottery** and **woodcarving** are still an important part of life; legendary figures such as the **Rain Queen** (see p.729) retain great potency, and even **witchcraft** is still encountered in many places.

The arrival of the **Voortrekker** ox-waggons in the early nineteenth century brought profound changes to the orientation of the region. Their route roughly followed what is now the N1, founding such towns as Warmbaths, Nylstroom and Pietersburg. Led by men such as Louis Trichardt, Hermanus and Piet Potgieter, Andries Pretorius and Paul Kruger, the Voortrekkers who ventured this far north were determined people, and their conflicts with the local peoples were notoriously bitter. At **Makapan's Cave** near Potgietersrus, several thousand Ndebele were starved to death by an avenging Boer commando, while further to the north, Venda troops forced the Voortrekkers to abandon the settlement they had established at **Schoemansdal** in the Soutpansberg.

In the twentieth century, the **apartheid years** saw several large chunks of the province hived off as homeland areas, with Venda becoming nationally independent and Lebowa and Gazankulu self-governing. Now reformed into one province again, the contrasts between the old homelands and the white farming areas are manifest throughout the province. Indeed, in recent elections the Northern Province produced the highest-percentage vote in the country for both the ANC and the right-wing Afrikaner Freedom Front.

The central region

The core of Limpopo province, at least in terms of density of settlement and land use, lies along the N1 **from Warmbaths to Polokwane**. The generally flat bushveld, together with the dominance of farming here, however, means there is little by way of sights or diversions until you leave the highway and head for the mountains, either westward to the Waterberg (see p.731), or eastwards along the R71 from Polokwane into the otherworldly **Letaba** area.

The Great North Road

Between Pretoria and Beitbridge, the N1 highway or **Great North Road** links a series of towns established by the Voortrekker settlers. Most of these are little more than service centres for the surrounding farmland, and few have any real attraction beyond what they offer on a practical level – somewhere to sleep or eat while en route somewhere else. Although all have significant black populations, the prevailing flavour of the towns is strongly Afrikaner, with little in the landscape to lighten the sometimes uncomfortable tone this sets.

The southernmost of the towns, **Warmbaths** and **Nylstroom**, make a valiant attempt to rise above their mundane roots by catering for weekend and holiday tourists from Gauteng with a glut of unexciting family-oriented resorts. Further north, **Potgietersrus** is an infamous example of a town struggling to come to terms with the New South Africa, while the larger provincial capital, **Polokwane** (formerly Pietersburg), offers a range of services but remains dominated by the highway. North of Polokwane, there is a 100-kilometre stretch to Louis Trichardt and the Soutpansberg Mountains, an area covered separately (see p.735).

For all its grand title, the highway has only recently seen a major upgrading, but by South African standards it is now fast and easy, if often busy. It becomes a **toll road** from just before Nylstroom to Polokwane, and then again from Polokwane to Louis Trichardt, and although it's possible to use alternative roads, the charges aren't crippling for a one-off journey, and don't merit skimping on.

Warmbaths (Bela-Bela)

The Great North Road passes into Limpopo approximately 40km north of Pretoria, with a flat and undistinguished landscape predominating all the way up to the town of **WARMBATHS**, lying a few kilometres to the west of the

---

Malaria in Limpopo

Parts of Limpopo are **malarial**; you will need to take prophylactics, and exercise caution against mosquitoes if you are travelling in the lowveld, including Kruger National Park, or north of the Soutpansberg Mountains. The Waterberg and Letaba areas are not at present affected; however, the situation may change, so it's a good idea to double-check before you go. For reliable local advice, contact the British Airways Travel Clinics in Cape Town (☏021 419 3172), Knysna (☏044 382 6366) or Johannesburg (☏011 807 3132).

highway. Other than as a pitstop on the N1 or as the gateway to Thabazimbi and the southern Waterberg, Warmbaths has little to attract visitors, many of whom consider it too close to Pretoria and too far from their ultimate destination to be much use as a base for exploring.

The town's one point of interest, from which it takes its name, is the **hot mineral spring**. This has now been engulfed by the sprawling Adventura Warmbaths watersports and leisure resort, which offers waterslides and a water-skiing lake, and can draw up to 10,000 people a day during the holiday periods. Beside the entrance gate to the resort on Voortrekker Road, the source of the spring pumps out 20,000 litres of water at 50°C every hour. In the area surrounding the town, in particular between it and Nylstroom, 30km to the north, the many smaller holiday resorts are dismal and deserted out of season, but at weekends and during school holidays become almost unbearably busy and noisy.

Gradually, however, the market is changing, and many farms in the area are transforming themselves into game reserves. While many of these offer luxury lodges, game-viewing drives and 4WD routes, you'll generally get a better experience in the game-rich lowveld, or in places combining the experience with more attractive scenery, in areas such as the Waterberg, Soutpansberg or the parks of Northwest Province.

Practicalities

The **layout** of Warmbaths is quite confusing, but the town isn't large. Arriving from the highway, the first group of buildings you come to contains the **tourist information** office (Mon–Fri 8am–5pm, Sat 9am–2pm, Sun 9am–noon; ☎014 736 3694), one of the thatched A-frame buildings comprising the Waterfront development. Here you can get help finding accommodation, but remember to be specific about what you want, especially if your idea of a pleasant place to stay doesn't involve waterslides, caravans and copious braai facilities.

Accommodation in town is generally quite pricey, and high-season rates (including weekends) are often more than double low-season rates. The cheapest option is holiday flats: you'll find a number of these along Moffat Street, parallel to Voortrekker, or ask at the tourist information office. Otherwise, the large, mustard-coloured *Protea Elephant Springs Hotel*, 31 Sutter Rd (☎ & ☎014 736 2101, ⊛www.proteahotels.com; ❹), is very central and quite characterful for a member of a large hotel chain. On the outskirts of town is an extravagantly grand B&B, *Chateau Annique*, off Swanepoel Street, (☎ & ☎ 014 736 2847; ❹). The *Adventura Warmbaths* resort itself on Voortrekker Rd (☎014 736 2200, central reservations ☎012 346 2277; ❹), has various chalets and hotel accommodation.

As a town by a main highway, Warmbaths has a wide selection of unexciting **eating places**: your best bet is the *Keg and Elephant* pub in the *Elephant Springs Hotel*, where you can get good, cheap pub grub or a fuller restaurant meal. At the Waterfront development there's an *O'Hagan's Irish Pub and Grill*; a couple of doors away is *Greenfields,* a restaurant serving breakfast from 7am, and other meals throughout the day. There are also various fast-food takeaways around the town centre.

Nylstroom (Modimolle)

The most entertaining thing about **NYLSTROOM**, 27km north of Warmbaths on the R101, is the story behind its name. The legend goes that the first Voortrekkers discovered a reed-lined river, consulted their Bibles (the only reference books they carried) and decided that they had been travelling north for so long that they must surely be at the source of the Nile. The presence of a pyramid-shaped hill, Kranskop, the large mountain you can see clearly beside the N1, only confirmed their theory.

The Little Nyl River (as it was dubbed) runs through the centre of the modern town, parallel to the wide main street, **Potgieter**. Along here, establishments like Ammo Africa and Trappers Trading Co, as well as an endless parade of orange dust-covered *bakkies*, proclaim the town's white farming roots. Interestingly, one of the more profitable local crops is table grapes, grown on large vineyards in the well-irrigated surrounding area.

Sights are few. A memorial **gateway** at the primary school (Laerskool) on Van Riebeeck Street commemorates the women and children who died in a concentration camp sited there during the Anglo-Boer War, while you can also visit the **house of J.G. Strydom**, a prime minister of South Africa during the dark days of apartheid in the 1950s, which is located at 145 Kerk St (Mon–Fri 9am–4pm, Sat 10am–4pm; R3). Less predictably, there is a **mosque** not far from the bridge over the river – testimony to the presence of an unexpectedly large Indian community.

Practicalities

Limited local **information** is available from a row of leaflets held at the library on Field Street. In town, the **accommodation** options are the *Eurosun* campsite (℡014 717 1328), beside the stadium on the northern side of the river, or a somewhat over-decorated but civilized guesthouse, *Pink Gables*, 3 De Beer St, by the hospital on the Warmbaths road (℡014 717 5076; ❹). A more upmarket country lodge, *Shangri-la* (℡014 717 5381, ⓦwww.proteahotels .com; ❹), stands at a turn-off 3km down the Eersbewoond road, a turning from the R33 between Nylstroom and the N1. It's pricey but comfortable; the surroundings are lush, and the lodge is filled with an eclectic mix of antique furniture and African memorabilia.

Mapungubwe and other archeological sites

As one of the early melting pots of southern Africa, Limpopo has a number of important **archeological sites** where excavations have helped piece together a picture of the different people who inhabited the land for thousands of years. Some of the most interesting sites are at places where iron was smelted, as the development from what was essentially a Stone Age culture to an Iron Age culture, with its associated improvement in tools for cultivation and war, was a vital part of the migration of black tribes into South Africa around 1500 years ago. Although the iron itself seldom survives the processes of erosion, the presence of slag and other wastes normally provide the strongest clues. Some of the most revealing excavations have taken place at **Thulamela**, inside Kruger National Park not far from the Punda Maria Gate, **Bakone Malapa** cultural village outside Polokwane, **Makapan's Cave** near Potgietersrus, and **Masorini**, also in the Kruger park, not far from Phalaborwa.

The single most important site in Limpopo province is at **Mapungubwe** (Hill of the Jackals), situated by the confluence of the Limpopo and Shashi rivers, where South Africa, Zimbabwe and Botswana meet. The site was only discovered in 1933, when a local farmer climbed the dome-shaped granite hill and found remains of stone walls, iron tools, graves, pottery and jewellery, including a tiny rhinoceros and a bowl, both made out of gold. It is now thought that the years 1000 to 1300AD were the heyday of a civilization centred at Mapungubwe, which later moved to the much more famous Great Zimbabwe. The area is now protected as part of the Limpopo National Park, although as yet there is no general access. An exhibition of the treasures of Mapungubwe can be seen at the University of Pretoria (see p.634).

A handful of rather unexciting **places to eat** in town along Potgieter and Voortrekker streets include *Pepe's*, located beside Ammo Africa on Potgieter or the slightly livelier *Mampoer Boer Pub and Grill* by the main crossroads on Potgieter. There's a classier dining room at *Shangri-la Country Lodge*, though you must book ahead (☎014 717 5381).

Naboomspruit and Nylsvlei Nature Reserve

To the east of the N1, midway between Nylstroom and **NABOOMSPRUIT**, another resort-encircled highway town situated at the foot of the Swaershoek Mountains, is **Nylsvlei** – a 160-square-kilometre nature reserve enclosing one of the most important wetland areas in South Africa. When the Nyl River is in flood, the *vlei* can spread out to as much as 7km in width, attracting over 150 species of bird, including a number of the country's rarest indigenous water birds. As well as picnic sites and bird- and game-viewing routes, there's also a simple campsite (☎014 717 2523). Right next to the nature reserve is a lovely place to stay, *Boekenhout* (☎014 743 0957, ⓦwww.boekenhout.southernafrica.com; full-board ❸), which has various cottages around the farm and offers game drives in a characterful old truck onto Nylsvlei itself.

Potgietersrus (Mokopane)

A further 50km north of Naboomspruit, also just off the N1, lies **POTGIETERSRUS**, named after the Voortrekker hero Piet Potgieter, who died during a famous siege at Makapan's Cave in the hills to the north of town. The N1 formerly ran right through the centre of town, but the new highway smoothly by-passes it, an act you should have few qualms about following, unless you are bound for parts of the northern Waterberg or have a perverse attraction to check out one of the country's racist hot-spots.

In the mid-Nineties, the town attracted worldwide publicity when white locals tried to prevent black children entering what had been all-white schools during the apartheid years. This display of dogged racism earned the town the unenviable title of racist capital of South Africa. There's little doubt that the old thinking still dies hard in the town and its agricultural hinterland – something you'll still pick up from such things as "Club Members Only" signs over white-filled bars and intolerant squabbling over local services and amenities. On the other hand, blacks crowd the main streets with stalls and, despite the continual crawl of traffic, give the place a bustling, lively feel.

The one place worth stopping at is the **Arend Dieperink Museum** (Mon–Fri 8am–4.30pm; R5), located in an old schoolhouse set back from Voortrekker Road (the main R101), behind the tourist information office. It has a substantial collection of ploughs, tractors, waggons and farm implements outside; inside is more interesting, with well-labelled displays on the significant archeological discoveries made at Makapan's Cave, 19km north of Potgietersrus, including that of three-million-year-old fossils of *Australopithecus africanus*, a predecessor of *Homo sapiens*. For the moment, access to the cave itself is only by arrangement with the museum (☎015 491 2244).

Practicalities

The local **tourist information** office (☎015 491 8458) is on Voortrekker Road as you come into the main part of town from the south, between Kruger and Van Riebeeck streets. Most of the **accommodation** in Potgietersrus is in the form of plain travellers' overnight rooms, and as a result rates drop at week-

The network of limestone caves northeast of Potgietersrus known as **Makapan's Cave** might be the repository of some of South Africa's most important paleontological finds, but to many locals it is better known for one of those incidents in South African history which is remembered in different ways by different sections of the population. In 1854, bent on revenge after a party of Voortrekkers had been ambushed, a Boer commando cornered the clan of Ndebele chief Makapan in the hills to the north of Potgietersrus. Led by Piet Potgieter, the nephew of Voortrekker leader Hermanus Potgieter who had been skinned alive not long before by kinsmen of Makapan, the Boers besieged the chief and an estimated three thousand of his followers inside the network of caves which ran through the hills. With little food and almost no water, the imprisoned Ndebele became increasingly desperate, and eventually seven hundred besieged men rushed out towards a nearby stream, only to be mown down by the patient Boers. When the siege was finally broken after four weeks, hundreds of rotting bodies were found inside. The Boers lost only two men, one of them Potgieter, whose body was "heroically" retrieved by a young Paul Kruger. A rather one-sided account of the siege is available at the museum in Potgietersrus.

ends. There is an unappealing municipal caravan park just off the N1 on the northern side of town, behind a parked steam locomotive. The cheapest place to stay is the block of apartment rooms at *Lonely Oak Lodge*, Van Riebeeck and Hodge streets (☎015 491 4560; room only ❷). On the northern edge of town, by the side of the main road, are a couple of travellers' hotels: *Oasis* (☎015 491 4124; ❷); and the ageing but respectable *Protea Park* (☎015 491 3101, ⓦwww .proteahotels.com; room only ❸), which has a pool and a decent restaurant. North of town, signposted after 32km along the N1, is the *Protea Ranch Hotel* (☎015 290 5000, ⓦwww.theranch.co.za; ❹), a well-run, pleasant but pricey modern resort-style hotel. On the southern side of the Nyl River, 10km south of Potgietersrus on the N1, is a homely B&B, *Jaagbaan* (☎015 491 7833; ❷).

Polokwane (Pietersburg)

Lying almost dead central in the province of which it is the capital, **POLOKWANE** is also the largest city on the Great North Road between Pretoria and the border. It's mostly an administrative and industrial centre, and much of its energy derives from the large volume of traffic moving through the city on the N1. But it does have a couple of quirky attractions, including an excellent museum, and if you're heading towards the Letaba area, the lowveld or central Kruger National Park, Polokwane is the point to connect with the R71 to Tzaneen and Phalaborwa.

Arrival and information

The city's former air-force base now operates as **Gateway airport**, located on the N1, 5km north of the city. The airport is serviced by both domestic flights (SA Airlink ☎015 288 0166 or 011 978 1111) and occasional international connections from neighbouring countries. All the city's **car rental firms** are located here: Avis (☎015 288 0171), Budget (☎015 288 0169) and Imperial (☎015 288 0097), and **taxis** are also available (☎015 297 4493).

Daily **trains** to and from Messina stop at the train station on the northern edge of the city centre, just off the R521 (an extension of Market Street). All the intercity **buses** pass through the centre of town: Translux stops at the *Big Bite* on Grobler Street and Greyhound at the Shell Ultra City.

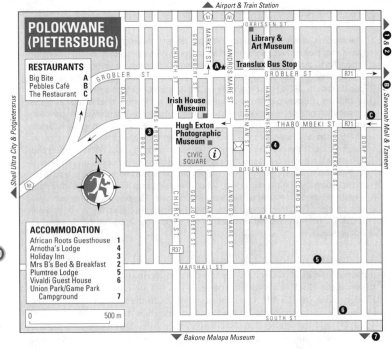

Airport & Train Station

POLOKWANE (PIETERSBURG)

RESTAURANTS
Big Bite **A**
Pebbles Café **B**
The Restaurant **C**

Library & Art Museum

Translux Bus Stop

Irish House Museum

Hugh Exton Photographic Museum

CIVIC SQUARE (i)

N

ACCOMMODATION
African Roots Guesthouse **1**
Arnotha's Lodge **4**
Holiday Inn **3**
Mrs B's Bed & Breakfast **2**
Plumtree Lodge **5**
Vivaldi Guest House **6**
Union Park/Game Park Campground **7**

0   500 m

Shell Ultra City & Potgietersrus

Savanah Mall & Tzaneen

Bakone Malapa Museum

The **tourist information** office is in the southeast part of Civic Square (Mon–Fri 8.30am–4pm; ☎015 290 2010, ⓦwww.pietersburg.org.za) – the best way to get to it is off Landros Mare Street. Away from the centre, there's a helpful budget travellers' tourist agent, SA Tours and Bookings, at 2 Voortrekker St (☎015 295 6162, ⓔesatours@mweb.co.za).

Accommodation

African Roots Guesthouse 58a Devenish St ☎015 297 0113. A relaxed, tasteful spot run by artists, with local and foreign artefacts and works of art in every room. ❸

Arnotha's Lodge 42 Hans van Rensburg St ☎015 291 3393. Open 24hr, and cheap but not especially cheerful, this lodge offers centrally located self-catering rooms. Room only ❶

Holiday Inn On the corner of Vorster and Bok streets ☎015 291 2030, ⓦwww.southernsun .com. A couple of blocks from Civic Square, with predictable but decent rooms and an outdoor pool. Room only ❸.

Mrs B's Bed and Breakfast 17 Welsford St, Bendor ☎015 296 1021. An unremarkable but inexpensive and hospitable suburban B&B with two twin bedrooms. ❶

Plumtree Lodge 138 Marshall St ☎015 295 6153, ⓔplumtree@pixie.co.za. Not far from the centre, probably the smartest and most comfortable lodge in town, with a pool, a big garden and cheaper rates over the weekend. ❸

Union Park campground Off Dorp Street. The town's camping and caravan park, with simple but adequate ablution facilities and some inexpensive rondavels. It's right beside the Pietersburg Game Reserve on the southern edge of town, but there's little sense of it being surrounded by nature.

Vivaldi Guest House 2 Voortrekker St (☎015 295 6162). A friendly, well-kept guesthouse with six rooms in a pleasant part of town. Known for its hearty breakfasts and the parrots in the garden. ❷

The City and around

Polokwane has a busy, compact CBD set out on a grid pattern (which includes lots of one-way streets), with layers of industry and suburbia tightly packed around it. It may not be the most inspiring spot, but much of Limpopo's drive and enterprise emanates from its capital. At its heart, the **Civic Square**, a park area bounded on two sides by Landros Mare and Vorster streets, has an incongruous but entertaining array of sculptures, statues and monuments, ranging from a family of giraffes to a fighter aircraft. In the middle of the park is a white church housing the small but absorbing **Hugh Exton Photographic Museum** (Mon–Fri 8.30am–3.30pm, Sun 3–5pm; free), which displays the early years of the town through the work of a local commercial photographer; the portraits are excellent. Opposite the park, on the other side of Vorster, is the old shop frontage of the decent **Irish House Museum** (Mon–Fri 8am–4pm, Sat 9am–noon, Sun 3–5pm; free), which includes displays on the city's past and natural history.

For those inspired by the sculptures of the Civic Centre, there's a small **art museum** above the library on Schoeman and Jorissen streets, together with an annexe of outdoor, industrial-type modern sculptures in a park on the left as you leave town on the N1 heading north.

However, the one sight in Polokwane really worth putting aside time to see is the **Bakone Malapa Museum** (daily except Mon afternoon 8.30am–12.30pm & 1.30–3.30pm; R3), 9km southeast of town on the R37. This is an open-air museum displaying the traditional way of life of the local Bakone people, a grouping within the Northern Sotho. A village of huts has been built in the traditional style, and fourteen people live permanently on site, working on crafts such as pottery and leatherworking through the day. One of them also acts as a guide, and will explain the different activities going on, as well as the architecture, history and legends of the site. It is a simple but genuine project, and one which succeeds in conveying some of the old way of life where many flashier examples have fallen short.

Eating and drinking

True to its functional role, Polokwane has no shortage of standard chain **restaurants and takeaways**. The largest collection of these can be found at the Savannah Mall, on the fringes of the city along the Tzaneen road – among the familiar names look out on the lower level for *Villa Italia*, part of a small local chain of Italian restaurants. There are also a couple of locally owned places in town, including *The Restaurant* (☎015 291 1918), serving quite classy meat and fish dishes, as well as curries, in an older house on the corner of Thabo Mbeki (formerly Vorster) and Dorp streets, and *Pebbles Café* (☎015 295 6999) in the Tom Naude homestead at 39 Grobler St, which serves breakfasts, snacks, lunches and, through the week, evening meals.

Letaba

The **Letaba** is a forested, lush, mountainous area east of Polokwane which contrasts very sharply with the hot lowveld immediately east and the wide, flat bushveld to its west. It marks the first dramatic rise of the Drakensberg Escarpment as it begins its sweep south through Mpumalanga, and in many ways is an attractive but less well-known alternative to the latter province's crowded highlands. The forestation begins around the mountain village of **Haenertsburg** and follows two very scenic parallel valleys to the largest centre in the area, **Tzaneen**. The valleys are filled with lakes surrounded by dark pine forests, sparkling rivers, misty peaks and, towards Tzaneen, subtropical crops such as tea, macadamia nuts and avocados. There are some very comfortable and beautifully located guesthouses, farmstalls and tea rooms, hiking trails and trout fishing, making the Letaba a soothing alternative to South Africa's more challenging environments.

Haenertsburg and around

Mellow **HAENERTSBURG** lies 60km from Polokwane, high on a hillside overlooking the R71 as it winds down into the thickly wooded Magoebaskloof Valleys. Once an old gold-rush village, Haenertburg has wonderful views over the area known as the Land of the Silver Mist. Along its **main street** you'll find a small pub, a friendly tea room called *The Elms* (closed Mon), which also has a gift shop and is the place to buy trout and ask about trout fishing, and a useful **tourist information** office, the Magoebaskloof Tourist Association (Mon–Fri 8am–5pm, Sat & Sun 9am–noon; ⓣ015 276 5047, ⓦwww.magoebaskloof.com). Here you can organize local accommodation or tours, or find out about good picnic spots and short walks in the area, including a tough one up to the **Iron Crown**, the peak above the village. Good **food**, including pancakes and big breakfasts, can be had during the day at *Picasso's Restaurant*, in a large wooden cabin beside the R71, and in the evenings at the *Atholl Arms* (ⓣ015 276 4712), on the main street beside *The Elms*.

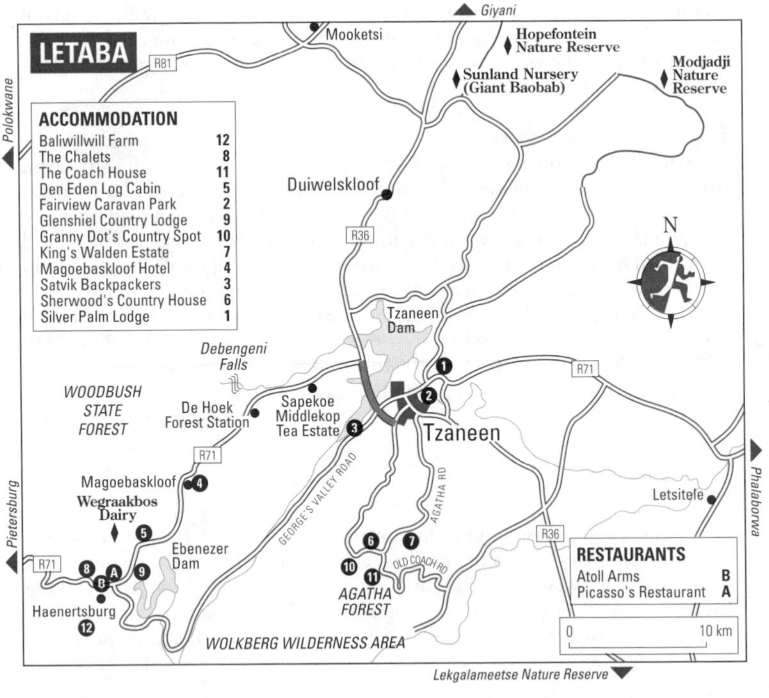

If you're planning to be in the area in May – a beautiful time with glorious
autumnal colours in the valley – get details from the tourist association about
the annual **music and cultural festival**, which sees national orchestras and
choirs performing in unusual venues locally.

Georges Valley Road and the Magoebaskloof Valleys

Just east of Haenertsburg is a turning to the right off the main R71, which
offers an alternative route to Tzaneen along the Georges Valley Road. There is,
in fact, little to choose between the two options in terms of both distance and
stunning scenery, and if you are spending any time in the area it's worth trying
both.

Along the Georges Valley Road lies a **memorial to John Buchan** (author
of *The Thirty-nine Steps*), who became captivated by the area when he visited
not long after the Anglo-Boer War, calling it "a place enchanted and consecrated." There's also the tranquil **Ebeneezer Dam**, an atmospheric spot for
swimming and picnicking.

Staying on the R71, you come to the **Magoebaskloof Valleys**, named after
the rogue chief Makgoba, who in 1895 had his head chopped off by native
warriors serving under the Boer leader Abel Erasmus. About 4km beyond
Haenertsburg is a turning to the **Cheerio Gardens**, which holds an annual
Cherry Blossom Festival at the end of September. If you miss the festival it still
isn't hard to imagine the lush subtropical landscape bursting into extravagant
colour; the Magoebaskloof Tourist Association (☎015 276 5047,
ⓦ www.magoebaskloof.com), can provide details of various private show gardens in the area. Along this same turning is another wonderful piece of backwoods life, at the tiny **Wegraakbos Dairy** (☎015 276 1811), where cheese is
made in traditional style over an open fire in a huge copper cauldron. A visit is
thoroughly recommended: tours, which cost a few rand, are at 9am, but you
can visit the dairy throughout the day, and taste the cheese and walk around
the farm and nearby woods.

As the R71 crosses the Magoebaskloof pass, it twists and turns impressively,
with dark forests and long views alternating on either side. A sideroad leads into
the **Woodbush State Forest**, where there is a network of roads (not all of
them passable), various multi-day hiking trails and the famous **Debegeni
Falls**, an attractive series of waterfalls and natural pools. There are some braai
sites by the river, and you can swim in various places if you're careful, but the
smooth, slippery rock is very dangerous and a sign indicates that a few folk
who tried the DIY waterslide didn't live to recommend it.

Between the turn-off to Debengeni and Tzaneen, the valley becomes
broader, with huge stands of citrus, avocado and banana trees, as well as the

rich green texture of tea bushes, covering the rolling hillsides. On the **Sapekoe Middlekop** tea estate not far from the junction of the R71 and R36, a winding road leads up to the **Pekoe View tea garden** (daily 10am–5pm) – the location of some of the best views in the whole valley. Tea and scones are always available, along with other snacks and drinks; packets of local tea and coffee can be bought in the shop, and there are also worthwhile factory tours (Tues–Sat 11am), on which you can see tea being picked, learn about different grades of tea, and take a look at the production process in the factory.

Accommodation

The area around Haenertsburg and Magoebaskloof, and indeed around Tzaneen as well, offers a lot of attractive **places to stay**. As well as the places listed below, the Magoebaskloof Tourist Association in Haenertsburg can help you find somewhere suitable.

BaliWillWill Farm Haenertsburg ☎ 015 276 2212. B&B rooms in the farmhouse or in a simple self-catering flat, 1500m into the hills from Haenertsburg past the police station. ❸

The Chalets Off the R71 just west of Haenertsburg, ☎ 015 276 4764. A collection of tall, Swiss-style self-catering chalets in a scenic wooded setting within walking distance of Haenertsburg village. ❷

Den Eden Log Cabin Den Eden farm, off the R71, ask for Meinie de Villiers on ☎ 015 276 4742 or 083 269 3552. Pleasant and secluded self-catering log cabin tucked away on its own under some tall pine trees. ❷

Glenshiel On R71 2km east of Haenertsburg ☎ 015 276 4335, ⓦ www.glenshiel.co.za. Top-of-the-range accommodation, and one of the finer country lodges in South Africa, with roaring fires, deep sofas, antiques and fine food. ❺

Magoebaskloof Hotel On the R71 10km east of Haenertsburg ☎ 015 276 4776, ⓦ www.magoebaskloof.co.za. Boasts what is probably the most spectacular view in the area from its front deck, but the rest, including a pub with an old red postbox outside, is fairly uninspired. ❹

Satvik 4km from Tzaneen on the George's Valley road ☎ 015 307 3920, 082 971 1171, ⓔ satvik@pixie.co.za. Unusual and appealing backpackers' lodge which makes use of a group of old whitewashed farmworkers' cottages set above a lake. The facilities, which include doubles and small dorms, are simple and rustic, but outdoor showers and a lakeside bar and cooking area make it is an atmospheric spot typical of Letaba, and one you could easily find yourself chilling out at for days on end. ❶

Tzaneen and around

The dams and soaring gum forests surrounding **TZANEEN** are graceful and attractive. However, the town itself is fairly scruffy, well-endowed with shops and a useful transport hub, but worth avoiding as a place to stay. The one thing to see here is the **Tzaneen Museum** (Mon–Fri 8.30am–4.30pm, Sat 8.30am–12.30pm; donation requested), situated in a tiny, four-roomed building in the grounds of the library at the top of Agatha Street. You'll need time: the dedicated curator and his assistants don't label any items, preferring to walk around with you and talk about the small but important collection, which includes sacred drums and other items associated with the Rain Queen (see opposite). It's almost impossible to make a quick, casual visit, but it's worth sparing the time if you want to dig a bit more deeply into the history and traditions of the region.

A **minibus** operated by Northlink Tours (☎ 015 307 2242), links Tzaneen with Polokwane and Johannesburg three times a week. The privately run **Tzaneen Tourism Information Centre** (Mon–Fri 8am–5pm, Sat 8am–11am; ☎ 015 307 1294), 25 Danie Joubert St, is a useful place to find out about local accommodation, as well as pick up advice on travelling to spots such as Modjadji, the Magoebaskloof Valleys and Kruger National Park. A couple of locals run **tours** to these: contact Letaba Active Tours (☎082 494 3970), or Yvonne Clarke (☎015 307 2000). There are also a number of good local **mountain-bike routes** – ask at the local bike shop, G Sport, for details.

Accommodation options in town aren't inspiring, especially in comparison to what is available in the surrounding countryside. It's better to head for the Magoebaskloof Valleys, or take the road leading out of town into the Wolkberg Mountains to Agatha, which has some high-class country lodges and spectacular views out over the valleys and peaks of the escarpment (see below).

If you're not inclined to do this, or don't have the time (or money), there's a decent caravan park on Old Gravelotte Road, *Fairview* (☎015 307 2679; ❶–❷), which has inexpensive chalets; otherwise *Silver Palm Lodge* (☎015 307 3092 or 083 635 0556; ❷) off Voortrekker Street beside the Malaria Research Institute, has some decent modern units around a pool.

As for **food**, Tzaneen has a smattering of familiar takeaways and a few chain restaurants. The best in town is the *Villa Italia,* corner of Danie Joubert and Lannie streets, while near the museum there's a pleasant coffee shop, *Gazebo Gardens*, 30 Agatha St, set in an old Victorian garden.

Agatha

AGATHA, the wife of an early mining commissioner, gave her name to a high plateau overlooking Tzaneen, now covered in forest, but a cool and attractive place, especially if you can rise to a night at one of the top-class guesthouses set along the edge of the ridge. The best value of these is *Kings Walden Estate*, 12km from Tzaneen up Agatha Road (☎015 307 3262, ⓦwww.kingswalden.co.za; ❹), a family-owned avocado farm with superbly lush gardens and four simple rooms. Turning left at the top of the hill, Old Coach Road leads to *The Coach House* (☎015 307 3641, ⓦ.www.coach-house.co.za; ❺), a classy, well-run establishment that's consistently quoted as one of the best small hotels in South Africa. It has 45 suites, a spa, great food and the views from the breakfast balcony and pool area are breathtaking. In the opposite direction from the top of Agatha Road, *Sherwood's Country House* (☎015 307 5512, ⓔesherc_h@mweb.co.za; ❹) is a more intimate but slightly less-well-bred rival. A less expensive, more down-to-earth alternative in the Agatha area is *Granny Dot's Country Spot* (☎015 307 5149 or 083 760 0983; ❸), a B&B close to the Rooikat Walking Trail (see box on p.730) with fine views and lush surroundings. Self-catering (❷) is also available here.

Modjadji Nature Reserve

The area around the rather downbeat village of **MODJADJI**, 32km north of Tzaneen off the R36, is the home of the famous **Rain Queen**, the hereditary female monarch of the Lobedu people, whom legend maintains has the power to make rain, a useful talent in these often parched northern areas. Suitably, her home village is up in the mists on a mountain where a special form of ancient cycad, or tree fern, flourishes. The **Modjadji Cycad Reserve** (daily 8.30am–4pm; R10) protects these plants in an area at the very top of the hill, and incorporates some fine views (often obscured by mist) and various short but pleasant, rather vaguely marked walking trails. There are a few facilities, such as a souvenir shop and information centre, which explains a bit more about the unique plants found here and, of course, the famous monarch. At the

One of the principal attractions of the Letaba area, especially given the spectacular scenery, deep forests and relatively cool air of the escarpment, is hiking. Of the **multi-day hikes**, the two most popular are the two-day Debegeni and three-day Dokolewa trails, which are well-marked and utilize well-kept forester's houses or log cabins (❶–❷) for the overnight stops – details from the state forestry organization, SAFCOL (☎012 481 3615, ⓦwww.safcolecotourism.co.za). The two large protected areas in the southern parts of the Letaba also offer excellent walking: Wolkberg Wilderness Area (☎015 276 1303) has a campsite at Serala Forest Station, which you get to from the Haenertsburg side, but few other facilities – it's meant to be wild and untamed; **Lekgalameetse Nature Reserve** (☎0152302/1514), reached from the R36 south of Tzaneen, encompasses the transition between lowveld and escarpment and has accommodation in simple log cabins (❶).

If you're not up for such serious hiking, there are good **day-walks** in various parts of the Letaba: around Haenertsburg, through some of the last remaining indigenous forest; along the waymarked four-kilometre Lesodi Trail, beginning at Sandford Heights Nursery on the R71 past the *Magoebaskloof Hotel*; along the Rooikat Walking Trail, a circular forest trail on the Agatha ridge, also marked and beginning near the *Coach House*; and at Modjadji Nature Reserve. For details of local guides, contact the Magoebaskloof Tourist Association (☎015 276 5047).

time of going to press, the death of the Rain Queen Modjadji V in the winter of 2001 had left a problematic succession, with the future of the monarchy and her hereditary powers surrounded in more mystery than ever before.

Around 20km away from the turning to Modjadji lies the **Sunland Nursery**. Here you'll find a massive baobab tree with a pub inside; the owner will serve you draught beer while relating a few of the strange stories attached to his odd location. He claims this is the largest baobab in the world, although a few other specimens around Limpopo also contend for the honour. Still, it's fun to visit, especially if you've got time for a few convivial drinks, though you have to pay to get in (R10). A few kilometres further down the same road is the five-hundred-hectare **Hopefontein Nature Reserve** (☎015 305 3607; ❷), where you can stay in one of two tree houses or a rustic farmhouse; phone beforehand if you want to stay.

Letsitele and around

LETSITELE is a small town 30km east of Tzaneen whose main function is as a waypoint to a few places of interest in the area of lowveld abutting the escarpment. To the south are the large nature and wilderness areas of **Lekgalameetse** and **Wolkberg** (see box above), places to explore if you have a few days and a penchant for empty green landscapes. Near Letsitele itself is one of the most interesting handicraft projects in the province, **Karosswerkers**, who produce intricate and striking embroidered ethnic place mats, cushion covers and wall hangings. You can arrange to see the workshops (☎015 345 1765), which employ over 150 locals, and their work is on sale at the excellent Monsoon Gallery on the R527 west of Hoedspruit (see p.679).

Waterberg

Even now. with the great gold-city belching its smoke almost within sight – even now, with invading civilization marching across the hills in seven-league boots, Waterberg still holds its charm.

Eugène Marais

Rising out of the plains to the west and north of the Great North Road, the **WATERBERG** is one of the least-known and most intriguing of South Africa's significant mountain massifs. Once an area of lakes and swamps – hence its name – the elevated plateau can often seem a place as dry and sparse of water as its surrounding northern bushveld, yet it harbours a diversity of vegetation and topography which supports cattle-ranching, hunting concessions and, increasingly, some of the country's foremost conservation projects.

Driven to a large degree by the efforts of Clive Walker of **Lapalala Wilderness**, the primacy of conservation in the region was recognized in 2001 when some 14,500 square kilometres of both private and publicly owned land in the Waterberg was declared a **UNESCO Savannah Biosphere Reserve**. As a game-viewing destination, the Waterberg is now being considered as an alternative to the lowveld areas around Kruger National Park, with the important advantage that malaria is not endemic to the Waterberg. However, while it has impressive credentials as a vast area of true wilderness, and is certainly less commercialized, the game is less dense than around Kruger. The best chance to see big game is in the **Marakele National Park** or in one of the upmarket private reserves which contain the Big Five; these are complemented by a patchwork of smaller and more affordable (but still very dedicated) private reserves gathered loosely in the area to the north of the town of **Vaalwater**. In these you'll find rhino often heads the list of game highlights, along with giraffe, large antelope and leopard. The area also offers some exciting **adventure activities**, including bush-hiking trails and some of the finest wilderness horse-riding in South Africa.

Eugène Marais (1872–1936)

One of the most gifted yet troubled South Africans of his time, the journalist **Eugène Marais** left South Africa during the 1890s to study law and medicine (simultaneously) in London. In the early 1900s, his poetry and short stories established Marais as one of the first writers to make a literary mark in the "new" Afrikaans language. However, he also suffered from depression and ill health, and retreated from his career as a lawyer to the remote Waterberg Mountains. His intense involvement with the natural world around him there led to the publication of two pioneering studies of animal behaviour: *The Soul of the Ape*, the result of some three-and-a-half years living in close proximity to a troop of baboons, and *The Soul of the White Ant*, a study of termites which argues that a termite nest is a single functioning composite similar to the human body. Still racked by ill health and increasingly addicted to morphine, he committed suicide in 1936.

Vaalwater and around

The only settlement of any size in the Waterberg is the small town of **Vaalwater**, which offers a couple of useful places to stay. The surrounding area, however, can offer absorbing bush experiences on most levels, from luxury lodges to inexpensive self-catering cottages and wilderness campsites. The scenery in this part of the Waterberg is subtle rather than dramatic: the way to appreciate it is to stay for a few days.

Vaalwater

The small farming town of **VAALWATER** offers the visitor little more than an orientation point on the R33, which connects Nylstroom, just off the N1, with Ellisras, and marks the junction with the tarred road to Melkrivier and Marken – along which the main conservation areas of the northeastern Waterberg are located. Waterberg Transfers (☎082 320 6515, ✉ab.farm@mweb .co.za) offers easy and efficient long-distance taxi links between places such as Johannesburg International Airport and the Waterberg

If you need **accommodation** in town, there's a great backpackers' lodge as well as comfy, tasteful B&B at the *Zeederberg Cottages* (☎014 755 3538 or 082 332 7088; ❶–❷), situated by the Total service station and the excellent *Black Mamba* crafts gallery on the northern side of town, at the junction where the R510 to Bulge River meets the R33 to Ellisras. As well as a useful stop-over, this makes a great base for activities such as hiking or game viewing, which can be organized locally. Otherwise, *Waterberg Game Lodge* (☎014 755 3686; ❷), on the right-hand side as you come into town from Nylstroom, offers rooms, a small restaurant and a lively locals' bar. It subtitles itself the *International Hunter's Hotel*, which says quite a lot about what you can expect. For **eating**, try the *Waterberg Game Lodge* or the *Waterhole Steakhouse* (☎014 755 3775), located in the Village Square complex, amongst the shops by the Melkrivier turn-off.

Hunting: a rough guide

To some it is barbaric blood lust, while to others it lies at the heart of conservation. The emotive issue of **hunting** is one you will encounter and hear vigorously debated in the Waterberg, as you will in many rural areas of South Africa where it is regarded as an essential part of life in the bush. It is also a multi-million-rand industry and, although you don't necessarily read about them in the guidebooks, there are many more hunting reserves in South Africa than there are eco-friendly game reserves.

In hunting reserves, the land is stocked with game specifically for the purpose of hunting, whereas in conservation-oriented game reserves the guiding principle is that tourists will pay simply to see the animals in their natural environment. However, wherever land has been fenced in (which is just about everywhere), the idea of a completely natural environment is inevitably compromised, and intervention is necessary to maintain a realistic balance and diversity of nature within that area. Such intervention – "management" is a common euphemism – takes place even in the most conservation-oriented reserves. What is more at issue is the extent to which this process is commercialized. Some game reserves, knowing that they need to cull a certain number of animals, will allow paying clients to hunt for that quota, providing a valuable source of income for the reserve and its conservation ideals. Inevitably, this leads to grey areas: how many animals need to be culled, for instance, when there is money at stake?

Waterberg game reserves

As with most game areas in South Africa, widely different experiences are available in the **Waterberg** depending on which reserve you head for and what level of accommodation you choose. The only national park in the area, Marakele, is essentially limited to those driving 4WD vehicles, and to gain access to any private reserve you'll almost always be expected to book into accommodation on the reserve, though such is the co-operative nature of many parts of the Waterberg that the owners of guesthouses located alongside a reserve have often negotiated access rights. As many of the lodges in the Waterberg are small and relatively remote, it's advisable to prebook somewhere to stay, at least for your first couple of nights. Upmarket lodges usually offer full board and include early-morning and late-afternoon game drives or walks in their programmes, so it's worth arriving at a time when you can take full advantage of these.

While game viewing from a vehicle or on foot is a mainstay of most of the lodges and private reserves in the Waterberg, the area is also an excellent place to come if you're interested in doing something a little more energetic. The Waterberg is recognized as one of South Africa's finest locations for **horse-riding safaris**, and offers a couple of well-established and highly professional outfits. The more upmarket of the two is Equus Horse Safaris (⊕011 788 3923, ⓦ.www.equus.co.za), based in the Lapalala Wilderness Area (see p.734), who offer top-class riding from an eight-bed luxury tented bush camp. Horizon Horse Trails (⊕014 755 4003, ⓦwww.ridinginafrica.com), based at *Triple B Ranch* (see p.734), is a fun place for horse-lovers: as well as outrides, overnight rides and trips to game areas, other activities include cattle-mustering, polocrosse and a cross-country course. Accommodation is offered in double rooms in the farmhouse at the steading where the horses are kept, or in rondavels next to it.

For other activities, including hiking trails and mountain biking, *Lindani* (⊕083 631 5579; ❸–❹) is a 28-square-kilometre farm with various attractive thatched houses including *Skebenga Lodge*, which overlooks a dam.

Luxury game lodges

In the Waterberg there are three large game reserves which hold the Big Five: **Marakele National Park** (see p.735) and **Welgevonden** and **Touchstone** private reserves. The latter two are very much in the upmarket bracket: Welgevonden, a reserve of 380 square kilometres to the west of Vaalwater which abuts Marakele, is in fact divided into hundreds of separate (unfenced) plots, but there are very tight regulations on the number of lodges which can be built and the number of vehicles allowed in the reserve. Only a handful of the lodges are open to the general public – of these, the exclusive *Makweti Safari Lodge* (⊕011 837 6776, ⓦwww.makweti.com; ❽), with five wood-and-thatch suites built into the natural rock formations of the mountains, is both spectacular and luxurious, its sense of isolation complemented by the fact that game drives can range anywhere over the reserve. North of Vaalwater, Touchstone Game Ranch (⊕011 7848022, ⓔtouchstone@icon.co.za; ❼) has a larger, less-stylized but extremely comfortable lodge sleeping forty, based on a 9000-hectare reserve.

Different again is the tranquil *Ant's Nest* (⊕083 287 2885 or 014 755 4296, ⓦwww.waterberg.net; ❽), a converted farmhouse set deep in the bush north of Vaalwater with rhino, giraffe, gemsbok and blesbok on the game farm, and drives, walks and, in particular, horse-riding offered. The sense of sheer escapism here is clinched by the fact that the owners only ever host one couple or party at a time.

Mid-range and self-catering accommodation

The Waterberg owes much of its credibility and profile to the conservation ideals of Lapalala Wilderness Area (see box below). The upmarket option here is to stay in the intimate and relaxed *Rhino Camp* (❺), a tented self-catering **bush camp** right by the Lapalala River. Less expensive are a series of basic but remote self-catering bush camps (❷) in different parts of the wilderness area, some of which have a wonderfully atmospheric setting – *Lookout Camp* in particular has safari tents perched on the edge of a hillside overlooking the Lephalala River Valley.

Although not all located on game reserves, there are a number of **self-catering chalets** and **cottages** in the Waterberg which often make arrangements with larger farms or reserves nearby for game walks or drives. As a result, they tend to be more affordable and flexible. The best of these include *Cattlelands Cottage* (☎014 755 4179; ❹), a tasteful, comfortable cottage sleeping two with a plunge pool and a secluded bush setting, and *Le Thabo Pioneer Settlement* (☎014 755 4178, or ☎082 635 8967; self-catering ❸, full-board ❺), a collection of small log cabins on the banks of the Melk River near Lapalala. On *Triple B Ranch*, next to the excellent Horizon Horse Trails (see p.733), pleasant self-catering accommodation is available in *Windsong Cottage*, one of the old farmhouses (☎014 755 4296; ❷). The ranch is one of the oldest in the region and is famous for its unusual-looking but hardy Bonsmara cattle, which you can find out more about on one of the farmer's fascinating **farm tours**. Not far from the *Triple B Ranch*, it's worth a detour to look at the tiny stone **church** at Twenty-Four Rivers (on the edge of the ranch), designed by Sir Herbert Baker (see p.602). He was commissioned by two maiden aunts, who expected that he would do it for free, since it was a place of worship; their

---

Lapalala – putting rhinos first

Established in 1981, the **Lapalala Wilderness Area** (☎011 453 7645, ⊛www .parksgroup.co.za) is a 400-square-kilometre reserve masterminded by Clive Walker, a highly regarded South African conservationist and artist. It provides sanctuary for endangered and rare animals, and has developed into one of the foremost conservation projects in South Africa. It was the first private game reserve in the country to obtain the highly endangered black rhino, when five were acquired from Natal Parks Board for R2.2 million. It has never been shy to commit itself to conservation: the Lapalala Wilderness School, for example, was established in 1985 and each year introduces some 3000 children from all over Africa to the principles and practice of conservation during week-long courses in the heart of the wilderness area. Lapalala is at the heart of the recently declared **Waterberg Biosphere Reserve**, founded on a close-knit association of local landowners inspired by its example in combining the conservation of wildlife and the ideals of wilderness with the benefits of tourism. Recognition by UNESCO as a biosphere means that the Waterberg is a protected environment of international importance in terms of both conservation and sustainable use of natural resources.

An excellent introduction to some of the achievements of Lapalala, and the personalities involved, is at the world's only dedicated **Rhino Museum** (Tues–Sun 9am–5pm; R5), based in the old Melkrivier School, about 6km along the road to Lapalala off the Vaalwater to Marken tarred road. It's also possible to arrange to see Lapalala's rhino **orphans**, including the young black rhino Bwana, who lives in Clive and Conita Walker's back garden. Next door to the Rhino Museum is the equally worthwhile **Waterberg Museum** (same hours), which explores the origins of man in the Waterberg and looks at the various peoples and traditions which have held sway here over the centuries.

assumption was, unsurprisingly, not shared by Baker. Although self-catering in this range is standard, most accommodation options will provide catering if requested beforehand; an excellent alternative if you want somewhere to **eat** is *Walker's Wayside* (☎014 755 4428; closed Mon), a pub and restaurant right next to the Rhino Museum near Lapalala. Here you'll find well-priced and tasty lunches and evening meals.

Marakele National Park

Southwest of Vaalwater, in the mountains to the northeast of the mining and hunting town of Thabazimbi, lies **Marakele National Park** (daily: May–Aug 8am–5pm; Sept–April 8am–6pm), one of South Africa's newest national parks, and already an impressive 600 square kilometres in size. At its core are the Kransberg, a striking assortment of odd-shaped peaks, plateaus and cliffs. The diversity of land and altitude means that a variety of interesting plants, including ferns, orchids, and even proteas and cycads are found here, while the fauna includes tsessebe, roan and sable antelope, red hartebeest and 800 breeding pairs of the endangered Cape vulture. Larger game such as elephant, rhino and lion have also been introduced, many of them from Kruger National Park.

While the park has a great deal of potential, for the moment **day visitors** (R10) are restricted to a small area – although this does include Kransberg, with its inspiring views. At present, the only place to **stay** is a tented camp situated on the banks of the Matlabas River, which requires a 4WD vehicle to get to. Bookings for this can be made through the National Parks Board (☎012 343 1991, ⓦwww.parks-sa.co.za).

The far north

The **northernmost part of Limpopo province** is a hot, green, undeveloped rural region with as much in common with Zimbabwe as with South Africa. The essential geographical features of the area are the **Limpopo River**, the border between South Africa and Zimbabwe (and, further west, Botswana), and the alluring **Soutpansberg mountain range**, aligned east–west just to the north of the area's main town, **Louis Trichardt**. Both landmarks lie in the path of the N1 highway, still the main route through the area, which crosses into Zimbabwe at **Beitbridge**.

As a first impression of South Africa for visitors arriving from Zimbabwe, the far north cannot compete with the lure of attractions further south. Yet it is an area where the lack of sophistication and isolated history of the people and culture make absorbing contrasts to other parts of the country. Perhaps the most distinctive area is the **Venda** region, formerly an "independent" homeland under the apartheid regime; although economically impoverished, it remains rich in tradition, art and legend. East of the Venda lands is the northern tip of **Kruger National Park**, a less-visited but intriguing part of the park (see p.708); there are two entry gates to the park here, at **Punda Maria** and **Pafuri**.

The Soutpansberg area

The **Soutpansberg Mountains** have an unusual claim to distinction, named as they are after a set of saltpans – one of the flatter natural features known to man. The name came about after Voortrekker pioneers, under the leadership of Louis Trichardt, established their first settlement by the pans on the northern side of the mountain range. While the settlement soon relocated to Schoemansdal, on the southern side, the moniker stuck.

An impressive range of hills, particularly from the south, the Soutpansberg attract sufficient rainfall to create a subtropical climate, and spectacularly lush green farms along the southern slopes produce a range of exotic crops such as avocados, mangoes, bananas and macadamia nuts. In other parts, the rocky *kloofs* and green hillsides offer some remote and unspoilt mountain retreats, shaded by up to 250 different species of tree, and the home of monkey, small antelope, foraging warthog and some noble raptors.

The N1 highway bisects the range, passing through the main town of the north, **Louis Trichardt**, situated in the southern shadow of the mountains, then climbing over a low pass and descending through a pair of tunnels on the northern side. Once over the escarpment, the highway runs north across mostly empty baobab plains to **Messina** and the **Limpopo River**.

Louis Trichardt

With the N1 running through town, it's easy to miss **LOUIS TRICHARDT**, basically a practical place to stop at the junction of the road leading into Venda and to the Punda Maria Gate of Kruger National Park. With little on offer further north at Messina, however, this is the last town with a reasonable selection of shops and services before you reach the border. A centre for the surrounding mountain and bushveld farms, it has hung onto its traditional role as a white bastion in the hostile north, and you'll find its white population overwhelmingly Afrikaans-speaking.

There is a well-organized and convenient **tourist information** office (Mon–Fri 8am–5pm, Sat 8am–1pm; ☎015 516 0040, ⓦwww.tourismsoutpansberg.co.za) beside the Caltex garage, just off the highway at the third junction (second four-way stop) on the N1 as you come past town. Note, however, that sometime in 2002 this is due to move to a custom-built tourist resource centre on the left-hand side of the middle junction (the one with traffic lights) as you travel north through Louis Trichardt. The **train station** is at the southern end of Kruger Street. **Minibus taxis** for links into Venda and up to Beitbridge rank near the corner of Trichardt and Kruger streets. Greyhound, Intercape and Translux **buses** stop at the information office.

The best **accommodation** in the area is out of town, mainly in the foothills of the Soutpansberg (see p.738), but there are a few inexpensive places you can stay here. The municipal caravan park is on Grobler Street near the centre of town – it offers a bit of gloomy shade and grass for camping. In town, the *Bergwater Hotel*, 5 Rissik St (☎015 516 0262; ❸), has some decent-sized and relatively modern rooms upstairs with views over a small lake. Off Rissik Street, the *Carousel Lodge*, Klein Street (☎015 516 4482; ❷), is an unglamorous alternative, but has adequate and inexpensive self-catering rooms and units, as well as a dorm.

Outside town, the small *Ben Lavin Nature Reserve*, signposted 8km south of town on the N1 (☎015 516 4534, ⓦwww.satis.co.za/benlavin ❶–❷), has a collection of larger antelope and giraffe, with a neat restcamp deep in the bush.

It has walking and mountain-bike trails (bikes can be rented), self-catering cottages, luxury tents and space to pitch your own tent. The *Plaas Guesthouse*, 21km east of town along the R524 (☎015 516 4717, ✉plaasgst@cis.co.za; ❸), is a very hospitable, friendly B&B on an avocado farm on the lush slopes of the Soutpansberg, with great breakfasts.

There are various familiar take-away **food** outlets around the grid-set town centre. For a sit-down meal, head to the *Shenandoah Spur* steakhouse on Krogh Street and Magistrate Avenue, while there is also a pricier restaurant at the *Bergwater Hotel*. More appealing are some of the alternatives out of town, including the tea garden at the *Inn on Louis Trichardt*, the *Ingwe Ranch Hotel* (for details on both, see p.738) or the *Elephant & Castle* pub, 14km south of Louis Trichardt on the N1.

Schoemansdal

Established by the first Voortrekkers reaching the Soutpansberg, **SCHOE-MANSDAL**, off the R522 towards Vivo (Mon–Sat 9am–4pm; free), was abandoned around thirty years later, after its inhabitants failed to stem attacks by Venda warriors, and was never again occupied. When control of the area was regained by the Zuid-Africaanische Republiek in 1898, a new settlement was established at Louis Trichardt, some 12km to the east, leaving Schoemansdal the only established Voortrekker settlement in the country not to become a modern town. Perhaps not surprisingly, the site of the historic village has been turned into an **outdoor museum of pioneering history**, with a number of old dwellings and buildings re-created and various aspects of settler life and domestic crafts on display. From the top of a wooden viewing platform you can make out the lines of grass where the streets of the settlement once were, as well as the archeological diggings which have been made on the site. It certainly paints a humble picture of pioneer Voortrekker life, and one that is not so readily evident in the collections of artefacts on display in dusty town houses. Having said that, the Schoemansdal museum is obviously dying a slow death of neglect, and has really become a place to absorb those interested in history rather than the wider audience it has the potential to attract.

Elim and around

Southeast of Louis Trichardt along the R578 lie some areas that used to form part of the self-governing homeland of Gazankulu (a Tsonga area). They boast the leftover scruffiness and vibrant roadside action typical of such rural areas – most notably at **ELIM**, a cluster of stalls, minibuses and hoardings on the site of a long-established Swiss mission hospital. A short way from here, along the road to Levubu, is the modest, but relaxing *Shiluvari Lakeside Lodge* (☎015 556 3406, ✉shiluvar@lantic.net; full-board ❹), with lawns running down to the edge of Albasini Dam and views over the water to the Soutpansberg.

Continuing on the R578 from Elim crossroads, towards the town of Giyani, there are a series of rural arts and crafts workshops. This isn't strictly in Venda (see p.740), but the traditions and skills in arts and crafts are not dissimilar, and most of the workshops and small factories have simple, rural roots, making the trip to see them quite an adventure, but definitely one well worth making.

The Soutpansberg Mountains

Lush, rounded mountains rising to a height of over 1700m and cut by some dramatic outcrops of pinky-orange rock, the **Soutpansberg** seem to form a final barrier of colourful relief before the long hot plains either side of the Limpopo River. Travelling north on the N1, you begin to climb immediately after leaving Louis Trichardt, up what becomes a narrow, winding road not easily negotiated by the heavy trucks plying the Great North Road. Along this stretch, you'll pass a number of **hotels and guesthouses** that have used the lush surroundings to create a mountain-resort-type atmosphere. The best of these can certainly be regarded as alternatives to a stopover in Louis Trichardt: try the *Mountain View Hotel* (☏015 517 7031; ❷), 9km north of town or, even better, *The Inn on Louis Trichardt* (☏015 517 7088, ⊛www.innsofzim.co.zw; ❹), 12km north of town, which has various rooms with an old colonial feel set around pleasant gardens and a pool, as well as an attractive craft shop and tea garden in the grounds. Of the guesthouses hidden in the folds of the Soutpansberg, one of the nicest is *Harnham House* (☏015 517 7260; ❸), 6km along the scenic "Bluegumspoort" road, which has rooms in the attractive main house as well as in a lovely remote cottage overlooking a dam. Backpacker beds and camping sites are also available here. Once over the low pass, on the much less dramatic northern slopes, you'll find the well-run *Ingwe Ranch Hotel* (☏015 517 7087; ❸), which offers a variety of rondavels and rooms, a coffee bar and one of the better restaurants in the area.

Mountain retreats

Beyond the well-worn route of the N1, you can get deeper into the more remote and wilder parts of the mountains if you have a couple of days to spare. Most of the options listed below are members of the Soutpansberg conservancy (⊛www.soutpansberg.co.za), which promotes the natural heritage of the area as well as developing the tourism potential within the mountain range. Just south of Waterpoort, is the Sand River gorge, through which the rail line passes through the mountains; here, approached from the southern side (29km west of Louis Trichardt on the R522) is the escapist *Medike Mountain Reserve* (☏015 516 0481; ❷), with **accommodation** in thatched stone cottages and trails to see the surrounding area's rock art, birds, wildlife and waterfalls. Further west along the R522, along a turn-off 46km from Louis Trichardt, *Lajuma Mountain Retreat* (☏015 593 0352 or 072 133 6208; ❷), situated by the top of Letjume, the highest point of the Soutpansberg, has two attractive thatched chalets perched on the mountainside, as well as simpler Victorian cottages tucked into the luxuriant tropical bush. Again, there are terrific opportunities to explore the slopes, with archeology trails a speciality here. On the north side of the mountains you can visit the salt pans that gave the range its name at *Bergpan Eco Resort* (☏015 593 0127) east of Waterpoort along the R523, where tours of the pans and a chance to experience salt-making are offered, along with hiking and a self-catering guesthouse (❷). The tourist information office in Louis Trichardt and its website (see p.736) hold details of other retreats.

North to the border

Once over the Soutpansberg, the N1 runs across hot, mostly featureless plains of dense bush and baobab trees for some 60km before reaching the town of **Messina**, the last settlement before the Zimbabwe border crossing at Beitbridge on the Limpopo River. There isn't anything much else in the region, although the famous Iron Age site at Mapungubwe (Hill of the Jackals) is around 80km west of Messina, close to the confluence of the Shashe and Limpopo rivers. This is set to become part of an ambitious Transfrontier Park, with links to adjacent nature reserves in Zimbabwe and Botswana, but as yet there's no public entry or facilities.

Messina (Musina)

Eighteen kilometres south of the border, **MESSINA** is above all a mining town, although it does attract a fair bit of the traffic passing through on the N1. The border at Beitbridge is not open 24 hours a day, so there's always call for accommodation and food, which Messina does offer, but without flourish.

The one thing of note around Messina is the **Baobab Tree Reserve** encircling the town. According to legend, God planted baobab trees upside down with their roots in the air. You don't find the trees in great stands but rather dotted around the bushveld, each one with a plate nailed onto it displaying its protected status. Many are over a thousand years old, and the largest have been hollowed out inside and used as houses, bars, shops and even toilets. There are quite a number of fine examples by the roadside on the N1, although many of these are covered in graffiti. The entrance to the reserve, which doesn't have any facilities, is a couple of kilometres south of town.

Practicalities

The town's reasonably well-run caravan and camping park is on the left when you enter the town from the south. Otherwise, **accommodation** is a choice between *Günter's Country House* (℡015 534 1019; ❷), 25 Irwin St (the R508 to Tshipise), a civilized, pleasant B&B with a pool; *Ilala Lodge* (℡015 534 3220; ❸), situated in the baobab reserve 8km northwest of town, with secluded stone chalets with a pool; or, least expensive, the *Limpopo River Lodge*, on the N1 in the centre of town (℡015 534 0204; ❶), a plain travellers' hotel with a certain creaking character.

When it comes to **eating**, there are various takeaways, including a *Nando's*, at the elbow in the road close to the mine entrance. For sit-down meals, the *Buffalo Ridge Spur* franchise is by the N1 off Sam Street; there's also a steakhouse at *Mudzwiri Lodge*, by the mine on the northern side of town.

Beitbridge

On the South African side of the Limpopo, there isn't much to **BEITBRIDGE** other than a tacky service station, a habitually long queue of trucks, some noisy minibus touts and the customs and immigration buildings (which include a duty-free shop). Two bridges cross the Limpopo (the river memorably described by Rudyard Kipling in *Just So Stories* as "great grey-green, greasy"), one for vehicles and one for pedestrians. The border is open 5.30am–10.30pm, but count yourself lucky if you get through without delay, hassle or hindrance. The only viable alternative if you want to get to Zimbabwe from South Africa is the Grobersbrug/Martin's Drift border (daily 8am–4pm), 150km northwest of Potgietersrus on the N11, although this means detouring through Botswana.

Venda

To the west and north of Louis Trichardt lies the intriguing land of the **VhaVenda** people, a culturally and linguistically distinct African grouping known for their mystical legends, political independence and their arts and crafts. Venda was demarcated as a homeland under the apartheid system in the Fifties, and became one of three nationally independent homelands in South Africa in the late Seventies. Of all the homelands, Venda was one of the least compromised, keeping both its geographic and cultural integrity, and largely being left to mind its own business during the dark years of apartheid. Its boundaries have regained their former fuzziness, within Limpopo, but the region has retained its strong, independent identity.

Like most of the other homelands of apartheid South Africa, Venda arrived in the new South Africa with a bloated and inefficient bureaucracy. Despite the restructuring of the provinces and tightening of budgets, many difficulties have lingered. Venda Tourism, ambitious even in its heyday, eventually crumbled in 1998, leaving vague promises of new provincial structures, but very little of substantive help to the visitor to Venda. For now, the best place to get **information** is from the tourist information office in Louis Trichardt (see p.736) or one of the established accommodation options such as the *Venda Sun*. Various tour guides offer trips round the area: good ones include the ebullient Chris Olivier of *Face Afrika Tours* (☎ & ☏015 516 2076 or ☎082 969 3270, ✆facaf @mweb.co.za) and Dries Bester (☎015 583 0299 or 082 964 2745), a specialist in the local plant-life. Otherwise, you'll find almost no tourist-oriented infrastructure whatsoever in Venda and a general lack of familiarity with visitors and what they might be looking for. However, it's a lot less dangerous to **travel independently** through Venda than many other places in South Africa, and the journey can be wonderfully rough, raw and rewarding – but be prepared for the fact that you will be very much on your own.

Venda history and culture

The people who today call themselves **VhaVenda** are descended from a number of ancient groupings who migrated from the Great Lakes area in east-central Africa in the eleventh and twelfth centuries. Their identity gelled when a group under Chief Dimbanyika arrived at Dzata (which means "peace" in Venda) in the northern Soutpansberg, where a walled fort was later built. From here, they consolidated their power in the region, fending off attack from a number of different African groupings (including the Voortrekkers, whom they drove from their settlement at Schoemansdal, just south of the Soutpansberg in 1867). Although the VhaVenda suffered a reverse at the hands of the Boers in 1898, the onset of the Anglo-Boer War prevented that victory being consolidated. The British had little interest in such a remote region, and were content to allow their administration to be run by the local chiefs, a system of self-government which, in one contrived form or another, lasted through the apartheid years until 1994.

The **culture** of the VhaVenda is a fascinating one, steeped in mysticism and vivid legend. One pervading theme is water – always an important concern in hot, seasonal climates, but in which Venda is unusually abundant. Lakes, rivers, waterfalls and lush forests all form sacred sites, while legends abound of *zwidutwane*, or water sprites, and snakes who live at the bottom of dark pools or lakes. You can still even find older people who hold a taboo against fish, partly because the animals live in water and partly because they believe that if you eat fish the crocodiles will go hungry and turn on other available food sources, such as humans.

Many VhaVenda **ceremonies** and **rituals** still hold great importance, with the most famous the python, or *domba*, dance performed by young female initiates. Naked but for jewellery and a small piece of cloth around their waist, the teenage girls form a long chain, swaying and shuffling as the snake winds around a fire to the sound of a beating drum – another sacred object in Venda – often for hours on end. Although it is well known, your chances of seeing it performed are limited – although dancing can always be arranged (at a price, and with advance notice). The genuine thing is most common during spring; Heritage Day around the end of August or the beginning of September is a good time for celebrations.

Thohoyandou

Following the southern edge of the Soutpansberg along the R524, 70km west of Louis Trichardt, lies the Venda capital of **THOHOYANDOU**. It's an ugly, dirty sprawl of broken concrete and undisciplined building glamorized by a casino. Situated among the last of the foothills at the eastern end of the Soutpansberg, it's not a place you'll want to spend time in if you can help it; if you're heading for Kruger, the R524 mercifully bypasses the centre of town altogether.

The highlight of the capital, at least according to the tourist authorities, is the **Venda Sun hotel and casino** (T015 962 4600 or 015 581 2101; ❹), a clone of the gambling dens tacitly encouraged in the homelands by the apartheid government and lapped up by South Africans denied such illicit entertainment in their own country. It is set in the heart of the downtown area, surrounded immediately by trees, but not far beyond the road and tatty shopping mall. To get to it, turn left off the R534 coming from Louis Trichardt at the Delta/Toyota service station, and right at the third set of traffic lights. The hotel has a pool and decent, if expensive, rooms and facilities; it also has an impressive record of supporting Venda arts and crafts, with useful maps and tours available here.

The only reasonable alternative in town to the *Venda Sun* is *Bougainvillea Lodge* (T015 962 4064; ❸), just up the hill from the *Venda Sun*, a simple motel-like travellers' stop. A good option for budget travellers keen to get a taste for the region is *Land of Legend Backpackers* (T083 430 0098 or 015 516 1077; ❶), a fairly basic, but friendly place, situated deep in the forests of the eastern Soutpansberg off the R524, about halfway between Louis Trichardt and

Animal magic

Along with their spiritual relationship with water-inhabiting creatures, the VhaVenda have an interesting affinity with a number of **animals** of the forests and mountains. The relationship is, in many ways, a lot less aggressive and more humanized than that found in other African peoples. With lions, the VhaVenda recall the story of their great leader Makado, who harried the Boer commandos from the north. He was captured and thrown into a lion pit in Pretoria but, rather like Daniel in the Old Testament, the lions chose not to eat him. Around the hot spring at Mphephu the legend runs that a leopard controls the hillside, and that it's always wise practice to keep him informed about who's in the area. And, towards the eastern end of the Soutpansberg range there stands a lion's head-shaped hill (there are nice views of it across Vondo Dam, on the Thate Vondo pass road) called Lwamondo. It is inhabited by baboons, who are protected because they once warned the VhaVenda of an imminent attack from their enemies.

Thohoyandou; free pick-ups from Louis Trichardt can be organized. Accommodation is in two dorms and a guesthouse sleeping four, and while facilities are for self-catering, meals can be arranged, and tours to the crafts and historic sites of Venda are also available.

There isn't a wide choice of **places to eat** in Thohoyandou. In the shopping centre next to the *Venda Sun* there are a number of take-away food shops, including a *Nando's* and *KFC*, and a pricier sit-down restaurant in the *Venda Sun* itself. **Minibuses** for Louis Trichardt leave from the large, chaotic taxi rank in front of the shopping centre.

Arts and crafts in Venda and Gazankulu

The Venda and Gazankulu regions have established a strong reputation in **arts and crafts**. The best known of these are clay pots distinctively marked with angular designs in graphite silver and ochre. Also growing in status are woodcarvings, ranging from abstract to practical; though, while the best of these can be imaginative and bold, many are unfinished and overpriced. You'll also come across tapestries, fabrics, basketwork and painting.

Finding your way to these villages can be quite an adventure, as they are widely scattered, the roads are poor, and directions can often be vague and confusing.

In the former homeland of **Gazankulu**, the main route is along the R578 between Elim and Giyani. Travelling southeast from Elim crossroads, look out for a track leading up to the **Rivoni** workshop (opposite the turn to Waterval), where blind and other handicapped people make sisal mats, furniture, candles and coffins – a line that evidently does a roaring trade. There isn't a great deal to see, but the place is industrious and there is a small shop. Back on the R578, turn left at the brow of the next hill, then up a right-hand fork, to reach **Tsonga Textiles**, where screen-printed fabrics are produced and turned into tablecloths, bedspreads and clothes.

The R578 then goes down a hill, at the bottom of which is a turning to Mbhokota village. Going along this, turning left at the T-junction and left again along a narrow track just past a small homestead with a busy garden, you'll find a run-down-looking collection of buildings where **Twananani** textiles are created – attractive, funky hand-painted and batik garments with traditional African designs, made by around twenty people.

At the next junction off the R578 to Riverplaats, then along a right-hand fork, is the house and small workshop of Shangaan woodcarver **Jackson Thugwane**. He's an almost mystical figure, with pieces exhibited in major galleries around the country and in Europe: if he isn't there you won't find much to see; if he is, be prepared for a few absorbing hours of philosophy, theology, art and the state of the modern world. There are a number of other, younger carvers nearby trying to emulate Jackson's success. If you take the left-hand fork after the Riverplaats sign, you will eventually come to a village called **Mashamba** where villagers make clay pots in the traditional way. This is, however, a trek deep into the rural areas of Gazankulu and road conditions are fairly unreliable, so ask around for the latest.

In **Venda**, the villages are even more scattered and hard to find. There are a number of sites situated to the south of Thohoyandou, including the workshop of **Noria Mabasa**, whose clay-and-wood sculptures have become widely recognized around South Africa. Another place to look out for is **Mutale**, to the north of Thohoyandou, where traditional decorative drums are made. You can pick up a hand-drawn **arts and crafts map** of Venda at the *Venda Sun* or the tourist information office at Louis Trichardt; another option is to contact **Annette and Martin Kennealy** (℡ 0159 32096 or 083 326 2922), two artists who are very knowledgeable about art (rather than crafts) in the area and can advise on what to look out for and where to find it.

Lake Fundudzi, the Sacred Forest and the Mabudashango Trail

Along the northern side of the Soutpansberg, through a valley traced by the R523 road from the N1 to Thohoyandou, is the most appealing core of VhaVenda history and legend. This is where you'll find the lush forests, waterfalls and mountains which give Venda its mystical atmosphere.

From Thohoyando, climb out of town to the north and then west, eventually leaving the suburbs to get amongst the elevated green scenery which lies enticingly ahead. You'll pass the **Vondo Dam**, created in the early Nineties and surrounded by pine forests, then climb over the **Thate Vondo Pass**, over the summit of which a small shack marks the entrance to a network of forest roads that take you into the area containing the most important lake in Venda, **Lake Fundudzi**, and the **Sacred Forest**, an area of dense indigenous forest which contains the burial ground of Venda chiefs. You can look at both from afar, but to get any closer is a matter of deep cultural sensitivity: you have to gain permission which, without local leads to the right people, is not easy to do. There isn't a readily available map showing you the network of roads around the forest, and some of the roads require 4WD; if you want to see the area, it's best to join a tour (see p.740) or make sure you've gathered information and advice beforehand.

One option well worth considering is the **Mabudashango Hiking Trail**, a four-day, fifty-five-kilometre walk that takes you as close as any road to the main highlights of the area, including Lake Fundudzi and the Sacred Forest. The trail offers spectacular views and lush vegetation, and navigation isn't always easy, but at each of the camps along the way you'll find a shelter with water and toilet facilities; for details, contact the tourist information office in Louis Trichardt (see p.736).

Mphephu and Dzata

Heading west, the R523 crosses over the crest of the Thate Vondo Pass before following the **Nzhelele River** down a valley of scattered but mostly unbroken settlement. About halfway along is **Aventura Mphephu** (☎011 207 3600, ⓦwww.aventura.co.za; ❸), a holiday resort with around twenty chalets based around a hot spring on the flanks of the Soutpansberg. Not far west of Mphephu, on the northern side of the road, are the **Dzata ruins**, the remains of the royal kraal of the kings of VhaVenda, dating from 1400. While interesting historically, as with the rest of the tourism infrastructure, the ruins are not very visitor-friendly. If you find the gate locked, you'll probably have to toot your horn to rouse the gateman, and even then you may find the place deserted.

Routes to the northern Kruger National Park

The R525 runs across the Messina plains towards **Pafuri Gate**, the most northerly of the Kruger entrances, past which is a border post to Mozambique, although there is little beyond unless you're well-equipped for adventure. If you need a **place to stay** over on your way to Kruger, there's another Aventura holiday resort at Tshipise (central reservations ☎011 207 3600, ⓦwww.aventura .co.za; ❸). An alternative is *Popallin Ranch* (☎01553 40644, ⓔecotours@mweb .co.za), an 80-square-kilometre farm with buffalo, giraffe and baobab trees right on the Limpopo River. You can camp here, or stay at the comfortable *De Wet's Camp* (❹), with game drives available as an extra. Even more rustic and escapist is *Pafuri Rivercamp* (☎082 785 0305, ⓦwww.pafuri.co.za; ❹), on the Mutale River just before you reach the Pafuri Gate. This incorporates a series of tree-top tents and an open self-catering bush camp, from where you can set off in pursuit of the profuse local plants and wildlife, or relax by the river or pool. There's no electricity, but arrangements for meals can be made in advance.

Travel details

Trains

One train travels every day in each direction between Johannesburg and Messina (a 15hr overnight journey), calling at Pretoria (1hr 30min), Warmbaths (3hr 30min), Nylstroom (4hr), Potgietersrus (6hr), Polokwane (8hr), Louis Trichardt (12hr) and Messina (15hr). Note that using this (very slow) service you will often arrive at the above destinations in the middle of the night.

Buses

Greyhound, Intercape and Translux buses ply the N1 between Johannesburg and Beitbridge, stopping at Warmbaths, Polokwane, Louis Trichardt and Messina; most services carry on to either Bulawayo and Victoria Falls or Harare in Zimbabwe. Northlink Tours connects Tzaneen and Johannesburg via Polokwane. These and other routes are also covered by minibus taxis from any moderately sized town; the best way to find out where they're going and when they depart is to enquire at the taxi rank.

Beitbridge to: Johannesburg (daily; 8–10hr).

Polokwane to: Johannesburg (daily; 4hr); Tzaneen (daily; 1hr 45min).

Tzaneen to: Johannesburg (6 weekly; 6hr 15min); Polokwane (daily; 1hr 45min).

Flights

Polokwane to: Johannesburg (4 daily Mon–Fri, 1–3 daily Sat & Sun; 50min).

Lesotho

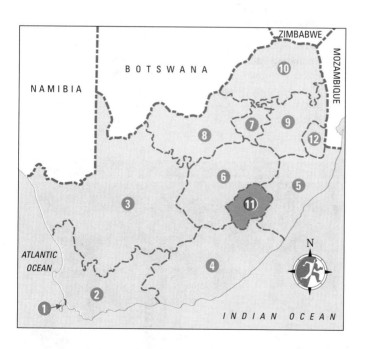

* **Pony trekking** The ideal way to see Lesotho following paths from village to village through spectacular high-level scenery. **See p.755**

* **Thaba Bosiu** The hill-top fortress from which Lesotho's greatest king, Moshoeshoe I, protected his kingdom against attackers. **See p.762**

* **Semonkong Falls** A remote 200-metre waterfall plunging into a vast gorge deep in the Highland region. **See p.767**

* **"Roof of Africa" road** A narrow, winding road from Butha-Buthe to Sani Pass though dramatic mountain passes and valleys. **See p.775**

* **Malealea Lodge** The friendliest and best-run of Lesotho's travellers' lodges, with terrific hiking, pony trekking and views. **See p.781**

* **Sehlabathebe National Park** A lonely mountain reserve with superb hiking and blissful solitude. **See p.787**

11

Lesotho

ntirely surrounded by South Africa and sometimes mistaken for one of apartheid's ill-conceived semi-states, the aptly named "mountain king-dom" of **Lesotho** (pronounced Le-sue-toe) is, in fact, proudly independent of and very different in character to its dominant neigh-bour. One refreshing physical (and psychological) contrast is the almost total absence of fences in Lesotho, which means you can hike into the upland regions at will, while meeting some of the most hospitable people of the region. The other thing you'll notice pretty quickly is that Lesotho is virtual-ly treeless, with the exception of the invasive and water-hungry eucalyptus and the peach trees introduced by French missionaries a century ago. Indeed, the country – once the grain basket of the region – is in deep ecological trou-ble, and acres of irreplaceable topsoil, loosened by decades of over-farming, are washed away down its rivers each year.

The **Lesotho lowlands** form an east-facing crescent around the country, and are where you'll find all the nation's major towns, including the busily practi-cal capital of **Maseru**, with its very African mix of new glass buildings and dusty streets, and a host of smaller, mostly nondescript settlements that began life as tax-collection centres for the British administration. There are plenty of interesting things to see in the lowlands – the weaving crafts of **Teya-Teyaneng**, the extraordinary caves at **Mateka**, and **Thaba Bosiu**, the moun-tain fortress of Lesotho's founder, King Moshoeshoe I – though in many ways the everyday bustle of life you'll encounter here is the most fascinating part of all. The true splendours of the country, however, lie in its ruggedly beautiful **Highlands**, an extended mountainous area characterized by plunging valleys, remote villages, improbable roads and inspiring vistas. Once up the steep, twist-ing roads which lead into the hills you can visit the engineering masterpieces of the **Katse and Mohale dams**, ski at **Oxbow**, fish from rivers everywhere, and above all wander through the countryside, dividing your time between remote villages of simple stone-and-thatch huts and the peaceful solitude of the mountains.

Although the tarred **road network** is good, many Sotho still travel by **pony**, particularly in the Highlands. You can do the same from pony-trekking lodges all over the country; a day trek or, better, a longer ride incorporating a night in a remote Basotho village, is *the* way to experience Lesotho. Most of Lesotho's four hundred or more **San rock-art sites** and the many more **dinosaur footprints** can only be visited this way – although there are still plenty close by the roads which you can reach with ease if travelling by car.

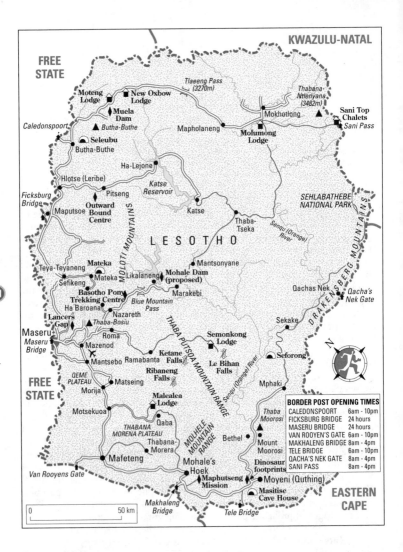

Tlaeeng Pass (3270m)

Thabana-Ntlenyana (3482m)

Moteng Lodge

New Oxbow Lodge

Muela Dam

Butha-Buthe

Caledonspoort

Mokhotlong

Sani Top Chalets
Sani Pass

Seleubu
Butha-Buthe

Mapholaneng

Molumong Lodge

Ha-Lejone

Hlotse (Leribe)

Ficksburg Bridge

Pitseng

Katse Reservoir

SEHLABATHEBE NATIONAL PARK

Maputsoe

Outward Bound Centre

Katse

Thaba-Tseka

Senqu (Orange) River

L E S O T H O

MALOTI MOUNTAINS

Teya-Teyaneng

Mateka

Mateka

Mantsonyane

Sefikeng

Likalaneng

Mohale Dam (proposed)

Marakebi

Qachas Nek

Qacha's Nek Gate

DRAKENSBERG MOUNTAINS

Basotho Pony Trekking Centre

Ha Baroana

Blue Mountain Pass

Nazareth

Lancers Gap

Thaba-Bosiu

Roma

Sekake

THABA PUTSOA MOUNTAIN RANGE

Maseru
Maseru Bridge

Mazenod

Mantsebo

Semonkong Lodge

Ramabanta

Ketane Falls

Le Bihan Falls

Seforong

FREE STATE

QEME PLATEAU

Matseing

Ribaneng Falls

Senqu (Orange) River

Mphaki

Morija

Motsekuoa

Malealea Lodge

MOHELE MOUNTAIN RANGE

Thaba Moorosi

Qaba

THABANA MORENA PLATEAU

Thabana-Morera

Bethel

Mount Moorosi

Mafeteng

Mohale's Hoek

Dinosaur footprints

Van Rooyens Gate

Maphutseng Mission

Masitise Cave House

Moyeni (Quthing)

EASTERN CAPE

Makhaleng Bridge

Tele Bridge

BORDER POST OPENING TIMES	
CALEDONSPOORT	6am - 10pm
FICKSBURG BRIDGE	24 hours
MASERU BRIDGE	24 hours
VAN ROOYEN'S GATE	6am - 10pm
MAKHALENG BRIDGE	8am - 4pm
TELE BRIDGE	6am - 10pm
QACHA'S NEK GATE	8am - 4pm
SANI PASS	8am - 4pm

0   50 km

N

Some history

Lesotho exists because of the determined efforts of one man, **Moshoeshoe I** (1786–1870), to secure land for his people in the face of intense social upheaval and the insatiable land-hunger of others. Before the arrival of Moshoeshoe's ancestors around 900 AD, the San inhabited Lesotho's hills and mountains unchallenged. Today the San are gone, exterminated by the British led by one Colonel Bowker, who led the last of many missions against them in the highland region of Sehonkong in 1873. However, they have left their mark through rock paintings, elements of their tongue in the Sotho language, and traces of their features in some Sotho people.

The Sotho first settled the fertile plains that today form the Lesotho lowlands and the Free State, before going on to colonize the mountains. They farmed these plains relatively peacefully for centuries, but by Moshoeshoe's time, bandit clans from elsewhere had already forced thousands of Sotho off their land. Moshoeshoe proved his own marauding skills in 1809, when he rustled so many cattle from another chief that he was judged to have "shaved his beard"; Moshoeshoe is the "praise name" he earned for that feat – pronounced "Moshwehshweh", the name is supposed to represent the sound of shaving. He became a chief in 1820, based on top of a mountain near Butha-Buthe, where he became patron to many refugees in search of safety. However, after a particularly vicious attack on Butha-Buthe in 1824, Moshoeshoe decided it was no longer safe and trekked south with his followers in search of a better mountain. He found one at Thaba Bosiu, which was subsequently attacked repeatedly, but never taken. Moshoeshoe meanwhile expanded his kingdom by securing other clan chiefs as clients, at the same time earning a reputation for wisdom and generosity amongst ordinary Sotho that is almost mythical today.

Moshoeshoe had heard from travellers that **missionaries** brought peace, and so welcomed the arrival in 1833 of three from the Paris Evangelical Missionary Society (PEMS), establishing them in Morija, and taking an active interest in their work, though he never officially converted. The missionaries established what is now the Lesotho Evangelical Church, second in size only to the Catholics in Lesotho, whose missionaries founded Roma in the 1860s (see p.764).

The kingdom was encroached upon by land-hungry whites from the 1840s, and the Orange Free State (OFS) government invaded in 1858, their soldiers destroying Morija and then launching a failed attack on Thaba Bosiu. They

11

LESOTHO

△ Pony-trekking, Lesotho

nonetheless captured plenty of farm land, whose acquisition was sanctioned by a British treaty in 1860. In 1865, the OFS government cited Sotho cattle theft as the pretext for a new war, though few could deny Moshoeshoe's bitter assertion that "my great sin is that I possess a good and fertile country". The ensuing Seqiti War resulted in the destruction of Sotho crops by Free State troops, forcing Moshoeshoe into a humiliating treaty in 1866 which signed over most of his remaining good land. The war resumed in 1867, and was halted only by the British taking over what was left of the kingdom as the protectorate of

Lesotho travel basics

Accommodation

This is reasonably priced in Lesotho; you can get a double room for under M100 per person in most parts of the country, and for around M150 per person in one of the mid-range hotels in Maseru. Be aware that most places to stay outside Maseru accept cash only. There are a handful of hotels, but very few guesthouses – "lodges" are the main accommodation option. Broadly, these fall into two categories: bland, conventional hotels that get most of their business from conferences or civil servants, and relaxed, well-run places which target travellers. The latter, such as *Malealea Lodge*, *Fraser's Semonkong Lodge*, *Molumong Lodge* near Mohkotlong and *New Oxbow Lodge*, offer a range of accommodation from backpacker dorms to well-appointed rondavels, and make for easy-going places that capture the feel of Lesotho very well. Independent camping is possible all over rural Lesotho (see p.753), while some lodges allow camping in their grounds.

Books and maps

The glossy brochures available from the tourist information have useful phone numbers, but are otherwise thin on facts. You should turn instead to Marco Turco's now quite dated *Visitor's Guide to Lesotho* (Southern, 1994), or the small *Backpackers' Guide to Lesotho*, an up-to-date booklet self-published by Russell Suchet, who runs the *Sani Lodge*; some South African backpacker lodges have copies. Some of the lodges stock a very good 1:250,000 topographical map of Lesotho, which you can also get at the Department of Land, Surveys & Physical Planning (see p.753), the only place where you can get detailed maps suitable for serious hiking.

Costs, money and banks

Costs are lower than in South Africa. Food and public transport are slightly less expensive, while imported items like film are more expensive and only reliably available in Maseru. Pony trekking costs about M120 a day at most of the lodges (see p.755). A ten percent sales tax is applicable, and often not added to marked prices on menus or in supermarkets and shops.

Most major **credit cards**, such as Visa, Mastercard and American Express, are of limited use. Hotels and lodges geared to foreign visitors accept them, as do a few Maseru restaurants and the craft shops of Teya-Teyaneng. Otherwise, you need cash for everything.

Lesotho's **currency** is the maloti (M), divided into 100 lisenti, which is tied to the South African rand (R1 = M1). You can use rand in Lesotho, so you don't need to convert them beforehand, but you cannot use or exchange maloti anywhere outside Lesotho, so make sure you use them up or exchange them before leaving.

There's no need to convert South African rand. **Banks** are found in all Lesotho's towns, but Maseru is the only place where it's easy to **change money** at them. Hours are Mon–Fri 8.30am–3.30pm, closing 1pm on Wed, Sat 8.30am–11am (avoid busy Saturdays). While a few ATMs exist, not all accept foreign cashcards. The larger hotels in Maseru and the lowland towns change money, but for ludicrously bad rates, making them very much a last resort.

Basotholand in 1868. The Treaty of Aliwal North in 1869 restored Moshoeshoe's land east of the Caledon but left the rest with the Free State, where it has remained to this day.

Moshoeshoe died in 1870 and the British handed Basotholand to the Cape administration a year later, which began taxing its new subjects, establishing a series of hut tax-collection points which have since grown into Lesotho's modest collection of small towns. In 1879, in a bid to tempt the OFS and Transvaal into federation, the Cape government decided to confiscate all Sotho firearms.

Passports and visas

Visa requirements for the kingdom of Lesotho were in the habit of changing fairly often, but currently seem a little more settled. Commonwealth citizens, except those from India, Pakistan, Nigeria and Ghana, do not need visas, and nor do citizens of France, Germany, Ireland, Israel, Italy, Japan, the Netherlands, Spain, Switzerland and the USA. You may find that border officials, particularly at smaller entry points, do not know the new rules, and will demand a visa from you even if you don't need one. There is not much you can do about this, but since visas are available on the spot, and are relatively inexpensive (M20/R20 single entry, M40 multiple entry), you may as well pay up. If you have travelled through a yellow fever zone, you will need an International Certificate of Vaccination against yellow fever. The standard entry permit is for fourteen days but, should you need an **extension**, contact the Department of Immigration and Passport Services, Kingsway, Maseru (☎31 7339).

Phone numbers

To phone Lesotho from anywhere apart from South Africa, the country code is ☎266, followed by the number (note that there are no area codes); from South Africa, dial ☎09266. To phone abroad from Lesotho, dial ☎00, followed by the country and area codes and then the actual telephone number. To phone South Africa, first dial ☎0027, then the area code and phone number. To call collect, first call the operator on ☎100. Where area codes are indicated in the text, the number in question is a South African number, and you will need to prefix it with ☎0027 if calling from Lesotho.

Security

Overall, Lesotho is a **safe country** for travellers. Internal strife of the kind seen in 1998 is very uncommon and was largely regarded as uncharacteristic of the Basotho. Muggings and opportunistic theft is on the rise in Maseru; be careful if you're wandering around the back streets here or after dark. In the Highlands, however, hikers and campers normally have little more to worry about than snarling dogs and persistent demands for sweets from children. However, it's unwise to show off your wealth too obviously, and don't leave valuables like cameras lying around unattended.

Tour operators

The Lesotho **tourist information office** in Maseru (☎31 9485) can arrange tailor-made tours of the country. *Thaba Tours* (ⓦwww.thabatours.de) is a German tour operator with an extensive knowledge of Lesotho. Alternatively, the *Malealea Lodge* (☎051 447 3200, ⓦwww.malealea.co.ls) offers some innovative options, often involving pony trekking or 4WDs, while *Hotel Maluti Lodge* (☎78 5224) also offers specialized 4WD trips.

Water

Tap water is safe to drink. Whilst Lesotho's rivers and streams are bilharzia-free, drinking from them is inadvisable without purifying the water first.

The result was two years of raids and skirmishes, known as the **Gun War**, an expensive and futile effort that brought down the Cape government and so outraged London that Britain resumed direct rule in 1884.

Along with Bechuanaland and Swaziland, Basotholand rejected incorporation into the union of South Africa in 1910, with **King Letsie II** instead helping found the South African Native National Congress (later the ANC) in 1912. During the following years, the monarchy and chiefs' position declined, partly because British reforms forced their uneasy conversion into a junior arm of the colonial civil service, but also because social changes at work in the region, like migration, urbanization and rising education levels, proved too much for chiefs and successive kings to adapt to. In 1960, when **Moshoeshoe II** was crowned king, independence politics were in full swing, spearheaded by Pan-Africanist Ntsa Mokhele's Basotho Congress Party (BCP), and rivalled by the more conservative Basotho National Party (BNP). The BCP easily won the 1960 elections, but the 1965 ones were narrowly won by the BNP, who duly led newly named Lesotho into independence on October 4, 1966. However, after losing the 1970 election, prime minister **Leabua Jonathan** annulled the result, declared a state of emergency, and carried on ruling until he was toppled in 1986 by **Major General Metsing Lekhanya**. Lekhanya ordered the expulsion of the ANC from Lesotho and signed an agreement that year with South Africa for the Lesotho Highlands Water Project (see p.778).

In 1990, Lekhanya sent Moshoeshoe into exile and installed his son **Letsie III** as king, but a year later Lekhanya was himself ousted by **Major General Phisona**, who then gave way to a democratically elected government led by Mokhele's BCP in 1993. There was no end to the turmoil, however, with Letsie dissolving the BCP government in August 1994 for alleged incompetence, although regional pressure soon forced the restoration of the government and constitution. Letsie stood down in favour of his father in 1995, but Moshoeshoe II died in a car crash the next year, and Letsie regained the throne rather sooner than he really desired.

The **elections** of 1998 were won in a landslide by Mokhele, this time at the head of the breakaway Lesotho Congress for Democracy (LCD), but opposition parties cried foul amid widespread allegations of vote-rigging. In July and August of that year, large crowds gathered outside the Royal Palace in Maseru demanding the results be overturned; these protests developed into a **mutiny** by Lesotho Defence Force soldiers, and in September, under the flag of a Southern African Development Community (SADC) **peacekeeping force**, South African troops crossed the border. Fierce fighting took place around military bases and at the strategically vital Katse Dam, but the delayed arrival of further peacekeeping troops from Botswana meant that Maseru was left unsecured, and demonstrators from the Royal Palace were joined by thousands of others from surrounding districts angry at what they regarded as South Africa's heavy-handed intervention. A large number of shops and offices in Maseru, as well as towns such as Mafeteng, were looted and burned. Though largely regarded as an aberration, the 1998 disturbances still loom large in local politics, and there is every evidence that political squabbling will continue.

When to go

The Lesotho **winter** runs from May to July, when it often snows in the Highlands and sometimes in the lowlands too, which is great for skiing and very picturesque. Although the days are usually clear and warm, it does get extremely cold at night and ice can make driving hazardous in Highlands areas. **Spring** (August–October) is a beautiful time, when the snow melts, new plants

Hospitable and almost entirely fenceless, Lesotho is a **hiker's paradise**. It's possible to set off into the hills and hike for as long as you like, with no prospect of an angry farmer yelling at you to get off his land – quite a change from South Africa. In the Highlands there is a vast network of informal tracks and paths between all the villages, and anyone you meet on the way is normally delighted to point you in the direction you want to go. If you're camping, it's important to ask permission, preferably from the chief, although it's normally fine just to pitch your tent if there's no one around. A cosier alternative, where its available, is to stay in a rondavel, for which you will definitely need to ask permission, and to pay a token fee – M10–20 per person.

Always prepare adequately before setting out, and bring supplies for at least a day more than you think the hike will take. Be warned that in the highest reaches of the Drakensberg there are very few villages, and you can walk for days without seeing anyone. Lovely as this is, it is also risky, so make sure someone knows where you have gone, and don't hike there on your own. Lesotho's weather is notoriously fickle, and you should bring a sunhat and sunblock, as well as warm clothing and waterproofs, whatever the season.

Other basics include a torch, plenty of food (there aren't many stores in very rural areas, and those there are usually poorly stocked), a water container, water purifying tablets, an all-weather cooker with fuel (don't count on finding firewood), a genuinely waterproof tent, a sleeping mat and a warm sleeping bag. Also invaluable is a decent map and a compass. The 1:250,000 map available from tourist outlets in Maseru (see p.758) marks most trails and topography, although the really detailed 1:50,000 **maps** of specific regions of Lesotho, available from the Department of Lands, Surveys and Physical Planning (☎32 2376), on Lerotholi Road, near the corner of Constitution Road in Maseru, are far better.

sprout up everywhere, and the fields are tilled again. November to January is **summer**, when Lesotho gets most of its rain, which is often torrential, turning dirt roads into mudslides. Still, when it isn't raining the weather is usually sunny and the landscape vivid shades of green. **Autumn** (February–April) is one of the best times to visit the country, as it doesn't usually rain too much and temperatures are moderate. Whatever the time of year, Lesotho can be very cold at night, particularly in the Highlands, and prone to rapid weather changes, for which it is always wise to be prepared.

Getting to Lesotho

There are fourteen **border posts** from South Africa into Lesotho – from the Free State, KwaZulu-Natal and the Eastern Cape. All the **Free State** border crossings, and **Tele Bridge** (daily 6am–10pm) in the Eastern Cape, cross over into the Lesotho lowlands and are much more accessible than the others, which enter via the Drakensberg. The latter include the famous **Sani Pass** (daily 8am–4pm), which requires a 4WD, although alternative transport is provided by local backpackers' lodges. The **Ficksburg Bridge** and **Maseru Bridge** crossings (both 24hr), are the busiest in the country.

The **drive** from Bloemfontein to Maseru is an easy 200km east along the N8. From Durban, turn off towards Ficksburg at Bethlehem, and then either cross the border at Maputsoe and drive down through Lesotho, or continue on to Ladybrand and cross the border at Maseru. Driving from the Eastern Cape to Maseru is more fiddly, and if you want to stay on tarred roads for as long as possible, remain in South Africa at least until Wepener, from where you can cross into Mafeteng through the Van Rooyen's Gate **border post** (daily

Lesotho public holidays

January 1 – New Year's Day	May 1 – Workers' Day
March 11 – Moshoeshoe Day	July 17 – King's Birthday
April 4 – Heroes Day	October 4 – Independence Day
Good Friday	December 25 – Christmas Day
Easter Monday	December 26 – Boxing Day
Ascension Day (Thursday)	

6am–10pm), or continue through Hobhouse on the Ladybrand road, taking the right-hand fork to Maseru.

Lesotho's only international **airport**, Moshoeshoe I, is 18km south of Maseru, but the only scheduled flights are the daily links to Johannesburg run by SA Airlink (☎011 978 1111).

Lesotho transport

Lesotho has a good tarred **road network**, though you can't avoid dirt roads when heading to more out-of-the-way places of interest. Wherever you travel, however, and especially when you make for the Highlands, twisting roads, fast minibus taxis and frequent encounters with road-side pedestrians and livestock make **driving** here tiring work. Of the main roads, the **northern route** is a continuous tarred road leading north from Maseru to Mokhotlong; the road to Sani from Mokhotlong is untarred but can be negotiated in a saloon car; and while the fearsome Sani Pass itself can be tackled in a saloon car by a good driver in good conditions, you should only consider doing it with a 4WD. Striking off the northern route, the **Katse dam road** from Hlotse is tarred and of very high quality, though it involves some punishing gradients. On the **central route**, the tar extends for a way beyond the site of the new Mohale Dam around Likalaneng, and then reverts to dirt and gravel as far as Thaba Tseka. The high-altitude route from here to Katse is also only for 4WD vehicles, although minibus taxis will tackle it. The **southern** route from Maseru is tarred as far as Mphaki, but is passable in an ordinary saloon car up to Qacha's Nek. The road to Sehlabathebe National Park is just about impassable without a 4WD, though again minibus taxis and buses somehow manage it.

If you've rented a car in South Africa, make sure the **insurance** covers you for travel in Lesotho. Some companies are reluctant to do this, because of the condition of many of the roads. **Fuel** costs roughly the same in Lesotho as it does in South Africa. The **speed limit** is 80kph, and 50kph in urban areas.

Public transport covers Lesotho well. **Buses** are slower but safer than **minibus taxis**, but they are both very inexpensive. **Timetables** do not exist as such; the rule of thumb is to check the day before, and get to the bus station early if you have a long way to go, as long-distance transport usually leaves around 6am. If you're travelling short distances on the main tar and dirt roads, you shouldn't have to wait too long for a minibus taxi going your way.

Hitching is much safer in Lesotho than in South Africa and is a good way to get around. Some drivers expect payment, so you should negotiate this before you've travelled too far.

For **internal flights** you can charter planes out of the old Maseru airport through Mission Aviation Fellowship based in Maseru (☎31 3640) which charges around M1600 per hour for planes that can carry four to five people; single seats are also sometimes available for less if the planes are flying anyway on a training flight or to drop off people or supplies.

Maseru and the central districts

The most convenient entry point from South Africa, and the country's most sophisticated urban centre by far, **Maseru** is a good place to start exploring Lesotho. Apart from a few elegant colonial sandstone buildings, there's not a great deal to see here. All but one or two of the buildings burnt in the 1998 riots have been replaced by ambitious new concrete edifices which threaten to sterilize what is still a fairly characterful town. The pervading atmosphere is not hostile, and travellers will probably feel more comfortable here than in most South African cities. While most visitors pass through fairly quickly on their way to the more appealing countryside, if you're in town for a few days there are plenty of excursions into the hills and plateaus surrounding the city, includ-

Pony trekking

Ponies were introduced to Lesotho from the Cape in the nineteenth century, with one of the first given as a present to King Moshoeshoe I by chief Moorosi in 1829. Moshoeshoe learnt to ride that year, and rapidly acquired further steeds, which he distributed to his family and followers. By the time of Moshoeshoe's death in 1870, ponies were widespread throughout the kingdom and the Sotho had become expert riders.

Lesotho's ponies are famously hardy, capable of slogging away for hours and negotiating slippery rock passes. The Sotho rarely groom their ponies, so they usually look pretty dishevelled, but that doesn't affect their performance in the hills, where for many locals they are the only form of long-distance transport.

A number of lodges offer pony trekking, for which no previous experience at all is needed. However, only a few are well-organized, with guides, routes and places to stay worked out in advance. Among the best places are the Basotho Pony Trekking Centre (☏31 7284; see p.767), *Malealea Lodge* (☏051 447 3200; see p.781), and the *Semonkong Lodge* (☏051 933 3106; see p.766). You might also consider trying the *Trading Post Guest House* (☏34 0202; see p.765) in Roma, the *Molumong Lodge* (☏033 355 1141; see p.776) near Mokhotlong, and the *Mount Maluti Hotel* (☏78 5224; see p.783) in Mohale's Hoek.

Of the three most professional outfits, the Basotho Pony Trekking Centre is cheapest, at around M100 for a day ride, although there are reports of declining standards. At *Malealea* and *Semonkong*, a close watch is kept on the standard of both ponies and guides, which cost around M120 a day. One way to decide which place to go for is to first choose what kind of countryside you want to trek in. Semonkong, Mokhotlong and the area around the Basotho Pony Trekking Centre are all high up, above the sandstone and into the basalt (see box on p.768); most of the others are lower down, where weather conditions are usually less variable for you, though the terrain is harder on the ponies.

Wherever you go, make sure you bring a wide-brimmed sunhat, sun protection cream and waterproof gear, and, if you are staying somewhere overnight, a sleeping bag and mat, food, and something to cook it on. A luxury, but one you'll definitely appreciate, is some kind of balm to ease your aching limbs and buttocks, which will certainly be sore after a day's trekking, even if you are used to riding.

ing the one to Lesotho's most famous mountain, Thaba Bosiu, the so-called Mountain of the Night where the founder of the nation, Moshoeshoe I, ruled for almost fifty years.

Roma, less than 40km from Maseru along good roads, is the academic centre of the country, surrounded by beautiful sandstone hills and with an historic Catholic mission – the ascent from Roma into the Highlands to Semonkong, through several mountain passes, is one of the most striking in the country. **Semonkong** is famous for its mighty waterfalls, and you can visit another set, the **Ketane Falls**, by trekking westwards by pony from the delightful *Semonkong Lodge*.

Any car can manage the drive from Maseru along Lesotho's **central route** to the Basotho Pony Trekking Centre and the Mohale Dam construction site some way beyond. However, continuing further on over the epic **Central mountain range** requires a rugged vehicle that can handle the poor and rocky roads. Though the final destination of **Thaba Tseka** is unspectacular, the journey more than compensates, and from Thaba Tseka it is possible to continue along a reasonably good dirt road to Katse and its massive new dam (see p.777).

Maseru

Sprawling **MASERU**, the nation's capital and only big town, spills east from the Caledon River, which marks the border with South Africa. Maseru's older buildings, as well as some stylish new ones, are built from well-crafted local sandstone, now recognized as the town's vernacular building material, though a number of ill-thought-out concrete box buildings diminish the effect, and unfortunately dominate the skyline. Most of the daytime action happens on or around the Kingsway, the road which runs through town, getting more and more downmarket and lively as it heads east towards the cathedral. It is along Kingsway, particularly in the less-affluent sections further up town, where you will see the charred shells of shopping centres looted in the riots of 1998. Some were quickly demolished and redeveloped into bright, modern malls, but others provide a backdrop to lively street stalls and hawkers, who have undoubtedly profited from the demise of their more institutionalized competitors. The tension that brought about the riots has dissipated, and as long as you take the precautions you would in any other city on the continent, you can walk around here comfortably.

Maseru is only a short drive from some beautiful walking country, although the true splendours of the country lie further east and into the Highlands. The capital is also the only place where you can book for the Sehlabathebe National Park (see p.787). If you need to stock up on supplies, you should do so in Maseru before heading off elsewhere, although it's not great for souvenirs, lacking the craft selection of Teya-Teyaneng.

Some history

Maseru, which gets its name from the local sandstone from which it was first built, was established by the British as their administrative centre in 1869. Britain had annexed Basotholand, as it was then known, a year earlier (see p.750) and needed somewhere close to the Sotho royal stronghold of Thaba Bosiu that was relatively accessible from the Cape Colony.

Britain put as little effort into developing Maseru as it did the rest of the country, no doubt expecting it to become just a minor South African town

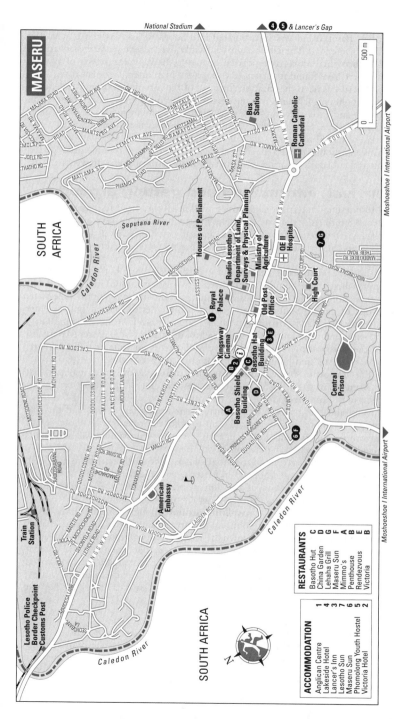

MASERU

National Stadium ▲   ▲ ❹,❺ & Lancer's Gap

SOUTH AFRICA

SOUTH AFRICA

Train Station

Lesotho Police Border Checkpoint Customs Post

Caledon River

Moshoeshoe I International Airport ▶

Moshoeshoe I International Airport ▶

Seputana River

Caledon River

Houses of Parliament

Radio Lesotho

Department of Land, Surveys & Physical Planning

Ministry of Agriculture

QE II Hospital

❶ Royal Palace

Kingsway Cinema

Basotho Hat Building

Old Post Office

High Court

❸ E

B ❷

ⓒ

Ⓓ

Basotho Shield Building

Ⓐ

❻ F

❼ G

Roman Catholic Cathedral

Bus Station

Central Prison

LESOTHO | Maseru

⓫

757

ACCOMMODATION
Anglican Centre	1
Lakeside Hotel	3
Lancer's Inn	4
Lesotho Sun	7
Maseru Sun	6
Phomolong Youth Hostel	5
Victoria Hotel	2

RESTAURANTS
Basotho Hut	C
China Garden	D
Lehaha Grill	G
Maseru Sun	F
Mimmo's	A
Penthouse	B
Rendezvous	E
Victoria	B

500 m

0

when Basotholand was incorporated into South Africa – which is what the British intended. The city has grown swiftly over recent years, the poverty in Lesotho's rural areas having driven people to the capital in search of a better life. Few have found it yet, and the city has a high unemployment rate.

Maseru has been the location for most of the turbulence of post-independence politics, including two successful coups and several more unsuccessful ones – and, most recently, the serious disturbances following the disputed elections in 1998. However, the ensuing destruction is fast being cleared up and Maseru has all the marks of an upwardly mobile African city, with slick fashions and mobile phones much in evidence – even if they're sometimes spotted alongside blanket-wearing villagers and the occasional horse-drawn cart.

Arrival, information and getting around

Moshoeshoe I international **airport** is 18km southeast of Maseru off the Main Road South (A2); there are frequent, inexpensive minibus taxis and buses (less than M10) into town during the day and early evening (arrivals and departures, ☎35 0418). Private taxis are available, but cost considerably more (around M40).

Public transport is chaotic and crazily unregulated, but does at least go everywhere in the country from Maseru, invariably cheaply. There are no **train** connections to Maseru; the nearest station is in Bloemfontein in the Free State. None of the big South African bus companies goes to Maseru, but there are always the daily **minibus taxis**, which travel from Johannesburg, Bloemfontein and Durban, as well as a host of smaller places nearer Maseru. All of them stop at the border, which you must cross on your own. From there, you can easily find public transport into the centre of town.

The **Lesotho tourist information office** (Mon–Fri 8am–5pm, Sat 8.30am–1pm; ☎31 9485) lies at the western end of the town centre, on Kingsway near the *Victoria Hotel*. Although it's under-resourced, the staff are helpful and can give you a town map, flyers from a few resorts and the odd glossy brochure, and reasonably up-to-date information on hotel costs. Lesotho's tourism structures are in a fairly constant state of upheaval, and there's regular talk of relocating the tourist office.

If you're planning on a visit to the Sehlabathebe National Park (see p.787), you'll need to arrange bookings in Maseru; contact either the tourist office or Sehlabathebe Reservations at the Ministry of Agriculture, 82 Constitution Rd, PO Box 24, Maseru 100 (☎31 6407, ✉agric@ilesotho.com).

Maseru is small enough for **walking around**, though some accommodation is too far to reach easily on foot, and the streets can be risky after dark. Plenty of **minibus taxis** go up and down the Kingsway and off into semi-urban areas, with each journey costing under M2. Otherwise, there are a few **taxi** companies you can try (see "Listings", p.761). **Driving** is straightforward in town, though often slow. Bear in mind that the Kingsway becomes a one-way street in the direction of the border from 7 to 9am each weekday morning. For **car rental** see p.761.

Accommodation

Maseru is the only place in the country where there's much choice of **accommodation**, offering everything from camping and grim dorms to luxury suites in plush hotels. The central options, on or near the Kingsway, are the most practical if you don't have your own transport.

Anglican Centre On the corner of Assisi and Lancers roads ☎ 32 2046. A large and fairly institutionalized centre reasonably close to the Kingsway, though tricky to find; it's principally used by church groups and visiting volunteers, but travellers can book into the spartan but adequate double rooms with communal showers and toilets. Normally closed for one month from mid-December. Ask for Mrs Mokoena if you want to stay. ❶

Lakeside Hotel Off Main Road North ☎ 31 3646. A big, ugly, brick building on the edge of an industrial estate, though the rooms are OK, with en-suite bath, soft mattresses and TVs with M-Net. The restaurant does solid and inexpensive meals, but the hotel's main attraction is its occasional choral music shows and competitions. Turn right off Main Road North at the junction marked for Mafeteng, and the hotel is 100m further on the left. ❷

Lancers Inn Kingsway ☎ 31 2114, ℱ 31 0223. A very central, pleasant, sandstone building that escaped burning in the 1998 riots but was looted bare. The renovations are impressive and tasteful, and with comfortable rondavels and chalets with en-suite bath, grassy areas and a pool, this is probably Maseru's most characterful and pleasant place to stay. There's also a good beer garden and restaurant. ❹

Lesotho Sun Off Nightingale Road, behind the QEII Hospital (☎ 31 3111, ℱ 31 0104). The smartest hotel in town, accommodating visiting dignitaries and wealthy businessmen. It has comfortable, if smallish, rooms with TVs and all sorts of sports facilities, a pool, casino, cinema, and one of the best restaurants in town. ❻

Maseru Sun Orpen Road ☎ 31 2434, ℱ 31 0158. The second of the town's two ageing Sun hotels, with decent, though box-like, rooms, in soothing well-tended garden surroundings that are popular with locals in the evening. There's a good restaurant, and also slot machines. ❺–❻

Phomolong Youth Hostel Lancers Gap Road ☎ 33 2900. Some way out of town, offering battered dorms with ancient mattresses. You can use the spartan kitchen, but meals are only provided for groups, and the doors close at 10pm. Take the Lancers Gap turn off Main Road North and carry on for 2.5km, where it's on the right in a low building surrounded by a fence. Not recommended unless you run out of alternatives. ❶

Victoria Hotel Kingsway ☎ 31 2922, ℱ 31 0318. This plain concrete high-rise hotel is a prominent city landmark offering unremarkable but reasonable rooms, a popular dining room and bar with a terrace attached, from which you can watch Maseru go by beneath you. ❹

The City

With little of architectural merit appearing from Maseru's recent rush of new building, the city's most famous landmark is still the appropriately shaped **Basotho Hat Building**, which stands on the corner of Kingsway and Orpen Road, opposite the *Victoria Hotel*. During the 1998 riots, the thatched roof of the original building made a spectacular bonfire, but a replacement was quickly erected, this time with room for an upstairs restaurant and balcony café as well as the established craft shop on the ground floor. A little way east along the Kingsway, you'll find more crafts, mostly woven grass Sotho hats, sold on the pavements outside the tourist office, though further down Orpen Road there's a more upmarket selection at Mohair Cottage, a foyer boutique in the *Maseru Sun*. See p.771 for more on Lesotho's craft industry.

Walking from the Basotho Hat Building up the Kingsway, into the main part of town, look out for the Alliance Française in the interesting old sandstone library, corner of Pioneer and Kingsway, and the former Anglican church in a scruffy park area in front of *Lancers Inn* on your right, and then, to the left, the striking **Post Office**, ready evidence of Maseru's intention to create an image of being a thoroughly modern African capital. Nearby are a number of single-storey sandstone buildings, many dating from the end of the last century, though few are treated with much veneration. A little further up on the left, it's worth pausing to look at the old **Resident Commissioner's House**, now a government department, built in sandstone in 1891 and now restored, making it one of Maseru's finest buildings once again. Across the road, look out for one of the world's very few prefabricated national libraries. The large Queen

Elizabeth II Hospital is a short distance further up, also on the right. From here on the Kingsway is busier, its low-priced shops thronged by shoppers, and informal traders touting everything from Sotho fast food to cutlery made of galvanized iron. In a new **mall** on the left-hand side, just past the Sales House store, the Lesotho Blanket Company sells the best-priced Sotho blankets (see p.771) in Lesotho, while J's Music Bar, next door, has the widest selection of Sotho and South African music cassettes in town.

The Kingsway comes to an end at the traffic circle by the impressively large, though architecturally unremarkable, **Roman Catholic Cathedral**, and splits into Main Road North and Main Road South. Continue along Main Road North, turning right a few kilometres further on to reach Lancers Gap (see p.762), where the particularly striking mountain pass has good views over the town.

Eating, drinking and nightlife

As you'd expect from the capital, Maseru has a better selection of **restaurants** than anywhere else in Lesotho. There's a range of familiar chain takeaways along Kingsway, including *KFC* and *Steers*, as well as plenty of inexpensive informal daytime takeaways and **snacks** to be had there and around the bus station. One place not to miss is the bakery beside *Lancers Inn*, where you can get delicious, freshly baked loaves, muffins and other treats. **Nightlife** is considerably more limited, though if you're just after a drink or two, there are plenty of hotel bars.

Restaurants

Basotho Hut Basotho Hat Building, Kingsway. For now the most glamorous restaurant in Maseru, on the upper floor of the famous landmark. The fairly pricey full menu includes steaks; you can also sit on the balcony for a lighter terrace menu.

China Garden Orpen Road ☏ 31 3915. A reasonably priced Chinese menu in a setting of faded opulence, but the food can take ages to appear on the table. Closed Sun.

Lehaha Grill *Lesotho Sun*, off Nightingale Road. A busy restaurant serving a tasty but somewhat pricey range of continental dishes.

Maseru Sun Orpen Road. A choice of buffet or a la carte, with the buffet probably the better and certainly the healthier bet.

Mimmos Maseru Club, UN Road. Serves decent pizzas and filling pastas popular with the expat community.

Penthouse *Victoria Hotel*, Kingsway. Right at the top of the hotel, with a bird's-eye view of the town, serving respectable Italian dishes, grills and seafood amidst great splurges of faded velvet decor. Closed Sat lunchtime & Sun.

Rendezvous *Lancers Inn*, Kingsway. Impressively renovated after the riots, with an African-themed, moderately priced menu. The outdoor seating is justifiably popular at lunchtimes and early evening.

Victoria *Victoria Hotel*, Kingsway. Unexciting meaty fare and pizzas are served at this spacious restaurant, which is usually busy in the evening. It's best visited when they serve curries (Mon) and traditional Sotho dishes (Wed afternoon).

Bars and nightlife

Maseru's **bars** are almost all attached to hotels or restaurants, with those at the *Victoria* and *Lancers* being among the most cheerful. If you want to drink in more typically Sotho surroundings, you need to head out of the town centre and make for any of the numerous informal bars scattered about the outskirts of town,

Maseru's **nightclub** options are limited to *Club G* (Thurs–Sun 9pm–late) under the *Victoria Hotel*, where Maseru's youth strut their stuff until the early hours. Otherwise, a **cinema** at the *Lesotho Sun* screens mostly action movies (☏31 3111), and there are one or two **jazz clubs** away from the centre, though you'll need to get a knowledgeable local to take you there.

If you're heading out of Maseru, orientation is fairly easy, as both **Main Road North** (A1) and **Main Road South** (A2), the two major roads out of town, begin life at the cathedral traffic circle, which is at the eastern end of Kingsway. There are a few fuel stations scattered along both for their first few kilometres. Public transport from Maseru to the rest of the country runs from the bus station off the Main Road North; just after the cathedral traffic circle, turn left into Pitso Road and you cannot fail to miss the huge sprawl in front of you. Rather than trying to work out the method in the madness, just ask around for where buses and minibuses to your destination currently run from. Many of the services to towns south of Maseru congregate a little way along the Main Road South.

Listings

Airlines Mission Aviation Fellowship ☏ 31 3640; SA Airlink, in Jo'burg ☏ 011 978 1111.
Airport Moshoeshoe I international airport ☏ 35 0418 or 0419.
Banks Main branches of Lesotho Bank, Nedbank and Standard Bank are on Kingsway.
Books The best of Maseru's small range of bookshops, called simply The Book Centre, is on Kingsway, just past the Lesotho Bank.
Car rental Avis, at the airport ☏ 31 4325 or 35 0328; Budget ☏ 31 6344.
Emergencies Ambulance ☏ 121; Fire ☏ 122; Police ☏ 123.
Hospitals Queen Elizabeth II Hospital, Kingsway ☏ 31 2501; Maseru Private Hospital, Thetsane Road ☏ 31 3260.
Internet facilities LEO (Lesotho Office Equipment), Orpen Road (Mon–Fri 8am–5pm; ☏ 32 2772); CBS in post office building (Mon–Fri 8am–5pm, Sat 8am–1pm).

Libraries American Cultural Centre, Options Building, Pioneer Road; British Council, corner of Kingsway and Lerotholi Road ☏ 31 2609; National Library, Kingsway.
Post office The grand new post office is prominent on Kingsway, and is open Mon–Fri 8am–4.30pm, Sat 8am–noon. Lesotho stamps are famous and highly prized; contact the philatelic bureau on the first floor here.
Radio A nearby transmitter provides Maseru with good evening reception for the BBC World Service at 90.2FM.
Swimming pool The pool at the *Maseru Sun* is normally open to non-residents. Check with reception and expect to pay around M10.
Taxis Max Taxis ☏ 32 5935; Moonlight Taxis ☏ 31 2695; Planet Taxis ☏ 31 7777; Silver Star ☏ 31 1603.
Travel agents Afric-Go-Tours ☏ 32 5367; Execu Travel ☏ 32 5113; UCS, *Victoria Hotel* ☏ 532 3706.

Around Maseru

Although you're unlikely to spend much of your time in Lesotho in Maseru itself, there are a number of rewarding places to visit within easy reach of the capital. A short excursion walkable from central Maseru is the ridge with three peaks known as the **Word, the Flesh and the Devil**, while **Lancers Gap** and the **Qeme Plateau** are further out of town, but as a result offer views over the city and its surrounding countryside. A little oddly in a country so dominated by towering mountain ranges, it is two of the smaller hills, **Thaba Bosiu**, Moshoeshoe I's impregnable hilltop fortress, and nearby **Qiloane**, model for the Basotho hat, which are the most famous, ranking as the most important historical sites in the country.

The Word, the Flesh and the Devil

Starting behind the *Lesotho Sun* hotel is an easily accessible climb to the three peaks, which were a favoured hangout for snipers during the Gun War (see p.752). Walk between the fences separating the hotel and Friebel Houses, and straight up the hill past a succession of large boulders. After less than twenty minutes, you'll reach the northernmost peak, the Word, where there's a survey beacon and excellent views of Maseru and the distant mountains. From here you can walk along the ridge to the other two peaks, the Flesh and then the Devil, though neither provide such good views.

Lancers Gap

Lancers Gap is an extraordinary ridge a short distance east from town, with a great gap in the middle through which the road passes, so named because a Lancers regiment was allegedly ambushed and defeated there during the Gun War. In fact, the regiment was ambushed somewhere else, but it doesn't really matter, as this is still a great place to scramble around and look out both on Maseru and the mountains to the east. To get there, take the Main Road North from Maseru, and turn right at the Lancers Gap turn. The ridge is a few kilometres further along, up a very steep incline which you ascend along a good-quality hairpin bend road.

Qeme Plateau

The large T-shaped **Qeme Plateau**, which measures over 25 square kilometres, and provides superb vistas into the Free State and east into Lesotho, is only a few kilometres south of Maseru, near the South African border. The usual way to get there is by going along the Main Road South as far as Mantsebo, turning right at the crossroads, then turning left after a Fraser's Store. Leave your transport there, look out for a diagonal line climbing the plateau from left to right and make for this. You soon hit a footpath which takes you to the top; there and back takes three or four hours.

Alternatively, take United Nations Road (the new ringroad, accessible from Kingsway along Pioneer Road) out of Maseru, and follow it until you meet the rise of Qeme. Here, a right turn along a dirt road heading towards Mokhalinyane takes you through beautiful countryside along the western part of the plateau. Look out for a cleft in the plateau's ridge, and park at its foot at the village of Ha Mapholo. Leaving your car here is quite safe. Walk through the village and make for the cleft; you'll find that the first part of the climb is pretty obvious, but two-thirds of the way up you'll need either inspired guess-work or the help of one of the many herd boys who are usually clambering around here with their cows and goats. The climb there and back takes about two hours.

Once at the top, the boulders and grasslands make for an excellent stroll and picnic spot, albeit not much else. Make sure you've left yourself enough time to get back down before dark. From Ha Mapholo, you can either return the way you came or carry on a few kilometres, at which point the road improves, finally taking you to Main Road South just north of Morija.

Thaba Bosiu

Thaba Bosiu is Lesotho's most important historical sight, a steep mountain with a large flat top about 20km east of Maseru that was the capital of the kingdom in the days of Moshoeshoe I. Although it has been declared a World Heritage Site by UNESCO, nothing has yet been done to develop it, and there's not that much to see once you reach the top. However, it is a place of great significance to the people of Lesotho, and the burial ground of the country's kings, and as such is well worth a visit.

Moshoeshoe I trekked with his followers to Thaba Bosiu in 1824, in a bid to settle somewhere far from the warrior clans then terrorizing the flat plains to the north and west, and somewhere that would be extremely hard for anyone to capture. Thaba Bosiu, with its good grazing and seven or eight freshwater springs on top, fitted the bill, although it wasn't long before warrior clans, including Afrikaner ones, found their way here – although none was able to take the mountain, which has earned it, and Moshoeshoe, a good deal of mystique.

The name means "Mountain of the Night", perhaps because, as the legend has it, Moshoeshoe first arrived there at night. A more compelling reason, and the one most Sotho prefer, is that the mountain, which does not look particularly high or impressive by day, seems to grow inexorably as night falls, becoming huge and unconquerable, before slipping back to more hill-like normality during the daytime.

Taking Thaba Bosiu

Fresh from conquering much of the flat land east of the Caledon in 1828, the Ngwane were the first to attack **Thaba Bosiu**, but were decisively beaten, after which they never troubled **Moshoeshoe** again. The mixed-race Kora people also harried Thaba Bosiu in 1831, often capturing and enslaving the villagers living beneath it, but always driven off the mountain proper by Moshoeshoe's warriors. **Mzilikhazi**, King of the Ndebele, who later conquered much of modern-day Zimbabwe, tried to take the mountain the same year, but his men were defeated by the mass of great boulders flung down from the top by the Sotho; Moshoeshoe is reputed to have sent the Ndebele a large number of fat oxen after their defeat, an unprecedented move for a victorious chief – as if to say that he understood that their attack had been inspired by hunger and that he wanted to help them out. At any rate, Mzilikhazi never came back that way.

There followed a twenty-year period of relative calm, during which time Moshoeshoe would receive visitors wearing a beautifully tailored dark-blue military uniform, complete with cloak, and offer them tea from a prized china tea service. He allowed the French missionary, Eugene Casalis, to establish a mission at the bottom of the mountain in 1837, and employed him as his secretary and interpreter. In 1852, a British punitive force led by the Cape governor, Sir George Cathcart, didn't even make it as far as the mountain, instead being attacked a short distance away by a well-armed mass of Moshoeshoe's troops, who forced their hasty withdrawal. Afrikaner forces fighting for the Orange Free State (OFS) made a brief attempt on Thaba Bosiu in 1858, but came back in 1865 in a more determined manner, armed with heavy artillery and began steadily shelling the mountain, launching two simultaneous assaults a few days later. Eight men made it to the top, but were seriously wounded as soon as they did so, and speedily retreated back down. A week later, more Afrikaner troops and the OFS president turned up, and another assault was launched. General Wepener led his men right to the top of the Khubelu Pass, but he was shot at the top and mortally wounded. The Sotho then pressed a counter-attack, and the Afrikaner forces withdrew. They continued the siege for a month, though, during which time most of the livestock on Thaba Bosiu died of hunger and the Sotho became so short of bullets that they melted down the shells being fired at them to make homemade ones.

Although they won this battle, the Sotho lost the war, and Moshoeshoe signed a humiliating treaty in 1866 which surrendered most of Lesotho's farmland to the OFS. Four years later, the old king died and was buried on the top of Thaba Bosiu. Since then, every Sotho king has been buried there, including the latest to die, Moshoeshoe II, in 1996.

There is a **tourist information** building (daily 8.30am–4pm) at the foot of the mountain, where you are charged a small fee for information leaflets and an official guide who will show you around. He takes you up the **Khubelu Pass**, a cleft in the cliffs marked by two flagpoles, where the Afrikaner General Louw Wepener was killed trying to storm the mountain in 1865 (see box on p.763), past the rock where Sotho warriors used to watch out for approaching enemy forces and to the remains of Moshoeshoe's European house, built for him by army deserters living on the mountain top. From there, it's a short walk to the slight remains of Moshoeshoe's royal court and then to the royal grave-yard. The tombs of Moshoeshoe I and most of his successors are marked with simple stone cairns, except the latest, of Moshoeshoe II, who was killed in a car crash in 1996, which is a more elaborate affair, adorned with plastic flowers.

To the east of the mountain, you get a great view of Qiloane, a strange cone-shaped mountain with a large nodule on the top, which apparently was the inspiration for the national headdress, the distinctive Basotho Hat. Around the other side of the mountain, is a kind of cave village where the royal household used to hide during attacks, but which were occupied and decorated with rock paintings by the San who lived there before them. A guide who usually hangs around the Khubelu Pass can take you to them, and include a visit to the traditional healer (*sangoma*) who lives in one of the caves. The caves are about a four-kilometre drive from the Khubelu Pass, followed by a short walk.

Practicalities

To get to Thaba Bosiu **by car**, take the Main Road South, turning right where Thaba Bosiu is signposted. Follow this road through a dip down into a riverbed where the road is temporarily untarred, and all the way to a T-junction. Turn left at the junction and Thaba Bosiu is about 3km further along on the right. During the day, a number of **minibus taxis** run between here and the main bus station in Maseru.

There is good **accommodation** next to the mountain at the *Mmelesi Lodge* (☎35 7215 or 35 7216, ℱ31 2369; ❷), probably the best-run Basotho-owned lodge in the country. Though often used for government conferences and more used by civil servants than travellers, it has a plush bar and pleasant restaurant serving moderately priced meat and fish dishes, along with comfortable ron-davels out the back with en-suite bathrooms.

Roma and Semonkong

Southeast of Maseru, the historic Catholic mission and university town of **Roma** is worth a stop, and the road from here to the town of **Semonkong** is an epic drive through the sandstone and stunning basalt peaks of the Thaba Pusoa range of the Lesotho Highlands, past a succession of remote and relaxed-looking villages filled with Lesotho's characteristic dry-stone-walled rondavels. The road ends at Semonkong, which offers the *Semonkong Lodge*, one of the best places to stay in the country, and only a short distance away are the spectacular Semonkong (LeBihan) Falls, which crash down from nearly 200m to the Maletsunyane River below.

Roma

About 30km from Maseru along a good road, the mission town of **ROMA** has a beautiful location in strangely sculpted sandstone foothills and is home to the unlovely campus of the **University of Lesotho**, which began life as Pius XII College, run by the Roman Catholic Church. Between 1964 and 1971 it was the university of all three of the former British southern African protectorates, now Lesotho, Botswana and Swaziland. Here you can also buy phonecards and make use of their public phone boxes, which are rare in Lesotho, but there's not much to see on campus. A kilometre or so further up the road from the university, past a succession of schools and colleges, is **Roma Mission**, most of which was built in 1862. Though its towers and exterior detail make it grander than its evangelical counterpart in Morija (see p.779), the mission is still a little run-down these days, and there's not much reason to linger – although its extension to accommodate the grave of one Father Gerard is a classic of Catholic kitsch. Father Gerard was a founder member of the Mission and celebrated for restoring a young girl's sight through prayer, for which he has recently and posthumously been beatified (he died in 1940).

Practicalities

Several **buses** and many more **minibus taxis** travel daily between Maseru and Roma, making this one of the busiest public transport routes in the country. The journey costs M5–10 whichever means you use. Once you're here, the Mission will reluctantly put you up if you beg them, but the best **accommodation** is undoubtedly at the *Trading Post Guest House* (☎34 0202, or 082 773 2180, ⊜tradingpost@leo.co.ls; ❶) at the western end of Roma. Built in 1903 as a trading store by the Thorn family, this self-catering guesthouse has been lived in by them ever since. You can camp, stay in rondavels, or in the house itself. They've added a swimming pool and can arrange pony trekking (M15 an hour) in the surrounding sandstone hills. To get there, look out for a sign on the right of the main road as you enter Roma from the Maseru side, marked "*Manonyane High School*" and the "*Trading Post*," and continue 100m up the dirt road.

The only place to **eat** in Roma is the accurately named *Speak Easy Liquor Restaurant*, opposite the university and used mainly by students. It serves inexpensive, good-value food that you can wash down with a spectacular selection of alcoholic beverages that far surpasses anywhere in Maseru for choice. Right next door is the last place you can buy **fuel** before Semonkong.

Semonkong and around

The road from Roma to Semonkong is one of the most spectacular in Lesotho, with superb views as you climb into the Highlands. Where the tarred road turns to gravel at Moitsupeli, look ahead towards the twin summits of the appropriately named **Thabana liMele** (Breast Mountains). The northern summit is climbable without special equipment, if you can find the cleft on its northern side. Just park at the next village of **Ha Dinzulu**, let people know where you are going, cross the Makhalaneng River and make your way up as far as you can. If you make it to the top, it's about seven hours there and back.

The road from Ha Dinzulu continues to climb, peaking at 2000m on Nkesi's Pass and then dropping down to the village of Ramabanta; here you can cross the Makhalaneng River and then drive up to 3000m by Thaba Putsoa itself, before descending gently to the curiously straggly town of **SEMONKONG**. Inhabited only by the San until the 1880s, Semonkong began life after the Gun War as a refuge for displaced Sotho from the lowlands. The town offers a few basic stores, plenty of **bars** stocking a remarkable selection of beers and ciders, and even a post office and bank, though you can't rely on either for vital business. The roads in town are bad but not impassable, and it's worth going to the

Dongas and soil erosion in Lesotho

Travelling around in Lesotho's scarred and treeless landscape, it's hard to believe that the country was once the grain basket of the region. Yet, during the nineteenth century, the kingdom exported food to the neighbouring Orange Free State (OFS) and to Kimberley and the Rand to feed the thousands of diamond- and gold-mine workers. The problems began with the expropriation of the best land by the OFS in the 1860s, which forced the Sotho to start farming hilly areas that had previously only been used for winter grazing. This process continues to this day, and you will even see crops being grown at over 2000m in districts like Semonkong and Mokhotlong. Mountains are no substitute for fertile plains, however, and Lesotho has been a net importer of food since the 1920s.

The ecological effect of the sustained and unrelenting cultivation of the Lesotho mountains has been devastating. The soil fertility has plummeted and, more seriously, huge quantities of topsoil are simply washed away with each summer rains, often ending up as silt in the rivers of the Eastern Cape. In many places, so much topsoil has gone that great ravines called **dongas** have opened up. These, though they often look green enough, in fact tend to be so close to the surface rock that they are useless for serious cultivation.

Efforts have been underway to slow this process for some time, most noticeably through the neat terracing of fields set on hillsides, with layers of grass interspersed with the crops. For one of the best examples of how simply *dongas* can be filled in or reclaimed, ask to be shown the way to the Musi family *donga* in the village beside *Malealea Lodge* (see p.781). It's not difficult to spot – on a hillside of degraded cropland and bare earth, it's an oasis of fertility, lush greenness and birdlife.

ubiquitous Fraser's Store just to check out the Wild West-style clientele, dressed mostly in blankets and gumboots, with their ponies hitched to a post at the entrance. If you're here in winter, try to catch the local **horse races** on the last weekend of every month.

Practicalities

Semonkong is about a four-hour **drive** in a car from Maseru; there are a couple of **buses** daily (around 6hr). If you miss the bus, you can always get public transport to Roma and then a minibus taxi from there, though these stop running by mid-afternoon. Alternatively, you can organize a **flight** from Maseru to the airstrip in town with the Mission Aviation Fellowship (T31 3640).

The place to **stay** here is the excellent *Fraser's Semonkong Lodge* (T051 933 3106, Wwww.placeofsmoke.co.ls; ❶–❷), tucked in a cut in the river valley on the outskirts of town. One of the best lodges in Lesotho, this laid-back but well-run place offers cosy doubles, a bunkhouse, camping sites and good facilities. There's a great bar area with a pool table and a decent selection of music, tasty meals are available (you can also self-cater) and you can organize local trips, including **pony trekking** for about M110 per day, guided hiking with a packhorse for about M80 per day, and overnight stays in villages. Unusually for accommodation outside Maseru, the lodge accepts some credit cards.

Around Semonkong: Ketane and Semonkong Falls

From Semonkong, it's a day's walk or pony trek west (see above) over some pretty high mountains to the pristine 120-metre **Ketane Falls**. The falls are inaccessible by any other means of transport, and the pony trek is considered one of the best in the country. They can also be visited on a popular four-day pony trek from *Malealea Lodge* (see p.781).

Rather easier to reach are the **Semonkong Falls**, a pretty five-kilometre walk from town through the maize fields and grazings that adorn the banks of the Maletsunyane River, though the path is slippery in parts. It's possible to drive, but you risk getting your car broken into if you go down to the bottom. Also known as the LeBihan Falls, after the French missionary who was the first European to see them, the dramatic Semonkong (Smoking Water) Falls drop nearly 200m down a sheer and scary cliff surrounded on all sides by natural vantage points, into an exotic and swimmable pool. The best views are from the plateau facing the falls – for such a spectacular and well-known sight, it's quite refreshing to feel yourself entirely surrounded by nature with no man-made facilities whatsoever, not even a car park, impinging on the experience. There's a path down to the bottom which takes three or four hours there and back, though it's well worth the journey, particularly if you fancy the swim, or if you want to camp. The water at the foot of the falls usually freezes by June, but the waterfall keeps going all winter, spraying the surrounding rocks with ice and forming an impressive ice cage over the pool. At other times of year, you can look out for birds such as the bald ibis or lammergeier soaring in the vast chasm which frames the falls.

The road to Thaba Tseka

Beyond the turn to Roma, the central A3 road runs over Lesotho's Central mountain range to the small district capital of Thaba Tseka, 175km from Maseru, and the countryside changes from cultivated lowlands to more sparsely populated mountains.

The small village of **NAZARETH** is the first settlement along this route. Here you'll find the *Tollgate Caravan and Camping Park* (☎37 0206), the only official campsite in the country, but there's little happening here and the surrounding scenery is easily surpassed by what comes later. A few kilometres north of Nazareth are what were once some of the finest rock paintings in the country at **Ha Baroana**. The paintings are still impressive, with clearly discernible figures of animals, dancers and hunters, but they have been vandalized and washed away by child guides who throw water at them to make them clearer for tourists. To get to the paintings, either walk or drive 3km north along a difficult dirt road to Ha Matela and walk the last 4km from there, or drive up the next turn to the left, also along a bad road, which takes you straight to the site.

After Nazareth, the main road then ascends steeply into the mountains through the 2268-metre-high **Bushman's Pass**. Along the way you may see young boys trying to sell lumps of quartzite and, more worryingly, Lesotho's national flower, the protected and rare spiral aloe. Don't be tempted to purchase one, as it will only sustain the market in these unique plants – if you haven't seen one, you'd be much better off hiking into the mountains and finding one in the wild. A short while after the pass you find the ageing *Molimo Nthuse Lodge* (☎37 0211, ⓕ31 0318; ❶), attractively perched by a stream in a tight fold in the surrounding hills. It's a comfortable place to stay, particularly good if you're interested in trout fishing or hikes in the surrounding hills, though the moderately priced meals are rather mediocre.

The lodge is a useful stopping-off point if you're on your way to the **Basotho Pony Trekking Centre** (☎31 7284), a short distance further up the road (2hr by bus from Maseru, less by car). One of Lesotho's original trekking centres, it's

Sandstone and basalt

Lesotho is the only country in the world that lies entirely above an altitude of 1000m, earning its name "the mountain kingdom". The Lesotho lowlands would be highlands anywhere else, and are made of **sandstone**. Right across the country, at about 1400m, the sandstone gives way to **basalt**, a dark grey rock thrown up by volcanic eruptions several million years ago. Roughly marking the beginning of the Lesotho Highlands, basalt is a hard rock that resists erosion, unlike the sandstone, which has been carved by the wind over the millennia into an infinite variety of shapes that have turned the hills into the kingdom's natural sculptures.

still about the least expensive place to pony trek in the country, with a two-day/one-night trek costing only M125 per person, plus M10 for overnight accommodation. However, it's not as efficiently run as other places in Lesotho, and you are advised to book a ride here – casual visitors may find the place deserted. As usual, you need to bring all your supplies with you. A shorter trek, and also suitable for hiking (2hr each way), is to the impressive Qiloane Falls on the Makhaleng River, due north of the *Lodge* and Trekking Centre; the latter can provide information and directions.

The road carries on from here over the epic **Blue Mountain Pass**, more than 2600m high, which offers commanding views of the surrounding mountains, though the views are even better if you climb the hills on either side. From there, the road descends into the village of **Likalaneng**, now dominated by the offices, shops and houses servicing the nearby **Mohale Dam**, the second phase of the Lesotho Highlands Water Project (see p.778). When the project is completed in 2004, water will flow by gravity from the dam down a forty-kilometre delivery tunnel to the Katse Dam. For now, however, there isn't much to see apart from heavy construction lorries and rows of new housing. For a good view of the progress of construction on the dam wall, take a left turn after the village, out towards the control building set prominently on a long spur of hillside.

Now a dirt road, the route rises once more to the village of **Marakabei** on the banks of the Senqunyane River. There is a pleasant lodge here which has been closed in recent years, but is due to reopen sometime in 2002. You can buy fuel at Marakabei, and also at **Mantsonyane**, about 20km further east, where there are also a few take-away restaurants serving Sotho dishes, and some sparsely filled trading stores. This is as far as you can safely go in a car without high clearance; if you want to press on further, there are buses going on to Thaba Tseka.

Thaba Tseka

The road into **THABA TSEKA** is a dramatic one, peaking in the heart of the Central mountain range at the Mokhoabong Pass (2880m) before descending to the town, which is over 2200m above sea level. Once here, though, you may wonder why you made the effort, as there is very little in this 1980s purpose-built administrative centre except buses to take you somewhere else. If you need somewhere to stay, try the *Mountain Star Hotel*, a locally owned place mostly used by civil servants and local contract workers. Otherwise, cheaper but more spartan accommodation is available at the self-catering *Agricultural Training Centre* (☎90 0304; ❶), a long prefabricated building that's often full during the week. The only restaurant in town is the very basic affair at the *Mountain Star Hotel*, though there are one or two stores in the centre of the town serving Sotho food to take away. There's no road south to Semonkong and the Sehlabathebe National Park, though there are hikeable trails (for maps, see 'box' on p.753). There's a spectacular road to Mokhotlong and Sani Pass from Thaba Tseka, but it's not one you should tackle in anything other than a 4WD vehicle.

The road to Katse is much better and, although you still shouldn't attempt it in an ordinary saloon car, there are a number of buses plying the route. From Katse there's a perfect tarred road to Hlotse in the north (see p.777). Otherwise, your only option is to go back the way you came, towards Maseru.

The northern districts

The route north from Maseru right the way round to Sani Pass takes in the best of both Lesotho's lowlands and highlands, from the wind-carved sandstone hills on the way to **Teya-Teyaneng**, a hill town famed for its woven crafts, to the epic mountain passes of the "Roof of Africa route" that runs from **Butha-Buthe** to the ramshackle town of **Mokhotlong** and on to Sani. There are a number of intriguing, out-of-the-way sights along the way, like the remarkable **cave houses** at Mateka, the **rock art** at Lipofung and the winter **skiing** runs near Oxbow. You'll find plenty of reasonable places to stay (though some take a little finding), particularly in the Highlands, where a succession of well-located lodges make perfect bases for hiking in the surrounding mountain countryside. A new attraction is the **Katse reservoir**, completed in 1997, which collects water from Lesotho's south-flowing rivers, thanks to a 185-metre dam wall. The road from Butha-Buthe is tarred all the way to Mokhotlong, deep amongst Lesotho's (and southern Africa's) highest mountains. A dirt road leads to the **Sani Pass**, a dramatic winding road down the western reaches of the mighty Drakensberg into South Africa.

Maseru to Hlotse

While most travellers speed through en route to the more spectacular Highlands, the lowland stretch between Maseru and Hlotse nonetheless offers a number of attractions. The caves at **Mateka** are the most fascinating in Lesotho and well worth a special trip, and the woven crafts in **Teya-Teyaneng** (the town is widely referred to simply as T.Y.) are of superb quality and design. The busy town of **Hlotse** has less of interest, but nearby is one of the largest collections of **dinosaur footprints** in the country.

There are two good roads from Maseru to Teya-Teyaneng. The most commonly used is the scenic **Main Road North**, which takes you through sandstone mountain-studded lowlands. Only a few kilometres after leaving Maseru, you'll come to the hexagonal, red-roofed *Palace Hotel* (☎86 4905; ❷), whose rooms have opulent beds and decent bathrooms, but the communal balconies make the rooms less secure than they should be. The hotel restaurant serves steaks, chops and fish for moderate prices. The *Galaxy Nightclub* next door opens on Fridays and Saturdays till late, and fills up when there's something special on. From the hotel, it's only an hour's drive to T.Y., though it takes a little longer by bus.

A good alternative to the Main Road North is the **Sefikeng Road**. Follow the Main Road North out of Maseru, and turn right after a short distance at the sign to Lancers Gap and Sefikeng; you soon find yourself on the Berea plateau, from where you can look down on the lowlands to your left. Strangely, there's a missing link in the tar roads at Sefikeng: when you come into the village, turn left at the Paradise General Dealer, head along a short patch of dirt track, and then join the tar road towards Mateka.

Mateka

Getting to **MATEKA** by public transport or hitching is possible, but requires considerable patience. If you're driving, leave your car at Mateka, and enlist one of the many children usually hanging around to take you on the half-hour walk down the hill to the cave houses. The seven inhabited **cave houses** here have been sculpted out of mud under a huge rock overhang, and look more like igloos or West African mud architecture than anything usually found in southern Africa. Their laid-back residents don't mind you taking photographs, or simply goggling at what are the best-kept architectural secrets in the country.

Due to the deaths of the chief and chief's son who were running it, the *Teng Lodge*, signposted from Mateka, is not officially open. However, if you make the tricky eight-kilometre journey here, across a seemingly impassable river (wade in first to check the depth, and take it at speed) and some dodgy stretches of dirt road, the new chief (who is the old chief's wife) will let you stay there for a donation, and send someone round to bring you hot water in the morning. You'll stay in a lovely rondavel looking out onto the Berea Mountains, but bring candles, food and cooking gear as the lodge has none of these. The chief can also provide a guide to take you to some remarkable, unvandalized San rock paintings about an hour's walk away, through gentle hills, maize fields and charmingly secluded villages.

Once you are back in Mateka, it's only a half-hour drive to T.Y. on a good tarred road. Travelling under your own steam, you'll find the occasional minibus taxi or private vehicle willing to take you, though you will probably have to wait a while.

Teya-Teyaneng and around

TEYA-TEYANENG, which means "place of shifting sands" after the way the nearby river changes its course from time to time, straggles out over a hill; it has a bustling, compact centre and suburbs that spread several kilometres north and east. T.Y. is the **crafts capital** of Lesotho, specializing in all manner of weavings, from luxurious jerseys to elaborately designed wall-hangings.

There are three **weaving outlets** in town. Setsotho Weaving (daily 8am–5pm) lies opposite the *Blue Mountain Inn* off a signposted road west of the main road; here you can see tapestries being made, and various woven products are sold at reasonable prices in the fairly uninspiring adjacent shop. Just before you reach T.Y., on the left of the main road from Maseru, look out for signs to the small showroom of Hatooa Mose Moasali (daily 8am–5pm), which translates as "women must stand up and work hard". This women's collective sells particularly beautiful weaving, though they keep a fairly limited range in stock; their catalogue displays some very special wall-hangings, which you need to order as they take a week or two to make. A short distance further on, also signposted but this time to the right off the main road, the pleasant sandstone Anglican St Agnes Mission is home to Helang Basali Handicrafts (daily 8am–5pm). The showroom has an excellent selection of woven crafts, again including some very elaborate items, and in the workshop next door you can watch the craftswomen working on the wall-hangings at great looms stretching nearly to the ceiling.

Practicalities

T.Y.'s **bus and taxi ranks**, as well as plenty of **fuel stations**, are all on the main road, alongside a number of undistinguished fast-food and takeaway stores. There is plenty of **public transport** from T.Y. to Maseru, and further north to Hlotse and Butha-Buthe, and you rarely have to wait long.

You'll find the **post office** off the main road to the left, on the road to the *Blue Mountain Inn* (☎ 50 0362; ❸), the only **accommodation** in town but a

---

Culture as fashion: the blanket and the hat

In a region of Africa where **traditional dress** has all but died out, Lesotho stands out as the exception. It's true that the **mokorotlo** (the Sotho traditional hat) is not widely worn these days, but you still occasionally see its distinctive cone and bobble in Lesotho, and in South Africa it is popular with Sotho migrant workers as a badge of ethnic distinction. Ironically, miners' hard-hats are sported in Lesotho as a fashion item, often by younger brothers of Basotho men working in the South African mines. Modelled on the shape of the Qiloane Mountain near Thaba Bosiu, and made of woven straw, the *mokorotlo* has become the standard Sotho souvenir, sold in every craft shop, usually for M25 or less.

More prevalent than the *mokorotlo* is the Sotho **blanket**, still worn all over the country. When King Moshoeshoe I was presented with a blanket by European traders in 1860, there were hardly any in his kingdom, the people wearing *karosses* made of animal hides instead. However, by 1872 traders were reporting insatiable demand for the blankets. Made from high-quality woven cloth, they were originally manufactured in Birmingham, England, and are today made in Port Elizabeth, South Africa. The ubiquitous Fraser's Stores, which you find all over the country, first established themselves by selling blankets, and still stock them today, although the Lesotho Blanket Company in Maseru (see p.760) is the cheapest place to buy them. Good ones (made of pure wool) cost about M250 – but don't forget to buy an outsized safety pin to tie the blanket with.

The blankets are very practical, keeping the body at an even temperature except when it's really hot outside (although the Sotho wear them whatever the weather); they don't absorb much water, and they do not easily catch fire, which is handy when you are dozing by an open fire. Blankets are also associated with fertility, which is why some carry the design of a maize cob, a Sotho symbol of fertility and prosperity. Young brides are supposed to wear a blanket around their hips until their first child is conceived, and boys wear different blankets before and after circumcision.

Most blankets have stripes designed to lie horizontally when you wear the blanket. A curious feature of the pattern of some blankets is their retention of British imperial symbolism. One popular design features a large crown at its centre; another shows warplanes with British military markings. However, although they have always been foreign imports, and are the commodities on which many European trader fortunes have been built, the blankets remain quintessentially Sotho, and a source of national pride.

decent enough place by Lesotho's standards. A spacious hotel with old-fashioned but comfortable cottages to stay in, the *Blue Mountain* also has T.Y.'s only proper **restaurant**, which serves tasty, inexpensive meals with a good wine selection to accompany them, and the town's only **nightclub**, which is busy and recommended on a Saturday night. Both the private and public bars are popular too, and the large surrounding garden is a fine place in which to drink and relax. It's also possible to camp in the garden and use the facilities.

Maputsoe

A rough, manufacturing-based border town opposite the South African town of Ficksburg, **MAPUTSOE** is not a good place to stay long, if you can avoid it. Fortunately, the border is open 24 hours a day, and there is plenty of public transport to Maseru and Hlotse and the north.

The town's main streets are filled with migrant workers commuting between Lesotho and South Africa, amongst them an uncomfortable number of hustlers who can spot strangers in town a mile off. Many seem to congregate at Maputsoe's only **accommodation**, the *Sekekete Hotel* (☎43 0621; ❷), near the border, usually filled with heavy drinkers and gamblers stuffing money into the slot machines. The hotel's plain but functional rooms are around the back, a short distance from the general commotion. The main street also has plenty of takeaways, of which the *Captain Dorego's* is probably the best. There's a 50kph speed limit leaving town and plenty of police about, so take care if you're driving.

Hlotse (Leribe)

A dilapidated but pleasant little lowland town named after the local river, **HLOTSE** was founded in 1876 by an Anglican missionary, Reverend John Widdicombe, and suffered repeated siege during the 1880 Gun War. Since then, it has kept a low profile and, apart from a few shops and department stores, the only thing to see in town are the battered remains of a small military tower built by the British and now practically falling down.

There are, however, one or two local attractions, including a set of **dinosaur footprints** a few kilometres south of the town, left off the Main Road North to T.Y., at the turn-of-the-century **Tsikoane Mission**. You'll need to climb up the rock overhang above the church, preferably with the help of a guide (ask at the mission), where you'll find over forty reasonably clear imprints. Rather more accessible is **Leribe Craft Centre** (daily 8am–5pm), on the right-hand side as you head north, where the exit road from Hlotse meets the main road. Here you can buy mohair scarves, blankets and table mats, along with a small selection of other crafts, made by a team of local women, about half of whom have disabilities.

On the road **north of Hlotse** towards Butha-Buthe, you will see on your right the **Leribe Plateau**, which gives the town its alternative name, with the **Leribe Mission**, founded in 1859 by François Coillard, at its foot. French and Sotho missionaries headed from here to modern-day Zambia in the 1870s, founding the Barotseland Mission there. The mission is only a short walk off the main road, although there's little to see there.

Practicalities

There's plenty of **public transport** in and out of Hlotse, stopping just near the post office. For **eating**, you'll find Sotho restaurants dotted all over the town, where you can buy inexpensive *pap* and stew or chicken. Otherwise, there's the *Pelican Bar and Steakhouse* just off the main road, which serves inexpensive big meat dishes, or the restaurant of the *Leribe Hotel* (☎50 0362; ❷), which is the town's main **accommodation**. At the hotel, you have a choice of rondavels or terraced rooms overlooking a pleasant garden, which are all fine except those with numbers in the thirties (they're next to a large and noisy water tank). The somewhat staid restaurant serves moderately priced meat and fish dishes and the occasional vegetarian pasta, and also, unusually for Lesotho, filter coffee. The only other place to stay in town is the Agricultural College (❶) on the old road from Hlotse to Butha-Buthe, just before it meets the new road. There are basic dorms here and, though the college isn't really geared to taking in outsiders, its staff will let you stay if you ask nicely.

Butha-Buthe to the Sani Pass

The road from **Butha-Buthe** to the Sani Pass is the most popular route into the Lesotho Highlands and travels through some of the highest and most dramatic mountain passes in the country. Though there's not much to do in Butha-Buthe except stock up for the continuing journey, the Butha-Buthe mountain, just beyond the town, was where **Moshoeshoe I** first ruled as chief before moving south (see p.749), and the great views are worth the steep climb.

Butha-Buthe and around

Not far from the Caledonspoort **border post** (daily 6am–10pm), and the last major town before the Highlands, **BUTHA-BUTHE** has a frontier feel. The main road is clustered with takeaway restaurants and stores, and the pavements are filled with Highlanders here for their monthly shopping trip. The town was founded in 1884 because the local chief refused to go to Hlotse to pay taxes, necessitating a new tax centre nearer his residence. Butha-Buthe attracted traders from the outset, and is one of the few towns in Lesotho with a sizeable Indian community.

The **Butha-Buthe** (Lie Down) Mountain, just north of town, is where Moshoeshoe I had his first stronghold before retreating to Thaba Bosiu in 1824 (see p.749). Though a stiff climb, it's not too difficult to ascend, which was one of the reasons the king felt obliged to move. The summit provides tremendous views of the surrounding area. Seven kilometres north of town on the Main Road is a turn-off the **Sekubu Caves**, another 9km away down a dirt track. They're worth a look if you have the time; guides will point out some pretty good rock paintings, but rather faint **dinosaur footprints**.

Practicalities

There is absolutely no shortage of **public transport** in Butha-Buthe, all of which congregates at the market in the centre of town. As well as buses and minibus taxis going to Maseru, Katse and Mokhotlong, you can also find buses heading for Bloemfontein and Johannesburg.

The only **accommodation** in town is at the run-down *Crocodile Inn* (☎46 0223; ❷), signposted off the main road on the left as you come in from Hlotse and the south. The hotel, which offers large rooms with thin walls but tolerable beds, has seen better days and fills up at weekends with dedicated drinkers who occupy its various bars until well into the next morning. Food at the restaurant is inexpensive, but unimpressive and pretty slow in coming.

More pleasant, but much trickier to get to, is the self-catering *Ramakantane's*

Youth Hostel (❶), affiliated to the HI, 3.5km from town in the village of Ha Sechele. The hostel is pretty basic, with no electricity but gas instead for lighting and cooking; but the management is friendly and it's a good place to meet Sotho villagers and hike into the hills nearby. You can't drive there without a high-clearance vehicle, so the best thing is to walk. Turn by the Guys'n'Gals store on the main road and it's about an hour's walk uphill from there. A further choice is the *Cindi Lodge & Supermarket* (☏ 46 0616; ❶), 14km north of town, just by the Main Road. Despite its rough appearance, rooms here are basic but perfectly adequate; there's a bar with a pool table and two restaurants, one serving Sotho food and the other, decorated exclusively with mirrors, serving steaks and chops. The lodge is the last place to get fuel before Oxbow.

The road to Mokhotlong: Muela, Oxbow and the Moteng Pass

Just over 20km past Butha-Buthe, immediately after the small settlement of **Khukhune**, a good tar road to the left leads up to **MUELA**, an integral part of the Lesotho Highlands Water Project (see p.778). Here the water flowing down the delivery tunnel from the Katse Reservoir powers an underground electricity station, which now supplies all of Lesotho, as well as a small surplus sold to South Africa. Previously Lesotho had to buy its electricity from South Africa, so in addition to the royalties received for water, this part of the scheme benefits the mountain kingdom to the tune of something like thirty million rand a year. At the **Muela Dam**, water enters a second delivery tunnel, which empties into the Ash River, near Clarens, which in turn feeds the Vaal Dam, the main water supply for Gauteng. There isn't a great deal to see here – the power station is well hidden inside the mountain and the reservoir is small, but the view of the surrounding mountains is worth pausing to admire. Tours of the hydro station and dam are advertised from the administration block beside *Muela Lodge*, though there isn't always anyone around to lead them. The *Muela Lodge* is an attractive new building overlooking the dam where you can stop for a drink or a **meal**; planned rondavels should offer a pleasant **place to stay**.

The road from here into the Highlands is one of the most dramatic in Lesotho, passing through some particularly striking sandstone cliffs before finally climbing into the basalt. Some 10km or so on from Muela is the well-signposted **Liphofung Heritage Site** (Mon–Fri 8.30am–4.30pm, Sat & Sun 9am–4.30pm; M15), based around a large overhang boasting a series of San rock paintings. More significant for the Basotho is its previous role as a hideout of the young Moshoeshoe I, and as a result the government has invested a lot of money developing the site, with special walkways, a rock-art museum, and a couple of overnight rondavels built alongside. To avoid any damage to the rock art, you're obliged to tour the site with a guide, who can provide some entertaining stories about Moshoeshoe's small army.

A further 20km, over the **Moteng Pass** (2820m) and through stunning mountains and ravines, each of which would make for perfect hiking (though there are no formal routes at all), you come to a mountain lodge popular with South African visitors, the *New Oxbow Lodge* (☏ 051 933 2247; doubles ❸), whose alpine-style buildings have comfortable, warm rooms. There's also camping facilities, a well-stocked bar, and a restaurant serving reasonably priced meals. You'll find good trout fishing on the Malimbamatso River, which flows by the lodge, and wonderful hiking in any direction. If you're coming here in winter, it's worth checking with the lodge about the state of the roads, as they tend to ice over from April onwards. In fact, temperatures up here sometimes drop to below -20°C, so come prepared. If you are driving on from the lodge, remember that this is the last place you can buy **fuel** before Mokhotlong.

There's **skiing** a few kilometres further along the road, in a wide basin below the Mahlasela Pass (3220m). Extravagant plans for a large development with proper lifts and chalets are occasionally rumoured, but for now the runs are short and the tows primitive – most visitors who venture this far in winter are South Africans simply intrigued to see snow. *Oxbow Lodge* rents skis for around M100 a day.

The road to Mokhotlong is often called "the Roof of Africa route", crossing a succession of ever higher passes, peaking at the **Tlaeeng Pass** (3270m), and passing through bleak, sparsely populated but entrancing mountain country-side. The road was recently tarred from *Oxbow Lodge* to Mokhotlong, which makes the journey a lot more feasible, although with the extremes of temperature experienced here the road is already breaking up in places. If you are adequately equipped, this district is tremendous hiking country, and you'll find the hardy locals who eke out a living here amongst the most hospitable in the country. About 40km from the Tlaeeng Pass, the descent to Mokhotlong begins, and most transport stops first at the small village of **Mapholaneng**, where there are two well-stocked bars. From here it's only 30km to Mokhotlong as the crow flies, though twists and turns in the road extend the journey to around 50km.

Mokhotlong

Perched on the banks of the Mokhotlong River, **MOKHOTLONG**, whose name means "place of the bald ibis" (although they are rarely seen these days), began life as a police post in 1905. Slowly, the post evolved into a trading centre for the Highlanders of the region, but remained cut off from the rest of Lesotho for years, with radio contact only established with Maseru in 1947. An airstrip was constructed in 1948 and a rudimentary road link built in the 1950s, but Mokhotlong continued to get the bulk of its supplies by pony from Natal, via Sani, for a long time afterwards. Even today it feels remote, with locals usually riding into town for a shop and a drink on ponies, resplendent in their blankets.

Not much happens in town, which is dominated by hurriedly built and decidedly plain breeze-block buildings that compare unfavourably with the immaculately constructed dry-stone-walled dwellings of the surrounding countryside. On Tuesdays things liven up a bit, when Mokhotlong has its livestock sales. Or you can pick up decent cassettes, or just listen to the music blasting out from the Mamolibeli Music Shop on the main road at the western edge of town near the *Senqu Hotel*. But otherwise, you'll find little to buy except for fast food from a few stores near the bus stops in the centre of town.

There's no public transport to Sani from Mokhotlong, but there are two daily **buses** that stop at Butha-Buthe, one leaving at around 6.30am and the other at 8.30am. Plenty of buses and **minibus taxis** run short distances, including the 15km or so to the *Molumong Lodge* (see overleaf), often marked in the direction of "Ha Janteau".

Accommodation

Farmers' Training Centre ☏ 92 0235. A friendly place with camping facilities and dorms, but with limited bedding, hot water only if they are running a course, and no kitchen. Situated at the far eastern end of town, past the hospital, with a bright-red roof; quite a walk, but you can get minibus taxis. ❶
Mokhotlong Hotel ☏ 92 0212. Reasonable though rather bare rooms with functional en-suite

bathrooms looking out onto the mountains, and a public bar popular for its TV but with hardly any chairs. The restaurant serves moderately priced, unadventurous meat meals. The hotel is at the end of the tarred section of the main road, just beyond the hospital, and unfortunately right next to an abattoir. ❷

Molumong Lodge ☎ 033 355 1141 or 083 254 3323. 15km southwest of town, on the dirt road to Thaba Tseka. A fairly rustic but characterful lodge with fantastic mountain views set on the slopes of the village of Ha Rafolatsane, and clearly marked "Molumong" on its red roof. The main house is self-catering, with very cosy doubles and a great

lounge to relax in, and there's also a bunkhouse alongside in one of the sheds. Meals can sometimes be arranged in advance, but there are virtually no supplies in the village so you have to bring everything in. The lodge offers inexpensive pony trekking, and is a good base for hiking. Either take a bus or minibus taxi from Mokhotlong or, if you're driving, take the junction just before Mokhotlong to Sani Pass and then the first right. ❶–❷

Senqu Hotel ☎ 92 0330. The smartest hotel in town, and the first you come to from the Butha-Buthe road, with comfortable rooms, poky corridors, a TV in the public lounge, and tolerable food in its high-ceilinged, echoing restaurant. ❷

Sani and around

Branching off from the Mokhotlong road, 5km before the town, the rough gravel-and-dirt road to **SANI** twists its way in spectacular fashion for nearly 60km along the Sehonkong River, peaking at the **Kotisephola Pass** (3240m) before dropping to 2895m at **Sani Top**. There are plenty of rewarding hikes from Sani Top, including the twelve-kilometre one to **Thabana Ntlenyana** (3482m), the highest peak in the region, which is walkable in a day if you start early enough, and the tough but stunningly beautiful forty-kilometre **Top-of-the-Berg** walk to the Sehlabathebe National Park, which takes about four days.

Although the descent from Sani, down the dramatic, hairpin-bend-filled Sani Pass, is just about possible in an ordinary car, you'd be much better off with a 4WD, and certainly the ascent of the pass from the South African side is not recommended without one. An ordinary saloon car could make it up, but this requires the rare collusion of perfect, dry conditions and a good driver. During the winter, the pass is frequently blocked with snow, and rain can often render it very slippery during the summer, so ring the chalet or lodge (see below) in advance to find out conditions.

The only **public transport** from Mokhotlong to Sani is the occasional minibus taxi. Otherwise you'll need to hitch, in which case you should make your way to the junction off the Mokhotlong Road as early as possible, or better still, arrange a lift in Mokhotlong the day before. From the South African side, Sani Pass Carriers (☎033 701 1017, or 083 555 5059, Ⓔsanipasscarriers @wandata.com) have scheduled links between *Sani Lodge* (see below) and Pietermaritzburg, Durban and Kokstad. At Kokstad it meets the Baz Bus (☎021 439 2323) travelling between Johannesburg, Durban and Cape Town.

The **border** is open daily (8am–4pm), and there's **accommodation** on both sides. On the Lesotho side is the popular *Sani Top Chalets* (☎082 574 5476 or 033 702 1158, ⓦwww.sanitopchalet.co.za; camping & dorms ❶, doubles with dinner and breakfast ❹). The setting is superb, with commanding views of the mountains, and it makes much of its claim to be the highest **pub** in Africa. It's recommended for the views and the hearty food on offer at lunchtime, while in the evenings you can drink in front of the fire or sit on the balcony and watch the sunset over the mountain tops. In winter, if there's enough snow, skis and boots are for rent, and at other times you can take an overnight pony-trekking trail with a guide. You can sometimes make use of the transport which runs regularly between the *Chalets* and Himeville, although it's also possible to hitch a lift or hop on one of the 4WD taxis which ply the route. Some way down the pass, on the KwaZulu-Natal side, is the excellent *Sani Lodge*, where Russel Suchet, the owner, has an extensive knowledge of Lesotho and will help organize transfers and tours up Sani Pass and beyond.

Katse and the Lesotho Highlands Water Project

The **Lesotho Highlands Water Project** is southern Africa's most ambitious engineering feat for decades. Its centrepiece, the **Katse reservoir**, with its huge dam, stands in stark contrast to the rural simplicity surrounding it. The road built for the dam from Hlotse to Katse is a remarkable journey almost worth doing for the drive alone. Once at Katse itself, you should also take a tour around the dam; such a large and incongruous expanse of water deep in the Highlands offers memorable views.

The road to Katse

Once amongst the most inaccessible parts of the country, Katse's future has been changed forever by the Lesotho Highlands Water Project, not least by the transformation of its **road**, which used to be a rough track, into one of the best tarred routes in the country. The road begins at Hlotse, from where it is a speedy, unexciting run through the lowlands to dreary **Pitseng**. After Pitseng, just before the road starts to ascend steeply, there's a police barrier. If you're in a private car, an official will ask you to stop and may, depending on their mood, pry further about where you're going and what you've got in your boot. From here the road climbs to over 3000m at the **Mafika-Lisiu Pass** in under 30km, making it a punishing journey for most cars, which are lucky to make it out of second gear. Thanks to some remarkable engineering, the road twists and turns around the mountains, sometimes cutting through them, sometimes leaving you suspended over terrifyingly long drops. There are plenty of places to stop and take in the view, though there have been reports recently of theft (in some cases armed) of tourists who have done just that, so keep a good look out if you stop, and your vehicle in view at all times.

After the Mafika-Lisiu Pass, you descend to the small village of **HA-LEJONE**, at the northern end of the massive Katse reservoir. Though signposted as if it offers accommodation, the *Marmeso Lodge* is in fact just a good bar with a pool table and customers likely to offer you illicit diamonds, which you're advised not to buy. From Ha-Lejone, the road follows the reservoir, and just after the unmissable **Intake Tower**, which marks the point where the long tunnel carrying water to Gauteng begins, it crosses the water on the impressive new **Malibamatso Bridge**. From here, it climbs once more, reaching 2600m at the **Laitsoka Pass**, descends to the small village of Seshote, and climbs again inexorably to the **Nkaobee Pass** (2510m), before descending to pass below the dam wall and reach the now burgeoning town of Katse.

Katse and the dam

The town of **KATSE** is drab and boring, with uniform box-like houses arranged in an uninspired suburban manner. But the massive dam really is

The Lesotho Highlands Water Project

Lesotho's abundance of water but its shortage of cash, and Gauteng's monetary wealth and water poverty, are the stark facts that have led to the stunningly ambitious **Lesotho Highlands Water Project**. The essence of the project is to dam Lesotho's major rivers, most of which flow into the Senqu River (which South Africans know as the Orange River); then divert the water through specially constructed tunnels, via a hydroelectric power station at Muela near Butha-Buthe, to South African rivers; which carry it to the Vaal Dam; which then supplies Gauteng. For this, South Africa presently pays Lesotho royalties of around R12 million a month.

The treaty that started the project was signed in 1986, when South Africa had a government fond of imposing draconian states of emergency on its people, and Lesotho had a military dictatorship; unsurprisingly, popular consultation never featured very strongly in the treaty. There wasn't much of an assessment of the environmental impact of the project either, which is worrying in view of recently reported "seismic activity" induced by the reservoir, though the engineers have been busy assuring everybody that things are OK. Various compensation arrangements have been put in place for villagers whose homes, fields or grazing areas have been flooded, or who can no longer get from one side of the Katse valley to the other, though not unexpectedly there are grumbles that these promises have not been met. Meanwhile, the project marches inexorably forward, and it was no surprise that when South African peacekeeping forces entered Lesotho in 1998, one of their main priorities was to secure the dam. The fighting here was heavy, and there were more casualties among the rebel Lesotho soldiers here than anywhere else.

The initial treaty only committed the two parties to complete the first of four proposed phases of the project, after which there would be fresh negotiations and agreements, and it seems likely that when these happen both countries will have much more accountable governments than were in place in 1986. Phase 1a, which is now pretty much completed, consisted of the construction of the Katse reservoir and dam wall, the tunnels to South African rivers, and all the road infrastructure. Phase 1b, involving the construction of the Mohale Dam on the Senqunyane River (see p.768), is due to be completed by 2003, though there has been unrest locally over the unsatisfactory resettlement plans for villagers affected by the dam. The final decision is yet to be made on further phases of the project, but by the original outline the Senqu will be dammed in three separate places, with the water repeatedly diverted into the Katse reservoir, and the whole thing will be finished some time in the 2020s.

impressive, even if you aren't usually interested in engineering. To find out more, make for the blue pre-fab **visitor centre** (Mon–Fri 8am–noon, 1–4pm, Sat & Sun 8am–noon), just before the town and dam, where you can take in a video about the development of the dam, as well as a rather bewildering relief model with flashing lights showing how water will be moved around the Highlands when (or if) the whole scheme, with five separate dams, is completed. The centre can also provide someone to take you around the dam wall and, if you're lucky, into some of its amazing network of tunnels. The wall itself is 185m high and up to 60m thick; it curves inwards for extra strength to such a degree that when you look down from the top, you can't see the rest of the wall, and experience the uneasy illusion of being suspended in space.

The only **place to stay** in Katse is the *Katse Lodge* (☎91 0202; ❶), with functional if well-kept rooms offering fine views of the reservoir and its impressive birdlife, and a surprisingly good restaurant serving a decent selection of inexpensive meals. Unfortunately, the lodge is small and still primarily intended for LHDA workers, so the staff only confirm your reservation a maximum of 48 hours before your arrival, and there's always a good chance that the place will be completely full. If it is, your only other option is to stay at the Agricultural Training Centre (☎90 0304; ➊), which is a long drive on a dirt road in Thaba Tseka (see p.768). At least there's a steady stream of private and public transport from Katse to Thaba Tseka, so you should be able to find something going there, though rarely after 2pm.

The southern districts

The **southern districts** of the country can't match for sheer scale the mountains of north and central Lesotho, but they nevertheless hold some dramatic countryside which is relatively easy to tour around. There is a reasonable network of tar roads linking a number of small towns, some based around missions founded by the British in the last century – **Malealea**, famous for its welcoming lodge and excellent pony trekking, is probably the most handsomely situated, **Morija** the most historic. Further south, you can see **dinosaur footprints** at **Mohale's Hoek** and, more accessibly, at **Moyeni**, before moving on east to **Qacha's Nek** and the isolated delights of the **Sehlabathebe National Park** beyond: Lesotho's only national park, but so remote as to make visits here a true adventure.

Morija to Malealea

The main road south from Maseru, past the airport and the Qeme Plateau (see p.762), soon takes you to historic **Morija**, with its small cluster of mid-nineteenth-century buildings and the only museum in the country. A further 45km away, along roads that get increasingly scenic as you near your destination, the easy-going and smoothly run lodge at **Malealea** is the most attractive of its type in Lesotho. Set amid wonderful countryside, it's a perfect spot for hiking and well-organized pony trekking in wind-carved sandstone hills.

Morija

Just 44km from Maseru, **MORIJA**, established in 1833 as the first mission in Lesotho, is a pleasant little town 1km off the main road at the foot of the Makhoarane Plateau. It's easy to get to Morija from Maseru with your own or public transport, with buses and minibus taxis running throughout the day in both directions. Morija is also a good spot to pick up transport going further south to Mafeteng and Mohale's Hoek.

Morija houses the country's only museum and Lesotho's oldest building, church and printing press. Granted by King Moshoeshoe I to three missionaries of the Paris Evangelical Missionary Society (PEMS), Eugene Casalis, Thomas Arbousset and Constant Gossellin, they gave the place the name that

Abraham bestowed on the mountain where he was reprieved from killing his son by God (it means "God will provide").

The large, red-brick **mission church**, with its impressive teak-beamed roof, is almost always open. Begun in 1847, this is the third church built on this site, using the labour of Pedi economic migrants on their way to the Cape Colony, though its tall steeple was only built in 1905. You have to make special arrangements to get in to see the historic **printing works** nearby, which have produced Sotho literature since the 1860s and the country's oldest newspaper, *Leselinyana la Lesotho* (Little Light of Lesotho), which has been in almost continual publication since 1863.

Most of Morija was razed to the ground by Afrikaner troops in 1858, and almost the only building left standing was the **Maeder House**, built in 1843 and now Lesotho's oldest building. Today, this simple stone house next to the mission church contains a small craft shop, selling inexpensive Sotho hats, dolls, carvings, tapestries and batiks. Close by, the **Morija Museum & Archives** (Mon–Sat 8am–5pm, Sun 2–5pm; M5) is a stimulating combination of a geological and fossil exhibition, ethnographic material and historic items of Moshoeshoe and his contemporaries, and a useful commentary on Lesotho's history and modern-day political issues. The geological and fossil displays are presented somewhat drily, although the dinosaur exhibits are striking, but you should find something of interest amongst the ethnographic and historical items, including a succession of treaties broken by the British, Moshoeshoe's china tea set, and a *khau*, the beautiful V-shaped neck ornament awarded to brave Sotho soldiers. The archives have yet to be fully organized and catalogued, but you are allowed to dip into them under supervision and see what you can unearth among the jumble of nineteenth-century missionary tracts and records and some valuable Africana. The museum also produces a **booklet**, *A Guide to Morija*, which tells you everything and more that you could possibly want to know about the town, including some pointers to nearby sites of interest. The museum's **tea shop** (Mon–Sat 9am–4.30pm, Sun 2–4.30pm) offers cold drinks and simple Basotho meals; you can sit either in the cool little rondavel or on the attractive lawns outside. In early October every year, the museum helps organize the **Morija Arts and Cultural Festival** (ⓦwww.morijafest.com), the largest and most significant event of its kind in the country, where traditional music, dancing and crafts mix with theatre, cinema, sport and children's events.

Linked to Morija Museum is a pleasant **place to stay** in the self-catering *Ha Matela Guesthouse* (ⓣ36 0308; ❷), set in a dramatic spot right at the top of the town on the way to the Makhoarane Plateau. The large thatched house has a number of comfortable rooms and a large verandah with great views out over the surrounding area. A simpler, smaller house in the village is also available to let. If you organize it beforehand, catering can be arranged with the tea room at the museum. The lodge can also arrange pony trekking for competitive rates.

The best of a number of **walking trails** marked out from Morija leads to a dinosaur footprint on one side of a large rock, halfway up the **Makhoarane Plateau**. To get there, make first for the *Ha Matela Guesthouse*, up the hill behind the museum, and from there head for the plateau, across a *donga*, following a succession of red arrows. Though a stiff climb to the rock, much of the path is sheltered by trees and the footprint itself is impressive, though rather faint; it takes about an hour there and back.

Malealea

A further 10km south of Morija you come to a dip in the road and the bustling minibus-taxi stop at Motsekuoa, which marks the turning for the road to the village of **MALEALEA**, one of the best-known spots in Lesotho thanks to the hugely popular *Malealea Lodge* (℡051 447 3200, ⓦwww.malealea.co.ls; camping and dorms ❶, doubles ❷, rondavels ❸). A little less isolated these days because of the tar road running most of the way to the village, it's still a spectacular spot set in the foothills of the Thaba Putsoa mountain range. The lodge was originally a trading store, established by the British adventurer Mervyn Bosworth-Smith in 1905, and it was he who wrote the inscription "Wayfarer, pause and look upon a gateway of Paradise" at the magnificent mountain pass taking you into the final stretch of the journey to the lodge. The current owners of the lodge, Di and Mick Jones, have done as much as anyone in recent years to promote Lesotho, not least because of the enthusiastic but laid-back way they run the lodge, which has grown significantly from its trading store origins to incorporate a cluster of huts, houses and rondavels with both backpackers' dorms and decent double rooms. It's always a lively place; next to the dining room is a great little bar and most evenings guests congregate round an open fire outside, occasionally with a band of local school children bashing out tunes on homemade instruments.

Many visitors come to Malealea to hike, and the lodge has mapped out a series of trails, but the main activity is **pony trekking**. The lodge doesn't own the ponies, but acts as an agent for local horsemen who receive the bulk of the money. It costs about M120–175 for a day trek, plus a small additional cost for staying in a village for overnight treks. Together with the horsemen, the lodge has worked out a series of guided trips, from short one-hour tours and half-days to as many days as your bottom and your wallet can stand. An excellent two-day adventure is the journey to the **Ribaneng Falls**, which takes you down and over steep sandstone valleys and hills. The lodge ensures that there is an empty, well-kept rondavel with a gas cylinder in the village for your overnight stop, offering a rough-and-ready, but nonetheless memorable, taste of life in the mountains. You do need to take your own food and sleeping gear with you. If you have the time for a four-day journey, your guide will take you all the way east to the impressive Ketane Falls (see p.766) and back, travelling over some particularly beautiful mountains, and through quiet, friendly villages. A good, less pricey alternative to the pony trekking, which is quite hard on the body if you are not used to it, is simply walking and using a pony as a pack animal. The pony can carry four people's packs, provided they're not excessively heavy.

To get to Malealea by **public transport** from Maseru, take a bus or minibus taxi to Motsekuoa, or to Morija and then on to Motsekuoa. During the day, there's plenty of transport from Motsekuoa towards Matelilie and the only possible slow bit is after you're dropped off at the junction to Malealea, which is about 8km away. However, almost all the vehicles going that way are likely to give you a lift to the lodge. There is frequently transport travelling between the lodge and Bloemfontein, via Wepener; ask about this when you make your booking. If you're travelling to or from the eastern Free State, it's possible to arrange a transfer with the **Lesotho Shuttle**, which runs from *Amphitheatre Backpackers* (℡036 438 6106, ⓦwww.amphibackpackers.co.za) in the Royal Natal National Park, and also provides a means of linking up with the **Baz Bus** route between Johannesburg and Durban.

Mafeteng, Mohale's Hoek and Moyeni

There's little to detain you between **Mafeteng** and **Moyeni** apart from some good walks in the surrounding sandstone hills, including some leading to interesting sets of **dinosaur footprints**. You'll also find the best meal for miles around at the *Hotel Mount Maluti*, where you can hire ponies to explore the beautiful and little-visited Mokhele mountain range east of the town of **Mohale's Hoek**. Mafeteng, Mohale's Hoek and Moyeni are all within half a dozen miles of the South African border, with Mafeteng the most practical for border crossings and with the most public transport.

Mafeteng and around

The bustling town of **MAFETENG**, 20km from the Van Rooyenshek **border post** (daily 6am–10pm), will be the first place you come to in Lesotho if crossing from Wepener in the Free State. It means "the place of Lefeta's people", after the son of a French missionary Emile Rolland, who was the district's first magistrate and was nicknamed Lefeta, or "he who passes", by locals, who regarded him as virtually Sotho except for the fact that he "passed by" initiation school.

Unfortunately, much of the town suffered in the 1998 riots, leaving the centre in quite a mess, but in any case the only building of interest in Mafeteng is the **council office** on the main street. It's worth a quick look for the animal heads studding its front wall, and a nice statue of a handlebar-moustached Cape Mounted Rifles soldier in the front garden. There are two good nearby excursions, though you'll need your own transport to get to them. The **Luma Pan**, 3km from town, attracts a good selection of birdlife; head for Wepener, and turn right down the first substantial dirt road you come to. About 20km east of Mafeteng, along a road that deteriorates past the village of Likhoele to the point that you're taking a risk in an ordinary saloon car, is the impressive **Thabana Morena Plateau**. Rising above a village of the same name, it rewards the steep climb with good views of the Free State plains to the west and the Thaba Putsoa Mountains to the east.

Practicalities

As befits a border town, Mafeteng has a very busy **bus station** where you can easily find transport north to Morija, Maseru and Malealea, and south to

---

Bog standard: the new pit latrine

A new feature of the Lesotho landscape are great numbers of improved **pit latrines** with white chimneys, which are easy to build and hygienic, but hardly to be found in neighbouring South Africa. Their main improvement on the old pit latrines, still in use in the Republic, is that they keep flies that have come into contact with human faeces away from humans and their food, thus helping prevent dysentery. With this design, once the flies are in the pit they never get out again.

Typically, flies enter the latrine when someone opens the door, and then fly down through the latrine seat and hole and then into the pit itself. With the old design, they would then escape the way they came in, but with the new latrines they're attracted by the light at the top of the chimney, which is sealed with gauze. As long as people remember to close the lavatory seat and keep the latrine door shut, thus keeping light out of the latrine, this is pretty foolproof, keeping the flies buzzing harmlessly in the pit and chimney.

Mohale's Hoek, Moyeni and beyond. There are various small **places to eat** by the bus station and on the main street, but otherwise the best choice is in the hotels. For **accommodation**, there is the *Golden Hotel* (℡70 0566; ❷), an anonymous-looking building offering adequate rooms and a small dining room serving meat dishes, to the right of the Main Road South from Maseru, just before you enter Mafeteng proper. A better choice, is the *Hotel Mafeteng* (℡70 0236; ❸), which looks like a 1960s airport control tower, but offers pleasant rooms and cottages in a secluded garden with a good swimming pool. The restaurant serves a limited range of moderately priced meat dishes. You'll find the hotel signposted off the Main Road South to Mohale's Hoek.

Mafeteng's **nightlife** centres around the rather seedy, mirrored *Las Vegas* disco in the grounds of the *Hotel Mafeteng*, which blasts out soul and South African *kwaito* sounds until 4am on Friday and Saturday nights. Alternatively, the *Golden Hotel* sometimes has *famo* music – a local style with accordions and singing – on Saturday nights.

Mohale's Hoek

MOHALE'S HOEK, a short distance from the little-used Makhaleng Bridge **border post** (daily 8am–6pm), is a rather bedraggled little town, but with one of the best hotels in the area and some interesting sites in the surrounding hills, including some well-preserved **dinosaur footprints**. Mohale was Moshoeshoe's younger brother, appointed to look after the area by the king as part of his bid to wrest control of the district from chief Moorosi. There are still quite a few of Moorosi's Baphuthi clan here though, whose language is in some ways closer to Xhosa than Sotho.

If you desperately need to do some banking, you'll find the Standard and Nedbank **banks** more efficient than most banks outside Maseru, although changing money and traveller's cheques can still take a long time. These are located on the main street, perpendicular to the main road through town. Otherwise, there's nothing to see or do here, but there's an excellent drive/walk to the **Mokhele Mountain**, about 10km east of town. Travel a short distance south on the main road to the little village of Mesitsaneng, and then head 7km east along a rough dirt track to the **Maphutseng Mission**. Just before this historic French mission, which once hid locals in its roof from attacking Boers, turn right down a smaller track, and you'll see a plateau to the right a short walk away, where you'll find some **dinosaur footprints** and an inscription marking their "discovery" in 1959.

Practicalities

You'll find it hard to work out the system at the busy **bus station** in the centre of Mohale's Hoek, so instead just ask where the bus for your destination is standing. **Minibus taxis** congregate on the main street, and between them and the buses you should be able to find transport heading both north and south throughout the day.

For **accommodation** in town, the place to go is the *Mount Maluti Hotel* (℡78 5224; ❸), owned by a white family who have lived in the area for years and can offer good advice about what to see and do there, as well as arranging inexpensive pony treks and guides. They've also plotted an adventurous 4WD route through the southern Highlands, though the closest 4WDs for rent are in Maseru (see "Listings" on p.761). The hotel rooms are comfortable, with TVs, and there's a tennis court, pool and small garden, and a small but pleasant **campsite** (ask at the hotel reception). The highlight is its restaurant, which offers decent cuisine, even for vegetarians, at reasonable prices. As usual, there are also plenty of inexpensive **places to eat** on the main street.

Moyeni and around

MOYENI (Place of the Wind), also known as Quthing, is a curious split-level town established by the British after the Gun War in 1884. The town itself is messy, though it has an attractive setting beside a river gorge, with views of the surrounding hills improving as you climb to the upper part of town. This is home to the police station, the main hotel, a large hospital and one or two pretty useless banks, while the lower half has most of the shops and fuel stations and is where you catch public transport. During the day, there are always plenty of **buses** and **minibus taxis** running north towards Maseru, far fewer running east towards Qacha's Nek, and one or two heading for the nearby Tele Bridge **border post** (daily 8am–6pm), where you can pick up transport to Sterkspruit in the Eastern Cape.

The most easily accessible **dinosaur footprints** in Lesotho are very near the western side of the lower section of Moyeni. Just continue a short distance up the Main Road from the Moyeni turn and look out for the simple **visitor centre** (daily 8am–4pm), an orange thatched building beside the road on the left. The man who works there will direct you towards the variety of clearly discernible prints in the hope of a small tip.

Also worth a visit is the **Masitise Cave House**, a few kilometres west of Moyeni to the right of the main road. Follow signs to the Masitise primary and high schools, and at the high school ask for someone to show you the house, built into the cave by the French Protestant missionary family who lived here in the 1870s.

A little further on, are some much-vandalized and greatly faded **rock paintings**. If you've made it this far, have a brief look also at the pleasant mission **church**, which has a fine bell tower but no bell.

Accommodation

The Catholic mission at Villa Maria is the only local budget **accommodation** option as you approach the town from the south, and there are two hotels in town. Neither is of a particularly high standard, though the *Mountainside* just about wins for its more intimate and friendly atmosphere.

Mountainside Hotel ☎ 75 0257. Halfway between upper and lower Moyeni, this small hotel has mostly adequate rooms (check the mattress before you accept a room), half of which overlook the street, while the others are more secluded and quieter. There's a pleasant and cosy private bar, a friendly public one and a good restaurant with a tasty fixed menu that normally has something for vegetarians. ❷

Orange River Hotel ☎ 75 0252. An ungainly building decorated in 1970s-style hessian and pine, which has the air of having seen little atten-

tion, and fewer guests, since. Rooms are reasonable but very stuffy, and some of the ceilings are in serious need of repair. The tolerable restaurant overlooks upper Moyeni and the surrounding countryside. To get to the hotel, follow the main road through town, almost to the top of the hill. ❷

Villa Maria Roman Catholic Mission ☎ 75 0364. Set in the grounds of the very grand two-towered church, the mission offers clean, inexpensive rooms with communal bathrooms. The complex is just west of Moyeni, to the right of the main road. ❶

Mount Moorosi, Qacha's Nek and the Sehlabathebe National Park

A far less-used route into the Highlands than the northern road from Butha-Buthe to Mokhotlong, the mountain road from **Mount Moorosi to Sehlabathebe** is ruggedly beautiful, with the added bonus of the mighty Senqu (Orange) River winding majestically alongside much of it. If the Katse dam builders have their way, the Senqu will in a few years be much reduced, but for now the chocolate-brown river is normally in full flood. Highlights along the route include **Thaba Moorosi**, the mountain where the outlawed chief Moorosi made his last stand against the British in 1879, the San caves at **Seforong**, and the remote, pristine national park of **Sehlabathebe** itself, the only national park in the country – perfect for fishing, bird-watching and kilometre-upon-kilometre of isolated hiking.

Mount Moorosi and around

Just over 40km on from Moyeni, along a decent tar road with fine views of the mountains and glimpses of the mighty Senqu (Orange) River, the small town of **MOUNT MOOROSI** clings to the mountainside and provides inhabitants of various local villages with a minibus taxi stop and shopping. The largest institution is Mitchell's Trading Store, which serves as the town's main store, garage and fuel station. Ask here if you want to park your car in the compound, where it should be safe, before taking the ferry across the Senqu to Bethel (see below).

Mount Moorosi is named after a chief, who moved to the region in the 1850s, living in the cliffs around the town. He was an ally of the San and had several San wives, but made an enemy of the British in the 1870s when they captured his son as a hostage and Moorosi promptly snatched him back. British troops retaliated by attacking his stronghold in 1879, but he held out for eight months, until finally captured when the soldiers used scaling ladders on the steep cliffs, and then cut off and publicly displayed Moorosi's severed head. **Thaba Moorosi**, where the main battle took place, is a kilometre or so further along the main road on the right, and you'll find if you climb it that some stone slabs still bear the inscriptions of the soldiers sent to catch the chief. It's quite a tricky climb, though, so be sure to let someone in Mount Moorosi know where you are going.

Bethel

On the other side of the Senqu River from Mount Moorosi is the village of **BETHEL**, where there is a large, rather neglected mission church and the much more proactive **Bethel Business and Community Development Centre** (@www.lesoff.co.za/bbcdc/). Despite its rather cumbersome name, this is an innovative training centre, teaching locals practical skills in solar technology, permaculture and market gardening. The centre is a thriving advertisement for the principles it expounds, with healthy crop fields and vegetable patches, rows of trees, well-designed buildings and solar power used for everything from the hot water to a satellite phone link-up for email. Facilities include a self-catering guest flat and dormitories (●), and meals are available if arranged beforehand. Short-term visitors are welcome, but if you would like to stay longer, write to the centre at PO Box 53, Mount Moorosi 750, or email them (©bbcdc@maf.org) as far in advance as you can. To get to Bethel, walk or catch a minibus from Mount Moorosi for two kilometres to the ferry point on the Senqu River, below the towering cliffs of Thaba Moorosi. There are hopes that a road crossing will be built, but meanwhile the rowing-boat crossing of the fast-flowing river is worth experiencing. Once on the other side, it's a further four-kilometre walk to the mission. If you have a 4WD vehicle, an alternative to crossing by ferry is a two-hour drive along a route that leaves the tarred road on the western side of the bridge over the Senqu, between Moyeni and Mohale's Hoek.

Mphaki and around

Shortly after rounding Thaba Moorosi, the main road leaves the Senqu River, and heads swiftly into the Highlands through the impressive **Quthing Gorge**, peaking after about 10km at the **Lebelonyane Pass** (2456m), with superb views. The road carries on through a series of attractive high-altitude valleys, before reaching the small village of **MPHAKI**, which has excellent accommodation at the Farmers' Training Centre (❷), which offers well-equipped self-catering rondavels and a pleasant guesthouse. If you don't fancy self-catering, the *Motsekuoa Liquor Restaurant* opposite the centre provides inexpensive and tasty Sotho **food** as well as a good bar.

The tarred road continues for another 10km out of Mphaki, where it reverts to decent gravel. You'll find some **San caves** a short hike off the road a few kilometres further on at **Seforong**, just before **Sekake**, though – unusually – they don't have rock paintings. At Sekake you can **camp** or **stay** at the atmospheric Christian Council of Churches Mission, a kilometre or so along a rocky track that leaves the main road at the *Hotline Restaurant*.

Qacha's Nek

Past Sekake, the road rejoins the southern banks of the Senqu, but deteriorates significantly in quality, though you can still make it with care in an ordinary vehicle. You'll find it a beautiful, undulating drive, amongst the loveliest in Lesotho, though once you reach the approach to **QACHA'S NEK** you'll see depressingly familiar soil erosion and *dongas*.

Qacha's Nek, named after chief Moorosi's son Ncatya, was an area famed for its banditry when the British founded the town in 1888, in an attempt to forestall the kind of trouble they'd experienced with chief Moorosi. Many of the "bandits" were in fact desperate San, hounded from their homes and now with no means of survival; this left the British unmoved, and they hunted them to extermination throughout the 1860s. Moorosi's Baphuthi people had started moving there in the 1850s, rapidly wiping out all the game, and turning the land over to grazing and cultivation instead. The area has unusually high rainfall, and the weather conditions favour conifers, including a few massive Canadian redwoods, giving Qacha's Nek an atmosphere completely different from most of virtually treeless Lesotho.

There's little to see in town, except the elegant **St Joseph's Church** at its eastern end, but the entire surrounding mountainous countryside is great for **hiking**. Qacha's Nek is also an important **border town** (daily 8am–6pm) and there's usually plenty of public transport heading west towards Moyeni from the Shell garage in the centre of town. You can hear the minibus taxis a mile off, thanks to the cowbells tied to their fronts. You'll also find transport just over the border heading for the Eastern Cape town of Matatiele, from where it is a simple matter to find buses and minibus taxis going on to Kokstad and beyond.

The best **accommodation** in town is the *Nthatuoa Hotel* (☎95 0260; ❷–❸), which is the first building you come to on the left as you enter Qacha's Nek from the south. The hotel offers four types of room, each more luxurious than the last, starting with a decent though smallish double and ending with a large, fancy suite. All tariffs include a substantial breakfast from a restaurant serving the finest **food** in town (unless you are vegetarian, in which case you'll go hungry). Just past the hotel, and opposite the Farmers' Training Centre, ask your way to the excellent *Narna's Guest House* (☎95 0374; ❶) close by. Though the owners don't speak much English and water supply is often a problem (as it is elsewhere in town, despite the high rainfall), this is a friendly place with a good kitchen where you can either do your own cooking or just provide the ingredients and let the owner cook them up, for a small extra charge. Turn left past the fuel station in town for the *Central Hotel* (☎95 0224; ❷) which, despite its name, is over a kilometre further on, nestled away next to the PEP department store. A sandstone building and full of character, the hotel has only six rooms and is often full. Even if you're not staying, it's worth visiting at weekends for live music. There's a small number of inexpensive **places to eat** in the centre of town, but for more substantial meals you're best off in one of the hotels.

Sehlabathebe National Park

The only national park in the country, **Sehlabathebe National Park** (free) is remote and almost inaccessible, but predictably peaceful and beautiful. Set on the border with South Africa, in the eastern reaches of the Drakensberg, the park has a few game animals but is better known for its birdlife, excellent trout fishing, waterfalls, and seemingly endless open spaces that make for perfect hiking. Once here (just turn up, and they'll let you in), you may not want to leave in a hurry, so bear this in mind when you book. Having said that, the weather can be so foul as to make you want to move on straightaway, with mists and rain emerging out of nowhere even on the finest days.

Sehlabathebe is managed by the Ministry of Agriculture, and is the subject of ongoing land disputes that primarily concern grazing access. The current state of affairs is a rather messy compromise, and you are likely to see herd boys grazing livestock all over the park, much to the irritation of environmentalists.

Practicalities

To **get to the park** from the Lesotho side you definitely need a 4WD. Failing that, there is a daily bus from Qacha's Nek to the village outside the park, which takes four to five hours; or you can sometimes hitch a lift from the junction about 11km from Qacha's Nek, but you are then faced with the problem of walking the very steep 17km up from the park entrance to the park's office. The only other way into the park from the Lesotho side is to walk the forty-kilometre "Top of the Berg" hike from Sani Top (see p.776). From South Africa, the only way in is a day's walk along the dramatic path starting at Bushman's Nek, which is a few hours' drive from Underberg and Himeville in KwaZulu-Natal.

To be sure of **accommodation** in Sehlabathebe's well-equipped and inexpensive lodge (❶), book in advance in Maseru through Sehlabathebe Reservations, Ministry of Agriculture, 82 Constitution Rd, PO Box 24, Maseru 100 (☎31 6407, ✉agric@ilesotho.com). The easiest way to do this is in person when you are in Maseru. During the week, however, the lodge is rarely full, and even if it is, you can always camp. Neither the Ministry of

Agriculture, nor the tourist information office or the park office itself have any maps of Sehlabathebe; if you want to do some serious hiking, go to the Department of Lands, Surveys and Physical Planning in Maseru (see p.753), where you should be able to pick up some detailed maps of the area.

Travel details

Buses

There is no such thing as a bus timetable in Lesotho, so the following information is intended to give a rough idea of frequencies and journey times. Minibus taxis supplement bus services everywhere and ensure that you can always find some form of public transport on major routes, though the story is very different on minor routes off the tarred roads, where you can expect long waits. Because public transport is so erratic, it's usually a better idea to just make for the next town on and find something from there rather than getting a ticket all the way to your destination (unless there's only one a day); your bus will stop at the next town anyway, and wait for more passengers, and you might be able to get a minibus taxi in the meantime.

Butha-Buthe to: Hlotse (4 daily; 30min); Maputsoe (4 daily; 45min); Mokhotlong (2 daily; 7hr).

Hlotse to: Butha-Buthe (4 daily; 30min); Maputsoe (5 daily; 30min); Maseru (8 daily; 2hr).

Mafeteng to: Maseru (5 daily; 1hr 30min); Mohale's Hoek (5 daily; 45min).

Maputsoe to: Butha-Buthe (4 daily; 45min); Hlotse (5 daily; 30min); Maseru (8 daily; 2hr).

Maseru to: Hlotse (8 daily; 2hr); Mafeteng (5 daily; 1hr 30min); Maputsoe (8 daily; 2hr); Qacha's Nek (1 daily; 10hr); Roma (4 daily; 1hr); Semonkong (4 daily; 5hr); Teya-Teyaneng (8 daily; 45min).

Mohale's Hoek to: Mafeteng (5 daily; 45min); Moyeni (5 daily; 45min).

Mokhotlong to: Butha-Buthe (2 daily; 7hr).

Moyeni to: Mohale's Hoek (5 daily; 45min); Qacha's Nek (1 daily; 7hr).

Qacha's Nek to: Maseru (1 daily; 10hr); Moyeni (1 daily; 7hr).

Roma to: Maseru (4 daily; 1hr); Semonkong (4 daily; 4hr).

Semonkong to: Maseru (4 daily; 5hr); Roma (4 daily; 4hr).

Teya-Teyaneng to: Maputsoe (8 daily; 45min); Maseru (8 daily; 45min).

Flights

Maseru to: Johannesburg (3 daily Mon–Sat, 2 daily Sun; 1hr 10min).

Swaziland

CHAPTER 12

Highlights

* **Royal festivals** The spectacular ceremonies of *Ncwala* and *Umhlanga* are colourful affirmations of Swazi national identity. **See p.805**

* **Mlilwane** A tranquil reserve where you can walk, cycle or ride horses amongst giraffe and antelope, or watch hippos from the bar. **See p.805**

* **Malandela's Homestead** A collection of buildings bursting with creativity and enterprise, including the funky performance space House on Fire, and Gone Rural, one of the best of Swaziland's many attractive arts and crafts outlets. **See p.807**

* **Horse-riding** Well-run horse treks combine stunning countryside and peaceful rural stopovers. **See p.806**

* **Myxo's Place** Get a true taste of life in rural Swaziland – this enterprising project allows backpackers to live as part of a village for a few days. **See p.809**

* **Whitewater rafting on the Great Usutu** As action-packed as anything south of the Zambezi – you can paddle a two-man croc raft down Swaziland's largest river. **See p.817**

* **Mkhaya Game Reserve** Swaziland's best wildlife experience, where you can walk with rhino and elephant before sleeping in the bush in open-sided cottages. **See p.818**

12

SWAZILAND | Highlights

12

Swaziland

A tiny landlocked kingdom, **Swaziland** lies in the spanner-like grip of South Africa which surrounds it on three sides, with Mozambique providing its eastern border along the Lubombo Mountains. Although South Africa's influence predominates, Swaziland was a British protectorate from 1906 until its full independence in 1968, and today the country offers an intriguing mix of colonial heritage and homegrown confidence, giving the place a friendlier, more relaxed and often safer feeling than its larger neighbour.

During the long years of apartheid, white South Africans regarded Swaziland as a decadent playground, where sinful opportunities (gambling, interracial sex and porn movies), forbidden by their Calvinist rulers, were freely available. This image is fading fast, and though Swaziland still feels a lot more commercialized than, say, Lesotho, its outstanding **scenery**, along with its commitment to **wildlife conservation**, makes it well worth a visit. With a car and a bit of time, you can explore some of the less-trampled reserves, make overnight stops in unspoilt, out-of-the-way settlements and, if you time your visit well, take in something of Swaziland's well-preserved **cultural traditions**.

In recent years, Swaziland has become something of a draw for **backpackers**, with useful transport links to different parts of South Africa as well as Mozambique, some good backpacker lodges and plenty of adventure activities from horse-riding to whitewater rafting.

Swaziland has six **national parks**, between them exemplifying the country's geographical diversity, and all offering good-value accommodation. While not as efficiently run as South African National Parks, the Swazi reserves are less officious, and many people warm to their easy-going nature. The best-known are those run by **Swazi Big Game Parks** (see p.807): Hlane Royal National Park in the lowveld, Mlilwane Wildlife Sanctuary near Mbabane, and the upmarket Mkhaya Game Reserve between Manzini and Big Bend. The Swaziland National Trust Commission, based in Lobamba (see p.804), manages Malolotja Nature Reserve in the northwest highveld, Mlawula Nature Reserve in the eastern lowveld and the tiny Mantenga Nature Reserve in the eZulwini Valley.

Despite encroaching political dissent, Swaziland remains one of the world's few absolute monarchies, and **King Mswati III**, educated at Britain's elite Sherbourne College, regularly appears in the country's sacred ceremonies, bedecked in the leopard skins of his office, participating in a ritual dance or assessing the year's crop of eligible maidens as they dance before him. He might even choose to add a few to his collection of wives, carefully drawn from a wide selection of clans in order to knit the nation more closely together. If you

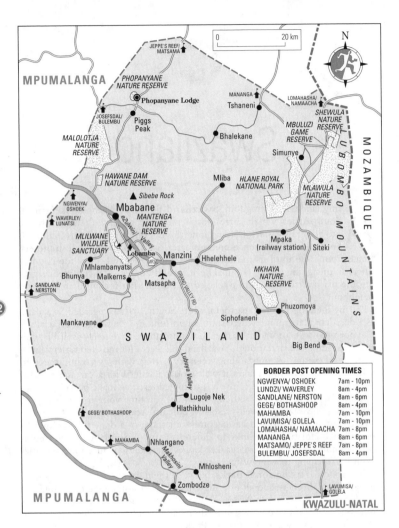

can, plan to come to Swaziland for **Ncwala** (around the end of December or the start of January) or **Umhlanga** (August or September); both ceremonies are as important to the Swazis as New Year is to the Chinese.

Laid-back **Mbabane**, the country's tiny capital city, makes a useful base from which to explore the attractive central **eZulwini Valley**, home to the royal palace and the **Mlilwane Wildlife Sanctuary**. With your own transport, or a bit of determination and public transport, you can venture further afield, heading into the highveld of the northwest, and up to the fantastically beautiful **Malolotja Nature Reserve**, with its fabulous hiking country, soaring valleys and cliffs.

If you are trying to get between northern KwaZulu-Natal and the Kruger National Park in South Africa, Swaziland offers a good, fully tarred **through**

route via the Matsamo border in the north and the Lavumisa and Mahamba borders in the south, passing by the Mkhaya Game Reserve and Big Bend. Approaching Kruger this way is a far more attractive option than skirting through the eastern parts of Mpumalanga.

Summers are hot, particularly in the eastern lowveld. **Winter** is usually sunny, but nights can be very chilly in the western highveld around the Malolotja Nature Reserve and Piggs Peak. In summer, rainfall is usually limited to short, drenching storms that play havoc with the smaller untarred roads. Note that Swaziland's eastern lowveld, including Hlane Royal National Park and Mkhaya Nature Reserve, is **malarial** during the summer months (November to May). For details on necessary precautions, see p.22.

Some history

The history of Swaziland dates back to the **Dlamini** clan and their king, **Ngwane**, who crossed the Lubombo Mountains from present-day Mozambique in around 1750. Pushed into southeast Swaziland by the Ndwandwe people of Zululand, the clan eventually settled at Mhlosheni and then Zombodze in the southwest, where Ngwane reigned precariously, under constant threat of Ndwandwe attack. His grandson, **Sobhuza I**, was forced to flee north from the Ndwandwe, but they in turn were defeated by the Zulu king Shaka in 1819. Sobhuza then established a new capital suitably far from Shaka in the eZulwini Valley, and made peace with the Ndwandwe by marrying the king's daughter.

Sobhuza's power grew as he brought more and more clans under his wing. His alliance with the newly arrived Afrikaners, forged out of mutual fear of the Zulu, was pursued by his son **Mswati II** (after whom the Swazi people are named), who stretched his kingdom north to the Sabi River and sent raiding parties as far as the Limpopo River and east to the Indian Ocean.

Europeans arrived in greater numbers throughout the 1880s, after the discovery of gold in neighbouring Transvaal and at Piggs Peak and Forbes Reef in Swaziland. Mswati's son, **Mbandzeni**, granted large chunks of his territory in concessions to the new arrivals, emboldening Britain to ignore his claims to most of the rest, and by the time Swaziland became a protectorate of South Africa in 1894, there was precious little land left. After their victory in the Second Anglo-Boer War, Britain assumed control of the territory and retained it until 1968.

After World War II the British invested in their protectorate, establishing enormous **sugar plantations** in the northeast, and an **iron-ore mine** at

Choosing the king

Swazi monarchs are always men of the **Dlamini** family, and over the course of their reign marry a number of women who are carefully selected from different clans to cement national unity. In theory, the king marries women from increasingly important families as he goes along, which means that the son of the last wife is always a strong contender for the succession. In practice, however, other wives with older sons are also in with a chance, resulting in unrest and power-struggles every time the king dies. After his death, the royal council, or *liqoqo*, selects the new **Queen Mother**, who rules as regent until her son is old enough to take charge. She usually has to work hard to ensure her position against ambitious uncles. The main advantage of this awkward process is that by the time the new king is old enough to rule, he and his mother have generally garnered enough support for him to do so effectively.

Ngwenya in the highveld (today, the country's major export is sugar). Meanwhile, **Sobhuza II**, who had become king of the Swazis in 1921, concentrated on buying back his kingdom, and had acquired about half of it by the time independence came in 1968. The Swazi aristocracy managed the transition to independence skilfully, with its Imbokodvo party winning every parliamentary seat in the first elections. In 1973, a radical pan-Africanist party won three seats, prompting Sobhuza to **ban political parties** and declare a state of emergency which has technically been in place ever since. A parliament governs Swaziland today, but final authority rests with the king, who continues to name the prime minister (who, by tradition, is always a Dlamini) and approve or veto important legislation.

After Sobhuza's death in 1982, a period of intrigue ensued, with the Queen

Swaziland travel basics

Accommodation in the mid- and upper range is generally better value than in South Africa, although there isn't a wide choice, particularly in the guesthouse and B&B sector. Backpacker and budget places are on a par with South Africa.

Banks are easily found in the major centres. Opening hours are generally Monday to Friday, 8.30am to 2.30pm, with some branches open on Saturday from 8.30am to 11am. Most banks and hotels should be prepared to change traveller's cheques, but usually at poor rates of exchange. Most ATMs in Swaziland accept international cards.

Camping in designated campsites is possible near almost every tourist attraction and in all the national parks except for Mkhaya.

Currency is the lilangeni – plural emalangeni (E) – which is tied to the South African rand (1 rand = 1 lilangeni). The rand is legal tender in Swaziland, so you won't have to change any money, but note that emalangeni are not convertible outside Swaziland. There is a shortage of change in Swaziland, so if you do exchange money ask for a good amount of low denomination notes.

Credit cards such as Visa, Mastercard and American Express are widely accepted in hotels, restaurants and shops. The national parks accept cards for larger payments such as accommodation, but you'd be well-advised to carry cash to pay for meals and guided walks.

Costs are similar to those in South Africa, with food and fuel somewhat less expensive.

Phone numbers The country code for Swaziland is ℡268, followed by the destination number (there are no area codes). The code for phoning out from Swaziland is ℡00, followed by the country and area codes and finally the destination number. To phone South Africa, dial ℡07. To arrange a collect call, dial ℡94. Country codes are the same as those dialled from South Africa (see p.52). If you experience difficulties, call enquiries on ℡919490. Swaziland has its own mobile phone network, which works well in the eZulwini Valley but can be patchy elsewhere. International roaming is possible with certain phones and contracts. All Swazi mobile phone numbers are seven figure and begin with 6.

Driving is the best way to see Swaziland; distances are small, all the main tourist sites are near good, tarred roads, and the major gravel roads are in decent condition. Most dirt roads are passable with an ordinary vehicle in dry months. Driving standards, however, leave a lot to be desired – highlighted by the fact that two of the last four ministers of transport have died in road accidents. The authorities permit a blood-alcohol level in drivers which is double that permitted in South Africa, which should make you think twice about long drives at night. Also, the general speed limit of 80kph outside towns is universally ignored and very rarely enforced. For Swazi car rental, see p.800.

Passports and visas see p.18

Mother Dzeliwe assuming the regency until deposed by Prince Bhekimpi, who ruled until 1985, purging all the opposition he could. The current king, **Mswati III**, the son of one of Sobhuza's seventy wives, was recalled from an English public school to become king in 1986, and parliamentary elections were held in 1987. New opposition began to emerge, most notably the **People's United Democratic Movement** (PUDEMO), which has strong support amongst Swazi workers, though in general Swazis are proud of their distinctive kingdom, and as a result calls for change are tempered by an unwillingness to show disloyalty to the king, or to expose Swaziland to what many see as the predatory ambitions of South Africa.

Thus the maintenance of tradition and appeals to broad nationalism have been key components of Swazi royalty's strategy to retain power. Relations

Swaziland on the internet
ⓦ **www.swazi.com**
Swaziland's official website is lively, colourful and packed with useful information, including hotel listings and alternative tours of Swaziland. You can also read the *Swazi Observer* newspaper online, or visit the "Artists on the Internet" page for a roundup of the country's arts scene.

ⓦ **www.biggame.co.sz**
Provides practical information on the country's most visited attractions, the Hlane, Mlilwane and Mkhaya parks, with links to the Swazi Trails site and details of tours.

ⓦ **www.swazitrails.co.sz**
The most important tour operator in the country, with details of a range of tours around Swaziland, including cultural, wildlife and adventure options.

Language

Siswati greetings and responses
Hello (to one)	*Sawubona*
Hello (to many)	*Sanibona*
How are you?	*Kunjani?*
I'm fine	*Ngikhoua*
Goodbye (said by person leaving)	*Sala kahle*
Goodbye (said by person remaining)	*Hamba kahle*

Basics
Yes	*Yebo* (also a casual greeting)
No	*Cha*
Thank you	*Ngiyabonga*
It's nice/tasty	*Kumnazdi*
Today	*Lamuhla*
Tomorrow	*Kusasa*
Yesterday	*Itolo*

Travel
Where is.. ?	*Iphi l.. ?*
Where can we stay?	*Singahlala kuphi?*
Where are you going?	*U ya phi?*
How much?	*Malini?*

January 1	August/September (*Umhlanga* Dance
Good Friday	Day)
Easter Monday	September 6 (Independence Day)
April 19 (King Mswati III's birthday)	December/January (*Ncwala* Day)
April 25 (National Flag Day)	December 25
May 24 Ascension Day	December 26
July 22 (King Sobhuza II's birthday)	

with the new South African regime are uneasy: the ANC remembers the expulsion of its activists during the Eighties and wants speedy political change. Although Mswati III is sometimes said to favour reform, so far none has materialized. The authorities work hard to keep dissent bottled up, by means of sporadic police repression; opposition leaders are prevented from speaking freely in the media, and poor turnouts marked the "elections" of 1993 and 1998. Currently, Swaziland is the only country in southern Africa not practising multiparty democracy. It seems only a matter of time before it is coerced by the other regional powers into doing so.

Getting there

Of the twelve border posts serving traffic from South Africa, the main ones are **Ngwenya/Oshoek** (7am–10pm), which is closest to Johannesburg and is the easiest route to Mbabane; **Jeppe's Reef/Matsamo** in the northwest (7am–8pm), which is handy if you're coming in from Kruger Park; **Mananga** in the northeast (8am–6pm); **Lavumisa/Golela** in the southeast (7am–10pm), close to the KwaZulu-Natal coast; and **Mahamba** in the southwest (7am–10pm), off the N2 from Piet Retief in the KwaZulu-Natal interior. The northern crossing via **Bulembu** (8am–4pm) to Piggs Peak is perhaps the most spectacular in the country, but the bad road makes this journey hard going in an ordinary car. Crossing the border is usually very straightforward: you simply have to show your passport and pay the token E5 (R5) **road tax**.

Transtate **buses** from Johannesburg enter Swaziland through the Ngwenya/Oshoek border, stopping at Ermelo en route to Mbabane; and through Mahamba, stopping at Nhlangano and Hlathikulu. The Baz Bus runs eastbound from Jo'burg to Durban via Mbabane and then Manzini on Monday, Wednesday, Saturday, departing for Durban the next morning; westbound, from Durban, it arrives on Tuesday, Friday and Sunday and sets off for Jo'burg the next morning.

Swaziland has one **international airport**, Matsapha (often referred to as "Manzini"), between Mbabane and Manzini. Airlink Swaziland (a partner of SAA) flies three times daily to and from Johannesburg. Swazi Express Airways flies in from Durban daily except Saturday.

Mbabane and around

Tucked in the jumble of granite peaks and valleys that make up the Dlangeni hills, Swaziland's administrative capital, **MBABANE** (pronounced "M-buh-ban"), is small, relaxed and unpretentious, with a population of only 90,000. The most popular route into Swaziland, through the Oshoek/Ngwenya border post, is only 20km west of Mbabane; the city roughly marks the point where the mountainous southern African highveld descends briefly into middleveld, before bottoming out further east as dry lowveld. This is a good base from which to start exploring Swaziland, especially if you're without your own transport: the **Mlilwane Wildlife Sanctuary** lies not far south, and the royal village of **Lobamba** makes an easy day-trip – vital if you're here when the *Umhlanga* or *Ncwala* ceremonies take place (see p.805). There's not much to do in the city, but many visitors find it more agreeable than hectic **Manzini**, especially if you need to change money, find a comfortable bed or plan your trip ahead.

An alternative route to Mbabane

While most visitors – and Transtate buses from South Africa – approach Mbabane from the Ngwenya/Oshoek border, a good **alternative route** is via the **Sandlane/Nerston** border post (8am–6pm), about 35km further south, and roughly 70km from the city. Although a longer journey, this road passes through some outstanding scenery and will take you past some excellent places to stay.

Once past Nerston, where there are some interesting San paintings (ask at the church for someone to show you the way), the road plunges deep into the vast and beautiful **Usutu Forest**, which covers over ten percent of Swaziland. After some steep climbs, you'll start a long descent to the factory town of **Bhunya**, whose hub is a belching pulp mill – reason enough not to linger. Press on for another 15km or so on the road to Mhlambanyatsi, taking care when crossing the single-lane bridge over the Usutu River. Just before Mhlambanyatsi is a fine **hotel**, *The Forester's Arms* (⊕4674377, ⊛www.swaziland.freeservers.com /foresters; half-board ➎), set in a picturesque clearing in the surrounding woodland. Cosy rooms with wonderful mountain views and hearty **meals** make this a good place to stop over; on Sundays, people from all over the country pour in to feast on the hotel's superb buffet and roast – you'll need to **book** ahead to be sure of a table.

Back on the road, **Mhlambanyatsi** itself has a small shopping centre and some filling stations, but little else. The road beyond it enters a beautiful, lush river valley dotted with traditional houses; this is prime **hiking** territory, and a particularly spectacular unmarked trail leads all the way to (but not into) the Mlilwane Wildlife Sanctuary (see p.805). Note that there are no facilities, and you have to be pretty self-sufficient, asking at villages for somewhere to stay. Eventually the road breaks through the hills to the plateau on which Mbabane stands, where you can connect with the main routes to the centre of the country.

Arrival and information

Matsapha airport (⊕518615), 35km southeast of Mbabane, just west of Manzini, is Swaziland's only international airport. There's no public transport from here into Mbabane, so if you haven't been able to arrange a pick-up with your hotel, be prepared to take a **taxi** or **rent a car** (see p.800). You cannot change money at the airport, so have some rands or emalangeni handy.

Transtate (Jo'burg ⊕011 773 6002) **buses** from South Africa terminate some way out of town at the intersection of Usutu and Manzini roads, from where you should call a taxi, as it's too far to walk into town. The main bus station is off the Western Distributor Road, beside the Swazi Plaza mall, and from here you can take a bus to almost anywhere in Swaziland. **Minibus taxis** ply the Mbabane–Manzini route and rank on the west side of the bus station – this is also where you can rent a **private taxi** for local travel.

Mbabane's **tourist office**, Swazi Plaza (Mon–Fri 8am–5pm, Sat 8.30am–12.30pm; ☏4042531) has a good supply of **maps** and brochures and a free *What's On?* guide – very handy for information on forthcoming events.

Central Mbabane empties out at night, and **muggings** are a risk for those wandering the streets alone. If you're going out after dark, arrange for a taxi to pick you up.

Accommodation

Mbabane's **accommodation** is somewhat limited, and some of the options in the lower price range are in a seedy part of town. However, there are a couple of backpackers' lodges near the centre and a handful of fairly decent **hotels** on and around Allister Miller Street. There are also various guesthouses on the fringes of the city, and it's worth remembering that most of the establishments in the eZulwini Valley (see p.801) are close enough to be considered as alternatives to those listed below. If you have trouble finding anywhere, staff at the tourist office should be able to help.

Cathmar Cottages 3km north of Mbabane on Pine Valley Road ☏4043387 or 6021364, ⓔcathmar@mailfly.com. Self-catering cottages and simpler wooden cabins in a lovely location north of town near Sibebe Rock. Facilities include cable TV in the cottages and a swimming pool. ❶–❷

Chillage Backpackers 18 Mission St ☏4048342, ⓔchillage@hotmail.com. A friendly if fairly scruffy backpacker lodge a 10min walk north of the city centre. It tends to have a large percentage of long-term residents, and doesn't tend to attract those just stopping for a night and moving on. ❶

City Inn Allister Miller St ☏4042406, ⓕ4045393. The oldest city-centre hotel, offering plain but spacious en-suite rooms, all with TV. It incorporates a small coffee shop facing the street. ❸

Hill St Lodge Hill St ☏4046342. Basic rooms with shared bath, in a quiet suburb west of Allister Miller St. ❶

Kapola Guest House 6km southeast of Mbabane off MR3 ☏4040906 or 6048962, ⓔtfc@iafrica.sz. Decent guesthouse accommodation in a large family home, at the bottom of the hill between

Mbabane and the start of the eZulwini Valley. There are six well-equipped en-suite guest rooms, with a quiet balcony and secluded garden. ❸

Mbabane Backpackers Gilfillan St ☏4043097. An apartment block converted into a backpacker lodge, with dorms, doubles and lounges; central, but a little lacking in character. The hostel can organize trips to Swazi villages. ❶

Mountain Inn 4km southeast of Mbabane off MR3 ☏4042781, ⓦwww.mountaininn.sz. A smart, efficiently run if slightly dated hotel, with sixty rooms and good facilities including a lovely pool and the *Friar Tuck* restaurant. Located on a spacious mountainside plot with wonderful views down eZulwini Valley. ❹

Thokoza Church Centre Mhlanhla St ☏4046681, ⓔanglicanchurch@iafrica.sz. Church mission centre some way east of the city centre, offering drab but cheap two-or three-bed rooms, with breakfast available as an extra. There is a 10pm curfew unless you make prior arrangements, and the area can be rough at night. ❶

The City

Mbabane's hilly **centre** is a pleasant jumble of office blocks, markets, plazas and shacks that you can very easily explore on foot – which is just as well, as driving here can be stressful without a sound grasp of the street layout. **Allister Miller Street** is the closest the city has to a main street; running south into the central business district (CBD), it's lined in parts by colonial administrative buildings which are attractive to look at, but can only be entered on official business. At the end of Allister Miller Street, on the banks of the Mbabane River, lies the **Swazi Market**, with neat rows of curio stalls with a colourful selection of handicrafts and, though prices aren't cheap, you can always haggle. It's just as interesting wandering further into the market, where fresh fruit and vegetable stalls make for a colourful scene (though prices here aren't negotiable).

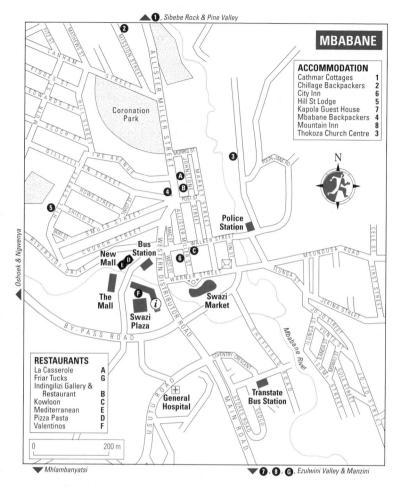

MBABANE

ACCOMMODATION

Cathmar Cottages	1
Chillage Backpackers	2
City Inn	6
Hill St Lodge	5
Kapola Guest House	7
Mbabane Backpackers	4
Mountain Inn	8
Thokoza Church Centre	3

Coronation
Park

Police
Station

Bus
Station

New
Mall

The
Mall

Swazi
Plaza

Swazi
Market

Mbabane River

RESTAURANTS

La Casserole	A
Friar Tucks	G
Indingilizi Gallery & Restaurant	B
Kowloon	C
Mediterranean	E
Pizza Pasta	D
Valentinos	F

General
Hospital

Transtate
Bus Station

0	200 m

Oshoek & Ngwenya

◀ Mhlambanyatsi

▼ 7 , 8 , G , Ezulwini Valley & Manzini

12

SWAZILAND | Mbabane

The main focus of the city centre, however, is the sprawl of shopping malls down the hill from Allister Miller Street. Most of Mbabane's main shops, banks and services are located in either the **Swazi Plaza** or the more upmarket **Mall** and **New Mall**. Alongside the Swazi Plaza is the busy bus and taxi rank.

Eating, drinking and nightlife

You'll find the ubiquitous *Spur*, *Steers*, *Debonairs* (pizza) and *KFC* in Mbabane, but the town also has a smattering of very good **restaurants**, as well as some lively **bars** and **clubs**.

Restaurants

Friar Tucks At the *Mountain Inn*, 4km southeast of the city centre ☏ 4042781. Serves reliable buffet lunches and a la carte dinners, in an intimate, rather dark interior; there's also outdoor seating.

Indingilizi Gallery & Restaurant 112 Johnstone St ☏ 4046213. A very pleasant place to come for lunch. The restaurant is in the gallery's back garden, and serves light, wholesome dishes at rea-

sonable prices. Mon–Fri 8am–5pm, Sat 8am–1pm.
Kowloon Fast Food New Mall ☎ 4048637. A reliable Chinese takeaway, open daily till 8pm. There's also a branch on Allister Miller Street.
La Casserole Omni Centre, Allister Miller St ☎ 4046426. Upmarket but good-value restaurant specializing in German dishes, with vegetarian selections.
Mediterranean Allister Miller St ☎ 4043212. Despite the name, this is an Indian restaurant

serving moderately priced wonderful dishes in a dark, cavernous setting.
Pizza Pasta New Mall ☎ 4048628. Reliable, well-priced if fairly predictable Italian fare and good coffee.
Valentino's Pub & Restaurant Swazi Plaza ☎ 4041729. Serves mostly mainstream food including burgers, grilled chicken and ribs – but it's worth looking out for the special curries and stir fry. Daily

Bars, clubs and entertainment

The city's liveliest **bars** are *Valentino's* and the *Plaza Bar*, both in the Swazi Plaza complex. The best bet for nightlife is the *West End Girls* **nightclub**, above the *Yemfo* bar, reached down Western Distributor Road or West Street, where a good local band can normally be found at weekends. Most locals think nothing of travelling to happening spots along the eZulwini Valley or in Manzini, and for the best nightlife it's not a bad idea to follow them. Check the daily *Times of Swaziland* for details. **Women travellers** on their own are likely to encounter some unwanted attention in bars and clubs, but the pestering probably won't be aggressive or persistent.

Listings

Airlines Airlink Swaziland ☎ 5186155 or in Johannesburg ☎ 011 978 1111, ✆ www.saairlink .co.za; Swazi Express Airlines ☎ 5186840 or in Durban ☎ 031 408 1115, ✆ www.swaziexpress.com.
Banks Most banks are lined along Allister Miller Street or in the Swazi Plaza. Branches include First National, Nedbank and Standard. Hours are generally Mon–Fri 8.30am–2.30pm, Sat 8.30–11am. The best time to bank is a weekday morning.
Bookshops Websters, at 120 Johnstone St and in the New Mall, has the best general selection. There is also an SNA newsagent (the Swazi equiv-

alent of South Africa's CNA) in the Swazi Plaza.
Car rental Avis (☎ 5186226) and Imperial (☎ 5184393) are located at Matsapha airport, and there's another Imperial agent at the Engen service station at the junction of the By-Pass Road and Main Road (☎ 4041384). Cheaper than either company is Affordable Car Hire (☎ 4049136 or 6020394) in the Swazi Plaza.
Embassies Mozambique, Princess Drive ☎ 404 3700; South Africa, New Mall ☎ 4044651; UK, Allister Miller St ☎ 4042581; USA, Warner St ☎ 4046442.

Sibebe Rock

About 10km north of Mbabane along the Pine Valley road, Swaziland's most famous geological feature, a huge granite dome called **Sibebe Rock**, can be found among the Mbuluzi Mountains. Rising 300m above the Mbuluzi River Valley, the vast slabs of granite are very steep and dangerous in places, but among the scattered boulders at the summit are Bushman paintings indicating that the rock was inhabited by humans thousands of years ago. While the hard, coarse surface of the granite offers more grip than other types of rock, it can be very dangerous if you slip, and any ascent should only be attempted in the company of a guide. Swazi Trails (see p.801) offers a challenge they describe as "the steepest walk in the world", which ascends an impossible-looking path up the front face of the dome. Swazi Trails also offers a **caving trip** in the same mountain range, which involves a lot of squeezing through narrow spaces and navigation by little more than a head torch and the encouraging words of your guide – it's a memorable adventure for those who don't mind enclosed spaces and a few bumps and scratches. Both the Sibebe Challenge and the caving trip are run on a half-day basis, each costing around E200 including transport to and from various points in the eZulwini Valley and Mbabane.

Emergencies Fire ☎4043333; Police ☎999 or 4042221.
Hospitals Mbabane Clinic Service (private), St Michael St ☎4042423; Government Hospital (public), Usutu Rd ☎4042111.
Internet facilities The Internet Café (✉box31@icafe.co.sz, or check out the website at ⱳ www.iafrica.sz.icafe), at the Omni Centre, opposite the cinema on Allister Miller Street. This isn't really a café – it's a room in a business centre – but it does offer internet access. You can also get online at the internet café beside the Post Office, upstairs in the Swazi Plaza (Mon–Fri 8am–6pm, Sat 8am–5pm, Sun 2–5pm).
Laundries Swaziland Steam Laundry & Dry, Allister Miller St, and in the Swazi Plaza.
Pharmacy Mbabane Pharmacy, Allister Miller St; Philani Pharmacy, in the Swazi Plaza; and Green Cross, in The Mall.

Post office The main post office is on Warner Street, and there's a smaller one in the Swazi Plaza. Mon–Fri 8am–4pm, Sat 8–11am.
Taxi Mbabane Taxis ☎4043084; SD Tel Taxis ☎4040965.
Tour operators The country's biggest and best tour operator is Swazi Trails (☎4162180, ⱳ www.swazitrails.co.za), located in the Mantenga Craft Centre (see p.802). It runs tours to the Lobamba royal village, game parks, nature reserves, craft centres, local villages and even a local *sangoma* (healer). They can also arrange horse-riding, hiking, mountain biking, caving and some great whitewater rafting trips (see p.817). There are also a handful of smaller local operations, including Nabo Bashoa, 37 Commercial Centre, Johnston St (☎605 6346, ✉phephelo @yahoo.com), who runs minibus tours to different parts of Swaziland. The tourist information office keeps information on other tour guides.

The eZulwini Valley

After passing through Mbabane, the smooth, new, four-lane **MR3** winds down the steep sides of Malagwane Hill in a series of sweeping curves, made hazardous by crawling lorries and reckless minibus taxis. The road then heads off southeast along the eZulwini Valley, but unless you're bound directly for Manzini and beyond, take the turning not long after the foot of the hill onto the older and quieter **MR103**: this links most of the main sights of the scenic **eZulwini Valley** (Place of Heaven). In the 1960s, a succession of casinos, strip joints, hotels and caravan parks sprang up here, all catering for mainly South African tourists. When gambling became legal in South Africa in the mid-1990s, however, the number of pleasure-seekers dropped; the tourist industry had to start looking beyond the noise of the slot machines and karaoke to the valley's cultural and natural assets, and in particular places such as the royal residences of **Lobamba** and **Ludzidzini**, the **Mantenga Nature Reserve** and **Mlilwane Wildlife Sanctuary**. The latter, in particular, is one of Swaziland's main attractions, with its range of accommodation from backpacker lodges to colonial guesthouses, as well as numerous activities, including hiking trails and game viewing from a mountain bike.

Malagwane Hill and along the eZulwini Valley Road

Soon after leaving Mbabane, the main Mbabane–Manzini road begins its giddy descent down **Malagwane Hill**. As the highway begins to level out at the bottom of the valley, the first main exit leads to the old eZulwini Valley road, the **MR103**, which runs parallel to the mountains on the southern side of the valley. A kilometre or so along the MR103, a right-hand turn leads to *Timbali Park* (☎4161156, ✉timbali@africaonline.co.sz), a well-maintained camping and caravan park which also has shaded self-catering cottages (❷), a pool, bar and coffee shop serving breakfasts. Next door to *Timbali* you'll find one of Swaziland's swankiest **restaurants**, the *Calabash* (☎4161187), which serves an excellent range of fresh seafood and specializes in German, Swiss and Austrian dishes. Further up this road, *Martin's Bar & Disco* becomes pleasantly raucous and drunken at weekends, and if you're in the mood for partying will doubtless deliver a night to remember.

Continuing along the MR103 valley road, you'll soon come to the Swazi Health and Beauty Studio, which incorporates the popular **Cuddle Puddle** (daily 6am–6pm; E10), a beautifully warm outdoor spa pool filled from a natural spring nearby and surrounded by tropical vegetation. Immediately beyond this lie three Sun **hotels** offering their usual blend of comfort and anonymity. The *Royal Swazi Sun* (℡4161001, ⓦwww.suninternational.com; ❻) is the smartest of the lot, with a fine swimming pool, a golf course, a good selection of restaurants and plenty of upmarket bars, as well as a swanky casino and a tatty adult cinema. The other Sun options offer slightly better value: the *Lugogo Sun* (℡4161550; ❻) provides a well-priced buffet that is particularly enticing at breakfast, and the *Ezulwini Sun* (℡4161201; ❻) has a beer garden open on Tuesday nights. In the same direction, just beyond the filling station and past the Sun hotels, the *1st Horse* **restaurant** (℡4161137) serves very good Chinese meals and has a large bar. Opposite the filling station stands an extended line of **craft stalls**, commonly signposted by one or two tour buses drawn up alongside. This is a good place for mainstream Swazi crafts such as wood and soapstone carvings, though you have to haggle to get the prices down to sensible levels.

Also on this section of the eZulwini Valley road is the *Happy Valley Motel* (℡4161061, ⓔhappyvalley@iafrica.sz; ❷), located a kilometre or so past the *1st Horse Restaurant*. A remnant of Swaziland's days as a place of temptation for repressed white South Africans, the motel has a casino, slot machines, pool tables, the *If Not?* go-go bar and the *Why Not?* disco, a popular nightclub and venue for local and touring bands. The rooms in the motel are predictable but neat, with air conditioning and cable TV; there's also the *Bella Vista Pizzeria* (6.30am–midnight weekdays, 6.30am–2am weekends), which is popular with locals stopping for a drink, meal or takeaway.

The Mantenga Valley

The Mantenga Valley follows the course of the Lusushwana (Little Usutu) River from the eZulwini Valley road up into the hills to the west, most prominent of which is the twin-peaked **Lugogo Mountain**, also known as "Sheba's Breasts", which featured in H. Rider Haggard's famous adventure novel *King Solomon's Mines*. Apart from a series of good **craft centres**, the valley is dominated by the **Mantenga Nature Reserve**, home of the **Swazi Cultural Village** and **Swazi River Café**. There's a fair amount of new development by the side of the eZulwini Valley road in this area, so the road layout is subject to change, but by following signs to the Mantenga Craft Centre or Mantenga Nature Reserve you should get onto the correct road.

Mantenga Craft Centre

The **Mantenga Craft Centre**, less than a kilometre from the turn-off from the eZulwini Valley road, consists of an attractive purpose-built village of craft shops. These specialize in more exclusive and individual crafts than are found in many other parts of Swaziland, including fabrics, artworks and better carvings. There's also a **tourist information** office (Mon–Fri 8am–5pm, Sat 8.30am–12.30pm) and the main booking office for **Swazi Trails**, the country's leading tour operator where you can organize a wide range of cultural and adventure trips including a half-day arts and crafts trail, whitewater rafting (see p.817) and caving. Just beyond the Mantenga Craft Centre is the beautifully located *Mantenga Lodge* (℡4161049, ⓔmantenga@iafrica.sz; ❹), a good choice for mid-priced **accommodation** in the eZulwini Valley. The lodge has 26 en-suite rooms, some in cosy chalets for two to four people each, nestled on the

△ Swazi crafts

hill rise, as well as a pool, terrace bar and **restaurant** with especially good views. Also on the road beyond the Mantenga Craft Centre is a long, terracotta-painted building where you can find more crafts worth checking out: in the *Jewellery Studio* (Tues–Sat 9am–5pm, Sun 10am–5pm), jewellery is hand-crafted on the premises out of gold, silver, semi-precious stones and even elephant and giraffe hair, while the adjoining *Guava Gallery* (same hours) sells some highly original local arts and crafts, including paintings, sculptures and woven mats.

Mantenga Nature Reserve

Not far past the Guava Gallery is the entrance to the **Mantenga Nature Reserve** (daily 6.30am–6pm; E10 plus E5 per car), which incorporates **Ligugu lemaSwati** (meaning "the pride of the Swazi people"), Swaziland's most authentic cultural village. This open-air living museum replicates a nineteenth-century Swazi homestead with sixteen beehive huts, all built in traditional style using wooden frames joined by leather strips, reed thatch, cow-dung and termite-hill earth. Cattle and goats wander about, and there are often demonstrations of traditional activities and crafts. Informative and enthusiastic guides will take you round on free tours, and you can even **stay** in one of three beehive huts if you're prepared to rough it, as there's no bedding, no electricity, and you cook on a campfire (☎4161013 or 4161151; ❶). Rather more comfortable accommodation is available a little further upriver in fifteen luxury tents, each located on a sturdy wooden platform and equipped with an en-suite toilet and hot shower (❷). All the platforms incorporate a deck in front of the tent – it's worth asking if tents no.5 or 6 are free, as these have the best view of the pretty 95-metre **Mantenga Falls**. The tents are grouped around the thatched *Swazi River Café* (daily, breakfast, lunch and dinner; ☎4161151 or 602 2183), a restaurant serving "Swazi fusion cuisine" which can include spicy chicken livers, ostrich stroganoff and locally grown vegetables. The café, which also serves teas and coffees, is open to everyone, and has established a good reputation both with locals and those staying elsewhere in the eZulwini Valley.

Although the café and the cultural village are the main attractions, the rest of the reserve shouldn't be ignored, as there are some pleasant **hikes** and a beautiful **picnic** and **swimming** spot with views of the Mantenga Falls, a five-minute walk from the café.

The royal villages of Lobamba and Ludzidzini

Some 20km south of Mbabane at the heart of the eZulwini Valley, **LOBAMBA** was originally built in 1830 for King Sobhuza I, and became the royal *kraal* of Sobhuza II. The Houses of Parliament are situated here, and must be one of the few in the world to have cattle grazing undisturbed in surrounding fields. Next door, fascinating exhibitions of Swazi life can be found in the **National Museum** (Mon–Fri 8am–1pm & 2–3.45pm, Sat & Sun 10am–1pm & 2–3.45pm; E10). They provide a helpful potted history of the country, with displays of cultural artefacts and wonderful old photographs of Swazi people and royalty, of Manzini and Mbabane when they were one-horse towns, of sweaty British administrators in full colonial regalia attending functions of the Swazi royal house, and much more. A natural history wing was also opened recently. The museum is the base of the **National Trust Commission**, PO Box 100 (Mon–Fri 8am–1pm & 2–3.45pm, Sat & Sun 10am–1pm & 2–3.45pm; ☎4161151, ⓦwww.sntc.org.sz), which handles bookings for the Mantenga, Malolotja and Mlawula nature reserves (see p.811 & p.814).

Outside the museum stands a life-size re-creation of a traditional Swazi homestead. Remarkably, given their size, these huts are actually portable. Across the road is **King Sobhuza II Memorial Park**, a peaceful open space dedicated to the much-loved late king. Nearby, Lobamba's **Somhlolo stadium** is the country's venue for major events and football matches, which are usually highly entertaining. For a few emalangeni on a Sunday afternoon, you can treat yourself to violence-free games of occasional great skill, with a good-humoured and vociferous crowd. Consult the local *Times of Swaziland* for details, or ask almost any male Swazi.

On the other side of the MR103 from Lobamba, the village of **LUDZIDZINI** is the royal *kraal* of the present king, Mswati III, and the Queen Mother. Unlike Lobamba, Ludzidzini cannot be visited or even photographed at all except during *Ncwala* (around New Year) and *Umhlanga* (end of Aug/early Sept), when permission must be obtained (see box below).

Mlilwane Wildlife Sanctuary

For many visitors to Swaziland, the highlight of the eZulwini Valley is **Mlilwane Wildlife Sanctuary** (daily dawn–dusk; E20), with its relaxed atmosphere and attractive, game-filled plains. The name Mlilwane refers to the "little fire" that sometimes appears when lightning strikes the granite mountains. As well as offering good game viewing and activities, Mlilwane is an easy alter-

---

Ncwala and Umhlanga

The most sacred of Swaziland's ceremonies, **Ncwala** celebrates kingship, national unity and the first fruits of the new year. Its timing is determined by royal astrologers; coinciding with the new moon in November, a group of selected men journey east to the ancestral home of the Ngwane on the shores of the Indian Ocean to collect foam from the waves. While they are there, the *Ncwala* ceremony begins, with songs and rituals performed until the afternoon of the full moon in December/early January, when the six days of the full *Ncwala* begin. Young Swazi men meet at **Lobamba** and are then sent away to gather branches of the *lusekwane* tree, from which they build a bower for the king. Warriors gather and sing songs that can only be sung at this time, while the king dances with them and eats the first fruits of the harvest. On the sixth day, objects representing the previous year are burnt on a massive bonfire, and prayers are offered to Swazi ancestors, asking them to put out the fire with rain. The ceremony ends amidst raucous singing, dancing and feasting. Visitors are allowed to attend most of *Ncwala*, but photography is prohibited during certain times (a free permit is also required; contact the Government Information Service, PO Box 338, Mbabane), so be sure to ask first to avoid having your camera smashed.

The **Umhlanga** is a **fertility dance** which gets its name from the large reeds gathered by young women and brought to the residence of the Queen Mother to repair her *kraal*, usually in late August or early September. The sixth and seventh days are the most spectacular, when you can watch the young women, dressed in elaborate and carefully coded costumes, sing and dance before the king and Queen Mother at Lobamba, giving the king an opportunity to pick a **new wife**. The former king, Sobhuza II, invariably plucked a new mate from the bevy of young beauties and racked up a total of seventy wives during his lifetime. His successor, Mswati III, now in his mid-thirties, has proved a little more restrained with only eight wives so far. In 2001 he caused some controversy by insisting that the young maidens parading in front of him at Umhlanga should continue to wear the *umcwasho*, a traditional regalia indicating that they were still virgins, for five years after the ceremony marking their passage from childhood to maidenhood. With HIV/AIDS spreading alarmingly in Swaziland, the king's pronouncement was seen as a fairly futile attempt to check the disease.

native to staying in Mbabane or on the eZulwini strip. Given its popularity, it's wise to book ahead if you intend to stay overnight.

The reserve holds a special place in the history of wildlife conservation in Swaziland; it was here that Ted Reilly (see below) first realized his dream of a sanctuary for Swaziland's fast-disappearing **wildlife**. Mlilwane's animals are mainly herbivorous, and include giraffe, zebra, bountiful numbers of antelope and the sanctuary's emblem, the warthog. There's also the occasional crocodile and hippopotamus, which means you still need to be cautious if viewing the game on foot, bike or horseback.

Over 100km of road enables you to drive through the park to view game. Alternatively, guided walks and drives are available through the park office at the main restcamp; the best of the self-guided **walking trails** is the Macobane Hill Trail, a gentle, three-hour hike through the mountains. The more adventurous can climb to the top of Nyonyane, the "Execution Rock", which rises so prominently in the north of the reserve. The office can supply maps for all these. There are also guided **mountain-bike tours** (E60 per hour) and **horse-back trails** (from E75 per hour), both fairly relaxed ways of taking in the park's attractions. For those with a little more horseback experience, various overnight trails involve camping in caves and rustic trail camps in the more remote parts of the reserve; for the really committed, the Lusoti "Real Africa" Horse Trails, organized by Swaziland Big Game Parks in association with Hawane Horse Trails, offer a seven-night cross-country expedition taking in Mlilwane, Mkhaya Game Reserve and remote rural homesteads. For details, contact Big Game Parks Central Reservations (see opposite). If you're feel-

Ted Reilly and the Swazi nature conservation story

Swaziland owes the creation and survival of three of its major wildlife sanctuaries – Mlilwane, Mkhaya and Hlane – to **Ted Reilly**, who was born in Mlilwane in 1938, the son of a British Anglo-Boer War soldier who had stayed on. As Reilly was growing up, Swazi wildlife and its natural habitats were coming under serious threat from poachers and commercial farmers. In 1959, Reilly lobbied the colonial government to set aside land for parks, but was defeated by farmers who wanted the land for commercial agriculture. Undeterred, he turned his Mlilwane estate into a park any-way, and set about cultivating a relationship with **King Sobhuza II**, who was having trouble himself with poachers at the royal estate in Hlane. After Swazi independ-ence, Sobhuza became much more powerful, and Reilly's relationship with him lent weight to his nature conservation efforts.

Despite rickety finances, the **Mlilwane Wildlife Sanctuary** opened in 1963, and the re-stocking and reintroduction of species has continued ever since (the reserve today is ten times the size of the original sanctuary). Meanwhile, Sobhuza asked Reilly to help stamp out poaching at Hlane. Reilly's tough approach resulted in shootouts with the poachers, earning him the praise of some, but the enmity of many. Matters came to a head in 1992 when, with the help of the South African Police Endangered Species Protection Unit, Reilly tracked down a poaching unit that had been operating in Mkhaya. In the ensuing gun-fight, one poacher was killed and another paralyzed; criticism of Reilly's tactics intensified.

Reilly's dependence on royal connections has also generated controversy: critics claim it has prevented the development of a single parks board and a participatory, grass-roots involvement in conservation that is the key to long-term success. Some also assert that Reilly subordinates wildlife management principles to the needs of the tourist industry. Reilly's answer to his critics is simply to point to the three game parks his company runs. It's a powerful argument – without Reilly, the parks would not exist, and Swaziland and its visitors would be much the poorer for it.

ing less energetic, you can pass the time watching **hippos** wallowing in the hippo pool, overlooked by the *Hippo Haunt* restaurant at the main restcamp. The hippos are fed every day at 3pm.

Practicalities

To get to Mlilwane, take the turning from the eZulwini Valley road, sign-posted off the MR103 about a kilometre beyond the turn-off to Ludzidzini. From here, it's 3.5km along a dirt road to the entrance gate, where there's a small exhibition and craft centre. The reserve offers a wide variety of **accommodation**; for all options except Sondzela, **bookings** should be made through Swaziland Big Game Parks Central Reservations (⌗5283944, ⓦwww.biggame.co.sz). In the **main restcamp**, about 1.5km from the gate, there's a campsite, dorms (❶), traditional beehive huts (❷) and two-person huts (❷), along with communal ablution facilities and a swimming pool. Situated in the northern part of the sanctuary is *Sondzela* **backpacker lodge**, a friendly place now firmly established on the backpacking circuit, where you can stay in dorms or doubles and relax in the lush garden by a large swimming pool (bookings ⌗5283117; ❶). At the other end of the scale is *Reilly's Rock Hilltop Lodge* (full-board; ❻), a lovely colonial home full of antiques and hardwood furniture situated on a hilltop surrounded by woodland and prolific birdlife. With only six rooms, it's more upmarket than a guesthouse but more rustic than a game lodge, and guests here can enjoy fantastic views from the balcony over the Mdzimba Mountains, wander round the gardens which surround the house, and take part in any of the activities offered elsewhere in the reserve. The only place to eat is at the inexpensive *Hippo Haunt* **restaurant**, at the main restcamp, where there's also a bar.

For those who don't have their own **transport**, it is possible to walk from Sondzela to the main restcamp, and there are occasional **shuttle buses** running between *Sondzela* and Malandela's Homestead (see below), where pickups for the **Baz Bus** are made.

Through the Malkerns Valley

Continuing on the road towards Manzini, a turn to the southwest at Mahlanya, roughly 5km beyond the road to Mlilwane (beside a row of shops and a petrol station), takes you to the scenic, pineapple-growing **Malkerns Valley**. About a kilometre along this road, look out on the right hand side for *Malandela's Homestead* (⌗5283423), a fascinating collection of buildings where you can find craft shops, a pub and restaurant, a theatre and an internet café. Situated under a large thatched roof, *Malandela's Restaurant* (⌗5283115) has a European-style menu with good-quality a la carte **meals** including stews, game and fresh fish dishes. The restaurant's outdoor dining area provides excellent views of the adjoining fields and distant mountains, while the adjoining **pub** has British beer on tap and is a popular spot for locals to watch big rugby and soccer games on cable TV. *Sigubhu Internet Café* (Mon–Sat 8am–5.30pm; ⌗5283423) is used by backpackers staying at *Sondzela* in Mlilwane (see above), and also operates as a useful **tourist information** point. Alongside *Sigubhu*, the funky designs of House on Fire, a gallery and amphitheatre-like performance space (⌗5282001), are worth checking out for contemporary African crafts and the sheer exuberance and imagination which has gone into creating the place. Next door, Gone Rural (⌗5283439) is one of the most successful and creative **local handicrafts projects** in Swaziland; the colourful and well-designed woven mats and baskets on sale here are made by a huge network of women working from villages all over the country.

A little further on, several more **craft shops** line the Malkerns–Manzini road: *Swazi Candles* (daily 9am–1pm) sells a bewildering array of brightly patterned wax candles; Baobab Batik, 2km further along, sells all manner of colourful batiks. Beside this is *Nyanza Cottage* (☎5283090, ⓔnyanza@africaonline.co.sz; ❹), a relaxing cottage set on an appealing cluttered working farm roamed by dogs, cats, geese, peacocks and jersey cows. The cottages are linked to Nyanza Horse Trails, which offers cross-country and mountain rides lasting from half an hour to a whole day.

Manzini

MANZINI is Swaziland's largest city and its commercial hub. Almost all the country's industrial and commercial sector is based in or around here, and the city is dominated by office blocks and malls obscuring its few attractive edifices. With a rising crime rate and an atmosphere far less relaxed than Mbabane, Manzini would be an eminently missable place were it not for its outstanding **market** on the corner of Mhlakuvane and Mancishane streets (daily except Sunday).

Much of Manzini's market is devoted to fruit and vegetables, household goods and traditional medicines, while an upper section that spills onto the steps below sells **crafts** and **fabrics**. The crafts selection is bigger, more varied and much better value than any other market in Swaziland, while the fabrics – from Zimbabwe, Congo and Mozambique – are hard to find elsewhere in the country.

Just north of the market, on Ngwane Street, stands **The Bhunu**, one of Manzini's new shopping malls. **The Hub**, south of the market, on Mhlakuvane Street, is smarter and has a good supermarket and several restaurants and takeaways. Manzini's only other point of interest is its original **Catholic mission**, an elegant stone building (not open to casual visitors) opposite the new cathedral on Sandlane Street (parallel to Mhlakuvane Street).

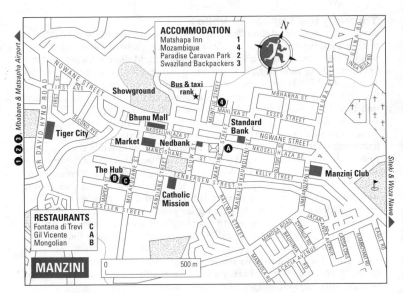

Practicalities

Buses from all over the country and South Africa pull in at Manzini's busy main bus station at the end of Louw Street, just north of Ngwane Street. **Matsapha airport** (℡5186155) lies 8km west of the city centre; if you're arriving here, you'll need to take a **taxi** into central Manzini. The centre itself is small enough to walk around.

Manzini has a limited selection of **places to stay**. In town, near the bus station, on the corner of Meintjies and Mahleka streets, the *Mozambique Hotel* (℡5052489, ℻5052586; ❷) offers tiny rooms with paper-thin walls, but has a friendly bar and an excellent restaurant. For backpackers, there's nothing in Manzini itself: east of town is the simple but fun *Woza Nawe* (see box below), while seven kilometres west of the city, on the road to Malkerns and eZulwini, is the recently upgraded *Swaziland Backpackers* (℡5187255, @info@swazilandbackpackers.com; ❶). This operates as the overnight stop for the **Baz Bus**, and consequently attracts a fair amount of passing travellers stopping off to check out Swaziland for a couple of days or arrange a side trip into Mozambique. The hostel, which has small dorms, decent doubles and some pleasant areas outside for lounging around, isn't all that convenient if you want to get to Manzini to do some shopping or banking, though minibus taxis are constantly passing on the main road outside. Otherwise, trips to different attractions including the game reserves and activities such as whitewater rafting can be organized, including pick-ups from the hostel. Across the road is the motel-like *Matshapa Inn* (℡5187481; ❸), and a sparse **campsite**, *Paradise Caravan Park* (℡5184935).

As well as the *Mozambique's* restaurant, other good **places to eat** in town include *Gil Vicente*, in the Ilanga Centre, Martin Street (℡5053874; closed Mon), which serves tasty Portuguese dishes; the *Mongolian*, Villiers Street, where you'll find the best Chinese food in town; and the *Fontana de Trevi Pizzeria*, The Hub, Mhlakuvane Street. The best **nightlife** is found at the *Oasis* nightclub, Tenbergen Street, which often attracts bands from South Africa at weekends and provides some no-holds-barred Swazi partying. The only **cinema** in Swaziland is at Tiger City (℡5056323) on Dr David Hynd Road.

Myxo's Place

Woza Nawe, a backpackers' lodge located about 6km southeast of Manzini on the Big Bend road, has quickly established itself on the backpacker circuit as a relaxed spot with a very different feel to most white-run lodges in South Africa and Swaziland. Run by a young Swazi, **Mxolisi Mdluli** (or Myxo for short), *Woza Nawe* is also used as a base for an ambitious community tourism project based in the village of KaPhunga, about 30km into the mountains southeast of Manzini. Here Myxo has built a mini-village of huts and rondavels specially for backpackers to experience a few days living as part of a local community. The authentic huts are separate from the main village, so that a certain amount of privacy is allowed both visitors and villagers, but you're encouraged to eat and sleep in the traditional Swazi way. During the day, visitors can join in whatever is going on in the village, such as building projects, farming work, brewing beer or teaching at the local school.

Two-day overnight trips to KaPhunga, including transport and contributions to the village, cost around E300 per person (extra nights are E50), while *Woza Nawe* hostel has both dorms and doubles (❶) and space for camping. For more details contact Myxo on ℡5058363 or 6044102, @wozanawe@realnet.co.sz.

Piggs Peak and the northwest

The highveld of **Piggs Peak** and the **northwest** is unquestionably the most beautiful region of Swaziland, with rolling hills perfect for hiking, countless sparkling streams, a sprinkling of waterfalls and some wonderful accommodation.

Approaches to Piggs Peak

Most visitors to the northwest enter Swaziland after going through the Kruger National Park (see p.693), but Piggs Peak is only 64km north of Mbabane and easily reached from there, too. The most spectacular – and rugged – entrance into the country is via the Bulembu road from Barberton in Mpumalanga (see p.685), which passes through Bulembu village on the way to Piggs Peak.

From Jeppe's Reef/Matsamo border

From the **Jeppe's Reef/Matsamo border** (8am–4pm), the road on the Swazi side is good all the way to Piggs Peak. Some 25km south of the border on this road is a good **place to stay**, the *Protea Piggs Peak Hotel & Casino* (℡4371104, ⓦwww.proteapiggspeak.sz; ❺), set in thousands of acres of mountainous pine forest. Despite the monolithic appearance of the hotel's exterior, the rooms have fabulous views, and there's an inviting swimming pool with a bar in the middle, plus a good buffet **restaurant**. You can buy hand-spun mohair products in the hotel lobby as well as from their source nearby. However, like most of the large hotels in Swaziland, the main focus of the place is the casino and slot machines.

For somewhere very different in style and atmosphere, continue another 3km; a sign on the right indicates the private **Phophonyane Nature Reserve** (℡4371319 or 4045006), which is five slow kilometres away from the road. The reserve is small, but carefully laid-out **trails** ensure there's plenty to see, including the Phopanyane Waterfall on the reserve's eastern side. The vegetation is subtropical and attracts hundreds of colourful **bird species**. Animals include mongooses, bushbabies, otters and numerous snakes, but all are hard to spot. The lodge in the reserve is one of the most beautiful places to stay in Swaziland, offering two-person safari tents next to the Phopanyane River, with a communal kitchen and washing facilities (❹), and cottages for four to six people, with private kitchens and gardens (❺). If you can't afford to stay, it's still worth stopping here for a short hike in the reserve and a meal in its secluded, mid-priced **restaurant**. The pool, although chilly, is cleverly blended into the rocks beside the tumbling river and has a stunning location, looking out onto endless mountains and surrounded by luxuriant vegetation.

A few kilometres south of Phophonyane, 1km north of Piggs Peak, the turn-off to Kuthuleni is the start of a scenic fifty-kilometre drive along a good dirt road to **Bhalekane**. There isn't much in Bhalekane (except a prison), but you can proceed from here to Tshaneni and the **northeast** (see p.813), or head south through fairly remote territory to Mafutseni and then Manzini.

From Bulembu

The road from Barberton in Mpumalanga, to Piggs Peak via **Bulembu border post** (8am–4pm), is briefly tarred out of Barberton, but soon deteriorates as it passes through some of the most rugged country imaginable, with the road near the border crossing in particularly poor shape. Looking up, you can see the Barberton–Havelock cableway, which carries asbestos from the nearby

Havelock mine to South Africa. Once in Swaziland, the road soon passes through Bulembu, with Piggs Peak a further 20km away.

Piggs Peak

PIGGS PEAK, a small straggling forestry town along the main road, was named after a French prospector called William Pigg, who discovered gold nearby in 1884, where it was mined until the site was exhausted in 1954. Apart from the attractive surrounding countryside, there's nothing much to see here, but if you're heading to Mallotja Nature Reserve this is a good place to stock up on supplies.

The town's **bus station** and **market** are near the Total garage at the northern end of town, where there is also a small shopping centre with a **supermarket**. There are a couple of **banks** in the centre of town, but they are unused to foreign transactions, so either summon your patience or hold out until Mbabane. For an **overnight stay**, the *Highland Inn* (℡4371144; ❸) offers simple, but comfortable, rooms in a pleasant colonial building on the main road on the southern edge of town. Inside, the *Woodcutter's Den* **restaurant** serves steaks and other meat dishes at fairly reasonable prices. For a quick snack, *The Ranch*, in the town's shopping centre, offers fast food, while the *Pholani* **bar** alongside does plenty of trade, rocking until late on weekends.

On to Malolotja Nature Reserve

Driving south, you soon leave the pine plantations behind and pass into rolling highveld grassland, peppered with rural dwellings, with the stretch across the Nkomati River Valley a particularly beautiful one. Alongside the road are curio stalls, often staffed by young children dressed in leaves to attract your attention. Also along this road is evidence of the construction work on the large **Maguga Dam** project on the Komati River, which will radically alter the scenery of the river valley through flooding by the time it is completed early in the twenty-first century. Near here are two **places to stay** set up by young Swazi men offering a taste of rural living. *Mthunzi's Paradise Village* (℡6080469, Ⓦwww.swaziplace.com/mthunzi; ❸) is near the Komati River, and provides a chance to stay in a small community and experience local life, from river-fishing to supporting the local football team. The price includes a tour, accommodation and meals. Alternatively, *Sobantu Guest Farm* (℡6053954; ❶) is a large modern farmhouse in an isolated spot near Mnyokane, where backpackers are encouraged to chill out for a few days. There are plenty of hiking trails, waterfall and rockpools nearby, and local Swazi food is often cooked in the evenings. Before making for either place you should contact them for precise directions.

About 30km from Piggs Peak, just after Nkhaba, you'll reach the entrance to the Malolotja Nature Reserve. The main road continues south from here to join the Ngwenya–Mbabane road at Motshane (see p.813), 20km further on.

Malolotja Nature Reserve

Swaziland's least touristy park, the easy-going **Malolotja Nature Reserve** (daily: May–Sept 6.30am–6pm, Oct–April 6am–6.30pm; E10 plus E5 per car; ℡4424241) offers awesome scenery and some of the finest hiking in southern Africa. This is a place to come for rugged, wild nature and tranquillity, rather than for game spotting. The mountains here, among the oldest in the world (3.6 billion years old), are covered in grassland and graced by myriad streams and waterfalls, including the 95-metre-high **Malolotja Falls**.

Nearly three hundred species of **birds** are found in Malolotja, with an impressive colony of the rare bald ibis just by the waterfalls. You'll have to look harder for **game**, although wildebeest, blesbok and impala are often visible, and there are leopards and two very retiring elephants lurking somewhere in the gaping tracts of mountain and valley; in the friendly spirit of the reserve, a leaflet is handed out on arrival asking hikers to help the park's research by reporting any signs of the elephants, or of the rare eland introduced a few years ago.

Malolotja also boasts **Ngwenya Mine**, the world's most ancient at 43,000 years old. The Stone Age Workers here once dug for specularite and haematite, which were used as cosmetics and for religious rituals. To visit you must book a **guide** at least one night beforehand, although there's always a guide on duty at weekends, at an entry point at the south of the reserve near to the Ngwenya Glass factory (see opposite); note that this gate gives access to the mine only. Nearby, the **Forbes Reef Gold Mine** can be visited alone, but take care on the slippery banks; you can find it using the map you get on arrival at the park entrance.

Malolotja's small network of roads pass some fine viewpoints and picnic sites, but to really savour this park's rugged wilderness and see its waterfalls you'll need to hike. A variety of **hiking trails** are laid out in the reserve, from easy half-day excursions to seven-day marathons, with accommodation available en route (see below).

Practicalities

Brochures and **maps** are available from the reserve's **office**, just inside the entrance gate. The office also issues permits for Hawane Dam Nature Reserve (see below), as well as the useful free *Hiking and Backpacking Guide*.

Accommodation should be booked in advance through the National Trust Commission (see p.804). The main restcamp has fifteen tent sites with hot water in a communal bath area and braai areas, but not much wind shelter. There is also an A-frame **chalet** (❶), which sleeps up to six people, and five well-located log **cabins** (❷), which can also house up to six people each. A small shop at the entrance sells basic **provisions**, but it's wiser to stock up in Piggs Peak or Mbabane. Twenty **campsites** without facilities are scattered around the reserve for those attempting longer hikes: you'll need to bring all your own equipment, including a cooker, as no fires are permitted.

If you're on a long hike during the summer, be prepared for blisteringly hot days; however, temperatures drop dramatically in winter, when the nights can be freezing.

Hawane Dam and horse trails

Around two kilometres south of Malolotja, on the Mbabane road, lies the **Hawane Dam Nature Reserve** (☎ 4424241; Mon–Fri free, Sat & Sun E10), a small area around the northern end of the Hawane Dam, designed to protect part of the Black Umbuluzi River wetlands. Hawane's main attraction is its wealth of **birdlife**, and there's an excellent trail for bird-watching.

A little further on is **Hawane African Adventure Trails** (☎ 4043375 or 6021911, ⓦ www.hawane.co.sz), signposted down a track, a good option if you fancy exploring the attractive surrounding countryside on horseback. They have a range of ponies and horses for trails lasting anything between a couple of hours and a week. There's also a base-camp, with around half-a-dozen comfortable bee-hive **huts** sleeping two people (full-board; ❸); this accommodation is available even if you're not riding.

Ngwenya

The road from Piggs Peak meets the main MR3 between the Ngwenya/ Oshoek border post and Mbabane at the small settlement of **Motshane**. A kilometre west of Motshane along this road is the Ngwenya Glass factory (daily 9am–4pm), where of one of Swaziland's best-known exports, **Ngwenya glass**, is made. Their products, which range from attractive wine glasses to endless trinkets in the shape of rotund animals, are made from recycled glass and are produced by highly skilled workers, and it's well worth stopping here just to see them blowing and crafting the glass from the viewing balcony above the roaring furnaces. The adjoining gift shop and **café** are usually swamped by coach-loads of tourists, who can further satisfy their craving for crafts a few hundred metres from the factory up the hill at **Endlotane Studios** (Mon–Fri 8am–4.30pm, Sat–Sun 9am–5pm), where large and colourful tapestries are painstakingly woven from mohair wool spun on the premises. Nearby, is an entrance to Malolotja Nature Reserve, allowing access to **Ngwenya Mine** (see opposite).

The northeast

Northeast Swaziland is dominated by sugar plantations stretching into the distance, shimmering from the constant water spray, wreaking havoc with the water table – and leaving many locals without – but earning the country valuable foreign exchange. Three large tracts of bush – **Hlane**, **Mlawula** and **Mbuluzi** – have been preserved as wildlife and nature reserves, and these are the main attractions for visitors to this region. Together with **Shewula Nature Reserve**, these form part of the **Lubombo Conservancy**, a grouping of protected land in the **Lubombo Mountains** that runs along Swaziland's eastern border and provides fantastic views of both Swaziland and the western fringes of Mozambique.

The most direct and obvious route to the reserves from Mbabane is to follow the signposted and tarred **Siteki road** for 100km. The **northern route** is a little over twice as long and is part gravel, but makes for a far more spectacular journey. Travel north to **Piggs Peak** from Mbabane, and turn right at the **Bhalekane** turn-off towards Bhalkane, roughly 1km later.

Tshaneni

The gravel road from Piggs Peak passes through some fabulous scenery before eventually winding up at the sugar town of **TSHANENI**. The one **hotel** here, the *Impala Arms* (☎3131244; ❷), has plain but comfortable rooms; the bar has a pool table, and is filled with exuberant Swazi at weekends. If you need supplies, Tshaneni's Score **supermarket** will come in handy, and there is a Caltex **garage** nearby for fuel.

The **Mananga border post** (8am–6pm) lies 5km north of here, from where the road leads to Komatipoort (see p.687). Heading south, however, the next town you'll meet is bougainvillea-festooned **Mhlume**. Twenty kilometres further on is a junction at Maphiveni: a left turn to the north takes you to the **Lomahasha/Namaacha border post** with Mozambique (7am–8pm), another 20km away, while a right turn followed almost immediately by a signposted left takes you to Mbuluzi Game Reserve and Mlawula Nature Reserve.

Mbuluzi Game Reserve

Privately owned and little-known, **Mbuluzi** (daily 8am–5pm; E10 per person, E20 per vehicle; @www.mbuluzi.co.sz) is about 1km off the Manzini–Lomahasha road, and straddles the road to Mlawula. Set in classic lowveld bush, it's filled with thorn trees and hot in the summer. Currently the park is being restocked with game, including hippo and giraffe, which you can view in your own vehicle – as long as it's 4WD. At the park entrance you can rent vehicles for E150 per day, and hire guides for a negotiable amount. The absence of predators in Mbuluzi's southern portion means that you can walk along a network of **trails** in this section.

Mbuluzi's self-catering **accommodation** (➏ for the whole lodge, which sleeps between 3 and 8 people), is its finest feature: three large and comfortable lodges with verandahs overlook the Mlwawula stream, whose luxuriant vegetation attracts birds and animals which you can watch from the verandahs.

Mlawula Nature Reserve

The largest single protected area in the Lubombo Mountains is the 165-square-kilometre **Mlawula Nature Reserve** (daily dawn–dusk; E10 per person, E5 per vehicle), south of the Mbuluzi River. The best reason to come to Mlawula is to stay at *Sara Bush Camp* (see below), but you can spend some time exploring a network of self-guided hiking **trails**. As well as climbing into the mountains and onto the plateau at the top of the Lubombo range where unique species of ironwood trees and cycads grow, the trails wend their way around the river heading for caves, a waterfall and a rhino pool (although there are no rhino left), and vary in length from two to eight hours. The bush throughout the reserve is quite dense, however, which largely prevents you from seeing much game. Guides are available to lead you on the hiking trails.

The Mlawula stream and more substantial Mbuluzi River both flow through some spectacular valleys in this reserve, and Stone Age tools over one million years old have been found along their beds. **Antelope**, **zebra** and **wildebeest** congregate near the water, but so do **crocodiles**, so resist the temptation to swim.

Practicalities

Buses from Manzini travel to the Mlawula Nature Reserve once a day very early in the morning. To get here by **car**, continue past the Mbuluzi Reserve for a few kilometres until you see a sign pointing to the Mlawula Reserve on your right. You can pick up various leaflets at the park gate, but no supplies, so stock up beforehand.

Accommodation should be booked through the National Trust Commission, in the National Museum at Lobamba (see p.804). Overnight **camping** on the trail has not been permitted since the camping hut was burnt down, apparently by Mozambican border-hoppers, but there is a shaded campsite in the Siphiso River Valley. Much more appealing is the self-catering *Sara Bush Camp* (➋ per double tent), which has three large safari tents on wooden decks perched on the very edge of a cliff. Surrounded by bush, each tent also has it's own bathing area, consisting of a tiny perch amongst the rocks on the cliff edge with a donkey-boiler shower and galvanized iron washtub, allowing you to bathe outside with a stunning view west over the reserve and beyond, making it perfectly positioned for sunset. Each tent has a braai site and there's a communal lounge and kitchen area.

Shewula

Situated on a plateau to the north of Mlawula, **Shewula Mountain Camp** (booking essential ☎4162180, ✉tours@swazitrails.co.za; ➊) is a new tourism development by the local Shewula community. Although it's isolated and time-consuming to reach, the camp has a spectacular site at one end of the plateau, with views west across northeast Swaziland and even, on a clear day, to the sky-scrapers of Maputo to the east. It also offers an interesting insight into the life of a rural community in Swaziland. Accommodation is in four rondavels (which sleep up to 8 people) with bunks or doubles around communal ablution and dining areas, but there's no electricity and cooking is done on gas. Activities include hiking through Shewula Nature Reserve and a visit to the nearby village. If you don't want to self-cater, meals can be arranged in advance.

Hlane Royal National Park

Some 67km northeast of Manzini is **Hlane Royal National Park** (daily dawn–dusk; E10), the largest of Swaziland's parks. Formerly a private royal hunting ground, the main attraction here is the presence of big game, including **elephant, rhino, lion, leopard** and **cheetah**. Hlane is also one of the best parks in southern Africa to view elephants and rhino **on foot** – an unforgettable experience – in the company of a guide (E15 per hour). These two species are in the northern area of the park, which you can also visit in your own vehicle, with or without a guide, and rhino-sighting is virtually guaranteed. Other animals in this section include giraffe, zebra and waterbuck.

Various **southern enclosures** contain lion, cheetah and leopard, along with some more elephant and rhino; walking here is out of the question, but you can drive with a guide in your own car. If you don't have your own transport, there's also a guided tour in one of the park's 4WD minibuses (E100). Although the enclosures guarantee lion sightings, the animals are well habituated to vehicles and look thoroughly bored by the whole experience – a pity, as the presence of lions in the country is meant to be the source of great pride to the Swazis, not least because they are the royal symbol.

Practicalities

The **entrance** to Hlane is roughly 4km south of Simunye, off the Manzini–Lomahasha road. **Buses** between Manzini and Simunye stop at the park gate.

Hlane has two **accommodation** options, both of which must be **booked** through Big Game Parks Central Reservations (☎5283944, ⊛www.biggame .co.sz). The main *Ndlovu* camp (➋), situated near the gate, offers large thatched cottages sleeping two to three people and camping spots, but no electricity (paraffin lamps are provided). Unless there's a large group staying, this camp is fairly relaxed, with plenty of trees and shady spots to sit. There's also a thatched restaurant and lounge area, with a wide deck overlooking a large nearby watering hole which attracts rhino, elephant and giraffe. The self-catering *Bhubesi* camp (➊), with its three comfortable stone cottages overlooking a dry river, is 18km from *Ndlovu* along a dirt track, and feels much more remote, though the cottages here have electricity.

Siteki

Perched spectacularly on a hillside and once the gateway to a busy border post with Mozambique, **SITEKI**, just over 30km south of Mlawula Nature Reserve, is a fairly lively regional centre. Although the border has now been closed for some years, Siteki remains busy, with a **bus station** that operates frequent services to Manzini, a colourful **market**, and a number of lively restaurants along the main street. Next door to the *Siteki* hotel, off the main road on the way out of town, is the headquarters of Litiko Letinyanga (☎3434512), a traditional healing organization, run by Dr Nhlavana Maseko, which seeks to improve the credibility of traditional healing with Western medical institutions. You may be able to arrange a session with a traditional healer, but you'll have to phone beforehand (ask for Betty).

There's only one **place to stay** – the *Siteki* (☎3434126; ❸), which is pleasant enough, though the rooms feel a bit spartan. Downstairs, the hotel **restaurant** serves steaks and other meat dishes, and there's a great bar attached, which is popular with locals and gets very lively at weekends.

At the beginning of the road ascending to the town, you'll pass through a foot-and-mouth disease control **checkpoint**; the guards only check you on the way out, to confiscate any meat products that you might have tucked away.

The south

Approaching Swaziland from one of its border crossings in the south is an excellent idea if you're travelling from northern KwaZulu-Natal through to the Kruger National Park or Mpumulanga. The scenery, particularly along the drive from **Mahamba** to Manzini through the **Grand Valley**, is really superb, and the road passes near most of the historical sites of the Swazi royal house. The south is also home to the **Mkhaya Nature Reserve**, Swaziland's most upmarket reserve and a sanctuary for the rare black rhino.

From Mahamba to Manzini

The **Mahamba border crossing** (7am–10pm) is the nearest to Piet Retief in South Africa. Mahamba means "the runaways", which refers to nineteenth-century pretenders to the royal throne who fled here twice to escape retribution. The nearest major town is **NHLANGANO**, only 16km from the border. Nhlangano (the name means "meeting place", commemorating the meeting of the British and Swazi monarchs George V and Sobhuza II in 1947) is a good place to change money and to catch **buses** to Mbabane and Manzini.

The town also has a couple of decent **places to stay**: the lively *Phoenix* (☎2078488; ❷) on the main street offers en-suite rooms, while the upmarket *Nhlangano Sun* (☎2078211, ⓦwww.suninternational.com; ❺), designed to resemble a ski resort, lies off a signposted turn-off just north of town and looks out onto the Makhosini Valley. The rooms are plush, and the hotel's reasonably priced **restaurant** is worth a visit if you're just passing through; there's also a casino.

The **Makhosini Valley**, 8km **east of Nhlangano** on the Mhlosheni road, is the site of the main **royal burial grounds**, guarded and tended by the Mduli clan. To avoid disturbing their rulers' eternal rest, the Mduli never cut the grass; consequently, the grounds now stand out as islands of forest in a sea of cultivated land. The Mduli also grind the king's medicines and snuff, and have the interesting task of preventing any part of his body (including his faeces, semen and toe-clippings) from being used for magical purposes.

A little further on is a turn to the south to **Zombodze**, King Ngwane I's first royal residence in modern-day Swaziland. It's badly signposted, so follow signs for the nearby Ngwane High School.

Another 28km **north of Nhlangano**, along on a good road, is the settlement of **HLATHIKHULU**, perched impressively on a hill and providing cool relief after the murderous heat below. Ngwane's grandson **Sobhuza I** fled near here from the attacks of the mighty Ndwandwe king Zwide, to a place called kaPhungalegazi ("place of the smell of blood"), though nothing is now left of the *kraal* he erected here. Sadly for the town, the main road steams right by it, leaving it forlorn on a diversion to the right.

The Ngwane clan fought a murderous but inconclusive battle with the Zulus under King Dingane in the nearby **Lubuya Valley** in 1839. This quiet valley is barely populated and, though there's nothing to remind you of the battle that once raged here, it's a good place for a picnic and a stroll. To get to the valley from Hlathikhulu, take the first turning right after heading north towards Manzini, towards Lugoje Nek, and a left turn at the fork here brings you to the valley. The battle left Dingane's army much reduced, making him an easy target for his brother Mpande the following year.

From Hlathikhulu, Manzini is 74km away, with the bulk of the drive passing along the **Grand Valley**, through which flows the sometimes mighty Mkhondvo River. The valley is hot, overgrazed and almost barren, but offers stunning hiking possibilities and stupendous views from a car.

From Lavumisa to Manzini

Travelling north from KwaZulu-Natal, you'll come to the **Lavumisa/Golela border post** (7am–10pm). The border is named after one of the wives of Sobhuza I, whose son Malambule tried to overthrow Sobhuza's successor, Mswati II. Golela, on the South African side, means "many animals", and indeed this area was once predominantly a hunting ground. Today, however, the animals have all but gone and there's little reason to linger, unless you're tempted by the prospect of a close encounter with one of the lions at a small, new game reserve, **Nisela Safaris** (daily 8.30am–4.30pm; ☏3030247, ✉nisela@iafrica.com). The reserve's animals, including giraffe, kudu, zebra and warthog, are for understandable reasons of preservation kept apart from the lions, who prowl their own separate enclosure. Accommodation is offered in thatched cabins (❹), each sleeping four, and a colonial-style guest house (❺); there's also a pool and restaurant. At the entrance to the reserve, a coffee shop and curio stall provide a rest stop for drivers making their way to or from the border.

Whitewater rafting

One of the most exhilarating things you can do in southern Swaziland is to **whitewater raft** on the beautiful Great Usutu River, located in the east of the country near the Mkhaya Nature Reserve. One of the best whitewater rivers in southern Africa, it's also one of the few where you can take a trip in a two-man "croc" raft. The route runs for 15km in summer (a bit less in winter), and crosses over rapids classed in grades two to four. Anyone can tackle these rapids once they have had a safety briefing.

The scenery along the route is stunning, but hard to appreciate once you hit the rapids, which leave you paddling like crazy and doing your best not to fall in the water. Most people do capsize, but careful supervision ensures that everyone lives to tell the tale. Trips include pick-ups from various points in the eZulwini Valley and cost around E350 a person, including a picnic lunch and evening sundowners. Contact Swazi Trails (☏4162180, ✇www.swazitrails.co.sz) for bookings and further information.

The road north crosses the Ingwavuma River just south of Nsoko, about 30km from the border, and then runs parallel to the **Lubombo Mountains**. A few kilometres before Big Bend, you'll pass **The Riverside**, a complex on the main road housing a functional **motel** (☎3636012; ❷), a good Portuguese restaurant and a scruffy nightclub; downstairs, Emoya Handicrafts offers a small selection of good-value pieces. Next door is the Bushlands Butchery, where prices are so good that many South Africans drive here to stock up on meat. A kilometre further on is an outstanding **restaurant**, *Lubombo Lobster* (☎3636613), which serves a wonderful seafood curry.

BIG BEND itself, dominated by a huge sugar mill, is only worth visiting for its **hotel**, the *New Bend Inn* (☎3636111; ❷), on a hill at the far end of town beyond the golf course. A slightly run-down colonial establishment with superb views of the valley and well-positioned bars, the sixteen-bedroom hotel is a lively Swazi haunt on weekends, when major parties take place. The rooms are spartan but air-conditioned and perfectly comfortable, and the hotel **restaurant** serves tolerable curries and grills for around E25–40.

From the centre of Big Bend, **buses** travel to Manzini, Mbabane and north to Siteki (see p.815).

Mkhaya Game Reserve

Roughly 30km north of Big Bend lies **Mkhaya Game Reserve**, situated along a turn-off from the wonderfully named village of **Phuzumoya** ("drink the wind") in classic lowveld scrubland, filled with acacia and thorn trees. A sanctuary for the rare **black rhino**, Mkhaya also accommodates **white rhino**, **elephant** and numerous antelopes such as nyala and eland. As well as a tourist attraction, Mkhaya also operates as a refuge where endangered species such as **roan antelope** and **tsessebe** are bred. Rubbing shoulders with them all are herds of **Nguni cattle** (see box below).

Day visits and overnight stays at Mkhaya must be booked in advance (see p.819), and you can't tour Mkhaya in your own vehicle, but must arrange to be met at the gate. Day visitors are taken on a game drive, where you have a high chance of encountering much of the big game, and a generous **lunch** is included in the price. For overnighters, morning and evening game drives are included in the accommodation price. Unlike game reserves in South Africa, Mkhaya's experienced Swazi rangers have few qualms about stopping in the middle of a game drive and inviting visitors to get out of the vehicle and walk quite close to white rhino and elephant. If you're staying overnight, early-morning game walks can also be organized.

Nguni cattle and Mkhaya

The long-horned **Nguni cattle**, herded by the African clans when Europeans encountered them in the nineteenth century, were descendants of the early Iron Age herds. Although they are hardy, disease-resistant and well-adapted to their environment, white beef-farmers regarded them as too puny and unproductive for their industry, and replaced them with imported stock. By the 1970s, pure strains of long-horned cattle had virtually disappeared from Swaziland, and **Ted Reilly** initially purchased Mkhaya (see p.806) to save them. The sharp increase in the price of cattle feed in the late 1970s made the long-horns increasingly attractive commercially, enabling Reilly to sell them as pure-bred breeding stock, using the money to fund the game acquisition programme at Mkhaya. Today, the cattle graze here alongside zebra, wildebeest and antelope, just as they always used to.

You'll need to **book** your visit to Mkhaya through Swazi Big Game Parks Central Reservations (☎5283944, ⊛www.biggame.co.sz). Day visits cost around E250, including lunch. The reserve's main camp, *Stone Camp*, makes up for the lack of elevation in the reserve with an atmospheric bush setting beside the dry Ngwenyane river bed. There are two types of full-board **accommodation** (including game drives ⑤): open-plan and open-sided thatched cottages which give you a wonderful sense of sleeping right in the bush; and luxury safari tents with en-suite toilets and showers. All of these are secluded but secure and lit by paraffin lamps; cooking is done on a large campfire in the main part of the camp under the shade of a massive sausage tree (its seed pods look like sausages), and staff have been known to treat guests to an after-dinner concert.

Travel details

Buses

Big Bend to: Manzini (13 daily; 1hr 30min); Siteki (2 daily; 1hr 30min).
Manzini to: Big Bend (13 daily; 1hr 30min); Hlatsi (2 daily; 1hr 30min); Johannesburg (3 weekly; 8hr); Lavumisa (2 daily; 5hr); Mbabane (27 daily; 45min); Nhlangano (12 daily; 3hr 15min); Siteki (15 daily; 1hr 30min).

Mbabane to: Johannesburg (3 weekly; 7hr 30min); Manzini (27 daily; 45min); Nhlangano (4 daily; 4hr); Piggs Peak (10 daily; 1hr).
Nhlangano to: Manzini (12 daily; 3hr 15min); Mbabane (4 daily; 4hr).
Piggs Peak to: Mbabane (10 daily; 1hr).
Siteki to: Big Bend (2 daily; 1hr 30min); Manzini (15 daily; 1hr 30min).

Baz Bus

Manzini to: Durban (3 weekly; 10hr); Johannesburg (3 weekly; 8hr).

Flights

Manzini to: Durban (daily except Sat, 1hr), Johannesburg (3 daily; 1hr), Maputo (1 daily Tues–Thurs; 45min).

contexts

contexts

History

Human history – or prehistory – probably began in South Africa. That, at least, is the story told by recent fossil finds, which show that *Homo sapiens* existed along Africa's southern coast over 50,000 years ago. The descendants of these nomadic Stone Age people – ochre-skinned San hunter-gatherers and Khoikhoi herders, still inhabited the Western Cape when the first European seafarers arrived in the fifteenth century. By the time of the first Dutch settlement at the Cape in the mid-seventeenth century, tall dark-skinned people, who had begun crossing the Limpopo around the time of Christ's birth, had occupied much of the eastern half of the country.

The stage was now set for the complex drama of South Africa's modern history, which in crude terms was a battle for the control of scarce and conflicting resources between the various indigenous people, African states and the European colonizers. The twentieth century saw the temporary victory of colonialism, the unification of South Africa and the attempts by whites to keep at bay black demands for civil rights, culminating with the implementation of South Africa's most notorious social invention – apartheid. The century ended with the ultimate victory of multiracialism and democracy.

Prehistory

When our ancestors climbed down from the trees, it is quite likely they did it in South Africa – if a growing body of scientific evidence is to be believed. In 1924, the world's **oldest hominid remains** and the first-ever evidence of human-like creatures to be discovered in Africa were dug up in the Northern Cape and identified as a "fossilized monkey skull". After a stint as a humble paperweight, the fossil came to the attention of Professor Raymond Dart at the University of the Witwatersrand, who identified the earthshaking find as an intermediate species between apes and humans, with a small brain but an upright posture. Still a little unsteady on its feet, our ancestor trod the plains of eastern and southern Africa, perhaps three million years ago. Dart called it *Australopithecus africanus*: **Africa's southern ape**. After the emergence of *A. Africanus*, hominids spent the next couple of million years or so perfecting bipedal walking, tool-making, speech and got big-headed (a huge expansion in brain size took place) until they finally strode forth as *Homo sapiens*: the modern humans. Another first for South Africa was the unearthing of the oldest fossil evidence of *Homo sapiens* in a cave at the Klasies River Mouth in the Eastern Cape, reckoned to be between 50,000 and 100,000 years old.

The first South Africans

Rock art provides evidence of human culture in the subcontinent dating back nearly 30,000 years and represents southern Africa's oldest and most enduring artistic tradition. The artists were hunter-gathers, sometimes called Bushmen but more commonly **San**, a relatively modern term from the Nama language with roots in the concept of "inhabiting or dwelling" to reflect the fact these were South Africa's aboriginals. The most direct descendants of the late Stone Age, San people have survived in tiny pockets, mostly in Namibia and Botswana, making theirs the longest-spanning culture in the subcontinent. At one time they probably spread throughout sub-Saharan Africa, having pretty well perfected their **nomadic lifestyle**, which involved an enviable twenty-hour week spent by the men hunting and the women gathering. This left considerable time for artistic and religious pursuits. People lived in small, loosely connected bands comprising family units and were free to leave and join up with other groups. In this egalitarian society, the concept of private property had scant meaning because everything required for survival could be obtained from the environment.

About two thousand years ago, this changed when some groups in northern Botswana laid their hands on fat-tailed **sheep and cattle** from northern Africa, thus transforming themselves into **herding communities**. The introduction of livestock had a revolutionary effect on social organization, creating the idea of ownership and accumulation. Animals became a symbol of both wealth and social status and those who were better at acquiring and holding onto their animals gradually became wealthier. Social divisions developed, political units became larger and centred around a chief, who had important powers, such as the allocation of pasturage.

These were the first South Africans encountered by Portuguese mariners, who landed along the Cape coast in the fifteenth century. Known as **Khoikhoi** (meaning "men of men"), they were not ethnically distinct from the San, as many anthropologists once believed, but simply represented a distinct social organization. According to current thinking it was possible for Khoi who lost their livestock to revert to being San and for San to lay their hands on animals to become Khoi, giving rise to the collective term "Khoisan". This dynamic view of history is significant because it throws out the nineteenth-century idea that race was an absolute determinant of history and culture – a concept that found great popularity among apartheid apologists.

Farms and crafts

Around two thousand years ago, tall, dark-skinned people who practised mixed farming – raising both crops and livestock – crossed the Limpopo River into South Africa. San paintings from some time in the intervening period depict small ochre people and larger black ones in a variety of hostile and harmonious relationships, indicating contact between the two groups. These **Bantu-speaking** farmers were the ancestors of South Africa's majority African population, who gradually drifted south, to occupy the entire eastern half of the subcontinent as far as the Eastern Cape, where they were first encountered by Europeans in the sixteenth century.

Today there are four main **Bantu language groups** in South Africa, **Nguni** (comprising Zulu, Swazi and Xhosa) and **Sotho** (Sotho and Tswana) being by far the largest. The other two are **Venda** and **Tsonga**. Apart from highly developed farming know-how and a far more sedentary life than the Khoisan, the early Bantu speakers were skilled craftworkers and knew about mining and smelting metals, including gold, copper and iron, which became an important factor in the extensive network of **trade** that developed.

The picture painted by the British of them as bloodthirsty Africans engaged in endemic internecine conflicts probably said more about the white colonizers than the Bantu speakers themselves. The nineteenth-century traveller Ludwig Alberti underlined this fact when he observed that the Xhosa of the Eastern Cape "cannot be regarded as a warlike people; a predominant inclination to pursue a quiet cattle-raising life is much more in evidence amongst them".

The Cape goes Dutch

In the fifteenth century, Portuguese mariners under the command of **Bartholomeu Dias** became the first Europeans to set foot in South Africa. Marking their progress, they left an unpleasant set of calling cards all along the coast – African men and women they had captured in West Africa and had cast ashore to trumpet the power and glory of Portugal to the locals. Little wonder that their first encounter with the Khoi along the Garden Route coast was not a happy one. It began with a group of Khoi stoning the Portuguese for taking water from a spring without asking permission and ended with a Khoi man lying dead with a crossbow bolt through his chest.

It was another 170 years before any European settlement was established in South Africa. In 1652, a group of white employees of the **Dutch East India Company**, which was engaged in trade between the Netherlands and the East Indies, pulled into Table Bay to set up a refreshment station to revictual company ships trading between Europe and the East. There was no thought at the time of setting up a colony; on the contrary, the Cape was a rather bum posting, given to the station commander **Jan van Riebeeck** because he had been caught with his hand in the till by the company bosses. Van Riebeeck dreamed up a number of schemes to isolate the Cape Peninsula from the rest of Africa, including a plan to build a canal that would cut it adrift. In the end, he had to satisfy himself with planting a **bitter almond hedge** (still growing in Cape Town's Kirstenbosch Gardens) to keep the natives at bay, symbolically representing an ambivalence about being European in Africa, which still haunts many white South Africans.

Despite van Riebeeck's view that the **Khoi**, who were already living at the Cape, were "a savage set, living without conscience", from the start the Dutch were dependent on them to provide livestock, which were traded for trinkets. As the settlement developed, van Riebeeck needed more **labour** to keep the show going, and bemoaned the fact that he was unsuccessful in persuading the Khoi to discard the freedom of their herding life for the toil of ploughing furrows for him. Much to his annoyance, the bosses back in Holland had forbidden van Riebeeck from enslaving the locals, and refused his request for slaves from elsewhere in the company's empire.

This led to the inexorable process of **colonization** of the lands around the fort, when a number of Dutch men were released in 1657 from their contracts to farm as **free burghers** on land granted by the company. The idea was that they would have to sell their produce to the company at a fixed price, thereby overcoming the labour shortage. The only snag with this was the land didn't belong to the company in the first place and the move sparked the first of a series of **Khoikhoi–Dutch wars**. Although the first campaign ended in stalemate, the Khoikhoi were ultimately no match for the Dutch, who had the tactical mobility of horses and the superior killing power of firearms. Campaigns continued through the 1660s and 1670s and proved rather profitable for Dutch raiders, who on one outing in 1674 rounded up eight hundred Khoi cattle and four thousand sheep.

Meanwhile, in 1658, van Riebeeck had managed to successfully purloin a shipload of **slaves** from West Africa, whetting an insatiable appetite for this form of labour. The Dutch East India Company itself became the biggest slave owner at the Cape and continued importing slaves, mostly from the East Indies, at such a pace that by 1711 there were more slaves than burghers in the colony. By the end of the eighteenth century there were almost 15,000 slaves and just under 14,000 burghers at the Cape. With the help of this ready workforce, the embryonic Cape Colony expanded outwards and trampled the Peninsula Khoikhoi, who by 1713 had lost everything. Most of their livestock (nearly 50,000 animals) and most of their land west of the Hottentots Holland Mountains had been gobbled up by the Dutch East India Company. Dispossession and diseases like smallpox, previously unknown in South Africa, decimated their numbers and shattered their social system. By the middle of the eighteenth century, those who remained had been reduced to a condition of miserable servitude to the colonists.

Impoverished whites living at the fringes of colonial society also had few options, but these included the real possibility of dropping out of its grindingly class-conscious constraints. Many just packed up their waggons and rolled out into the interior, where they lived by the gun, either hunting game or taking cattle from the Khoi by force. Beyond the control of the Dutch East India Company, these nomadic **trekboers** began to assume a pastoral niche previously occupied by the Khoi. By the turn of the nineteenth century, trekboers had penetrated well into the Eastern Cape, pushing back the Khoi and San in the process. Not that the indigenous people gave up without a fight. As their lives became disrupted and living by traditional means became impossible, the Khoisan began to prey on the cattle and sheep of the trekboers. The trekboers responded ruthlessly by hunting down the San as vermin, killing the men and often taking women and children as slaves, bringing them to virtual extinction in South Africa.

After the **British occupation of the Cape** in 1795, the trekboer migration from the Cape accelerated. Britain was now undisputed as the world's dominant naval power. In the ferment that followed the French Revolution, Britain feared for the security of the Cape sea route to the East and therefore sent a few war sloops into Table Bay and informed the Dutch officials there that they were no longer in charge.

Rise of the Zulus

While in the west of the country white trekboers were migrating from the Cape Colony, in the east equally significant movements were under way. Throughout the seventeenth and eighteenth centuries, descendants of the first **Bantu speakers** to penetrate into South Africa had been swelling their numbers and had expanded right across the eastern half of the country, where the rainfall was high enough for their mixed farming economy. By the turn of the nineteenth century, the territory was brimming with people and cattle who were fast grazing it out, the limits of expansion having been reached. Exacerbating this was a sustained period of drought.

Nowhere was this more marked than in **KwaZulu-Natal**, where chiefdoms survived by subduing and absorbing their neighbours to gain control of pasturage, thus creating larger and more powerful groupings. By the early part of the nineteenth century, two chiefdoms, the **Ndwandwe** and the **Mthethwa**, dominated the eastern section of South Africa around the Tugela River. During the late 1810s a major confrontation between them ended in the defeat of the Mthethwa.

Out of their ruins emerged the **Zulus**, who were to become one of the most powerful polities in southern Africa. Prior to the defeat of the Mthethwa, the Zulus had been a minor clan under their domination. Around 1816, **Shaka** assumed the chieftaincy of the Zulus, whose fighting tactics he quickly transformed, supplementing the Nguni's traditional long javelin with the **assegai**, a short stabbing spear suitable for close combat. The throwing spear rendered a warrior unarmed once he had thrown it and was relatively easily deflected by a cowhide shield, but with a stabbing spear he could keep on fighting indefinitely. Shaka also introduced the tactic known as the "horns of the bull" by which the enemy were outflanked by highly disciplined formations spreading out to engulf them by means of two wings. The manoeuvre was used to devastating effect against the British at the Battle of Isandlwana in 1879.

By 1820, the Zulus had incorporated the fragments of the Mthethwa and had defeated the Ndwandwe. By the middle of the decade they had formed a **centralized military state** with a 40,000-strong standing army. The nature of war in the east changed from the almost symbolic skirmishes that characterized Nguni raids up to the end of the eighteenth century to decisive battles in which massacres of women and children weren't unknown. Nevertheless, the real strength of the system lay in its ability to absorb the survivors, who became members of the expanding Zulu state. Throughout the 1820s, Shaka sent out his armies to attack his neighbours and take their cattle. In 1828, in a palace coup, he was stabbed to death by a servant and his two half-brothers, one of whom, **Dingane**, succeeded him. Dingane continued with his brother's ruthless policies and tactics.

The rise of the Zulu state reverberated right across southern Africa and led to the creation of a series of **centralized Nguni states** as well as paving the way for Boer expansion into the interior. In a movement known as the **mfecane**, or forced migrations, huge areas of the country were laid waste and people across eastern South Africa were displaced, dispossessed and driven off their lands, either attempting to survive in small groups or banding together in larger political organizations to survive. To the north of the Zulu kingdom, another Nguni group with strong cultural and linguistic affinities with the Zulus came together under Sobhuza I and his son Mswati II, after whom their new state **Swaziland** took its name. A few hundred Zulus under the leadership of **Mzilikazi** had taken refuge in Northwest Province after rebelling against Shaka. By 1829, their numbers had swelled to around seventy thousand, but in 1838 they were routed by encroaching Voortrekkers, against whose firearms they proved no match. They relocated to southwestern Zimbabwe, where they re-established themselves as the **Matabele** kingdom. In the Drakensberg, on the west flank of KwaZulu-Natal, **Moshoeshoe I**, another chief with humble origins, used diplomacy and cunning to build up his state from the ruins of the *mfecane*. By providing a haven to refugees, he was able to build up a substantial state from disparate Sotho groupings. Believing that "peace is like the rain which makes the grass grow", he kept no standing army, relying instead on opportunism and good-neighbourliness to survive.

C

The Great Trek

Back in the Cape, many Afrikaners were becoming fed up with British rule. Their principal grievance was the way in which the colonial authorities were tampering with labour relations and destroying what they saw as a divine distinction between blacks and whites. In 1828 the **Cape Ordinance 50** gave Khoi residents and free blacks equality before the law, while the **abolition of slavery** in 1834 was the last straw. One Voortrekker wrote: "it's not so much their freedom that drove us to such lengths, as their being placed on an equal footing with Christians, contrary to the laws of God and the natural distinction of race".

In this spirit, 15,000 Afrikaners (one out of every ten living in the colony) set out to leave the Cape and once and for all shake off the meddlesome British. When they arrived in the eastern half of the country, they were delighted to find vast tracts of apparently unoccupied land. In fact, they were merely stumbling into the eye of the *mfecane* storm – areas that had been temporarily cleared either by war parties or by fearful people hiding out to escape detection. As they fanned out further they encountered the Nguni states and a series of battles followed. By the middle of the nineteenth century, the Voortrekkers had consolidated control and established the two Boer states of the **South African Republic** (now Mpumalanga, Northwest and Northern provinces) and the **Orange Free State** (now Free State), both of whose independence was recognized by Britain in the 1850s.

Britain wasn't too concerned about the interior of South Africa. Apart from its strategic position, South Africa was a chaotic and undeveloped backwater at the butt-end of the Empire that was of scant interest back in London. At this time, the United States, which was first settled by Britons a mere thirty years before the Dutch hit South Africa, had a population of over thirty million people of European extraction and 80,000km of railways compared with South Africa's 250,000 whites and 120km of railways. Things changed first in the 1860s, with the **discovery of diamonds** (the world's largest deposit) around modern-day Kimberley and even more significantly in the 1880s, with the **discovery of gold** at Witwatersrand (now Gauteng). Together, these discoveries were the catalyst that transformed South Africa from a down-at-heel rural society to an urbanized industrial one. In the process great fortunes were made by capitalists like **Cecil Rhodes**, traditional African society was crushed and the independence of the Boer republics ended.

Although the **Gauteng goldfields** were exceptionally well-endowed with ore, they were also particularly difficult to mine, requiring the sinking of deep shafts, which necessitated capitalist intervention. Exploiting the mines required costly equipment and cheap labour to operate it. Capital quickly flowed in from Western investors eager for profit: even today the West retains strong links with the South African mines, and South Africa remains the world's largest producer of gold.

Despite the benefits it brought, the discovery of gold was also one of the principal causes of the **Second Anglo-Boer War**. Gold-mining had shifted the economic centre of South Africa from the British-controlled Cape to a Boer republic, while at the same time, Britain's European rival, Germany, was beginning to make political and economic inroads in the Boer republics. Britain feared losing its strategic Cape naval base, but perhaps even more important were questions of international finance and the substantial British investment in the mines. London was at the heart of world trade and was eager to see a flourishing gold-mining industry in South Africa, but the Boers seemed rather sluggish about modernizing their infrastructure to assist the exploitation of the mines.

In any case, a number of Britons had for some time seen the unification of South Africa as the key to securing **British interests** in the subcontinent. To this end, under a wafer-thin pretext, the Empire had declared war and subdued the last of the independent African kingdoms by means of the **Zulu War** of 1879. This had secured KwaZulu-Natal and meant that all the coastal territories of South Africa from Namibia round to Mozambique were under British control. All that remained was to bring the two Boer republics under the Union Jack.

The Anglo-Boer War

During the closing years of the nineteenth century, Britain demanded that the South African Republic grant voting rights to British miners living in the country – a demand that, if met, would have meant the end of Boer political control over their own state. The Boers turned down the request and war broke out in October 1899. The British command, which had been used to fighting colonial wars against enemies armed with spears, believed they were looking at a walkover; in the words of Lord Kitchener, "a teatime war" that would get the troops home in time to open their Christmas presents.

In fact, the battle turned into the most expensive campaign since the Napoleonic Wars. During the **early phase** of the war, the Boers took the imperial power by surprise and penetrated into British-controlled KwaZulu-Natal and the Northern Cape, inflicting a series of humiliating defeats. By June a reinforced British army was pushing the Boers back and once again the high command was talking about being home in time for their Christmas pudding. But the Boers fought on for another two years of protracted guerrilla war. **Lord Kitchener** responded ruthlessly with a scorched-earth policy that left the countryside a smouldering wasteland and thousands of women and children homeless. To house these thousands of dispossessed, the British introduced the **concentration camp**, in which 26,370 Boer women and children died. For some Afrikaners, this episode remains a major source of bitterness against the British today. Less widely publicized were the **African concentration camps** which took 14,000 lives. By 1902, the Boers were demoralized and split between those who couldn't face another winter of near starvation (the so-called "hands-uppers") and those who wanted to fight on ("the bitter-enders"). In May that year, the Boer republics signed a treaty surrendering their independence in exchange for British promises of reconstruction. By the end of the so-called "teatime war", Britain had committed nearly half a million men to the field and lost 22,000 of them. Of the 88,000 Boers who fought, 7000 died in combat. With the two Boer republics and the two British colonies under imperial control, the way was clear for the federation of the **Union of South Africa** in 1910.

Migrant labour and the Bambatha Rebellion

Between the conclusion of the Anglo-Boer War and the unification of South Africa, the mines suffered from a shortage of **unskilled labour**. Most Africans still lived by agriculture, either as tenant farmers on white farms or in reserves created by the colonial government. They had no need to desert their traditional farming way of life for a thankless existence in shantytowns far away from home. To counter this, the government took measures to compel them to supply their labour. One method was the imposition of **taxes** that had to be paid in coin, thus forcing Africans from subsistence farming and into the cash economy, where they would have to earn a wage. Responding to one such tax, a group of Zulus protested in 1906 and refused to pay up. The authorities declared martial law and dealt mercilessly with the protesters, burning their huts and seizing all their possessions. This provoked a full-blown rebellion led by Chief Bambatha, which was ruthlessly put down by the colonial authorities, with 4000 rebels dying in the process. This marked an end to armed resistance by Africans for over half a century. After the defeat of the **Bambatha Rebellion**, the numbers of African men from Zululand working in the Gauteng mines shot up by sixty percent. By 1909, eighty percent of adult males in the territory were absent from their homes and working as migrant labourers. **Migrant labour**, with its shattering effects on family life, became one of the foundations of South Africa's economic and social system, and was a basic cornerstone of apartheid.

Kick-starting Afrikanerdom

In a parallel development, large numbers of **Afrikaners** were forced to leave rural areas in the early part of the twentieth century. This was partly due to the aftermath of British scorched-earth tactics during the Anglo-Boer War, but also a result of overcrowding, drought and pestilence. Many Afrikaners joined the ranks of a swelling **poor white working class** that felt itself caught in a vice: victimized and despised on the one hand by the English-speaking capitalists who commanded the economy, and on the other under pressure from lower-paid Africans who were competing for their jobs.

In 1918 (the year Nelson Mandela was born) a group of Afrikaners formed the **Broederbond** ("the brotherhood"), a secret society to promote the interest of Afrikaners and to forge an Afrikaner republic in South Africa. It aimed to uplift impoverished members of the *volk* ("people") and to develop a sense of pride in their language, religion and culture. Ultimately, the Broederbond was to dominate every aspect of the way the country was run for close on half a century.

During the 1930s, a number of young Afrikaner intellectuals travelled to Europe, where they were inspired by the jackbooted march of **fascism** in Portugal, Spain, Italy and Germany. This extreme manifestation of nationalism appeared to hold the key to realizing Afrikaner nationhood. It was around this time that Afrikaner intellectuals began using the term **apartheid** (pronounced "apart-hate", not "apart-hide").

Among the leading lights of apartheid who could be found kicking their heels in Germany in the 1930s were **Nico Diederichs**, who became minister of finance under the National Party government; **Hendrik Frensch Verwoerd**, apartheid's leading theorist and prime minister from 1958 to 1966; and **Piet Meyer**, controller of the state broadcasting service, who named his son Izan ("Nazi" spelled backwards – but he later claimed this was sheer coincidence). Meanwhile, in 1939, the Broederbond kicked into action with a scheme that launched 10,000 Afrikaner businesses in the space of a decade. Some of these, such as Rembrandt Tobacco, Volkskas (the country's third-largest bank), the Santam insurance company and Gencor (one of the five largest mining houses) are still among the leading players in South Africa's economy.

Africans' claims

Despite having relied on African co-operation for their victory in the Anglo-Boer War and having hinted at enhanced rights for blacks after the war, the British excluded blacks from the cosy deal between Afrikaners and Britain that resulted in the unification of South Africa in 1910. It wasn't long, in fact, before the white Union government began eroding African rights. In response, a group of middle-class mission-educated Africans formed the **South African Native National Congress** (later to become the ANC) in 1912. The founders weren't interested in overthrowing the white government; they simply wanted recognition by white society. Middle-class blacks already enjoyed the vote in the Cape Province (now the Western, Northern and Eastern capes) on the basis of a **qualified franchise** according to education and property ownership, and the early African leaders wanted this to be extended to the rest of the country. Taking as their model the evolutionary growth of democracy in Britain, they hoped that this would eventually lead to universal suffrage.

In 1914, the leaders set off as a deputation for London, to protest against the **1913 Natives' Land Act**, which severely restricted property ownership by blacks. The trip was unsuccessful and the Land Act came into force, providing the legal foundation stone for the subsequent formalization of apartheid some 35 years later. The Act provided for the division of South Africa into distinct African and white areas, with blacks – despite constituting the overriding majority of the population – confined to less than ten percent of the land surface.

Through the early half of the twentieth century, the ANC remained a conservative organization, unwilling to engage in active protest. This led to accusations that its leaders were "good boys tied to the apron strings of the white liberals". In response, a number of alternative mass organizations arose. Among the largest was the mighty **Industrial and Commercial Union**, an African trade union founded in 1919, which at its peak in 1928 had gathered an impressive 150,000 members. But in the 1930s it ran out of steam. The first political movement in the country not organized along ethnic lines was the **South African Communist Party**, which was founded in 1921 with a multiracial executive. While it never itself gained widespread membership, it became an important force inside the ANC.

Throughout the 1930s, the ANC plodded on with speeches, petitions and pleas, which proved completely fruitless. They suffered a major setback in 1936 with the **termination of the African franchise** in the Cape Province. The

ANC's response was to send a deputation to Prime Minister Hertzog to protest; Hertzog treated them abominably, not even offering them seats. These events left the ANC crippled and hobbling impotently into the 1940s.

World War II split Afrikanerdom. There were those like Prime Minister **Jan Smuts** who stood firmly in favour of joining the war alongside Britain. But for others, like **John Vorster**, Britain was the old enemy, so they supported Germany, some signing up with the **Ossewa Brandwag** (the "Ox-Wagon Torch Commando"), which carried out sabotage against the government. After the war there were hopes of reform from Prime Minister Smuts, who at the time was playing a leading role in the formation of the **United Nations**. Smuts even had a part in penning the Preamble to the Charter on Human Rights, but while his work for abstract "human rights" earned him a statue next to Winston Churchill outside Britain's parliament, he was in no hurry to grant such rights to the majority of South Africans. Even conservative African leaders were losing patience: one, Councillor Paul Mosaka, complaining that "we have been asked to co-operate with a toy telephone. We have been speaking into an apparatus which cannot transmit sound."

Young Turks and striking miners

In 1944, a young hothead called **Nelson Mandela** got together with his friends **Oliver Tambo** and **Walter Sisulu** under the leadership of **Anton Lembede** to form the **ANC Youth League**. Strict Africanists, they refused to work with any other organizations – such as the Indian Congress. The League's founding manifesto criticized the ANC leadership as a group who regarded themselves as "gentlemen with clean hands". Lembede's radical brand of politics was based on his idea that "Africa is the black man's country". He continued: "We have inhabited Africa, our motherland, from time immemorial. Africa belongs to us."

The 1945 annual conference of the ANC adopted a document called "**Africans' Claims in South Africa**", which reflected an emerging politicization resulting from the experiences of the war and especially the defeat of fascism. The document demanded **universal franchise** and an end to the **colour bar**, which reserved most skilled jobs for whites. The Youth League was influenced by the industrial militancy it had witnessed during the war. Despite a ban on industrial action, between 1942 and 1944 there were sixty strikes. In 1946 the African Mineworkers' Union launched one of the biggest strikes in the country's history in protest against falling living standards. Virtually the entire Gauteng gold-mining region came to a standstill as 100,000 workers downed tools. Smuts sent in police who forced the workers back down the shafts at gunpoint.

In 1947, the ANC Youth League was thrown into confusion when Lembede died suddenly. He was succeeded by **A.P. Mda**, and **Nelson Mandela** took his first step into public life when he was elected general secretary of the organization. At the same time, the Smuts government was under pressure for change. Meanwhile, **European decolonization** was beginning in earnest, with Britain withdrawing from India in the same year. This seemed to have implications for political rights for black South Africans. But more important still was demography, with the relentless **influx of Africans** into the urban areas breaking the traditional stereotype of them as rural tribespeople.

For years, the white government had been hinting at easing up on segregation, and even Smuts himself, who was no soft liberal, had reckoned that it was untenable and would have to end at some point. His deputy, **J.H. Hofmeyr**, had thrown caution to the winds and committed himself to scrapping job reservation, which excluded blacks from skilled jobs. "I take my stand on the ultimate removal of the colour bar", he went on record as saying. Playing for time, the government appointed the **Fagan Commission** to look into the question of the Pass Laws, which controlled the movement of Africans and sought to keep them out of the white cities unless they had a job. The laws led to millions of black South Africans being condemned to a ghetto existence in the rural areas, where there were no jobs, poverty reigned and infant mortality was high.

When the Fagan Commission reported its findings its 1948, it concluded that "the trend to urbanization is irreversible and the Pass Laws should be eased". While some blacks may have felt heartened by this hint of reform, this was the last thing many whites wanted to hear. For Afrikaners, the threat seemed particularly acute, and raised all sorts of fears about losing their identity and being swamped by blacks. For **white workers**, the threat of losing their jobs to lower-paid African workers was a real one, while **Afrikaner farmers** were alarmed by the idea of a labour shortage due to Africans leaving the rural areas for better prospects in the cities.

Against this background of black aspiration and white fears, the Smuts government called a **general election**. The opposition **National Party** campaigned on a *swart gevaar* or "black peril" ticket which played on white insecurity and fear. The Afrikaner nationalists promised to satisfy a range of conflicting interests. With an eye on the vote of Afrikaner workers and farmers, they promised to reverse the tide of Africans coming into the cites and send them all back to the reserves. For white business they made the conflicting promise to bring black workers into the cities as a cheap and plentiful supply of labour.

On Friday May 28, 1948, South Africa awoke to the unthinkable reality of a **National Party victory** at the (whites-only) polls. Party leader **D.F. Malan** was summoned to Pretoria by the governor-general to form a cabinet. On arriving by train at Pretoria station he told a group of ecstatic supporters: "For the first time, South Africa is our own. May God grant that it always remains our own. We Afrikaners are not a work of Man, but a creation of God. It is to us that millions of barbarous blacks look for guidance, justice and the Christian way of life."

Meanwhile, the ANC was riven by its own power struggle. Fed up with the ineffectiveness of the old guard, and faced with the rabid D.F. Malan, the Youth League staged a putsch, voted in their own leadership with Nelson Mandela on the executive and adopted the League's radical **Programme of Action**, with an arsenal of tactics that Mandela explained would include "the new weapons of boycott, strike, civil disobedience and non-cooperation".

The 1950s: peaceful protest

During the 1950s, the National Party began putting in place a barrage of laws that would eventually constitute the structure of apartheid. Some early onslaughts on black civil rights included: the **Coloured Voters Act**, which stripped coloureds of the vote; the **Bantu Authorities Act**, which set up pup-

The Freedom Charter

- The people shall govern.
- All national groups shall have equal rights.
- The people shall share the nation's wealth.
- The land shall be shared by those who work it.
- All shall be equal before the law.
- All shall enjoy equal human rights.
- There shall be work and security for all.
- The doors of learning and culture shall be opened.
- There shall be houses, security and comfort.
- There shall be peace and friendship.

pet authorities to govern Africans in the reserves; the **Population Registration Act**, which classified every South African at birth as "white, native or coloured"; the **Group Areas Act**, which divided South Africa into ethnically distinct areas; and the **Suppression of Communism Act**, which made any anti-apartheid opposition (Communist or not) a criminal offence.

The ANC responded in 1952 with the **Defiance Campaign**, which kicked off with a letter to the government demanding the same civil rights for blacks that whites enjoyed. During the campaign, eight thousand volunteers deliberately broke the apartheid laws listed above and were jailed. The campaign rolled on through 1952 until the police provoked violence in October by firing on a prayer meeting in East London. A riot followed in which two white people were killed, thus appearing to discredit claims that the campaign was non-violent. The government used this as an excuse to swoop on the homes of the ANC leadership, resulting in the detention and then banning of over one hundred ANC organizers. **Bannings** were designed to restrict a person's movement and political activities. A banned person was prohibited from seeing more than one person at a time or talking to another banned person; prohibited from entering certain buildings; kept under surveillance; was required to report regularly to the police, and could not be quoted or published.

The most far-reaching event of the decade was the **Congress of the People**, held near Johannesburg in 1955. At a mass meeting of nearly three thousand delegates, four organizations, representing Africans, coloureds, whites and Indians, formed a strategic partnership called the **Congress Alliance**. Explaining the historic significance of the meeting, ANC leader Chief **Albert Luthuli** commented that "for the first time in the history of our multiracial nation its people will meet as equals, irrespective of race, colour and creed to formulate a freedom charter for all the people of our country". The **Freedom Charter** (see box above), which was adopted at the Congress of the People, became the principal document defining ANC policy.

The government found the breadth of the movement and its principles of freedom and equality too much to stomach and they sent in the police to round up 156 opposition leaders who were charged with treason. Evidence at the **Treason Trial** was based on the Freedom Charter, which was described as a "blueprint for violent Communist revolution". Although all the defendants were acquitted, the four-year trial disrupted the ANC and splits began to emerge. From within the organization, a group of Africanists criticized the Freedom Charter because it promoted co-operation with white activists. At the 1958 ANC national conference they attempted to hijack the leadership, but when they failed they walked out and formed the **Pan Africanist Congress** under the leadership of the charismatic **Robert Mangaliso Sobukwe**. Upstaging the ANC, the PAC launched an anti-pass campaign ten days before a similar one planned by the ANC.

Sharpeville

On March 21, 1960, Sobukwe and thousands of followers left home to present themselves without passes to police stations. Sobukwe gave strict instructions to keep the demonstrations peaceful and not to be provoked by anyone. Across Gauteng and the Western Cape there were demonstrations which in due course dispersed, but at **Sharpeville** police station, south of Johannesburg, the crowd refused to leave, despite being buzzed by low-flying Sabre jets. A scuffle broke out, the police panicked and opened fire, killing 69 and injuring nearly 200. Most were shot in the back.

In a rapid sequence of events, demonstrations swept the country on **March 27**, and ANC activist Oliver Tambo (later to become the ANC leader in exile until the release of Mandela) illegally left the country. The following day, Africans staged a **total stay-away** from work and thousands followed Nelson Mandela and Albert Luthuli in a public pass-burning demonstration. The day after that, the government declared a **state of emergency** and rounded up 22,000 people. One day later, the United Nations Security Council resolution called for the government to abandon apartheid, to which it reacted swiftly with bans on the ANC and PAC. It was now illegal to be a member of either organization. Among white South Africans there was near hysteria as the value of the rand slipped, shares slumped and some feared an imminent and bloody revolution.

Later that month, Prime Minister **Hendrik Verwoerd** was shot twice in the head by a half-crazed white farmer and many people hoped his death would provide a speedy retreat from apartheid. But Dr Verwoerd survived, with his prestige enhanced and his appetite for apartheid stronger than ever. More than anyone else, Verwoerd made apartheid his own and formulated it into a coherent system based around the idea of **notionally independent bantustans**, in which Africans were to exercise their political rights away from the white areas. The underlying aim of the scheme was to divide Africans into distinct ethnic groups, thereby dismantling the black majority into several separate "tribal" minorities, none of which on its own could outnumber whites.

After the banning of opposition in 1960, Dr Verwoerd pressed ahead with his cherished dream of an all-white **Afrikaner republic**, which he succeeded in achieving in March 1961 through a referendum. For his pains, the Commonwealth Prime Ministers' Conference in London kicked the republic out of the British Commonwealth and Mandela called for a national convention "to determine a non-racial democratic constitution". Instead, Verwoerd appointed one-time neo-nazi **John Vorster** to the post of justice minister. A trained lawyer, Vorster eagerly set about passing a succession of repressive laws that circumvented normal legal procedures and flouted all principles of natural justice.

Some in the ANC realized that the rules of the game had changed irrevocably. "The time comes in the life of any nation when there remain only two choices: submit or fight. That time has now come to South Africa. We shall not submit", Mandela told the world, before going underground as commander-in-chief of **UmkhontoWe Sizwe** (Spear of the Nation, aka MK), a newly formed armed wing involving ANC and Communist Party leaders. The organization was dedicated to economic and symbolic acts of sabotage and was under strict orders not to kill or injure people. Mandela operated clandestinely for a year, travelling in disguise, leaving the country illegally and popping up unexpectedly at meetings – all of which earned him the nickname, the "Black Pimpernel". In August 1962, he was finally arrested, tried and imprisoned. He was let out again briefly in 1963 to defend himself against charges of treason at the **Rivonia Trial**. Mandela and nine other ANC leaders were all found guilty and handed life sentences.

Apartheid: the dark days

With the leadership of the liberation movement behind bars, the Rivonia Trial marked the beginning of the decade in which everything seemed to be going the white government's way. Resistance was stifled, the state grew more powerful and for white South Africans, businessmen and foreign investors life seemed perfect. The panic caused by the Sharpeville massacre soon became a dim memory and confidence returned. For black South Africans, poverty deepened – a state of affairs enforced by apartheid legislation.

There was a minor setback in 1966 when Dr Verwoerd was stabbed to death (and failed to return from the dead this time) in parliament by a messenger who went off the rails after a tapeworm had ordered him to do it, as he told doctors. The breach was filled by **John Vorster**, whose approach was more pragmatic than that of Verwoerd. Not averse to travelling to Africa to shake hands with tame black leaders like Hastings Banda of Malawi in the interests of detente, his approach to black South Africans was rather less chummy. His premiership was characterized by an increased use of the **police** as an instrument of repression, while bannings, detentions without trial, house arrests and deaths of political prisoners in detention became commonplace.

The ANC was impotent, and resistance by its armed wing MK was virtually nonexistent. This was partly because up to the mid-1970s South Africa was surrounded by sympathetic white regimes – in neighbouring Rhodesia and Mozambique – making it close to impossible to infiltrate combatants into the country. But as South Africa swung into the 1970s, the uneasy peace began to fray, prompted at first by **deteriorating black living standards**, which reawakened industrial action. **Trade unions** came to fill the vacuum left by the ANC and neither Vorster nor any of his National Party successors proved able to stem the escalation of strikes, despite all the repressive resources at their disposal.

However, it was the Soweto Revolt of June 16, 1976, that signalled the transfer of protest from the workplace to the townships, when black youths took to the streets in protest against the imposition of Afrikaans as a medium of instruction in their schools. The protest spread across the country after police opened fire and killed thirteen-year-old Hector Peterson during one march. By the following February, 575 people (nearly a quarter of them children) had been killed in the rolling series of revolts that followed.

Even in the face of naked violence, protest spread to all sections of the community. The government was forced to rely increasingly on armed police to impose order. Even this was unable to stop the mushrooming of new liberation organizations, many of them part of the broadly based **Black Consciousness Movement**. As the unrest rumbled on into 1977, the Vorster government responded by banning all the new black organizations and detaining their leadership. In September 1977, **Steve Biko** (one of the detained), became the 46th political prisoner to meet his end in jail at the hands of the security police. In place of the banned organizations, a fresh crop had sprung up by the end of the 1970s. The government never again successfully put the lid on opposition which escalated through the 1980s. There were rent, bus and school **boycotts**, **strikes** and **campaigns** against removals. By the end of the decade, business was complaining that apartheid wasn't working any more, and even the government was starting to agree. The growth of the black population was outstripping that of whites; from a peak of 21 percent of the population in 1910, whites now made up only 16 percent. This proportion was set to fall to 10 percent by the end of the century. The sums just didn't add up.

Total strategy

It was becoming clear that Vorster's deployment of the police couldn't solve South Africa's problems, and in 1978 he was deposed by his defence minister **Pieter Willem (P.W.) Botha** in a palace coup. Under Vorster's premiership, Botha had turned the **South African Defence Force** into the most awesome military machine on the African continent and it became central to his strategy for maintaining white power. Botha realized that the days of old-style apartheid were over, and he adopted a two-handed strategy of reform accompanied by unprecedented repression. Believing there was a total onslaught on South Africa from both inside and outside the country, he devised his so-called **Total Strategy**.

In June 1980, MK, the ANC's armed wing, made an unscheduled reappearance when it successfully attacked the heavily guarded strategic oil refinery at **Sasolburg**, taking the government by surprise. The 1980s saw the growing use of sabotage against the apartheid state. During 1981, there were over ninety **MK armed actions** against police stations, railway lines, power plants, military bases and army recruiting offices. Attacks were often co-ordinated with protest campaigns: for example, buildings at the British Leyland plant were bombed when workers were on strike there. Botha began thinking about reforms and moved **Nelson Mandela** and other imprisoned ANC leaders from Robben Island to Pollsmoor Prison in mainland Cape Town.

At the same time, he poured ever-increasing numbers of troops into African townships to stop unrest, while using economic incentives to attempt to draw neighbouring countries into a **"constellation of Southern African states"** under South Africa's leadership. Between 1981 and 1983, the army was used to enforce compliance on every one of the country's neighbours. An undeclared war against **Angola** reduced a potentially oil-rich country to war-ravaged ruins, while a South African-sponsored conflict in **Mozambique** brought a poverty-stricken country to its knees. Nor was Botha averse to sending commando units across the borders into **Botswana**, **Zimbabwe**, **Swaziland** and **Lesotho** to attack and bomb South African refugees.

Botha hoped that by making a few reforms that tinkered with apartheid and by creating a black middle class as a buffer against the ANC, he could get the world off his back and stem internal unrest. On both counts he was wrong.

Unrest continued unabated and he found himself having to rely increasingly on force. Detentions and executions of political activists increased (in contravention of the Geneva Convention) and heavy sentences were handed down in political trials. Used to maintaining control through the barrel of a gun, Botha was lost for any real political initiatives. Nevertheless, in 1983 he concocted what he believed was a master plan for a so-called **New Constitution** in which coloureds and Indians would be granted the vote. But before anyone got too excited he qualified this with the revelation that each group would be represented in separate chambers, which would have no executive power. Meanwhile, for Africans, apartheid would continue as usual.

Botha hoped for a tactical alliance between whites, coloureds and Indians in opposition to Africans. The scheme was a dismal failure that only served to alienate right-wingers, who saw it as selling out white privilege. As Botha was punting this ramshackle scheme, 15,000 anti-apartheid delegates met at Mitchell's Plain in Cape Town to form the **United Democratic Front** (UDF) at the biggest opposition gathering since the Congress of the People in 1955. Under a leadership that included ANC veterans, the UDF was a multiracial umbrella for 575 organizations. It endorsed the Freedom Charter and became a proxy for the ANC. Two years of strikes, protest and boycotts followed. But there were sinister stirrings when **Mangosuthu Buthelezi**, chief minister of the KwaZulu *bantustan* and leader of the Zulu nationalist **Inkatha** movement, told a rally of migrant workers in Soweto that "the UDF seems to be another force for disunity and cannot succeed without Inkatha. From now on Inkatha will adopt the attitude of an eye for an eye." Attacks by Inkatha members on the now defunct UDF and ANC supporters became commonplace, and have continued to the present, although on a far diminished scale. (Evidence in the 1990s pointed to support for Inkatha from elements in the apartheid security forces, including the supply of weapons.)

In the face of intensifying protest, the government looked for ways to respond, and between March and December it offered to **release Mandela** no fewer than five times, provided he agreed to banishment to the Transkei *bantustan*. Five times he refused and this cat-and-mouse game continued right through the 1980s as the pressure mounted and South Africa's townships became ungovernable. Towards the end of the decade, the world watched as apartheid troops and police were shown regularly on TV beating up and shooting unarmed Africans. The **Commonwealth**, despite the concerted efforts of British Prime Minister Margaret Thatcher to stop them, condemned the apartheid government. The United States and Australia **severed air-links** and Congress defied President Reagan and passed the comprehensive Anti-Apartheid Act which promoted **disinvestment**. In 1985, the **Chase Manhattan Bank** announced that it would no longer be prepared to roll over its loan to South Africa. Over the next two years, ninety US firms closed down their South African operations. An increasingly desperate Botha now modified his conditions for releasing Mandela, offering to "release Mandela if he renounces violence".

Mandela issued a moving reply, read by his daughter Zinzi to a crowd at Jabulani Stadium, in Soweto: "I am surprised by the conditions the government wants to impose on me. I am not a violent man. It was only when all other forms of resistance were no longer open to us that we turned to armed struggle. Let Botha show that he is different to Malan, Strijdom and Verwoerd. Let him renounce violence. I cherish my own freedom dearly but I care even more for yours."

As events unfolded, a subtle shift became increasingly apparent: Botha was the prisoner and he desperately needed Mandela to release him. On the one hand **black resistance** wasn't abating, while on the other Botha was facing a white **right-wing backlash**. At every by-election the ultra right-wing Conservative Party had been eroding government majorities. In the **1987 general election**, the government polled just 52 percent while, so far to the right that it had slid off the political spectrum, the **Afrikaner Weerstand Beweging** (Afrikaner Resistance Movement, aka AWB) broke up National Party meetings and threatened civil war.

Crisis

In 1986, Botha declared yet another **state of emergency** and unleashed a last-ditch storm of tyranny. **Bannings** of people and meetings followed, and **shootings** by the police were carried out with impunity. There were **mass arrests**, **detentions**, **treason trials** and **torture**. Sinister hit squads were deployed to assassinate the UDF leadership. Alarmed by the spiral of violence that was engulfing the country, a group of South African businessmen, mostly Afrikaners, flew to Senegal in 1987 to meet an ANC delegation headed by **Thabo Mbeki**. A joint statement pressed for unequivocal support for a negotiated settlement.

Weeks after the world celebrated **Mandela's seventieth birthday** in July 1988 with a huge bash at London's Wembley Stadium, Mandela was rushed off to Tygerberg Hospital, suffering from tuberculosis. Although he was better by October, the government announced that he wouldn't be returning to Pollsmoor Prison. Instead he was moved to a warder's cottage at Victor Verster Prison in Paarl. Outside the prison walls, Botha's policies had hit the buffers and even the army top brass were pushing for change. They told Botha that there could be no decisive military victory over the anti-apartheid opposition and the undeclared war in Angola was bleeding the treasury dry.

At the beginning of 1989, Mandela wrote to Botha from Victor Verster Prison calling for negotiations. "I am disturbed by the spectre of a South Africa split into two hostile camps – blacks on one side, whites on the other," he wrote. An intransigent character, Botha found himself with little room to manoeuvre. He had brought South Africa to a state of unprecedented crisis, yet he refused to change direction. When he was weakened by a stroke, his party colleagues moved swiftly to oust him and replaced him with **Frederik Willem (F.W.) De Klerk**.

Drawn from the conservative wing of the National Party, from the start De Klerk made it clear he was totally opposed to majority rule. But he inherited a massive pile of problems that could no longer be ignored: the economy was in trouble and the cost of maintaining apartheid prohibitive; the illegal influx of Africans from the country to the city had become an unstoppable flood; blacks hadn't been taken in by Botha's constitutional reforms; and even South Africa's friends were beginning to lose patience. In September 1989, US President **George Bush** let De Klerk know that if there wasn't progress on releasing Mandela within six months, he would extend US sanctions against South Africa.

De Klerk made a strategic calculation that the ANC was organizationally weak, having little internal base and having lost all its external support as a result of the enforced closure of its bases in Angola and Zambia, as well as having lost aid from eastern Europe with the collapse of the Iron Curtain regimes. He gambled on his own party's five-decade track record in gerrymandering and on his own ability to outmanoeuvre the ANC. In February 1990, De Klerk announced the **unbanning** of the ANC, the PAC, the Communist Party and 33 other organizations, as well as the **release of Mandela**. On Sunday February 11, at around 4pm, Mandela stepped out of Victor Verster Prison and was driven to City Hall in Cape Town, from where he spoke publicly for the first time in three decades. He told his supporters that the factors which necessitated armed struggle still existed, but that he believed that "a climate conducive to a negotiated settlement will exist soon".

That May, Mandela and De Klerk signed an **agreement** in which the government agreed to repeal repressive laws and release political prisoners, while Mandela persuaded the ANC to suspend the armed struggle. As events moved slowly towards full-blown negotiations it became clear that De Klerk still clung to race-based notions for a settlement. "Majority rule is not suitable for South Africa", he said, "because it will lead to the domination of minorities."

Negotiations

The **negotiating** process which took place between 1990 and 1994 was fragile, and at many points a descent into chaos looked likely. Obstacles included ongoing violence linked to a sinister "**Third Force**" – elements in the apartheid security forces who were working behind the scenes to destabilize the ANC; **threats of civil war** from heavily armed right-wingers and a low-key war of attrition in KwaZulu-Natal between Zulu nationalists and ANC supporters had already claimed three thousand lives between 1987 and 1990.

In August 1990, this violence burst into the Johannesburg townships when gunmen opened fire on black commuters on a train. In June 1992, forty people were hacked to death in a midnight attack on a squatter camp near Johannesburg. Eyewitnesses reported seeing police trucks ferrying alleged Inkatha supporters to the area. When Mandela arrived at the scene a crowd of youths sang: "Mandela, you behave like a lamb while we are being slaughtered." This response was very much to the advantage of the National Party as it gave the impression of an impotent ANC unable to protect its supporters and with no power to stop the violence. Mandela responded by breaking off negotiations and launching a **campaign of mass action** to pressurize the government. On August 3 and 4, 1992, the ANC called the largest **strike** in South African history, when four million people stayed away from work. Subsequently negotiations between the government and the ANC resumed and in October 1992, President De Klerk apologized (conditionally) for apartheid.

But in April 1993, it looked like the whole process was going to unravel with the **assassination of Chris Hani**, the most popular ANC leader after Mandela. Hani's slaying by a right-wing gunman touched deep fears among all South Africans. A descent into civil war loomed and for three consecutive nights the nation watched as Mandela appeared on prime-time television appealing for calm. This marked the decisive turning point as it became apparent that the ANC president was able to hold the country together, while De Klerk kept his head down. Pushing his stategic advantage, Mandela swiftly called for the immediate setting of an **election date**. On June 3, 1993, the poll was proposed for April 27, 1994, and Mandela was able to tell his followers that "the countdown to democracy has begun".

By December 1993, South Africa had its first multiracial administration in 350 years, when the **Transitional Executive Authority** was installed. But this did nothing to stop the violence, which continued to endanger the transition, while Chief Buthelezi and the white right-wing continued to threaten civil war unless KwaZulu-Natal was given autonomy and the Afrikaners a *volkstaat* (homeland). Bloodshed and mayhem continued in KwaZulu-Natal and it looked as if the election was going to be disrupted. In February 1994, the negotiating parties held fresh discussions to accommodate Chief Buthelezi and the right-wingers. But concessions accepting the principle of self-determination failed to draw either into the elections.

In March 1994, a popular uprising against the government of the **Bophuthatswana** *bantustan* resonated across South Africa. The territory's army and police mutinied and, in an attempt to shore up his regime, Chief Mangope asked the white right wing to help. Hundreds of armed AWB neo-nazis converged on the capital, Mmabatho, and South Africa watched as they were routed by the *bantustan* army. Television images of armed white neo-fascists being ingloriously defeated by Africans put paid to any ideas about white invincibility and laid to rest the threat of a right-wing rebellion.

In response, the fractionally less right-wing **Afrikaner Volksfront** (Afrikaner Peoples' Front), an alliance of whites who wanted their own self-governing homeland, announced that it would take part in the election, thus leaving Buthelezi isolated. Yet Buthelezi still insisted on boycotting the poll and threatened to lead a KwaZulu-Natal secession from South Africa. His supporters were whipped up into a frenzy of violence that swept across the province. The transitional government declared a **state of emergency** in KwaZulu-Natal and swamped the province with troops. One week before the election was due, the mercurial Inkatha leader agreed to take part.

The 1994 election

Despite a last attempt by right-wingers to disrupt the election by bombing Johannesburg International airport, the **election** of April 27, 1994 passed peacefully. At the age of 76, Mandela, along with millions of his fellow citizens, voted for the first time in his life in his country's elections. On May 2, De Klerk conceded defeat after an ANC landslide, in which they took 62.7 percent of the vote. Of the remaining parties, the National Party fared best with 20.4 percent, followed by the Inkatha Freedom Party with 10.5 percent; trailing way behind were the Freedom Front with 2.2 percent, the Democratic Party with 1.7 percent and the Pan Africanist Congress with 1.2 percent. The ANC was dominant in all but two of the provinces, the National Party taking the **Western Cape** decisively and Buthelezi's Inkatha achieving a tight 50.3 percent majority in its **KwaZulu-Natal** heartland. However, one of the disappointments for the ANC was its inability to appeal broadly to non-African racial groups. Ironically, the National Party won an overwhelming proportion of this Indian, coloured and white support.

For the ANC, the real struggle was only beginning. It inherited a country of 38 million people. Of these it was estimated that six million were unemployed, nine million were destitute, ten million had no access to running water, and twenty million had no electricity. Among adult blacks, sixty percent were illiterate and fewer than fifty percent of black children under 14 went to school. The gap between black and white was still gaping. One indicator of this, infant mortality, ran at eighty deaths per thousand among Africans, compared with just seven among whites.

The Mandela years: 1994–1999

Few people in recorded history have been the subject of such high expectations; still fewer have matched them; Mandela has exceeded them. We knew of his fortitude before he left jail; we have since experienced his extraordinary reserves of goodwill, his sense of fun and the depth of his maturity. As others' prisoner, he very nearly decided the date of his own release; as president, he has wisely chosen the moment of his going. Any other nation would consider itself privileged to have his equal as its leader. His last full year in power provides us with an occasion again to consider his achievement in bringing and holding our fractious land together.

Mail & Guardian, December 24, 1998

South Africa's first five years of democracy are inextricably linked to the towering figure of **Nelson Mandela**, who had the unenviable task of presiding over attempts to redress the atrocities and imbalances of racial oppression while simultaneously fostering reconciliation. On one hand he had to mollify the fears of many whites who, having seen their political privileges stripped away, imagined an imminent collapse of lifestyle. And on the other, he had to temper the impatience of a black majority that, having finally achieved civil rights, found it hard to understand why economic advancement wasn't following quickly. The achievements of the government, however, were more uneven than those of its leader.

Soon after taking power, Mandela announced the **Reconstruction and Development Plan** (RDP), which set health, housing, education and economic growth as its priorities. This was to be realized in the electrifying of 350,000 homes in the ensuing year, the provision of decent education for all children, and in the building of 2.5 million houses by the end of the decade. But in August 1994, Mandela's keynote address, outlining the government's progress in its first hundred days of office, was greeted by industrial action protests at the slow pace of change. By the end of 1997, only 350,000 houses had been built, though the introduction of clean, piped water and electricity to over a million homes were significant successes.

Despite the victory of liberal democratic principles embodied in the 1994 election, South Africa still displayed a singular lack of the trappings associated with civil society. **Crime**, sensationalized daily in the media, continued to dog the country. In the closing stages of the ANC's first five years, the police were reporting an average of 52 murders a day, a rape every half hour (including a frightening rise in child rape), and one car theft every nine minutes. Simmering behind the scenes was a less obvious threat to the social fabric, a culture of **non-payment of municipal rates**. This had begun as a form of anti-apartheid political action during the 1980s, but by the post-apartheid era it had become a way of life, with nearly eighty percent of township residents witholding payment.

In response, Mandela called for a **"new patriotism"** and attacked the "culture of rapacity" that appeared to underlie these problems. But a popular sense that whites weren't doing enough to redress the imbalances, and that many officials had forgotten about liberation and were simply riding the gravy train, did little to encourage a climate of probity. One well-publicized, but by no means isolated, example of **corruption** involved the Reverend **Allan Boesak**. A founding member of the United Democratic Front and a stalwart of the liberation struggle, in 1999 he was found guilty of misappropriating over a million rands of Danish donor funding. That March, at a Human Rights Day rally, the then deputy president Thabo Mbeki acknowledged the extent of the problem and pledged to root out "those who have smuggled themselves into the ANC not to serve the people, but to pursue their own ends."

The overriding theme of the Mandela presidency was that of **reconciliation**. In 1995, Mandela hosted a symbolic lunch for the wives of liberation leaders and ex-prime ministers and presidents, as well as taking tea with Betsie Verwoerd, widow of Hendrik Verwoerd. Perhaps the highlight of this policy was in May and June 1995, when the rugby union **World Cup** was staged in South Africa. The Springboks – for many years an international pariah due to their whites-only membership – won, watched by Mandela, sporting Springbok colours. Rapprochement was also pursued with the **Inkatha Freedom Party (IFP)**, leading to a reduction in political violence in KwaZulu-Natal. The most significant side-show of the period was the **Truth and Reconciliation Commission**, which began sitting in 1996, set up to examine gross human rights abuses in South Africa between 1960 and 1993 (see box on pp.844–45).

The **New Constitution**, approved in May 1996, ensured that South Africa would remain a parliamentary democracy with an executive president. One of the most progressive constitutions in the world, it incorporated an extensive bill of rights. The main points were the outlawing of discrimination on the grounds of race, gender, pregnancy, ethnic or social origin, sexual orientation, disability, religion, belief, culture or language; protection of freedom of religion, belief, movement, association, expression and artistic creativity; prohibition of slavery, servitude, forced labour, torture, detention without trial, violence or cruel punishment; guarantee of the right to life, banning capital punishment but permitting abortion; and the appointment of a public protector to defend individuals against maladministration.

The post-Mandela era

One of Mandela's most skilful achievements was to initiate the post-Mandela era while still in office, ensuring a seamless political transition for South Africa as it moved into the twenty-first century. By the middle of Mandela's presidency, his deputy, **Thabo Mbeki**, had taken charge of the nuts-and-bolts running of the country, having already assumed the chairmanship of the ANC in 1993. At the 1997 ANC national congress he succeeded Mandela as the leader of the party and after the 1999 general election, which the ANC won by a landslide, he became president of South Africa.

Mbeki was never going to be another Mandela, and he knew it. Soon after taking over from the great man, Mbeki had joked that he had no intention of stepping into Mandela's shoes as they were "too ugly". Despite his formidable intellect – possibly because of it – Mbeki has failed endear himself to South Africa's citizens. He certainly lacks Mandela's common touch and most South

As you type, you don't know you are crying until you feel and see the tears on your hands. Chief typist of the transcripts of the TRC hearings, as told to Archbishop Tutu

By the time South Africa achieved democracy in 1994, it was internationally accepted that **apartheid** was, in the words of a UN resolution, "a crime against humanity," and that atrocities had been committed in its name. But no one could have imagined how systematic and horrific these atrocities had been.

This was only to emerge at the hearings of the **Truth and Reconciliation Commission** (TRC), set up to investigate gross abuses of human rights under apartheid. Under the chairmanship of Nobel Peace laureate, Archbishop **Desmond Tutu**, the commission was mandated to examine acts committed between March 1960, the date of the Sharpeville massacre, and May 10, 1994, the day of Mandela's inauguration as president.

The objective of the TRC was to discover the **secret history of apartheid** (not to punish wrongdoers) and to gain "as complete a picture as possible of the nature, causes and extent of human rights violations". The main means of achieving this was through evidence given by victims and perpetrators. To facilitate this, there was provision for **amnesty** to be granted in exchange for "full disclosure of all the relevant facts relating to acts associated with a political objective committed in the course of the conflicts of the past".

The commission began sitting in April 1996 under the glare of international TV cameras, and completed its hearings on July 31, 1998 (with investigations continuing until June 2000). Unique among the truth commissions of the late twentieth century, including those held in Latin America, the South African TRC operated **in public**, allowing all South Africans to share a knowledge of what had actually happened. Among the deeply moving **testimonies** given by over 21,000 people were individual stories from parents, siblings and friends of those who had disappeared. Others gave gruesome accounts of torture, bombings and murders on an extensive scale. In his foreword to the TRC report, Tutu recalls "how at one of our hearings a mother cried out plaintively: 'Please cannot you bring back even just a bone of my child so that I can bury him?'"

Leading members of the former government and the ANC appeared before the TRC, among them former president **F.W. De Klerk**. In May, 1996, he told the commission that he had not been aware of any atrocities committed under apartheid – a statement Archbishop Tutu said he found difficult to believe, especially given the avalanche of information available to De Klerk as president.

Further evidence of a systematic and brutal campaign of repression by the government came to light during a trial (incidental to the TRC) in September 1996 of

Africans find him remote, an impression reinforced by the feeling that he jet-sets around the world promoting **Third World issues**, rather than dealing with South Africa's domestic problems. But Mbeki believes South Africa's economic prospects are inextricably tied to those of the Third World. Part of this agenda entails pushing his cherished **African Renaissance**, a slightly vague idea that seems to bring together the promotion of black empowerment at home with an attempt to foster pride among the worldwide African diaspora.

At home Mbeki and his cabinet have followed a neo-Thatcherite **economic policy**, framed in the language of budget-deficit reduction, wage restraint and privatization. The unflinching implementation of the policy by the highly competent finance minister, **Trevor Manuel**, has won applause internationally and at home from most centrist and centre-right economists. However, it has former police colonel, **Eugene De Kock**, who was pleading in mitigation after being convicted on 89 charges of murder, gun-running and fraud. He revealed that his activities were not the work of a rogue unit, but part of a well-coordinated campaign by the security forces, carried out with the full knowledge of the government, including presidents Botha and De Klerk.

After two-and-a-half years of hearings across the country, the TRC released its 3,500-page **report** on October 29, 1998. Unsurprisingly, the commission found that "the South African government was in the period 1960–94 the primary perpetrator of gross human rights abuses in South Africa, and from 1974, in Southern Africa". The TRC heard overwhelming evidence that from the 1970s to the 1990s the state had been involved in criminal activities including "extra-judicial killings of political opponents." Among the violations it listed were torture, abduction, sexual abuse, incursions across South Africa's borders to kill opponents in exile, and the deployment of hit squads. It also found that the ANC (and a number of other organizations, including the PAC and Inkatha) was guilty of human rights violations, though on nowhere near the scale of the government. The report acknowledged that the ANC had been waging a just war against apartheid but drew "a distinction between a 'just war' and 'just means'".

There was considerable **criticism of the TRC** from all quarters. Many people felt that justice would better have been served by a Nuremberg-style trial of those guilty of gross violations, but Tutu argued that this would have been impossible in South Africa, given that neither side had won a military victory. Defending the amnesty provisions, he pointed out that "members of the security establishment would have scuppered the negotiated settlement had they thought they were going to run a gauntlet of trials for their involvement in past violations."

The South African media has tended to give the impression that the Truth and Reconciliation Commission has led to a deterioration of race relations in South Africa (as if that were possible). However, a market research survey carried out for *Business Day* in August, 1998, found that attitudes to the TRC split along racial lines; eighty percent of black respondents believed that "the people in South Africa will now be able to live together more easily", while ninety percent of whites felt that the commission would not bring the races closer.

Responding to the lack of support for the TRC, and sometimes even active obstructivism from white leaders, Tutu remarked: "I have been saddened by a mean-spiritedness in some of the leadership of the white community. They should be saying: 'How fortunate we are that these people do not want to treat us how we treated them. How fortunate that things have remained much the same for us except for the loss of some political power.'"

also drawn a predictable barrage of fire from South Africa's left for a policy that they see as quite inappropriate to a country beset by one of the world's most inequitable distributions of wealth and growing unemployment. This has exposed **tensions in the tripartite alliance** – the ANC and its two junior partners: the South African Communist Party and the Congress of South African Trade Unions. Although there are frequent rumblings about a split and the formation of a left-wing opposition party, this seems unlikely since, despite the yawning ideological divide, the three are painfully aware that they will probably have to sink or swim together.

It therefore seems probable that for the forseeable future, the most effective opposition to government policies will come from inside the governing alliance. This is reinforced by the weakness of the parliamentary opposition. In

2000, the **official opposition** in parliament, an alliance between the New National Party and the Democratic Party known as the **Democratic Alliance (DA)** split. The **New National Party**, led by Marthinus van Schalkwyk, was the reinvented National Party – the party of apartheid – which now drew most of its support from the coloureds it had formerly oppressed, as well as Afrikaans-speaking whites. The **Democratic Party** under Tony Leon was the successor to the liberal Progressive Party, which for decades had been the only party in parliament to oppose apartheid. After this unlikely marriage ended on the rocks, the NNP entered into an even more unlikely liaison with the ANC, the party whose members it had previously banned, murdered or imprisoned on Robben Island. What is left of the DA lacks broad electoral support, most notably among the vital constituency of Africans, and gets most of its votes from some coloureds and English-speaking and Afrikaner whites.

Mbeki's handling of the crisis in neighbouring **Zimbabwe**, in which President Robert Mugabe's government unrolled a barrage of laws to curtail civil rights and unleashed violence on its own citizens during the run-up to that country's 2002 presidential election, has also done little for Mbeki's reputation, particularly in the light of his patter about an "African Renaissance". In dealing with the recalcitrant Mugabe, Mbeki has insisted on following a policy of "quiet diplomacy" rather than confrontation, which has failed utterly to produce any positive results.

South Africa's **rand crisis** of 2001, which saw the South African currency lose forty percent of its value in less than a year against sterling and the dollar, was blamed by economists on events in Zimbabwe, Mbeki's failure to strongly condemn them and investor fears that a Zimbabwe-style situation could develop in South Africa. The economists kept predicting that the rand would soon stabilize since "the economic fundamentals were in place". When the currency continued to slide, these same economists blamed the rand's rapid decline on events in Argentina, amongst other factors. They eventually had to admit they had no idea why the rand continued to reach new record lows week after week. It did finally stabilize at around R11 to the dollar and R16 to the pound at the end of 2001.

But as South Africa faces the twenty-first century, no issue is more important or more divisive than Mbeki's stance on **AIDS**. According to South Africa's Medical Research Council, AIDS is the biggest killer in the country. It also threatens to undermine the gains achieved by the Mbeki government's economic successes. Despite pressure from the medical establishment, trade unions and opposition parties – as well from inside his own party – the president has stolidly clung to his unconventional ideas about the disease, and has rejected the provision of anti-retrovirals in state hospitals. Particularly emotive has been the withholding of drugs to AIDS-infected pregnant women to combat mother-to-child transmission, which is widespread in South Africa. Mbeki's greatest failure has been to treat AIDS as an intellectual conundrum rather than a human catastrophe. When asked in November 2000 by *Time* magazine whether he was prepared to acknowledge a link between HIV and AIDS, he replied: "No, I am saying that you cannot attribute immune deficiency solely and exclusively to a virus."

Mbeki's views on AIDS have seriously damaged his international reputation; the *Mail & Guardian* reported in 2001 that "he is known even in small-town United States as 'the African leader with funny views on AIDS'". When Mbeki convened a panel of scientists, comprising mainstream researchers and AIDS dissidents to look into the causes of AIDS, his detractors likened this to someone about to be consumed by a blazing fire setting up an enquiry into the causes of the conflagration rather than fighting it. In 2000, the DA-controlled provincial government of the Western Cape began dispensing anti-retrovirals in state hospitals; in 2002, KwaZulu-Natal followed suit, and it looked like a number of ANC-controlled provinces were going to defy their party's official policy and do likewise.

Perhaps the brighter side of all this is that it demonstrates that **democratic debate** is alive in South Africa, even in the ruling party. South Africa bears more resemblance to a liberal democracy like Britain than to a near-dictatorship like Mugabe's Zimbabwe. Despite the ANC's overwhelming political dominance, views opposing those of the president can be expressed freely. Although South Africa entered the twenty-first century laden with problems, it stands a better chance than virtually any country in sub-Saharan Africa of dealing with them.

Wildlife

There's nowhere better than South Africa to encounter African mammals. Kruger National Park, the biggest of several major reserves along the northern and eastern extremes of the country, is rated among the world's top wildlife areas, both for its ease of access and its range of mammal species. Apart from offering thrilling experiences, the major South African reserves are islands of living archeology, hinting at the teeming life that moved across the subcontinent as far south as present-day Cape Town, before European settlers with firearms swept it to the margins of the country. Apart from Kruger, Kalahari-Gemsbok, Hluhluwe-Umfolozi and Pilanesberg parks, where you'll see the Big Five (lion, leopard, buffalo, elephant and rhino), over a hundred other reserves offer numerous smaller predators and dozens of herbivores, including endangered species, in invariably beautiful settings.

This account supplements the colour fieldguide to "The Wildlife of East and Southern Africa" in the colour section at the start of the book (to which bracketed page numbers refer), and will help you get the most from watching both big game and smaller species. It aims to inspire you to go beyond checklists, to appreciate the interactions of the bush and help you get more out of your safari. Beyond the scope of this account are the hundreds of colourful bird species that are an inseparable part of the South African landscape and whose calls are a constant element of its soundtrack. An interest in these will add immeasurably to your experience. Some outstanding field guides are listed on pp.894–95.

Primates

Southern Africa has the lowest diversity of **primates** on the continent, a mere five species (compared with Kenya's twelve) excluding *Homo sapiens*. They include two varieties of bushbaby, two monkeys and one species of baboon – the largest and most formidable of the lot. Great apes such as gorillas and chimpanzees aren't found in the wild in southern Africa.

> Page numbers below refer to the **colour guide** to "The Wildlife of East and Southern Africa" in the colour section at the start of this book.

Chacma baboons

Chacma baboons, *Papio ursinus* – cynocephalus – (see p.xviii), the local subspecies of common savannah monkeys, are the primates most widely found in South Africa. Males can be somewhat intimidating in size and manner and are frequently bold enough to raid vehicles or accommodation in search of food, undeterred by the close presence of people. Baboons are highly gregarious and are invariably found in troops, which can number as few as fifteen to as many as a hundred, though around forty is common. Social relations are complex, revolving around jockeying to climb the social ladder and avoiding being toppled from its upper rungs. Rank, gender, precedence, physical strength and family ties determine an individual's position in this mini society, which is led by a dominant male. Males are unreconstructed chauvinists, and every adult male enjoys dominance over every female. Days are dominated by the need to forage and hunt for food; baboons are highly opportunistic omnivores who will as happily tuck into a scorpion or a newborn antelope in the bushveld as they will clean up the entire crop from an orange tree on a Garden Route citrus farm. Grooming is a fundamental part of the social glue during times of relaxation. When baboons and other monkeys perform this massage-like activity on each other, the specks which they pop into their mouths are sometimes parasites – notably ticks – and sometimes flecks of skin.

Vervet monkeys

Another widespread primate you're likely to see in the eastern half of the country, and along the coastal belt as far west as Mossel Bay, are **vervet monkeys**, *Cercopithecus aethiops* (see p.xviii). Although happy foraging in grasslands, they rarely venture far from woodland, particularly along river courses. You can see them outside reserves, where they often live around farms and even come into suburban fringes, where opportunities for scavenging are promising. In the Eastern Cape, KwaZulu-Natal and along the Garden Route you might see them hanging about along the verges of the coastal roads, risking their lives "playing chicken" with the traffic. Vervets are principally vegetarians but they are not averse to eating inverterbrates, small lizards, nestlings and eggs, as well as processed foods like biscuits and sweets – when they can snatch them from visitors. Vervet society is made up of family groups of females and young defended by associate males and is highly caste-ridden. A mother's rank determines that of her daughter from infancy, and lower-ranking adult females risk being castigated if they fail to show due respect to these "upper crust" youngsters.

Samango monkeys

In striking contrast with the cheekier, upfront disposition of vervets, the rarer **samango monkeys**, *Cercopithecus mitis*, are shy animals that may only give themselves away through their loud explosive call or the breaking of branches as they go about their business through the canopy. Although they bear a passing resemblance to vervets, samangos are larger and have long cheek hair that gives the passing appearance of Darth Vader. Found only in isolated pockets of KwaZulu-Natal, the Eastern Cape and Mpumalanga, they tend to hang out in the higher reaches of gallery forest, though on occasion they venture into the open to forage. Like vervets, they're highly social and live in troops of females under the proprietorship of a dominant male, but unlike their relatives they are more inclined to fan out when looking for food.

Bushbabies

With their large soft, fluffy pelts, huge, saucer-like eyes, large, rounded ears and superficially cat-like appearance, **bushbabies** are the ultimate in cute, cuddly-looking primates. Of the half-dozen or so species endemic to Africa, only the thick-tailed bushbaby, *Otolemur crassicaudatus,* and, about half the size, the lesser bushbaby, *Galago moholi*, are found south of the Limpopo. The former is restricted to the eastern fringes of the sub-continent, while the latter overlaps its range in the northeast and extends across the north of the country into Northwest Province.

South Africa's **ecological zones** encompass a range of climate, topography and vegetation supporting a rich diversity of animal life. There are thornveld deserts, pockets of forest, tangles of subtropical vegetation, grassy savannahs, mountainous peaks and several distinct coastal habitats. Geographically, South Africa is divided in two by successive mountain ranges that run in a huge arc from the Cape Peninsula to Mpumalanga, approximately parallel to the coast. This Great Escarpment divides the vast, drier interior plateau from the wetter marginal zone merging with the coastal belt. The plateau and coastal margin can each be divided into a series of ecological zones, or biomes, which share a climate and similar vegetation.

The lowveld

The **lowveld**, or bushveld, is the stereotypical African landscape of great plains, forming a backdrop for thousands of animals. It stretches down across a third of Africa, from Malawi into South Africa; here it forms a large, crescent-shaped swathe running parallel to the Limpopo River, then sweeps down between the Drakensberg and the sub-tropical coastal strip runing from the northern KwaZulu-Natal coast into the Eastern Cape as far as Port Elizabeth. Typical vegetation consists of mixed **savannah** and **dry woodlands** and includes deciduous broad-leafed trees such as **marulas**, whose fruit is highly sought-after by elephants.

The moister subtropical section of the lowveld, along the Mpumalanga and northern KwaZulu-Natal borders, contains thorny **acacias**, green-barked **fever trees** and thick-set **baobabs**, with **palm** trees thriving in the river valleys. In the drier transitional zones to the west, bordering the arid zone, succulent species such as **aloes** (with their red-hot poker flowers) and massive candelabra-tree **euphorbias** dominate a harsher landscape.

Subtropical lowland

South of the Mozambique border, to the Great Fish River in the Eastern Cape, lies the narrow **coastal plain**, at an altitude of below 400m. Once thickly forested, cane fields have replaced indigenous woodland, particularly in KwaZulu-Natal. However, one of the wildest environments in the country survives in Maputaland, where extensive **dunes** and **wetlands** constitute a transitional zone between the Mozambique tropics and subtropical KwaZulu-Natal. Some 21 ecosystems have been identified here.

With the notable exception of lions, you can see a terrific array of wildlife, including aquatic and semi-aquatic species such as crocodile, hippo, terrapin, clawless otter, reedbuck and water monitor lizard. Giant forests on the protected west flank of its dunes are home to red duiker, bushpig, and vervet and samango monkeys.

From southern KwaZulu-Natal into the Wild Coast of the Eastern Cape, dozens of major river courses have etched deep valleys that protect the remnants of dwindling forests. Nowhere is it more dramatic though, than at Oribi Gorge Nature Reserve, near Port Shepstone, where a twenty-four-kilometre-long and five-kilometre-wide gorge is part of an environment descending from **clifftop grasslands**, down **sandstone cliffs**, to dense **riverine forests**. Here you'll find leopards, bushbuck, vervets, samango monkeys and two species of the small duiker antelope.

The fynbos region

Confined to a shallow southwestern corner of South Africa, the **fynbos region** extends in an inverse arc from the Olifants River in the north to Port Elizabeth in the east, and includes the Cape Peninsula. The region consists of the smallest and richest of the world's six floral kingdoms. A **heathland** system, it grows on the back of the Cape fold mountains that cut off the coastal belt from the semi-arid Karoo interior. Despite its diversity, fynbos is extremely poor in nutrients and is unable to support a large biomass (it can't feed large organisms in great quantities). Although a reasonable cross-section of mammals, including lion and elephant, inhabited the zone when the first settlers arrived, they were soon wiped out in the localized area. One, the blue antelope, a large species related to the sable, was totally extinguished.

Most exciting of its mammals are the fairly numerous but infrequently seen Cape mountain leopards. The same species as those elsewhere in the country, they're smaller here – an adaptation to the scarcity of nutrients. Other predators include caracals, African wild cats, and jackals. The Cape of Good Hope Nature Reserve is one of the best places to get an idea of the fynbos ecological zone and is one of the areas where the endangered bontebok still survives, alongside baboons, porcupines and Cape mountain zebras. For more on fynbos, see p.147.

The western arid zone

The **western arid zone** creeps down from the north and includes the entire section of the Kalahari ecological zone entering the Northern Cape from Botswana, as well as the succulent Karoo zone along the west coast and the Nama Karoo zone in the extensive interior. Permanent surface water is almost totally absent throughout the vast zone – the Orange River is its only perennial watercourse. The succulent Karoo coastal zone contains succulents which explode into swathes of colourful flowers in August and September after the winter rains; the South African Kalahari is a lonely region of **red sandveld** punctuated with **camelthorn acacia** trees; and the Nama Karoo consists mainly of wiry **dwarf shrubs** in flat country fringed with low **hills**.

Kalahari-Gemsbok National Park is the most notable game reserve in the western arid zone, rated by some as a rival to Kruger because of its wilder ambience and excellent wildlife. It's the one of the few places in the country to see gemsbok, and you might also encounter lion, cheetah, jackal and bat-eared foxes among an impressive list of mammals. Only elephant and buffalo are notably absent.

The Karoo once hosted great herds of migrating antelope including springbok and bontebok. Now they're only seen behind fences, raised for their meat alongside millions of sheep. However, some species that once roamed the Karoo, including gemsbok, hartebeest and black wildebeest, have been reintroduced into the National Park, where they co-exist with baboon, reedbuck, klipspringer and caracal.

The highveld

The high-lying central plateau (generally 1200–1829m) of South Africa, known as the **highveld**, takes in the territory south of Johannesburg, including the Free State east of Bloemfontein, and is defined in the south and east by the Great Escarpment. The ecological zone varies from flat grassy, treeless **plains** to the rugged **peaks** of the Drakensberg, where you'll find alpine-type vegetation above an altitude of 3000m. Most of the region is now covered by **semi-desert** scrub and **maize fields**, with indigenous vegetation surviving only around the peaks and in the rugged valleys. Of the mammals that once thrived here, only smaller species, such as caracal, mongoose and hare, have survived the massive agricultural onslaught. However, at Suikerbosrand Nature Reserve, just south of Johannesburg, you can see once-endangered species such as blesbok, as well as cheetah, springbok, hartebeest, oribi, zebra, mountain reedbuck, rhebok, duiker, steenbok, kudu and brown hyena. One bird you could well see amongst cultivated fields is the blue crane, South Africa's national bird, which feeds on the seeds of standing crops. In the reserves of the Drakensberg, mountain-adapted antelope, such as klipspringer and mountain reedbuck, and baboon, porcupine and jackal all thrive.

Afro-montane forest

South Africa is one of the least forested countries in the world, a tiny fraction of one percent of its surface carrying indigenous woodland. **Afro-montane forest**, which requires high annual rainfall, exists only in isolated pockets, most famous of which is the Knysna Forest on the southern slopes of the Western Cape's Outeniqua Mountains. Best known for its **giant trees**, including yellowwood, stinkwood and ironwood, it also has leopard, bushpig, bushbuck, caracals and mongoose. Similar forest survives in the Eastern Cape in the Katberg-Hogsback area, where baboon, vervet and samango monkeys, duiker, bushbuck and porcupine are common.

If you're staying at any of the KwaZulu-Natal reserves, you stand a fair chance of seeing a bushbaby after dark as they emerge from the dense forest canopy, where they rest in small groups, for spells of lone foraging for tree gum and fruit. Even if you don't see one, you're bound to hear their piercing scream cut through the sounds of the night. Unlike other bushbabies, including the lesser, which leap with ease and speed, *crassicaudatus* (thick tails) is a slow mover that hops or walks along branches, often with considerable stealth. Bushbabies habituate easily to humans and will sometimes come into lodge dining rooms, scavenging for tidbits; at *Rocktail Bay Lodge*, on the northern KwaZulu-Natal coast, Gremlin, a semi-tame bushbaby, periodically joins guests in their beds and has developed a penchant for sugar and booze.

Carnivores

Almost three dozen species of **carnivore** are found in South Africa, ranging from mongooses and weasels to dog-relatives, hyenas and seven species of cat.

Dog-relatives

South Africa's five **dog-relatives**, *Canidae*, consist of two foxes, two jackals and the wild dog. The member of the *Canidae* you're most likely to see is the **black-backed jackal**, *Canis mesomelas* (see p.xx), found especially, though not exclusively, in the country's reserves. It bears a strong resemblance to a small, skinny German Shepherd, but with a more fox-like muzzle, and is distinguished from the grey **side-striped jackal**, *Canis adjustus*, by the white-flecked black saddle on its back, to which it owes its name. In South Africa, the side-striped is found only in and around Kruger and the extreme north of KwaZulu-Natal, and this is the only region where any confusion can arise. The fact that the black-backed seeks a drier habitat, in contrast to the side-striped's preference for well-watered woodland, is an additional identification pointer. Both are omnivorous, with diets that take in carrion, small animals, reptiles, birds and insects, as well as wild fruit and berries; and both are most commonly spotted alone or in pairs, though family groups are occasionally sighted.

The **bat-eared fox**, *Otocyon megalotis* (see p.xx), is found throughout the western half of the country and along the Limpopo strip and can be easily distinguished from the jackals by its outsized ears, its shorter, pointier muzzle and its considerably smaller size. The bat-eared's black Zorro mask helps distinguish it from the similar sized **Cape fox**, *Vulpes chama*, which inhabitats an overlapping range. Like other dogs, the bat-eared fox is an omnivore, but it favours termites and larvae, which is where its large radar-like ears come in handy. With these it can triangulate the precise position of dung beetle larvae up to 30cm underground and dig them out. Bat-eareds tend to live in pairs or family groups, an arrangement that affords mutual protection.

Once widely distributed hunters of the African plains, **wild dogs**, *Lycaon pictus* (see p.xx), have been brought to the edge of extinction. For many years they were shot on sight, having gained an unjustified reputation as cruel and wanton killers of cattle and sheep. More recent scientific evidence reveals them to be economical and efficient hunters – and more successful at it than any other African species. They have only survived in the Kruger, and have been reintroduced into Hluhluwe-Umfolozi, though you'd be extremely lucky to see a pack trotting along for a hunt. Capable of sustaining high speeds (up to 50kph) over long distances, wild dogs lunge at their prey en masse, tearing it to pieces – a gruesome finish, but no more grisly than the suffocating muzzle-bite of a lion. The entire pack of ten to fifteen animals participates in looking after the pups, bringing back food and regurgitating it for them.

Hyenas

The largest carnivores after lions are **hyenas**, and apart from the lion, the **spotted hyena**, *Crocuta crocuta* (see p.xxi), is the meat-eater you will most often see. Although considered a scavenger *par excellence*, the spotted hyena is a formidable hunter, most often found where antelopes and zebras are present. Exceptionally efficient consumers, with immensely strong teeth and jaws, spotted hyenas eat virtually every part of their prey, including bones and hide and, where habituated to humans, often steal shoes, unwashed pans and refuse from tents. Although they can be seen by day, they are most active at night – when they issue their unnerving whooping cries. Clans of twenty or so animals are dominated by females, who are larger than the males and compete with each other for rank. Curiously, female hyenas' genitalia are hard to distinguish from males', leading to a popular misconception that they are hermaphroditic. They occur in Kruger, Hluhluwe-Umfolozi and Kalahari-Gemsbok parks, and north into East and West Africa.

The **brown hyena**, *Hyaena brunnea*, is restricted to parts of Namibia, Botswana, Zimbabwe and South Africa, where it's generally seen only in the northernmost regions. That it's usually seen singly also distinguishes this shaggier, slightly larger hyena from its spotted cousin.

The hyena-like **aardwolf**, *Proteles cristatus*, is smaller than the spotted hyena and far lighter (about two-thirds the height at the shoulder and roughly a tenth of its weight) as well as being less shaggy with vertical dark stripes along its tawny body. It is further distinguished from hyenas by its insectivorous diet and its particular preference for harvester termites, which it laps up en masse (up to 200,000 in one night) with its broad sticky tongue. Far more widely distributed in South Africa than the hyenas, this nocturnal animal is sometimes active in the cooler hours just before dusk or after dawn. Although they aren't often seen, keep an eye open at the Cape of Good Hope, Karoo, Mountain Zebra, Pilanesberg, Kruger, Hluhluwe-Umfolozi and Kalahari-Gemsbok reserves.

Cats

Apart from lions, which notably live in social groups, **cats** are solitary carnivores. With the exception of the cheetah, which is anatomically distinct from the other cats, remaining members of the family are so similar that, as Richard Estes comments in *The Safari Companion*, big cats are just "jumbo versions" of the domestic cat, "distinguished mainly by a modification of the larynx that enables them to roar."

Perhaps it's just a question of size, but the most compelling of the *Felidae* for most people on safari are **lions**, *Panthera leo* (see p.xxii) the largest cats, and indeed, the most massive predators in Africa. It's fortunate then that despite having the most limited distribution of any cat in South Africa, lions are the ones you're most likely to see. Of the public reserves, the Kruger and Kalahari-Gemsbok parks have healthy populations, and prides have been reintroduced into Hluhluwe-Umfolozi, where numbers are relatively limited. Lazy, gregarious and sizeable, lions rarely attempt to hide, making them relatively easy to find, especially if someone else has already spotted them – a gathering of stationary vehicles frequently signals lions. Seeing them hunt is another matter, and you're less likely to see David Attenborough-esque enactments of the chase. In fact, their fabled reputation as cold, efficient hunters is ill-founded, as lions are only successful around thirty percent of the time, and only then if operating as a group. Males don't hunt at all if they can help it and will happily enjoy a free lunch by courtesy of the females of the pride.

The lion may be king, but most successful and arguably most beautiful of the large cats is the **leopard**, *Panthera pardus* (see p.xxii), which survives from the southern coastal strip of Africa all the way to China. Highly adaptable, they can subsist in extremes of aridity or cold, as well as in proximity to human habitation, where they happily prey on domestic animals – which accounts for their absence in the sheep-farming regions of central South Africa, due to extermination by farmers. They're present in the rugged, mountainous southern areas of the Western Cape, but you are most unlikely to encounter these secretive, solitary animals here. Your best chance of a sighting is at the private lodges in Sabi Sands, abutting Kruger, which trade on their leopards being highly habituated to people. You'll need greater luck and sharper eyes to see them in the public reserves they inhabit, including the Kruger, Kalahari-Gemsbok, Hluhluwe-Umfolozi and Mkhuze. Powerfully built, they can bring down prey twice their mass and drag an impala their own weight up a tree. The chase is not part of the leopard's tactical repertoire; they hunt by stealth, getting to within two metres of their target before pouncing.

In the flesh, the **cheetah**, *Acionyx jubatus* (see p.xxii), is so different from the leopard that it's hard to see how there could ever be any confusion. Cheetahs are the lightly built greyhounds of the big-cat world, with small heads, very long legs and an exterior decor of fine spots. Unlike leopards, cheetahs never climb trees, being designed rather for activity on the open plains. They live alone, or sometimes briefly form a pair during mating. Hunting is normally a solitary activity, down to eyesight and an incredible burst of speed that can take the animal up to 100kph for a few seconds. Because they're lighter than lions and less powerful than leopards, cheetahs can't rely on strength to bring down their prey, instead having to resort to tripping or knocking the victim off balance by striking its hindquarters and then pouncing. Once widespread across South Africa, now you'll only see them in a few reserves including Kruger, Kalahari-Gemsbok and Hluhluwe-Umfolozi.

The other *Felidae* are usually classified as small cats, although the **caracal**, *Caracal caracal* (see p.xxii), is a substantial animal. An unmistakeable and awesome hunter, with great climbing agility, it's able to take prey, such as adult impala and sheep, which far exceed its own mass of eight to eighteen kilogrammes. More commonly it will feed on birds, which it pounces on, sometimes while still in flight, as well as smaller mammals, including dassies. Found across most of South Africa, excluding KwaZulu-Natal, but not often seen, caracals live in the Mountain Zebra National Park (one of the best places to see them), Kruger, Giant's Castle, the Cape Peninsula, Karoo and Kalahari-Gemsbok parks.

Long-legged and spotted, **servals**, *Felis serval* (see p.xxiii), are higher at the shoulder but lighter than caracals, and are equally rarely seen, although they are present in Mpumalanga and KwaZulu-Natal in the Kruger, Hluhluwe-Umfolozi and Giant's Castle. Efficient hunters, servals use their large rounded ears to pinpoint prey (usually small rodents, birds or reptiles), which they pounce on with both front paws after performing impressive athletic leaps.

Of the genuinely small cats, the **African wild cat**, *Felis lybica*, is distributed throughout South Africa and is easily mistaken for a domestic tabby, although its legs are longer and it has reddish ears. First domesticated six thousand years ago by the Egyptians, wild cats are so closely related to the domestic version that the two are able to interbreed freely. You're unlikely to encounter the compact small **spotted cat**, *Felis nigripes* (also known as the black footed cat), a beautifully spotted fluffy animal, which is so rarely seen that little is known about its behaviour in the wild.

Smaller carnivores

Among the smaller predators is the unusual **honey badger**, *Mellivora capensis* (see p.xx), related to the European badger and with a reputation for defending itself extremely fiercely. Primarily an omnivorous forager, it will tear open bees' nests (to which it is led by a small bird, the honey guide), its thick, loose hide rendering it impervious to stings.

Small-spotted (or common) genets, *Genetta genetta* (see p.xxi), are reminiscent of slender elongated cats, and were once domesticated around the Mediterranean (but cats turned out to be better mouse hunters). In fact, they are viverrids, related to mongooses, and are frequently seen after dark around national park lodges, where they live a semi-domesticated existence. Found throughout the country, apart from KwaZulu-Natal, they're difficult to distinguish from the **large-spotted genet**, *Genetta tigrina*, which has bigger spots and a black (instead of white) tip to its tail. These are found in northeastern parts of the country, KwaZulu-Natal and along the coastal margin as far west as the Cape Peninsula.

Most species of **mongoose** (see p.xxi), of which there are nearly a dozen in South Africa, are also tolerant of humans and, even when disturbed, can usually be observed for some time before disappearing. Their snake-fighting reputation is greatly overplayed: in practice they are mostly social foragers, fanning out through the bush like beaters on a shoot, rooting for anything edible – mostly invertebrates, eggs, lizards and frogs.

One of the best places to see Cape **clawless otters**, *Aonyx capensis*, a large heavily built species, is in the Tsitsikamma National Park, where it feeds on crabs, fishes and octopuses and will commonly forage on cliff faces and in tidal pools. They are also common in the KwaZulu-Natal reserves and the Kruger.

The **civet** (or African civet), *civettictis civetta* (see p.xxi), is a stocky animal resembling a large, terrestrial genet. It was formerly kept in captivity for its musk (once an ingredient in perfume), which is secreted from glands near the tail. Civets aren't often seen, but they're predictable creatures, wending their way along the same path at the same time, night after night.

Antelope

Antelope are the most regularly seen family of animals in South Africa's game reserves, and you'll even spot some on farmland along the extensive open stretches that separate interior towns. South Africa has roughly a third of all antelope species in Africa. South African antelope can be sub-divided into a number of tribes, and like buffalo, giraffe and domestic cattle, they are ruminants.

Bushbuck tribe

Among the bushbuck tribe, it's generally only males that have horns, which are curved and spiralled. The exception is the eland, in which both sexes have straight horns (but still marked by distinctive spiralling). Bushbuck are the only non-territorial African antelope, and you'll see them in the shadows of thickets and bush cover, which they use for defence against predators.

Largest of the tribe, and indeed, the largest living antelope is the **eland**, *Taurotragus oryx* (see p.xxx), which is built like an ox and moves with the slow deliberation of one, though it's a great jumper. Once widely found, herds survive around the Kruger, Kalahari-Gemsbok and a tiny enclave in northern KwaZulu-Natal Drakensberg, plus they've been reintroduced to a number of other reserves throughout the country.

The magnificent **kudu** (known as the greater kudu in east Africa), *Tragelaphus strepsiceros* (see p.xxx), is more elegantly built, and males are adorned with sensational spiralled horns that can easily reach 1.5m in length – it's these that you'll often see mounted in old-fashioned country hotels. Female groups usually include three or more members and will sometimes combine temporarily to form larger herds; males form similarly sized but more transient groupings, although it's not uncommon to encounter lone bulls.

Despite a distinct family resemblance you could never confuse a kudu with a **bushbuck**, *Tragelaphus scriptus* (see p.xxx), which is considerably shorter and has a single twist to its horns, in contrast to the kudu's two or three turns. They also differ in being the only solitary members of the tribe, one reason why you're less likely to spot them. Apart from the major reserves, they're found in Addo Elephant and Greater St Lucia parks.

Nyalas, *Tragelaphus angasi* (see p.xxix), are midway in size between the kudu and bushbuck, with which they could be confused at first glance. Telling pointers are their size, the sharp vertical white stripes on the side of the nyala (up to fourteen on the male, eighteen on the female) and in the males a short stiff mane from neck to shoulder. Females tend to group with their two last offspring and gather with other females in small herds of rarely more than ten. Males become more solitary the older they get. You'll tend to see males and females separately, as they only deliberately congregate for mating.

Horse antelope

Restricted mainly to the Kruger, the **sable**, *Hippotragus niger* (see p.xxxi), is easily as magnificent as the kudu. A sleek, black upper body set in sharp counterpoint to its white underparts and facial markings, as well as its massive backwardly curving horns, make this the thoroughbred of the ruminants, particularly when galloping majestically across the savannah (though they prefer woodland). Highly hierarchical female herds number between one and three dozen, while territorial bulls frequently keep their distance, remaining under cover where you could easily miss them.

The **roan**, *Hippotragus equinus* (see p.xxxi), is very similar-looking, but larger than a sable (it's Africa's second-largest antelope), with less impressive horns and lighter colouring. You're more likely to see them in open savannah than sables.

Geographically more restricted, **gemsbok** (also known as the oryx), *Oryx gazella* (see p.xxxi), are only seen in South Africa in Kalahari-Gemsbok, the southernmost part of their range which stretches down from the deserts of Namibia and Botswana. If you encounter a herd of these highly gregarious grazers, you should be left in no doubt as to what they are. Like the roan and sable they have thick-set bodies and superficially similar facial markings, but their greyish-fawn colouring, black and white underbody markings and long, slender, almost straight backward-pointing horns make them unmistakable. Gemsbok are highly adapted for survival in the arid country they inhabit, able to go for long periods without water, relying instead on melons and vegetation for moisture. They tolerate temperatures above 40°C by raising their normal body temperature of 35°C above that of the surrounding air, losing heat by conduction and radiation; at the same time they keep their brains cool by using cool blood from their noses as a coolant.

Hartebeests

With their bracket-shaped, relatively short horns and ungainly appearance, **hartebeest** look vaguely like elongated cows – particularly their faces. All hartebeest are gregarious, but the exemplar of this is the **blue wildebeest**, *Connochaetes taurinus* (see p.xxvi) which, in East Africa, gather in hundreds of thousands for their annual migration. You won't see these numbers in South Africa, but you'll see smaller herds if you go to any of the reserves in the northern half of the country or KwaZulu-Natal, as well as a number in the southern half, where they've been reintroduced. A particularly photogenic sight is wildebeest mingling with zebras, a habit said to be for mutual defence, though it may simply reflect the fact that they are both grazers and therefore hang around similar terrain. You're less likely to see **black wildebeest**, *Connochaetes gnou*, which were brought to the edge of extinction in the nineteenth century and now number around 3000 in South Africa, though you may find them in the Karoo and Mountain Zebra parks as well as Giant's Castle. You can tell them apart from their blue cousins by their darker colour (brown rather than the black suggested by their name) and long white tail.

Rather inelegant, like the wildebeests, the **red hartebeest**, *Alcelaphus buselaphus* (see p.xxvi), the extremely rare **Lichtenstein's hartebeest**, *Sigmocerus lichtensteinii*, and the **tsessebe**, *Damaliscus lunatus* (see p.xxvi), are all highly similar in appearance, but confusion is only likely to arise at the Kruger, the one place Lichtenstein's are found in the same range as tsessebes. The key distinction is in the horns, which in the hartebeest curve round to almost touch each other, while the tsessebe's are more splayed. Parks where you can see red hartebeests include Mountain Zebra, Karoo, Addo and Kalahari-Gemsbok.

The **blesbok**, *Damaliscus dorcas phillipsi*, and **bontebok**, *Damaliscus dorcas dorcas*, are near identical sub-species of the same animal and resemble darker, better-looking versions of the tsessebe. The largest bontebok population is at De Hoop Nature Reserve, with other members of the sub-species at the Cape of Good Hope Nature Reserve. Good places to see blesbok include Mountain Zebra National Park and Suikerbosrand Nature Reserve. After springboks, blesboks are the most important game-farm species in the country, and you may see them on Karoo farms.

Duiker and dwarf antelope

Duiker and the dwarf tribe are non-herding antelope that are either solitary or live in pairs. Despite their size, or perhaps because of it, males tend to be highly aggressive and are able to use their straight, stiletto-sharp horns to deadly effect.

The smallest South African antelope, the **blue duiker**, *Philantomba monticola*, weighs in at around 4kg, has an arched back and stands 35cm at the shoulder (roughly the height of a cat). Extremely shy, it is seldom seen in the southern and eastern coastal forests (as well as Ndumo Game Reserve) where it lives.

The slightly larger **red duiker**, *Cephalophus natalensis*, is three times heavier, and enjoys a similar environment to the blue, but only inhabits the woodlands and forest of KwaZulu-Natal.

The member of this tribe you're more likely to see, though, is the **common duiker** (sometimes called the grey duiker, reflecting its colouring), *Sylvicapra grimmia* (see p.xxix), which occurs all over South Africa and is one of the antelope most tolerant of human habitation. When under threat it freezes in the undergrowth, but if chased will dart off in an erratic zigzagging run designed to throw pursuers off balance.

This type of fast darting movement is also characteristic of **dwarf antelope**, particularly the **Cape grysbok**, *Raphicerus melanotis* (see p.xxxii), and **Sharpe's grysbok**, *Raphicerus sharpii*, which bear a close resemblance to one another, but can't be confused because their ranges don't overlap. The Cape grysbok lives in the Western Cape fynbos belt (including Cape of Good Hope Nature Reserve and Addo), while Sharpe's occur in the northeastern corner of the country around the Kruger. Both are nocturnal and so are not often sighted.

A relative of the grysbok, the **steenbok**, *Raphicerus campestris* (see p.xxii), is by far the most commonly sighted of all the dwarf antelope, and you can spot them by day or night all over the country (except parts of KwaZulu-Natal). Its large, dark eyes, massive ears and delicate frame give this elegant half-metre-high antelope an engaging Bambi-like appearance.

Another dwarf antelope you could well see is the **klipspringer**, *Oreotragus oreotragus* (see p.xxxii), whose Afrikaans name (meaning "rock jumper") reflects its goat-like adaptation to living on *kopjes* and cliffs – the only antelope to do so, making it unmistakeable. It's also the only one to walk on the tips of its hooves. Keep your eyes peeled at Kruger or Mountain Zebra parks (and other wilderness areas where there are rocky outcrops) for their large, bounding movements to scale steep inclines or their hopping from rock to rock.

The largest of the dwarves is the **oribi**, *Ourebia ourebi* (see p.xxxii), which could be taken for an outsized steenbok or a small gazelle, to which its faster smoother movements, when compared to other dwarves, are more akin. Only found in small pockets of KwaZulu-Natal, they live in small parties of a ram and several ewes. You may hear their short sharp warning whistle as you approach, before you see them, although they will frequently stop after fleeing a little way to look back at you.

Gazelle

Springbok, *Antidorcas marsupalis* (see p.xxvii), are said to have once migrated in their millions across the drylands of South Africa, but today their numbers are greatly reduced and the network of fences segmenting the country has ended such mass movements. South Africa's only gazelle, they are the most populous members of this tribe, whose several other species are found in East Africa. Their characteristic horns and dark horizontal patch on their sides, separating their reddish tawny upper body from their white underparts, are definitive identifiers. Tolerant of a wide range of open country from deserts to wetter savannah, you'll see these medium-sized antelope in reserves in the western arid zone of the country. The symbol of the national cricket and rugby teams, they're also raised on farms in this region for venison and hides. Springbok are recorded as having reached nearly 90kph and are noted for "pronking", a movement in which they arch their backs and straighten their legs as they leap into the air.

Impala

Larger and heavier than springbok, which they superficially resemble, **impala**, *Aepyceros melampus* (see p.xxviii), are a one-off antelope in a tribe of their own. Elegant and athletic, they are prodigious jumpers that have been recorded leaping distances of 11m and heights of 3m. Only the males carry the distinctive lyre-shaped horns. They are so common in the reserves of the northeast and of KwaZulu-Natal that some jaded rangers look on them as the goats of the savannah – a perception that carries more than a germ of truth as these flexible feeders are both browsers and grazers. Ewes and lambs form tight herds that can number over a hundred, moving about in a home range that may overlap the territory of several rams. During the rut, which takes place during the first five months of each year, these males will cut out harem herds of around twenty and expend considerable amounts of effort herding them and driving off any potential rivals.

Near-aquatic antelope

Of the near-aquatic Kob tribe, only the males have horns, but all species live close to water. Largest of the tribe, **waterbuck**, *Kobus ellipsiprymnus* (see p.xxviii), are sturdy antelope – 1.3m at the shoulder – with shaggy reddish-brown coats and a white horseshoe marking on their rumps. They're found sporadically in the northeastern reserves, always in proximity to permanent water close to woodland. Sociable animals, they usually gather in small herds of up to ten, and occasionally up to thirty.

Two closely related species, the **common reedbuck**, *Redunca arundinum* (see p.xxviii), and the slightly smaller **mountain reedbuck**, *Redunca fulvorufula*, both roughly two-thirds the height of waterbuck, are tan-coloured antelope. The common reedbuck favours a habitat of tall grass or reedbeds for refuge, while the mountain reedbuck inhabits hilly country with trees or grassy slopes.

All three species can be seen in suitable habitat in the Kruger, while the waterbuck and common reedbuck will also be sighted in the wetland reserves of KwaZulu-Natal, and the mountain reedbuck in the Mountain Zebra, Giant's Castle and Pilanesberg parks.

Other hoofed ruminants

Alongside cattle, sheep, goats and antelope, buffalo and giraffe are also **hoofed ruminants** – animals that have four stomachs and chew the cud. Bacteria in their digestive systems process plant matter into carbohydrates, while the dead bacteria are absorbed as protein – a highly efficient arrangement that makes them economical consumers, far more so than non-ruminants such as elephants, which pass vast quantities of what they eat as unutilized fibre. Species that concentrate on grasses are grazers; those eating leaves are browsers.

Buffalo

You won't have to be in the Kruger or most of the other reserves in South Africa for long to see **buffalo**, *Syncerus caffer* (see p.xxvi), a common safari animal that, as one of the Big Five, appears on every hunter's shopping list. Don't let their resemblance to domestic cattle or water buffalo (to which they are not at all closely related) or apparent docility lull you into complacency; lone bulls, in particular, are noted and feared even by hardened hunters as dangerous and relentless killers. In other words, don't assume that because there are no carnivores about in some reserves that it's safe to go walking without a guide.

Buffalo are non-territorial and highly gregarious, gathering in hundreds or even sometimes thousands. Herds under one or more dominant bulls consist of clans of a dozen or so related females under a leading cow. You'll be able to spot such distinct units within the group: at rest, clan members often cuddle up close to each other. There are separate pecking orders among females and males, the latter being forced to leave the herd during adolescence (at about three years) or once they're over the hill, to form bachelor herds, which you can recognize by their small numbers. Evicted old bulls (sometimes called "*daga* boys" on account of their penchant for mud baths), stripped of their social position and sex lives, understandably become resentful and embittered loners and are to be avoided at all costs. To distinguish males (as shown in the colour guide) from females, look for their heavier horns bisected by a distinct boss, or furrow.

Giraffe

Giraffe, *Giraffa camelopardalis* (see p.xxv), are among the easiest animals to spot because their long necks make them visible above the low scrub. The tallest mammals on earth, giraffes spend their daylight hours browsing on the leaves of trees too high for other species; combretum and acacias are favourites. Their highly flexible lips and prehensile tongues give them almost hand-like agility and enable them to select the most nutritious leaves while avoiding deadly-sharp acacia thorns. At night they lie down and spend the evening ruminating. Non-territorial, they gather in loose, leaderless herds; if you encounter a bachelor herd look out for young males testing their strength with neck wrestling. When the female comes into oestrus, which can happen at any time of year, the dominant male will mate with her. She will give birth after a gestation period of approximately fourteen months. Over half of all young, however, fall prey to lions or hyenas in their early years. Kruger, Pilanesberg and KwaZulu-Natal parks are all good places to see them.

Non-ruminants

Non-ruminating mammals have more primitive digestive systems than animals that chew the cud. Although both have bacteria in their gut that convert vegetable matter into carbohydrates, the less efficient system of the non-ruminants means they have to consume more raw material and to process it faster. The upside is they can handle food that's far more fibrous.

Elephants

Elephants, *Loxodonta africana* (see p.xxiii), were once found throughout South Africa. Now you'll only see them in a handful of reserves, notably the Kruger, Pilanesberg, Hluhluwe-Umfolozi, Tembe and Addo, the last of which protects the only population to survive naturally in the southern two-thirds of the country. Apart from this, one or two elephants may still survive in the Knysna Forest, but their days are numbered and they are rarely, if ever, seen. Elephants are the most engaging of animals to watch, perhaps because their interactions, behaviour patterns and personality have so many human parallels. Like people, they lead complex, interdependent social lives, growing from helpless infancy through self-conscious adolescence to adulthood. Babies are born with other cows in close attendance, after a 22-month gestation. Calves suckle for two to three years.

Basic family units are composed of a group of related females, tightly protecting their young and led by a venerable matriarch. It's the matriarch that's most likely to bluff a charge – though occasionally she may get carried away and tusk a vehicle or person. Bush mythology has it that elephants become embarrassed and ashamed after killing a human, covering the body with sticks and grass. They certainly pay much attention to the disposal of their own dead relatives, often dispersing the bones and spending time near the remains. Old animals die in their seventies or eighties, when their last set of teeth wears out and they can no longer feed.

Seen in the flesh, elephants seem even bigger than you would imagine. You'll need little persuasion from those flapping warning ears to back off if you're too close, but they are at the same time amazingly graceful. Silent on their padded, carefully placed feet, in a matter of moments a large herd can merge into the trees and disappear, their presence betrayed only by the noisy cracking of branches as they strip trees and uproot saplings.

Dassies (hyraxes)

Dassies look like they ought to be rodents, but amazingly, despite being fluffy and rabbit-sized, their closest relatives (some way back) are elephants rather than rats. Their name (pronounced like "dusty" without the "t") is the Afrikaans version of *dasje*, meaning "little badger", given to them by the first Dutch settlers. **Tree dassies**, *Dendrohyrax arboreus*, a rarely seen, solitary species, live along the Eastern Cape and southern KwaZulu-Natal coastal plains, where they take refuge in forest and thick bush.

In contrast, **rock dassies**, *Procavia capensis* (see p.xxiii), are widely distributed, having thrived with the elimination of predators. They hang out in suitably rocky habitat all over the country apart from north of the Orange River in the western half of the country and in the east along the northern KwaZulu-Natal coast. One of the most dramatic places you'll see them is sunning themselves along the rocky shore of the Tsitsikamma National Park, as breakers crash down ahead.

Like reptiles, hyraxes have poor body control systems and rely on shelter against both the cold and hot sunlight. They wake up sluggish and seek out rocks to catch the early morning sun – this is one of the best times to look out for them. One adult stands sentry against predators and issues a low-pitched warning cry in response to a threat. Dassies live in colonies of a dominant male and eight or more related females and their offspring.

Rhinos

Two species of rhinoceros are found in Africa: the hook-lipped or **black rhino**, *Diceros bicornis* (see p.xxiv), and the much heavier square-lipped or **white rhino**, *Ceratotherium simum* (see p.xxiv). Both have come close to extinction in the African wild and have all but disappeared. Happily, South Africa has bucked this continental trend and, due to timely conservation measures (especially in KwaZulu-Natal), it's the best place in the world to see both. Spend a day or two at Itala, Hluhluwe-Umfolozi or Mkuzi reserves and you're bound to see one species or the other. Elsewhere, look for white rhinos at Addo and both varieties at Kruger and Pilanesberg.

"Hook-lipped" and "square-lipped" are technically more accurate terms for the two rhinos. "Black" and "white" are based on a linguistic misunderstanding – somewhere along the line, the German *weid*, which refers to the square-lipped's wide mouth, was misheard as "white". The term has stuck, despite both rhinos being a greyish muddy colour.

The shape of their lips is highly significant as it indicates their respective diets and consequently their favoured habitat. The cantankerous and smaller black rhino has the narrow prehensile lips of a browser, suited to picking leaves off trees and bushes, while the wide, flatter mouth of the twice-as-heavy white rhino, is more like a lawnmower and well-suited to chomping away at grasses. Diet and habitat also account for the greater sociability of the white rhino, which relies on safety in numbers under the exposure of open grassland; the solitary black rhino relies on the camouflage of dense thickets, which is why you'll find them so much more difficult to see.

Rhinos give birth to a single calf after a gestation period of fifteen to eighteen months, and the baby is not weaned until it is at least a year old, sometimes two. Their population growth rate is slow compared with most animals, another factor contributing to their predicament.

Hippos

Hippopotamuses, *Hippopotamus amphibius* (see p.xxv), are highly adaptable animals that once inhabited South African waterways from the Limpopo in the north to the marshes of the Cape Peninsula in the south. Today they're restricted to the northeastern corner of the country, with the most southerly indigenous population living in KwaZulu-Natal. You will find them elsewhere, in places where they've been reintroduced, such as the Double Drift Reserve in the Eastern Cape. Hippos need freshwater deep enough to submerge themselves in, with a surrounding of suitable grazing grass. By day, they need to spend most of their time in water to protect their thin, hairless skin. After dark, hippos leave the water to spend the whole night grazing, often walking up to 10km in one session.

Their grunting and jostling in the water may give the impression of loveable buffoons, but throughout Africa they are feared and rightly so, as they are reckoned to be responsible for more human deaths on the continent than any other animal. When disturbed, lone bulls, and cows with calves, can become extremely aggressive. Their fearsomely long incisors can slash through a canoe with ease, and on land they can charge at speeds up to 30kph and have a tight turning circle.

Zebras

Zebras are closely related to horses and, together with wild asses, form the equid family. Of the three species of zebra, two live in South Africa.

The Burchell's or **plains zebra**, *Equus burchelli* (see p.xxiv), has small ears and thick, black stripes, with lighter "shadows" and survives in Mpumalanga, KwaZulu-Natal and along the Limpopo. Elsewhere it has been widely introduced and you'll see them in many reserves across the country.

The **Cape mountain zebra**, *Equus zebra zebra*, only narrowly escaped extinction, but now survives in healthy but limited numbers in the Mountain Zebra National Park in the Eastern Cape and other reserves in the southwest wherever there is suitably mountainous terrain. Distinguishing characteristics of the mountain zebra are the dewlap on its lower neck, the absence of shadow stripes, its larger ears, and stripes that go all the way down to its hooves – in contrast to the Burchell's whose stripes fade out as they progress down its legs.

Zebras congregate in family herds of a breeding stallion and two mares (or more) and their foals. Unattached males will often form bachelor herds. Among plains zebras, offspring leave the family group after between one and two years, while mountain zebras are far more tolerant in allowing adolescents to remain in the family.

Pigs

Two **wild pigs** are found in South Africa. If you're visiting the Kruger, Pilanesberg or the KwaZulu-Natal parks, families of **warthogs**, *Phacochoerus aethiopicus* (see p.xxv), will become a familiar sight, trotting across the savannah with their tails erect like communications antennae. Family groups usually consist of a mother and her litter of two to four piglets, or occasionally two or three females and their young. Boars join the group only to mate; they're distinguished from sows by their prominent face warts, which are thought to be defensive pads protecting their heads during often violent fights. Warthogs shelter in holes in the ground, usually porcupine or aardvark burrows, although they are quite capable of making their own – in fact, they are supreme diggers who routinely dig up nutritious bulbs.

Bushpigs, *Potamochoerus porcus*, are slightly more widely distributed than warthogs in South Africa, but because they're nocturnal forest dwellers, they aren't as often seen. Their northerly range overlaps with that of the hogs, but they also extend along the southern coastal woodlands of the Eastern Cape as far west as Mossel Bay. Much like hairier versions of domestic pigs, they live in harems called "sounders", consisting of a boar with several females and their piglets. Fathers drive out male offspring when they approach adolescence.

Other mammals

Despite their common taste for ants and termites, their nocturnal foraging and their outlandish appearance, aardvarks and pangolins are quite unrelated. The **aardvark**, *Orycteropus afer* (see p.xix), is one of Africa's – indeed the world's – strangest animals, a solitary mammal weighing up to 70kg. Its name, Afrikaans for "earth pig", is an apt description, as it holes up during the day in large burrows that are excavated with remarkable speed and energy. It emerges at night to visit termite mounds within a radius of up to 5km, digging for its main diet. It's most likely to be common in bush country that's well scattered with termite mounds. Holes dug into the base of these are a tell-tale sign of the presence of aardvarks.

Pangolins, *Manis temminckii*, are equally unusual – scale-covered mammals, resembling armadillos and feeding on ants and termites. Under attack they roll themselves into a ball. Pangolins occur widely in South Africa, north of the Orange River.

A number of species of rabbits and hares bounce about the South African landscape, but the **scrub hare**, *Lepus saxatilis*, distinguished by its exceptionally long ears, is the commonest and one you'll undoubtedly see in scrubby, wooded country throughout the region. Wherever there's rocky terrain south of the Orange River and in KwaZulu-Natal, keep an eye open for **rock rabbits**, which look just like brown- and white-speckled domestic bunnies.

If you go on a night drive you'd be most unlucky not to see the glinting eyes of **springhares**, *Pedetes capensis* (see p.xix), which, despite their resemblance to rabbit-sized kangaroos, are in fact true rodents. In the western arid zone you'll spot **ground squirrels**, *Xerus inauris*, scurrying about during the day looking for roots, seeds and bulbs, while in the northeast, **tree squirrels**, *Paraxerus cepapi*, enjoy a similar diet. The most singular and largest of the African rodents is the **porcupine**, *Hystrix africae-australis* (see p.xix), which is quite unmistakable with its coat of many quills. Porcupines are widespread and present in most reserves, but because they're nocturnal, you may only see shed quills lying along the path or in front of their burrows.

Scores of different **bats**, either fruit or insect eaters, leave their roosts each night and take off into the South African night, but all you're likely to see of them is some erratic flying against a moonlit sky. The foxy-faced **Egyptian fruit bat**, *Rousettus aegyptiacus*, is virtually single-handedly responsible for pollinating baobab trees, thus keeping them from extinction. And while **rats and mice** are probably not what brought you on safari, it's worth noting that over forty different species are found in South Africa.

Literature

Without apartheid, some critics have argued, there would have been little modern South African literature. Apartheid has delivered ready-made plots and subject matter for gifted and mediocre artists alike. Stories of the white minority's psychological and political alienation versus the legitimate struggle of the oppressed majority, illegal and clandestine interracial relationships, and possibilities of reconciliation, revenge or revolution abound. With all these, apartheid and its colonial precursors have provided a truth stranger than many fictions. Produced by people with vastly different life experiences and subject to different political pressures over centuries, it is difficult to avoid distinctions between the literature of white and black South Africans.

The story of South African writing

During pre-colonial times there were a variety of oral literary forms, sometimes known as **orature**, in the southern African region. Orature was male–dominated, but women played a significant part in genres such as **praise poems**, equivalent to the heroic epic and folk tales. In contemporary South African orature there has been a further blurring of the boundaries of genre and gender. Women produce oral works at political gatherings, traditionally a male prerogative, while men and women participate in the **toyi-toyi**, a direct descendant of the war songs originally performed only by women to exhort men in battle, now most commonly associated with resistance and political rallies.

Early settlers and travellers

From the sixteenth century onwards, explorers such as Drake, Houtman and Hakluyt provided descriptions of the Cape, and in 1572, the Portuguese poet **Luis de Camoens** described his voyage (partly mythologized) in *The Lusiads*. **Jan van Riebeeck**, governor of the Dutch East India's station wrote a *Daghregister* (Journal), as did **Adam Tas**, one of the station's more rebellious subjects. As the territory passed between the various Dutch, French and British administrators, so different residents and visitors arrived. One such person was **Francois La Valliant**, an admirer of Rousseau, whose *Travels* is an example of how travellers of the past (and today) can live out their preconceptions for themselves and for their metropolitan audiences.

Colonialism and transition

Published in 1883 under a male *nom de plume*, **Olive Schreiner**'s *The Story of an African Farm* is widely regarded as the first novel rooted in South Africa. It stands in marked contrast to the frontier tales of **Percy Fitzpatrick**'s *Jock of the Bushveld* (1907) and **Henry Rider Haggard**'s *Boy's Own*-style tales of colonial penetration and subjugation such as *King Solomon's Mines* (1885) or *She* (1887). Today, these find direct and indirect descendants in Wilbur Smith, literary doyen of airport departure halls, and the late Sir Laurens van der Post, spiritual mentor to Prince Charles.

Christian mission education, the only early route to literacy for black South Africans, favoured men and prioritized the translation of biblical and religious texts, such as John Bunyan's *Pilgrim's Progress*, which appeared in Sesotho, Zulu and Xhosa. As a result, African women did not enjoy the educational opportunities open to the playwright **H.I.E. Dhlomo**; the writer **Thomas Mofolo**, whose historical novel *Chaka* (1925) originally appeared in Sesotho and was translated into English, French, Italian, German, Yoruba and Afrikaans; or the journalist, translator and novelist **Sol Plaatje**. A founder member of the ANC, Plaatje's best-known works are *Mhudi* (1930) and *Native Life in South Africa* (1916). The former is the story of an African society in transition as it deals with the implications of the Afrikaner Great Trek and the social upheaval caused by the Zulu military state's raids and conquest. In *Native Life* Plaatje documented the disastrous effects on Africans of the 1913 Land Act, a law denying them access to the land of their birth.

Jim-comes-to-Jo'burg

The discovery of minerals and the growing urbanization and industrialization of South African society had a detrimental effect on African and Afrikaner rural society alike. From the white perspective, removal from the land threatened the "natural order" of race relations for landless Afrikaners and Africans arrived in the city as "equals". While the perceived threat to white civilization was greatly exaggerated, it had four significant consequences for white writers at the time: it shifted literary attention away from rural concerns towards urban-based issues, it provided the context for fears of miscegenation; it encouraged a re-examination of the image of Afrikaners; and it opened up new forms of narration.

Movement towards the city fostered what Nadine Gordimer later termed the "**Jim-comes-to-Jo'burg**" novel, in which a naive young African man moves from a protected and stable rural environment to city life and a variety of urban experiences and temptations. **Peter Abrahams**' contribution was *Mine Boy* (1946), often regarded as South Africa's first proletarian novel, while for **Alan Paton** the true nature of African culture was to be found in a rural setting and the *status quo ante*. Much later **Mtutuzeli Matshoba**'s short story "Three Days in the Land of a Dying Illusion", from his collection *Call Me not a Man* (1979), would invert and parody the genre.

Miscegenation and archetypes

Roy Campbell (*Adamastor*, 1930), subsequently associated with Spanish fascism, is the best-known poet of the interwar years. Like **Guy Butler** after him, he tended to equate Europe with history, development and rationalism, and Africa with unchanging archetypes. During this period **Sarah Gertrude Millin**'s fiction, particularly *God's Stepchildren* (1924), provided the starkest articulation of differences between Europe and Africa and white anxiety about the consequences of **miscegenation**. The basis for Millin's views lay in the notion of "good" and "bad" blood, and in the fear that the (male) colonizer's possession and control of the colonial territories would simultaneously confirm his dominance and open him to control by the "heart of darkness". Millin of course did not even begin to contemplate "the horror" of miscegenation involving a black man and a white woman. **Ethelreda Lewis** offered a problematic variant on the theme of blood and civilization in *Wild Deer* (1933), the story of an African-American singer, modelled on Paul Robeson, who visits

South Africa in search of spiritual renewal. He decides to uplift the "pure" and pre-urban African by impregnating "a carefully chosen virgin mate" and so pass on the benefits of his civilization while protecting the "kernel of primitive life".

With the repeal of the so-called Immorality Act in 1985, which forbade interracial sexual relations, miscegenation has lost its literary and political significance, though repackaged in the form of theories of hybridity and difference it is now making a fashionable return. **Stephen Gray**'s *Time of our Darkness* (1988) may well be the last serious work on the "immorality" subject tackled by **William Plomer** in *Turbott Wolfe* (1926), **Peter Abrahams** in *The Path to Thunder* (1948), **Alan Paton** in *Too Late the Phalarope* (1953), **Nadine Gordimer** in her short story "The Country Lovers" (1967), and **Athol Fugard**, one of South Africa's most famous playwrights, in *Statements After an Arrest Under the Immorality Act* (1974).

From dispossession to apartheid

The separation of **Afrikaners** from "their" land, and their participation in an industrializing economy largely controlled by English speakers, encouraged pathos-filled representations of Afrikaners. **Pauline Smith**'s work, such as *The Beadle* (1926) and her short story collection *The Little Karoo* (1925), inadvertently fostered the myth of the Boer as a landless, economically oppressed victim denied his language and culture. While **Herman Charles Bosman**'s short stories such as "Mafeking Road" (1947) and "A Cask of Jerepigo" (1964) also focus on rural Afrikaner life, they display far more irony. Narrated by one Oom Schalk Lourens, who in Mark Twain-like fashion is never fully aware of the implications of the stories that he tells, Bosman's humorous tales of backveld ambition, betrayal and desire presage the concerns and doubts about writing and the control of history, truth and identity that would increasingly characterize what the novelist **J.M. Coetzee** has called "white writing" – writing that articulates the "concerns of people no longer European, not yet African".

Alan Paton's *Cry, the Beloved Country* appeared in 1948, the year in which the Nationalist government came to power, and has been filmed twice. Probably the most famous of all South African novels, and still a best-seller, Paton's account of an inter-racial murder did more than any other work to bring South Africa's racial plight to the attention of the rest of the world. The book has often been criticised for its liberal paternalism, but with the benefit of hindsight it can also be read as a one-man Truth and Reconciliation Commission in which Paton details the devastation caused by white dominance in South Africa, and tries to promote a vision in which justice and love co-exist.

The Drum generation

In the 1950s, predominantly male **black writing and journalism** centred on the Johannesburg-based **Drum magazine**. The publication was one of the few outlets for black creative writers such as **Can Themba**, **Es'kia Mphahalele**, **Bloke Modisane** and **Todd Matshikiza**, many of whom chose to write short stories or autobiographical novels. Favoured because of its flexibility and compatibility with their fast-paced and fractured lifestyles under oppressive conditions, the short story has remained a popular medium for black and white South African fiction. The so-called **Drum generation** articulated black urban experience and aspirations, often in an Americanized B-movie style in journalism, fiction and drama such as *King Kong*, a musical based on the life of an actual boxer-gangster that helped to launch the singing careers of Thandi Klaasen, Dolly Rathebe and Miriam Makeba. **Z.B. Molefe**'s *A Common Hunger to Sing* (1997) gives them and successors such as Brenda Fassie, Sibongile Khumalo and Yvonne Chaka Chaka the recognition they deserve.

In general, there was little space for **women's journalism and fiction** at this time. Covering her pre-Botswana years in South Africa, **Bessie Head**'s posthumously published *The Cardinals* (1993) is a rare exploration of the problems faced by one of the few black women journalists during this period who made the transition to novel-writing.

While many of the Drum generation died relatively young and in exile, **Es'kia Mphahalele** has been a survivor. His *Down Second Avenue* (1959) is often viewed as the definitive text of an era characterized by black male autobiographies such as *Tell Freedom* (1954) by **Peter Abrahams**, **Bloke Modisane**'s *Blame me on History* (1963) and **Todd Matshikiza**'s *Chocolates for my Wife* (1961). Mphahalele's subsequent novels, *The Wanderers* (1971) and *Afrika my Music* (1984) recorded the fragmented experience of exile, that "soul-mutilating process" that has affected so many South Africans in the last sixty years.

Sophiatown, the last area in Johannesburg where Africans had freehold property rights, was the heartbeat of the Drum generation. **Jurgen Schadeburg**'s photographs, and a host of reminiscences of Drum and Sophiatown by figures ranging from **Anthony Sampson** in *Drum: An African Adventure and Afterwards* to **Father Trevor Huddleston**'s *Naught for your Comfort*, are testimony to the fascination it held.

Its nearest equivalent in Cape Town was District Six, a multiracial but predominantly coloured inner-city slum that provided the backdrop for the early work of three Cape Town writers: **Richard Rive** (*Buckingham Palace* and *District Six*; 1986), **Alex La Guma** (*A Walk in the Night*; 1962), and **Achmat Dangor** (*Waiting for Leila*; 1981). Of more recent works, **Nomvuyo Ngcelwane**'s *Sala Kahle, District Six* (1998) recounts the life of its African residents, a community ignored or marginalized in most accounts, while **Linda Fortune**'s *The House in Tyne Street* (1996) is more idyllic. Set in the 1960s, but with little reference to the main political developments of the time, the autobiographical novel *The Party is Over* (1997) by veteran poet and novelist **James Matthews** recounts the frustrations of a black writer in a paternalistic, white-dominated world of arts and letters. Poetry of note in this period can be found in *Sirens, Knuckles, Boots* (1963) and *Letters to Martha* (1968), by **Dennis Brutus**, who devoted considerable energy to ensuring South Africa's sporting isolation during the apartheid years, and **Arthur Nortje** in *Dead Roots* (1973). Like the short-story writer **Zoe Wicomb** in her collection of short stories, *You Can't Get Lost in Cape Town* (1987), Nortje was prepared to explore the more ordinary and less obviously political aspects of life in South Africa. He did this by focusing on inner worlds and on the issue of coloured identity as marginal to larger political and national questions, as **Mphahalele**, in *Man Must Live* (1947), and **Njabulo Ndebele**, in *Fools and Other Stories* (1983), had done for African township life.

Rive also wrote several Cape Town-based novels such as *Emergency* (1964), the latter about the events surrounding the declaration of a state of emergency in 1960. Several other novelists have set works in this and subsequent periods of repression: **Jonty Driver**'s *Elegy for a Revolutionary* (1969), **Lewis Nkosi**'s *The Rhythm of Violence* (1964) and **Alex La Guma**'s *In the Fog of the Seasons' End* (1972) for the 1960s; **Sipho Sepamla**'s *A Ride on the Whirlwind* (1981),

Mongane Serote's *To Every Birth Its Blood* (1981) and **Miriam Tlali**'s *Amandla* (1981) for the Soweto period; **Menan du Plessis**'s *A State of Fear* (1983), **Hein Grosskopf**'s *Artistic Graves* (1993), **Mandla Langa**'s *A Rainbow on the Paper Sky* (1989) and **Bridget Pitt**'s *Unbroken Wing* (1998) which continues the theme on a more personal note, for the late 1980s.

Prison writings

Many intellectuals and writers were jailed during the apartheid years. Among many books on the subject, **Albie Sachs**' *Jail Diary* (1966) and **Ruth First**'s *117 Days* (1982) record their detentions without trial in the early 1960s, while **Indres Naidoo**'s *Island in Chains* (1982) deals with his ten years on Robben Island after being arrested and charged with sabotage. Most prisoners served out their sentences, but Tim Jenkin, Alex Moumbaris and Stephen Lee managed to escape from Pretoria Central Prison where most white political prisoners were held. **Tim Jenkin**'s tale, *Escape from Pretoria* (1987) reads like a thriller, while in *The True Confessions of an Albino Terrorist* (1983) **Breyten Breytenbach** manages to combine political critique with grim humour. Not surprisingly, fictional accounts of prison such as **Alex La Guma**'s *The Stone Country* (1974) and **D.M. Zwelonke**'s *Robben Island* (1973) rely heavily on their authors' own experiences, but are complex narratives. In the realm of non-political prison writings, **Herman Charles Bosman**'s *Cold Stone Jug* (1971) provides an ironic and beautifully written foil to the seriousness of "correct" accounts.

South African writers are gripped by what Mphahalele has described as "the tyranny of place". All but one of **Alex La Guma**'s five novels are set in Cape Town, and they are linked by a steady evolution of political consciousness and organization. A journalist, writer and political activist from the 1960s until his death in 1985, where he was the ANC's Chief Representative, his early works, *A Walk in the Night* (1962) and *And a Threefold Cord* (1964) explore individual acts of defiance against the state. His later novels, *In the Fog of the Seasons' End* (1972) and *Time of the Butcherbird* (1979), display more complex narrative structures and deal with collective resistance.

White liberal writing

If La Guma's concerns have been with the disenfranchised and the dispossessed, **Nadine Gordimer**'s novels and short stories stand as dispassionate and coldly sensual chronicles of the interior voice of white liberal and radical opposition to apartheid. They represent an alternative to Paton's stress on individual responsibility as the key to political change. Over the years, Gordimer has moved from confessional, though not necessarily autobiographical, narratives such as *The Lying Days* (1953), to bolder and more complex explorations of time and psychological make-up, such as *July's People* (1991).

While the former explores the growing political awareness of her typical main character, a white middle-class woman resident in Johannesburg's prosperous suburbs, the latter is set in a post-revolutionary South Africa in which Maureen Smales, wife and mother to a white middle-class family, has become heavily dependent on July, their former "houseboy". The novel explores her search for political and personal liberation, part of which involves her efforts to confront and break with the emotionally fraught and contradictory personal and political dynamics so often associated with domestic service relationships in a colonial context. Her more recent *The House Gun* (1998) continues the exploration of white liberal consciousness and conscience in the post-liberation period.

Gordimer is not the only white writer to explore the dilemmas of privilege and conscience. The **Sestigers** were an innovative group of Afrikaans writers prominent in the 1960s that included Breyten Breytenbach and **André Brink**, who acquired the reputation of being the foremost white literary opponent of apartheid. Brink explored notions of truth, history and freedom in the colonial setting through books such as *An Instant in the Wind* (1976); *A Chain of Voices* (1982); *The Wall of the Plague* (1984); *An Act of Terror* (1991); and *Devil's Valley* (1998). In this his work has much in common with Booker Prize winner and literary critic **J.M. Coetzee**'s first novel, *Dusklands* (1974). This book establishes psychological and behavioural parallels between America's presence in Vietnam and the behaviour of one Jacobus Coetzee during his South African frontier experience in 1760. Several of J.M. Coetzee's subsequent novels have used the perspective of a borderline psychotic narrator to explore the political and psychological damage caused by colonialism and apartheid. His *In the Heart of the Country* (1976) is narrated by an isolated spinster and plays ironically with the tradition of farm novels as represented by Olive Schreiner and others. *Waiting for the Barbarians* (1980), which takes its title from Cavafy's poem of the same name, occupies a more allegorical domain, with a narrator who is a bumbling magistrate wrestling with moral concerns in the outpost of an unnamed empire. *His Life and Times of Michael K* (1983) foregrounds the concern with allegory by making it a concern of one of the novel's characters.

An intellectually brilliant postmodern critic of apartheid, Coetzee has always distanced himself and his writing from the demands of publishing in order to function as a "weapon of struggle". Though by describing himself in *Dusklands*, even parodically, as "one of the 10,000 Coetzees ... that Jacobus Coetzee begat", his work invites parallels with the self-hatred and self-obsession of Rian Malan's *My Traitor's Heart* (1990), which establishes its author in Calvinist style as the seventh-generation inheritor of the founding fathers' sins.

While white writing became increasingly introspective and its ventures into the interior shifted from geographical to psychological terrain, black writing faced an entirely different situation. Impeded by the exile of many artists, intimidated by trials and arrests, and censored by the state during a period of severe repression in the early 1960s, it was largely dormant until the late 1960s and early 1970s. This period saw the growth of the Black Consciousness Movement and the increasingly effective organization of black workers, followed by the Soweto riots and the independence of Angola and Mozambique.

Beyond social realism

The dawn of the 1970s saw both white and black writing beginning to look beyond the conventions of social realism, but for very different reasons. In the case of white writing, **interiority** was a response to the dilemmas imposed by a conscience that could not be ignored and privileges that could not be sacrificed. For black writers, **poetry**, and free verse in particular, became popular because it facilitated indirect forms of political expression. Among the names associated with this phase, the most prominent are **Oswald Mtshali**, *Drum* survivor **Casey Motsisi**, **Mafika Gwala**, **Don Mattera**, **Njabulo Ndebele**, **Mongane Serote**, **Mandla Langa**, **Gladys Thomas** and **James Matthews** from Cape Town. In subsequent decades, many of these also wrote short stories and novels.

Oswald Mtshali was working as a motorbike courier when his path-breaking *Sounds of a Cowhide Drum* appeared in 1971. For Mtshali and many of his contemporaries, a cultural nationalism that rejected "white" standards and asserted a specifically "black" aesthetic and identity was the route to political nationalism. They sharply criticized the self-destructive nature of township violence, and used the perspectives and experiences of children to point out the injustices and inequalities of apartheid. Like many of their predecessors, Ndebele, Serote and Langa were forced to leave the country, but James Matthews stayed, and *Cry Rage* (1972), co-written with Gladys Thomas, still remains a powerful statement of black consciousness and protest poetry. Along with **Gcina Mhlope** and **Jennifer Davids**, Thomas was able to modify the traditional role of black women as significant but secondary figures in the national liberation struggle, typified by the idea of the powerful black woman as mother figure.

The early 1970s also saw a resurgence of **drama**. There were escapist and exploitative musicals such as *Ipi Tombi*, nostalgic and utopian works such as **Credo Mutwa**'s *uNosilimela* and **Gibson Kente**'s *Too Late* and *Survival*, both with strong political messages. For international audiences, however, **Athol Fugard** remains the most prominent South African playwright. Fugard would be the last to claim full responsibility for several of his works, which were produced under workshop conditions with actors such as John Kani and Winston Ntshona contributing their views and experiences to *Sizwe Bansi is Dead*, a play about strategies to avoid pass law controls, and *The Island*, based on Sophocles' *Antigone*. Continuing the tradition of collaborative production, *Ubu and the Truth Commission* (1998) combines the talents of writer Jane Taylor, artist William Kentridge and puppeteers Basil Jones and Adrian Kohler in a work that explores some of South Africa's less enviable qualities – evil, ultra-violence, cowardice and self-pity – in a work that reflects on a country dealing with the consequences of the Truth and Reconciliation Commission. This is also the subject of **Antjie Krog**'s *Country of My Skull* (1998), a multileveled and many layered account of more than two years' reporting on the Commission, from its legislative origins to testimonies of victims and perpetrators.

People's history

Launched in 1977, and capitalizing on the limited cultural and political space occasioned by the apartheid government's moves towards a policy of "repressive reform" in the post-Soweto period, **Staffrider magazine** was the most important literary development of the late 1970s. Taking its name and image from township slang for people (frequently black youth) who rode the overcrowded African sections of the racially segregated commuter trains by hanging onto the outside or sitting on the roofs, the magazine had two main objectives: to provide publishing opportunities for community-based organizations and young writers, graphic artists and photographers; and to oppose officially sanctioned state and establishment culture. Selections from the magazine between 1978 and 1988 appeared in *Ten Years of Staffrider* (1988). Initially based on a hands-off editorial policy, the magazine focused on "**people's history**", helping to retrieve hidden aspects of South Africa's past for a wider audience. The *Staffrider* tradition continues; Charles van Onselen's tome *The Seed is Mine* (1996) and Isabel Hofmeyr's *We Spend Our Years as a Tale That is Told* (1994) have been outstanding contributions to this genre.

The magazine also popularized a return to traditional conventions and forms of oratory such as **Nongenile Zenani** and **Harold Scheub**'s *The World and the Word* (1992) and **Sandile Dikeni**'s *Guava Juice* (1992). Much of the latter's poetry was delivered at opposition mass rallies and trade union launches. By contrast, **Mongane Wally Serote**'s *Third World Express* (1992), his first published work since his return from exile, retains links with an oral tradition but is more introspective than Dikeni's poetry. More recently, praise poets performed at the inauguration of President Mandela and the opening of the country's first democratically elected parliament.

From the 1980s onwards, debates around the political relevance of poetry became even more intense than those dealing with prose. Some of the more politically committed poets included **Kelwyn Sole** (*Blood of Our Silence*; 1988) and **Jeremy Cronin**, whose anthology *Inside* (1983) asks readers "To learn how to speak/With the voices of the land", return to introspective themes of language and the poet's sense of place. In *Even the Dead* (1997) Cronin searches for a moral community that incorporates the past and takes issue with the "smug rainbowism" of the new South Africa. Others, such as **Christopher van Wyk** with *It is Time to Go Home* (1979) and **Achmat Dangor** in *Bulldozer* (1983), retain a strident anger mixed with Cape Town's acerbic slang.

Contemporary writing

By the mid-1980s, international condemnation of apartheid and support for the liberation movement coincided with the growth of feminist theory and an expanding **feminist** publishing industry. These developments favoured the emergence of black South African women's autobiographies such as **Ellen Kuzwayo**'s *Call Me Woman* (1985) and **Emma Mashinini**'s *Strikes Have Followed me All my Life* (1989). This form has seen little development since the appearance of **Noni Jabavu**'s *Drawn in Colour* (1960) and *The Ochre People* (1963), in the early 1960s, and Sindiwe Magona's two autobiographical works *To My Children's Children* (1990) and *Forced to Grow* (1992) retain an American connection. In *Mother to Mother* (1998), she deals with the death of visiting American scholar Amy Biehl, killed by black youths stirred up by "anti-white" slogans, through an address from one of the mothers of Biehl's killers to the mother of his victim. The late 1980s was also a favourable period for the publication of black women's poetry in anthologies such as *Siren Songs* (1989) and *Breaking the Silence* (1990) and in individual collections such as Sobhna Poona's *In Search of Rainbows* (1990).

As the 1990s took hold, however, the politicized approach that saw publishers, writers and readers going for the "struggular" had to acknowledge the less dramatic and more byzantine process of negotiations towards a relatively peaceful transfer of power, and the emergence of splits and disagreements in the cultural sphere between the ANC and some of its internal supporters. In this context, **Phyllis Ntantala**'s *A Life's Mosaic* (1992) acknowledged personal concerns, **Mamphela Ramphele**'s *A Life* (1995) criticized ways in which the liberation struggle had been male-dominated, and **Barbara Schreiner**'s *A Snake with Ice Water* (1992), a collection of interviews, stories and poems by women about their prison experiences from the 1960s onwards, confronted the shame and sense of incapacity to which many women in the liberation struggle had been subjected.

Exile and **return** are themes which several writers have dealt with. **Breyten Breytenbach**'s *Dog Heart* (1998) recalls present and past Bonnievale, the village of his birth. In *The Naked Song and Other Stories* (1996) **Mandla Langa** explores the transition from exile to "home", while **Barry Feinberg**'s *Gardens of Struggle* (1992) covers thirty years of the poet's life, from exile in 1961 to return in 1991.

Good insights into the troubled psyche of the white South African male in a period of political transition include **Ivan Vladislavic**'s short-story collection

Missing Persons (1989), his novels *The Folly* (1993) and *Propaganda by Monuments and Other Stories* (1996); **Etienne van Heerden**'s *Mad Dog and Other Stories* (1992) and *Casspirs and Camparis* (1993) – casspirs are armoured personnel carriers used by the police and army; and **Mark Behr**'s *The Smell of Apples* (1995), which attached significance to the death of Hendrik Verwoerd, architect of apartheid, during their fictionalized childhoods. Behr's subsequent disclosure that he was a police informer during his days as an anti-apartheid student activist doubtless adds interest to this confessional narrative.

Political autobiography and biography

The tradition of **political autobiography** is now well-established. *Let my People Go* (1962) by the late **Albert Luthuli**, former leader of the ANC, remains as compelling an explanation of the struggle for majority rule as Nelson Mandela's *Long Walk to Freedom* (1994). Dramatic political change and the acquisition of freedom has seen many politicians and public figures come and go. Inevitably this has encouraged several to write stories of the life they would like us to believe they led or, in the case of those involved in clandestine work such as **Ronnie Kasrils** (*"Armed and Dangerous": My Undercover Struggle Against Apartheid*; 1993), **Joe Slovo** (*Unfinished Autobiography*; 1995) and **Natoo Babenia** (*Memoirs of a Saboteur: Reflections on my Political Activity in India and South Africa*; 1995), of the life they could not previously talk about in public. National secretary of the non-racial Federation of South African Women in the 1950s, **Helen Joseph** was banned four times, jailed four times, on trial for four years and periodically unbanned. Her autobiography *Side by Side* appeared in 1986. Centrally involved in many of the inquests of the political detainees who died in South African jails, *No one to Blame?* (1998) by Advocate **George Bizos** provides a grim if illuminating complement to the life stories of those who survived torture and interrogation. **Bram Fischer**, member of an eminent Afrikaner family and a lawyer who defended Mandela and Sisulu in the Rivonia trial and member of the then banned South African Communist Party, was one of those who did not survive. Stephen Clingman tells his story *Bram Fischer: Afrikaner Revolutionary* (1998).

Post-apartheid writing

South Africa's recently acquired political respectability has meant that writers of the formerly international pariah state can now, in Michael Ondaatje's phrase, become "international bastards" if they wish, as postmodernism and magical realism, sometimes in combination with autobiography, have become more popular and politically acceptable. **Ashraf Jamal** in *Love Themes for the Wilderness* (1996) has been quick to capitalize on the space available. Two novels by **Zakes Mda**, already recognized as a major playwright, *She Plays with the Darkness* (1995) and *Ways of Dying* (1995), can also be classified as **magical realism**. While the former may rely upon aspects of a traditional African culture with which many urbanized black South Africans have no contact, the latter explores some of the country's more bizarre forms of death from the perspective of a self-styled "professional mourner". With the differences between official and personal histories a subject of continuous negotiation, **Mike Nicol**'s *This Day and Age* (1992) makes a strong case for the integration of magical realism and **postmodern** techniques in pursuit of a new perspective on South African history. **Rayda Jacobs'** novel *The Slave Book* (1998), set on the eve of slave emancipation, returns to earlier moments of political and personal freedom that invite comparison with the present. **Etienne van Heerden**'s *Kikuyu* (1999) is set on that sign of the times (but rarer in the 1960s) – a holiday farm in the Karoo. In *On Soebatsfontein*, **Fabian Latsky**'s sheltered world of eccentric characters comes into contact with the rumblings of an increasingly unstable South Africa. **Tony Spencer-Smith**'s *The Stooping of Aquila* (1999) is an erotic thriller set in Cape Town's Hout Bay, focusing on environmental issues, their growing prominence a sign of the region's tourist potential and of a shift in values away from overtly political concerns.

Roger Field

South African writers

There's no better way to get under the skin of South Africa than through its writing. And, while no five extracts can ever hope to convey South African literature's richness and diversity, the ones we've selected are intended as a useful taster. What the writers below have in common is that, although they are well-known in South Africa, none is internationally a big-name author. For a more comprehensive survey of South African writing, see p.865.

Steve Biko

Charismatic Black Consciousness activist **Steve Biko** (1946–77) died after police torture. These words, extracted from an interview some months before his death, give insight into Biko's extraordinary commitment to political change. The extract is taken from "I Write What I Like", a collection of non-fiction writing from 1969 to 1972. In 1973, Biko was banned and could no longer travel, speak in public or write for publication.

On Death

You are either alive and proud or you are dead, and when you are dead, you can't care anyway. And your method of death can itself be a politicizing thing. So you die in the riots. For a hell of a lot of them, in fact, there's really nothing to lose – almost literally, given the kind of situations that they come from. So if you can overcome the personal fear for death, which is a highly irrational thing, you know, then you're on the way.

And in interrogation the same sort of thing applies. I was talking to this policeman, and I told him, "If you want us to make any progress, the best thing is for us to talk. Don't try any form of rough stuff, because it just won't work." And this is absolutely true also. For I just couldn't see what they could do to me which would make me all of a sudden soften to them. If they talk to me, well I'm bound to be affected by them as human beings. But the moment they adopt rough stuff, they are imprinting in my mind that they are police. And I only understand one form of dealing with police, and that's to be as unhelpful as possible. So I button up. And I told them this: "It's up to you." We had a boxing match the first day I was arrested. Some guy tried to clout me with a club. I went into him like a bull. I think he was under instructions to take it so far and no further, and using open hands so that he doesn't leave any marks on the face. And of course he said exactly what you were saying just now: "I will kill you." He meant to intimidate. And my answer was: "How long is it going to take you?" Now of course they were observing my reaction. And they could see that I was completely unbothered. If they beat me up, it's to my advantage. I can use it. They just killed somebody in jail – a friend of mine – about ten days before I was arrested. Now it would have been bloody useful evidence for them to assault me. At least it would indicate what kind of possibilities were there, leading to this guy's death. So, I wanted them to go ahead and do what they could do, so that I could use it. I wasn't really afraid that their violence might lead me to make revelations I didn't want to make, because I had nothing to reveal on this particular issue. I was operating from a very good position, and they were in a very weak position. My attitude is, I'm not going to allow them to carry out their programme faithfully. If they want to beat me five times, they can only do so on condition that I allow them to beat me five times. If I react sharply, equally and oppositely, to the first clap, they are not going to be able to systematically count the next four claps, you see. It's a fight. So if they had meant to give me so much of a beating, and not more, my idea is to make them go beyond what they wanted to give me and to give back as much as I can give so that it becomes an uncontrollable thing. You see the one problem this guy had with me: he couldn't really fight with me because it meant he must hit back, like a man. But he was given instructions, you see, on how to hit, and now these instructions were no longer applying because it was a fight. So he had to withdraw and get more instructions. So I said to them, "Listen, if you guys want to do this your way, you have got to handcuff me and bind my feet together, so that I can't respond. If you allow me to respond, I'm certainly going to respond. And I'm afraid you may have to kill me in the process even if it's not your intention."

Reprinted by permission of Bowerdean Publishers.

Herman Charles Bosman

Herman Charles Bosman (1905–51), one of South Africa's most widely read writers, is best known for his wry and amusing short stories about Afrikaner life in the Groot Marico district of the then Western Transvaal, where he spent six months as a schoolteacher in 1925.

A Bekkersdal Marathon

At Naudé, who had a wireless set, came into Jurie Steyn's voorkamer, where we were sitting waiting for the railway lorry from Bekkersdal, and gave us the latest news. He said that the newest thing in Europe was that young people there were going in for non-stop dancing. It was called marathon dancing, At Naudé told us, and those young people were trying to break the record for who could remain on their feet longest, dancing.

We listened for a while to what At Naudé had to say, and then we suddenly remembered a marathon event that had taken place in the little dorp of Bekkersdal – almost in our midst, you could say. What was more, there were quite a number of us sitting in Jurie Steyn's post office, who had actually taken part in that non-stop affair, and without knowing that we were breaking records, and without expecting any sort of a prize for it, either.

We discussed that affair at considerable length and from all angles, and we were still talking about it when the lorry came. And we agreed that it had been in several respects an unusual occurrence. We also agreed that it was questionable if we could have carried off things so successfully that day, if it had not been for Billy Robertse.

You see, our organist at Bekkersdal was Billy Robertse. He had once been a sailor and had come to the bushveld some years before, travelling on foot. His belongings, fastened in a red handkerchief, were slung over his shoulder on a stick. Billy Robertse was journeying in that fashion for the sake of his health. He suffered from an unfortunate complaint for which he had at regular intervals to drink something out of a black bottle that he always carried handy in his jacket pocket.

Billy Robertse would even keep that bottle beside him in the organist's gallery in case of a sudden attack. And if the hymn the predikant gave out had many verses, you could be sure that about halfway through Billy Robertse would bring the bottle up to his mouth, leaning sideways towards what was in it. And he would put several extra twirls into the second part of the hymn.

When he first applied for the position of organist in the Bekkersdal church, Billy Robertse told the meeting of deacons that he had learnt to play the organ in a cathedral in northern Europe. Several deacons felt, then, that they could not favour his application. They said that the cathedral sounded too Papist, the way Billy Robertse described it, with a dome three hundred feet high and with marble apostles. But it was lucky for Billy Robertse that he was able to mention, at the following combined meeting of elders and deacons, that he had also played the piano in a South American dance hall, of which the manager was a Presbyterian. He asked the meeting to overlook his unfortunate past, saying that he had had a hard life, and anybody could make mistakes. In any case, he had never cared much for the Romish atmosphere of the cathedral, he said, and had been happier in the dance hall.

In the end, Billy Robertse got the appointment. But in his sermons for several Sundays after that the predikant, Dominee Welthagen, spoke very strongly against the evils of dance halls. He described those places of awful sin in such burning words that at least one young man went to see Billy Robertse, privately, with a view to taking lessons in playing the piano.

But Billy Robertse was a good musician. And he took a deep interest in his work. And he said that when he sat down on the organist's stool behind the pulpit, and his fingers were flying over the keyboards, and he was pulling out the stops, and his feet were pressing down the notes that sent the deep bass tones through the pipes – then he felt that he could play all day, he said.

"I don't suppose he guessed that he would one day be put to the test, however."

It all happened through Dominee Welthagen one Sunday morning going into a trance in the pulpit. And we did not realise that he was in a trance. It was an illness that overtook him in a strange and sudden fashion.

At each service the predikant, after reading a passage from the Bible, would lean forward with his hand on the pulpit rail and give out the number of the hymn we had to sing. For years his manner of conducting the service had been exactly the same. He would say, for instance: "We will now sing Psalm 82, verses I to 4." Then he would allow his head to sink forward on to his chest and he would remain rigid, as though in prayer, until the last notes of the hymn died away in the church.

Now, on that particular morning, just after he had announced the number of the psalm, without mentioning what verses, Dominee Welthagen again took a firm grip on the pulpit rail and allowed his head to sink forward on to his breast. We did not realise that he had fallen into a trance of a peculiar character that kept his body standing upright while his mind was a blank. We learnt that only later.

In the meantime, while the organ was playing over the opening bars, we began to realise that Dominee Welthagen had not indicated how many verses we had to sing. But he would discover his mistake, we thought, after we had been singing for a few minutes.

All the same, one or two of the younger members of the congregation did titter, slightly, when they took up their hymn books. For Dominee Welthagen had given out Psalm 119. And everybody knows that Psalm 119 has 176 verses.

This was a church service that will never be forgotten in Bekkersdal. We sang the first verse and then the second and then the third. When we got to about the sixth verse and the minister still gave no sign that it would be the last, we assumed that he wished us to sing the first eight verses. For, if you open your hymn book, you'll see that Psalm 119 is divided into sets of eight verses, each ending with the word "Pouse".

We ended the last notes of verse eight with more than an ordinary number of turns and twirls, confident that at any moment Dominee Welthagen would raise his head and let us know that we could sing "Amen".

It was when the organ started up very slowly and solemnly with the music for verse nine that a real feeling of disquiet overcame the congregation. But, of course, we gave no sign of what went on in our minds. We held Dominee Welthagen in too much veneration.

Nevertheless, I would rather not say too much about our feelings, when verse followed verse and Pouse succeeded Pouse, and still Dominee Welthagen made no sign that we had sung long enough, or that there was anything unusual in what he was demanding of us.

After they had recovered from their first surprise, the members of the church council conducted themselves in a most exemplary manner. Elders and deacons tiptoed up and down the aisles, whispering words of reassurance to such members of the congregation, men as well as women, who gave signs of wanting to panic.

At one stage it looked as though we were going to have trouble from the organist. That was when Billy Robertse, at the end of the 34th verse, held up his black bottle and signalled quietly to the elders to indicate that his medicine was finished. At the end of the 35th verse he made signals of a less quiet character, and again at the end of the 36th verse. That was when Elder Landsman tiptoed out of the church and went round to the Konsistorie, where the Nagmaal wine was kept. When Elder Landsman came back into the church he had a long black bottle half-hidden under his manel. He took the bottle up to the organist's gallery, still walking on tiptoe.

At verse 61 there was almost a breakdown. That was when a message came from the back of the organ, where Koster Claassen and the assistant verger, whose task it was to turn the handle that kept the organ supplied with wind, were in a state near to exhaustion. So it was Deacon Cronje's turn to go tiptoeing out of the church. Deacon Cronje was head warder at the local gaol. When he came back it was with three burly Native convicts in striped jerseys, who also went through the church on tiptoe. They arrived just in time to take over the handle from Koster Claassen and the assistant verger.

At verse 98 the organist again started making signals about his medicine. Once more Elder Landsman went round to the Konsistorie. This time he was accompanied by another elder and a deacon, and they stayed away somewhat longer than the time when Elder Landsman had gone on his own. On their return the deacon bumped into a small hymn book table at the back of the church. Perhaps it was because the deacon was a fat, red-faced man, and not used to tiptoeing.

At verse 124 the organist signalled again, and the same three members of the church council filed out to the Konsistorie, the deacon walking in front this time.

It was about then that the pastor of the Full Gospel Apostolic Faith Church, about whom Dominee Welthagen had in the past used almost as strong language as about the Pope, came up to the front gate of the church to see what was afoot. He lived near our church and, having heard the same hymn tune being played over and over for about eight hours, he was a very amazed man. Then he saw the door of the Konsistorie open, and two elders and a deacon coming out, walking on tiptoe – they having apparently forgotten that they were not in church, then. When the pastor saw one of the elders hiding a black bottle under his manel, a look of understanding came over his features. The pastor walked off, shaking his head.

At verse 152 the organist signalled again. This time Elder Landsman and the other elder went out alone. The deacon stayed behind on the deacon's bench, apparently in deep thought. The organist signalled again, for the last time, at verse 169. So you can imagine how many visits the two elders made to the Konsistorie altogether.

The last verse came, and the last line of the last verse. This time it had to be "Amen". Nothing could stop it. I would rather not describe the state that the congregation was in. And by then the three Native convicts, red stripes and all, were, in the Bakhatla tongue, threatening mutiny. "Aa-m-e-e-n" came from what sounded like less than a score of voices, hoarse with singing.

The organ music ceased.

Maybe it was the sudden silence that at last brought Dominee Welthagen out of his long trance. He raised his head and looked slowly about him. His gaze travelled over his congregation and then looking at the windows, he saw that it was night. We understood right away what was going on in Dominee Welthagen's mind. He thought he had just come into the pulpit, and that this was the beginning of the evening service. We realised that, during all the time we had been singing, the predikant had been in a state of unconsciousness.

Once again Dominee Welthagen took a firm grip of the pulpit rail. His head again started drooping forward on to his breast. But before he went into a trance for the second time, he gave out the hymn for the evening service. "We will," Dominee Welthagen announced, "sing Psalm 119."

Alex La Guma

Alex La Guma (1925–85) was the son of one of the leading figures in the black liberation movement. He was politically active against the apartheid government – among other things, helping with the Freedom Charter in 1956 – until he was put under house arrest in 1962. He and his wife fled the country in 1967 to the UK, then moved to Cuba where he was the ANC representative. His writing was banned by the white minority government.

This extract is from La Guma's first work, a collection of short stories set in Cape Town's District Six, before the area was razed to the ground and declared an area for whites only.

A Walk in the Night

Up ahead the music shops were still going full blast, the blare of records all mixed up so you could not tell one tune from another. Shopkeepers, Jewish, Indian, and Greek, stood in the doorways along the arcade of stores on each side of the street, waiting to welcome last-minute customers; and the vegetable and fruit barrows were still out too, the hawkers in white coats yelling their wares and flapping their brown paper packets, bringing prices down now that the day was ending. Around the bus-stop a crowd pushed and jostled to clamber onto the trackless trams, struggling against the passengers fighting to alight.

Along the pavements little knots of youths lounged in twos and threes or more, watching the crowds streaming by, jeering, smoking, joking against the noise, under the balconies, in doorways, around the plate-glass windows. A half-mile of sound and movement and signs, signs, signs: Coca-Cola, Sale Now On, Jewellers, The Modern Outfitters, If You Don't Eat Here We'll Both Starve, Grand Picnic to Paradise Valley Luxury Buses, Teas, Coffee, Smoke, Have You Tried Our Milk Shakes, Billiard Club, The Rockingham Arms, Chine … nce In Korea, Your Recommendation Is Our Advert, Dress Salon.

Michael Adonis moved idly along the pavement through the stream of people unwinding like a spool up the street. A music shop was playing shrill and noisy, "Some of these days, you gonna miss me honey"; music from across the Atlantic, shipped in flat shellac discs to pound its jazz through the loudspeaker over the doorway.

He stopped outside the big plate window, looking in at the rows of guitars, banjoes, mandolins, the displayed gramophone parts, guitar picks, strings, electric irons, plugs, jews-harps, adaptors, celluloid dolls all the way from Japan, and the pictures of angels and Christ with a crown of thorns and drops of blood like lipstick marks on his pink forehead.

A fat man came out of the shop, his cheeks smooth and shiny with health, and said, "You like to buy something, sir?"

"'No man," Michael Adonis said and spun his cigarette-end into the street where a couple of snot-nosed boys in ragged shirts and horny feet scrambled for it, pushing each other as they struggled to claim a few puffs.

Somebody said, "Hoit, Mikey," and he turned and saw the wreck of a youth who had fallen in beside him.

"Hullo, Joe."

Joe was short and his face had an ageless quality about it under the grime, like something valuable forgotten in a junk shop. He had the soft brown eyes of a dog, and he smelled of a mixture of sweat, slept-in clothes and seaweed. His trousers had gone at the cuffs and knees, the rents held together with pins and pieces of string, and so stained and spotted that the original colour could not have been guessed at. Over the trousers he wore an ancient raincoat that reached almost to his ankles, the sleeves torn loose at the shoulders, the body hanging in ribbons, the front pinned together over his filthy vest. His shoes were worn beyond recognition.

Nobody knew where Joe came from, or anything about him. He just seemed to have happened, appearing in the District like a cockroach emerging through a floorboard. Most of the time he wandered around the harbour gathering fish discarded by fishermen and anglers, or along the beaches of the coast, picking limpets and muscles. He had a strange passion for things that came from the sea.

"How you, Joe?" Michael Adonis asked.

"Okay, Mikey."

"What you been doing today?"

"Just strolling around the docks. York Castle came in this afternoon."

"Ja?"

"You like mussels, Mikey? I'll bring you some."

"That's fine, Joe."

"I got a big starfish out on the beach yesterday. One big, big one. It was dead and stank."

"Well, it's a good job you didn't bring it into town. City Council would be on your neck."

"I hear they're going to make the beaches so only white people can go there," Joe said.

"Ja. Read it in the papers. Damn sonsabitches."

"It's going to get so's nobody can go nowhere."

"I reckon so," Michael Adonis said.

They were some way up the street now and outside the Queen Victoria. Michael Adonis said, "You like a drink, Joe?" although he knew that the boy did not drink.

"No thanks, Mikey."

"Well, so long."

"So long, man."

"You eat already?"

"Well ... no ... not yet," Joe said, smiling humbly and shyly, moving his broken shoes gently on the rough cracked paving.

"Okay, here's a bob. Get yourself something. Parcel of fish and some chips."

"Thanks, Mikey."

"Okay. So long, Joe."

"See you again."

"Don't forget the mussels," Michael Adonis said after him, knowing that Joe would forget anyway.

"I'll bring them," Joe said, smiling back and raising his hand in a salute. He seemed to sense the other young man's doubt of his memory, and added a little fiercely, "I won't forget. You'll see. I won't forget."

Then he went up the street, trailing his tattered raincoat behind him like a sword-slashed, bullet-ripped banner just rescued from a battle.

Michael Adonis turned towards the pub and saw the two policemen coming towards him. They came down the pavement in their flat caps, khaki shirts and pants, their gun harness shiny with polish, and the holstered pistols heavy at their waists. They had hard, frozen faces as if carved out of pink ice, and hard, dispassionate eyes, hard and bright as pieces of blue glass. They strolled slowly and determinedly side by side, without moving off their course, cutting a path through the stream on the pavement like destroyers at sea.

They came on and Michael Adonis turned aside to avoid them, but they had him penned in with a casual, easy, skillful flanking manoeuvre before he could escape.

"*Waar loop jy rond, jong?* Where are you walking around, man?" The voice was hard and flat as the snap of a steel spring, and the one who spoke had hard, thin, chapped lips and a faint blonde down above them. He had flat cheekbones, pink-white, and thick, red-gold eyebrows and pale lashes. His chin was long and cleft and there was a small pimple beginning to form on one side of it, making a reddish dot against the pale skin.

"Going home," Michael Adonis said, looking at the buckle of this policeman's belt. You learned from experience to gaze at some spot on their uniforms, the button of a pocket, or the bright smoothness of their Sam Browne belts, but never into their eyes, for that would be taken as an affront by them. It was only the very brave, or the very stupid, who dared look straight into the law's eyes, to challenge them or to question their authority.

The second policeman stuck his thumbs in his gun-belt and smiled distantly and faintly. It was more a slight movement of his lips, rather than a smile. The backs of his hands where they dropped over the leather of the belt were broad and white, and the outlines of the veins were pale blue under the skin, the skin covered with a field of tiny, slanting ginger-coloured hair. His fingers were thick and the knuckles big and creased and pink, the nails shiny and healthy and carefully kept.

This policeman asked in a heavy, brutal voice, "Where's your dagga?"

"I don't smoke it."

"*Jong*, turn out your pockets," the first one ordered. "Hurry up."

Michael Adonis began to empty his pockets slowly, without looking up at them and thinking, with each movement, You mucking boers, you mucking boers. Some people stopped and looked and hurried on as the policemen turned the cold blue light of their eyes upon them. Michael Adonis showed them his crumbled and partly used packet of cigarettes, the money he had left over from his pay, a soiled handkerchief and an old piece of chewing gum covered with the grey fuzz from his pocket.

"Where did you steal the money?" The question was without humour, deadly serious, the voice topped with hardness like the surface of a file.

"Didn't steal it, baas (you *mucking boer*)".

"Well, muck off from the street. Don't let us find you standing around, you hear?"

"Yes (you *mucking boer*)."

"Yes, what? Who are you talking to, man?"

"Yes, baas (you *mucking bastard boer with your mucking gun and your mucking bloody red head*)."

They pushed past him, one of them brushing him aside with an elbow and strolled on. He put the stuff back into his pockets. And deep down inside him the feeling of rage, frustration and violence swelled like a boil, knotted with pain.

Reprinted by permission of Heinemann.

Antjie Krog

Antjie Krog is an Afrikaans poet, novelist and journalist who reported on the Truth and Reconciliation Commission for the South African Broadcasting Corporation. She blends introspection and meditations on her Afrikaner origin, some of which she describes as "lies in this book about the truth", with reflections on the content and texture of experiences of a reporter on this harrowing 'beat'.

Country of my Skull

… And suddenly it is as if an undertow is taking me out … out … and out. And behind me sinks the country of my skull like a sheet in the dark – and I hear a thin song, hooves, hedges of venom, fever and destruction fermenting and hissing underwater. I shrink and prickle. Against. Against my blood and the heritage thereof. Will I forever be them – recognizing them as I do daily in my nostrils? Yes. And what we have done will never be undone. It doesn't matter what we do. What De Klerk does. Until the third and fourth generation.

Famished. Parched, one waits for Constand Viljoen's party [Freedom Front] to make its submission. They form a modest group.

Viljoen speaks as if he wants to capture something, bring something back, confirm some essence of Afrikanerhood that is wholesome. I want it too – but at the same time know it not to be. When Viljoen talks about how the British took away the land of the Boers, an English-speaking journalist mutters sarcastically, 'Ah shame!'

I cannot help it, I spit like a flame: 'Shut up, you! You didn't utter a word when De Klerk [leader of the National Party] spoke . . . Viljoen is at least trying.'

'You must be joking – this poor man is an anachronism.' My anger shrivels before his Accent. And his Truth.

Viljoen was the only political leader who requested that a special Reconciliation Commission be set up in future to deal with 'the hardening of attitudes I experience daily.'

After the first political submissions in August 1996 I interviewed Archbishop Tutu. 'Weren't you irritated that you had to listen to four versions of South Africa's past?'

He spreads his four skinny fingers under my nose. 'Four versions . . . four . . . exist of the life of Christ. Which one would you have liked to chuck out?'

I try another question. 'Why did the last part of the ANC's submission sound so paranoid? As if the whole world is in a conspiracy against Thabo Mbeki.'

Tutu tilts his head in surprise. 'You should be the last person to ask me this. You are sitting with me daily, listening to what happened in the past. Many people are the second and third generation of being persecuted. And if you don't know the past, you will never understand today's politics.'

A friend who has emigrated visits me in the office. She answers a call for me: 'It's your child. He says he's writing a song about Joe Mamasela and he needs a word to rhyme with "Vlakplaas".' She lowers the phone. 'Who is Joe Mamasela?'

A massive sigh breaks through my chest. For the first time in months – I breathe.

The absolution one has given up on, the hope for a catharsis, the ideal of reconciliation, the dream of a powerful reconciliation policy . . . Maybe this is all that is important – that I and my child know Vlakplaas and Mamasela. That we know what happened there.

When the Truth Commission started last year, I realized instinctively: if you cut yourself off from the process, you will wake up in a foreign country – a country that you don't know and that you will never understand."

Reprinted by permission of Random House SA.

Mtutuzeli Matshoba

Mtutuzeli Matshoba is a black writer who is well known in South Africa. The extract below gives an idea of the conditions of life in the Transkei, the first artificially created homeland or *bantustan*, after it was notionally given "independence" in 1976. Kaiser Matanzima, the repressive first leader of the Transkei, imprisoned political opponents without trial and imposed emergency regulations which he renewed annually.

Three Days in the Land of a Dying Illusion

"Heh, heh," he had chuckled at my ignorance of the present world. "You don't know that Transkei is independent?"

"Independent from what, of what?"

"Of South Africa," and his eyes had completed the sentence with "bloody fool!"

"That's news to me," I said as sincerely as I could.

"You must have been in jail. Were you not in prison when Transkey got independence? Or maybe you were mad, at Sterkfontein."

"Maybe. If that's what you want – your fellow blacks to be in prison. What's the red tape?"

"Give me your pass."

Fortunately, for once I had it for identification purposes. What with everybody looking for "terrorists" under every stone. I gave it to him and he pages through it before throwing it back at me.

"You're Xhosa, neh?"

I nodded.

"Then go and apply for Transkei citizenship at Counter Six. Next!"

I could not suppress my indignation anymore. "When you look at me you imagine I could make an ideal Transkei citizen? When you arrive home this evening you tell your mother to apply for it so that she can go and learn witchcraft if she is not a professional already." I turned and stomped for the door without waiting for his reaction.

So there I was, rolling into Qamata with my third denomination comrades. The discussion petered out to a noticeable hush as everybody was diverted from the articulate lady by the crossing of an invisible Iron Curtain.

The soil was red, ironically reminding me of Avalon and Doornkop cemeteries back home, the land parched and scarred with erosion. In the first fields that we passed the maize had grown hardly a metre high. The weeds, blackjack outstanding, outgrew it. A woman in dusty traditional attire with a baby strapped to her back and two boys in inherited clothes following her, was searching for stems that might have been overlooked at harvest time.

We passed two cows shaving the roadside of sun-scorched grass.

"*Kakade*, what's the use of buying cattle that end up short of grass?" remarked one of my travelling companions.

"*Imfuyo* [stock] is no longer an investment these days," added another.

I had thought the animals looked acceptable. Perhaps that was due to my inability to judge good beef. However you looked at it, some of the animals that we saw were scrawny and others well-nourished. Probably the latter belonged to people who could afford to buy hay.

The mountains rose high, solid, silent and motionless until they melted into blue-grey and hazy horizons, the only sight that appealed magnificently to my eyes. Below them there were picturesque villages of perfectly circular, thatched rondavels whitewashed for about a foot just below the edges of the thatch and around the windows and doors. This architecture dotted the elevated parts of the landscape on both sides of the road for endless acres.

"*Awu*," someone ventured, "*esikaDaliwonga! Ilizwe lembalela* [a land of drought]. That is why he has left it to pick out the richest parts of the land for himself elsewhere; to bulldoze the people out of land that they inherited from their fathers."

"*Ewe. Nathi uyokusixina ngaphaya.*" [Yes. He also crowds us into the parts that remain ours.]

I was confounded by those words because they came from simple people. Things being taken for granted as they generally are, who could have expected them to nurture any misgivings concerning their share of that wilderness? I say wilderness because that was the most suitable description of what was unfolding before my eyes compared with the white-owned Free State country I had seen the previous day. Proof of its being wasteland lay in the fact that they had surrendered to the inhuman migratory way of life rather than stay and try to eke out a living in their "homeland". It showed there was just no way to suck blood out of a stone. The illusion of freehold in a free land had long faded in the imagination of my cheated people. Independence, *uhuru*, had come, avowedly to break the chains of blackness and drive away poverty. Instead it had brought an ominous fog of helplessness that hung over a land marred with eroded ravines which gave one a clear picture of what the earth might look like after an earthquake. From the silvery trickles that traced erratic courses on the sandy beds of some of the shallow dongas, I concluded that they had been rivulets many aeons ago.

The maize refused to grow higher than a foot without water and scientific agricultural methods. It would cost decades in time and billions of rands in the form of irrigation, fertilizer and technology before one would see any advance beyond cross-plantation on the slopes, which was the only scientific land treatment about which I could write home. Where would the billions come from? Obviously from "white South Africa" with her own sick economy.

If anybody out there had figured that he could temporarily depend on South Africa by sending people there as slaves, hoping that they would earn enough to be self-sufficient after some time, he had dreamt up a nightmare. Slaves don't earn anything; they live from hand to mouth. His country would forever remain both a labour reservoir and a vacuum to suck discarded human labour units out of the South African economy.

We passed a village with a dusty filling station or garage that might have been constructed from the home-made mudbricks of the rondavels. Even if I had a car and happened to have a breakdown near that place, I would never risk taking it there.

Reprinted by permission of Ravan Press in association with Rex Collings.

Books

For a country with such a low proportion of its population reading regularly, South Africa generates a huge amount of literature, particularly about subjects the literate feel guilty about – namely, politics and history. Almost all the books listed below are in print, and those that are not, and which are published in either the UK or US, should be fairly easy to track down in secondhand bookshops. Those books only published in South Africa may prove hard to find outside South Africa itself. Where two publishers are given, the first is British, the second US unless otherwise indicated. Titles marked ⊡ are particularly recommended.

History and anthropology

William Beinart *20th Century South Africa* (OUP, UK). A useful and concise account of South African history, with an emphasis on economic history that manages to emphasize the essential without descending into tedium. His predictions for the future seem wobbly now, but there's nothing unusual about that.

Axel-Ivar Berglund *Zulu Thought Patterns and Symbolism* (Hurst, UK). A sensitive and knowledgeable account of rural Zulu world views, related as they have been described to the author, with the minimum of interpretation. He does, however, set the scene well, and make thought-provoking connections between the various views expressed, whilst bending over backwards to avoid tedious judgementalism.

Philip Bonner *Kings, Commoners and Concessionaries* (CUP, UK). The definitive history (so far) of nineteenth-century Swaziland, by a skilled historian with a gratifying grasp of the source material and mostly reliable judgement. Its one weakness is a lack of oral historical research, though fortunately useful work has been done on this recently by the Swazi Oral History Project, based at the university there.

Emile Boonzaier, Candy Malherbe, Andy Smith and Penny Berens *The Cape Herders, A History of the Khoikhoi of Southern Africa* (David Philip, SA; Ohio University Press, US). A recently published and accessibly written account of the Khoikhoi people of southern Africa, successfully exploding the many prejudices and myths that surround them and exploring their way of life, their interaction with Europeans, and what remains of them today.

Jane Carruthers *The Kruger National Park: A Social and Political History* (University of Natal, SA). A specialist history that deals with broad issues. By examining the scientific and ideological forces that gave rise to the Kruger National Park, this fascinating book asks important questions about our notions of nature and conservation.

Rodney Davenport *The Transfer of Power in South Africa* (Toronto University Press, Canada). An eminent liberal historian examines reconciliation in South African society since 1990 and explains how potential obstacles have been overcome.

Stephen Gill *A Short History of Lesotho* (Morija, Lesotho). A thoughtful and well-informed account of Lesotho's history and the best single volume you'll find, written by the chief archivist at the Morija Museum. Gill clearly loves Lesotho and has little sympathy for its many invaders but is a little over-generous in his account of Lesotho's missionaries.

Barbara Hutton *Robben Island – Symbol of Resistance* (Sached Books UK; Mayibuye Books, SA). A fast, straightforward and illustrated account of Robben Island from pre-historic times to the present, with a good overview of prison conditions in the apartheid years.

★ **Antjie Krog** *Country of My Skull* (Jonathan Cape; Times Books). A deeply personal and gripping account of the hearings of the Truth and Reconciliation Commission by Afrikaner SABC radio journalist and poet. Krog reveals the complexity of horrors committed by apartheid, and also paints an admiring tribute to Commission Head Desmond Tutu.

Hilda Kuper *The Swazi, A South African Kingdom* (Saunders College Publishing, US). A combination of anthropology and history, written in the 1960s, whose theoretical perspectives seem pretty dated now, though Kuper's observations still sound sharp. Her political insight was often astute too, though she was too fond of the Dlamini royal house to provide much of a critical perspective on them.

★ **Ben Maclennan** *A Proper Degree of Terror – John Graham and the Cape's Eastern Frontier* (Ravan, SA). A riveting account of the early nineteenth century in the Eastern Cape, written with the cracking narrative pace of a novel.

Candy Malherbe *Men of Men* (Shuter and Shooter, SA). A brief, simple and highly readable primer on the earliest inhabitants of the Cape, the Khoikhoi, who were systematically dispossessed, but have nevertheless left their mark on modern South Africa.

Hein Marais *South Africa, Limits to Change* (Zed Books, SA). A readable assessment of why the privileged classes remain just that, and why the new government has followed relatively conservative economic policies.

Shula Marks and Stanley Trapido (eds) *The Politics of Race, Class and Nationalism in 20th Century South Africa* (Longman, UK). A seminal collection of Marxist and left-leaning analyses of South African social and political trends, with an emphasis on the micro-study that stands in deliberate contrast to the sweeping liberal histories that have preceded it.

★ **Noel Mostert** *Frontiers – The Epic of South Africa's Creation and the Tragedy of the Xhosa People* (Pimlico, UK). An academically solid and brilliantly written history of the Xhosa of the Eastern Cape and their tragic fate in the frontier wars fought against the British.

Credo Mutwa *Indaba, My Children* (Payback Press; Grove Atlantic). Many of Africa's most enduring and entertaining legends, myths and stories vividly retold – and some would say reinvented – by enigmatic Zulu spiritualist Mutwa.

★ **Dougie Oakes (ed)** *Illustrated History of South Africa* (Reader's Digest, SA). Physically weighty, but written in a delightfully light style, this illustated history is an essential volume on the shelves of anyone seriously interested in the democratic history of South Africa.

Thomas Pakenham *The Boer War* (Abacus, UK). The definitive liberal history of the Anglo-Boer War that reads grippingly like a novel, managing to maintain a panoramic sweep of events while homing in on the quirks and foibles of the individuals involved.

Jeff Peires *The Dead Will Arise* (Ravan, SA) and *The House of Phalo* (Ravan, SA). The leading historian of the Xhosa people tells in beautifully readable prose the stories of the Eastern Cape before the arrival of whites, as well as the impact of colonialism on their lives and society.

Marjorie Shostak *Nisa* (Earthscan, UK). A fascinating book – both bawdy and romantic – based on the life of a San woman in a hostile Kalahari environment.

Leonard Thompson *A History of South Africa* (Yale University Press, UK/US). Reliable and elegantly written, this is among the best introductions to its subject.

Desmond Tutu *No Future Without Forgiveness* (Rider Books, UK). The Truth and Reconciliation Commission as described by its chairman. There are better accounts of the hearings, but the book offers essential insight into one of South Africa's most unlikely heroes.

Laurens van der Post *The Lost World of the Kalahari* (Penguin, UK). The author's almost spiritual quest to find, and film, San people still existing as pure hunter-gatherers. *The Heart of the Hunter* (Penguin, UK) is the sequel, although it can be read on its own, dwelling on the San van der Post met and their mythology.

Nigel Worden, Elizabeth van Heyningen and Vivian Bickford-Smith *Cape Town: The Making of a City* (David Philip, SA). The definitive and highly readable illustrated account of the social and political development of South Africa's first city from 1620 to 1899, written by three leading historians based at the University of Cape Town. A companion volume covers the twentieth century.

Autobiography and biography

Breyten Breytenbach *True Confessions of an Albino Terrorist* (Faber & Faber, UK). In vividly poetic language, the exiled Afrikaner poet tells the entertaining story of his return to South Africa in 1975 – to be arrested and jailed for seven years.

Wilfred Cibane *Man of Two Worlds* (Kwela Books, SA). The autobiography of Cibane, from his life as a rural goatherd to cosmopolitan man of means and the cultural clashes that accompanied it.

Robin Denniston *Trevor Huddleston, A Life* (Macmillan, UK). An inspiring biography of the English

churchman who worked among Johannesburg's urban blacks in the 1950s and later founded the Anti-Apartheid Movement.

Mark Gevisser *Portraits of Power* (David Philip, SA). Forty profiles of South Africa's movers and shakers in the era of transition.

Sindiwe Magoma *To my Children's Children* (David Philip, SA). A fascinating autobiography, initially started so that her family would never forget their roots – that traces Magoma's life from the rural Transkei to the hard townships of Cape Town, and from political innocence to wisdom born of bitter experience.

Greg Marnovich and Joao Silva *The Bang Bang Club* (Arrow, UK). The compelling story of four news photographers who snapped the country's most violent townships in the late 1980s and early 1990s. Two survived to tell the tale; Ken Oosterbroek was killed in cross-fire days before the 1994 elections and Ken Carter committed suicide not long afterwards.

Mike Nicol *Sea-Mountain, Fire City: Living in Cape Town* (Kwela Books, SA). One of the most recent books in that rare category, a non-fiction documentary, on living in Cape Town at the beginning of the new millennium. Basing his narrative on the apparently prosaic business of moving house from one part of the city to another, Nicol maps many of those fissures, not to say abysses, that make Cape Town such a divided city.

Nelson Mandela *Long Walk to Freedom* (Abacus, UK). The superb best-selling autobiography of the South African president, which is wonderfully evocative of his early years and intensely moving about his long years in prison. However, when it comes to his love life, the byzantine intricacies of ANC politics during its long years as an illegal organization, and the story behind the negotiated settlement, Mandela is more diplomatic than candid. Mandela's generosity of spirit and tremendous understanding of the delicate balance between principle and tactics come out very strongly, and the book is without doubt essential reading for the new South Africa.

Emma Mashinini *Strikes Have Followed me All my Life* (Women's Press, UK). The moving account of this diminutive but unstoppable trade unionist, who defied both

injustice in the labour market and the deep sexism of her colleagues during her tireless struggles from the 1950s to the 1980s.

William Plomer *Cecil Rhodes* (David Philip, SA). There are countless books on Rhodes, most of which feed the legend, although the distance of time has made some historians ready to regard him as a flawed colossus. This is a re-publication of one of the most critical accounts, written several decades ago, against the grain, by a South African poet-novelist, when colonialism was still regarded by many whites as a good thing. It pulls no punches in presenting Rhodes as an immature person driven by his weaknesses.

Richard Rosenthal *Mission Improbable* (David Philip, SA). A fascinating account of an attempt to set up "talks about talks" between the ANC and P.W. Botha's government in Switzerland during December 1988, which were cut short by the latter's stroke.

Albie Sachs *The Soft Vengeance of a Freedom Fighter* (David Philip, SA). The ANC veteran relates the story of how, in exile in Mozambique, he was almost killed by a South African security police bomb. The book vividly traces his recovery and the mental difficulties he went through to emerge with a new vision of the struggle.

Anthony Sampson *Mandela, The Authorised Biography* (Harper Collins; Knopf). Released to coincide with Mandela's retirement from presidency in 1999, Sampson's authoritative volume can compete with *A Long Walk to Freedom* in both interest and sheer poundage. Firmly grounded in the author's long association with his subject, as well as exhaustive research and interviews, it offers a broader perspective and sharper analysis than the autobiography.

Travel

Gavin Bell *Somewhere Over the Rainbow* (Abacus, UK). A British foreign correspondent during the apartheid years returns in the mid-1990s to provide an astute commentary on the fortunes and foibles of the new South Africa.

Dan Jacobson *The Electric Elephant* (Hamish Hamilton, UK). Jacobson, who left South Africa in the 1950s, returned in 1993 to travel from Kimberley in the Northern Cape to Victoria Falls, along the old "Great North Road", built by Rhodes and since trodden by generations of missionaries, colonists and freebooters.

Dervla Murphy *South from the Limpopo: Travels through South Africa* (John Murray, UK). A fascinating bike journey through the new South Africa with a writer who isn't afraid to explore the complexities and paradoxes of this country.

Marco Turco *Visitor's Guide to Lesotho* (Southern, SA). An exhaustive account of nearly every town and village on the main routes through Lesotho, accompanied by constant exhortations for readers to get out and meet the Sotho. Helpful in places, though rather indiscriminate.

Marco Turco *Visitor's Guide to Swaziland* (Southern, SA). Turco travelled everywhere to write this book, including some really out-of-the-way places, though his account is marred by his tendency to recommend everything, no matter how dull it turns out to be when you get there.

Fiction

Tatamkhulu Afrika *The Innocents* (Africasouth, SA) Set in the struggle years, this novel examines the moral and ethical issues of the time from a Muslim perspective.

Mark Behr *The Smell of Apples* (Abacus, UK). A best-selling novel about a small white boy growing up in a military family under apartheid in the 1970s, and painfully resonant for many.

★ **Herman Charles Bosman** *Unto Dust* (Human & Rousseau, SA). A superb collection of short stories from South Africa's master of the genre, all set in the tiny Afrikaner farming district of Groot Marico in the 1930s, with the narrator Oom Schalk Lourens revealing with delicious irony the passions and foibles of his community.

André Brink *A Chain of Voices* (Minerva, UK). The superbly evocative tale of Cape eighteenth-century life, exploring the impact of slavery on one farming family, right up to its dramatic and murderous end.

★ **J.M. Coetzee** *Age of Iron* (Penguin, UK/US). Voted by writers in a *Mail & Guardian* poll to be the finest South African novel of the last ten years, this depicts a white female classics professor dying from cancer during the political craziness of the 1980s. She is joined by a tramp who sets up home in the garden, and thus evolves a curious and fascinating relationship that transforms her.

Achmat Dangor *The Z Town Trilogy* (Ravan, SA). One of the best Cape Town writers, Dangor sets this trilogy in a town much like it, during one of apartheid South Africa's many states of emergency, which have started to burrow in intricate ways into the psyches of his characters.

Modikwe Dikobe *Marabi Dance* (Heinemann, UK). A short novel celebrating the bittersweet nature of black Johannesburg life in the 1930s, where the daily humiliations of life are tempered by the prospect of wild *marabi* parties when the weekends come.

Nadine Gordimer *July's People* (Penguin, UK/US). A liberal white family is rescued by its gardener July from revolution, and taken to his home village for safety, where Gordimer teases out the power dynamics of this fraught situation with customary insight and eloquence.

Dan Jacobson *The Trap, and a Dance in the Sun* (David Philip, SA). Two taut novellas written in the 1950s in one volume, skilfully portraying the developing tensions and nuances of the white-versus-black lives of the era.

Douglas Killam and Ruth Rowe *The Companion to African Literature* (James Currey). As its title implies, this book, published in 2000, comprises details of significant African writers, as well as more general articles on issues such as Negritude or publishing in Africa. There are bibliographies, plus brief critical commentaries on individual authors. If you want to know who wrote what and when, this is the book for you.

★ **Alex La Guma** *A Walk in the Night* (Heinemann, UK). An evocative collection of short stories by this talented political activist/author, set in District Six, the ethnically mixed quarter of Cape Town razed by the apartheid government,

Anne Landsman *The Devil's Chimney* (Granta; Penguin). A stylish and entertaining piece of magic realism about the Southern Cape town of Outshoorn in the days of the ostrich-feather boom.

Zakes Mda *Ways of Dying* (OUP, UK). Winner of the 1997 M-Net Book Prize, this brilliant tale of a professional mourner is full of sly insights into the culture of black South Africa.

Thomas Mofolo *Chaka* (Heinemann, UK). Thomas Mofolo was Lesotho's first great fiction writer, who wrote this epic tale in Sotho of the Zulu king Shaka in 1909, here portrayed as a man fatally controlled by his strong passions. The original English translation gave the text a misleadingly biblical slant, which has been corrected in this newer translation by Daniel Kunene.

Isaac Mogotsi *Alexandra Tales* (Ravan, SA). Delightful tales of family life in the run-down, lively homes of Johannesburg's Alexandra township, all with a clever and provocative twist in the tail.

★ **Es'kia Mpahalele** *Down Second Avenue* (Faber & Faber, UK). A classic autobiographical novel set in the 1940s in the impoverished township of Alexandra, where Mpahalele grew up as part of a large extended family battling daily to survive the problems and injustices of the age.

★ **Alan Paton** *Cry, the Beloved Country* (Penguin, UK). Classic novel by one of South Africa's great liberals, describing with tremendous lyricism the journey of a black pastor from rural Natal to Johannesburg, depicted as a veritable Sodom and Gomorrah, to rescue his missing son from its clutches.

Kathy Perkins *Black South African Women – An Anthology of Plays* (Routledge, UK) Groundbreaking collection of ten plays by a wide range of known and unknown playwrights such as Gcina Mhlope, Sindiwe Nagona, Muthal Naidoo and Lueen Conning.

Sol Plaatje *Mhudi* (Heinemann, UK). The first English novel by a South African writer, *Mhudi* is the epic story, set in the 1830s, of a young Barolong woman who saves her future husband from the raids of the Ndebele, at a time when the Afrikaner Great Trek had just begun. Plaatje was also a political activist and was one of the founder members of the ANC.

Linda Rode *Crossing Over* (Kwela, SA) Collection of 26 stories by new and emerging South African writers on the experiences of adolescence and early adulthood in a period of political transition.

★ **Olive Schreiner** *Story of an African Farm* (Penguin, UK/US). The first-ever South African novel, Schreiner wrote this in 1883 under a male pseudonym. Though subject to the ideologies of the era, the book nonetheless explores with genuinely open vision the tale of two female cousins living on a remote Karoo farm whose young lives are disrupted by an Irish traveller.

Sipho Sepamla *A Ride on the Whirlwind* (Heinemann, UK). Set in the terrifying times of 1976 in riot-swept Soweto, Sepamla's novel examines the psychology of resistance and defiance amongst the angry township youth.

Mongane Wally Serote *To Every Birth Its Blood* (Heinemann, UK). Serote's only novel is a powerfully turbulent affair that traces the evolution of a township man from someone interested only in jazz, drinking and sex, to political consciousness through the humiliations he is subjected to by the forces of authority.

★ **Martin Trump and Jean Marquard (eds)** *A Century of South African Short Stories* (Ad Donker, SA). A selection of South Africa's finest short stories, including contributions from *Drum* writer Can Themba, Charles Bosman and Nadine Gordimer.

Marlene van Niekerk *Triomf* (Johnathan Ball, SA; Little, Brown & Co, UK). Award-winning Afrikaans novel translated into South African English as well as a less idiomatic form for the overseas market. Tells the colourful and tragic story of a family of poor whites living in the emblematic Johannesburg suburb of Triomf, built on the ruins of the black enclave of Sophiatown.

Ivan Vladislavic *The Restless Supermarket* (David Philip, SA). A dark and intricate urban satire about Johannesburg's notorious Hillbrow district during the last days of apartheid.

Zoe Wicombe *You Can't Get Lost in Cape Town* (David Philip, SA 1987). Wicombe's short stories are remarkable for her sense of realism and the subtle way in which she produces work where social concern is transparent, humour is demonstrable, and yet which avoids the heavy-handedness of most anti-apartheid protest literature.

Poetry

Guy Butler (ed) *A Book of South African Verse* (OUP, UK); **Jack Cope and Uys Krige** (eds) *The Penguin Book of South African Verse* (Penguin, UK). Early anthologies that, for better or for worse, "mapped" South African poetry. Butler's comment in his introduction – "Most of our poets have tried to belong to Africa and, finding her savage, shallow and uncooperative, have been forced to give their allegiance, not to any other country, but to certain basic conceptions" (read Europe) – remains controversial.

⊟★ **Roy Campbell** *Selected Poems* (OUP, UK). Very much a figure from a period of South Africa's literary colonialism, Roy Campbell, despite his sometimes politically repellent views, remains a major figure, and one of the most lyrically gifted and satirically sharp poets that South Africa has ever produced.

Tim Couzens and Essop Patel (eds) *Return of the Amasi Bird* (Ravan, SA). Comprehensive collection of black South African poetry, which stretches right back to the early colonial era and extends to the cries of liberation and beyond.

Jeremy Cronin *Inside/Outside* (David Philip, SA). Written by a leading member of the South African Communist Party, *Inside,* first published in 1983, is probably the most inventive work of South African prison poetry. *Outside* charts Cronin's reaction to post-apartheid South Africa, and continuing resistance to the many forms of betrayal of South Africa's larger populace.

⊟★ **Ingrid de Kok** *Transfer* (Snail Press, SA) Probably the most

poetically intelligent of South Africa's feminist poets. Technically adroit, and always moving.

Peter Horn *The Rivers which Connect us to the Past* (Mayibuye, SA). Horn was one of SA's most prolific protest poets during the 1970s, with strong socialist convictions.

Ingrid Jonker *Selected Poems* (Human & Rousseau, SA). One of the few Afrikaans language poets whose English translation does justice to her work. The poems display a remarkable rawness in depicting the outrage of 1960s apartheid, as well as a grief-stricken lyricism from a poet who drowned herself in 1965 off Sea Point.

⊟★ **The Lava of this Land: South African Poetry 1960–1996** (David Philip, SA). This most recent and comprehensive anthology of South African poetry includes work from the oral period, as well as translations from Afrikaans and other languages. The most useful introduction to date.

Mongane Wally Serote *Selected Poems* (Ad Donker, SA). The leading light amongst South Africa's many protest poets, with a work that ranges from early rage to incantations of freedom, leavened with humour and startling imagery.

⊟★ **Stephen Watson** *The Other City* (David Philip, SA). No one better evokes Cape Town's changeable beauty, though Watson also writes of the heart and the great universal themes that make him a first-rate poet of the world, rather than just of his native city.

The arts

Marion Arnold *Women and Art in South Africa* (David Philip, SA). Pioneering work that reinterprets South African art history.

Basil Beakey *Beyond the Blues: Township Jazz of the Sixties and Seventies* (David Philip, SA) Portraits of the country's jazz greats such as Kippie Moeketsi, Basil Coetzee and Abdullah Ibrahim (Dollar Brand).

Ian Berry *Living Apart* (Phaidon, SA). Superbly evocative and moving photographs spanning from the 1950s to 1990s, which chart a compelling vision of the politics of the nation, but at the level of the individual.

Clive Chipkin *Johannesburg Style* (David Philip, SA). Perhaps a contradiction in terms, but a fascinating study of architecture and society in the South African city.

J. Christopher *The Atlas of Apartheid* (Routledge, UK). Detailed but accessible study of the policy and implementation of urban and regional planning that gave South African towns and cities their current form.

S. Francis and H. Dugmore *Madam and Eve* (Penguin, SA). One of South Africa's leading cultural exports conveys the daily struggle between an African domestic worker and her white madam in the northern suburbs of Johannesburg in various volumes of telling and witty cartoon strips that say more about post-apartheid society than countless academic tomes.

★ J.D. Lewis-Williams *Discovering Southern African Rock Art* (David Philip, SA), and *Images of Power: Understanding Bushman Rock Art* (David Philip, SA). Short, concise books written by an expert in the field, full of drawings and photos. It concludes that most of the paintings depict images seen while in a state of shamanic trance, and reflect a San world-view in which the spiritual and material were both a part of everyday life.

Z.B. Molefe *A Common Hunger to Sing* (Kwela, SA). Large format, well-illustrated tribute to the achievements of the country's black women singers and the obstacles they have overcome.

Jurgen Schadeberg *Sof'town: Images from the Black '50s* (Jurgen Schadeberg, UK). Classic black-and-white photographic studies of the *Drum* era of swinging Johannesburg, where, if Schadeberg is to be believed, every black woman was a beauty and every black man a dude in a zoot suit.

Sue Williamson *Resistance Art in South Africa* (David Philip, SA), and *Art in South Africa: The Future Present* (David Philip, SA). Taken together, these two volumes map the course of South African art from the early 1980s to the present day, with a thoughtful text that's minimal enough to let the artists' works speak for themselves.

Zapiro *End of Part One* (David Philip, SA). Third collection of cartoons by the country's leading exponent, preceded by *The Hole Truth* and *The Madiba Years*.

Specialist guidebooks

G.M. Branch *Two Oceans* (David Philip, SA). Don't be fooled by the coffee-table format; this is a comprehensive guide to southern Africa's marine life.

David Bristow *Best Hikes in Southern Africa* (Struik, SA). Well-written and reliable guide that does your homework for you, selecting the best trails from a confusingly extensive lot.

David Bristow *Drakensberg Walks: 120 Graded Hikes and Trails in the 'Berg* (Struik, SA). An indispensable paperback for anyone exploring the Drakensberg, with detailed route instructions and informative background about the natural history of the massif.

Shirley Brossey *A Walking Guide for Table Mountain* (self-published, SA). Useful and inexpensive guide to trails around the Table Mountain, with handy hand-drawn maps and down-to-earth text.

Duncan Guy *The Very Best of Johannesburg and Surrounds* (Struik, SA). A rare book which delights in the diversity and colour of Johannesburg – lots of photographs and some good detail on the nooks and crannies of Gauteng.

Judith Hopley *On Foot in the Garden Route* (self-published, SA). Excellent little guide that's perfect if you're planning on exploring the coasts and forest of the Garden Route on foot.

⭐ **Jaynee Levy** *The Complete Guide to Walks & Trails in Southern Africa* (Struik, SA). Encyclopedic hiker's bible covering over 500 trails suitable for all abilities, with useful practical information about what to take and where to book. One to invest in if you're a keen trailist spending time in the country, but definitely not light reading to take on a walk.

⭐ **Mike Lundy** *Best Walks in the Cape Peninsula* (Struik, SA). Handy, solidly researched guide to some of the Peninsula's many walks, and small enough to fit comfortably in a backpack while you are walking them.

Tony Pooley and Ian Player *KwaZulu-Natal Wildlife Destinations* (Southern, SA). Comprehensive directory of every game and nature reserve in the province, with useful practical and background information.

Charles Stewart *Rock and Surf Fishing* (Southern, SA). Uninspiringly written, but the author does appear to have tried his luck from nearly every available vantage point on the South African coast, and the book is a useful guide to what he has found out on the way.

Cornel Truter *West Coast* (UCT, SA) The history, flora, industry, agriculture and tourism of this gaunt but beautiful stretch that is the opposite of the lush Garden Route.

Birds

Hugh Chittenden *Top Birding Spots of Southern Africa* (Southern, SA). Essential companion-guide for any keen bird-watcher, with information on spots and how to access them as well as a rundown on the common species and any specials to look out for.

Gordon Lindsay Maclean Roberts *Birds of Southern Africa* (New Holland, UK). The definitive reference work on the subcontinent's entire avifauna population: if it's not in Roberts, it doesn't exist. Alas the weight of this tome makes it more of a book to consult in a library than to take on your trip.

Ian Sinclair *Southern African Birds – A Photographic Guide* (Collins, UK; Struik, SA). Pocket-sized volume full of photos to help you bird-spot your way around the country, with pretty minimal textual accompaniment, rather short on interesting little facts about the birds in question.

Mammals

⭐ **Richard D. Estes** *Safari Companion* (Russell Friedman Books, SA). A long-needed guide on how to understand African wildlife, with interesting and readable information on the behaviour and social structures of the major species.

Chris and Tilde Stuart *Field Guide to the Mammals of Southern Africa* (New Holland, UK). One of the best books on this subject providing excellent background and clear illustrations to help you recognize a species.

Trees and plants

L. McMahon and M. Fraser *A Fynbos Year* (David Philip, SA). Exquisitely illustrated and well-written book about South Africa's unique floral kingdom.

Keith Coates Palgrave *Trees of Southern Africa* (Struik, SA). The authoritative book on the subject,

but too big and heavy to carry around.

Eve Palmer *A Field Guide to the Trees of Southern Africa* (Collins, UK). Covers South Africa, Botswana and Namibia and is small and more practical to carry than Coates Palgrave.

Wine

David Biggs *South African Plonk Buyer's Guide* (Ampersand, SA). Annually updated survey of the best of the cheap wines (under R20).

James Seely *The Wines of South Africa* (Faber & Faber, UK). Almost as definitive as it claims, this book tackles South African wine region by region, estate by estate, complete with tasting notes and recommendations. Written by an author who

once imported wine to the UK for Harvey's, but now does so for himself, it's a useful and inexpensive reference guide.

⭐ **Philip van Zyl (ed)** *John Platter South African Wines* (Andrew Mcdowall, SA). Annually updated pocket guide to South Africa's current output, with reviews and rating by one of the country's top wine writers.

Music

South Africa has a deserved following, with the continent's most diverse recorded music output and its most developed music industry. Paradoxically, judging by what you tend to hear pumping from the nation's radios, clubs and car stereos, more of the population listens to American rather than home-brewed sounds then anywhere else on the continent. African American music has been popular with black South Africans for over one hundred years, and jazz, R&B, hip hop and Chicago house have all been critical in the development of local sounds. Thirty years later than in the rest of Africa, Congolese music is finally making its mark, now that the Congolese are in South Africa in numbers, and apartheid bureaucrats no longer police radio playlists. Despite some excellent local bands, most South African whites also prefer to look outside the country for inspiration, in their case to the British and American rock and house scene. Yet, as the saying here goes, "local is *lekker* (sweet)". Despite countless predictions of its demise, local music and musicians continue to innovate and survive.

South African music compilations released abroad usually ignore recent material in favour of *mbaqanga* or township jive, so Western fans could be forgiven for thinking that this style, made famous by Paul Simon's *Graceland* album, and touring South African artists like the Soul Brothers and Mahlathini back in the 1980s, remains at the local musical cutting edge. In South Africa, however, *mbaqanga* is popular but old-fashioned – a safe bet for a DJ at a wedding, but not the thing to play to an urban party crowd.

Far and away the most popular music in the country, – and consistently outselling every other genre – is gospel. Among urban black youth, much the biggest local sound is *kwaito*, South Africa's house music, followed some distance behind by hip-hop and reggae. Older people tend to prefer the country's great jazz artists, like Abdullah Ibrahim and Winston "Mankunku" Ngozi, and artists like Jabu Khanyile, who play a kind of contemporary folk, which draws consciously on rural styles but also skilfully blends in jazz and *mbaqanga*. In the rural areas and in the hostels, neo-traditional music still holds sway, with songs accompanied by the accordion, guitar and a thumping bass line, constantly reworking themes of marriage, dowries, betrayal and village gossip. Young whites, meanwhile, continue to have plenty of alternative rock bands to choose from, including the very successful and recently disbanded Springbok Nudegirls and the bizarre self-styled munki-punk Boo!.

Gospel

Choral harmony and melody are perhaps black South Africa's greatest musical gifts to the world, and nowhere are they better manifested than in its **churches**. In the mainstream Catholic, Anglican and Methodist denominations a tradition of choral singing has evolved that has taken the style of European classical composers but loosened it up, added rhythm and, as always, some great dance routines. This type of choral singing is immensely popular, with regular competitions involving amazingly attired choirs – some of which are over one

Rebecca Malope

Diminutive **Rebecca Malope** is South Africa's biggest selling music star, enjoying years at the top of the gospel scene, with only stadia able to hold her fans, every album going gold or platinum, popular magazines full of her photos, views and story, and everyone knowing the lyrics of her songs. Well, nearly everyone that is, for Rebecca Malope is virtually unknown outside the black community.

Rebecca's musical formula, engineered by her lynchpin keyboard player **Zako**, who also producers the music, rarely varies. Her songs are anthems characterized by swirling keyboards and excellent backing singers, delivered in Rebecca's tremendous, soaring and sometimes husky voice, accompanied by dramatic gestures as she becomes possessed by the spiritual power her lyrics unleash.

The daughter of a Sotho father and Swazi mother, Rebecca was born in Nelspruit, Mpumalanga in 1969, and soon began singing in the local Assemblies of God church, where her grandfather was a pastor. Her initial recordings were mostly forgettable pop, but in Johannesburg she was spotted by Zako, and under his tutelage and because, she says, of letters from fans pleading that she sing God's songs, Rebecca returned to gospel in 1990, where she has since been amply rewarded. Denying that she is apolitical, Rebecca says she does sometimes sing at rallies, but will select songs that tell the politicians what she believes they need to hear.

Huge in South Africa, Rebecca has a growing fan base elsewhere in Africa, but has had little impact in Europe and the US. Back home, Rebecca has scaled back her recording activity, and increasingly concentrated on talent spotting and development. The result is a string of very Rebecca-influenced new stars like **Vuyo** and **Lundi**.

hundred strong. If you can't make it to a competition, you can watch the choirs every Sunday on television's SABC 1.

In the **Pentecostal** churches, the music is more American-influenced, yet the harmonies and melodies remain uniquely South African and intensely moving. Pentecostal gospel music is the main recorded style; look out for groups like **Lord Comforters**, and the powerful **Rebecca Malope** (see box above).

Also worth seeking out is **Zionist gospel**. The Zionist churches have more members than any other denomination in the country; devotees are required to donate ten percent of their income to the church, live an ultra-clean life and attend all the services and conventions, in distinctive long robes, often adorned with sashes. Zionist music is an extraordinary mix of mournfulness and fervour, with a tonality all of its own, rendering it perfect for the moving night vigils that precede funerals, as well as regular church services. Services are held outside and often in parks, where you are welcome to watch as long as you do so respectfully. Zionist gospel cassettes and CDs are easily spotted, as their covers invariably feature the substantial performing choir in full robes, often with the preacher out in front in some suitably religious pose.

Kwaito

South Africa's definitive youth sound, **kwaito,** has been in existence for about a decade. Apparently, DJs importing dance music in the early 1990s found that white clubs were unresponsive to Chicago house and so tried it in black nightclubs instead. Here the DJs found that people preferred it when they slowed the records from 45 to 33rpm. Soon producers tried their own versions,

Kwaito killed the careers of many of the 1980s bubblegum stars, but **Brenda Fassie** has managed not only to survive the new music, but to thrive on it. Brenda is South Africa's true pop queen and the one local artist whose music is pretty much guaranteed to get things going on the dance floor, wherever you are in the country. Brenda began her career in the early 1980s as lead singer for **Brenda and the Big Dudes**, enjoying a string of bubblegum hits, including the classic *Weekend Special*, which for years was a South African disco anthem. Brenda never was one for politics, but skilfully caught the mood of the time in the tense year of 1989 with a moving song about police brutality on the album *Too Late for Mama* called *Good Black Woman*.

During the 1990s, while contemporaries like her one-time arch rival **Yvonne Chaka Chaka** produced comfortable material aimed more at middle-class and middle-aged audiences, Brenda made a point of hanging out with the youth in Soweto and Hillbrow, Johannesburg's fastest-paced and most dangerous patch of inner city. The result was a lesbian love affair that thrilled the tabloids, a bad crack habit, a tendency to lose the plot completely on stage, and the best music she had ever produced. Brenda mixed *kwaito*, *mbaqanga*, gospel and her own extraordinary persona into her sound, earning massive and deserved success with tunes like *Vul'Ndlela* and *Nomakanjani*. Brenda's most recent album *Mina Nawe* makes for good listening, but nearly all the tunes are shameless reworkings of her earlier songs, suggesting that she is short of new ideas for now. However, as with great football clubs, you can never write off Brenda, and the chances are good that she has more great material in store for us.

deliberately thinning the production to give their music the tinny sound township dwellers were familiar with from **bubblegum**, South Africa's 1980s disco-inspired pop music. Innovative producers soon began to experiment, incorporating South African melodies, and DJs singing doggerel verses of the latest, wickedest phrases of *tsotsi taal* – ghetto rude boy slang. This trend has continued, and in addition, *kwaito* today has become more heavily produced, with strong bass lines designed for maximum impact through a powerful sound-system. In an accurate reflection of the depressed and nihilistic mood of township youth culture, *kwaito*'s vibe tends to be downbeat, and the music carries a strong association with gangsterism and explicit sexuality. *Kwaito* is often condemned by older and God-fearing South Africans but this matters nix ("nothing") to its young township fans, to whom *kwaito* embodies the style and groove of the new South Africa.

Few *kwaito* tunes or performers last long in the limelight, though some *kwaito* artists like **Arthur** have managed to prolong their careers by also working as producers. Major artists to look out for include the funky **Trompies**, hard-rock-influenced **Mandoza**, and the matchstick-chewing, gangster-styled **Zola**. Zola starred in the hit South African drama series **Yizo Yizo** about the interplay between a township school and local young gangsters, and its two soundtrack CDs are a virtual who's who of the *kwaito* scene.

Rap and reggae

While **rap and reggae** are very popular in South Africa, particularly in the coloured community, credible local performers are thin on the ground. By far the best South African rap group is still the **Prophets of Da City**, who hail from the coloured townships of Cape Town, and have a distinctly political slant to their lyrics, while a good up-and-coming act are **Max Normal**, headed by **Watkin Tudor Jones**. The unquestioned king of the local reggae scene for over a decade now is **Lucky Dube**. Originally a township jive singer, his switch to Peter Tosh-style roots reggae in the early 1990s was an inspired one, and his album *Prisoner* became the biggest-selling South African album of all time. An energetic, disciplined and talented live performer, Lucky Dube can also come up with a falsetto like Smokey Robinson's, which adds a distinctly new twist to his otherwise familiar roots sounds.

Neo-traditional music

The best way to see South African **neo-traditional music**, unless you're lucky enough to find yourself at an event where it's being performed live, is on SABC TV Channel 1's *Ezodumo*, which is compulsory viewing in the few rural homesteads and hostels that have a television. The programme is a great showcase for the bands, all dressed in vaguely traditional attire, and usually consisting of a male lead vocalist, female backing singers and a small rhythm section, which often includes a concertina player. As with *kwaito*, the instrumentation is really just a backdrop to the lyrics – usually shouted at great speed – and the graceful dance routines.

One of the major stars of neo-traditional music is the Shangaan singer **Thomas Chauke**, who is an *Ezodumo* regular, and probably the best seller in

Ladysmith Black Mambazo and the iscathamiya sound

The most famous of all South Africa's neo-traditional music is the great Zulu tradition of **iscathamiya**, or *mbube*. Iscathamiya is an unaccompanied and distinctive choral singing style made famous in the West by **Ladysmith Black Mambazo**. The style began in the migrants' hostels after World War I, with the first hit going to Solomon Linda and the Original Evening Birds, whose song *Mbube* sold 100,000 copies, and has been used many times since, including in the Disney movie *The Lion King*, where it was the basis of the song *The Lion Sleeps Tonight*.

Although it enjoyed pan-ethnic popularity in the 1940s and 1950s, in the 1960s *iscathamiya* reverted to its role as the defining sound of Zulu men's hostels. This was cleverly used by Radio Zulu to promote the apartheid concepts of rigid ethnic identity and ruralism, and the station encouraged and recorded songs that dwelt on Zulu-ness, and the need to leave the cities and return to the rural areas. In 1973, Ladysmith Black Mambazo recorded their first album, *Amabutho*, which quickly sold 25,000 copies and have since recorded about forty others, all of which have gone gold. Following their collaboration with Paul Simon on *Graceland*, he produced their album *Shaka Zulu*, which sold 100,000 copies around the world, and took *iscathamiya* to the international stage.

Having flirted with the Inkhatha Freedom Party's Zulu nationalist politics in the late 1980s, today Ladysmith Black Mambazo prefer to dwell on religious matters, and keep their politics to calls for peace. Though non-Zulu speakers can appreciate the group's smooth dance steps, immaculate singing and vocal arrangements, the true glory of their music for the Zulu is the beauty of the lyrics, composed by Black Mambazo's gentle lead singer **Joe Shabalala**, who is surely one of South Africa's greatest living poets.

any of the neo-traditional genres, making heavy use of a drum machine, an electric keyboard and some often intricate lead-guitar work to complement his vocals.

Sotho neo-traditional styles have shown the least development over the years, largely because of a particularly conservative music policy on Radio Sotho during the apartheid era. Nevertheless, the basslines are good, and while you can take or leave the concertinas, the shouting is definitely first-class. **Tau Oa Matshela** and **Tau Oa Linare** are groups to look out for.

Xhosa and Tswana neo-traditional music rarely makes it to the national scene, but **Zulu music** is everywhere, both in its instrumental and a cappella form, known to the Zulu as *iscathamiya* (see box on p.899). A unique guitar-picking style (*ukupika*) is central to the instrumental sound, though it's often overshadowed these days by a hammily played electric keyboard. Each song starts with the *izihlabo* (an instrumental flourish), followed by the main melody, which is interrupted by the lead singer's *ukubonga*, a fast-spoken declamation, usually in deep rural Zulu, that always used to be some kind of praise poem, but could just as well in modern songs be a denunciation of a woman's cooking pot. For particularly fine examples of the art, look out for **Phuz'khemisi** and the late, great **Mfaz'Omnyama**. Another star of the neo-traditional scene, and also an *Ezodumo* regular, is the queen of Ndebele music, **Nothembi.** As well as being a talented and veteran performer, Nothembi is also known for her sensational outfits, decorated with intricate bead and metalwork.

Jazz

Ever since its main exponents went into self-imposed exile in the 1960s, **South African jazz** has been the music most associated with the struggle against apartheid. Musically, though, the sound of the exiles represented a departure from the indigenous *marabi* jazz of the 1950s (see below), and a move in the direction of the American avant-garde, as personified by Thelonious Monk, Sonny Rollins and John Coltrane. The two prime exponents of this new fusion were the **Jazz Epistles**, featuring Hugh Masekela, Jonas Gwangwa, Abdullah Ibrahim (then called Dollar Brand) and the great Kippie Moeketsi, and the **Blue Notes**, who included in their line-up Chris McGregor and Dudu Pukwana. Most of the Epistles left South Africa in 1960, and the Blue Notes left in 1964. During their exile, South African jazz musicians sought to reincorporate South African styles, and *mbaqanga* in particular, into their repertoire. Today, the exiled artists, including **Miriam Makeba** and **Hugh Masekela** are back home, at last receiving the recognition and respect they have long deserved. Some, like **Ibrahim** and **Winston "Mankunku" Ngozi**, continue to perform fairly regularly and you should catch them if you get the chance.

Ironically, you may find more opportunity to hear **marabi jazz** than the old new-wave, thanks to the dedicated gigging of the elderly but tireless **African Jazz Pioneers** and **Elite Swingsters**, often featuring Dorothy Rathebe on vocals. When it first emerged in the 1920s, *marabi* was the music of the black Johannesburg slums, played on pianos in *shebeens*. Always revolving around a simple three-chord structure, *marabi* developed in the 1930s, with guitars, banjos and concertinas added to the line-up. In the 1940s, American swing jazz hit

South Africa and it was the fusion of swing and *marabi* that led to *marabi* jazz.

A new generation of jazz musicians has emerged in South Africa, keen to move beyond nostalgia, *marabi* and 1960s-style avant-garde, often drawing instead for inspiration on American West Coast fusion. Virtuoso pianist **Bheki Mseleku** has elected to stay in London, but hard at work back home are artists like the talented young bassist **Sipho Gumede** and ultra-smooth keyboard player **Don Laka**. Pianist **Moses Taiwa Molelekwa** pursued an interesting route, fusing jazz with techno beats, but his career was tragically cut short by his suicide in early 2001. You can almost always find jazz performances in Johannesburg, Pretoria or Cape Town on virtually any weekend of the year, and sometimes midweek too – check the press for details.

Political music

With the collapse of apartheid and the accession to power of the ANC, the heyday of South African **political song** has passed. With lyrics singing the praises of Umkhonto weSizwe (the armed wing of the ANC), or stating bluntly that "*uMama uyajabula uma ngibulala iBhunu*" ("My mother is happy when I kill a Boer"), the songs were performed during marches, demonstrations, rallies and most of all at the funerals of slain activists, usually accompanied by the *toyi-toyi*. This combination of a march and a dance is performed on the spot or on the move, with knees brought high, and is still widely used, but the old songs don't really fit any more, and you rarely hear them today.

Mzwakhe Mbuli made his name in the 1980s as "the people's poet", performing his articulate and angry political poetry at countless rallies around the country. His house was firebombed by the authorities, and Mzwakhe himself was harassed and detained, but his poetry remained defiant, with titles like *Unbroken Spirit* and *Now is the Time*. In 1989, Mzwakhe correctly discerned the signs of the times, proclaiming in one poem that "the bull is dying at last, kicking at random", and in the following year, while celebrating Mandela's release, he urged prophetically: "When you vote and get elected, think of those who died."

After the 1994 elections, Mzwakhe was for a time a contented man, asking disillusioned compatriots, "if this is not the time for happiness, when is?", while also using his poetry to urge an end to social ills like criminality and drug addiction. However, Mzwakhe is today serving a long sentence in a maximum security prison in the company of apartheid mass murderers like Eugene de Kock, after being convicted of armed robbery. Mzwakhe insists he has been framed; most of his former comrades have failed to visit him in prison, and he is reported to have prepared some incisive poetry for them when he is eventually released.

Boeremusiek

Boeremusiek is what is left of Afrikaans folk music, originating in Dutch and French folk music, but heavily influenced over the years by American country and hillbilly music, with the legendary **Jim Reeves** standing out as a major hero of the scene. These days, it's definitely easy listening and deeply sentimental, with the style's most successful practitioner **Bles Bridges** famous for throwing roses, Barry Manilow-style, into the arms of his adoring fans. The jazz-tinged concertina virtuosity of the veteran **Nico Carstens** can be interesting, and particularly his experimental fusions with *mbaqanga*, which he calls *Boereqanga*. **Koos Kombuis** champions a blend of rock and Afrikaans music, though the lyrics are the key thing here and just listening to the rather average instrumentation is not much compensation.

White rock

It has long been the lament of **white rock** musicians in South Africa that no one in Europe or America will take them seriously, and that 95 percent of South Africans will never be interested in what they are up to. However, the wonderfully named, but sadly disbanded, **Springbok Nude Girls** did manage to build a solid overseas following to add to their adoring fan base at home, and hard-rock act **Saron Gas** have recently signed a lucrative US recording contract. Also of interest are the funky **Wonderboom**, Pearl Jam sound-alikes **Zen Arcade**, Gauteng-based punk rockers **Diesel Arcade**, and one of the country's best experimental acts, the fast-paced "munki-punkers" **Boo!**. New bands spring up all the time in all the major cities, and even though most of their music is derivative and poorly executed, every so often you hit upon a gem.

Discography

Bubblegum

Yvonne Chaka Chaka *The Best Of...* (Teal, SA). Pretty much all the 1980s disco-style Yvonne you need, including her biggest hit *Umqombothi*.

Sello "Chicco" Twala *The Best Of...* (Teal, SA). A fair selection of Chicco's biggest bubblegum.

Contemporary folk

Bayete *Umkhaya-Lo* (Polygram, SA). A seminal fusion of South African sounds with laid-back soul and funk, blended by lead singer Jabu Khanyile's unique mixing talent and spiced with his beautifully soothing vocals.

Yvonne Chaka Chaka *Bambani* (Teal, SA). The album bombed commercially, yet is Yvonne's most adult,

intricate and interesting ever release, mixing a range of traditional styles and featuring wonderful melodies.

Ringo *Sondelani* (CCP, SA). A superb modern reworking of traditional Xhosa sounds by this bald Capetonian heart throb, including the hit track *Sondela*, which has become one of South Africa's most popular love songs.

Gospel

Amadodana Ase Wesile *Morena U Ba Elele* (Gallo, SA). A representative offering of spiritual anthems from this popular Methodist male choir, who wear blazers and red waistcoats, keep time by thumping a Bible, and can make huge congregations sway and sing as one.

Choirs of South Africa *Choirs of South Africa* (Roi Music, SA). Stirring gospel anthems delivered by mass choirs with exuberance and power. All that's missing is the visual spectacle of their members dressed in flowing garments and swaying to the mighty sounds.

Imvuselelo Yase Natali *Izigi* (BMG, SA). One of the most extraordinary gospel acts in South Africa, fronted by the charismatic and, at times, plain bizarre Reverend Makitaza. If you ever get the chance to see this group, don't miss them.

IPCC *Ummeli Wethu* (Gallo, SA). An excellent offering from one of South Africa's most popular gospel choirs, replete with charisma, powerful sounds and stunning melodies.

Joyous Celebration *Volumes 1–5* (Sony, SA). Five albums of classic gospel from some of South Africa's

finest gospel artists, taken from their seemingly endless roadshow around the country, where they play to packed audiences everywhere.

Lord Comforters *Ubukhulu Bakho* (CCP, SA). Gentle, moving mid-tempo gospel sounds from this strong-voiced, popular gospel choir.

Lundi *Phaphamani* (EMI, SA). The latest release of heart-rending tunes from this young Malope protégé, who is slowly beginning to develop his own sound.

Rebecca Malope *Shwele Baba* (CCP, SA). One of Rebecca's finest albums, with the title track a strong contender for her best-ever song and the rest of the cuts all pretty good too.

Solly Moholo *Motlhang ke Kolobetswa "Die poppe sal dans"* (CCP, SA). A beautiful release from the country's finest Sotho gospel artist.

Various Artists *Gospel Spirit of Africa* (Gallo, S A). An excellent compilation of most of South Africa's top current gospel choirs, including Ladysmith Black Mambazo, the Holy Cross Choir, and the Holy Brothers.

Jazz

Dollar Brand *Voice of Africa, African Sun, Tetenya* and *Blues for a Hip King* (Kaz, UK). Virtually definitive four-album compilation of the best of Abdullah Ibrahim's (Dollar Brand) prodigious output, including the seminal *Mannenberg (Is Where It's Happening). Township One More Time* (EMI, South Africa) is Ibrahim's latest offering, and as the title suggests, is a return to his older, more accessible ways. It includes a superb version

of the anthem *Shosholoza*.

Errol Dyers *Sonesta* (Nkomo, S A). Dyers is a smooth, fusion-oriented guitarist, who tends to be too laid-back for his own good, but who comes to life for the superb Latin-influenced title track.

Sipho Gumede *Down Freedom Avenue* (B&W, UK). Intriguing jazz fusion from this accomplished bassist at the cutting edge of the new South African jazz sound.

Jazz Epistles *Verse One* (Celluloid, France). Seminal recordings of this great South African jazz band, featuring Hugh Masekela, Kippie Moeketsi, Jonas Gwangwa and Dollar Brand.

Jazz Pioneers *Sip 'n' Fly* (Flametree, UK). Well-paced old-style *marabi* jazz by the veterans of the art.

Sibongile Khumalo *Ancient Evenings* (Sony, SA). Though a classically trained opera singer, Khumalo takes on both jazz and a variety of traditional melodies in this wonderful album that demonstrates clearly why she is currently one of South Africa's best-loved singers.

Don Laka *Destiny* (Sony, SA). Smooth, sophisticated sounds from this talented, sharp-dressing young pianist.

Miriam Makeba and the Skylarks *Miriam Makeba and the Skylarks* (Teal, SA). Two-CD set of 32 great recordings of South Africa's queen of song, from the 1950s.

Winston Mankunku *Yakal'Inkomo* (Polygram, SA). Coltrane's influence on this stalwart of the jazz scene is palpable, and successfully fused by Mankunku on this release with some classic township melodies.

Hugh Masekela *The Collection* (Connoisseur, UK). Good budget-price compilation of Masekela's 1960s and 1970s hits. Masekela scored a deserved hit in the late 1990s with *Black to the Future* (Sony, SA), which includes the excellent track *Chileshe* – an impassioned plea to his countrymen to discard their intense xenophobia towards African immigrants.

Moses Taiwa Molelekwa *Genes and Spirits* (Melt2000, UK). Fascinating jazz/drum'n'bass fusion by this talented young pianist.

Philip Tabana and Malomobo *Unh!* (Elektra Nonesuch), *Ke a Bereka* (Tusk, SA). The masterful guitarist with a sound and a style entirely his own does his individualistic take on Afro-jazz. The second release veers in a more traditional direction, but is still unmistakably Tabana.

Kwaito

Alaska *Most Wanted* (Sony, SA). Well-produced, ultra-stylish *kwaito* from this well-dressed foursome, featuring great beats and some particularly impenetrable ghetto lyrics.

Arthur *Die Poppe Sal Dans* (CCP, SA). One of the best releases of this prolific artist and producer who came to fame with the controversial hit *Don't call me Kaffir*, this time stirring up a storm once more with *Voetsek* ("fuck off" in Afrikaans).

Bongo Muffin *Bongolution* (Sony, SA). The latest release from this popular artist who combines Jamaican-style ragga lyrics with more typical *kwaito* beats, including the catchy hit single, *The Way Kungakhona*.

Brenda Fassie *Mama* (CCP, SA); Great late-1980s tunes from South Africa's very own Madonna. *Memeza* (CCP, SA) features the massive hit *Vul'Ndlela*, and is Brenda's most successful ever album, closely followed by the compelling *Nomakanjani?* (CCP, SA). Brenda's latest, *Mina*

Nawe (CCP, SA), is less original, but still very danceable.

Makhendlas *Jammer* (CCP, SA). Features two massive hits, *Emenwe* and *Ayeye Aho*, from Arthur's brother, who tragically shot himself immediately after killing a troublesome fan after a gig in late 1998.

Mandoza *Godoba* (EMI, SA). The follow-up to Mandoza's massively successful *Nakalakata*, featuring more of his trade-mark hard rock-*kwaito* fusion.

M'Du *No Pas No Special* (Sony, SA). A popular though somewhat downbeat album from one of *kwaito*'s most enduring stars.

TKZee *Halloween* (BMG, SA). A solid early offering from these popular *kwaito* artists, complete with their trademark catchy anthems and R&B-based sounds, and unmatched by their recent more disappointing output.

Trompies *Boostin' Kabelz* (Sony, SA). Kicking sounds from one of the coolest *kwaito* acts on the circuit, including the irresistible *Di Potsotso*. A perfect follow-up to their earlier hit release *Mapantsula*.

Various Artists *Yizo Yizo Volumes 1&2* (CCP, SA). The soundtrack to South Africa's hippest TV drama, with cuts from virtually every major *kwaito* artist.

Zola *Mdlwembe* (EMI, SA). The first solo album of "Mr Ghetto Fabulous", full of menacing rhythms and including the surprise gospel hit *Mzione*.

Mbaqanga

Mahlathini and the Mahotella Queens *Thokolize* (Earthworks, UK). Perfect introduction to the 1980s sound of this most stomping of *mbaqanga* outfits.

Soul Brothers *Jive Soweto* (Earthworks, UK). Good compilation of all the Soul Brothers tunes that matter, including their masterly title track that still goes down a storm in South Africa.

Various Artists *Zulu Jive* (Earthworks, UK; Carthage, US). Good selection of early 1980s cuts, mostly from Zulul *mbaqanga* ace Joshua Sithole, as well as more traditional stompers from Aaron Mbambo and Shoba.

Neo-traditional

Amampondo *Drums for Tomorrow* (Melt2000, UK). South Africa's most famous marimba (xylophone) band deliver a fine and well-produced set here, full of their distinctive Xhosa melodies and powerful polyrhythms.

Ladysmith Black Mambazo *The Best of...* (Shanachie, US). Respectable introduction to a group who have never put a musical foot wrong, and whose back catalogue is gratifyingly mostly available.

Ladysmith Black Mambazo Ne Nzalabantu *Ukuzala-Ukuzelula* (Gallo, SA). The album features Ladysmith in combination with some great female singers, providing a rare recorded showcase for the powerful Zulu women's choral sound.

Mfaz'Omnyama *Ngisebenzile Mama* (Gallo, SA). The title means "I have been working, Mum", and is amply justified by this superb set, featuring some of the best-ever recorded *maskanda*.

Busi Mhlongo *UrbanZulu* (Melt2000, UK). Classic Zulu *maskanda* from this powerful *sangoma* (traditional healer), immaculately produced by an innovative British label fast making a name for itself as one of the best sources of contemporary South African music around.

Nothembi *Akanamandl' Usathana* (Gallo, SA). Beautiful guitar-driven sounds from the Ndebele music queen, with a cover showing

Nothembi in one of her impressive traditional outfits.

Phuz'khemisi *Nginenkinga* (Gallo, SA). The latest offering from the reigning *maskanda* champion, complete with stunning guitar work, great vocals and murderous bass lines.

Various Artists *The Heartbeat of Soweto* (Shanachie, US). Misleading title for this fine collection of Zulu, Shangaan and Tsonga traditional styles.

Various Artists *Singing in an Open Space* (Rounder, US). Superb compilation of Zulu traditional styles by Gallo's guru Rob Allingham.

Political music

Mzwakhe Mbuli *Resistance is Defence* (Earthworks, UK). Great sample of the militant lyricism of the

people's poet, including a moving ode to Mandela's release.

Rap and reggae

Lucky Dube *Prisoner* (Shanachie, US). South Africa's biggest-selling album ever, full of stirring Peter Tosh-style roots tunes.

Prophets of Da City *Ghetto Code* (Polygram, SA). South Africa's rap supremos' finest release, full of tough but articulate rhymes and some seriously funky backing tracks to wash them down with, all in true Cape Flats style.

White rock

James Phillips *Made in SA* (Shifty/Tic Tic Bang, SA). A collection of the best of this seminal singer, songwriter and bandleader, who died in 1995, from late-1970s punk-style protest to 1980s rock and 1990s R&B, tackling the complexities and nuances of South African society.

Pressure Cookies *Swallow!* (Shifty/Tic Tic Bang, SA). All-grrrl group with sharply observed songs delivered in refreshingly bouncy manner.

Springbok Nude Girls *Afterlife Satisfaction* (Sony, SA). One of South Africa's most popular white bands deliver a powerful, if not particularly original, belting rock set.

Wonderboom *Never Ever Ever* (David Gresham, SA). Medium-paced and grungy funk rock from this danceable though somewhat derivative outfit.

Compilations

Various Artists *From Marabi to Disco* (Gallo, SA). Quite simply the best South African music compilation around, with superb tracks and informative sleeve notes taking you from the 1930s to the 1980s.

Various Artists *The Indestructible Beat of Soweto Volumes 1–4* (Earthworks, UK). Superb compilation, mainly featuring 1980s *mbaqanga*, along with a few more traditional samples. As the compiler Trevor Herman writes, "best heard loud and standing up".

language

language

Language

South Africa has eleven official languages, all of which have equal status under the law. In practice, however, English is the *lingua franca* that dominates politics, commerce and the media. If you're staying in the main cities and national parks you'll rarely, if ever, need to use any other language. Afrikaans, although a language you seldom need to speak, nevertheless remains very much in evidence and you will certainly encounter it on official forms and countless signs particularly on the road; for this reason we give a comprehensive list of written Afrikaans terms you could come across.

With nine official indigenous African languages and several unofficial ones, unless you're planning on staying a very long time, there's little point trying to get to grips with the whole gamut, and even progressing beyond the absolute fundamentals of one of these languages is likely to be a challenge. Having said this, it's always useful to know a few phrases of the local indigenous language, especially greetings – a gesture that will always be appreciated even if you aren't able to carry your foray through to a proper conversation. For basic greetings in English and of the six other most commonly used languages, see the box on p.914.

The nine official African languages are split into four groups. Nguni, which consists of Zulu, Xhosa, siSwati and Ndebele; Sotho, which comprises Northern Sotho, Southern Sotho (or Sesotho) and Tswana; and Venda and Tsonga. Most people speak languages in the first two groups. In common with all indigenous southern African languages, these operate under very different principles to European languages in that their sentences are dominated by the noun, with which the other words, such as verbs and adjectives, must agree in person, gender, number or case. Known as concordal agreement, this is achieved by supplementing word stems (the basic element of each word) with prefixes or suffixes to change meaning.

If you're in KwaZulu-Natal, it's worth investing in one of the Zulu language cassettes available in bookshops. These can easily help you to master the basic phrases we've listed. Tapes for other languages can be more difficult to come by, but it's always worth checking out bookshops.

English

South African English is a mixed bag, one language with many variants. Forty percent of whites are mother-tongue English speakers, many of whom believe that they are (or at least should be) speaking standard British English. In fact, South African English has its own distinct character, and is as different from the Queen's English as is Australian. Its most notable characteristic is its huge and rich vocabulary, with unique words and usages, some drawn from Afrikaans and the indigenous African languages. The hefty *Oxford Dictionary of South African English* makes an interesting browse.

As a language used widely by non-native speakers, there is great **variation in pronounciation** and usage – largely a result of mother-tongue interference from other languages. Take for example the sentence "The bad bird sat on the bed", which speakers of some African languages (in which distinctions between English vowel sounds don't exist) might pronounce as "The bed bed set on the bed". While some English-speaking whites feel that their language is being mangled and misused, linguists argue that it is simply being transformed.

Afrikaans

Contrary to popular belief outside South Africa, the majority of **Afrikaans** speakers are not white but coloured, and the language, far from dying out, is in fact understood by more South Africans than any other language. It's the predominant tongue in the Western and Northern Cape provinces, and in the Free State is the language of the media.

Broadly speaking, Afrikaans is a dialect of Dutch, which became modified on the Cape frontier through its encounter with French, German and English settlers, and is peppered with words and phrases from indigenous tongues as well as languages used by slaves. Some historians argue, very plausibly, that Afrikaans was first written in Arabic script in the early nineteenth century by Cape Muslims.

Despite this heritage, the language was used by Afrikaners from the late nineteenth century onwards as a key element in the construction of their racially exclusive ethnic identity. The attempt by the apartheid government in 1976 to make Afrikaans the medium of instruction in black schools, which led to the Soweto uprising, confirmed the hated status of the language for many urban Africans, which persists to this day.

Afrikaans signs

Bed en Ontbyt Bed and breakfast
Derde Third
Dankie Thank you
Doeane Customs
Drankwinkel Liquor shop
Droe vrugte Dry fruit
Eerste First
Fruit Vrugte
Geen ingang No entry
Gevaar Danger
Grens Border
Hoof Main
Hoog High
Ingang Entry
Inligting Information
Kantoor Office
Kerk Church
Kort Short
Links Left
Lughawe Airport
Mans Men
Mark Market
Ompad Detour
Pad Road
Padwerke voor Road works ahead

Pastorie Parsonage
Perron Platform (train station)
Plaas Farm
Poskantoor Post office
Regs Right
Ry Go
Sentrum Centre
Singel Crescent
Slaghuis Butcher
Stadig Slow
Stad City
Stad sentrum City/town centre
Stasie Station
Straat Street
Strand Beach
Swembad Swimming pool
Toegang Admission
Tweede Second
Verbode Prohibited
Verkeer Traffic
Versigtig Carefully
Vierde Fourth
Vrouens Women
Vyfde Fifth

The Nguni group

In common with Southern Sotho, the **Nguni language group** contains a few clicks adopted from San languages, which are difficult for speakers of European languages, but can be mastered with practice.

Zulu (or isiZulu), the most widely spoken black African language in South Africa, is understood by around twelve million people. It's the mother tongue of residents of the southeastern parts of the country, including the whole of KwaZulu-Natal, the eastern Free State, southern Mpumalanga and Gauteng. Some linguists believe that Zulu's broad reach could make it an alternative to English as a South African *lingua franca*. Don't confuse Zulu with **Fanakalo**, which is a pidgin Zulu mixed with other languages. Still sometimes spoken on the mines, it is not popular with most Zulu speakers, though many white South Africans tend to believe it is.

For all practical purposes, **siSwati**, the language spoken in Swaziland, is almost identical to Zulu, but for historical reasons has developed its own identity.

The same applies to **Ndebele**, which shares around 95 percent in common with Zulu. It broke off from Zulu (around the same time as siSwati), when a group of Zulu-speakers fled north to escape the expansionism of Shaka. Ndebele is now spoken in pockets of Gauteng and Northwest provinces as well as throughout southern Zimbabwe.

Xhosa is Nelson Mandela's mother tongue, which he shares with seven million other South Africans, predominantly in the Eastern Cape, but the language is also spoken by Africans in the Western Cape, most of whom are concentrated in Cape Town.

The Sotho group

Northern Sotho, Southern Sotho (or Sesotho) and Tswana are members of the **Sotho language group**. As with the Nguni languages, the distinctions between these owe more to history, politics and geography than to pure linguistic factors; speakers of some Northern Sotho dialects can understand some dialects of Tswana more readily than they can other Northern Sotho dialects.

Northern Sotho dialects, which are numerous and diverse, are spoken by around 2.5 million people in a huge arc in the northwestern region of South Africa that takes in the country around the Kruger National Park, around to the Botswana border and south from there to Pretoria. **Southern Sotho**, one of the first African languages to be written, is spoken in the Free State, parts of Gauteng, as well as Lesotho and the areas of the Eastern Cape bordering it.

Tswana, also characterized by a great diversity of dialects, is geographically the most widespread language in southern Africa. The principle language of Botswana, in South Africa it's dialects are dispersed through the Northern Cape, the Free State and Northwest provinces.

Basic greetings and farewells

ENGLISH	AFRIKAANS	NORTHERN SOTHO	SESOTHO	TSWANA	XHOSA	ZULU
Yes	Ja	Ee	Ei	Ee	Ewe	Yebo
No	Nee	Aowa	Tjhe	Nnyaa	Hayi	Cha
Please	Asseblief	Hle.../...hle	(Ka kopo) hle	Tsweetswee	Nceda	Uxolo
Thank you	Dankie	Ke a leboga	Ke a leboha	Ke a leboga	Enkosi	Ngiyabonga
Excuse me	Verskoon my	Tshwarelo	Ntshwaerele	Intshwarele	Uxolo	Uxolo
Good morning	Goiemore	Thobela/dumela	Dumela (ng)	Dumela	Molo/bhota	Sawubona
Good afternoon	Goeiemiddag	Thobela/dumela	Dumela (ng)	Dumela	Molo/bhoto	Sawubona
Good evening	Goeinaand	Thobela/dumela	Fonaneng	Dumela	Molo/bhota	Sawubona
Goodbye	Totsiens	Sala gabotse/ sepele gabotse	Sala(ng) hantle	Sala sentle	Nisale kakuhle	Sala kahle
See you later	Sien jou later	Re tla bonana	Re tla bonana	Ke tla go bona	Sobe sibonane	Sizobanana
Until we meet again	Totsiens	Go fihla re kopana gape	ho fihlela re bonana	Go fitlhelela re bonana gape	De sibonane kwakhona	Size sibonane
How do you do?	Aangename kennis?	Ke leboga go le tseba	Ke thabela ho o tseba	O tsogile jang?	Kunjani	Ninjani?
How are you?	Hoe gaan dit?	Le kae?	O/le sa phela?	O tsogile jang?	Kunjani?	Ninjani?
I'm fine, thanks	Goed dankie	Re gona	Ke phela hantle	Ke tsogile sentle	Ndiphilile, enkosi	Ngisaphila

Glossary

African Indigenous South African, distinct from "black"

Apartheid Term used from the 1940s for the National Party's official policy of "racial separation"

Arvie Afternoon

Assegai Short stabbing spear introduced by Shaka to the Zulu armies

Baai Afrikaans suffix meaning "bay", used in place names eg Stilbaai

Bakkie Light truck or van

Bantustan Term used under apartheid for the territories such as Transkei reserved for members of the African linguistic groups

Bergie A vagrant living on the slopes of Table Mountain in Cape Town

Biltong Sun-dried salted strip of meat, chewed as a snack

Boerekos Farm food, usually consisting of loads of meat and vegetables cooked using butter and sugar

Boerewors Spicy lengths of sausage that are *de rigueur* at braais

Bokkoms Dried fish, much like salt fish or fish *biltong*

Boland Southern part of the Western Cape

Boy Offensive term used to refer to an adult African man who is a servant

Braai Barbecue

Bredie Vegetable and meat stew

Bundu Wilderness or back country

Bush See *bundu*

Bushveld Country composed largely of thorny bush

Cape Dutch Nineteenth-century, white-washed, gabled style of architecture

Ciskei Eastern Cape region west of the Kei River declared a "self-governing territory" for Xhosa speakers in 1972 and now fully reincorporated into South Africa

Cocopan Small tip truck on rails used to transport gold ore

Coloured Mulattos or people of mixed race

Dagga Marijuana

Dagha Mud used in traditional indigenous construction

Dankie Thank you (Afrikaans origin)

Dassie Hyrax

Dominee Reverend (abbreviated to DS)

Donga Dry, eroded ditch

Dorp Country town or village (Afrikaans origin)

Drift Fording point in a river (Afrikaans origin)

Egoli Zulu name for Johannesburg (lit: "city of gold")

Fanakalo Unfashionable pidgin mixture of English, Zulu and Afrikaans taught to facilitate communication between white foremen and African workers on the mines or farms

Frikkadel Fried onion and meat balls

Fundi Expert

Fynbos Term for vast range of fine-leafed species that predominate in the southern part of the Western Cape (see p.850)

Gem squash Orange shaped (and sized) marrow

Girl Offensive term used to refer to an African woman who is a servant

Gogga Creepy crawly or insect

Group Areas Act Now defunct law passed in 1950 that provided for the establishment of separate areas for each "racial group"

Hanepoort Delicious sweet dessert grape

Highveld High-lying areas of Gauteng and Mpumalanga

Homeland See *bantustan*

Hottentot Now unfashionable term for indigenous Khoisan herders encountered by the first settlers at the Cape

Impi Zulu regiment

Indaba Zulu term meaning a group discussion and now used in South African English for any meeting or conference

Inkatha Fiercely nationalist Zulu political party, formed in 1928 as a cultural organization

Is it? Really?

Jislaaik! Exclamation equivalent to *geez!* or *crikey!*

Jol Party

Just now In a while

Kaffir Highly objectionable term of abuse for Africans

Karoo Arid plateau that occupies a large proportion of the South African interior

Khoikhoi Self-styled name of South Africa's original herding inhabitants

Kloof Ravine or gorge

Knobkerrie Wooden club

Koeksister Deep-fried plaited doughnut, dripping with syrup

Kopje Dutch spelling of *koppie*

Koppie Hillock

Kraal Enclosure of huts for farm animals or collection of traditional huts occupied by an extended family

Kramat Shrine of a Muslim holy man

Krans Sheer cliff face

Lapa Courtyard of group of Ndebele houses; also used to described an enclosed area where *braais* are held at safari camps

Lebowa Now defunct homeland for North Sotho speakers

Lekker Nice

Location Old-fashioned term for segregated African area on the outskirts of a town or farm

Lowveld Low-lying subtropical region of Mpumalanga and Northern Province

Malay Misnomer for Cape Muslims of Asian descent

Mealie See *mielie*

Melktert Traditional Cape custard pie

Mielie Maize

MK Umkhonto we Sizwe (Spear of the Nation), the armed wing of the ANC, now incorporated into the national army

Naartjie Tangerine or mandarin

Nek Saddle between two mountains

Nguni Group of southeastern Bantu-speaking people comprising Zulu, Xhosa and Swazi

Nkosi Sikelel 'i Afrika "God Bless Africa", anthem of the ANC and now of South Africa

Nyanga Traditional healer

Pawpaw Papaya

Pastorie Parsonage (Afrikaans origin)

Platteland Country districts (Afrikaans origin)

Poort Narrow pass through mountains along river course

Pronk Characteristic jump of springbok or impala antelope

Protea National flower of South Africa

Qwaqwa Now defunct homeland for South Sotho speakers

Raadsaal Council or parliament building

Restcamp Accommodation for visitors to national parks

Robot Traffic light

Rondavel Circular building based on traditional African huts

Rooibos tea Indigenous herbal tea

SABC South African Broadcasting Authority

Shebeen Unlicensed tavern

Shell Ultra City Clean, bright stops along major national roads, with a filling station, restaurant, shop and sometimes a hotel.

Sjambok Rawhide whip

Skelm Villain

Snoek Large fish that features in many traditional Cape recipes

Spaza shops Small temporary stalls/shops

Sosatie Spicy skewered mince

Stoep Verandah

Tackie Sneakers or plimsolls

Township Areas set aside under apartheid for Africans

Transkei Now defunct homeland for Xhosa speakers

Tsostsie Villain

Van der Hum South African *naartjie*-flavoured liqueur

Velskoen Rough suede shoes

Vetkoek Deep-fried doughnut-like cake

Vlei Swamp

VOC Verenigde Oostindische Compagnie, the Dutch East India Company.

index

and small print

Index

Map entries are in colour

INDEX

N

O

Twenty Years of Rough Guides

In the summer of 1981, Mark Ellingham, Rough Guides' founder, knocked out the first guide on a typewriter, with a group of friends. Mark had been travelling in Greece after university, and couldn't find a guidebook that really answered his needs.There were heavyweight cultural guides on the one hand – good on museums and classical sites but not on beaches and tavernas – and on the other hand student manuals that were so caught up with how to save money that they lost sight of the country's significance beyond its role as a place for a cool vacation. None of the guides began to address Greece as a country, with its natural and human environment, its politics and its contemporary life.

Having no urgent reason to return home, Mark decided to write his own guide. It was a guide to Greece that tried to combine some erudition and insight with a thoroughly practical approach to travellers' needs. Scrupulously researched listings of places to stay, eat and drink were matched by careful attention to detail on everything from Homer to Greek music, from classical sites to national parks and from nude beaches to monasteries. Back in London, Mark and his friends got their Rough Guide accepted by a farsighted commissioning editor at the publisher Routledge and it came out in 1982.

The Rough Guide to Greece was a student scheme that became a publishing phenomenon. The immediate success of the book – shortlisted for the Thomas Cook award – spawned a series that rapidly covered dozens of countries. The Rough Guides found a ready market among backpackers and budget travellers, but soon acquired a much broader readership that included older and less impecunious visitors. Readers relished the guides' wit and inquisitiveness as much as the enthusiastic, critical approach that acknowledges everyone wants value for money – but not at any price.

Rough Guides soon began supplementing the "rougher" information – the hostel and low-budget listings – with the kind of detail that independent-minded travellers on any budget might expect. These days, the guides – distributed worldwide by the Penguin group – include recommendations spanning the range from shoestring to luxury, and cover more than 200 destinations around the globe. Our growing team of authors, many of whom come to Rough Guides initially as outstandingly good letter-writers telling us about their travels, are spread all over the world, particularly in Europe, the USA and Australia. As well as the travel guides, Rough Guides publishes a series of dictionary phrasebooks covering two dozen major languages, an acclaimed series of music guides running the gamut from Classical to World Music, a series of music CDs in association with World Music Network, and a range of reference books on topics as diverse as the Internet, Pregnancy and Unexplained Phenomena. Visit **www.roughguides.com** to see what's cooking.

Rough Guide credits

Text editor: Fran Sandham
Series editor: Mark Ellingham
Editorial: Martin Dunford, Jonathan Buckley, Kate Berens, Ann-Marie Shaw, Helena Smith, Judith Bamber, Orla Duane, Olivia Eccleshall, Ruth Blackmore, Geoff Howard, Claire Saunders, Gavin Thomas, Alexander Mark Rogers, Polly Thomas, Joe Staines, Richard Lim, Duncan Clark, Peter Buckley, Lucy Ratcliffe, Clifton Wilkinson, Alison Murchie, Matthew Teller, Andrew Dickson (UK); Andrew Rosenberg, Stephen Timblin, Yuki Takagaki, Richard Koss, Hunter Slaton, Julie Feiner (US)
Production: Susanne Hillen, Andy Hilliard, Link Hall, Helen Prior, Julia Bovis, Michelle Draycott, Katie Pringle, Zoë Nobes, Rachel

Holmes, Andy Turner
Cartography: Melissa Baker, Maxine Repath, Ed Wright, Katie Lloyd-Jones
Cover art direction: Louise Boulton
Picture research: Sharon Martins, Mark Thomas
Online: Kelly Cross, Anja Mutic-Blessing, Jennifer Gold, Audra Epstein, Suzanne Welles, Cree Lawson (US)
Finance: John Fisher, Gary Singh, Edward Downey, Mark Hall, Tim Bill
Marketing & Publicity: Richard Trillo, Niki Smith, David Wearn, Chloë Roberts, Demelza Dallow, Claire Southern (UK); Simon Carloss, David Wechsler, Kathleen Rushforth (US)
Administration: Tania Hummel, Julie Sanderson

Publishing information

This 3rd edition published June 2002 by
Rough Guides Ltd,
62–70 Shorts Gardens, London WC2H 9AH.
Penguin Putnam, Inc. 375 Hudson Street, NY 10014, USA.
Distributed by the Penguin Group
Penguin Books Ltd,
80 Strand, London WC2R ORL
Penguin Putnam, Inc.
375 Hudson Street, NY 10014, USA
Penguin Books Australia Ltd,
487 Maroondah Highway, PO Box 257, Ringwood, Victoria 3134, Australia
Penguin Books Canada Ltd,
10 Alcorn Avenue, Toronto, Ontario, Canada M4V 1E4
Penguin Books (NZ) Ltd,
182–190 Wairau Road, Auckland 10, New Zealand
Typeset in Bembo and Helvetica to an original design by Henry Iles.

Printed in Italy by LegoPrint S.p.A

©Tony Pinchuck, Barbara McCrea, Donald Reid and Greg Mthembu-Salter 2002

976pp includes index
A catalogue record for this book is available from the British Library

ISBN 1-85828-853-3

The publishers and authors have done their best to ensure the accuracy and currency of all the information in **The Rough Guide to South Africa, Lesotho & Swaziland**, however, they can accept no responsibility for any loss, injury, or inconvenience sustained by any traveller as a result of information or advice contained in the guide.

Help us update

We've gone to a lot of effort to ensure that the 3rd edition of **The Rough Guide to South Africa, Lesotho & Swaziland** is accurate and up-to-date. However, things change – places get "discovered", opening hours are notoriously fickle, restaurants and rooms raise prices or lower standards. If you feel we've got it wrong or left something out, we'd like to know, and if you can remember the address, the price, the time, the phone number, so much the better.

We'll credit all contributions, and send a copy of the next edition (or any other Rough Guide if you prefer) for the best letters. Everyone who writes to us and isn't already a subscriber will receive a copy of our full-colour thrice-yearly newsletter. Please mark letters: "**Rough Guide South Africa, Lesotho & Swaziland Update**" and send to: Rough Guides, 62–70 Shorts Gardens, London WC2H 9AH, or Rough Guides, 4th Floor, 345 Hudson St, New York, NY 10014. Or send an email to:
mail@roughguides.co.uk or
mail@roughguides.com

Acknowledgements

Barbara and Tony would like to thank our editor, Fran Sandham, for his tireless efforts, good humour and patience in dealing with pesky authors and a huge project, and a special thanks to Donald Reid for being all one could hope for from a co-author and for being a good friend. Thanks too, to our mothers for their support, especially Lily for many afternoons of child-minding; Peta Lee, Bron Kaplan and Robert McCrea for great work on the KwaZulu-Natal chapter; Martie Malan and Dina Fisher at SA National Parks for arranging accommodation at the Kruger National Park; Erick van Zyl at SA Tourism for his efficiency in arranging flights through SA Express airline; Stephen Watson for his comments and additions to the literature section; the inexhaustible Japie for intelligence on Bloemfontein; Dave Bristow for his ever-cheerful and well-informed advice; the Beckers at *Nkorho Bushcamp*; *Chitwa Chitwa Camp*; Inathi Mqoboli at East London Tourism; Off Beat Safaris for a memorable horse ride; Stanley Singer for help with Cape Town restaurants; Ida Cooper; Beneta Bester for West Coast and Cederberg arrangements; Pam Nel at Nelshof in Hermanus; the Fenwicks at *Agulhas Guest House*; Nina Mackenzie at *Drift Water Lodge*; Koos and Petro Pieters at Paternoster; Grant and Marie Burton at *The Retreat*, Groenfontein; Isabe Fourie at Busy Bee, Oudtshoorn; Monkeyland; Richard and Stella Sohn at Narnia Farm; Brandon at Port St Johns; Marylin at Zoete Inval, Hermanus; the Holmans at *Wetlands Guest House*; Judy Meeser; William and Liezel Ross; Steve Roberts at Cremorne Estate; Jeff Rosenberg at *Sabi Sun Hotel*; Bea Struwig at Veldrif Tourism; Marianne Wicht at *Blue Bay Lodge*, Saldanha; Bill Mitchell at Ou Drif Farm; Don at the Jetty, Port St Johns; Hugh Tyrell; Ben Maclennan; Michelle Broster; Eleanor Kulain at Clanwilliam; *The Point Hotel*, Mossel Bay; Nita Ross for her invaluable help on the Transkei section; Inathi Mqoboli at East London Publicity; *Trennery's Hotel* at Qolora Mouth; *Ocean View Hotel*, Coffee Bay; Tanya Wilson; Jessica Wilson; Guy Berger; Yvette Thomas at the *Lodge on the Bay*; Steve Jaffe for information about the Cape Town theatre scene, Dr Debbie Young at the MTN Centre for Dolphin Studies; finally, all the unmentioned friends, readers and people we met on our travels who gave us their time and information.

Dedicated to our son, Gabriel, who put up with seemingly interminable journeys and managed to restrict his requests for "treats" to about fifteen-minute intervals; and for developing his new accommodation grading system based on the number of fans in the bedrooms.

Donald would like to thank all those who bring colour to the Deep South, including Oranje Jane, Joubs, Susan (and Teresa, though it's early days yet); Tracey, Isabella and Daniel (kings and queens of the castle); Derek in exile, Tony, Barbara and Gabriel for their whales, but just as much their continued inspiration and friendship; in eGoli, thanks for the loyal support and down-to-earth hospitality of Duncan, Trish, Owen and Wendy; to Helen, Ivan, Amy and Justin Suzor, and Ivy, for Base Camp a mile high; Janine and everyone at Penguin SA; Dirk and Johaan in Kimberley, Niel Stemmet, Henriette Engelbrecht, Vanessa and Heidi in Upington; Hendrick van Zyl in Nieuwoudtville; Gracia de Beer in Port Nolloth; His Excellency Jopie Kotze of Namaqualand; equally excellent Darron and Anita Raw in Swaziland; Ann Reilly, her bakkie and gang at Mlilwane; the Baz guys; Nthikeng Mohlele and colleagues at Gauteng Tourism Authority; Neil Fraser and Johannes van Breda (the only place I was mugged in Jo'burg); Di and Mick Jones at *Malealea Lodge*; Paul Middleton and Paul Jefferson in Maseru; Claire Beith, Andrea Rowlands, Tessa, Ant, Nina and Charles Baber, Mariska and Dawn at Makweti; Karen in Louis Trichardt; Dougie and Pam and Cammy in Pietersburg; Chris Lucas and Jaci van Heteren at Madikwe; and everyone else who helped along the way with beds, meals, wine, coffee, ideas, good leads, top tips and stories. Most of all, thanks and love to Mo, as ever, for ever.

The editor would like to thank Tony, Barbara and Donald for their consistently good work throughout the project, Andy Turner and Michelle Bhatia for typesetting, Sharon Martins for picture research, Jo Mead for proofreading, Katie Lloyd-Jones for cartography, Louise Boulton for covers, and Helena Smith for all her helpful suggestions.

SMALL PRINT

Readers' letters

Thanks to all the readers who took the trouble to write in with their comments and suggestions (and apologies to anyone whose name we've misspelt or omitted):

Sylvia M. Arber, James and Christine Atkins, Daniel Barber, Julia Bohanna, Melahat Behlil, Ursula Brown, Guy Bristow, Fran Cave, Andrew Clare, Dr Christie Clark, Gary Coleman, Neville Cornwell, Carolyn Cumming, Clive Cutter, Debs Cooke, P. Crusbridge, Cian Dean, Sarah de Rycke, Colin Dilland, Meg Edwards, Rosaline Erskine, Julia Ford, N. Fox, Lawrence Geary, Jim Godfrey for a mammoth letter; Sharon Harris (for two exceptional letters), Martin Hogg, Christine Kitch, Indra Jackson, Catherine Junor, Colin Little, Stephen Mendel, Dr Ursula Nusgen, Rosalinde Schut, Stephanie Shea, J. Shone, D. Stapleton-Cotton, Denise Stevens, M. Taylor, Tee Taylor, Philip Theo, Margaret van der Merwe, Monique Weschta, Sadie Wilcox, Beth Wooldridge.

Photo credits

Cover Credits

Main front image Kaaimans Bridge ©Image Bank
Front (small top image) Lesotho ©Robert Harding
Front (small bottom image) Quiver tree, Richtersveld National Park ©Robert Harding
Back (top) Giraffe ©Images Colour Library
Back (lower) Cederberg Mountains, South Africa ©Robert Harding

Colour introduction

Trumpeter in township ©Per-Anders Pettersson/iAfrika Photos
Cactus in front of traditional house ©Graeme Robinson/Cape Photo Library
Springbuck, Kgalagadi Transfrontier Park ©South African Tourism
White-painted Xhosa boys walking on road ©Per-Anders Pettersson/iAfrika Photos
Abseiling at Storm's River ©Jennifer Stern/Cape Photo Library
Bushman paintings, Drakensberg Battle Cave ©David Rogers/Cape Photo Library
Muizenberg Beach on a misty morning ©Alain Proust/Cape Photo Library

Things not to miss

1. Namaqualand ©South African Tourism
2. Drakensberg peaks ©Richard Van Tyneveld/Cape Photo Library
3. Aerial view of Robben Island with Table Mountain in background ©South African Tourism
4. Bo-Kaap ©Eric Miller/iAfrika Photos
5. Woman making pot ©Tian Wessels
6. Rafting on the Great Usutfu river ©Darron Raw/Swazi Trails
7. Wild dogs, Madikwe Game Reserve ©Ken Woods/Cape Photo Library
8. Jazz group in Rosebank ©Per-Anders Pettersson/iAfrika

9. Cape Point, Cape Peninsula ©South African Tourism
10. Whale breaching ©South African Tourism
11. Table Mountain Cableway ©Christophe Armand/Cape Photo Library
12. Skull of Mrs Ples ©Shaun Harris/iAfrika Photos
13. Private lodges in Londolozi Game Reserve, Greater Kruger National Park© Alain Proust/Cape Photo Library
14. Cape Dutch House ©Alain Proust/Cape Photo Library
15. Lesotho from the saddle ©Richard Van Ryneveld/Cape Photo Library
16. Pounding surf at sunset, Wild Coast ©South African Tourism
17. "Jimmy's face to face tours", Soweto ©Per-Anders Pettersson/iAfrika Photos
18. Basotho house ©South African Tourism
19. Hippos swimming at Umfolozi ©South African Tourism
20. Cabins on Storms River coastline ©South African Tourism
21. Swartberg Pass with car ©Christophe & Diana Heierli/Cape Photo Library
22. Cato Manor Temple, Durban ©South African Tourism
23. Gemsbok, Kgalagadi Transfrontier park ©by Alain Proust/Cape Photo Library
24. Hiking in the Kruger National Park ©Alain Proust/Cape Photo Library

Wildlife section

All images ©Bruce Coleman Library

Black and white photos

Penguins on Boulders Beach ©Alain Proust/Cape Photo Library (p.76)
Fishermen and catch, Hout Bay ©Alain Proust/Cape Photo Library (p.138)
Cape Dutch House ©South African Tourism (p.176)
Goat tower ©Donald Reid (p.195)

Watching whale from rocks, Hermanus
©South African Tourism (p.235)
Halfmens Tree ©South African Tourism
(p.300)
Windmill on farm ©Eric Miller/iAfrika Photos
(p.305)
Pounding surf at sunset, Wild Coast ©South
African Tourism (p.346)
Church exterior, Graaff-Reinet ©Alain
Proust/Cape Photo Library (p.390)
Nelson Mandela Museum, Umtata ©David
Rogers/Cape Photo Library (p.432)
Rhino drinking water ©Gert Lamprecht/Cape
Photo Library (p.446)
Mweni valley ©Richard Van Ryneveld/Cape
Photo Library (p.504)
Fisherman in Kosi Bay lagoon carrying pack
of sticks ©Sasa Kralj/iAfrika Photos
(p.536)
Clarens landscape ©Gert Lamprecht/Cape
Photo Library (p.556)

Taxi rank in Johannesburg ©Shaun
Harris/iAfrika Photos (p.578)
Ponte City Tower, Hillbrow ©Shaun
Harris/iAfrika Photos (p.585)
Township tour leader ©Per-Anders
Pettersson/iAfrika Photos (p.619)
Tourist trucks, Pilanesberg National Reserve
©Jean du Plessis/Cape Photo Library
(p.642)
Waterval-Boven Valley ©Chad Henning/Cape
Photo Library (p.668)
Leopard on branch ©Alain Proust/Cape
Photo Library (p.694)
Baobab tree ©South African Tourism (p.714)
Hut in highlands ©Donald Reid (p.746)
Silhouette of rider on mountain top ©Graeme
Robinson/Cape Photo Library (p.749)
King Mswati leading tribal dance ©Jesper
Strudsholm/iAfrika Photos (p.790)
African crafts by roadside ©Donald Reid
(p.803)

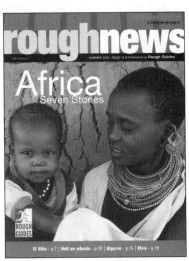

Visit us online
roughguides.com

Information on over 25,000 destinations around the world

- **Read** Rough Guides' trusted travel info
- **Share** journals, photos and travel advice with other readers
- Get exclusive Rough Guide **discounts** and travel **deals**
- Earn membership points every time you contribute to the
  Rough Guide **community** and get **free** books, flights and trips
- Browse thousands of CD reviews and artists in our **music** area

around the world

in twenty years

London Mini Guide ★ London Restaurants ★ Los Angeles ★ Madeira ★ Madrid ★ Malaysia, Singapore & Brunei ★ Mallorca ★ Malta & Gozo ★ Maui ★ Maya World ★ Melbourne ★ Menorca ★ Mexico ★ Miami & the Florida Keys ★ Montréal ★ Morocco ★ Moscow ★ Nepal ★ New England ★ New Orleans ★ New York City ★ New York Mini Guide ★ New York Restaurants ★ New Zealand ★ Norway ★ Pacific Northwest ★ Paris ★ Paris Mini Guide ★ Peru ★ Poland ★ Portugal ★ Prague ★ Provence & the Côte d'Azur ★ Pyrenees ★ The Rocky Mountains ★ Romania ★ Rome ★ San Francisco ★ San Francisco Restaurants ★ Sardinia ★ Scandinavia ★ Scotland ★ Scottish Highlands & Islands ★ Seattle ★ Sicily ★ Singapore ★ South Africa, Lesotho & Swaziland ★ South India ★ Southeast Asia ★ Southwest USA ★ Spain ★ St Lucia ★ St Petersburg ★ Sweden ★ Switzerland ★ Sydney ★ Syria ★ Tanzania ★ Tenerife and La Gomera ★ Thailand ★ Thailand's Beaches & Islands ★ Tokyo ★ Toronto ★ Travel Health ★ Trinidad & Tobago ★ Tunisia ★ Turkey ★ Tuscany & Umbria ★ USA ★ Vancouver ★ Venice & the Veneto ★ Vienna ★ Vietnam ★ Wales ★ Washington DC ★ West Africa ★ Women Travel ★ Yosemite ★ Zanzibar ★ Zimbabwe

also look out for our maps, phrasebooks, music guides and reference books

ROUGH GUIDES TWENTY YEARS

NOTES

The ideas expressed in this code were developed by and for independent travellers.

Learn About The Country You're Visiting

Start enjoying your travels before you leave by tapping into as many sources of information as you can.

The Cost Of Your Holiday

Think about where your money goes - be fair and realistic about how cheaply you travel. Try and put money into local peoples' hands; drink local beer or fruit juice rather than imported brands and stay in locally owned accommodation. Haggle with humour and not aggressively. Pay what something is worth to you and remember how wealthy you are compared to local people.

Embrace The Local Culture

Open your mind to new cultures and traditions - it will transform your experience. Think carefully about what's appropriate in terms of your clothes and the way you behave. You'll earn respect and be more readily welcomed by local people. Respect local laws and attitudes towards drugs and alcohol that vary in different countries and communities. Think about the impact you could have on them.

Exploring The World – The Travellers' Code

Being sensitive to these ideas means getting more out of your travels - and giving more back to the people you meet and the places you visit.

Minimise Your Environmental Impact

Think about what happens to your rubbish - take biodegradable products and a water filter bottle. Be sensitive to limited resources like water, fuel and electricity. Help preserve local wildlife and habitats by respecting local rules and regulations, such as sticking to footpaths and not standing on coral.

Don't Rely On Guidebooks

Use your guidebook as a starting point, not the only source of information. Talk to local people, then discover your own adventure!

Be Discreet With Photography

Don't treat people as part of the landscape, they may not want their picture taken. Ask first and respect their wishes.

We work with people the world over to promote tourism that benefits their communities, but we can only carry on our work with the support of people like you. For membership details or to find out how to make your travels work for local people and the environment, visit our website.

www.tourismconcern.org.uk

TourismConce
Campaigning for Ethical and Fairly Traded To

NO TIME TO PACK?

When disaster or war strike, there is no time to pack your bags.

very year hundreds of thousands of people in Africa are forced to flee heir homes and literally run for their lives.

IEDAIR, specialising in emergency humanitarian aid, provides life-saving are to over 3 million victims of disaster and conflict worldwide, regardless f race, sex, religion or age.

ut with MEDAIR it's life that counts, not statistics.

e're committed to making our assistance as personal as possible. That's hy our programmes are made to suit individual needs, from healthcare, ealth education and trauma counselling, to reconstruction, food-istribution and improving water supplies.

oin us on the frontline nd see how you can help y visiting www.MEDAIR.org r e-mailing info@MEDAIR.org.uk